Footprint Chile

Toby Green and Janak Jani
4th edition

*I can see how puzzling a country can be that starts at the frozen
South Pole and stretches upwards to salt mines and deserts where
it hasn't rained for eons.*
Pablo Neruda, *Memoirs*

Chile Highlights

See colour maps at back of book

1 Altiplano National Parks
Shy vicunas set against a background of snowcapped volcanoes.

2 La Tirana
Dance for a week at the famous fiesta.

3 San Pedro de Atacama
A desert town surrounded by geysers and salt pans.

4 Parque Nacional Pan de Azúcar
Where sea lions hang out on beautiful beaches.

5 Elqui and Limarí Valleys
Star-filled skies and wild countryside.

6 Valparaíso
The city's *cerros* are a UNESCO world heritage site, just waiting to be explored.

7 Cerro La Campana
Some of Chile's most stunning views can be enjoyed from the summit in winter.

8 Ski resorts
The best skiing and boarding in Latin America, within easy reach of Santiago.

9 Wine routes
Chile's finest vintages come from the Central Valley.

10 Pucón
One of the top destinations in the Lake District, with volcanoes, fishing and whitewater rafting all nearby.

11 Lago Llanquihue
The third largest lake in South America is a haven of peace and tranquillity.

12 Lakes route to Bariloche
Travelling by boat and bus to Argentina is one of the region's most beautiful journeys.

13 Parque Pumalín
Native temperate rainforest preserved for posterity.

14 Chiloé
A magical island of fishing, forests and mythical creatures.

15 Futaleufú
The country's mecca for whitewater rafting.

16 Carretera Austral
Cycle, hike or fish your way through spectacular scenery between Puerto Montt and Villa O'Higgins.

17 Laguna San Rafael
Cruise to the mighty glacier before it disappears.

18 Torres del Paine
Quite simply one of the world's greatest national parks.

19 Isla Navarino
Trek through wild forests and beaver dams south of Tierra del Fuego.

20 Easter Island
A remote dot in the Pacific ocean with a fascinating cultural heritage.

4

Contents

Tierra del Fuego

Chilean Pacific Islands

Background

Footnotes

Inside front cover
Sleeping and eating
price codes

Inside back cover
Authors' biographies

Piercing the sky
A candelabra cactus lights up the scenery of the Atacama Desert.

A foot in the door

With an almost comical geographical shape, virtually every climate imaginable, and the political earthquake of the Pinochet affair to compliment its geological shudders, Chile is a country that, in recent years, has forced the world to sit up and take notice. Here you can ski in the mountains in the morning and be drinking *pisco sours* on the beach come sundown. This beautiful, memorable corner of the world is a place of extremes and contradictions, in terms of geography – and politics.

For a start, few countries in the world have quite such a split geographical personality. Here, you can often glimpse the snows of the high Andes from the Pacific Ocean. To the south, the country is hemmed in by thick temperate rainforest, while to the north is the uniquely memorable Atacama Desert, with its endless spaces and pristine skies. The desert's geoglyphs bear testament to the ingenuity of some of prehistoric America's most complex civilisations, while an intermingling of the old world with the new has led to some of the most enduring aspects of ancient and modern Chilean culture: these range from the legend of the Inca princess La Tirana, which spawned the country's biggest religious fiesta, to the political militancy, which arose among the nitrate mines in the early 20th century and played a big part in forging Salvador Allende's Popular Unity government of 1970-1973, later to be overthrown by Augusto Pinochet.

Politics and poetry

Like it or not, Chile is most famous today for the legacy of the Pinochet government. A decade ago, the very mention of politics was likely to lead to an embarrassed silence but, these days, people are much freer with their opinions. The constraints of the military government on people's conversations have gone and the result is an increasing cultural dynamism. Many avant-garde writers (such as Roberto Bolaño and Raul Zurita) hail from Chile, perpetuating the country's long and distinguished artistic tradition. With its remarkable geography and an enduring sense of isolation, it is perhaps no surprise that poetry has flourished here. The country is rightly proud of its two Nobel laureates, the poets Gabriela Mistral and Pablo Neruda, whose writings reveal something of the essence of Chile. But the country's poetic output is not limited to these two international names: Chileans have a saying that there is a poet hidden under every stone ...

All at sea
Colourful boats line up for a day's fishing at Ancud on Chiloé.

Isolation and identity

It has long been said (in Chile and elsewhere) that the Chileans are the 'English of South America'. The roots of this surprising assertion cut to the heart of much of what it once meant to be Chilean. Inaccessible for centuries, except by sea or over the passes of the high Andes, Chileans developed a highly distinct and slightly isolationist identity: an insularity and indomitable national pride that meant that they could empathize all too easily with a place such as England. These days, however, with the collapse of the dictatorship and the resulting cultural liberation, Chileans are increasingly self-confident and outward-looking. They might still call their high tea *'onces'* (Chilean for 'elevenses'), but other vestiges of supposed 'Englishness' – old-fashioned ceremoniousness and the modelling of the Chilean Navy on the British one – are of less and less importance to the psyche. This is an increasingly confident nation, with no need to look elsewhere for its national pride.

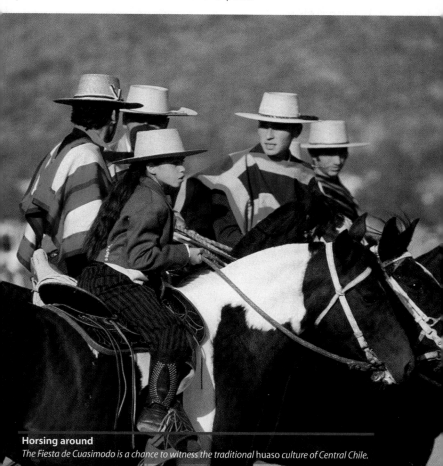

Horsing around
The Fiesta de Cuasimodo is a chance to witness the traditional huaso *culture of Central Chile.*

1 Chile's markets sell crafts and products from all over South America, including textiles, basketwork and musical instruments. ▸▸ See page 59.

2 A startling sculpture reaches towards the sky, interrupting the emptiness of the Atacama Desert. ▸▸ See page 202.

3 Located in a beautiful spot at the northern end of a fjord, the village of Puyuhuapi is a tranquil stopping place between Chaitén and Coyhaique. ▸▸ See page 413.

4 Santiago's 18th-century cathedral creates a baroque reflection in the sleek high-rises of the modern capital. ▸▸ See page 83.

5 Chile's varied climates and landscapes can be thanked for a wide range of fresh produce, from Pacific seafood to Easter Island pineapples. ▸▸ See page 53.

6 A masked protestor highlights the plight of those who 'disappeared' under the Pinochet regime. ▸▸ See page 522.

7 The Parque Nacional Conguillio is the best place in the country to see the distinctive monkey puzzle tree, Chile's national emblem. ▸▸ See page 313.

8 An ancient textile testifies to the cultural vibrancy of early civilisations in northern Chile. ▸▸ See page 513.

9 The dry, cracked earth of the Atacama Desert belies the fascinating natural and manmade sights to be found in this unique landscape. ▸▸ See page 202.

10 Even the llamas dress up for festivities on Chiloé Island, famous for its fantastic myths and legends. ▸▸ See page 379.

11 The seemingly lifeless semi-desert bursts into bloom in a rare but unmissable phenomenon known as 'el desierto florido'. ▸▸ See page 188.

12 Volcán Parinacota looms up from the glassy surface of Lago Chungará in Parque Nacional Lauca. ▸▸ See page 261.

In a microcosm

If there are many reasons to come to Chile, it is most often for its serenity and natural beauty that visitors are attracted here. Travelling from north to south and with only a little exertion it is possible to see the highest geyser, the driest desert and one of the highest lakes in the world; a flowering desert; schools of dolphins; the Andes; forests of monkey puzzle trees; temperate rainforest; the Patagonian ice-field; the glaciers of Tierra del Fuego and the islands near Cape Horn. More vigorous visitors can climb active volcanoes where the crater bubbles away beneath them, ride galloping horses along wild and empty beaches, ski in some of South America's finest mountain resorts, go whitewater rafting, canoeing or kayaking and trek in one of the world's finest national parks, Torres del Paine in Patagonia.

Highs of metropolitan life

This cornucopia of wilderness should be reason enough to come to Chile. Yet while the country wears its beautiful scenery on its sleeve, peel away the layers of urban life and an equally intriguing animal lurks below. Chile is perhaps more 'European' than some of its Andean neighbours and it possesses some fascinating cities. Santiago is a sophisticated capital with a vibrant cultural life, including an underground rock scene and some of South America's most experimental modern artists. The nearby port city of Valparaíso, with its warrens of streets and brightly painted houses, is a place where it is possible to spend weeks and not even scratch the surface.

Circles in the sand. The ruins of Tulor village, dating from 100 BC to AD 100, are just one of the intriguing archaeological sites around the desert town of San Pedro de Atacama.

Torres del Paine National Park in Patagonia is one of the undisputed highlights of a trip to Chile, with an abundance of wildlife, fresh air and incredible views.

To the south, Chillán has wonderful galleries and museums that provide an insight into life in Chile's heartland, while Iquique – one of the driest cities on earth – gives a sense of life on a forbidding frontier.

Mapuche to Moai

Away from material considerations, one of Chile's greatest attractions is its people – warm, courteous and generous to a fault. You will find an effusive welcome all over the country, especially if you speak Spanish. In the south, particularly in the region around Temuco, you can also gain first-hand experience of the fierce pride of the Mapuche people and understand something of their heritage and tragic history. Meanwhile, to confirm the strength of Chile's indigenous cultures, it is only necessary to look westwards to Easter Island, where the mysterious *moai* figures have fascinated anthropologists for decades.

Doubts and witches

But just in case you are still doubtful that Chile is anything more than a European country disguised as a South American one, take a short boat trip to the island of Chiloé in the south-west of the country. Here the islanders have developed an entire mythology all of their own, peopled with goblins, ghost ships and mermaids, not to mention witches, who fly to the graveyards at night and eat the bodies of the recently interred.

Los Penitentes
Taking their name from the traditional white pointed hats worn by penitent Christians, these sculpted spears of ice are formed by the action of the wind and sun. They can be seen at the Guataquina Pass on the border with Argentina.

Planning your trip

Chileans say that, when God had almost completed the act of creation, there was a little of everything left, so God threw it all down in a narrow strip of land and called it Chile. The national pride is justifiable, for this is a fantastically diverse country, but so much choice can be confusing for the visitor. Chile is hemmed in by the Pacific Ocean, the Atacama Desert and the Andes. When combined with the country's shape, these geographical barriers rule out circular routes within the country – the choice therefore comes down to whether to go north or south. A word of advice is try not to do too much: you will get more out of your travels by covering a small area properly than by flitting from one place to another.

Where to go

With such variety to explore, this guide makes no attempt to be prescriptive. There are, however, a number of places that stand out. These itineraries are suggested for those who want to see as much of the country as they can in the time available; but those with more time to spare could easily devote several weeks to each area of the country without running out of things to see and do.

The south
One week Those with just a week to see something of the south are probably best advised to use a **LanChile** airpass (see page 45) to fly straight from Santiago to Puerto Montt, allowing two days to visit the beautiful island of Chiloé: perhaps the penguins at **Pumillahue** and the town of **Ancud**. Visiting Chiloé in 1835, Charles Darwin found that the rolling hills reminded him of England. Chiloé has changed little since and, with its rich mythology and close-knit agricultural communities, it still evokes a bygone age. Just north of Chiloé and Puerto Montt is the Lake District, where another two days could be spent visiting the area around **Lago Llanquihue**, where the Osorno volcano provides a spectacular backdrop to the third biggest lake in South America. Travellers could then fly south to Punta Arenas, where three days could be spent visiting the mountains and eerie blue glaciers of the **Parque Nacional Torres del Paine**, one of the world's great national parks, before flying back to Santiago.

Two weeks With a little more time available, several great additions could be made to the one-week itinerary. Rather than flying straight to Puerto Montt, travellers might want to travel by bus, spending a few days in the Central Valley. This is the heart of Chile and is essential for a deeper understanding of the country. The high mountains around **Vilches**, east of Talca could be visited, or the **Parque Nacional de las Siete Tazas**, near San Fernando. Wine-buffs might want to sample some of Chile's best wines on the **Ruta del Vino**, also near San Fernando, while beach lovers might prefer surfing at **Pichilemu**, or visiting beautiful and deserted resorts such as **Iloca** or **Curanipe**. After four or five days move on to the famous forests and hills around **Lago Villarrica**, perhaps climbing the famous volcano nearby, before flying from Puerto Montt to Punta Arenas to visit the Torres del Paine (as above) and then heading straight back to Santiago.

One month A month is enough time for a truly memorable trip. Spend a further two or three days on Chiloé, visiting the **Parque Nacional de Chiloé** at Cucao, and **Castro**. A boat could then be caught to **Chaitén**, from where you could spend the next eight or

Futaleufu and hike around **Chile Chico** or **Cochrane**, before making for Puerto Chacabuco and (if money is no object) taking a two-day cruise to the **Laguna San Rafael glacier**. After this you could sail down to Puerto Natales, and complete the itinerary at Torres del Paine (see above), before flying back to Santiago.

The north

One week With just a week to see the best of northern Chile, you will again probably want to take advantage of the **LanChile** airpass, flying first to La Serena in order to spend perhaps three days exploring the area around that city. Pick two attractions from among the Elqui Valley **observatories**, the **Parque Nacional Fray Jorge**, the cave paintings at the **Valle del Encanto** or the **Limarí Valley**. Fly on to Calama, gateway to the Atacama, to visit the small town of **Chiu Chiu**. The next day, travel to the oasis of **San Pedro de Atacama** and spend three days visiting the geysers, the salt lake and the Valley of the Moon, before flying back to Santiago.

Two weeks Those with a fortnight to spend in the north will probably want to avoid flying. A bus north to **Ovalle** provides a good introduction to the beauties of the mountains of the semi-desert, before visiting the attractions around La Serena mentioned above. From La Serena, it's worth travelling to Chañaral to visit the spectacular **Parque Nacional Pan de Azucar**, before moving on to Calama to continue with the itinerary suggested above. After exploring the area around San Pedro, travel to **Arica**, and spend two days visiting the spectacular **Parque Nacional Lauca** and the world's highest lake, **Chungará**, before the flight back to the capital.

One month A month allows you to visit some fascinating additional destinations in the north of the country. Two or three days should be spent exploring the hinterland around Illapel, Salamanca and Combarbalá, for example, which is spectacularly rugged country and full of minerals and ancient rock art. Heading north from Chañaral, break your journey at the eerie, attractive coast town of **Taltal** and then use one of your extra days to visit **Chuquicamata**, the largest open-cast copper mine on earth. With two extra days at San Pedro de Atacama, you should tour the beautiful *altiplano* villages, before travelling north to the city of **Iquique**, where you can relax on the beach for a couple of days. Then head into the interior, visiting the thermal baths at **Mamiña**, and the spectacular natural park at **Surire**, before completing the itinerary at Arica as suggested above.

The two-week itineraries could be combined into a one-month exploration of the country as a whole.

Other options

The itineraries suggested above incorporate the most popular destinations for visitors to Chile, but those who have several months available (or who want to experience other aspects of the country) will find their travel plans equally busy. Since over one third of Chileans live in **Santiago**, it is a shame to avoid the capital completely; travellers who enjoy nightlife and/or urban living will thrive here, though it is best to try to avoid the incapacitating heat of summer and the worst days of the winter smog. Nearby, **Valparaíso** is perhaps the most interesting city in Chile, while the summit of the **Cerro La Campana** offers some of the best views in the whole country. The beach resorts to the north and south of Valparaíso are also attractive, though busy in summer.

Two final suggestions would be the **Juan Fernández Islands,** where Alexander Selkirk was marooned for almost five years, and **Easter Island,** with its famous archaeological heritage; both are easy (if expensive) to reach from Santiago by plane.

Essentials Planning your trip

When to go

When planning your trip you should take into account the time of year. High season throughout the country is during the summer (especially January and February), when most areas are open to visitors, though the *altiplano* (the high plain of the Andes east of the Atacama) can experience heavy rain. It is also worth bearing in mind that many destinations are busy with Chilean and Argentine tourists at this time, especially in the far south, and bus fares and hotel prices are higher by around 20%. The north of the country has another high season in June, July and August, but these are winter months in the south, meaning that many services here are closed and transport links are reduced. Probably the ideal seasons for a visit, therefore, are spring (October-November) and autumn (March-April) when many facilities in the south are open, but less crowded, and temperatures in the northern and central regions are lower.

It is also worth arranging your travel plans to coincide with certain festivals (see page 104); although in all cases it is best to book transport and accommodation in advance. The period around the national Independence festivals on 18th September will be especially busy wherever you are.

Tour operators

In the UK and Ireland
Austral Tours, *20 Upper Tachbrook Street, London SW1V 1SH, T020-7233 5384, www.latinamerica.co.uk* Specialist company with a wide range of activity holidays.
Condor Journeys and Adventures, *2 Ferry Bank, Colintraive, Argyll, PA22 3AR, T01700-841318, www.condorjourneys-adventures.com* A wide range of specialist tours available – website in French.
Cox & Kings Travel, *Gordon House, 10 Greencoat Place, London SW1P 1PH, T0207-873500 F0207-6306038, www.coxandkings.co.uk* Exclusive set tours all over the continent.
Destination South America, *51 Castle Street, Cirencester, Glos, GL7 1QD, T01285-885333, www.destinationsouthamerica.co.uk* Tailor-made tours.
Exodus Travels, *Grange Mills, Weir Road, London SW12 0NE T, T020-87723822, www.exodus.co.uk* Experience in adventure

travel around the world; good trips to all parts of Chile.
Hayes and Jarvis, *Sandrocks, Rocky Lane, Haywards Heath, West Sussex RH16 4RH, T0870-333-1952, F0870-333-0069, www.hayesandjarvis.co.uk* Long-established operator. Offers tailor-made itineraries as well as packages.
Journey Latin America, *London office: 12-13 Heathfield Terrace, Chiswick, London W4 4JE, T020-8747 8315, F742 1312; Manchester office: 12 St Ann's Square (2nd Floor), Manchester M3 7HW, T0161-832 1441, F832 1551, www.journeylatinamerica.co.uk* Long established company, running escorted and bespoke tours throughout the region, and offering a wide range of flight options.
Last Frontiers, *Fleet Marston Farm, Aylesbury, Buckinghamshire HP18 0QT, T01296-658650, www.lastfrontiers.co.uk*
Pura Aventura, *18 Bond Street, Brighton, East Sussex BN11 1RD, T01273-676712, F676774,*

enquiries@pura-aventura.com Small Chilean specialist with a wide range of organised and tailor-made tours.

Scott Dunn (formerly Passage to South America), *Fovant Mews, 12a Noyna Road, London SW17 7PH, T0208-7678989, www.scottdunn.com* Wide range of tailor-made packages throughout the region including the lost kingdom of the Incas.

South American Experience, *47 Causton Street, Pimlico, London SW1P 4AT,* *T020-79765511, F9766908.* Apart from booking flights and accommodation, also offers tailor-made trips.

Steppes Latin America, *51 Castle St, Cirencester, Glos GL7 1QD, T01285-885333, www.steppeslatinamerica.co.uk* Tailor-made holidays including Patagonia escorted tours, riding trips and bird watching.

Trips Worldwide, *14 Frederick Place, Clifton, Bristol, BS8 1AS, T0117-311 4400, www.tripsworldwide.co.uk* Specialists in tailor-made holidays.

4 Star South America, *3003 Van Ness, NW Ste S-823, Washington, DC 20008, T1-800 747 4540 (US)/0871-711 5370 (UK)/+49-700-4444 7827 (rest of the world), http://4starSouth America.com (tours to South America), http://4starFlights.com (flight consolidator tickets to South America).* Tour operator and flight consolidator with internet- and catalogue-based marketing.

Discover Chile Tours, *5775 Blue Lagoon Drive Suite 190, Miami, Florida 33126. T305-2665827 (local), T1-800-826-4845 (toll-free), www.discover-chile.com* Has a range of tours, including good ski trips.

International Expeditions, *1 Environs Park, Helena, AL35080, USA, T1-800-6334734, www.internationalexpeditions.com* Travel company specializing in nature tours.

Ladatco Tours, *3006 Aviation Ave, Suite 4C, Coconut Grove, FL33133, T1-800-327 6162, www.ladatco.com* Specialist tour operator based in Miami, runs explorer tours themed around mysticism, wine, etc.

Mila Tours, *T1-800-3677378, F1-847-2492772, www.milatours.com* Arrange a wide range of tours from rafting to photography.

Mountain Travel Sobek, *6420 Fairmount Ave, El Cerrito, CA 94530, T1-888-MTSOBEK (toll-free)/T1-510-527 8100, www.mtsobek.com* A specialist in Chile, with a wide range of tours on offer.

Myths and Mountains, *976 Tee Court, Incline Village, NV 89451, T1-800-670-6984/ 775-832 5454, F775-832 4454, www.mythsandmountains.com* Cultural, wildlife and environmental trips.

South American Explorers Club, *126 Indian Creek Road, Ithaca, New York 14850, USA, T(USA)607-2770488, F2776122, www.samexplo.org* Can give good advice.

Wilderness Travel, *1102 Ninth St, Berkeley, CA 94710-1211, T510-5582488 or toll-free on T1-800-3682794, www.wildernesstravel.com* Organises trips worldwide, including very good tours of Patagonia.

In Australia and New Zealand
Australian Andean Adventures, *33 Imperial Arcade, Pitt Street Mall, Sydney, T02-92351889, www.andeanadventurescom.au* The specialists in trekking in South America for Australians.

South America Travel Centre, *104 Hardware St, Melbourne, T03-96425353, www.satc.com.au* Good, individual tailor-made trips to Chile.

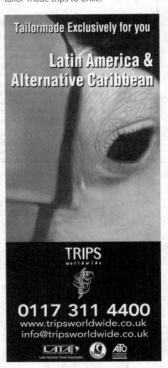
Finding out more

For general information contact the **Tourism Promotion Corporation of Chile** ⓘ *Antonio Bellet 77, Oficina 602, Providencia, Santiago, T02-2350105, F02-2362166.* The **Latin American Travel Advisor** ⓘ *PO Box 17-17-908, Quito, Ecuador; USA and Canada toll-free F888-2159511, international F593-2562566, www.amerispan.com/lata/,* offers a travel information service including a quarterly newsletter (free sample available), country reports by email or fax, and a wide selection of travel maps. Travel planning assistance is also offered to subscribers. Credit card payment is required for fax or mail orders.

There are a great many sites about Chile that surfers may wish to explore, but note that you may have to weed out the sites related to chile peppers! Three useful sites specifically covering Chile are www.visit-chile.org, www.sernatur.cl, and www.gochile.cl Two sites of general interest on Latin America are the Latin American Travel Advisor (see below) and **El Planeta Platica**, www.txintinet.com/mader/ecotravel/schools

Sites geared specifically to Patagonia include www.chileaustral.com and www.patagoniachile.cl, while www.rapanui.cl deals exclusively with Easter Island. Other sites dealing with specific destinations in Chile include: www.chiloeisland.cl, www.chiloeweb.cl, www.iquique.co.cl, www.laserena.cl, www.pucon.com, www.puertomonttchile.cl, www.puertovaras.org, www.valparaisochile.cl (the best map of the city available) and www.vinadelmarchile.cl

Reservations for many hotels in Chile (particularly upmarket ones) can be made at www.chile-hotels.com Those wanting to enjoy the outdoors will want to look at www.chile-outdoors.cl; wine enthusaists will want to look at www.ccv.cl, the website of the Chilean winemaking association, and surfers will be interested in www.surf.cl There is up-to-date information on environmental issues at www.greenpeace.cl, while www.desaparecidos.org/chile and www.remember-chile.org give background on the Pinochet years and the human rights situation. A website devoted to disseminating information on Chile's Mapuche people is www.mapuche.cl

Language

Although English is understood in many major hotels, tour agencies and airline offices (especially in Santiago), travellers are strongly advised to learn some Spanish before setting out. Chilean pronunciation – very quick and lilting, with final syllables cut off – can present difficulties to the foreigner. Chileans have a wide range of unique idioms that even other Latin Americans find difficult to understand. Visitors may want to buy *How to Survive in the Chilean Jungle* by John Brennan and Alvaro Taboada, a handbook for English speakers on Chilean colloquialisms and slang available in bookshops in Santiago. In rural areas of the IX Region and in the interior of the I and II Regions travellers will encounter indigenous languages – Mapudungu (the Mapuche language) in the south; Aymará in the north – but some people usually also speak Spanish. ▶▶ *For a list of Spanish words and phrases, see page 558.*

For Spanish courses in Chile contact **Amerispan** ① *PO Box 58129, Philadelphia, PA19102, T1-800 879 6640/215 751 1100, www.amerispan.com*, or **Spanish Abroad**, ① *5112 N 40th Street, Suite 103, Phoenix, AZ85018, T1-888 722 7623 (toll free)/1-602 778 6791/0800-028 7706 (UK freephone), www.spanishabroad.com*, which offers courses in Santiago, with tailor-made programmes, airport pickup and excursions.

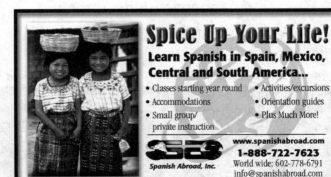

Disabled travellers

Chileans are usually very courteous, and disabled travellers will be helped and assisted where possible. The 1992 census found that 288,000 Chilean citizens had some form of disability, but the **National Fund for the Handicapped (FONDIS)** estimates that the actual number is closer to one million (figures for the 2002 census were not yet available as this book went to press). Congress passed a law in 1994 to promote the integration of people with disabilities into society and **FONDIS** has a US$1.5 mn budget. However, the disabled still suffer some forms of legal discrimination; for example, blind people cannot become teachers or tutors. Although the law now requires that new public buildings provide access for the disabled and the more expensive hotels usually have dedicated facilities, transport provision is a different matter. The Linea 5 subway line in Santiago has no facilitated access for the disabled and, although bus companies will certainly be helpful, they do not have any dedicated services. Where possible, disabled travellers might therefore be better off hiring their own transport, especially since reserved parking for the disabled is now becoming more common.

Useful organizations

Directions Unlimited,*123 Green Lane, Bedford Hills, NY 10507, T800-533-5343.* A tour operator specializing in tours for disabled US travellers.
Disability Action Group, *2 Annadale Ave,* Belfast BT7 3JH, T01232-491011. Information about access for British disabled traveller.

Disabled Persons' Assembly, *PO Box 27-524, , Wellington 6035, New Zealand, T04-801-9100, gen@dpa.org.nz.* Has lists of tour operators and travel agencies catering for the disabled.

Gay and lesbian travellers

In a macho culture, it is no surprise that there is quite a lot of homophobia in Chile, and gay and lesbian travellers should be aware that derogatory jokes about homosexuals (especially men) are widespread. Having said that, attitudes are beginning to loosen up. A mine of information is the website **www.gaychile.com**, where you can make gay-friendly hotel reservations and seek out gay-friendly shops and establishments up and down the country. There is also a specialist travel agency for gays and lesbians in Chile called **Novellus** ① *Almirante Pastene 7, Of 54, Providencia, Santiago, T02-2518547, novellus@tempotravel.cl*

Student travellers

If planning to study in Chile for a long period it is essential to get a student visa in advance, which you obtain by contacting a Chilean consulate (see page 31); you will be asked for proof of affiliation to a Chilean university. Note that students are not allowed to undertake paid employment in Chile.

If you are in full-time education you are entitled to an International Student Identity Card, which is distributed by student travel offices and travel agencies in 77 countries. The **ISIC** gives you special prices on all forms of transport, and access to a variety of other concessions and services. To find the location of your nearest ISIC office look at www.istc.org or contact: the **ISIC Association** ① *Box 9048, 1000 Copenhagen, Denmark, T+45-33939303.* In Chile, student ID cards can be obtained from Providencia 2594, Local 421, Santiago, and cost US$8 (photo and proof of status required). If you are a holder of an ISIC card and get into trouble, you can make a reverse-charge call to the helpline on T+44-20-8762-8110. If travelling with a student card, it is always worth asking for discounts for museum entry and bus tickets, although all student ID cards must carry a photograph if they are to be of any use.

Travelling with children

Chile is a good place for travelling with children as there are few health risks and children are very popular. Officials tend to be more amenable where children are concerned, and even thieves and pickpockets seem to have retained the traditional respect for families and may leave you alone because of it.

However, a lot of time can be spent waiting for **transport**. On bus journeys, if the children are good at amusing themselves, or can readily sleep while travelling, the problems can be considerably reduced. Train journeys are easier, as they allow more scope for moving about, but there are few of these in Chile. On all long-distance buses you pay for each seat; there are no half-fares, so it is cheaper, if less comfortable, to seat small children on your knee for shorter trips. On urban and local buses, small children generally do not pay a fare, but are not entitled to a seat if paying customers are standing. On sightseeing tours you should always bargain for a family rate; often children can go free. All civil airlines charge half price for children under 12.

Food can be a problem if your children are not adaptable. It is easier to take biscuits, drinks, bread etc with you on longer trips than to rely on meal stops. A small immersion heater and jug for making hot drinks is invaluable. You will find that people will be very friendly to children in restaurants. As far as **health** is concerned, remember to be very careful about sunburn in the south, due to the lack of ozone.

In **hotels**, try to negotiate family rates. If charges are per person, always insist that two children will only occupy one bed, therefore counting as one tariff. If rates are per bed, the same applies. You can always get a reduced rate at cheaper hotels.

> ● Note that a child travelling free is not always covered by the operator's travel insurance; it is advisable to pay a small premium to arrange extra cover.

Women travellers

Chile presents no special problem to women travellers. Most Chileans are courteous and helpful. The following useful tips have been supplied by women (although most apply to any single traveller).

When you set out, err on the side of caution until your instincts have adjusted to the customs of the country. If you can befriend a local woman, you will learn a great deal. Unless actively avoiding foreigners like yourself, don't go too far from the beaten track; there is a very definite 'gringo trail' that you can join. This can be helpful when looking for safe accommodation, especially if arriving after dark . Remember that a taxi at night can be as dangerous as wandering around on your own, particularly in Santiago. At borders dress as smartly as possible. Buses are much easier than trains for a person alone; on major routes your seat is reserved and your bags are locked in the hold.

Women may, though, be subject to much unwanted attention. To help minimize this, do not wear suggestive clothing. Some readers advise not flirting. By wearing a wedding ring and carrying a photograph of your 'husband' and 'children' you may dissuade an aspiring suitor. If politeness fails, do not feel bad about showing offence and departing. When accepting a social invitation, make sure that someone knows the address and the time you left. Ask if you can bring a friend (even if you do not intend to do so). A good rule is always to act with confidence, as though you know where you are going, even if you do not. Someone who looks lost is more likely to attract unwanted attention. Finally, be aware that anywhere calling itself a 'nightclub' is in fact a brothel.

Working in Chile

It is not difficult to find short-term or temporary work as a foreigner in Chile. The most obvious opening is as a teacher of English as a foreign language; even those without the appropriate TEFL qualification should be able to find this kind of work, especially in Santiago, but also in other cities such as Viña del Mar, Concepción and La Serena. Teachers are expected to be clean-cut and well-dressed, and to have the correct paperwork. The pay is often poor; as low as US$3 per hour after tax for those without the appropriate qualification. Prospective English language teachers should apply in mid-February/early March with a full CV and photo. A work visa should be obtained as soon as you have found a contract (see below); beware that, without this, you will be liable to deportation and fines if discovered. We have received reports of more unscrupulous institutes employing teachers with 90-day tourist visas and then 'discovering', as this expires, that the teacher is not entitled to work, at which point unpaid wages may be withheld. The best paid work for English language teachers is almost invariably private, one-to-one tuition, mainly found through word of mouth (although it may be worth placing an advertisement in *El Mercurio* as well).

Opportunities for work are not limited to language teaching. There is considerable scope for volunteer work in Chile, both in inner cities and on environmental projects. Those with appropriate skills and experience may also find work by approaching foreign companies (especially engineering or financial service firms) with offices in Chile (usually in Santiago). There is a large expatriate community in Santiago; try visiting some favourite local haunts, particularly **The Phone Box Pub**, Providencia 1670, Santiago; Metro Manuel Montt, and asking around. Casual manual labour will not be worth most travellers' while, as the wages are so low.

Working visas

The main obstacle to anyone seeking to work in Chile is the problem of obtaining and maintaining a working visa. All sorts of extraordinary pieces of paper may be asked for (one woman was asked for her grandfather's birth certificate when trying to open a bank account) and, at the very least, you will need proof of employment and proof of need before the visa is issued. Those planning to work may enter Chile on a tourist visa and then get a working visa on presentation of a contract with a minimum wage of 100,000 Chilean pesos per month after tax (approx US$150).

Business people face no special problems when doing business in the country, and may enter on a tourist visa. It is recommended to carry a good supply of business cards, as the first thing which many business people will do at a meeting is ceremoniously present you with their card. Business visas are required for those who are buying a going concern, or are investing a minimum of US$5000 in Chile. ▶▶ *For further information, see Visas and immigration, page 30.*

Volunteer organizations

Earthwatch, *126 Bank Street, South Melbourne, Victoria 3205, Australia, T03-96826828, www.earthwatch.org* Organises volunteer work on scientific and cultural projects around the world (also has associated offices in Oxford, UK).

Project Trust, *The Hebridean Centre, Isle of Coll, Argyll PA78 6TE, T01879-230441, www.projecttrust.org.uk* One of several UK organizations offering volunteer work for foreigners.
Raleigh International, *27 Parsons Green Lane, London SW6 4HZ, T0207-3718585, www.raleigh.org.uk* Volunteer projects for young travellers.

Essentials Planning your trip

Bank exchange rates: October 2003

Currency	Chilean peso	Currency	Chilean peso
US$1	633	S African	
UK£1	1074	Rand 1	91
Euro 1	745	Israeli New	
Aus $1	443	Shekel 1	141
Can $1	485	Yen ¥100	578
NZ $1	397		

Before you travel

Getting in

Visas and immigration

Regulations change frequently, so it is imperative to check visa requirements before you travel. At the time of writing, **visas** are required by citizens of Cuba, Guyana, Haiti; all African and Middle-Eastern countries, except Israel and South Africa; all Asian and Pacific countries, except Fiji, Indonesia, Japan, Malaysia, Singapore, Tonga and Turkey; all former Communist countries except for Croatia, the Czech Republic, Estonia, Hungary, Lithuania, Poland, the Slovak Republic, Slovenia and Yugoslavia.

A **passport**, valid for at least six months, and a **tourist card** are required for entry by all other foreigners, except for citizens of Argentina, Brazil, Colombia, Paraguay and Uruguay, who require national identity cards only. Those entering with just a passport and tourist card may all stay for a period of 90 days, except for citizens of Belize, Costa Rica, Malaysia and Singapore (30 days only), and citizens of Greece, Indonesia and Peru (60 days only). Tourist cards are handed out as a matter of routine at immigration offices at major land frontiers and Chilean airports. It is essential that you keep the tourist card safe, since you must surrender it on departure. Onward travel tickets are officially required for entry but these are rarely asked for. On arrival you may be asked where you are staying in Chile; just give the name of any hotel. Remember that it is your responsibility to ensure that your passport is stamped in and out when you cross frontiers. The absence of entry and exit stamps can cause serious difficulties, so seek out the proper immigration offices if the stamping process is not carried out as you cross. The vast majority of border crossings, though, are trouble-free.

Ninety day **visa extensions** (costing US$100) can be obtained from the **Ministerio del Interior** (Extranjería) in Santiago or from any local *gobernación* (government) office. The procedure is often time-consuming and is officially supposed to include providing proof of funds and having an international record check (although these are sometimes missed out in smaller regional offices). To avoid hours of queuing and excessive punctiliousness when you are finally dealt with, you are advised to obtain extensions from small provincial offices rather than from Santiago; every provincial capital has a *gobernación*. If you must get the extension in Santiago, arrive at **Extranjería** before 7.30 am and consider bringing lunch. If you wish to stay longer than 180 days as a tourist, it is easier to make a short trip into Argentina, or Peru if near Arica, and return with a new tourist card, rather than to apply for a residency visa; however, if you do this once too often officials may become difficult. Usually, after nine months or so of obvious one-day trips to Argentina, you will be given a final warning to get a residency visa within the next 90 days or leave.

for nationals of Mexico (US$15), Australia (US$34), Canada (US$55) and the USA (US$100); however, in practice, this tax is only charged at airports and the tax is valid for the lifetime of the passport.

Finally, on a general note, Chilean officials are very document-minded, but also often exceptionally hospitable and helpful. In remote areas, you should register your documents with the *carabineros* (police), not only as a matter of courtesy, but also because the local police are usually a mine of information about local conditions and may be able to help you find accommodation and transport. If staying for a while, it is also worth registering at your embassy or consulate. Then, if your passport is stolen, the process of replacing it is simplified and speeded up. Keeping photocopies of essential documents, including your flight ticket, and some additional passport-sized photographs, is recommended; you should always carry a photocopy of your passport on your person.

Chilean embassies and consulates

For the latest information, see
www.minrel.cl/pages/misiones/index.html

Argentina, *Tagle 2762, Buenos Aires 1425, T54-11-48027020, F54-11-48045927, data@embajadadechile.com.ar* Also consulates up and down the country.
Australia, *10 Culgoa Circuit, O'Malley Act 2606, PO Box 69, Canberra, T61-6-62862430, F61-6-62861289, chilemb@embachile australia.com* Also in Melbourne and Sydney.
Austria, *Lugeck 1/3/10, Vienna A-1010, T43-1-5129208, F43-1-512920833, echileat1@chello.at*
Belgium, *40 Rue Montoyer, 1000 Brussels, T32-2-2801620, F32-2-2801481, embachilebelgica@skynet.be*
Bolivia, *Av Hernando Siles 5873, Esq. Calle 13, Sector Obrajes, La Paz, T279-1203, F2126491, cgchilp@ceibo.entelnet.bo*
Brazil, *Ses-Avda Des Nacoes, q.803, Lote 11, CEP 70.407-900, Brasília, T55-61-3225781, F55-61-3222966, embchile@embchile.org.br*
Canada, *50 O'Connor Street, Suite 1413, Ottawa, Ontario K1P 6L2, T1-613-2354402, F1-613-2351176, echileca@chile.caglobalx.net* Also in Montreal, Toronto and Vancouver.
Colombia, *Calle 100 Nro 11 B-44, Santa Fe de Bogotá, T57-1-2147990, F57-1-6193863, embajadadechile@colomsat.net.co*
Croatia, *Smiciklasova 23/2, 10.000, Zagreb, T (385-1) 4611958, F (385-1) 4610328, embajada@echile.hr*
Czech Republic, *U Vorliku 623/4, 16000, Prague 6, T (420-2) 24315064, F (420-2) 24316069, echilecz@mbox.vol.cz*

Denmark, *Kastelsvej 15, III 2100, Copenhagen, T45-35261535, F45-31384201, embassy@chiledk.dk*
Ecuador, *Juan Pablo Sanz 3617 y Amazonas, 4 Piso, Edificio Xerox, Piso 3, Quito, T593-2-2256947, F593-2-2258348, conchile@punto.net.ec*
El Salvador, *Pasaje Bellavista 121, 9 Calle Poniente, Colonia Escalón, T503-2634285, F503-2634308, embachile@embachile.org.com*
Finland, *Erottajankatu 11, 2nd Floor -0130 Helsinki, T358-9-611699, F358-9-611399, echilefi@kolombus.fi*
France, *64 Bd de la Tour Maubourg, 75007 Paris, T33-1-47054661, F33-1-45511627, cgparifr@aol.com*
Germany, *Mohrenstrasse 4263, 10117 Berlin, T49-30-7262035, F49-30-726203-603, embachilealemania@echileberlin.de* Also consulates in Bonn, Frankfurt, Munich.
Greece, *Vassilisis Sofias 25, 2º Piso, 10674 Athens, T30-1-7252574, F30-1-7252536, embachilegr@ath.forthnet.gr*
Ireland, *44 Wellington Road, Ballsbridge, Dublin 4, T (353-1) 6675094 F (353-1) 6675156, embachileirlanda@eircom.net*
Israel, *Beit Sharbat, 8 Piso, kaufman 4 st., Tel Aviv, T972-3-5102750, F972-3-5100102, consulad@inter.net.il*
Italy, *Via Po No 23, 00198 Roma, T39-6-8841449, F39-6-8412348, cnromait@flashnet.it*
Japan, *Nihon Seimei Akabanebashi Bldg 8F, 3-1-14 Shiba, Minato-ku, Tokyo 105-0014, T81-3-34527561, F81-3-34524457, consulado@chile.or.jp*
Mexico, *Andres Bello 10, Edificio Forum, Piso 18, Colonia Polanco, CP11560, Delegación Miguel Hidalgo, Mexico DF, T52-5-2809681,*

F52-5-2809703, echilmex@prodigy.net.mx
Also a consulate in Cancún.
Netherlands, *Mauritskade 51, 2514 HG, The Hague, T31-70-3123640, F31-70-3616227, echilenl@echilenl* Also in Amsterdam.
New Zealand, *19 Bolton Street, Wellington, T64-4-4716270, F64-4-4725324, echile@embchile.co.nz*
Norway, *Meltzers Gate 5, 0244 Oslo, T47-22445496, F47-22442421, embassy@chile.no*
Paraguay, *Capital Emilio Nudelman 351, Esquina Campos Cervera, Asuncion, T595-21-662 756, F595-21-662755, echilepy@consexion.com.py*
Peru, *Avda Javier Prado Oeste 790, San Isidro, Lima, T51-1-6112200, F51-1-6112224, congechilelima@embachileperu.com.pe*
Portugal, *Avda Miguel Bombarda 5-1000, Lisbon, T351-1-3148054, F351-1-3150909, echile.pt@mail.telepac.pt*
South Africa, *West Quay Building, Block 1, 1st Floor, West Quay Road, Waterfront, Cape Town, 8001 – (PO Box 50668, Waterfront 8002), T(27-021)-4212344, F(27-021)4253034,*

chilecpt@iafrica.com
Spain, *Rafel Calvo 18–5° D, 28010 Madrid, T34-91-3190763, F34-1-3193278 cgmadres@interbrook.net*
Sweden *Vasagatan No 36, 3 Piso, Stockholm 111 20, T(46-8)53480030, F(46-8) 4060355, info@sthlmconsulado.com*
Switzerland, *Eigerplatz 5, 12 Piso, 3007 Berne, T41-31-3717050, F41-31-3710748, consuladoberna@embachile.ch*
UK, *12 Devonshire Street, London, W1N 2DS, T44-207-5801023, F44-207-3234294., cglonduk@congechileuk.demon.co.uk*
Uruguay, *Calle Andes 1365, Piso 1, Montevideo, T598-2-9082223/9082616, F598-2-9021649, cgideouy@netgate.com.uy*
USA, *1732 Massachusetts Ave NW, Washington DC 20036, T1202-7851746, F1202-8875579, embassy@embassyofchile.org* Also consulates across the Union.
Venezuela, *Av Venezuela, Edifcio Venezuela, Piso 3, Oficina 31, El Rosal, Caracas, T58-2-9531485, F58-2-9531501, congechiccs@cantv.net*

Customs, duty free and export allowances

The following may be brought into Chile duty free: 500 cigarettes or 100 cigars or 500 g of tobacco, plus three bottles of liquor, and all articles for personal use, including vehicles, radios, portable tape recorders, cameras, personal computers, and similar items. Unlike its neighbouring countries, Chile's agricultural sector is free of many diseases, and so fruit, vegetables, meat, flowers and milk products may not be imported; these will be confiscated at all borders, where there are thorough searches. This applies even to those who have had to travel through Argentina in the far south to get from one part of Chile to another. There are also internal customs checks for all travellers going south from Región I. This is mainly to inspect for duty-free goods from Iquique but fruit, vegetables, meat, flowers and milk products will also be confiscated.

Vaccinations

Before you travel make sure the medical insurance you take out is adequate. Have a check-up with your doctor, if necessary, and arrange your immunisations well in advance. Try ringing a specialist travel clinic if your own doctor is unfamiliar with health in the region. No vaccinations are demanded by immigration officials in Chile, but you would do well to be protected by vaccination against typhoid, polio, hepatitis A and B, and tetanus; children should, of course, also be up-to-date with any immunisation programmes in their country of origin. It is also advisable to know your blood group. There is no malaria in Chile. ▶▶ *For further information, see Health, page 65.*

What to take → *Take twice as much money as you think you might need.*

Everybody has their own list but here are a few suggestions to help you pack for your trip to Chile. As far as clothing is concerned, be prepared for the desert heat and mountain snow. You'll need fully waterproof clothing (essential for the south at any time of year), very warm clothes for the northern highlands and the far south, light clothing for the summer, plus a sun hat, a pair of strong shoes/boots and a pair of sandals (outside Santiago size 10½/44 is very hard to find!). A sarong is very useful as it can be used as a skirt, curtain, bedsheet or a towel.

Other items that you might want to take (especially budget travellers) include air cushions for slatted seats, inflatable travel pillow for neck support, a small first-aid kit and handbook, earplugs and airline-type eye mask to help you sleep in noisy and poorly curtained hotel rooms, a sheet sleeping-bag and pillow-case, a clothes line, a nailbrush (useful for scrubbing dirt off clothes as well as off oneself), a universal plug, a Swiss Army knife, an alarm clock or watch and a torch. If you use an electric shaver, take a rechargeable type. Remember not to throw away spent batteries containing mercury or cadmium; take them home to be disposed of, or recycled properly. There is no point in bringing extensive supplies of basic toiletries, as these are readily available; good clothes are also avilable in Chile, usually at prices which are half those in Europe or North America.

In addition to the useful medical provisions suggested on page 66, take pre-moistened wipes (such as Wet Ones) and toilet paper – cheap hotels and restaurants do not supply it.

Insurance

It is vital to take out fully comprehensive travel insurance (including medical insurance) for the duration of your stay overseas. Numerous companies offer travel insurance, including many high-street travel agents. As well as full medical insurance (including evacuation by air ambulance where necessary), it is important to check that you are covered for any special activities, as many policies exclude so-called dangerous sports (including, in some cases, trekking). Also, many policies have a limit of cover per item, so, if you are taking something valuable and want it fully insured, you may need to pay extra.

If you do have the misfortune to be robbed (or even just to lose something), you need to make a report to the police and get a police certificate within 24 hours in order to make a successful claim on your insurance. Note also that every policy will have an excess amount, which you will have to pay, and that this varies from policy to policy. There is no substitute for reading the small print of a policy before signing up to it.

Money

Currency and currency exchange
The unit is the peso, its sign is $. Notes are for 500 (being phased out of circulation as this book goes to press), 1,000, 2,000, 5,000, 10,000 and 20,000 pesos (this last almost never seen outside Santiago); coins come in denominations of 1, 5, 10, 50, 100 and 500 pesos. Inflation is low. Official exchange rates for many currencies are quoted in *La Tercera*, and the best rates are to be had in Santiago. Travellers to rural areas should carry supplies of 500 and 1,000-peso notes; higher denominations are difficult to change. In many cities and towns changing cash and/or travellers' cheques is simpler and quicker at *casas de cambio* than at banks, although exchange rates vary and are not necessarily better, so shop around.

ATMs
The easiest way to obtain cash in Chile is by using automatic telling machines (ATMs). These are situated at the major banks and often in other locations, especially in shopping malls, bus stations, at the larger supermarkets and at most Esso petrol

stations. You can choose to be guided through the transaction in English. ATMs operate under the sign **Redbanc**; both Cirrus (Mastercard) and Plus (Visa) are accepted for daily transactions of up to US$400. A full list of **Redbanc** machines in Chile is listed by town at www.redbanc.cl

Cash

Most major currencies can be readily exchanged in tourist centres, but rates for the US dollar remain much better than for any other currency. US dollars are widely accepted by banks, *casas de cambio* (exchange shops) and some hotels, but rarely if ever by shops and other establishments. Outside Santiago, currencies other than the US dollars are rarely accepted anywhere. Dollar bills are often scrutinized carefully and rejected if torn or marked in any way. Before changing any currency check whether any commission is charged. If crossing to Argentina take some low-value US dollar bills: the Argentine currency crisis means that the 'greenback' remains widely accepted.

Credit cards

Visa, Mastercard and Diners' Club are readily accepted (**Bancard**, the local card, is affiliated to both Mastercard and Visa), but American Express is less useful. Credit card use does not usually incur a commission or higher charge in Chile, but in parts of Argentina commission of 10% is often charged. In shops, identification is usually necessary to use credit cards; places accepting Visa and Mastercard usually display a 'Redcompra' sticker in the window. In case of loss or theft of your card make sure that you carry the phone numbers necessary to report this; make a photocopy of the numbers and keep them in a safe place. Some travellers have reported problems with their credit cards being frozen by their bank when a charge is incurred in a foreign country. To avoid this problem, notify your bank before departure that you will be making charges in Chile (and other countries, where applicable). To avoid charges from your bank, top up your credit card account with sufficient cash before departure. If you will need to make very expensive one-off purchases, you may want to specify that your daily spending limit should not be applied to the amount by which your account is in credit, although this will prove dangerous if your card is stolen.

Travellers' cheques

Exchanging travellers' cheques is possible in most large cities, although the rate will be about 2% lower than for cash. In Santiago, **American Express Bank**, Andres Bello 2711, Piso 9, will change AmEx travellers' cheques to dollars without commission. However, it is generally not advisable to change cash or travellers' cheques in banks as the rate is much worse.

Transferring money

Before leaving your home country, find out which Chilean bank is correspondent to your own bank. Then, when you need funds, telex your own bank and ask them to telex the money to the local bank (confirming by fax). Be sure to provide the exact details of the routing number of the receiving bank. Funds can be received within 48 banking hours. Otherwise, money can be sent within minutes through **Western Union** (Santiago number: T02-6968807); if collecting money in a city with more than one Western Union agent, you can go to any one of them to receive the money.

Cost of living

The minimum wage in Chile is approximately US$150 per month, while the wage for relatively senior office workers may be around US$500 per month. This is low considering the general cost of living in the country. The cost of accommodation or rent is higher in Santiago than elsewhere – around US$150 per month for a basic two-room unfurnished flat as compared to half that in the provinces. Many office workers eat out for lunch and basic meals can usually be had for US$1.50 or US$2. City bus fares are US$0.50 in Santiago, less in the provinces. Someone living in Santiago and earning a reasonable salary (by Chilean standards) will find that they have little spare change at the end of the month and that holidays and weekends away are a definite luxury.

Cost of travelling

Prices for food and other consumables tend to rise in proportion to the distance from Santiago (being highest in Arica and Punta Arenas), although accommodation is cheaper outside the capital. In Santiago itself, Las Condes and Providencia are much more expensive than the rest of the city.

Chile is more expensive than much of South America , and you should budget on a minimum of US$200 per week per person for basic accommodation, food, overland transport and an occasional tour. Cheap accommodation in Santiago costs over US$6 per person, while north and south of the capital *alojamiento* in private houses (bed, breakfast and often use of the kitchen) costs US$6-10 per person (bargaining is possible off-season). *Colaciones* can be had for about US$2-3 in most places. Bus fares are reasonable (around US$2.50 per 100 km). Southern Chile is more expensive from 15 December to 28 February. With a budget of US$400 a week, you will be able to stay in nice hotels, eat in smart restaurants and not stint yourself on excursions and nightlife.

Getting there

Air

On long-haul flights, airlines now generally allow two pieces of luggage neither of which may weigh more than 32 kilogrammes; but these limits are often not strictly enforced when it is known that the plane is not going to be full. If you know you are over the limit, arrive early. Weight limits for internal flights are usually 30 kilogrammes for first class and 20 kilogrammes for economy class.

Flights from the UK

Flights from the UK take 16 to 20 hours, including a change of plane. It is impossible to fly directly to Santiago from London, so connections have to be made on one of the following routes: **Aerolineas Argentinas**, www.aerolineas.com.ar, via Buenos Aires, three per week; **Air France**, www.airfrance.com, via Paris, three per week; **British Airways**, www.british-airways.com, connecting through **LanChile** in Buenos Aires, daily; **Iberia**, www.iberia.com, via Madrid, daily; **LanChile**, www.lanchile.com, via Madrid, daily; **Lufthansa**, www.lufthansa.com, via Frankfurt, 6 per wee; **Varig**, www.varig.com.br, via Rio or São Paolo, daily.

Alternatively, there are daily connecting flights on one of the American carriers via New York or Miami (see below).

Flights from North America

Flights from Miami to Santiago take nine hours and are operated by **American Airlines**, www.aa.com, direct from Miami, daily; **LanChile** direct from Miami, two per day; **LanPeru**, www.lanperu.com, from Miami via Lima.

LanChile also has two daily flights to Santiago from New York, 12 hrs, and from Los Angeles (via Mexico City and Lima) with onward connections to Boston, Chicago, Dallas, San Francisco and Washington. **American Airlines** flies from Dallas Fort Worth to Santiago three times a week, while **Delta**, www.delta.com, connects daily through Atlanta to Santiago. Additional flights from Los Angeles and Miami to Santiago are operated by **Copa** (via Panama City), www.copaair.com; **Lacsa** (via Mexico City, San José and Lima, http://centralamerica.com/cr/lacsa/lacsa.html, and **Mexicana** (via Mexico City and Bogotá), www.mexicana.com).

From Canada, **LanChile** offers connections with sister airlines from Vancouver to Los Angeles and thence to Santiago, or from Toronto to New York and on to Santiago.

Flights fom Australia and New Zealand

LanChile flies once or twice a week, depending on season, from Tahiti (connections to Japan, Australia and New Zealand) to Santiago, with a stop over at Easter Island. **Air New Zealand**, www.airnz.co.nz, and **LanChile** have a code-sharing agreement on weekly flights between Auckland, Sydney and Santiago. For excursion fares between Australia/New Zealand and Chile, the stopovers at Easter Island now carry a surcharge of about US$125. There are also several weekly flights from Auckland to Santiago via Buenos Aires with **Aerolineas Argentinas**.

Flights from the rest of Europe

There are direct flights from many European destinations to Santiago. From Paris with **Air France** (three per week); from Madrid with **Iberia** and **LanChile** (each daily); from Frankfurt with **Lufthansa** (six per week) and **LanChile** (daily); from Lisbon with **Varig** via Rio or São Paolo (daily); from Rome with **Varig** via São Paolo.

Flights from South Africa

From South Africa it is possible to connect to Santiago through Rio de Janeiro or São Paolo on **South African Airways** (twice weekly from Johannesburg). **Varig** also has flights from some African destinations connecting to Santiago through São Paolo, including **Luanda** (Angola), **Maputo** (Mozambique) and **Sal** (Cape Verde).

Flights from other Latin America countries

There are about about 75 flights per week to Santiago from Buenos Aires (Argentina), operated by **LanChile, Aerolíneas Argentinas, Air France, American** or **Avianca** (many depart at the same time, check carefully). There are also two daily flights by **LanChile** from Córdoba, Mendoza and Rosario. **LanChile** and **Pluna** run eight weekly flights from Montevideo (Uruguay). **Lapsa** has four flights a week from Asunción (Paraguay). Flights from Rio de Janeiro (Brazil) are run by **Iberia** (four weekly), **LanChile** (two daily), or **Varig** (three daily). There are also services from São Paulo by **LanChile** (three non-stop daily), **Varig** (four daily). Flights from La Paz (Bolivia) are offered by **Lloyd Aéreo Bolivia**no (LAB; five weekly) and daily with **LanChile**. LAB also has flights from Cochabamba and Santa Cruz; LanChile three a week from Santa Cruz. There are 23 flights per week from Lima (Peru) by **LanPeru, Lacsa, United** and **LanChile**. (**LanChile** also flies daily from Arequipa, Cusco, Juliaca and Puerto Madlonado through its sister airline **LanPeru**.) From Ecuador, **LanChile, Tame** and **Saeta** fly non-stop from Guayaquil (Saeta and Tame's flights start in Quito). **Avianca, Mexicana** and **LanChile** have nine weekly services between them from Bogotá (Colombia). **LanChile** and **Viasa** both have two weekly flights each from Caracas (Venezuela). There are also two weekly flights from Havana (Cuba) with **LanChile** and **Cubana**; six flights weekly from Mexico City with **Mexicana** and **LanChile** and two weekly from Cancún with **LanChile**.

Flights to other Chilean destinations

There are flights to Arica and Iquique from La Paz and Santa Cruz by **LAB** and **LanChile,** and to Antofagasta from Santa Cruz with **LanChile**. **TAM** may have direct flights connecting Iquique to Asunción in Paraguay (these have been discontinued, but may be reinstated). **LanChile** flies to Santiago from Port Stanley on the Falkland

Prices and discounts

The very busy seasons are 7 December to 15 January and 10 July to 10 September. If you intend travelling during those times, book as far ahead as possible. Between February to May and September to November special offers may be available. Fares vary from airline to airline, destination to destination and according to time of year. In the low season it may be possible to get a return flight from London to Santiago for as little as £520 (plus over £50 airport departure taxes), but in the high season this may rise to £750 return. Prices are comparable for flights from the US, but from Australia and New Zealand they may rise to £1000 return or more. Most airlines offer discounted fares of one sort or another on scheduled flights. These are not offered by the airlines direct to the public, but through agencies who specialize in this type of fare. If you buy discounted air tickets always check the reservation with the airline concerned to make sure the flight still exists. Other fares fall into three groups and are all on scheduled services.

Excursion (return) fares Restricted validity eg seven to 90 days. Most carriers have introduced flexibility into these tickets, permitting a change of dates on payment of a fee.

Yearly fares May be bought on a return basis. Some airlines require a specified return date, changeable upon payment of a fee. If staying for a whole year, you may find that the airline is not yet booking return flights that far ahead; in that case it may be possible to secure one free change of date on your ticket, even if buying through a discount operator. To leave the return completely open is possible for an extra fee. You must fix the route (some of the cheapest flexible fares now have six months' validity). If you foresee returning home at a busy time, such as Christmas or August, a booking is advisable on any type of open return ticket.

Student (or under 26) fares Do not assume that student tickets are the cheapest; though they are often very flexible, they are usually more expensive than excursion or yearly fares. Some airlines are flexible on the age limit, others strict.

Round-the-world fares Many airlines now offer code-sharing round-the-world fares. Although the cheapest ones tend to miss out South America, the Buenos Aires-Wellington and Santiago-Tahiti-Sydney flights mean that, for around £1200, it is possible to include Chile on a round-the-world trip.

Open jaw fares For people intending to travel a linear route, arriving and departing from different airports. Open-jaws are available as student, yearly or excursion fares. Many require a change of plane at an intermediate point, and a stopover may be permitted, or even obligatory, depending on schedules. Simply because a flight stops at a given airport does not mean you can break your journey there; the airline must have traffic rights to pick up or set down passengers between points A and B before it will be permitted. This is where dealing with a specialized agency (like **Journey Latin America**) will really pay dividends. On multi-stop itineraries, the specialized agencies can often save clients hundreds of pounds.

Flight agents

In the UK

Just the Ticket, *Level 2, 28 Margaret Street, London W1W 8RZ, T020-7291 8111, www.justtheticket.co.uk* All-purpose cheap ticket agency, often with excellent deals.
STA Travel, *Priory House, 6 Wrights Lane,* *London W8 6TA, T08701-600599/ T0161-8307413 (northern telesales).*

Trailfinders, *194 Kensington High Street, London W8 7RG, T020-7938 3939.* Sometimes has good deals to Latin America, especially at peak times. Also at *48 Earl's Court Road, London, W8 6EJ, T020-7938 3366.*

Also check out websites such as www.cheapflights.com; www.dialaflight.com; www.ebookers.com; www.flynow.com; and www.lastminute.com

Online agents include www.expedia.com; www.priceline.com; www.travelocity.com; www.cheaptickets.com, and www.etn.nl/discount.htm

In North America
Air Brokers International, *323 Geary Street, Suite 411, San Francisco, CA 94102, T01-800-883273, www.airbrokers.com* Specialist on RTW and Circle Pacific tickets.
Airtech, *588 Broadway, Suite 204, New York, NY 10012, T212-219.7000, www.airtech.com*
Exito Travel, *1212 Broadway Suite 910, Oakland CA 94618, T1-800-6554053(toll-free), www.exitotravel.com*
Ladatco Tours, *3006 Aviation Ave, Suite 4C, Coconut Grove, FL33133 T1800-327-6162.*
STA Travel, *10 Downing St, New York, NY 10014, T(toll-free)1-800-777-0112.*
Travel CUTS, *234 College Street, Toronto, ON M5T 1P7, T(toll-free)1-866-246 9762, www.travelcuts.com* Also in many other Canadian cities.

In Australia and New Zealand
Anywhere Travel, *345 Anzac Parade, Kingsford, Sydney, T02-96630411.*
Budget Travel, *600 Hurtsmere Road, Takapuna, Box 336620, Auckland, T09-366-4665.*
Destinations Unlimited, *13 Clyde Road, PO Box 35-573, Browns Bay, T09-4785042, F09-479-7968.*
Flight Centre, *82 Elizabeth Street, Sydney, T02-92353522, www.flightcentre.com.au* Also at *350 Queen Street, Auckland, T09-3584310* and in many other antipodean cities.
STA Travel,*702 Harris St, Ultimo, Sydney T1300-360960, www.statravel.com.au* Also in other major cities and towns.
Travel.com.au, *80 Clarence Street, Sydney, T02-92901500, www.travel.com.au*

Road and rail

There are good **road** connections between Chile and Argentina, from Santiago to Mendoza, and from Osorno and Puerto Montt to Bariloche; there is also a reasonable road from Arica to La Paz in Bolivia, and a good road from Arica to Tacna in Peru. All of these routes are served by buses. Less good road connections north and south of Santiago are described in the relevant chapter of the book, along with details of border crossings. Note that any of the passes across the Andes to Argentina can be blocked by snow from April onwards (including the main Mendoza crossing, where travellers are occasionally stranded at the border posts). Travelling to or from Argentina anywhere north of Mendoza is likely to be an adventure you will not forget in a hurry. Chile only international **rail** link is from Calama to Uyuni and Oruro in Bolivia; for further details see page 223.

Sea

Enquiries regarding sea passages to Chile should be made through agencies in your own country. In the UK, try **Strand Voyages,** Charing Cross Shopping Concourse, The Strand, London WC2N 4HZ, T020-7836 6363, or **The Cruise People**, 88 York Street, W1H 1DP, T020-7723 2450 (reservations T0800-526313). In the USA contact **Freighter World Cruises**, 180 South Lake Ave, Pasadena, CA 91101, T818-4493106, www.freighterworld.com

✦ Touching down

Business hours Banks: Mon-Fri
0900-1400. Government offices:
Mon-Fri 1000-1230 (the public is
admitted for a few hours only).
Businesses: Mon-Fri 0830-1230,
1400-1800. Shops (Santiago):
Mon-Fri 1030-1930, Sat 0930-1330.
International dialling code +56

Official time GMT minus 4 hours;
minus 3 hours in summer. Clocks
change from mid-September or
October to early March.
Voltage 220 volts AC, 50 cycles.
Weights & measures The metric
system is obligatory but the quintal
of 46 kilos (101.4 lb) is used.

Touching down

Airport information

Aeropuerto Arturo Merino Benitez ① *26 km northwest of Santiago at Pudahue,
international terminal information To2-6901900/6018758, flight information
To2-6763149/6763297,* handles both international and domestic flights, and is the
only airport in Chile with intercontinental connections. It is a modern, safe and
efficient terminal, recently voted the best airport in Latin America from a sample of
70,000 international businessmen. Domestic and international flights leave from
different sections of the same terminal. Procedures at customs (*aduana*) are quick
and efficient. Facilities include banks (with ATMs), fast food outlets, a Sernatur tourist
information office which offers an accommodation booking service, a *casa de cambio*
for changing money near the baggage reclaim area and several car hire offices. Left
luggage is US$2.50 per item per day (much more expensive than in the city centre)
and items can be left for a maximum of 60 days. Outside customs there are kiosks for
bus and taxi companies serving Santiago, as well as car hire companies; you are
likely to be approached by people offering taxi and bus services as you emerge from
the customs area. ▶▶ *For further details, see Ins and outs, page 78.*

Airport departure information

Check-in time for international flights is two hours before departure, one hour for
domestic flights. Some airlines will perform check-in at their offices in the city the
previous day, after which they require you to be at the airport just 45 minutes before
departure. Remember that you must reconfirm bookings on international flights 72
hours in advance. Airport **departure tax** is US$18 for international flights; US$8 for
domestic flights (credit cards not accepted). There is also a tourist tax of 2% on single
air fares and 1% on return fares beginning or ending in Chile, and a sales tax of 5% on
all transport within Chile. All these taxes will be included in the price of the ticket
when bought by the traveller.

Tourist information

The national secretariat of tourism, **Sernatur** ① *Head office: Av Providencia 1550
(Casilla 14082), Santiago, To2-2362420, Fo2-2518469,* has offices throughout the
country (addresses are given throughout this guide). Most tourist offices around the
country are run by **Sernatur** and can provide town maps, leaflets and other useful

information, otherwise contact the head office. **CONAF** (Corporación Nacional Forestal) ① *Presidente Bulnes 291, piso 1, Santiago, T/F02-697-2273*, manages national parks throughout Chile (see box page 64). CONAF's staff are dedicated and knowledgeable, and their offices in the parks themselves are usually extremely helpful. CONAF also publishes a number of leaflets and has documents and maps about the national park system that can be consulted or photocopied in its Santiago office; but these are not very useful for walking. For general information on travel in the region, consult the **Latin American Travel Advisor**, see page 24. **Ancient Forest International** ① *Box 1850, Redway, CA 95560, T/F707-3233015, USA, www.ancientforests.org*, can be contacted regarding Chilean forests. ▸▸ *For details of other useful organizations and their publications, see also page 555.*

Local customs and laws

Courtesy

Politeness – even a little ceremoniousness – is much appreciated in Chile. Men should always remove any headgear and say "permiso" when entering offices, and be prepared to shake hands; always say "Buenos días" (until midday) or "Buenas tardes" (in the afternoon and evening) and wait for a reply before proceeding further. Remember that the traveller from abroad has enjoyed greater advantages in life than most Chilean minor officials, and should be friendly and courteous in consequence. Never be impatient, and do not criticize situations in public: the officials may know more English than you think (especially when it comes to swearwords) and they can certainly interpret gestures and facial expressions. You should be aware that the stereotype of the corrupt Latin American official does not apply in Chile, where most officials are scrupulously honest.

Politeness should also be extended to street traders; saying "No, gracias" with a smile is better than an arrogant dismissal. Bargaining is not as commonplace in Chile as in some other South American countries, and very low offers will be seen as contemptuous, even in markets. Begging is rare outside Santiago. Whether you give money to beggars is a personal matter, but locals may provide an indication of whether people are begging out of genuine need. In Santiago, beggars get onto buses and sing or sell tiny religious calendar cards; Santiaguinos are often generous towards them. There are occasions where giving away food in a restaurant may be appropriate, but first inform yourself of local practice.

Tipping

In restaurants 10% is a good tip, but you should only leave about 100 pesos (US$0.15) in bars and *fuentes de soda*. A tip of US$0.50 per piece of luggage is appropriate for railway porters; airport porters now charge US$1. Cloakroom attendants should get about US$0.20. Taxi drivers are not tipped.

Clothing

Urban Chileans are very fashion conscious. You should dress reasonably smartly in the towns and cities as scruffiness will make things needlessly difficult. People tend to dress smartly at nightclubs in urban centres – Santiago, Viña del Mar, La Serena and Iquique being particularly swish. Away from the cities, though, and in areas where there are many foreign tourists, people are less concerned about such matters.

Prohibitions and getting out of trouble

There are several types of police operating in Chile: *carabineros* (green uniforms) handle all tasks except immigration; *Investigaciones* (in civilian dress) are the detectives, and deal with everything except traffic; while the *Policía Internacional*, a division of the *Investigaciones*, handle immigration.

⁑ How big is your footprint?

1 Where possible choose a destination, tour operator or hotel with a proven ethical and environmental commitment, and if in doubt ask.

2 Spend money on locally produced (rather than imported) goods and services and use common sense when bargaining – your few dollars saved may be a week's salary to others.

3 Consider staying in local, rather than foreign owned, accommodation – the economic benefits for host communities are far greater – and there are far greater opportunities to learn about local culture.

4 Use water and electricity carefully – travellers may receive preferential supply while the needs of local communities are overlooked.

5 Don't give money or sweets to children – it encourages begging – instead give to a recognized project, charity or school.

6 Learn about local etiquette and culture – consider local norms and behaviour – and dress appropriately for local cultures and situations.

7 Protect wildlife and other natural resources – don't buy souvenirs or goods made from wildlife unless they are clearly sustainably produced and are not protected under CITES legislation.

8 Always ask before taking photographs or videos of people.

If you get into trouble with the police, the worst thing that you can do is offer a bribe to get you out of trouble. Chilean police are very proud of their office, and will assume any attempt to bribe them is both an insult and an admission of guilt. Legal penalties for most offences are fairly similar to what you might expect in a western European or North American country, although be advised that the attitude towards possession of soft drugs, such as cannabis, is very strict. If you get into trouble, your first call should be to your consulate, which should be able to put you in touch with a lawyer who speaks your language.

Responsible tourism

Travel to the furthest corners of the globe is now commonplace and the mass movement of people for leisure and business is a major source of foreign exchange and economic development in Chile. Towns such as Puerto Natales, San Pedro de Atacama, Villarrica and Viña del Mar depend almost exclusively on tourism for their livelihoods, while every town south of Temuco is awash with people letting out private rooms in their homes.

The benefits of international travel are self-evident for both hosts and travellers: employment, increased understanding of different cultures, business and leisure opportunities. At the same time there is clearly a downside to the industry. Where visitor pressure is high and/or poorly regulated, adverse impacts to society and the natural environment may be apparent. This is as true in undeveloped and pristine areas (where culture and the natural environment are less 'prepared' for even small numbers of visitors) as in major resort destinations.

⁑ *Offset your flight's carbon emissions by paying to have the appropriate number of trees planted in sustainable forests through Future Forests www.futureforests.com*

The travel industry is growing rapidly and its impact is becoming increasingly apparent: air travel is clearly implicated in global warming and damage to the ozone

Essentials Touching down

layer, while resort location and construction can destroy natural habitats and restrict traditional rights and activities. Although these effects can seem remote and unrelated to an individual trip or holiday, a traveller's attitude and choices can make a big difference to his or her own impact on the region (see box page 41). And, collectively, travellers have a significant role in shaping a more responsible and sustainable industry.

Travel and tourism in a region can also have beneficial effects; many National Parks, for example, are part funded by receipts from visitors. Travellers can promote the patronage and protection of important heritage sites through their interest and contributions via entrance and performance fees. They can also support small-scale enterprises by staying in locally run hotels and hostels, eating in local restaurants and by purchasing local goods, supplies and arts and crafts.

In an attempt to promote awareness of responsible tourism, UK organizations such as **Green Globe** (T020-7930 8333, greenglobe@compuserve.com), the **Centre for Environmentally Sustainable Tourism** (CERT; T01268-795772) and **Tourism Concern** (T020-7753 3330, www.tourismconcern.org.uk) now offer advice on destinations and sites that have made certain commitments to conservation and sustainable development. Generally these are larger mainstream destinations and resorts, although efforts are being made to also provide information on smaller operations.

Ecotourism

Ecotourism has expanded astronomically in Chile over the past decade, and is probably the fastest growing sector of the travel industry today, providing access to a vast range of destinations and activities, from the Atacama to Tierra del Fuego. While the eco authenticity of some operators needs to be interpreted with care, there is clearly both a huge demand for this type of activity and also significant opportunities for travellers to support worthwhile conservation and social development initiatives. Organizations such as **Tourism Concern** (see above), **Planeta** (www.planeta.com), the **Eco-Tourism Society** (T001-802-447 2121, http://ecotourism.org) and **Conservation International** (T001-202-429 5660, www.ecotour.org) have begun to develop and/or promote ecotourism projects and their websites are an excellent source of information about initiatives throughout Chile. Additionally, **Earthwatch** (T01865-311601, www.earthwatch.org) and **Discovery International** (T020-7229 9881, www.discoveryinitiatives.com) offer opportunities to participate directly in scientific and development projects throughout the region.

Safety

While Chileans will delight in building up the prowess of Chilean thieves to nervous visitors, Chile is generally a safe country to visit. Police stations in rural areas very rarely have people in their one cell. Like all major cities, though, Santiago and Valparaíso do have crime problems. Avoid the *poblaciones* (shanty towns) of Santiago – especially Pudahuel and parts of the north (such as Conchali) – especially if you are travelling alone or have only recently arrived. The following suggestions are particularly applicable in central Santiago, in some of the hills of Valparaíso and in Coquimbo, which has a reputation for theft.

Keep valuables out of sight Cameras should be kept in bags when not in use, and expensive watches or jewellery should not be worn. It is best, if you can trust your hotel, to leave any valuables you don't need in the safe deposit there when sightseeing locally. Always keep an inventory of what you have deposited. If you lose valuables, always report to the police and note details of the report for insurance purposes.

Quake, rattle and roll

It is impossible to spend much time in Chile without becoming aware of the fragility of the land beneath your feet. Earth tremors and violent quakes are a part of everyday life, and raising the matter with Chilean friends tends to lead to quick changes of the subject. The most severe earthquake in recent decades occurred in 1960, causing devastation to the Lake District around Valdivia, see box page 338.

Quite apart from the terror of the earthquakes, tremors really are common- place. These are most often felt at night, owing to the fact that everything is quieter. If sleeping, your first feeling may be that someone is gently shaking your bed and interfering with your dream. The vibrations of crockery and swaying flowers should alert you that this is something more. Once the tremor has passed, dogs burst into frightened barks, thought to be because, owing to their more sensitive hearing, they can hear the creaks and groans of the earth below.

While it is likely that visitors passing through the region will experience nothing more sinister than tremors, they should be aware that a severe earthquake is expected in the Iquique/Arica region at some point in the next 10 to 15 years. There is no way of telling, at the beginning of a tremor, whether it will develop into a full-scale earthquake. If you are unfortunate enough to experience an earthquake, do not panic. Rushing outside into the street leaves you open to falling masonry and objects such as flower pots. In fact, the safest place to hide really is beneath the lintel of a doorway, as in the old wives' tale.

Keep all documents and money secure When travelling with all your gear hide your main cash supply in different places or under your clothes; you may wish to use extra pockets sewn inside shirts and trousers, pockets closed on the outside with a zip or safety pin, moneybelts (best worn under clothes, below the waist rather than around the neck), neck or leg pouches or elasticated support bandages for keeping money and cheques above the elbow or below the knee.

Try not to appear nervous Nervous behaviour is a clear sign to any thief that you are carrying valuables or that you are unsure where you're going. Walking confidently, but without excessive speed, is a sure way of showing that you are at home in a place – even if you are not.

Look out for tricks Petty thieves may employ tricks to distract your attention and separate you from your possessions. One common ruse in large city centres is 'the mustard trick': the victim is sprayed with mustard, ketchup or some other substance, apparently accidentally, and an accomplice offers sympathy and helps to clean your jacket, removing your wallet at the same time.

Don't fight back If you are attacked, remember your assailants may well be armed, so it is better to hand over your valuables rather than risk injury.

Finally, bear in mind that safety awareness is not just a matter of avoiding theft or violent attack. While Chile is no worse than any other South American country as far as sexually transmitted diseases are concerned, travellers should always practise safe sex (see page 70).

Getting around

Internal transport is usually straightforward. Most of Chile is linked by one road, the paved **Pan-American Highway** (or Panamericana), marked on maps as Ruta 5, which runs from the Peruvian frontier south to Puerto Montt and the island of Chiloé. However, some of the most popular destinations in Chile lie to the south of Puerto Montt, and travelling to this part of the country requires careful planning. Though much of this area can be reached by the **Carretera Austral**, a gravel road marked on maps as Ruta 7, bus services here are far less reliable than elsewhere in the country. Furthermore, the Carretera Austral is punctuated by three ferry crossings, with a further crossing at Villa O'Higgins for those on the direct overland route from the Carretera to the far south; the latter is only available in the summer. Alternatives are to travel by sea and air from Puerto Montt. Ferries provide vital links in this region, notably from Chiloé to both Puerto Montt and Chaitén for the Carretera Austral; from Puerto Montt to Puerto Chacabuco (and Coyhaique); and from Puerto Montt to Puerto Natales in the far south.

Major domestic air routes

✷ *For the best views of the Andes sit on the left when flying south and on the right when flying north.*

Air → *Confirm domestic flights at least 24 hrs before departure.*

Travellers with very limited time to spare should consider flying. Air travel can offer fantastic views stretching from the Andes to the sea, but the disadvantage, of course, is that it reduces your knowledge of the bits in between. **LanChile** (www.lanchile.cl) flies between Santiago and major cities under the banner **Lan Express**. The budget Peruvian airline **Aerocontinente** used to provide much cheaper fares than **LanChile**, but in July 2001 its planes were impounded and its executives arrested on charges of drug running and money laundering. A year later the company was declared bankrupt, and it now operates only international flights to Lima and Miami. A new budget operator called **Sky** (www.skyairline.cl) has opened up, but as yet it serves only a few destinations. Details of useful flights are given throughout the guide.

Check with the airlines for matrimonial, student and other discounts. Both **LanChile** and **Ladeco** sell cut-price tickets with up to 50% off either as part of special promotions or to standby passengers, though the availability of standby fares is often limited. Passengers travelling to Chile with **LanChile** can obtain reductions on subsequent internal flights. Note that with some fares it may be

cheaper to fly long distance than take a *salón cama* bus, and also that flight times
may be changed without warning; always double check the time of your flight when
reconfirming. You should book several months in advance for flights to Easter Island
in January and February; if flying from Australia or New Zealand, note that some
airlines offer a free stopover at Easter Island (see also page 508).

Visit Chile Airpass

LanChile sells a **Visit Chile Airpass** which can be used on all **LanChile** routes within Chile
with the exception of Easter Island. The airpass can only be purchased abroad at the
same time as a transatlantic ticket to Chile and is valid for one month after the first flight
coupon has been used. If bought with a **LanChile** transatlantic flight the airpass costs
US$250 for three coupons, plus US$50 per extra coupon up to six. If bought with a
transatlantic flight with another carrier the pass costs US$350 for three coupons plus
US$80 for each additional coupon up to six. Domestic air taxes (US$8) must be paid in
addition for each flight. Reservations should be made well in advance since many flights
are fully booked. Flight dates can be altered without penalty, but route changes incur a
penalty of US$30 per change. A refund (minus 10%) can be obtained prior to travel.

Road

About half of the 79,593 km of roads in Chile can be used all year round, though a
large proportion is unimproved and only about 11,145 km are paved. Many other
roads are described as *ripio*, meaning the surface is unmade gravel and/or stones;
speed limits on these roads are usually slower. The region round the capital and the
Central Valley have the best road connections. The main road is the Pan-American
Highway (Ruta 5; see also page 44), which is now dual carriageway from La Serena to
Puerto Montt. This is a toll road; the toll includes towing to the next city and free
ambulance in case of an accident. A paved coastal route running the length of Chile is
under construction, and should be ready by 2007.

Bus

Bus services in Chile are frequent, and on the whole, good. Buses tend to be
punctual, arriving and leaving when they say they will. Apart from at holiday times,
there is little problem getting a seat on a long-distance bus and there is no need to
reserve far in advance out of season. Services are categorised as *salón-cama*
meaning 25 seats, *semi-cama* meaning 34 seats and *salón-ejecutivo* meaning 44
seats. *Salón-cama* services run between main cities and stops are infrequent; **TurBus**
and **Pullman Bus** are highly recommended operators.

Since there is lots of competition between bus companies, you may be able to
bargain for a lower fare, particularly just before departure, out of season. Prices are
highest between December and March, while fares from
Santiago double during the Independence celebrations in
September. Students and holders of Hostelling International
cards may get discounts, which vary in amount, but these are not
usually available in high season; discounts are also often
available for return journeys. Most bus companies will carry bicycles, but may ask for
payment; on **TurBus** payment is mandatory.

> **Avoid back seats near the toilet due to the smell and the disruption of passing passengers.**

The best way of sending luggage around Chile is by "Encomienda": your package
is taken by bus from terminal to terminal and stored for up to one month at the
destination (**TurBus** can deliver to a specified address). This means you can
Encomienda bags when you don't need them, and pick them up when you do, which
is great if you only need camping or cold weather gear for, say, Torres del Paine .

⁉ Bus fares in Chile

The following is intended to provide an idea of single bus fares from
Santiago. Fares given are for standard services; other services such as *salón
cama* and *semi cama* are more expensive. Lower fares than those shown are
often available, especially at the last minute, but much higher fares are
charged in summer (January-February) and during the Independence
celebrations in September. Prices quoted are in US dollars.

Northbound		Southbound	
La Serena	10-15	Talca	5-7
Copiapó	17-20	Temuco	9-13
Antofagasta	32-35	Valdivia	10-16
Iquique	45-47	Puerto Montt	12-18
Arica	45-50	Ancud	20-25
		Castro	21-29

Driving

Documents Always carry your passport and driving licence. According to the
Chilean **Ley de Tránsito**, a national driver's licence is acceptable, but *carabineros*
may demand an international driver's licence (in the north especially). To avoid
problems, obtain one before leaving home. Car drivers require a Chilean *Relaciones
de pasajeros* document, available at borders, and the original registration document
of their vehicle. Motorcyclists require the bike registration document and are also
advised to carry an international *carnet de passages* (see below). In the case of a car
registered in someone else's name, carry a notarized letter of authorization.

Taking a vehicle into Chile Officially, if you wish to take a vehicle into South
America you must have one of the following three documents, although in practice,
none is required: an *carnet de passages* issued by the **Fedération Internationale de
l'Automobile** (FIA – Paris); a *carnet de passages* issued by the **Alliance Internationale
de Tourisme** (AIT-Geneva), or the *Libreta de Pasos por Aduana* issued by the
Féderación Interamericana de Touring y Automóvil Clubs (FITAC). The *carnet de
passages* is available only in the country where the vehicle is registered. In the UK it
can be obtained from the **RAC** and the **AA**. In the USA the **AAA** seems not to issue the
carnet, although the organization's headquarters in Washington DC may be able to
give advice. It is, however, available from the **Canadian Automobile Association**
ⓘ *1775 Courtwood Crescent, Ottawa, K2C 3JZ, T613-2267631, F2257383*, from whom
full details may be obtained.

Buying a vehicle in Chile It is possible to buy a vehicle through an agent in Chile,
although prices tend to be higher and you will be responsible for repairs, maintenance
and road taxes. Buying through an agent will usually involve a 'buy-back' guarantee.
Reports of the efficiency of companies offering this service are mixed. All Chilean cars
have to undergo an annual technical revision ('*revision técnica*') to ensure
road-worthiness; the month when this is due will be shown on a sticker on the
windscreen. If your vehicle fails the technical revision you are given one month to carry
out repairs. Technical revisions can be carried out in any of the larger cities; it is worth
enquiring locally about the best centres as standards vary. If hiring a car, or buying
through an agent with buy-back arrangements, check when its technical revision is due
and who is responsible for it. In most cases it will be the hire company. Note also that all
Chilean car taxes are payable in March each year; again, check who is responsible for
paying tax. Failure to keep the tax up to date can lead to trouble with the police.

Car hire Car hire is an increasingly popular way of travelling around Chile,
although it tends to reduce your contact with Chileans. Many agencies, both local and international, operate in the country. Note that the **Automóvil Club de Chile** (see below) has a car-hire agency (with discounts for members or affiliates), although the office may not be at the same place as the Club's regional delegation. Vehicles may be rented by the day, the week or the month, with or without unlimited mileage. Rates quoted should include insurance and 18% VAT, but always check first. A small car, with unlimited mileage costs about US$500 a week in high season, a pick-up much more, but shop around for a deal, as there is plenty of competition. In some areas rates are much lower off-season, while at peak holiday times, eg for the Independence celebrations, car hire is very difficult. If intending to leave the country in a hired car, you must obtain an authorization from the hire company, otherwise you will be turned back at the frontier. When leaving Chile this is exchanged for a quadruple form, one part of which is surrendered at each border control. If you plan to leave more than once you will need to photocopy the authorization.

Insurance This is obligatory and can be bought at borders. It is very expensive and increasingly difficult to insure against accident, damage or theft. If the car/motorbike is stolen or written off you will be required to pay very high import duty on its value. Get the legal minimum cover, not expensive, as soon as you can, because if you should be involved in an accident and are uninsured, your vehicle could be confiscated. If anyone is hurt, do not pick them up (you may become liable). Seek assistance from the nearest police station or hospital if you are able to do so.

Information and maps Members of foreign motoring organizations may join the **Automóvil Club de Chile** ① *Av Andres Bello 1863, Santiago, T02-431-1000, acchinfo@automovilclub.cl, US$58 for 3 mths,* and obtain hotel discounts. Road maps are available at the Santiago headquarters, or from other regional offices. Several individual maps provide greater detail than the Club's road atlas. **Turistel** maps mark police posts; make sure you are not speeding when you pass them, as *carabineros* are strict about speed limits. For details of other maps, see page 556.

Fuel Petrol (sold in litres) costs about US$0.60 per litre, but becomes more expensive the further north and further south you go. Unleaded fuel, 93 octane, is available at many service stations in the major cities, but unleaded 95 and 97 octane are less common. Diesel fuel is widely available and much cheaper. All service stations usually accept credit cards, except perhaps those in isolated rural areas, and the standard of facilities is generally good. When driving in the south (on the Carretera Austral particularly), and in the northern desert, always top up your fuel tank and carry spare fuel in a steel container; a siphon pipe is also essential for those places where fuel is sold out of the drum. Car hire companies may not have fuel cans and they are not obtainable from service stations, although some supermarkets may stock them.

Preparing a car This is largely a matter of common sense: obviously any part that is not in first-class condition should be replaced. Tyres need to be hard-wearing (avoid steel belt) and to have tubes, since air plugs are hard to find. Always take spare tubes, an extra spare tyre, spare plugs, fanbelts, radiator hoses and headlamp bulbs. Driving a *ripio* road usually requires a four-wheel-drive vehicle, and the number of *ripio* roads outside the main cities means that normal street cars are of limited use in Chile, although they should be able to cope with roads designated as *buen ripio*. If you intend to drive on *ripio* roads, especially the Carretera Austral, fit a good windscreen protector. It is also wise to carry a spade, jump leads, tow rope, an air pump, spare fuel (see above), water and a neon light, and to fit tow hooks. In Santiago car parts are available from many shops on Calle 10 de Julio. For car and motorcycle tyres try Calle Serranos 32, Santiago, reported to have the best stock in South America.

Preparing a motorbike The bike should be off-road capable. Fit heavy duty front fork springs and the best quality rebuildable shock absorber you can afford. Fit lockable luggage or make some detachable aluminium panniers. Fit a tank bag and tank panniers for better weight distribution. A large capacity fuel tank is essential if going off the beaten track. A washable air filter is a good idea, also fuel filters, fueltap rubber seals and smaller jets for high altitude Andean motoring. A good set of trails-type tyres as well as a high mudguard are useful. If riding a chain driven bike, a fully enclosed chaincase is useful. A hefty bash plate/sump guard is invaluable.

Motorbike luggage and equipment Take oil filters, fork and shock seals, tubes, a good manual, spare cables (taped into position), a plug cap and spare plug lead. A spare electronic ignition is a good idea. A first class tool kit is a must and, if riding a bike with a chain, then a spare set of sprockets and an 'o' ring chain should be carried. Spare brake and clutch levers should also be taken as these break easily in a fall. Recommended mechanics are given throughout the guide. You should wear a tough waterproof jacket, comfortable strong boots, gloves and a helmet with which you can use glass goggles. If you're going to camp, take the best quality tent and camping gear that you can afford and a petrol stove that runs on bike fuel. For details of documentation, see above.

Security Chile is much safer than most South American countries, and you need do no more to protect your vehicle than you would at home. Remove all belongings and leave the empty glove compartment open when a car is unattended. Try not to leave a fully laden bike on its own, and always secure your bike with a D-lock or chain. Be sure to note down key numbers and carry spares of the most important ones (but don't keep all spare keys inside the vehicle). Wheels should be secured by locking nuts.

Safety Driving at night is not recommended; be especially careful on major roads into and out of cities in the early evening because people tend to cross the highway without warning. Watch out for cyclists without lights at night in rural areas.

Taxis and colectivos and taxis

Taxis usually have meters and can be engaged either in the street or by phoning, though they tend to be more expensive when booked from a hotel. A minimum fare is shown on a large sticker in the windscreen, with increments (usually per 100 m) below. A 50% surcharge is applied after 2100 and on Sunday. Agree beforehand on fares for long journeys out of city centres or for special excursions; also compare prices among several drivers for this sort of trip. There is no need to give a tip unless some extra service is performed. Bear in mind that taxi drivers may not know the location of streets away from city centres.

Colectivos (collective taxis) operate on fixed routes (identified by numbers and destinations) and are a good way of getting around cities. They are usually flagged down on the street corner, although in some cities such as Puerto Montt there are signs. The fixed charges are normally advertised in the front windscreen, and increase at night and weekends. It is best to use small denominations when paying, as the driver takes the money and offers change while driving along. *Colectivos* also operate on some interurban routes (especially in the north), leaving from a set point when full. On interurban routes they compete favourably with buses for speed but not for comfort.

Cycling

At first glance a bicycle may not appear to be the most obvious vehicle for a major journey, but given ample time and reasonable energy it is certainly one of the best. It can be ridden, carried by almost every form of transport from an aeroplane to a canoe, and lifted across your shoulders over short distances. Cyclists can be the envy of travellers using more orthodox transport, since they can travel at their own pace, explore more remote regions and meet people who are less commonly in contact with tourists.

Choosing a bicycle A mountain bike is essential. Good quality mountain bikes (and the cast iron rule is never to skimp on quality) are incredibly tough and rugged, with low gear ratios for difficult terrain, wide tyres with plenty of tread for good road-holding, cantilever brakes, and a low centre of gravity for improved stability. Although imported spares are available in the larger cities, locally manufactured parts are of a lower quality and rarely last. Buy everything you possibly can before you leave home.

Luggage and equipment Be sure to have a small but comprehensive tool kit, a spare tyre and inner tubes, a puncture repair kit, a set of brake blocks, brake and gear cables and all types of nuts and bolts, at least 12 spokes, a light oil for the chain, tube of waterproof grease, a pump secured by a pump lock, a Blackburn parking block (a most invaluable accessory, cheap and virtually weightless), a cyclometer, a loud bell, and a secure lock and chain. Strong and waterproof front and back panniers are essential, and must be mounted on the strongest racks available. A top bag-cum-rucksack makes a good addition for use on and off the bike. A front bag (or any other bar bag) is good for maps, camera, compass, etc. Waterproof and wind-resistant goretex jacket and overtrousers are invaluable. All equipment and clothes should be packed in plastic bags to give extra protection against dust and rain.

Useful tips Wind, not hills, is the enemy of the cyclist. Try to make the best use of the times of day when there is little; mornings tend to be best but there is no steadfast rule. Take care to avoid dehydration. In northern Chile, where supplies of water are scarce between towns, be sure to carry an ample supply. Give your bicycle a thorough daily check for loose nuts or bolts or bearings, and to see that all parts run smoothly. A good chain should last 2,000 miles, 3,200 km or more but be sure to keep it as clean as possible and to oil it lightly from time to time. Most towns have a bicycle shop of some description, but it is best to do your own repairs and adjustments whenever possible. Most cyclists agree that the main danger comes from other traffic. A rearview mirror has been frequently recommended to forewarn you of vehicles which are too close behind. Make yourself conspicuous by wearing bright clothing and a helmet. *Bicycle Expeditions*, by Paul Vickers (1990), is available direct from the **Expedition Advisory Centre** ① *Royal Geographical Society, 1 Kensington Gore, London SW7 2AR*. In the UK there is also the **Cyclist's Touring Club** (CTC) ① *Cotterell House, 69 Meadrow, Godalming, Surrey, GU7 3HS, T0870 870-0060, cycling@ctc.org.uk*, for touring and technical information.

Hitchhiking
Hitchhiking in Chile is relatively easy and safe, and when a lift does come along it is often in the shape of an exhilarating open-air ride in the back of a pick-up truck. However, in some regions – especially in the south – traffic is sparse, and roads in places like Tierra del Fuego rarely see more than two or three vehicles per day. Drivers will sometimes make hand-signals if they are only going a short distance beyond – this is not a rude gesture.

Sea

In the south of Chile, maritime transport is very important. Vital routes are, from north to south: Puerto Montt to Chiloé (many daily); Puerto Montt to Chaitén (three times weekly in summer) and Puerto Chacabuco (twice weekly); Puerto Montt to Puerto Natales (twice weekly in summer); Castro to Chaitén (four weekly in summer, fewer in winter); Castro to Puerto Chacabuco (once weekly); Punta Arenas to Porvenir (five times weekly); Punta Arenas to Puerto Williams (twice monthly). The main operators are **Transmarchilay** and **Navimag**. Reservations are essential for the ferries in high summer. Details of all routes and booking information are given under the relevant chapters.

Rail

There are 4,470 km of line, of which most are state owned. Most of the privately owned 2,130 km of line are in the northern deserts where only one line, from Calama to Uyuni (Bolivia) carries passengers (see page). The main passenger service south from Santiago runs to Temuco; this journey is more tranquil than travelling by road along the Panamericana, and between Santiago and Chillán it is faster than the bus President Lagos has promised to extend the line to its original terminus, Puerto Montt, by 2009. There are also suburban passenger trains around Santiago and inland from both Concepción and Valparaíso, as well as the scenic line from Talca along the valley of the Río Maule to Constitución (see page). The **Ferrocarriles del Estado** publishes an annual *Guía Turística*, available in various languages from the larger stations.

Trains in Chile are moderately priced, and dining car food is inexpensive. There is a 15% discount on return tickets and a 10% discount for senior citizens aged 60 or over. For further information on all lines except for Calama-Uyuni, visit the railway information office ① *Universidade de Chile metro station, Santiago, level 1, T02-6883284*, where English is spoken.

Maps

A good map of **Santiago** is the *Plano de Santiago*, published annually by **Publiguías**, ① *Av Santa María 0792, Providencia, Santiago*; this contains sectional maps of the city and a street index. **Publiguías** also publishes a *Guía Comercial y Profesional de Providencia*. Maps of the major tourist areas are published by **Mapas JLM**, ① *Gral del Canto 105 T/F02-2364808*; these are sold at newpaper kiosks and elsewhere.

Geophysical and topographical maps (US$11) are available from **Instituto Geográfico Militar** ① *Dieciocho 369, T6987278, open Mon-Fri 0900-1800 Mar-Dec; Mon-Fri 0800-1400 Jan and Feb*. The **Instituto Geográfico** has published a *Guía Caminera*, with roads and city plans (not 100% accurate). It is only available at IGM offices, although the **Biblioteca Nacional** in Santiago has an excellent collection of IGM maps, sections of which can be photocopied. The **Turistel** guidebooks contain good general maps (see page 556).

Stanfords, ① *12-14 Long Acre, Covent Garden, London, WC2E 9LP, T020-7836 1321, www.stanfords.co.uk*, with over 80 well-travelled staff and 40,000 titles in stock, is the world's largest map and travel bookshop. It also has branches at 29 Corn Street, Bristol, BS1, and at 39 Spring Gardens, Manchester, M2.

• Hotel price codes explained

LL Top-of-the-range hotels with all amenities, mainly in Santiago. US$150 and above.
L Very luxurious business-style hotels. US$100-150.
AL Good city or resort hotels, sometimes with gym, pool and restaurant. US$66-99.
A Upper-range hotels with most facilities in minor cities and smaller resorts. US$46-65.
B Mid-range hotels with mod cons, private bathrooms and TV. US$31-45.

C Comfortable small hotels with few luxuries but decent facilities. US$21-30.
D Lower-end hotels or expensive *hospedajes* in small towns. US$16-20.
E *Hospedajes* in expensive resorts, with good breakfasts and facilities. US$12-15.
F Most *hospedajes* are in this category. Quality is variable, prices are per person. US$7-11.
G Remote *hospedajes*, resort dormitories or very basic *albuergues*. Prices per person. USS$6 and under.

Sleeping

In most parts of Chile accommodation is plentiful and finding a room to suit your budget should be easy. During the summer holiday months of January and February, rooms can be more scarce – especially in upmarket hotels in the more popular holiday venues of the south. This is also true during Easter, and at the time of the Independence Day holidays in mid-September. Even so, you should rarely have a problem in finding a roof over your head.

Types of accommodation

The term **hotel** implies an expensive establishment in the south (but not in the north). Top class hotels are available in Santiago and major cities, but elsewhere choice is more limited. **Hosterías** tend to be in rural areas and may have many of the facilities of a hotel, while the terms **hostal**, **residencial** and **hospedaje** usually refer to a small family-run establishment with limited facilities and services. A **motel**, especially if it is situated on the outskirts of a city, is likely to rent rooms by the hour unless it is described as a *motel turístico*: usually the name or sign outside will indicate what type it is. In the south, many families offer bed and breakfast, which may be advertised by a sign in the window. People here often meet buses to offer rooms, but the quality is variable. In larger cities, the cheapest and often the nastiest hotels tend to be situated around bus terminals. If you arrive late and are just passing through, they may be OK, but better quality accommodation is often to be found near the main plaza. Taxi drivers can be useful sources of information about accommodation, but, especially in tourist centres, they may try to take you to a place where they know they will get a commission. Note that even in small villages there is often someone who will rent out a room for a very reasonable price; ask around.

Backpackers (especially those with little Spanish) would do well to consult www.backpackersbest.cl and www.backpackerschile.com for information on suitable accommodation around the country. The former features lots of hostels in a broad price range, while the latter focuses on hostels that charge around US$10 per person. For people who want to learn Spanish while they travel, a group of hostels offer the same syllabus in different parts of the country; consult www.spanish-for-travellers.com for further details.

Accommodation is more expensive in Santiago than in most other parts of the country, although prices also tend to be higher the further south you go from Puerto Montt, as well as in some northern cities such as Antofagasta. In tourist areas, prices rise in the high season (January/February, plus any local festivity), but off-season you can often bargain for a lower price, though you will usually have to stay for two or more days to be successful: ask politely for a discount (*descuento*). Single travellers do not come off too badly in Chile compared to other Latin American countries such as Mexico. In the south, *hospedajes* charge per person (although you may have to share your room), while in the north, single rooms are about 60-70% the price of a double.

Value Added Tax (known as **IVA**) at 18% is charged on hotel bills and should be included in any price quoted in pesos. The government waives the VAT charge for hotel bills paid in dollars (cash or travellers' cheques) but only for hotels that have an agreement (*convenio*) with the government. As a result, larger hotels (but few other establishments) can offer you much lower tariffs if you pay in dollars than those advertised in pesos. Establish clearly in advance what is included in the price rather than relying on prices or services displayed on notices in the reception area.

Rooms and facilities

Many hotels, but few budget places, have restaurants serving lunch and dinner. Most *hospedajes* offer breakfast, which usually consists of instant coffee or tea with bread and jam; but in the north, very few hotels offer breakfast. An increasing number of cheaper establishments have kitchen facilities for guest use, but if you are relying on these you should check them out first. Most establishments will not allow you to wash and dry clothes in your room, but some offer facilities for you to do your own laundry. Many hotels have parking facilities, though in large cities this may be a few blocks from the hotel itself. Motorcycle parking is widely available.

Reception areas in hotels can be very misleading, so it is a very good idea to see the room before booking. If you are shown a dark room without a window, ask if there are rooms with windows (*ventana*). In large cities the choice may be between an inside room without a window and a room with a window over a noisy street. Many middle-range establishments have rooms with private bathroom (*con baño privado*) and without (*con baño compartido*) so it is often worth asking whether there is anything cheaper than the price initially quoted. If you are not satisfied, do not be afraid of walking away and trying elsewhere.

Many hotels, restaurants and bars have inadequate water supplies. Without exception used toilet paper should not be flushed down the pan, but placed in the receptacle provided. This applies even in expensive hotels. Failure to observe this custom will block the pan or drain, causing a considerable health risk. If you are concerned about the hygiene of the facility, put paper on the seat, or else bring your own portable toilet seat. Remember to carry toilet paper with you, as cheaper establishments as well as restaurants, bars, etc frequently do not supply it.

Camping → *Turistel publishes an annual guide, listing campsites.*

Camping is not always cheap at official sites. A common practice is to charge US$10 for up to five people, with no reductions for fewer than five; however, if a site is not full, owners will often give a pitch to a single person for around US$4. Camping Gaz International stoves are recommended, since green replaceable cylinders are available throughout the country (white gas – *benzina blanca* – is available in hardware shops; for good value try the **Sodimac** or **Tricot** chains of DIY stores). Cheap gas stoves can be bought in camping shops in Santiago and popular trekking areas. **Copec** runs a network of 33 'Rutacentros' along Ruta 5 which have showers, cafeterias and camping. Free camping is also available at many filling stations. Campsites are very busy in January and February.

Camping wild is easy and safe in remote areas of the far south and in the *cordillera* north of Santiago. However in much of central and central-southern Chile the land is fenced off, and it is often necessary to ask permission to camp. In Mapuche and Aymará communities it is both courteous and advisable to make for the primary school or some other focal point of a village to meet prominent members of the community first. Camping wild in the north is difficult, because of the absence of water.

Albuergues (youth hostels)

Albuergues spring up in summer all over the south of Chile. These are usually schools earning extra money by renting out floor space. They are very cheap (rarely more than US$3-4 per person) and are excellent places to meet young Chileans. Do not go to them if you want a good night's sleep, though; guitars often play on into the small hours. There is no need for an International Hostelling card to stay in *albuergues*, but there is rarely much in the way of security either.

Official youth hostels throughout Chile cost about US$8-15 per person. The Hostelling International card (US$15) is usually readily accepted, but as an alternative you can obtain a Chilean YHA card (US$5) from the **Asociación Chilena de Albergues Turísticos Juveniles** (ACHATJ) ① *Hernando de Aguirre 201, Oficina 602, T2333220, achatj@hostelling.co.cl www.hostellingcl.achatj.html*, together with a useful guidebook of all youth hostels in Chile, *Guía Turística de los Albergues Juveniles*.

Eating

The main meals are breakfast (*desayuno*), lunch (*almuerzo*) and dinner (*cena*). Lunch is eaten any time from 1300 to 1530, and dinner between 2000 and 2300. *Las onces* (literally elevenses) is the name given to a snack usually including tea. In cafés and restaurants this is served at around 1700 but many Chileans also call their evening meal *once*. Breakfast usually consists of bread, butter and jam, served with coffee or tea. Lunch tends to be the main meal of the day, and by law restaurants have to serve a cheaper fixed-price meal at lunch time; this is often called *la colación* or *el menu*. In more expensive places, this may not be referred to on the menu. When ordering from the menu note that vegetables, other than potatoes, are not usually included in the price. ▸▸ *For simple vocabulary related to food and drink, see Basic Spanish for travellers, page 558.*

Food

Chile's cuisine is varied and often delicious. The Mediterranean climate of the central regions is perfect for growing a wide variety of fruit and vegetables – avocados are especially delicious. The semi-tropical climate of northern Chile supplies mangoes, papayas, *lúcumas* and *chirimoyas* (custard apples). The lush grasslands of the south are ideal for dairy and beef farming as well as for growing apples, cherries, plums and (in the far south) rhubarb.

Although Chilean cuisine is mostly rooted in the Spanish tradition, it has also been influenced by the immigrant groups who have settled in the country. The pastry making skills of the Germans have produced '*onces Alemanas*', a kind of high tea with *Küchen*. *Pan de Pascua*, a traditional Christmas fruit loaf, also derives from Germany.

Seafood

Perhaps the most outstanding ingredient is the seafood. Although there are good fish restaurants in Santiago, and fine seafood can be found at the Mercado Central, naturally the best seafood and fish is found on the coast. The excellent fish

66 99 It may be very disconcerting to be presented with a plate containing a rock with feathery fins, but it is well worth taking up the challenge of eating it...

restaurants between Playa Ancha and **Concón**, near Valparaíso, are especially popular with Santiaguinos. Almost every port on the Chilean coast has a small market or a row of seafood restaurants where excellent seafood can be eaten very cheaply; in smaller harbours, it is often possible to eat with the fishermen. Most of these seafood restaurants receive their supplies of fish and shellfish from local fishing boats which land their catch every morning in the harbours. Watching the unloading at a port such as **Talcahuano** can be fascinating. If you have the courage to bargain you may be able to pick up some delicious, fresh fish from the boats or from the stalls along the harbour; whole crates of shellfish go for the equivalent of a few dollars.

In the north, great seafood can be had at **Caleta Hornos**, north of La Serena, and at **Huasco**. In the centre and south the best seafood is to be had at Valparaíso, **Constitución**, Talcahuano, **Angelmo** (Puerto Montt) and on **Chiloé**, where you should try the famous *curanto*, a stew of shellfish, pork, chicken and other ingredients. Beware of eating seafood that you have bought unofficially in the far south because of the poisonous '*marea roja*' (see page 445).

The most popular fish are *merluza* (a species of hake inferior to European hake), *congrio* (ling), *corvina* (bass), *reineta* (a type of bream), *lenguado* (sole) and *albacora* (sword fish). *Merluza*, which is usually fried, is an inexpensive fish, found in ordinary restaurants. *Congrio* is very popular, and particularly delicious served as *caldillo de congrio*, a soup containing a large *congrio* steak. *Albacora* is a delicious fish, available mainly in quality restaurants. *Ceviche*, fish marinated in lemon juice, is usually made with *corvina*.

There is an almost bewildering array of shellfish. Look out for *choritos* (mussels), *ostiones* (queen scallops), *ostras* (oysters) and *erizos* (sea-urchins). Prawns are known as *camarones*, but these are often imported from Ecuador and can be tasteless and expensive. Chile's most characteristic products are the delicious *erizos*, *machas, picorocos* and *locos*, which are only found in these seas. *Machas a la parmesana* are prepared in their shells with a parmesan cheese sauce, grilled and served as a starter, or as a canapé with *pisco sour*. *Picorocos* (giant barnacles), which are normally boiled or steamed in white wine, are grotesque to look at but have a very intense taste: it may be very disconcerting to be presented with a plate containing a rock with feathery fins but it is well worth taking up the challenge of eating it. *Locos* are the most popular Chilean mollusc, but because of overexploitation its fishing is frequently banned. This situation has led to an extensive illegal trade, both nationally and internationally, with *locos* being exported illegally to parts of Asia (especially Japan). The main crustaceans are *jaiva* (crab), *langosta* (lobster) and the local *centolla*, an exquisite king crab from the waters of the south.

Packages of dried seaweed, particularly *cochayuyo* (which looks like a leathery thong), are sold along coastal roads. Both *cochayuyo* and *luche* are made into a cheap, nutritious stew with vegetables, and eaten with potatoes or rice; these dishes are rarely available in restaurants. Until recently salmon was available only in the south where the rivers and lakes are full of 'wild' salmon that has escaped from farms. It is now farmed extensively in the south and can be found on menus in many parts of the country.

Empanadas de pino

Although other fillings are used nowadays for *empanadas*, the traditional filling is pino, a mixture of meat, onions, and spices. Most Chilean families have their own recipes: this one was kindly supplied by Manuel and Ximena Fernández.

Ingredients (to make 20 *empanadas*)

Pastry: 1 kilogram flour; 125 grams margarine, butter or lard; 1 level spoonful salt; cold water.

Filling: 600 grams meat, chopped into small pieces (or lean minced meat); 2 large onions; 4 or 5 teaspoons cooking oil; teaspoon each of cumin, black pepper and chilli powder; 1 teaspoon paprika; 3 cloves garlic, finely chopped; salt to taste; 4 hard boiled eggs; 1 teaspoon flour; 20 black olives; 40 raisins.

Methods

Pastry: in a bowl mix the flour and margarine, add salt (dissolved in ½ a cup water), gradually add more water to make soft but consistent pastry and leave it for at least 1 hour, then knead it for 10 minutes, before replacing it in the bowl and leaving it covered with a clean cloth.

Filling: heat the cooking oil in a large frying pan or pot, then add the onion and fry for about 8 minutes. Add spices and salt, then fry for 2 minutes. Add meat and fry for 15 minutes, stirring continuously, until the onions are crystal-like and softly cooked. Add the flour, lower the heat and simmer for 5 minutes. Leave the mixture overnight. Shell the eggs and cut each lengthwise into 5 pieces.

Making the empanadas: Divide the pastry into 20 pieces, then roll each piece into a thin round shape. On one "hemisphere" of each piece of pastry place the following: 1 piece of egg; one heaped teaspoon of the filling; 2 raisins and 1 olive. Carefully paint the rim of each piece of pastry with water, then fold the empty "hemisphere" over to enclose the filling; press the rim down. You should now have a semicircular turnover: paint the outer rim again with water and fold it again towards the centre of the *empanada*.

Bake the *empanadas* in a preheated oven (200°C). After about 5 minutes reduce the heat to 150°C and bake for a further 14 minutes until the *empanadas* are nicely browned. To improve their appearance paint the *empanadas* with a thin coat of cold water as soon as you remove them from the oven. Serve hot with Chilean red wine.

Other specialities

Away from seafood, savoury Chilean dishes tend to be creative. Specialities include *humitas* (mashed sweetcorn mixed with butter and spices and baked in sweetcorn leaves), *pastel de papas* (meat pie covered with mashed potatoes), and *cazuela de vacuno* (meat stew with pumpkin, potato, coriander and a twist of lemon – the most common everyday dish). In central and southern Chile stews with beans (*porotos*) are common. A typical (and unhealthy) dish from Valparaíso is the *chorillana*: chips covered with sliced steak, fried onions and scrambled eggs. A very typical dish is *cazuela de ave*, a nutritious stew containing chicken, potatoes, rice, and maybe onions and green peppers; best if served on the second day. *Valdiviano* is another stew, common in the south, with beef, onion, sliced potatoes and eggs. *Pastel de choclo* is a casserole of meat and onions with olives, topped with polenta, baked in an earthenware bowl. *Prieta* is a blood sausage stuffed with cabbage leaves. *Bife* or *Lomo a lo pobre* (a poor man's steak) is just the opposite: it is a steak topped by two fried eggs, chips, onions and salad. A *paila* can take many forms (the *paila* is simply a

Essentials Eating

kind of serving dish), but the commonest are made of eggs or seafood. In the north, *paila de huevos* (two fried eggs with an *hallulla*) is common for breakfast. *Paila chonchi* is a kind of bouillabaisse, while a *mariscal* is a delicious shellfish stew.

Chileans tend to have a very sweet tooth, and their **desserts** can be full of *manjar* (caramelised condensed milk).

Snacks

Among the many snacks sold in Chile, the most famous are *empanadas*, pastry turnovers made *de pino* (with meat, onions, egg and an olive) , *de queso* (with cheese), or *de mariscos* (with shellfish). The quality of *empanadas* varies: many are full of onions rather than meat. In the south there are *empanadas* filled with seafood, which are delicious and usually better value.

Chilean sandwiches tend to be fairly substantial: the *chacarero* contains thinly sliced steak and salad; *barros lucos* have steak and grilled cheese; and *barros jarpas* have grilled cheese and ham.

Completos are the cheapest and most popular snacks, betraying the German influence on everyday food: these are hot dogs served with plenty of extras, including mustard, sauerkraut, tomatoes, mayonnaise and *ají* (chilli sauce). An *Italiano* is a *completo* with avocado and without the sauerkraut. Avocado is very popular at family *onces*, mashed up and served on bread. Bread itself is plentiful and cheap, and comes in pairs of fluffy rolls (*maraquetas*) or as a crisper slim roll (*hallullas*). Central Santiago has many ice cream stands doing a roaring trade.

Drink

Coffee and tea While Argentine cafés have excellent real coffee, if you ask for **coffee** in many places in Chile you will get a cup of boiling water and a tin of instant coffee, even in quite high-class restaurants. There are espresso bars in major cities, elsewhere specify *café-café*, *espresso*. **Tea** is usually served with neither milk nor lemon. If you order '*café*, or *té, con leche*', it will come with all milk; to have just a little milk ask for a *cortado*. After a meal, instead of coffee, try an *agüita* – hot water in which herbs such as mint, or aromatics such as lemon peel, have been steeped. A wide variety of refreshing herbal teas is available in sachets.

Wine Chilean wine is excellent, and even the cheapest wines are very drinkable. The best are from the central areas. The bottled wines are graded, in increasing excellence, as *gran vino*, *vino especial* and *vino reservado*. Champagne-style wines are also cheap and good (especially those from the Casablanca area). Even quite good wine is commonly sold in litre cartons, which are cheaper than bottles. ►► *For more on wine, see page 552.*

Beer Chilean beer is cheap but hardly for connoisseurs; draught lager is known as *Schop*; also try *Cristal Pilsener* (nationwide; not bad), or *Royal Guard* in the central regions, *Kunstmann* (very good) around Valdivia, and *Escudo Austral* and *Polar* in the south. *Baltica* is good, stong and cheap. *Heineken* is also good, but *Dorada* is best left for the drunks. *Malta*, a dark beer, is recommended for those wanting a British-type beer; however, there are different breweries, and the *Malta* north of Temuco is more bitter than that to the south. European-style lager is brewed by **HBH**, a company which began life in Temuco and which has bars in Santiago. European beers are increasingly available. As with wine, a deposit is required for beer bottles (about US$0.50); it may be worth buying some bottles and using them to exchange for new bottles up and down the country, as bottled beers are cheaper than cans.

Pisco and other spirits The most famous spirit is *pisco*, made with grapes, usually drunk with lemon or lime juice as *pisco sour* (see box page 57). *Pisco* is also often mixed with coca cola or sprite. *Pisco* is graded in strength from 30-46°; paradoxically, the stronger brands are much more pleasant and easy to drink.

Pisco sour

What is important in making pisco sour is the balance between the ingredients; once the mixing is done you can add extra sugar, pisco or lemon to taste. The egg white is purely for presentation. Most Chileans have their own recipe for this famous drink: this one was kindly supplied by Jaime Baez.

Ingredients (for 450 millilitres of pisco sour): 200 millilitres refrigerated 30° pisco; 150 millilitres lemon juice; 2 teaspoons granulated sugar; ½ teaspoon egg white.
Method: Put all the ingredients in liquidizer and mix for a few seconds, until the sugar is well dissolved, then place in refrigerator until cold.

Recommended brands of *pisco* are *Alto del Carmen* and *Capel*; avoid the ironically named *Pisco Control*, especially at 30°. Reasonably good brandy, *anís* and crème de menthe are all bottled in Chile, and good gin is also produced.Local rum is very cheap and tends to lead to poisonous hangovers. *Manzanilla* is a local liqueur, made from *licor de oro* (like Galliano); *crema de cacao*, especially Mitjans, has been recommended. Two delicious drinks are *vaina*, a mixture of brandy, egg and sugar and *cola de mono*, a mixture of *aguardiente*, coffee, milk and vanilla served very cold at Christmas. There are many seasonal fruit liqueurs which are delicious; *eguindado*, made from cherries, is particularly recommended. *Chicha* is any form of alcoholic drink made from fruit; *chicha cocida* is three-day-old fermented grape juice boiled to reduce its volume and then bottled with a tablespoonful of honey. Cider (*chicha de manzana*) is popular in the south.

Other drinks Away from alcoholic drinks, Chile does not perhaps take as much advantage of its variety of fruits as it should. Unlike in Mexico, say, cheap and freshly squeezed juices are uncommon, though of course there is nothing to stop you buying a job lot of fruit from the market and preparing juices for yourself. *Chicha fresca* is plain apple juice, while *Mote con huesillo*, made from wheat hominy and dried peaches, is very refreshing in summer. Families tend to drink a lot of sugary soft drinks, picking up on the usual international brands.

Eating out

Those on a budget will want to stick to the cheaper eateries, where simple and very tasty meals can be had at a very reasonable price; a *colación* need not cost you more than US$2-3. The cheapest restaurants in urban areas tend to be by the transport terminals and markets or, in coastal areas, by the port. These restaurants may well have a wide choice of food for very reasonable prices, and often there is very little difference in the quality of the food between cheaper and more expensive places, the main differences being the service and the elegance (or pretensions) of the surroundings. More expensive places will, though, have a wider range of starters and desserts, which are often non-existent in cheaper eateries. The focal point

Waiting staff should be referred to as señor/señorita, never as mozo.

for life in towns is the plaza, in which there will typically be a number of slightly upmarket cafés, where people tend to have a beer and snacks, but rarely go for a full meal. If you are travelling in small villages off the beaten track, it is usually possible to find someone who will cook for you; ask around. Among the cheaper eating places are the *casinos de bomberos* (firemen's canteens) in most towns. Fire stations are not paid for by the state, and firemen are all voluntary. Eating at a canteen helps fund their work, and the food is usually cheap and good.

With such a range of inexpensive alcoholic drinks on offer , Chile does have quite a severe alcoholism problem, especially on Chiloé and in the far south. There are numerous bars in every town, and often many bars even in small villages; finding one to suit your purpose (however sober or otherwise it may be) is rarely a problem.

Vegetarians Although there are vegetarian restaurants in major cities, vegetarians will find that their choice of food is severely restricted, especially in smaller towns and away from tourist areas. To confuse matters, '*carne*' is understood to mean red meat, so asking if a dish has meat in it is likely to lead to disaster; or chicken, at the very least. Vegetarians should explain which foods they cannot eat rather than saying '*Soy vegetariano*' ('I'm a vegetarian') or '*No como carne*' ('I don't eat meat'). To make matters worse, the bread known as *hallulas* is often made with lard (*manteca*); ask first. There are fewer problems for vegetarians if they can cook for themselves, and they may be best off looking for accommodation which has cooking facilities.

❢ *Those who suffer from diabetes or high blood pressure are advised, where possible, to cook their own food, as Chilean cuisine tends to have a high salt and sugar content.*

Eating in
It is certainly much more economical to prepare your own food in Chile, especially if you shop in markets, where fruit and vegetables can be absurdly cheap. For non-perishable supplies, though, supermarkets are very good, and they are now ubiquitous in decent-sized towns up and down the country. In large villages there will always be one or two smaller stores with many things that you might want, although little in the way of fruit and vegetables.

Entertainment

Chile's centre for cultural and nocturnal entertainment is, naturally, Santiago. Here both visitors and residents will find their diaries can get frenetically full.

Santiago and around
Bohemian nightlife in Santiago centres around Barrio Bellavista, below Cerro San Cristóbal, where clubs do not really get going until after 1, and the streets are crowded with night birds until after 5 in the morning. It is best to just turn up and go with the flow, as there are countless bars and clubs here, all with something to offer. More upmarket clubs are in the Providencia and Barrio Alto areas of Santiago; these tend to be expensive and posy. There are, though, good (but expensive) bars throughout the whole Providencia district, particularly on Calle Suecia (near Pedro de Valdivia). Away from the streets, house parties have similar norms throughout the country: arrive much before 11.30 and you will be the first person there – and don't worry about getting home, as you will probably be up until the first morning buses run.

Santiago also has a thriving cultural scene, with numerous small theatres, arts' cinemas and a pulsating underground music scene (especially big in 'progressive rock'); the university campuses are good sources of information.

Going to watch a football match at one of the big stadia – Universidad Católica in Lo Barnechea, Colo Colo off Vicuña Mackenna or Universidad de Chile in the Estadio Nacional – is highly recommended. ▸▸ *For details of venues in Santiago, see pages 93-118.*

Elsewhere
Away from the capital, the scene is understandably less busy. Cities renowned for being lively are Iquique, Viña del Mar and La Serena, but everywhere – even very small towns and villages – has a *discoteca*. These do not get going until after midnight, people tend to

dance in couples (unlike in Santiago), and the music is a mixture of mainstream Latin American and North American rock music, with occasional salsa and merengue. The cities with the biggest cultural scenes are those with a significant student population, particularly Concepción and La Serena; but even here, cinemas tend to show only the latest Hollywood blockbusters (usually with subtitles, not dubbed).

Festivals and events

Regional festivals

Festivals are held in all of Chiloé's towns, rotating from week to week, Jan and Feb (p380).

Fiesta de la Piedra Santa Mapuche festival of the Holy Stone in the Lake District, 20 Jan (p298).

Fiesta de la Candelaria One of northern Chile's most important religious festivals, 1st Sun in Feb (p191).

Festival de la Canción Viña del Mar hosts the dreaded (and often dreadful) international music festival, Feb (p).

Campeonato Nacional de Rodeo National rodeo competition in Rancagua, Mar (p275).

La Tirana This festival near Iquique, celebrating the Virgin del Carmen, is an exhilarating combination of indigenous and Catholic folklore, attended by people from all over Chile and from neighbouring Bolivia and Peru, 16 Jul (p247).

La Pampilla The week-long independence celebrations in Coquimbo are the biggest in the country, 13-20 Sep (p180).

Día de la Virgen Pilgrimage to Quinchao, off Chiloé, 8 Dec (p390).

Fiesta Grande Vast pilgrimage to Andacollo, 23-27 Dec (p167).

Public holidays

New Year's Day 1 Jan
Easter 2 days in Mar/Apr
Labour Day 1 May
Navy Day 21 May
Assumption 15 Aug
Day of National Unity 1st Mon in Sep
Independence 18, 19 Sep
Columbus Day 12 Oct
All Saints Day 1 Nov
Immaculate Conception 8 Dec
Christmas Day 25 Dec

Shopping

What to buy → *VAT is charged at 18%.*

There is an excellent variety of handicrafts: woodwork, pottery, copperware, leatherwork, Indian woven goods including rugs and ponchos. However, many of the goods sold in main handicraft markets are from elsewhere in South America, in some cases with the country of origin labels cut off; if going on a wider South American tour, these goods are almost always cheaper in the northern Andean countries. Among the most interesting purchases will be jewellery made with the semi-precious lapis lazuli stone, found only in Chile and Afghanistan. There are also less well known stones unique to Chile (such as the *combarbalita*, found around Combarbalá, near Illapel), and many fine jewels and knick-knacks (such as paperweights) made with stones such as onyx. People returning home may want to buy typical Chilean foods or drinks: *pisco*, *aji Chileno* or *manjar*, for instance.

Tips and trends

Bargaining is rare in Chile, and often seen as impolite. You can't try the usual 'offer a half, go up to two thirds' formula, and will often do well to knock more than the equivalent of US$1 off the asking price. If you want to get the cheapest possible price your best bet is to go directly to the area where the object you have in mind is made, since craft specialities tend to be specific to particular places in Chile (see page 529); once there, do not go to the first craft shop you find (those nearest to the entry to the town), but look for those that are tucked away. The past decade has seen the growth of mall culture, especially in Santiago; Las Condes is brimful of malls (such as Parque Arauco), to which families descend en masse at weekends.

Sport and activities

Chile might well have been designed for adventure tourism. In a country where you can often see the Andes from the coast, you are never more than a few hours' drive away from mountains, so a wide range of adventure activities can be practised year-round. In the high summer month of January, for instance, although Parinacota volcano in the north is shrouded in cloud, the Torres del Paine in Patagonia enjoy their main season. Some destinations possess unusual versatility: the mountain resorts near Santiago are famous for their skiing, but they are also good for mountain biking and trekking in high summer.

The infrastructure for 'soft' adventure tourism, such as a half-day's rafting on a Grade 3 river (quite a thrill), or a day spent climbing a volcano, is quite good in Chile, particularly in the Lake District. Agencies in centres such as Pucón, Puerto Varas and Puerto Montt organize combinations of activities, many for one day but some for longer durations. Parapenting and hang-gliding can be organized from Santiago, and there is a parapenting centre at the Antillanca ski resort. Santiago is well placed for short trips, especially for horse riding in the central *cordillera* and visits to the ski resorts nearby. Some of the world's top rafting and fishing is also easily accessible.

'Tougher' adventure tourism, often involving camping at high altitudes, is also possible. Chile offers boundless opportunities for well-equipped independent adventurers: the best way to see the Atacama Desert is in your own in a rented four-wheel drive vehicle; and a mountain bike is the best form of transport on the Carretera Austral. It is important to check the experience of agencies offering expeditions to remote areas.

Organizations and information

Among the organizations involved in adventure tourism several deserve special mention: **CATA** (Consejo de Autorregulación de Aventura) ① *Arzobispo Casanova 3, Providencia, Santiago, T02-7358034, F7772375*, is an organization formed by the more reputable agencies to try (with mixed success) to regulate adventure tourism, ensure safety and exclude 'cowboy' operators. It works closely with **CONAF** ① *T02-2361416; see also box page 64*), which regulates adventure activities within the national parks, following CATA's written guidelines on matters such as guide experience, types of activity, size of groups and safety requirements. **Sernatur** (the National Tourist Board) has a separate section in its head office in Santiago specializing in adventure tourism and ecotourism (see page 39). ▸▸ *For further information, see also Further reading, page 555.*

Climbing

Types of climbing

Rock climbing This is not organized on a national basis, though **ENAM** (Escuela Nacional de Montaña de Santiago) runs courses in rock and ice climbing, and adventure tourism agencies are beginning to offer rock climbing activities. The three granite towers in the **Parque Nacional Torres del Paine** are the best known and most difficult climbs, but they are in such demand that a climbing fee is levied. There are also very high cliffs (800 m) at the eastern en end of **Lago Todos Los Santos** and at Cerro Picada (800 m) on the northwest shore.

Mountain climbing High mountains such as **Tupungato** and **Ojos del Salado** rival the Argentine peak of Aconcagua for climbers. Like the latter they pose few technical difficulties, but the weather can be vicious and the altitude should be taken very seriously. Moreover, Ojos del Salado is not easily accessible.

Ice climbing Some of the most important high-altitude ice climbs are easily reached from Santiago: the **Loma Larga** and **Plomo** massifs are two to three hours drive from the capital. The **Federación de Andinismo** can advise on the better known and more difficult climbs such as El Plomo, El Altar and El Morado, though it is less useful for information of mountains further afield and its offices are often closed.

Volcano climbing There are hundreds of volcanoes to choose from, ranging from the high-altitude **Parinacota** in the far north and remote **Licancábur** on the Bolivian frontier near San Pedro, to the chain of much lower cones in the Lake District and along the Carretera Austral. Some of these, such as **Puntiagudo** and **Corcovado** with their precipitous plugs, are difficult climbs. The easiest and most popular are **Villarrica** and **Osorno**, though CONAF rightly controls access to these because the crevasses are hazardous. Osorno, with its seracs and ice caves is a more attractive climb, but Villarrica has the dubious advantage of being more active and hiring guides for this trek is much cheaper. Note that Osorno and Villarrica are still not easy climbs, and even well-equipped and experienced climbers have suffered fatal accidents on them.

Canyoning The southern bank of the **Río Petrohué** in the Lake District offers many fantastic canyons for climbing. Nearby *Aquamotion* have fixed rope ladders in the canyon of the Río Leon, 30 minutes by boat from Petrohué on the southern shore of **Lago Todos Los Santos**.

Formalities

To climb some mountains in frontier areas, notably Ojos del Salado and Parinacota, permission must be obtained from the **Dirección de Fronteras y Límites** ① *piso 5, Ministerio de Relaciones Exteriores, Bandera 52, Santiago, T02-6714210, F6971909*. Preferably apply three months in advance; Chilean embassies abroad can help. In addition, climbers require permits for some mountains, such as Torres del Paine and Volcàn Osorno; further information from the **Federación de Andinismo** (see below).

Mountain rescue services are provided by the **Cuerpo de Socorro Andino**, based in Santiago, and by rescue groups in popular climbing areas: if organizing a climb register with them, often at the entry control to the mountain and with the local *carabineros*. Away from the popular areas you are on your own, which can also be one of Chile's main attractions.

Further information

The national climbing club is the **Federación de Andinismo de Chile** ① *Almte Simpson 77A, Santiago, T02-2220888, www.feach.cl, office open daily in theory but frequently closed, especially in Jan/Feb; museum daily 1100-1330, 1700-2000, free; library Mon, Tue, Thur-Sat 1930-2100*. It organises training for local climbers. runs some expeditions and hires out equipment to members. The shop in the foyer sells climbing guides and equipment and is often open when the office is closed. **Escuela Nacional de Montaña** (ENAM), is based at the same address (T02-2220799). It holds seminars and conferences on climbing, runs rock- and ice-climbing courses, plus qualification courses for guides in Santiago and elsewhere. It also administers the *Carnet de La Federación de Chile*, a card which is often required to climb mountains especially where CONAF control access. The *carnet* can be renewed through CONAF offices.

Essentials Sport & activities

Fishing

The lakes and rivers of Regions IX (Araucanía), X (Los Lagos) and XI (Aisén) offer great opportunities for fishing, especially trout (rainbow, brown and fario) and salmon (coho and chinook). The season runs from 15 November to the first Sunday in May except on Lago Llanquihue where it starts on 15 September. Organized fly fishing with a guide can be expensive: trolling and spinning are the more widely practised methods.

The Lake District is popular for **trout** fishing. Both rainbow and fario trout are found in all the major lakes; the largest fish are found in Lago Llanquihue, while Lago Todos Los Santos, on which very few boats are permitted, is noted for quantity. Apart from the main lakes, Lago Maihue and Lagunas El Toro, El Encanto and Paraíso (all in the Parque Nacional Puyehue) have been recommended. In the southern Lake District the main rivers for **salmon** fishing include the Ríos Pescado, Petrohué, Puelo, Maullín and, on Chiloé, the Chepu and Pudeto.

The greatest fishing area in Chile lies along the Carretera Austral: Lago Yelcho and the Ríos Futaleufú and Palena are important areas for **fly fishing**, while further south the rivers and lakes around Coyhaique offer some of the best fishing in the world; Lago Blanco on Tierra del Fuego is also a good destination. Santiago and Valparaíso residents fish at the mountain resort of Río Blanco.

Sea fishing is popular between Puerto Saavedra in the IX Region and Maullín in the X Region: the main centres are Mehuín, the coast from Niebla to Curiñanco near Valdivia, Maicolpue, Llico and Maullín itself, where salmon may be caught in the sea. In Villarrica a lot of fishing guides offer trips down the Tolten river.

Formalities and further information

A licence is required, whether for one day or a longer period, and is usually obtained from the local Municipalidad, though some tourist offices also sell them. For details on licences and local conditions, contact the **Asociación de Pesca y Caza** (Sernap) ① *San Antonio 427, piso 8, Santiago, T02-639 1918, www.sernapesca.cl, Mon-Fri 0900-1400*. Check with **Sernatur** about closed seasons.

Horseriding

There is more of an equine culture south of Santiago than further north, but some of the best riding country is to the north and east of Santiago, where the narrow tracks over mountain passes provide spectacular terrain. Saddles are narrow and covered with sheepskins, but Argentine saddles are wider and tend to be more comfortable.

Horse treks are organized in Santiago, in the Elqui and Hurtado valleys, in the Lake District and on Chiloé, and in numerous remote areas of the south. One of the best places for hiring and riding horses is along the west coast of Chiloé; expect to pay US$5 per hour. The biggest danger to riders is from cars and trucks

Buying a horse

A good horse costs from US$350 upwards; anything cheaper is likely to be a nag. The best horses are to be found in the area around Osorno. In rural areas, everyone will know who has horses for sale; if arriving at a city ask in a vet's for help in finding a reputable seller of horses. Horse sales are frequent in Puerto Montt's livestock market, where horses are sold by weight. A good saddle costs at least US$300 (including tack). Pack-saddles cost a similar price; when buying a pack-saddle, make sure that the wooden cross is not cut low, as these press on the horse's withers and lead to sores. Saddlebags (*alforjas*) can be made up in saddlers (*talabarterías*) for about US$40; make sure that the stitching is strong as they are liable to rip. A bale of

Mountain biking

Mountain biking is a popular activity, particularly on descents from the Andes and from *refugios* on volcanoes such as Antillanca and Osorno. Touring the length of the **Carretera Austral** by mountain bike is also an excellent way of seeing this part of the country. Bikers might also wish to explore coastal areas anywhere between Valparaíso and Puerto Montt. In resorts such as Pucón and San Pedro, reasonable quality mountain bikes can be hired (prices from US$8 per half day). The best place in Santiago for bikes is on Calle San Diego, south of the Alameda.

Sailing and yachting

Sailing, both wind and motor powered, is popular in Chile. Protected harbours, yacht clubs and racing fleets can be found at most sizeable coastal towns. The biggest regatta in Chile's sailing calendar is the biennial event in January (2004, 2006 etc) from Puerto Montt around the coast of **Chiloé**. There are also important annual regattas, plus weekly events on **Lagos Llanquihue** and **Villarrica** every Saturday, racing Lasers, Vagabonds and catamarans. Sailing is best south of Puerto Montt. You should allow at least a week to begin to do justice to Chiloé and the islands off its eastern shore. Three weeks or more are required to reach the glaciers of **Laguna San Rafael**.

Chartering

A variety of sail and power boats can be chartered from **MDS Charters** in **Puerto Montt** (see page 368). Most charters are skippered: unusually good sailing credentials are required for a bareboat charter. For the really adventurous a dozen or more sailing yachts are based in **Ushuaia/Puerto Williams**: these are blue water sailing yachts doing charters to Cape Horn and Antarctica. They advertise in sailing magazines and are often booked a year in advance.

Yacht facilities

There are three travel lifts in **Valdivia**, among them a 35-tonne lift and complete yacht repair facility at the modern **Awolplast** boatyard. The Valdivia yacht club often has slips available. **Puerto Montt** has the new **Marina del Sur**, with 65 slips, hydraulic lift, showers and laundry. Budget minded sailors can pick up a mooring at the **Club Náutico** here. South of Puerto Montt there are no marina facilities. Complete re-provisioning can be carried out in Puerto Montt, Castro, Puerto Aisén, Puerto Natales and Ushuaia; odds and ends can be found at Melinka and Puerto Aguirre, but fuel and other supplies are virtually unobtainable between Puerto Aguirre and Puerto Natales.

Navigation

The yachting season runs from November to March in these southern waters. South of 45S the weather is significantly worse than at corresponding latitudes in the northern hemisphere. Reasonably accurate weather forecasts are provided by the Chilean Navy and are updated twice daily: they are broadcast over HF radio by voice and weatherfax map. Complete chart portfolios are stocked at the Navy administration offices in Puerto Montt and Puerto Williams. Individual charts cost US$23 each and are generally superior to the US charts. A high quality colour chart atlas containing 28 cm by 43 cm reductions of the entire Chile chart portfolio was published in 1997.

! Chilean national parks

Chile has an extensive system of protected natural areas, covering seven million hectares in all. These areas are divided into national parks, forest reserves, natural monuments and natural sanctuaries, but these distinctions are of little importance for the visitor. Most of these areas have public access and details of the majority are given in the text. Camping areas are usually clearly designated, especially in the major natural areas, and wild camping is discouraged and frequently banned.

The first forest reserve was the Reserva Forestal Malleco in 1907; the first national park was the Parque Nacional Vicente Pérez Rosales in 1926. The expansion of the system has been based on the desire to preserve natural resources that may be under threat and to provide access for the public to areas of outstanding beauty.

All of these protected areas are managed by CONAF (the Corporación Nacional Forestal), a dependency of the Ministry of Agriculture which also has responsibility for forestry development. The address of CONAF's head office in Santiago is given below. It maintains an office in each of the regions of the country and kiosks in some natural areas and other locations. It publishes an illustrated guide to the parks and maps of the major protected areas which can be obtained from its head office and from some regional offices, the addresses of which are given in the text. CONAF publishes a useful little book on native trees, *Arboles nativas de Chile, Guía de Reconocimiento*, by Claudio Donoso Zegers (1983).

Skiing

Chile's major international ski resorts lie in the Andes near Santiago (see page 121), but skiing is possible from Santiago to Punta Arenas. **Sernatur** produces a leaflet on all Chilean ski resorts. Skiing elsewhere is mostly on the volcanoes to the south of Santiago, although back-country ski-mountaineering is quite possible on the volcanoes of the northern *altiplano* where a guide is essential and expertise required. The larger resorts in the south are **Termas de Chillán**, **Villarrica/Pucón** and **Antillanca**, all of which have accommodation on or near the slopes. There are, however, alternatives to these: many suitable volcanoes close to towns have a small base lodge and a lift which functions at weekends or peak periods (eg Antuco near Los Angeles; Llaima and Lonquimay further south). Here prices tend to be very reasonable and basic equipment rental is usually possible in the nearest town. Hitching is often the only form of transport, though it is sometimes possible to arrange transport with the local **Club Andino**. After all the effort to reach the snow, the atmosphere is happy-go-lucky and the skiing is great.

In the southern resorts skiing is for the laid-back and adventurous only. Snow conditions tend to become more slushy the further south you go. Lift systems are not the most modern, fast or well-maintained, piste preparation is mediocre and the weather is often more rainy than snowy. Despite all these disadvantages skiing on an active volcano looking down onto five huge lakes, as is the case at Villarrica/Pucón, is a memory which will truly last a lifetime.

Trekking

Chile offers limitless possibilities for both short and long treks in vastly differing landscapes: a one-day hike to the **Valle de la Luna** near San Pedro de Atacama is half

Over 1,000 km of hiking opportunities have been opened up by the building of
the Carretera Austral, though the heavy rainfall in this area can be a drawback. Within
the national parks there are often short two- to three-hour sign-posted nature trails,
starting from a visitor's centre, supplemented, in season, by lectures (usually only in
Spanish), on flora and fauna and other highlights of the park.

The latest plan is the **Sendero de Chile**, a walking route stretching all the way
from the Peruvian border to Tierra del Fuego, which is due to be completed by 2010.
Whether this ambitious undertaking will ever be finally realised remains to be seen: it
seems likely that the authorities in the Atacama and Aysen regions may have
particular difficulties, although certain sections are now open in the far north of the
country, and also in the Central Valley. For more information, see www.visit-chile.org
or www.senderodechile.cl, or ask at any **Sernatur** office.

Watersports

Water sports, such as diving and surfing, are generally practised in northern Chile. An
exception is **Pichilemu**, a resort three hours to the south-west of Santiago, which is
famous for surfing. ⟫ *For Sailing and yachting, see page 63.*

Rafting

Over 20 rivers between Santiago and Tierra del Fuego are excellent for white-water rafting.
Apart from the Maipo, which is the most easily accessible from Santiago, the main ones
are the Cachapoal, Teno, Claro, Maule and Biobío; the Trancura, Fuy, Bueno, Rahue and
Petrohué; the Yelcho, Futaleufú; Corcovado, Palena and Baker and the Serrano and
Tyndall. One of the most beautiful rivers is the Río Petrohué, which flows between the
Osorno and Calbuco volcanoes with lush temperate rainforest along its banks.

Rafting is generally well organized and equipment is usually of high quality. Access
to the headwaters of most rivers is easy. Agencies, particularly in Santiago, Pucón and
Puerto Varas, offer half-day trips to Grade 3 rivers for beginners, US$40-69 per person.
Rafts should ideally carry six people and certainly no more than seven plus guide.

Kayaking

The most attractive waters for sea kayaking are around the islands off eastern **Chiloé** or
around **Hornopirén** in the fjords of the sheltered Gulf of Ancud. Adventurous and
experienced sea kayakers will be tempted by the prospect of circumnavigating the island
of Cape Horn in the far south. The highlight for lake kayaking is the open competition on
Lago Llanquihue, involving five stages totalling 310 km around the lake shore.

Kayaks can be hired from **Oceanic** ① *Isidora Goyenehcea, 3120, Piso 7, T02
244-2020 , info@oceanic.cl*, and **Kayak Equipment** ① *San Vicente de Paul 5831, La
Reina, T/F02-2775288*, both in Santiago, and from **Canoas Tours** ① *Rosario 1305,
T02-233587* in Puerto Varas. Courses are available at the **Chiloé Sea Kayaking Centre**
near Dalcahue and are bookable through **Altué Expeditions** in Santiago.

Health

Local populations in Chile are exposed to a range of health risks not encountered in
the western world. Many of the diseases are major problems for the local poor and
destitute. The risk to travellers is more remote but cannot be ignored.

Obviously five-star travel is going to carry less risk than back-packing on a
minimal budget. The health care in the region is varied. There are many excellent

private and government clinics/hospitals. As with all medical care, first impressions count. If a facility is grubby, staff wear grey coats instead of white ones then be wary of the general standard of medicine and hygiene. A good tip is to contact the embassy or consulate on arrival and ask where the recommended clinics (those used by diplomats) are. Diseases you may be exposed to are caused by viruses, bacteria and parasites. The key viral disease is **Dengue fever**, which is transmitted by a mosquito that bites in the day, see page 68. Bacterial diseases include tuberculosis (**TB**) and some causes of traveller's **diarrhoea**. Tropical South American countries pose a greater disease risk than Temperate South American countries such as Chile. Other health problems, such as altitude sickness, may affect you along the entire length of the Andes and travellers should be aware that certain areas of the country are prone to extreme drops in temperature; take local advice as to what additional clothing or protection may be required.

Before you go

Ideally see your GP or travel clinic at least six weeks before departure for general advice on travel risks, malaria and **vaccinations**. Get a **dental check**, know your own **blood group** and if you suffer a long-term condition such as diabetes or epilepsy make sure someone knows or that you have a Medic Alert bracelet/necklace with this information. Take out medical **insurance**. Make sure it covers all eventualities, especially evacuation to your home country by a medically equipped plane. Obtain a spare glasses prescription, a spare oral contraceptive prescription (or enough pills to last) and, if you suffer from a chronic illness (such as diabetes, high blood pressure, ear or sinus troubles, cardio-pulmonary disease or nervous disorder) arrange for a check up with your doctor, who can at the same time provide you with a letter explaining the details of your disability in English and if possible Spanish. If you are on regular **medication**, make sure you have enough to cover the period of your travel.

Vaccinations for Chile

Hepatitis A Recommended as the disease can be caught easily from food/water.
Polio Recommended if nil in last 10 years.
Rabies Recommended if travelling to remote areas.
Tetanus Recommended if nil in last 10 years (but after 5 doses you have had enough for life).
Typhoid Recommended if nil in last 3 years.
Yellow Fever Not required for Chile. However, if you are travelling more extensively around South America it is best to get this vaccine since you will need it for the northern areas.

What to take

For longer trips involving jungle treks take a clean needle pack, clean dental pack and water filtration device. **MedicAlert** bracelets, or an equivalent, should be carried or worn by anyone with a significant medical condition. **Travel With Care** ⓘ *Homeway, Amesbury, Wiltshire, SP4 7BH, T0870 7459261, www.travelwithcare.co.uk,* provides a large range of products for sale.

Antibiotics Ciproxin (Ciprofloxacin) is a useful antibiotic for traveller's diarrhoea (which can affect up to 70% of travellers). It can be obtained by private prescription in the UK, which is expensive, or bought over the counter in South American pharmacies, but if you do this check that the pills are in date. You take one 500 mg tablet when the diarrhoea starts and if you do not feel better in 24 hours the diarrhoea is likely to have a non-bacterial cause and may be viral. Viral causes of taking the right mixture of salt and water. This is available as rehydration salts in ready made sachets or can be made up by adding a teaspoon of sugar and a half teaspoon of salt to a litre of clean water. Flat carbonated drinks can also be used.

Diarrhoea treatment Immodium is a great standby for those diarrhoeas that occur at awkward times ie before a long coach/train journey or on a trek. It helps stop the flow of diarrhoea and in the author's view is of more benefit than harm. It was believed that letting the bacteria or viruses flow out had to be more beneficial. However, with Immodium they still come out but in a more solid form. Pepto-Bismol is used a lot by the Americans for diarrhoea. It certainly relieves symptoms but like Immodium it is not a cure for underlying disease. Be aware that it turns the stool black as well as making it more solid.

Insect bite relief If you are prone to insects' bites or develop lumps quite soon after being bitten, carry an Aspivenin kit. This syringe suction device is available from **Boots Chemists** in the UK and draws out some of the allergic materials and provides quick relief.

Mosquito repellents Remember that DEET (Di-ethyltoluamide) is the gold standard. Apply the repellent every 4-6 hours but more often if you are sweating heavily. If a non-DEET product is used check who tested it. Validated products (tested at the London School of Hygiene and Tropical Medicine) include Mosiguard, Non-DEET Jungle formula and non-DEET Autan. If you want to use citronella remember that it must be applied hourly to be effective.

Painkillers Paracetomol or another suitable painkiller can have multiple uses for symptoms, but always remember that more than eight paracetomol a day can lead to liver failure.

Soap Biodegradable soap for jungle areas or ordinary soap for emergencies. Handwashing is the safest way of preventing unwanted muck to mouth transmission before you eat.

Sun block The Australian's have a great campaign, which has reduced skin cancer. It is called 'Slip, Slap, Slop': as in slip on a shirt, slap on a hat, slop on sun screen. SPF stands for Sunscreen Protection Factor. It is measured by determining how long a given person takes to burn with and without the sunscreen product on. If it takes 10 times longer with the sunscreen product then that product has an SPF of 10. If it only takes twice as long then that product has an SPF of 2. In reality, the testing labs don't really burn the test subjects. They give them just enough UVR to cause the skin to turn barely red. This minimum dose is called the MED (minimal erythemal dose). The higher the SPF the greater the protection. However, do not just use higher factors just to stay out in the sun longer. 'Flash frying' (desperate bursts of excessive exposure), as it is called, is known to increase the risks of skin cancer.

When you arrive

When you arrive in each country let the Embassy or Consulate know. The information can be useful if a friend/relative gets ill at home and there is a desperate search for you around the globe. You can also ask them about locally recommended medical facilities and do's and don'ts.

Medical facilities

Medical facilities in Chile are generally perfectly adequate. There are English (or other foreign language) speaking doctors in most major cities. Your embassy representative will often be able to give you the name of local reputable doctors, and most of the better hotels have a doctor on standby. If you do fall ill and cannot find a recommended doctor, try the Outpatient Department of a hospital – private hospitals are usually less crowded and offer better standards of care. Though there are state hospitals (who may perform minor tasks such as changing dressings, etc., free of charge), these are generally overcrowded and underfunded (something which travellers from the UK, at any rate, will be able to relate to). All large towns will have private clinics, and most small provincial centres should do as well – for anything remotely serious, it is probably best to go here and rely on the insurance to pick up the tab. Pharmacies are widespread. Addresses of hospitals are given in the text.

An A-Z of health risks

Altitude sickness

Symptoms This can creep up on you as just a mild headache with nausea or lethargy. The more serious disease is caused by fluid collecting in the brain in the enclosed space of the skull and can lead to coma and death. A lung disease with breathlessness and fluid infiltration of the lungs is also recognised.

Prevention and cure Get acclimatized. Do not try to reach the highest levels on your first few days of arrival. Climbers like to take treatment drugs as protective measures but this can lead to macho idiocy and death. The peaks are still there and so are the trails, whether it takes you personally a bit longer than someone else does not matter as long as you come back down alive. The best cure is to descend as soon as possible.

Chagas disease

Symptoms The disease occurs throughout South America, affects locals more than travellers, but travellers can be exposed by sleeping in mud-constructed huts where the bug that carries the parasite bites and defaecates on an exposed part of skin. You may notice nothing at all or a local swelling, with fever, tiredness and enlargement of lymph glands, spleen and liver. The seriousness of the parasite infection is caused by the long-term effects which include gross enlargement of the heart and/or guts.

Prevention and cure Sleep under a permethrin-treated bed net and use insect repellents. To cure it, early treatment is required with toxic drugs.

Dengue fever

Symptom This disease can be contracted throughout South America. In travellers this can cause a severe flu like illness with fever, lethargy, enlarged lymph glands and muscle pains. It starts suddenly, lasts for two to three days, seems to get better for two to three days and then kicks in again for another two to three days. It is usually all over in an unpleasant week. The local children are prone to the much nastier haemorrhagic form of the disease, which causes them to bleed from internal organs, mucous membranes and often leads to their death.

Prevention and cure The mosquitoes that carry the Dengue virus bite during the day unlike the malaria mosquitoes. Sadly this means that repellent and covered limbs are a 24 hr issue. Check your accommodation for flower pots and shallow pools of water since these are where the Dengue-carrying mosquitoes breed. The traveller's disease is self limiting and forces rest and recuperation on the sufferer.

Diarrhorea/intestinal upset

Symptoms Diarrhoea can refer either to loose stools or an increased frequency; both of these can be a nuisance. It should be short lasting. Persistence beyond two weeks, with blood or pain, require specialist medical attention.

Prevention and cure The standard advice is to be careful with water and ice for drinking. Ask yourself where the water came from. If you have any doubts then boil it or filter and treat it. There are many filter/treatment devices now available on the market. Food can also transmit disease. Be wary of salads, re-heated foods or food that has been left out in the sun having been cooked earlier in the day. There is a **69** simple adage that says 'wash it, peel it, boil it or forget it'. Also be wary of unpasteurised dairy products these can transmit a range of diseases from brucellosis (fevers and constipation), to listeria (meningitis) and tuberculosis of the gut (obstruction, constipation, fevers and weight loss). Ciproxin will cure many of the bacterial causes but none of the viral ones. Immodium and Pepto-Bismol provide symptomatic relief. Dehydration can be a key problem especially in hot climates and is best avoided by taking oral rehydration salts (at least one large cup of drink for each loose stool).

A bout of diarrhorea/ intestinal upset is almost inevitable. A study showed that up to 70% of travellers may suffer during their trip.

Essentials Health

Hanta virus

Some forest and riverine rodents carry hanta virus, epidemics of which have occurred in Argentina and Chile, but do occur worldwide. Symptoms are a flu-like illness which can lead to complications. Try as far as possible to avoid rodent-infested areas, especially close contact with rodent droppings. Campers and parents with small children should be especially careful.

Hepatitis

Symptoms Hepatitis means inflammation of the liver. Viral causes of Hepatitis can be acquired anywhere in South America. The most obvious sign is if your skin or the whites of your eyes become yellow. However, prior to this all that you may notice is itching and tiredness.

Prevention and cure Pre-travel Hepatitis A vaccine is the best bet. Hepatitis B is spread by a different route by blood and unprotected sexual intercourse, both of which can be avoided. Unfortunately there is no vaccine for Hepatitis C or the increasing alphabetical list of other Hepatitis viruses. Early on, depending on the type of Hepatitis, a vaccine or immunoglobulin may reduce the duration of the illness.

Leptospirosis

Various forms of leptospirosis occur throughout Latin America, transmitted by a bacterium which is excreted in rodent urine. Fresh water and moist soil harbour the organisms, which enter the body through cuts and scratches. If you suffer from any form of prolonged fever consult a doctor.

Malaria

Malaria is not a concern in Chile.

Marea Roja

The *marea roja*, or 'red tide', is a maritime phenomenon that affects the whole of Chile from the south of Chiloé to Tierra del Fuego. This affects certain types of shellfish, and the result of an infected mollusc can be instant death – there is no cure. Though shellfish in reputable restaurants will have been checked, it is best to avoid eating seafood in private homes or fresh from the beach in these areas.

Marine bites and stings

Certain tropical sea fish when trodden upon inject venom into bathers' feet. This can be exceptionally painful. Wear plastic shoes if such creatures are reported. The pain can be relieved by immersing the foot in extremely hot water.

Prickly heat

A very common intensely itchy rash is avoided by frequent washing and by wearing loose clothing. It is cured by allowing skin to dry off (through use of powder and spending two nights in an air-conditioned hotel!).

Rabies

Remember that rabies is endemic throughout Latin America, so avoid dogs that are behaving strangely and cover your toes at night from the vampire bats, which also carry the disease. If you are bitten by a domestic or wild animal, do not leave things to chance: scrub the wound with soap and water and/or disinfectant, try to at least determine the animal's ownership, where possible, and seek medical assistance at once. The course of treatment depends on whether you have already been satisfactorily vaccinated against rabies. If you have (this is worthwhile if you are spending lengths of time in developing countries) then some further doses of vaccine are all that is required. Human diploid vaccine is the best, but expensive: other, older kinds of vaccine, such as that derived from duck embryos may be the only types available. These are effective, much cheaper and interchangeable generally with the human derived types. If not already vaccinated then anti rabies serum (immunoglobulin) may be required in addition. It is important to finish the course of treatment.

Sexual health

Unprotected sex can spread HIV, Hepatitis B and C, Gonorrhea (green discharge), chlamydia (nothing to see but may cause painful urination and later female infertility), painful recurrent herpes, syphilis and warts, just to name a few. You can cut down on the risks by using condoms, a femidom or if you want to be completely safe, by avoiding sex altogether.

Snake bite and other animal bites and stings

It is a very rare event indeed for travellers, but if you are unlucky (or careless) enough to be bitten by a venomous snake, spider, scorpion or sea creature, try to identify the creature, without putting yourself in further danger. What you might expect if bitten are: fright, swelling, pain and bruising around the bite and soreness of the regional lymph glands, perhaps nausea, vomiting and a fever. Symptoms of serious poisoning would be: numbness and tingling of the face, muscular spasms, convulsions, shortness of breath or a failure of the blood to clot, causing generalized bleeding.

Treatment of snake bite Victims should be taken to a hospital or a doctor without delay. Commercial snake bite and scorpion kits are available, but are usually only useful for the specific types of snake or scorpion. Most serum has to be given intravenously so it is not much good equipping yourself with it unless you are used to making injections into veins. It is best to rely on local practice in these cases, because the particular creatures will be known about locally and appropriate treatment can be given. Reassure and comfort the victim frequently. Immobilize the limb by a bandage or a splint and get the person to lie still. Do not slash the bite area and try to suck out the poison. If you are not experienced, do not apply a tourniquet.

Precautions Do not walk in snake territory in bare feet or sandals – wear proper shoes or boots. If you encounter a snake stay put until it slithers away and do not investigate a wounded snake. Spiders and scorpions may be found in the more basic hotels, especially in the Andean countries. If stung, rest and take plenty of fluids and call a doctor. The best precaution is to keep beds away from the walls and look inside your shoes and under the toilet seat every morning.

Sun burn

People with white skin are notorious for becoming red in hot countries because they like to stay out longer than everyone else and do not use adequate skin protection factors (see What to take, above). This can lead to sunburn, which is painful, followed by flaking of skin. Aloe vera gel is a good pain reliever for sunburn. Long-term sun damage leads to a loss of elasticity of skin and the development of pre-cancerous lesions. Many years later a mild or a very malignant form of cancer may develop. The milder basal cell carcinoma, if detected early, can be treated by cutting it out or freezing it. The much nastier malignant melanoma may have already spread to bone and brain at the time that it is first noticed.

Tapeworms

Acquired through eating the cysts of the worm in undercooked beef or pork. Humans can also get the cystic stage of the pork tape worm (cysticercosis) through food or water contaminated by human faeces. The cysts get into the muscle and brain, and cause fits months or years later.

Ticks

Ticks usually attach themselves to the lower parts of the body often after walking in areas where cattle have grazed. They take a while to attach themselves strongly, but swell up as they start to suck blood. The important thing is to remove them gently, so that they do not leave their head parts in your skin because this can cause a nasty allergic reaction some days later. Do not use petrol, vaseline, lighted cigarettes etc to remove the tick, but, with a pair of tweezers remove the beast gently by gripping it at the attached (head) end and rock it out in very much the same way that a tooth is extracted. Certain tropical flies which lay their eggs under the skin of sheep and cattle also occasionally do the same thing to humans with the unpleasant result that a maggot grows under the skin and pops up as a boil or pimple. The best way to remove these is to cover the boil with oil, vaseline or nail varnish so as to stop the maggot breathing, then to squeeze it out gently the next day.

Tuberculosis (TB)

Symptoms TB can cause fever, night sweats and a chronic cough. Some people cough up blood. You may not know you have it but your friends will remark on your gradual weight loss and lack of energy. The lung type of TB is spread by coughs. Sometimes TB causes swelling of the lymph glands. TB can be spread by dairy products. Gut or pelvic TB can cause abdominal lumps, gut obstruction and even infertility. All parts of the body can be affected by TB.

    Prevention and cure Unfortunately BCG vaccine may not protect against lung TB. The best you can do is avoid unpasteurised dairy products and do not let anyone cough or splutter all over you. After diagnosis at least six months continuous treatment with several drugs is required to effect a cure.

Typhoid fever

Symptoms This is a gut infection that can spread to the blood stream. You get it from someone else's muck getting into your mouth. A classic example would be the waiter who fails to wash his hands and then serves you a salad. The fever is an obvious feature, occasionally there is a mild red rash on the stomach and often you have a headache. Constipation or diarrhoea can occur. Gut pain and hearing problems may also feature. Deaths occur from a hole 'punched' straight through the gut.

    Prevention and cure The vaccine is very effective and is best boosted every three years. Watch what you eat and the hygiene of the place or those serving your food.s: Antibiotics are required for a cure and you are probably best managed in hospital.

Typhus

This can still occur and is carried by ticks. There is usually a reaction at the site of the bite and a fever. Seek medical advice.

Underwater health

If you go diving make sure that you are fit do so. The **British Scuba Association** (BSAC) ① *Telford's Quay, South Pier Road, Ellesmere Port, Cheshire CH65 4FL, UK,*

T0151 350 6200, F0151 350 6215, www.bsac.com, can put you in touch with doctors who do medical examinations. Check that the dive company knows what it is doing, has appropriate certification from **BSAC** or **PADI** (the Professional Association of Diving Instructors; www.padi.com) and that the equipment is well maintained. Protect your feet from cuts, beach dog parasites (larva migrans) and sea urchins. The latter are almost impossible to remove but can be dissolved with lime or vinegar. Treat secondary infections with antibiotics. Serious diving injuries may need time in a Decompression Chamber.

Water

There are a number of ways of purifying water. Dirty water should first be strained through a filter bag and then boiled or treated. Bringing water to a rolling boil at sea level is sufficient to make the water safe for drinking, but at higher altitudes you have to boil the water for a few minutes longer to ensure all microbes are killed. There are sterilizing methods that can be used and there are proprietary preparations containing chlorine (eg Puritabs) or iodine (eg Pota Aqua) compounds. Chlorine compounds generally do not kill protozoa (eg Giardia). There are a number of water filters (available in personal and expedition size) that work either on mechanical or chemical principles. Make sure you take the spare parts or spare chemicals with you and do not believe everything the manufacturers say.

Further information

Useful websites

Blood Care Foundation,
www.bloodcare.org.uk Charity 'dedicated to the provision of screened blood and resuscitation fluids in countries where these are not readily available.' It will dispatch certified non-infected blood of the right type to your hospital/clinic from various centres around the world.

British Travel Health Association
www.btha.org Official website of an organization of travel health professionals.

Centers for Disease Control and Prevention (USA), *www.cdc.gov* The US Government gives excellent advice on travel health, has useful disease maps and has details of disease outbreaks.

Department of Health Travel Advice
www.doh.gov.uk/traveladvice Excellent site, also available as a free booklet, the T6, from Post offices. Lists vaccine advice requirements for each country.

Fit for Travel, *www.fitfortravel.scot.nhs.uk* Scottish site provides a quick A-Z of vaccine and travel health advice requirements for each country.

Foreign and Commonwealth Office (FCO), *www.fco.gov.uk* A key travel advice site, with useful information on the country,

people, climate and a list of UK embassies/consulates. Also promotes the concept of 'Know Before You Go', and encourages travel insurance and appropriate travel health advice. Links to the Department of Health travel advice site, listed below.

Medic Alert, *www.medicalalert.co.uk* The foundation produces bracelets and necklaces for those with existing medical problems. You write your key medical details on paper inside the bracelet/necklace, so that if you collapse, a medical person can identify you as someone with epilepsy or allergies etc.

NetDoctor, *www.Netdoctor.co.uk* General health advice site with a useful section on travel and an ask-the-expert chat forum.

Public Health Laboratory Service
www.phls.org.uk Malaria advice guidelines for travel around the world. It gives specific advice about the right drugs for each location. It also has useful information for those who are pregnant, suffering from epilepsy or planning to travel with children.

Travel Screening Services,
www.travelscreening.co.uk The Health author's website. A private clinic dedicated to integrated travel health. The clinic gives vaccines, travel health advice, email and SMS text vaccine reminders, as well as screening returned travellers for tropical diseases.

Tropical Medicine Bureau, *www.tmb.ie*
Irish-based site with a good collection of travel health information and disease risks.
World Health Organization, *www.who.int*
Links to the *WHO Blue Book* on travel advice, which lists the diseases in different regions, describes vaccination schedules and makes clear which countries have Yellow Fever Vaccination certificate requirements.

Books and leaflets

The Travellers Good Health Guide by Dr Ted Lankester (ISBN 0-85969-827-0)
Expedition Medicine (The Royal Geographic Society) Editors David Warrell and Sarah Anderson. (ISBN 1 86197 040-4)

Organisation, Geneva (ISBN 92 4 158026 7)
The World's Most Dangerous Places by Robert Young Pelton, Coskun Aral and Wink Dulles. (ISBN 1-566952-140-9)
The Travellers Guide to Health (T6) can be obtained by calling the Health Literature Line on 0800 555 777.

Advice for travellers on avoiding the risks of HIV and AIDS (Travel Safe) is available from Dept of Health, PO Box 777, London SE1 6XH.

The health section was written by **Dr Charlie Easmon** MBBS, MRCP, MPH, DTM&H, DOCCMed, who runs **Travel Screening Services** based at 1 Harley Street (www.travelscreening.co.uk).

Keeping in touch

Communications

Internet
The rise of the internet café is inexorable, in Chile as elsewhere. Whereas five years ago you would have been lucky to find one in each large city, there is now fierce competition in most tourist centres, which, of course, means that prices are competitive as well, ranging from US$0.80-US$3 per hour. Other than dealing with slow connection speeds (in rural areas) and Spanish keyboards, the services are perfectly adequate, and should suit most people's needs. To access the @ symbol, you usually press the ctrl and alt keys together with q. Website addresses are given wherever possible throughout the guide.

Post
The Chilean postal system is usually efficient. Airmail takes around a week from both the UK and the US. Seamail takes eight to 12 weeks from the UK. There is a daily airmail service to Europe. Letters to Europe/North America cost US$0.65. To register a letter costs US$0.80. Surface mail rates for parcels to Europe cost US$16 for less than one kilo; US$20 for one to three kilos; US$350 for 10 kilos. The poste restante service ('*lista de correo*') only holds mail for 30 days, then returns it to sender. The *Lista de Correo* in the Central Post Office in Santiago is good and efficiently organized, but letters are kept separately for men and women so envelopes should be marked Sr or Sra/Srta.

Telephone
National and international calls have been opened up for competition in Chile. For those with their own phoneline, there are eight main companies (*carriers*) offering competing rates, which are widely advertised. If you do not have your own phone, though, it is best to make a call from a **Centro de llamados**, or call centre. The cheapest call centres tend to be run by **CTC** or by small, private independent operators. National calls cost around US$0.10 per minute. However, **telephone boxes** can be used for making local, long-distance and collect calls and for receiving calls. They are programmed to direct calls via one carrier: to make a local call, simply dial the number you require and pay the rate charged by the carrier who owns the booth. To make an inter-urban call, dial 'o' plus the

Telephone access codes for long-distance calls

Entel 123
CTC Mundo 188
CNT 121 (in north)
Telefónica del Sur 121 (in south)
VTR 120

Chilesat 171
Bell South Chile 181
Isutel 155
Transam 113

area code (DDD) and the number; if you wish to select a carrier, dial its code before the area code (leaving out 'o'), then the number. To make an international call, dial 'oo' before the country code. Yellow phones accept only 50 peso coins. Blue phones accept pre-paid phone cards costing 5,000 pesos (*tarjeta telefónica*); available from kiosks. Booths taking **CTC** cards are more widespread than others. Phone cards only charge for the duration of the call rather than for the normal three-minute minimum. There are also special phones for long-distance domestic calls, which accept Mastercard and Visa credit cards. **Entel** has strategically-placed, self-dialling white phones; users press a button and are instantly connected with an operator from their own country. A call to a mobile costs US$0.25-0.30 per minute.

❖ *Area codes are given throughout this guide; the prefix 09- indicates a mobile phone.*

Media

Newspapers and magazines

Santiago daily papers are *El Mercurio* (centre-right, a heavyweight broadsheet), *La Nación* (liberal-left), *La Segunda* (middle-market tabloid), *La Tercera* (more serious tabloid), *La Quarta* (salacious and gossip-mongering), *Las Últimas Noticias* and *La Hora. News Review* ① *Casilla 151/9, Santiago, T02-2361423, F2362293; newsrevi@mcl.cl, US$1.20*, a weekly in English is published on Fridays, and is on sale at selected kiosks. Recent international newspapers can be bought at kiosks on the Paseo Ahumada in Santiago. Magazines published weekly include *Hoy, Qué Pasa, Ercilla, Rocinante* (art, culture, society).

❖ *Look out for 'The Clinic', a satirical weekly paper named after the hospital at which General Pinochet was arrested in 1998.*

Radio

South America has more community radio stations than practically anywhere else in the world. Visitors to the region are recommended to bring or buy a compact portable radio, with digital tuning and a full range of short-wave bands, as well as FM, long and medium wave, as a practical means to brush up on the language, sample popular culture and absorb some regional music. International broadcasters such as the **BBC World Service** (17.8h or 15.19 MHz), the **Voice of America** (6130 or 7370 KHz), **Monitor Radio International** (operated by Christian Science Monitor in Boston, Mass (15.30 or 9.755 MHz) and the Quito-based evangelical station, **HCJB**, keep the traveller abreast of news and events, in both English and Spanish. In small regional centres, the local radio station is a very effective medium for sending a message to someone else in the area; go to the studio and make the request in person.

Television

TV channels include **TVUC** (Universidad Católica) on Channel 13, the leading station; **TVN** (government operated) on Channel 7; **Megavisión** (private) on Channel 9 and **La Red** (private) on Channel 4. Soap operas (*teleseries*) and soccer constitute the most popular programmes.

Santiago Region

Introduction

If you are flying into Chile, you will probably arrive in Santiago. No one can deny that the Chilean capital has a dramatic setting, in a hollow surrounded by mountains, with peaks over 5,000 m visible on clear days. They are most dramatic just after rainfall in winter, when the smog clears and the new snows glisten.

Santiago is a vibrant, progressive city. With its many **parks**, interesting **museums**, glittering **high-rises** and **boutiques**, it bursts with possibilities. As far as **entertainment** goes, there are popular scenes in everything from techno to progressive rock, via bohemian hang-outs and most of the bits in between. Certainly, those who spend an extended period of time in Santiago soon find plenty of things to do at night and at the weekends.

The region near the capital is in many ways a microcosm of the country as a whole. Not only are the resorts on the coast less than two hours away, but the city is within easy reach of the best **ski resorts** in South America, which are also great spots for **weekend hikes** in summer. Meanwhile, the area south of Santiago is perhaps the best wine-producing area in Chile. Autumn, when the grapes are being harvested, is a particularly good time to visit the **vineyards**.

★ **Don't miss...**

① **Cerro San Cristóbal** Take in a panoramic view of the city and the Andes (smog permitting) from the top of Cerro San Cristóbal, page 88.

② **Mercado Central** Have lunch at this market and discover weird and wonderful varieties of shellfish, page 107.

③ **Museo de Arte Precolombino** Visit one of the world's most important collections of Native South American artefacts at this museum, page 84.

④ **Ski resorts** Take to the slopes on skis at any of the modern resorts in the Andes, just a stone's throw from Santiago, page 121.

⑤ **Maipo Valley** Take a tour then sip wine at some of Chile's best vineyards, page 119.

Santiago → *Phone code: 02. Colour map 3, B3. Population: 6 mn.*

Situated in the Central Valley, Santiago has grown to become the sixth largest city in South America, as well as the political, economic and cultural capital of Chile. The city is crossed from east to west by the long-suffering Río Mapocho, into which most of the city's sewage is dumped; however, the magnificent chain of the Andes provides a more appropriate natural landmark.

It is easy to see Santiago as just another westernized Latin American city but, away from the centre and wealthier suburbs, the reality is more complicated. Street vendors are often newly arrived from rural areas, many living in appalling **villas misérias** *on the city's outskirts (Pudahuel and La Pintana are both especially chastening* **barrios** *for those who claim that "poverty does not exist in Chile"). Some* **barrios** *in the south of the city even have a higher concentration of Mapuche people than the Mapuche heartlands of the south.*

If just passing through, Santiago is unlikely to be the highlight of your trip to Chile – it can take a while to get a real feeling for the city's pulse. However, it does still warrant a visit of a few days. On top of its setting and nightlife, there are excellent museums, and you will find that the contrast with the rest of the country is stark; over a third of Chileans live in Gran Santiago, so, if you want to understand the country you are visiting, Santiago is a must. ►► *For Sleeping, eating and other listings, see pages 93-118.*

Ins and outs

Getting there

Air International and domestic flights arrive at the **Aeropuerto Arturo Merino Benitez** at Pudahuel, 26 km northwest of the city centre (see page 39). Frequent **bus** services between the international and domestic terminals and the city centre are operated by two companies: **Tur Bus** ① *to/from Moneda y San Martín, every 30 mins, US$2.50;* and **Centropuerto** ① *to/from Metro Los Héroes (just round the corner from Tur Bus), To2-6019883, first from centre 0600, last from airport 2230, US$2.50.* Return tickets are cheaper than two singles. En route to the airport, the buses also pick up at Estación Central and Terminal Santiago. Do not confuse these buses with the bus marked 'Aeropuerto', which stops 2 km short of the airport. **Minibus** services between the airport and hotels or other addresses in the city are operated by four companies with offices in the airport: **Transfer,** To2-7777707; **Delfos,** To2-6011111; **Turismo Bar-C** and **Navett,** To2-6956868. These charge US$5 to/from the city centre, US$7 to/from Las Condes. Minibuses to the airport should be booked the previous day, but taxis are cheaper if flagged down in the street. There is a **taxi** office inside the international terminal. Taxis to/from centre should cost around US$17, to/from Providencia US$20; agree the fare beforehand. It is also possible to negotiate taxi fares from the airport to quite distant cities such as Melipilla and Valparaíso; rates to Valparaíso can be as low as US$50.

Bus and train Buses arrive at one of four terminals, all located close to each other, just west of the centre and not far from the train station, along Avenida O'Higgins. This is the main east-west avenue through the city and is within easy reach of Line 1 of the metro. ►► *For further details, see Transport, page 111.*

Getting around

The city's main avenue, Avenida O'Higgins, is almost always referred to as the Alameda, while Plaza Baquedano, one of the city's main squares, is almost always known as Plaza Italia (in both instances, this book follows suit). Most of the more expensive accommodation is situated in the city centre or further east in the neighbourhoods of

⁝ Moving mountains

While Santiago's smog is not too bad in spring, summer and autumn, those who arrive here during winter could be in for an unpleasant shock. It might not take more than half an hour for your throat to begin to itch and your eyes to water due to one of Santiago's biggest problems – pollution. In 2001, it was rated the eighth most polluted city in the world. When Pedro de Valdivia founded the city in 1541, between the coastal mountains and the Andes, it must have seemed like a perfect site; he could never have imagined that the city would one day engulf the whole valley, and that the mountains would become a serious problem.

The principal reason for Santiago's high levels of pollution is that it lies in a bowl, encircled by mountains, which means that the smog is trapped. This, combined with the

centralization of Chilean industry in Santiago, the fact that many buses are not equipped with catalytic converters and the sheer volume of cars that choke the city's highways, conspires to create a problem that cannot easily be resolved. It is a serious issue: asthma rates are high and older people sometimes die during the winter *emergencias*, when the pollution gets particularly bad.

Over the years, all sorts of solutions have been proposed. A team of Japanese scientists once even suggested blowing up the part of the Andes nearest the city, so that the pollution could disperse more easily. Each weekday, cars that have number plates ending in one of two digits are prohibited from circulating. But, until the government finds a means of dispersing the population more widely throughout the country, the problem is likely to remain.

Santiago Region Ins & outs

Providencia and Las Condes. Most budget accommodation is located in the city centre or further west in the vicinity of the bus terminals. Although parts of the centre can be explored on foot, you will need to master the city's transport system, which is well organized, if crowded and slow in peak periods. ▸▸ *For a map of the metro, see page 113.*

Tourist information

Sernatur (Servicio Nacional de Turismo), *Av Providencia 1550, next to Providencia Municipal Library, T02-7318336, info@sernatur.cl, Mon-Fri 0845-1830, Sat 0900-1400*. The national tourist board has maps, many brochures and posters. English, German and some French are spoken. Good notice board. There is also an information office at the airport ① *0900-2100 daily*. **Municipal Tourist Board** ① *Casa Colorada, Merced 860, T02-336700*, offers walking tours of the city, on Wednesdays at 1500. There is also a good free booklet on historical buildings in the city available in English and Spanish, *Historical Heritage of Santiago: A Guide for Tourists*. Many tourist offices in small towns, particularly in the south, are closed in winter, so stock up on information here. Excellent road maps (US$2.50) and information may be obtained from the **Automóvil Club de Chile** ① *Vitacura 8620, T02-2125702, www.aclub.cl, Metro Pedro de Valdivia then bus to Vitacura, or a US$6 taxi ride from the centre, Mon-Fri 0845-1815, Sat 0900-1300*, which also gives discounts to members of affiliated motoring organizations; very helpful. **CONAF** (Corporación Nacional Forestal) ① *Presidente Bulnes 291, piso 1, T02-3900126, www.conaf.cl*, publishes a number of leaflets and has documents and maps about the national park system that can be consulted or photocopied (not very useful for walking). **CODEFF** (Comité Nacional Pro-Defensa de la Fauna y Flora) ① *Bilbao 691, Providencia, T02-2510262, www.codeff.cl*, can also provide information on environmental questions.

Security

Like all large cities, Santiago has problems of theft. However, it has to be said that these tend to be exaggerated by Santiaguinos. While the central area is frequented by pickpockets and bagsnatchers (who are often well-dressed) – operating mostly on the metro, around the Plaza de Armas, in Barrio Brasil, near Cerro Santa Lucía and around the restaurants in Bellavista – these are easily avoided with a little common sense. The biggest risk is in unwittingly entering a dangerous *barrio* away from the centre. Parts of Pudahuel in the west, Conchalí in the north and Macul and La Pintana in the south have a big drug and crime problem and can be dangerous. At night, it is best to take a public bus (*micro*) rather than a taxi, as you will be watched over by your fellow passengers; better still, call for a radio taxi.

Climate

The Santiago area enjoys a Mediterranean climate, with long dry summers and daytime temperatures rising to over 30°C, when the heat can be uncomfortable. Rainfall is heaviest in autumn and winter and almost unknown in summer. Long spells of rain are unlikely, storms being heavy and brief. Snowfall is rare, although frost is not uncommon, and, as houses in Santiago rarely have central heating, you will feel the cold more in winter. There is usually less wind in winter, making smog a more serious problem over the city (forecast levels of smog are published in the daily papers). Pollution levels vary; the west and the old 'city centre' are much worse affected than the more expensive areas around Las Condes. Pollution is usually at its worst in July and at its lightest in September and October and after rainfall.

Santiago orientation

⁝ 24 hours in the city

First, try to make sure you are here on a Saturday. Assuming you are staying in the centre, get up early and walk down to Calle San Diego for breakfast. Afterwards, walk down San Diego to the **Iglesia de los Sacre- mentinos** – Santiago's answer to Sacré Coeur – and then west through gardens until you reach the **Palacio Cousiño** in time for the first tour at 0930. This extraordinary building (see page 86) gives a real insight into the lives, customs and belief systems of the Chilean aristocracy and the opulence to which the upper classes became accustomed. Once the tour has finished, stroll to Toesca metro and head a few stops south to Franklin. Here you will find swarms of people all making their way to the **Mercado Bío Bío**. This market will show you how most of Santiago lives and it provides a striking contrast to Palacio Cousiño.

When you start feeling hungry, head back to Franklin metro and take the train north to **Cal y Canto**. On the opposite side of the Río Mapocho is the **Mercado Central**, where you will find some of the best **seafood restaurants** in Santiago. Don't be put off by the choice – take your time and enjoy some of the best shellfish the world has to offer.

After lunch, it's time to remind yourself that Santiago has one of the most dramatic settings of any of the world's major cities. Cross back over the Río Mapocho and stroll east towards the conical hill of **Cerro San Cristóbal**. If it's summer, the heat may be making you feel a little tired by now – if so, you could go up the hill on the **funicular railway**. If you are lucky and it is a clear day, you will have an unforgettable view of the Andes. Here you can stroll through lanes that are lined with trees – a world away from the clutter of the city. There are even swimming pools to cool off in and the chance to do some wine tasting. Towards dusk, have a drink in the café near the funicular railway station and watch the sun go down over the coastal mountain range, lighting up the snows of the Andes.

After dark, go back down the hill by funicular railway (it's not advisable to walk here in the evening) in time to sample Santiago's nightlife. At the foot of Cerro San Cristóbal is **Barrio Bellavista**. Here you can take your pick of any one of dozens of excellent (and expensive) restaurants, before going out to one of the area's buzzing *salsotecas*. These don't really get going until midnight and you'll usually find that you don't leave much before five, so perhaps head back to your hotel room for some sleep after dinner and then go out dancing later on.

Santiago was founded by Pedro de Valdivia in 1541 on the site of a small indigenous settlement between the southern bank of the Río Mapocho and the Cerro Santa Lucía. During the colonial period, it was only one of several Spanish administrative and cultural centres; also important were Concepción to the south and La Serena in the north. Nevertheless, by 1647 there were 12 churches in the city but, of these, only San Francisco (1618) survived the earthquake of that year. A further earthquake destroyed most of the city in 1730.

Following Independence, the city became more important. In the 1870s, under the Intendente (Regional governor) Benjamín Vicuña MacKenna, an urban plan was drafted, the Cerro Santa Lucía was made into a public park and the first trams were introduced. As the city grew at the end of the 19th century, the Chilean elite, wealthy from mining and shipping, built their mansions west of the centre around Calle Dieciocho. One of these families were the Cousiños, who built the Palacio Cousiño and later donated this and what became the Parque O'Higgins to the city. Expansion east towards Providencia began in 1895. Until the 1930s, much of the city centre had colonial buildings in the style of Quito or Lima, but expansion and modernization meant that these were gradually replaced. In the latter part of the 20th century, like most Latin American capital cities, Santiago spread rapidly. Many older Santiaguinos who live in areas that are now relatively central tell how, when

Santiago centre

0 metres 300
0 yards 300

affluent moved east into new neighbourhoods in the foothills of the Andes and poorer neighbourhoods were established to the west of the centre. This geographic division of wealth continues today.

Sights

The centre of the old city lies between the Río Mapocho and the city's main avenue, Alameda. From **Plaza Italia**, in the east of the city's central area, the river flows to the northwest and the Alameda runs to the southwest. From Plaza Italia, Calle Merced runs due west to the **Plaza de Armas**, the heart of the city, which lies five blocks south of the Río Mapocho. ▸▸ *For Sleeping, Eating and other listings, see pages 93-118.*

Around the Plaza de Armas

The shadiness and tranquillity of the Plaza de Armas has been disturbed by a recent remodelling of the square. Some of the taller trees were stripped away to make way for new stonework but most Santiaguinos are unhappy with the barer plaza that has resulted. On the eastern and southern sides of the Plaza de Armas, there are arcades with shops; on the northern side is the post office and the Municipalidad; and on the western side the cathedral and the archbishop's palace. The **cathedral**, much rebuilt, contains a recumbent statue in wood of San Francisco Javier and the chandelier that lit the first meetings of Congress after Independence; it also houses an interesting museum of religious art and historical pieces. In the Palacio de la Real Audiencia is the **Museo Histórico Nacional**, ① *Plaza de Armas 951, T02-638 1411, www.museohistoriconacional.cl, Tue-Sun 1000-1730, US$0.80, free on Sun,* which covers the period from the Conquest until 1925 and contains a model of colonial Santiago.

A block west of the cathedral is the **former Congress** building, now occupied by the Ministry of Foreign Affairs (the

Café Brasil **2** C4
Café Caribe **3** D4
Café Colonial **4** D5
Café Haiti **5** D4
Café Ikabaru **11** C5
Círculo de Periodistas **19** D3
Congreso **6** B3
Da Carla & San Marco **7** B5
El 27 de Nueva York **8** D4
El Naturista **9** D4

El Vegetariano **10** C4
Fra Diavolo **14** E5
Govindas **22** C2
Les Asasins **15** C6
Lung Fung **12** D5
Masticón **21** E4
Mermoz **20** C4
Natural Green **23** C3
Salon de Té
  Cousiño **13** D4

new Congress building is in Valparaíso). Nearby are the law courts and the **Museo Chileno de Arte Precolombino** ⓘ *Bandera 361, www.precolombino.cl, Tue-Sun 1000-1800, US$3, students and kids free, booklet, US$0.35*. Housed in the former Real Aduana, this is one of the best museums in Chile with an excellent representative exhibition of objects from the pre-Columbian cultures of Central America and the Andean region. Displays are well labelled in English. A visit is highly recommended. A further two blocks west is **Palacio de la Alhambra** ⓘ *Compañía 1340, T02-6890875, www.snba.cl, Mon-Fri 1100-1300, 1700-1930*, a national monument sponsored by the Society of Arts. It stages exhibitions of paintings as well as having a permanent display.

A few metres east of the Plaza de Armas is the Casa Colorada. Built in 1769, it was the home of the Governor in colonial days and then of Mateo de Toro, first President of Chile. It now holds the **Museo de Santiago** ⓘ *Merced 860, Tue-Sat 1000-1800, Sun and holidays 1100-1400, US$2, students free, booklet US$0.35*, which covers the history of Santiago from the Conquest to modern times with excellent displays, models and guided tours.

From the Plaza de Armas, Paseo Ahumada runs south to the Alameda, four blocks away. **Ahumada** is a pedestrianized street and is the commercial heart of the centre. This is always an interesting place to come for a stroll, especially at night, when those selling pirated CDs or playing the three-card trick mix with evangelist preachers and satanists. One block south of the Plaza de Armas, Ahumada crosses **Calle Huérfanos**, which is also pedestrianized and presents a similar spectacle.

Four blocks north of the Plaza de Armas is the interesting **Mercado Central** ⓘ *Av 21 de Mayo y San Pablo*. The central market is the best place to come in Santiago for seafood (see page 99), and is so prominent in the Chilean psyche that it was the setting for a recent national soap opera, *Amores del Mercado*. The building faces the **Parque Venezuela**, on which is the Cal y Canto metro station, the northern terminus of Line 2, and, at its western end, the former Mapocho railway station, now a cultural centre and concert venue. If you head east from Mapocho station, along the river, you arrive at the **Parque Forestal**. Although the park is prettily laid out, the proximity of many busy roads means that few people stroll here for long. The **Museo Nacional de Bellas Artes** ⓘ *www.mnba.cl, Tue-Sun 1000-1845, US$0.80*, is located in the wooded grounds and is an extraordinary example of neo-classical architecture. Inside is a large display of Chilean and foreign painting and sculpture; contemporary art exhibitions are held several times a year. In the west wing of the building is the **Museo de Arte Contemporáneo** ⓘ *US$0.80*.

Along and around the Alameda

The Alameda runs through the heart of the city for over 3 km. It is 100 m wide, choked full of *micros*, taxis and cars day and night and ornamented with gardens and statuary. The most notable are the equestrian statues of generals O'Higgins and San Martín; the statue of the Chilean historian Benjamín Vicuña MacKenna who, as mayor of Santiago, beautified Cerro Santa Lucía; and the great monument in honour of the battle of Concepción in 1879.

At the eastern end of the Alameda is **Plaza Italia**, where there is a statue of General Baquedano and the Tomb of the Unknown Soldier. Four blocks south is the **Museo Nacional Benjamín Vicuña MacKenna** ⓘ *Av V MacKenna 94, Tue-Sat 0930-1300, 1400-1800, US$0.80*, which records the life and works of the 19th-century Chilean historian and biographer who became one of Santiago's most important mayors. It also has occasional exhibitions.

The population density of the area around Santiago is over 300 people per sq km, though it is much lower in the valleys around Los Andes.

⁝ Huevón, Señor?

If you spend any time in Chile, it is almost impossible not to come across 'huevón'. This versatile word is unique to Chilean Spanish and is used by all classes of society to describe a person. Literally meaning 'big egg', it is by turns an expression of endearment ('mate', 'buddy') and a slang expression of disgust ('idiot', 'fool'), and is used equally often in both senses. In some conversations, virtually every other word mayseem to be huevón.

Confusion arises for the visitor because of the similarity of huevón to 'huevo', the Spanish word for egg. Legend has it that an expatriate living in Santiago a few years ago made the mistake of ordering a sandwich with huevón rather than huevo – the waiter was so overcome that he had to finish his shift early. The hilarity with which mistakes of this sort are greeted can work to the visitor's advantage, however: tell any Chilean acquaintance that you have been to the shop to buy huevón and your friendship will be secured for life.

The use of huevón is symptomatic of the distinctiveness of Chilean Spanish, which has an unusually wide range of idioms and slang not used elsewhere in Latin America. Those spending any length of time in Chile, or who are serious about getting to grips with Chilean Spanish, should get hold of a copy of How to Survive in the Chilean Jungle by John Brennan and Alvaro Taboada (Ventriloc Dolmen Editores, 2001), a handbook of Chilean colloquialisms.

Between the Parque Forestal, Plaza Italia and the Alameda is the **Lastarria** neighbourhood (Universidad Católica metro). For those interested in antique furniture, pieces of art and old books, the area is worth a visit, especially the **Plaza Mulato Gil de Castro** (Calle Lastarria 305). Occasional shows are put on in the plaza, and surrounding it are restaurants, bookshops, handicraft and antique shops, an art gallery, the **Instituto de Arte Contemporáneo** and the **Museo Arqueológico de Santiago** ⓘ *Lastarria 307, Mon-Fri 1000-1400, 1530-1830, Sat 1000-1400, free*, with temporary exhibitions of Chilean archaeology, anthropology and pre-Columbian art. The museum also houses the **Museo de Artes Visuales** ⓘ *Tue-Sun 1030-1830, free*.

Nearby on Calle Lastarria are the **Jardín Lastarria**, a cul de sac of craft and antique shops (No 293); **Gutenberg, Lafourcade y Cía**, an antiquarian bookseller (No 307), the **Ciné Biógrafo** (No 131) and, at the corner with Calle Merced, the **Instituto Chileno-Francés**.

From here, the Alameda skirts, Cerro Santa Lucía, on the right, and the Catholic University, on the left. **Cerro Santa Lucía**, a cone of rock rising steeply to a height of 70 m, can be scaled from the Caupolicán esplanade, on which, high on a rock, stands a statue of that Mapuche leader, but the ascent from the northern side of the hill – where there is an equestrian statue of Diego de Almagro – is easier. There are views of the city from the top, which is reached by a series of stairs. There is a fortress, the **Batería Hidalgo** (closed to visitors) on the summit, but only its platform survives from the colonial period. The hill closes at 2100; visitors must sign a register at the entrance, giving their ID card number. It is best to descend the eastern side, to see the small **Plaza Pedro Valdivia** with its waterfalls and **statue of Valdivia**. The area is known to be dangerous after dark. Travellers should beware of thieves here, although, with the new need to register ID cards, security in the area has been tightened up.

⁝ On clear days you can see across to the Andes from cerro Santa Lucía. Even on smoggy days, the view of the sunset is good.

Past the hill, on the right, the Alameda goes past the **Biblioteca Nacional** ⓘ *Moneda 650, www.dibam.cl, Mon-Fri 0900-1900, Sat 0900-1400, free*, which contains the national archives as well as exhibitions of books, book illustrations, documents and posters. Concerts and lectures also take place here, entry to which is often free.

Beyond, on the left, between Calle San Francisco and Calle Londres, is the oldest church in Santiago: the red-walled church and monastery of **San Francisco** (1618). Inside is the small statue of the Virgin that Valdivia carried on his saddlebow when he rode from Peru to Chile. Free classical concerts are sometimes given in the church in summer; arrive early for a seat. Annexed to the church, near the cloisters, is the **Museo Colonial** ① *Londres 4, T02-6398737, www.museosanfransisco.cl, Tue-Sun 1000-1300, 1500-1800, US$1.50.* Containing displays of religious art, one of the rooms here has 54 paintings of the life of Saint Francis. In the cloisters is a room containing Gabriela Mistral's Nobel Prize medal and there is also a collection of locks. Some of the information is in English.

South of San Francisco is the attractive **Barrio París-Londres**, built in 1923-29, now restored and pedestrianized, while two blocks north of the Alameda is the **Teatro Municipal** ① *Calle Agustinas, guided tours Tue 1300-1500 and Sun 1100-1400, US$3.* A little further west along the Alameda is the **Universidad de Chile** and the **Club de la Unión**, an exclusive social club founded in 1864. The current building dates from 1925 and houses a restaurant where wonderful meals are served at exorbitant prices. Nearby, on Calle Nueva York, is the **Bolsa de Comercio** (stock exchange). The public are allowed access to view the trading, but you will have to show your passport to get inside.

One block further west there are three plazas: **Plaza de la Libertad** to the north of the Alameda, **Plaza Bulnes** in the centre and **Plaza del Libertador O'Higgins** to the south. To the north of Plaza de la Libertad, hemmed in by the skyscrapers of the Centro Cívico, is **Palacio de la Moneda** (1805), the Presidential Palace containing historic relics, paintings, sculptures and the elaborate Salón Rojo used for official receptions. Although the Moneda was damaged by air attacks during the military coup of 11 September 1973 it has been fully restored. The courtyards are open to the public, ① *Mon-Fri 1000-1800, guided tours of the palace 0900-1300 final Sun of every month.* In front of the palace is the statue of former President Arturo Alessandri Palma. Ceremonial changing of the guard every other day at 1000.

South of the Alameda

Four blocks south of Plaza del Libertador O'Higgins is **Parque Almagro**, notable for the **Iglesia de los Sacramentinos**, a gothic church loosely designed in imitation of Sacré Coeur in Paris, which is best viewed from the nearby Palacio Cousiño against the backdrop of the *cordillera*. **Palacio Cousiño** ① *C Dieciocho 438, admission by guided tour only (Spanish or English), Tue-Fri 0930-1330, 1430-1700 (last tour 1600), Sat, Sun and holidays 0930-1330, US$2.40,* on the west side of the Parque Almagro and five blocks south of the Alameda, is a large mansion in French rococo style. It was built by Luis and Isadora Cousiño, part of a wealthy Chilean dynasty that made its money in the mining and wine industries. Furnished with tapestries, antiques and pictures imported from France, the palace startled Santiago society with its opulence and its advanced technology, including its own electricity generators and the first lift in the country. Even today, the word luxurious falls short when describing the palace: one of the chandeliers is made with 13,000 pieces of crystal and the superb Italian staircase was built using 20 different types of marble. Look out also for the '*indiscretos*', three-seater armchairs designed for courting couples and a chaperone. The family monogram can be seen on the curtains, mirrors and doors. Now owned by the Municipalidad, the palace is used for official receptions but is also open as a museum. A visit is highly recommended.

❧ *Try to get to Palacio Cousiño in time for the first tour of the morning or afternoon, as later groups tend to be rushed.*

Parque O'Higgins lies about 10 blocks south of the Alameda. It has a small lake, playing fields, tennis courts, a swimming pool (open from 5 December), an open-air stage for local songs and dances, a disco, the racecourse of the **Club Hípico**, and an amusement park, **Fantasilandia** ① *daily in summer, Sat and Sun only in winter, adults*

US$9, children US$7, unlimited rides. There are kite-flying contests on Sundays and, during the Independence celebrations around 18 September, there are many good *peñas*. There is also a group of about 20 basic restaurants, some craft shops, and three small museums: **Acuario Municipal** ① *Local 9, T02-5565680, daily 1000-2000, small charge;* **Museo de Insectos y Caracoles** ① *Local 12, daily 1000-2000, small charge,* with a collection of insects and shellfish; and **Museo del Huaso** ① *T02-5561927, Mon-Fri 1000-1700, Sun and holidays 1000-1400, free,* which houses a small, interesting collection of *criollo* clothing and tools. Cars are not allowed in the park, which can be reached by Metro Line 2 to Parque O'Higgins station or by bus from Parque Baquedano via Avenida MacKenna and Avenida Matta.

Barrio Brasil

On the northern side of the Alameda, immediately to the west of the Panamericana, is the Barrio Brasil, a tranquil area in which many of the houses are brightly painted. This historic part of the city, lying was the first area to be colonized by Santiaguinos away from the centre, at the end of the 18th century. The area is rich in colonial architecture and is also a centre for nightlife with many underground bars, clubs and restaurants and Santiago's most radical shop, **La Lunita**, stocking feminist books and Santiago's only gay monthly, *Lambda News*.

The heart of the *barrio* is **Plaza Brasil**, easily reached by walking straight up calle Concha y Toro from the República metro stop. This is a narrow, winding cobblestone street that passes elegant old stone homes in rococo and German Gothic styles, before reaching the plaza, which is shaded by palms, lime trees and silk cottons. Just west of the plaza, on Compañía, is the **Basilica del Salvador**, a striking yellow- and rose-coloured church built between 1870 and 1872, with stained glass and a statue of the Virgen del Carmen. A little further along Compañía is the **Iglesia Preciosa Sangre**, a bright red church of neo-classical design, with impressive reliefs and twin towers. You could then walk one block north to calle Catedral, where there are some fine old buildings with tall double windows, wooden balconies and stone pallisades.

Around Estación Central

The Alameda continues westwards across the Pan-American Highway towards the impressive railway station, **Estación Central**, which is surrounded by several blocks of market stalls. Opposite Estacíon Central is the **Planetarium** ① *US$4.50,* while to the north on Avenida Matucana y Diego Portales is **Parque Quinta Normal**. The park founded as a botanical garden in 1830, and is a pleasant, popular spot, which gets very crowded on Sundays with families and the street entertainers who vie with one another to get their pesos.

The park contains several museums. **Museo Ferroviario** ① *www.corpdicyt.cl, Tue-Fri 1000-1800, Sat and Sun 1100-1900, US$1.20, free to over 60s, photography US$2,* contains the former Presidential stagecoach and 13 steam engines built between 1884 and 1953, including a rare surviving Kitson-Meyer. The **Museo Nacional de Historia Natural,** ① *www.mnhn.cl, Tue-Sat 1000-1730, Sun and holidays 1100-1830,US$0.80, Sun free, students free,* was founded in 1830 and is one of Latin America's oldest museums. Housed in a neo-classical building, it has exhibitions on zoology, botany, mineralogy, anthropology, ethnography and aeology. **Museo Artequín** ① *Av Portales 3530, Tue-Fri 0900-1700, Sat, Sun and holidays 1100-1800, US$1,* is housed in the Chilean pavilion built for the 1889 Paris International Exhibition. It contains prints of famous paintings and explanations of the techniques of the great masters. Recommended. Two blocks east of the park is the **Museo de la Solidaridad Salvador Allende,** ① *Herrera 360, T02-6817542, www.mssa.cl, Tue-Sun 1000-1900, US$0.80.*

● ● *In 1981, a thief made off with the statue of the Virgen del Carmen, but hastily returned it the next day after an earthquake rocked the city.*

Located in a beautiful listed building with a cobbled patio and palm trees with nesting birds, it houses a collection of over 400 art works produced by Chilean and foreign artists in support of the Unidad Popular government and in opposition to the Pinochet dictatorship. Artists include Alexander Calder, Joan Miró, Oswaldo Guayasamín and Roberto Matta. There are also videos of interviews (in Spanish) with survivors of the 1973 coup and an information sheet in English. You need to give four days' notice for guided tours, but they are recommended. The good café serves a cheap set lunch.

Bellavista and Cerro San Cristóbal

Santiago's bohemian face is most obvious in the **Bellavista** district, on the north bank of the Río Mapocho at the foot of **Cerro San Cristóbal**. This is the main focus of nightlife in the old city; the area around Pío Nono and López de Bello hums and buzzes, especially at weekends. In the bars you can see everything from live Cuban music to local imitations of Georges Brassens, while eating options range from classic Italian dishes to sushi and West African palm-nut stew. There are also theatres, art galleries and craft shops specializing in lapis lazuli, as well as **La Chascona** ① *F Márquez de la*

Bellavista

0 metres 200
0 yards 200

Sleeping 🛏
Bellavista Hostel **8**
Casa Condell **7**
Hostal Del Parque **2**
Montecarlo **3**
Posada del Salvador **4**
Presidente **5**
Principado **6**
Residencial Providencia **1**

Eating 🍴
Azul Profundo &
   Tragaluz **22**
Casa en el Aire **1**
Cava de Dardignac & Zen **2**
Cipriani **3**
Como Agua para
   Chocolate **23**
Dulcería Las Palmas **4**
El Antojo Gaugin **5**

El Otro Sitio **6**
El Rincón Español **7**
Eladio **8**
Etnico **25**
Evelyn **9**
Gatopardo **10**
HBH Bar **11**
Il Siciliano **12**
Kilometre 11.680 &
   Sommelier **24**

1000-1300, 1500-1800, US$2 guided visits only, English guides can be booked. This is the house of the poet Pablo Neruda. There are really three houses, built on a steep hillside and separated by gardens. It was completed in 1955 and thereafter Neruda lived here whenever he was in the capital. It is basically in the same condition as when he lived here (it was restored after being damaged in the 1973 coup) and is also now the headquarters of the Fundación Pablo Neruda.

Parque Metropolitano

The sharp, conical hill of **San Cristóbal** to the northeast of the city, forms the **Parque Metropolitano** ① *daily 0900-2100, vehicles US$3*, the largest and most interesting of the city's parks. On a clear day it provides excellent views over the city and across to the Andes. More usually, however, the views provide a graphic demonstration of Santiago's continuing smog problem. There are two sectors, **sector Cumbre** on Cerro San Cristóbal and, further east, **sector Tupahue**. There are two entrances: west from Pío Nono in Bellavista and east from Pedro de Valdivia Norte. When the weather is good, the walk up the access road from Bellavista is very pleasant, providing unexpected views of distant and little-visited northern parts of the city. On Cerro Cumbre (300 m above the city), there is a colossal statue of the Virgin, which is floodlit at night; beside it is the astronomical observatory of the Catholic University, which can be visited on application to the observatory's director. Near the Bellavista entrance is the **Jardín Zoológico** ① *Tue-Fri 1000-1300, 1500-1800, Sat, Sun and holidays 1000-1800, US$2*, which has a well cared-for collection of animals.

The Tupahue sector is reached by taxi either from the Bellavista entrance (much cheaper from inside the park as taxis entering the park have to pay entrance fee), or from the Pedro de Valdivia metro. Alternatively you could walk the kilometre from Pedro de Valvivia metro. This section of the park contains terraces, gardens and paths. One building houses the **Camino Real** (T02-2321758), a good, expensive restaurant with a splendid view from the terrace, especially at night, and an **Enoteca** or exhibition of Chilean wines from a range of vineyards. You can taste one of the six 'wines of the day' | *US$1.50 per glass*, and buy if you like, although prices are higher than in shops. Nearby is the **Casa de la Cultura**, which has art exhibitions and free concerts at midday on Sunday. There are also two good **swimming pools** in the park (see page 109. East of Tupahue are the **Botanical Gardens** ① *daily 0900-1800, guided tours available*, with a collection of Chilean native plants.

La Bodega de Julio 13
La Divina Comida 14
La Máquina 30
La Pergola de la Plaza 21
La Tasca Mediterránea 26
Les Assasins 15
Libro Café
  Mediterraneo 16
Mare Nostrum 28
Michelle's 17

San Fruttuoso 18
Sarita Colonia 27
Tercera Compañía de
  Bomberos 29
Venezia 19
Viejo Verde &
  Le Coq au Vin 20

Funicular railway ┼┼┼

If you don't want to walk to the top of Cerro San Cristóbal, you can take the **funicular** ① *from Plaza Caupolicán at the northern end of Calle Pío Nono, every few minutes 1000-2000 daily, US$1.50 return, US$1 one way*. Or, from the Tupahue sector, take the **teleférico** ① *from Estación Oasis, Avenida Pedro de Valdivia Norte via Tupahue, summer only, Mon 1430-1830, Tue-Fri 1030-1830, Sat and Sun 1030-1900, US$3 combination ticket including funicular*. An open bus also operated by the *teleférico* company runs to San Cristóbal and Tupahue from the Bellavista entrance with the same schedule.

Cementerio General

From the top of Cerro San Cristóbal the Cemeterio General can be see, situated in the *barrio* of La Recoleta to the north. This cemetery contains the mausoleums of most of the great figures in Chilean history and the arts, including Violeta Parra, Victor Jara and Salvador Allende. There is also an impressive monument to the victims of the 1973-90 military government; their names, ages and dates of detention or disappearance are listed in two sections: those who disappeared and those executed for political reasons. The cemetery can be reached by any Recoleta bus from Calle Miraflores.

East to Providencia and Los Condes

East of Plaza Italia, the main east-west axis of the city becomes known as **Avenida Providencia**, as it heads out towards residential areas at the eastern and upper levels of the city. On the south bank of the Mapocho, beneath Parque Metropolitano is **Parque Baquedano**, also known as Parque Gran Bretaña. It is one of the more attractive parks in

Providencia

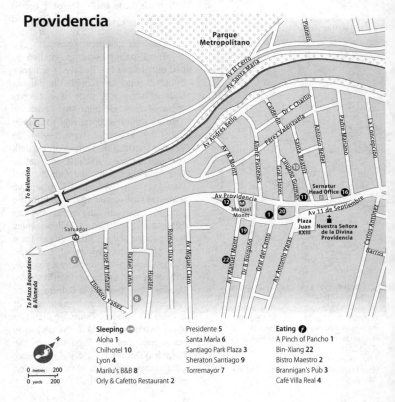

Sleeping	Presidente **5**	Eating
Aloha **1**	Santa María **6**	A Pinch of Pancho **1**
Chilhotel **10**	Santiago Park Plaza **3**	Bin-Xiang **22**
Lyon **4**	Sheraton Santiago **9**	Bistro Maestro **2**
Marilu's B&B **8**	Torremayor **7**	Brannigan's Pub **3**
Orly & Cafetto Restaurant **2**		Café Villa Real **4**

0 metres 200
0 yards 200

Santiago with well laid-out gardens and fountains. The park houses the **Museo de los** **Tajamares** ⓘ *Av Providencia 222, Mon-Fri 0900-1400 and 1500-2100*, an exhibition of the 17th- and 18th-century walls built to protect the city from flooding by the river and of the subsequent canalization. There is also an exhibition of photographs.

Providencia

The neighbourhood of Providencia is the upmarket commercial centre of Santiago, a busy area of shops, offices and smart restaurants, mostly congregated around Pedro de Valdivia and Los Leones metro stations. The national offices of Sernatur, the national tourist board, are located here. **Calle Suecia**, near Los Leones, is the focal point for nightlife in this part of the city, with over a dozen 'pubs' offering European beers on tap, Tex-Mex food and live music.

Las Condes

At Tobalaba metro, Avenida Providencia becomes **Avenida Apoquindo**, which heads on past Avenida Amérigo Vespuccio – Santiago's ring road – and out towards the exclusive neighbourhoods of Las Condes, Lo Curro and La Dehesa. Here you will find walled residential compounds, houses with servants and several brand new cars, and very expensive US-style shopping centres, such as **Alto Las Condes** and **Parque Arauco**. Anyone who is anyone in Chilean society lives in this part of town.

Las Condes is home to two museums. **Museo de la Escuela Militar** ⓘ *Los Militares 4500, Mon-Fri 0830-1330, 1500-1730*, has displays on Bernardo O'Higgins, the Conquest and the Pacific War. **Museo Ralli** ⓘ *Sotomayor 4110, Vitacura, Tue-Sun 1000-1600, closed in summer, free,* is an excellent museum with a collection of works

Carousel **5**
Centre Catalá **7**
Copelia **8**
Da Renato **21**
El Giratorio & Eladio **14**
El Huerto **9**

El Rincón Brasileiro **19**
Gatsby & Lomit's **6**
Kimomo **11**
La Pez Era **20**
La Pizza Nostra **13**
Oradia **15**

Phone Box Pub
  & Café El Patio **16**
Red Pub **17**
River Pub **18**
Salvaje **12**

by modern European and Latin American artists, including Dalí, Chagall, Bacon and Miró. Recommended. There are art galleries on Avenida Nueva Costanera and Alonso de Cordova, Vitacura, in the Barrio Alto. Here, four or five private galleries showcase contemporary Chilean and Latin American art. All galleries are within a couple of blocks of each other. Try **Galeria Tomas Andreu** ① *Av Nueva Costanera 3731, T02-2289952;* **Galeria de Arte Isabel Aninat** ① *Alonso de Cordoba 3053, T02-2632729;* and **AMS Marlborough** ① *Av Nueva Costanera 3723, T02-2288696.*

South of Las Condes

Parque de la Paz, the new peace park in the southwestern suburb of Peñalolén, stands on the site of **Villa Grimaldi,** the most notorious torture centre during the Pinochet regime. The Irish missionary, Sheila Cassidy, has documented the abuses that she underwent when imprisoned without trial in this place. The walls are daubed with human rights' graffiti and the park makes a moving and unusual introduction to the conflict that has eaten away at the heart of Chilean society for the past 30 years. To reach the park, take a metro to Tobalaba and then any bus marked Peñalolén heading south down Tobalaba. Get off at the junction of Tobalaba y José Arrieta and then walk five minutes up Arrieta towards the mountains.

Las Condes

0 metres 200		
0 yards 200		

Sleeping 😴	Santa Magdalena	Delmónico **1**	Flannery's **4**
Hyatt Regency	Apartments **4**	Diego Pizza **2**	Isla Negra & Coco
Santiago **1**		El Club **15**	Loco **5**
Montebianco **2**	**Eating** 🍴	El Madroñal **11**	La Cascade **13**
Radisson Royal **3**	Cuerovaca **10**	El Mesón del Calvo **3**	Le Fournil **12**

Maipú

The suburb of Maipú, 10 km southwest of Santiago, is worth the 45-minute bus ride, caught from Teatinos y O'Higgins. Here, a monument marks the site of the Battle of the Maipú, 5 April 1818, which resulted in the final defeat of the Spanish royalist forces in mainland Chile. Nearby is the interesting **National Votive Temple of Maipú** ① *open to visitors daily 0830-2000; in summer mass Mon-Fri 1700, Sat and Sun 1200 and 1700; in winter mass Mon 1830, Tue-Sun 1200 and 1830.* This temple is a fine example of modern architecture and stained glass (best viewed from the inside). It is located on the site of a 1818 temple, built on the orders of Bernardo O'Higgins to commemorate the battle. The walls of the old temple stand in the forecourt, having fallen into ruin due to successive earthquakes. Pope John Paul II gave a mass here on his visit to Chile in 1987. **Museo del Carmen** ① *Mon-Fri 1000-1300, 1500-1800, Sat and Sun 0900-1300, 1500-1800,* is part of the same building and contains carriages, furniture, clothing and other colonial and later items.

⬤ Sleeping

Most of the more expensive accommodation is situated in the city centre or further east in the neighbourhoods of Providencia and Las Condes. The expensive hotels listed tend to be slightly characterless but with good service. Most budget accommodation is located in the city centre or further west in the vicinity of the bus terminals. There are many basic hotels on Morandé, Gral MacKenna, San Martín and San Pablo in the centre, particularly on Gral MacKenna 1200 block, but bear in mind that this is the red light district. Another good option is to stay in a family-run guesthouse; see box, p.

Accommodation here is generally about 30% more expensive than elsewhere in the country. Check if breakfast is included in the price quoted. Most 3-, 4- and 5-star hotels do not charge the 18% tax to foreigners who pay in US$ cash. However, the exchange rate given is often so harsh that it may be cheaper to pay in pesos. Several websites offer hotel booking services for Santiago and the rest of Chile, but most charge a sizeable commission.

If you are staying for weeks or months rather than days, staying with a family is an economical and interesting option. For private rentals, see the classified ads in *El Mercurio* – where flats, homes and family *pensiones* are listed by district – or in *El Rastro* (weekly), or try the notice board at the tourist office. Rates for 2-bed furnished apartments in a reasonable neighbourhood start at around US$200 per month, or

Pinpilinpausha 14
Praga 6
Puerto Marisko 18
Route 66 7
Sakura 16

Shoo Gun 8
Wok House 17
You 9

US$130 if unfurnished. Note that you cannot install a phone line unless you have permanent Chilean residence; you may need to get a friend to put the line in their name.

Estate agents handle apartments, but often charge half of the first month's rent as commission, while a month's rent in advance and 1 month's deposit are required. Some apartments are listed below. The 3 agencies here are recommended:

Edificio San Rafael, *Miraflores 264, T02-6330289, F02-2225629*. Apartment costing US$30 a day single, US$46 a day double, minimum 3 days, longer periods discounted.

Nancy Lombardo, *MacIver 175, of 42, T02-6382009, F02-6330210*, offers apartments with 1, 2 or 3 bedrooms, fully furnished.

Tempo Rent, *Santa Magdalena 116, T02-2311608, F02-3340374, tempo.rent@chilnet.cl* Recommended apartment rental agency.

It's worth getting a list of YH addresses around the country from the Chilean Youth Hostel association, the **Asociación Chilena de Albergues Turisticas Juveniles** (ACHATJ), *Hernando de Aguirre 201, of 602, T02-2333220, www.hostelling.cl*

Around the Plaza de Armas
p 83, map p82

LL Carrera, *Teatinos 180, T02-6982011, www.carrera.cl* Huge, art deco 5-star hotel, slightly faded grandeur, historical location opposite Moneda Palace, rooftop pool, 3

Santiago west of centre

Sleeping	Hostelling Internacional	Residencial Mery 11
Conde de Anzúrez 2	Santiago 8	Residencial Vicky 15
Ducado 16	Huérfanos 2842 4	San Patricio 13
Hostal Americano 5	Imperio 17	Santiago Adventure 14
Hostal Internacional	La Casa Roja 9	SCS Habitat 18
Letelier 6	Residencial Alemana 10	Tokyo 3
Hostal Río Amazonas 7	Residencial Gloria 1	Turhotel Express 12

0 metres 200
0 yards 200

good restaurants, one of the most expensive hotels in Santiago, outstanding.

LL Fundador, *Paseo Serrano 34, T02-6322566, hotelfundador@hotelfundador.cl* In a nice area, central with helpful staff and charming staff, conference rooms and banqueting halls. Pool, bar, restaurant, internet connections.

L-AL Hostal del Parque, *Merced 294, opposite Parque Forestal, T02-6392694, hotelhostade002@chilnet.cl* Comfortable, quiet, friendly. Recommended.

L-AL Tupahue, *San Antonio 477, T02-756 2587, www.tupahue.cl* Comfortable, large with a pool and restaurant. Nothing out of the ordinary. Cheaper to book online.

AL Majestic, *Santo Domingo 1526, T02-6958366, www.hotelmajestic.cl* With breakfast, pool, US-chain standard. Internet

connection port in rooms. Excellent Indian restaurant. English spoken. Recommended.

A-B Montecarlo, *Subercaseaux 209, T02-6391569, www.hotelmontecarlo.cl* At foot of Cerro Santa Lucía in quiet street, modern but with "nice art deco touches", restaurant, stores luggage, helpful. Recommended.

B Lira, *Lira 314, T02-2222492, www.hotellira.co.cl* Old fashioned, friendly.

B Santa Lucía, *Huérfanos 779, Piso 4, T02-6398201, santalucia@terra.cl* Garage 2 blocks away, clean, comfortable, good, small, quiet restaurant.

B Tokyo, *Almte Barroso 160, Los Héroes metro, T02-6714516, www.hoteltokyo.cl* Helpful and friendly but rundown and overpriced, with breakfast, manager speaks English and Japanese, nice garden, no credit cards.

C Santa Victoria, *Santa Victoria 6, T02-2220031, F02-6345753.* Quiet, small, safe, family run.

F-G Res San Antonio, *San Antonio 811, T02-6384607, ressnant@ctcinternet.cl* Price per person. Good place, decent value.

F-G Santo Domingo, *Santo Domingo 735, T02-6396733, sto.dgo@bcimail.cl* Cleanish, basic, gloomy.

G Indiana *(no sign), Rosas 1339, T02-6880008, hostal_indiana@hotmail.com* Price per person. Very basic, kitchen facilities, friendly, internet.

G Olicar, *San Pablo 1265, T02-6983683.* Price per person. Very basic, cooking facilities.

G Nuevo Valparaíso, *Morandé y San Pablo, T02-6715698.* Price per person. Simple, central, erratic hot water, poor beds, safe, basic, use of kitchen (no utensils), cable TV, popular.

G Res Sur, *Ruiz Tagle 055, T02-7765533.* Clean, meals available.

G San Felipe, *Gral MacKenna 1248, T02-6714598.* Cheap laundry service, kitchen, noisy (2nd floor quieter), luggage stored.

Along and around the Alameda *p84, maps p82, p88 and p94*

LL Fundador, *Paseo Serrano 34, T02-3871200, www.hotelfundador.cl* Helpful, good service, charming staff. Some rooms are small. **LL-L Galerías**, *San Antonio 65, T02-4707400, www.hotel-galerias.cl* Large rooms, good location, good breakfast, 5-star. **A El Marqués del Forestal**, *Ismael Valdés Vergara 740, T02-6333462, www.apart-hotel-elmarques.cl* Good value, apartments.

Eating 🍽

Bella China **2**
El Puente de Chabuca **3**
Las Vacas Gordas **1**
Los Chinos Ricos **4**
Mansión de la Novia **5**
Ocean Pacific **6**

Keeping it in the family

Family-run guesthouses tend to be found slightly further out of the centre but the rewards – getting more of a feel for family life and having a more authentic Santiago experience – often outweigh the distance.

Amigos de Todo el Mundo, *Av Pdte Bulnes, Paseo, 285, dept 201, T02-6726525*. Run by Señor Arturo Navarrete, prices from US$10 with breakfast, other meals extra, monthly rates available, also transport to/from airport. Recommended.

Antonio & Ana Saldivia, *Guillermo Tell 5809, La Reina, a long way from the centre, near Las Condes, T02-2266267*. Price per person, including breakfast. Dinner on request US$6 per head including wine. Hospitable.

Ceclia Parada, *Llico 968, 1 block from Departamental metro, T02-5229947, F02-5216328*. Price per person. Laundry service, gardens, quiet.

Fidela Monge, *San Isidro 211, dept H, 3 blocks from Santa Lucía metro, T02-2221246, residenciamonge@latinmail.com* Price per person. Kitchen and laundry facilities.

Rodrigo Sauvageot, *Gorbea 1992, dept 113, T02-6722119*. Price per person. With breakfast, reservation essential.

Sra Lucía, *Catedral 1029, piso 10, dept 1001, T02-6963832*. Price per person. Central, friendly, safe, cooking facilities, basic.

A **Principado**, *Vicuña MacKenna 30, 1 block south of Plaza Baquedano, T02-2228142, www.hotelesprincipado.com* Good standard.

A **Vegas**, *Londres 49, T02-6322498, www.hotelvegas.net* Nice location, very convenient for centre.

A-B **Libertador**, *O'Higgins 853, T02-6394212, www.hotellibertador.cl* Helpful, stores luggage, good restaurant, bar, rooftop pool. Recommended.

C-D **París**, *C París 813, T02-6640921, www.hotelparis.cl* With bath, quiet, clean, good meeting place, good value, breakfast extra, luggage store. Recommended. Book in advance in summer.

F **Residential Gloria**, *Latorre 449 (no sign), T02-6988315. Toesca metro*. Price per person. Including breakfast, clean, popular, meals, difficult to use kitchen.

F **Residential Londres**, *Londres 54, T02-6382215, unico54@ctcinternet.cl* Price per person. Near San Francisco Church, former mansion, large old-fashioned rooms and furniture, some rooms with bath, few singles, no heating, English spoken, book exchange, great value, very popular, highly recommended, usually full, no advance bookings, arrive early.

Santiago Region Sleeping

Barrio Brasil *p87*

B Ducado, *Augustinas 1990, T02-6961948, hotelducado@entelchile.cl* With breakfast. Reasonable value, clean, quiet at back, nice area just west of the Panamericana. Secure parking.

B Hostal Río Amazonas, *Rosas 2234, T02-698 4092, www.hostalrioamazonas.cl* With breakfast and bath, internet, good value. Recommended.

C Hostal Americano, *Compañia 1906, T02-6981025, hostal@mi.terra.cl* Shared bathrooms, breakfast not included (US$2 extra), clean, safe, friendly atmosphere. Recommended.

F Hostal Internacional Letelier, *Cumming 77, T02-9656861*. Price per person. Internet, without breakfast, also Spanish classes.

G La Casa Roja, *Agustinas 2113, T02-6964241, info@casaroja.tie.cl* Price per person. Huge old house slowly being restored. Dormitories, no breakfast, kitchen facilities, internet. Australian run. Rowdy. Recommended if you want to party, not if you want to sleep. Camping available.

G San Patricio, *Catedral 2235, T02-6954800*. Price per person. Basic, clean, hot showers, quiet location in Barrio Brasil, good value.

Around Estación Central *p87, map p94*
Staying in this area is convenient for those on a lightening visit or for those with an early or late start.

A Conde de Anzúrez, *Av República 25, T02-6996368, F02-6718376. República metro.* Convenient for airport, central station and bus terminals, clean, helpful, safe, luggage stored.

B Tur Hotel Express, *O'Higgins 3750, piso 3, in the Turbus Terminal, T02-6850100.* Comfortable business standard with breakfast, cable TV, air-conditioning, free internet. Particularly useful if you need to take an early flight as buses leave for the airport from here.

C Res Mery, *Pasaje República 36, off 0-100 block of República, T02-6968883, m.mardones@entelchile.net* Big green building down an alley, hot showers, quiet, good value. Recommended.

E Santiago Adventure, *Cabo Arestey 2468 (off C España), T02-6715529. ULA metro.* Price per person. Family run, friendly, tours, airport pick-up, English spoken. Recommended.

F Residential Alemana, *República 220 (no sign), T02-6712388, residencial.alemana@usa.net República metro.* Price per person. Without bath, clean, with breakfast, pleasant patio, central, heating on request, good cheap meals available. Recommended.

G Federico Scoto 130, *on north side of Alameda opposite bus terminals, T02-7799364.* Price per person. Use of phone and fax, good meals, cooking facilities, hot water, large rooms, clean, good meeting place. Recommended.

G Res Vicky, *Sazie 2105, T02-6984507*. Price per person. Kitchen and laundry facilities, good dormitory accommodation, good beds.

G SCS Habitat, *San Vicente 1798, T02-6833732, scshabitat@yahoo.com* Price per person. English spoken, lots of information, hot showers, laundry facilities, bicycle rental, internet, maps, guidebooks and camping equipment sold/rented, safe parking for bikes and motorbikes, book exchange, not central, frequently recommended but some mixed reports. Camping available.

Bellavista and Cerro San Cristóbal *p88, map p88*

AL Presidente, *Eliodoro Yáñez 867, almost at Providencia, Bellavista, T02-2358015, www. presidente.cl* Good value and good location.

F Bellavista Hostel, *Dardignac 0184, T02-7328737.* Price per person. In the heart of the lively Bellavista area. European-style hostel, sheets provided but make your own bed. With breakfast. Kitchen facilities, free internet. Good meeting place.

F Residential Providencia, *Vicuña MacKenna 92B, Bellavista, T02-2220533. Baquedano metro.* Price per person. With bath, quiet.

East towards Providencia and Las Condes

Providencia *p91, map p90*

LL-L Sheraton Santiago, *Santa María 1742, T02-2335000, www.sheraton.cl* 5 star, one of the best in town, good restaurant, good buffet lunch, all facilities.

L Santiago Park Plaza, *Av Ricardo Lyon 207, T02-3724000, www.parkplaza.cl* 5 star, another typical 'luxury hotel' geared towards business travellers.

AL Santa María, *Santa María 2050, T02-2326614, hotelsantamaria@entel chile.net* 3 star, excellent, friendly, small, good breakfast, other meals. Mixed reports as to value for money.

AL Torremayor, *Av Ricardo Lyon 322, T02-2342000, www.hoteltorremayor.cl* Clean, modern, good service, restaurant, good location.

AL-A Orly, *Pedro de Valdivia 027, T02-231 8947, www.orlyhotel.com* *Pedro de Valdivia metro.* Small, comfortable, convenient location. Also smaller and cheaper rooms, small café attached with cheap food. Recommended.

AL-A Providencia (ex Aloha), *Francisco Noguera 146, T02-2332230, www.panameri canahoteles.cl* Helpful, good restaurant.

A Lyon, *Av Ricardo Lyon 1525, T02-2257732, hotelyon@gmr.met* With breakfast, small, intimate, good value, also has annex **B** with breakfast.

A Marilú's Bed and Breakfast, *Rafael Cañas 246 C, T02-2355302, tradesic@intermedia.cl* Comfortable, no credit cards, very friendly, good beds, English and French spoken. Warmly recommended.

A-B Chilhotel, *Cirujano Guzmán 103, T02-2350713, www.chilhotel.cl* Basic but comfortable.

C Casa Condell, *Condell 114, T02-2092343 Salvador metro.* Also 4-bed dorms, **F** per person. Pleasant old house, central, quiet, nice roof-terrace. Shared baths, no breakfast, kitchen facilities, free local phonecalls, friendly, English spoken. Recommended.

Las Condes *p91, map, p92*

LL Hyatt Regency Santiago, *Av Las Condes 4601, T02-2181234, www.hyatt.cl* Superb, beautifully decorated, large outdoor pool, gymnasium, Thai restaurant. Highly recommended.

LL Ritz Carlton Santiago, *El Alcalde 15, T02-4708500, www.ritzcarlton.com/hotels/ santiago* New 5-star plus hotel. All services. The most luxurious hotel in Santiago and also the most expensive.

LL-L Radisson Royal, *Av Vitacura 2610, T02-2036000, radisson@radisson.ia* 5 star, excellent, disabled access.

L-AL Parinacota, *Av Apoquindo 5142, T02-2126366, www.hotelparinacota.cl* 4 star, small, all services, no pool.

AL Manquehue, *Esteban Dell'Orto 6615, T02-2128862, www.hotelmanquehue.com* Very good with new wing and new pool, 4 star.

AL Montebianco, *Isidora Goyenechea 2911, T02-2330427, www.hotelmontebianco.cl* Small, smart motel.

AL Santa Magdalena Apartments, *office at Helvecia 244, Las Condes, T02-3746875, www. santamagdalena.cl* Apartment rental (for 1-4 people) 1 block from metro stations, air-conditioning.

A Atton, *Alonso de Córdova 5199, T02-4227979, www.atton.cl* Comfortable, 4 star, disabled-friendly, good value.

D Urania's Bed and Breakfast, *Boccaccio 60, T02-2012922, uraniae@hotmail.com* Price per person. Comfortable, friendly, good beds, English and French spoken. Good value. Recommended.

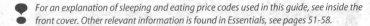

For an explanation of sleeping and eating price codes used in this guide, see inside the front cover. Other relevant information is found in Essentials, see pages 51-58.

Luxury hotels have computerized information on the more expensive restaurants, particularly useful if you are not sure what to eat. There is also an excellent guide to the more exclusive restaurants at www.emol.com, *El Mercurio*'s online entertainment guide.

Budget travellers should make the *almuerzo* their main meal. For cheap meals in the evening try the *fuentes de soda* and *schoperias* scattered around the centre.

Around the Plaza de Armas *p83, map p82*

For excellent cheap seafood lunches make for the Mercado Central (Cal y Canto metro), or the Vega Central market on the opposite bank of the Mapocho.

$$$-$$ **Da Carla**, *Maclver 577*. Traditional Italian restaurant, good, expensive.

$$$-$$ **Majestic**, *Santo Domingo 1526*. This hotel has an excellent Indian restaurant, good range of vegetarian dishes.

$$$-$$ **San Marco**, *2 doors from Don Carler*, another Italian. Manages to pip its next-door neighbour to the post.

$$ **Congreso**, *Catedral 1221*. Good meat and wines, popular at lunchtime.

$$ **El 27 de Nueva York**, *Nueva York 027, a stone's throw from the Alameda*. International cuisine, good and varied menu.

$$ **El Lugar de Don Quijote**, *Morandé y Catedral*. Bar/restaurant, *parilladas*, good wines, popular, good.

$$ **Faisan d'Or**, *Plaza de Armas*. Good *pastel de choclo*, pleasant place to have a drink and watch the world go by.

$$ **Guimas**, *Huérfanos y Teatinos*. Good, reasonable prices, good-value *almuerzo*.

$$ **Les Assassins**, *Merced 297*. French, very good. Highly recommended.

$$ **Los Adobes del Argomedo**, *Argomedo 411 y Lira*. Good Chilean food, floor show (Mon-Sat) includes *cueca* dancing, salsa and folk.

$$ **Lung Fung**, *Agustinas 715*. Delicious Oriental food, pricey, large cage in the centre with noisy parrots.

$ **Bar Central**, *San Pablo 1063*. Popular, noisy, good specialities, good value.

$ **Bar Nacional No 1**, *Huérfanos 1151*. Similar to sister restaurant, below.

$ **Bar Nacional No 2**, *Bandera 317*. Good restaurants, popular, local specialities.

$ **Bella China**, *Compania 2280*. Large portions of Oriental food.

$ **Círculo de Periodistas**, *Amunátegui 31, piso 2*. Unwelcoming entrance, good-value lunches. Recommended.

$ **El Naturista**, *Moneda 846*. Vegetarian, excellent, closes 2100.

$ **El Rápido**, *next door to Bar Nacional No 2*. Specializes in *empanadas*, cheap, quick service, popular.

$ **El Vegetariano**, *Huérfanos 827, Local 18*. Popular vegetarian, good juices.

$ **Govindas**, *Compañía 1489*. *Santa Ana metro*. Indian vegetarian food.

$ **Mermoz**, *Huérfanos 1048*. Good for lunches.

$ **Natural Green**, *Huérfanos 1188, T02-3609689*, also at *Puente 689, Local 314*. Good vegetarian.

$ **Nuria**, *Agustinas y Maclver*. Wide selection.

$ There are several more cheap eateries along Huérfanos 700-900.

Cafés

Bon Bon Oriental, *Merced 345*. Superb Turkish coffee, savouries and cakes.

Café Caribe and **Café Haití**, *Paseo Ahumada*, institutions among Santiago's business community and good places to see the people who make Chile tick; also branches throughout the centre and in Providencia.

Café Colonia, *Maclver 133*. Splendid variety of cakes, pastries and pies, fashionable and pricey, excellent. Recommended.

Café Ikabaru, *Huérfanos 709*, another good coffee bar, popular and intimate.

Gelato's, *Agustinas 941*. Very good. For ice-cream in the centre try here.

New York Café, *Moneda y Tenderine*. Helpful staff, good coffee.

Salón de Té Cousiño, *Cousiño 107*. Good coffee, snacks and *onces*, very popular, not cheap.

Tip-Top Galletas. Recommended for freshly baked biscuits, branches throughout the city, take-away only.

Along and around the Alameda *p84, maps p82, p88 and p94*

$$ **Acuario**, *París 817*. Excellent seafood and attentive service, good-value set lunch. Highly recommended.

$$ **Fra Diavolo**, *París 836 (near Res Londres)*. Lunches only, excellent food and service.

$$ **El Bar Escondida**, *Lastarria*, a small but pleasant bar.

$$ **El Rincón Español**, *just off Rosal, Lastarria*. Spanish, good, reasonably priced, try the paella.

$$ **Gatopardo**, *next door to El Rincón Español, Lastarria*. Mediterranean, good value. Highly recommended.

$$ **La Pérgola de la Plaza**, *Plaza Mulato Gil de Castro, Lastarria*, French specialities.

$ **Confitería Torres**, *O'Higgins 1570*. Traditional bar/restaurant, good atmosphere, live music at weekends. Cheap lunches are served in a large underground *comedor*.

South of the Alameda *p86*

Those on a very tight budget should make straight for C San Diego, where there are the following:

$ **La Caleta de Don Beno**, *No 397*. Excellent *parrilladas*, also seafood, popular, recommended. A little more expensive than the ones listed below. At *No 260* is a Peruvian restaurant with live salsa music on Fri and Sat nights.

$ **Las Tejas**, *No 234*. Lively, rowdy crowd, very cheap cocktails and drinks such as *pisco sour* and *pipeño*, excellent *cazuelas* and other typical dishes.

$ **Masticón**, *No 152*. Good service, excellent value, popular, wide range.

$ **Tercera Compañia de Bomberos**, *Vicuña Mackenna 097, near the junction with Diagonal Paraguay*. Good food, very cheap, recommended.

Barrio Brasil *p87*

$$ **El Puente de Chabuca**, *Brasil 72*. Average Peruvian fare in an impressive colonial building.

$$ **Las Vacas Gordas**, *Cienfuegos 280, T02-6736962*. Excellent *parrillada*. Very popular, so book in advance.

$$ **Los Chinos Ricos**, *Brasil 373, on the plaza*. Good Chinese.

$$ **Mansión de la Novia**, *Agustinas 2859*. Chilean food, elegant.

$$ **Ostras Azócar**, *Bulnes 37*. Specializes in oysters. Several reasonable seafood restaurants on the same street.

Cafés

Café Universitario, *Alameda 395 y Subercaseaux (near Santa Lucía), Lastarria*. Good, cheap *almuerzos*, lively at night, separate room for lovers of rock videos, very pleasant.

Bellavista *p88, map p88*

Most restaurants are closed for lunch in Bellavista, but this is one of the liveliest places to come out and eat at night, with many excellent and costly restaurants.

$$$ **Azul Profundo**, *Constitución 111, Bellavista*. Typical Chilean food with a touch of invention.

$$$ **Como Agua Para Chocolate**, *Constitución 88, Bellavista*. Mexican and Mediterranean.

$$$ **El Otro Sitio**, *López de Bello 053, Bellavista*. Peruvian, excellent food, good service, elegant.

$$$ **El Viejo Verde**, *López de Bello 94, Bellavista*. Excellent vegetarian food.

$$$ **Il Siciliano**, *Dardagnac y Constitución, Bellavista*. High-class pasta and seafood.

$$$ **Kilometre 11.680**, *Dardignac 145, Bellavista*. French restaurant with one of Chile's best wine lists.

$$$ **La Divina Comida**, *Purísima 093, Bellavista*. Italian with 3 rooms - Heaven, Hell and Purgatory. Highly recommended.

$$$ **Le Coq au Vin**, *No 0110, Bellavista*. French, excellent cuisine, reasonably priced.

$$$ **Nuevo Cipriani**, *Pinto Lagarrigue 195, Bellavista*. Italian, elegant atmosphere, very expensive, top class.

$$$ **Off the Record**, *López de Bello 153, Bellavista*. Period design, nice atmosphere, cheaper set lunch.

$$$ **San Fruttuoso**, *Mallinckrodt 180, Bellavista*. Italian, elegant. Recommended.

$$$ **Sommelier**, *Dardignac 163, Bellavista*. Modern cuisine. Excellent wine list.

$$$ **Zen**, *Dardignac 175, Bellavista*. Sushi restaurant. Recommended.

$$ **Aji Verde**, *Constitución 284, Bellavista*. Specializes in Chilean food, open for lunch.

$$ **Cava de Dardignac**, *Dardignac 0191, Bellavista*. Portuguese cuisine with live *fado* music at night.

$$ Eladio, *Pío Nono 251, Bellavista*. Argentine cuisine, good steaks, bingo.

$$ El Antojo de Gaugin, *Pío Nono 069, Bellavista*. Arabic. Good *brochetas a la plancha*.

$$ Etniko, *Constitución 172, Bellavista*. Inventive Japanese cuisine.

$$ La Tasca Mediterránea, *Purísima 163, Bellavista*. Extensive menu including fish, seafood, good value, good food. Recommended.

$$ Michelle's, *Arzobispo 0615, Bellavista*. Bistro with excellent seafood and fish dishes, recommended.

$$ Sarita Colonia, *Dardignac 50, Bellavista*. Peruvian, popular.

$$ Tragaluz, *Constitución 124, Bellavista, T02-738 2011*. Good Chilean food, not cheap.

$$ Venezia, *Pío Nono y Lopez de Bello, Bellavista*. Large servings, good value.

Cafés

Café de la Dulcería Las Palmas, *López de Bello 190*. Good pastries and lunches.

Cafetería La Nona, *Pío Nono 099*. Real coffee, good *empanadas* and cakes, fresh fruit juices. Recommended.

Empanatodos, *Pío Nono 153*. Serves 25 different types of *empanadas*.

Green, *Constitución 042*. Excellent healthy sandwiches and snacks.

East towards Providencia and Los Condes

Providencia *p91, map p90*

$$$ Cafetto Restaurant, *Pedro de Valdivia 030, next to Hotel Orly*. Italian specializing in haute cuisine, very smart.

$$$ Carousel, *Los Conquistadores 1972*. Fine French cuisine, exceptionally smart, nice garden, very expensive.

$$$ Centre Català, *Av Suecia 428 near Lota*. Good, quiet street, nice decor, cheaper set lunch.

$$$ Da Renato, *Mardoqueo Fernández 138. Los Leones metro*. Good Italian.

$$$ El Giratorio, *11 de Septiembre 2250, piso 16*. Good French food eaten while the whole city rotates outside your window. Recommended.

$$$ El Huerto, *Orrego Luco 054, T02-2332690*. Recommended. Open daily, live music Fri and Sat evenings, varied menu, very good, popular.

$$$ La Pizza Nostra, *Av Las Condes 6757*. Pizzas and good Italian food, real coffee, pricey. Also at *Av Providencia 1975* and *Luis Thayer Ojeda 019*.

$$$ Lomit's, *Av Providencia 1980*. Good, attentive service.

$$$ Oradia, *Tobalaba 477*. Celebrated French restaurant, very expensive.

$$$ Oriental, *M Montt 584*. One of the best Chinese restaurants in Santiago.

$$$ Salvaje, *Av Providencia 1177*. Excellent international menu, open-air seating, good-value lunches. Warmly recommended.

$$$ Valerio, *Coronel Pereira 139*. Smart Italian, good wines, not cheap.

$$ A Pinch of Pancho, *Gral del Canto 45*. Seafood and fish specialities, very good.

$$ Bin-Xiang, *M Montt 155*. Chinese.

$$ Bistro Maestro, *Las Urbinas y Providencia*, Russian food, good.

$$ Café El Patio, *Providencia 1652, next to Phone Box Pub*. Tofu and pasta as well as fish dishes, nice sandwiches, popular.

$$ Eladio, *11 de Septiembre 2250, piso 5*. Reasonably priced, good meat dishes.

$$ Gatsby, *Providencia 1984*. American food, as-much-as-you-can-eat buffet and lunch/dinner, also coffees and snacks, open till 2400, tables outside in warm weather, good.

$$ Jardín de Bambú, *Salvador 1827*. Vietnamese.

$$ La Pez Era, *Providencia 1421*. Seafood, smart but reasonably priced.

$ Kimomo, *Av Providencia 1480*, Vegetarian. Tofu, miso soup, good snacks.

$ La Máquina, *C Seminario, Salvador metro*. Nice atmosphere, music in the evening.

$ Unicornio, *Plaza Lyon, Local 49*. Decent vegetarian.

Cafés

There are several good places for snacks and ice-cream on Av Providencia including: **Copelia**, *No 2211*; **Bravissimo**, *No 1406*; **El Toldo Azul**, *No 1936*. Also, **Salón de Té Tavelli**, *Drugstore precinct, No 2124*.

Las Condes *p91, map p92*

This area has many first-class restaurants, including grills, serving Chilean (often with music), French and Chinese cuisine. They tend to be more expensive than central restaurants. Lots of expensive eateries are located on El Bosque Norte, near the Tobalaba metro stop.

$$$ **Benyarong**, *Américo Vespucio Norte 2970*. Thai.

$$$ **Coco Loco**, *El Bosque Norte 0215*. Fish, seafood, good.

$$$ **Cuerovaca**, *El Mañío 1659, Vitacura, T02-2468936*. Serves fantastic steaks, both Argentinian and Chilean cuts. Recommended.

$$$ **El Club**, *El Bosque Norte 0380*. Popular, very smart, good.

$$$ **El Madroñal**, *Vitacura 2911, T02-2336312*. Excellent, Spanish cuisine, one of the best restaurants in town, booking essential.

$$$ **El Mesón del Calvo**, *El Bosque Norte y Roger de Flor*. Seafood specials.

$$$ **Isla Negra**, *next door to Coco Loco, El Bosque Norte*. Seafood a speciality.

$$$ **La Cascade**, *Isadora Goyenechea 2930*. French, expensive, long established, closed Sun.

$$$ **München**, *Isadora Goyenechea 204*. German. Pricey but recommended.

$$$ **Pinpilinpausha**, *El Bosque Norte 2900*. Basque specialities, good.

$$$ **Sakura**, *Vitacura 4111*. Excellent sushi. Recommended.

$$$ **Shoo Gun**, *Enrique Foster Norte 172*. Japanese.

$$$ **You**, *El Bosque Norte 036*. Japanese restaurant, good sushi.

$$$-$$ **Diego Pizza**, *El Bosque Norte y Don Carlos*. Friendly, good cocktails, popular. Recommended.

$$$-$$ **Mare Nostrum**, *La Concepción 281*. Fine seafood.

$$$-$$ **Puerto Marisko**, *Isadora Goyenechea 3471*. Good seafood.

$$ **Delmónico**, *Vitacura 3379*. Excellent, reasonably priced.

$$ **Jabri**, *Vitacura 6477*. Arab cuisine.

$$ **Le Fournil**, *Vitacura 3841, opposite Cuerovaca, T02-2280219*. Excellent French bakery and restaurant. Particularly popular at lunchtime.

$$ **Praga**, *Vitacura 3917*. Czech.

$$ **The Wok House**, *Vitacura 4355, T02-2074757*. Good Chinese food, takeaway available.

⊕ Bars and clubs

As in most of South America, a night out in Santiago begins late. Arrive in a restaurant before 2100 and you may be eating alone, while bars and clubs are often empty before midnight. Clubs and bars playing live music will generally charge an entry fee of between US$2 (for student-orientated places) and US$10 (for upmarket clubs), usually with some sort of drink included in the price.

Santiago has a good selection of varied restaurants, bars, discos and *salsotecas* from reasonably priced in Bellavista (Baquedano metro) to the smarter along Av Suecia and G Holley in Providencia (Los Leones metro).

In Las Condes, El Bosque Norte is lined with chic bars and expensive restaurants for the Chilean jetset (Tobalaba metro).

Barrio Brasil has a number of bars and restaurants dotted around Plaza Brazil and on Av Brazil and Cumming. The area is popular with Chilean students (República metro).

In the middle-class suburb of Nuñoa is Plaza Nuñoa, around which a number of good bars are dotted.

Clubs in Las Condes and Providencia can be expensive, up to US$20 or more to get in. Clubs in Bellavista are cheaper and more downmarket than those in Providencia.

Bellavista *p88, map p88*

Bogart, *López de Bello 34*. Rock music.

Caribbean, *López de Bello 40*. Reggae.

Club 4-40, *Santa Filomena 081*. Named after popular singer Juan Luis Guerra's backing group from the Dominican Republic, live Cuban music, packed at weekends.

Disco Salsa, *Pío Nono 223*. Good atmosphere, also salsa dance classes downstairs.

Emmanuelle, *Andrés Bello 2857*. Shows at 0100 and 0300.

HBH Bar, *Purísima y López de Bello*. Good beer, good atmosphere.

La Bodega de Julio, *Constitución 256*. Cuban staff and Cuban cocktails, excellent live music and dancing possible, very popular, free entry before 2300, very good value. Highly recommended.

La Casa en el Aire, *López de Bello 125*. Pleasant atmosphere, live music. Recommended.

La Chimenea, *Passaje Principe de Gales 90*. Hidden away up stairs in a street in the close to the centre of downtown, an atmospheric and slightly dingy pub serving meals during the day. No airs and graces, but lively.

La Otra Puerta, *Pío Nono 348*. Lively *salsoteca* with live music. Recommended.

Libro Café Mediterraneo. Popular with students, lively, expensive. US$4.50 charge on Mon nights, when a local man does good Georges Brassens impressions.

Peña Nano Parra, *San Isidro 57*. Good folk club, cheap.

Restaurant/Pub Evelyn, *Purísima 282*. Austrian beers on tap, good atmosphere, not cheap.

Tu Tu Tanga, *Pío Nono 127*. Busy at night, cheap, good value.

East towards Providencia and Los Condes

Providencia *p91, map p90*

Brannigan Pub, *Suecia 35*. Good beer, live jazz, lively.

Café Mistral, *C Arzobispo 0635, T02-7776173*. Owned by French mountain-climber, free climbing wall, internet.

Flannery's Irish Geo Pub, *Encomenderos 83*.

Irish pub, serving Guinness on draft, good lunches, popular among gringos and Chileans alike.

Golden Bell Inn, *Hernando Aguirre 27*. Popular with expats.

Louisiana River Pub, *Suecia y General Holley*. Live music.

Phone Box Pub, *Providencia 1670, T02-496627*. Very popular with expats, serves numerous European beers including Pilsener Urquell, and canned British beers including Newcastle Brown Ale, Beamish Stout and Old Speckled Hen. A good place to go if you are missing home.

Las Condes *p91, map, p92*

Country Village, *Av Las Condes 10680*. Mon-Sat from 2000, Sun from lunch onwards, live music Fri and Sat.

Heaven, *Recoleta 345*. Thu, Fri, Sat 2330-0500, US$12 per person.

Ilé Habana, *Bucaré just off Suecia*. Bar with salsa music, often live, and a good dance floor.

Las Urracas, *Vitacura 9254*. US$15 but free before 2300 if you eat there.

Morena Pizza and Dance Bar, *Av Las Condes 10120*. Good sound system, live music at weekends, happy hour before 2200.

Tequila, *Av Las Condes at Paseo San Damián*, One of a few popular bar-restaurants in the area.

⊙ Entertainment

For all entertainment, nightclubs, cinemas, restaurants, concerts, *El Mercurio Online* website has listings and a good search feature. Look under the *tiempo libre* section of the site: www.emol.com There are also listings in weekend newspapers, particularly *El Mercurio* and *La Tercera*, and in *Santiago What's On*.

Cinemas

A good guide to daily cinema listings across the city is provided by the 2 free newspapers, *La Hora* and *tmg*, which are given out at metro stations early on weekday mornings. Seats cost US$4-6 with reductions on Wed (elsewhere in the country the day varies). Some cinemas offer discounts to students and over 60s (proof required).

There are many mainstream cinemas showing international films, usually in original English with Spanish subtitles. Multiplex cinemas include:

Cinemark Alto Las Condes, *Av Kennedy 9001, Las Condes, T02-6002463*, and

Showcase Parque Arauco, *Av Kennedy 5413, Las Condes, T02-2247707*, both attached to respective shopping malls.

Cinehoyts Huérfanos, *Huérfanos 735, T02-6641861*.

Cinehoyts San Agustín, *San Antonio 144, T02-6329566*.

Cinehoyts Estación Central, *in the shopping mall next to the train station*.

'Ciné Arte' (arthouse cinemas that show quality foreign films), are also very popular and include the following:

Casa de Extensión Universidad Católica
Av B O'Higgins 390, T02-6351994.
Cine Arte Normandie, *Tarapacá 1181,
T02-6972979.* Varied programme, altered
frequently, films at 1530, 1830 and 2130
daily, students half price.
El Biógrafo, *Lastarria 181, T02-6334435.*
Tobalaba, *Av Providencia 2563, T02-2316630.*

Cultural centres

**Instituto Cultural del Banco del Estado de
Chile**, *Alameda 123.* Regular exhibitions of
paintings, concerts, theatrical performances.
Instituto Cultural de Providencia, *Av 11 de
Septiembre 1995. Pedro de Valdivia metro.* Art
exhibitions, concerts, theatre, worth checking
out the programme.
Instituto Cultural Las Condes, *Av
Apoquindo 6570, near beginning of Av Las
Condes.* Also with art exhibitions, concerts,
lectures, etc.

Performing arts

Teatro Municipal, *Agustinas y San Antonio.*
Stages international opera, concerts by the
Orquesta Filarmónica de Santiago and
performances by the Ballet de Santiago,
throughout the year; on Tue at 2100 there
are free operatic concerts in the Salón
Claudio Arrau; tickets range from US$7 for a
very large choral group with a symphony
orchestra, and US$8 for the cheapest seats at
the ballet, to US$70 for the most expensive
opera seats. Some cheap seats are often sold
on the day of concerts.
Teatro Universidad de Chile, *Plaza
Baquedano.* Home of the Orquesta y Coro
Sinfónica de Chile and the Ballet Nacional
de Chile.

A great number of more minor theatres
around the city stage plays in Spanish, either
in the original language or translations,
including **Abril**, *Huérfanos 786*; **Camilo
Henríquez**, *Amunátegui 31*; **Centro Arrayán**,
Las Condes 14891; **El Galpón de los Leones**,
Av Los Leones 238; **El Conventillo**, *Bellavista
173* and **La Comedia**, *Merced 349.* Events are
listed in *El Mercurio* and *La Tercera.*

For Folies Bergères-type revues, try:
California, *Irarrázaval 1546*; **Humoresque**,
San Ignacio 1249; **Opera**, *Huérfanos*; or
Picaresque, *Recoleta 345.*

● Festivals and events

Religious festivals and ceremonies continue
throughout **Holy Week**, when a priest
ritually washes the feet of 12 men.

A food festival towards the end of **May**
called **Expo gourmand**. Its location changes
every year.

The image of the **Virgen del Carmen**
(patron saint of the Armed Forces) is carried
through the streets by cadets on **16 Jul**.

18 Sep is Chile's **National Day** when
many families get together.

19 Sep is **Armed Forces Day**, celebrated
with an enormous military procession
through the Parque O'Higgins.

In **Oct** or **Nov**, **Parque Cerrillos** hosts a
sumptuous flower show and an annual
agricultural and industrial show known as
Fisa.

A free **art fair** is held in the Parque
Forestal on the banks of the Río Mapocho
during a fortnight in **Nov**.

○ Shopping

There are many shopping areas in Santiago.
The shops in the centre and to the north of
the Plaza de Armas are cheaper and more
downmarket than the countless arcades and
boutiques strung along Providencia,
especially near Av Ricardo Lyon. Specialist
shops tend to be grouped together, eg bikes
and second-hand books on San Diego, new
bookshops on Providencia, opticians on Mac
Iver, lapis lazuli in Bellavista. Many stalls on
Paseo Ahumada/Huérfanos sell overseas
newspapers and journals.

66 99 Santiaguinos say that if there was a market for souls, someone would be selling them off at cost price in the Bío Bío.

Bookshops

Book prices are very high compared with Europe, even for second-hand books. There are many bookshops in the Pedro de Valdivia area on Av Providencia. Much better value but with a smaller selection are the bookshops in the shopping mall at Av Providencia 1114-1120. Those looking for cheap English-language books should also try the many second-hand book kiosks on San Diego, 4 blocks south of Plaza Bulnes, next to the Iglesia de los Sacramentinos.
Apostrophes, *Merced 324*, specializes in French publications including literature.
Books, *Providencia 1652, Local 5, in a court-yard beside the Phone Box Pub and Café El Patio*. Wide selection of English-language books for sale or exchange, English spoken.
Feria Chilena del Libro, *Huérfanos 623*. Largest bookstore in Santiago, good for travel books and maps; also in Drugstore precinct, Providencia 2124.
Librairie Française, *Estado 337*. French books and newspapers.
Librería Chile Ilustrado, *Providencia 1652 local 6, next door to Books, T02-2358145, chileil@tnet.cl* Specializes in books (nearly all in Spanish) relating to Chile, particularly flora and fauna, history and anthropology.
Librería Eduardo Albers, *Vitacura 5648, Las Condes, T02-2185371, F2181458*. Spanish, English and German – good selection, cheaper than most, helpful, also German and Swiss newspapers.
Librería Inglesa, *Huérfanos 669, Local 11, Pedro de Valdivia 47, Vitacura 5950, Providencia 2653, T02-2319970, www.libreriainglesa.cl* Sells only books in English, good selection, sells the *South American Handbook*.
Librería Lila, *Providencia 1652, Local 3*. Mind/body/spirit specialists, best in Santiago for this field.
Librería Universitaria, *Av O'Higgins 1050, T02-6951529, F02-6956387*. Particularly for books in Spanish.

LOM Ediciones, *Estación Mapocho*. Mon-Fri 1000-2000, Sat 1000-1400. Sells a stock of literature, history, sociology, art and politics from its own publishing house. Also a bar and a reading room with recent Chilean newspapers and magazines.
South American Way, *Av Apoquindo 6856, Las Condes, T02-2118078*. Sells books in English.

Camera repairs and film

Many developers on Ahumada offer 24-hr service of varying quality (some develop, but do not mount, slides, slow service).
Black Box, *Pérez Valenzuela 1503. Manuel Montt metro*. Highly recommended.
Carmen Pérez Gúzman, *MacIver 148*. Good quality, helpful, some English spoken.
Harry Müller, *Ahumada 312, of 402*. Good, quick and inexpensive. Recommended. Speaks German and English.
Moretto, *Merced 753*. Recommended as cheap and good.
Prontofoto, *Ahumada 264, T02-6721981*. Good-quality developing and printing.
TecFo, *Nueva York 52, piso 2, T02-6952969*. For Minolta and Canon repairs. Recommended.
Tecnofoto, *Ahumada 131, piso 7, of 719, T02-6725004*. Recommended as quick and efficient. For camera batteries and other spares.

Camping and outdoors equipment

Bertonati Hnos, *Manuel Montt 2385*. Equipment for camper vans
Casa Italiana, *Tarapacá 1120*. Repairs camping stoves.
Club Andino and **Federación de Andinismo** (see p). Expensive camping goods because these articles are imported.
Fabri Gas, *Bandera y Santo Domingo*. Camping gas cartridges.
Juan Soto, *Silva Vildosola 890, Paradero 1, Gran Avenida, San Miguel, T02-5558329*. For tent repairs.

Industria Yarur, *Rosas 1289 y Teatinos, T02-6723696*. Good value for money, discounts available.

La Cumbre, *Apoquindo 5258, Las Condes, T02-2209907, la_cumbre@email.com* Climbing equipment.

Luz Emperatriz Sanhuela Quiroz *Portal de León, Loc 14, Providencia 2198. Los Leones metro*. Second-hand equipment.

Outdoors & Travel, *Encomeneros 206, Las Condes, T02-3357104*. For wide range of imported and locally made camping goods.

Patagonia, *Helvecia 210, Providencia, T02-3351796*. Good range of clothing and equipment, comparatively expensive.

Unisport, *Av Providencia 2503*. Camping gas cartridges.

Handicrafts

Those wishing to spend a reasonable amount of money buying good-quality crafts may wish to travel to Pomaire (see p118), where goods from all over Chile are for sale at cheaper prices than those in Santiago.

The gemstone, lapis lazuli, can be found in a few expensive shops in Bellavista but is cheaper in the arcades on the south side of the Plaza de Armas. Antique stores can be found in Plaza Mulato Gil de Castro and elsewhere on Lastarria (Merced end).

Plaza Artesanos de Manquehue, *Av Manquehue Sur, block 300-600, just off Apoquindo in Las Condes*. This is the biggest craft market in Chile. A good range of modern Chilean crafts from ceramics to textiles, a pleasant central piazza, and places where the artisans can be seen working on wood, silver, glass and so on. Although more expensive than, for instance, the market in Santa Lucía, this is a good and attractive place to come; take any bus east from Providencia or Escuela Militar which goes via 'Apoquindo'.

Aldea de Vitacura, *Vitacura 6838, T02-7353959*. 1000-2000.

Amitié, *Av Ricardo Lyon y Av Providencia. Los Leones metro*. Recommended.

Centro Artesanal Santa Lucía *Santa Lucía metro, south exit*. Lapis lazuli can be bought here cheaply. Also has a wide variety of woollen goods, jewellery etc.

Chile Vivo, *Dardignac 15, Barrio Bellavista, T02-7350227, chilevivo@latinmail.com* Shopping centre with café, handicraft shop, internet, art gallery and jewellery workshop.

Dauvin Artesanía Fina, *Providencia 2169, Local 69. Los Leones metro*. Recommended.

El Almacén Campesino, *Purísima 303, Bellavista*. Co-operative association in a colonial building. Sells handicrafts from all over Chile, including attractive Mapuche weavings, wood carvings, pottery and beautiful wrought copper and bronze. Prices similar to those in Temuco. Ask about shipping.

El Pueblo de Artesanos, *daily except Mon, 1130-1900*. All types of ware on sale, classes given in some shops, interesting.

Marita Gil, *Los Misioneros 1991, Pedro de Valdivia Norte, T02-2326853*. A cheaper craft market is next to the bridge of Pio Nono in Bellavista, best at weekends.

Prisma de los Andes, *Santo Domingo 1690, T02-6730540. Santa Ana metro*. A women's social project, sells distinctive high-quality textiles made in the organization's co-operative workshops (which can be visited).

Other craft stalls can be found in an alleyway, *1 block south of Av O'Higgins between A Prat and San Diego*; on the *600 to 800 blocks of Santo Domingo* and at *Pío Nono y Av Santa María* in Bellavista..

Maps

Automóvil Club de Chile, *Vitacura 8620*. Route maps of Chile. US$6 each or US$3 each if affiliated to motor organization.

CONAF, *see p79*. Maps of the national parks.

Instituto Geográfico Militar, *Dieciocho 369, near Toesca metro, T02-4608222*. Detailed geophysical and topographical maps of the whole of Chile, very useful for climbing. Expensive (about US$11 each), but **Biblioteca Nacional**, *Alameda 651, T02-3605200*, stocks them and will allow you to photocopy parts of each map.

Librería Australis, *Av Providencia 1670, local 5*. All sorts of local, regional and trekking maps.

Markets

For details of the city's craft markets, see Handicrafts, above.

Bío Bío flea market, *C Bío Bío*. Every Sat and Sun morning. This is the largest and cheapest flea market in the city and sells everything from spare parts for cars and motorbikes to second-hand furniture. Those trying to do up a new flat on the cheap, a car on the hoof, or who are simply interested in sharing a street with tens of thousands of others, should find their way here, just go to Franklin metro and follow the crowds. Beware rip-offs.

Mercado Central, *Puente y 21 de Mayo by the Río Mapocho. Cal y Canto metro*. Brilliant for seafood, with many places to eat cheaply, **Don Agusto** is recommended. Otherwise an excellent range of goods, but quite expensive.

Vega Central, *on the opposite bank of the river*, is cheaper than Mercado Central.

Music

Feria del Disco, *Paseo Ahumada*. The biggest chain. Also sell tickets for rock concerts. Branches in numerous malls.
Musimundo, *Huérfanos 930 (complete with listening stations) and Providencia 2266*. Music megastores.

Opticians

Those needing to have a new set of glasses made up should head for MacIver 0-100 block, where there are many opticians to choose from, and prices are lower than comparable rates in Europe or North America.

Wine

There's also a good selection of wines at **Jumbo, Líder** and **Ekono** supermarkets.
El Mundo del Vino, *Isidora Goyenechea 2929*. Also in the Alto Las Condes and Plaza Vespucio malls.
Vinopolis, *El Bosque Norte 038 and Pedro de Valdivia 036*. Mon-Fri 0900-2300, Sat 1000-2300, Sun 1000-2200. Exclusively Chilean wines. Good selection and various prices.
The Wine House, *Vitacura 2904*.

Shopping malls

These are generally open 7 days a week 1000-2100.
Apumanque, *Apoquindo y Manquehue, Las Condes*. Large shopping centre.
Centro Comercial Alto Las Condes *Av Kennedy, east of Las Condes*. This is the largest and most modern mall in the city.
Mall del Centro, *C Rosas 900-block, just north of the Plaza de Armas*. Brings US mall culture to the centre of Santiago.
Parque Arauco, *Av Kennedy, north of Escuela Militar metro, Las Condes*. More of the same.
Plaza Vespucio, *at the terminus of Metro line 5, Bellavista de La Florida*. The next most convenient after Mall del Centro.

● Sport and activities

Bowling
Bowling Center, *Av Apoquindo 5012*. Ten-pin bowling, lots of alleys. Recommended.

Cricket

Club Príncipe de Gales, *Las Arañas 1901, right by the junction of Bilbao and Vespuccio*. Matches held on Sat in summer at this snooty ground. Admission US$5, membership not required (just tell the doorman you are there for the cricket), lots of drinks included in the price.

Football

There are 3 big clubs; see also box p108.
Colo Colo, play at the Estadio Monumental, reached by any bus to Puente Alto; tickets from *Cienfuegos 41, T02-6883244*.
Universidad de Chile, play at Campo de Departes, *Nuñoa, T02-2392793*. Estadio Nacional is the nearest metro station.
Universidad Católica, play at San Carlos de Apoquindo, reached by bus from Escuela Militar metro; tickets from *Andrés Bello 2782, Providencia, T02-2312777*.

If you decide to visit the Estadio Nacional, where international matches are played, find a space high up on the terraces and you will be able to watch the sun set over the mountains behind Santiago.

⁝ Soccer nation

Football arrived in Chile towards the end of the 19th century, courtesy of the British. The role of British workers – most of whom were employed in the construction of the railway system – is reflected in the names of several of the leading teams, notably Santiago Wanderers (who are based in Valparaíso), Everton (based in Viña) and Rangers (based in Talca). The game's popularity grew rapidly; by the 1940s most large towns boasted their own team and stadium. In 1962, Chile's importance as a soccer nation was recognized internationally when it hosted the World Cup and the national side finished third. The quarter final between Chile and Italy became known as the 'Battle of Santiago', one of the most vicious games in the sport's history (Chile won 2-1).

Although Chilean football may not enjoy the worldwide recognition given to Argentina and Brazil, Chileans follow 'the beautiful game' with as much passion as their illustrious neighbours. Chile played well in the qualifying round for the 1990 World Cup, and the decisive match saw them having to draw with Brazil to go through to the finals. Chile lost 1-0 and nearing the end of the game the Chilean goalkeeper, 'El Condor' Rojas, collapsed with blood falling from his cheek, claiming to have been hit by a missile from the crowd; the Chilean team walked off in protest. It later emerged that Rojas had cut himself with a razor blade; Chile were disqualified and banned from the 1994 World Cup. Chile's performance in the 1998 World Cup – when they reached the last 16 – was therefore a source of great national pride. In truth, the 1998 adventure was somewhat typical of Chilean football; the national side flattered for a moment (being only eight minutes away from an

unlikely victory against Italy in their first match), before going out 4-1 to Brazil.

The last few years have seen a rapid demise in the fortunes of the national team, the low point being a home loss to Venezuela in qualifying for the 2002 World Cup – the first time that Venezuela had won away from home in a competitive game for nearly 40 years. The last time a Chilean side reached the final of the *Copa Libertadores* (the South American club championship) was in 1993, when Universidad Católica somewhat let things slip by losing 5-1 to Sao Paolo in the away leg of the final, before waking up belatedly and winning the home leg 2-0.

The local season is split into two tournaments, the *apertura* running from March to June and the *clausura* from August to December, the winners of each competition being decided by a playoff. Most of the support (and money) goes to the big three clubs, all based in Santiago: Universidad de Chile (known as 'La U'), Colo-Colo and Universidad Católica (which tends to be favoured by the well-off). The greatest rivalry is between La U and Colo-Colo (who are also known as Los Indios, as their strip carries an image of the great Mapuche leader after whom they were named). The most fervent supporters of the former are known as *los de abajo* (the underdogs), while those of the latter are called *la garra blanca* (the white claw).

A visit to a match, especially either an international game or a *clásico* (local derby), is an unforgettable experience. Watching football is still very much a family affair and the supporters dance, sing and wave their team colours beneath a non-stop rain of confetti, fireworks and coloured smoke. Cheap tickets cost around US$5.

Gymnasiums

Gimnásio Alicia Franché, *Moneda 1481, T02-6961681*. Central location for aerobics and fitness classes (women only). Another at *Huérfanos 1313, T02-6711562*.
Sesame, *Los Leones 2384, Providencia*. With pool, aerobics. Highly recommended.

Racecourses

Betting is a growing industry, with increasing numbers of **Teletrak** betting shops around the city.
Club Hípico, *Blanco Encalada 2540*. Racing every Sun and every other Wed afternoon, worthwhile even if only to watch dusk fall over the Andes, entry to main stand US$5, card of up to 18 races.
Hipódromo Chile, every Sat afternoon. Pari-mutuel betting.

Skiing and climbing

The 2 main climbing areas near Santiago are the Grupo Loma Larga near the Cajón del Maipo and the Grupo Plomo near the ski resort of La Parva. For ski resorts in the Santiago area, see p121. Ski equipment hire is much cheaper in Santiago than in the resorts.
Club Alemán Andino, *El Arrayán 2735, T02-2425453*. Tue and Fri 1800-2000, May-Jun.
Club Andino de Chile, *Enrique Foster 29*. 1900-2100 on Mon and Fri. Ski club.
Federación de Andinismo de Chile, *Almte Simpson 77A, T02-2220888, www.feach.cl* Open daily. It has the addresses of all the mountaineering clubs in the country and has a mountaineering school.

La Cumbre Ltda, *Av Apoquindo 5258, T02-2209907, www.lacumbreonline.cl* Dutch proprietors very helpful, good climbing and trekking equipment.
Mountain Service, *Santa Magdalena 75, T02-2343439, www.mountainservice.cl* English spoken, tents, stoves, clothing, equipment rental. Recommended.
Panda Deportes, *Paseo Las Palmas 2217, T02-2321840. Los Leones metro*.
Skitotal, *Av Apoquindo 4900, of 40-42, T02-2460156*. Rents equipment, organizes accommodation and lessons. English and German spoken. Transport also provided to the ski resorts of Farellones, El Colorado, La Parva and Valle Nevado.

Swimming pools

Antilen, *Cerro San Cristóbal*. Open Tue-Sun 1000-150 in summer; closed Apr-Oct, US$10. Fine panoramic view over the city.
Parque Araucano, *near Parque Arauco Shopping Centre, Escuela Militar metro*. Open Nov-Mar Tue-Sat 0900-1900. Olympic pool.
Parque O'Higgins, *T02-5569612*. Two pools (one for children), open summer only, US$4.
Tupahue, *Cerro San Cristóbal*. Large pool with cafés, US$7; 2 for the price of 1 on Wed.

Tennis

There are municipal courts in Parque O'Higgins; the national stadium, **Estadio Nacional**, *Av Grecia con Av Marathon*, has a tennis club that offers classes.

⋒ Tour operators

Adventure tours and trekking

Altue Expediciones, *Encomenderos 83, piso 2, Las Condes, T02-2321103, F02-2336799, altue@entelchile.net* For wilderness trips including tour of Patagonia and sea-kayaking in Chiloé.
Andina del Sud, *Bombero Ossa 1010, piso 3, of 301, T02-6971010, www.andinadelsud.com* Climbing and trekking in the Lake District and other areas.

Azimut 360, *Arzobispo Casanova 3, Providencia, T02-7358034, www.azimut.cl* Low prices. Adventure and eco-tourism throughout Chile, including tours to the Atacama Desert. Aconcagua base camp services and mountaineering expeditions to Parinacota and Sajama.Highly recommended.
Cascada Expediciones, *Orrego Luco 040, Providencia, T02-2342274, www.cascada-expediciones.com* Specializse in activity tours in remote areas.

Mountain Service, *Paseo Las Palmas 2209, T02-2330913. Los Leones metro.* Recommended for climbing trips.

Patagonia Connection SA, *Fidel Oteíza 1921, of 1006, Providencia, T02- 2256489, www.patagonia-connection.com, Pedro de Valdivia metro.* For cruises to Patagonia.

Rapa-Nui, *Huérfanos 1160.* Specializes in trips to Easter Island.

Racies, *Plaza Corregidor Zañartu 761, T/F02-6382904.* Cultural tours, including Robinson Crusoe Island and Antarctica.

Southern Cross Adventure, *Jose Miguel de la Barra 521, T02-6396591, www.scadventure.com* Offers mountaineering, biking, horseriding, trekking, high-altitude archaeology, visits to volcanoes, fishing in the Andes. English, French, German and Spanish-speaking guides, camping gear provided. Branch office also at *Caracoles 119* in San Pedro de Atacama.

Sportstours, *Moneda 970, piso 14 T02-5495200, www.sportstour.cl* German-run, helpful, 5-day trips to Antarctica (offices also at hotels **Carrera** and **San Cristóbal**).

Turismo Cabo de Hornos, *Agustinas 814, of 706, T02-6338481, F02-6338486.* For **DAP** flights and Tierra del Fuego/Antarctica tours.

Local tours

Ace Turismo, *O'Higgins 949, T02-6960391.* City tour, US$12 for ½ a day.

Maysa, *Paseo Ahumada 6, of 43, T/F02-6964468.* Good tours of wine bodegas and Valparaíso, US$30.

Nicole Aventuras, *T02- 225 6155/T8241277 (mob), wwwfis.puc.cl/~gtarrach/ avenic* Excursions in Santiago region, including wildlife and glacier tours.

Travel agents

4 Star South America, *T1-800 747 4540 (US)/ 0871-711 5370 (UK)/+49-700-4444 7827 (rest of the world), http://4starSouthAmerica.com (tours to South America), http://4starFlights.com (flight consolidator tickets to South America).* Tour operator and flight consolidator with internet- and catalogue-based marketing.

All Travels, *Huérfanos 1160, Local 10, T02-6964348.* Good for flight tickets.

Asatej Student Flight Centre, *Hernando de Aguirre 201, of 401, T02-3350395, chile@asatej.com.ar* For cheap flights and youth travel, also tours, car rental, ISIC cards, medical insurance and hotels.
Eurotur, *Huérfanos 1160, Local 13, www.eurotur.com* For cheap air tickets to a variety of European destinations.
Passtours, *Huérfanos 886, of 1110, T02-6393232, F02-6331498, www.finam.cl/ passtour* Many languages spoken, helpful.

Turismo Grant, *Huérfanos 863, of 516, T02-6395524.* Helpful, English spoken.
Turismo Tajamar, *Orrego Luco 023, Providencia, T02-3368000, www.tajamar.cl* Good for flights, helpful. Recommended.
USIT Andes, *Av 11 de Septiembre 2305, Local 13, T02-3351415, www.travelandes.cl* Student travel agency.
VMP Ltda, *Huérfanos 1160, Local 19, T/F02-6967829.* For all services. Many languages spoken, helpful. Recommended.

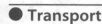 # Transport

Air

For details of the Aeropuerto Arturo Merino Benitez, see p39. For domestic flights from Santiago see under relevant destinations. Airline offices are listed in Directory, below.

Bus

Local

In Santiago, buses are known as *micros*, with each *micro* displaying its particular route on a board in the window. Over the past decade, the system has progressed from one of utter chaos (in which buses could stop anywhere at all and no routes were numbered) to a curious combination of chaos and efficiency. Now routes are all numbered and, on most main roads, buses will only stop at bus stops. On the Alameda, Providencia and Apoquindo, different bus stops serve different destinations (eg Pudahuel, Las Condes, Maipú) – these destinations are clearly marked on the stops. The chaos is provided by the new ticket machines. Theoretically, on getting onto the bus, you are supposed to put exact change into the machine to get a printed ticket, but in practice any one of several things may happen: you may give the money to the driver who will then arrange a printed ticket; or you may give the money to the driver who will give you a paper ticket of the type that were used before the machines were brought in. Whatever happens, the driver will expect you to be expecting his particular way of doing things. The fare is about US$0.50, but there are frequent rises.

Long distance

There are frequent, good inter-urban buses to all parts of Chile. Prices are much lower outside the peak summer season. You should always book ahead in Jan and Feb, July, and other peak times such as Easter and on and around Chile's National Day (18 Sep). At other times of the year, departures are so frequent that it is usually possible to just turn up and go. Check if student rates are available, or reductions for travelling on the same day as purchasing the ticket; it is worth bargaining over prices, especially shortly before departure and out of the summer season. Also take a look at the buses before buying the tickets (there are big differences in quality among bus companies); ask about the on-board services, as many companies offer drinks, sometimes complimentary, and luxury buses have meals and videos. Reclining seats are the norm and there are also *salón cama* sleeper buses. Fares from/to the capital are given in the text, see Transport sections in each destination.

There are 4 terminals, all located close to each other near the city centre. **Tur Bus** has a booking office in the centre, *Bulnes 96, T02-6973541*, and at *Av Apoquindo* for those beginning their journeys in Las Condes. Bear in mind that on Friday evenings in summer, when the night buses are preparing to depart, the terminals are nightmarishly chaotic and busy in the extreme.

Terminal Alameda, *O'Higgins 3712, T02-27071500, Universidad de Santiago metro*, has a modern extension with a shopping centre called Mall Parque Estación, several Redbanc ATMs and internet. This has the best left luggage facilities in the city, and is a good choice as two of the best companies, **Tur Bus** and **Pullman Bus**, leave from here (serving all main destinations from **Arica** to **Puerto Montt**), and there are also **Pullman del Sur** buses to less frequented parts of the central valley, eg **Chanco** (US$6), **Iloca** (US$4.50).

Terminal Santiago, *O'Higgins 3878, T02-3761755, 1 block west of Terminal Alameda, Universidad de Santiago metro.* Sometimes referred to as the 'Terminal Sur', this terminal is used by services to and from the **south**, as well as buses to **Valparaíso** and **Viña del Mar**. It is the only terminal with services to **Punta Arenas** (48 hrs), and is also the centre for most international services (see below). There is a Redbanc ATM.

Terminal San Borja, *O'Higgins y San Borja, T02-7760645, 1 block west of Estación Central, 3 blocks east of Terminal Alameda. Estación Central metro.* There are buses to destinations in the **Santiago area**, such as **Melipilla**, and to most of the coastal towns (these are very frequent), and many companies serving **northern Chile**. Booking offices are arranged according to destination. The entrance is, inconveniently, located through the shopping centre next to the station, and is not immediately apparent from the Alameda.

Terminal Los Héroes, *Tucapel Jiménez, just north of the Alameda, T02-4200099. Los Héroes metro.* A smaller terminal with 8 companies, but useful destinations such as **Vicuña** with **Diamantes de Elqui** and **Chiloé** with **Cruz del Sur**. Note also that some long-distance bus services also call at **Las Torres de Tajamar**, which is much more convenient if you are planning to stay in Providencia.

International
Almost all international buses leave from the Terminal Santiago.

To Argentina There are frequent services through the Cristo Redentor tunnel to **Mendoza**, 6-7 hrs, US$12, many companies, eg Ahumada (recommended), Andesmar, CATA, TAC (recommended), Tas Choapa, departures around 0800, 1200 and 1600, touts approach you in Terminal Santiago. Most of these services continue on to **Buenos Aires**, 24 hrs, US$35. There are also *colectivos* to **Mendoza** from the Terminal Santiago, 5 hrs, US$17; Chi-Ar Ltda is recommended (pick up

from hotels), shorter waiting time at customs. Companies in the Terminal Santiago have connections to many other Argentine cities: Andesmar to **Bahía Blanca**, US$40, change in Mendoza, 24 hrs; TAC and Tas Choapa direct to **Córdoba**, US$25, 18 hrs (*El Rápido* not recommended); to **San Juan**, TAC, Tas Choapa, US$18. If going to destinations such as **Bariloche** or **Neuquén** in Argentine Patagonia, it is better to travel south to Temuco or Osorno and connect there.

To other destinations To **Montevideo** (Uruguay), most involving a change in Mendoza, **Tas Choapa** and others, 27 hrs, including meals. To **São Paulo** and **Rio de Janeiro** (Brazil), Chilebus and Pluma, Tue, Thu, Sat, 72 hrs, US$80. To **Asunción** (Paraguay), 4 a week, 28 hrs, US$60. The biggest company serving Andean destinations is the Peruvian company **Ormeño** in Terminal Santiago, whose buses leave on Tue and Fri at 0900 to **Lima** (Peru), where connections are made to **Guayaquil** and **Quito** (Ecuador), **Cali** and **Bogotá** (Colombia) and **Caracas** (Venezuela) – buses are good and comfortable and there are meal stops. To **Lima**, 51 hrs, US$60 (it is cheaper to take a bus to Arica, a *colectivo* to Tacna (US$3), then bus to Lima); to **Guayaquil**, 80 hrs, US$100; to **Quito**, 88 hrs, US$110; to **Cali**, 4½ days, US$140; to **Bogotá**, US$150, 5 days; to **Caracas**, US$165, 7 days. Those heading for Bolivia are best advised to travel to one of the northern cities and then go by frequent bus from Iquique or Arica, or via the weekly train from Calama.

Car

As in most cities of its size, traffic and pollution are major problems: driving in the city is restricted according to licence plate numbers; each day, plates ending in 1 of 2 digits are prohibited from circulating (prohibited registration numbers are published in the press). For car hire, see Directory, below.

Colectivo

Collective taxis, which operate on fixed routes between the centre and the suburbs, are a convenient form of transport. They ply the streets and carry destination signs and route numbers. Fares vary, depending on the length of the journey, but are usually between US$0.75 and US$1.50. Higher fares at night.

Hitchhiking

To **Valparaíso**, take the metro to Pajaritos and walk 5 mins to west – no difficulty. Alternatively, take bus 'Renca Panamericana' from MacIver y Monjitas.

To hitch **south**, take Buses del Paine from outside the Terminal San Borja as far as possible on the highway to the toll area, about US$1, 75 mins.

To hitch **north** is not easy, but take blue Metrobus marked 'Til-Til' (frequent departures from near the Mercado Central as far as the toll bridge (*peaje*), 40 mins, US$1), then hitch from just beyond the toll bridge; you may be better off getting a bus north to the town of La Calera, 2 hrs, and trying from there.

To **Buenos Aires** (and Brazil) take a bus to Los Andes (**Buses Los Andes** leave from Tucapel Jimenez y Moneda, behind the Terminal Los Héroes), then go to Copec station on the outskirts (most trucks travel overnight).

Line 1 of the underground railway system runs west-east between San Pablo and Escuela Militar, under the Alameda. Line 2 runs north-south from Cal y Canto to Lo Ovalle. The connecting station is Los Héroes. Line 5 runs north-south from Santa Ana on Line 2, via Baquedano on Line 1 to La Florida. Work is under way to extend Line 2 both north and south, and Line 5 west to the Parque Quinta Normal (works due to be completed in 2004). The new Line 4 linking the south and east of the city is also under constuction, but will not be completed before the end of 2005.

The trains are fast, quiet and very full. The first train is at 0630 (Mon-Sat), 0800 (Sun and holidays), the last about 2245. Fares vary according to time of journey; there are 2 charging periods: high 0715-0900 and 1800-1930, US$0.55; low all other times, US$0.40. The simplest solution is to buy a *boleto valor*, US$4.70, a charge card from which the appropriate fare is deducted; there are often queues for the ticket office, but bigger stations also have ticket machines. Metrobus

Santiago metro

Line 1	
Line 2 (Extensions due for completion 2004)	
Line 4 (Due for completion 2005)	
Line 5 (Extentions due for completion 2004)	
Under construction	
Bus terminal	
Train station	

Not to scale

services (blue buses, fare US$0.40) connect the metro stations of Lo Ovalle, San Pablo, Las Rejas, Cal y Canto, Salvador, Escuela Militar, Pedrero and Bellavista de la Florida with outlying parts of Gran Santiago. For more information on the metro, see www.metrosantiago.cl

Taxi

Taxis (black with yellow roofs) are abundant, and not expensive, with a minimum charge of US$0.30, plus US$0.10 per 200 m. Taxi drivers are permitted to charge more at night, but in the daytime check that the meter is set to day rates. Taxis are more expensive at bus terminals and from taxi ranks outside hotels – best to walk a block and flag down a cruising taxi. Avoid taxis with more than 1 person in them, especially at night. For journeys outside the city arrange the charge beforehand. The private taxi service that operates from the bottom level of **Hotel Carrera** has been recommended (same rates as city taxis).

Also recommended: **Radio Taxis Andes Pacífico**, *T02-2253064/2888*, **Rigoberto Contreras**, *T02-6381042, ext 4215*, but rates are above those of city taxis.

Train

All trains leave from **Estación Central**, *Alameda O'Higgins 3322*. There are no passenger trains to northern Chile, Valparaíso or Vína del Mar. The line runs south to **Rancagua**, **San Fernando**, **Curicó**, **Talca**, **Linares**, **Parral** and **Chillán**, thereafter services go to **Concepción** and **Temuco**. The line south from Temuco to Puerto Montt is scheduled to be reopened by 2006. There are 6 trains daily to **Chillán** (first 0830, last 2230, 4½ hrs, US$10), 1 overnight to **Concepción** (2245, 8¼ hrs, US$10 *turista*, US$14 *clase preferente*) and 1 overnight to **Temuco** (2130, 12 hrs, US$10 *turista*, US$13 *salón*, US$27 sleeper, US$63 compartment (sleeps 2)). *Dormitorio* carriages were built in Germany in the 1930s, bunks (comfortable) lie parallel to rails, US-Pullman-style (washrooms at each end, one with shower-bath – often cold water only); an attendant for each car. Cars can be transported on the service to Temuco (US$80). Trains are still fairly cheap and generally very punctual, although 1st class is generally more expensive than buses; meals are good though not cheap. Cycles can be carried, but check in advance. There are family and senior citizen discounts. No student discounts. Trains can be cold and draughty in winter and spring. There are also frequent local **Metrotren** services south to **Rancagua** and **San Fernando**. Booking offices: *Alameda O'Higgins 853 in Galería Hotel Libertador, Local 21, T02-6322801*, Mon-Fri 0830-1900, Sat 0900-1300; *Escuela Militar metro, Galería Sur, Local 25, T02-2282983*, Mon-Fri 0830-1900, Sat 0900-1300; or *Estación Central, T02-6895718/ 6891682, www.efe.cl*, open till 2230. Left-luggage office at Estación Central.

● Directory

Airline offices

Aerocontinente, *Huérfanos 801, of 430, T02-6386940*; **Aerolíneas Argentinas**, *ofs Generales Tenderinoi 82, piso 6, T02-6393922*; **Aero Mexico**, *Isidora Goyenechea 2939, of 602, T02-3901000, www.aeromexico.com*; **Air France**, *Alcantara 44, piso 6, Las Condes, T02-2909330, F02-2909340*; **Alitalia**, *El Bosque Norte 0101, of 21, T02-3788230*; **American**, *Huérfanos 1199, T02-6790000*; **British Airways**, *Isidora Goyenechea 2934, of 302, T02-3308600, airport T02-6010721*; **Continental**, *Nueva Tajamar 481, T02-2002100*; **Delta**, *Isidora Goyenechea 2939, of 601, T02-2002700*; **Iberia**, *Bandera 206, piso 8,* *T02-8701010*; **KLM**, *San Sebastián 2839, of 202, T02-2330011 (sales), T02-2330991 (reservations)*; **LACSA**, *Dr Barros Borgoño 105, piso 2, T02-2355500*; **LanChile**, *Américo Vespuccio 901, T02-526 2000, www.lanchile.cl*, other offices, including: *Huérfanos 926* and *Centro Comercial Alto Las Condes*; **Lufthansa**, *Moneda 970, piso 16, T02-6301655, www.lufthansa.cl*; **South African Airlines**, *11 de Septiembre 1881, of 713, T02-3769040*; **Sky Airline**, *Fuenzalida 55, Providencia, T600-6002828, www.skyairline.cl*; **United**, *El Bosque Norte 177, T02-3370000.*; **Varig**, *El Bosque Norte 177, piso 9, T02-7078001*.

Banks are open from 0900 to 1400, but close on Sat. Official daily exchange rates are published in *El Mercurio* and *La Nación*. Some *casas de cambio* reduce their rates slightly when banks are closed. There is never a problem in finding a Redbanc ATM. Look for **Banco Santander** and **Banco de Santiago** and others with Redbanc sign, for Cirrus ATMs.

American Express, *Andrés Bello 2711, piso 9, T02-3506700, Tobalaba metro*, also at *Blanco Viajes, Gen Holley 148, T02-2336164,*, no commission, poor rates (better to change TCs into dollars – no limit – and then into pesos elsewhere); **Banco de Chile**, *Ahumada 251*, demands the minimum of formalities, but may charge commission; **Banco Santander**, *Av Providencia y Pedro de Valdivia*, for Visa, no commission; **Citibank**, *Av Providencia 2653 and branches elsewhere in the city*, currency exchange; **Corp Banca**, *Huérfanos y Bandera*, for Visa but beware hidden costs in 'conversion rate'; **Transbank**, *Huérfanos 770, piso 10*, for stolen or lost Visa cards; **Turismo Tajamar**, *Orrego Luco 023, T02-3368000*, Thomas Cook/Mastercard agent.

Casas de cambio

Some in the centre open Sat morning (but check first). Most *casas de cambio* charge 3% commission to change TCs into dollars. Always avoid street money changers (particularly common on Ahumada and Agustinas). They will show you a figure that is fractionally more than the going rate, before pulling a number of tricks, eg using the MR button on calculators to do a false calculation giving much less than you should have, asking you to accompany them to somewhere obscure; the passing of forged notes and muggings have also been reported.

Afex, *Moneda 1140*, good rates for TCs; **Alfa**, *Agustinas 1052*; **Cambios Andino**, *Ocho, Agustinas 1062*; **Cambios Manquehue**, *Huérfanos 1160, Local 5 (Galeria Alessandri)*; **Exprinter**, *Bombero Osso 1053*, good rates, low commission; **Inter**, *Andrés de Fuenzalida 47, Providencia*; **Intermundi**, *Moneda 896*. Also several around *Av Pedro de Valdivia, Providencia, eg at Gral Holley 66*, good rates; **Casa de Cambio Blancas**, *opposite Hotel Orly on Pedro de Valdivia*; **Mojakar**, *Pedro de Valdivia 072*; **Guínazu**, *Pedro de Valdivia 048*, all major currencies can be bought or sold.

For parts and repairs the only place to go is C San Diego, south of the Alameda. The 800 and 900 blocks have scores of bicycle shops with spare parts, new models and repairs all offered at prices much cheaper than you will find in Providencia or Las Condes.

Bicicletas Wilson, *C San Diego 909*; **El Supermercado de las Bicicletas**, *C San Diego 921*, good stock; **Importadora Caupolicán**, *C San Diego 863, T02-6972765*, wide range, helpful, has been recommended; **Luis Cabalin**, *Coquimbó 1114, T02-6984193*, is good for maintenance and repairs; **Terrabike**, *C San Diego 896*, does repairs.

Car hire

Prices of car hire vary widely so shop around first. Tax of 18% is charged but check if it is included in the price quoted. A credit card is usually asked for when renting a vehicle. **Hertz**, **Avis**, **Budget** and others are available from the airport; **Alameda**, *O'Higgins 4332, T02-7790609, Pila del Ganso metro*, very good value; **ANSA**, *Irarrázaval 4369, T02-2762551*; **Automóvil Club de Chile**, *Marchant Pereira 122, Providencia, T02-2744167*, discount for members of associated motoring organizations; **Avis**, *San Pablo 9900, T02-6019757*, poor service reported; **Full Famas**, *Diego Portales 506, T02-258060*; **Hertz**, *Costanera Andrés Bello 1469, T02-6010477 and at Hotel Hyatt T02-2455936*, has a good network in Chile and cars are in good condition; **Rosselot**, *Francisco Bilbao 2032, Providencia, T02-3813690, www.rosselot.cl*, and airport, *T02-6901374*, reputable Chilean firm with national coverage; **Seelmann**, *Las Encinas 3057, T02-398849*; **Verschae**, *Manquehue Sur 660, T02-2027266, www.verschae.cl*, good value, branches throughout the country.

Dentists

Antonio Yazigi, *Vitacura 3082, apto 33, T02-2087962/2085040*, English spoken, recommended; **Dr Torres**, *Av Providencia 2330, dept 23*, excellent, speaks English.

Embassies

Argentina, *Miraflores 285, T02-6331076*; Australia, *Isidora Goyenechea 3261, T02-5503500*; Austria, *Barros Errázuriz 1968, piso 3, T02-2234774*; Belgium, *Av Providencia 2653, dept 1103, T02-2321070*; Bolivia, *Av Santa María 2796, T02-2328180. Los Leones metro.*; Brazil, *Alonso Ovalle 1665, piso 15, T02-6982496*; Canada, *Nueva Tajamar 481, Torre Norte, piso 12, T02-3629660.*; Colombia, *Errázuriz 3943, T02-2061999*; Denmark, *Jacques Cazotte 5531, Vitacura, T02-2185949*; Ecuador, *Av Providencia 1979, piso 5, T02-2315073*; Finland, *Alcántara 200, of 201, T02-2634947, embajada@finlandia.co.cl*; France, *Condell 65, T02-3749300*; Germany, *La Hualtatas 5677, T02-4632500*; Greece, *Jorge VI 306, T02-2127900*; India, *Triana 871, T02-2352633.*; Israel, *San Sebastian 2812, piso 5, T02-7500500*; Italy, *Clemente Fabres 1050, T02-4708400*; Japan, *Av Ricardo Lyon 520, piso 1, T02-2321807*; Mexico, *Félix de Amesti 128, T02-2066133*; Netherlands, *Las Violetas 2368, T02-2236825*; New Zealand, *El Golf 99, of 703, T02-2909802*; Norway, *San Sebastian 2839, T02-2342888*; Panama, *Lota 2257, T02-2311641*; Paraguay, *Huérfanos 866, of 510, T02-6394640*; Peru, *Av Andrés Bello 1751, T02-2356451*; South Africa, *Av 11 de Septiembre 2353, Edif San Román, piso 16, T02-2312862*; Spain, *Av Andres Bello 1895, T02-2352755*; Sweden, *11 de Septiembre 2353, Torre San Ramón, piso 4, Providencia, T02-9401700, www.embajadasuecia.cl*; Switzerland, *Av Vespucio Sur 100, piso 14, T02-2634211*; UK, *El Bosque Norte 0125, Casilla 72-D, T02-3704100, F3704160.will hold letters*; Uruguay, *Pedro de Valdivia 711, T02-2744066*; USA, *Av Andrés Bello 2800, T02-2322600, www.embajadaeeuu.cl*

Consulates

For the consulate contact the embassies above with the exception of the following: Argentina, *Vicuña MacKenna 41, T02-2226947, F2226853*, open 0900-1400 (visa US$25, free for US citizens), if you need a visa for Argentina, get it here or in the consulates in Concepción, Puerto Montt or Punta Arenas, there are no facilities at the borders, Australians will need a letter from their embassy to get an Argentinian visa here; Brazil, *Maclver 225, piso 15*, open Mon-Fri 1000-1300, visa takes 2 days, US$10, take passport, 2 photos, ticket in and out of Brazil, photocopy of 1st 2 pages of passport, tickets, credit card and tourist card; Paraguay, *Huérfanos 886, of 514, T02-6394640*, open 0900-1300, 2 photos and copy of 1st page of passport required for visa; United States, *Merced 230, T02-710133*, visa obtainable here.

Hospitals

If you need to get to a hospital, it is better to take a taxi than wait for an ambulance. Clínica Central, *San Isidro 231, T02-2221953*, open 24 hrs, German spoken; Emergency hospital, *Marcoleta 377*, costs US$60, for yellow fever vaccination and others (but not cholera); Hospital de Urgencia, *Portugal 125*, from US$125, cheapest hospital open to the public; Hospital San Salvador, *J M Infante 551, T02-2256441*, Mon-Thu 0800-1300 and 1330-1645, Fri 0800-1300 and 1330-1545; Vaccinatoria Internacional, *Hospital Luis Calvo, MacKenna, Antonio Varas 360*.

Other medical services

Dr Sergio Maylis, *T02-2320853.*, physician available 1430-1900; Emergency pharmacy, *Portugal 155, T02-382439*.

Internet

Internet cafés are ubiquitous. Prices around US$0.75 to US$1.50 per hr. 463@café, *Av Brasil 463, Barrio Brasil*; Anditel, *Bandera y Catedral, 1 block from the Plaza de Armas*, quiet; c@fe.com, *O'Higgins 0145, near Plaza Italia*, good snacks; Café Phonet, *San Sebastián 2815, Providencia*, also very cheap international phonecalls; Ciberia, *Pío Nono 015, Bellavista*; Cybercafe, *Santa Lucía 0120, next to Instituto Chileno-Británico*; Cybercafe, *Cienfuegos 161, near junction with Moneda, just west of Panamericana, Barrio Brasil*, cheap; easy@net, *Ricardo Lyon y Providencia, Providencia*; ES Computación, *Salvador Sanfuentes 2352, Barrio Brasil, Republica metro*, helpful staff; Internet Virtual, *Santo Domingo 1091.* also very cheap call centre; Sonnets Ltda, *Londres 043*, tea, coffee, book exchange, owner speaks Spanish, English, Dutch and German, helpful. There is also access at the Terminal de Buses Alameda, on the upper floor of the terminal building.

Language schools

AmeriSpan Unlimited, *PO Box 40513, Philadelphia, PA 19106, USA, T02-215 985 4522, F215 985 4524, info@amerispan.com*, provides information about the affiliated AmeriSpan school in Santiago; **Carolina Carvajal**, *T/F02-381000, ccarvajal@interactiva.cl*, Spanish taught to individuals and small groups, intensive/ business courses offered; **Centro de Idiomas Bellavista**, *Crucero Exeter 325, Bellavista, T02-7375102, www.cib.in.cl*; **Escuela de Idiomas Violeta Parra**, *Ernesto Pinto Lagarrigue 362A, Recoleta-Barrio Bellavista, T02-7358240, vioparra@chilesat.net*, courses aimed at budget travellers, information programme on social issues, arranges accommodation and visits to local organizations and national parks; **Instituto Chilena de la Lengua**, *Miraflores 590, piso 2, of 4, T02-6643114, www.cmet.net/ichil*; **Instituto Chileno Suizo de Cultura**, *San Isidro 171, T02-6385414, chilenosuizo@tie.cl*, courses in Spanish, French, German and English taught by native speakers, also computer courses, internet access, café, library, art gallery, accommodation can be arranged; **Lucía Araya**, *T02-7318321, www.espanolentrenos.cl*; **Natalislang Language Centre**, *Vicuña Mackenna 06, piso 7, of 4, T02-2228721, info@natalislang.com*, 2-wk courses are recommended as good value; **Pacifica**, *Guillermo Acuña 2884, Providencia, T02-2055129, pacifica@netline.cl*, Anglo-Chilean agency offering cultural programmes to students. Will also find accommodation with families and arrange Spanish classes either in language schools or with private teachers, minimum 1 month, US$70 commission charged; **Top Language Services**, *Huérfanos 886, of 1107, T/F02-6390321*, offers Spanish in groups and individually, accommodation organized.

Many private teachers: **Carolina Carvajal**, *Miraflores 113, dept 26, T02-3810000*, highly recommended; **Patricia Vargas Vives**, *José Manuel Infante 100, of 308, Providencia, T02-2442283*, qualified and experienced (US$12.50 per hr); **Lucía Araya Arévalo**, *Puerto Chico 8062, Villa Los Puertos, Pudahuel, T02-2360531*, phone after 1800, speaks German and English.

Laundry

Dry cleaning

At the corner of Providencia and Dr Luis Middleton there are several self-service dry cleaners (*Pedro de Valdivia metro, 11 de Septiembre exit*). Also several just south of Universidad Católica metro including **American Washer**, *Portugal 71, Torre 7, local 4*. 0900-2100 including Sun, US$3, can leave washing and collect it later.

Wet-wash

Lava Fácil, *Huérfanos 1750*, Mon-Sat 0900-2000, US$4 per load; **Lavandería Lola**, *Av Ricardo Cumming y Monedo*, cheapest wet-wash in the centre, very busy so get there before 1100, US$4.50 per load; **Laverap**, *Av Providencia 1600 block, Manuel Montt 67*; **Marva**, *Carlos Antúñez 1823, Pedro de Valdivia metro*, wash and dry US$8; *Av Providencia 1039*, full load, wet-wash, US$5, 3 hrs; **Nataly**, *Bandera 572*.

Post office

The main office is on the Plaza de Armas (open 0800-1900), poste restante is well organized (though only kept for 30 days), passport essential, list of letters and parcels received in the hall of central post office (one list for men, another for women, indicate Sr or Sra/Srita on envelope).

Also sub offices in Providencia, *Av 11 de Septiembre 2092, Manuel Montt 1517, Pedro de Valdivia 1781, Providencia 1466*, and in *Estación Central shopping mall*. These are open Mon-Fri 0900-1800, Sat 0900-1230.

If sending a parcel, the contents must first be checked at the post office. Paper, tape etc on sale, Mon-Fri 0800-1900, Sat 0800-1400.

Shipping offices

Check shipping schedules with shipping lines rather than the national tourist office, Sernatur. **Cruceros Australis**, *El Bosque Norte 0440, T02-4423110, www.australis.com*, for trips from Punta Arenas to Puerto Williams, Cape Horn and Ushuaia; **M/N Skorpios**, *Augusto Leguía Norte 118, Las Condes, T02-2311030, www.skorpios.cl*, for luxury cruise out of Puerto Montt to Laguna San Rafael; **Navimag**, *Av El Bosque Norte 0440, of 1103,*

T02-4423120, www.navimag.cl For services from Puerto Montt to Puerto Natales and vice versa; **Patagonia Connection SA**, *Fidel Oteíza 1921, of 1006, Providencia, T02-2256489, www.patagonia-connection.com*, Pedro de Valdivia metro, for services Puerto Montt-Coyhaique/ Puerto Chacabuco- Laguna San Rafael; **Transmarchilay**, *Agustinas 715, of 403, T02-6335959, www.transmarchilay.cl*, for services between Chiloé and the mainland and ferry routes on the Camino Austral.

Telephone

The cheapest call centres are on C Bandera, Catedral and Santo Domingo, all near the Plaza de Armas. International calls from here are half the price of the main company offices: to the US, US$0.25 per min, to Europe, US$0.35 per min, eg at Catedral 1033 and Santo Domingo 1091. The main compancy offices are **Telefónica CTC**, *Moneda 1151*, closed Sun, and **ENTEL**, *Huérfanos 1133*, Mon-Fri 0830-2200, Sat 0900-2030, Sun 0900-1400, calls cheaper 1400-2200, fax upstairs.

Fax also available at the Telefónica office in **Mall Panorámico**, *11 de Septiembre, 3rd level* (phone booths are on level 1). There are also **Telefónica** phone offices at some metro stations including La Moneda, Escuela Militar, Tobalaba, Universidad de Chile and Pedro de Valdivia for local, long-distance and international calls.

Useful address

Ministerio del Interior, *Departamento de Extranjería, Teatinos 950 (near Estación Mapocho), T02-6744000*. Mon-Fri 0900-1200. For extension of tourist visa or any enquiries regarding legal status. They can give you the information you need, but to get the paperwork done you will then have to go round the back of the building and queue. The office to which this queue leads is open from 0900-1300. Make sure you are in the queue before 0800 and take a good book.

Around Santiago

This region can be divided into three: to the east are the peaks of the Andes; to the west is the coastal range; and between is the Central Valley. On the eastern edge of the Central Valley lies Santiago, its more affluent suburbs spreading east into the foothills of the Andes. Some of the highest peaks in the range lie in this region; just over the border in Argentina, Aconcagua is the highest mountain in the world outside Asia, rising to 6,964 m. There is a mantle of snow on all the high mountains, while the lower slopes are covered with dense forests. Between the forest and the snowline there are pastures; during the summer, cattle are driven up to these pastures to graze. In this area you can ski down the slopes in winter, hike in the summer and soothe your limbs in thermal springs year round. The less energetic may opt for a tour of the vineyards, sampling the yield as you go.

❗ *Note that prices on the outskirts of town are up to twice as high as those charged in the centre.*

Pomaire → *Colour map 3, B3.*

A small town, 65 km west of Santiago, Pomaire is in a charming setting surrounded by tall hills dotted with algarrobo bushes and covered in green grass. The town is famous for its ceramic work; the main street is brimful with shops selling dark clay pots and kitchenware, as well as diverse *artesanía* from all over Chile including fine basketwork from the Central Valley and some lovely items made from the *combarbalita* stone from the north. There are probably few better places in Chile in which to buy general souvenirs and presents (although bargaining is not really entered into); pottery can be bought and the artists can be observed at work, before visitors retire to any one of numerous restaurants serving traditional dishes such as *humitas*, giant *empanadas* and *pastel de choclo*. ➤➤ *For details on how to get to Pomaire, see Transport, page 125.*

Reserva Nacional Río Clarillo → *Colour map 3, B3.*

This reserve covers 10,185 ha and is situated 45 km south of Santiago in the *precordillera* at between 850 m and 3,000 m. It offers excellent views of the higher mountains and of the surprisingly green pastures of the foothills. Administration is at the entrance, 2 km southeast of El Principal. There is an information centre, guided trails and wildlife, including the endangered Chilean iguana, salamanders and the endangered bird, Torcaza. The reserve is also the only remaining home to *sclerophyllous* (hard leaved) trees in central Chile. In summer it is very hot and horse flies are a nuisance. There are no places to stay and camping is forbidden. If you are in the city for a while it is a good place to get away from the bustle for a day. The park is reached by paved road via San Bernardo and Pirque and is open all year.

Santuario de la Naturaleza Yerba Loca → *Colour map 3, B3.*

ⓘ *Park administration office, Villa Paulina, 4 km north of Route G21, reached by a dirt road, 45 km northeast of Santiago, T02-3216285, Sep-Apr, US$3.*

Reached on the paved Route G21 towards Farellones, this park covers 39,000 ha of the valley of the Río Yerba Loca, ranging in altitude between 900 and 5,500 m. It was founded in 1973. From the park administration office a four-hour walk leads north to **Casa de Piedra Carvajal**, which offers fine views. Further north are two hanging glaciers, **La Paloma** and **El Altar**. You may spot eagles and condors in the park. Native tree species include the mountain olive. Maps and information available from CONAF. There is no accommodation here.

Maipo Valley vineyards → *Colour map 3, B3.*

The Maipo Valley is considered by many experts to be the best wine-producing area in Chile. Several vineyards in the area can be visited and this makes a good excuse to get away from the smog.

Cousiño-Macul, ⓘ *Av Quilin 7100, on the eastern outskirts of the city, T02-2841011, vtaparticular@cousinomacul.cl, free, wine tasting from US$1 per glass.* This vineyard offers tours in English and Spanish at 1100 from Monday to Friday. Call in advance if you wish to visit.

Concha y Toro ⓘ *Virginia Subercaseaux 210, Pirque, near Puente Alto, 40 km south of Santiago, T02-8217069, rpublicas@conchaytoro.cl, US$4, wines US$1 per glass,* offers short tours in Spanish, English, French, German and Portuguese (daily). Reserve two days in advance and enquire about the specific time of tours in your language of choice.

Undurraga ⓘ *Santa Ana, 34 km southwest of Santiago, T02-3722800, sproduccion@undurraga.cl, free,* allows vistors who have made a prior reservation two days in advance. Tours are given by the owner-manager, Pedro Undurraga on weekdays, 1000-1600.

Viña Santa Rita, ⓘ *Padre Hurtado 0695, Alto Jahuel, Bin, 45 km south of Santiago on the Camino a Padre Hurtado, T02-3622520, rrivas@santarita.cl, US$6,* offers good tours in both English and Spanish (Tuesday to Friday at 1030, 1130, 1215 and 1630, Saturday and Sunday at 1230 and 1530). You must reserve three days in advance. The vineyard has a good restaurant. Weekend tours only available to those with reservations at the restaurant (lunch US$30 per head).

Cajón del Maipo → *Colour map 3, B3.*

This rugged and green valley southeast of Santiago provides an easy escape from the smog and bustle of Santiago. The valley is lined by precipitous mountains and the snows of the high Andes can easily be seen. There are many interesting and beautiful sidetracks, such as to Lagunillas (see page 122) or Los Maiténes but the upper reaches of the valley around El Volcán and Baños Morales are amazingly deserted.

The road into the valley runs east from Puente Alto via Las Vizcachas, where the most important motor racing circuit in Chile is located, towards **San José de Maipo**. The mountain town of **Melocotón** is 6 km south of San José de Maipo and **San Alfonso** is 4 km further on. The walk from San Alfonso to the **Cascada de las Animas** is pleasant; ask at the campsite for permission to cross the bridge.

The road continues up the valley and divides 14 km southeast of San Alfonso. One branch forks northeast along a very poor road (four-wheel drive essential) via Embalse El Yeso to **Termas del Plomo**, Km 33, thermal baths with no infrastructure, but stunning scenery. The other branch continues and climbs the valley of the Río Volcán. At **El Volcán** (1,400 m), 21 km from San Alfonso, there are astounding views, but little else. It is possible to cross the river and camp in the wild on the far side, surrounded by giant rock walls and with a real sense of isolation. If visiting this area or continuing further up the mountain, be prepared for military checks: passport and car registration numbers may be taken. From El Volcán the poor road runs 14 km east to **Lo Valdés**, a good base for mountain excursions. Nearby are warm natural baths at **Baños Morales** ① *open from Oct, US$2.* This is a wonderful area to come and get away from it all and it is possible to spend days here exploring the paths that lead high into the mountains. (This is the old southerly horse trail linking Santiago and Mendoza, with a path still leading over into Argentina.) Some 12 km further east up the mountain is **Baños Colina** (not to be confused with Termas de Colina, see above) with free, hot thermal springs and horses for hire. This area is popular at weekends and holiday times, but is otherwise deserted. There are no shops so take food. Try the local goat's cheese if you can, it may be sold by the roadside or at farmhouses.

Situated north of Baños Morales, **Parque Nacional El Morado** ① *Oct-Apr, US$2, administration near the entrance,* covers an area of 3,000 ha including the peaks of El Morado (5,060 m), El Mirador del Morado (4,320 m) and El Morado

Cajón del Maipo

glacier. It is in an exceptionally secluded and beautiful place, well worth making the effort to reach. There is a good day hike from the park entrance to the glacier and back. Great views. Lakeside camping is possible near the glacier. ►► *For Sleeping, Eating and other listings, see pages 124-126.*

Ski resorts → *Colour map 3, B3.*

There are six main ski resorts near Santiago, four of them around the mountain village of Farellones. All have modern lift systems, international ski schools, rental shops, lodges, mountain restaurants and first-aid facilities. The season runs from June to September/October, weather permitting, although some resorts have equipment for making artificial snow. Many professional skiers from the northern hemisphere come here to keep in practice during the northern summer. Altitude sickness can be a problem, especially at Valle Nevado and Portillo, so avoid over-exertion on the first day or two. ►► *For details of Sleeping, Eating and other listings, see pages 124-126.*

Farellones

ⓘ *32 km east of Santiago, daily lift ticket US$22, combined ticket for all 4 resorts US$40-50.* The first ski resort built in Chile, Farellones is situated on the slopes of Cerro Colorado at 2,470 m and is reached by road in under 1½ hours. It is a service centre for the three other resorts and provides affordable accommodation and several large restaurants. It also has a good beginners' area and is connected by lift to El Colorado. Perhaps the most popular resort for residents of Santiago, it is busy at weekends. One-day excursions, US$5, are available from **Ski Club Chile** ⓘ *Goyenechea Candelaria 4750, Vitacura (north of Los Leones Golf Club), T02-2117341.*

> ⸙ *From Farellones there are incredible sunsets and beautiful views for 30 km across 10 Andean peaks.*

El Colorado

ⓘ *8 km from Farellones, www.elcolorado.cl, daily lift ticket US$26.* Further up Cerro Colorado along a circuitous road, El Colorado has a large but expensive ski lodge at the base, which offers all facilities, and a mountain restaurant higher up. There are nine lifts giving access to a large intermediate ski area with some steeper slopes. *La Cornisa* and *Cono Este* are two of the few bump runs in Chile. This is a good centre for learning to ski.

La Parva

ⓘ *daily lift ticket US$26.* Situated nearby at 2,816 m, La Parva is the upper-class Santiago weekend resort with 30 pistes and 14 lifts, running from 0900 to 1730. Accommodation is in a chalet village and there are some good bars in high season. Although the runs vary, providing good intermediate to advanced skiing, skiers face a double fall-line so it is not suitable for beginners. Connections with Valle Nevado are good. Equipment rental is from US$10-15 depending on quality. In summer, this is a good walking area, with a trail that leads to the base of Cerro El Plomo, which can be climbed.

Valle Nevado

ⓘ *16 km from Farellones, T02-206 0027, www.vallenevado.com, daily lift ticket US$30 Mon-Fri, US$42 Sat and Sun.* Owned by **Spie Batignolles** of France, Valle Nevado was the site of the 1993 Pan American winter games and offers the most modern ski facilities in Chile. It has been described as a deluxe hotel complex high up in the mountains. Although not to everyone's taste, it is highly regarded and efficient. There are 40 km of slopes accessed by 41 lifts. The runs are well prepared and are suitable for intermediate skiers and beginners. There's also a ski school and excellent heli-skiing.

ⓘ *145 km north of Santiago, www.skiportillo.cl, daily lift ticket US$20*. Situated at 2,855 m, Portillo lies 62 km east of Los Andes, near the customs post on the route to Argentina and is one of Chile's best-known resorts. The 23 pistes are varied and well prepared, equipped with snow machines and connected by 12 lifts, two of which open up the off-piste areas. This is an excellent family resort, with a very highly regarded ski school, and there are some gentle slopes for beginners near the hotel. The major skiing events are in August and September. Cheap packages can be arranged at the beginning and out of season; equipment hire costs US$21.

Nearby, at an altitude of 2,835 m, is the **Laguna del Inca**, 5½ km long, 1½ km wide and surrounded on three sides by accessible mountain slopes. This lake, frozen over in winter, has no outlet and its depth is not known. From **Tío Bob's** there are magnificent views of the lake and condors may be spotted from the terrace. There are boats for fishing; but beware, the afternoon winds often make the homeward pull three or four times as long as the outward pull. Mules can be hired for stupendous expeditions to the glacier at the head of the valley or to the Cerro Juncal.

Lagunillas

ⓘ *67 km southeast of Santiago, www.skilagunillas.cl, tow fees US$15, daily lift ticket US$17*. Lagunillas lies in the Cajón del Maipo (see page 120), 17 km east of San José de Maipo, along a beautiful *ripio* road clinging to a chasm with stunning views of the far reaches of the Andes. It is more basic than the other ski centres in the region, with less infrastructure but the skiing is good. It is owned by the **Club Andino de Chile**, and is the only not-for-profit ski centre in Chile. There are 13 pistes and four ski lifts. In winter, the *carabineros* insist that drivers have snowchains, and rent them out at US$6. Being lower than the other resorts, its season is shorter but it is also cheaper.

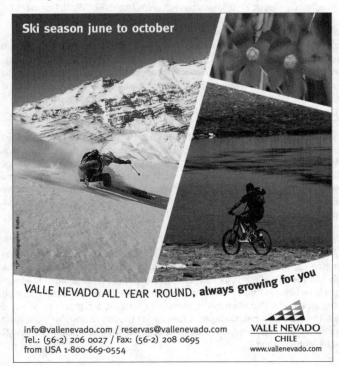

From Santiago to Argentina

The route across the Andes via Los Andes and the Redentor tunnel is one of the major crossings into Argentina. Route 5 runs north of Santiago through the rich Aconcagua Valley, known as the Vale of Chile. The road forks at the Santuario de Santa Teresa, the west branch going to San Felipe, the east branch going to Los Andes and Mendoza. Before travelling, you should always check on weather and road conditions beyond Los Andes. It is difficult to hitchhike over the border, and Spanish is essential; try on trucks from Aduana building in Los Andes. ▸▸ *For details of buses, see Transport, page 112.*

Termas de Colina → *Colour map 3, B3. Altitude: 915 m.*

Based at Hotel Termas de Colina, 43 km north of Santiago (see page 125), this is an attractive, popular spa in the mountains. The temperature of the water is on the cool side (25°C) but it is supposedly good for rheumatism and nervous disorders. There is a large swimming pool, plus individual baths that can be filled with the thermal water and a sauna. There are some pleasant short walks in the area. The springs are in a military-controlled area, so do not take photos or even show your camera when passing the military base.

San Felipe and around → *Phone code: 034. Colour map 3, A3. Population: 42,000.*

The capital of Aconcagua Province, 96 km north of Santiago, San Felipe is an agricultural and mining centre with an agreeable climate. Part of the Inca highway has recently been discovered in the city; previously, no traces had been found further south than La Serena. **Curimón**, 3 km southeast of San Felipe, is the site of the Convento de Santa Rosa de Viterbo (1727), which has a small museum attached. A paved road (13 km) runs north from San Felipe to the old town of **Putaendo**; in its church there is an 18th-century Baroque statue of Christ. Situated high in the *cordillera*, **Termas de Jahuel** lies 18 km by road northeast of San Felipe; see Sleeping for details. The mountain scenery includes a distant view of Aconcagua.

Los Andes → *Phone code: 034. Colour map 3, B3.*

Some 16 km southeast of San Felipe and 77 km north of Santiago, Los Andes is situated in a wealthy agricultural, fruit-farming and wine-producing area, but is also the site of a large car assembly plant. It is a good place for escaping from Santiago and a convenient base for skiing at nearby Portillo (see page 122). There are monuments to José de San Martín and Bernardo O'Higgins in the Plaza de Armas and a monument to the Clark brothers, who built the Transandine Railway to Mendoza (now disused). There are good views from El Cerro de la Virgen, reached in an hour via a trail from the municipal picnic ground on Independencia.

The road to the border: Los Libertadores

The road to Argentina follows the Aconcagua Valley for 34 km until it reaches the village of **Río Blanco** (1,370 m), where the Ríos Blanco and Juncal meet to form the Río Aconcagua. There is a fish hatchery with small botanical garden at the entrance to the Andina copper mine. East of Río Blanco the road climbs until Juncal where it zigzags steeply through 29 hairpin bends at the top of which is the ski resort of Portillo (see page 122). This is the location of the Chilean border post. If entering Chile, there may be long delays during searches for fruit, meat and vegetables, which may not be imported. Put all camera film in your hand luggage as this is not X-rayed.

Traffic crosses the border through the 4-km **Redentor tunnel** ① *open Sep-May 24 hrs, Jun-Aug daily 0700-2300, toll US$3.* Note that this pass is closed after heavy snowfall, when travellers are occasionally trapped at the customs complex on either side of the border.

Above the tunnel is the old pass, used before the tunnel was built, and above this again, at 3,854 m, is the statue of **El Cristo Redentor** (Christ the Redeemer), which was erected jointly by Chile and Argentina in 1904 to commemorate King Edward VII's decision in the boundary dispute of 1902. It is completely dwarfed by the landscape. The old road over the pass is in a very poor state, especially on the Chilean side, and is liable to be blocked by snow even in summer. When weather conditions permit, the statue can be reached on foot from **Las Cuevas**, a modern settlement on the Argentine side (4½ hours up, two down). There are also 12-hour excursions to the statue from Mendoza.

Into Argentina → *Argentine phone code: +54*

Just beyond Argentine customs and immigration is **Puente del Inca**, a sports resort named after the natural bridge which crosses the Río Mendoza. The bridge, apparently formed by sulphur-bearing hot springs, is 19 m high, 27 m wide and has a span of 21 m. At the resort are **Hostería Puente del Inca** and **Residencial Vieja Estación** (much cheaper), as well as camping, transport to Mendoza and information and access for climbing **Aconcagua** (6,959 m), the highest mountain peak on earth outside Asia.

Some 17 km further east is **Punta de Vacas**, from where there is a good view of Tupungato (6,550 m). The only town of any size between the border and Mendoza is **Uspallata**, from where two roads lead to Mendoza: the paved, southern branch of Route 7, via Porterillos; and the unpaved, northern branch via Villavicencio.

● Sleeping

Cajón del Maipo *p120, map p120*
A **Cabañas Corre Caminos**, *Estero Morales 57402, Baños Morales, T6992002, daniella piccoli@hotmail.com* Sleeps 4, comfortable.
A-B **Refugio Alemán Lo Valdés**, *Lo Valdés, T02-2454424, T09-8242123.* Stone-built chalet accommodation. Price per person for full board. Good food. Recommended.
B **Millahue**, *Melocotón, T/F02-8611856.* Price per person in *cabañas* with full board.
C **Hostería Los Ciervos**, *Camino al Volcan 31411, San Alfonso, T/F02-8611581.* With breakfast, full board also available, good.
C-D **Res España**, *San Alfonso, T02-8611543.* Clean, comfortable, with restaurant.
E **Res El Tambo**, *Baños Colina.* Price per person for full board, restaurant, also camping.
E **Res Los Chicos Malos**, *Baños Morales, T02-2885380.* Price per person. Comfortable, fresh bread, good meals. Free campsite.
F **Alojamento Inesita**, *Comercio 301, San José.* Price per person. Good, excellent chips.
F **Residencial Pensión Diaz**, *Río Maipo s/n, T02-8611496.* Price per person. Basic, friendly.

Camping
Comunidad Cascada de las Animas, *500 m off the main road, San Alfonso, T02-8611303.* US$30 per site (up to 6 people). Also cabins with hot water, cooking equipment etc, sauna and horseriding.

Farellones *p121*
L **La Cornisa**, *Las Cóndores 636, T02-2207581, www.lacornisa.cl* Half board. Reasonably basic but comfortable, chalet style.
L **Posada de Farellones**, *T02-2013704, www.skifarellones.com* Cosy and warm, Swiss style, satellite TV and games room. Transport service to slopes. Decent restaurant.
B **Refugio Club Alemán Andino**, *see* p109. Price per person. Hospitable, good food.

El Colorado *p121*
LL **Colorado Apart Hotel**, *Av Apoquindo 4900, of 43, Santiago, T02-2467398, www.skiandes.co.cl* Fully furnished apartments with half board.
L **Edificio Monteblanco**, *bookings from A Apoquindo 5555, of 905, T02-2073700, www.ceciliawilsonpropiedades.cl* Apartments that can be rented by the day or week. Food and room service available at extra cost.

La Parva *p121*
L **Condominio Nueva La Parva**, *reservations in Santiago, La Concepción 266, of 301, T02-2641574, www.laparva.cl* Good hotel and restaurant. Three other restaurants.

Valle Nevado *p121*
LL **Apart Hotel Mirador del Inca**, *T02-3813000, www.miradordelinca.cl* Fully furnished apartments and 2 restaurants serving everything from gourmet to fast food.

LL **Valle Nevado**, *T02-4777000, F02-2080695, www.vallenevado.com* 5-star resort, full board, lift ticket included.

Portillo *p122*

Cheaper accommodation can be found in Los Andes but the road is liable to closure due to snow.

LL **Hotel Portillo**, *reservations with Renato Sanchez 4270, Las Condes, T02-2630606, www.skiportillo.cl* On the shore of Laguna del Inca. Accommodation ranges from lakefront suites with full board and fabulous views, to family apartments, to bunk rooms without bath (much cheaper, from **B** up). Parking charges even if you go for a meal, self-service lunch, open all year, minibus to Santiago US$50 each. Cinema, nightclub, swimming pool, sauna and medical service.

Lagunillas *p122*

A **Cabañas Pura Vida**, *Camino a Lagunillas, T02-2084234, Km 4 from San José on the Lagunillas road.* Beautiful spot in a fantastic gorge, swimming pool, completely calm and off-the-beaten track. Highly recommended. C **Club Andino de Chile**, *bookings at O'Higgins 108, loc 205, Santiago, T02-6380497.* Price per person. Cabins for rent.

Termas de Colina *p123*

B **Hotel Termas de Colina**, *T/F02-8440990.* Modern, expensive thermal baths, a beautiful swimming pool (closed Fri), US$6. Formal restaurant. Facilities open to public, crowded at weekends.

San Felipe and around *p123*

L **Termas de Jahuel**, *T034-511240, northeast of San Felipe,* has a thermal pool and tennis courts. Good but often closed. F **Hotel Reinares**, *Condell 75, San Felipe, T034-510359.* Price per person.

Los Andes *p123*

L **Baños El Corazón**, *San Esteban 2 km north of Los Andes, T034-482852.* Full board, swimming pool, thermal baths, take bus San Esteban/El Cariño (US$0.50). B **Plaza**, *Esmeralda 367, T034-421929.* Good, expensive restaurant. D **Central**, *Esmeralda 278, T034-421275.* Reasonable and very friendly (excellent bakery opposite, try the *empanadas*).

F **Estación**, *Rodríguez 389, T034-421026.* Price per person without breakfast. Basic. Cheap restaurant. F **Res Italiana**, *Rodríguez 76, T034-423544.* Price per person. Clean rooms without bath. G **Res Maruja**, *Rancagua 182.* Price per person. Clean.

The road to the border *p123*

See above for accommodation in Portillo. B **Hostería Guardia Vieja**, *8 km east of Río Blanco.* Expensive but untidy, campsite. C **Hostería Luna**, *T034-421026, 4 km west of Río Blanco.* Good value, clean, helpful, good food.

🍴 Eating

For details of alternative restaurants, see Sleeping, above.

Cajón del Maipo *p120, map p120*

$$ **El Rancho del Ché**, *on the road between Puente Alto and San José, El Canelo.* Excellent Argentine meat dishes. $$ **La Petite France**, *on the road between Puente Alto and San José, nearer San José.* Good French food, not cheap. $$ **Restaurant El Campito**, *Camino al Volcán 1841, San José.* Very good. $$ **Restaurant La Isidora**, *on the plaza, San José.* Smart, good, meat dishes.

Portillo *p122*

Restaurant La Posada, *opposite Hotel Portillo.* Cheaper than the hotel, but open evenings and weekends only.

San Felipe and around *p123*

$$ **La Piedra del Molino**, *in the Almendral sector, a couple of kilometres east of the San Felipe on the road to Santa María.* Excellent traditional food

🚌 Transport

Pomaire *p118*

From Santiago take the Melipilla bus from behind Estación Central metro station, every few mins, US$1 each way, Rutabus 78 goes on the motorway, 1 hr, other buses via Talagante take 1 hr 25 mins. Alight at the side road to Pomaire, 2-3 km from town; from here there are *colectivos* and *micros* every 10-15 mins (there are also *colectivos* linking Pomaire and Melipilla) – this route is easier than taking one of the direct buses from Santiago. En route, delicious *pastel de choclo* can be obtained at **Mi Ranchito**.

Santuario de la Naturaleza Yerba Loca *p119*
Colectivos with **Taxis Transarrayán Ltda** leave from Plaza San Enrique in Lo Barnechea. Take any bus for Barnechea from Alameda or Providencia in Santiago.

Reserva Nacional Río Clarillo *p119*
Bus from Puente Alto in Cajón del Maipo (see below) to El Principal, 1 hr, US$2.50.

Maipo Valley *p119*
For **Cousiño-Macul**, take either bus 390 from Alameda or bus 391 from Merced, both marked to Peñalolén. For **Concha y Toro**, take the metro to La Florida, then catch Metrobus 74 to Pirque and ask the driver to let you off by the vineyard, or take the *colectivo* from Plaza Baquedano, US$2.50. For **Undurraga**, take a Talagante bus from the Terminal San Borja to the entrance. For **Viña Santa Rita**, get a bus direct to Alto Jahuel from Terminal San Borja, *T02-7760645:*

Cajón del Maipo *p120, map p120*
Buses leave Santiago from Parque O'Higgins metro, Av Norte-Sur, or west side of Plaza Ercilla, every 15 mins to **San José**, 2 hrs, US$1; or else take Linea 5 metro to Bellavista de la Florida and wait for the bus on Av Vicuña Mackenna. *Línea 27 colectivos* also run from the plaza in Puente Alto as far as **San Alfonso**. On weekdays hitching from San José is possible on quarry trucks.

From Parque O'Higgins metro, to **El Volcán** and to **Baños Morales**, 1 bus daily, leaves Parque O'Higgins at 1200 (San José at 1345), returns at 1745; buy return on arrival to ensure seat back. This service goes through **San José**, **El Melocotón** and as far as San Gabriel. Between Baños Morales and **Baños Colinas** you may be able to arrange a lift on one of the summer tour buses.

Ski resorts *p121*
Air
Helicopter services are run by **Alfa Helicópteros**, *T02-2739999, www.alfa-helicopteros.com*, 45 mins.

Bus
Services from Santiago to **Farellones**, **El Colorado**, **La Parva** and **Valle Nevado** are run by **Ski Total**, *Av Apoquindo 4900, Edificio Omnium, ofs 40-42, T02-2466881, www.skitotal.cl*, and leave from outside their offices, daily from 0730 in season, book in advance, US$9 return. **Centro de Esqui El Colorado**, *T02-2463344, www.elcolorado.com*, departs from here to **Farellones** and **El Colorado** daily from 0800 in season. **Manzur Expediciones**, *T02-7774284, www.vermail.net*, leave for **Farellones**, **Valle Nevado**, **El Colorado**, **Lagunillas** and **Portillo**, Wed, Sat and Sun 0830 from Baquedano metro. Except in bad weather, **Portillo** is also reached by any bus from Santiago or Los Andes to Mendoza; you may have to hitch back.

It is easy to hitch from the junction of Avenida Las Condes/El Camino Farellones (YPF petrol station in the middle).

Termas de Colina *p123*
From Santiago take the bus from Av La Paz 302 (40 mins). From here a rough road leads through countryside 6 km; last return bus at 1900. Taxi from Colina to the hotel, US$5.

Los Andes *p123*
The bus terminal, 1 block east of the Plaza de Armas, has services to **Mendoza** (Argentina) with **Tas Choapa**, **Fenix Pullman Norte**, **Cata** and **Ahumada**. Any of these will drop passengers off at **Portillo**, US$6.

The road to the border *p123*
Saladillo buses run hourly from Los Andes to **Río Blanco**; there are also services from Santiago, **Ahumada**, 1930 daily, direct, 2 hrs, US$2. For Transport into Argentina, see p112.

---

❻ Directory

San Felipe has similar facilities to Los Andes, but there is little infrastructure elsewhere.

Los Andes *p123*
Banks ATMs on the Plaza de Armas. **Cambio Inter**, *Plaza Hotel*, good rates, changes TCs, also *casa de cambio* in Portillo customs building and at **Ingeniero Roque Carranza**, 13 km from tunnel. **Telephone** Telefónica, *O'Higgins 405*. **Useful address** Automovil Club de Chile, *Chacabuco 33, T034-422790*.

Valaparaíso and Viña del Mar

Introduction

The coastal strip west of Santiago is one of the most popular destinations for regional tourists. Midway along the coast is **Viña del Mar**, one of the most famous resorts in South America, and awash with Argentines and Chileans strutting their stuff in summer. Near Viña are other popular resorts, such as **Reñaca** and **Concón**, plus a host of more secluded spots, including **Horcón** to the north and **Quintay** to the south. While the beaches on this stretch of coast are attractive, the water is very cold and swimming is dangerous in many places because of a heavy undertow.

The place that makes this part of Chile really worth visiting is **Valparaíso**, once the south Pacific's most important port and now the most beguiling city in the country, the capital of V Región and seat of the Chilean lower house of parliament. Nearer by is the lumpy summit of **Cerro La Campana**, a tall hill between the coast and the central valley, which offers some of the best views in Chile and which can be climbed in a day. South of Valparaíso, towards the mouth of the Río Maipo, are a number of other centres, including **Algarrobo**, perhaps the most affluent resort along this coast, and **Isla Negra**, a village famous as the home of Pablo Neruda, in which the Nobel laureate gathered together a collection of objets d'art from around the world.

★ Don't miss...

❶ **Cerros Alegre and Concepción** Enjoy the architectural anarchy of Valparaíso's hills, page 133.

❷ **Cerro La Campana** Climb to the top for some of the best views in Chile, page 136.

❸ **Horcón** Watch horses towing the fishing boats ashore, ready for the catch to be unloaded at this small fishing village on the coast, page 147.

❹ **Concón** Enjoy some of the best cuisine in Chile at one of the resort's many restaurants, page 146.

❺ **Viña del Mar** Sun yourself along with the rich and famous on the beach at Chile's premier resort, page 145.

Valparaíso & Viña del Mar

Background

This was one of the earliest areas settled by the Spanish, the lands being assigned to prominent *conquistadores* during the 16th century. For most of the colonial period this region was an important exporter of wheat and other foodstuffs to Peru. During the 19th century Valparaíso rose to become the most important port on the Pacific coast of South America, but there were few other large centres of population along this coastline until the 1880s, when the fashion for holidaying near the sea spread from southern Europe. Viña del Mar was established in 1880 and several other resorts followed between 1880 and 1900: Algarrobo, Cartagena, Las Cruces, Zapallar and Papudo, all owing part of their popularity to the building of railway lines linking them to the capital.

Today, this area is one of the major economic centres of the country. Valparaíso and San Antonio are important ports, between them handling much of the country's trade. The region is also a major producer of agricultural products, particularly soft fruit such as avocados, tomatoes, grapes and peaches. The coastline enjoys a Mediterranean-style climate: the cold sea currents and coastal winds produce much more less extreme temperatures than in Santiago and the central valley; rainfall is moderate in winter and the summers are dry. Although the influence of European resorts can still be seen in some of the buildings, especially in Viña del Mar and Zapallar, most of the older buildings have not withstood earthquakes and bulldozers.

Valparaíso → *Phone code: 032. Colour map 3, B2. Population: 300,000.*

Sprawling over a crescent of 42 hills (cerros) that rear up from the sea 116 km west of Santiago, Valparaíso is a one-off. The main residential areas here are not divided into regimented blocks, as in all other Chilean cities; instead Valparaíso is really two cities: the flat, vaguely ordered area between the bus terminal and the port known as 'El Plán', and the chaotic, wasp-nest cerros, in which most porteños (people from Valparaíso) live. It is possible to spend weeks exploring the alleyways of the cerros, where packs of dogs lie sunning themselves, brightly painted houses pile on top of one another and half forgotten passageways head up and down the hills, offering fantastic views of the Pacific, the city and – on a clear day – right over to the snowcapped cordillera. The bohemian and slightly anarchic atmosphere of the cerros reflects the urban chaos of the city as a whole. Here you will find such unusual sights as a 'monument to the WC' (calle Elias) and a graveyard from which all the corpses were shaken out during a severe earthquake. Valparaíso is all about contradictions – the fact that both Salvador Allende and Augusto Pinochet were born and raised here expresses this fact more eloquently than anything else – but the oppositions can also be seen in the juxtaposition of the flat Plán against the labyrinthine cerros; the sea against the views of Aconcagua; and the city's grandiose mansions mingling with some of Chile's worst slums.

Ins and outs

Getting there   There are inter-urban buses to Valparaíso from every major Chilean city (even including connections through to Punta Arenas), and it makes an interesting change to most travellers' itineraries to get a bus to Valparaíso instead of Santiago. Valparaíso also has international connections to Mendoza, Córdoba, Buenos Aires and as far as Rio de Janeiro.

Getting around   You should never have to wait more than 30 seconds to travel anywhere within 'El Plán' (between Plaza Aduana and Avenida Argentina): 'Pedro Montt' buses are cheap but slow; 'Errázuriz' buses are faster. Valparaíso is the only city in Chile still to have trolleybuses. These machines (mostly Swiss and from the 1950s) ply the length of El Plán and cost the same as a local bus fare. Buses to Cerro Alegre and the top of Cerro Concepción leave from Plazuela Ecuador (Nos 142 and D3). Taxis and *colectivos* usually wait around at the bottom of each *cerro*; otherwise, you can use the *ascensores* (funicular railways). If you are going to Viña or one of the nearby towns to the north, catch a *micro* from Errázuriz or Brasil; *colectivos* to Viña leave from the same place. Taxis seldom use their meters but are generally reasonable and, if there are three or four of you, sharing a taxi can be cheaper than taking a *colectivo*. ▸▸ *For further details, see Transport page 143.*

Security Robbery is an occasional problem in El Puerto and around the *ascensores*. The upper outskirts of town, while offering amazing views, are not the safest of places. The poorer and rougher districts tend to be those furthest from the centre. Also beware that Calle Chacabuco (on which some hotels are located) is the pick-up point for local rent boys. Beware of the mustard trick (see page 43).

Cerro Concepción, Cerro Alegre and El Puerto were awarded UNESCO World Heritage Site status in June 2003.

Tourist information Offices are located in the Municipalidad building ① *Condell 1490, Of 102, open Mon-Fri 0830-1400, 1530-1730*, and at Muelle Prat ① *open Nov-Mar only, Mon-Fri 1030-1430, 1600-2000*. There are also two information offices in the bus terminal, but these are privately run on a commission basis and hence do not give impartial advice. ▸▸ *For Sleeping, Eating and other listings see pages 137-145.*

Background

Founded in 1542, Valparaíso became, in the colonial period, a small port used for trade with Peru. It was raided at least seven times during the colonial era by pirates and corsairs, including Drake. The city prospered from Independence more than any other Chilean town. It was used in the 19th century by commercial agents from Europe and the US as their trading base in the southern Pacific and became a major international banking centre as well as the key port for shipping between the northern Pacific and Cape Horn. Until the 1840s, the journey from the port to El Almendral (site of the congress and the old road to Santiago) took several hours and passed over wild hills but, as the city's wealth and importance grew, part of the original bay was filled in, creating the modern day 'El Plán'. Fine buildings were erected here, including several banks, South America's first stock exchange and offices of *El Mercurio*, the oldest newspaper in the Spanish language, first printed in 1827 and still in publication. (The impressive Mercurio building, built in 1900, stands on the site of a famous pirates' cave.) Wealthy European merchants began to populate Cerro Concepción and Alegre in this period, building churches and fine mansions in every conceivable architectural style.

The city's decline was the result of two factors: the development of steam ships, which stopped instead for coaling at Punta Arenas and Concepción, and the opening of the Panama Canal in 1914. Since then, it has declined further owing to the development of a container port in San Antonio, the shift of banks to Santiago and the move of the middle classes to nearby Viña del Mar. Little of the city's colonial past survived the pirates, tempests, fires and earthquakes of the period, but a remnant of the old colonial city can be found in the hollow known as 'El Puerto', grouped round the low-built stucco church of La Matriz. Very few wooden buildings predate the devastating earthquake of 1906, which was followed by a series of fires.

Sights

The lower part of the city, known as **El Plán**, is the business centre, with fine office buildings on narrow streets that are strung along the edge of the bay and cluttered

⁙ Neruda on Valparaíso

"The hills of Valparaíso decided to dislodge their inhabitants, to let go of the houses on top, to let them dangle from cliffs that are red with clay, yellow with gold thimble flowers, and a fleeting green with wild vegetation. But houses and people clung to the heights, writhing, digging in, worrying, their hearts set on staying up there, hanging on, tooth and nail, to each cliff. The port is a tug-of-war between the sea and nature, untamed on the *cordilleras*. But it was man who won the battle little by little. The hills, and the sea's abundance gave the city a pattern, making it uniform, not like a barracks, but with the variety of spring, its clashing colours, its resonant bustle. The houses became colours: a blend of amaranth and yellow, crimson and cobalt, green and purple."

Pablo Neruda, Memoirs,
Penguin, 1978.

with buses. Above, covering the hills or '*cerros*' is a fantastic agglomeration of buildings in every conceivable shape that seem literally to tumble down the slopes. Part of the charm of the *cerros* is the lack of order. It is as if every individual bought a plot of land and decided to build whatever they saw fit, resulting in buildings that are a unique hotchpotch of size, style and colour. Spanish colonial mansions lie side by side with adobe shacks and neo-classical monoliths.

Superb views over the bay are offered from most of the *cerros*, each of which offers its own unique view and distinct atmosphere. It is enjoyable to spend an afternoon exploring the hills and, however lost you might feel, a few minutes' walk downhill will always lead you back to El Plán. The lower and upper cities are connected by steep winding roads, flights of steps and 15 *ascensores* or funicular railways dating from the period 1883-1914.

Plaza Sotomayor and El Puerto

The old heart of El Plán is the **Plaza Sotomayor**, dominated by the former **Intendencia** (Government House), now the seat of the admiralty. Be careful when crossing the plaza, which, although it appears pedestrianized, is in fact criss-crossed by busy roads.

⁙ *The area around Plaza Echaurren in El Puerto can be dangerous at night, and it is inadvisable to seek accommodation here.*

Opposite is a fine monument to the 'Heroes of the Battle of Iquique', which also serves as a mausoleum housing the bodies of all who fought in the battle. Visitors are allowed inside on 21 May of each year (the anniversary of the battle), following a massive procession of the armed forces through the city. While excavating under Plaza Sotomayor in order to build a new underground car park, parts of Valparaíso's original **old quay** were uncovered; they can be viewed from above ground through the glass ceiling, although the glass tends to mist up. Look out, too, for the bronze plaques on the ground illustrating the movement of the shoreline over the centuries.

One block away from Plaza Sotomayor is the port entrance (take a boat trip from here around the bay; see Tour operators) and the **railway station**, from which passenger services run on the metropolitan line to Viña del Mar and Limache. In the evening the station is a gathering place for chess players; join in if your Spanish and chess are up to it.

One block northwest of Plaza Sotomayor, on Calle Serrano, is the **Ascensor Cordillera** and the *escalera de la muerta* (the stairs of death; just try climbing them to find out why). At the top, on Plazuela Eleuterio Ramírez, take Calle Merlet to the left and you will find the **Museo del Mar Almirante Cochrane** ① *Merlet 195, Tue-Sun 1000-1800, free*, which hosts temporary art exhibitions in a small colonial house with excellent views over the bay (the New Year fireworks are filmed from here).

Back in El Plán, continue another block along Serrano into the heart of El Puerto to reach **Plaza Echaurren**, Valparaíso's oldest square, tree-lined and with a picturesque fountain. It was once the height of elegance but is now surrounded by cheap restaurants and frequented by a sizeable population of local drunks. Near Plaza Echaurren stands the church of **La Matriz**, built in 1842 on the site of the first church in the city and unusual for its sloping nave and stained-glass windows all depicting Valparaíso themes. Further northwest, along Bustamante, lies **Plaza Aduana**, named after the customs building, from where the **Ascensor Artillería** takes you up to the **Mirador 21 de Mayo** and the imposing **Museo Naval y Marítimo** ⓘ *Tue-Sun 1000-1730, US$1*, in the old Naval Academy, which documents naval history 1810-80, and includes exhibitions on Chile's two naval heroes, Lord Cochrane (see box, page 340) and Arturo Prat.

Playa Ancha and around
To the west of **Cerro Artillería**, the Avenida **Playa Ancha** runs to the municipal stadium on Cerro Playa Ancha, which seats 20,000 people and is home to the local football team Santiago Wanderers. The buildings on Avenida Gran Bretaña are a good example of the suburb's eccentric architecture. Avenida Altamirano runs along the coast at the foot of Cerro Playa Ancha to **Las Torpederas**, a picturesque bathing beach. Just beyond the beach is a promontory topped by the **Faro de Punta Angeles**, which was the first lighthouse on the west coast of South America. Closer to town, **Caleta Membrillo** has a number of good seafood restaurants.

Around Cerros Alegre and Concepción
Southeast of Plaza Sotomayor, calles Prat, Cochrane and Esmeralda run through the old banking and commercial centre to **Plaza Aníbal Pinto**, around which are some of the city's oldest bars and cafes. Above this part of El Plán are **Cerro Alegre** and **Cerro Concepción**, for many the undisputed symbols of the city. Both are filled with mansions and high-ceilinged 19th century houses, some falling down but many now being restored to their former glory. Cerro Concepción is as posh as Valparaíso gets, while Cerro Alegre has a more artistic, bohemian feel: brightly coloured murals abound, most of the shops seem to double as art galleries and, during university term, students can be seen on practically every street corner sketching buildings or the panoramic views. The two hills are connected to El Plán by three *ascensores*, of which **Ascensor Concepción**, inaugurated on 1st December 1883, is the oldest in Valparaíso. Three *miradores* (Paseos Atkinson and Gervasoni in Cerro Concepción, and Paseo Yugoslavo in Cerro Alegre) offer views of the bay, over to Viña and beyond.

The **Museo Municipal de Bellas Artes** ⓘ *Paseo Yugoslavo, closed for refurbishment till mid-2004, then Tue-Sun 1000-1800, free,* is housed in Palacio Baburizza, and has displays of Chilean land- and seascapes and some modern paintings. A visit is highly recommended and, if you are lucky, you may get to see the whole of this interesting rococo mansion; the games room, drawing room, shower and servants' quarters provide an insight into the contrasting lifestyles of *porteños* in the early part of the 20th century.

Also worth a visit is the **Casa de Lukas** ⓘ *Paseo Mirador Gervasoni 448, Cerro Concepción, www.lucas.cl, summer Tue-Sun 1100-2200; winter Tue-Sun 1030-1400, 1530-1830, US$0.70,* dedicated to the work of Chile's most famous caricaturist. Lukas (real name Renzo Pecchenino) was originally from Italy but spent most of his life in Valparaíso. The museum holds a permanent exhibition of his work, which gives a humorous insight into the political and social history of Valparaíso and Chile.

● *Porteños call the commune of Playa Ancha an "independent republic", owing to its reputation for self-sufficiency.*

A walking tour of Cerros Alegre and Concepción

From the **Plaza Aníbal Pinto** walk up Calles Cumming and Elias and take the *ascensor* **Reina Victoria** up to a viewing point. Walk along Paseo Dimalow to the end, then head down Urriola (opposite). After one block, turn right onto **Calle Templeman**. On the left are two alleyways: Pasaje Templeman has a couple of art workshops, while Pierre Loti has typical English-style houses. Further along Calle Templeman is the Anglican church of **San Pablo**, built in 1858, which has organ recitals every Sunday at 1230. Follow the church round past the entrance on Pilcomayo and head down to the end of that street, where steps lead down to **Paseo Pastor Schmidt**, with views of the cemetery opposite. Carry on past the Lutheran church (1897) and along the revamped **Paseo Atkinson**, once home to merchants and ships' captains and with expansive views. At the end of the walkway, turn right onto Papudo. The next right leads to the **Paseo Gervasoni**, overlooking the port and the Turri clocktower, and

home to the Lukas museum. Following the paseo round, take the steps down to the labyrinthine **Pasaje Galvez**, past restaurants, bars and art galleries.

Cross Calle Urriola, and head up **Pasaje Bavestrello**, ahead and to the right. At the top is an unusual building, four storeys high and 3 m wide. Turn right here onto the **Paseo Yugoslavo** and the Palacio Baburizza, with views of the Cochrane museum to the left and Playa Ancha beyond. Walk past the *ascensor* Peral and follow the road up and round into **Pasaje Leighton**. The second road on the right is Miramar. Climb 100 m and turn left onto **Lautaro Rosas**, an avenue lined with fine houses and mansions. After two blocks the road crosses the stair-lined **Calle Templeman**, boasting one of Valparaíso's classic views.

If you still have any energy left you can climb three blocks to the **Plazuela San Luis** and begin exploring other hills along the Avenida Alemania.

Avenida Alemania and around

Walking uphill along any of the main streets of Cerro Alegre will lead you to the Plazuela San Luis, from where **Avenida Alemania** runs southeast, following the contours of Valparaíso's hills. This is the only road that connects all the hills above Valparaíso and

makes a pleasant walk, with ever-changing views, one of the best of which is to be had from **Plaza Bismark**. Calle Cumming heads back down to the Plán from Plaza Bizmarck passing the former prison (now a cultural centre and worth a visit) and three cemeteries, all of which can be visited: **Cementerios I** and **II** are the city's two oldest Catholic cemeteries, while the third **Cementerio de los Disidentes** holds the graves of immigrants. Back on Avenida Alemania, meanwhile, a 20-minute walk will

❖ The best way to enjoy Av Alemania is aboard the 'O' bus, between Av Argentina and El Puerto, which winds up and down the cerros for an unforgettable rollercoaster ride.

bring you to the former home of Pablo Neruda, **Casa La Sebastiana** ① *Ferrari 692, off Av Alemania, Altura 6900, Cerro Florida, T032-256606, www.lasebastiana- neruda.cl, Tue-Sun 1030-1430, 1530-1800 (until 1900 in summer), US$2.80, students half price Tue-Fri, bus O from Av Argentina, US$0.35, or colectivo from Plazuela Equador, US$0.60*. It now houses an art gallery, showing his eccentric tastes to the full, and there is a small café in the garden, with fine views.

Plaza de la Victoría and around

From Cerro Florida, walk down **Cerro Bellavista** along Calle Ferari and Calle Hectór Calvo to arrive at the **Museo al Cielo Abierto**. Opened in 1992, this open-air museum consists of large-scale murals painted on the outside walls of buildings throughout Cerro Bellavista by 17 of Chile's leading artists. Look out in particular for the 6 m by 3 m mural by Chile's most famous contemporary artist, Roberto Matta, which is situated just before you reach the Ascensor Espíritú Santo; it's a typical example of Matta's later work with sharp-toothed, monsters hurtling through space. At the bottom of the *museo*, in El Plán, is **Plaza de la Victoria** with the Cathedral on its east side and the municipal library on Plaza Simon Bolívar just to the north. Plaza Victoria is the official centre of Valparaíso and commemorates Chile's victory in the War of the Pacific; the statues and fountain were looted from Peru during the war. One block west, on calle Condell in the 19th-century Palacio Lyon is the **Museo de Historia Natural** ① *Condell 1546, Tue-Fri 1000-1300, 1400-1800, Sat 1000-1800, Sun 1000-1400, US$1,* which hosts exhibitions. Next door is the **Galería de Arte Municipal** ① *Condell 1550, T032-220062, Mon-Sat 1000-1900, free.*

Plaza O'Higgins and further east

East of Plaza de la Victoria, Pedro Montt leads to the Parque Italia and **Plaza O'Higgins**. The latter is dominated by the imposing **Congreso Nacional**, a monolithic arch in neo-fascist style, thoroughly out of keeping with the rest of the city. (Now that the congress is possibly about to return to Santiago, the municipality are in a quandary as to what to do with the construction.) Opposite is the bus terminal, while four blocks north on Errázuriz is the Barón train station and the **Muelle Barón**, the new terminal for cruise ships. A walk to the end of this pier, past kite-flying children, gives a different view of Valparaíso, clearly showing the amphitheatre-like form of the city. Just off the pier is a small colony of sea-lions.

To the east of the congress, Avenida Argentina runs south past four *ascensores* including **Ascensor Polanco** (entrance from Calle Simpson, off Avenida Argentina a few blocks southeast of the bus terminal). This is the most unusual *ascensor* in the city as it is in two sections: walk along a 160-m horizontal tunnel through the rock, then take a vertical lift to the summit on which there is a *mirador*. Note that the lower entrance is in an area that can be unsafe after dark: do not go alone and do not take valuables. Beyond Polanco the road branches left towards Santiago or continues straight on to Cerro O'Higgins, where **El Jardin Suizo** ① *closed Sun and holidays, green bus J from Av Argentina,* can be found. Also known as El Pümpin, this botanical garden incorporates a nursery near the entrance, where you can buy all sorts of plants, while beyond are hills clad in almost-untouched native forest, giving a glimpse of what Valparaíso must have looked like before it became a port. It's a good place for a picnic. Nearby is the **Mirador O'Higgins**, from which the Supreme Director, Bernardo O'Higgins, saw the arrival of Cochrane's liberating squadron (see box, page 340) and proclaimed "On those four craft depends the destiny of America".

South of Valparaíso

Laguna Verde, 12 km south of Valparaíso, is a picturesque bay with a huge beach that's peaceful and perfect for picnics, although the wind can get quite fierce in the afternoons and strong undercurrents make swimming dangerous.

Further south, **Quintay** is the least known of the villages on the central *littoral* (there is no direct route here from Santiago) and also one of the most picturesque. In its heyday, the village's whaling station, which is open to visitors ① *Tue-Sun 0900-1800, US$0.50,* employed over 1,000 workers, mostly from Chiloé, but now only the fishermen remain. Most people ignore the threatening sign warning you not to climb up to the lighthouse. If you take the risk, the view is worth the short climb; sit on the rocks and watch the sunset.

Quintay has two beaches, the larger of which is being overrun by a housing development. The other, **Playa Chica**, is accessed via an unsignposted route through a eucalyptus wood (entry by the *carabineros*). It is wild and deserted off season and is definitely worth the 20-minute walk. ▸▸ *For Sleeping, Eating and other listings see pages 137-145. For details of the resorts further south, see page 152.*

East of Valparaíso

Towards Santiago
Reserva Nacional Peñuelas encompasses 9,260 ha around the artificial Lago Peñuelas and is open to visitors (US$2) for walking and fishing. The park, which is covered by pine and eucalyptus forest, is situated 30 km southeast of Valparaíso near the main road to Santiago (Route 68). Buses between the two cities pass the entrance where the park administration is located. Beyond the park, Route 68 passes through two tunnels, the first of which is 51 km southeast of Valparaíso and charges a US$3 toll. On the journey east, this can be avoided by turning off about 1 km before the tunnel onto the old road over the mountains, which has good views of the surrounding countryside (toll US$0.50). There is another tunnel with a toll further east, 56 km west of Santiago.

Towards Argentina
Route 62 (better known as *'El Troncal'*) runs through Viña del Mar, climbs out of the bay and passes through **Quilpué**, Km 16, a dormitory town for Valparaíso and Viña, with an interesting municipal zoo. It crosses a range of hills and reaches the Aconcagua Valley at **Limache**, a sleepy market town, famous for its tomatoes, 40 km from Valparaíso. Route 62 joins Route 60 just before **Quillota**, another fruit-growing centre, continuing to La Calera, Km 88, where it joins the Pan-American Highway; turn southeast and east for Llaillay, San Felipe, Los Andes and the Redentor tunnel to Mendoza.

Parque Nacional La Campana
Situated north of Olmué (8 km east of Limache), the park (entry US$2 per person) covers 8,000 ha and includes Cerro La Campana (1,828 m), which Darwin climbed in 1835, and Cerro El Roble (2,200 m). It is divided into three main sections, each with its own entrance: in the south are **sector Granizo** ① *paradero 45, 5 km east of Olmué*, from which the Cerro La Campana is climbed, and **sector Cajón Grande**, ① *paradero 41, reached by unpaved road off the Olmué-Granizos road*, while to the north is **sector Ocoa** ① *reached by unpaved road (10 km) off the Pan-American Highway between Hijuelas and Llaillay*, which is where the main concentration of Chilean coconut palms (*kankán*) can be found. This native species is now found in natural woodlands in only two locations in Chile. The park can be crossed on foot (six hours) between Ocoa and Cajon Grande along well-marked trails through the gamut of Chilean natural vegetation, from cactuses and palm trees to southern beech and lingue. A number of shorter trails lead from all three entrances.

A fair amount of agility is required to climb **Cerro la Campana**; visitors without much climbing and scrambling experience may wish to seek advice or take a guide. Allow a whole day there and back from Olmué, although fit and experienced hikers could probably do it in around seven hours. There are three places where fresh water is available on the climb, but you should take your own food and drink. From the entrance at Granizo, a path leaves the road to the left just past the CONAF *guardería*, and climbs steeply through forest, fording a clear, rushing stream and providing increasingly fine views of the Andes until reaching an old mining area (two hours from the *guardería*). From here the path is well marked, but becomes more testing; after passing a plaque dedicated by the British community to Charles

Darwin on the centenary of his visit, it climbs over loose rock to a pass to the northeast, before doubling back and rising over rocks (where scrambling and a little very basic climbing is required) to the summit. The wonderful views from the top of the Cerro la Campana take in a 300-km stretch of the Andes (including Aconcagua), as well as the rugged outline of the central *cordillera* losing itself in the haze to the north, the gentler scenes of the southern hills, and, when the haze is not too great, Valparaíso and the Pacific Ocean to the west. It is also possible to ascend La Campana from Quillota, but this route is more difficult and definitely requires a guide.

▸▸ *For Sleeping, Eating and other listings see pages 137-145.*

Sleeping

Plaza Sotomayor and El Puerto
p132, map p138

C Reina Victoria, *Plaza Sotomayor 190, T032-212203*. With breakfast, noisy, dingy, run down and with only a single bathroom on each floor, poor beds, overpriced; don't be fooled by the façade.

F-G Garden, *Serrano 501, T032-252776*. Price per person. Friendly, large rooms, gloomy and rundown but central, use of kitchen.

Playa Ancha *p133*

F Villa Kunterbunt, *Av Quebrada Verde 192, T032-288873*. Lovely building – the tower room has panoramic views – breakfast, very friendly, Chilean-German run, garden, English and German spoken. Highly recommended. Buses 1, 2, 5, 6, 17, 111, N, and *colectivos* 150, 151, 3b all pass by.

Around Cerros Alegre and Concepción *p133, map p138*
There are several *hostals* in the neighbourhood, shop around.

A Brighton, *Paseo Atkinson 151, Cerro Concepción, T032-223513, brighton-valpo@entelchile.net* Bills itself as a typical building in an historic part of Valparaíso, although it's not even 10 years old. Small rooms, mixed reports on service, one room has a balcony with excellent views. There is live tango and bolero music in the bar at weekends.

B Templeman Apartments, *Pierre Loti 65, Cerro Concepción, T032-257067/09-5194811, chantalderementeria@hotmail.com* Fully equipped, stylish, self-contained apartments sleeping 3-4, one uses an old weaving loom as table and has a wardrobe painted Mondrian style, good if you want a little peace away from the gringo trail. Book in advance for weekends. Highly recommended.

C-F Luna Sonrisa, *Templeman 833, Cerro Alegre, T032-734117, www.lunasonrisa.cl* Price per person with shared bath, also doubles with bath. Newly restored, bright, comfortable, large kitchen, patio, lots of information, excellent breakfast, tours arranged, English and French spoken, friendly and helpful, and run by one of the authors of this guide. Highly recommended – of course!

F Casa Aventura, *Pasaje Galvez 11, off Calle Urriola, Cerro Concepción, T032-755963, www.casaventura.cl* In restored traditional house, with good breakfast, German and English spoken, Spanish classes offered, tours, helpful, friendly, informative, kitchen facilities. Highly recommended.

F La Biciclette, *Almte Montt 213, Cerro Alegre. T032-222215*. Basic, bright rooms, lovely patio, French run, hires out bicycles.

F Sr Juan Carrasco, *Abtao 668, Cerro Concepción, T032-210737*. Price per person. Good location, but dark rooms. Terrace with fine views, good meeting place.

Avenida Alemania and around
p134, map p138

F Res Dinamarca, *Dinamarca 539, Cerro Carcel, T032-259189*. Unfortunately located between the cemetery and the old prison (from Plazuela Ecuador take any *micro* marked 'Cárcel'; or climb 10 mins up Av Ecuador). Price per person with breakfast, clean, good value, parking.

Plaza de la Victoria and around
p135, map p142

AL Robinson Crusoe, *Hector Calvo 389, Cerro Bellavista, T032-495449,*

www.hotels.tk/robinson Down the hill from the Sebastiana museum in a large restored old house. Lovely roof terrace with views, peaceful, nice suites with bathrooms, but most rooms have shared bathrooms and these are overpriced.

A Puerta de Alcalá, *Piramide 524, T032-227478*. Probably the best accommodation in the city. Without being outstanding, it has everything you would expect of a hotel in this bracket, together with a reasonable restaurant.

C Condell, *Pasaje Pirámide 557, T032-212788*. Without breakfast, comfortable, clean, central, television, no singles.

C Prat, *Condell 1443, T032-253081*. Comfortable rooms, central, restaurant has good value *almuerzo*. Under same management as **Condell**, see above.

Plaza O'Higgins and further east
p135, map p142

The area near the bus terminal can be unsafe, especially at night.

Valparaíso west

B-C Lancaster, *Chacabuco 2362, T032-217391*. 2-star hotel; surprisingly the only hotel in the city to be officially given starred status. The quality is OK, but the hotel's location is more notable for its rent-boys than its views.

C Hostal Kolping, *Vergara y Independencia, Valdes Vergara 622, T032-216306, kolpingvalparaiso@yahoo.es* Rooms without bath, pleasant, quiet, a nice choice in the Plán.

C-F Austral, *Las Heras 622, T032-216306*. Rooms with or without bath, without breakfast, kitchen facilities, central.

F Res El Rincon Universal, *Argentina 825, T032-235184, www.elrinconuniversal.cl* Price per person. With breakfast, laundry, study, cable TV and internet access, a good, reasonably priced alternative in this part of town; the area can be a little intimidating at night, though.

G Casa Patricia, *12 de Febrero 315, T032-220290*. Price per person. Family accommodation, hot showers, good local knowledge.

Hamburg **8**	Terra Nostra **15**
La Colombina **9**	Turri **16**
La Costeñita **10**	
La Tertulia **11**	**Bars & clubs**
Le Filou de	La Piedra Feliz **19**
Montpelier **12**	Vinilo **17**
Los Porteños **13**	

G Elena Escobar, *Chacabuco 2340, Casa No 7, T032-214193*. Next door to María Pizarro's and same price. Recommended.

G María Pizarro, *Chacabuco 2340, Casa No 2, T032-230791*. Price per person. Clean, lovely rooms, central, quiet, kitchen. Recommended, although in a somewhat seedy street.

G Res Eliana, *Av Brasil 2146, T032-755872*. Price per person. Large old house, without breakfast. Recommended, despite the slightly rough area.

G Sra Mónica Venegas, *Av Argentina 322, Casa B, T032-215673*. Price per person, 2 blocks from, bus terminal, often booked up.

G Sra Silvia, *Pje La Quinta 70, Av Argentina, 3 blocks from Congress, T032-216592*. Price per person. Clean, quiet, kitchen facilities.

South of Valparaíso *p135*
Camping is possible in Laguna Verde at **Camping Los Olivos**, which has good facilities and is well run and friendly.

Parque Nacional la Campaña *p136*
There are places to stay in all price categories in Olmué for easy access to the Granizo sector of the park.

A El Copihue, *Diego Portales 2203, Olmué, T033-441544, www.copihue.cl* Small resort set in pleasant gardens, with gym, games room, indoor and outdoor pools. Half- and full-board available.

E Sarmiento, *Blanco Encalda 4689, Olmué, T033-442838*. Cheap and cheeful.

F La Alondra, *Granizo 8459, Olmué, T033-441163*. A reasonable budget choice

Camping
It is possible to camp in all sectors of the park, US$9 per site with cold showers. In summer reserve in advance, *T033-441342*.

🍴 Eating

Plaza Sotomayor and El Puerto
p132, map p138
$$$ Bote Salvavidas, *Muelle Prat s/n, piso 2*. Seafood restaurant overlooking the port.

$$ La Costeñita, *Blanco 86*. Good seafood restaurant, with incredibly kitsch decor. Try the *Pastel de Jaivas*.

$$ Los Porteños, *Valdivia 169 and Cochrane 102*. Perennial favourite for fish and shellfish, terse service but good food.

Valparaíso & Viña del Mar Valparaíso

There are countless *fuentes de soda* throughout El Plán and in the market, where the portions are large (closed in the evenings).

$ **Calaguala**, *2nd floor of the market (off Plaza Echaurren)*. Excellent.

$ **Sandrita**, *2nd floor of the market (off Plaza Echaurren)*. Good *carbonada de mariscos*, friendly, recommended.

Playa Ancha and around *p133*

There are several good fish restaurants at Caleta Membrillo, 2 km west of Plaza Sotomayor (take any *Playa Ancha* bus).

$$ **Club Social de Pescadores**, *Altamirano 1480*. A concrete monstrosity by the harbour, redeemed by views. Busy at weekends.

$$ **El Membrillo**, *Caleta Membrillo*. The oldest restaurant in the Caleta. Opposite the Club Social.

Around Cerros Alegre and Concepción *p133, map p138*

$$$-$$ **La Colombina**, *Paseo Yugoslavo 15, Cerro Alegre, T032-236254*. Good food, wide range of wines, fine views, recommended.

$$$-$$ **Turri**, *Templemann 147, on Cerro Concepción, T032-259198*. Wonderful views, reasonable food but a bit of a tourist trap.

$$ **Bar Inglés**, *Cochrane 851 (entrance also on Blanco Encalada), El Plán*. Historic bar/restaurant dating from the early 1900s; a chart shows the ships due in port. Good food and drink, traditional, not cheap. Recommended.

$$ **El Rincón Sueco**, *Lautaro Rosas 510*. Swedish food including good salmon.

$$ **Terra Nostra**, *Esmeralda 978, next to Mercurio building, El Plán*. Italian/Argentinian. Good pasta dishes.

$$-$ **Cinzano**, *Plaza Aníbal Pinto 1182, El Plán*. The oldest bar in Valparaíso, also serving food. Flamboyant live music at weekends, noted for tango performances but no dancing by guests allowed. Service can be awful.

$$-$ **La Tertulia**, *Esmeralda 1083, El Plán*. Good vegetarian options.

$$-$ **Michelangelo**, *Esmeralda 1099, El Plán*. New Italian restaurant. Good service, great value and possibly the best pizzas in Chile. Highly recommended by Italian visitors.

$ **El Dominó**, *Cumming 67, El Plán*. Traditional basic *porteño* restaurant serving *empanadas*, *chorillanas* and the like. Recommended.

$ **El Gremio**, *Pasage Galvez 173*. Ultra-modern bar serving inventive lunches. Vegetarian options available.

$ **Gloria Vuscovic**, *Montealegre 280*. Good set lunches in a delightful old house.

$ **Le Filou de Montpellier**, *Almte Montt 382*. French run. Set menu very popular and deservedly so.

Cafés

Both the **Turri** restaurant and the **Hotel Brighton** have terraces where you can drink coffee while enjoying the views.

Color Café, *Papudo 526, Cerro Concepción*. Cosy, eclectic, arty café with a wide selection of teas and real coffee, fresh juice, good cakes, snacks and all-day breakfasts, regular live music, art exhibits, and local art and craft for sale.

Pan de Magia, *Almte Montt 738 y Templemann, Cerro Alegre, T09-4268626*. Cakes, cookies and by far the best wholemeal bread in town, all take away.

Riquet, *Plaza Aníbal Pinto, El Plán*. One of the oldest cafes in Valparaíso, good coffee and breakfast. Recommended.

Plaza de la Victoria and around *p135, map p142*

$$$-$$ **Gato Tuerto**, *Héctor Calvo 205, Cerro Bellavista*. Thai food, great views. Downhill from La Sebastiana, or take *ascensor* Espíritu Santo from the Plán.

$$$-$$ **Hamburg**, *O'Higgins 1274*. Owned by an elderly German emigré. Right-wing military memorabilia abounds but the food is apparently good.

$$ **Hon San**, *Donoso y Huito*. Chinese. Nothing special, but the best of the bunch nevertheless.

$ **Bambú**, *Pudeto 450*. Vegetarian lunches only, closed Sun.

$ **Casino Social JJ Cruz**, *off Calle Condell*. A Valparaíso institution: restaurant-cum-museum, famous for its *chorillanas*, and for being open when everything else is not. Not to be missed unless you are vegetarian.

$ **Empanadas Famosas's de Adali**, *S Donoso 1379-81*. Best *empanadas* in Valparaíso.

$ **Gioco**, *Molina 586-B (in yoga centre)*. No sign. Excellent-value vegetarian set lunches with fruit juices. Recommended.

Cafés

Bogarín, *Plaza Victoria*. Great juices and good sandwiches.
Café do Brasil, *Condell 1342*. Excellent coffee, juices, sandwiches.
Cioccolata, *Condell 1235*. Good coffee, excellent cakes.

Plaza O'Higgins and further east
p135, map p142

$$$ **Coco Loco**, *Blanco 1781, pisos 21 y 22*, *T032-227614*. Plush revolving restaurant 70 m above the bay. Extensive menu.
$$$ **Portofino**, *Bellamar 301, Cerro Esperanza (above caleta Portales)*, *T032-629939*. Fine restaurant with excellent views. Best in Valparaíso. Take *colectivo* 6 from Plaza Victoria.
$$$-$$ **Caleta Portales**, *Av España s/n, T032-625814, www.restaurantcaletaportales.cl* Good seafood restaurant on the road to Viña.
$$ **La Otra Cocina**, *Yungay 2250*. Seafood specialities, cosy, good food and service.
$$ **Nuevo Restaurant O'Higgins**, *Almte Barroso 506, behind the congress*. Not to be confused with Restaurant O'Higgins around the corner, specializes in meat and *parrilladas*, good.
$$-$ **La Mangiata**, *Rodríguez 538, off Pedro Montt*. Italian, simple decor, very good food.
$$-$ **Pizza Napoli**, *Pedro Montt 2935, near bus terminal*. Very good pizzeria.
$ **La Puerta del Sol**, *Pedro Montt 2033*. Traditional Chilean dishes, great chips are served outside.

Cafés

Cafe Claudia, *Calle Rawson, opposite bus terminal*. A good place for a sandwich while waiting for your bus.
Hesperia, *Victoria 2250*. A classic old-time coffee emporium, the internet annexe makes a strange contrast.

South of Valparaíso *p135*

El Galeón restaurant in Laguna Verde serves good simple food. In Quintay try the local speciality *congrio arriero* (fish stew with chips on top!) at any of the reasonably priced restaurants on the harbour (**Miramar** is especially recommended)

Plaza Sotomayor and El Puerto
p132, map p138

La Playa, *Serrano 567*. An old-fashioned bar, similar to **Bar Inglés**, but cheaper, frequented by students and run by slightly snooty staff. There are several bars attracting a similar crowd nearby.
Liberty, *Almte Rivero 9, Plaza Echaurren*. A real dingy old-timers' bar, where you can see local characters drinking and singing all day. Good cheap food is served.
Pagano, *Blanco 236, El Puerto*. 80s music and 'anything-goes' atmosphere.
Proa Al Canaveral, *Errázuriz 304*. Seafood restaurant downstairs, bar upstairs with dancing from 0100, poetry reading on Thu, Latin pop music, mostly students.
Valparaíso Eterno, *Almte Senoret 150, near Plaza Sotomayor*. Three floors of live latin music (mostly folk/traditional) only at weekends, performances start about 2300 hrs, US$2 cover charge and cheap drinks, open till 0400.

Playa Ancha and around *p133*

Bar Roma, *Playa Ancha*. The unofficial drinking hole of the crazier students from the university down the street. Bags are searched at the entrance to stop anyone smuggling in beer and the urinal is regularly smashed up by inebriated students. Despite all this, the atmosphere is relaxed and friendly; if you have something you want to get off your chest, you can write it on the wall.

Around Cerros Alegre and Concepción *p133, map p138*

Hotel Brighton (see Sleeping, above) has a small bar with live music at weekends 2300 to 0300. There are also good bars at **Cinzano** and **Bar Inglés** (see Eating, above).
Axe Bahía, *Errázuriz 1084*. Cuban *salsoteca*.
El Cielo, *Errázuriz 1152*. Disco for the technopop generation.
El Gremio, *Pasage Galvez 173*. Ultra-modern trendy bar in a typical winding alley. Art gallery upstairs.
La Piedra Feliz, *Errázuriz 1054*. Incorporates 3 areas, each with different decor: a large pub, a live music area and a dance floor, serving up everything from jazz to salsa, bossanova and tango depending on the evening, entrance US$7.

Vinilo, *Almte Montt 448*. New bar attracting a friendly 20- and 30-something crowd, good place to meet locals and other travellers. Extensive vinyl record collection and occasional live music at weekends. Serves food.

Plaza de la Victoria and around
p135, map p142

There are many bars on *Subida Ecuador*, but be careful which ones you go into, as in some of them you risk being eaten alive (only enter **El Muro** and **La Viuda**, for example, if you are into methylated spirits and the sordid elements of life).

⊚ Entertainment

It is worth checking out the website www.granvalparaiso.cl for the latest listings information, as well as the 'Invita' supplement, inside the *Mercurio de Valparaíso* every Fri. For live music venues, see Bars and clubs, above.

Cinema
Cinehoyts, *Pedro Montt 2111, T032-594709*. Mainstream movies, most from Hollywood.

The **Instituto Chileno-Norteamericano de Cultura** (see below) also shows films, but for a wider choice of cinemas you need to go to Viña del Mar.

Galleries
In addition to the **Galería de Arte Municipal** and the **Museo Municipal de Bellas Artes**, occasional free exhibitions are held at the following galleries:

Cult-Art, *Almte Montt y Galos, Cerro Alegre*. Contemporary art by local artists.

El Gremio, *Pasage Galvez 173, 2nd floor, Cerro Alegre*. Features work by Valparaíso artists.

Fundación Valparaíso, *Héctor Calvo, Cerro Bellavista (between La Sebastiana and the ascensor Espiritu Santo)*. Local contemporary art.

Instituto Chileno-Norteamericano *Esmeralda 1069*. Temporary exhibitions of photos and paintings from all over Chile.

Valparaíso east

Sleeping 😴		
Austral 1	Lancaster 6	Sra Mónica Venegas 12
Casa Patricia 2	Prat 7	Sra Silvia 13
Condell 3	Puerta de Alcalá 8	
Elena Escobar & María	Residencial El Rincón	**Eating** 🍴
Pizarro 4	Universal 9	Bambú 1
Hostal Kolping 5	Residencial Eliana 10	Bogarín 13
	Robinson Crusoe 11	Café Claudia 2

☻ Festivals and events

The **New Year** is celebrated by a 3-day festival culminating in a superb 40-minute firework display on the bay, which is best seen from the *cerros*. Over a million visitors and locals take supper and champagne to celebrate from vantage points around the bay. Accommodation can double or even triple in price at this time and needs to be booked well in advance.

○ Shopping

Books
CHAOS, *Pedro Montt by the bus terminal*. An excellent new and second-hand bookshop.
Librería Ivens, *Plaza Aníbal Pinto*. The oldest bookshop in Valparaíso with periodicals in English, French and German, and lots of literature about the city and its history.
Librería Universitaria, *Esmeralda 1132*. Good selection of regional history.

To Viña del Mar & Caleta Portales

Ascensor Barón
Ascensor Lechero
Ascensor Larraín
Congreso Nacional
Wed/Sat Fruit & Veg Market, Sun Flea Market
Ascensor Polanco
Simpson
To Santiago
To El Jardín Suizo

Casino Social JJ Cruz **3**
Coco Loco **4**
Empanadas Famosas's de Adali **5**
Gioco **6**
Hon San **7**
La Mangiata **8**
La Otra Cocina **9**
La Puerta del Sol **10**
Nuevo O'Higgins **11**
Pizza Napoli **12**

Crafts
Handicraft shops on the quay are expensive and poor quality.

Department stores
Falabella and **Ripley**, both by the Plaza Victoria.

Food
Emporio Echaurren, *Plaza Echaurren*. A delicatessen that stocks unlikely provisions; if you are hankering after Coleman's mustard or mint sauce, this is the place to come.

Markets
The **fruit and veg** market on *Av Argentina*, Wed and Sat, is colourful and well worth a visit; a **flea market** is held on the same site on Sun. There is also a large **antiques market** around *Plaza O'Higgins* on Sun mornings.

▲▲ Activities and tours

Casa Aventura, *see Sleeping, above*. City tours on foot and trips to La Campana national park.
Luna Sonrisa, *see Sleeping, above*. Trips to local vineyards and tours of historic parts of the city.
Valparaíso Mágico, *T/F032-911972*. A variety of tours, US$24 to US$50 per person, overpriced.

Boat trips
Launches run trips around the harbour from Muelle Prat, 30 mins, US$1 per person or US$15 to hire an entire boat, offering a pleasant view of the city, especially when it is sunny. Beware that groups of foreign tourists are liable to be overcharged. Other boats can be hired for fishing. Don't photograph naval ships or installations.

Parque Nacional la Campaña *p136*
Paredón, *Granizo sector, T033-443741, paredonadventure@hotmail.com* Good tours of the park in Spanish, English and French.

⊖ Transport

Ascensores
Very cheap at US$0.10-0.20 per journey; going uphill is slightly more expensive; sometimes you pay on entrance, sometimes on exit.

For boat services from Valparaíso to the Juan
Fernández Islands, see p501.

Bus

Urban Buses and trolley buses, US$0.25
within the Plán, US$0.35 to the *cerros*. There
are plenty of buses between the
long-distance terminal and Plaza Sotomayor.

Local An excellent and incredibly
frequent bus and *colectivo* service from Plaza
Aduana, passes along Av. Errázuriz to **Viña
del Mar**, 25 mins, $0.45. Buses serving **Lago
Peñuelas**, **Isla Negra**, **San Antonio** and
Llolleo leave every 15 mins, US$2.

Long distance The terminal is at *Pedro
Montt y Rawson*, 1 block from Av Argentina.
To **Santiago**, frequent, 1¾ hrs, shop around
for the best prices, book on Sat to return to
the capital on Sun. There are also frequent
daily services to the following destinations:
to **Chillán**, 7 hrs, US$9; to **Concepción**, 8 hrs,
US$10; to **Puerto Montt**, 14 hrs, US$17; to
La Serena, 7 hrs, US$9 *semi cama*; to
Calama, 24 hrs, US$23 *semi cama*; to **Arica**,
30 hrs, US$25 *semi cama*. Buses **Norte** run a
service to **Punta Arenas**, Wed and Thu 1800,
US$50. La Porteña and **Intercomunal** run
several buses daily north to **Pichidangui** and
Los Vilos, Intercomunal continuing on to
Illapel and **Salamanca**, although it may be
easier to catch any bus to **La Calera** from
Errázuriz/Brasil (every few minutes) and
make a connection there.

To Argentina To **Mendoza**, 3
companies, 6-7 hrs, US$12, **Pluma**
continuing on Tue, Fri and Sun to Buenos
Aires, Florianopolis, Sao Paolo and Rio. To
Córdoba, Tas Choapa, daily, US$25.

Taxi

Colectivos, which pick up and set down
passengers anywhere en route, operate
along the same routes as buses and offer a
cheap and quick form of transport. Taxis are
more expensive than Santiago.

Train

Regular service on **Merval**, the Valparaíso
metropolitan line, to **Viña del Mar**, every 30
mins, 15 mins, US$0.30, and on to **Quilpué**
and **Limache**. Some disruption is expected
until 2005 due to the construction of a
railway tunnel through the centre of Viña.

South of Valparaíso *p135*
Buses to **Laguna Verde** can be caught from
Pedro Montt via Playa Ancha every 30 mins,
40 mins, US$0.70. A yellow *colectivo* from
calle 12 de Febrero behind the bus terminal
in Valparaíso runs to **Quintay**; it won't go
until it's full, but if you're in a hurry you can
pay for the extra seats, 45 mins, US$1.60.

Parque Nacional Campaña *p136*
The entrances at **Granizo** (paradero 45) and
Cajón Grande (paradero 41) are reached by
Euro Express bus from Calle Errazuriz in
Valparaíso, via Viña and Limache, or by local
bus/*colectivo* from Limache. There is no
public transport to the entrance at **Palmar
de Ocoa** to the north; bargain with
colectivo/taxi drivers in La Calera, expect to
pay around US$10-15 for the trip, arrange
return transport if necessary.

⊙ Directory

Airline offices LanChile, *Esmeralda 1048,
T032-251441*. **Banks and currency
exchange** Banks open 0900 to 1400, but
closed on Sat; many **Redbanc** ATMs on Prat,
also in **Santa Isabel** supermarkets and one in
the bus terminal; best exchange rates from
Marin Orrego, *3rd floor of the stock exchange
building, Prat y Urriola*, only changes US$ cash;
for other currencies, there are several casas de
cambio along Prat and Esmeralda. **Car hire**
Bert Rent A Car, *Victoria 2681, T032-254842*;
Colón Rent a Car, *Colón 2581, T032-256529*;
Suzuval, *Colón 2537, T032-255505*; many more
options in Viña. **Consulates** Argentina,
Blanco 890, Of 204, T032-213691; Belgium,
Prat 827, Piso 12, T032-213494; Bolivia, *Serrano
579, T032-259906*; Brazil, *Blanco 951, Piso 2,
T032-217856*; Denmark, *Errazuriz 940,
T032-268379*; Ecuador, *Blanco Encalada 1623,
of1740, T032-222167*; Germany, *Blanco 1215,
Of 1102, T032-256749*; Guatemala, *Blanco
1199, Local 4, T032-255214*; Norway, *Freire 657,
T032-252219*; Panama, *Blanco 1623, Of 1103,
T032-213592*; Peru, *Errazuriz 1178, Of 71,
T032-253403*; Spain, *Brasil 1589, piso 2,
T032-214466*; Sweden, *Errázuriz 940,
T032-250305*; UK, *Blanco 1199, piso 5,
T/F032-213063*. **Internet** There are dozens,
scattered all over El Plán; in Cerro Alegre, on
Templemany Urriola. **Laundry** Las Heras 554,
good and cheap; Lavanda Café, *Almirante*

Montt 454, Cerro Alegre, enjoy a coffee while you wait for your clothes, US$2.50 wash, US$2.30 dry, full service US$1 extra.
Medical services Dr Walther Meeden Bella, *Condell 1530, Depto 44, T032-212233,* dentist; Hospital Alemán, *G Munich 203, Cerro Alegre,* often has English-speaking staff on duty. **Post office** *North side of Pedro Montt, between San Ignacio & Bolivar.*

Telephone There are cheap call centres around the bus terminal, eg on Calle Rawson; also CTC, on the *Plaza Aníbal Pinto* or *Pedro Montt 2023*; Entel, *Condell 1491.*
Useful addresses YMCA (Asociación Cristiana de Jóvenes), *Blanco Encalada 1117*; YWCA (Asociación Cristiana Feminina), *Blanco 967*; Valparaíso Seamen's Institute, *Blanco Encalada 394.*

Viña del Mar and the coastal resorts → *Phone code: 032. Colour map 3, B2. Population: 300,000.*

Nine kilometres northeast of Valparaíso via the Avenida España, which runs along a narrow belt between the shore and precipitous cliffs, is Viña del Mar, one of South America's leading seaside resorts. Viña is also famous throughout Chile for its annual international music festival, during which the attention of the entire country is focused on the city; the festival used to bring in some top performers from all over Latin America, but this is no longer the case. In fact, neither the festival nor Viña itself are as wonderful as Chileans like to make out. This is the only place in Chile where road signs are in English as well as Spanish and much of the city feels like suburban North America. That said, with pleasant beaches and shady parks, Viña is a nice enough city to visit, especially if you have some pesos to burn, and makes an interesting contrast to nearby Valparaíso.

North of Viña strung along the coast are several smaller settlements. Reñaca, now a suburb of Viña del Mar is a well-to-do resort with extensive beaches, while further north, Maitencillo and Zapallar are fashionable seaside destinations, overflowing with tourists in summer. In between are the fishing towns of Concón, famous for its seafood, and Horcón, where horses are still used to tow the fishing boats onto land.

Ins and outs
Getting there There are inter-urban buses to Viña del Mar from many Chilean cities. The city also has daily connections through to Mendoza in Argentina. **Getting around** Frequent *micros* linking Viña and Valparaíso depart from Plaza Vergara. *Colectivos* also serve this route, as well as running to many of the city's outlying neighbourhoods and there are numerous buses along the coast. Taxis are plentiful and usually reasonably priced. ▶▶ *For further details, see Transport, page 151.* **Tourist information** Sernatur is at ⓘ *Valparaíso 507, Of 303, T032-683355, infovalparaiso@sernatur.cl* The municipal tourist office is on the corner of Plaza Vergara and can arrange the rental of private homes in the summer season; there's also a kiosk on Calle Valparaíso y Villanelo.

Sights
The older part of Viña del Mar is situated on the banks of a creek, the Marga Marga, which is crossed by bridges. Around Plaza Vergara and the smaller Plaza Sucre are the **Teatro Municipal** (1930) and the exclusive **Club de Viña**, built in 1910. It's a private club, but sometimes hosts public concerts and events. The municipally owned **Quinta Vergara**, formerly the residence of the shipping entrepreneur Francisco Alvarez, lies two blocks further south. The superb grounds include a double avenue of palm trees and encompass a children's playground and a large outdoor amphitheatre where the music festival takes place in February; it also hosts concerts

and events throughout the year. Also here is the **Palacio Vergara** ① *T032-680618, Tue-Sun 1000-1400, 1500-1800, US$0.50*, which houses the Museo de Bellas Artes and the Academia de Bellas Artes.

Calle Libertad runs north from the plaza, lined with banks, offices and shops. At the junction with 4 Norte is the **Palacio Carrasco**, now a cultural centre housing temporary exhibitions. In the same grounds is the **Museo Sociedad Fonk** ① *Calle 4 Norte 784, Tue-Fri 1000-1800, Sat and Sun 1000-1400, US$1*, an archaeological museum, with objects from Easter Island and the Chilean mainland, including Mapuche silver. East of this is the **Palacio Rioja** ① *Quillota 214, T032-689665, Tue-Sun 1000-1400, 1500-1800*, built in 1906 by a prominent local family and now used for official municipal receptions. The ground floor is preserved in its original state and is well worth a visit. Four blocks further east is the **Valparaíso Sporting Club** with a racecourse and playing fields, while to the north, in the hills, are the **Granadilla Golf Club** and a large artificial lake, the **Laguna Sausalito** ① *US$2.50, children under 11 US$1.75, colectivo 19 from Viana*, which has an excellent tourist complex with swimming pools, boating, tennis courts, sandy beaches, water skiing and restaurants. Nearby is the **Estadio Sausalito**, home to Everton football club.

West of the plaza, on a headland overlooking the sea is **Cerro Castillo**, the president's summer palace; its gardens can be visited. Below, on the coast, Castillo Wolff houses the **Museo de la Cultura del Mar** ① *T032-62542, Tue-Sat 1000-1300, 1430-1800, Sun 1000-1400*, which contains a collection devoted to the life and work of the novelist and maritime historian, Salvador Reyes. Just north, on the other side of the Marga Marga, is the **casino** ① *open all year, US$1.50*, built in the 1930s and set in beautiful gardens. North of this are the main beaches, **Acapulco** and **Las Salinas** (see below), while south of Cerro Castillo is another popular stretch of sand at **Caleta Abarca**.

Jardín Botánico Nacional ① *8 km southeast of the city, US$1, bus 20 from Plaza Vergara* was formerly the estate of the nitrate magnate Pascual Baburizza and is now administered by CONAF. Covering 405 ha, it contains over 3,000 species from all over the world and a collection of Chilean cacti; it's very pretty, but unfortunately the different species are not labelled. ▸▸ *For Sleeping, Eating and other listings, see pages 147-152.*

Resorts north of Viña del Mar

North of Viña del Mar the coast road runs past **Las Salinas**, a popular beach set between two towering crags. The suburb of **Reñaca** is a popular resort with access to excellent beaches, while to the north at Cochoa, there are giant sand dunes and a large sea-lion colony 100 m offshore. This route affords lovely views over the sea, but there is also a much faster inland road between Viña del Mar and Concón. ▸▸ *For Sleeping, Eating and other listings, see pages 147-152.*

Concón → *Phone code: 032. Colour map 3, A2.*

Concón lies on the southern shore of a bay 18 km north of Viña del Mar at the mouth of the Río Aconcagua. The town claims to be the oldest settlement in Chile, having been founded by Pedro de Valdivia in 1541, prior to his arrival at what is now Santiago. Concón is famous for its restaurants and is rightly known as the culinary capital of the V region. The area is very popular among Santiaguinos, who often come here for the weekend. A series of six beaches stretches along the bay between Caleta Higuerilla at the western end and La Boca at the eastern end. These beaches include **Playa Amarilla**, which is good for sunbathing; the very peaceful **Playa Higuerillas**, where there are lots of shells; **Playa Los Lilenes**, backed by sand dunes, and **Playa La Boca** itself, which is by far the largest of the six, and excellent for beach sports (horses US$3 for 30 mins; also

‼ *Most buses to Concón drop passengers off at the main roundabout near La Boca. The Nandu bus from Viña follows the coast road and passes all six beaches.*

helpful **tourist office** ① *annexed to the municipal museum, Maroto 1030, www.concon.cl,* can provide maps of the resort.

Quintero → *Phone code: 032. Colour map 3, A2.*

Another 23 km north of Concón, Quintero is a fishing town situated around a rocky peninsula with 16 small beaches, all of varying character and quality. The path running along the north side of the peninsula offers a good view of the sunset over the ocean from the Cueva del Pirata at its western end. Good fishing and windsurfing are available at **Playas Loncura** and **Ritoque** to the north of the town, while horses can be hired on **Playa Albatros**. Note that there are many touts and beggars in Quintero in the high season, when the atmosphere can become a little tense. On the opposite side of the bay is **Las Ventanas**, where a power station and copper processing plant rather spoil the outlook from the beach.

Horcón → *Phone code: 032. Colour map 3, A2.*

Set back in a cove surrounded by cliffs, Horcón, also known locally as Horcones, is a pleasant small village, mainly of wooden houses. Although overcrowded in season, during the rest of the year it is a charming place, populated by fishermen and artists, with a tumbledown feel unlike the more well-to-do resorts to the north and south. Sadly, a condominium development is underway on the northern side of the bay, which will surely take away some of Horcón's secluded charm. Across the headland to the south of the village is **Playa Cau Cau**; scramble down a steep flight of log steps to reach the sandy, frequently deserted, tree-lined cove.

Maitencillo → *Phone code: 032. Colour map 3, A2.*

Maitencillo, 19 km north of Las Ventanas, is an upmarket resort consisting mainly of chalets and frequented mainly by well-to-do Santiaguinos. There is a wonderful long beach here but the sea is notorious for its strong undercurrents.

Zapallar → *Phone code: 033. Colour map 3, A2.*

A fashionable resort with a lovely beach, 33 km north of Las Ventanas, Zapallar is an expensive place to stay. The number of fine mansions along Avenida Zapallar are a clue to its luxurious heritage. At **Cachagua**, 3 km south, there are clear views of a colony of penguins on an offshore island from the northern end of the beach; take binoculars.

Papudo → *Phone code: 033. Colour map 3, A2.*

Ten kilometres further north is the site of a naval battle in November 1865, in which the Chilean vessel *Esmeralda* captured the Spanish ship *Covadonga* during the War of Independence. Following the arrival of the railway Papudo rivalled Viña del Mar as a fashionable resort but it has declined a great deal since its heyday in the 1920s. Among the buildings surviving from that period is the **Casa Rawlings**, now the Casa de la Cultura. There are two fine beaches, which are empty except in high summer .

● Sleeping

Viña del Mar *p145, map p148*

There are a great many more places to stay in addition to those listed here, particularly in the **AL-B** range, some with private beach access. In season, it is generally cheaper to stay in Valparaíso and commute to the beaches around Viña. Note that during the music festival in Feb, accommodation is almost impossible to find. Out of season, furnished apartments can be rented through agencies (with commission).

LL Hotel del Mar, *Av Perú y Los Héroes, casino complex, T032-500600, www.casino.cl/vina* Luxurious 5 star with all facilities and panoramic views over the bay.

L-AL Gala, *Arlegui 273, Local 10, T032-321500, www.galahotel.cl* Excellent, suites, all mod cons.

AL Albamar, *San Martín 419, T032-975274, F032-970720*. Tastefully decorated.

AL Cap Ducal, *Av de la Marina 51, T032-626655, www.capducal.cl* Old mansion charm, good restaurant (see below).

AL-A Alcázar, *Alvarez 646, T032-478000, www.alcazar.cl* Good restaurant, 4 star.

AL-A San Martín, *San Martín 667, T032-689191, www.hotelsanmartin.cl* Small rooms, some with sea view. Also café, bar, sauna.

B Andalue, *6 Poniente 124, T032-684147, F684148*. With breakfast, central, recommended.

B Español, *Plaza Vergara 191, T032-685145, hotelespanol@elhostal.cl* Large rooms, run down.

B Offenbacher Hof, *Balmaceda 102, Cerro Castillo, T032-621483, residoff@vtr.net* Clean, friendly. Recommended.

B-C Genross, *Paseo Monterrey 18, T032-661711, genrosshotel@hotmail.com* Located in a beautiful old mansion, clean airy rooms with bath, garden patio and sitting room, very friendly and informative, English spoken, highly recommended.

C Balia Casino, *von Schroeder 36, T032-976307, hotelbaliacasino@entelchile.net* With parking, overpriced.

C El Escorial, *4 Norte 535, T032-907919, escorial@directo.cl* With breakfast, shared bath, clean, central.

C Petit Palace, *Paseo Valle 387, T/F032-663134*. Small rooms, good, central, quiet.

C Quinta Vergara, *Errázuriz 690, T032-685073, hotelquinta@hotmail.com* Clean, friendly, large rooms, beautiful gardens. Recommended.

C-D Res Capric, *von Schroeder 39, T032-978295*. Rooms with bath and TV, breakfast included, special rates for YHA members.

D Res Agua Santa, *Agua Santa 36*. Hot shower.

E Res Magallanes, *Arlegui 555, T032-685101*. Breakfast, clean, mixed reports.

F Res Blanchart, *Valparaíso 82A, T032-974949, celsolr@entelnet.cl* Price per person, with breakfast, hot water, clean, good service.

F Res Villarica, *Arlegui 172, T032-881484, F032-942807*. Price per person, without bath.

Viña del Mar

To Mall & Hypermarket
To Beaches, Reñaca & Concón

Pacific Ocean

Museo de la Cultura del Mar
Casino
La Marina
Palacio Presidencial
Caleta Abarca
Cerro Castillo
Floral Clock
Balmaceda
To Valparaíso

Museo Sociedad Fonk
Palacio Carrasco
Palacio Rioja
Automóvil Club de Chile
Municipalidad
Plaza Vergara
Teatro Municipal
Plaza Sucre
Viña del Mar
Palacio Vergara, Academia & Museo de Bellas Artes
Quinta Vergara

To Limache & Parque Nacional La Campana
To Jardín Botánico Nacional

N
0 metres 200
0 yards 200

Good, friendly.

F-G Res Victoria, *Valparaíso 40, T032-977370*. Price per person with bath and breakfast, clean, central.

G Res de Casia, *Von Schroeder 151, T032-971861*. Price per person.

Camping

Reñaca Center, *town centre, T032-833207*. Good facilities on the river bank, US$20 per site.

Reñaca p146

Accommodation here is much cheaper out of season.

L Cabañas Don Francisco, *Torreblanca 75, T032-834802*. Helpful service, *cabañas* only available for week-long bookings.

AL Montecarlo, *V MacKenna 136, T032-830397*. Very modern and comfortable.

A Piero's, *Av Central y Segunda, T032-830280*. Comfortable, with café, pool, some rooms with sea view.

Concón p146

AL-A Hostería Edelweiss, *Av Borgoño 19200, T032-814043, www.edelweiss.cl* Modern *cabañas* sleeping 2-6, clean, sea views, pool, kitchenette (cheaper cabins without), including breakfast, excellent food in attached restaurant, German spoken. Recommended.

C Cabañas Los Romeros, *T032-813671*. Cabins for up to 3 people.

C Cabañas Río Mar, *T/F032-814644*. Many other *cabañas* in this price range.

Camping

Matagua, *3 km north, T032-811415, www.mantagua.cl*. Well equipped but very expensive, also *cabañas*.

Quintero p147

There are lots of cheap *residenciales* here.

A Yachting Club, *Luis Acevedo 1736, T032-930061, www.hotelyachting.cl* Hotel with large gardens on the seafront.

C Monaco, *21 de Mayo 1530, T032-930939*. Rundown but interesting, good views.

C Res Brazilian, *21 de Mayo 1336, T032-930590, clilo3@msn.com* With breakfast, large windows but no view, clean, well maintained, warm seawater baths for US$4.

There are many *cabañas* around the village; shop around for the best price, especially off season. Rooms are also available in private houses and, although there's no campsite, camping is possible in people's gardens.

C El Ancla, *by the harbour*. Pleasant *cabañas*, also serves good food.

C-D Cabañas Arancibia, *T032-796169*. Cabins with or without bath, pleasant gardens, good food, friendly. Recommended.

D-F Juan Esteban, *Pasaje Miramar, Casa 2, T032-796056, T09-4384388, www.geocities.com/jestebanc* English, Portuguese and Italian spoken, nice terrace with view. Recommended. Also fully equipped *cabañas* (B) for 4 people.

Maitencillo p147

LL Marbella Resort, *2km south, T032-772020, www.marbella.cl* 5-star resort, conference centre, restaurants, golf course, tennis courts, pools, and everything else you would expect.

B Cabañas La Mar, *Av de la Mar 524, T032-771036*. There are several others in the same price range.

Zapallar p147

Accommodation is expensive especially in the centre where it is sparse. There is no campsite.

L Isla Seca, *T033-741224, islasec@ctcinternet.cl* Small, with pool and very expensive suites, good restaurant.

AL César, *T033-741259*. Nice but expensive.

B Hostal Villa Real. Large rooms, with breakfast. Recommended.

B Residencial Villa Alicia, *Moises Chacón 280, T033-741176*, good, and one of the cheapest.

Papudo p147

There are several cheap *residenciales* on Chorillos 100-150.

B Carande, *Chorrillos 89, T033-791105*. Best in town.

B De Peppino, *No 609, T033-791108*. *Cabañas* for 4-6 people.

F-G Armandini, *F Concha 525*. Price per person.

🍽 Eating

Viña del Mar p145, map p148

$$$ Cap Ducal, *in the Cap Ducal hotel (see above)*. Good seafood, elegant surroundings, excellent views.

$$$ **Flavia**, *6 Poniente 121*. Good Italian food, polished service, tasty desserts and decent wine selection.

$$$ **Punto Verde**, *Arlegui 346, Local A*. Expensive vegetarian food.

$$$ **Savinya**, *Peru 199*. Elegant restaurant above the casino.

$$$-$$ **Diego Pizza**, *San Martín y 8 Norte*. Good pizzas but overpriced.

$$$-$$ **Las Delicias del Mar**, *San Martín 459*. Award-winning seafood restaurant. Recommended.

$$$-$$ **Mastrantonio**, *3 Norte 155*. Good Italian.

$$$-$$ **Ruby Tuesdays**, *in the mall, 14 Norte*. For those of you who can't do without a US-style sports bar.

$$ **Africa**, *Valparaíso 324*. Extraordinary façade, good food.

$$ **Guarak**, *5 Poniente 441*. Arabic specialities.

$$ **Las Gaviotas**, *14 Norte 1248*. Chilean meat dishes, inexpensive.

$$ **Pau San**, *Quinta 122*. Chinese.

$$ **Pizzería Mama Mía**, *San Martín 435*. Good, reasonably priced.

$ **Café Aleman**, *Arlegui 228*. Good set lunch.

$ **Café Journal**, *Agua Santa y Alvarez*. Excellent-value set lunch, recommended.

$ **El Guatón**, *Valparaíso, on the corner of plaza Vergara*. Super-sized fast food.

$ **Jerusalem**, *Quinta 259*. Kebabs and felafel.

$ **La Flor de Chile**, *8 Norte 607 y 1 poniente*. Good, typically Chilean food.

Cafés
Alster, *Valparaíso 225*. Elegant, but pricey.

Café Big Ben, *Galería Fontana, Valparaíso 469*. Good coffee, good food.

Samoiedo, *Valparaíso 637*. Old-time café.

Reñaca *p146*
$$$ **Hotel Oceanic**, *Av Borgoño*. Very good.

$$$ **Rincón Marino**, *Av Borgoño 17120*. Good seafood.

$$ **El Pancho**, *Av Borgoño 16180*. Excellent seafood and service.

Concón *p146*
Seafood is the name of the game here. Both Caleta Higuerilla and La Boca are renowned for their restaurants.

$$$ Among the most upmarket are located along Av Borgoño, one side fronting onto the road, the other onto the beach, including the excellent **La Perla del Pacifico**, in La Boca; and the following in Caleta Higuerilla: **Albatross**, *No 21295*; **Aqui Jaime**, *No 21303*; **Bellamar**, *No 21505*; **Don Chico**, *No 21410*; **Edelweiss**, *No 19200*; and **Vista al Mar**, *No 21270*.

$$-$ Mid-range options include **La Picá de Emeterio**, and **Las Deliciosas**, both on Borgoño in La Boca, while cheaper eateries are to be found in Alto Higuerillas, where *picadas* have been converted by the fishermen into good-value restaurants; try **La Cava de Franz**, *San Pedro 345*; **La Picá de Juan Segura**, *Illapel 15*; **La Picá El Horizonte**, *San Pedro 120*, and **La Picá Los Delfines**, *San Pedro 130*. Look out, too, for tasty seafood *empanadas* served in the resort's bars.

Quintero *p147*
There are several cheap seafood restaurants down by the harbour.

Horcón *p147*
Seafood lunches made from the catch of the day are sold at any number of stalls on the seafront, where there also a number of restaurants.

$$ **Bahía**. Good food, pleasant atmosphere.

$$ **El Ancla**. Recommended.

$$ **Santa Clara**. Try the *chupe de mariscos* (cheesy shellfish soup) and *pastel de jaivas* (crabmeat cooked in cheese and breadcrumbs). Recommended.

$ **Reina Victoria**. Cheap and good quality.

$ **Roty Schop**. Acclaimed for its *empanadas*.

Maitencillo *p147*
$$$ **Bar Rest La Canasta**, *Av del Mar 592*. Mediterranean and Moroccan cuisine served in elegant surroundings, expensive but worth it.

$$ **Bar Tsunami**, *Av del Mar 1366*. Mid-range seafood.

$ **Café Entre Rocas**, *Av del Mar s/n*. Good drinks and snacks.

Zapallar *p147*
$$$ **Isla Seca**, *see Sleeping above*. Expensive, excellent seafood.

$$ **César**, *see Sleeping above*. Good food and reasonable prices.

$ **La Culebra**. Cheap eatery.

$ **Los Troncos**. Good-value grub.

$ **Natón**, *Cachagua, south of Zapallar*. Cheap restaurant with disco.

Papudo *p147*

$$$ **Cava del Mar**. Pricey international cuisine.
$$$ **Gran Azul**. Expensive seafood.
$$ **La Abeja**. Mid-range.
$$ **La Maison des Fous**, *Blanco 151*. Unusual bar-restaurant in lovely old house. Friendly staff, good food and atmospheric candlelit piano bar with graffiti-covered pillars.
$ **Don Rota**. Cheap seafood.

🜚 Bars and clubs

Viña del Mar *p145, map p148*
Barlovento, *2 norte y 5 poniente*. The designer bar in Viña, set over 3 floors with a roof terrace, serves great pizzas and Kunstmann beer.
Café Journal, *Agua Santa y Alvarez*. Good beer. Full of students at night.
La Grua, *by the pier off San Martín*. An old cargo crane has been converted into a very popular nightlife centre with bars and clubs, a beach location and good views.
Oh! Cerveza, *7 norte y 3 poniente*. Wide variety of draught beer.
Twister, *Av Borgoño*. One of many discos. Also try **Kamikaze** and **Neverland** east of town.

Reñaca *p146*
El Ciervo, *Av Central y Segunda*. Bar/café with live music in evenings. Recommended.

Papudo *p147*
Help, *Glorias Navales 409*. Disco with music from techno to salsa.
La Maison des Fous, *see Eating above*.

🜚 Entertainment

Viña del Mar *p145, map p148*
Cinemas
Cine Arte, *Plaza Vergara 42*. Also a multiplex in the shopping mall on Libertad (see Shopping).

Galleries
Fodigliani, *5 Norte 168*.
Mar Pau, *Valparaíso 595, local 18*.
Palacio Carrasco, *Libertad 250*.
Sala de Arte Viña del Mar, *Arlegui 683*.

🜚 Festivals and events

Viña del Mar *p145, map p148*
The **Festival Internacional de la Canción** takes place in Feb and attracts an audience from all over Chile. Tickets are available from the Municipalidad and should be bought ahead of time; you should also reserve any accommodation well in advance.

Resorts north of Viña del Mar *p146*
Since this area comprises coastal communities, it is no surprise that the **Fiesta de San Pedro** (the patron saint of fishermen) on **29 Jun** is an important event.

🜚 Shopping

Viña del Mar *p145, map p148*
The **market** is held on Wed and Sat at the intersection of Av Sporting and the river. There is a huge new **mall** on Libertad between 14 and 15 Norte, open till 2300.

⛰ Activities and tours

Viña del Mar *p145, map p148*
Bowling
Available in the shopping mall on Libertad y 14 Norte (see Shopping above).

Diving
Octopus, *Libertad 1154, T032-973857, octopus@entelchile.net* Scuba-diving along the central coast, with lots of shipwrecks to explore. Courses for US$200.

Maitencillo *p147*
Paragliding
Parapente Aventura, *Maitencillo, T09-2330349, www.parapente.cl* Single tandem flight, US$50; 13 classes, US$350.

Surfing
Café Entre Rojas, *see Eating above*. Surfing classes and biplane tours (US$35 for 20 mins).

🜚 Transport

Viña del Mar *p145, map p148*
Bus
Bus terminal is 2 blocks east of Plaza Vergara at *Av Valparaíso y Quilpué*. To **Santiago**, frequent, 1¾ hrs, many companies, US$3-4, heavily booked in advance for travel on Sun afternoons, at other times some buses pick up passengers opposite the train station; to **La Serena**, 6 daily, 7 hrs, US$9; to **Antofagasta**, 20 hrs, US$20 (*semi-cama*); to **Temuco**, 9 hrs,

US$10. To **Mendoza** (Argentina), El Rápido, Fenix and TAC, all leave in the morning, 7 hrs, US$12. Buses north from Valparaíso for destinations **La Calera**, **La Ligua**, **Cabildo**, **Pichidangui** and **Los Vilos** all pass through Viña, and can be caught on Libertad.

Train

Services on the Valparaíso Metropolitan line (**Merval**) stop at Viña (see p143).

Resorts north of Viña del Mar *p146*

Buses run from Av Errázuriz in Valparaíso and from Av Libertad in Viña del Mar: to **Concón**, bus 1 or 10, very frequent, 20-30 mins, US$0.50; to **Quintero** and **Horcón**, Sol del Pacífico, every 30 mins, 2 hrs, US$1; to **Zapallar** and **Papudo**, Sol del Pacífico, 4 a day (2 before 0800, 2 after 1600), US$3.

● Directory

Viña del Mar *p145, map p148*
Airline offices Air France, *Equador 125, T032-710976*; American, *8 Norte 492, T032-990997*; LanChile, *Equador 74, T032-251441, www.lanchile.cl* **Banks and currency exchange** Several casas de cambio on calles Arlegui and Valparaíso; shop around for best rates, and avoid changing money on the street; many banks (with ATMs) on Arlegui, Valparaíso and Libertad; ATMs also in the mall; **Western Union** money transfer, *Libertad 715* (also has DHL). **Car hire** Euro Rent-A-Car, in Hotel O'Higgins, clean cars, efficient; **Flota Verschae**, *Libertad 10, T032-267300, www.verschae.cl*, good value, recommended; Hertz, *Quillota 766, T032-971625*; Rosselot, *Libertad 892, T032-382373, www.rosselot.cl*, well regarded nationwide agency. **Car mechanic** Luis Vallejos, *13 Norte 1228*, recommended. **Cultural centres** Casa Italia (cultural centre, consulate, restaurant), *Alvarez 398*; Instituto Chileno-Aleman de Cultura, *Goethe Haus, Alvarez 2950, T/F032-677249*; Instituto Chileno-Británico de Cultura, *3 Norte 824, T032-971061*; Instituto Chileno-Francés de Cultura, *Alvarez 314, T032-685908*; Instituto Chileno-Norteamericano de Cultura, *2 Oriente 335, T/F032-686191*. **Internet** Several all along Calle Valparaíso, prices around US$0.60-US$0.80 per hour. **Post office** North of Plaza Vergara, by the bridge. **Telephone** several on Calle Valparaíso. **Useful address** Automóvil Club de Chile, *1 Norte 901, T032-689509*.

Resorts south of Valparaíso

This cluster of resorts stretches along the coast from the mouth of the Río Maipo north towards Valparaíso. There are two good routes from Santiago, one leading from the main Santiago-Valparaíso highway to Algarrobo and the other, Route 78, direct from Santiago to San Antonio. The resorts here are not as upmarket as those north of Viña, but every summer tens of thousands of Chileans flock to them from the capital. Beaches range from classic wide white-sand affairs to secluded coves, and a wild, rocky zone around Isla Negra; off season, most are deserted.

Ins and outs

Getting there Road links between Valparaíso and the resorts to the south are poor, but there are two good routes from Santiago: one from the main Santiago-Valparaíso highway to Algarrobo and the other, Route 78, to San Antonio. **Getting around** Buses link the resorts in this area, but a hire car will allow you to explore more secluded coves.

San Antonio → *Phone code: 035. Colour map 3, B2. Population: 74,742.*

Situated near the mouth of the Río Maipo, 112 km south of Valparaíso, San Antonio was at the epicentre of a large earthquake in 1985. Subsequently, the harbour was rebuilt and has now taken over from Valparaíso as the main container port for this part of the coast. It is the terminal for the export of copper brought by rail from the large mine at El Teniente, near Rancagua (see page 272) as well as being an important fishing port. Many restaurants buy their fish and seafood here and a visit to the docks just after the catch has been unloaded is an interesting experience. The **Museo Municipal de Ciencias Naturales y Arqueología** ⓘ *Av Barros Luco, Mon-Fri 0900-1300, 1500-1900*, has displays on nature, precolonial culture and geology. There is also a botanical garden.

Nearby to the south are two resorts: **Llolleo**, 4 km, famous for the treatment of heart diseases, and 7 km further **Rocas de Santo Domingo**, the most attractive and exclusive resort in this area with 20 km of beaches and a golf course; even in high season it is not very crowded. ▶▶ *For Sleeping, Eating and other listings, see page 154.*

Cartagena → *Phone code: 035. Colour map 3, B2. Population: 10,318.*

Eight kilometres north of San Antonio, Cartagena is the biggest resort on this part of the coast, but is a quieter place than San Antonio. It is filled with fish restaurants and ice cream shops and has lovely views sweeping north around the bay towards Isla Negra. In the early years of this century, it was a fashionable summer retreat for the wealthy of Santiago; a number of mansions survive, notably the **Castillo Foster** overlooking the bay. The centre lies around the **Plaza de Armas**, situated on top of the hill. To the south is the picturesque **Playa Chica**, overlooked by many of the older hotels and restaurants; to the north is **Playa Larga**. Between the two a promenade runs below the cliffs; high above hang old houses, some in disrepair but offering spectacular views. Cartagena is a very popular resort in summer but out of season it is a good centre for visiting nearby points of interest; there are many hotels and bus connections are good. For more information on Cartagena, look at www.cartagena.cl

North of Cartagena

The road to Algarrobo runs north along the coast through several small resorts including **Las Cruces**, **El Tabo** and **El Quisco**, a small fishing port with two beautiful white-sand beaches (crowded during Chilean holidays). Just south of Las Cruces is **Laguna El Peral** ⓘ *Sep-Apr daily 0900-1400, 1500-1800; May-Aug daily 0900-1300, 1400-1800*, a nature reserve that protects a wide range of aquatic birds.

Isla Negra → *Phone code: 035. Colour map 3, B2.*

Four kilometres south of El Quisco in the village of Isla Negra is the beautifully restored **Museo-Casa Pablo Neruda** ⓘ *T035-461284, Tue-Sun 1000-2000 in summer; Tue-Fri 1000-1400, 1500-1800 rest of year, US$4, students US$1.50, guided tours in Spanish, English or French US$5, call in advance for opening hours or to book an English guide*. Bought by Neruda in 1939, this house, overlooking the sea, was the poet's writing retreat in his later years, and became the final resting place of Neruda and his last wife Mathilde. The house contains artefacts gathered from all over the world and the café specializes in Neruda's own recipes. The museum conveys a powerful sense of the poet and is well worth a visit. However, some Chileans feel that the **Fundación Pablo Neruda** should not be charging such high admission prices. For further information about Pablo Neruda, visit his Santiago house, La Chascona, page 88, and La Sebastiana in Valparaíso, page 134; see also box page 539.

Algarrobo → *Phone code: 035. Colour map 3, B2.*

Algarrobo is the largest resort north of Cartagena and the most chic, with large houses, a yacht club and a marina. Conveniently located for Santiago, it was the retreat of politicians in the 1960s; both Salvador Allende and Eduardo Frei had summer residences here. Today, it remains one of the most popular spots on the

● ● *The celebrated 1994 film 'Il Postino' was based on Antonio Skármeta's novel 'Ardiente Paciencia', which is set in Isla Negra during the last years of Neruda's life. After the success of the film the novel was retitled 'El Cartero de Neruda' (Neruda's Postman).*

central coast: its shallow waters and sheltered bay ensure that sea temperatures here are much warmer than at most other resorts along the central Chilean coast, while good beaches are supplemented by activities such as fishing, surfing and sailing. From **Playa Canelo** there are good views of pelicans and boobies in a seabird colony on an offshore island. Boat tours circle round it in summer, departing from the jetty.

> *Algarrobo's population of 4,000 is swamped by 100,000 summer visitors.*

Valparaíso & Viña del Mar Resorts south of Valparaíso

⬤ Sleeping

San Antonio and around *p152*
A **Rocas de Santo Domingo**, *La Ronda 130, Santo Domingo, south of San Antonio*, T035-444356, F035-444494. Clean, friendly, with restaurant, cable TV. Good breakfast included in price. Also suites.
B **Jockey Club**, *21 de Mayo 202*, T035-211777, F035-212922. Best accommodation in town, good views, restaurant.
F **Res El Castillo**, *Providencia 253, Llolleo, south of San Antonio*, T035-373821. Price per person.

Cartagena *p153*
D **Violeta**, *Condell 110*, T035-450372. With swimming pool, good views.
E **Res Carmona**, *Playa Chica*, T035-450485. Small rooms, basic, clean, good value.
F **El Estribo**, *just off Plaza de Armas*. Rooms with breakfast, basic, cheap *comedor*.
F **Residencial Paty's**, *Alacalde Cartagena 295*, T035-450469. Nice spot, good value.

North of Cartagena *p153*
Accommodation is generally more expensive in El Quisco.
A **Motel Barlovento**, *El Quisco*, T035-471030. 3-star accommodation.
C **Gran Italia**, *Dubournais 413, El Quisco*, T/F035-481631. Good beds and pool. Recommended.
C **Hotel El Tabo**, *El Tabo*, T035-433719. Good accommodation.
C **La Posada**, *Las Cruces*, T035-421280. With bath and breakfast, good birdwatching.
D **Cabañas Pozo Azul**, *Capricornio 234, El Quisco*, T035-471401. Southeast of town, quiet.
D **El Quisco**, *Dubournais 166, El Quisco*, T035-481923. With breakfast, clean, open weekends only, with seafood restaurant.
D **Motel El Tabo**, *next door to the hotel, El Tabo*, T035-212719. Very crowded in Jan-Feb
D **Res Julia**, *Aguirre 0210, El Quisco*, T035-471546. Very clean, quiet, good value..
E **Res Oriental**, *near the beach, El Quisco*,

T035-471662. Price per person with breakfast, good, clean, hot water.

Isla Negra *p153*
B **Hostería Santa Elena**, T035-213439. Beautiful building and location, but some rooms damp and gloomy, also restaurant.
F **Casa Azul**, *Av Santa Luisa*, T035-461154. Price per person with breakfast, kitchen and living room, English spoken, camping. Recommended.

Algarrobo *p153*
A **Uribe**, *behind Costa Sur*, T035-481035. Pleasant, quiet.
E-F **Res Vera**, *Alessandri 1521*, T035-481131. Price per person with breakfast, good.
G **Res San José**, *Av Principal 1598*, T035-481131. Price per person. Basic, no hot water.

▲▲ Activities and tours

Tours to the seaside resorts from **Santiago**, depart at 0900 from Plaza de Armas (Compañia y Ahumada), US$20 and include seaside resorts, T02-2322574.

⊖ Transport

Bus
Pullman Lago Peñuelas operates direct buses from Valparaíso to **San Antonio**, every 30 mins until 2000, 2hrs, US$3. The coastal service from Valparaíso to **Algarroba** and **Isla Negra**, every 30 mins, 2 hrs, US$3, also continues to San Antonio. **Empresa de Buses San Antonio** and **Empresa Robles** run frequent services from Algarroba to **San Antonio**, until 2000, 30 mins.

Pullman Bus runs services from Santiago to **San Antonio**, every 20 mins in summer, US$3. There are also frequent services from the capital with **Pullman Bus** (from Terminal Alameda) and other companies (from Terminal Sur) to **Isla Negra** and **Algarrobo** (via Cartagena and other resorts).

From Santiago to La Serena

Introduction

This is a little-known part of Chile, stretching 500 km from Santiago north to La Serena and the fertile Elqui Valley. While some of the coastal towns are popular, the interior between La Ligua and Vicuña is almost universally overlooked. Yet here there are rich rewards for those prepared to rough it and take a few risks – one of the world's highest concentrations of **petroglyphs**, spectacular mountainsides speckled different colours by rich mineral deposits and desolate tracks winding through some of Chile's best high mountain scenery.

The largest resort is **La Serena**, the usual centre for visiting the pisco distilleries of the **Elqui Valley**. This valley is one of the world's most important astronomical centres, with four **observatories**, including one built especially for visitors – it is also the focal point of Chile's New Age movement, and was the birthplace of Nobel laureate Gabriela Mistral. South of La Serena is the lively city of **Ovalle**, an ideal centre for forays into the cordillera and for visiting the **Parque Nacional Fray Jorge**, a temperate rainforest that survives in this dry region due to the sea mists that hang almost constantly over its hills.

★ Don't miss...

❶ La Pampilla Take in Chile's biggest independence day celebrations in Coquimbo, a week of constant revelry in September, page 180.

❷ Parque Nacional Fray Jorge A temperate rainforest amid semi-desert that survives due to dense fogs, page 164.

❸ Observatories Budding astronomers and those who are simply curious will want to visit at least one of the star-gazing institutes near La Serena, page 171.

❹ Petroglyphs Explore and imagine the pre-Hispanic past of the Diaguitas and Molle people, etched poignantly into the area's beautiful mountainsides, page 158.

❺ Pacific beaches Get away from it all in places such as La Herradura, Tongoy and Pichidangui, pages 174 & 159.

❻ Reserva Nacional Pingüino de Humboldt Take a boat trip among dolphins, penguins and the sea-lions, page 177.

Background

Stretching north from the Río Aconcagua to the Río Elqui, this area is a transitional zone between the fertile heartland and the northern deserts. Rainfall is rare, and only occurs in winter, while temperatures are relatively stable, with little seasonal variation. North of the

> ❧ *The average temperature on the coast is 14°C, compared to 16-17°C inland. Visitors should note that it gets very cold at night inland, especially in winter.*

Aconcagua, the Andes and the coastal *cordillera* merge in a spectacular lattice of mountains and are crossed by river valleys separated by high ridges. The valleys of the Choapa, Limarí and Elqui rivers are green oases, where the land is intensively farmed using irrigation to produce fruit and vegetables. Elsewhere, the vegetation is characteristic of semi-desert (dry scrub and cactus), except in those areas where frequent sea mists provide sufficient

moisture to support temperate rainforest. The coastline is generally flat, with many beautiful coves, both rocky and sandy, and good surf, although the water is very cold.

Archaeological finds indicate that the river valleys were inhabited at an early stage in prehistory. The rise of the Molle culture happened around the same time as the rise of Christianity in Europe; sharing links with northern Argentina, the Molle people produced intricate ceramics and worked with copper. They were superseded by the Diaguitas, who crossed the Andes around AD 900 and settled throughout the area. The pre-Hispanic peoples left their mark in the form of petroglyphs (rock carvings).

Soon after the arrival of the Spanish and the foundation of Santiago, Pedro de Valdivia attempted to secure control over northern Chile by founding La Serena in 1544. Due to the arid climate and the more testing living conditions, the indigenous people here were less numerous than the Mapuche in the south and, despite a few setbacks for the Spanish, they were soon subjugated and wiped out. Throughout the colonial period, La Serena dominated the rest of the region; although small, it was the only city in the north and its leading families had close ties to the main Spanish landowners in the other valleys. After Independence, the area became an important mining zone, producing large amounts of silver, copper and gold.

Mining remains an important industry in this area: El Indio, inland from La Serena is the biggest gold producer in Chile, as well as a source of copper, and El Romeral, north of La Serena, is the most important iron ore deposit in the country. Quartz and the semi-precious stones lapis lazuli and combarbalita are also mined. Despite the dry climate, much of the region's industry is linked to its agricultural produce, notably the distilling of *pisco* from grapes; by law, only grapes grown in the regions of Copiapó and Coquimbo can be used to make *pisco*.

North of Santiago

The first stretch of the Pan-American Highway from Santiago heads inland through green valleys with rich blue clover and wild artichokes. North of La Ligua, it follows the coast, and the first intimations of the northern deserts appear. From Los Vilos, a paved road turns off the Panamericana towards Illapel, climbing steeply up to a pass, from which there are staggering views of the Andes and the Choapa River.

Illapel is surrounded by barren hills, with good views of the cordillera to the east. While the town is not wildly interesting in itself, it is close to wonderful mountain country, best explored by the adventurous or those with their own transport. The Illapel region is largely ignored by travellers, yet it has some worthwhile attractions. This is the narrowest part of Chile, between Arica and Aysén, and the Andes are never far away, with valleys carving right up towards the snowline. There are many examples of pre-Hispanic petroglyphs for those who take the trouble to find them.

Ins and outs

Getting there Illapel is easily reached by regular buses from Los Vilos, Santiago, La Serena and other destinations as far north as Calama. However, those travelling by bus in this region should note that bus companies take advantage of the remoteness of the Choapa Valley and double their prices for the return journey from Illapel to Los Vilos – unfortunately, without your own transport, there's no alternative means of leaving the area. ▸▸ *For further details, see Transport, page 162.*

Los Vilos and the coast → *Phone code: 053. Colour map 3, A2. Population: 9,422.*

Los Vilos, a former mineral port 216 km north of Santiago, is now a small seaside resort. Set in a wide bay, it is a peaceful, windswept place, disturbed mainly by the noise of the kelp gulls and the waves. There are several attractive *plazuelas* on the *costanera*, with stone benches from which you can watch the fishing boats bobbing in the sea; the water is cold for bathing. Offshore are two islands reached by frequent launches: **Isla de Los Huevos**, situated in the bay, and, 5 km south, **Isla de Los Lobos**, where there is a colony of seals. There is a **tourist office** ① *Caupolicán 278, www.losvilos.cl, open summer only.*

> ⊛ *In the evenings, there is a craft market in Los Vilos at Caupolicán y Purén selling relatively cheap woollens and semi-precious stones.*

Pichidangui, 26 km south, is a popular resort on a rocky peninsula, with a beautiful beach to the north. **Los Molles**, 10 km south of Pichidangui, is a fishing village where many wealthy residents of Santiago have their summer homes. Nearby are the **Puguén blow holes** ① *US$1, free off-season*, and the **Piscina Los Molles**, a natural swimming pool. ▸▸ *For Sleeping, Eating and other listings, see pages 161-163.*

Illapel → *Phone code: 053. Colour map 3, A3. Population: 18,900.*

Nearly 480 km north of Santiago, Illapel is a poor town that depends on mining in the surrounding mountains for its survival. The lives of the *pilquineros* (see box page 160) in the nearby hills provide a sobering illustration of the lifestyle that miners in the north of Chile have endured since colonial times. The workers drag rocks from the mine-face in rusting wheelbarrows, living without power, fresh water or even public transport, and many of them die tragically young from lung cancer or chagas disease. If you do venture up into these remote areas, bring gifts and humility in abundance.

Illapel

N	0 metres 100 / 0 yards 100	**Sleeping** 🛏	**Eating** 🍴	
		Alameda **1**	Domingo Ortíz de Rojas **4**	Bufett Estación **3**
		American **2**	Londres **6**	Bamby **6**	Luz My Pan **7**
		Diaguitas **3**	Los Tilos **7**	Bistro Quiet **1**	Nicco's **4**
			María Elena **8**	Bomberos **2**	Speed Lunch **5**

Mineral heaven

If you are at all interested in geology, you could spend months in this part of Chile and still not be satisfied. The mountains of the *cordillera* here are brimful of minerals that are easily visible to the naked eye. Near Combarbalá, the colours are white and red, showing that the combarbalita – a marble-type rock found nowhere else in the world – is nearby. In the high mountains inland from Ovalle is one of the world's two mines of the brilliant blue stone, lapis lazuli; while at Andacollo, you may have your only chance in Chile to see small-scale gold mining in operation, although the number of miners working here has declined rapidly in recent years.

Miners in these areas often work independently and they are known as *pilquineros*. They process their findings in two types of small mills. The *trapiche* consists of two heavy vertical wheels in a container half filled with water. As the ore is ground between the wheels, the mineral sticks to mercury, which is spread on the sides of the container. The other type of mill, the *maray*, resembles a large mortar and pestle and is hand driven. Both the *trapiche* and the *maray* are rented by the miner, the rent being paid as a share of the ore.

Illapel is a small town, and can easily be covered on foot. There is a small archaeological museum next to the library in the **Casa de la Cultura** ① *Valdivieso y Constitución, just off the Plaza de Armas, Mon-Fri 0900-1300 and 1400- 1800, free,* with a bizarre and disordered collection of arrowheads, jewellery, pottery, miners' boots and newspapers so dusty you almost choke. There is no tourist office (although you could try asking for information at the Municipalidad on the Plaza), but there is a very helpful office run by **CONAF** ① *Vicuña Mackenna 93, open Mon-Sat 0830-1730.*
▶▶ *For Sleeping, Eating and other listings, see pages 161-163.*

Salamanca and around

This small, friendly town lies 32 km southeast of Illapel along the Río Choapa. It is surrounded by the dusty foothills of the Andes and has a shady plaza where craftspeople display their goods in the evenings. Halfway along the road from Illapel is the **Los Cristales Pass**, from where there are views of distant snowy mountains.

Some 2 km north of Salamanca on the Illapel road is a turning for the small town of **Chalinga,** with a church dating from 1750 (ask at the nearby convent if entry is possible). A dusty road continues from Chalinga up into the Chalinga valley, passing plantations of *pisco* grapes, fruit orchards and irrigated vegetable patches before heading up into barren mountain scenery around **Zapallar**. The teacher at the school here has made a study of the petroglyphs in the surrounding area – of which there are many – and may be able to help interested parties seek them out.

North to Combarbalá

From Illapel, a paved road leads 15 km north to the **Reserva Nacional Las Chinchillas** ① *daily 0900-1700 (or until 1800 in summer), US$2.50,* passing impressive mountains speckled with cacti and minerals. The reserve covers 4229 ha and protects the last remaining colony of chinchillas in this region. The chinchillas and six related species can be viewed from behind two-way mirrors.

After Las Chinchillas, the asphalt disappears, the mountainsides close in – red, purple and white with minerals, and covered with cacti. The bad road climbs the **Cuesta El Espino** to a height of over 2000 m, from where there are unforgettable views of the multicoloured mountains and the white snows of the Andes. A much worse

Chinchillas and follows the old railway track on an even more remote and dramatic route to Combarbalá, via mining settlements at Farellón Sánchez and Matancillas. Eventually, it rejoins the main road below Cuesta El Espino and reaches the small town of Combarbalá, 73 km north of Illapel.

Combarbalá is set in a dusty bowl surrounded by mountains. The town is famous as the home of the *combarbalita*, a semi-precious stone that was declared the National Stone of Chile in 1993. However, the town is little known, even to Chileans – the Senatur office in Santiago told a caller to "phone the appropriate embassy" when asked about Combarbalá in 2001. *Combarbalita* is similar in appearance to marble and is found nowhere else in the world. There are lots of workshops on the north side of town, particularly on Calle Flores, where you can see the craftsmen at work and buy their goods.

Sleeping

Los Vilos and the coast *p159*
A **Pichidangui**, *Francis Drake s/n, Pichidangui, T053-531114, www.hotelpichdangui.cl* Hotel with swimming pool and restaurant.
B **American Motel**, *Km 224, T053-541163.* Right on the highway and a convenient stopping place between Viña del Mar or Santiago and La Serena, good value. There are several other motels here as well.
C **El Conquistador**, *Caupolicán 210, Los Vilos, T053-541663.* Very nice rooms with bath, TV and refrigerator, big breakfast, pleasant patio, sauna, friendly, worth bargaining off season, excellent value, highly recommended. Also *cabañas*.
C **Lord Willow**, *Hostería 1444, Los Vilos, T053-541037, information T02-8572930.* Overlooking beach and harbour, collection of old firearms, with breakfast and bath, pleasant, friendly, parking, weekend disco next door.
F **Bellavista**, *Rengo 20, Los Vilos, T053-541073.* With breakfast, bath and TV in carpeted rooms, hot water, sea views, no curtains. Price per person.
F **Hostería Puquen**, *2 Poniente s/n, Pichidangui, T053-531104.* Attractive and good value.
F-G There are 3 cheap, central *residenciales* (price per person) on Caupolicán in Los Vilos, **Drake**, at No 435, **Turismo**, No 437, and **Res Angelica**, at No 627. The latter is cold and has lumpy beds.

Pichidangui has various hotels and *pensiones* at every price.

Camping
Bahía Marina de Pichidangui, *Pichidangui, T053-531120.* Sports facilities and *cabañas*.

Campomar, *Campusano s/n, Los Vilos, T053-541049.* Campsite plus *cabañas* near the town centre.

Illapel *p159, map p159*
B **Diaguitas**, *Constitución 276, T/F053-522587, hdiaguitas@entelchile.net* Noisy, with swimming pool.
B **Domingo Ortíz de Rozas** *Ignacio Silva 241, T/F053-522127.* All mod cons at this attractive 3-star.
C **American**, *Carrera 128, T053-523361.* Nice courtyard, with breakfast, bath and TV.
C **Los Tilos**, *Ignacio Silva 45, T053-523335.* With bath, breakfast and TV, friendly, but small rooms, overpriced.
E **Londres**, *Mackenna 21, T053-211906.* Basic, quiet, friendly, worth bargaining.
F **Alameda**, *Ignacio Silva 20, T053-522355.* With bath and TV, without breakfast, friendly, clean, nice patio with lemon and orange trees, cheap laundry service, recommended. Price per person.
G **Pensión María Elena**, *Esmeralda 54.* Best of the cheapies, very basic but warm and friendly.

Salamanca and around *p160*
B **Hostal Vasco**, *Bulnes 120, T053-551119.* With bath and breakfast, swimming pool.
G **Residencial O'Higgins**, *O'Higgins 430.* Breakfast extra, friendly, clean, basic, patio.

Camping
There are several basic campsites in the Chalinga valley, including one at Zapallar.

North to Combarbalá *p160*
C-D **Yagnam**, *1 block from the plaza, Combarbalá.* Clean, new hotel, friendly, room service, recommended.

F Reserva Nacional Las Chinchillas
Well-equipped *cabañas*, with kitchen
facilities, also a campsite.
G Residencial La Golondrina, *Chacabuco y
Libertad, Combarbalá*. Price per person.

🍴 Eating

Los Vilos and the coast *p159*
$$ **Alisio**, *Caupolicán 298, Los Vilos*. Seafood
and fish, good value.
$$ **Restaurant Turistico Costanera**, *Purén,
Los Vilos*. Good views over ocean, good
meals and choice of wines, nice warm bread.
Also serves a cheap menu.
$ **El Rey de la Paila Marina**, *Purén, Los Vilos*.
Good-value seafood.
$ **El Rey de la Paila Marina Vileña**, *Purén,
Los Vilos*. Fish and seafood.
$ **Pastelería/Heladería Roma**, *Caupolicán
712, Los Vilos*. Excellent cakes and ice creams.
The very helpful owners both speak English.
$ **Restaurant Crucero del Amor**, *Los Vilos*.
One of countless places on the seafront.
  Restaurants in Pichindangui tend to be
pricey, although there is a food shop.

Illapel *p159, map p159*
$$ **Bistro Quiet**, *Constitución 200 block*.
Smart, fills up at weekends.
$$ **Bufett Estación**, *Buín 452*. Smartest in
town, good food.
$$ **Nicco's**, *Ignacio Silva 219*. Good pizzas,
fancy decor, vegetarian options.
$ **Bamby Restaurant**, *Constitución 340*. Not
great quality but very cheap.
$ **Casino de Bomberos**, *Buín 590*. Incredibly
friendly, excellent value, good views of the
town, highly recommended.
$ **Luz My Pan**, *San Martín, opposite the bus
station*. Good bread and cakes.
$ **Speed Lunch**, *Constitución 160*. Friendly,
some vegetarian possibilities (ask for lentils),
not as bad as the name suggests.

Salamanca and around *p160*
$ **El Americano**, *O'Higgins y M de Montepio*.
Good lunches, also has information on the
surrounding area.
$ **Restaurant Crillón**, *on the Plaza on Calle M
de Montepio*. Friendly, excellent value
almuerzos, serves Grolsch.
$ **Restaurant Salamanca**, *Echavarría 340*,
seafood and meat, clean.

There are cheap ice creams at a shop next
to **ENTEL** on the plaza.

🍷 Bars and clubs

Los Vilos and the coast *p159*
Piel Morena, *Rengo s/n*. Summer only.
Dino's Disco, *Caupolicán*. Popular.
Zone Beach, *Rengo 86*. A favourite hangout
in summer.

Illapel *p159, map p159*
Pub Marabú, *Ignacio Silva 260*. US$3.
Bar with free drink, salsa and merengue at
the weekends.

🎉 Festivals and events

Salamanca *p160*
Holy Week is a big event in Salamanca, with
horse races *à la Chilena* and costumed
processions through the town.

🥾 Activities and tours

Illapel *p159, map p159*
Turismo Libuca, *Independencia 099,
T053-522155*. Specializes in tours of the
south for those from Illapel, but can also
arrange visits to Las Chinchillas.

🚌 Transport

Los Vilos *p159*
Bus
The main companies serving Los Vilos are
Pullman Bus, **Turbus** and **Tas Choapa**, each
with at least 5 buses daily to **Santiago**, 3½
hrs, US$4, and **La Serena** (usually at night),
6 hrs, US$6.50, as well as frequent buses to
Illapel, 1 hr, US$0.80, and **Salamanca**,
US$1.60. There is only 1 bus daily between
Pichidangui and Santiago, but north-south
buses on the Highway (for example **Inca
Bus**) also pass Los Vilos and Pichidangui.

Illapel *p159, map p159*
Bus
The bus station is at San Martín, on the 200
block. Illapel is best served by **Pullman Bus**,
which has services to **Santiago**, US$4.75,
and **La Serena**, US$5.20, via Los Vilos.
Intercomunal have 4 buses daily to **Viña**
and **Valparaíso**, US$5.20. Buses to rural

destinations leave from Independencia y Ignacio Silva; the timetables are posted at the greengrocer's at the bottom end of Ignacio Silva.

Salamanca p160
Bus
The bus company offices are on O'Higgins. Two buses an hour, from 0800 to 1800, US$0.80, run to **Illapel**, continuing either north to **La Serena** or south to **Santiago**. There are one or two rural buses daily from Salamanca to the mountain communities, as well as *colectivos* to Illapel and Chalinga.

North to Combarbalá p160
At present, there is no transport from Illapel to Combarbalá. However, the road is due to be paved by 2004, when public transport services should commence. For now, Combarbalá is reached by buses from **Ovalle** (p168), or with **Buses Combarbalá** from **Santiago**, **La Calera**, **La Ligua** and **Los Vilos**. For now, the best way to visit **Las Chinchillas** is to hire a taxi from Illapel, costing approximately US$20.

Los Vilos *p159*
Dentist Juan Rubio, *Lautaro 435, T053-541683*. **Film** *Caupolicán 667*. Also at *Rengo y Lautaro*. **Post office** *Lincoyán*. **Telephone** ENTEL, *Caupolicán 873*.

Illapel *p159, map p159*
Banks Exchange is not possible in Illapel and there are no Redbanc ATMs. **Dentist** *Vicuña Mackenna 183, T053-521010*. **Hospital** *Independencia s/n, T053-522312*. **Laundry** Alondra, *Ignacio Silva 370*, only one in town. **Post office** *Plaza de Armas*, Western Union money transfers. **Telephone** ENTEL *San Martín y Constitución*, and at *Constitución 161*.

Salamanca *p160*
Post office *Bulnes, on the plaza*. **Telephone** CTC Veronica, *Salamanca, on the plaza*. ENTEL, *M de Montepio y Bulnes, on the plaza*.

The Limarí Valley

The Limarí Valley contains much of the north of Chile in a microcosm: beaches at Tongoy, the mysteriously lush Parque Nacional Fray Jorge, countless examples of ancient rock art and wonderful mountain scenery. With remote tracks through the mountains and giant hillsides sprinkled with cacti and multicoloured minerals, it is a fine place to wander for a week or more.

Ins and outs
Getting there and around Ovalle is easily reached by regular buses: north from La Serena and destinations as far north as Arica; south from Illapel and Santiago. Note that, although Ovalle is a small city, confusingly it has two bus terminals: the **Terrapuerto Limarí** and the **Terminal Media Luna**. The Terrapuerto Limarí is by far the more important and is the only one used by all major companies. Numerous local buses link Ovalle with outlying communities. Most *colectivos* leave from Avenida Ariztía. ▸▸ *For further details, see Transport, page 168.*

Ovalle and around → *Phone code: 053. Colour map 2, C1.*
Situated inland in the valley of the Río Limarí – a fruit-growing and mining district – this lively town is a focal point for the numerous communities in the surrounding mountains. Edged by dusty hills, which are lined with vines for *pisco* grapes and orchards of avocado trees, it gets busy on market days, when local *campesinos* throng around the market area. It is famous for its *talabarterías* (saddleries) and for its products made of locally mined lapis lazuli, as well as *queso de cabra* (goat's cheese)

and dried fruits (sold in the market). The central part of town can easily be covered on foot. The **Museo del Limarí** ⓘ *Covarrubias y Antofagasta, Tue-Fri 0900-1300, 1500-1900, Sat and Sun 1000-1300, US$1, Sun free,* is housed in the old railway station and has displays of petroglyphs and a good collection of Diaguita ceramics and other artefacts (replicas on sale). There is an unofficial **tourist information** kiosk on the Plaza de Armas.

Embalse La Paloma, the largest reservoir in Chile, is 26 km southeast. On the northern shore is the small town of **Monte Patria,** with a *pisco* distillery that can be visited. From Monte Patria, a paved road leads to Chilecito and Carén, where there is the **Parque Ecológico La Gallardina** ⓘ *T053-726009, US$1.50 (US$2.20 at weekends),* containing a beautiful collection of roses and other plants and flowers amid the dry mountains.

Monumento Nacional Valle del Encanto ⓘ *about 22 km southwest of Ovalle, open all year 0800-1800, US$1,* is one of the most important archaeological sites in northern Chile. Artefacts from hunting peoples from over 2000 years ago have been found, but the most visible remains date from the Molle culture (AD 700). There are over 30 petroglyphs as well as great boulders, distributed in over sites.

Termas de Socos ⓘ *Pan-American Highway, 35 km southwest of Ovalle, US$5, bus US$2,* is a very popular resort among Chileans. There are swimming pools and individual bath tubs fed by thermal springs, as well as a sauna, Jacuzzi and water massage. ▸▸ *For Sleeping, Eating and other listings, see pages 166-168.*

Parque Nacional Fray Jorge

ⓘ *T053-620058, open Sat, Sun and public holidays only 0900-1800, last entry 1600, US$2.50.* Situated 90 km west of Ovalle and 110 km south of La Serena at the mouth of the Río Limarí, this UNESCO Biosphere Reserve covers 9959 ha and contains original temperate rainforests, which contrast with the otherwise barren surroundings. Receiving no more than 113 mm of rain a year, the forests survive because of the almost constant fog and mist covering the hills, the result of the discharge of the warm waters of the Río Limarí into the cold waters of the Pacific. The increasingly arid climate of this part of Chile has brought the habitat under threat and

Ovalle

Sleeping 🛏
Americana 1
Gran 2
Residencial Socos 4
Roxy 5
Turismo 6
Venecia 7

Eating 🍴
Bavaria 1
Café Haiti 2
Club Comercial 3

Club Social Arabe 4
D'Oscar 5
El Quijote 6
El Rincón Marino 10
Lucerna 7
Yum Yum 8

hence visits are closely controlled by **CONAF**, although scientific groups may obtain permission to visit from the Director of CONAF in La Serena ① *Córdovez 281, T051-211124*. All visitors should take particular care to leave no trace of their presence behind them. The park is reached by a dirt road leading off the Pan-American Highway. The entrance and administration are at Km 18, from where it is 10 km further to the summit of the coastal hills (known as the Altos de Talinay), which rise to 667 m. Waterproof clothing is essential. ➤➤ *For Sleeping, Eating and other listings, see pages 166-168.*

Along the Río Limarí

From Ovalle, a road leads 77 km northeast, following the course of the Río Limarí to the village of Hurtado. The route passes the Recoleta Reservoir and then follows the valley, where fat horses graze on alfalfa, vines with *pisco* grapes are strung out across what flat land there is, and the glades are planted with orchards of orange and avocado trees.

The road is paved as far as Samo Alto; shortly after is the turn-off (to San Pedro) for the **Monumento Natural Pichasca** ① *open daily 0800-1800, US$3*. Some 47 km northeast of Ovalle at an altitude of 1350 m, this park contains petrified tree trunks and archaeological remains, including a vast cave, comparable to the Cueva Milodón outside Puerto Natales, with remnants of ancient roof paintings. Gigantic rock formations can be seen on the surrounding mountains. Encouraged by the local mayor, a bright green model of a dinosaur has been erected here. Sure to be a magnet for groups of local schoolchildren, the dinosaur is supposed to be the north's answer to the sloth in the Milodon Cave near Puerto Natales, but as yet it is too early to claim that Jurassic Park has come to Pichasca. Note that it is 3 km to the park from the turn-off and about 2 km further to sites of interest.

Beyond the village of **Pichasca** are several plantations, where rickety wooden suspension bridges cross to the far side of the Río Limarí. It is a further 32 km to Hurtado and the road continues winding along the side of the valley, with the Andes now easily visible at the head of the valley. At Vado Morrillos, 4 km before Hurtado, is the **Hacienda Los Andes** ① *T053-691 822, www.haciendalosandes.com*, a centre for horseriding excursions in the area, set in a very pretty location, with a 7 km nature trail. The Hacienda is run by a German/Austrian couple with previous experience of running horseback trips, English and German spoken. Horseriding tours from one to three days are offered in the surrounding mountains, starting at US$80. If coming by bus to the hacienda, ask the driver to let you off at the bridge at Vado Morrillos – the entrance to the hacienda is just before the bridge on the right.

The road continues on to **Hurtado**, a village set at 1300 m. Excellent accommodation is available at **Tambo de Limarí** (see Sleeping below), a *hospedaje* owned by Sra Orieta. Near Hurtado is the only petroglyph in Chile depicting the sun, hinting at possible links to the Incas, and it is also possible to climb the Cerro Gigante (2825 m) and visit the site o a Diaguita cemetry.

The extremely adventurous may consider continuing from Hurtado into **Argentina** (permission must be sought from the *carabineros* in Hurtado). It is three days on horse to the pass into Argentina (4229 m); near the pass are the corrals of El Ternero, where a wall built by pre-Hispanic peoples climbs up into the snows. On the far side of the frontier, the path descends to the Laguna de los Patos, where the Argentines have a police post. However, it is then a further seven to 10 days by horse to the nearest settlement in Argentina and there is no road. It may be possible to find guides for this trip in the village of Las Breas, 22 km beyond Hurtado, where there is a small restaurant.

An easier option is to continue from Hurtado north to **Vicuña** in the Elqui Valley (see page 174) only 46 km away. This is a desolate road; there is very little traffic and no public transport, but pick-ups can be hired in Hurtado to make the trip for US$20-25. ▶▶ *For Sleeping, Eating and other listings, see pages 166-168.*

To Andacollo → *Phone code: 053. Colour map 2, C1. Population: 10,216.*

The good road inland between Ovalle and La Serena makes an interesting contrast to Ruta 5, the Pan-American Highway, with a fine pass and occasional views of snowcapped Andes across cacti-covered plains and semi-desert mountain ranges. Some 66 km north of Ovalle, a winding side road runs 27 km southeast, to **Andacollo**.

Situated in a gorge, Andacollo has been a mining centre since before the arrival of the Spanish (see box, page 160). Ruins of mines and waste tips dot the area. Two mines, one copper and one gold, still operate and there are many independent mines and *trapiches*, small processing plants, which can be visited; the gold has, however, begun to run out and, in recent years, many miners have moved away. Andacollo, however, is more famous as one of the great pilgrimage sites in Chile. In the enormous **Basilica** (1893), 45 m high and with a capacity of 10,000, is a small, carved wooden statue of the Virgen del Rosario de Andacollo, brought from Peru in the 17th century and credited with miraculous powers. Nearby is the **Templo Antiguo**, smaller and dating from 1789. There is also a museum, **Museo de Andacollo** ① *open daily 0900-1300, 1500-1900.* The tourist office on the Plaza de Armas can arrange tours to the Basilica and to mining operations.

● Sleeping

Ovalle and around *p163, map p164*
AL **Termas de Socos**, *T053-1982505.* Reasonable hotel offering full board.
A **Hotel Hacienda Juntas**, *near Monte Patria, km 41, T053-711290.* Stands in 90 ha of vineyards, with spectacular views and a swimming pool.

Accommodation is poor in Ovalle itself; try
B **Hotel Turismo**, *Victoria 295, T053-623258, F053-623536.* Parking, modern, friendly.
B-C **Gran Hotel**, *Mackenna 210 (entrance through Galería Yagnam), T053-621084, yagnam@terra.cl* Decent rooms. Bargain, ask to be away from the main road.
C **Hotel American**, *Mackenna 169, T053-620159, F053-620722.* Friendly, small rooms, overpriced.
D **Roxy**, *Libertad 155, T053-620080.* Constant hot water, big rooms, clean, friendly, patio, slightly run down. Recommended.
G **Hotel Venecia**, *Libertad 261, T053-620968.*

Clean, safe, friendly. Recommended. Price per person.
G **Res Socos**, *Socos 22, T053-629856.* Clean, family run, breakfast extra. Price per person. There are several other cheap *residenciales* in Calle Socos (short stay).

Camping
There are camping facilities at **Monumento Nacional Valle del Encanto** (price per tent) and near the **Termas de Socos**.

Parque Nacional Fray Jorge *p164*
B There is 1 *cabaña* sleeping 5 people, which may be hired.
F Basic accommodation is also available in an old hacienda, price per person, and at 2 campsites in the national park, one is at the administration centre,

Along the Río Limarí *p165, map p167*
C **Hacienda Los Andes**, *Vado Morrillos, T053-691 822,*

www.haciendalosandes.com All the rooms have a private bath and there is a sauna and a Jacuzzi that overlooks the river. Price per person for bed and breakfast. Camping (including hot showers) is also available.

F Tambo de Limarí, *Caupolican 27, Hurtado, T053-1982121.* Excellent *hospedaje* with wonderful breakfast. Owner Sra Orieta is very friendly and there is an interesting collection of ancient riding spurs, stirrups and Spanish padlocks. Recommended.

To Andacollo *p166*
There are no hotels, but some *pensiones.* During the festival, private houses rent beds and some let you pay for a shower. Contact the tourist office for details.

🍴 Eating

Ovalle and around *p163, map p164*
$$ Bavaria, *MacKenna 161.* Usual range of plastic-tasting sandwiches and main dishes, overpriced.
$$ Club Social Arabe, *Arauco 255.* Spacious glass-domed premises, limited selection of Arab dishes, not cheap.
$ Casino La Bomba, *Aguirre 364.* Very good-value *almuerzos*, run by the fire brigade.
$ Club Comercial, *Aguirre 244 (on plaza).* Open Sun for general Chilean fare.
$ El Quijote, *Arauco 294.* Intimate atmosphere, good seafood, inexpensive, Ovalle's 'bohemian' hangout.
$ La Bocca Restaurant, *Benavente 110.* Specializes in shellfish.
$ El Rincón Marino, *Victoria 400-block.* One of the better seafood restaurants beside the market.
$ Restaurant Lucerna, *Independencia 339 (opposite the market).* Opens early for breakfast, popular, interesting place doubling as a doss house for *campesinos.* Next door is **Las Tejas**, of a similar ilk.

Cafés
Café Caribe Express, *MacKenna 241.* For drinks and snacks.
Café Haiti, *Victoria 307.* Opens early for breakfast.
D'Oscar Bar, *Plaza de Armas.* Serves good real coffee and is open late.

Panadería Victoria, *MacKenna 60.* Mouthwatering cakes.
Pastelería Josti, *Libertad 427.* Good cakes.
Yum Yum, *MacKenna 21.* Good, cheap, lively.

Along the Río Limarí *p165, map p167*
$ Restaurant Flor del Valle, *Pichasca.* Cheap meals and basic accommodation.

🎭 Entertainment

Ovalle and around *p163, map p164*
Cine Cervantes, *Centro Comercial G Corral.* Cinema on the plaza.
Eskla Discotheque, *Mackenna 100-block.* Nightclub, often featuring live music.

✴ Festivals

To Andacollo *p166*
Fiesta Grande takes place **23-27 Dec** (most important day 26 Dec) and attracts 150,000 pilgrims from northern Chile. The ritual dances date from a pre-Spanish past. Transport is available from La Serena and Ovalle but 'purists' walk (torch and good walking shoes essential). Two villages are passed on the route, which starts on the paved highway, then goes along a railway track and lastly up a steep, dusty hill.

Fiesta Chica is a smaller festival on the 1st Sun of **Oct**.

Valley of the Limarí

Sleeping
Hacienda Juntas 1
Hacienda Los Andes 2
Tambo de Limarí 3

Eating 🍴
Flor del Valle 1

Ovalle and around *p163, map p164*
Market days are Mon, Wed, Fri and Sat, till
1600; the market, feria modelo, is off
Benavente, east of the town centre. There
are many *talabarterías* nearby on Benavente.

For articles made of lapis lazuli, try **Sr
Wellington Vega Alfaro**, *T053-620797*,
although his workshop, on the northern
outskirts, is difficult to reach without
transport. Phone ahead for directions.

▲ Activities and tours

Ovalle and around *p163, map p164*
Tres Valles, *Libertad 496, T053-629650*.
Worth a try for trips to Fray Jorge, Valle del
Encanto and other destinations in the area.

● Transport

Bus
Long distance Ovalle's 2 bus terminals
are the **Terrapuerto Limarí** (next to the *feria
modelo* near Benavente 500-block) and the
Terminal Media Luna (by the rodeo ring on
Ariztía Oriente). The Terrapuerto Limarí is the
only one used by all major companies (most
buses using the Terminal Media Luna have
departed from the Terrapuerto Limarí).

There are buses to **Santiago**, mostly
mid-morning or late at night, 6½ hrs, US$7;
to **La Serena**, 20 a day, 1½ hr, US$2.50
(Horvitur and Via Elqui); also to **Valparaíso**,
6 hrs, US$8, **Antofagasta**, 14 hrs, US$16, and
Arica, 24 hrs, US$21, mostly at night (**Tur
Bus, Pullman Bus, Fenix Norte**). Pullman
and **Expreso Norte** serve Illapel, US$3.

Local Rural buses – of which there are
many – leave from a terminal outside the *feria
modelo*, next to the Terrapuerto Limarí. Hourly
buses to Carén serve the **Parque Ecológico
La Gallardina**. However, there is no service
to the **Nacional Valle del Encanto**; instead
you must take a long-distance southbound
bus and ask to be dropped off; it's a 5 km
walk to the valley; flag down a bus to return.

Buses M&R, *T053-1982121, T09-8220320*,
have an erratic schedule linking Ovalle with
Hurtado. On Ovalle's market days (Mon, Wed,
Fri, Sat), 3 buses leave Hurtado between 0600
and 0630; on Tue and Thu, the buses leave
Hurtado at 1000 and 1015, on Sun, at 1230 and
1245. From Ovalle, there are three buses to
Hurtado on market days (1200, 1230 and 1500),
except for Sat, when there is just one bus at
1400. On Tue and Thu, buses leave Ovalle at
1615 and 1645, on Sun at 1700 and 1730. The
fare is US$2. These buses pass the turn off to
the **Monumento Natural Pichasca** about
42 km from the city.

The journey from Ovalle to **Andacollo**
costs US$2 by *colectivo* and US$1.40 by bus.

Taxi
Abel Olivares Rivera, *T053-620352*.
Recommended. The round trip to **Parque
Nacional Fray Jorge** costs US$30.

● Directory

Ovalle *p163, map p164*
Banks Many Redbanc ATMs on the Plaza de
Armas, including **Banco de Chile** and **Banco
Santander**. **Cycle repairs** Cycles Penna,
Benavente 360. **Internet** BigD@ddy, *Centro
Comercial Jofre, MacKenna 200-block, local 21.*
Also **Chilesat** in the same Centro Comercial.
Post office *MacKenna on the Plaza de Armas.*
Telephone CTC, *Victoria y Vicuña MacKenna,
on the Plaza de Armas.* **Useful address**
Automóvil Club de Chile, *Libertad 144,
T053-620011,* helpful, with overnight parking.

The Elqui Valley

*A dramatic cleft in the heart of the mountains, the Elqui Valley is home to two of the
north's most important cities, Coquimbo and La Serena. Inland, you will find star-filled
nights lit up by shooting stars, pisco distilleries and villages in the mountains. The
valley of the Río Elqui is one of the most attractive oases in this part of Chile. There are
mines, orchards and vineyards set against imposing arid mountains. The contrast
between the immense rock formations and the lush valley floor is overwhelming.*

Ins and outs

Getting there The cities of Coquimbo and La Serena are easily reached by countless buses from both north and south, from any one of more than 10 companies. Several flights daily from Santiago to Copiapó, Antofagasta and Iquique stop off at La Serena. For transfers to the airport, call T051-295058, or take any Vicuña-bound bus and get off at airport entrance. **Getting around** La Serena and Coquimbo are linked by buses that pass down Av Francisco de Aguirre in La Serena before travelling along the Panamericana. Taxis are plentiful and cheap. ▶▶ *For further details, see Transport, page 181.*

La Serena → *Phone code: 051. Colour map 2, C1. Population: 120,000.*

Situated nearly 500 km north of Santiago, La Serena is the capital of Región IV and is one of the most attractive cities in northern Chile. Built on a hillside 2 km inland from the Bahía de Coquimbo, the city is famous for its numerous churches, while the centre is made up of white buildings of neo-colonial style. Beneath this façade, however, La Serena has a more ancient history and residents often claim to stumble across indigenous burial sites in their back yards. The city has rapidly become a major tourist centre, being popular for its long sandy beach and its proximity to the Elqui Valley – it is full of Chilean holidaymakers in January and February.

Ins and outs

Tourist information Helpful advice is available from **Sernatur** ① *Edificio de Servicios Públicos (next to the post office on the Plaza de Armas), T/F051-225199, infocoquimbo@sernatur.cl, Mon-Fri 0845-1830 (0845-2030 in summer), Sat and Sun 1000-1400 (1000-1400 and 1600-2000 in summer). There are also kiosks at the bus terminal (summer only) and at I Balmaceda y Prat, open in theory Mon-Sat 1100-1400, 1600-1900, which are helpful and have accommodation information.*

History

La Serena was founded by Juan de Bohón, aide to Pedro de Valdivia, in 1544, destroyed by the Diaguita in 1546 and rebuilt by Francisco de Aguirre in 1549. The city was sacked by the English pirate Sharpe in 1680. In the colonial period, it was the main staging-post on the route north to Peru; many of the religious orders built churches and convents here providing accommodation for their members. In the 19th century, the city grew prosperous from copper-mining; the neo-classical mansions of successful entrepreneurs from this period can still be seen. The characteristic neo-colonial style of architecture in the centre, however, dates only from the 1950s, when the city was remodelled under the instructions of President González Videla, a lawyer, diplomat and Radical party politician, who was eager to leave his mark on his native city. González Videla ordered the drafting of an urban plan, under which Avenida Francisco de Aguirre was modernized and the Pedro de Valdivia gardens, west of the city, were built. All new buildings in the centre were constructed in Californian colonial style, although his regulation has since been modified, permitting the erection of some modern buildings.

Sights

Around the attractive Plaza de Armas, most of the official buildings can be found, including the post office and the **Casa González Videla**, the great man's residence from 1927 to 1977, which now houses the **Museo Histórico Regional** ① *Mon-Fri 1000-1800, Sat 1000-1300, US$0.80 (ticket also valid for Museo Arqueológico)*, with several rooms dedicated to his life and the history of La Serena. Opposite is the **cathedral**, built in 1844 and featuring a carillon which plays every hour. There are 29 other churches, several of which have unusual towers. **Santo Domingo**, half a block southwest of the Plaza de Armas, built in 1755 with a clock tower dating from 1912, is fronted by a small garden with statues of sea-lions. Southeast of the plaza, on Balmaceda y de La Barra, is **San Francisco,** built between 1586 and 1627, which has a baroque façade and faces a small plaza with arcades. It is home to the **Museo De Arte Religiosa** ① *Mon-Fri 1000-1300, 1600-1800, Sat 1000-1300, US$0.50,* which includes the funeral mask of Gabriela Mistral.

San Augustín, northeast of the plaza at Cantournet y Rengifo, originally a Jesuit church, dates from 1755 but has been heavily modified. Opposite this church is **La Recova,** the market, which includes a large display of handicrafts and, upstairs, several good seafood restaurants. One block south is the **Museo Arqueológico** ① *Cordóvez y Cienfuegos, muarse@entelchile.net, Tue-Fri 0930-1750, Sat 1000-1300, 1600-1900, Sun 1000-1300, US$0.80,* which has an outstanding collection of Diaguita and Molle Indian exhibits, especially of attractively decorated pottery, although they are poorly labelled. There are also some exhibits from Easter Island. Further from the centre, in the University of La Serena, is the **Museo Mineralógico Ignacio Domeyko** ① *A Muñoz 870, Mon-Fri 0930-1230, US$0.50,* for those with a particular interest in geology.

La Serena

N

0 metres 100
0 yards 100

Sleeping
Alameda **1** *B2*
Backpacker Lodging **25** *C2*
Berlín **2** *B2*

Brasilia **3** *A2*
Casa Alejandro
  Muñoz **4** *A3*
Casablanca **5** *A3*
Casa de Huéspedes **26** *C2*
Celia Rivera & María
  Pizarro **7** *C2*
Costa Real **8** *B1*
El Cobre **9** *A2*

El Escorial I **10** *A3*
Francisco de
  Aguirre **11** *B2*
Gregoria Fernández **12** *C2*
Hostal El Punto **6** *C2*
Hostal Croata **13** *A3*
Hostal Joffre **14** *C2*
Lido **15** *B2*
Londres **16** *B2*

Los Balcones de
  Aragón **17** *A3*
Mediterráneo **18** *B3*
Pucará **19** *A2*
Residencial Chile **20** *B2*
Residencial El Loa **21** *B3*
Residencial Carvajal **22** *C2*
Residencial Petit **23** *B2*
Residencial Suiza **24** *A3*

⁞ Buccaneers of the Chilean coast

Sir Francis Drake was one of the first Europeans to commit piracy along the west coast of South America but his example was soon widely followed. By the second half of the 17th century, free-booting renegades – mostly English, French and Dutch – were roaming the South Seas preying on Spanish coastal towns and shipping in the hope of getting rich quick.

Basil Ringrose has a special place among these desperadoes because he left a fascinating first-hand account of his activities. Towards the end of 1679, he set out, under the command of a Captain Sharp, to take and plunder what Ringrose describes as the "vastly rich town of Arica". On finding the Spanish defence of Arica too strong to overcome, however, they had to continue south to nearby Hilo where they managed to land and occupy the sugar factory. The besieged Spaniards agreed to supply Ringrose and his comrades "four score of beeves" on the condition that they didn't burn the sugar factory to the ground. After several days of waiting for the "beeves" to arrive, the pirates began to smell a rat and decided to burn the factory

down regardless and retreated to their ship. It was as well they did because they had no sooner re-embarked than they saw 300 Spanish horsemen advancing on their encampment. But Ringrose was still impressed by Hilo, describing it as "a valley very pleasant being all over set with figs, olives, oranges, lemons, and lime trees, and many other fruits agreeable to the palate". What Ringrose most remembered Hilo for, however, was its "good chocolate" of which they "had plundered some small quantity".

After the double disappointment of Arica and Hilo, the pirates continued south to the Bay of Coquimbo where they discovered the city of La Serena, "most excellent and delicate, and far beyond what we could expect in so remote a place". Ringrose was particularly impressed by the town's seven churches which he and his companions hoped to loot, but again news of their activities preceded them and the Spaniards had already removed the churches' treasures. Instead they "found strawberries as big as walnuts and very delicious to the taste".

From Santiago to La Serena The Elqui Valley

One block west of the Plaza de Armas is the **Parque Pedro de Valdivia** ① *1000-2000, US$1.25*, with the Parque Japonés just south of it. Avenida Francisco de Aguirre, a pleasant boulevard lined with statues and known as the **Alameda**, runs from the centre to the coast, skirting the Parque Japonés and terminating at Faro Monumental, a neo-colonial mock-castle and lighthouse, now a pub. A string of beaches stretch from here to **Peñuelas**, 6 km south, linked by the Avenida del Mar. Many apartment blocks, hotels, *cabañas* and restaurants have been built along this part of the bay. ▶▶ *For Sleeping, Eating and other listings, see pages 177-182.*

Visiting the observatories

The clear skies and dry atmosphere of the valleys around La Serena have led to the area becoming one of the astronomical centres of the world (see box, page 172). There are four observatories, one built specially to receive visitors. Personal applications for visitors' permits to the other three observatories can be made at the office at Colina Los Pinos, on a hill behind the new university ① *T051-207301*. It is critical to reserve all tours in advance – up to three or four months ahead during holiday periods. Travel agents in La Serena and Coquimbo including **Ingservtur, Gira**

⁞ The clear skies of northern Chile

With its large expanses of uninhabited desert and its dry, relatively thin atmosphere, northern Chile has become one of the great astronomical centres of the world. In the Elqui Valley alone, there are no fewer than three large observatories, built by inter-national organizations with important backing from Europe or the USA.

One, **La Silla**, is owned by European Southern Observatory (ESO), which is financed by the governments of some 10 European governments. The other two are **El Tololo**, which belongs to a consortium of US and Chilean universities, and **Las Campanas**, which is owned by the Carnegie Institute. Visitors are welcome at all these sites, but are not allowed to use the telescopes (see page 171). For this experience, you should go to **Mamalluca**, a smaller observatory in the valley built specifically for the public. It offers night-time visits and provides an opportunity to view the southern skies from the vantage point of the Elqui Valley.

The great powers of astronomy have continued to expand their operations in northern Chile. A new observatory was opened by ESO in March 1999 at **Cerro Paranal**, 120 km south of Antofagasta (see page 208). Known as the VLT ('very large telescope'), it consists of four 8-m telescopes that together are capable of picking out items on the moon as small as 1 m long. When the lenses arrived at the port of Antofagasta, the entire city centre had to be closed down to allow them to be transported to their final destination. Planning is now under way on an even larger project at Chajnantor, over 5000 m up in the Andes; this giant observatory, with 64 12-m radio telescopes, is being financed by ESO along with the governments of the USA and Japan.

These new developments are not without controversy, however. Construction of Cerro Paranal was held up by local landowners, who refused to renounce their rights to permit mining activity on their land (which would threaten the observatory with increased dust). Eventually, the Chilean government was forced to introduce some new legislation permitting it to buy out the landowners to enable the project to go ahead.

Tour and **Turismo Cristóbal**, receive tickets from the observatories and arrange tours to Mamalluca, as well as occasionally to El Tololo (US$22 per person) and La Silla. If you can arrange tickets directly with the observatory, taxi drivers will provide transport. ▶▶ *For further details, see Transport, page 181.*

Some visitors to the large observatories complain that they do not get as much of an insight as they had expected. Bear in mind that trained astronomers have to reserve years in advance to use the equipment and that a day tour will not be the beginning of your astronomical career – it will, though, give you a window onto the workings of some of the most important telescopes on earth.

El Tololo ⓘ *www.ctio.noao.edu, open to visitors by permit only Sat 0900-1200, 1300-1600. For permits (free), write to Casilla 603, La Serena, T051-205200, F051-205212, then pick your permit up before 1200 on the day before your visit from the office at Colina Los Pinos.* Situated at 2200 m, 87 km southeast of La Serena in the Elqui valley, 51 km south of Vicuña, this observatory belongs to Aura, an association of US and Chilean universities. It possesses what was until recently the largest telescope in the southern hemisphere (diameter 4 m), six other telescopes and a radio telescope. During holiday periods apply for a visitor's permit well in advance; at other times it is worth trying for a cancellation the day before. The administration will insist that you have private transport; you can hire a taxi, US$33, but you will require the registration number when you book. Motorcycles are, apparently, not permitted to use the access road.

La Silla ⓘ *www.ls.eso.org, open Sat except in Jul and Aug, 1430-1730. For permits, register in advance at Alonso de Córdoba 3107, Santiago, To2-2285006, or write to Casilla 567, La Serena, To51-224527.* Located at 2400 m, 156 km northeast of La Serena, this belongs to ESO (European Southern Observatory), is financed by eight EU countries and comprises 14 telescopes. To reach La Silla, head north from La Serena for 120 km along the Panamericana to the turn-off, then another 36 km.

Las Campanas ⓘ *www.lco.cl, open Sat 1430-1730. For permits, write to Casilla 601, La Serena, To51-224680.* This observatory is at 2510 m, 162 km northeast of La Serena, 30 km north of La Silla. It belongs to the Carnegie Institute, has five telescopes and is altogether a smaller facility than the other two. To get to Las Campanas, follow the Panamericana, take the turning for La Silla and then turn north after 14 km.

Mamalluca ⓘ *Visitor bookings from Gabriela Mistral 260, La Serena, To51-411352, obser_mamalluca@yahoo.com, visits daily at 2100, 2300, 0100 in summer, 1800, 2000, 2200 in winter, US$5.50 plus transport (US$2) per person.* Situated at 1500 m, 6 km north of Vicuña, this new observatory was built specifically for the public and is the only one where visitors can actually look through a telescope at the night sky. The first telescope, diameter 30 cm, was donated by El Tololo. There is also a multimedia centre here. Advance booking is strongly recommended. Spanish- and English-speaking guides are available for groups of five or more with advance notice.

Coquimbo and the coast

Coquimbo → *Phone code: 051. Colour map 2, C1. Population: 122, 000.*

On the same bay as La Serena and only 84 km from Ovalle, Coquimbo was used during the colonial period as a port for La Serena, attracting attention from English pirates, including Francis Drake, who visited in 1578. A statue to Drake was erected in the city in 1998. Legends of buried treasure at Bahía la Herradura de Guayacán persist to this day. From these small beginnings, Coquimbo grew into a city in the 19th century, when it – and the separate centre of Guayacán – became important in the processing of copper. By 1854, there were two large copper foundries in Coquimbo and in 1858 the largest foundry in the world was built in Guayacán.

Today, the city depends on the port for its vitality and economic solvency. It has one of the best harbours on the coast and several major fish-processing plants. The city is strung along the north shore of a peninsula, with most of the commercial life centred on three streets that run between the port and the steep hillside on which are perched many of the poorer houses. On the south shore of the peninsula lies the suburb of **Guayacán**, where there is an iron-ore loading port, a steel church designed by Eiffel, an English cemetery and a huge cross, the **Cruz del Tercer Milenio**, erected to mark the millennium. It is possible to climb the 83-m cross for a charge of US$1.50. In 1981, heavy rain uncovered 39 tenth-century burials of humans and llamas, which had been sacrificed; the exhibits are on display in the **Museo del Sitio** ⓘ *Plaza Gabriela Mistral, Jan and Feb only, Mon-Sat 0930-2030, Sun 0930-1400, free.* It doubles as a tourist information office. Travellers should be aware that Coquimbo has a reputation for theft. In summer, it is possible to take boat trips around the harbour and to Punta Lobos on the bay ⓘ *regular departures, US$3.* ▸▸ *For Sleeping, Eating and other listings, see pages 177-182.*

The coastal resorts

The coast around Coquimbo has some great beaches; the closest is at **La Herradura**, 2½ km from Coquimbo, a slightly upmarket suburb that has the best beaches in the bay and numerous *cabañas* and restaurants. Also nearby is a resort complex called **Las Tacas**, with beach, swimming pool, tennis and apartments. Heading south, there are good swimming beaches at **Totoralillo**, 12 km beyond Coquimbo, and a 10-km beach east of **Guanaqueros**, a fishing village on the southern coast of a large bay, 37 km south of Coquimbo. **Tongoy**, 13 km further on is an old fishing port occupying the whole of a small peninsula. It is now a rapidly growing resort and well worth a visit, with two large beaches: the Playa Grande to the south (14 km long) and the Playa Socos to the north.

Upper Elqui Valley

Vicuña, the main town in the Elqui Valley, lies 66 km east of La Serena. The road is paved for another 37 km beyond, as far as Pisco Elqui. Most of the tiny towns here have but a single street. Many tour operators in La Serena offer day trips as far as Pisco Elqui, but you really need to stay overnight to experience the wonder of the upper valley.

The valley is the centre of *pisco* production: of the nine distilleries in the valley, the largest is Capel in Vicuña. *Huancara*, a delicious fortified wine introduced by the Jesuits, is also produced in the valley. The Río Elqui has been dammed east of El Molle, 30 km east of La Serena. This has forced the relocation of five small towns in the valley and has also led to increased winds in the valley, according to locals.

Coquimbo

Sleeping		Eating
Iberia 1	Prat 3	La Bahía 1
Lig 2	Vegamar 4	Sol y Pimienta del Capitán Denny 2

0 metres 200
0 yards 200

The Elqui Valley in the words of its poet

"It is a heroic slash in the mass of mountains, but so short as to be little more than a green-banked torrent, yet small as it is one comes to love it as perfect. It contains in perfection all that man could ask of a land in which to live: light, water, wine and fruit. And what fruit! The tongue which has tasted the juice of its peaches and the mouth which has eaten of its purple figs will never seek sweetness elsewhere.

The people of the Elqui take remarkable pride in their green soil.

Whenever there is a hump, a ridge or bare patch without greenery, it is because it is naked rock. Wherever the Elquino has a little water and three inches of soil, however poor, he will cultivate something: peaches, vines or figs. That the leafy, polished vines climb only a little way up the mountainsides is because if they were planted higher, they would wither in the pitiless February sun."

Gabriela Mistral, quoted in Jan Reed, *The Wines of Chile* (Mitchell Beazley, 1994).

Vicuña → *Phone code: 051. Colour map 2, C2. Population: 7,716.*

This small, friendly town was founded in 1821. On the west side of the plaza is the Municipalidad, built in 1826 and topped in 1905 by a medieval-style tower – the **Torre Bauer** – prefabricated in Germany and imported by the German-born mayor of the time. Inside the Municipalidad is a gallery of past local dignitaries. Also on the plaza are the **Iglesia Parroquial**, dating from 1860, and the **tourist office** ⓘ *Mistral 200, T051-209125*.

Museo Gabriela Mistral ⓘ *Gabriela Mistral 759, Mon-Sat 1000-1900, Sun 1000-1800, shorter hrs off season, US$0.75, students half price,* contains manuscripts, books, awards and many other details of the poet's life. Next door is the house where the poet was born. **Museo Entomológico** ⓘ *Calle Chacabuco 334, daily 1000-2100 in summer; Mon-Fri 1030-1330 and 1530-1930, Sat-Sun 1030-1900 in winter, US$0.50,* has over 3000 insect species displayed. **Solar de los Madariaga** ⓘ *Gabriela Mistral 683, open Jan, Feb and holidays only, Mon-Fri 1000-1900, US$0.70,* is a former residence containing artefacts belonging to a prominent local family. There are good views from Cerro La Virgen, north of town.

Vicuña

Sleeping ●		
Cabañas Yunkai **7**	La Elquina **1**	Sol del Valle **5**
Hostería Vicuña **2**	Residencial Mistral **3**	Valle Hermosa **6**

0 metres 300
0 yards 300

From Santiago to La Serena The Elqui Valley

The **Capel Pisco distillery** ① *open Dec-May Mon-Sat 1000-1800, no booking required, free, guided tours (in Spanish)*, lies 1½ km east of Vicuña, to the right of the main road. The new observatory of **Mamalluca** is 6 km north of Vicuña. ⟩⟩ *For Sleeping, Eating and other listings, see pages 177-182.*

The valley

From Vicuña a *ripio* road runs south via Hurtado (Km 46), Pichasca (Km 85) and the Monumento Natural Pichasca to Ovalle (Km 120); for details, see pages 163- 165. The main road through the Elqui Valley continues east another 18 km to **Rivadavia**, where the rivers Turbio and Claro meet. Here the road divides, the main route (Route 41) winds through the mountains on a good, partly paved road to the Argentine frontier at **Paso Agua Negra** (4775 m). Chilean immigration and customs ① *open 0800-1700*, are at Juntas, 84 km west of the frontier (88 km east of Vicuña), where there is also a turning to Baños del Toro and the **Mina el Indio**. The mine can be visited only with a permit (obtainable from **Compañía Minería del Indio**, Baño Industrial Piñuelas, La Serena), and may be forced to close in the coming years because of pollution concerns.

The other branch of the road runs through Paihuano to **Monte Grande**, where the schoolhouse in which Gabriela Mistral lived and was educated by her sister is now a museum ① *C Principal s/n, T051-415015, Tue-Sun 1000-1300, 1500-1800 (until 1900 in Jan and Feb), US$0.50*. The poet's tomb is situated at the edge of town, opposite the **Artesanos de Cochiguaz** *pisco* distillery, which is open to the public. Here the road forks, one branch leading to the **Cochiguaz valley**. There is no public transport along this road, but there are several New Age settlements – it is said that the valley is an important energy centre – and a number of campsites. At night, there is no better place on earth to star gaze. When the moon is new, or below the horizon, the stars seem to be hanging in the air; spectacular shooting stars can be seen every couple of seconds, as can satellites crossing the night sky.

Pisco Elqui, with a population of 500, is situated 2 km south of Monte Grande along the main road. It is an attractive village with the newly restored Iglesia de Nuestra Señora Rosario fronting onto a shady plaza. Here is the **Tres Erres** *pisco* distillery, which is open to the public for free; the vineyards themselves are now covered by nets to protect them from the winds caused by the new dam. Pisco Elqui is famous for its night skies and beautiful scenery and is also a New Age centre, where all sorts of alternative therapies and massages are available. Horses can be hired, $4 per hour with guide, for exploring the surrounding area – ask at the Hotel Elqui (see Sleeping below).

North of La Serena

Heading north

It is 218 km north from La Serena to Vallenar, through a sparsely populated district usually bypassed by travellers. Thirty-five kilometres north of La Serena is **Caleta Hornos**, an impoverished fishing village with several restaurants where excellent seafood is served (*locos* are sometimes available). The Panamericana then climbs to an arid plateau; 21 km beyond Caleta Hornos is a turning eastwards to **La Higuera**, a small town that once thrived from the iron ore mine at **El Tofo** on the opposite side of the valley. This was once one of the largest iron ore mines in the world; the mine stacks can clearly be seen from the Panamericana, as can the eerie eucalyptus trees on top of the hill, kept alive by the coastal fog. Only the guardian of the mine lives here now, but it is worth driving up to El Tofo to see the ghost town and for the spectacular views down to the coast. ⟩⟩ *For Sleeping, Eating and other listings, see pages 177-182.*

Reserva Nacional Pinguino de Humboldt

Sixteen kilometres north of the turn-off for El Tofo, a road heads westwards from the Panamericana, signposted for **Punta de Choros**. This *ripio* road leads through a rugged dry river valley for 20 km before reaching the small village of **Los Choros Bajos**, where the main activity is growing olives; the groves of olive trees provide a beautiful green backdrop to the harshness of the desert. There is a restaurant serving basic meals here, but it is better to continue a further 22 km towards the coast to Punta de Choros, the departure point for visiting the **Reserva Nacional Pinguino de Humboldt**.

This reserve consists of three islands: Chañaral, Choros and Damas. It was founded to preserve the coast's marine life, which includes many penguins, sea-lions and dolphins, as well as wonderful birdlife. The combination of this and the coast's rugged isolation means that visits here will not be quickly forgotten. To visit the reserve, tours are available from La Serena and Vallenar or you can hire a boat with the local fishermen (around US$50 for up to 10 people). Isla Damas is the only island at which it is possible to disembark (entrance to the island costs US$2.50) and here camping is allowed, but before visiting or camping on the island you must seek permission from CONAF in Punta de Choros (T051-272798); there is also a toilet on Isla Damas but no drinking water. From the turning to Punta de Choros, the Panamericana continues north, passing several small mining towns. At Domeyko, 165 km north of La Serena, a *ripio* road leads west to the coast towards the northern sector of the Reserva Nacional, based around the small *caleta* at Chañaral.

● Sleeping

La Serena *p169, map p170*

La Serena is suffering from the lack of Argentinian tourists, hence prices are much more reasonable than they once were, and discounts are often offered. The Panamericana from La Serena to Coquimbo is lined with cheaper accommodation and restaurants. There are also hotels and other accommodation along Av del Mar, 500 m off the highway.

AL Costa Real, *Av de Aguirre 170, T051-221010, www.costareal.cl* 5-star hotel with restaurant, bar, pool and conference centre.

AL Francisco de Aguirre, *Córdovez 210, T051-222991, www.hotelfranciscodeaguirre.tie.cl* 4-star, with breakfast, shower, good rooms, reasonable restaurant.

A Los Balcones de Aragón, *Cienfuegos 289, T051-212419, www.losbalconesdearagon.cl* Parking, breakfast, modern.

A Mediterráneo, *Cienfuegos 509, Casilla 212, T/F051-225837*. Recommended by readers for its good breakfast.

A Pucará, *Balmaceda 319, T051-211966, F051-211933*. Modern, clean, helpful, quiet, with bath and breakfast.

B Berlín, *Córdovez 535, T051-222927, F051-223575*. Clean, safe, efficient, good value. Recommended.

B El Escorial I, *Colón 617, T051-224793, hotelescorial@entelchile.net* Good, reasonably priced, with breakfast and all mod cons.

B-C Londres, *Córdovez 550, T051-219066, hotellondres@hotmail.com* With bath or without, restaurant, old fashioned.

C Alameda, *Av de Aguirre 452, T051-213052*. Run down, but clean and comfortable.

C Brasilia, *Brasil 555, T051-225248, brasilia@entelchile.net* Friendly, small rooms.

C Lido, *Matta 547, T051-213073*. Hot water, clean, friendly.

C Res Suiza, *Cienfuegos 250, T051-216092, residencial.suiza@terra.cl* With bath and breakfast, good beds, recommended.

C-E Hostal Croata, *Cienfuegos 248, T/F051-224997, hostalcroata@entelchile.net* With bath or without, with breakfast, laundry facilities, cable TV, patio, hospitable, good value. Recommended.

C-F El Punto, *Andres Bello 979, T051-228474, www.punto.de* Recently refurbished rooms with or without bath, with breakfast, tasteful, comfortable, café, laundry, parking, English and German spoken, highly recommended.

D El Cobre, *Colón y Matta, T051-221457*. Large rooms, clean.

D Res Chile, *Matta 561, T051-211694*. Basic, without bath, small rooms, clean, hot water morning only, overpriced.

D Rosa Canto, *Cantournet 976, T051-213954*. Kitchen, comfortable, family run, good value.

D San Juan, *Balmaceda 827*. Clean, central.
F *Amuñategui 315*. With bath, kitchen facilities, patio, good beds. Recommended. Price per person.

F Backpacker Lodging, *El Santo 1058, T051-227580*. Kitchen facilities, central, also camping. Price per person.

F Casa Alejandro Muñoz, *Brasil 720, T051-211619*. Accommodation in family home in old part of town, hot showers, good breakfast, garden, English and French spoken, friendly atmosphere. Price per person.

F Casa de Huéspedes, *El Santo 1410, T051-213557*. Convenient for bus terminal, hot water, cable TV, clean, friendly. Price per person including breakfast. Recommended.

F Casona de Cantournet, *Vicuña 414, T051-217162, casablancahotel@123.cl* With bath, huge rooms in old mansion, comfortable. Price per person.

F Gregoria Fernández, *Andrés Bello 1067, T051-224400, gregoria_Fernández@hotmail.com* Clean, friendly and very helpful (good local information), good beds, some rooms with bath, 3 blocks from bus terminal, garden, excellent breakfast, price per person. Highly recommended. Fills up quickly so book ahead; if full she will divert you to her mother's house, also good but less so for the bus station.

F Hostal Joffre, *Rgto Coquimbo 964 (entre Peni y Amuñátegui), T051-222335, hostaljofre@hotmail.com* With bath and breakfast, good beds, garden, near bus terminal. Recommended. Tours of Elqui valley arranged; Hector is the best guide. Price per person.

F Res Carvajal, *Av Santo 1056, T/F051-224059*. Family home, kitchen facilities, central camping. Price per person.

F Res El Loa, *O'Higgins 362, T051-210304*. Without bath, with breakfast, good inexpensive home cooking, friendly, good value. Price per person.

F Res Lorena, *Cantournet 950, T051-223380, hostal_lorena@msn.com* Quiet, pleasant. Price per person.

F Res Petit, *de la Barra 586, T051-212536*. Hot water. Price per person.

G Celia Rivera, *Las Rojas 21, T051-215838*. Near terminal, use of kitchen, clean, friendly. Price per person.

G Maria Pizarro, *Las Rojas 18, T051-229282*. Very welcoming, near bus terminal, laundry facilities, garden, camping, very helpful. Recommended repeatedly.

Youth hostel
F Res Limmat, *Lautaro 914, T/F051-211373*. With breakfast, central, patio, tours offered, English and German spoken. Price per person; Hostelling International reduction. Recommended.

Motels and cabañas
A-C Cabañas Los Papayos, *Gonzalez Videla, Huertos 66/67, 2 km south of city (Vista Hermosa bus), T051-294153, F051-293233*. Cheaper out of season, 2 bedroom cabins, pool, gardens. Recommended.

A/B Canto del Agua, *Av del Mar 2200, T051-216630, F051-241767*. Very good, pleasant *cabañas*, also apartments.

A/B Hostal Del Mar, *Cuatro Esquinas 0680 (near beach), T051-22559*. Also apartments, clean, friendly.

A/B La Fuente, *Av del Mar 5665, T051-245755, F051-541259*. Apartments, cable TV, parking, very good. Several more motels along Av del Mar.

A/B Les Mouettes, *Av del Mar 2500, T051-225665, F051-226278*. Good restaurant, includes breakfast. Recommended.

B Motel/Cabañas El Palmar, *Av del Mar 5700, T051-247983, F051-231576*.

Camping
Antares, *Los Pescadores 4655, Peñuelas, T/F051-243753*. Price for up to 6 people.
Hipocampo, *Av del Mar, 4 km south of La Serena, T/F051-241316*. Reached by Coquimbo bus (get off at Colegio Adventista). English spoken.
Maki Payi, *153 Vegas Norte, 5 km north of La Serena, T051-213628*. Near sea, friendly, also *cabañas*. Recommended.
Sole di Mare, *Peñuelas Vega Sur, T051-312531*. On seafront, fully equipped.

Coquimbo *p173, map p174*
Accommodation is cheaper than La Serena.
C Lig, *Aldunate 1577, T051-311171, F051-313717*. Comfortable, friendly, with breakfast, overpriced, near bus terminal.
D Prat, *Bilbao y Aldunate, T/F051-311845*. Comfortable, with breakfast, pleasant.
D-E Iberia, *Lastra 400, T051-312141, F051-326307*. Cheaper without bath. Friendly. Recommended.
E Vegamar, *Las Heras 403, T051-311773*. Shared bath, basic.

The coastal resorts *p174*

C **Cabañas Bahia Club**, *Guanaqueros, T051-395819, camping1@entelchile.net* Cabañas for three people with kitchens, on the waterfront. Recommended. Camping also available.

D **La Herradura**, *Av La Marina 200, La Herradura, T/F051-261647*. Rooms with bath, restaurant attached.

Camping
Camping Oasis, *Guanaqueros, T051-395319*. On the beach; price per site.
Camping La Herradura, *La Herradura, T051-263867, mac-food@ctcinternet.cl* Price for up to 5 people.

Vicuña *p175, map p175*
AL-A **Cabañas Yunkai**, *O'Higgins 72, T051-411195, yunkai@latinmail.com* Cabañas for 4/6 persons, pool, restaurant.
A-B **Hostería Vicuña**, *Sgto Aldea 101, T051-411144, www.hosteriavicuna.cl* Swimming pool, tennis court, restaurant, parking.
D **La Elquina**, *O' Higgins 65, T051-411317*. Lovely garden, laundry and kitchen facilities.
D **Valle Hermoso**, *Gabriela Mistral 706, T/F051-411206*. Clean, comfortable, parking. Recommended.
F **Sol del Valle**, *Gabriela Mistral 741. T051-411078*. With breakfast, bath, TV, vineyard, restaurant, swimming pool, recommended. Price per person.
G **Residencial Restaurant Mistral**, *Gabriela Mistral 180, T051-412853*. Gardens very run down, basic, hot water, clean. Price per person.

Camping
G *Gabriela Mistral 152, T09-4286158*. Hot showers, kitchen.
G **Las Tinajas**, *east end of Chacabuco*. Swimming pool, restaurant.

The valley *p176*
Accommodation in the valley is much cheaper outside Jan and Feb. If you're heading for the Argentine border, there is basic, clean accommodation at **Huanta** (Guanta on many maps), Km 46 from Vicuña; ask for Guillermo Aliaga. Huanta is also the last chance to buy food. The following options are all in Pisco Elqui.
AL **Los Mistérios de Elqui**, *A Prat s/n, Pisco*

Elqui, T051-1982544, www.misteriosdeelqui.cl Plush *cabañas*, sleep 4, swimming pool, good expensive restaurant.
A-B **El Tesoro del Elqui**, *Pisco Elqui, T/F1982609, www.pisco.de* Cabañas for up to 4, pleasant gardens, pool, German spoken.
A-B **Los Dátiles**, *A Prat s/n, Pisco Elqui, T051-1982540, elqui_datil@yahoo.com* Cabañas sleep 5, swimming pool, good restaurant.
C **Elqui**, *O'Higgins s/n, Pisco Elqui, T051-1982523*. Hot shower, good restaurant. Recommended.
F **Casa Valentina**, *Rodriguez s/n, Pisco Elqui, fampintz@hotmail.com* With breakfast, friendly, helpful, informative, English and German spoken, recommended.
G **Hospedaje**, *Prat 27, Pisco Elqui*. Cheapest option, friendly, watch out for fleas.

Camping
El Olivo, *Pisco Elqui*. Small restaurant, pool, excellent facilities. Well-stocked supermarket 1 block from the plaza.
Sol de Barbosa, *Pisco Elqui*. Showers, open all year, price per site.

North of La Serena *p176*
C **Cabañas Los Delfines**, *Pilpilen s/n, sitio 33, Punta de Choros, T09-6396678*. Cabins for up to 6 people. There are other eating and accommodation options in the area.

⦿ Eating

La Serena *p169, map p170*
Eating tends to be expensive in La Serena – Coquimbo is cheaper. For good cheapish fish lunches, try the restaurants on the upper floor of the Recova market where you will be immediately assailed by numerous waiters. The quality of restaurants, especially on Av del Mar, varies considerably; often many dishes on the menu are not available.
$$ **Bavaria**, *E de la Barra 489*. International menu, good service, plastic restaurant chain.
$$ **Ciro's**, *Av de Aguirre 431, T051-213482*. Old fashioned, good lunch. Recommended.
$$ **Donde El Guatón**, *Brasil 750*. Parrillada, paradise for meat eaters, also good seafood, expensive.
$$ **El Cedro**, *Prat 572*. Serves expensive Arabian cuisine.
$$ **La Mía Pizza**, *O'Higgins 360, T051-215063*. Italian, good value (another branch on Av del Mar 2100 in summer, T051-212232).

Pastissima Limitado, *O'Higgins 663*. $$
Wide variety of pizzas and delicious
pancakes, not cheap, live music and dancing
at the weekends.
Diavoletto, *Prat 565 and O'Higgins 531*. $$-$
Fast food, popular.
Mai Lai Fan, *Cordóvez 740*. Good $$-$
Chinese, reasonably priced *almuerzo*.
Plaza Royal, *Prat 465*. Light meals and $$-$
snacks, pleasant. Recommended.
Qahlûa, *Balmaceda 655*. Good fish, $$-$
seafood, popular, cheap.
Taiwan, *Cantournet 844*. Cantonese, $$-$
good quality, reasonably priced.

Cafés
Bocaccio, *Prat y Balmaceda*. Good cakes,
modern, smart, popular.
Bravissimo, *Balmaceda 545*. The best spot
for ice cream.
Café do Brasil, *Balmaceda 461*. Good coffee.
Tahiti, *Córdovez 540, local 113*. Real coffee,
pastries. Recommended.

Coquimbo *p173, map p174*
According to the tourist office in La Serena,
the best seafood is to be had at Coquimbo; it
is especially cheap in the municipal market,
Melgarejo, entre Bilbao y Borgoño.
Sal y Pimienta del Capitán Denny, $$$-$$
Aldunate 769. One of the best in town:
pleasant, old fashioned, mainly fish cooked
in Chilean style.
Crucero, *Valera*. Excellent seafood. $$
La Picada, *Costanera*. Excellent, good $$
pebre. Near statue of O'Higgins.
Mai Lai Fan, *Av Ossandón 1*. Reasonable $$
Chinese food.
La Bahía, *Pinto 1465*. Excellent, good value. $
La Barca, *Ríos y Varela*. Modest but good. $

Vicuña *p175, map p175*
Club Social de Elqui, *Gabriela Mistral 435*. $$
Very good, attractive patio, good-value
almuerzo, real coffee.
Halley, *Gabriela Mistral 404*. Good meat $$
dishes, swimming pool (US$5 entry).
Pizzería Virgos, *Plaza*. Mid-range pizzas. $$
Mistral, *Gabriela Mistral 180*. Very good, $
popular with locals, good-value *almuerzo*.
Yo Y Soledad, *Gabriela Mistral 364*. $
Inexpensive, good.

Bars and clubs

La Serena *p169, map p170*
Most of the clubs are on the Av del Mar and
in Peñuelas but in town, you should try:
Afroson Taberna, *Balamceda 824*. Salsa and
frequent live music, good food and fun
company. Recommended.
Bar Real, *on the plaza, Los Carrera y Cordovez*.
Nice bar with colonial-style interior.
B-Cool, *Av 4 Esquinas s/n*. Recommended.
Café del Patio, *Prat 470*. Café-bar with 'Tijuana
Blues' live music from 2100 to the early hours,
and the 'Beatles Club' from 2300 on Sat. Also
tour agency (see Activities and tours below).
El Faro, *Av del Mar y Av Francisco Aguirre*.
A pricey but good pub.
Pub-Discosalsa Kamanga, *Costanera 4785*.
University crowd, fun, recommended.
VIP, *Edo de la Barra 645*. Popular night spot,
intimate atmosphere. Recommended.

Entertainment

La Serena *p169, map p170*
Cine Centenario, *Córdovez 399*. There is also
a multiplex cinema complex in the Mall
Plaza (see Shopping below).

Festivals and events

Coquimbo *p173, map p174*
Coquimbo hosts **La Pampilla**, by far the
biggest Independence Day celebrations in
Chile. Between 200,000 and 300,000 people
come from all over the country for the fiesta,
which lasts for a week. Things get going on 14
Sep, and the partying does not stop until 21
Sep. It costs a nominal US$1.50 to gain access
to the area where the main dancing tents are
to be found, as well as much typical Chilean
food and drink. You have to pay to enter the
peñas, but there also free communal areas. Big
bands such as Illapu and La Ley have played
here in recent years, as well as *cumbia* bands
from Argentina and Colombia.

Shopping

La Serena *p169, map p170*
For handicrafts try **Cema-Chile**, *Los Carrera 562*,
or **La Recova** handicraft market on Cantournet
and Cienfuegos, though many items sold here
are imported from Peru and Bolivia.

Good supermarkets include **Las Brisas**, *Cienfuegos y Cordóvez*, open 0900-2200, and **Rendic**, *Balmaceda 561*, open 0900-2300. There is also a big new shopping centre, the **Mall Plaza**, on the Panamericana, next to the bus station.

▲▲ Activities and tours

Several agencies offer similar tours of the region. Approximate tour prices: Valle del Elqui US$20, Parque Nacional Fray Jorge US$28, Tongoy US$24, city tour US$9, Mamalluca observatory US$16, Reserva Nacional Los Pingüinos and the Isla Damas US$35. **Gira Tour**, *Prat 689, T051-221992, giratour@ctcinternet.cl*, and **Ingservtur**, *Matta 611, T/F051-220165, www.ingservtur.cl*, also offer tours to Valle del Encanto, Andacollo and Isla Chañaral.

The following offer a range of local tours including trekking and climbing options: **Elquitour**, *Matta 522, T051-214846*. **Friends**, *Los Carrera 515, T051-215517, www.turismofriends.cl* **Talinay Adventure Expeditions/Inca Travel**, *both at Café del Patio (Prat 470)*. **Tourandes**, *Prat 595, T051-210931, www.tourandes.cl* **Valle Mar**, *Los Carrera 594, T051-213784, agvallemar@123.com*

⊙ Transport

La Serena *p169, map p170*
Air
Aeropuerto La Florida, *5 km east of the city, T051-271812*. To **Santiago** and **Copiapó**, Lan Chile, 45 mins.

Bus
Local The bus terminal is at *El Santo y Amunátegui* (about 8 blocks south of the centre). City buses cost US$0.25. To **Coquimbo**, bus No 8 from Av Aguirre y Cienfuegos, US$0.45, every few mins; to **Vicuña**, with **Via Elqui** and **Megal Bus**, every ½ hr, 1 hr, US$1.75, the buses continue to **Pisco Elqui**, US$2.50, last one at 2000.

Colectivos to **Coquimbo** from Av Aguirre y Balmaceda; to **Vicuna** from Domeyko y Balmaceda, US$2.50; to **Andocollo**, yellow *colectivos* from Domeyko. *Colectivos* also operate on fixed routes throughout city.

La Silla and Las Campanas **observatories** can be reached without private transport by taking any bus towards Vallenar (see below) getting out at the junction (*desvío*) and hitching from there.

Long distance Buses daily to **Santiago**, several companies, 7-8 hrs, US$8 classic, US$10 *semi cama*, US$13 *cama*; to **Arica**, 20 hrs, US$24; to **Calama**, 16 hrs, US$20; to **Vallenar**, 3 hrs, US$4; to **Valparaíso**, 7 hrs, US$10; to **Caldera**, 6 hrs, US$7; to **Antofagasta**, several companies, 12 hrs, US$15, and to **Iquique**, 17 hrs, US$22.

Taxi
City taxis charge a flat rate of US$0.75 plus US$0.20 for every 200 m. A recommended firm is **Cecilia Cruz**, *T051-222529, T09-5510579*, which charges US$63 to La Silla.

Coquimbo and the coast *p173, map p174*
Bus
Terminal at Varela y Garriga. To **La Serena**, every few mins, US$0.45; to **Guanaqueros**, 45 mins, US$0.80; to **Tongoy**, 1 hr, US$1, with **Ruta Costera**, frequency varies according to day (more on Sun) and season. There are also *colectivos* to **Guanaqueros**, US$1.40 and to **Tongoy**, US$1.70.

Upper Elqui valley *p174*
Bus
Buses depart from Pisco Elqui to **La Serena**, US$2.50, 6 a day, via Vicuña. From Vicuña to **La Serena**, about 10 a day (more in summer), mostly with **Via Elqui** or **Megal Bus**, 1st 0800, last 1930, 1 hr, US$1.75, also *colectivo* from Plaza de Armas, US$2.50; to **Santiago** via La Serena, with **Via Elqui** and **Turbus**, US$10; to **Pisco Elqui**, 10 a day, with **Vía Elqui** and **Frontera Elqui**, 1 hr, US$2. Also local buses from the plaza in Vicuña to **Monte Grande**. There is no public transport beyond Rivadavia, although El Indio mine transport may give lifts as far as Juntas.

North of La Serena *p176*
There is no public transport to Punta de Choros, but tours are readily available from La Serena; traffic on the road between Punta de Choros, and the Panamericana is relatively frequent, especially at weekends, so hitching is also possible.

La Serena *p169, map p170*

Airline offices LanChile, *Prat y Balmaceda, T051-315099*, also an office in the Mall Plaza.

Banks If heading north note that La Serena is the last place to change TCs before Antofagasta. **Corp Banca**, *O'Higgins 529*, Visa. ATMs at **Banco Santander**, *Córdovez 351*; **Banco Sud Americano**, *Córdovez 699*; **Banco Santiago**, *Balmaceda 1015*; **Banco de Chile**, *Prat 481*; **Banco BHIF**, *Prat 528*; **Banco BCI**, *Prat 614*; also at the **Las Brisas** supermarket. **Car hire** Avis, *Av de Aguirre 063, T051-227171*; **Budget**, *Balmaceda 3820, T051-290241*; **Daire**, *Balmaceda 3812, T051-226933*, recommended, good service; **Flota Verschae**, *Fransisco de Aguirre 0240, T051-27645*, good value, recommended; **Hertz**, *Av de Aguirre 068, T051-227171*, prices range from US$40 to US$80 per day; **La Florida**, *at airport, T051-271947*. Cheapest is **Gala**, *Balmaceda 1785, T051-221400*. **Casas de Cambio** **Intercam**, *E de la Barra 435B, Prat 515*, changes TCs; **Cambio Fides**, *Caracol Colonial, Balmaceda 460*, good rates, changes TCs; **Gira Tour**, *Prat 689, basement,* building closed 1400-1600. **Cycle repairs** Mike's Bikes, *Av de Aguirre 004, T051-224454*, sales, hire, repairs, English spoken, helpful. **Cultural centres** Centro Latino- Americano de Arte y Cultura, *Balmaceda 824, T051-229344*. Offers music and dance workshops, art gallery, handicraft workshops, also **Taverna Afro Son** (see Bars and clubs). **Nueva Acropolis**, *Benavente 692, T051-21214*. Lectures, discussions, free entry. **Internet** Cyber-Bazaar 2000, *Fco de Aguirre 343-A*; **Cybercafe**, *Cordovez 285 y Matta, T051-212187*; **Ingservitur**, *Matta 611, T/F051-220165*;. **Shalom**, *Fco de Aguirre 343*; The Electric Net, *Domeyko 560, T051-212224*. **Laundry** La Universal, *Balmaceda 851*, also *Av de Aguirre 411* and *Colón 560*; **Laverap**, *Av de Aguirre 447*; **Nevada**, *Los Carrera y Av de Aguirre*; **Ro-Ma**, *Los Carrera 654*. **Telephones** Long-distance calls from *Cordóvez 446* and *La Recova* market; **Entel**, *Prat 571*; CTC administration on Plaza de Armas sells *Turistel*. **Useful address** Automóvil Club de Chile, *E de la Barra 435, T051-225279*.

Coquimbo and the coast *p173, map p174*

Casa de cambio Cambios Maya, *Portales 305*. Also many Redbancs in the centre. **Internet** Aldunate 1196, open until 2330, US$1.50 per hr. **Telephone** CTC, *Aldunate 1633*.

Upper Elqui valley *p174*

Useful information CODEFF, the environmental organization, has an office on the outskirts of Vicuña.

For an explanation of sleeping and eating price codes used in this guide, see inside the front cover. Other relevant information is found in Essentials, see pages 51-58.

Introduction

From La Serena, the shrubs and cacti of the semi-desert stretch north as far as the mining and agro-industrial centre of **Copiapó**. Beyond this city, the **Atacama Desert** begins. The main population centres are in the valleys of the rivers Huasco and Copiapó, which are oases of olive groves and vineyards, and in the Salado valley, where the most important economic activity is mining, especially inland at El Salvador.

Although much of this region appears lifeless and of limited interest to visitors, the area around **Vallenar** is famous for the flowering of the desert following the rare occasions when there is heavy rainfall; the upper reaches of the **Huasco Valley** are beautiful and tranquil, and make a good resting point en route to/from the Atacama, while the port of **Huasco** itself has excellent seafood. There are also three national parks: one, the **Parque Nacional Pan de Azúcar**, protects a wide range of marine life; the second, the **Parque Nacional Llanos de Challe**, safeguards the habitat of one of the very rare flowers that bud with rainfall; and the third, the **Parque Nacional Tres Cruces**, covers extensive areas of salt flats northeast of Copiapó. East of the Parque Nacional Tres Cruces is the Paso San Francisco, a border crossing into Argentina; near the pass are some of the highest peaks in the Andes, although most are best tackled from the Argentinian side.

★ Don't miss...

① **Desierto florido** When it rains, go to the desert around Vallenar and witness the kaleidoscopic assortment of flowers, whose buds lie dormant in the sand waiting for moisture. An unforgettable sight, page 188.

② **Tránsito Valley** Explore the high Andean valleys, page 187.

③ **Pisco** Sample Chile's best liqueur at the Alto del Carmen and Horcón Quemado distilleries in the upper Huasco Valley near Vallenar, page 187.

④ **Ojos del Salado** Climb the tallest mountain in Chile and the highest volcano in the world, page 192.

⑤ **Pan de Azúcar** Visit a park with stunning beaches and a wide variety of wildlife, page 197.

Background

History

Although small groups of Spanish settlers took over the fertile lands in the Huasco and Copiapó valleys in the 16th century, no towns were founded in this area until late in the colonial period. Even the valleys were sparsely populated until the 19th century when the development of mining led to the creation of the ports of Caldera, Chañaral and Huasco and encouraged the building of railways between the mines and the ports. Mining remains a major economic activity in this region: one of the largest copper mines is at El Salvador and over 50% of all Chilean iron ore is mined around Vallenar. Agriculture is limited to the river valleys; the Copiapó valley is an important producer of grapes, while the lower Huasco valley is Chile's biggest olive-growing area. Fishing, centred on Caldera and, on a smaller scale, Chañaral and Huasco, is also important.

Geography and climate

This part of the country can be divided into two: between the Río Elqui and the Río Copiapó the transitional semi-desert zone continues; north of the Copiapó the Atacama desert begins and drivers should beware high winds and blowing sand. The valleys of the rivers Huasco, Copiapó and Salado form oases in this barren landscape. On the coast, temperatures are moderated by the sea and mist is common in the mornings. Inland temperatures are higher by day and cooler by night; Vallenar and the upper valleys of the Copiapó and Huasco can be especially cold on winter evenings. Rainfall is sparse and occurs in winter only, with amounts decreasing as you go north.

East of Copiapó the Andes divide: between the eastern range (Cordillera de Claudio Gay) and the western range (Cordillera de Domeyko) a basin collects the waters from the Andes. Here there are salt flats, the most extensive being the Salar de Pedernales. The eastern range has some of the highest peaks in Chile: Ojos del Salado (6879 m/6864 m; see page 192), Incahuasi (6615 m), Tres Cruces (6749 m) and San Francisco (6020 m).

The Huasco Valley

This valley is an oasis of olive groves and vineyards. It is rugged and spectacular, somewhat reminiscent of the Cajón del Maipo near Santiago. At Alto del Carmen, 39 km east of Vallenar, the valley divides into the Carmen and Tránsito valleys. There are pisco distilleries at Alto del Carmen and San Félix, both of which have basic residenciales. A sweet wine known as Pajarete is also produced.

Ins and outs

The Huasco Valley's main town and **transport** hub is Vallenar, which is easily reached by regular buses from both north and south. ▸▸ *For further details see Transport, page 189.* **Tourist information** for the valley is available from the Municipalidad on the Plaza de Armas in Vallenar and from a kiosk on the Panamericana.

Vallenar → *Phone code: 051. Colour map 2, B2. Population: 47,000.*

Nearly two hundred kilometres north of La Serena is Vallenar, the chief town of the Huasco Valley. It was founded in 1789 as San Ambrosio de Ballenary to commemorate the birthplace in Ireland of Ambrosio O'Higgins. The town is centred on a pleasant Plaza de Armas, in which all the benches are made of Chile's purest marble, extracted from the Tránsito Valley. **Museo del Huasco** ① *Sgto Aldea 742, Tue-Fri 1500-1800, US$0.70,* contains historic photos and artefacts from the valley. Opposite is the northernmost Chilean palm tree in the country. ▸▸ *For Sleeping, Eating and other listings, see pages 188-189.*

West of Vallenar

Freirina is easily reached by *colectivo*, 36 km west of Vallenar. Founded in 1752, this was the most important town in the valley, its prosperity based upon the nearby Capote goldmine and on later discoveries of copper. On the main plaza are the Municipalidad (1870) and the Santa Rosa church (1869).

Situated at the mouth of the river, **Huasco** lies 56 km west of Vallenar. West of the town is a terminal for loading iron ore from Algarrobal, 52 km north of Vallenar. Destroyed by an earthquake in 1922, Huasco is a modern town with a large beach that is popular in summer. The port is interesting, as the fishermen unload their catches and hundreds of pelicans hover, waiting to snatch the fish that slip off the crates into the sea. The best reason to come to Huasco is undoubtedly the seafood.

Nine kilometres east of Huasco, a road branches north at the old settlement of Huasco Bajo, near which are the Humedal de Huasco wetlands, known for their variety of marine birdlife. Fifty kilometres further north (37 of them *ripio*) is the small *caleta* of **Carrizal Bajo**. Carrizal Bajo is the best place from which to visit the **Parque Nacional Llanos de Challe**, a national park set up to preserve the habitat of the *garra de león* flower during the rare occasions when the desert is in bloom. For those with their own transport, tracks follow the coastline north of Carrizal Bajo, passing a series of small *caletas* en route to Caldera, including the beautiful beach at Puerto Viejo, near Copiapó.

East of Vallenar

East of Vallenar, a paved road leads 39 km to **Alto del Carmen**, the site of the distillery of one of the best *piscos* in Chile. The road clings to arid hillsides sprinkled with cacti and *maitén* bushes, passing the Santa Juana Reservoir, which was created following the damming of the Río Huasco in 1995 and has transformed agriculture in the area. The valley is filled with grapevines for *pisco*, and with groves of pepper and eucalyptus trees.

At Alto del Carmen, the road forks: left for the **Tránsito Valley**, right for the **Carmen Valley**. The Tránsito Valley is wilder and extends further into the heart of the mountains, while the Carmen Valley is greener and more populous: both valleys are unlikely clefts in the rocky Andes and reward the traveller who is prepared to make the effort to get to

Vallenar

Sleeping
Camino del Rey 1
Cecil 2
Hostería de Vallenar 3
Mary 2 4
Residencial Oriental 5
Vall 6
Viña del Mar 7

Eating
Bavaria 1
Corona del Inca 3
La Pica 4
Pizza Il Boccato 2
Shanghai 5

⁞ The flowering of the desert

The average annual rainfall in this region declines as you travel northward: in Vallenar it is 65 mm, in Copiapó 20 mm. Most years, the semi-desert appears to support only bushes and cacti and these become sparser as you continue north. However, in years of heavier than usual winter rainfall, this semi-desert breaks into colour as dormant seeds and bulbs germinate to produce blankets of flowers, while insects that normally hide underground emerge to enjoy the foliage.

Although the *desierto florido* 'flowering of the desert' used to occur every seven years or so, changing climatic conditions have led to a sharp increase in the phenomenon. The most recent years in which it has occurred include 1983, 1987, 1991, 1997, 2000 and 2002. In 1997, a record 76 mm of rain fell in the space of 15 hours on 12 June; by July and August much of the region was covered with expanses of green; by September and October areas of different colours could be seen in unexpected places.

Although the first traces of the *desierto florido* can be seen as far south as La Ligua and Los Molles, it is particularly worth seeing around **Vallenar**. From La Serena northwards, the Pan-American Highway is fringed with expanses of different colours: there are great stretches of violet Pata de Guanaco, yellow Corona del Fraile and blue Suspiro del Campo. Not all of these species can be seen at the same time: as the brief spring unfolds, the colours change and new species push through to replace others.

Around Vallenar, however, the colours are more varied as different species compete to celebrate this ever more frequent coming of spring: the Pan-American Highway north of the city as far as Copiapó and the coastal road north of Huasco are both recommended for a prime view. For guided tours, contact **Roberto Alegría**, T051-613865, Vallenar. For further information, contact Vallenar **tourist office** (see page 186).

know them. The Tránsito Valley, 20 km beyond Alto del Carmen, has marble mines; the village of El Tránsito (where there is a cheap, small restaurant) is a further 10 km on. The Carmen Valley stretches 25 km from Alto del Carmen to **San Félix**, the largest town of the valley, and the site of the distillery for Horcón Quemado *pisco*.

● Sleeping

Vallenar *p186, map p187*

A **Hostería de Vallenar**, *Ercilla 848, T051-614379, hotval@ctc.cl* Excellent accommodation with pool, parking, good breakfast and Hertz car hire office. Worth bargaining.

B **Cecil**, *Prat 1059, T051-614071, F051-614400*. Modern and clean with bath and hot water, and swimming pool. Recommended.

B/C **Hostal Real Quillahue**, *Plaza de Armas 70, T/F051-619992*. With breakfast, modern, friendly. Recommended.

C **Hostal Camino del Rey**, *Merced 943, T/F051-613184*. Clean, cheaper rooms

without bath; friendly, good value. Worth bargaining for longer stays. Recommended.

D **Vall**, *Aconcagua 455, T051-613380*. Rooms with breakfast and bath; friendly, parking, good value.

F **Residencial Mary 2**, *Ramirez 631*. With private bath, friendly. Price per person.

F **Viña del Mar**, *Serrano 611, T051-611478*. Clean, *comedor*, nice rooms. Highly recommended. Price per person.

G **Res La Oriental**, *Serrano 720, T051-613889*. Pleasant, friendly, cheap meals, decent value. Price per person. There are also several *residenciales* in the town.

West of Vallenar *p187*

There is no accommodation in Freirina but you'll find options in Huasco, including:

B Hostería Huasco, *Carrera Pinto 110, T051-531026*. Parking, conference room, with TV and all mod cons.

D Cabañas Skitniza, *Craig 833, T051-531596*. Parking available.

F Hostal San Fernando, *Pedro de Valdivia 176, T051-531726*. Parking, restaurant.

Camping

Tres Playitas, *12 km north along the coast towards Carrizal Bajo*. Also in Huasco near the post office, US$2 per site.

East of Vallenar *p187*

F Cabañas Camino al Oro, *Serrano y Larraín, San Felix, T051-983173*. Cabins, price per person.

F Residencial El Azadón del valle, *Alonso Garcia s/n, Alto del Carmen, T051-617695*. Price per person.

There is no accommodation in the Tránsito Valley but camping wild is easy.

● Eating

Vallenar *p186, map p187*

$$ Bavaria, *Serrano 802*. Reasonable chain, attentive service.

$$ Pizza Il Boccato, *Plaza de Armas*. Good coffee, good food, popular.

$ Corona del Inca, *Prat 900-block in local set aside from road*. Cheap meals, good cocktails.

$ La Pica, *Brasil y Faez*. Seriously cheap but good, serves meals, cocktails and seafood. There are other cheap places along the south end of Av Brasil.

$$ Moros y Cristianos, *Panamericana, junction with Huasco road*. A good choice outside town.

$ Shanghai, *Ramírez 1267*. Chinese.

West of Vallenar *p187*

Aficionados of Chile's seafood should take a trip to **Huasco** for lunch; the journey takes only 45 mins from Vallenar. Some of the best seafood in the country is served at many cheap restaurants near Huasco's port. Heading north up the coast, there is also a seafood restaurant at **Carrizal Bajo**.

$$ Restaurant Escorial, *Huasco*. Highly recommended.

● Entertainment

Vallenar *p186, map p186*

Billboard Pub, *Prat 920*. Popular with locals. It is also worth checking out the **Centro Cultural Vallenar**, *Vallenar y Colchagua*, for cultural events.

▲ Activities and tours

Agrotur, *Plaza de Artesanos 18, Vallenar, T051-617549*. Tours of the Huasco Valley as well as the northern section of the Reserva Nacional Humboldt.

● Transport

Bus

Operators to/from Vallenar include **Tur Bus**, *Merced 561*, and **Pullman Bus**, located opposite. Next door is Vallenar's bus terminal, from which **TasChoapa** and **Flota Barrios** depart. To **Copiapó**, 2 hrs, US$4; to **Chañaral**, 5 hrs, US$8,; to **La Serena**, 2 hrs, US$4. Buses to **Junta de Valeriano** (Tránsito Valley) and **San Félix** (Carmen Valley), as well as the intermediate points such as **Alto del Carmen**, leave from *Marañon 1289*, at 0730, 1100, 1430, 1630, 1730.

There are also *colectivos* in Vallenar, which may be useful for those with heavy luggage making their way to the bus terminals (catch them on Serrano).

● Directory

Vallenar *p186, map p191*

Banks Banco de Chile, *Prat 1010*, with ATM; BCI, *Prat y Brasil*; Corpbanca, *Prat 1070*, with ATM, exchanges dollars. **Internet** *Prat 862*. **Laundry** Lavaseco Rodier, *Verdaguer y Ramirez*. **Medical emergencies** Consulta Médico y Laboratorio Clinico, *Pje Nicolas Naranjo 341, T051-616012*. **Telephone** ENTEL *Prat 1000-block*.

 For an explanation of sleeping and eating price codes used in this guide, see inside the front cover. Other relevant information is found in Essentials, see pages 51-58.

The Copiapó Valley

From Vallenar, it is 148 km north to Copiapó, the largest city in the valley of the Río Copiapó, which is generally regarded as the southern limit of the Atacama desert. This valley is a surprisingly green cleft in the desert, an oasis of farms, vineyards and orchards that is about 150 km long.

Ins and outs

Getting there The Copiapó Valley's main centre is Copiapó, which is easily reached by regular buses from both north and south. There are several daily flights serving Copiapó from Santiago and La Serena, continuing on to El Salvador. For a transfer to the airport call T052-231488. ▶▶ *For further details, see Transport, page 196.* **Getting around** There are many *colectivos* and public buses in Copiapó, which may be useful for those heading for some of the out-of-town sites, such as the Santuario de la Candelaria; the fare for buses is US$0.30. **Tourist information** The **Sernatur** office in Copiapó is on the north side of Plaza de Armas ① *Los Carrera 691, T052-212838, infoatacama@sernatur.cl, open Mon-Fri 0830-1930, Sat 1030-1430, 1630-1930, Sun 1030-1430; out of season Mon-Fri 0830-1730 only*, and is extremely helpful. English is spoken. There is also a **CONAF** office in Copiapó ① *Juan Martinez 55, T052-210282.*

Copiapó and around → *Phone code: 052. Colour map 2, B2. Population: 127,000.*

The capital of Región III, Atacama, Copiapó is an important mining centre with a big mining school. Founded in 1744, Copiapó became a prosperous town after the discovery in 1832 of the third largest silver deposits in South America at Chañarcillo. The wealth from Chañarcillo formed the basis of the fortunes of several famous Chilean families – most notably, the Cousiños – and helped finance the first railway line in South America, linking Copiapó to Caldera (1851). Although quite a poor city in itself, Copiapó's economy thrives on the large numbers of lone miners who descend to the city in order to seek distraction and spend their pay cheques. On cool summer nights, people flock to the pleasant, shady Plaza de Armas to flirt and watch the world go by.

Sights

The neo-classical **cathedral**, on Plaza Prat, dating from 1851, was designed by William Rogers. Mass is held here every evening. The **Museo Mineralógico** ① *Colipí y Rodríguez, one block east of the Plaza, Mon-Fri 1000-1300, 1530-1900, Sat 1000-1300, US$0.80*, is the most impressive museum of its type in Chile. The museum possesses a collection of weird, beautiful minerals from Chile and also from Asia, Europe and North America, plus a decent set of fossils. There is an unfortunate lack of narrative or explanation but a visit is highly recommended nonetheless; it is extraordinary how, although there are minerals from all over the world, the most colourful or striking are almost always Chilean.

❧ *On Plaza Prat, at the corner of Colipi y Los Carrera, is a stall selling exquisite minerals from the Atacama – a uniquely Chilean souvenir.*

Three blocks further north, at Infante near Yerbas Buenas, is the colonial Jesuit **Iglesia de Belén** ① *Mon-Fri 1630-1830*, remodelled in 1856. Further west, at Atacama y Rancagua, you'll find the **Museo Regional del Atacama** ① *murea@entelchile.net, Mon 1400-1745, Tue-Fri 0900-1745, Sat 1000-1245, 1500-1745, Sun 1000-1245, US$1 (free Sun)*, containing collections on local history, especially from the 19th century up to the time of the War of the Pacific; it is also notable for its collection of artefacts from the Huentelauquén people, thought to have flourished 10,000 years ago. On the opposite corner of the same block, at Matta y O'Higgins is the **Monument to Juan Godoy**, the muleteer, who, in 1832, discovered silver at Chañarcillo. Behind, is the **Iglesia de San Francisco**, built in 1872 (the nearby convent is from 1662), which is a good example of a 19th-century construction using Pino Oregón and Guayaquil cane (see box, page 192). The wealth of the 19th-century mining families is reflected in the **Villa Viña de Cristo**, built in Italian renaissance style, three blocks northwest on Calle Freire. A few blocks further on, the Norris Brothers steam locomotive and carriages used in the inaugural journey between Copiapó and Caldera in 1851 can be seen at the **Universidad de Atacama**; also at the university is an example of an old *trapiche* (see box, page 160). Nearby, in the old railway station on Calle Ramirez, is the **Museo Ferroviario**, which has photos and artefacts from the railway age, but it opens only sporadically.

On the other side of the city, 3 km southeast of the centre, the **Santuario de la Candelaria** is the site of two churches, the older built in 1800, the other in 1922; inside the latter is the Virgen de la Candelaria, a stone image discovered whole in the Salar de Maricunga by the muleteer Mariano Caro in 1780. The Virgin is said to protect miners, hence her local importance, and is celebrated in the Fiesta de la Candelaria every February (see page 195). ►► *For Sleeping, Eating and other listings, see pages 194-196.*

Around Copiapó

The **Centro Metalúrgico Incaico** is a largely reconstructed Inca bronze foundry, 90 km up the Copiapó Valley by paved road. There is no accommodation in the nearby villages of Villa Hermoso or Las Juntas but there are *cabañas* at Los Loros, which was the site of a clinic for pulmonary diseases at the beginning of the 20th century, attended by the rich and unhealthy from Santiago.

South of Copiapó, about 59 km on the Pan-American Highway, is a signpost for the turning to the ghost town and former silver mine of **Chañarcillo**, along a very poor road. When Chañarcillo was at its peak, the town had a population of 7000; the mine was closed in 1875 but the tips have been reworked and this has destroyed many of the ruins. Now that the silver has gone, only a few goatherds live here.

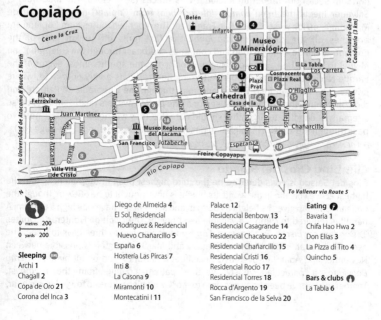

Copiapó

0 metres 200
0 yards 200

Sleeping
Archi 1
Chagall 2
Copa de Oro 21
Corona del Inca 3

Diego de Almeida 4
El Sol, Residencial
  Rodríguez & Residencial
  Nuevo Chañarcillo 5
España 6
Hostería Las Pircas 7
Inti 8
La Casona 9
Miramonti 10
Montecatini I 11

Palace 12
Residencial Benbow 13
Residencial Casagrande 14
Residencial Chacabuco 22
Residencial Chañarcillo 15
Residencial Cristi 16
Residencial Rocío 17
Residencial Torres 18
Rocca d'Argento 19
San Francisco de la Selva 20

Eating
Bavaria 1
Chifa Hao Hwa 2
Don Elias 3
La Pizza di Tito 4
Quincho 5

Bars & clubs
La Tabla 6

⦂ The churches of Copiapó

The Age of Silver, which followed the discovery of Chañarcillo, has left an unmistakable if subtle mark on the architecture of Copiapó's churches. New building materials, brought in to build railway stations and bridges, were used on houses and churches. Chief among these materials was Pino Oregano: neither a pine nor from Oregon (it is native to northern California), it offered the size and strength of timber required for the new buildings. Guayaquil cane, a type of large diameter bamboo from the Ecuadorean coast, was also introduced: sliced lengthways and flattened, it made strips of light fibre which could be used to make thin walls. At the same time, builders and carpenters from Britain and the United States, attracted by opportunities in railway and mine development, employed their skills on the new buildings of the city.

Church building in Copiapó was influenced by all these factors: architects such as William Rogers designed churches that reflected English neo-classicism. Particularly noticeable is the design of the tower, positioned in the centre of the church and decorated with columns and wooden cornices. Built of wood and using strips of Guayaquil cane covered with clay, in an almost rainless climate, they have withstood earthquakes to become the oldest buildings in Copiapó.

East to Paso San Francisco

The Argentine frontier can be crossed at **Paso San Francisco** (4726 m), which is situated just north of **Ojos del Salado** (see below). The pass can be reached by three poor *ripio* roads (high-clearance vehicle advisable) from Copiapó and by another *ripio* road that runs south and east from El Salvador. All these routes meet up near the northern sector of the **Parque Nacional Tres Cruces** (see below). The road from El Salvador meets the main *camino internacional* from Copiapó near the Salar de Maricunga, 96 km west of Paso San Francisco. The other two routes from Copiapó are branches off the *camino internacional*: the first forks off 10 km east of the Copiapó-Diego de Almagro road and continues southeast through the Quebrada San Miguel to reach the Laguna del Negro Francisco in the southernmost sector of the Parque Nacional Tres Cruces, before turning north. This is a very poor road, where drivers can easily get lost. The second runs through the Quebrada de Paipote and then on through the northernmost sector of the park. Travellers taking either of these alternatives en route to Argentina should note that they will need to deviate north to pass through the Chilean immigration post at the Salar de Maricunga (see page 193).

▸▸ *For Sleeping, Eating and other listings, see pages 194-196.*

Climbing Ojos del Salado

Ojos del Salado is considered to be the third highest peak in the Americas and the highest active volcano in the world. Its height is now thought to be 6864 m, though the Chilean IGM map gives its height as 6879 m and some maps have it as high a 6893 m. A permit is required to climb it, available free from the **Dirección de Fronteras y Límites** ⓘ *Bandera 52, piso 4, T02-6714110, F6971909*, taking two to three days to issue. The ascent is best attempted between January and March, though it is possible between November and April. In November, December and April it can be hit by the *Invierno Boliviano*, a particularly nasty weather pattern coming from the northeast. Temperatures have been known to drop to -40°C with high winds up to 150 km per hour.

Access to the volcano is via a turning off the main Chile-Argentina road at the former Hostería Murray (burned down). Base camp for the climb is at the old Argentine frontier post (4500 m). There are two refugios: Refugio Atacama (four to six beds) at 5100 m and Refugio Tejos (better, 12 beds) at 5750 m. The spur to the former is not easy to find, but can be reached with a high clearance four-wheel-drive vehicle. From Refugio Tejos it is ten to 12 hours' climb to the summit. The climb is not very difficult (approx grade three), except the last 50 m, which is moderate climbing on rock to the crater rim and summit. Take large quantities of water for the ascent. Guides and equipment can be hired in Copiapó.

Parque Nacional Tres Cruces

Extending over 59,082 ha, this newly designated park is in two sectors: the largest part, the northern sector, includes **Laguna Santa Rosa** and parts of the **Salar de Maricunga**, an expanse of salt flats covering 8300 ha at 3700 m; the southern sector covers the area around **Laguna del Negro Francisco**, a salt lake covering 3000 ha at 4200 m. The lakes are home to some 47 bird species, including all three species of flamingo ound in Chile, as well as guanacos and vicuñas. The park is stunningly beautiful and, owing to its isolation, rarely visited. The park administration is located at a *refugio* southeast of Laguna del Negro Francisco ① *open 0830-1230 and 1400-1800, summer only, US$5 (US$2 for Chileans)*.

Paso San Francisco

Although officially open all year, this pass is liable to closure after snow in winter. Call T052-1981009 for reports of the road's condition. Chilean customs are near the Salar de Maricunga, 100 km west of the frontier, ① *open 0900-1900, US$2 per vehicle for crossing Sat, Sun and holidays*. From here a *ripio* road continues along the southern shore of Laguna Verde, where there are thermal springs and a reasonable campsite, en route to the border. On the Argentine side, a paved road continues to Tinogasta. The Argentine border post is at Fiambalá, 210 km beyond the frontier, ① *open 0700-1900*, but there is also a police post at La Gruta, 24 km after the border.

Caldera and around → *Phone code: 052. Colour map 2, B2. Population: 12,000.*

Situated 73 km northwest of Copiapó, **Caldera** is a port and terminal for the loading of iron ore. In the late 19th century, it was a major railway engineering centre and was the terminus of the first railway in South America. The train station has recently been restored to its former glory and now houses a cultural centre and tourist information office. The **Iglesia de San Vicente de Paul** (1862), on the revamped Plaza de Armas, was built by English carpenters working for the railway company. Caldera is home to the earliest non-denominational cemetery in Chile, where vestiges of a prouder past can be glimpsed in the crumbling graves of European settlers.

Bahía Inglesa

Six kilometres south of Caldera and 6 km west of the Pan-American Highway, this resort is popular with Chileans for its beautiful, white sandy beaches and unpolluted, crystal clear sea; the bay is now dominated by an oyster farm but this is not too noticeable from the beach. In the sheltered bay, the water is warmer than around the neighbouring coast and it is safe to swim. Bahía Inglesa is rather expensive and can get crowded in January and February and at weekends, but off-season makes a perfect, deserted retreat. It was originally known as Puerto del Inglés after the visit in 1687 of the English pirate, Edward Davis. ►► *For Sleeping, Eating and other listings, see pages 194-196.*

Copiapó and around *p190, map p191*
A **Chagall**, *O'Higgins 760, T052-213775, F052-211527, chagall@ctcinternet.cl* Modern, comfortable, central.

A **Diego de Almeida**, *Plaza Prat, T052-212075, F052-218688, dalmeida@tnet.cl* Cable TV, good restaurant, spacious bar, pool.

A **Hostería Las Pircas**, *Copayapu 95, T052-213220, F052-211633, hostería.laspirca@chilnet.cl* Bungalows, nice rooms, pool, good breakfast and good restaurant.

A **Miramonti**, *Freire 731, T/F052-210440, miramont@entelchile.net* All facilities.

B **Hotel Copa de Oro**, *Infante 530, T052-211309, F052-217604*. Big rooms with all mod cons.

B **Inti Hotel**, *Freire 180, T/F052-217756*. Nice modern rooms, friendly.

B **La Casona**, *O'Higgins 150, T052-217278, lacasona@entelchile.net* Clean, friendly, good modern art in the lounge, nice rooms (but ask to be off the road), worth bargaining. Recommended. Tours organized.

B **Hotel San Francisco de la Selva**, *Los Carrera 525, T052-217013, F213255, hosanco@entelchile.net* Nice rooms, central, with breakfast, modern cafetería/bar.

B/C **Corona del Inca**, *Las Heras 54, T052-217019, F052-213831*. With breakfast, big rooms, friendly, quiet, good value, worth bargaining. No restaurant.

B/C **España**, *Yerbas Buenas 571, T/F052-217198*. With breakfast, friendly, small rooms, a little overpriced.

B/C **Montecatini I**, *Infante 766, T052-211363, F052-217021, hotelmontecatini@123click.cl* Large rooms set around beautiful green courtyard with hibiscus, pool, helpful, best value in the more expensive price bracket.

C **El Sol**, *Rodriguez 550, T052-230760, F052-215672*. With breakfast, parking, small rooms with cable TV, quiet, overpriced.

C **Palace**, *Atacama 741, T052-212852*. Comfortable, good breakfast, parking, central, nice patio.

E **Hotel Archi**, *Vallejos 111, T/F052-212983*. Without bath, ugly setting, convenient for bus terminal.

F-G **Res Chañarcillo**, *Chañarcillo 741, T052-213281*. With breakfast, central, parking, rooms with and without bath. Price per person.

F-G **Res Nuevo Chañarcillo**, *Rodríguez 540, T052-212368*. Pleasant lounge, small rooms, more expensive with bath. Price per person.

G **Res Benbow**, *Rodriguez 541, T052-217634*. Basic rooms but the best value of the many *residenciales* on this part of Rodriguez.

G **Res Casagrande**, *Infante 525, T052-244450*. With breakfast, friendly, with TV in big rooms, set in a beautiful old house with bougainvillaea in the courtyard, excellent value. Highly recommended. Price per person.

G **Res Chacabuco**, *O'Higgins 921, T052-213428*. With bath. Near bus terminal, quiet, clean. Price per person.

G **Res Cristi**, *Maipú 739, T052-219650*. Friendly, simple rooms, good beds, decent choice. Price per person.

G **Res Rocío**, *Yerbas Buenas 581, T052-215360*. More expensive with bath, good value, clean, attractive patio. Recommended. Price per person.

G **Res Rodríguez**, *Rodríguez 528, T052-212861*. Basic, poky rooms, good *comedor*. Price per person.

G **Res Torres**, *Atacama 230, T052-240727*. Without bath, hot water, friendly, quiet. Recommended. Price per person.

There are also several cheap places (**G**) around the local bus terminal.

East to Paso San Francisco *p192*
F There are two **CONAF** *refugios* in the Parque Nacional Tres Cruces; a very basic one southeast of Laguna Santa Rosa, and another southeast of Laguna del Negro Francisco, with bunk beds, heating, electric light and hot water. Price per person.

Caldera and around *p193*
AL **Rocas de Bahía**, *El Morro 888, Bahía Inglesa, T/F052-316005, www.rocasdebahia.cl* 4-star hotel with all facilities and good restaurant.

A **Los Jardines de Bahía Inglesa**, *Av Copiapó, Bahía Inglesa, T052-315359*. *Cabañas*, open all year, good beds, comfortable.

A/B **Hostería Puerta del Sol**, *Wheelwright 750, Caldera, T052-315205, F052-315507*. *Cabañas* with kitchen, all mod cons, laundry service, view over bay.

A/B **Portal del Inca**, *Carvallo 945, Caldera, T052-315252*. Fully equipped 4-star *cabañas* with kitchen, English spoken, restaurant not bad, order breakfast on previous night.

B **Costanera**, *Wheelwright 543, Caldera, T/F052-316007*. Takes credit cards, simple rooms, friendly.

B **El Coral**, *Av El Morro, Bahía Inglesa, T052-315331*. Overlooking sea, good seafood, open all year. Also *cabañas*.

B-E **Blanco Encalada**, *Copiapó y Pacífico, Bahía Inglesa, T/F052-315345*. Comfortable, some rooms with balcony, roof terrace with great view, English spoken. Cheap per person deals in low season. Recommended.

C **Cabañas**, *Playa Paraíso, Bahía Inglesa, T052-315363, F052-315507*. On beach, solar heating. Recommended.

D **Restaurant Hospedaje Mastique**, *Panamericana Norte Km 880, outside Caldera*. Cabin accommodation, hot showers, breakfast included, comfortable.

F **Res Millaray**, *on main plaza, Cousiño 331, Caldera, T052-315528*. Friendly, good value, basic. Price per person.

Camping
Camping Bahía Inglesa, *Playa Las Machas, T052-315424*. Price per site. Also fully equipped *cabañas* for up to 6 persons.

Eating

Copiapó and around *p190, map p191*
$$ **Bavaria**, *Plaza Prat*. Pricey restaurant upstairs, cafeteria downstairs (open 0800 for breakfast), salon de té around the corner in Los Carrera.

$$ **El Corsario**, *Atacama 245*. Good food in shaded patio, reasonably priced.

$$ **La Carreta**, *Av Copayapu*. Expensive *parrillada*.

$$ **Nuevo Restaurante Quincho**, *Atacama 109*. Range of meat, dancing on Fri and Sat.

$ **Benbow**, *Rodriguez 543*. Very good value *almuerzo*, extensive menu. Recommended.

$ **Chifa Hao Hwa**, *Colipí 340 and Yerbas Buenas 334*. One of several cheap *chifas* (Chinese restaurants) in town.

$ **Don Elias**, *Los Carrera y Yerbas Buenas*. Excellent seafood, popular. Recommended.

$ **La Pizza di Tito**, *Infante y Chacabuco*. Pizzas with good fillings, sandwiches, cheap *almuerzos*.

$ **Tebuk**, *in the Cosmocentro Plaza Real*. Self service, good range, reasonably priced, good views overlooking Plaza Prat.

$ **Willy Beer**, *Maipú 386*. Restaurant/bar serving very cheap *almuerzo*, popular with locals.

Cafés
Café Haiti, *Cosmocentro Plaza Real 215*. Real coffee, snacks, overlooks Plaza Prat, popular meeting place.

El Bramador, *Paseo Julio Aciares (part of Casa de la Cultura)*. Real coffee, good meeting place. Recommended.

Panadería La Industrial, *O'Higgins 984*. Good cakes.

Caldera and around *p193*
$$-$$$ **Belvedere**, *in Hotel Rocas de Bahía, Bahía Inglesa*. Reasonably elegant Italian/ Chilean restaurant, with good service and appealing views.

$$ **Charles**, *Ossa Cerda, Caldera*. Slow service.

$$ **El Pirón de Oro**, *Cousiño 218, Caldera*. Good but not cheap.

$$ **El Plateao**, *on the Costanera, Bahía Inglesa*. Local specialities, excellent.

$ **Miramar**, *Gana 090, Caldera*. Good seafood at the pier.

Bars and clubs

Copiapó and around *p190, map p191*
El Sótano, *Panamericana Norte on the way out of town*. The best disco in Copiapó.
La Tabla, *Los Carrera y Salas*. Good pub, very popular with locals.

Entertainment

Copiapó and around *p190, map p191*
Alhambra, *Atacama 455*. Cinema.
Casa de la Cultura, *Plaza Prat*. This colonial-style mansion has a gallery devoted to plastic arts, weekly film screenings and also organizes workshops. An annex houses the **Café El Bramador**, and hosts theatre productions and recitals.

Festivals and events

Fiesta de la Candelaria begins on the 1st **Sun in Feb** and lasts for 9 days. Up to 50,000 pilgrims and 3000 dancers congregate at the

Santuario de la Candelaria (p191) in Copiapó from all over the north of Chile for this important religious festival.

⚒ Activities and tours

Alejandro Aracena, *Tierra Amarilla, near Copiapó, T052-320098*. Personal tours of small working mines, starting from a small town in the valley.
Aventurismo, *Tupac Yupanqui 16, Bahía Inglesa, T/F052-316395, www.aventurismo.cl*
Azimut 360, *Arzobispo Casanova 3, Providencia, Santiago, T02-7358034, F02-7772375, www.azimut.cl* Based in the capital, this adventure and ecotourism company offers mountaineering expeditions to Ojos de Salado and Incahuasi.
Cristian Irribarren, *T09-884 5836*. Sandboarding trips. Based in Copiapó.
Océano Aventura, *Gabriela Mistral 57, Caldera, T095469848*. Diving trips.
Turismo Cobre, *O'Higgins 640, Copiapó, T/F052-211072*. Sells air tickets and arranges good regional tours.

A full list of guides, specializing in mountain trekking and climbing, is available from **Sernatur** in Copiapó (p190).

⊖ Transport

Air
Chamonate Airport is 12 km north of Copiapó (taxi US$7 to the centre). LanChile flies daily to/from **Santiago**, also to **El Salvador**.

Bus and colectivo
Long distance Copiapó's main bus terminal is 3 blocks southwest of the centre on Freire y Chacabuco. To **Santiago** 12 hrs, US$15; to **La Serena** 5 hrs, US$6.50; to **Antofagasta** 8 hrs, US$13; to **Calama** 11 hrs, US$17. Pullman Bus has its own terminal next door, where there is a good left-luggage store. Turbus and Tas Choapa are 1 block away in Chañarcillo.

There are bus services from Caldera to **Santiago**, several daily, and to **Antofagasta**, 7 hrs, US$11, although to travel north it may be better to take a bus to **Chañaral** (Inca-bus US$2), then change.

Local Although the major companies run between Copiapó and **Caldera**, the cheapest service is provided by Buses **Recabarren**, every 30 mins, US$1, leaving from the street 1 block west of the main bus terminal in Copiapó. *Colectivos* to **Caldera** also leave from this point. They are much quicker than the bus, cost US$2, and will take you to **Bahía Inglesa** for an extra US$0.75. Otherwise, *colectivos* between Bahía Inglesa and Caldera cost US$1.50. There are also buses in summer for $US0.50. *Colectivos* run from Copiapó to **Chañaral** and **Vallenar** and regular buses serve the upper valley as far as the **Tranque Lautaro**; get off at Valle Hermoso to reach the Inca foundry, 1-km walk from the main road. Note that there are no public transport connections to the **Parque Nacional de Tres Cruces**

➊ Directory

Copiapó *p190, map p191*
Airline offices LanChile, *Colipí 484, T052-213512, F052-217224, airport T052-214360*. **Banks** Cambio Fides, *Atacama 541, Galeria Coimbra local 3, 2 piso. Mon-Fri 1000-1400, 1600-1900 (closed Sat/Sun)*. Finandes, *Colipí 484*. Mastercard agent. Corp Banca, *Chacabuco 481 (on plaza)*, visa agent; next door is BCI, with a Redbanc – other Redbancs in the Plaza Real shopping centre and at the Banco de Chile, *O'Higgins y Colipí*. **Car hire** Avis, *Peña 102, T/F052-213966*. Budget, *Freire 466, T052-218802*. Flota Verschae, *Luis Flores y Copayapu, T052-227898*. Hertz, *Copayapu 173, T052-213522*. Rodaggio, *Colipí 127, T052-212153*. **Cycle repairs** Bicicleteria Biman, *Las Carrera 998A, T052-217391*. Sales, repairs, parts. Recommended.
Dentist Eduardo Cáceres, *Salas 385, T052-211902*. **Film and camera equipment** Foto Master, *Chacabuco 355*. **Hospital** *Los Carrera s/n, T052-212023*. **Laundry** Lavandería Añañucas, *Chañarcillo 612*. **Internet** Cybercafé Zona Virtual, *Rodriguez/Colipí, T052-240308, www.zonavirtual.cl* Terra, *Chacabuco 380*, US$1per hr. **Post office**, *Los Carrera y Colipí, on Plaza Prat. Mon-Fri 1000-1400, 1600-2000*. **Telecommunications** Entel, *Colipí 484*. CTC, *O'Higgins 531*.

The Salado Valley

It is 93 km north from Caldera to Chañaral, the port of the valley of the Río Salado. Until Chañaral, there are some vestiges of vegetation in the desert, but thereafter there is nothing but unremitting pampa until Antofagasta. The course of the Río Salado itself is always dry and the valley is less fertile and prosperous than the Copiapó or Huasco valleys to the south.

Chañaral → *Phone code: 052. Colour map 2, B2. Population: 12,000.*

This is a small, sad town with wooden houses perched on the hillside. In its heyday, Chañaral was the processing centre for ore from the nearby copper mines of El Salado and Las Animas, but those mines have declined, and the town now ekes out a living processing the ores from other mines in the interior. Stone walkways climb steeply up the desert hills behind the main street, Merino Jarpa, reaching platforms where you'll find several stone benches from which to watch the sea; behind the benches are religious murals daubed with the graffiti of impoverished, angry urban youth. There is a huge, beautiful and often deserted white-sand beach just beyond the Panamericana, created by waste minerals from the old copper processing plant, and stained green by its pollution. Swimming is dangerous here.

The **Museo de Historia Natural** ① *Buín 818, Mon-Fri 0900-1300 and 1530-1900, free,* has exhibits on the mineralogy, hydrobiology and entomology of the region; interesting for naturalists. There is a **tourist information** kiosk on the Panamericana, south of town, in summer.

There are two alternative routes from Copiapó to Chañaral: west to Caldera and then north along the coast, 167 km; or the inland route, known as the Inca de Oro, via Diego de Almagro and then west to meet the Pan-American Highway near Chañaral, 212 km. ▸▸ *For Sleeping, Eating and other listings, see page 198-200.*

Parque Nacional Pan de Azúcar

① *CONAF office, Caleta Pan de Azúcar, open daily 0830-1800, park admission US$5 (US$2.75 for Chileans).* This glorious national park north of Chañaral consists of the **Isla Pan de Azúcar**, home to Humboldt penguins and other sea birds, plus some 43,754 ha of coastal hills rising to 800 m and fantastic white-sand beaches, which are popular at weekends in summer. The park is inhabited by 103 species of birds as well as guanacos and foxes, and a sea-lion colony can be observed by following the signs marked 'loberías' from the park entrance. The *camanchaca* (coastal fog) ensures that the park has a unique set of flora that belies its desert location; after rain tall *alstroemerias* of many colours bloom in some of the gullies. As well as extremely rare species of cacti, the park is also one of the best places in Chile to see the flowering desert (see box, page 188).

There are two entrances to the park: either along a side road 20 km from the Pan-American Highway, 45 km north of Chañaral, or by a good secondary road north from Chañaral, 28 km to the village of **Caleta Pan de Azúcar**. The **CONAF** office here has an exhibition room and cactarium. Basic maps are available, as well as entrance tickets to the park. Two hours' walk from the office is a *mirador* giving extensive views over the southern section of the park but, to experience the park fully, transport is needed. Although the penguins are sometimes visible from the mainland, for a closer look take a boat trip round Isla Pan de Azúcar from Caleta, US$50 for up to 18 people.
▸▸ *For Sleeping, Eating and other listings, see page 198-200.*

Towards El Salvador → *Phone code: 052. Colour map 2, A2.*

Some 67 km from Chañaral on the El Salvador road is the smaller mining town of **Diego de Almagro**. Twelve kilometres north of here, on a mining track through the desert, is the interesting **Pampa Austral** project, where Codelco, the state mining company, has used water resulting from the process of extracting copper from nearby mines to irrigate the desert, producing a 4-ha extension of plantations in the middle of the desert pampa.

El Salvador itself is a modern town, built near one of the biggest copper mines in Chile. Located 120 km east of Chañaral, just north of the valley of the Río Salado, it is reached by a road that branches off the Pan-American Highway, 12 km east of Chañaral. All along the valley people are extracting metal ore from the water with primitive settling tanks. Further east, 60 km by unpaved road is the Salar de Pedernales, salt flats 20 km in diameter and covering 30,000 ha at an altitude of 3350 m, where pink flamingos can be seen.

Taltal and around → *Phone code: 055. Colour map 2, grid A2.*

Situated 25 km off the Pan-American Highway and 146 km north of Chañaral, Taltal is the only town between Chañaral and Antofagasta, a distance of 420 km. Along Avenida Prat are several wooden buildings, including the impressive church, dating from the late 19th century when Taltal prospered as a mineral port of 20,000 people, exporting nitrates from 21 mines in the area. The town is now a fishing port with a mineral processing plant. **Museo Augusto Capdeville** ① *Avenida Prat 5*, free, is a good local museum in the former *gobernación*, with rooms on prehistory, local history and the saltpetre industry, European immigration, and an exhibition on the Paranal observatory. The curator is very friendly. On Calle O'Higgins is an old steam engine with a pair of carriages. The pleasant tree-lined plaza is laid out in the form of the Union Jack in honour of the historical importance of the British community in the town. Just north of town is the cemetery, where the European influence can clearly be seen.

Excellent and deserted beaches line the coast both north and south of Taltal, the best known of which is **Cifuncho**, some 40km south. There's no accommodation here, but camping is easy. North along the coast by 72 km is the **Quebrada El Médano**, a gorge with ancient rock paintings along the upper valley walls. *For Sleeping, Eating and other listings, see page 198-200.*

⏺ Sleeping

Chañaral *p197*
C **Hostería Chañaral**, *Müller 268, T052-480055, F052-480554*. Very spacious and attentive, excellent restaurant in beautiful dining room, pool room, parking. Recommended.
C-D **Carmona**, *Costanera 402, T052-480522*. With bath and TV, friendly, decent value.
C-D **Nuria**, *Costanera 302, T052-480903*. Breakfast, parking, friendly, but a little basic and overpriced. Worth bargaining.
F **Residencial Sutivan**, *Comercio 365, T052-489123*. Very friendly, clean, nice rooms, good beds, excellent value. More expensive rooms with bath also available. Highly recommended. Also arranges tours to Pan de Azúcar. Price per person.
G **Hotel Jiménez**, *Merino Jarpa 551, T052-480328*. Friendly, patio with lots of birds, clean rooms, modern shared bathrooms, good value restaurant,

convenient for Pullman Bus. Recommended. More expensive rooms with bath also available. Price per person.
G **La Marina**, *Merino Jarpa 562*. Basic, many parakeets. Price per person.

Parque Nacional Pan de Azúcar *p197*
A-C **CONAF cabañas**, *T052-213404/ 480323 (reservations advised)*. Cabañas behind the *caleta*. Cheaper off-season.

Camping
There's a campsite on the beach with showers and 20 litres of drinking water. Price per person. Book through **CONAF**.

Towards El Salvador *p197*
AL **Camino del Inca**, *El Tofo 330, T052-475252, F475207*. The upmarket choice.
C-G **Hostería El Salvador**, *Potrerillos 003, T052-475749*. Cheaper rooms here are without bath.

Taltal *p198*

BCabañas Caleta Hueso, *Camino a Paposo 2 km from Taltal, T055-612251, m.finger@entelchile.net* Good cabins, just outside town.

CHostería Taltal, *Esmeralda 671, T055-611173, F611625, btay@entelchile.net* Sea view, excellent restaurant, good-value *almuerzo*.

CMi Tampi, *O'Higgins 138, T055-613605.* Recommended.

C-DHostal del Mar, *Carrera 250, T/F055-611612.* Modern, comfortable.

F-GRes Paranal, *O'Higgins 106.* Next door to Hostal del Mar. Good. Price per person.

GSan Martín, *Martínez 279, T055-611088, F055-268159.* Without bath, good *almuerzo*.

● Eating

Chanaral *p197*

$**Restaurant Nuria**, *Yungay y Buín, on the Plaza.* Not bad, open at night.

$**Restaurante de los Pescadores**, *La Caleta.* Good fish, clean, cheap. Recommended.

$**Rincón Porteño**, *Merino Jarpa 567.* Good and inexpensive.

There are also a couple of cheap stalls serving coffee and sandwiches early in the morning, next to the **Pullman Bus** terminal.

Parque Nacional Pan de Azúcar *p197*

In Jan and Feb, there is a restaurant in **Caleta**. Otherwise, buy fish straight from the boats at around 1700 Tue-Sun and prepare it yourself. Take all other food with you into the park.

Taltal *p198*

$$**Club Social Taltal**, *Torreblanca 162.* Excellent, good value. The former club of the British community, with poker room, billiard table and ballroom.

$**Caverna**, *Martínez 247.* Good seafood.

$**Las Brisas**, *by the caleta.* Large servings, good and cheap.

✵ Festivals and events

On the night of **15 Jul**, the people of Chañaral celebrate the **Fiesta of the Virgen del Carmen** (the same fiesta for which La Tirana is so famous, p247). This is a scaled-down version of La Tirana, but still involves plenty of drumming and dancing around the plaza. The religious groups are dressed in elaborate costumes and vie with one another for the loudest band and the most complex dance; it's a moving manifestation of the faith of this impoverished but proud town.

▲ Activities and tours

Chañaral *p197*

Chango Turismo, *Panamericana Norte s/n, T052-480484, changoturismo@hotmail.com* Offers tours and transfers to the Parque Nacional Pan de Azúcar as well as kayak trips to the island. Tours of the park are also offered by **Residencial Sutivan** (see Sleeping, above), and by **Sergio Molina**, *T09-7542888/ 09-5236549*, both of whom have been recommended.

● Transport

Chañaral *p197*

There is no main **bus** terminal. The **Pullman Bus** terminal is at Los Baños y Costanera, **Tur Bus** is on the Panamericana, opposite Copec. Frequent services to **Antofagasta**, US$10 *semi cama*, 5 hrs, and **Santiago**, US$18. To **Copiapó**, US$3. To **Taltal**, 3 daily, US$3; *colectivos* to Copiapó depart from Merino Jarpa y Los Baños, US$5, try to leave early in the morning.

Parque Nacional Pan de Azúcar *p197*

Taxi from Chañaral, US$15, or transfer with **Chango Turismo** (see above). Gates control vehicles in the park, but keys are available from the **CONAF** office. There are fines for driving in 'restricted areas' of the park.

Towards El Salvador *p197*

Lan Chile flies to/from **Santiago** and **Copiapó**. There are **Pullman Bus** services daily to **Santiago**, **Copiapó** and **Chañaral**.

Taltal *p198*

Bus services to **Santiago**, 3 a day; to **Antofagasta**, Tur Bus, US$5. There are many more bus services from the Pan-American Highway (taxi US$8).

Chañaral p197

Banks Poor rates for cash in **BCI** on the plaza. Nowhere to change Tcs; **Redbanc** ATMs in the supermarket and ESSO; in summer, money exchange is offered at the ironmonger's, *Consuelo y Merino Jarpa*.

Telephone CTC, *Merino Jarpa 506*; **ENTEL** *Merino Jarpa 700-block*, next to the municipal health centre.

For an explanation of sleeping and eating price codes used in this guide, see inside the front cover. Other relevant information is found in Essentials, see pages 51-58.

Antofagasta, Calama and San Pedro de Atacama

Introduction

This desolate region is one of the most striking in Chile. The Atacama Desert is punctuated by small oases in the all-encompassing yellowness; clefts of green such as the beautiful **Quebrada de Jerez**, near Toconoa, or the **Alto Loa**, in which the lifelessness of the desert seems somehow impossible.

The main cities are **Antofagasta** and **Calama**, both of which are service centres for the mining industry that dominates the region's economy. Calama is the departure point for the sole remaining passenger train service in northern Chile, the 'tren de la muerte' to Uyuni in Bolivia. Most visitors, however, head first for **San Pedro de Atacama**, an ancient centre of civilization in the region since well before the Spanish conquest, and the base for excursions to spectacular desert landscapes such as the **Valle de la Luna** and the **Salar de Atacama**, as well as to the **El Tatio geysers**. San Pedro is home to one of the north's most important archaeological museums, and excursions can also be made over the frontier into **Bolivia** to the Salar de Uyuni and to two beautiful lakes, Laguna Colorada and Laguna Verde.

★ Don't miss...

❶ La Portada The rock arch near Antofagasta is famous throughout the country, page 206.

❷ Chuquicamata The enormity of the mine makes for a very interesting trip, page 218.

❸ El Tatio geysers Set at over 4,000m, these are the highest geysers in the world, page 227.

❹ Hiking a volcano Adventurous and well-equipped trekkers and mountain climbers can choose one of many remote routes through the altiplano. The Volcán Licancábur, is very popular, page 230.

❺ Quebrada de Jerez A beautiful green oasis that provides a memorable contrast with the desert. The Río Loa, near Lasana, is equally lovely, pages 219 and 227.

❻ Valle de la Luna Extraordinary desertscape near San Pedro, page 227.

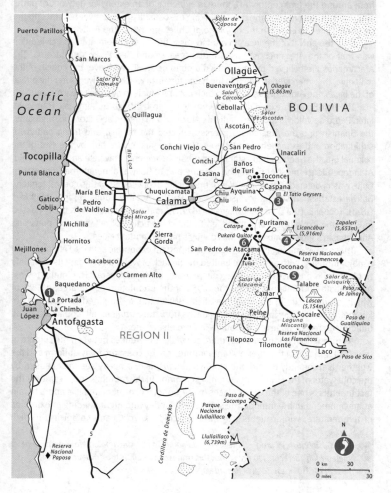

Background

The Atacama Desert stretches 1,255 km north from the Río Copiapó to the Chilean frontier with Peru. The Cordillera de la Costa, at its highest in this region (the highest peak is Cerro Vicuña (3114 m), runs close to the coast, an inhospitable and spectacular cliff face rising sheer from the waters to a height of up to 900 m. Below this cliff, on the edge of the Pacific, is a ledge on which the city of Antofagasta and some smaller towns are situated. In the eastern branch of the Andes, several peaks rise to around 6000 m: Llullaillaco (6739 m), Socompa (6051 m), Licancábur (5916 m), Ollagüe (5863 m). The western branch of the Andes ends near Calama. In between these two ranges the Andean Depression includes several salt flats, including the Salar de Atacama and the smaller Salar de Ascotán.

Before the Spanish conquest, this part of Chile was populated both on the coast and inland. The Chango people fished in the Pacific out of boats made from the pelts of sea-lions. They traded fish with the peoples of the interior, from whom they bought coca leaves and quinoa (the staple grain before the arrival of those from Europe); from around the first century AD, there is evidence of an extensive network of paths and trade routes crossing the desert, linking the coastal areas between Taltal and the estuary of the Río Loa with the *altiplano* of Chile, Argentina and Bolivia.

Until the arrival of the Incas in around 1450, the most important inland civilization was that of the Atacameños, based in the area around San Pedro de Atacama. The Atacameños are believed to have arrived around 9000 BC, and, over the course of the millennia, they managed to adapt to the harsh terrain in which they lived. After the arrival of the Incas, the Atacameños adapted their cultural rituals to suit their new masters.

The first Spanish expedition arrived in 1536, led by Diego de Almagro. Four years later, Pedro de Valdivia took San Pedro de Atacama and the fort at Quitor and, thereafter, the Spanish and the Atacameño peoples enacted the familiar and tragic pattern of subjugation and extinction. San Pedro was the colonial centre but, by the end of the colonial era, the Spanish had established urban settlements only here and in Chiu Chiu. At independence most of the region became part of Bolivia, although the frontier with Chile was ill-defined. Before the War of the Pacific deprived her of this coastal territory, Bolivia established several towns along the Pacific, notably Cobija (1825), Mejillones (1841), Tocopilla (1843) and Antofagasta (1872). After the war, when the territory passed to Chile, the exploitation of nitrates led to the construction of railways and ports and Antofagasta's growth into one of the country's most important cities.

These days, mining is by far the most important economic activity. Fishing is also a major industry, with agriculture limited by the lack of water and poor soils to mainly tropical fruit production on the coast south of Antofagasta. The main towns, Antofagasta and Calama, account for 87% of the population of the area, 98.8% of which is urban. Life in the area is artificial. Water has to be piped for hundreds of kilometres to the cities and the mining towns from the *cordillera*; all food and even all building materials have to be brought in from elsewhere.

As throughout northern Chile, there are major differences between the climate of the coast and that of the interior. Temperatures on the coast are fairly uniform and the weather is frequently humid and cloudy; *camanchaca*, a heavy sea mist caused by the cold water of the Humboldt current, is common in the morning and, in spite of the fact that this is one of the driest places in the world, it can seem that it is about to rain at any moment. In the interior ,the skies are clear day and night, leading to extremes of temperature; winter nights can often be cold as -10°C, and colder in the high

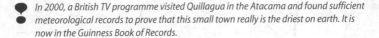

In 2000, a British TV programme visited Quillagua in the Atacama and found sufficient meteorological records to prove that this small town really is the driest on earth. It is now in the Guinness Book of Records.

⦂ Archaeology of the Atacama

From early times, people settled along the northern coast of Chile, sustained by the food supply from the Pacific Ocean. Since about 7600 BC, fisherfolk and foragers lived in large groups in permanent settlements, such as the Quebrada de Conchas, just to the north of Antofagasta. They fished with fibre nets, sometimes venturing inland to hunt for mammals.

About 2000 years later, the successors of these people, the 'Chinchorros', developed one of the deepest characteristics of Andean cultures, veneration for their ancestors. The role of the dead in the world of the living was vital to the earliest Andean people. As a link between the spiritual and the material world, the ancestor of each local kin group would protect his clan. The expression of these beliefs came in the form of veneration of the ancestors' bodies; sacrifices were made to them, funeral rites were repeated, and precious grave offerings were renewed. In the arid climate of the Atacama, the people observed how bodies were naturally preserved. The skilled practice of mummification was thus developed, over a period of 3,000 years, preserving the dead as sacred objects and spiritual protectors.

Another major cultural practice of northern Chile was the use of hallucinogens. Grave remains found in the region, dating from about AD 1000, include leather bags containing organic powder, wooden tablets and snuffer tubes. The tablets and snuffers were often decorated with supernatural figures, such as bird-headed angels, winged humans, star animals and other characters familiar in *altiplano* cultures. Although the origins and function of taking hallucinogens is not known for certain (see page 512), it is thought that the practice may have been brought down to the coast by traders from the highlands. There were also 'medicine men' who travelled throughout the central and south central Andes dispensing the drugs and healing the sick. As with cures practised in the Andes and Amazonia, it is possible that the drugs were taken as part of religious rituals, and often for a combination of spiritual and physical healing.

altiplano. Strong winds, lasting for up to a week, are common, especially, it is said, around the full moon, while between December and March there are often violent storms of rain, snow and hail in the *altiplano*, a phenomenon known as *invierno altiplánico* (highland winter) or *invierno boliviano* (Bolivian winter).

Antofagasta and around

→ *Phone code: 055. Colour map 1, C1. Population: 225,316.*
Situated on the edge of a bay, nearly 700 km south of Arica, Antofagasta is the largest city in northern Chile and the fourth largest in the country. It is not a terribly attractive place, although the combination of the tall mountains and the ocean is dramatic. Apart from the lack of rain, the climate is pleasant; the temperature varies from 16°C in Jun and Jul to 24°C in January and February, never falling below 10°C at night. The city's economy depends on the enormous mine at La Escondida in the interior, where 8,000 people work, doing week-long shifts at the mine before spending a week in the city; the city's port also acts as the processing point for the copper from La Escondida and Chuquicamata. As well as being the capital of Region II, Antofagasta is also an important commercial centre and the home of two universities.

Getting there Antofagasta is served by many regular buses from both north and south. All major companies serving the north stop here and there are frequent flights with **LanChile** and **Sky** south to Santiago and north to Calama, Iquique and Arica. Taxis to/from the airport cost US$7 but are cheaper if ordered from a hotel. For airport transfers, call To55-262727. **Getting around** Antofagasta is one of Chile's largest cities, and you may need to take some of the *colectivos* or buses to get to more out-of-the-way places, particularly the discos and bars in the south and the university campuses. ▶▶ *For further details, see Transport, page 210.* **Tourist office** ① *Prat 384, in the intendencia on Plaza Colón, To55-451818, infoantofagasta@sernatur.cl, Mon-Fri 0830-1300, Mon-Thu 1500-1930, Fri 1500-1930.* There is also a kiosk on Balmaceda near **Hotel Antofagasta** ① *open Mon-Fri 0930-1300, 1530-1930, Sat and Sun 0930-1300,* and a kiosk at the airport (open summer only).

Sights

In the main square, Plaza Colón, there is a clock tower donated by the British community in 1910. It is a miniature of Big Ben with a carillon that produces similar sounds. Two blocks north of Plaza Colón, near the old port, is the former **Aduana**, built as the Bolivian customs house in Mejillones and moved to its current site after the War of the Pacific. Inside is the recommended **Museo Regional de Antofagasta** ① *Balmaceda y Bolívar, www.dibam.cl, Tue-Fri 1000-1830, Sat, Sun and holidays 1100-1400, US$1, children half price,* which includes displays on the geology and natural history of the north, as well as sections on the War of the Pacific and the nitrate era. Explanations are in Spanish only. Opposite are the former offices of the **Capitanía del Puerto** (harbourmaster) and the **Resguardo Marítimo** (coastguard).

East of the port are the buildings of the **Antofagasta and Bolivia Railway Company** (FCAB) dating from the 1890s and beautifully restored, but still in use and difficult to visit. These include the former railway station, company offices, workers' housing and the **Museo del Ferrocarril a Bolivia** ① *Bolívar 255, To55-206311, jlyons@fcab.cl (reservations must be made 48 hours in advance),* which has an interesting collection relating to the history of the Antofagasta-Bolivia railway, with photographs, maps, instruments and furniture. Just north of the port is the **Terminal de Pescadores**, where there are markets selling seafood, fruit and vegetables. Pelicans sit on the fish market roof and sea-lions swim in the harbour; there are half-hour tours of the port available from **La Cabaña de Mario** ① *Anibal Pinto s/n, US$3.50.*

The former main plaza of the **Oficina Vergara**, a nitrate town built in 1919 and dismantled in 1978, can be seen in the campus of the University of Antofagasta, 4 km south of the centre (take *colectivo* 3 or 33 from the town centre). Also on the university campus is the **Museo Geológico de la Universidad Católica del Norte** ① *Angamos 610, gchong@socompa.ucn, Mon-Fri 0930-1300, 1530-1800, free.* On a hill to the south of town (reached by bus B) are the ruins of **Huanchaca**, a Bolivian silver refinery built after 1868 and closed in 1903. From below, the ruins resemble a fortress rather than a factory. ▶▶ *For Sleeping, Eating and other listings, see pages 208-211.*

Around the coast

La Portada, 16 km north of the city, is a natural arch with fantastic rock formations that are the symbol of Region II and are often seen on postcards up and down the country. From the main road it is 2 km to the beach which, although beautiful, is too dangerous for swimming. However, a number of bathing beaches are within easy reach.

A windsurfers' paradise, **Juan López**, is 38 km north of Antofagasta. The sea is alive with birds, including Humboldt penguins, especially opposite Isla Santa María. If you have your own transport, follow the road out of Juan López to the beautiful cove at Conchilla. Keep on the track to the end at Bolsico.

Sleeping
Aliro 1 D2
Antofagasta 3 B1
Brasil 4 D1
Chillán 5 C3
Ciudad de Avila 6 B3
Colón 7 B2
Costa Marfil 8 C3
Dakota 9 B2
Diego de Almagro 10 B2
Frontera 11 B3
Hostal del Norte 12 A3
Marsal 13 C3
Nadine 14 B2
Parina 15 C2
Plaza 17 B2
Rawaye 18 C3
Residencial El Cobre 19 C3
Residencial La
   Riojanita 20 B2
San Marcos 21 B3
San Martín 22 B2
Sol del Horizonte 23 C2
Tatio 24 E1

Eating
Bavaria 2 C2
Café Caribe
   & Café Haiti 3 B2
Club de la Union 4 B2
Club de Yates 9 B1
D'Alfredo 5 B2
Panda 6 C2
Regatta's Pub 7 E1

Bars & clubs
Picadillo 1 E1
Wally's Pub 8 E1

0 metres 100
0 yards 100

To Universidad de Antofagasta, Huanchaca & Pan-American Highway south

ⓘ *Cerro Paranal, T055-435000, www.eso.org/paranal/site/visitors, open Jan-Nov on the last 2 weekends in the month 1400-1700, reservations essential.* Located on a hill in the coastal *cordillera*, 132 km south of Antofagasta, this is, at present, the most powerful telescope in the world, although it will soon be usurped by a rival telescope that is currently being built near La Serena. The site at Cerro Paranal was chosen as 350 clear nights a year were guaranteed (see also box, page 172).

● Sleeping

Antofagasta *p205, map p207*
Budget hotels are scarce and of poor quality. The tourist office does not maintain a list of cheaper places.
AL Antofagasta, *Balmaceda 2575, T/F055-228811.* 5-star, garage, pool, lovely view of port and city, good but expensive restaurant (bar serves cheaper snacks), with breakfast (discount for Automóvil Club members), beach, rooms facing the city are noisy due to all-night copper trains.
A Diego de Almagro, *Manuel Verbal 1632, T055-354600.* Good for the money although a bit tatty.
A Plaza, *Baquedano 461, T055-269046, hplaza@chilesat.net* Pool, squash court, parking. TV, *salon de té*, exchange, also has apartments. Recommended.
A Tatio, *Av Grecia 1000, T055-419111.* Modern building, out of old town on the beach, good restaurant.
B Astore, *Matta 2537, T055-261203, F267439.* All mod cons, friendly.
B Colón, *San Martín 2434, T055-261851, F260872.* With breakfast, local phone calls free, quiet, clean.
B Marsal, *Prat 867, T055-268063, F221733, marsalhotel@terra.cl* Modern, very comfortable, Catalan owner, friendly atmosphere, recommended.
B Nadine, *Baquedano 519, T055-227008, F265222.* TV, bar, café, parking.
B Parina, *Maipú 446, T055-223354, F266396.* Modern, comfortable, friendly, restaurant, conference centre, good value.
B San Martín, *San Martín 2781, T055-263503, F268159.* With bath, TV, parking, clean, safe.
B Sol del Horizonte, *Latorre 2450, T055-221886, hotelsoldelhorizonte@123click.cl* Cable TV, bar, friendly and pleasant, good value, recommended.
C Costa Marfil, *Prat 950, T055-225569, F264806.* With breakfast, friendly, English spoken.

C Dakota, *Latorre 2425, T055-251749.* With breakfast and cable TV, friendly, popular, good value, recommended.
C San Marcos, *Latorre 2946, T055-251763, F221492.* Comfortable, parking, avoid rooms at the back (loud music), overpriced.
D Chillán, *Sucre 823, T055-227237.* Friendly, with bath and breakfast.
D Ciudad de Avila, *Condell 2840, T/F055-221040.* Very clean, TV, restaurant, excellent value. Warmly recommended.
D Hostal del Norte, *Latorre 3162, T055-251265, F267161.* Without bath, clean, comfortable, quiet.
D Maykin, *Condell 3130, T/F055-259400.* With bath, modern, helpful, good value.
F Brasil, *Ossa 1978, T055-267268.* Basic, dark.
F Frontera, *Bolívar 558, T055-281219.* Without bath, poky rooms, basic, overpriced.
F Res Aliro, *Ossa 2275, T055-410505.* Basic.
G Rawaye, *Sucre 762, T055-225399.* Very basic, hot water morning only, no towels.
G Res El Cobre, *Prat 749, T055-225162.* Without bath, clean, dingy, unattractive.
G Res La Riojanita, *Baquedano 464, T055-226313.* Friendly, basic, very helpful, noisy but recommended.

Camping
Las Garumas, *Km 6, south of the city on the road to Coloso, T055-247763 ext 42.* Also cabins (sleep 4), cold showers and beach. For reservations contact *Av Angamos 601, Casilla 606.* Price per site (bargain for lower price out of season), wild camping is possible on the beach nearby.
Rucamóvil, *Km 11, south of the city on the road to Coloso, T055-223929.* Open year round. Price per site.

Around the coast *p206*
A La Rinconada, *10 km from Juan López, T055-261139.* This is a *cabaña* and camping complex, prices for up to five people.
C Hostería Sandokan, *Juan López, T055-223022.* Standard facilities.

❼ Eating

Antofagasta *p205, map p207*
Note that many bars and restaurants are
closed on Sun.
$$$ Club de la Unión, *Prat 474, 2 piso*.
Excellent *almuerzo*, good service, traditional
atmosphere. Recommended.
$$$ Club de Yates, *on the costanera beside
Hotel Antofagasta*. Exclusive, great sea views
and great seafood.
$$$ Marina Club, *Av Ejército 909*. Good fish
and seafood dishes and a view, expensive
but worth it.
$$ Bavaria, *Ossa 2428*. Excellent meat and
German specialities, cheaper cafeteria
downstairs, real coffee.
$$ Chifa Pekín, *Ossa 2135*. Chinese, smart,
reasonable prices.
$$ D'Alfredo, *Condell 2539*. Pizzas, good.
$$ El Arriero, *Condell 2644*. Good service,
cheaper set lunch, popular, live music.
$$ Panda, *Condell y Baguedano*. Self-service,
all you can eat for US$8.
$$ Pizzante, *Carrera 1857*. Good pasta
and seafood.
$$ Puerto Caliche, *Ejercito 0809*. Excellent
food and service.
$$ Rincón Oriental, *Washington 2432*.
Excellent Cantonese, pricey, 'over the top'
jolly atmosphere.
$$ Tío Jacinto, *Uribe 922*. Friendly and serves
good seafood.
$ Bundes Schop, *Latorre 2655*. Cheap and
open late.
$ Casa Vecchia, *O'Higgins 1456*. Good value.
$ Chicken House Center, *Latorre 2660*.
Chicken, beef and daily specials. Open till 2400.
$ La Selecta, *Sucre 720*. Basic food, but
cheap and open for *cenas*.
$ La Yugoslava, *Matta 2341*. Fast food,
cheap *almuerzo*, snacks.
$ Oliver Café Plaza, *Plaza Colón*. Self-service,
modern, reasonably priced. Recommended.
    Above the market are several good places
selling cheap seafood *almuerzos* and
super-cheap set lunches, including **El
Mariscal** and **Toledo**. Good fish restaurants
are also to be found in *terminal pesquero
centro* and at *Caleta Coloso*, 8 km south.

Cafés
Note that it is difficult to find coffee or
breakfast before 0900.
Café Bahía, *Prat 474*. Open 0900 for real coffee.
Café Haiti, *Galeria, Prat 482*. Serves real coffee.
Cafetería, *Hotel Nadine, Baquedano 519*.
Serves real coffee, pastries and ice cream.
Chez Niko's, *Ossa 1951*. Bakery, *pastelería*,
good pizzas, *empanadas* and bread.
Heladería Latorre, *Baquedano y Latorre*.
For ice creams.
Panadería El Sol, *Baquedano 785*. Serves
good bread and cakes.
Pastelería La Palmera, *Ossa 2297*. Good
cakes, pastries, bread.

Along the coast *p206*
$$$ La Portada, *Camino a la portada*,
T055-226423. Excellent, expensive seafood
restaurant and café, open lunchtime only.

❼ Bars and clubs

Antofagasta *p205, map p207*
Thanks to Antofagasta's large student
population, the nightlife is thriving. The most
popular bars and clubs are 16 km south of
the town in Balneario El Huascar. Take Micro
2 from C Matta to get there.
Bar Picadillo, *Av Grecia 1000*.
Recommended, lively atmosphere, also
serves good food.
Castillo Pub, *Pasaje Carrera 884*. Live music,
tasty food and good-value *almuerzo*, fun.
Recommended.
Pub En Vivo, *O'Higgins 1998*. Often has live
music, popular.
Wally's Pub, *Toro 982*. British expat-style
with pool, darts and beer, closed Sun.
Club Happy, **Entre Negros**, **La Terraza**, **Vox**,
Camino Coloso. Popular clubs on the road
south along the coast past the universities.

❼ Entertainment

Antofagasta *p205, map p207*
Teatro Municipal, *Sucre y San Martín*,
T055-264919. Modern, state-of-the-art theatre.
Teatro Pedro de la Barra, *Condell 2495*. Run
by University of Antofagasta, this theatre has
a regular programme of high-quality plays,
reviews, concerts and more; details in press.

⊕ **Sport and activities**

Antofagasta *p205, map p207*
Club de Tenis Antofagasta *Av Angamos 906, T055-247756*. Phone for details of temporary membership.
Geyser, *Chillán 1245, T055-255278*. Genuine sauna plus Turkish bath, hydromasssage, health suite.
Olympic Swimming Pool, *Condell y 21 de Mayo*. For when the sea is too cold.

⊛ **Festivals and events**

Antofagasta *p205, map p207*
On **29 Jun** the image of San Pedro, patron saint of the fishermen, is taken out by launch to the breakwater to bless the first catch of the day.

On the last weekend of **Oct**, the city's immigrant communities put on a joint festival on the seafront with national foods, dancing and music.

O **Shopping**

Antofagasta *p205, map p207*
Antiques
Galería de Arte Imagen, *Uribe 485*, sells antiques including artefacts from former nitrate plants.

Bookshops
Libreria Andres Bello, *Condell 2421*. Excellent selection.
Librería Universitaria, *Latorre 2515*. Mainly technical books.
Multilibro, *opposite the Librería Universitaria*. Contemporary Latin American literature, also English-language authors. Recommended.

Food and drink
See also Markets, below.
Korlaert, *Ossa 2400-2500 block*. Supermarket.
Las Brisas, *Baquedano 750*. Supermarket with ATM.
Lider *A Pinto, north of the port*. Supermarket.
Naturista, *Condell 2394*. Healthfood specialist.
Tricot, *Ossa 2450*. Supermarket with ATM.

Markets
Feria Modelo O'Higgins, *Av Pinto, next to the fish market*. Excellent fruit and vegetables as well as restaurants.

Fish market, *Av Pinto, next to the Feria Modelo*.
Municipal market, *Matta y Uribe*.

▲ **Activities and tours**

Antofagasta *p205, map p207*
Tour companies in Antofagasta offer general adventure tourism, including packages to the Atacama, but, on the whole, it is much better value to book directly with an operator in San Pedro (p233).
Atacama Wüstereisedienst, *Apartado Postal 55, T055-243322, F259132*. Alex Joseph Valenzuela Thompson guides German-speakers around the area.
Intitour, *Baquedano 460, T055-266185, F260882, intitour@dtl.net* English-speaking guides.
Tatio Travel, *Washington 2513, T055-263532, F263532*. English spoken, tours arranged for groups or individuals. Highly recommended.

⊖ **Transport**

Air
Cerro Moreno Airport, is 22 km north of the city. LanChile and Sky fly daily to **Santiago**, **Iquique** and **Arica**. No main terminal; each company has its own office in town, some at quite a distance from the centre (see Directory, below).

Bus
Long distance Except for services to Mejillones (p216), buses depart from the company offices as follows: **Flota Barrios**, *Condell 2682, T055-268559*; **Géminis**, *Latorre 3055, T055-251796*; **Pullman Bus**, *Latorre 2805, T055-262591*; **Tur Bus**, *Latorre 2751, T055-264487*.

Numerous companies run services to **Santiago**, 18 hrs, US$20 *semi-cama*, US$30 *cama*, 30% reduction on **Inca**, **Tramaca**, and **Géminis** for students once you have secured a seat, book 2 days in advance. If all seats to the capital are booked, catch a bus to **La Serena**, 12 hrs, US$15 *semi-cama*, US$20 *cama*; or **Ovalle**, 14 hrs, US$15, then re-book.

To **Valparaíso**, 16 hrs, US$20 *semi-cama*; to **Arica**, 11 hrs, US$11 *semi-cama*, **Tur-Bus**; to **Chuquicamata**, frequent, 3 hrs, US$5; to **Calama**, several companies, 3 hrs, US$4.50;

to **San Pedro de Atacama**, Tur Bus, 3 daily, 5 hrs, US$5.50, or via Calama; to **Copiapó**, US$12; to **Iquique**, 6 hrs, frequent, US$10.

To **Salta and Argentina**, Tur Bus, Pullman Bus and **Géminis**, Wed at dawn, change at Calama, via San Pedro, Paso Sico and Jujuy, US$35/US$38. Immigration check at San Pedro de Atacama. Book in advance for this service, take food and as much warm clothing as possible. There is nowhere to change Chilean pesos en route; take small denomination dollar bills to use in Argentina.

Local **La Portada** is reached by minibuses from Latorre y Sucre (US$4 return), or on any bus for Mejillones from the Terminal Centro. Taxis charge US$11. Hitching is easy. Buses go to **Juan López** at weekends in the summer only; there are also minibuses daily in summer from Latorre y Sucre.

Hitchhiking
If hitching south from Antofagasta, go to the checkpoint, restaurant and gas station at **La Negra**, about 15 km south of the city. If hitchhiking to Mejillones or Tocopilla try starting at the police checkpoint on the Mejillones road north of Antofagasta.

❶ Directory

Antofagasta *p205, map p207*
Airline offices LanChile, *Prat 445, T055-265151, F222526*; American, *Washington 2507, T055-410781*; Lufthansa, *Copiapó 654, T055-263399*; Sky, *Velaquez 890, T055-459090*. **Banks** It is impossible to change TCs south of Antofagasta until you reach La Serena; major banks around Plaza Colón include **Corp Banca**, visa agents, **Banco Santiago** and **Banco BCI**; all have ATMs; there are also ATMs at the Tricot and Las Brisas supermarkets (see Shopping above). **Bicycle** spares Rodrigo Baez Banda, *Condell 3071*, also repairs; Cicles Miranda, *Matta 2795, T055-223867*. **Car mechanic** Andrés Ljubetic Romo, *Atacama 2657, T055-268851*, recommended. **Car** rental Avis, *Balmaceda 2499, T055-221073*;

Budget, *Balmaceda 2584, Of 6, T055-251745*; First, *Bolívar 623, T055-225777*; Hertz, *Balmaceda 2492, T055-269043*, offers city cars and jeeps (group D, Toyota Landcruiser) and does a special flat rate, with unlimited mileage; IQSA, *Latorre 3033, T055-264675*. **Casas de cambio** These are mainly on Baquedano, such as Ancla, *Baquedano 524*, open Mon-Fri 0900-1400, 1600-1900, Sat 0900-1400, poor rates (if closed try the ice cream shop next door); several exchange agents in the shopping centre at Baquedano 482-498; nearby is also **Nortour**, *Baquedano 474*; AFEX, *Latorre 668*, open Mon-Fri 0830-2000, Sat 0830-1400, better rates for TCs than Ancla. **Consulates** Argentina, *Blanco Encalada 1933, T055-220440*; France and Belgium, *Baquedano 299, T055-268669*; Bolivia, *Washington 2675, piso 13, of 1301, T055-225010*; Germany, *Pérez Zujovic 4940, T055-251691*; Holland, *Washington 2679, of 902, T055-266252*; Italy, *Matta 1945, of 808, T055-227791*; Spain, *Rendic 4946, T055-269596*. **Cultural centres** Centro Cultural Nueva Acropolis, *Condell 2679, T055-222144*, talks Wed 2100, also Tai Chi, yoga, archaeological and philosophical discussions; Instituto Chileno-Alemán de Cultura, *Bolívar 769, T055-225946*; Instituto Chileno-Norte americano de Cultura, *Carrera 1445, T055-263520*. **Customs agent** Luis Piquimil Bravo, *Sucre 363, Of 28, T055-251789, F6385727*, excellent, fast service, efficient. **Internet** Cheapest is Intitour (see Activities and tours, above), US$0.60 per hr; also try Cybercafé, *Maipú y Latorre*, US$1/hr, or *Sucre 671*, US$0.80/hr. **Laundry** Clean clothes, *G Lorca 271*; La Ideal, *Baquedano 660*; Laverap, *14 Febrero 1802*, efficient, not cheap; París, *Condell 2455*, laundry and dry cleaning, expensive, charges per item. **Post office** Plaza Colón, 0830-1900, Sat 0900-1300.
Telephones CTC, *Condell 2529*; Entel Chile, *Condell 2451*; on Sun, the only call centre to open is CTC, *Condell 2750*. **Useful addresses** Automóvil Club de Chile, *Condell 2330, T055-225332*; CONAF, *Argentina y Baquedano*.

● *For an explanation of sleeping and eating price codes used in this guide, see inside the*
● *front cover. Other relevant information is found in Essentials, see pages 51-58.*

░ Nitrates

The rise and fall of the nitrate industry played an important role in opening up the northern desert areas between Iquique and Antofagasta to human settlement. In the second half of the 19th century, nitrates became important in Europe and the USA as an artificial fertilizer and for making explosives. The world's only known deposits of nitrates were in the Atacama Desert provinces of Antofagasta in Bolivia and Tarapacá in Peru. After the War of the Pacific, Chile gained control of all the nitrate fields, giving her a monopoly over world supply. Ownership was dominated by the British who controlled 60% of the industry by 1900. Taxes on the export of nitrates provided Chilean governments with around half their income for the next 40 years.

The processing of nitrates was labour intensive: at its height over 60,000 workers were employed. Using a combination of dynamite and manual labour, the workers dug the nitrate ore from the desert floor. It was then transported to nitrate plants, known as *oficinas*, crushed and mixed with water, allowing pure nitrates to be extracted. The mining and refining processes were dangerous and cost many lives. Wages were relatively high, but workers were paid in special tokens valid only for the particular *oficina* in which they worked. This not only meant that they had no means of leaving the *oficina* with ready cash, but also that they had to buy all their goods from the company stores which were, of course, controlled by the *oficina*.

The development of the Haber-Bosch process, a method of producing artificial nitrates, in Germany during the First World War, dealt a severe blow to the nitrate companies and many mines closed in the 1920s. New techniques were introduced by the Guggenheim company, but the world depression after 1929 led to a collapse in demand and with it the Chilean nitrate industry. Traces of the nitrate era can, however, still be seen: the mining ghost towns of Chacabuco, north of Antofagasta, and Humberstone, near Iquique, can be visited, as can Baquedano, the most important junction of the nitrate railways; most of the other *oficinas* are marked only by piles of rubble at the roadsides north of Antofagasta. Only one mine survives today, at María Elena; paradoxically, its future is secure, as the nitrates from the Atacama are believed to be much better for the soil than those created by the artificial process and demand has increased in recent years.

North of Antofagasta

There are two routes north from Antofagasta: to Iquique along the Pan-American Highway or along the coastal road, Ruta 1, towards Tocopilla and beyond. The coastal route is more picturesque and makes a beautiful alternative to the sterility that accompanies large stretches of the Panamericana.

Along the Pan-American Highway

From Antofagasta, the Highway continues north via Baquedano (Km 72) and **Carmen Alto** (Km 98), where there is a turning to Calama. Four kilometres' walk from the junction is **Chacabuco** (100 km northeast of Antofagasta), a large abandoned nitrate town, opened in 1924 and closed in 1938. It was used as a concentration camp by the

Pinochet government between 1973 and 1975. Workers' housing, the church, theatre, stores and the mineral plants can be visited and there is a free guided tour in Spanish. If you visit Chacabuco, be sure to take water and set out early in the morning as you will probably be hitching back.

Another turning 69 km north of Carmen Alto leads to **Pedro de Valdivia**, a nitrate town abandoned in 1996, which has been declared a National Monument and can be visited. From here, a road runs north, parallel to the Pan-American Highway, crossing the Salar del Mirage to **María Elena**, the only nitrate town still functioning. After a half-century or more in the doldrums, the nitrate business is now profitable once again, because the nitrates extracted from the Atacama desert are thought to be better for the soil than the chemical version (see box, page 212). The **Museo Arqueológico y Histórico** ⓘ *on the main plaza, US$1,* has exhibits on pre-Hispanic cultures.

Some 22 km southeast of María Elena, on the Pan-American Highway, is the **Balneario Chacance**, also known as the Parque El Loa, where bathing and camping are available on the banks of the Río Loa. North of María Elena, meanwhile, the Highway crosses the Tocopilla-Calama road 107 km north of Carmen Alto. At **Quillagua**, Km 81, there is a customs post where all vehicles heading south are searched. Situated 111 km further north is the southernmost and largest section of the **Reserva Nacional Pampa del Tamarugal**, which contains the **Geoglifos de Pintados**, about 400 figures of humans, animals and geometric shapes on the hillside 3 km west of the highway; the other sections are near La Tirana (see page 246) and 60 km north of Pozo Almonte (see page 220).

Along the coastal road → *There is no fuel between Mejillones and Tocopilla.*

Mejillones and beyond → *Phone code: 055. Colour map 1, C1. Population: 5,500.*
Located 60 km north of Antofagasta, Mejillones stands on a good natural harbour protected from westerly gales by high hills. Until 1948, it was a major terminal for the export of tin and other metals from Bolivia. Remnants of that past include a number of fine wooden buildings: the Intendencia Municipal, the Casa Cultural, built in 1866, and the church, 1906, as well as the Capitanía del Puerto. The town has been transformed in recent years by the building of the largest port in South America here – on completion the port will link Argentina, southern Brazil and Paraguay with the lucrative markets of the Asian Pacific Rim. Although the large port buildings now dominate the northern end of the town, fishing remains important, and Mejillones comes alive in the evening when the fishermen prepare to set sail. The sea is very cold around Mejillones because of the Humboldt current.

From Mejillones, the road runs at the foot of 500-m cliffs, with constantly shifting views of the mountains and of the glistening ocean. Where the cliffs break down into jagged rocks on the shoreline, hundreds of cormorants can be seen swarming all over the pinnacles. There are good weekend beach resorts at **Hornitos**, 88 km north of Antofagasta, and **Poza Verde**, 117 km north.

Behind the mountains, the coastal sierra is extensively mined for copper, often by *pilquineros*, small groups of self-employed miners. There are larger mines, with the biggest concentration inland at Michilla. Reminders of the area's mining past can be seen, principally at the ruins of **Cobija**, 127 km north of Antofagasta, founded by order of Simón Bolívar in 1825 as Bolivia's main port. A prosperous little town handling silver exports from Potosí, it was destroyed by an earthquake in 1868 and again by a tidal wave in 1877 before losing out to the rising port of Antofagasta. Adobe walls, the

● *The only significant river in this part of Chile is the Río Loa, the longest river in the country.*
● *It has been dammed at Conchi to provide irrigation for several oases around Calama and, when it finally reaches the sea, south of San Marcos, it is barely 2 m wide.*

rubbish tip right above the sea and the wreckage of the port are all that remains. The haunting ruins of the port of **Gatico** are at Km 144, just a little way beyond, and about 4 km further north there is an amazing ransacked cemetery. About 152 km north of Antofagasta, a very steep zigzag road winds up the cliffs a further 18 km to the mine at **Mantos de la Luna**. At the top, there are rather dead-looking groves of giant cactus living off the sea mist that collects on the cliffs. Wildlife includes foxes, or *zorros*.

Tocopilla → *Phone code: 055. Colour map 1, C1. Population: 24,574.*

Tocopilla lies 187 km north of Antofagasta via the coast road (or 365 km via the Pan-American Highway), and has one of the most dramatic settings of any Chilean town, sheltering at the foot mountains that loom inland at heights of 500 m. There are some interesting early 20th-century buildings with wooden balustrades and façades, while the sloping plaza is an unlikely fiesta of palms and pepper trees amid the otherwise unremitting desert. Tocopilla is dominated by a thermal power station, which supplies electricity to the whole of northern Chile, and by the port facilities used to unload coal and to export nitrates and iodine from María Elena and Pedro de Valdivia. There are two good beaches: **Punta Blanca**, 12 km south, and **Caleta Covadonga**, 3 km south, which has a swimming pool. There is also fine deep sea fishing here, if you can find a boat and a guide. For a spectacular view, head up Calle Baquedano as far as possible until you reach a stone stairway. Walking up this, you reach a minor road, which climbs up behind the town, giving views of the cliffs to the north, the mountains reaching inland and the fishing boats bobbing up and down in the harbour.

> ✿ *A colony of some 20-30 sea turtles can often be seen about 3 km north of the town.*

Routes north and east of Tocopilla

The coastal road runs north from Tocopilla to Iquique, 244 km away, and is a highly recommended journey, offering views of the rugged coastline, sea-lions and tiny fishing communities. The customs post at Chipana-Río Loa (Km 90) searches all southbound vehicles for duty-free goods; this can take up to half an hour. Basic accommodation is available at **San Marcos**, a fishing village (Km 131). At **Chanaballita** (Km 184), there is a hotel, *cabañas*, camping, restaurant, shops. There are campsites at the former salt mining town of **Guanillos** (Km 126), **Playa Peruana** (Km 129) and **Playa El Aguila** (Km 160).

East of Tocopilla a good paved road climbs a steep and narrow valley 72 km to the Pan-American Highway. From here, the road continues eastwards to **Chuquicamata** (see page 218); the first 62 km east of the Pan-American Highway is in good condition, the last part is very poor. Chuquicamata lies 16 km away from Calama, the main city of the interior.

Tocopilla

To Calama & Chuquicamata

To Iquique

O'Higgins

Cienfuegos

M Rodríguez

Freire

Washington

Flota Barrios

Colón

Pullman Carmelita

A Pinto

Plaza de Armas

Bolívar

BCI Bank & Redbanc   Tur Bus

Baquedano

Pullman
Tequila Disco

Serrano

Pacific Ocean

To Antofagasta & Mejillones

N

0 metres 100
0 yards 100

Sleeping	Eating
América 1	Bela Napoli 9
Atenas 2	Chifa Fu Zhou Lou 1
Casablanca 4	Club de la Unión 2
Chungará 5	El Chilenito 3
Colonial 6	Los Dos Leones 4
Croacia 3	Luciano's Pizzas 5
Hostal Central 7	Oasis 8
Residencial Royal 8	Piero's Place 6
Sucre 9	Pizzería Vittorio 7
Vucina 10	

Along the Pan-American Highway
p212

F **Posada Los Arbolitos**, *122 km north of Carmen Alto*. Rooms, *cabañas* and meals but no running water.

E/F **Residencial Chacance**, *María Elena, T055-632749*. Run down but the same owners provide nicer rooms round the corner and cheap meals are available at **Casino Social**, nearby.

Mejillones *p213*

A **Hotel Mejillones**, *M Montt 86, T055-621590*. New 4-star.

C **Paris**, *Pje Iquique 95, T055-623061*. Clean, modern, good.

G **Res Elisabeth**, *Alte Latorre 440, T055-621568*. Friendly, basic, with restaurant. Price per person.

G **Res Marcela**, *Borgoño 150, T055-621464*. With bath, pleasant. Price per person.

There's no campsite here, but wild camping is possible on the beach.

Tocopilla *p214, map p214*

B-C **Atenas**, *21 de Mayo 1448, T/F055-813650/1*. Good restaurant, overpriced.

C **Vucina**, *21 de Mayo 2069, T/F055-813088*. Modern, good restaurant.

C-D **Chungará**, *21 de Mayo 1440, T055-811036*. With all mod cons.

C-F **Croacia**, *Bolívar 1332, T055-812783*. Modern, helpful. Cheaper without bath. Opposite on Bolívar is the **Sucre**, same ownership, same price.

D **Hotel Colonial**, *21 de Mayo 1717, T055-811621, F811940*. With bath, breakfast and cable TV, friendly, helpful.

F **Casablanca**, *21 de Mayo 2054, T055-813222*. Friendly and helpful, good restaurant, good value. Price per person.

G **América**, *Serrano 1243*. Without bath, clean. Price per person.

G **Hostal Central**, *A Pinto 1241*. Huge rambling place like something out of a Hitchcock film, very basic, friendly, vast rooms, no hot water.

G **Residencial Royal**, *21 de Mayo 1988, T/F055- 811488*. Helpful, basic, without breakfast or bath, parking. Price per person.

Mejillones *p213*

$$-$ **Sion-Ji**, *Alte Latorre 718*. Good-value Chinese cuisine.

$ **Juanito**, *Las Heras 241*. Excellent *almuerzo* and cheap eats.

Tocopilla *p214, map p214*

$$ Good meals are available in the restaurants of **Hotel Vucina** and **Hotel Casablanca** (see above).

$$ **Bela Napoli Pizzas**, *Bolívar 1324, T055-813569*. Pizza deliveries.

$$ **Club de la Unión**, *Prat 1354*. Pleasant atmosphere. Good value *almuerzo*.

$$ **Echikhouse**, *21 de Mayo 2132*. Good value 4-course *almuerzo*.

$$ **Luciano's Pizzas**, *21 de Mayo 1995*. Fairly good.

$$ **Oregón**, *Rodriguez 1280*. Cafeteria, fine sea views from veranda.

$$ **Piero's Place**, *21 de Mayo 1395*. Fast-food café, lively, good music with video screen. Recommended.

$ **Caleta Boy**, *Caleta Covadonga*. Good seafood. Recommended.

$ **Chifa Fu Zhou Lou**, *21 de Mayo 1842*. Chinese restaurant, pleasant.

$ **El Chilenito**, *21 de Mayo 2042*. Few places open early for breakfast; this is the first up.

$ **La Caleta**, *opposite the old wooden clock tower*. Good seafood.

$ **Los Dos Leones**, *21 de Mayo 1993*. Sandwiches, good value *almuerzo*, popular with locals.

$ **Oasis**, *21 de Mayo 2072A*. Good value.

$ **Pizzeria Vittorio**, *21 de Mayo 1759*. Good atmosphere, good value.

Bars and clubs

Tocopilla *p214, map p214*

The town can get quite rowdy on Sat night. **Tequila Pub**, *21 de Mayo y Serrano*. Dancing Thu-Sat.

Shopping

Tocopilla *p214, map p214*

Basar e Artesano Lastato, *21 de Mayo y Washington*, has varied crafts. There's also a **craft market** on 21 de Mayo outside the post office.

Supermercado Colón, *Colón y 21 de Mayo*.
Supermercado Loconómico, *Bolívar y Sucre*.

▲ Activities and tours

Tocopilla *p214, map p214*
Munditour, *Sucre 1228, T055-813523, 09-540519*. Mostly fixes trips to the south but may also arrange local excursions.

⊜ Transport

Pan-American Highway *p212*
Buses between Antofagasta and Calama stop at the **Carmen Alto** junction, 1½ hrs, US$2. **María Elena** is served by **Tur Bus** from Iquique, 6 hrs, US$6.

Mejillones *p213*
Buses depart from the Terminal Centro, *Riquelme 513* in Antofagasta for Mejillones, 45 mins, US$1.50, continuing on to Tocopilla. There are also **minibuses** to Mejillones departing from *Latorre 2730*.

Tocopilla *p214, map p214*
There is no bus terminal in Tocopilla. Bus offices are located on *21 de Mayo*, including Pullman Bus, Tur Bus, Barrios and Pullman Carmelita, all serving the following destinations: **Antofagasta**, many daily, 2½ hrs, US$3; **Iquique**, frequent, 3 hrs, US$4. **Tur Bus** also runs services to **Chuquicamata** and **Calama**, 3 a day, 3 hrs, US$4.50. All the above companies also serve Santiago.

Note that most buses to southern destinations are en route from Iquique, so you're unlikely to be able to leave Tocopilla before mid-morning.

⊕ Directory

Tocopilla *p214, map p214*
Banks BCI, *Baquedano y Prat*, has a Redbanc ATM. **Internet** *21 de Mayo 1721*, US$1.20 per hr. **Post office** *21 de Mayo y A Pinto*. **Telephone** CTC call centre near the post office; also ENTEL, *21 de Mayo 2066*.

Calama and around

→ *Phone code: 055. Colour map 1, C2. Population: 121,300.*
Calama is a seedy city, set at 2,265 m in the oasis of the Río Loa, with beautiful views of volcanoes in the Ollagüe area. It is an expensive modern town, roughly 200 km northeast of Antofagasta, which acts as a service centre for the large nearby mines of Chuquicamata and Radomiro Tomic. Initially a staging post on the silver route between Potosí and Cobija, Calama superseded San Pedro de Atacama in importance with the development of mining activities at Chuquicamata. Most travellers use Calama as the departure point for San Pedro de Atacama and the weekly train to Bolivia, however, football fans will certainly want to make sure that their visit coincides with a home match of Cobreloa, the most successful Chilean football team outside Santiago in the past 20 years or so.

Ins and outs
Getting there Calama is easily reached by regular buses from Antofagasta and by less frequent buses from Iquique and Arica, which often travel overnight. For those heading to Uyuni in Bolivia, there is a weekly train (see box, page 223) and two weekly buses. There are also three weekly buses to Salta in Argentina. The airport is served by daily flights to/from Antofagasta and Santiago. Taxis to/from the airport cost US$6. There are also courtesy vans for hotels in Calama, Alfa and Lican Antai. Airport transfers are also offered by **Alberto Molina** ⓘ *T055-324834, US$3*, recommended. ►► *For further details, see Transport, page 222*. **Getting around** The central part of Calama is relatively compact and you should not need to take public transport. There are, however, many *colectivos*, most of which pick up on Abaroa or Vargas. **Tourist office** ⓘ *Latorre 1689, T055-345345, calamainfotour@entelchile.net, Mon-Fri 0830-1300, 1500-1900 (1830 on Fri)*. Provides map of town, English spoken, helpful staff.

The centre of Calama is Plaza 21 de Mayo, a shady spot in which to relax. The peach-coloured **Catedral San Juan Bautista** on the west side makes a pleasant contrast to the colours of the desert. On the northeastern side, the pedestrian walkway of Ramirez continues two blocks east, where visitors will not be able to miss the bright red, phallic statue of **El Minero**, erected as a tribute to the bravery of the region's miners, but also an unlikely piece of kitsch in the Atacama.

This area comes alive at night. In the plaza, teenagers flirt with one another, while Argentine backpackers down on their luck ponder their next move. The pedestrian walkways of Ramírez are awash with young and old, beggars and hippies, not to mention an old man winding a barrel organ, watched by his pet parakeet.

On Avenida B O'Higgins, 2 km from the centre, is the **Parque El Loa** ① *daily 1000-1800*, which contains a reconstruction of a typical colonial village built around a reduced-scale reproduction of Chiu Chiu church. In the park is the **Museo Arqueológico y Etnológico** ① *Tue-Sun 1000-1300, 1500-1930, US$0.40*, which has an exhibition of pre-hispanic cultural history. Nearby is the new **Museo de Historia Natural** ① *Wed-Sun 1000-1300, 1430-2000, US$0.65*, which has an interesting collection devoted to the *oficinas* and the region's ecology and palaeontology. ▸▸ *For Sleeping, Eating and other listings, see pages 220-224.*

Calama

Antofagasta, Calama & San Pedro de Atacama · Calama & around

Sleeping ●
Alfa **1**
Atenas **2**
Casablanca **5**
Casa de
  Huéspedes **6**
Cavour **23**
Claris Loa **7**
El Loa **8**

Génesis **9**
Hostal
  Internacional **11**
Hostal Splendid **12**
Hostería Calama **13**
John Kenny **14**
Lican Antai **15**
Los Andes **16**
Mirador **17**

Olimpo **18**
Palermo **19**
Paradise Desert **20**
Quitor **21**
Valle de la Luna **22**

Eating ●
Bavaria **1**
Club Croata **2**

Di Giorgio **3**
Los Adobes de
  Balmaceda **4**
Mariscal JP **5**
Nueva Chong Hua **6**
Pollo Scout **7**
Pukará **8**
Tropicana **9**

Farewell to Chuqui

The town of Chuquicamata has always been famous in Chile. Quite apart from the fact that the mine is responsible for a large part of Chile's GDP, miners at "Chuqui" are treated differently, with free healthcare in a special modern hospital and guaranteed housing close to the mine. The decision to move all those living in Chuqui down to Calama is very sad for those who have grown up and lived in the town, and will have a severe impact on both the people of Chuqui and on those living in nearby Calama.

Some 2,500 families are to be moved from Chuqui to Calama. New neighbourhoods are being built on the outskirts of the town, near the road to Chiu Chiu. The town's famous hospital has already been transferred to Calama, which will be of great benefit to the city. By the end of 2004, the move is expected to be complete. The two reasons for the change are the reserves of copper lying beneath the town of Chuqui and the pollution risks for those living there. Certainly, anyone approaching Calama only has to look at the great cloud that hangs to the north to appreciate the dangers of pollution in Chuqui. Nevertheless, the death of the town is a momentous and sad event in the history of northern Chile.

Chuquicamata → *Phone code: 055. Colour map 1, C2. Population: 12,722.*

A visit here is truly memorable. Sixteen kilometres north of Calama, Chuquicamata is the site of the world's largest open-cast copper mine, employing 8,000 workers and operated by **Codelco**, the state copper corporation. Although copper has been mined here since pre-Inca times, it was the Guggenheim brothers who introduced modern mining and processing techniques after 1911 and made Chuquicamata into the most important single mine in Chile. In other parts of the plant, 60,000 tonnes of low-grade ore are processed a day to produce refined copper of 99.98% purity. Since 1986, output has been over 500,000 tonnes a year, but the diggers are having to cut ever deeper into the desert, making the extraction process increasingly expensive. In 2004 the town that surrounds the mine is to be closed and the families moved to Calama, leaving only a small historical centre for visitors (see box, page 218). This will enable Codelco to exploit the copper that is buried in the earth beneath the houses and will make Chuquicamata the latest and the largest in the Atacama's long line of ghost towns.

A visit to the mine at Chuquicamata is highly recommended for the insight it gives into the industry that bankrolls Chile's economy. It also gives fantastic views of the desert pampa and the volcanoes to the east. Guided bus **tours** ① *Mon-Fri 0945 (less frequently in low season), 1 hr, US$1.50 donation, passport essential,* depart from the office of Chuqui Ayuda (a local children's charity) near the entrance at the top end of the plaza. The tours are in Spanish (also in English if enough people) and no filming is permitted. To join a tour, catch a *colectivo* from Calama at 0800 and register at the office of Chuqui Ayuda half-an-hour in advance. Consult the tourist office in Calama for further details.

● *Everything about the Chuquicamata mine is huge: the pit is 4 km long, 2 km wide and 630 m deep; the trucks have wheels over 3 m high, their tyres are worth over US$6,000 each and they carry 255-tonne loads, working 24 hours a day.*

Chiu Chiu was one of the earliest centres of Spanish settlement in the area. Set in the shadow of the Volcán San Pedro, it is a peaceful oasis village and a nice contrast to the bustle of Calama. In the glades nearby, horses graze on surprisingly lush grasses and the local people cultivate alfalfa. Chiu Chiu's plaza, fringed with pepper trees and opposite the church, is a pleasant place to while away a few hours. The church of **San Francisco**, dating from 1611, has roof beams of cactus and walls over 1 m thick – please leave a donation. Some 10 km distant on the road to Caspana is a unique, perfectly circular, very deep lake, also called **Chiu Chiu** or **Icacoia**.

From Chiu Chiu, the road continues north towards Ollagüe. Just beyond the oasis, a small turning branches off the main road and follows the course of the Río Loa. Here the canyon is green with crops, and donkeys plough the earth – it seems like a secret valley. This area has been settled for millennia and petroglyphs are clearly visible in the rocks on the right-hand side of the road heading towards **Lasana**. This small hamlet, 8 km north of Chiu Chiu, has striking ruins of a pre-Inca *pukará*, a national monument; drinks are on sale.

At **Conchi**, 25 km north of Lasana, the road crosses the Río Loa via a bridge dating from 1890; there is a spectacular view over the river from the bridge, but it is a military zone, so no photographs are allowed. Access to the river is by side tracks, best at Santa Bárbara. There is interesting wildlife and flower meadows and trout fishing in season; you can obtain a permit from Gobernación in Calama.

From Conchi, a road branches east following the valley of the **Río San Pedro**, which has been a route for herders and silver caravans for centuries, to **Inacaliri**, from where a very poor road (four-wheel drive essential) runs south to Linzor and the **El Tatio geysers** (see page 232). While there are several direct routes east from Chiu Chiu towards the geysers, only one is in good condition: just north of Chiu Chiu, turn right off the Ollagüe road and continue until you reach a fork some 22 km east of Chiu Chiu. Take the right fork, ignoring the large sign pointing left to El Tatio (this leads to another very bad track via Linzor). At Km 47 a track turns off north to Caspana; again, ignore this turning and continue along the main road as it climbs steeply up the Cuesta de Chita. At about Km 80, branch left to Tatio; this branch meets the main Tatio-San Pedro road some 5 km further north.

Caspana is beautifully set among hills with a tiny church dating from 1641 and a **museum** ① *Tue-Sun 1000-1300, 1500-1730*, with interesting displays on Atacameño culture. Basic accommodation is available. A poor road runs north and east of Caspana through valleys of pampas grass with llama herds to **Toconce**, which has extensive pre-Hispanic terraces set among some interesting rock formations. There are many archaeological sites nearby and the area is ideal for hiking, with the **Cerros Toconce, León** and **Paniri** – all over 5,500 m – within reach. A community **tourism project** ① *toconce@mixmail.com, T055-321828*, has recently been set up in Toconce, designed to help stem the flow of people moving away to an impoverished urban existence in Calama. Further information on the project can be had from the tourist office in Calama, which may also help with arranging transport. Given the fragility of these Andean communities and the fact that this is the community's first foray into tourism, please exercise as much sensitivity as possible during your visit. You should also check in with the *carabineros* in the plaza.

Twenty kilometres west of Toconce is **Ayquina**, in whose ancient church is enshrined the statue of the Virgin of Guadalupe. Her feast day is 8 September, when pilgrims come from far and wide to celebrate and worship. ▸▸ *For further details, see Festivals and events, page 222.* Six kilometres north of Ayquina are the lukewarm thermal waters of the **Baños de Turi** and the ruins of a 12th-century *pukará* that was once the largest fortified town in the Atacama mountains. Close to the village of **Cupo** is a large, ruined pre-Hispanic settlement at **Paniri**, with extensive field systems, irrigation canals (including aqueducts) and a necropolis. Some of the fields are still in use. The area around Cupo is one of the best for seeing the Atacama giant cactus (*Notocereus atacamensis*); flamingos are also visible on the mudflats. Surrounding the *baños* is an oasis of ancient pastoral land, the **Vega de Turi**, now drying up due to the water consumption of the mines. It remains an important site for the llama- and sheep-herders, who believe it has curative properties. At several times in the year, especially September, herders from a wide area congregate here with their flocks.

Ollagüe → *Phone code: 055. Colour map 1, B3. Population: 433.*

Situated 198 km north of Calama on the dry floor of the Salar de Ollagüe at 3696 m, **Ollagüe** is surrounded by a dozen volcanic peaks of over 5000 m. It is a cold, dusty, windswept place, but remarkable for its sense of remoteness. At this altitude, nights are cold, while the days are warm and sunny, there are only 50 mm of rain a year and water is very scarce.

The road to Ollagüe from Chiu Chiu runs north to Estación San Pedro. This first section is in poor condition, however, from Estación San Pedro to a *carabinero* checkpoint at **Ascotán**, it is worse. This is the highest point of the road at 3900 m. Ask at Ascotán or Ollagüe about weather conditions before setting out, especially in December

❖ *Do not deviate from the road, as the desert to the east is covered with minefields.*

and January or August. North of Ascotán, the road improves as it crosses the Salares de Ascotán and de Carcote and Ollagüe. There are many llama flocks along this road and flamingos on the *salares*. There is no petrol between Calama and Uyuni in Bolivia, although if you completely run out, you could try buying some from the *carabineros* at Ollagüe or Ascotán, the military at Conchi or the mining camp at Buenaventura.

Five kilometres south of Ollagüe is the sulphur mining camp of **Buenaventura**, which is situated at an altitude of 5800 m, only 150 m short of the summit of Ollagüe Volcano. Camping is possible and there are amazing views over the volcanoes and salt flats. A road leads to the sulphur camp but be wary of walking the route if not coming from Bolivia, as you will not yet be acclimatized for exercise at this altitude. You should also bear in mind that temperatures can drop as low as -37°C.

A road runs west from Ollagüe to the sulphur mines, now closed, of **Aucanquilcha**, where there are the ruins of an aerial tram system. A high-clearance vehicle is needed to drive to the mine but from there you can scramble to the summit of Aucanquilcha, at 6176 m, from which there are superb views. An interesting excursion can also be made north from Ollagüe to the village of **Coska** with its traditional agriculture and herds of llamas and alpacas.

Into Bolivia → *Bolivian phone code: +591. Immigration and customs are open 0800-2000*

A poor road leads across the Bolivian frontier from Ollagüe and runs to **Uyuni**, 170 km east. Trucks take a more northerly route across the Salar de Uyuni but motorists are warned against using this latter route into Bolivia. As well as the danger of getting lost on the many tracks leading over the salt lakes, there's no petrol between Calama and Uyuni and little hope of help with a breakdown on the Bolivian side, unless you don't mind waiting for days. After rain the route is impassable and even experienced guides get lost. Maps give widely differing versions of the route. Where the road has been built up, **never** forsake it for the appealing soft salt beside it. The salt takes a person's weight but a vehicle breaks through the crust into unfathomable depths of plasticine mud below.

⬤ **Sleeping**

Calama *p216, map p217*

L Park, *Camino Aeropuerto 1392, T055-319900, F319901 (Santiago T02-2338509)*. First class, pool, bar and restaurant.

L-AL Hostería Calama, *Latorre 1521, T055-310306, hcalama@directo.cl* Comfortable, good food and service.

L-AL Lican Antai, *Ramírez 1937, T055-341621, hotellicanantai@terra.cl* With breakfast, central, good service and good restaurant, TV. Recommended.

AL Hotel Paradise Desert, *Ramirez 1867, T/F055-341618, paradise_hotel@ hotmail.com* Internet, more expensive rooms with jacuzzi, excellent views, nice terrace, good for business people.

AL-A Alfa, *Sotomayor 2016, T055-314187, hotelalfa@terra. cl* Comfortable and with good service.

AL-A El Mirador, *Sotomayor 2064, T/F055-340329, hotelelmirador@ hotmail.com* With bath, good atmosphere, clean, helpful. Recommended.

A Quitor, *Ramirez 2116, T055-341716, hotelquitor@terra.cl* Central, pleasant, helpful. Good.

B John Kenny, *Ecuador 1991, T055-341430.* Modern, clean, friendly, parking.

C Atenas, *Ramirez 1961, T055-342666, F316399.* With bath and cable TV, small rooms, pricey laundry service, breakfast extra, overpriced.

C El Loa, *Abaroa 1617, T055-341963.* Cheaper rooms without bath. English spoken.

C San Sebastián, *Pinto 1902, T055-343810.* With bath (cheaper without), good beds, meals available, decent choice, family run.

C-D Res Splendid, *Ramirez 1960, T055-341841.* Central, clean, friendly, hot water, often full, good, cheaper without bath.

F Genesis, *Granaderos 2148, T055-342841.* Without bath, near Géminis bus terminal, clean. Recommended. Price per person.

F Gran Chile, *Latorre 1474, T055-317455.* With bath, good value. Price per person.

F Palermo, *Sotomayor 1889, T055-341283.* Friendly, dark, central. Price per person.

G Casa de Huéspedes, *Sotomayor 2073.* Poor beds, basic but reasonable, pleasant courtyard, clean, hot shower. Price per person.

G Cavour, *Sotomayor 1841, T055-314718.* Simple, basic, friendly. Price per person.

G Claris Loa, *Granaderos 1631, T055-311939.* Clean, quiet. Price per person.

G Los Andes, *Vivar 1920, T055-341073.* Good beds, noisy. Price per person.

G Valle de la Luna, *Sotomayor 2326, T055-312114.* Clean, central. Price per person.

North and east of Calama *p219*

C Hostal Chiu Chiu, *Esmeralda s/n, Chiu Chiu, T055- 326386.* Friendly and helpful. Three rooms are also available at the community tourism project in **Toconce**, providing accommodation for up to 12 people, with full board.

Ollagüe *p220*

There is nowhere official to stay in Ollagüe, but police and border officials will help travellers to find unofficial lodgings.

🍴 Eating

Calama *p216, map p217*

$$ Bavaria, *Sotomayor 2095.* Good restaurant with cafeteria downstairs, real coffee, open 0800, very popular, also at Latorre 1935.

$$ Los Braseros de Hans Tur, *Sotomayor 2030.* Good ambience, good food.

$$ Mariscal JP, *Félix Hoyos 2127.* Best seafood in town, not cheap but worth it.

$$ Mexico, *Latorre 1986.* Mexican cuisine, fairly expensive, live music at weekends.

$$ Osorno, *Espinosa y Granaderos.* Grill, with live Chilean folk music.

$$ Patagonia, *Granaderos 2549.* Lots of meat. Good wine list.

$$-$ Continental, *Vargas 2180.* Good seafood and fish, cheaper than Mariscal JP but less charm.

$$-$ Club Croata, *Abaroa, Plaza 23 de Marzo.* Excellent value 4-course *almuerzo*.

$$-$ D'Alfredo Pizzeria, *Abaroa, Plaza 23 de Marzo.* Vast and uninviting but good pizzas and *almuerzos*.

$$-$ Di Giorgio, *Abaroa, Plaza 23 de Marzo.* Pizzas, good coffee, ice cream, fancy building with a nice outlook, opens 0900.

$$-$ Nueva Chong Hua, *Abaroa 2006.* The best Chinese. Recommended.

$$-$ Plaza Restaurant, *Abaroa, Plaza 23 de Marzo.* Good *almuerzos*, opens early, good service. Recommended.

$ Jugo Camelot, *Abaroa 1968.* Good fruit juice.

$ Lascar, *Ramirez 1917.* Good value *almuerzo*. Recommended.

$ Pollo Scout, *Vargas 2102.* Clean, friendly, popular, reasonable.

$ Pukará, *Abaroa 2054B.* Typical local food. Highly recommended.

$ Tropicana, *Sotomayor 2043.* Good fruit juice.

There are also many very cheap eateries in the **Féria modelo** (see below).

Chuquicamata *p218*

$ Cheap lunches are available at the **Club de Empleados** and at **Arco Iris** both facing the bus terminal – although these will both close when the town is shut down.

$$ **Café Tambo**. A nice place with old wooden furniture. Mid-range meals.

⏵ Bars and clubs

Calama *p216, map p217*
Karka's Pub, *Latorre 1986B*. Swish, good.
Schoperia Ché Carlitos, *Abaroa 1901*.
Central, popular.

Calama's nightclubs are all out of town on Av Circunvalación. There are over 10 of them, including **Kamikaze**, very expensive, and **Vox**, both recommended.

⊛ Festivals and events

Calama *p216, map p217*
Calama's **annual festival** in early Feb is a riot of activities and celebrations – recommended for those in the area.

North and east of Calama *p219*
The feast day of the **Virgin of Guadalupe** on 8 Sep is celebrated in Ayquina, with day-long group dancing to Indian rhythms on flute and drum. Towards sunset the Virgin is carried up a steep trail to a small thatched shrine, where the image and the people are blessed before the dancing recommences, continuing all the way back to the village. The poor people of the hills gather stones and make toy houses all along the route: miniatures of the homes they hope to have some day.

Southwest of Ayquina is Cupo, which celebrates the fiesta, of **San José**, on 19 Mar.

Ollagüe *p220*
Fiesta de San Antonio de Padua on the 19 Jun celebrates the patron saint of Ollagüe, with dancing and Quechua customs, such as the sacrifice of llamas.

○ Shopping

Calama *p216, map p217*
Económico, *Grecia 2314*. Supermarket.
El Cobre, *Vargas 2148*. Supermarket.
Féria Modelo, *Antofagasta between Latorre and Vivar*. The market sells fruit juices and crafts. There are also craft stalls on *Latorre 1600-block*.
Shopping mall, *Baquedano, north of centre*. Reached by bus 1M, *colectivos* 11B and 18B.

▲ Activities and tours

Calama *p216, map p217*
Several agencies in Calama run 1-day and longer tours to the Atacama region, including San Pedro; these are usually more expensive than tours from San Pedro and require a minimum number for the tour to go ahead. Reports of tour quality are mixed – watch out for poorly maintained vehicles and poor guides – but the following have received positive recommendations. The tourist office (see above) also offers tours of the area.
Atacama Explorer, *Lascar 4182, Villa Ayquina, 055-335527*. Atacama tours, plus trips to the old nitrate mines and the upper Loa valley.
Atacama Park Adventure, *Camino al Aeropuerto 1392, T055-440100*. Atacama tours and other expeditions.
Azimut 360, *T/F055-333040, www.azimut.cl* Tours to the Atacama desert, plus mountaineering to Licanábur and Llullaillaco.
Colque Tours, *Caracoles, T055-851109, colquetours@terra.cl* 4WD tours of Andes and salt plains into Bolivia, good guides, vehicles, food and accommodation. Main office is in San Pedro de Atacama.
Turismo Buenaventura, *T/F055-341882, buenventur@entelchile.net* Recommended for tours of Atacama region.

⊖ Transport

Calama *p216, map p217*
Air
LanChile to **Santiago** via Antofagasta, 5 daily, US$150. **Sky Airline** is slightly cheaper.

Bus
No main terminal, buses leave from the company offices: **Tur Bus**, *Granaderos, about 12 blocks north of centre*; tickets from *Ramirez y Balmaceda*; **Pullman Bus**, *Balmaceda 1802*; **Géminis**, *Latorre 3055*; **Kenny Bus**, *Vivar 1954*; **Flota Barrios**, *Ramírez 2298*.

To **Santiago**, 22-24 hrs, US$23 (*sálon cama* US$35); to **Antofagasta**, 3 hrs, several companies, US$4; to **Arica**, usually overnight, 9 hrs, US$11, or change in Antofagasta; to **Valparaíso/Viña del Mar**, US$23; to **Iquique**, Tur Bus, 3 daily, 6 hrs, via Chuquicamata and Tocopilla, US$10. To **La Serena**, usually with delay in Antofagasta, 16 hrs, US$15. To **Chuquicamata** (see below). To **San Pedro de**

⁙ The 'tren de la muerte' from Calama to Uyuni

The line between Calama and Uyuni in Bolivia is the only section of the old Antofagasta and Bolivia railway line still open to passenger trains. It is a long journey, often taking up to 36 hours to Uyuni,. It is one of the world's great train journeys but uncomfortable – if your idea of fun is standing still at a border post for up to 10 hours, this is the trip for you. The journey is cold, both during the day and at night (-15°C). From Calama the line climbs to reach its highest point at Ascotán (3960 m); it then descends to 3735 m at Cebollar, skirting the Salar de Ascotán. Chilean customs are at Ollagüe, where there is a delay of five to six hours while an engine is sent from Uyuni. Immigration formalities are conducted on the train but passengers are required to disembark with their luggage, to be searched on the Bolivian side. There are money changers on the train but beware of forged notes. From the border, the line runs to Uyuni, 174 km northeast, crossing the Salar de Chiguana and running at an almost uniform height of 3,660 m. Uyuni is the junction with the line south to the Argentine frontier at Villazón.

A personal account: "A few years back, I was travelling with two friends in Bolivia and decided to take the train back from Uyuni to Calama. We were told that the train would arrive in Uyuni at 2300, so we sat in the waiting room until 0230, when the train finally arrived. The 'train' in fact consisted of several different sections, each heading in a different direction – some carriages only to Potosí, others on to Villazón, and only two carriages to Chile. After running frantically up and down in the freezing temperatures, we finally found the right carriage. However, the train went nowhere until dawn, when the driver awoke and decided to continue.

We reached Ollagüe at 1000, and then spent the entire day waiting there as the Chilean border guards searched every bag of every passenger for contraband goods – Bolivians travel with a lot of bags and so the train did not leave Ollagüe until 2000.

As we pulled out, the Chilean border guard remarked that the train was ahead of schedule. It arrived in Calama at 0300 the next morning, when, of course, most of the hotels were shut."

Atacama, 1½ hrs, US$1.50, **Tur Bus**, several daily, **Atacama 2000**, 3 a day from Abaroa y Antofagasta, **Frontera**, 9 a day from Antofagasta 2142, last bus 2030.

To **Salta** (Argentina), 22 hrs, **Tur Bus** services leave at 0915 on Wed, US$30, **Géminis** on Wed and Sun, US$35, **Pullman Bus** on Wed at 1000.

To **Bolivia**, Buses Manchego, *Alonso de Ercilla 2142, T055-31642*, midnight on Wed and Sun to Uyuní, US$10, also serving Ollagüe for US$5 (see below).

Driving

Car hire is not reliable in San Pedro de Atacama, so you're better off picking up a vehicle in Calama. A high-clearance vehicle (necessary for the desert) costs US$70-100

per day. Rates are sometimes much lower at weekends. A hired car, shared between several people, is an economic alternative for visiting the Atacama region.

Train

To **Uyuni** (Bolivia), weekly service, departing Wed 2300 (in theory), up to 36 hrs, US$10.50. Remember that between Oct and Mar, Chilean time is 1 hr later than Bolivian. Station closes for lunch 1300 to 1500, no luggage store. Book seats in advance (passport essential) from railway station after 1500 on the day of travel. Catch the train as early as possible: although seats are assigned, the designated carriages may not arrive; passengers try to occupy several seats to sleep on but will move if you politely show your ticket. Sleeping bag and/or blanket essential. Restaurant car serves cheap food and drinks, with waiter service; food is also available at Ollagüe (see also box, p223).

Chuquicamata *p218*

Yellow *colectivos* (marked 'Chuqui') depart from the corner of the Plaza 23 de Marzo in Calama, US$0.75. Chuqui is on the main road north from Calama and is served by buses to **Arica** at 2200 (weekends at 2300), 9 hrs, US$9; to **Antofagasta**, US$5; to **Iquique**, US$7; to **Santiago**, 24 hrs, US$26.

Chiu Chiu *p219*

Served by **Línea 80** *colectivos* to/from **Calama**, about 8 a day, US$2. To catch one, either ring ahead in Calama, *T055-362523*, or take the Línea 80 *colectivo* on Abaroa to the end of the line in Calama and then catch the next vehicle to Chiu Chiu. If arranged in advance, the *colectivos* will continue on to Lasana for an extra charge – you will have to book the return trip, or walk back to Chiu Chiu.

Ollagüe *p220*

There is no fuel in Ollagüe. **Buses Manchego** from **Calama**, Wed & Sun at 2400, 5 hrs, US$5; returns next day. Ollagüe can also be reached by taking the **Calama-Uyuni train** (see above) but, if you stop off, you will have to hitch back as the daily freight trains are not allowed to carry passengers. Hitching by road is difficult but the police may help you to find a truck.

● Directory

Calama *p216, map p217*
Airline offices LanChile, *Latorre 1726, T055-341477/341494 and airport, T055-311331*; Sky, Latorre 1497, T055-310190.
Banks Rates are generally poor especially for TCs. Corp Banca, *Sotomayor 2041*, Visa, ATM; **Finandes**, *Latorre 1763*, Mastercard; many Redbanc ATMs on Latorre and Sotomayor. **Car hire** Alamo, *Hoyos 2177, T055-364543*, good value; **Avis**, *Gallo 1985A, T055-319757*; **Budget**, *Granaderos 2925, T341076*; Hertz, *Latorre 1510, T055-341380*; IQSA, *O'Higgins 877, T055-310281*. **Casas de Cambio** Moon Valley Money Exchange, *Vivar 1818*, and also another exchange at *Sotomayor 1837*; also on Ramirez, next to Centro Comercial Gala, most open Sat.
Consulates Bolivia, *Centro Boliviano, Latorre 1395, T055-341976*, open (in theory) 0900-1230 Mon-Fri, friendly, helpful. **Cycle spares** Cicles Miranda, *Sotomayor 2271, T055-342769*. **Internet** Centro Internet, *Vargas 2054*, US$1.50 per hr; **Cybercafé**, *Vargas 2014, piso 2, T055-318925*, US$1.50 per hr; **Cybercafé Machi**, *Vivar 1944*.
Laundry Universal, *Vargas 2178* (cheapest); **Lavexpress**, *Sotomayor 1887*, good, speedy. **Post office** *Granaderos y V Mackenna*, open 0830-1300, 1530-1830, Sat 0900-1230, will not send parcels over 1 kg.
Telecommunications CTC, *Sotomayor 1825*; Entel, *Sotomayor 2027*. **Useful address** Automóvil Club de Chile, *Av Ecuador 1901, T/F055342770*.

San Pedro de Atacama and around → Phone code: 055. Colour map 1, C3. Population: 2,824.

Situated 103 km by paved road southeast of Calama, San Pedro is an oasis town in the valley of the Río San Pedro at 2,436 m. While San Pedro is now famous among visitors as the base for excursions in this part of the Atacama, it was important as the centre of the Atacameño culture long before the arrival of the Spanish. There is a definite sense of history in the shady streets and the crumbling ancient walls that drift away from the town into the fields and on into the dust. Owing to the clear atmosphere and isolation, there are wonderful views of the night sky from just outside town. Despite being in the desert, it does rain in San Pedro about three or four times a year, usually around March, as a a result of the invierno altiplánico.

Ins and outs

Getting there San Pedro can be reached by 16 buses a day to/from Calama. There are three companies – **Atacama 2000, Frontera** and **Tur Bus**. If you are driving, note that there is no food, water or fuel along the Calama-San Pedro road. ▶▶ *For further details see Transport, page 234.* **Getting around** San Pedro is small so taxis (from by the football field) are only needed for out-of-town trips. ▶▶ *For further details see Activities and tours, page 233.* **Tourist office** Sernatur has an office in the plaza. It is worth going there to check out previous travellers' observations on the merits of the various tour companies in the suggestions book. **Climate** Be prepared for the harsh climate and high altitudes of the interior. Gloves, a hat and a warm coat are essential for excursions from San Pedro, especially for the early morning trip to El Tatio. High factor sun cream and (again) a hat are necessary for the burning daytime sun. Take plenty of water on any excursion.

Background

The main centre for the Atacameño culture, which flourished in this region before the arrival of the Incas around 1450, San Pedro was defended by a *pukará* (fortress) at Quitor, 3 km north. The cultivable land around was distributed in 15 *ayllos* (socio-economic communities based on family networks) and irrigation channels were built. San Pedro was visited by both Diego de Almagro and Pedro de Valdivia and the town became a centre of Spanish colonial control; a mission was established in 1557. After

San Pedro de Atacama

Sleeping
Camping Kunza 1
El Tatio 2
Hostal Edén Atacameño 3
Hostal Inti-Kamac 4
Hostal Takha-Takha 5
Hostería San Pedro 6
Katarpe 7
Kimal 8
La Casa de Don Tomás 9
Putitama 20
Residencial Chiloé 10
Residencial Don Rául 11
Residencial Florida 12
Residencial Juanita 13
Residencial
  Licancábur 14
Residencial Rayko 15
Residencial Vilacoyo 16
Tambillo 17
Terrantai 18
Tulor 19

Eating
Adobe & Casa
  Piedra 1
Café Export 2
El Viaje 3
Flamenco 4
La Casona 5
La Estaka 6
Todo Natural 7

Independence, the town became an important trading centre on the route between Cobija on the coast and Salta in Argentina, but the decline of Cobija and the rise of copper-mining led to San Pedro being superceded as an economic centre by Calama.

In the early 20th century, San Pedro's economy was based around mining, with salt mines in the Valle de la Luna (whose ruins are easily visible today) and sulphur mines in the high mountains. Since the 1970s, tourism has been of increasing importance and the town is now dependent on the annual influx of Chilean and foreign visitors. However, travellers should be aware that tourism is a somewhat divisive issue in San Pedro. The tour companies are often run by outsiders and the glut of travel agencies has led to a tenfold increase in rents in the past ten years. Many of the local people still work in agriculture, having lower incomes than those who work with tourism, and, with 25 tour companies and not enough tourists to go round, there are dark (and doubtless somewhat exaggerated) rumours that some of these operations are fronts for money laundering and drug running, especially with Bolivia so close.

The road from Calama

At Paso Barros Arana (Km 58) there is an unpaved turning to the left, which leads through interesting desert scenery to the small, mud-brick village of **Río Grande**. Look out for vicuñas and guanacos on the pass. The main road continues skirts the Cordillera de la Sal about 15 km from San Pedro. There are spectacular views of the sunset over the western *cordilleras*. The old unpaved road to San Pedro turns off the new road at Km 72 and crosses this range through the Valle de La Luna (see Excursions below), but should only be attempted by four-wheel drive vehicles. This road is partly paved with salt blocks.

Sights

The **Iglesia de San Pedro**, dating from the 17th century, is supposedly the second oldest church in the country. It has been heavily restored and the tower was added in 1964. The roof is made of cactus; inside, the statues of Mary and Joseph have fluorescent light halos. Nearby, on the Plaza, is the **Casa Incaica**, the oldest building in San Pedro.

The **Museo Arqueológico** ① *www.ucn.cl/map-spedro.htm, Mon-Fri 0900-1200, 1400-1800, Sat and Sun 1000-1200, 1400-1800, US$1.50*, contains the collection of Padre Gustave Paige, a Belgian missionary who lived in San Pedro between 1955 and 1980. It is now under the care of the Universidad Católica del Norte. One of the most important museums in northern Chile, it traces the development of pre-Hispanic Atacameño society. It is well organized; the labels (in Spanish only) on displays are good and there is a comprehensive booklet in Spanish and English. Graham Greene observed "the striking feature of the museum is the mummies of Indian women with their hair and dresses intact dating from before the Conquest, and a collection of paleolithic tools which puts the British Museum in the shade". No heating: wear warm clothing.

San Pedro is a good base from which to visit **Toconao**, the **Salar de Atacama** and the **geysers of El Tatio**, see below. From 2004, entry charges will be levied at many of the natural attractions. There are also interesting destinations closer to the town, including the **Pukará de Quitor**, three kilometres north of San Pedro along the river. This pre-Inca fortress was restored in 1981 and covers 2.5 ha on a hillside on the west bank of the river. It was stormed by the Spanish under Pedro de Valdivia, 1,000 defenders being overcome by 30 horsemen who vaulted the walls. The road to Quitor involves fording the river several times, until the *pukará* comes into view on the hill on the left-hand side of the valley. There is a new plaza here, built as a homage to the indigenous people of the region and set amid thorn trees. The road continues along the valley of the Río San Pedro as the canyon climbs further into the Atacama, passing a couple of small farmsteads sheltered by pepper trees where sheep graze in the desert sun. A further 4 km up the river, there are ruins at **Catarpe**, which was the Inca administrative centre for this region. The ruins are on top of a hill on the east side of the valley, and are difficult to find without a guide; archaeological tours are offered in San Pedro.

There's another archaeological site 12 km southwest of San Pedro at **Tulor**, where parts of a village (dated 500-800 BC) have been excavated. The road is *ripio*, and fine for four-wheel-drive vehicles. You can sleep in two reconstructed huts or take a tour, US$5. Nearby are the ruins of a 17th-century Spanish-style village, abandoned in the 18th century because of the lack of water.

Valle de la Luna

Twelve kilometres west of San Pedro, this is a valley of fantastic landscapes caused by the erosion of salt mountains. The valley is crossed by the old San Pedro-Calama road. Although buses on the new road will stop to let you off, where the old road branches off 13 km northwest of San Pedro (signposted to Peine), it is far better to travel from San Pedro on the old road, either on foot (allow three hours there, three hours back), by bicycle or high-clearance vehicle. The Valle is best seen at sunset. Take water, hat, camera and a torch. Also consider spending the night to see the sunrise (take warm clothes and plenty of water). Agencies in San Pedro offer tours, departing around 1530, returning after sunset, US$4-6 per person, but make sure the agency departs in time for arrival in the Valle before sunset as they do not always do so. Tours usually include a visit to the **Valle de la Muerte**, a crevice in the Cordillera de la Sal near San Pedro, with red rock walls, contorted into fantastic shapes.

The geysers of El Tatio

At an altitude of 4,321 m, the geysers of El Tatio are a popular attraction. From San Pedro, they are reached by a maintained road that runs northeast, past the **Baños de Puritama** (28 km), then on for a further 94 km. The geysers are said to be at their best in the morning between 0630 and 0830, although the spectacle varies: locals say the performance is best when weather conditions are stable. A swimming pool has been built nearby. From here, you can hike to surrounding volcanoes if you are adapted to altitude, although it is advisable to take a guide because of the dangers of minefields.

There is no public transport and hitching is impossible. If going in a hired car, make sure the engine is suitable for very high altitudes and is protected with anti-freeze; four-wheel-drive is advisable. If driving in the dark, it is almost impossible to find your way: the sign for El Tatio is north of the turn-off. Following recent accidents a series of stone walls and wooden walkways has been built around the geysers, which some say has taken away from the spectacle. From 2004, visitors will be charged to enter the site.

South of San Pedro de Atacama

From San Pedro to Toconao, 37 km south, the paved road runs through groves of acacia and pepper trees. There are many tracks leading to the wells (*pozos*), which supply the intricate irrigation system. Most have thermal water but bathing is not appreciated by the local farmers. The groves of trees are havens for wildlife, especially rheas (*ñandu*) and Atacama owls; there are also some llamas.

Toconao and around → *Phone code: 055. Colour map 1, C3. Altitude: 2,600 m.*

This village is on the eastern shore of the Salar de Atacama. Unlike San Pedro, Toconao's economy is based on agriculture, not tourism. All houses are built of bricks of white volcanic stone, which gives the village an appearance totally different from San Pedro. The 18th-century church and bell tower are also built of volcanic stone.

East of the village is a beautiful gorge called the **Quebrada de Jerez**, ① *US$0.80*, which is almost unimaginably verdant and filled with fruit trees and grazing cattle. At the bottom of the gorge a crystal-clear stream cuts down towards Toconao. Nearby is the quarry where the stone *sillar* is worked; it can be visited. The stones sound like bells when struck. Also worth visiting are the vineyards, which produce a unique sweet wine.

About 4 km before Toconao, vehicle tracks head east across the sand to a hidden valley 2 km from the road where there is a small settlement called **Zapar**. There are some well-preserved pre-Hispanic ruins on the rocky cliffs above the cultivated valley here. The sand is very soft and a four-wheel-drive vehicle is essential.

Around the Salar de Atacama

South of Toconao is one of the main entrances to the Salar de Atacama. At 300,000 ha in extent, this is the third largest expanse of salt flats in the world; the air is so dry here that you can usually see right across the Salar. Rich in minerals, including borax, potassium and an estimated 40% of world lithium reserves, the Salar is home to three of the world's five species of flamingos – the Andean, Chilean and James – as well as other birds (although these can only be seen when lakes form in winter). The flamingos live by eating algae and tiny shellfish that subsist in the small saline pools in the Salar. Three areas of the Salar are part of the seven-sector **Reserva Nacional de los Flamencos** ① *US$3*, totalling 73,986 ha, administered by **CONAF** in San Pedro.

From Toconao, a road runs 67 km along the eastern edge of the Salar de Atacama to the attractive village of **Peine**, where you'll find the offices of the lithium extraction company. It is worth asking if the company's access road can be used to visit the Salar de Atacama's spectacular salt formations. There is also a thermal pool where you can swim. Woollen goods and knitwear are made here. To the east of the village lies a group of beautifully coloured hills, whose colours are more vibrant at sunset, with good views over the Salar de Atacama. A path leads across these hills to **Socaire**; allow two days. Other villages worth visiting include **Tilomonte** and **Tilopozo**, south and west of Peine.

South of San Pedro de Atacama

Minefields: Beware

An indication of the nature of General Pinochet's geopolitics in the 1970s and 1980s is provided by the numerous minefields that were placed along Chile's border with Bolivia and northern Argentina at that time. The minefields were put down to forestall any possible invasion from Chile's neighbours, which was then perceived to be a very real threat.

Following the Ottawa convention, Chile has begun the slow process of dismantling its extensive minefields. Meanwhile, the danger remains. It is not unknown for people to have been killed or maimed (often while attempting to smuggle drugs across the border). It is very unwise to make any lone forays into the *altiplano* without a knowledgeable local guide.

Minefields are known to affect the new **Parque Nacional Llullaillaco** (see page 229) and the Chilean side of **Volcán Licancabur** (see box page 230), to give just two examples – and there may be other areas that are not known about. Always ask first before heading off into the northern wilderness, keeping in mind that local people are often more knowledgdable than officials.

From Peine, a road (64 km) crosses the Salar de Atacama and joins the road that runs from San Pedro down the west side of the Salar, continuing south to **Pan de Azúcar**, an abandoned railway station. Here it meets the paved road that runs east-west from the Pan-American Highway south of Antofagasta to Socompa on the Argentine border, via the vast **La Escondida** copper mine, which has an output of copper higher than any other mine in the world. Ten kilometres east of La Escondida at Imilac, a poor road turns off south to the **Parque Nacional Llullaillaco**. This recently created park covers 263,000 ha and includes **Cerro Llullaillaco** at 6,739 m, the second highest peak in Chile, as well as three other peaks over 5,000 m: Cerro de la Pena at 5,260 m, Guanaqueros, 5,131 m, and Aguas Calientes, 5,070 m. The park is inhabited by large numbers of guanacos and vicuñas. Visits are by arrangement only with CONAF in Antofagasta, owing to the dangers of minefields in the area. Further along the Pan de Azúcar-Socompa road (poor condition) is **Monturaqui**, the source of the green onyx that is used for carving.

Southeast of Toconao

From Toconao, another road heads south through the villages of **Camar**, where handicrafts made from cactus may be bought, and **Socaire**, which has llama wool knitwear for sale; the road is paved as far as Socaire. About 20 km south of Socaire, a rough road leaves the main route to the Paso Sico and climbs a hill to the beautiful **Laguna Miscanti**, a lake that is part of the Reserva Nacional Los Flamencos. 'Miscanti' means 'toad' in Atacameño, and refers to when the lake was full of toads. In the 1940s and 1950s, trout were introduced for American fishermen working in Chuquicamata, resulting in the decline of the toad population; today there are none left.

Nearby is the **Laguna Miñiques**. The lakes are on the site of ancient Atacameño hunting grounds and arrowheads can still be found on the shores, which are edged with whorls of calcium salt crystals. There are clear views of the volcanoes behind the lakes, as well as fantastic views down to the Salar.

After the turning to the lakes, the road goes on to the mine at Laco, before proceeding to the **Paso de Sico**, which has replaced the higher, more northerly Guaytiquina pass, at 4,295 m (also spelt Huaytiquina) to Argentina (see below).

 The algae consumed by the flamingos on the Salar de Atacama contain chemicals that give the birds their distinctive pink colour.

Into Bolivia: the Salar de Uyuni and other sights

East of San Pedro, on the border with Bolivia, lies **Volcán Licancábur** (5,916 m), a sacred site for the Incas and the focal point of three Inca paths that crossed the *altiplano* and the Salar de Atacama. The volcano can be climbed only from the Bolivian side, at any time of the year except January and February. At the foot of the volcano on the Bolivian side is **Laguna Verde** (4,400 m), which extends over 17 sq km; its wind-lashed waters are an impressive jade, the result, it is said, of magnesium, calcium carbonate, lead or arsenic. There is a *refugio* near the lake (US$2, small, mattresses, running water).

Further north is the equally impressive **Laguna Colorada** (4,278 m), which covers 60 sq km; its flaming red waters are the result of the effects of the wind and afternoon sun on the numerous micro-organisms that live in it (up until midday the water is a fairly ordinary colour). The water is less than a metre deep but the mud is very soft,

and the shores are encrusted with borax, which provides an arctic white contrast with the waters of the lake. The pink algae in the lake provides food for the rare James flamingos, along with the more common Chilean and Andean flamingos. Some 40 other bird species can also be seen.

Further north still, beyond Ollagüe, is the **Salar de Uyuni**, the largest and highest salt lake in the world and an increasingly popular attraction for visitors. Situated at an altitude of 3,650 m and covering 9,000-12,000 sq km (depending on who you believe), the Salar is twice as big as the Great Salt Lake in the United States. The depth of the salt varies from 2 to 20 m. Driving across it is one of the most fantastic experiences in South America, especially in June/July when the bright blue skies contrast with the blinding-white salt (be sure to bring good sunglasses). After particularly wet rainy seasons the Salar is covered in water, which adds to the surreal experience.

Ten kilometres south of Toconao, the old road branches east towards Guaytiquina. In a deep *quebrada* below Volcán Láscar is the now deserted settlement of **Talabre**, with terracing and an ancient threshing floor. Above the *quebrada* is an isolated, stone-built cemetery. Large flocks of llamas graze where the stream crosses the road below the Láscar Volcano at 5,154 m. After a steep climb, you reach the **Laguna Lejía** at 4,190 m, once full of flamingos. Mysteriously, the colony declined rapidly immediately after the eruption of Volcán Láscar in 1993. You then pass through the high plains of **Guaytiquina** (4,275 m), where only a few herdsmen are found. The Guaytiquina crossing to Argentina is not open to road traffic.

Argentine border crossings from San Pedro

There are three crossings; the best is the most northerly, the **Paso de Jama** at 4,200 m, 165 km southeast of San Pedro, which is reached by a paved road that runs via the Salar de Tara, which forms a sector of the Reserva Nacional de los Flamencos. The main alternative to this, **Paso de Sico** at 4,079 m, lies further south, 207 km southeast of San Pedro, and is reached by a very poor road which runs via Toconao and Socaire (see above, page 229). This pass has replaced the higher **Paso de Guaytiquina** at 4,275 m. The most southerly crossing is **Paso de Socompa**, 3,865 m, which is reached by another very poor road from Pan de Azúcar (see page 229).

There is a Chilean post for **immigration and customs** ① *open 0800-2300*, at Paso de Socompa. Immigration and customs formalities for Paso de Jama and Paso de Sico are dealt with in San Pedro de Atacama ① *open 0800-2300*. Incoming vehicles are searched for fruit and dairy products.

If crossing by private vehicle, check road conditions with the *carabineros* and at immigration in San Pedro, as these crossings are liable to be closed by heavy rain in summer and blocked by snow in winter. If hitching, try the immigration post in San Pedro; Spanish is essential. ▸▸ *For bus services from Antofagasta, Calama and San Pedro to Jujuy and Salta, see the relevant Transport sections above.*

On the Argentine side of the border, all these roads link up and continue to **San Antonio de los Cobres** (where Argentine customs and immigration formalities take place) and **Salta**. Transport using the Paso de Jama crossing usually follows a more northerly alternative via **Susques**, where there is accommodation, and **Jujuy**. The most southerly route via Paso de Socompa is perhaps the most spectacular, crossing salt flats and wide expanses of desert, but this route is virtually unused.

> ‡ *The Escondido-Pan de Azúcar-Peine route is a good way of travelling from Antofagasta to San Pedro for those with their own transport.*

Bolivian border crossings from San Pedro

There are two crossings, the more northerly of which, via Ollagüe, is described above (see page 220). The more southerly crossing is at **Hito Cajones**, 45 km east of San Pedro via a poor road that turns off the paved road towards Paso de Jama at La Cruz, 8 km southwest of the frontier. Laguna Verde (see box, page 230) is 7 km north of Hito Cajones. Chilean **immigration and customs** are in San Pedro ① *open 0800-2300*. Incoming vehicles are searched for fruit, vegetables and dairy products.

There is no public transport: do not be tempted to hitch to the border as you risk being stranded without water or shelter at sub-zero temperatures. The most practical method of crossing this border is on a tour from San Pedro (see page 233). If you intend to travel independently in this region do not underestimate the dangers of getting stuck without transport or accommodation at this altitude. Do not travel alone and seek full advice in advance.

● Sleeping

San Pedro de Atacama *p224, map p225*
San Pedro is an expensive town; accommodation rates rise in Jan and Feb when it may also be scarce.
L Explora, *Av Américo Vespucio Sur 80, 5 piso, Santiago, T055-2066060, explora@entelchile.net* Luxury full board and excursion programme, 3 nights, 4 nights and 8 nights, advance booking only.
L Hostería San Pedro, *Toconao 460, T055-851011, hsanpedro@chilesat.net* Pool (residents only), petrol station, cabins, hot water supply, restaurant (good *almuerzo*) and bar. Accepts AmEx but not TCs.
L Terrantai, *Tocopilla 411, T055-851045, F851032 (Casilla 10), terrantai@adex.cl* Comfortable, but only offers all-inclusive packages, good restaurant.
L Tulor, *Atienza 523, T/F055-851027, tulor@chilesat.net* Good service, swimming pool, heating, parking, laundry service, excellent restaurant. Recommended.

L-AL Kimal, *Atienza y Caracoles, T055-851159, kimal@entelchile.net* Comfortable, nice living room, now expanding with an excellent restaurant.
AL La Casa de Don Tomás, *Tocopilla, T055-851055, dontomas@rdc.cl* Good accommodation, very pleasant inside, quiet and friendly, swimming pool, good restaurant. Recommended.
A El Tatio, *Caracoles 219, T055-851263, F851092, hoteleltatio@usa.net* Comfortable, parking, small rooms, overpriced, bargain off season, English spoken.
B Hotel Tambillo, *on Le Paige opposite Casa Corvatsch, T/F055-851078.* Pretty, benches on the patio, 24-hr hot water, good value.
B-C Katarpe, *Atienza 441, T055-851033, katarpe@galeon.com* Comfortable and quiet, nice patio, good value for money, friendly. Recommended.
B-F Casa Corvatsch, *Le Paige 178, T/F055-851101, corvatsch@entelchile.net* Pleasant views, but several bad reports about the owner. Also has much cheaper rooms.

B-F **Hostal Puritama**, *Caracoles 113, T055-851540*. Simple but comfortable, with large patio, kitchen facilities, good showers, camping available. Price per person for cheaper rooms. Recommended.

B-F **Hostal Takha-Takha**, *Caracoles, T055-851038*. Pretty, lovely garden, pleasant patio, nice rooms and camping. Laundry facilities. Price per person for cheaper rooms. Recommended.

B-F **Residencial Don Rául**, *Caracoles, T055-851138*. With bath and mod cons, small rooms, or price per person for basic rooms.

B-F **Residencial Licancábur**, *Toconao 495, T055-851007*. Clean, nicely furnished, friendly, a little basic. Much cheaper rooms available (price per person).

C **Hostal Inti Kamac**, *Atienza, T055-851200*. Pleasant veranda, with bath. Friendly and good value.

C-F **Hostal Mamatierra**, *Pachamama 615, T055-851418*. Price per person for cheaper rooms without bath. Kitchen, friendly, good.

F **Casa de Nora**, *Tocopilla, T055-851114*. Family accommodation, simple rooms, lovely patio. Recommended.

F **Hostal Edén Atacameño**, *Toconao, T055-851154*. Basic with laundry facilities. Price per person. Also camping.

F **Residencial Chiloé**, *Atienza, T055-851017*. Hot water, sunny veranda, good clean bathrooms, good meals, laundry facilities, good beds but no single rooms, luggage store, good value. Price per person. F **Residencial Vilacoyo**, *Toconao*. Friendly, kitchen facilities, recommended. Price per person.

G **Res Florida**, *Tocopilla, T055-851021*. Without bath, basic, hot water evenings only, laundry facilities, no singles. Price per person.

G **Res Juanita**, *on the plaza, T055-851039*. Without bath, dormitories, hot water, rundown, restaurant. Price per person.

Camping

Camping Kunza, *Antofagasta y Atienza, T055-851183*. Disco next door at weekends. Also **Camping Los Perales** and **Camping Terracota**.

El Tatio *p227*

There is a workers' camp at El Tatio, which is empty apart from one guard, who might let you sleep in a bed in one of the huts; bring food and a sleeping bag.

Toconao *p227, map p228*
There are basic *residenciales* in the village. Cheap accommodation is also offered at the **Restaurant Lascar**, which has good, simple food. Camping is possible along the Quebrada de Jérez.

Eating

San Pedro de Atacama *p224, map p225*
Few places are open before 1000. Drink bottled water as, owing to its high mineral content, the local supply is not recommended for those unaccustomed to it.

$$ **Adobe**, *Caracoles*. A good meeting place with an open fire, where you can watch the moon rise. Loud music and somewhat supercilious service. Greenwich Village/ Islington in the Atacama.

$$ **Café Export**, *Toconao y Caracoles*. Nice decor, vegetarian options, real coffee, English spoken, loud music.

$$ **Casa Piedra**, *Caracoles s/n*. Open fire, friendly service, also has a cheap menu, many of the waiters are musicians who, if in the mood, will play Inti Illimanni or Victor Jara songs on panpipes and *queñas* late at night, good food and cocktails. Warmly recommended.

$$ **Hostería San Pedro**, *see Sleeping, above*. Good value *almuerzo*.

$$ **La Casona**, *Caracoles*. Good food, vegetarian options, cheap lunchtime menu, large portions, interesting Cubist-style paintings of the desert, popular. Warmly recommended.

$$ **Milagro**, *Caracoles*. Good food, vegetarian options, attentive service.

$$ **Tulor**, *Atienza*. A la carte menu, real coffee.

$ **Café El Viaje**, *on Tocopilla in the Casa de la Arte*. Pleasant patio, good for vegetarians.

$ **Flamenco**, *Calama y Caracoles*. Friendly service, bad food.

$ **Quitor**, *Licancabur y Domingo Atienza, T055-851056*. Good, basic food, inexpensive (3 courses for US$3).

Cafés

Café Tierra Todo Natural, *Caracoles*. Much the best choice for breakfast, serving excellent fruit juices and the best bread in the Atacama, plus real coffee and yoghurt. It also opens earliest.

🌙 Bars and clubs

San Pedro de Atacama *p224, map p225*
Many San Pedro restaurants double as bars late at night.
Estaka, *Caracoles*. Lively watering hole after 2300, where the Chilean New Age scene congregates. Also very good cuisine and service. Recommended.

🛍 Shopping

San Pedro de Atacama *p224, map p225*
There is a good craft market on the plaza. Also try **Bazar Shaman**, on Le Paige opposite the church, for excellent cheap goods and friendly service.

🔺 Activities and tours

San Pedro de Atacama *p224, map p225*
San Pedro is awash with tour operators and, with competition so stiff, prices are low. Approximate prices for tours are as follows:
Valle de la Luna US$4-6; **Salar de Atacama** US$7-9; **Geysers of Tatio** US$14-16; **Altiplano Lakes** (including **Toconao** and **Salar de Atacama**) US$25-30.

The following advice should help those trying to pick through the glut of operators: avoid cut-price operators and try to check out vehicles and guides before booking; if travelling to high altitude make sure that oxygen is being carried; report any complaints to the Municipalidad or to Sernatur; if in doubt, check through the book with travellers' complaints at the Sernatur office.

Spanish speakers may prefer to go with one of the smaller operators to experience better the vastness of the desert, although all the more responsible operators do try to stay away from the well-trodden routes used by the majority. There are about 25 agencies, but some are temporary and/or open for only part of the year.
Atacama Inca Tour, *Plaza, T055-581034, F851062*. Recommended but not always open.
Ázimut 360, *Caracoles, T055-851469, www.azimut.cl*. A long-establishe,d nationwide operator that also offers adventure tours.
Cactus Tour, *Atienza 419*. Good reports.
Cosmo Andino Expediciones, *Caracoles, T/F055-851069, cosmoandino@entelchile.net*

One of the best tour agencies. English, French, German, Dutch spoken, good vehicles, good drivers, experienced guides, excellent book exchange for tour customers only, highly recommended for non-Spanish speakers. Dutch owner Martin Beeris is very knowledgeable about the region.
Desert Adventures, *Caracoles s/n, T/F055-851067, deserts@ctcinternet.cl*. Offers excursions to all the major sites, modern fleet of vehicles, large numbers, various reports that guides do not speak good English.
Expediciones Corvatsch, *Tocopilla, T055-851087, ccorvatsch@entelchile.net* Operated by Res Corvatsch and Res Florida, good vehicles, casual service, offer discounts for package tours with accommodation.
Labra Turismo, *Caracoles, T055-851137*. English, German spoken, reliable, owner Mario Banchón an expert guide who accompanies trips, good for visiting the altiplano lakes.
La Herradura, *Tocopilla s/n, laherraduraatacama@hotmail.com* Horseback tours with good local guides, repeatedly recommended.
Pachamama Tours, *Toconao, T055-851064*. Open for part of the year.
Southern Cross, *Caracoles 119, www.scadventure.com* Good vehicles, recommended.
Turismo Colque, *Caracoles, T055-851109, www.colquetours.com* Specialists for tours to Bolivia, including 1-day tour to Laguna Verde (US$90 per person) and 3-day tours to Laguna Colorado and the Salar de Uyuni (see below); TCs, Visa and Mastercard all accepted, reliable, hires sleeping bags, often recommended but some mixed reports. Has agencies in Uyuni and La Paz. Two or three other tour companies in San Pedro offer similar tours.
Turismo Ochoa, *Caracoles y Toconao, T055-851022*. Oldest operator in San Pedro, knowledgeable local guides who are a bit taciturn, inexpensive.
Vulcano, *Caracoles, 055-851023*. Mountain climbs and other adventure tours to infrequently visited areas, also hire out mountain bikes, recommended.

El Tatio *p227*
Tours to El Tatio depart around 0400, arriving at the geysers at 0700, US$12-14, including breakfast. There are opportunities to swim in

the hot thermal pool and to visit the Baños de Puritama on the return journey. Take warm clothing and a swimming costume. Some agencies offer tours to El Tatio and on to Calama, via the villages of the *altiplano*.

Around the Salar de Atacama *p228*

Agencies in San Pedro offer excursions to Toconao and the Salar, returning via the Quebrada de Jérez, US$8-10 plus park entry, usual departure 1530, but note that the flamingos are best seen in the morning, so try to get a morning tour, or combine with visiting the *altiplano* lakes.

Into Bolivia *box p230*

The Salar de Uyuni, Laguna Colorada and Laguna Verde are usually visited by tours from the Bolivian town of Uyuni, where accommodation, money exchange and transport to La Paz, Oruro and Potosi are all available. However, **Turismo Colque** (among others) in San Pedro (see above) also offers this tour and will drop passengers off in Uyuni, although some report that, to see the colour changes on Laguna Colorada, the trip is best done from Uyuni.

⊖ Transport

San Pedro de Atacama *p224, map p225*

Bus

To **Calama**, Tur Bus, several daily (3 continue on to Antofagasta), also **Frontera** 7 a day, 1½ hrs, first 0900, last 1900, US$1.50. Frequencies vary with more departures in Jan/Feb and some weekends, fewer out of

season. Book in advance if you want to return from San Pedro on Sun evening.

Frontera also run to **Toconao**, 4 daily at 1240, 1600, 1930, 2030, US$0.80, and to **Peine** at 1600, returns 0600 next day, US$2.

To **Arica**, daily direct service with **Tur Bus** and **Pullman Bus**, US$15. **Géminis** services from Calama to **Salta**, Argentina (see p222) also stop in San Pedro.

❶ Directory

San Pedro de Atacama *p224, map p225*

Banks   No banks or ATMs. **Cambio Atacama**, *Toconao, open daily 1030-1800*, rates posted outside, good rates for US$ cash, poor rates for Tcs; best not to try changing TCs in San Pedro; bring Chilean pesos from Calama. **Bicycle hire**   Several agencies offer cycle hire, check prices and condition of bicycles carefully, as quality varies. **Car hire**   Some agencies in San Pedro offer vehicle hire, but you should check vehicle condition and insurance very carefully as there are reports of accidents involving uninsured and badly serviced vehicles; it is better to hire cars in Calama. **Internet**   Ubiquitous, including **Café Adobe** and **Café Étnico**, both on Tocopilla, book exchange. **Laundry**   Alana, *Caracoles, near Atienza*. **Post office** *Padre Le Paige, opposite Museo Archaeológico*. **Telephone**   CTC, *Caracoles y Toconoa*; **Entel** *on the plaza, F055-851052*, open Mon-Fri 0900-2200, Sat 0930-2200, Sun 0930-2100.

For an explanation of sleeping and eating price codes used in this guide, see inside the front cover. Other relevant information is found in Essentials, see pages 51-58.

Introduction

The far north of Chile is equally as forbidding as the region around Antofagasta and Calama. North of the attractive city of **Iquique**, transport arteries head inland into the desert pampa. There is a palpable sense of antiquity here in the few oases and settlements that are sprinkled across the Atacama; the profusion of geoglyphs are testament to the fact that, wherever there is water, people have been living for millennia. These geoglyphs of peoples now vanished and the countless ghost towns of former nitrate *oficinas* both stand witness to the harshness and fragility of life in the region.

Further inland still, towards the *altiplano*, are some beautiful spots. **Mamiña** and **Pica** are two thermal springs resorts near Iquique, each of them remarkable for their tranquillity. There are four remote national parks in the high Andes, the northernmost of which – the **Parque Nacional Lauca** – offers some of the most stunning scenery in Chile, with a necklace of high lakes, snow-capped volcanoes, lava fields and varied birdlife. It is easily reached from **Arica**, Chile's northernmost city, along the international road to Bolivia. Near Parque Nacional Lauca are small Andean villages, such as Visviri and Parinacota, where most people speak Aymará, and Spanish remains a foreign language.

★ Don't miss...

① **Iquique** Wander among the city's well preserved 19th-century architecture built with the wealth of the nitrate era, page 239.

② **Humberstone and Santa Laura** These abandoned towns are ghostly reminders of the region's nitrate industry, page 245.

③ **A thermal bath** At the hot springs of Mamiña. This small Andean village is famous for the restorative powers of its waters, page 246.

④ **Cerro Unitas, Pintados or Tiliviche** Be amazed by the geoglyphs carved in the desert by prehispanic people at three of the best-known sites, page 248.

⑤ **The altiplano national parks** Escape the modern world in unforgettable, pristine natural environments, page 260.

Background

As elsewhere in northern Chile, there was a widespread and highly developed network of pre-Hispanic cultures in this region. The geoglyphs at sites such as Pintados and Tiliviche are thought to have been markers for caravans of traders making their way from the *altiplano* to the coast and back again. Circles marked in the hillsides signalled the presence of water. The coastal peoples traded furs and fish with the more highly developed cultures of the interior, maintaining links with Tiahuanaco and the Incas.

Even after the Spanish conquest, the early Spanish settler population was small in numbers. Settlement was concentrated largely in the oases of the sierra, where the climate was easier and where malaria, the scourge of the coast, was not found. From an early date, Arica became one of the principle ports for the silver trade from Potosí, but the coast remained sparsely inhabited until the 19th century. At the time of Independence, the whole of this area became the Peruvian provinces of Tarapacá and Arica, with the provincial capital at the now ruined city of Tarapacá, near Huara. The region became the focal point for the War of the Pacific (1879-83), with decisive naval battles fought at Iquique on 21 May 1879, and at Angamos, near Mejillones, on 8 October of the same year (see box, page 520). After the war, the area as far north as Tacna came under Chilean control, and became the country's economic powerhouse following the sudden growth of the nitrate industry (see page 212).

The poor conditions of workers in the nitrate mines led to the development of early left-wing and trade unionist movements in the far northern part of Chile. In 1907, a group of miners from one of the nitrate *oficinas* was executed by the army in the Santa María school in Iquique for campaigning to be paid in hard cash instead of *oficina* tokens. The legacy of the far north's radicalism can be seen in the now infamous 'caravan of death' executed in seven northern cities by one of General Pinochet's henchmen in the days following the 1973 coup (see page 524).

The region's borders were finally delineated in 1929: Tacna voted in a referendum to return to Peru, while Arica opted to remain Chilean. The collapse of the nitrate industry in the 1930s and 1940s was a regional crisis but the quick growth of the fishing industry saved the area from disaster.

The sea still provides the main source of wealth in this region: Iquique is the principal fishing port in Chile, unloading 35% of the total national catch, and has important fish processing industries. Nowadays, mining is much less important than in other parts of northern Chile; however, silver and gold are mined at Challacollo and copper at Sagasca, near Tarapacá, while the new copper mine at Collahuasi has made a big difference to the region's economy. Over 90% of the population lives in the two coastal cities, Arica and Iquique.

Geography and climate

The Atacama Desert extends over most of the far north. The Cordillera de la Costa slowly loses height north of Iquique, terminating at the Morro in Arica: from Iquique northwards it drops directly to the sea and, as a result, there are few beaches along this coast. Inland, the central depression, the *pampa*, 1,000-1,200 m high, is arid and punctuated by salt flats south of Iquique. Between Iquique and Arica, it is crossed from east to west by numerous gorges, formed by several rivers flowing west from the sierra; the more northerly of these, the Ríos Lluta and San José, provide water for Arica and for the Valle de Azapa, where fruit is grown. On the coast, temperatures are moderated by the Pacific Ocean but, in the *pampa*, variations of temperature between day and night are extreme, ranging between 30°C and 0°C. Coastal regions receive *camanchaca* (sea mist) but the *pampa* is permanently rainless.

East of the central depression lies the sierra, the western branch of the Andes, beyond which is a high plateau, the *altiplano* (3,500-4,500 m), from which rise volcanic peaks, including Parinacota (6,350 m), Pomerape (6,250 m), Guayatiri (6,064 m), Acotango (6,050 m), Capurata (5,990 m), Tacora (5,988 m) and Tarapacá (5,825 m). There are also a number of lakes in the *altiplano*, the largest of which, Lago Chungará, is one of the highest in the world. The main river draining the *altiplano*, the Río Lauca, flows eastwards into Bolivia. Temperatures in the sierra average 20°C in summer and 9°C in winter. The *altiplano* is much colder, averaging just 10°C in summer and -5°C in winter. Both the sierra and the *altiplano* are affected by storms of rain, snow and hail (*invierno boliviano*), usually between January and April.

Iquique → *Phone code: 057. Colour map 1, B2. Population: 200,000.*

Located 492 km north of Antofagasta, Iquique is the the capital of Región I (Tarapacá) and one of the main ports of northern Chile. The city is situated on a rocky peninsula at the foot of the high coastal mountain range, sheltered by the headlands of Punta Gruesa and Cavancha. Iquique is perhaps the most attractive city in northern Chile, with a well-preserved collection of historical buildings in the centre, whose bright wooden façades make a surprising contrast to the lifeless desert and the grey coastal mist.

Ins and outs

Getting there Iquique is served by all major bus companies from the south and from Arica – most southbound buses take the coastal road to Tocopilla. There are also daily buses up to Oruro and La Paz in Bolivia. National flights to Arica, Antofagasta and Santiago; international to La Paz. The airport transfer service ① *T057-310800, US$3.20 per person*, is unreliable; if there are three or more passengers, it is just as cheap to get a taxi, US$10. **Getting around** The best way to get around in Iquique is by *colectivo*. ►► *For further details, see Transport, page 244.* **Tourist information** Sernatur ① *Aníbal Pinto 436, T057-312238, infoiquique@sernatur.cl, Mon-Fri 0830-1630*, is very helpful.

History

Although the site was used as a port in pre-Hispanic times, it remained sparsely populated throughout the colonial period. Even in 1855, when Iquique had begun to export nitrates, the population was only about 2,500. The nitrate trade transformed the city, bringing large numbers of foreign traders and creating a wealthy elite. Although partly destroyed by an earthquake in 1877, the city became the centre of this trade after its transfer from Peru to Chile at the end of the War of the Pacific.

Sights

In the centre of the old town is **Plaza Prat** with a clock tower and bell dating from 1877. On the northeast corner is the **Centro Español**, built in Moorish style by the local Spanish community in 1904, and unique in Chile. The ground floor is a restaurant but the upper floors show paintings of scenes from Don Quixote and from Spanish history by the Spanish artist, Vicente Tordecillas. The extravagance of its construction shows the fabulous wealth that nitrates once brought to the region. On the south side of the Plaza is the **Teatro Municipal**, built as an opera house in 1890 with a façade featuring four women representing the seasons; in its heyday it played host to such famous names as Carruso. Three blocks north of the Plaza is the old **Aduana** (customs house) built in 1871 and the scene, in 1891, of an important battle in the Civil War between supporters of President Balmaceda and congressional forces. Part of it now houses the **Museo Naval de Iquique**

 The name of the town is derived from the Aymará word 'ique-ique', meaning 'place of rest and tranquillity'.

ⓘ *Esmeralda 250, Tue-Sat 0930-1230, 1500-1800, Sun 1000-1300, US$0.60,*
dedicated to the War of the Pacific, and more specifically, to the naval battle of
Iquique. Nearby, is the harbour; there are **cruises** from the passenger pier ⓘ *45 mins,
US$2.50, minimum 10 people,* and sea-lions and pelicans can be seen.

Iquique

Sleeping
Anakena 1 *D2*
Arturo Prat 2 *B1*
Barros Arana 3 *E3*
Belén 4 *B3*
Buenos Aires 5 *B2*
Caiti 6 *C2*
Cano 7 *C2*
Carani 8 *C1*
Carlos Condell 9 *C1*
Casa de Huéspedes
  Profesores 10 *C2*
Hostal América 14 *E2*
Hostal Catedral 21 *B2*
Hostal Cuneo 15 *D1*
Hostal Jean IV 16 *A3*
Hostal JJ Pérez 650 17 *E2*
Hostal Li-Ming 18 *C3*
Inti-Llanka 20 *C2*
Oregón 11 *B1*
Residencial Danny 22 *D2*
Residencial
  Nan-King 23 *B2*
Riorsa 24 *E2*
Wilson 25 *C2*

Eating
Bavaria 1 *C1*
Boulevard 7 *C1*
Casino Español 6 *B1*
Cioccolata 2 *B1*
Club de la Unión 3 *B1*
El Barril del Fraile 4 *D2*
La Picada Curicana 5 *C1*

Five blocks east along Calle Sotomayor is the **railway station**, now disused, built in 1883 and displaying several old locomotives. Two blocks south of the railway station, on Bolívar, is the **cathedral**, dating from 1885. It is painted bright yellow and blue and has interesting stained-glass windows. On Amunátegui, behind the **Escuela Santa María** on Zégers, there is a memorial to the workers from the nitrate mines who were killed by the army while sheltering in the school during the strike of 1907.

On Calle Baquedano, which runs south from Plaza Prat, is the highly recommended **Museo Regional** ① *Baquedano 951, T057-411214, Mon-Fri 0830-1300, 1530-1830, Sat 1030-1300, Sun (in summer) 1000-1300 and 1600-2000, free,* which has an excellent collection of pre-Hispanic artefacts (including several mummies). The archaeological section is very well set out, although explanations are in Spanish only, tracing the development of pre-Hispanic civilizations in the region and containing an important ethnographical collection of the Isluga culture of the *altiplano* (circa AD 400) and of contemporary Aymará cultures. There is also a section devoted to the nitrate era, with exhibits including a collection of *oficina* tokens, a model of a nitrate *oficina* and the collection of the nitrate entrepreneur, Santiago Humberstone.

Elsewhere on the street are the attractive former mansions of the 'nitrate barons'. Adorned with columns, balconies and impressive old doors, these buildings date from between 1880 and 1903 and were constructed from timber imported from California. The finest of these is the **Palacio Astoreca** ① *O'Higgins 350, Tue-Fri 1000-1300, Sat 1000-1330, Sun 1100-1400, US$0.60,* built in 1903, subsequently the Intendencia and now a museum with fine late 19th-century furniture and exhibitions of shells. Continuing south towards the beach at Playa Cavancha, along Baquedano, Lynch or Obispo Labbé, you'll pass many beautiful old wooden houses painted blue, green, yellow and pink, with white columns and large wooden shutters and doors.

Playa Cavancha is very popular in summer – in spite of the Humboldt Current, the water is almost warm – although surfers and other watersports enthusiasts make for the pounding waves of **Playa Brava** further south (see page 244). Those who enjoy walking or sandboarding may want to climb the large sand dune, **Cerro Dragón**, which rises behind Iquique and gives fantastic views of the city and the sea; take a *colectivo* to Chipana y La Tirana and then walk to the base of the hill.

Iquique is a major duty-free centre. North of town is the Free Zone, the **Zofri**, ① *Amuñategui, Mon-Sat 1100-2100, limit on tax free purchases US$1,000,* colectivo *from the centre US$0.50.* It is a giant shopping centre selling a wide range of duty-free imported products, including electronic and leather goods, perfumes, new and used cars, motorcycles and good-quality camping equipment. At Christmas, people come from all over Chile to do their shopping, as the Zofri is said to be cheaper than Punta Arenas' equivalent, the Zona Franca. Drivers should note that all vehicles travelling south from Iquique are searched for duty-free goods at Quillagua on the Pan-American Highway and at Chipana on Route 1, the coastal road.

● Sleeping

Accommodation is scarce in the weeks before Christmas as many Chileans visit Iquique to shop at the Zofri. At other times, it is always worth bargaining for better rates. There's no campsite in Iquique but wild camping is possible on La Brava beach.
L-AL Terrado Suites, *Los Rieles 126, Península de Cavancha, T057-488000, www.terrado.cl* Good sea-view suites with balconies, most expensive, rooftop restaurant, all mod cons.

AL Gavina, *Prat 1497, T057-413030, www.gavina.cl* Very exclusive, central.
AL-A Arturo Prat, *Aníbal Pinto 695, T057-427000, www.hotelarturoprat.cl* 4-star, pool, health suite, expensive restaurant, tours arranged.
A Cavancha, *Los Rieles 250, T057-434800, hostcav@entelchile.net* 4-star, expensive restaurant, pleasant inside but ugly exterior, south of city on the water's edge; outside is a giant chessboard.
B Atenas, *Los Rieles 738, T057-431100, atenashotel2000@yahoo.es* Pleasant,

personal, good value, good service and food, pool. Recommended.

B Barros Arana, *Barros Arana 1302, T057-412840, hotelba@entelchile.net* Clean, modern, swimming pool, friendly, good value. Recommended.

B Cano, *Ramirez 996, T057-315580, www.iqq.cl/hotelcano* Big rooms, friendly, nice atmosphere, good value.

B Carani, *Latorre 426, T057-399999, F399998.* Smart, modern, helpful.

B Carlos Condell, *Baquedano 964, T/F057-3113027, hotel-carlos-condell@ entelchile.net* Friendly, in the historic centre, negotiable for longer stays, with parking and mod cons.

B Majestic , *Playa Brava 3115, T057-441068, hotelmajesticiquiqe@entelchile.net* With breakfast, good.

B-C Riorsa, *Vivar 1542, T/F057-420153.* Friendly, modern, near beach, worth bargaining.

C Anakena, *Orella 456, T/F057-510182, paoa@entelchile.net* Nice old armchairs, friendly, good.

C Belén, *Tarapacá 1002, T057-421774, F413644.* Friendly, laundry, in a bad area.

C Hotel Caiti, *Gorostiaga 483, T/F057-423038.* Pleasant, with bath, breakfast and all mod cons, recommended.

C Inti-Llanka, *Obispo Labbé 825, T057-311104, www.inti_llanka.cl* Nice rooms, clean, helpful, good value.

C Playas, *Gral Hernán Fuenzalida 938, T057-423706.* Small, friendly.

C Wilson, *Wilson 422, T057-423789.* Good-sized rooms, with telephone and mod cons, worth bargaining.

D Hostal Catedral, *Labbé 253, T057-426372.* With bath, quiet, nice balcony, interesting building, also cheaper rooms.

F Buenos Aires, *Esmeralda 713, T/F057-413288.* With breakfast and cable TV, clean, modern, helpful, convenient for Tur Bus, excellent value. Price per person.

F Casa de Huéspedes Profesores *Ramirez 839, T057-475175, inostrozaflores@entelchile.net* With breakfast, helpful, old building with lots of character. Recommended. Price per person.

F Hostal Cuneo, *Baquedano 1175, T057-428654, hostalcuneo@hotmail.com* Modern, clean, nice rooms with bath, helpful, pleasant, good value. Price per person.

F Hostal Jean IV, *Esmeralda 938, T/F057-429904/510855, mespina@entelchile.net* With breakfast, clean, friendly, nice lounge and nice patio, with bath, convenient for buses to Bolivia, excellent value. Highly recommended. Price per person.

F Hostal JJ Pérez 650, *JJ Perez 650.* With breakfast, rooms with bath and cable TV, good value, simple and clean. Price per person.

F Oregón, *San Martín 294, T057-410959.* Central, hot water, friendly, helpful, breakfast included. Recommended. Price per person.

F Residencial, *O'Higgins 963-T057-422896.* Big rooms, good breakfast. Recommended. Price per person.

F Res Nan-King, *Thompson 752, T057-423311.* Clean, small but nice rooms.

G Hostal América, *Rodríguez 550, T/F057-427524.* Near beach, shared bath, unhelpful. Price per person.

G Hostal Li Ming, *Barros Arana 705, T057-421912, F422707.* Clean, simple, good value, kitchen and laundry facilities, small rooms. Recommended.

G Hostal San Francisco, *Latorre 990, T057-427524.* Clean, hot water, noisy. Price per person.

G Res Danny, *Vivar 1266, T057-390439.* Shared bath, with breakfast. Price per person.

⚫ Eating

Beware of the expensive and poor-value tourist restaurants on the wharf on the opposite side of Av Costanera from the bus terminal. Several good, cheap and super-cheap seafood restaurants can be found on the 2nd floor of the central market, Barros Arana y Latorre. There are a number of restaurants near Cavancha beach in Caleta Cavancha, including **Neptuno**, in Hostería Cavancha, see Sleeping, above.

$$$ Club Náutico, *Los Rieles s/n.* Seafood, exclusive. Recommended.

$$$ El Sombrero, *Los Rieles 704.* Quality fish and seafood cuisine, elegant setting, not cheap.

$$$ Otelo, *Valenzuela 775.* Italian specialities, seafood, pricey.

$$ Bavaria, *Pinto 926.* Expensive restaurant, reasonably priced café, serving real coffee, snacks and *almuerzo*.

$$ **Boulevard**, *Baquedano 790*.
Excellent French food.

$$ **Casino Español**, *Plaza Prat*. Good meals well served in a 1904 Moorish-style palace, which in itself is a reason to eat there.

$$ **Club de la Unión**, *Plaza Prat*. Roof terrace with panoramic views, open lunchtimes only, pricey but worth it.

$$ **Colonial**, *Plaza Prat*. Fish and seafood, popular, good value.

$$ **El Barril del Fraile**, *Ramírez 1181*. Good seafood, nice atmosphere.

$$ **Las Tejas de Barros Arana**, *Barros Arana 684*. Peruvian *parrillada*.

$$ **La Tarantella**, *Tarapacá y Baquedano*. Small portions, Italian-style, smart, cheap *almuerzo*.

$$ **Pizzeria d'Alfredo**, *Los Molles 2290 (Playa Brava)*. Large variety of pizzas, well-prepared pastas, not cheap, reasonably priced *almuerzo*.

$ **Bolivia**, *Serrano 751*. *Humitas* and *salteñas*. Recommended.

$ **Compañía Italiana de Bomberos**, *Serrano 520*. Authentic Italian cuisine, excellent value *almuerzo*, otherwise more expensive. Recommended.

$ **Esquis Schop**, *Bolivar 446B*. Fruit juices, nice ambience, good.

$ **La Picada Curicana**, *Pinto y Zegers*. Good local cuisine, good-value *menu de la casa*.

$ Many Chinese *chifas* on Tarapacá 800/900 blocks, including **Win Li**, *San Martin 439*, and **Sol Oriental**, *Martínez 2030*.

$ **Schopería Las Tejas**, *Barros Arana 680*. Seriously cheap, near the market.

Cafés

There are several excellent cafés in the centre of Iquique.

Cioccolata, *Pinto 487 (another branch in the Zofri)*. Good coffee and cakes.

Jugos Tarapacá, *Tarapacá 380*. Good fruit juices.

Salon de Té Ricotta, *Vivar y Latorre*. Very popular for *onces*, quite expensive.

Splendid, *Vivar 795,*. Good *onces*, inexpensive.

Tropical, *Baquedano y Thompson*. Juices and snacks. Recommended.

Via Pontony, *Baquedano y Zegers*. Fruit juices and *empanadas*. Recommended.

Bars and clubs

Most discos are out of the town on the road south to the airport.

Hotel Gavina (see Sleeping, above) has a good club on Fri and Sat nights, quite smart.

La Caldera del Sabor, *Bajo Molle, south of the city*. Most popular Iquique club, open Thu-Sat. Plays salsa and merengue, with dance classes.

Pharo's, *Av Costanera Sur 3607, Playa Brava*. Enormous club with an elaborate design, popular, good.

Santa Fé, *Mall Las Américas, locales 10-11-193*. Mexican, live music, great atmosphere, very popular. Highly recommended.

Taberna Barracuda, *Gorostiaga 601*. Nice decor, good atmosphere, recommended for late night food, drink, video entertainment, dancing.

Entertainment

Casino, *Balmaceda 2755*. Open nightly, entry to salóns US$0.50.

Cine Tarapacá, *Serrano 202*. Shows foreign films.

Mall las Américas, *Av Héroes de la Concepción, T057-432500*. Six-screen cinema.

Teatro Municipal, *Plaza Prat, T057-411292*. Plays, ballet, dance and concerts. There are also occasional recitals in the Cathedral.

Festivals and events

For details of the festival of the **Virgen del Carmen** in La Tirana, 70 km east of Iquique, see p247. There are numerous other, smaller religious festivals in the area – ask in Iquique's tourist office for information.

Shopping

Most of the city's commerce is in the **Zofri** duty-free zone. There is also the **Mall Las Américas**, south of the centre on *Avenida Héroes de la Concepción*. For books try **Andrés Bello**, *Héroes de la Concepción 2855*, which stocks an excellent range. Camping equipment is sold at **Tunset**, *Zofri*, and **Lombardi**, *Serrano 447*.

Fishing

Fishing for broadbill swordfish, striped marlin, yellowfin tuna and bonito is a popular pastime from Mar till end of Aug. Equipment can be bought from: **Ferretería La Ocasión**, *Sgto Aldea 890*. **Ferretería Lonza**, *Vivar 738, T057-415587*.

Paragliding

The cliffs directly behind Iquique are a great place from which to launch off down towards the coast. Two hang-gliding clubs: **Altazar**, *Serrano 145, of 702, T057-431382*. **Manutara**, *T057-418280*.

Surfing

Iquique offers some of the best surfing in Chile with numerous reef breaks on **Playa Brava**, south of the city; not for beginners. **Club de Surf**, *Av Héroes de la Concepción 1939, T057-447070*.

Swimming

The beach at **Cavancha**, just south of the town centre, is good, and popular between Nov and Mar. There is another bathing beach at **Huaiquique**, 5 km south, and a freshwater swimming pool, **Piscina Godoy**, *on Av Costanera at Aníbal Pinto and Riquelme*, open evening, US$1.

Tennis

Club de Tenis Tarapacá, *Bulnes 140, T057-412489*. Temporary membership available.

Tour operators

Avitour, *Baquedano 997, T057-473775, www.aviyours.cl* Tours to Pintados, La Tirana, Humberstone, Pica, etc, some bilingual guides, day tours start at US$20.
Iquitour, *Lynch 563, T/F057-412415*. Tours of saltpeter *oficinas* and Pica oasis. English spoken.
Viatours, *Baquedano 736, T/F057-417197, viatours@entelchile.net* Local tours.

Tours are also offered by the **Hotel Arturo Prat** (see above). The tourist office maintains a list of other operators.

Air

Diego Aracena International Airport, *35 km south at Chucumata*. **Sky** and **LanChile** fly south to **Santiago**, via Antofagasta, and north to **Arica** – some flights continue on to **La Paz** in Bolivia.

Bus

The bus terminal is at the north end of Patricio Lynch but not all buses leave from here; **Tur Bus** have their own terminal, *Ramírez y Esmeralda*, with a Redbanc ATM and a good luggage store. Bus company offices are near the market on Sgto Aldea and Barros Arana. All southbound buses are stopped for a luggage check on leaving the duty-free zone of Region I at Quillagua on the Pan-American Highway and at Chipana/Río Loa on the coastal Route 1. For local/regional services, see p251.

To **Arica**, buses and *colectivos*, frequent, 4½ hrs, US$4.50; to **Antofagasta**, 6 hrs, US$9.50; to **Calama**, 6 hrs, US$9.50; to **Tocopilla** along the coastal road, 3 hrs, US$4; to **La Serena**, 18 hrs, US$18; to **Santiago**, 25 hrs, US$21 (US$32 for *salón cama*).

International Most bus companies for services to **Oruro** and **La Paz** (Bolivia) leave from Esmeralda, near the junction of Juan Martínez (note that some buses go via Arica and Tambo Quemado to La Paz, not via Colchane and Oruro). **Litoral Buses**, T057-423670, daily at 2200 to **Oruro**, US$8, to **La Paz**, US$12; **Salvador Buses**, at 2300, same price; **Géminis** from the bus terminal to **La Paz**, via Oruro, more expensive. **Delta**, **Tata Sabaya** and **Comet** all leave from *Esmeralda y Juan Martínez* 2100-2300 to **Oruro** (via Colchane), bargain for a good price.

Colectivos/taxis

Any car that looks like a taxi serves is a *colectivo* unless it says *'sólo taxi'*. Tell the driver where you are going and, if your destination can combine with that of other passengers, he will take you; if you are the first passenger, tell the driver you want to hire the car as a *colectivo* and he will fit the journeys of subsequent passengers around your destination. The fare is US$0.50 (a little more late at night). Taxi fares are US$1.50 for journeys within the city centre.

❶ Directory

Airline offices Iberia, *Vivar 630,*
T057-411878; KLM, *Pinto 515, T057-423009.*
LAB, *Serrano 442, T057-407015;* LanChile,
Tarapacá 465, T057-427600, and in the Mall
Las Américas; Sky, *Ramírez 411, T057-415013;*
TAM, *Serrano 430, T057-390600.* **Banks**
Finandés, *Tarapacá 441,* Mastercard; Corp
Banca, *Serrano 343,* Visa; numerous Redbanc
ATMs in the centre; lots of ATMs in the Zofri.
Bicycles, Redolfi, *Latorre 786,* sales, parts,
repairs; try also the Zofri. **Car hire**
Continental, *18 de Septiembre 105,*
T057-441426; Hertz, *A Pinto 1303,*
T057-510432; airport office *T057- 407020;*
IQSA, *Labbé 1089, T057-417068.* Jofamar,
Libertad 1156, T057-411639; Procar, *Serrano*
796, T057-413470, at airport *T057-410920.*
Motorcycle mechanic Sergio Cortez,
Civet, Bolívar 684, highly recommended.
Casas de cambio AFEX, *Serrano 396,*
changes TCs; Cambio Cambio's, *Lynch 548,*
Local 1-2; Wall Street, *in the Zofri,* sells AmEx
TCs and changes them.
Consulates Bolivia, *Gorostiaga 215,*
Departamento E, T057- 421777, Mon-Fri
0930-1200; Netherlands, *Tarapacá 123,*
T057-390900; Italy, *Serrano 447,*
T057-421588; Paraguay, *O'Higgins 480,*
T057-419040; Peru, *Zegers 570, T057-411466;*
Spain, *Manzana 2, Sitio 5 y 9, ZOFRI, T057-*
422330. **Dentist** Clínica Dental Lynch,
Lynch y Orella, T057-413060.
Hospitals Centro Médico, *Orella 433,*
T/F057-414396; also at *Héroes de la*
Concepción 502, T057-415555. **Internet**
Fassher Internet, *Vivar 1497, piso 2,*
US$0.80/hr; same price is PC@NET
Computación, *Vivar 1373;* more central is the
cybercafé on *Obispo Labbé y Serrano,*
US$1/hr. **Language schools** Academia
de Idiomas del Norte, *Ramírez 1345,*
T057-411827, F429343, idiomas@chilesat.net
Swiss run, Spanish classes, accommodation
for students. **Laundry** Central Dry Clean,
Serrano 772; Laverap, *San Martín 490* – both
self-service laundries; also King Service
Lavandería, *Thompson 666.* **Post office**
Correo Central, *Bolívar 485,* beware
overcharging. **Telephone** CTC, *Serrano 620;*
Entel, *Tarapacá 476;* Correos, CTC,
Chilexpress, Chilesat and Entel all have
offices in the Plaza de Servicios in the Zofri.
Useful address Automóvil Club de Chile,
Serrano 154, T057-426772.

Around Iquique

Inland from Iquique are several small towns that were the early centres of Spanish
colonial settlement. They are less crowded than villages near Calama and Arica and
are well worth visiting. The rainy season in this area is mainly in January.

Nitrate towns

Humberstone ① *T057-751213, visits possible 0830-1830, US$1.50, leaflets*
available, is a large nitrate town, now abandoned, at the junction of the
Pan-American Highway and the road to Iquique. At its height in 1940, the town had a
population of 3,700. Although closed since 1961, you can see the plaza, the church,
a very well-preserved theatre, the *pulpería* (company stores) and the Olympic-size
swimming pool complete with grandstand (built of metal plating from ships' hulls).
An application has been made to UNESCO for Humberstone to be granted World
Heritage status, and the town is being slowly restored by former residents who are
more than happy to reminisce with visitors. Nearby are the ruins of several other
mining towns, including **Santa Laura** ① *2 km from Humberstone, T057-751981,*
visits possible daily 1000-1800, voluntary donation, which has the skeleton of a
nitrate processing plant, the machinery used to crush the minerals and a small,
somewhat disorganized mining museum. Both Humberstone and Santa Laura can
be visited on tours arranged by local agencies (see below). If you're travelling
independently from Iquique, take any bus to Arica or a *colectivo* for Pozo Almonte

from Sgto Aldea y Barros Arana, US$2 (there is a phone for contacting a taxi company for the return journey or you could probably flag down an Iquique-bound bus or minibus from the highway).

Situated on the Pan-American Highway, 5 km south of the turning to Iquique, Pozo Almonte was the main service centre for the nitrate fields of the area. The **Museo Histórico Salitrero** ① *on the plaza, Mon-Fri 0830-1300, 1600-1900*, displays artefacts and photographs of the nitrate era.

South along the Pan-American Highway

South of Pozo Almonte, the Pan-American Highway runs to **Quillagua**, 172 km, where there is a customs post. All southbound vehicles, including buses, are searched. The road continues towards Antofagasta. At Km 24, the road runs through the largest section of the **Reserva Nacional Pampa del Tamarugal** (the other two sections are around La Tirana and north of Huara), which is administered by CONAF. Covering a total of 100,650 ha, the reserve includes plantations of tamaruga, a tree species adapted to the dry climate and saline soils.

The **Geoglifos de Pintados**, some 400 figures on the hillsides, representing humans, animals and birds, as well as abstract designs, are situated some 3 km west of the Pan-American Highway; take any bus south, US$2.50, and get off at Km 43. Many other sites around Iquique, including the Gigante del Atacama (see box, page 248), are difficult to visit without a vehicle.

Mamiña → *Phone code: 057. Colour map 1, B2.*

A very popular thermal springs resort, Mamiña is reached by a good paved road, which runs 74 km east from Pozo Almonte. Situated on a ridge at 2,750 m, this is a delightful and very friendly village and would be an ideal place to relax for a few days after more strenuous activities in Bolivia or San Pedro de Atacama.

Mamiña has pre-Hispanic origins – its name means 'the girl of my eyes' in Aymará – and is inhabited mainly by people of Aymará origin. If you stand on the hill above the village, a circular geoglyph indicating the presence of water is clearly visible on the opposite side of the valley. The Aymará cultural centre, **Kaspi-Kala** ① *daily 1000-1400, 1600-2000*, near the **Hotel Los Cardenales** (see page 250), includes an *artesanía* workshop and a sales outlet. Legend has it that one of Mamiña's thermal pools once cured an Inca princess; an Inca *pukará* stands on a hilltop 3 km east marked by a white cross that can be seen from the village (it's probably best to hire a guide if you want to visit it). There are also said to be the ruins of a pre-Hispanic settlement further down the valley towards the *pampa*.

The church, built in 1632, is the only colonial Andean church in Chile with twin towers, each topped by a bell tower; ascend the church by steps at the side for a view of the bells linked together by a single rope. Mamiña's abundant thermal springs and unique mud spring have meant that it has been a popular health resort since the nitrate era; the **Hotel Termas** dates from this period. The thermal springs, classified as being radioactive, are rich in sodium, potassium, sulphur, chlorides and silicates, and are acknowledged to be valuable in treating ailments, such as rheumatoid arthritis and sciatica, as well as respiratory and digestive problems. There is also a mud bath, the **Baño Los Chinos** ① *daily 0930-1300*, which is considered valuable in the treatment of many skin diseases, such as psoriasis. The bath contains radioactive mud with natural deposits of vegetal mineral mud activated by the fermentation of certain algae; the mud is allowed to dry on the skin after the bath and then washed off in one of the thermal springs. ›› *For Sleeping, Eating and other listings, see pages 250-251.*

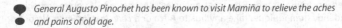

General Augusto Pinochet has been known to visit Mamiña to relieve the aches and pains of old age.

⁝ La Tirana

The legend of La Tirana is an intriguing mix of Andean traditions and Catholicism. It is said that, when Diego de Almagro made the first Spanish foray into Chile, one of his companions was an Inca princess. She was a fierce warrior who loathed everything to do with the Spanish and escaped into the pampa to wage war against them. She was so fierce that she became known as 'La Tirana' (the tyrant).

La Tirana's techniques were overthrown when she fell in love with Vasco de Almeyda, a Portuguese soldier enlisted by the Spanish, who persuaded her to convert to Christianity. When her companions discovered her treachery, both the Inca princess and the warrior were killed. The legend goes that a priest, coming some years later to the area to evangelise, discovered a cross on the spot where the couple had died, and built a church there.

Today, the fiesta treads a fine line between commercialism and maintaining these hybrid traditions.

The most important day and night occur on 16 July but, for up to a week beforehand, the town is awash with travelling salesmen, who come from all over Chile to sell everything that you could possibly need – clothes, music, bags, hats, cheap meals, ice creams and so on. At the same time, troupes of religious dancers and their accompanying brass bands come from as far away as Peru and Argentina to pay homage to the Virgen del Carmen. Eclecticism is the order of the day: as well as traditional Andean groups, there are also dancers who imitate the Sioux Indians from North America, as well as the 'Ali Baba Christians' dancing with imitation wooden sphinxes. The noise is deafening, day and night, as the brass bands vie with one another to produce the greatest racket. There is even an office set up by the church to perform marriages, and one of the most touching sights at the fiesta is that of happy couples being carried towards the church, amid the dancing, music and the chaos.

La Tirana → Population: 558.

Situated 10 km east of the Pan-American Highway, on a turning 9 km south of Pozo Almonte, La Tirana is famous for a religious festival dedicated to the **Virgen del Carmen**, held annually from 10 to 16 July (see box, page 247), which attracts some 150,000 pilgrims and merrymakers. Over 100 groups dance night and day decked out in colourful costumes and spectacular masks, starting on 12 July. All the dances take place in the main plaza in front of the church; no alcohol is served.

At other times of year, the church is well worth a visit, and there are two small museums: the **Museo de la Virgen de La Tirana** ① *Mon-Fri 0900-1300, 1600-1930, Sat-Sun 0900-2100, US$0.15*, which contains gifts to the virgin; and the privately owned **Museo de La Tirana** ① *open most days, free*, which houses a collection of artefacts from the nitrate era.

Matilla

Some 38 km east of La Tirana, Matilla is an oasis settlement founded in 1760 by settlers from Pica (see below). The village declined after 1912 when the waters of the Quebrada de Quisma were diverted to Iquique. The church (1887) is built of blocks of borax and rears up from over the arid plain like a version of the Sacré Coeur in the desert. Nearby is a **museum** ① *Lagar de Matilla, daily 0900-1700*, used in the 18th century for fermenting wine. Get a key from the kiosk in the plaza. Near Matilla, an unpaved, rough road runs southwest to meet the Pan-American Highway. ▶ *For Sleeping, Eating and other listings, see pages 250-251.*

: Geoglyphs

Found as far south as the Río Loa and as far north as the Río Azapa near Arica, as well as along the Peruvian coast as far as Nazca, geoglyphs or *geoglifos* are one of the most visible traces left by ancient civilizations in the Atacama. Dating from an estimated AD 1000-1400, these designs were made on the rocks using two different techniques: by scraping away the topsoil to reveal different coloured rock beneath or by arranging stones to form a kind of mosaic. They exhibit three main themes: geometrical patterns; images of animals, especially camelids, birds and snakes; and humans, often holding or carrying instruments or weapons, such as a bow and arrows. They are easily visible because they were intended to be seen. They are generally located on isolated hills in the desert, on the western slopes of the Cordillera de la Costa or on the slopes of *quebradas* (gorges). Their significance is thought by some experts to be ritual, but the more current theory is that they were often a kind of signpost pointing out routes between the coast and the sierra.

The largest site is at **Pintados**, 96 km south of Iquique, reached by turning off the Pan-American Highway towards Pica and then following a 4 km track from which several panels can be seen, including representations of animals, birds and a large number of humans dressed in ponchos and feather head-dresses, as well as geometrical designs.

Although there are several more sites, the other most important ones are at **Tiliviche**, 127 km north of Iquique, some 600 m south of the Pan-American Highway, where, on the southern side of the *quebrada*, a 300 m panel can be seen representing a drove of llamas moving from the *cordillera* to the coast; at **Cerro Rosita**, 20 km north of Huara near the Pan-American Highway, where the 'Sun of Huara' (an Aymara sun emblem) is visible on the eastern side of the hill; and at **Cerro Unitas**, 15 km east of Huara, where geoglyphs are visible on the western and southern sides of an isolated hill. On the western slope of Cerro Unitas is the *Gigante del Atacama* or Giant of the Atacama, probably the most famous of all the images: 86 m high, this is a representation of an indigenous leader with a head-dress of feathers and a feline mask; to his left is a reptile, thought to link him to the earth god Pachamama, to his right is his staff of office.

Pica → *Phone code: 057. Colour map 1, B2. Population: 3,000.*

Four kilometres northeast of Matilla, Pica was the most important centre of early Spanish settlement in this region. In colonial times, it produced a famous wine sold as far away as Potosí. Most of the older buildings, including the church, date from the nitrate period when it became a popular resort. It is a leafy oasis, famous for its thermal baths and the fruit grown here – one of the highlights of a stay is drinking fresh fruit juices from any one of numerous stalls near the thermal springs, which lie about 1 km from the centre of the town at **Cocha Resbaladero** ① *0700-2000 all year, US$2.* There are changing rooms, a snack bar and a beautiful pool on site and a small tourist information office opposite.

From Iquique to the Bolivian border

Thirty three kilometres north of Pozo Almonte, **Huara** was once a town of 7,000 people, serving as a centre for the nearby nitrate towns. Today, the population is reduced to 400 and little evidence remains of the town's former prosperity, apart from the railway station, which is a national monument, and a small museum preserving a pharmacy from the nitrate era with all the cures and remedies that were then on offer. The church is also worth a look.

At Huara, a road turns off the Pan-American Highway and runs to Colchane, 173 km northeast on the Bolivian frontier. Some 13 km east of Huara, the road passes, on the right, the **Geoglifos de Cerro Unitas**, the most outstanding of which is the **Gigante del Atacama**, a human figure 86 m tall, reported to be the largest geoglyph in the world and best viewed from a distance (see box, page).

At Km 23, an unpaved road branches off south to **Tarapacá**, settled by the Spanish around 1560 and capital of the Peruvian province of Tarapacá until 1855, now largely abandoned except for the **Fiesta of the Virgen de la Candelaria** on 2 and 3 February. The major historic buildings, the Iglesia de San Lorenzo and the Palacio de Gobierno, are in ruins. At **Chusmisa** (Km 77), there are thermal springs producing water that is bottled and sold throughout northern Chile. The forlorn and windy border town of **Colchane** livens up for the market, which takes place every other Saturday, and provides access to the southern entrance of the **Parque Nacional Volcán Isluga**, some 6 km northwest. The border is open 0800-2000 daily; on the Bolivian side, an unpaved road leads to Oruro, 233 km northeast. ▸▸ *For Sleeping, Eating and other listings, see pages 250-251.*

North towards Arica

The Pan-American Highway runs across the Atacama Desert at an altitude of around 1,000 m, with several steep hills, best tackled in daylight. At night, sea mist, *camanchaca*, can reduce visibility.

At Zapiga, 47 km north of Huara, a road heads west for 41 km to **Pisagua**, formerly an important nitrate port, now reduced to a small fishing village. Several of the old wooden buildings are national monuments, including the **Municipal Theatre** (1892) and the **Clock Tower** (1887), but the town is now largely abandoned, although a handful of fish restaurants make it a pleasant stop for a meal. Pisagua was the site of a detention centre after the 1973 military coup; mass graves from that period were discovered near here in 1990.

Heading east from Zapiga, meanwhile, a poor road (deep sand and dust) leads 67 km to **Camiña**, a picturesque village in an oasis. From here, a terrible road runs to the **Tranque de Caritaya**, a dam 45 km further northeast, which supplies water for the coastal towns and which is set in splendid scenery with lots of wildlife and interesting botany (especially *llareta*).

Ten kilometres north of Zapiga is an interesting British cemetery dating from the 19th century: note the fine wrought-iron gates. Nearby, stop for a view of the **Geoglifos de Tiliviche**, representing a group of llamas (signposted to the left and easily accessible). Further north at Km 111, the **Geoglifos de Chiza** can be seen from the bridge that carries the highway over the Quebrada de Chiza. At Km 172, a road runs east to **Codpa**, an agricultural community in a deep gorge surrounded by interesting scenery, with poor roads continuing north and east towards Putre (see page 261), through Tignamar and **Belén**.

This tiny village was founded by the Spanish in 1625 on the silver route between Potosí and the coast. It has two colonial churches: the older one, the **Iglesia de Belén** is one of the oldest (and smallest) churches in Chile; the other, the **Iglesia de Carmen**, dates from the 18th century. There are many pre-Hispanic ruins in the area, with four *pukarás* and a well-preserved stretch of the Camino del Inca. At Tignamar Viejo, an abandoned village 14 km south, there is another colonial church.

● Sleeping

Pozo Almonte *p246*

D **Estancia Inn**, *Calle Comercial*. Basic accommodation geared towards mineworkers.

D **Hotel Anakana**, *Comercio 053, T057-751201, F751621*. More of the same.

Mamiña *p246*

All the following are recommended, and all have rooms with private bath and thermal water available. Prices are for full board; as there are so many hotels in Mamiña, it is always worth bargaining.

A **Refugio del Salitre**, *T057-751203, tmami@chilesat.net* Secluded, pretty terrace, lovely views, swimming pool, nice rooms, games room, helpful, interesting older part where the top brass from the nitrate *oficinas* stayed. Recommended. Price per person.

B **Los Cardenales**, *T057-438182, T09-5451091*. 4-star, thermal baths, swimming pool with spring water, excellent cuisine in attractive restaurant, games room, lovely gardens and outlook, English, German spoken, delightful. Highly recommended. Price per person.

C **Bellavista**, *T057-474506*. Secluded, aviary in garden, games room, friendly, good cooking (including vegetarian options), sun terrace, basic but good rooms, worth bargaining. Price per person.

C **Hotel Kusy Tambo**, *Postal enquiries to Casilla 621, Iquique, T057-420436*. Friendly, clean, modern, table tennis available. Recommended.

C **La Coruña**, *T09-5430360*. Good Spanish cuisine, games room, swimming pool, very friendly and helpful, lots of local knowledge, parking and cable TV. Highly recommended. Price per person; children half price.

C **Llama Inn**, *T057-419893, pierangelam@hotmail.com* Pool tables, casino table, massage, terrace, friendly, cook will produce vegetarian meals if asked. Highly recommended. Price per person.

La Tirana *p247*

During the festival, accommodation is difficult to find, other than in organized campsites (take your own tent), which have basic toilets and showers, and through a few families who rent out rooms for over US$20 a night.

Matilla *p247*

Complejo Turístico El Parabien, *T057-431645*. Fully furnished *cabañas* and a swimming pool.

Pica *p248*

The hotels get full at weekends and at holidays, as well as during La Tirana – it is best to ring ahead. The following places are all near the Cocha Resbaladero.

C **Hostal Suizo**, *Ibañez 210, T057-741551*. With bath, popular, modern, very comfortable.

F **Hostal Casablanca**, *Ibañez 075, T057-741410*. Friendly, comfortable, cooking facilities, pool, parking. Price per person.

G **Res El Tambo**, *Ibañez 68, T/F057-741041*. Without bath, meals served, very popular, hospitable. Also 4-person *cabañas*. Warmly recommended.

G **Res Milton**, *No 188 opposite entrance to thermal baths, T057-741105*. Excellent breakfast, basic, friendly, good, canaries on patio.

Options in the town centre include:

F **Camino El Inca**, *Esmeralda 014, T/F057-741008*. With breakfast, shady patio, table football, good value. Recommended. Price per person.

F **Hostería O'Higgins**, *Balmaceda 6, T057-741524*. With bath, modern. Price per person.

F **Los Emilios**, *Cochrane 213, T/F057-741126*. With bath and breakfast, friendly, nice lounge, small swimming pool, interesting old building with photos of the nitrate era, lovely patio. Highly recommended. Price per person.

F **San Andrés**, *Balmaceda 197, T057-741319*. With bath and breakfast, basic but clean, good restaurant with cheap 4-course *almuerzos*. Price per person.

Iquique to the Bolivian border *p248*

Basic accommodation is available in the **Restaurant Frontera** in Huara and in 4 simple *residenciales* in Colchane.

North towards Arica *p249*
There is a campsite at the northern end of the beach in Pisagua and the friendly
G **Restaurant Acuario** also has beds.

A simple hostal on the plaza provides accommodation in Camina.

Accommodation and food is available in Belén with **María Martinez**, *General Lagos y San Martín*.

❼ Eating

Mamiña *p246*
Most hotels (see Sleeping above) operate on a full-board basis only, but there are also some cheap independent eateries.
$ **Cafetería Ipla**. Excellent fruit juices, vegetarian options.
$ **Los Chacras de Pasquito**. Clean, good.
$ **Restaurant Cerro Morado**. Good variety, traditional dishes, including rabbit.

Pica *p248*
Pica is famous for its *alfajores* filled with cream and honey and you cannot leave without trying some of the fruit juices. Hotels **San Andrés** and **El Tambo** (see Sleeping, above) both have good cheap restaurants.
$$ **El Edén de Pica**, *Riquelme 12*. Best in town, speciality dishes, fine ice cream, lovely surroundings.
$$ **Los Naranjos**, *Esmeralda y Barbosa*. Nice decor, good.
$ **La Mía Pappa**, Balmaceda. Good selection of meat and juices, attractive location near plaza.
$ **La Palmera**, *Balmaceda 115*. Excellent *almuerzo*, popular with locals, near plaza.
$ **La Viña**, *Ibañez 70, by Cocha de Resbaladero*. Good cheap *almuerzo*.
$ **Oasis**, *Balmaceda, by the plaza*. Ridiculously cheap. Recommended for *alfajores* and fruit juice.

☉ Transport

Mamiña *p246*
Two companies run minibuses between **Iquique** and Mamiña; best to book the day before: **Transportes Tamarugal**, *Barros Arana 897*, departs Iquique daily 0800, 1600, 2½ hrs, US$4 one-way, returns from Mamiña 0800, 1800; **Turismo Mamiña**, Latorre 779, departs Iquique Mon-Sat 0800-1600, also Sun 1600, 2½ hrs US$4, returns from Mamiña Tue-Sat 0830, Mon-Sat 1800.

La Tirana *p247*
In ordinary times, buses from Iquique to Pica stop here; during the festival, virtually every taxi and *colectivo* in Iquique seems to be making 'special' trips to La Tirana, leaving from Sargento Aldea by the market; some bus companies also have direct services from Antofagasta and Arica.

Pica *p248*
Three bus companies run between **Iquique** and Pica: **Santa Rosa**, Barros Arana 777, departs Iquique daily 0830 and 0930, 2 hrs, US$2.50, returns from Pica 1700 and 1800; **San Andrés**, Sgto Aldea y Barros Arana, departs Iquique daily 0930, returns from Pica daily 1800, US$2.50; **Pullman Chacón**, Barros Arana y Latorre, many daily, US$2.50, first return bus from Pica leaves at about 1100.

To the Bolivian border *p248*
From Iquique, **Pullman La Paloma** runs daily bus services to **Colchane** at 2300 from Esmeralda y Juan Martínez, US$5.

North towards Arica *p249*
From Arica, **Buses La Paloma**, *German Riesco 2071,T058-222710*, run a service to **Belén**, departing Tue and Fri at 0645, US$3.

❶ Directory

Mamiña *p246*
Communications   There are a couple of call centres on the plaza, and one supermarket (only open sporadically).

● *For an explanation of sleeping and eating price codes used in this guide, see inside the*
● *front cover. Other relevant information is found in Essentials, see pages 51-58.*

Arica and around

→ *Phone code: 058. Colour map 1, A1. Population: 169,456.*

Arica is the northernmost city in Chile, just 19 km south of the Peruvian border. With Peru so close and Arica being the main port for Bolivian trade, the city has a distinct half-way house sort of feel. It is less ordered than most Chilean cities, with hundreds of street vendors and indoor markets selling cheap, imported goods. The city centre itself is quite attractive, with long beaches, pleasant gardens and extensive networks of sand dunes all nearby. Rearing up to the south is El Morro, the rock that marks the end of the Chilean coastal range.

Ins and outs

Getting there Arica is a long way from most of Chile. All major bus companies serving the north make this their final stop; buses take up to 30 hrs to reach Santiago to the south. Arica is a centre for connections to Bolivia and Peru, with frequent *colectivos* north to Tacna in Peru and buses east to La Paz in Bolivia. There is also quite a wide-ranging bus service to villages in the sierra and the *altiplano*. **Sky** and **LanChile** fly south to Santiago via Iquique and Antofagasta, with some flights continuing on to La Paz in Bolivia. A taxi to town from the airport costs US$6, *colectivos* to the airport cost US$3.50 per person from Lynch y 21 de Mayo. ▶▶ *For further details, see Transport, page 258.* **Getting around** Arica is quite a large city, and you may need to take some of the *colectivos* or buses to get to more out-of-the-way places, particularly the nightclubs, many of which are on the road out to the Azapa Valley. **Tourist information** Sernatur ① *Marcos 101 y Parque Baquedano, T058-232101, Mon-Fri 0830-1300, 1500-1830,* is very helpful and can supply a list of tour companies and a good map.

Background

During the colonial period, Arica was important as the Pacific end of the silver route from Potosí. Independence from Spain and the re-routing of Bolivian trade through Cobija led to a decline, but the city recovered with the building of rail links to Tacna (1855) and La Paz (1913). The city came under Chilean control at the end of the War of the Pacific (see page 520). The Morro in Arica was the site of an important Chilean victory over Peru on 7 June 1880.

Arica remains an important route centre and port. Now linked to the Bolivian capital La Paz by road and an oil pipeline, it handles a large proportion of Bolivia's foreign trade and attracts Bolivians, as well as locals, to its beaches. There are also road connections with the Peruvian city of Tacna, 54 km north. Most of the large fishmeal plants have moved to Iquique, leaving several rusting hulks of trawlers in the bay, now home to a significant local crow population. Regrettably, there are indications that Arica is also becoming a key link in the international drugs trade.

Sights

The city is centred around **Plaza Colón**, on which stands the gothic-style cathedral of **San Marcos**, built in iron by Eiffel. Although small, it is beautifully proportioned and attractively painted. It was brought to Arica from Ilo in Peru as an emergency measure after a tidal wave swept over Arica in 1868 and destroyed all its churches; inside the cathedral is a Christ figure dating from the 12th century. Eiffel also designed the nearby Aduana (customs house), which is now the **Casa de la Cultura** ① *daily 0830-2000.* Just north of the Aduana is the La Paz railway station; outside is an old steam locomotive (made in Germany in 1924) once used on this line, while inside is a memorial to John Roberts Jones, builder of the Arica portion of the railway.

Arica

Arica centre

To Airport, Pan-American Highway (North) to Peru, Parque Nacional Lauca & Bolivia

Diego Portales · Buses & Colectivos to Tacna
Buses south & to Bolivia

Río San José

J A Ríos

Cemetery

Casino

Parque Brasil

Parque General C Ibáñez del Campo

Trains to Tacna

La Paz Station

Casa de la Cultura (Former Aduana)

Harbour

Plaza Colón

Cathedral

7 de Junio

Plaza Vicuña Mackenna

Museo Histórico y de Armas

El Morro

Bolivian Consulate

Peruvian Consulate

To Poblado Artesanal & Pan-American Highway (South) to Museo Arqueológico de San Miguel & Azapa Valley

Iquique, Arica & the Far North · Arica & around

0 metres 200
0 yards 200

To La Lisera, Playa Brava & El Laucho Beaches

Sleeping

Americano **21** *D2*
Aragón **28** *Arica centre*
Arica **1** *E1*
Diego de Almagro **2** *D2*
El Paso **4** *C1*
Hostal Casa Mia Nona **22** *D3*
Hostal Chez Charlie
  & La Ciboulette
  Restaurant **5** *Arica centre*
Hostal Jardín del Sol **7** *D3*
King **26** *Arica centre*
Las Palmas **27** *Arica centre*
Lynch **29** *D2*

Plaza Colón **10** *Arica centre*
Residencial América **11** *D2*
Residencial Blanquita **12**
Residencial Caracas **13** *D3*
Residencial Chillán **14** *D1*
Residencial Ecuador **6** *C3*
Residencial El Sur **15** *D2*
Residencial Española
  24 *Arica centre*
Reidencial Leiva **25**
  Arica centre
Residencial Madrid **9** *D2*
Residencial Stagnaro **19** *D3*

Residencial Velásquez **3** *D1*
Residencial Venecia **8** *D2*
San Marcos **23** *Arica centre*
Savona **17** *E2*
Sunny Days **20** *A2*
Tarapacá **16** *Arica centre*

Eating

Bavaria **2** *Arica centre*
Caffelatte & Di Mango **3**
  Arica centre
Chin Huang Tao **4** *D2*
D'Aurelio **5** *Arica centre*
Don Floro **6** *C3*

El Rey del Marisco **7**
  Arica centre
Kau Chea & Shaolin **9** *D1*
La Bomba **10** *Arica centre*
La Jaula **11** *Arica centre*
Los Aleros del 21 **12** *D3*
San Fernando **16**
  Arica centre
Scala **17** *Arica centre*
Yuri **20** *D2*

Bars & clubs

France Tropicale **8**
  Arica centre

To climb **El Morro**, 110 m high, walk to the southernmost end of the Calle Colón, and then follow the pedestrian walkway up to the summit; there are fine views of the city from here. The **Museo Histórico y de Armas** ① *0830-2000, US$1*, on the summit, contains weapons and uniforms from the War of the Pacific. ▸▸ *For Sleeping, Eating and other listings, see pages 255-245*

Valle de Azapa

A highly recommended excursion is up the Azapa Valley, a beautiful oasis east of Arica. At Km 12 is the **Museo Arqueológico San Miguel de Azapa** ① *T058-205555, museo@uta.cl, 0900-2000 (2 Jan-28 Feb), 1000-1800 (1 Mar-31 Dec), US$2*, part of the University of Tarapacá and well worth a visit. Set in a pleasant, shady part of the valley, the museum contains a fine collection of pre-Columbian weaving, pottery, woodcarving and basket work from the coast and the valleys as well as seven mummified humans from the Chinchorro culture (8,000-10,000 BC), the most ancient mummies yet discovered. In the forecourt of the museum are several boulders with pre-Columbian petroglyphs and opposite is a garden full of tropical plants and birds. Comprehensive explanations are provided by booklets in English, French, German and Spanish, loaned free at the entrance.

On the road between Arica and San Miguel several groups of geoglyphs of humans and llamas can be seen to the south of the road. On the opposite side of the valley at San Lorenzo are the ruins of a *pukará* (pre-Inca fortress) dating from the 12th century.

In the nearby village of San Miguel, there is a very friendly super-cheap restaurant serving good food and Peruvian Arequipeña beer. A good walk in the area is to climb the desert hill behind the valley, 45 minutes, giving wonderful views of the green oasis and the desolation beyond – running back down the hill takes 3 minutes and is an exhilarating experience.

Into Peru → *Peruvian phone code: +51.*

Chilean immigration at the border post of **Chacalluta** ① *open Sun-Thu 0800-2400, 24 hrs Fri and Sat*, is usually fairly uncomplicated, although crossing the border into Peru with a hire car is difficult: make sure you have the correct papers. The Peruvian side of the border is open 0900-2200. There are exchange facilities at the border but better rates are reported in Tacna.

▪ Chilean time is 1 hour behind Peruvian time between October and March, and 2 hours behind from October to February or March (varies annually).

Drivers of private vehicles entering Chile are required to file a form, *Relaciones de Pasajeros* (four copies; eight if planning to return to Peru via this crossing), giving details of passengers. The form can be obtained from a stationery store in Tacna, or at the border in a kiosk near customs. You must also present the original registration document for your car from its country of registration. The first checkpoints outside Arica on the road to Santiago also require the *Relaciones de Pasajeros* form, but the form is not required when travelling south of Antofagasta. If you can't buy the form (available from some service stations), write the details on a piece of paper.

Tacna is 36 km north of the border. The city was in Chilean hands from 1880 to 1929, when its citizens voted by plebiscite to return to Peru. There is a wide variety of hotels and restaurants here, as well as bus and air services to the rest of Peru. Many Chileans travel to Tacna for optical and dental treatment, which is much cheaper than in Chile. There is a **tourist office** ① *Avenida Bolognesi 2088*.

Into Bolivia → *Bolivian phone code: +591*

Via Chungará and Tambo Quemado There are two routes from Arica to the Bolivian border. **Route 11** (paved to La Paz, although seriously worn in places by overloaded juggernauts) turns off the Pan-American Highway, 12 km north of Arica, and runs through the Lluta Valley, where the **Geoglifos de Lluta** – four groups of geoglyphs representing llamas and humans – can be seen on the hillsides between Km 14 and Km 16. The road continues via Putre and Parinacota through the Parque Nacional Lauca to the border at Chungará. This is the route followed by most transport to Bolivia, including buses and trucks. Estimated driving time to La Paz is six hours. Chilean immigration formalities are 7 km west of the border ⓘ *open 0800-2000*. Bolivian immigration and customs are at Tambo Quemado, just over the border (where there is a local barter market every other Fri). This is a relatively speedy crossing, but very cold; if you're travelling by bus (see page 258), take a blanket or sleeping bag, food, water and a sense of humour.

Via Visviri and Charaña The road to Oruro and La Paz (Route 108) is unpaved and should not be attempted in wet weather. It follows the La Paz–Arica railway line to the Chilean immigration post at **Visviri** (altitude 4,069 m) ⓘ *3 km from the Bolivian frontier and 12 km from Peru (no crossing), T058-261486, 0800-2000*. There is no fuel or accommodation here. Bolivian formalities are conducted behind the railway station at **Charaña**, 10 km east. Accommodation is available at Alojamiento Aranda (H). There are two routes, both poor, continuing from Charaña towards La Paz, both of which meet at Viacha. Over the border, the route passes through the **Parque Nacional Sajama**, which covers 60,000 ha and contains the world's highest forest,

‡ Visviri can also be reached by road from Putre, see page 261.

consisting mainly of the rare Kenua tree, which survives at altitudes of up to 5,200 m. The scenery is wonderful and includes views of three volcanos: Parinacota (6,342 m) and Pomerape (6,282 m), both of which are on the frontier, and Sajama (6,530 m), which is Bolivia's highest peak, but can be seen from the Lauca national park in Chile. Park administration is at Sajama village, 14 km off Route 108 (altitude 4,200 m), where there is basic accommodation. There is also accommodation at Carahuara de Carangas, 111 km northeast of Tambo Quemado, and at **Patacamaya**, 104 km south of La Paz, where Route 108 joins the main Oruro-La Paz highway.

● Sleeping

Arica *p252, map p253*
In Jan and Feb the municipality supplies cheap basic accommodation, ask at the tourist office.
AL Americano, *Lagos 571, T058-257752, www.hotelamericano.cl* Cable TV, sauna, gymnasium.
AL Arica, *San Martín 599, 2 km south on coast (frequent buses and colectivos), T058-254540, www.panamericanahoteles.cl* Lower rates off season, good value, excellent restaurant, tennis court, pool, lava beach (not safe for swimming).
AL Azapa, *Sánchez 660, Valle de Azapa, T058-244537, www.azapainn.cl* Attractive grounds, pleasant location, also cheaper *cabañas*, good restaurant.
AL El Paso, *Gen Velásquez 1109, T/F058-231965, www.hotelpaso.cl* Bungalow style, excellent restaurant, lovely gardens, tennis court, pool.
AL Star Apart Hotel, *Av Consistorial y Ramón Carnicer, Playa Chinchorro 2928, T058-214691, www.staraparthotel.cl* Fully furnished apartments for up to 6.

A-B Savona, *Yungay 380, T058-231000, F231606.* Comfortable, 3-star, friendly, quiet. Highly recommended.
B Aragón, *Maipú 344, T/F058-252088.* Rooms with breakfast.
B Plaza Colón, *San Marcos 261, T058-254424, www.hotelplazacolon.cl* Modern, comfortable.
B San Marcos, *Sotomayor 387, T058-232970, F251815.* 3-star, comfortable, good value.
B Saucache, *Sanchez 621, Valle de Azapa, T/F058-241458, desierto300@123click.cl* Fully equipped *cabañas*, sleep 2 or 4.
B Sol de Arica, *Avalos 2041, T058-246050, www.hotelsoldearica.cl* Sauna, jacuzzi, pool. Recommended.
B-C King, *Colón 376, T058-232094, hotelking@chilenet.cl* With bath, central.
B-C Las Palmas, *Prat 528, T/F058-232994, laspalmas@hotmail.com* Central, modern.
C Diego de Almagro, *Sotomayor 490, T058-224444, F221240.* With breakfast, helpful, comfortable, parking, stores luggage. Recommended.
C Res Las Condes, *MacKenna y Maipú.* Kitchen facilities, hot showers, clean.

C-D **Lynch**, *Lynch 589, T058-231581*. Rooms with bath.

D **Hostal Casa Mia Nona**, *21 de Mayo 660, T058-250597*. With bath, without breakfast.

F **Hostal Chez Charlie**, *Paseo Thompson 236, T/F058-250057, latinor@entelchile.net* Comfortable, without breakfast, good value. Recommended. Price per person.

F **Hostal Jardín del Sol**, *Sotomayor 848, T058-232795*. With bath, with breakfast, comfortable, friendly, good value. Highly recommended. Price per person.

F **Hostal Sammy**, *Lagos 1066*. With breakfast. Price per person.

F **Res Caracas**, *Sotomayor 867, T058-253688*. Clean, with breakfast. Price per person.

F **Res Chillán**, *Velásquez 749, T058-251677*. Noisy, poor beds. Price per person.

F **Res Ecuador**, *Juan Noé 989, T/F058-251934*. With bath and breakfast, kitchen and laundry facilities, recently renovated. Recommended. Price per person.

F **Res El Sur**, *Maipú 516, T058-252457*. Clean but grim. Price per person.

F **Res Leiva**, *Colón 347, T/F058-232008*. Without bath, French spoken, cooking facilities, cycle hire. Price per person.

F **Res Stagnaro**, *Gallo 294, T058-231254, stagnaro@arica.cl* With breakfast, very good value. Recommended.

F **Res Venecia**, *Baquedano 739, T058-252877, hostal_venecia@hotmail.com* Spotless, hot water, small rooms, good value. Recommended. Price per person.

F **Sra Gloria Martinez**, *Pasaje 7, No 1026, Población Juan Noé, T058-241971*. Friendly, helpful. Price per person.

F **Sunny Days**, *Tomas Aravena 161 y Pedro de Valdivia, población Chinchorro, T058-241038*. Run by New Zealander, laundry facilities, some rooms with bath, English spoken, nice atmosphere, lots of information on the area, book exchange, bike rental, will pick you up from the terminal. Highly recommended. Price per person.

F **Tarapacá** , *Maipú 455, T058-252680*. With bath, clean, friendly, helpful.

G **Res América**, *Sotomayor 430, T058-254148, viosa_40@hotmail.comrnet.cl* With bath, clean, hospitable, good value. Price per person.

G **Res Blanquita**, *Maipú 472, T058-233548, residencialblanquita@hotmail.com* Clean, pleasant, good value. Price per person.

G **Res Española**, *Bolognesi 340, T058-231703*. Without breakfast, central, basic, quiet. Recommended. Price per person.

G **Res Madrid**, *Baquedano 685, T058-231479*. Without bath or breakfast, laundry, hot water, poor beds, good value, reductions for Hostelling International cards. Price per person.

G **Res Pacífico**, *Velásquez 611, T058-230567*. With breakfast, cooking facilities. Price per person.

G **Res Velásquez**, *Velásquez 669, T058-231989*. Basic, friendly, laundry facilities, cable TV. Price per person.

Camping

El Refugio de Azapa, *3½ km from Arica, T058-227545*. Full facilities including a restaurant. Also *cabañas*.

Gallinazos, *Villa Frontera, 15 km north of Arica, T058-232373*. One of many campsites at Villa Frontera. Full facilities, pool.

Basic camping (no water or facilities) is also possible at **Playa Las Machas**, 5 km north, **Playa Chinchorro**, north of town, and **Playa Corazones**, 8 km south, but this is risky as there have been reports of daylight mugging and robbery.

● Eating

Arica *p252, map p253*

$$ **Bavaria**, *Colón 613*. Good restaurant, coffee and cakes.

$$ **Casanova**, *Baquedano 397*. Excellent but not cheap.

$$ **Chifa Chin**, *Patricio Lynch 224*. Good-value Chinese food, diners welcome to take away 'leftovers'.

$$ **Chin Huang Tao**, *Lynch 317*. Excellent Chines, pricey but worth it.

$$ **D'Aurelio**, *Baquedano 369*. Italian specialities, good pasta, seafood.

$$ **Don Floro**, *V MacKenna 847*. Good seafood and steaks, good service. Recommended.

$$ **El Arriero**, *21 de Mayo 385*. Parrillada, also seafood and fish. Warmly recommended.

$$ **El Rey del Marisco**, *Maipú y Colón*. Excellent seafood, pricey, not always welcoming.

$$ **Las Tejas de Azapa**, *Valle de Azapa Km 2, No 4301*. Parrillada, seafood, pool, expensive.

$$ **Los Aleros del 21**, *21 de Mayo 736*. Recommended for seafood and service.

$$ **Maracuyá**, *San Martín 0321*. Seafood, splendid location on the coast, pricey.

$ **Acuario**, *Muelle Turístico*. Good food in fishy environment, good-value *menu de casa*.

$ **Capricho Latino**, *18 de Septiembre 250*. Good-value *almuerzo*.

$ **Cyclo**, *Lynch 224*. Seafood, pasta, reasonably priced. Recommended.

$ **El Tambo**, *Poblado Artesanal, Hualles 2025*. For lunches, folk music and dancing on Fri/Sat evenings.

$ **Kau Chea**, *18 de Septiembre y Prat* . Cheap Chinese.

$ **La Bomba**, *Colón 357, at fire station*. Good value *almuerzo*, friendly service.

$ **La Ciboulette**, *Paseo Thompson 238*. Good food, pleasant atmosphere, not expensive. Recommended.

$ **La Jaula**, *21 de Mayo 293*. Snacks, meals, not expensive.

$ **San Fernando**, *Baquedano 601*. Simple breakfast, good-value *almuerzo*. One of several cheap restaurants on this block.

$ **Shaolin**, *18 de Septiembre 601*. Cheap Chinese.

$ **Snack Suceso Inn**, *18 de Septiembre 250*. Good set meal and coffee.

$ **Yuri**, *Maipú y Lynch*. Good service, cheap Chinese lunches. Recommended.

Cafés

There are three good places on 21 de Mayo, all offering real coffee and outdoor seating: **Caffelatte**, No 248; **Carlos Díaz León Snack Place**, No 388; and **Di Mango**, No 244, which also serves juices and ice cream.

Also try **Mi Viejo**, *Maipú 436*, for cheap meals and snacks, and **Scala**, *21 de Mayo 201*, for excellent fruit juices and real coffee.

❶ Bars and clubs

Arica *p252, map p253*

Carpaccio, *Velásquez 510*. Restaurant and bar with live music from 2330 Wed-Sat.

Encuentros, *Velásquez 510*. Also serves pizzas.

France Tropicale Pub, *21 de Mayo y Baquedano*. Open till dawn, live music weekends. French and English spoken.

Puerto Navarrón, *Paseo Bolognesi*. Open till 0400, live music at weekends.

Soho, *Buenos Aires 209*. For rock 'n' roll.

Sunset and **Swing**, *both 3½ km out of town, Valle de Azapa*. Open weekends 2300-0430 (taxi US$3).

Arica *p252, map p253*

Casino

Casino Municipal de Arica, *Velásquez 955*. Daily 1200-0300. Formal dress not required.

Cinemas

Cine Arte, *Biblioteca Publíca , Yungay*.

Colón, *7 de Junio 190, T058-231165*.

Music

A *peña folklorica* of Andean music is held in the **Poblado Artesanal**, Fri and Sat 2130.

Theatre

Teatro Municipal de Arica, *Baquedano 234*. Theatrical and musical events, exhibitions.

☻ Festivals and events

Arica *p252, map p253*

In Jan Arica hosts a miniature version of the **Festival de la Canción** famous in Viña del Mar, with performances by Andean musicians. The **annual festival** of Arica and the national **Cueca championships** take place in Jun.

❍ Shopping

Arica *p252, map p253*

Cameras and film

Profonor, *18 de Septiembre y Lynch*. Recommended. Avoid **Megaclor** on 21 de Mayo for developing film.

Crafts

Feria Turística Dominical, *Chacabuco between Velásquez and Mackenna*, Sun market, good prices for llama sweaters.

Poblado Artesanal, *Plaza Las Gredas, Hualles 2825 (take bus 2, 3 or 7)*. Expensive but especially good for musical instruments, open Tue-Sun 0930-1300, 1500-1930.

Markets

Mercado Central, *Sotomayor y Sangra*. Recently renovated, fruit and vegetables, mornings only.

Terminal del Agro, *southeastern edge of town; take bus marked 'Agro' along 18 de Septiembre*. Fruit, vegetables and old clothes.

There are supermarkets at *Baquedano y 18 de Septiembre*, *San Martín y 18 de Septiembre* and at *Chacabuco y Lagos*.

Into Bolivia *p254*

There are markets in **Visviri** on Wed and Sat mornings; a Sun morning market is held from 0900 north of the town at the frontier of the 3 countries.

▲▲ Activities and tours

Arica *p252, map p253*
Golf
18-hole course in the **Valle de Azapa**, open daily except Mon.

Paragliding
Paragliding is practised on the mountains overlooking the city.
Escuela Profesional de Parapente Termica, *Av La Tirana 3441, Depto C-37, T/F058-450675*.

Surfing
There's good surfing at **Playa Las Machas** and **Playa Chinchorro**, north of the city, and at **La Isleta** and **Playa Corazones**, 9 km south along coast road (take bus or *colectivo*).

Swimming
The best beach for swimming is **Playa Chinchorro**, north of town (bus 24). **Playa Las Machas**, further north, has strong currents. Buses 7 and 8 run to beaches south of town; the first two, **La Lisera** and **El Laucho**, are both small and mainly for sunbathing. **Playa Brava**, also south, is popular for sunbathing but is too dangerous for swimming.

There's an Olympic pool in **Parque Centenario**, Tue-Sat; bus No 5A from *18 de Septiembre* (buy a ticket on Thu mornings).

Tennis
Club de Tenis Centenario, *Av España 2640*. Open daily.

Tour operators
Most of the following offer local tours and excursions to the *altiplano* at similar prices:
city tour US$10; **Valle de Azapa** US$12; **Parque Nacional Lauca**, 1 day US$20, 2 days US$60 including accommodation; Lauca and Isluga **national parks**, 3 days US$180.

Agencies pay up to 25% commission to hotels and *residenciales* that refer travellers; to get a lower price form a group of 5 or 6 travellers and negotiate direct with agencies.
AYCA Tour, *Covadonga 312, T/F058-240404, ayca@tnet.cl* Archaeological and historical tours of the area.
Ecotour Expediciones, *Bolognesi 370, T/F058-250000, eco-tour@ctcinternet.cl*
Globo Tour, *21 de Mayo 260, T/F058-232909*. Good for international flight bookings.
Kijo Tour and Travel, *Bolognesi 357, T/F058-232245*. Good for international travel.
Latinorizons, *Bolognesi 449, T/F058-250007, latinor@entelchile.net* Specializes in tours to Lauca National Park. Recommended.
Parinacota Expeditions, *Prat 386, T/F058-256227, parinacotaexpediciones@hotmail.com*
Transtours, *Bolognesi 421, T058-253927*.
Turismo Payachatas, *Sotomayor y Bolognesi, T/F058-256981*.

✈ Transport

Arica *p252, map p253*
Air
Arica airport, *18 km north of city, Chacalluta, T058-211116*. Flights to **La Paz**, LanChile; to **Santiago**, Sky and LanChile all via Iquique (some via Antofagasta), book well in advance; to **Lima**, LanPerú and others from Tacna (Peru), enquire at travel agencies in Arica.

Bus
Local City buses run from Maipú, US$0.25. *Colectivos* run on fixed routes within city limits, US$0.30 per person (US$0.50 per person after 2000). To reach **Valle de Azapa**, take a yellow *colectivo* from P Lynch y Chacabuco, US$1.

Long distance There are two terminals, both northeast of the centre at *Av Portales y Santa María*, reached by many buses, *colectivos* (including No 8 and 18, US$0.20 or US$0.45) and taxis, US$1.50 (terminal tax US$0.25).

The main terminal is for national services and services to La Paz with Chilean companies (see p259). Next door is the terminal for *colectivos* to Tacna (see p259) and Bolivian services to La Paz. It is advisable to arrive 30 minutes before departure for all services.

Apart from the following, bus company offices are located at the bus terminals:
Buses La Paloma, *Germán Riesco 2071* (bus U from centre); **Martínez**, *21 de Mayo 575*,

T058-232265; **Bus Lluta**, *Chacabuco y V Mackenna*. **Litoral**, *Chacabuco 454, T058-254702*; **Andes-Mar**, *Galerin Río San José, Av Santa María 2010, T058-248200/232265*.

To **Antofagasta**, 11 hrs, US$11; to **Calama** and **Chuquicamata**, 10 hrs, US$11, several companies, all between 2000 and 2200; to **San Pedro de Atacama**, daily 2200, 11½ hrs, US$12; to **Iquique**, frequent, 4½ hrs, US$4.50, also *colectivos*, several companies, all with offices in the terminal; to **Santiago**, 30 hrs, a number of companies, including **Carmelita, Turbus, Pullman Bus, Fénix** and **Flota Barrios**, US$22, also *salón cama* services, US$33 (most serve meals though these vary in quality; generally better on more expensive services; student discounts available); to **La Serena**, 23 hrs, US$17 (*salon cama* US$26); to **Viña del Mar** and **Valparaíso**, 29 hrs, US$22. Note that all southbound luggage is carefully searched for fruit prior to boarding and is then searched again at Cuya on the Pan-American Highway.

Car

Hertz (see Directory, below) provides the most reliable vehicles but check any rental vehicle for jack and lug wrench, and check the condition of both the fan belt (often dry and cracked) and the spare tyre.

It is illegal to take fruit and dairy products south of Arica: all vehicles are searched at Cuya, 105 km south, and at Huara, 234 km south. There are service stations between the Peruvian border and Santiago at Arica, Iquique, Pozo Almonte, Oficina Victoria, Tocopilla, Oficina María Elena, Oficina Blanco Encalada, Chuquicamata, Calama, Carmen Alto, Antofagasta, La Negra, Agua Verde (also fruit inspection post), Taltal, Chañaral, Caldera, Copiapó, Vallenar, La Serena, Termas de Soco, Los Vilos, and then every 30 km to the capital.

Hitchhiking

It's not easy to hitch south: try the **Terminal del Agro** off the Pan-American Highway (trucks leave Mon, Thu and Sat before 0700) and the **Copec station** opposite (reached by bus from Arica marked 'Agro' or *colectivo* No 8).

Taxi

Taxis cost US$1.50 within the city centre. Try **Radiotaxis Chacalluta**, *T058-254812*, for journeys to/from the airport.

Into Peru *p254*

Car

Crossing to Tacna with a hire car can be difficult; the hire firm **Klasse** (see Directory, below) can arrange the paperwork for this.

Colectivo

Regular service from the international terminal in Arica, *Diego Portales 1002*, to **Tacna**, 1½ hrs, drivers take care of all the paperwork. Bargaining is fierce. Chilean operators generally charge US$3 per person, while Peruvians charge US$2. Supply and demand means that lower prices than these are often on offer. A bus from the terminal, US$1, takes much longer than a *colectivo*.

Train

The service has been interrupted while repairs are carried out; Arica train station is on Maximo Lira, by the port, and, in normal times, a train leaves Mon-Fri 1000 and 2000, Sat 1500, US$1.50.

Into Bolivia *p254*

Bus

There are 3 or 4 buses daily between Arica and **La Paz**, via the border towns of Chungará (Chile) and Tambo Quemado (Bolivia), 8-10 hrs: **Humire**, Tue-Fri at 0900, US$15; **Geminis**, Mon, Wed, Fri 1000, US$15 without lunch; **ChileBus**, daily 1000, US$15; **Transalvador**, Tue, Thu, Sat, 0900, US$11.

Humire buses also run services from Arica to **Visviri**, Tue and Fri at 1030, US$6.50, from where you can take a jeep across the border to **Charaña**. From Charaña, buses to **La Paz** leave before 1000, US$4, 6 hrs.

Hitchhiking

The Chungará frontier post is a good place for hitching to La Paz; truck transport leaves in the afternoon. Trucks from Arica to La Paz rarely give lifts, and in any case are excruciatingly slow, but another place to try is at the **Poconchile** control point, 37 km from Arica.

⊕ Directory

Arica *p252, map p253*

Airline offices   LanChile, *21 de Mayo 345, T058-251641, F252600*; **Lloyd Aéreo Boliviano**, *P Lynch 371, T058-216411*; **Sky**, *Chacabuco 314, local 52, T058-251816*.

Banks Banco Santander, *21 de Mayo*, open 24 hrs; **Corp Banca**, *Bolognesi 317*, Visa, ATM; **Finandes**, *21 de Mayo 560*, Mastercard, many Redbanc ATMs. **Bicycles** Bicicletas Wilson, *18 de Sept 583*, repairs, parts, sales, ATB specialists. **Car hire** American, *Gen Lagos 571, T/F058-257752*; Cactus, *Baquedano 635, Loc 40, T058-257430, F258353*; GP, *Copacabana 628, T058-252594*, good reports; **Hertz**, *Baquedano 999, T058-231487*; **Klasse**, *Velásquez 760, Piso 2, Loc 25, T/F058-254498*. **Casas de cambio** Marta Daguer, *San Martín 258*, slow service, high commission for TCs; **Yanulaque**, *21 de Mayo 175*, Mon-Fri 0900-1400, 1600-2000, Sat 0930-1330; most large hotels also change cash; rates for TCs are universally better in Iquique. **Consulates** Bolivia, *Lynch 270, T058-231030*; Peru, *San Martín 235, T058-231020*; Germany, *Prat 391, of.101, T058-254663*; **Cultural centres** Instituto Chileno-Alemán de Cultura, *Camino Azapa 3727*; Instituto Chileno – Británico de Cultura, *Baquedano 351, T058-232399, icbc-ari@ctcreuna.cl*, library open Mon-Fri 0900-1230, 1630-2000, also has newspapers; Instituto Cultural Chileno Norteamericano,

San Marcos 581; Instituto Francés de Cultura, *Población Juan Noe, Psje 15, No 841, T058-242429*. **Hospital** *18 de Setiembre 1000, T058-232242*. **Internet** Several in centre, US$.75/hr. **Laundry** Lavandería A Kilo, *Santa Isabel shopping centre*, $6 per 5 kilos; Lavandería La Moderna, *18 de Septiembre 457*, US$4 per kg, open Sat till 2200. **Motorcycle repairs** Pablo Fernández Davils, *El Salitre 3254, T058-212863, F212823*. **Post office** *Prat 375*, to send parcels abroad, contents must be shown to Aduana (1st floor of post office), Mon-Fri 0800-1200, packaging sold but take your own tape. **Service stations** Shell, *Panamericana Norte 3456*; Esso, *Portales 2462*; Autocentro, *Azola 2999, T058-241241*. **Telephone** CTC, *Colón 430 and at 21 de Mayo 211*; **Entel-Chile**, *21 de May 345*, open 0900-2200; **VTR Telecommunications**, *21 de Mayo 477 and Colón 301*, telex, fax, telegrams. **Useful addresses** Automóvil Club de Chile, *Chacabuco 460, T058-252878, F232780*; CONAF, *MacKenna 820, T/F058-250570*, Mon-Fri 0830-1730.

Altiplano National Parks

Situated in the Andes and stretching from the entrance to the border with Bolivia, Parque Nacional Lauca is one of the most spectacular national parks in Chile. Declared a Biosphere Reserve by UNESCO, it is renowned for its birdlife, but is equally remarkable for the extraordinary views of snow-capped volcanoes set against the backdrop of Lago Chungará, one of the world's highest lakes, and the profusion of vicuñas and viscachas that live here. The brilliant quality of the light gives colours an intensity that is not easily forgotten and there are many deserted tracks across the altiplano, which provide a unique sense of the space and beauty of this remote corner of the world.

South of Parque Nacional Lauca are three further parks, covering areas of the western range of the Andes. They are best visited from Arica or Putre, as this permits acclimatization in Putre (Colchane and Enquelga, the alternatives, are too high). Tours in this area, lasting two or four days, can also be arranged here.

In and outs

Getting there and around Access to Parque Nacional Lauca is easy as Route 11, the main Arica-La Paz road, runs through the park. From mid-December to mid-March, during the rainy season, and in August, when snowfall occurs, some roads in the park may be impassable; check in advance with **CONAF** or the *carabineros* in Arica or Putre. Maps are available from the **Instituto Geográfico Militar** in Santiago. Water in the park is not drinkable; take bottled water.

⦂ Acclimatization for the *altiplano*

Unless you are entering Chile from Bolivia, the high altitude of the *altiplano* encountered in the Parque Nacional Lauca presents specific health problems for the traveller. The risks should not be underestimated; anyone with circulation or respiratory problems should avoid the area. Visitors to the park are advised to spend at least one night, preferably more, in Putre before moving on to higher altitudes. Drinking lots of water and/or *mate de coca* is also advised to compensate for the loss of body fluid. You should, of course, take it easy, limiting exercise before you get that familiar headache associated with *soroche* (altitude sickness), avoid smoking and take steps to get as much

fresh air as possible, particularly if spending the night in a *refugio*. In popular *refugios* there can be six to 10 people breathing the same air all night in a small room: to avoid the 3am headache that often develops in such conditions leave a window open and keep the water bottle nearby. Sleeplessness is a common first night problem but is not a cause for concern. One-day trips to the national park from Arica cannot really be recommended, either for health or for enjoyment: what should be an unforgettable trip amid incredible scenery can become an unpleasant endurance exercise in a minibus full of passengers all suffering from the dreaded *soroche*.

Parque Nacional Lauca → *Colour map 1, A2.*

Situated 145 km east of Arica, the park covers 137,883 ha and includes a large lake, Lago Chungará, a system of smaller lakes, the lagunas Cotacotani, and lava fields. Ranging in altitude from 3,200 m to four peaks of over 6,000 m, Lauca brings significant risks of *soroche*, or altitude sickness; beware, unless you are coming from Bolivia. Because of the extreme height, it is best to rise in stages, spending a night in Putre before going on to Lago Chungará; for this reason one-day tours from Arica are not the best way of seeing the park.

Often, when climbing the road from Arica, it may seem as though the weather is overcast; but vehicles soon gain altitude, climbing through the mist into a sort of lost world above, where the sky is a piercing blue colour and you can gaze down at the grey clouds huddled in the valley as if looking into a different plane of reality. On the way from Arica, at Km 90, there is a pre-Inca *pukará* (fortress) and, a few kilometres further, there is an Inca *tambo* (inn).

Putre → *Population 1,200.*

Putre is a scenic Aymará village, 15 km west of the park entrance at 3,500 m, and provides an ideal base for exploring and acclimatization. Situated at the base of **Volcán Taapacá** (Spanish name Nevadas de Putre, 5,824 m), it is surrounded by terracing dating from pre-Inca times, which is now used for cultivating alfalfa and oregano. It has a church dating from 1670. The village is a good centre for hiking: an extensive network of trails lead to numerous villages in the mountains, which provide great opportunities to explore, for those with the necessary time and fitness. In the vicinity, there are four archaeological sites with cave paintings up to 6,000 years old. Some 11 km east by road are the hot springs of **Jurassi** ⓘ *US$1.50*, with very hot water, a red mud bath, and views of vicuñas and alpacas. Transport can be organized in Putre. Note that weather can be poor in January and February, with fog and rain. Putre has a **tourist office** in the main plaza, which will help arrange tours; some English is spoken. ➽ *For Sleeping, Eating and other listings see pages 264-266.*

Wildlife of Parque Nacional Lauca

Although the park lies very close to the lifeless Atacama desert, its altitude ensures it receives more rain, which creates a fairyland of volcanoes and highland lakes surrounded by brilliant-green wetlands and vast expanses of puna grassland. The Río Lauca rises near Lago Chungará, then laces slowly through the park leaving marshy cushion bogs and occasional raceways and providing an array of habitats for the varied wildlife of the *altiplano*.

The **camelids** are the stars of the park; thousands of domesticated llamas and alpacas, as well as the dainty, graceful, wild vicuña which now number over 18,000. The charming viscacha, seemingly a long-tailed rabbit, but in fact belonging to the chinchilla family, can be seen perched sleepily on the rocks in the mornings, backside toward the rising sun.

Pumas, huemules (deer), foxes, skunks and armadillos are the more elusive **mammals**, some nocturnal, occupying the more remote reaches.

Lauca **birdlife** is spectacular with more than 120 species either resident or migrant here. Lago Chungará is home to more than 8,000 giant coots, distinguished by their bright orange legs, never-ending nest building and primordial cackling. In addition to coots, ducks and grebes, the wetlands provide a fine habitat for the puna plover, the rare diademed sandpiper plover, the puna ibis, Andean species of avocet, goose and gull, and an assortment of migratory shorebirds. Occasionally three species of flamingo can be seen at once: the Andean, the James (locally called *parinas*) and the more common Chilean flamingo.

Trips through the drier grasslands can produce glimpses of the puna tinamou, always in groups of three, and the puna rhea, seen in October and November with 20 or 30 miniatures scooting along behind. Passerines occupy all the habitats in the park, some to 5,000 m and above. There are also Sierra finches, black siskins, earthcreepers, miners, canasteros, cinclodes, tit-spinetails – new names for most birders. And in the skies above, keep your eyes peeled for Andean condors, mountain caracaras, aplomado falcons, black chested buzzard eagles and buteo hawks.

Exploring the park

From Putre, the road continues to climb and soon enters the park. **Parinacota** (4,392 m), a small village of whitewashed adobe houses, lies 26 km into the park and 41 km from Putre on two ancient trading routes, one from Potosí to Arica and the other from Belén into Bolivia. The interesting **17th-century church** – rebuilt in 1789 – has frescoes, silver religious objects and the skulls of past priests. Señor Sipriano keeps the key: ask for him at the kiosks and make sure you leave a donation. The **CONAF** office, ① *daily 0900-1200, 1230-1700*, which administers the national park is also here. There is a small shop in Parinacota with basic supplies, but most of the handicrafts sold in Parinacota are from Bolivia or Peru: a better place to buy locally made products is **Chucuyo**, 36 km further east, where local residents weave and knit from their own high-quality alpaca wool.

Cerro Guaneguane (5,300 m) can be climbed from Parinacota; ask one of the villagers to accompany you as a guide (and pay them). There is also a path to the **Lagunas de Botacotani**, a walk that would make a good day hike. CONAF maintains a nature trail that covers most plant and bird habitats, beginning at the CONAF pond in Parinacota and ending back in the village. Some 20 km southeast of Parinacota is

66 99 Climb through the mist into a sort
of lost world above, where the sky is a
piercing blue colour, and gaze down at the
grey clouds huddled in the valley as if
looking into a different plane of reality.

Lago Chungará, one of the highest lakes in the world, at 4,512 m, a must for its views
of the Parinacota, Pomerape, Sajama and Guallatire volcanoes. Overlooking the lake,
there is a CONAF refugio and campsite; vicuñas, llamas and alpacas can be seen
grazing nearby. From here, it is 3 km to the Chilean passport control point at Chungara
and 10 km to the Bolivian frontier at Tambo Quemado (see page 254). The border can
also be reached via an unpaved road from Parinacota to **Visviri**, 90 km further north.
▸▸ *For Sleeping, Eating and other listings, see pages 264-266.*

Heading south

A dirt road (A235) turns south off the Arica–La Paz highway, 1 km past **Las Cuevas**, a
park ranger post at the western end of the park, and ends at Huara on the
Pan-American Highway, near Iquique (see page 248). There is no public transport on
this route and frequently no traffic of any sort passes for days on the stretch between
Las Cuevas and Isluga. The road is open all year round but, between January and
March and in August, it may be impassable because of deep mud and water, which
can wash out the bridges. Four-wheel drive is essential; take sleeping bags and stock
up on fuel, drinking water and food for emergencies.

Although many maps show roads descending from the *altiplano* from Surire to
the Pan-American Highway and from Colchane to Camiña, do not be tempted to
follow them. These roads are terrible in the dry season, dangerous and impassable in
the rainy season; if stranded you could wait weeks for help to arrive. The only two safe
routes between the *altiplano* and the Pan-American Highway are the international
routes from Arica through Parque Nacional Lauca (see page 254) and from Huara to
Colchane (see page 248). ▸▸ *For Sleeping, Eating and other listings, see pages 264-266.*

Reserva Nacional Las Vicuñas
Split off from Parque Nacional Lauca in order to permit mining, this reserve, reached by
Route A235 (entrance free), stretches across 209,131 ha, most of it rolling *altiplano* at an
average altitude of 4,300 m. The reserve is bisected by the Río Lauca, along which
riverine vegetation alternates with puna tola/grasslands and many camelids can be
seen. Keep an eye open, too, for condors, rheas and migrating peregrine falcons. **Mina
Choquelimpie** (not operating), one of the world's highest gold and silver mines, can be
reached by a 7 km detour (clearly marked) off Route A235. The park administration is in
Guallatire , a village 96 km south of Las Cuevas at the foot of the smoking Guallatire
Volcano (6,060 m); the village has a lovely 17th-century *altiplano* church and a
carabinero control post. At Km 139, the road reaches the Salar de Surire.

Monumento Natural Salar de Surire
Situated at 4,300 m and covering 17,500 ha, the Salar de Surire is a drying salt lake with
thermal springs and a year-round population of 12,000-15,000 flamingos of three species
(nesting season is January). It is open all year, but see advice above. Administration is in

Surire, 45 km south of Guallatiri and 138 km south of Putre. About half of the *salar* is mined for borax; sometimes Surire may be reached by getting a ride in a borax truck from Zapahuira, a road junction at Km 100 on the road from Arica to La Paz.

Parque Nacional Volcán Isluga

This park includes some of the best volcanic scenery of northern Chile and covers 174,744 ha at altitudes above 2,100 m. Although the lower parts of the park, at its southwestern end, lie in the hills of the *precordillera*, the heart of the park is situated between **Laguna Aravilla** with its flamingoes and the village of **Isluga**, where there is an 18th-century Andean church and bell tower. Route A235 crosses the park, from the northern entrance, 40 km south of Surire, to the southern near Isluga. Northeast of Isluga under the smoking **Volcán Isluga** (5,501 m) is the village of **Encuelga**, where Aymaran weavers can be seen working in the sand behind wooden wind breaks. This is also the location of the park administration but there are seldom *guardaparques* there. Three other peaks over 5,000 m are Quimsachata (5,400 m), Tatajachura (5,252 m) and Latamara (5,207 m). Wildlife varies according to altitude; there are large numbers of camelids and birds but fewer than in Parque Nacional Lauca.

● Sleeping

Putre *p261*
B Hostería Las Vicuñas, *T/F058-228564*. Half board, bungalow-style, heating, restaurant, does not accept TCs, US$ cash or credit cards.
C-F Res La Paloma, *O'Higgins 353, T09-1979319, lapalomahugopaco@hotmail.com* Newly renovated, indoor parking, no heating, also restaurant, friendly. Price per person.
E Hostal Calí, *Baquedano s/n, by supermarket*. Clean, more expensive for room with bath.
F Res Rosamel, *Putre*. Clean, pleasant, with hot water and restaurant. Price per person.
G *Baquedano 250, no sign (blue garage door)*. Basic, clean, hot water, good value. Recommended. Price per person.
G Res Oasis, *Putre*. Basic, no showers, good food, very friendly.

Camping
Sra Clementina Caceres, *blue door , Lynch*, Camping in the garden and lunch.
Turismo Taki, *Copaquilla, 45 km west of Putre (100 km east of Arica)*. Campsite with a restaurant (serving homemade bread). English and Italian spoken. Also runs excursions to nearby *pukarás*, the Inca *tambo* and cemetery and the Inca trail, which connected the highlands with the coast.

Parque Nacional Lauca *p261*
E Casa Barbarita, *Parinacota, T058-300013, F222735*. 2 bedrooms, cooking facilities, heating, naturalist library.

F CONAF refugio, *Parinacota*. Many beds, cooking facilities. Price per person. Also camping, reserve in Putre.
F CONAF refugio, *Lago Chungará*. 8 beds, cooking facilities, camping, prices as in Parinacota, reserve in Putre. Take a sleeping bag, food and candles. CONAF *refugios* do not provide sheets or blankets.
G Res Copihue de Oro, *Chucuyo*. 1 room, 4 beds, no showers, restaurant.
G Res Doña Mati, *Chucuyo*. 1 room, 5 beds, no shower, restaurant.
G Sra Francisca, *Parinacota*. 3 beds, cooking facilities.
G Sr Gumercindo Gutierrez, *Lagunillas, 10 km north of Parinacota on road to Visviri, turn left near lake*. Accommodation and guide.
G Uta Maillko, *Parinacota*. The name means 'home of the condor' in Aymara. Dormitory, home-cooked Aymara food.

Reserva Nacional Las Vicuñas *p263*
There is accommodation for up to 7 people at the park administration in Guallatire, *T058-250570*. Imperative to reserve at least five days in advance or it will be closed.
G Sra Clara Blanca, *1 km east off A235, 10 km after Chuquelimpie turnoff*. An Aymaran weaver offers overnight accommodation, food typical of the region and allows travellers to help with llamas and alpacas.

Salar de Surire *p263*
G CONAF refugio, *Surire, 8 km past the borax mine*. 15 beds and cooking facilities, advance booking at CONAF in Arica essential (p260).

Camping
Polloquere, *17 km south of Surire*. No facilities, no water. Price per site.

Parque Nacional Volcán Isluga *p264*
CONAF refugio, *Encuelga*. Six beds and cooking facilities, reservation in Arica essential (p260).

There are also several basic *residenciales* in Colchane, which lies 6 km south of the southern entrance (p249).

🍴 Eating

Other eating options are given under Sleeping, above.

Parque Nacional Lauca *p261*
$ **Restaurant Kuchamarka**, *Baquedano s/n, Putre*. Serves local specialities including alpaca and vegetarian options, good value.
$ **Restaurant Los Payachatas**, *Chucuyo*. Tasty alpaca dishes.

Reserva Nacional Las Vicuñas *p263*
$ **Restaurant Sanchez**, *(no sign), 1 block from* carabineros, *Guallatire*. Good lunch stews in an *altiplano* truckstop.

⊕ Festivals and events

Putre *p261*
The **Feria de la voz Andina** takes place in Putre every year in **Nov**, attracting top Andean groups, as well as cultural exhibitions. If going, book accommodation in advance.

O Shopping

Putre *p261*
Buy all food for the park in Putre, which has markets where bottled water, fresh bread, vegetables, meat, cheese and canned foods can be obtained. The **Cooperativo** on the plaza is usually cheapest. Fuel is available from the **Cali** and **Paloma** supermarkets, but is cheaper at **ECA**, next to the post office. **Sra Daria Condori**'s shop on Calle O'Higgins sells locally made *artesanía* and naturally coloured alpaca wool. Organically grown vegetables are available from **Freddy Blanco**, opposite the Banco del Estado.

▲ Activities and tours

Putre *p261*
Birding Alto Andino, *Baquedano 299, Putre, T058-300013, bernapton@hotmail.com* Specialist birdwatching tours of the area and also walking tours along the Camino del Inca. English spoken, owner is an Alaskan biologist/naturalist, recommended.
Freddy Torrejón, *Gonzalo Cerda 1366, Arica, T/F058-253361, www2.gratisweb.com/losandeschileno* Accommodation in Putre and tours of the surrounding area, including Lago Chungará and the village of Parinacota, as well as trips to the more out-of-the-way places, such as the Salar de Surire and ancient rock paintings.

Parque Nacional Lauca *p261*
Tours are offered by many agencies in **Arica** (p258), daily in season, according to demand at other times, US$20 with light breakfast and lunch; all 1-day tours make Parinacota their last stop. It is better to spend more than 1 day in the Lauca National Park, but if limited to a 1-day tour choose carefully. Longer tours are also available. You can leave the tour and continue on another day as long as you ensure that the company will collect you when you want (tour companies try to charge double for this).

Climbing
The best season for climbing is Aug to Nov; avoid Jan to Feb. Permits are required for climbing Parinacota, Pomerape, Tarapacá and Guallatire volcanoes; these can be obtained from the Governor's office in Putre. The procedure is routine (passport required) but expect a delay of 1 or 2 days. To obtain a permit in advance, contact **Departamento de Fronteras y Limites (DIFROL)**, *Banderas 52, piso 5, Santiago, T02-6794200*, listing the mountains you wish to climb.

Arturo Gomez, who lives next to the Lipigas propane shop in Putre, is a climbing guide and local plant expert.

⊖ Transport

Bus
La Paloma leave Arica from their own terminal daily at 0630 for **Putre**, US$2.50, returning from Putre at 1330. The bus often

leaves full, so buy your ticket the day before. The journey takes you through several villages on the way. Alternatively, any bus heading to **La Paz** (p259) will drop you on the main road, 3km from Putre. Hitching from here is usually easy with the army or *carabineros*. If you walk, take it easy until you have acclimatized to the altitude.

Jurasi *colectivos, T058-222813*, leave Arica daily at 0700, picking up at hotels, US$5.

Buses Humire run services 1030 Tue and Fri from Arica to **Parinacota**, US$4.75, slow.

Car

For 5 or more, the most economical proposition is to hire a vehicle in Arica but take at least 1 spare fuel can with a tightly fitting cap. During the climb from Arica, you should stop several times to release excess pressure in fuel cans. For tyre repairs, ask for Andrés in Putre. For the Parque Nacional Lauca, 4WD and antifreeze are essential; if you wish to cross from the park into Bolivia you will need a permit from the hire company.

Hitchhiking

Most trucks for Bolivia pass **Parinacota** between 0700-1100. Hitching back to Arica is not difficult and you may be able to bargain with one of the tour buses.

The **Salar de Surire** can sometimes be reached by getting a ride in a borax truck from Zapahuira, Km 100 on the Arica–La Paz road; trucks run sporadically depending on rainfall. The drop-off point is on the mine side of the Salar, 30 km from the hot springs.

❶ Directory

Putre *p261*
Bank Changes TCs and cash to pesos, but commission on TCs is very high.

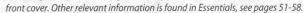
For an explanation of sleeping and eating price codes used in this guide, see inside the front cover. Other relevant information is found in Essentials, see pages 51-58.

The Central Valley

Introduction

The Central Valley is the heart of Chile. Stretching from just north of Santiago south to the **Río Biobío**, this wonderful region ranges from secluded tracks and beaches along the coast to the **high Andes** in the east, with the fertile valley itself in between.

On clear days, the snowy mountains can easily be seen from the coast, across the woods, fields and vineyards of Chile's agricultural heartland. It is here that the most enduring images of Chilean village life can be found: *huasos* (cowboys) with their long spurs, green valleys speckled with grazing horses and whitewashed houses in colonial style, hinting at that bygone age before cars and motorbikes sounded the death knell for the horse.

★ **Don't miss...**

❶ **The beach at Pichilemu** One of the best surfing strands in Chile, page 274.

❷ **Vineyards** Wine tasting is a pleasure in the vineyards around Santa Cruz and the Maule Valley, page 282.

❸ **Pacific coast resorts** Curanipe, Iloca and Lebu are the favourites, but there are countless others along the beautiful and largely deserted Pacific coast, pages 278, 285 and 296.

❹ **Trekking** Trek in the mountains near the resort of Vilches, east of Talca, page 283.

❺ **Rodeos** The highlight being the National Rodeo championships in Rancagua at the end of March, page 273.

The Central Valley

Background

The peoples of the Central Valley did not prove as fierce as their Mapuche neighbours. They were conquered by the Incas in about 1470. On his second visit to Chile, Pedro de Valdivia led an expedition southwards, founding Concepción in 1550 and a further seven cities south of the Río Biobío. The Mapuche insurrection of 1598 and the Spanish defeat at Curalabo in 1599 led the Spanish to withdraw north of the Río Biobío and concentrate their efforts in the Central Valley.

Here, the land and its inhabitants were divided up among the colonists to create the forerunner of the hacienda, which was to dominate social and economic life in Chile. The hacienda was a self-contained unit, producing everything it needed. There were no towns in the area but, from the 1740s, the Spanish crown attempted to increase its control over the region by founding settlements, including Rancagua (1743), San Fernando (1742), Curicó (1743), Talca (1742), Cauquenes (1742) and Linares (1755).

After Independence, the Río Biobío continued to be the southern frontier of white settlement until, in 1862, Colonel Cornelio Saavedra led an army south to build a line of 10 forts, each 4 km apart, between Angol and Collipulli. Following the occupation of the coast around Arauco in 1867, another line of forts was built across the Cordillera de Nahuelbuta. By 1881, the railway from Santiago had reached Angol, from where Chilean troops set out on the final campaign against the Mapuche.

Today, the Central Valley is the agricultural heartland of Chile, transformed in the past 30 years by the growth of commercial export agriculture and wine production. Since 1974, over 1,000,000 ha of trees have been planted in Regions VII, VIII and IX, mostly Monterrey Pine. Climatic conditions for forestry are particularly favourable inland from Arauco. The coast between Dichato and Arauco has also seen growth in fishing and fish-processing since the 1980s. Despite the decline of coal mining in the 1980s, Concepción and the surrounding area constitute an important industrial area in Chile.

Geography and climate

Encompassing three of the administrative regions of Chile, Regions VI (O'Higgins), VII (Maule) and VIII (Biobío), the Central Valley is a wide depression located between the Andes to the east and the Cordillera de la Costa to the west. The Andes gradually lose height as they continue southwards, although there are a number of high peaks east of Rancagua: Alto de los Arrieros (5,000 m), El Palomo (4,986 m), Tingiririca (4,280 m). The northern parts of the region enjoy a Mediterranean climate, with a prolonged dry season, but with more rain than Santiago. In general, rainfall increases gradually from north to south, until around Concepción there is usually some rainfall each month. The Central Valley receives less rain than the coastal mountains, but temperatures vary more inland than in coastal areas. The Coastal Range is generally under 500 m, but south of the Río Biobío it forms a range of high peaks known as the Cordillera de Nahuelbuta. Five major rivers cross the Central Valley: from north to south these are the Ríos Rapel, Mataquito, Maule, Itata and Biobío.

The Rapel Valley

The damming of the Río Rapel has created Lago Rapel, the largest artificial lake in Chile, and a very popular destination for Santiaguinos taking their summer holidays. There are numerous small and pleasant towns, and several large fundos (farms) south of the town of Rapel, in an area of green hills and stunted thorn trees. Open roads by the coast have wonderful views of the high Andes east of Rancagua, while the beach at Pichilemu is one of the best in Chile for surfing.

Rancagua → *Phone code: 072. Colour map 3, B3.*

The capital of Región VI, Rancagua lies 82 km south of Santiago, on the Río Cachapoal. The city was founded in 1743 and in October 1814 was the scene of an important battle during the Wars of Independence, when Bernardo O'Higgins and his 1,700 Chilean patriots were surrounded in the centre of the town by 4,500 Royalist (pro-Spanish) troops. O'Higgins managed to break out and escape but was forced into exile in Argentina, only to return within a few years finally to defeat the Spanish forces in Chile (see also page 518).

Ins and outs

Getting there Rancagua is accessible by bus and train from Santiago (both hourly). There are also connections to the towns further south, especially Talca, Chillán, Concepción, Temuco and Puerto Montt (several daily). ▶▶ *For further details, see Transport page 275.* **Getting around** While the centre of Rancagua is compact, some of the outlying *barrios* are quite a distance and you may wish to take one of the numerous *colectivos.*
Tourist information ① *Germán Riesco 277, T072-230413, info_ohiggins@sernatur.cl, English spoken. Also municipal office in the Municipalidad on Plaza de los Héroes.*

Sights

At the heart of the city is an attractive tree-lined plaza, the **Plaza de los Héroes** and several streets of single-storey colonial-style houses. In the centre of the plaza is an equestrian statue of O'Higgins. The double-spired cathedral on the south side of the plaza was restored in the 1860s, the original building having been destroyed in the battle of Rancagua, together with most of the other buildings around the plaza. There are several plaques in the city centre marking the sites of the battle and a diagram in the plaza shows the disposition of the troops. One block north is the **Merced** church, from where O'Higgins commanded his beleaguered forces. It dates from 1758 but has

The Central Valley The Rapel Valley

Rancagua

To Pan-American Highway (North)

To Pan-American Highway (South)

0 metres 200
0 yards 200

Sleeping ⊜		Eating ❷	
Aguila Real 1	Hostal Yaiman 4	Bravissimo 1	La Cocina
Camino del Rey 2	Rancagua 5	Geo Algas 2	Artesana 6
España 3	Residencial Ahumada 7	Guy 3	Lasagna 4
	Santiago 6		Le Gourmet 5

been restored several times. The main commercial area lies along Avenida Independencia, which runs west from the plaza towards the bus and rail terminals. The **Museo Histórico** ① *Estado y Ibieta, T/F072-221524, www.museorancagua.cl, Tue-Fri 1000-1800, Sat and Sun 0900-1300, US$1 (Tue free)*, housed in a colonial mansion, contains collections of religious art and late 19th-century furniture. There is also a **Casa de la Cultura** ① *corner of Milán and Cachapoal, T072-230976, daily 0830-1330, 1500-1700,,* directly south of Plaza de Los Héroes, which houses temporary exhibitions. In the station there is a small gallery with paintings by local artists for sale. ▸▸ *For Sleeping, Eating and other listings, see pages 274-276.*

Around Rancagua

Lago Rapel
West of Rancagua, this lake is 40 km long and feeds the Rapel hydroelectric plant. Most facilities at this popular summer resort are on the east shore around El Manzano, the main town, while the tourist information office is in Las Cabras. There are watersports at Bahía Skorpios, including windsurfing, yachting, waterskiing and fishing.

East of the city
The **El Teniente** copper mine, one of the biggest in the country, is 67 km east of Rancagua. Owned by **Codelco**, it can only be visited by prior arrangement with the company. Nearby, on a private road above El Teniente, is the small **Chapa Verde** ski resort ① *T072-294255, www.chapaverde.cl, lift tickets US$18 per day Mon-Fri, US$25 per day Sat, Sun, obtainable only from resort office, Del Sol shopping centre, north of Rancagua*. The resort is owned by **Codelco**, but is open to the public in season (June-September). Equipment can be hired, but there's no accommodation. ▸▸ *For details on how to get there, see Transport, page 276.*

South of El Teniente and 28 km east of Rancagua are the thermal springs of **Cauquenes**, visited by Charles Darwin in 1835. A bath in the springs costs US$5, massages start at US$7.50 and a Jacuzzi costs US$14. Some 5 km north is the village of **Coya**, where the Chilean President has a summer residence, while to the south is the **Reserva Nacional Río de los Cipreses** ① *T072-297505, entrance US$3*. Situated 50 km southeast of Rancagua, the Reserva Nacional covers 36,882 ha of the valley of the Río de los Cipreses at altitudes ranging from 900 m to 4,900 m. Park administration is at the entrance at the north end of the park.

San Fernando and around → *Phone code: 072. Colour map 3, B3. Population 44,500*
San Fernando lies on the Río Tingiririca, 51 km south of Rancagua. Founded in 1742, it is capital of Colchagua Province and a service town for this fertile valley. There is a small local museum in the **Casa Patronal de Lircunlauta** ① *Jiménez y Alameda, closed Mon, US$2.50*, a 17th-century colonial mansion, with local history exhibits.

From San Fernando, a road runs east towards the *cordillera* and divides: the southern branch of the road goes to the resort of **Sierra Bellavista**, a private *fundo* where many Santiago businesspeople have holiday houses, and where there are rodeos in October and November. The northern branch, a treacherous 75 km, runs to the **Termas del Flaco** near the Argentine border, where there is a poor campsite, *cabañas* and hotels. The thermal springs (US$1.40) are open only in the summer when they attract large numbers of visitors. Some 500 m from the Termas del Flaco

● *In 1984, Rosie Swale rode from Antofagasta to Caleta Tortel on two horses lent to her by the owner of Hacienda Los Lingues; she recorded her experiences in 'Back to Cape Horn', see page 554.*

Ride 'em cowboy

During the summer months, rodeo is one of the most popular sports in central and southern Chile, second only to the inevitable: football. Teams (or *colleras*) of two riders on horseback compete throughout the season, culminating in the national championships in Rancagua at the end of March. Eliminatory rounds are held in Osorno, Temuco, San Carlos, San Fernando, Vallenar and Los Andes, but most small towns in central southern Chile have their own *media lunas* (stadia, with their own corrals and horseboxes), often used once a year only.

Rodeo owes its origins to the colonial period, when cattle roamed openly and were rounded up once annually to be identified and marked by their owners in a rodeo. Based on the traditional view that heifers need to be broken in, the modern sport of rodeo is a test of the ability of two horses and their riders to work together and control the cattle.

The event takes place inside a stockade of thick upright timbers; although now circular, this is known as a *media luna* (crescent) after the design of the early rings: at two points the walls of the ring are covered by padded sections, with a flag at either end of the section. Each *collera* competes by manoeuvring a heifer around the edge of the ring between the padded sections, stopping it at each padded section by pinning its hindquarters against the fence, before turning it in the opposite direction. This is done three times before the animal is released from the ring.

Three judges give points (on a scale of one to seven) for elegance and horsemanship. It is one of the principles of rodeo that no heifer should be put through this performance more than once; the event should come as a complete surprise to the animal.

Rodeo is a good opportunity to see traditional Chilean rural customs: the *huasos* (cowboys) wearing brightly coloured ponchos, wide-brimmed hats and carved wooden stirrups that were common in the 19th century; the fine horses, and the *cuecas* (traditional dances) that sometimes follow the main event.

are 'Las huellas de dinosaurios', dinosaur footprints preserved in the rock, dating from over 120 million years ago. There are good one-day treks starting from the baths, and a two-hour horseride leads to the site of the Uruguayan plane crash immortalised in the film *Alive*.

Los Lingues ① *Contact: Torre C de Tajamar, Of 205, Santiago, T02-2352458, www.loslingues.com*, is a private *hacienda*, 20 km northeast of San Fernando, where the 'best' horses in Chile are bred. Visits can be arranged to the 17th-century house, a gift of the King of Spain, and one-day tours, including transport, rodeo and lunch, are also available. ▸▸ *For Sleeping, Eating and other listings, see pages 274-276.*

Heading west

West of San Fernando, tracks branch off the main road to Pichilemu southwards through quiet hill country towards **Lago Vichuquén** (see page 278). Dry thorn trees gradually give way to more fertile land, with the first signs of *copihues* and forests, while ridges high above the valleys provide beautiful routes for cyclists, walkers and horseriders.

Fifty kilometres southwest of San Fernando, Santa Cruz is surrounded by some of the country's best vineyards and is the site of the offices of the **Ruta de Vino del Valle de Colchagua** ① *Plaza de Armas 140, Of 6, T072-823199, rv@uva.cl* Also in the town is the **Museo de Cochagua** ① *Errazuriz 145, T072-821050, www.museocolchagua.cl, Tue-Sun 1000-1900, US$3.50, concessions US$0.75,* an excellent small museum with exhibits on local history and prehistory as well as winemaking.

Pichilemu

Pichilemu is a coastal resort with a great many hotels and *residenciales*, 120 km west of San Fernando. It was founded by Agustín Ross Edwards in the 19th century in the style of a European resort. Among several beaches is **Punta Los Lobos**, where international surfing competitions are held. The former train station, made of wood in 1925, is a national monument. There is also a small museum, the **Museo del Niño Rural de Ciruelos**, a few kilometres south of town, with three rooms of interesting exhibits from the pre-Hispanic cultures of the region. Fishing is good in nearby lakes.

⊜ Sleeping

Rancagua *p271, map p271*
AL **Camino del Rey**, *Estado 275, T072-232314, hotelcaminodelrey@terra.cl* 4-star, suites, full facilities, best in town.
AL-A **Santiago**, *Brasil 1036, T072-230860, hsantiago@entelchile.net* Poorly maintained but friendly.
A-B **Aguila Real**, *Brasil 1045, T072-222047, hsamour@ctcinternet.cl* 3-star. With breakfast, cable TV, laundry, restaurant.
B **Rancagua**, *San Martín 85, T072-232663, F072-241155.* Bath, quiet, clean, secure parking. Recommended.
C **España**, *San Martín 367, T072-230141, F072-234196.* Bath, cheaper without, central, hot water, pleasant, clean, laundry.
E **Hostal Yaiman**, *Bueras 655, T072-641773.* Price per person. Laundry facilities, food served.
F **Res Ahumada**, *Mujica 125, T072-225892.* Price per person. Kitchen facilities, secure.

Lago Rapel *p272*
L-AL **Punta Verde**, *Bahía Skorpios, T072-591434, F072-591442.* Full facilities.
F **Hostería Playa Llallauquén**, *Llallauquén Viejo s/n, T072-561474.* Also *cabañas*.

Camping
The eastern shore of Lago Rapel around El Manzano is lined with campsites.
Camping Punta Arenas, *3 km north of El Manzano.* Basic and cheap.

East of the city *p272*
AL-A **Hotel Termas de Cauquenes**, *Cauquenes, T072-899010, www.termasdecauquenes.cl* Excellent food is served in the hotel restaurant (full board available). It also has a chapel and gardens.

Camping
There is a site at **Los Maitenes**, 12 km south of the entrance to the Reserva Nacional Río de los Cipreses, prices per site.

San Fernando and around *p272*
LL **Hacienda Los Lingues**, *22 km north of San Fernando (see p273).* The very expensive accommodation starts at US$250 with an extra charge for breakfast or full board. The *hacienda* is a member of the French **Hotels et Relais et Chateaux**.
B **Español**, *Av Rodríguez 959, San Fernando, T072-711098.* 3-star, with parking and pool.
C **Imperio**, *Av Rodríguez 770, San Fernando, T072-714595.* With breakfast and bath (cheaper without), clean, cable TV, parking.
F **Pérez**, *Av Rodríguez 1028, San Fernando, T072-713328.* Price per person, without bath.

Pichilemu *p274*
There are dozens of cheap places to stay in Pichilemu.
B-C **Cabañas Lugano**, *Calle Santiago s/n, T072-842200, www.geocities.com/ eduardomarti* Cabin accommodation with TV, private bath and kitchen, various outdoor activities organized.
E **Rex**, *Ortúzar 34, T072-841003.* Price per person. Good breakfast, good value.

E-F **Chile-España**, *Ortúzar 255, T072-841270, hotelchileespana@terra.cl* Price per person; cheaper off season. Friendly, helpful, excellent restaurant, good value.
F **Bahía**, *Ortúzar 262*. Price per person with breakfast, clean.

Camping
Pichilemu has several campsites, but at US$12 per site, these are more expensive than the cheaper *residenciales*.

Eating

Rancagua *p271, map p271*
$$ **Guy Restaurante**, *Astorga 319*. Decent French cuisine.
$ **Bravissimo**, *Astorga 307*. Recommended for ice cream.
$ **Geo Algas**, *Independencia 677, 2nd floor*. Vegetarian food
$ **La Cocina Artesanal**, *O´Carrol 60*. Traditional meat and seafood dishes.
$ **Lasagna**, *west end of plaza*. Good for bread and *empanadas*.

San Fernando and around *p272*
$ **Club Social San Fernando**, *Rodríguez 787*. Good local food.
$ **Restaurante La Carreta**, *Rancagua 759*. Traditional cuisine.
$ **Rigoletto**, *Rodríguez 751*. Pizzas.

Bars and clubs

Rancagua *p271, map p271*
La Notta, *Illanes 303-A*. Bar with restaurant.
Pub Restaurant Puerto Girón, *Bueras 358*. Expensive.
Varadero, *O'Carrol 1109*. Disco.

San Fernando and around *p272*
Toscano Pub Disco, *Quechereguas 966*. Fri and Sat night disco.

Pichilemu *p274*
Many people come here for the nightlife; there is a good atmosphere after dark.
Bar Pub Pepe Cuervo, *Avda Costanera 1*. Bar with restaurant.
Disco Club 127, *Angel Gaete 127*. Popular nightspot.
Fabrica, *Acevedo 125*. Disco.
Vivo, *Ross 136*. Disco.

Festivals and events

Rancagua *p271, map p271*
National Rodeo Championships are held at the end of **Mar** in the Complejo Deportivo, north of the centre, US$10 per day. There are plenty of opportunities for purchasing cowboy items; watch out especially for the fantastic spurs, which are much more important to horsemanship in Chile than elsewhere in Latin America.

Beans are the most important staple food for *campesinos* in the area and are celebrated at the **Festival del Poroto** (Bean Festival) at the beginning of **Feb**.

Santa Cruz *p274*
Fiesta de la vendimia (harvest celebration) is held in the first weekend in **Mar** in Santa Cruz around the town's main plaza, where local wine and food can be sampled.

Shopping

Rancagua *p271, map p271*
There's a **shopping mall** at *Cuevas 483*, and a supermarket at **Hipermercado Independencia**, *Av Miguel Ramírez 665*.

Activities and tours

Rancagua *p271, map p271*
Andes Sur Expediciones, *T072-491157, www.andes-sur.cl* Regional operator specialising in mountaineering, trekking, horseriding and fishing in the Andes.
Ruta del Vino del Valle del Cachapoal
Panamericana, km110, (20 km south of Rancagua), T072-522085, www.chileanwineroute.com See box p282.

Transport

Rancagua *p271, map p271*
Bus
Main terminal in Rancagua is at *Doctor Salinas y Calvo* just north of the market but most buses for **Santiago** leave from the **Tur Bus** terminal at *Calvo y O'Carrol*. Many services from further south stop on the Pan-American Highway, 2 km outside town.

Local There are far too many local buses to list here, but destinations include **Lago Rapel** with **Sextur**, *T072-231342*, or **Galbus**

T072-230640, every 20 mins, US$2; **Pichilemu**, US$4 one-way, many companies; and **Termas Del Flaco**, US$12 return with Buses Amistad, *T072-229358*, booking required 2 days in advance.

Long distance Frequent services to **Santiago**, 1¼ hrs, US$3. To **Valparaíso** and **Viña del Mar**, Tur Bus, US$6. Viatur, *T072-234502*, have a nightly bus to **Valdivia, Osorno** and **Puerto Montt** (US$14), and another to **Chillán** and **Los Angeles** (US$7). Buses Lit, *T072-239800*, also run southbound services.

Train

Rancagua station is at *Av La Marina*, *T072-230361*. Mainline services between **Santiago** and **Chillán** stop here. Also regular services to/from **Santiago**, 1¼ hrs, and **San Fernando**, 35 mins, on **Metrotren**, 10-19 a day, US$2.

East of the city *p272*

The **Chapa Verde** ski resort can only be reached by mine-transport bus from **Del Sol** shopping centre on the northern outskirts of Rancagua, daily 0900, plus every 15 mins 0800-0930 during weekends in season. The thermal springs of **Cauquenes** are served by 5 daily buses from Rancagua with **Buses Termas**, US$1, or a *colectivo* from Rancagua market.

San Fernando and around *p272*

Bus

Many companies have buses to **Santiago**, US$2.50, including **Andimar**, *T072-711817* and **Pullman del Sur**, *T072-714076*. To **Pichilemu**, US$2.50, with **Nilahue**, *T072-711937* and **Galbus**, *T072-712983*; to **Termas del Flaco**, US$8 return, with

Amistad, *T072-710348*, **Andibus**, *T072-711817*, and others. Lots of competition to the south, with services running as far as **Chiloé**, US$15, with **Cruz del Sur**, *T072-710348*, and most intermediate destinations with **Turbus**, *T072-712923*, and **Buses Lit**, *T072-711679*.

Train

The station is at *Quecheregua s/n*, *T072-711087*. **Metrotren** runs 10 trains daily to Santiago.

Pichilemu *p274*

Andimar and **Nilahue** buses to **Santiago**, 4 hrs, US$5.

⊙ Directory

Rancagua *p271, map p271*

Airline offices Iberia, Lacsa and United Airlines, *Cuevas No 744*, *T072-220288 F072-237054*; LanChile, *Astorga 223B*, *T072-235573*, *F072-244392*. **Banks** Exchange at Cambios Afex, *Av Campos 363*, open every day; also several banks on Independencia. **Car hire** Weber Rentacar, *Membrillar 40*, *Of 2*, *T072-226005*, *autorentasweber@tie.cl*; Comercial O'Carrol, *O'Carrol 1120*, *T072-230041*, *ocarrolrentacar@yahoo.com* **Cycle repairs** Spares at Gustavo Sepúlveda, *Bueras 481*, *T072-241413*. **Car servicing** For parts try Aucamar, *Brasil 1177*, *T072-223594*, and several others around Brasil 1100-1200, although the selection and prices are better in Santiago. **Internet** Ciber Space, *Alcázar 376*. **Useful address** **Automóvil Club de Chile**, *Ibieta 09*, *T072-239930*, *F239907*.

The Mataquito Valley

The Río Mataquito, formed by the confluence of the Ríos Lontué and Teno, flows through the peaceful heart of Chilean wine country, reaching the Pacific at a wide and serene estuary near Iloca. The Andes can clearly be seen from the cliffs above the largely deserted coast.

Curicó → *Phone code: 075. Colour map 3, C2. Population: 103,919.*

Curicó, which means 'black water' in the Mapuche language, lies between the rivers Lontué and Teno, 54 km south of San Fernando. Founded in 1743, it is the only town of

any size in the Mataquito Valley and is the service centre for the region's vineyards.
The bustling town centre offers good views towards the mountains and a friendly atmosphere after dark.

Ins and outs

Getting there Curicó is easily accessible by bus from Santiago (many times daily). There are also some connections to the towns further south, especially Talca, Chillán, Temuco and Puerto Montt (several daily). ▶▶ *For further details, see Transport page* . **Getting around** While the centre of Curicó is quite compact, some of the outlying *barrios* are quite a distance away, and you may wish to take one of the numerous *colectivos*. **Tourist information** Gobernación Provincial ⓘ *Plaza de Armas, Mon-Fri 0900-1330, 1600-1800*, helpful, has street map. **CONAF** ⓘ *Gobernación Provincial building, piso 1, Plaza de Armas, daily 0900-1430*.

Sights

The **Plaza de Armas** is surrounded by about 40 Canary Island palms and has lovely fountains with sculptures of nymphs, black-necked swans and a monument to the Mapuche warrior, Lautaro, carved from the trunk of an ancient beech tree. The steel **bandstand** was built in New Orleans in 1904 and is now a national monument. On the western side of the plaza is the church of **La Merced**, which was badly damaged by an earthquake in 1986, and is slowly being restored. Five blocks east is the neo-Gothic church of **San Francisco**, a national monument, which contains the 17th-century Virgen de Velilla, brought from Spain. At the junction of Carmen and Avenida San Martín is the imposing **Iglesia del Carmen**.

Curicó

Sleeping	Residencial Central 5	Turismo 11	Centro Italiano
Comercio 1	Residencial Colonial 6		Club Social 3
Palmas Express 2	Residencial Ensueño 7	**Eating**	Club de la Unión 4
Prat 3	Residencial Montt 8	American Bar 1	El Fogón Chileno 5
Residencial Alemana 4	Residencial Rahue 9	Café-Bar Maxim 2	Los Cisnes 6

To the east of the city is the Avenida Manso de Velasco, with statues of various national heroes, and also a bust of Mahatma Gandhi. Nearby is **Cerro Condell** offering fine views of the surrounding countryside and across to the distant Andes; it is an easy climb to the summit, from where there are a number of short walks.

The **Miguel Torres bodega** ① *5 km south of the city, T075-564100, www.torres.es/esp/asp/vav_curico.asp, daily 1000-1700 in autumn and winter, daily 1000-1900 in spring and summer, tours in Spanish only*, is one of the biggest wine *bodegas* in Chile and well worth a visit. To get there, take a bus for Molina from the local terminal or from outside the railway station and get off at Km 195 on the Pan-American Highway. There's a good restaurant on the site, open Tuesday to Sunday. For details of other *bodegas* and vineyards in the area, contact the **Ruta del Vino del Valle de Curicó** ① *Merced 331, piso 2, T075-328972, www.rvvc.cl*

Around Curicó

Area de Proteccíon Radal Siete Tazas

① *Oct-Mar, US$2*. This park is in two sectors, one at **Radal**, 65 km east of Curicó, the other at **Parque Inglés**, 9 km further east and the site of the park administration. The most interesting sector is at Radal, where the Río Claro flows through a series of seven rock 'cups' (the *siete tazas*), each with a pool emptying into the next by means of a waterfall. The river then passes through a canyon, 15 m deep but only 1½ m wide, which ends abruptly in a cliff and a beautiful waterfall. There are several well-marked trails in the area.

Towards the coast

From Curicó, a road runs west through the small town of **Licantén** towards the mouth of the Río Mataquito and the popular resort of **Iloca**, set in a wide bay with great views south along the coastline. Some 5 km north of Iloca is **Puerto Duao**, a fishing village with a good campsite, while beyond is the resort of **Llico**, which has a pleasant beach and windsurfing facilities. It is reached either by the coastal route or by an unpaved inland road, which branches off at Hualañe, 74 km east of Curicó.

Six kilometres west of Licantén a bridge crosses the Río Mataquito, leading to a road south along the coast to **Putú**, past kilometres of rolling sand dunes, a kind of mini Sahara. Further south, the road reaches the Río Maule, where a ferry crosses to Constitución (see page 284).

Lago Vichuquén and around

Just east of Llico and 114 km west of Curicó, Lago Vichuquén is a large, peaceful lake, set in a bowl surrounded by pine woods. It is very popular with the wealthy and with watersports enthusiasts and, although parts of the eastern shore of the lake are inaccessible by road, there are full facilities on the western shore, particularly at Aquelarre. The nearby town of **Vichuquén** has some well-preserved colonial architecture and a recommended small **museum** ① *US$1.50*, set in a beautiful porticoed house in the town centre.

Just north of Lago Vichuquén, 120 km west of Curicó, is the **Reserva Nacional Laguna Torca** ① *administration and campsite 4 km east of Llico, open Sep-Apr*. The reserve covers 604 ha and is a natural sanctuary for over 80 species of birds, especially black-necked swans and other water fowl. To get there take any bus from Curicó to Llico and get out near the administration.

The Central Valley The Mataquito Valley

⬤ Sleeping

Curicó *p276, map p277*

A Turismo, *Carmen 727 y Prat, T075-310552, www.hotelturismocurico.cl* Modern, with breakfast, suites, restaurant, pleasant garden.

A-B Comercio, *Yungay 730, T075-310014, www.curicochile.cl/hotelcomercio* 3-star, clean.

C-G Res Ensueño, *Rodríguez 442, T075-312648.* Cheaper rooms without bath.

D Res Central, *Prat 669.* Good value, but not in the centre.

D-G Res Rahue, *Rodriguez 296, T075-312194.* Basic, with bath, meals, hot water, the cheaper annex rooms without bath have no ventilation.

F Prat, *Peña 427, T075-311069.* Price per person. With bath (cheaper without). Pleasant patio with grapevines and fig trees, friendly, clean, hot water, laundry facilities, breakfast extra, parking. Recommended.

F Res Montt, *M Montt 432, T075-312929.* Price per person, without bath or breakfast.

G Res Colonial, *Rodríguez 461, T075-314103.* Price per person. Clean, patio, friendly, some rooms with bath.

Area de Proteccíon Radal Siete Tazas
p278

C Hostería La Flor de la Canela, *Parque Inglés, T075-491613.* Breakfast extra, good food. Highly recommended.

Camping
There's a dirty campsite near the entrance with a shop, US$1 per person. Inside the park is **Camping Las Catas**, US$13 per site, no shop.

Towards the coast *p278*

B Hostería Atlántida 2000, *Llico, T075-400264, F312089.* Near beach, small rooms, with breakfast.

B-C Hostería Iloca, *Besoain 260, Iloca, T075-247035/09-3200244.* Full board, price per person.

C-G Res Miramar, *Carrera Pinto 48, Llico, T075-400032.* Price per person. Good seafood restaurant, small rooms with bath, excellent value, full board available.

D Hotel Iloca, *Besoain 221, Iloca, T075-1983751.* Price per person. Breakfast, good views, run down. Several *cabañas*, many open in summer only.

E Hospedaje El Capricho del Corazón, *35 km west of Curicó on road to Hualañe and Iloca, T09-6391086.* Price per person. Swiss run, English, French and German spoken, tours arranged. Recommended.

Camping

El Peñon, *6 km south of Iloca, T072-471026, T02-6336099.* US$12 per site. Phone ahead for reservation.

La Puntilla, *2 km north of Iloca, T09-7415585.* US$10 per site, also *cabañas*.

Lago Vichuquén and around *p278*

AL Hotel Playa Aquelarre, *Lago Vichuquén, T075-400018.* Well-equipped, with good food.

AL Marina Vichuquén, *T075-400265, www.marinavichuquen.cl* Fully equipped resort, good.

Camping

Vichuquén, *east shore of lake, T075-400062.* Full facilities.

El Sauce, *north shore of lake, T075-400203.* Good facilities, US$25 per site.

⬤ Eating

Curicó *p276, map p277*
There are several seriously cheap restaurants with varying standards of cleanliness outside the market on Calle Donoso.

$$$-$$ Club de la Unión, *Plaza de Armas.* Good, expensive, elegant.

$$ American Bar, *Yungay 647.* Real coffee, small pizzas, open daily morning to evening.

$$ El Fogón Chileno, *M Montt 399.* For meat and wines.

$$ Los Cisnes, *Rodríguez 1186.* Parilladas and cheaper *almuerzos*.

$ Café-Bar Maxim, *Prat 617.* Light meals, beer and wine.

$ Centro Italiano Club Social, *Estado 531.* Good, cheap meals.

$ Sant' Angelo, *Prat 430.* Excellent patisserie.

⬤ Bars and clubs

Curicó *p276, map p277*
The following are fairly basic drinking holes, and are likely to be shut during the day:

Bar Deportivo, *Montt 446.*

Crazy Horse, *Manso de Velasco.*

Scram Pub, *Velasco 451.*

Festivals and events

Curicó *p276, map p277*
Fiesta de la Vendimia (harvest festival) in mid-Mar has displays on traditional winemaking and the chance to try local food and wine. A similar event is also held in nearby Molina at the same time.

● Transport

Curicó *p276, map p277*
There is a toll (US$3) on the Pan-American Highway south of Curicó.

Bus
The **main bus terminal** is on *Prat y Maipú*. Local buses, including those to coastal towns as well as some long-distance services use **Terminal Plaza**, *Prat y Maipú*. **Turbus** stop on *M De Velasco;* their office is also on M De Velasco, 1 block south. **Pullman del Sur** have their own terminal at *Henríquez y Carmen*. Many southbound buses by-pass Curicó, but can be caught by waiting outside town.

To **Santiago** several companies, frequent, 2½ hrs, US$3. To **Temuco**, Alsa and **Tur Bus**, US$6. To **Llico**, Buses Díaz, regular in summer, 3 hrs, US$2.50. To **Iloca**, every hour in summer, less frequently off season, 2 hrs, US$2.50.

Train
The railway station is at the west end of *Prat, 4 blocks west of Plaza de Armas*, T075-310028. To/from **Santiago**, 6 a day, 2 hrs, US$6; to/from **Chillán**, 6 a day, 2¼ hrs, US$6.

Area de Protección Siete Tazas *p278*
Access by car is easy as the road through the park is paved. If you're travelling by public transport, take a minibus from Terminal Plaza to **Molina**, 26 km south of Curicó; from Molina 4 buses run daily to the **Parque Inglés** in summer (last return 1700), 3 hrs, US$2. There's also a daily bus from Curicó in summer at 1330 Mon-Sat (returns 0745) and at 0700 Sun (returns 1900), 4½ hrs.

● Directory

Curicó *p276, map p277*
Banks Major banks located around Plaza de Armas. *Casa de Cambio, Merced 255, Local 106*, no TCs. **Internet** *Carmen y Argomedo*; M y T Computación, *Peña 430, Montt 440, Prat 291* and *Yungay 665*.
Laundry Ecológico, *Yungay 411*; Lavacentro, *Yungay 437*; expensive, good.
Motorcycle spares Chaleco López Motos, *San Martín 171, T075-316191*. **Post office** *Plaza de Armas*. **Telephones** Call centres are expensive in Curicó, but try *O'Higgins 877* or *Prat 74*; also CTC, *Peña 650-A*. **Useful address** Automóvil Club de Chile, *Chacabuco 759, T311156*.

The Maule Valley

The Río Maule flows for 240 km from Laguna Maule in the Andes to the sea at Constitución. Its waters have been dammed east of Talca, providing power for the region and creating Lago Colbún. The river itself is particularly beautiful near the coast at Constitución.

Talca → *Phone code: 071. Colour map 3, C2. Population: 175,000.*

Situated on the south bank of the Río Claro, a tributary of the Maule, Talca lies 56 km south of Curicó. The most important city between Santiago and Concepción, it is a major manufacturing centre and the capital of Region VII, Maule. Founded in 1692, it was destroyed by earthquakes in 1742 and 1928. Today, it is a busy, dusty town, with a lively atmosphere day and night.

Ins and outs

Getting there Talca is easily accessible by bus and train from Santiago (both many times daily). There are also frequent connections to the towns further south, especially Chillán, Concepción, Temuco and Puerto Montt (several daily). ►► *For further details, see Transport, page 287.* **Getting around** Talca is a sizeable city, and some of the *barrios* are quite a distance from the centre. Buses and *colectivos* ply the routes to these areas, with their destinations marked in the window. **Tourist** information **Sernatur** ① *1 Poniente 1281, T071-233669, infomaule@sernatur.cl, winter Mon-Fri 0830-1730, summer Mon-Fri 0830-1930.*

Sights

In the **Plaza de Armas** are statues that were looted by the Talca Regiment from Peru during the War of the Pacific. Just off the Plaza is a colonial mansion that belonged to Juan Albano Pereira, tutor to the young Bernardo O'Higgins, who lived here as a child. The house was later the headquarters of O'Higgins' Patriot Government in 1813-14, before his defeat at Rancagua and is now the **Museo O'Higginiano** ① *1 Norte y 2 Oriente, Tue-Fri 1030-1300, 1430-1845, Sat and Sun 1000-1300, US$1.* In 1818, O'Higgins signed the declaration of Chilean Independence here: the room Sala Independencia is decorated and furnished in period style. The museum also houses a collection of regional art. The **Casino de Bomberos** ① *2 Sur y 5 Oriente*, has a small museum room with two old fire engines, old firefighting equipment and, for those with an interest in little-known conflagrations, information on important fires in Talca's history.

About 8 km southeast of the centre is **Villa Huilquilemu** ① *T071-242474, Tue-Fri 1500-1830, Sat 1600-1830, Sun 1100-1400, US$1, San Clemente bus,* a 19th-century *hacienda*, now part of the Universidad Católica del Maule, housing four museums of religious art, handicrafts, agricultural machinery and wine. It is also the office for the **Ruta de Vino del Valle del Maule.** ►► *For Sleeping, Eating and other listings, see pages 285-288.*

Talca

Sleeping ⊜
Amalfi 1
Cordillera 2
Hostal Alcázar 3
Hostal Balcones
  del Maule 4
Hostal del Puente 11

Hostal del Río 12
Marcos Gamero 6
Plaza 8
Residencial Maule 9
Terrabella 10
Terranova 5

Eating ⊕
Bavaria 1
Casino Club
  Deportivo 2
Casino de Bomberos 3
Casino Sociedad
  de Empleados 4

La Casa del
  Esquina 7
Posada de la
  Luna Sonrisa 6
Rubén Tapia 8
Taipei 5

0 metres 200
0 yards 200

⁝ Wine tasting in the Central Valley

The Central Valley offers ample scope for visits to vineyards and winetasting, whether independently, or on a tour on one of several "*rutas del vino*" (wine routes). There are four main areas producing quality wines here, each with distinctive characteristics, based on slight variations in soil and climate. Independent visits can be made to a number of vineyards, although a day's notice is usually required. Most give free tours with bilingual guides, or charge a small fee, with visitors paying for each wine they taste; some may provide lunch for an additional charge. For further information, consult the vineyard's own website.

The **Cachapoal Valley** (around Rancagua) produces a wide variety of wine, especially fruity Merlot and Carmenère. Tours of the valley's wine route start from km 109 of the Panamericana, some 16km south of Rancagua, T072-522085, www.chileanwineroute.com, and mix visits to local vineyards with local food and culture. They are not cheap, starting at about US$100 per person (less for large groups or if you have your own transport). Vineyards offering independent tours include:
Chateau Los Boldos, *Camino Los Boldos s/n, Requínoa, 072-551230, www.chateaulosboldos.com*
Gracia, *Camino Totihue s/n, Requínoa, 02-2067868, www.gracia.cl*
La Roncière, *Cousiño s/n, Graneros, 072-471571, www.laronciere.com*
Santa Mónica, *Camino Doñihue km5, Rancagua, 072-231444, www.santamonica.cl*
Torreón de Paredes, *Camino Las Nieves s/n, Rengo, 072-512551, www.torreon.cl*

The **Colchagua Valley** (around San Fernando and Santa Cruz) is one of the great success stories of modern Chilean wine, with the Apalta region producing some world-beating Cabernet Sauvignons. The Colchagua valley wine route's office is on the plaza at Santa Cruz, 37 km west of San Fernando, T072-823199, rv@uva.cl, and offers tours of three, four or six hours, from around US$40 to US$70 per person. The longer tours include lunch or a visit to the wine museum in Santa Cruz. Vineyards offering independent tours include:

East of Talca

Lago Colbún and around

From Talca a road runs 175 km southeast along **Lago Colbún** and up the valley of the Río Maule, passing through some of the finest mountain scenery in Chile to reach the Argentine border at **Paso Pehuenche** ⓘ *open Dec-Mar 0800-2100; Apr-Nov 0800-1900*. On the Argentine side the road continues to Malargüe and San Rafael.

At the western end of Lago Colbún is the town of Colbún, from where another road leads south and west to eventually join the Pan-American Highway at Linares.

⁝ *There is a cycle path much of the way between Linares and Panimávida.*

After 5 km it passes through **Panimávida**, where there are thermal springs. While at Panimávida, try the local 'Bebida Panimávida', made from spring water, still or sparkling, flavoured with lemon or raspberry. Artesanal goods are better and cheaper here than in Linares. Further on towards Linares is **Quinamávida**, 12 km south of Colbún, where there are more thermal springs, and an upmarket hotel.

La Posada, *R Casanova 570, Sta Cruz, 072-822589, www.puebloantiguo.cl*
Pueblo Antiguo, *F Valdez 236, Nancagua, 072-858296, www.puebloantiguo.cl*
Selentia, *Villa Angostura s/n, San Fernando, 072-913081, www.vinaselentia.cl*
Viu Manent, *San Carlos de Cunaco s/n, Sta Cruz, 072-858350, www.viumanent.cl*

The **Curico Valley** is where the Chilean wine revolution began in 1980. It now produces fruity reds, and quality Sauvignon Blancs. The valley office is in Curico's plaza, on the second floor of the Club de la Unión, T075-328972, www.rvvc.cl There are various circuits, ranging from basic half-day tours, taking in a couple of wineries, to multi-day tours including trips to thermal springs or horseriding. Vineyards offering independent tours include:
Miguel Torres, *R5 sur, km 195, 075-564100, www.torres.es/eng/asp/vav_curico.asp*
San Pedro, *R5 sur, km 205, 075-491517, www.sanpedro.cl*

The **Maule Valley** (around Talca and San Javier), traditionally the home of the insipid *Pais* grape, has now been replanted with noble varieties, and produces well-balanced reds of a decent standard. The wine route's offices are in the Villa Cultural Huilquilemu, 7km southeast of Talca, on the road to San Clemente, T071-246460, www.chilewineroute.cl

Tours cost US$14 per person for half a day (two vineyards) and US$38 for a full day (two vineyards, plus lunch and museum visit). Vineyards offering independent tours include:
Balduzzi, *Av Balmaceda 1189, San Javier, 072-322138, www.balduzzi.cl*
Casa Donoso, *Camino Palmira km3.5, Talca, 071-241980, www.casadonoso.cl*
Gillmore Estate, *Camino Constitución, km20, S J, 073-1975539, www.gillmore.cl*
Hugo Casanova, *Camino Las Rastras s/n, Talca, 071-266540, vcasanov@ctcinternet.cl*
Martínez de Salinas, *Camino Cauquenes a Parral, 073-512505, www.martinezdesalinas.cl*

Vilches and around

Some 63 km east of Talca, Vilches is the starting point for the climb to the volcanoes **Quizapu** (3,050 m) and **Descabezado** (3,850 m). For walks on Descabezado Grande and Cerro Azul, ice axe, crampons and an experienced guide are required (see page 287). There is also great horseriding in this area.

Situated just east of Vilches, the **Reserva Nacional Altos del Lircay** ① *US$1*, covers 12,163 ha and includes peaks up to 2,228 m as well as several small lakes. Much of the park is covered with mixed forest including lenga, ñirre, coigüe, roble, raulí and copihue. Near the entrance are the administration and visitors' centre; nearby are the **Piedras Tacitas**, a stone construction supposedly built by the indigenous inhabitants of the region, and the **Mirador Del Indio** from where there are fine views over the Río Lircay. There are also two good hikes: to **Laguna del Alto**, eight hours via a lagoon in a volcanic crater; and to **El Enladrillado**, 12 hours, a high basalt plateau from where there are great views. ►► *For Sleeping, Eating and other listings, see pages 285-288.*

South of Talca

Linares → *Phone code: 073.*

Fifty-three kilometres south of Talca on the Panamericana, Linares is a peaceful town with a distinctly *huaso* feel. It boasts the remarkable **Cathedral de San Ambrosio**, built between 1934 and 1967 in a Byzantine romantic style. On Letelier 572, in the middle of a row of colonial houses, is the **Museo de Arte y Artesania Nacional** ⓘ *Tue-Fri 1000-1730, Sat 1000-1700, Sun 1200-1700, US$1, Sun free.* Here there are exhibits of local, military and prehistoric history, including a 2-ft-long decorative curved spanner, an exploded cannon, horsehair artefacts from the village of Rari, local paintings, petrified wood, old toys and everyday utensils. In the **Mercado Municipal** on Chacabuco, it is possible to buy horsehair art from Rari. Tourist information is available from the Gobernación and Municipalidad, both on the plaza.

▶▶ *For Sleeping, Eating and other listings, see pages 285-288.*

West of Talca

Constitución → *Phone code: 071. Colour map 3, C2*

Lying west of Talca at the mouth of the Río Maule, Constitución is reached by road (89 km) and by a **narrow gauge railway** line from Talca, which offers fine views over the wooded Maule Valley. The railway, packed with chatting locals (and as often as not their goats and chickens) is unique in Chile and offers travellers a microcosm of life in the Central Valley. It is not unusual for trains to be flagged down like buses and for the driver to stop in order to share gossip and a coffee with a farmer.

‣ *On the Pan-American Highway, 88 km south of Talca, is the small town of Parral, celebrated as the birthplace of the Nobel Prize-winning poet Pablo Neruda (see box, p539).*

Founded in 1794, the city is situated in a major commercial logging area; there are naval shipyards here and a giant cellulose factory, whose pungent odour hangs over the town on windless days; fishing is also important. Constitución's main appeal, however, is as a seasonal seaside resort. While the town itself is relatively uninteresting, the beach, an easy walk from the centre, is surrounded by picturesque rocks, and the coast both to the north and south is beautiful.

There are good views from **Cerro Mutrún**, at the mouth of the river, accessed via Calle O'Higgins; the **Playa El Cable**, with *cabañas*, is 5 km south. For a pleasant walk or drive, take the quiet track along the south bank of the Maule 8 km east of Constitución to a disused railway bridge over the river; the bridge is open to vehicles, and has great views of the river valley. ▶▶ *For Sleeping, Eating and other listings, see pages 285-288.*

Chanco and around

A paved road runs from Constitución along the coast, through thick forest and past a large logging factory, via deserted beaches and fishing villages to the small, peaceful town of Chanco. Chanco is famous for its cheese and its traditional colonial architecture, including the charming **Iglesia San Ambrosia**. There is a pleasant 3 km walk to the coast and the unspoilt **Playa Monolito** (camping facilities).

The land just north of Chanco is the prettiest in this area, with rolling hills, small farmsteads and two small parks: the **Area Silvestre Laguna Reloca** ⓘ *8 km north of Chanco, Mon-Fri 1430-1800, Sat and Sun 0830-1800, free*, is a private park covering 245 ha. Some 130 bird species have been identified including flamingoes and black-necked swans. Closer to Chanco, the **Reserva Nacional Federico Albert** ⓘ *Apr-Nov 0830-1800, Dec-Mar 0830-2000, US$1*, covers 145 ha of dunes planted with eucalyptus and cypresses in experiments to control the shifting sands. It has a visitors' centre and campsite.

‣ *Chanco and Pelluhue are both popular with surfers.*

South of Chanco are two more small resorts at **Pelluhue** and **Curanipe**, 83 km south of Constitución. One kilometre south of Pelluhue a path leads down to a hidden beach, beautiful and deserted even in summer, while Curanipe has a lovely stretch of black sand. From Curanipe a poorly maintained track leads 50 km through wild country to the small seaside town of **Cobquecura**. A tranquil, friendly town, it has a good beach, a pretty plaza, several good seafood restaurants and well-preserved colonial-style houses. About 5 km to the north is an impressive *portada* or arch in the cliffs. There are also a few good surfing beaches nearby.

This coast can also be reached by paved road from Parral via Cauquenes. Just north of the road between Cauquenes and Chanco is the **Reserva Nacional Los Ruiles** ① *Dec-Mar 0830-2000, Apr-Nov 0830-1800, US$1, buses from Constitución or Cauquenes*, which covers 45 ha of native flora, including the *ruil* (Nothofagus alessandri), an endangered species of southern beech. ▸▸ *For Sleeping, Eating and other listings, see pages 285-288.*

● Sleeping

Talca *p280, map p281*
AL-A Plaza, *1 Poniente 1141, T071-226150, www.amarillas.cl/hotelplaza* Commercial standard, overpriced.
AL-A Terrabella, *1 Sur 641, T071-226555, terrabella@hotel.tie.cl* The best hotel in town.
A Marcos Gamero, *1 Oriente 1070, T071-223100, F224400.*
A Terranova,*1 Sur 1026, T071-239608, F239603.*Fully equipped, with conference room and sauna.
A-B Cabañas Entre Ríos, *Panamericana, km 245 (8 km north of Talca), T071-223336, www.turismoentrerios.cl* Very good value, excellent breakfast, pool, restaurant, very helpful owner. Highly recommended.
B Cordillera, *2 Sur 1360, T071-221817, www.cordillerahotel.cl* Decent, serves good breakfast.
B-D Amalfi, *2 Sur 1265, T071-239292.* Old-fashioned, central, good breakfast, cheaper rooms do not have bath.
B-F Casa Chueca, *Camino Las Rastras, 4 km from city centre, T071-1970097, casachueca@hotmail.com* European-run colonial-style house with swimming pool, great views, large gardens, mountain bikes, games room. Price includes breakfast, nice rooms with private bathrooms or cheaper rooms with shared bath. Good dinner on request. Trekking and horseriding tours organized, Spanish classes also available (www.spanish-for-travellers.com). English, German, French, Portuguese and Swedish spoken. Highly recommended. Call for instructions on how to get there.

C Hostal del Puente, *1 Sur 407, T071-220930, hostaldelpuente@terra.cl* Lovely gardens, English spoken, parking, with bath, cable TV, breakfast extra.
C Hostal del Río, *1 Sur 411, T071-225448, hostaldelrio@hotmail.com* Recently opened by the feuding brother of the owner of the Hostal del Puente next door, and designed to be just a little better and a little cheaper.
F Hosp Santa Margarita, *Pellarco, 18 km northeast of Talca, T09-3359051.* Swiss-run, meals served, open Dec-Mar only, reservation advised. Price per person.
F Hostal Alcázar, *6 Oriente 1449, T071-233587.* Price per person. Without bath, quiet, good value.
F Res Maule, *2 Sur 1381, T071-220995.* Price per person. Without breakfast, overpriced.

Lago Colbún and around *p282*
L Hotel Quinamávida, *Quinamávida, T073-213887, www.termasdequinamavida.cl* In the hotel there are thermal baths, Turkish baths, reflexology, and massage.
AL Casas El Colorado, *north shore of Lago Colbún, T071-221750, www.hotelcasaselcolorado.cl* Full board. Resort with restaurant, pool, 6 hole golf course, sauna, horseriding.
B Hotel Termas de Panimávida, *Panimávida, 073-211743.* A once grand hotel now partly restored but retaining a feeling of decaying grandeur. In the grounds is a small fountain, where you can drink the sulphourous 'agua de la mona'. Price per person.
C-E Posada Campesina, *km 10 on Linares-Rabones road, Quinamávida, T09-7520510.* Price per person. Large *estancia*

with forest trails and beaches, offering full board and bed-only deals. English spoken. Highly recommended.

Camping

There are several campsites around 12 km east of Colbún on the south shore of Lago Colbún. There are also 3 sites near Panimávida.

Vilches and around *p283*

AL **Complejo Turístico El Roble**, *Vilches (sector seminario)*, *T071-242148/09-7411065*, *www.turismoelroble.com* Fully furnished comfortable *cabañas* with swimming pool.
AL **Hostería Vilches**, *T071-621463*. With breakfast, use of kitchen, good food, knowledgeable and hospitable family. Also have *cabañas* for 4 people and a pool.

South of Talca *p284*

A **Hotel Curapalihue**, *Curapalihue 411, Linares*, *T/F073-212516*. Breakfast and bath, cable TV, conference facilities.
B **Hotel Turismo**, *Manuel Rodríguez 522, Linares*, *T073-210636, F214128*. Breakfast and bath, restaurant, cable TV.
C **Hotel Real**, *Freire 482, Linares*, *T/F073-210834*. Bath, without breakfast, cable TV.
G **Hotel Londres**, *Rodríguez 456, Linares*, *T073-210177, F213720*. Price per person. Without bath or breakfast.
G **Hostal Linares**, *Freire 442, Linares*, *T073-210695*. Price per person. With breakfast.
If you need to stay the night in **Parral**, try
C **Brescia**, *Igualdad 195, T073-462675*. With bath and clean, good restaurant.
F **Res do Brasil**, *Dieciocho 140, T073-462555*. Price per person, with breakfast, clean, quiet.

Constitución *p284*

B **Hostería Constitución**, *Echeverria 460*, *T071-671450, F673735*. Overpriced and not as good as it was, but still the best equipped hotel in town. Good lunches.
C **Avendaño**, *O'Higgins 681*. Pleasant patio, restaurant, friendly, safe.
D **Res Urrutia**, *Freire 238*. Breakfast, some rooms gloomy, laundry facilities.
E **Res Cristina**, *Portales 368*. Good.
E **Ruta Verde**, *12km east of town, off the road to Talca, T071-674824, T09-7448224, www.rutaverde.cl* Price per person. Call for free pick up from Constitución. Pleasant house in the woods powered by solar panels.

Very friendly and helpful, English and Italian spoken, excellent tours of the region on horse or in a 4WD. Highly recommended.

There are many other *residenciales* on Freire 100-300 blocks, including **Res López** at No 153; **Res Familiar** at No 160 and **Res Ramírez** at No 209. Book in advance from Jan to Mar.

Further south *p285*

A **Cabañas Campomar**, *north of Curanipe*, *T073-541000, campomar@ctcinternet.cl* Prices for up to 6 people, kitchen, English spoken.
B **Hostería Blanca Reyes**, *Prat 615, Pelluhue*, *T073-541061, blancareyes@123mail.cl* With good restaurant, best in town.
C **Pacífico**, *Comercio 509, Curanipe*, *T073-556016*. Pleasant, clean.
F **Pensión Rocas**, *Condell 708, Pelluhue*, *T073-541017*. Price per person, basic.
F **Res La Playa**, *Prat 510, Pelluhue*, *T09-8714538*. Price per person, food available. Also lots of *cabañas*.

⑦ Eating

Talca *p280, map p281*
$$ **Bavaria**, *1 Sur 1370*. Plastic Chilean chain serving reasonable steaks and sandwiches.
$$ **El Toro Bayo**, *Camino Las Rastras, 2 km east of town, T071-247643*. The best in the area, offering a wide and inventive menu, closed Sun evenings, recommended.
$$ **La Casa del Esquina**, *1 Poniente 708*. Spanish food, good.
$$ **Los Ganaderos**, *Panamericana, 10 km south of Talca*. Great food, a good place to stop for lunch for those with transport.
$$ **Posada de la Luna**, *1 Sur 626*. Slightly upmarket restaurant with attractive garden, good seafood.
$$ **Rubén Tapia**, *2 Oriente 1339*. Excellent modern cuisine.
$$ **Taipei**, *4 Oriente y 2 Sur*. Decent Chinese.
$ **Café al Grano**, *Galería Zaror, local 10*. Cosy, good coffee and snacks.
$ **Casino de Bomberos**, *2 Sur y 5 Oriente*. Good value.
$ **Casino Sociedad de Empleados**, *1 Norte 1025*. Cheap lunches.
$ **Las Viejas Cochinas**, *on the banks of the Río Claro, just over the bridge*. Famous *picada* serving very good typical Chilean food. Large portions and more than reasonable prices. Lots of others nearby.

There are many cheap restaurants in the **municipal market**, 3 blocks east of the plaza and several kiosks selling *completos* on 5 Oriente 900 block; some are open 24 hours.

Linares *p284*
$$ **Fay Chy**, *Rodríguez 398*. Chinese.
$$ **Las Parrillas de Linares**, *Lautaro 350*. Typical grill.
$ **Estadio Español**, *León Bustas 01242*. Traditional food.

Constitución *p284*
Some of the town's *posadas* and *hosterías* provide meals. In addition, you should try $$ **El Rancho Astillero**, open in summer only, on the banks of the river and accessible only by boat. Wonderful fish cooked over hot coals between 2 terracotta tiles.

Further south *p285*
Pelluhue is more expensive than Curanipe; it has lots of seafood restaurants and **Omas Küchen**, which sells wonderful cakes.

🍷 Bars and clubs

Talca *p280, map p281*
Varadero, *5 Oriente 985*. Good Cuban-themed pub.
Wurlitzer, *5 Oriente 960*. Deservedly popular pub above a pool hall.

Linares *p284*
El Tablón, *Ibáñez y Chacabuco*. Basic bar.
Refugio, *V Letelier 480*. Basic bar.

☺ Entertainment

Talca *p280, map p281*
Mainstream **cinema** at *1 Sur 1271* and *Sur 770*. Arts cinema at *1 poniente 685*. Also in Mall *Plaza Maule, east of centre*.

✹ Festivals and events

Talca *p280, map p281*
Regional folklore festival takes place during 1st week of **Jan**.
Fiesta San Francisco, an important *huaso* festival, takes place on **4 Oct** in Huerta del Maule (southwest of Talca).
Feria del Vino y la Viticultura (TECVIN), held in the 1st week of **Nov** is enjoyable for those with an interest in Chilean wine.
Feria Regional de Folklore y Artesanía is held at Villa Cultural Huilquilemu during the last week in **Nov**

⛰ Activities and tours

Talca *p280, map p281*
Carlos Verdugo Bravo, *Población Brilla El Sol, Pasaje El Nickel 257*. Mountain guide recommended for volcano treks east of Vilches. Spanish only.
La Casa Chueca, *see Sleeping, above and www.trekkingchile.com* Excellent touring information, plus kayaking, trekking and horseriding trips.
Leonardo Cáceres Rencoret, *T09-8923625*. Good mountain guide, works for **CONAF**.

Vilches and around *p283*
For trekking in the nearby volcanoes, contact mountain guide **Carlos Verdugo Bravo** or **La Casa Chueca** in Talca (for both, see above). Two recommended horse guides in Vilches are **Don Pancho**, *T09-7635447*, and **Don Eladio**, *T09-3418064*.

Linares *p284*
Achibueno Expediciones, *8 km southeast of Linares, T073-375098, www.achibueno expediciones.cl* Bespoke horseriding trips in the *cordillera* starting at US$100 per day per person.
Expediciones Cordillera, *Rodríguez 712, T073-210240, calesi@mi.terra.cl* Tours around the region in a 4WD.

⊖ Transport

Talca *p280, map p281*
Bus
Talca bus terminal is at *12 Oriente y 2 Sur*.
  Long distance To **Chillán**, frequent service, US$2. To **Puerto Montt**, US$11, 10 hrs. To **Temuco**, US$7, 5½ hrs. Many buses to **Santiago**, US$4, 3½ hrs, and direct services to destinations as far north as Copiapó.
  Local To **Lago Colbún**, Pullman del Sur, 2 daily, US$1; to **Vilches**, Buses Vilches, 5 daily, 2-2½ hrs, US$1.80; to **Linares**, many companies, frequent, US$1; to **Constitución**, Empresa O'Higgins and Contimar, every 20 mins, 2 hrs, US$1.20. There are hourly buses to **Chanco**, **Curanipe** and **Pelluhue** with

Buses Bonanza, US$3, also 3 daily with
Contimar, US$3, and 10 daily with **Pullman
del Sur**, US$2.50.

Train
Talca railway station is at *2 Sur y 11 Oriente,
T071-226254*. Trains run to **Santiago**, 5 a day,
US$5; to **Chillán**, 3 a day; to **Temuco**,
nightly; to **Concepción**, nightly; to
Constitución, 2 a day, 2½ hrs, US$2.

Lago Colbún and around *p282*
Buses Villa Prat run direct services to
Quinamávida from Santiago's Terminal Sur.
For services to/from **Talca** see above.

Linares *p284*
Bus
Linares' bus terminal is at *Espinoza 530*. To
Colbún via Quinimávida and Panimávida,
US$1. For services to/from **Talca**, see above.

Train
The railway station is at *Brasil y
Independencia, T073-216352*. Trains run to
Santiago, 6 a day, 3¼ hrs, US$7; to **Chillán**, 6
a day, 1 hr, US$3.50.

Constitución *p284*
Empresa Amigo runs buses to **Cauquenes**,
2½ hrs, US$2. For services to/from **Talca**,
see above.

⊙ Directory

Talca *p280, map p281*
Banks Banco Santander, *1 Sur y 4 Oriente*;
Edificio Caracol, *Oficina 15, 1 Sur 898*. For US$
cash. **Cycle repairs** Bicimotora Burgos, *5
Oriente 1185*. **Internet** *1 Poniente 1282*,
opposite Sernatur; also at *2 Sur 1661,
T216636*, free, but reservation essential; and *7
Oriente 1180*. **Laundry** Lavaseco Donini, *6
Oriente 1120*; Lavaseco Flash, *1 Norte 995*.
Post office *1 Oriente s/n*. **Telephone**
CTC, *1 Sur 1156 and 1 Sur 835*. **Useful
address** Automóvil Club de Chile, *1
Poniente 1267, T071-2232774*.

Linares *p284*
Banks Banco A Edwards, *on plaza*; Banco
Santander, *Independencia 555*. **Internet**
Chacabuco 491. **Post office** *Rodríguez 610*.
Telephone Call centre, *Independencia 488A*.

The Itata Valley

*The Río Itata and its longer tributary, the Río Ñuble, flow west reaching the Pacific
some 60 km north of Concepción. This is a tranquil valley with some native woods
along the banks near the mouth of the river at the tiny hamlet of Vegas de Itata. There
is no bridge here, although boats can be hired to make the short crossing in summer;
in winter the river swells and no one attempts the crossing.*

Chillán → *Phone code: 042 Colour map 3, C2. Population: 146,000.*

One hundred and fifty kilometres south of Talca, Chillán is a busy but friendly place.
Founded in 1580 and destroyed by the Mapuche, the city has been moved several times,
most recently following an earthquake in 1833. Although the older site, now known as
Chillán Viejo, is still occupied, further earthquakes in 1939 and 1960 ensured that few old
buildings have survived. Nevertheless, this is one of the most interesting cities south of
Santiago and has a shady plaza, numerous interesting churches and several museums,
as well as a mural of the life of Bernardo O'Higgins. Pleasantly hot in summer, the city is
filled with local *campesinos* on market days, creating an atmosphere that is the essence
of the Central Valley. In 2003, the centenary year of the birth of the local pianist Claudio
Arrau, Chillán was made American city of culture. Two good books on Chillán are
Iconografía de Chillán, by Marco Aurelio Reyes (1989), which describes the history of
Chillán up to the 1939 earthquake; and *Chillán me persigue*, by Luis Guzmán Molina et al
(1995), which contains drawings, poetry and prose about the city.

Ins and outs

Getting there Chillán is served by several trains and buses daily from Santiago. There are also frequent connections to the towns further south, especially Concepción, Temuco and Puerto Montt. ▸▸ *For further details, see Transport page 292.*

Getting around Chillán is an important city, and some of the outlying *barrios* and attractions are quite a distance from the centre. Buses and *colectivos* are numerous, with their destinations marked in the window, but taxis are most useful for arranging excursions out of the city. **Tourist information** The municipal office ① *18 de Sept 455, at side of Gobernación, T042-223272*, can provide a street map of the city and various leaflets on skiing, Termas de Chillán etc.

Sights

Chillán was the birthplace of Bernardo O'Higgins and today's city is centred around the Plaza O'Higgins and its modern **cathedral**, designed to resist earthquakes. The

Chillán

To Talca & Santiago via Pan-American Highway (north)

The Central Valley The Itata Valley

Sleeping		Paso Nevado 9	Eating
Claris 1		Quinchamalí 10	Arcoiris 1
Cordillera 2		Residencial Chi-Can 11	Café de París 2
Floresta 3		Residencial Su Casa 12	Café Europa 3
Gran Isabel Riquelme 7		Residencial Vem-Sau 13	Club Comercial 4
Hostal 5 de Abril 4		Rucamanqui 14	Fuente Alemana 5
Hostal Canadá 5		Ruiz de Gamboa 15	Jai Yang 6
Hostal de la Avenida 6		Sonia Segui 17	La Cosa Nostra 8
Libertador 8			La Masc'a 7

0 metres 200
0 yards 200

San Francisco church, three blocks northeast contains a **museum** ⓘ *Tue-Sun 1600-1800, US$1,* of religious and historical artefacts. Above the main entrance is a mural by Luis Guzmán Molina, a local artist, which is an interpretation of the life of San Francisco but placed in a Chilean context. The adjoining **convent** (1835) was a big centre for missionary work among the Mapuche.

Five streets west of the plaza is the neo-Gothic **Iglesia Padres Carmelita**, while to the northwest, on Plaza Héroes de Iquique, is the **Escuela México** ⓘ *daily 1000-1300, 1500-1830,* donated to the city after the 1939 earthquake. In its library are outstanding murals by the great Mexican artists David Alvaro Siqueiros and Xavier Guerrero depicting allegories of Chilean and Mexican history. Three blocks further south is the **Museo Naval El Chinchorro** ⓘ *Collin y I Riquelme, Tue-Fri 0930-1200, 1500-1730,* which contains naval artefacts and models of Chilean vessels.

In Chillán Viejo, southwest of the centre, is a monument and park marking the birthplace of Bernardo O'Higgins; a 60-m-long mural depicts his life (an impressive, but sadly faded mosaic of various native stones), while the **Centro Histórico y Cultural** ⓘ *0830-2000* has a gallery of contemporary paintings by regional artists. Halfway between the centre and Chillán Viejo on Avenida O'Higgins is the **Capilla San Juan de Dios,** a small chapel dating from 1791. ▸▸ *For Sleeping, Eating and other listings, see pages 291-292.*

Around Chillán

Quinchamalí

Quinchamalí is a small village of little houses hidden under large fruit trees, located 27 km southwest of Chillán, at the halfway point of the new motorway to Concepción. The village is famous for the originality of its crafts in textiles, basketwork, guitars, primitive paintings and especially black ceramics (see box page 291). These are all on sale in Chillán market and at a handicraft fair in the village during the second week of February. A **Museo Histórico Artesanal** is currently being developed in the village.

Termas de Chillán

Situated 82 km east of Chillán by good road (paved for the first 50 km), 1,850 m up at the foot of the double-cratered Chillán volcano, are two open-air thermal pools, officially for hotel guests only, and a health spa with Jacuzzi, sauna, mud baths and other facilities. There are several trekking oportunities from the *termas,* including a good one- or two-day return hike past some natural hot mud baths (free of charge) to the **Valle de Aguas Calientes,** where there are yet more hot springs, spectacular scenery and solitude.

Above the thermal baths is the largest **ski resort** in southern Chile, with 10 ski lifts and 28 ski runs (the longest is 13 km in length), rental shops, restaurants, bars, ski school, first aid and a nursery. Experienced skiers can take advantage of nordic skiing, alpine randonnée and heli-skiing, but Chillán is also suitable for families and beginners and is cheaper than centres nearer Santiago. For further information, contact the **Chillán Ski Centre** ⓘ *Barros Arana 261, www.termasdechillan.cl, lift pass US$30 per day, US$20 half day, equipment hire US$25 per day.*

San Fabián de Alico

This pleasant mountain village on the banks of the Río Ñuble lies 67 km northeast of Chillán (via San Carlos, daily buses). In summer it is very lively and full of young Chileans. There are several campsites and *hospedajes,* and many opportunities for trekking up the valley. Horses can readily be hired for about US$10 per day. Tourist information is available in the plaza or from the Municipalidad. ▸▸ *For Sleeping, Eating and other listings, see pages 291-292.*

Quinchamalí ceramics

Quinchamalí is one of the two most famous villages in Chile for producing black ceramic ware; the other, Pomaire, near Santiago, is much more influenced by tourism. While the men work on the land, women work with clay, mixing it with sand to make it porous and to prevent it breaking when it is heated. The mixture is worked in two halves, which are then joined and allowed to dry. The characteristic white patterns are made by incising with an old needle before the piece is wrapped in straw and heated over an open fire. Apart from items for domestic use, the women produce a wide range of other pieces, including roosters, three legged pigs and women with children, but the most popular object is the *guitarrera* (a woman playing the guitar).

Sleeping

Chillán *p288, map p289*

A-B Quinchamalí, *El Roble 634, T042-223381, www.hotelquinchamali.cl* Central, quiet, clean, hot water, heated lounge.

B Gran Hotel Isabel Riquelme, *Constitución 576, T042-213663, hotelir@termaschillan.cl* A decent option for the price, with cable TV, restaurant, laundry and parking.

B Hostal de la Avenida, *O'Higgins 398 y Bulnes, T042-230256.* 2-star facilities, including cable TV, café, bar and laundry.

B Paso Nevado, *Libertad 219, T042-237666, www.hotelpasonevado.cl* Nice rooms, internet, conference room, bar.

B Rucamanqui, *Herminda Martín 590 (off Plaza de Armas), T042-222927, F217072.* Clean but spartan.

C Cordillera, *Arauco 619, on Plaza de Armas, T042-215211, hotelcordillera@entelchile.net* 3-star, small, good.

C Floresta, *18 de Septiembre 278, T/F042-222253.* Quiet, old fashioned, friendly.

F Hostal 5 de Abril, *5 de Abril y Constitución.* Price per person. Without bath.

F Hostal Canadá, *Libertad 269, T042-234515.* Price per person. Without breakfast or bath.

F Libertador, *Libertad 85, T042-223255.* Without breakfast, parking, clean, good.

F Res Su Casa, *Cocharcas 555, T042-223931.* Price per person. Clean, parking.

F-G Claris, *18 de Septiembre 357, T042-221980.* Price per person. Clean, friendly, run down, with bath or without.

F-G Res Chi-Can, *Constitución 34.* Basic and noisy, but near the central terminal.

F-G Res Vem-Sau, *Constitución 96, T042-210958.* Near the central terminal. There are lots more cheap *hospedajes* on Constitutión 1-300.

G Sonia Segui, *Itata 288, T042-214879.* Price per person. Good beds, good breakfast, huge *almuerzo* but dirty bathrooms, friendly, noisy.

Termas de Chillán *p290*

The following are all located at Las Trancas on the road to the Termas, 70 km southeast of Chillán. Several *cabañas* are also available in the village, usually **A** for up to 6 people, see www.vallelastrancas.cl for more details. Camping is available 2 km from the slopes.

LL Gran Termas de Chillán, *information T02-2331313, www.termaschillan.cl* 5-star, sports facilities, sauna, thermal pool and spa centre.

L Pirigallo, *information T02-2331313, www.termaschillan.cl* 3-star. Same ownership as above.

AL Parador Jamón, Pan y Vino, *T042-222682, www.nevadosdechillan.cl* Arranges recommended horseriding trips.

AL Robledal, *T042-214407, hotelrobledal.cl* Pleasant rooms, including some suites, bar, restaurant, sauna and Jacuzzi. Wide variety of tours offered.

A Los Pirineos, *T042-293839.* Fully furnished cabins.

E Hostelling International, *T042-244628, j.bocaz@ctcinternet.cl* Price per person. Basic European-style youth hostel.

Chillán *p288, map p289*

The Chillán area is well known for its *pipeño* wine (very young) and its *longanizas* (sausages).

$$ **Arcoiris**, *El Roble 525*. Vegetarian.

$$ **Café de París**, *Arauco 666*. Good bar and fine restaurant upstairs.

$$ **Café Europa**, *Libertad 475*. Recommended.

$$ **La Cosa Nostra**, *Libertad 398*. Italian cuisine, German and Italian spoken, very good and reasonably priced.

$$ **Los Adobes**, *Parque O'Higgins, Chillán Viejo*. Tasty food and good service at reasonable prices.

$ **Club Comercial**, *Arauco 745*. Popular at lunchtime, good value *almuerzo*, popular bar at night. Recommended.

$ **Jai Yang**, *Libertad 250*. Good value Chinese.

$ **La Copucha**, *18 de Septiembre y Constitución*. Inexpensive meals and sandwiches.

$ **La Masc'a**, *5 de Abril 544*. Excellent cheap meals, *empanadas de queso*, drinks. Recommended.

There are also many cheap and seriously cheap restaurants in and around the **mercado municipal**.

❂ Festivals and events

Chillán *p288, map p289*

Encuentro International de Teatro takes place in **Jan**, with plays being performed in public spaces around the city.

Fiesta de la Vendemia is an annual wine festival held in the 3rd week in **Mar**.

◐ Shopping

Chillán *p288, map p289*

Mercado y Feria Municipal, *Riquelme y Marpón*. This large market sells regional arts and crafts.

Plaza El Roble, *El Roble y Riquelme*. A modern shopping centre.

◷ Transport

Chillán *p288, map p289*

Bus

Long distance There are 2 terminals: Tur Bus, Línea Azul, Tas Choapa and Alsa-LIT all use the central terminal at *Brasil y Constitución*. Other companies use the modern northern terminal at *O'Higgins y Ecuador*. To **Santiago**, 5 hrs, US$7; to **Concepción**, Tur Bus and Línea Azul every 30 mins, 1¼ hrs, US$3; to **Curicó**, US$4; to **Tecumo**, US$5.

Local Buses to **Yumbel** and **Quinchamalí**, 30 mins, US$1, leave from the terminal near the market, *Maipóa y Sgto Aldea*.

Train

The station is on *Brasil opposite Libertad, 5 blocks west of Plaza de Armas, T042-222424*. To **Santiago**, 6 daily, 4¼ hrs, US$10.

Termas de Chillán *p290*

Dedicated ski buses run Jun-Sep from *Libertador 1042* to the slopes at 0800 and from Chillán Ski Centre, subject to demand, US$30 (including lift pass). In summer (Jan-mid Mar) there's a bus service from **Anja**, *5 de Abril 594*, Thu, Sat, Sun only at 0730, US$5 return, book in advance. Taxis cost US$30 one way, 1½ hrs. At busy periods hitching may be possible from Chillán Ski Centre.

❶ Directory

Chillán *p288, map p289*

Banks On the Plaza de Armas are **Banco BCI**, **Banco Santander** and **Banco de Chile**, all with ATMs; there is also **Banco Sudamericano**, *Arauco y El Roble*, poor rates; Banco Santiago, *El Roble 580*, better rates than banks at **Casa de cambio**, *Constitución 550*. **Internet** Gateway, *Libertad 360*; Planet Cybercafe, *Arauco 683, 2nd floor*. **Motorcycle spares** Roland Spaarwater, *Ecuador 275, T/F042-232334*. **Post office** *Gobernación, Plaza de Armas*. **Telephone** Entel, *18 de Septiembre 746*; CTC, *Arauco 625*; also call centre at *5 de Abril 607*. **Useful address** Automóvil Club de Chile, *O'Higgins 677, T042-212550*.

For an explanation of sleeping and eating price codes used in this guide, see inside the front cover. Other relevant information is found in Essentials, see pages 51-58.

The Biobío Valley

The Río Biobío flows northwest from the Andes to reach the sea near Concepción. At 407 km, it is the second longest river in Chile. Its more important tributaries include the Ríos Laja, Duqueco and Renaico. Apart from Concepción and Talcahuano on the coast, the valley includes several other important cities, notably Los Angeles.

Concepción and around → *Phone code: 041. Colour map 3, C1.*

The capital of Región VIII (Biobío), Concepción is the third biggest city in Chile, with a population of nearly a quarter of a million. Founded in 1550, it was a frontier stronghold in the war against the Mapuche after 1600. The city was destroyed by an earthquake in 1751 and moved to its present site in 1764, but suffered another destructive earthquake and a tidal wave in 1835. Today, although it is one of the country's major industrial centres, Concepción is not in itself a wildly beautiful or fascinating place. Those staying for a long period or getting involved with students at the important university will find doors opening, but otherwise a visit to the port of Talcahuano, Chile's most important naval base (15 km north), is the highlight.

> ‼ *The weather is very pleasant in Concepción during the summer months, but from April to September it rains heavily.*

Ins and outs

Getting there Concepción is 15 km from the estuary of the Río Biobío, 516 km south of Santiago. There are flights daily to Concepción from Santiago and Puerto Montt, one or two of which continue on to Punta Arenas. Taxi to airport US$6. Concepción is the transportation hub of the region, and is served by buses to and from Santiago, Temuco, Valdivia and Puerto Montt, as well as to and from other smaller destinations such as Cañete and Lota. There are two long-distance bus terminals and neither is located in the city centre. ▸▸ *For further details, see Transport, page 303.* To get to nearby destinations such as Dichato and Talcahuano, it is easiest to take a *colectivo*. **Getting around** *Colectivos* and buses abound; the destinations are signed on the window or roof. Fares are US$0.30 for buses, slightly more for *colectivos*. **Tourist information** **Sernatur** ① *Aníbal Pinto 460 on Plaza de la Independencia, T041-741337, infobiobio@sernatur.cl,* provides regional information. ▸▸ *For Sleeping, Eating and other listings, see pages 299-304.*

Sights

In the centre of the city is the attractive **Plaza de la Independencia**, where, in January 1818, Bernardo O'Higgins proclaimed the Independence of Chile. Nearby are many official buildings, including the modern cathedral, the Municipalidad and the Palacio de la Justicia. Also on the plaza is the **Museo de Arte Sagrado** ① *Caupolicán 441, Tue-Fri 1000-1330, 1600-2000, Sat-Sun, 1100-1400, US$0.50,* containing many fine sacred Christian objects, including priests robes embroidered with gold, and a marble Christ. Southeast of the plaza is the **Parque Ecuador**, where the **Galería de la Historia** ① *Tue-Sun 1000-1330, 1500-1830, free* contains a pictorial history of the region; upstairs is a collection of Chilean painting. A few blocks north is the **Casa del Arte** ① *Roosevelt y Larenas, Tue-Fri 1000-1800, Sat 1000-1600, Sun 1000-1300, free,* which contains the University art collection; the entrance hall is dominated by *La Presencia de América Latina*, by the Mexican Jorge González Camerena (1965), an impressive allegorical mural depicting Latin American history, famous throughout

The 1835 earthquake that devastated Concepción was so severe that some cows, grazing on an island in the bay, rolled into the sea.

Chile and often depicted on postcards. Note especially the pyramid representing the continent's wealth, the figures of an armoured warrior and an Indian woman and the wounded cactus with parts missing, representing Mexico's defeat by the USA in 1845-48. University art students are on hand to provide explanations. There is

Concepción

The Central Valley The Biobío Valley

Sleeping	Hostal Casablanca **6**	Ruca Ray **12**	El Rancho de Julio **4**
Alborada **1**	Maquehue **7**	Silvia Uslar **17**	El Rincón de
Alonso de Ercilla **2**	Residencial Central **10**		Pancho **9**
Cecil **3**	Residencial Colo Colo **11**	**Eating**	Le Château **5**
Concepción **4**	Residencial O'Higgins **13**	Big Joe Saloon **1**	Mar y Tierra **6**
El Dorado **5**	Residencial San	Casino de	Piazza **7**
Hostal Antuco **9**	Sebastián **14**	Bomberos **2**	Waya's Gyros **10**
Hostal Bianca **8**	Ritz **15**	Chung Hwa **3**	Yiet-Xiu **8**

0 metres 300
0 yards 300

another fine mural in the entrance hall of the railway station, *La Historia de*
Concepción by Gregorio de la Fuente. From the Parque Ecuador you can climb **Cerro Caracol**, to the south, from where there are views over the city and the river.

Sixteen kilometres from Concepción, **Museo y Parque Hualpen** ① *Tue-Sun 1000-1300, 1400-1900, free,* is a house and garden that is now a national monument. Built around 1885, the house contains beautiful exhibits from all over the world. To get there take a city bus to Hualpencillo from Freire; ask the driver to let you out then walk for 40 mins (or hitch) along Av Las Golondrinas to the Enap oil refinery, turn left, then right (it is signed). Further west in the park, near the mouth of the Río Biobío, there are good opportunities for walking on the hills and several fine beaches including **Playa Rocoto**. ▸▸ *For Sleeping, Eating and other listings, see pages 299-304.*

North of Concepción

A road (nightmare for cyclists) runs north from Concepción along the coast through the suburbs of **Penco** (Km 12), where there is a fine beach, and **Lirquén**, Km 15, a small, old, pretty town of wooden houses with a beach that can be reached by walking along the railway. There is plentiful cheap seafood for sale here. **Tomé**, 13 km further north, is a small town set in a broad bay with long beaches and an interesting cemetery, Miguel Gulán Muñoz, on the cliff overlooking the ocean.

Dichato, 9 km further north along a hilly road offering fine views, is a beautiful fishing village and a busy summer holiday resort. It is also the site of the oceanographic centre of the University of Concepción. From Dichato you can take a local bus around the wide horseshoe bay to the tiny village of **Cocholgüe**.

Talcahuano → *Colour map 3, C1. Population: 244,000.*

Situated at the neck of Península de Tumbes, Talcahuano has the best harbour in Chile. It is Chile's main naval station and an important commercial and fishing port, where crowds of fishermen unload their catches of seafood before a seething mass of buyers, *stevedores* and hoary, old sailors, snaffling molluscs as they are carried past. In the naval base you can visit the great ship **Huáscar** ① *Tue-Sun 0900-1300, 1400-1700, US$1.50,* a relic of the War of the Pacific. Photography is permitted, but passports must be handed in at the main gate. Along the peninsula is **Parque Tumbes** ① *Information from Codeff, Caupolicán 346, Of east, p 4, T041-226649, admission free,* with paths leading along the coast. ▸▸ *For Sleeping, Eating and other listings, see pages 299-304.*

The coastal route south of Concepción

South of the Río Biobío is the **Costa del Carbón**, until recently the main coal-mining area of Chile. The road is busy, noisy and polluted by trucks plying to and from the numerous local industries; it is linked with Concepción by two bridges over the Biobío.

Towards Lota → *Colour map 4, A1. Population: 52,000.*

Just across the Río Biobío from Concepción is the **Laguna Grande**, a watersports centre, and **Laguna San Pedro Chica**, which is good for swimming. **Coronel**, 29 km from Concepción, was the scene of a British naval defeat in 1914, when the *Good Hope* and *Monmouth* were sunk by the German ship *Scharnhorst*. A monument commemorating the defeat was erected in November 1989. The defeat was later avenged at the Battle of the Falklands/Malvinas with the destruction of the German squadron. Close to town on the Bahía de Coronel are the small **Playa Negra**, which has few people and black sand, and **Playa Blanca**, which is bigger with white sand and more crowds, as well as bars, cafés, seafood restaurants and a free campsite.

The church on the main plaza in Lota contains a statue of the Virgin made of coal.

Forty-two kilometres south of Concepción, **Lota** was, until recently, the site of the most important coal mine in Chile, originally the property of the Cousiño family (see page 86). Even before the mine's closure in April 1997, the town was known to be one of the poorest in Chile and, although the government has invested in retraining for the miners and in trying to open up Lota to tourism, the city still suffers greatly from poverty and neglect. The town is in two parts: **Lota Alto**, on the hill, is the original mining town, while **Lota Bajo**, below, is more recent.

The **Parque de Lota Isidora Cousiño** ① *daily 1000-1800, till 2000 in summer, US$2.50*, covering 14 ha on a promontory to the west of the town, was the life's work of Isadora Cousiño. Laid out by English landscape architects in the 19th century, it contains plants from all over the world, ornaments imported from Europe, romantic paths and shady nooks offering views over the sea; peacocks and pheasants roam freely; no picnicing allowed. The mansion, which was Isadora's home during her stays in Lota, was destroyed in the 1960 earthquake. Near the entrance to the park is the **Museo Historíco de Lota** ① *daily 1000-2000 Nov-Mar, 1000-1800 Apr-Oct, US$1*.

The tunnels of the **coal mine** ① *T041-870682, daily 1000-1700, US$5*, run almost entirely under the sea (the longest is 11 km) and can be visited on guided tours led by former miners; at the entrance is a small Museo Minero. Offshore is an island, **Isla Santa María**, which has basic accommodation and good beaches. ▸▸ *For Sleeping, Eating and other listings, see pages 299-304.*

Towards Lebu

South of Lota the road runs past the seaside resort of **Laraquete**, where there are miles of golden sands and lots of Chilean holidaymakers in summer. The road passes a large cellulose factory and then, at Carampangue, Km 64 south of Concepción, it forks: one branch running west to **Arauco**, the site of a great beach but also two pungent cellulose factories; the other branch continuing south, 52 km, to Tres Pinos, where there is a turning towards Lebu.

A fishing port and coal washing centre, **Lebu** lies at the mouth of the Río Lebu, 149 km south of Concepción, and is the capital of Arauco province. There are enormous beaches to both the north and south, popular on summer weekends. About 3 km north, at **Playa Millaneco**, are steep hills and caves offering good walks and majestic views.

Cañete, Contulmo and Lago Lanalhue

Twenty-four kilometres south of Tres Pinos is the small town of Cañete. It is located on the site of the historic **Fort Tucapel** (now being restored), where Pedro de Valdivia and 52 of his men were killed by Mapuche warriors in 1553. About 1 km south on the road to Contulmo, in a modern building supposedly inspired by the traditional Mapuche *ruca*, is the **Museo Mapuche Juan Antonio Ríos** ① *summer Mon-Fri 0930-1830, Sat and Sun 1100-1900, closed Mon in winter, US$1.25*. Displays include Mapuche ceramics and textiles. Behind the museum is a reconstruction of a *ruca*.

South of Cañete, **Lago Lanalhue** is surrounded by forested hills from which there has been extensive logging. Much less popular than the Lake District, this area offers good opportunities for walking. A road runs south from Cañete along the north side of the lake to **Contulmo**, a sleepy village at the foot of the *cordillera*. The **Monumento Natural Contulmo**, 8 km south of the village and administered by CONAF, covers 82 ha of native forest. Access to the lake shore is restricted, as much of it is private property, but **Playa Blanca**, 10 km north of Contulmo, is a popular beach in summer (take any bus between Contulmo and Cañete). The wooden **Casa y Molino Grollmus**, 3 km along the southern side of the lake, are well worth a visit. The splendid garden has a fine collection of *copihue*, the national flower, and the mill, built in 1928, still contains its original wooden machinery. From here, the track runs 9 km north to the **Posada Campesina Alemana**, an old German-style hotel in a fantastic spot at the water's edge.

Twenty kilometres further east, **Purén** is reached by crossing the *cordillera* through dense forest (do this journey in daylight). Located in a major logging area, Purén was the site of a fortress built by Pedro de Valdivia in 1553 and destroyed soon after. It was again a key stronghold of the Chilean army in the last campaign against the Mapuche (1869-81) and there is now a full-scale reconstruction of the wooden fort on the original site. ▸▸ *For Sleeping, Eating and other listings, see pages 299-304.*

Lago Lleulleu and Tirúa

Lago Lleulleu lies 34 km south of Cañete. It is a peaceful lake covering 4,300 ha and offers sandy beaches, many opportunities for camping, fine views of the coastal mountain range and the chance to interact with the local Mapuche community, but there are few facilities. Further south, at the mouth of the Río Tirúa is the town of **Tirúa**, unremarkable in itself, but close to some wonderful country for walking and riding and with a beach that is calm and deserted. The island of **Mocha**, visited by Juan Bautista Pastenes in 1544 and later by Sir Francis Drake, lies 32 km offshore. Most of the island's 800 inhabitants live around the coast, the interior being forest. The main settlement is La Hacienda where accommodation is available with families.

Los Angeles and around → *Phone code: 043. Colour map 4, A2.*

Situated on the Pan-American Highway, 110 km south of Chillán, Los Angeles is the capital of Biobío province and lies at the heart of a wine, fruit and timber-producing district. Founded in 1739 as a fort, it was destroyed several times by the Mapuche.

Ins and outs

Getting there Los Angeles is easily accessible from north and south by bus; the most common destinations are Santiago, Puerto Montt and Concepción, but all intermediate destinations are also served. ▸▸ *For further details, see Transport page 304.*
Getting around Los Angeles is not as big as some of the other cities of the central valley, and as a result it is not necessary to take public transport quite as often as in, say, Chillán or Talca. **Tourist information** The tourist office is on Caupolicán close to post office; also try **CONAF** ① *Ercilla 936, daily 0900-1300.*

Los Angeles

To Long Distance Bus Terminal
& Pan-American Highway (North)

N

0 metres 100
0 yards 100

Sleeping 🛏
De Villena 2
Gran Müso 3
Residencial Santa María 4

Eating 🍴
Bavaria 4
Di Leone 5
El Arriero 2
Julio's Pizzas 3
Rancho de Julio 1

⁝ Fiesta de la Piedra Santa

The ancient festival of the Holy Stone is celebrated in Lumaco, near Purén every year on 20 January. The women dress in their traditional costumes, with colourful belts and silver jewellery. Each family carries a fowl, which is sacrificed, covering the stone with blood, while they ask for favours or give thanks for favours received. A few drops of wine are also poured onto the stone before the rest is drunk. The stone is illuminated by hundreds of candles and crosses made of straw or grass are placed over the blood, which sticks to them. *Machis* (shamans), surrounded by people from their communities, go up to the stone and, accompanied on their sacred instrument, the *kultrung*, they sing, dance and recite, while passing their knives over the diseased parts of the bodies of the sick. The festival continues through the night with singing, dancing, music and prayers.

Abridged and translated from *Lengua y Costumbres Mapuches* by Orietta Appelt Martin, Temuco, 1995.

Sights

Most visitors find themselves in Los Angeles on their way to Parque Nacional Laguna de Laja and, although there isn't much here in the way of sights, it is a pleasant, expanding city, with a large Plaza de Armas. Colón is the main shopping street and there is a good daily market. The **Museo de la Alta Frontera** ① *Colón 195, Mon-Fri 0815-1830, free,* has some Mapuche silver and colonial artefacts. Swimming is possible in the nearby **Río Duqueco**, 10 minutes south by bus, US$0.80.

Salto del Laja, 25 km north of Los Angeles, is a spectacular waterfall where the Río Laja plunges 15 m over the rocks. Numerous tour groups stop here, and the place is filled with tourist kiosks selling pap. Boat trips are available in the *Buenaventura* ① *T09-4181247.* ▸▸ *For Sleeping, Eating and other listings, see pages 299-304.*

Parque Nacional Laguna de Laja → *Colour map 4, A2.*

A road, paved for the first 64 km, runs east from Los Angeles for 93 km, past the impressive rapids of the Río Laja, to the Parque Nacional Laguna de Laja. Covering 11,600 ha, the park is dominated by the scree slopes of the **Antuco Volcano** (2,985 m), which is still active, and the glacier-covered **Sierra Velludac**. There is no clear path to the summit of Antuco. Start out early (0500) from the Refugio Digeder at 1,400 m to allow about six hours to ascend and leave plenty of time for the descent, which is exhausting. The volcano slopes are made of black scorias blocks, which are razor sharp, so wear good strong boots and take water; be warned that this sort of terrain is very demanding and can catch out those who are unaware of its severity. From the sulphur fume-cloaked summit of the volcano are fine views over the glaciers and south to the smoking Villarrica Volcano. The valley below is green and wooded, very pleasant and sparsely visited, even in high season. The **visitors' centre** is 1 km from the park administration (4 km from the entrance).

The **Club de Esquí de los Angeles** ① *open May-Aug*, has two ski-lifts, giving a combined run of 4 km on the Antuco Volcano. Passing the ski station, the road reaches the turquoise waters of the **Laguna de la Laja**, with views of the Andes stretching towards Argentina; note, however, that it is a walk of several hours from the park entrance to the lake and there is very little passing traffic. The laguna was created by the damming of the Río de Laja by a lava flow and is surrounded by stark scenery. Trees include a few surviving araucarias, and there are 47 species of birds including condors and the rare Andean gull. From the lake, the road continues to the Argentine border at **Paso Pichachén** ① *open Oct-Apr, depending on amount of snow.*

Angol → Phone code: 045 Colour map 4, A2.

Although of limited interest to travellers, Angol is the main base for visiting the Parque Nacional Nahuelbuta, further west. Reached from the Pan-American Highway by roads from Los Angeles and Collipulli, the town is situated at the confluence of the Ríos Rehue and Picolquén, at the foot of the Cordillera de Nahuelbuta, and is the capital of the province of Malleco. It was founded by Pedro de Valdivia in 1552 and was destroyed seven times by the Mapuche.

Northwest of the attractive Plaza de Armas is the church and convent of **San Bueneventura**. Built in 1863, it became the centre for missionary work among the Mapuche. Also worth visiting is **El Vergel** ① *5 km southeast of Angol, Mon-Fri 0900-1900, Sat and Sun 1000-1900, US$1, colectivo No 2*, which was founded in 1880 as an experimental fruit-growing nursery but now incorporates an attractive park with a wide range of trees and the Museo Dillman Bullock with displays on archaeology and natural history. There's an excellent **tourist office**① *O'Higgins s/n, across bridge from bus terminal, T045-711255*, and an office of **CONAF** ① *Prat 191, piso 2, T045-711870.* ▶▶ *For Sleeping, Eating and other listings, see pages 299-304.*

Parque Nacional Nahuelbuta

① *Open all year (snow Jun-Sep).* Situated in the coastal mountain range at an altitude of 800-1,550 m, the park covers 6,832 ha of forest and offers views over both the sea and the Andes. There are some good walks: one heads 4 km west of visitors centre to the **Piedra el Aguila** at 1,158 m, where there is a *mirador* on top of a huge boulder; another goes to **Cormallín**, 5 km north of visitors' centre, from where you may continue to Cerro Anay, 1,402 m, and another *mirador*. Although the forest includes many species of trees, the araucaria is most striking; some are over 2,000 years old, 50 m high and with trunks 2 m in diameter. There are also seven species of orchid. Animals include pudu, Chiloé foxes, pumas, kodkod, black woodpeckers and parrots. There is a **visitors' centre**① *spring and summer daily 0800-1300, 1400-2000*, at Pehuenco, 5 km from the entrance. Rough maps are available for US$0.25.

● Sleeping

Concepción *p293, map p294*
Good budget accommodation is hard to find.
A Alborada, *Barros Arana 457, T041-911121, www.hotelalborada.cl* Good 4-star with all mod cons. Disabled friendly. Tours offered.
A Alonso de Ercilla, *Colo Colo 334, T041-227984, www.hotelalonsodeercilla.co.cl* With breakfast, modern, heating, internet access, bar, conference room.
A-B El Dorado, *Barros Arana 348, T041-229400, hoteleldorado.co.cl* Comfortable, central, cafeteria, parking.
B Concepción, *Serrano 512, T041-620851, hotelconcepcion@entelchile.net* Central, comfortable, heating, English spoken.
B-C Maquehue, *Barros Arana 786, p 8, T041-911966, www.hotelmaquehue.co.cl* Clean, with restaurant, laundry service, parking. Recommended.
C Hostal Bianca, *Salas 643-C, T041-242103, hostalbianca@surnet.cl.* With breakfast, food available, parking, student discounts.

C-D Cecil, *Barros Arana 9, near railway station, T041-226603.* With bath and breakfast, clean, quiet. Highly recommended.
C-D Hostal Casablanca, *Cochrane 133, T041-226576.* With bath, cheaper without, clean.
C-D Hostal Antuco, *Barros Arana 741, apart 31-33 (entry via the Galería Martínez), T/F041-235485.* Recommended.
F Res San Sebastián, *Barros Arana 741, apart 35 (entry via the Galería Martínez), T041-910240.* Central, Hostelling International reductions. Price per person.
F Res Central, *Rengo 673, T041-227309.* Price per person. A little rundown, with breakfast.
F Res Colo Colo, *Colo Colo 743, T041-227118.* Price per person with breakfast. Some singles with bath.
F Res O'Higgins, *O'Higgins 457, T041-221086.* Price per person with breakfast, comfortable.
F Ruca Ray, *Barros Arana 317B, T041-238942.* Price per person. With breakfast, slightly old fashioned but comfortable and clean. Cable TV in room.

F **Silvia Uslar**, *Edmundo Larenas 202,*
T041-227449. Price per person. Good
breakfast, quiet, clean, comfortable.

North of Concepción p295
A-C **Chamaruk**, *Daniel Vera 912, Dichato,*
T041-683022. Clean and pleasant, cheaper
rooms are without bath.
B **Kalifa**, *Daniel Vera 813, Dichato,*
T041-683027, F229019. With bath, restaurant.
B **Manantial**, *Aguirre Cerda 201, Dichato,*
T041-683946, www.hotelmanantial.cl
Balconies with sea view, restaurant, bar,
parking, tours arranged, bike hire.
C **Vista Hermosa**, *Costanera 1135, Tomé,*
T041-650280. On the seafront, with bath,
without breakfast.
D **El Edén**, *7 km before Tomé, on a hill.*
Restaurant, bar and *cabañas*.
F **Chicki**, *Ugarte 410, Dichato, T041-683004.*
Price per person. Cheaper without bath.
F **De la Costa**, *M Montt 923, Tomé,*
T041-653379. Price per person. With
bath and breakfast.
F-G **Res Santa Inés**, *República 540, Dichato.*
Price per person. Without bath.

Talcahuano p295
B **De La Costa**, *Colón 630, T041-545913.*
Rooms with breakfast.
B-C **France**, *Av Pinto 44, T041-542230,*
hfrance@entelchile.net Rooms
with breakfast.
B-F **Res San Pedro**, *Rodríguez 22,*
T041-542145. With breakfast. Cheaper prices
per person without bath.

Lota p295
D **Angel de Peredo**, *Alessandri 169, Lota,*
T041-876824. With bath and breakfast.
F-G **Res Roma**, *Galvarino 233, Lota,*
T041-876257. Price per person. Clean,
friendly, some rooms with bath.
No breakfast.

Towards Lebu p296
AL-A **Hostería Millaneco**, *Playa Millaneco,*
Lebu, T041-511540. Offers *cabañas* for up to 7
people, good restaurant. Recommended.
B **Hostería Arauco**, *Esmeralda 80, Arauco,*
T041-551131, itafesa@hotmail.com Café, bar
laundry and parking.
C-F **Plaza**, *Chacabuco 345, Arauco,*
T041-551265. Cheaper rooms without bath.

E-F **Central**, *Pérez 183, Lebu, T/F041-511904.*
Price per person. With bath, clean, parking.
Recommended.
F **Gran**, *Pérez 309, Lebu, T041-511939.* Price
per person. With bath, old fashioned,
clean, *comedor*.
F **Hostal La Quinta**, *Laraquete, T041-571993.*
Price per person. Helpful, basic,
good breakfast.
G **Res Alcázar**, *Alcázar 144, Lebu.* Price per
person. With breakfast, cold water, friendly.
G **Res Los Abedules**, *Los Abedules 144,*
Laraquete, T041-571953. Price per person.
Friendly, small rooms, poor bathrooms.

Cañete, Contulmo and Lanalhue p296
Lanalhue Turismo, *T041-613537,*
www.lanalhueturismo.cl, is an agglomeration
of local hotel and *cabaña* owners who also
offer tours and information. There are
several *cabañas* on the lakeshore. Real
coffee is served at **Café Nahuel**, off the
plaza in Cañete.
L-AL **Hostería Lanalhue**, *Lago Lanalhue,*
T041-234981. On the south side of the lake,
many facilities, good.
C **Hotel Licahue**, *Lago Lanalhue, 4 km north*
of Contulmo, T09-8702822. Price per person.
Full board, attractively set overlooking lake,
with pool. Highly recommended. Also owns
cabañas nearby (connected by boat).
C **Nahuelbuta**, *Villagrán 644, Cañete,*
T041-611073, hotelnahuelbuta@
lanalhueturismo.cl. Clean, pleasant, parking.
Cheaper without bath.
D **Central**, *on the plaza, Purén.* Excellent
meals, rooms in tourist season only.
F **Derby**, *Marián y Condell, Cañete,*
T041-611960. Price per person. Without bath,
clean, basic, restaurant.
F **Gajardo**, *7 de la Línea 817 (1 block from*
plaza), Cañete. Price per person. Without
bath, old fashioned, friendly, pleasant.
F-G **Central**, *Millaray 131, Contulmo,*
T041-618089, hotelcentral@lanalhueturismo.cl
Cheaper without bath, no sign, hospitable.
F-G **Contulmo**, *Millaray 116, Contulmo,*
T041-894903. Price per person. Cheaper
without bath, an attractive retreat, friendly
and hospitable. Highly recommended.
G **Don Juanito**, *Riquelme 151, Cañete.* Price
per person. Very good, friendly.
Recommended by the locals, cheap.

Camping

Camping Elicura, *Contulmo*. Clean, US$6. Recommended.

Camping Huilquehue, *15 km south of Cañete*. Lakeside site.

Camping Playa Blanca, *Lago Lanalhue*.

Lago Lleulleu and Tirúa *p297*

F **Residencial Elimar**, *T041-894902*. 1 of 3 *hospedajes* in Tirúa.

Los Angeles *p297, map p297*

A **Gran Hotel Müso**, *Valdivia 222 (Plaza de Armas)*, *T043-313183*. Good restaurant open to non-residents.

A **Hostería Salto del Laja**, *T043-321706*, *www.saltodellaja.cl* With fine restaurant, 2 swimming pools and chalet-type rooms on an island overlooking the falls, also cabañas, for up to 6.

B **Complejo Turístico Los Manantiales**, *Salto del Laja, T/F043-314275*. Also camping.

B-C **Hospedaje El Rincón**, *Panamericana Sur Km 494, El Olivo, 2 km east,18 km north of Los Angeles, T09-4415019*, *www.contactchile.cl/elrincon/* Beautiful property beside a small river, restful. Good breakfast. South American and European cuisine, including vegetarian, tours arranged, Spanish classes, horseriding, rafting, English, French and German spoken, kitchen facilities.

C **Res Santa María**, *Plaza de Armas*, *T043-328214*. Hot shower, TV, friendly but rundown and overpriced.

D **Hotel de Villena**, *Lautaro 579*, *T043-321643*. With breakfast.

F *Caupolicán 651*. Private house offering good value rooms and large breakfast. Price per person. Opposite is another, also No 651, basic, cheaper.

There are also several cheap *residenciales* around *Colo Colo* and *Almagra*.

Parque Nacional Laguna de Laja *p298*

In Antuco, most places are fully occupied by local workers. Take your own food as little is available in Abanico or inside the park. Camping is not permitted on lake shore.

B **Cabañas Lagunillas**, *T043-321086, 2 km from park entrance*. Open all year, cabins sleep 6, lovely spot close to the river among pine woods, restaurant, also camping US$2.50 per person.

B **Refugio Chacay**, *21 km from the lake, T043- 222651*. Food, drink and beds, closed in summer.

F **Hostería El Bosque**, *Abanico*. With restaurant and good campsite.

F **Refugio Digeder**, *11 km from the park entrance, T041-229054*. *Refugio* on slopes of Antuco Volcano.

F **Refugio Universidad de Concepción**, *Of O'Higgins 740, T041-229054*. *Refugio* on slopes of Antuco Volcano.

Angol *p299*

C **Josanh-Paecha**, *Caupolicán 579, T045-711771*. With breakfast, clean, good food.

D **La Posada**, *El Vergel, T045-712103*. Price per person for full board, clean, friendly.

F **Casa de Huéspedes**, *Dieciocho 465*. Price per person with breakfast, friendly.

F **Res Olimpia**, *Caupolicán 625, T045-711162*. Price per person. Good.

G *Vergara 651*. Price per person. Chaotic.

Camping

There are 2 campsites on the road to Parque Nacional Nahuelbuta at Km 21 and Km 20.

The Central Valley The Biobío Valley

Parque Nacional Nahuelbuta *p299*
There's a campsite near the visitors' centre, US$9, and many free campsites along the road from El Cruce to the entrance.

🍴 Eating

Concepción *p293, map p294*
$$$ **Le Château**, *Colo Colo 340*. French, seafood and meat, closed Sun.
$$$ **Rincón de Pancho**, *Cervantes 469*. Excellent meat, also pasta and *congrio*, good service and ambience, closed Sun.
$$ **Big Joe Saloon**, *O'Higgins 808, just off plaza*. Popular at lunchtime, open Sun evening, good breakfasts, vegetarian meals, snacks and pizzas.
$$ **El Rancho de Julio**, *O'Higgins 36*. Argentine *parrillada*.
$$ **Novillo Loco**, *Portales 539*. Traditional food. Good, efficient service.
$$ **Piazza**, *Barros Arana 631, 2nd floor*. Good pizzas.
$ **Casino de Bomberos**, *O'Higgins y Orompello*. Good-value lunches.
$ **Chicki**, *Portales 531*. Spanish.
$ **Mar y Tierra**, *Colo Colo 1182*. Seafood and fish.
$ **Waya's Gyros**, *Angol 441*. Excellent value kebabs. Recommended. Also on Plaza Perú.
$ **Yiet-Xiu**, *Angol 515*. Good, cheap Oriental food.

Cafés and snack bars
Café Colombia, *Aguirre Cerda*. Good coffee, pleasant atmosphere.
Café El Dom, *Caupolicán 415*. One of several cafés near the Plaza de Armas. Open Sun morning.
Café Haiti, *Caupolicán 515*. Open Sun morning, good coffee.
Fuente Alemana, *Caupolicán 654*. Recommended *fuente de soda* near the Plaza de Armas.
La Capilla, *Vicuña MacKenna 769*. Good *ponches*, popular, crowded.
Nuria, *Barros Arana 736*. Very good breakfasts and lunches, good value.
QuickBiss, *O'Higgins between Tuscapel and Castellón*. Salads, real coffee, good service, good lunches.
Royal Pub, *O'Higgins 790*. Posh snack bar.
Saaya 1, *Barros Arana 899*. Excellent *panadería/pastelería/rotisería*.

Treinta y Tantos, *Prat 356*. Nice bar, good music, wide selection of *empanadas*, good breakfasts and lunches. Recommended.

North of Concepción *p295*
$$ **Casino Oriente**, *Penco*. Good seafood restaurant.
$$ **Munot**, *Baquedano 1690, Tomé*. Swiss food.
$$ **Villa Marina**, *Riquelme 55, Tomé*. Traditional food.
There are several seafood restaurants on *P Aguirre Cerda 600 and 700 blocks* in Dichato.

Talcahuano *p295*
The market abounds with fine seafood.
$$ **Club Talcahuano**, *Colón 446*. For meat.
$$-$ **Benotecas**, *on seafront*. A row of 4 restaurants facing the harbour. Superb fish and seafood. Recommended.
$$-$ **Domingo Lara**, *Aníbal Pinto 450*. Seafood specialities, excellent.
$$-$ **La Aguada**, *Colón 912*. Shellfish dishes.

Lota *p295*
$ **El Greco**, *P Aguirre Cerda 422, Lota*. Traditional food, cheap.

Los Angeles *p297, map p297*
$$ **Di Leone**, *Av Alemania 606*. Italian with good lasagne on the menu.
$$ **El Arriero**, *Colo Colo 235*. Good *parrillas* and international dishes.
$$ **Rancho de Julio**, *Colón 720*. Excellent *parrilla*. Recommended.
$ **Julio's Pizzas**, *Colón 542*. Good pizzeria.

Angol *p299*
$ **Carloncho**, *Lautaro 447*. Simple food, popular with locals.

🍸 Bars and clubs

Concepción *p293, map p294*
El Caríno Malo, *Barros Arana y Salas*. Popular bar and disco with live music, not cheap.

🎉 Festivals and events

Cañete, Contulmo and Lanalhue *p296*
Semana Musical (music week) is held in Contulmo in Jan.
Fiesta de Piedra Santa is a major Mapuche festival, held in Lumaco (see box, p298).

⊙ Shopping

Concepción *p293, map p294*
Feria Artesanal, *Freire 757*. Craft market.
Galería Internacional, *Caupolicán y Barros Arana*. Worth a visit; El Naturista vegetarian restaurant is at local 22.
Las Brisas, *Freire y Lincoyán*. Supermarket.
Mercado Municipal, *1 block west of the Plaza de Armas*. Excellent seafood, fruit and vegetables.
Plaza del Trebol, *near the airport*. Large modern shopping mall and multiplex cinema. Take any bus for Talcahuano.

▲ Activities and tours

Concepción *p293, map p294*
Alta Luz, *S Martín 586, Piso 2, T041-217727*. Tours to national parks.
Aventuratur, *Ejército 599, T041-819634*. Tours.
Chile Indomito Adventure, *Serrano 551, Of 3, T041-221618*. Trekking.
Ram, *T041-256161*. City and local tours.
South Expeditions, *O'Higgins 680, piso 2, Of 218D, T/F041-232290*. Rafting, horseriding, fishing and trekking expeditions.
Viajes Publitur, *A Pinto 486, Of. 202, T041-240800*. City and local tours.

Los Angeles *p297, map p297*
Senderos Chile Expediciones, *T09-7143958*. Trekking, mountain biking.
Strong Visión, *Caupolicán 506, T09-312295*. Trekking, mountain biking, rafting, kayaking, bungee-jumping, fishing.

⊝ Transport

Concepción *p293, map p294*
Air
Concepción airport is north of the city, off the main road to Talcahuano. In summer, flights daily to and from **Santiago** (fewer in winter) and connections to **Temuco**, **Puerto Montt** and **Punta Arenas**.

Bus
Long distance The main terminal is known as **Terminal Collao**, *2 km east, Av Gen Bonilla, next to athletics stadium*. To reach the city centre take a bus marked 'Hualpencillo' from outside the terminal and get off in Freire, US$0.40, taxi US$3.

Tur Bus, **Línea Azul** and **Buses Bío Bío** services leave from **Terminal Camilo Henríquez**, *2 km northeast of main terminal on J M García*, reached by buses from Av Maipú in centre, via Terminal Collao.

To **Santiago**, 8 companies, 6½ hrs, US$8; to **Valparaíso**, 8 hrs, US$10 (most go via Santiago). Estrella del Sur have buses to **La Serena** and **Iquique**. To **Loncoche**, 5½ hrs, US$7; to **Puerto Montt** several companies, about 9 hrs, US$10 (*cama* US$20); to **Pucón** direct, 8 hrs, US$8, in summer only; to **Valdivia**, 7 hrs, US$8, Tur Bus only; to **Los Angeles**, every ½ hr, US$3.

Best direct bus to **Chillán** is Línea Azul, 2 hrs, US$2. For a longer, more scenic route, take the Costa Azul bus, which follows the old railway line, through Tomé, Coelemu and Nipas on to Chillán (part dirt-track, takes 5½ hrs).

Local Línea Azul and Costa Azul buses from Concepción pass through the villages north of the city, which can also be reached cheaply by *colectivo* (every 15-20 mins).

To **Talcahuano**, frequent service from Plaza de Armas (bus marked 'Base Naval'), 1 hr, US$0.30, express 30 mins, US$0.50; *colectivos* leave San Martín every 2 mins.

Services to **Coronel**, US$0.45, **Lota**, **Lebu**, **Cañete**, **Tirúa** and **Contulmo** are run by J Ewert (next to railway station on Prat), Los Alerces (terminal at Prat y Maipú) and Jeldres, who leave from the main terminal.

Train
The station is at *Prat y Barros Arana, T041-226925*. To **Santiago**, Rápido del Bío Bío overnight, 10 hrs, US$10; *clase preferente* US$15. Also local services to **Laja** and **Yumbel**, and suburban trains to **Talcahuano** and **Chiguayante**. Booking offices at the station and at Galería Alessandri, *Aníbal Pinto 478, local 3, T041-225286*.

Towards Lota *p295*
Buses to **Concepción**, 1½ hrs, US$0.50. Many buses bypass the centre of Lota: catch them from the main road. See also above.

Cañete, Contulmo & Lanalhue *p296*
There are 2 bus terminals in Cañete: J Ewert, Inter Sur and Thiele use the terminal at *Riquelme y 7° de la Línea*; Jeldres, Erbuc and other companies use the **Terminal Municipal**, *Serrano y Villagrán*.

To **Santiago**, Inter Sur, daily, 12 hrs; to **Contulmo**, frequent, US$1; to **Purén**, US$1.50, sit on right for views of Lago Lanalhue; to **Concepción**, 3 hrs, US$3.50; to **Lebu** US$1.50; to **Angol** US$3.50; to **Tirúa**, Jeldres, frequent, and J Ewert, 3 a day, 2 hrs, US$2.

Contulmo is also served by buses to/from **Concepción**, Thiele, 4 hrs, US$4.50, and **Temuco**, Thiele and Erbuc, US$4, see above.

Tirúa *p297*
Buses run from Cañete to Tirúa, from where there are ferries to **Mocha**, 0600 daily, US$14. Alternatively, you can also ask the police to radio the plane to Mocha, US$56.

Los Angeles *p297, map p297*
Long-distance bus terminal on northeastern outskirts of town, local terminal at *Villagrán y Rengo* in centre (most services to Ralco and Santa Bárbara).

To **Santiago**, 6½ hrs, US$8, *cama* US$20. To **Viña del Mar** and **Valparaíso**, 8 hrs, US$11; to **Concepción**, US$2.50, 2 hrs; to Valdivia, US$6; to **Chillán**, US$2.50. To **Temuco**, US$4, hourly; to **Curacautín**, daily, 3 hrs, US$4. **Salto del Laja** is served by Bus Biobío from Los Angeles, frequent, 30 mins, US$1, and from Chillán, US$2.

Parque Nacional Laguna del Laja *p298*
Take ERS Bus, *Villagrán 507*, from Los Angeles to **Abanico**, then walk 4 km to park entrance. Alternatively take a bus to **Antuco**, 2 hrs, 5 daily Mon-Sat, 2 daily Sun, US$1.35, then hitch the remaining 24 km to the park.

Angol *p299*
Long-distance bus terminal is at *Chorrillos y Caupolicán*. Local buses use **Terminal Rural**, *Ilabaca y Lautaro*. To **Santiago**, US$6.50; to **Los Angeles**, US$1.20; to **Temuco**, Trans Bío-Bío, frequent, US$2.50.

Parque Nacional Nahuelbuta *p299*
There is a direct bus to park entrance from Angol, Dec-Feb, Sun 0800, return 1700. Otherwise, take a bus to **Vegas Blancas** (27 km west of Angol) 0700 and 1600 daily, return 0900 and 1600, 1½ hrs, US$1.20, and get off at El Cruce, for a 7-km walk to the park entrance (US$4.50). Access is also possible via a dirt road from Cañete, 4WD only Jun-Sep.

Directory

Concepción *p293, map p294*
Airline offices LanChile, *Barros Arana 560, T041-248824;* Aerolíneas Argentinas, *O'Higgins 650, Of 602*. **Banks and currency exchange** ATMs at banks on *Av O'Higgins;* high commission; several *cambios* in Galería Internacional, *Barros Arana 565 and Caupolicán 521,* check rates first: Afex, *local 57,* no commission on TCs; Cambios Fides, *local 58,* good rates for TCs; Inter-Santiago, *local 31, T041-228914*. **Bicycle repairs** Martínez, *Maipú y Lincoyán,* very helpful. **Car hire** Avis, *Chacabuco 726, T041-235837;* Budget, *Castellón 134, T041-225377;* Dollar, *at airport, T041-483661;* Full famas, *O'Higgins 1154, T041-248300, F041-242385, airport T09-4403300;* Hertz, *Prat 248, T041-230341*. **Consulates** Argentina, *San Martín 472, Of 52, T041-230257*. **Cultural centres** Alliance Française, *Colo Colo y Lamas,* library, concerts, films, cultural events; Chilean-British Cultural Institute, *San Martín 531,* British newspapers, library; Chilean-North American Institute, *Caupolicán 301 y San Martín,* library. **Internet** *Barros Arana 541, Caupolicán 567, T041-245409, admin@ cyberconce.cl,* English spoken. **Laundry** American Cleaning, *Freire 817;* Lavandería Radiante, *Salas 281,* open 0900-2030, very good; also at Lincoyán 441. **Post office** *O'Higgins y Colo Colo*. **Telephone** CTC, *Colo Colo 487, Angol 483;* Entel, *Barros Arana 541, Caupolicán 567, piso 2, Colo Colo 487*. **Useful addresses** Automóvil Club de Chile, *O'Higgins 630, Of 303, T041-245884;* Codeff, *Caupolicán 346, p 4, T041-226649*.

Los Angeles *p297, map p297*
Banks Banco Santander, *Colón 500.* Mastercard; Corp Banca, *Colón 300,* Visa. ATMs at banks; reluctant to change TCs or cash; best rates at Agencia Interbruna, *Caupolicán 350*. **Post office** *Plaza de Armas*. **Telephone** CTC, *Colo Colo;* Entel, *Colo Colo 393*. **Useful address** Automóvil Club de Chile, *Villagrán y Caupolicán, T043-322149*.

Angol *p299*
Banks Banco Bice, *Chorrillas 364;* Banco Santander, *Lautaro 399*. **Car hire** Christopher Car, *Ilabaca 421, T/F045-715156*.

The Lake District

Introduction

Extending from the Río Biobío south to the city of Puerto Montt, the Lake District is one of the most popular destinations for both Chileans and visitors. The main cities are **Temuco**, **Valdivia**, **Osorno** and **Puerto Montt**, but the most attractive scenery lies further east where a string of lakes stretches down the western side of the Andes. Much of this region has been turned into national parks and the mixture of forests, lakes and snow-capped volcanoes is unforgettable.

Between Temuco and the Pacific coast, meanwhile, is the indigenous heartland of Chile, home to the largest Mapuche communities. Here you will find traditional thatched houses (*rucas*) and communities still fiercely proud of their traditions, hinting at the sort of country that the first *conquistadors* might have found.

The major resorts include **Pucón** on Lago Villarrica and **Puerto Varas** on Lago Llanquihue. The cities of Temuco and Puerto Montt are also popular: **Temuco** for excursions into the Mapuche communities towards the coast and **Puerto Montt** as a base for longer voyages south to Puerto Natales, Puerto Chacabuco and the San Rafael glacier, as well as east across the lakes and mountains to the Argentine resort of Bariloche.

★ Don't miss...

❶ The journey from Puerto Montt to Bariloche in Argentina Cross the emerald waters of the Lago Todos Los Santos, overlooked by the Osorno volcano, and then take a narrow pass over the Andes, page 365.

❷ Parque Nacional Conguillío The best place in Chile to see the araucarias (monkey puzzle trees), in the shadow of Volcán Llaima, page 313.

❸ Volcán Villarrica An active volcano where molten lava bubbles in the crater, page 322.

❹ Eating at Angelmó This harbour near Puerto Montt has some of the best seafood in Chile (and, by extension, in the world), page 368.

❺ Temuco's feria This is one of the biggest and most fascinating markets in Chile, filled with Mapuche men and women who have come by ox cart to the city to sell their produce, page 318.

❻ Corral Visit this old fortified settlement near Valdivia and then take the coastal path south through wild forest clinging to cliffs above the ocean, page 341.

The Lake District

Background

After the Mapuche rebellion of 1598, Spanish settlement south of the Río Biobío was limited to Valdivia, although the Spanish had a right of way north from Valdivia along the coast to Concepción. At independence the only other Spanish settlement in this region was Osorno, refounded in 1796. The Chilean government did not attempt to extend its control into the Lake District until the 1840s. In 1845, all land south of the Río Rahue was declared the property of the state and destined for settlement and, in 1850, Vicente Pérez Rosales was sent to Valdivia to distribute lands to arriving European colonists.

The southern Lake District was settled from the 1850s onwards, mainly by German immigrants (see box, page 355). Further north, Chilean troops began occupying lands south of the Biobío after 1862, but the destruction of Mapuche independence did not occur until the early 1880s when Chilean forces led by Cornelio Saavedra founded a series of forts in the area including Temuco (1881), Nueva Imperial (1882), Freire (1883) and Villarrica (1883). A treaty ending Mapuche independence was signed in Temuco in 1881.

White settlement in the area was further encouraged by the arrival of the railway, which reached Temuco in 1893, reducing the journey time from Santiago to 36 hours; the line was later extended to Osorno (1902) and Puerto Montt (1912). In the 1930s the area became popular as a destination for rich Santiaguinos, and also as an important fishing destination for foreigners.

Today, agriculture is the most important sector of the local economy and the main industries are connected to the region's produce. Proof of Chile's position as a timber producer of international standing is provided by the wood-chip mountains of Puerto Montt. Fishing is particularly important in the south of the region, where farmed salmon regularly appears on restaurant menus. Tourism is a mainstay in summer (from mid-December to mid-March), when Chileans flock to the Lake District resorts, prices are high, and it is best to book well in advance, particularly for transport. Out of season, however, many facilities are closed.

The Lake District

Geography

The region between the cities of Temuco and Puerto Montt is one of the most picturesque lake regions in the world. There are 12 great lakes, and dozens of smaller ones, as well as imposing waterfalls and snowcapped volcanoes. This landscape has been created by two main geological processes: glaciation and volcanic activity. The main mountain peaks are volcanic: the highest are Lanín (3,747 m) and Tronador (3,460 m), both on the Argentine border. The most active volcanoes include Llaima and Villarrica, which erupted 22 and 10 times respectively in the 20th century.

❧ *Enormous horse-flies (tábanos) are a problem between mid-December and mid-January, especially in the Parque Nacional Vicente Pérez Rosales: cover up as much as possible and do not wear dark clothes.*

Seven main river systems drain the Lake District, from north to south the ríos Imperial, Toltén, Valdivia, Bueno, Maullín, Petrohué and Puelo. The Río Bueno drains Lago Ranco and is joined by the ríos Pilmaiquén and Rahue, thus receiving also the waters of Lagos Puyehue and Rupanco: it carries the third largest water volume of any Chilean river. In most of the rivers there is excellent fishing.

Rain falls all the year round, most heavily further south, but decreases as you go inland: some 2,500 mm of rain fall on the coast compared to 1,350 mm inland. There is enough rainfall to maintain heavy forests, mostly of southern beech and native species, though there are increasingly large areas of eucalyptus and other introduced varieties to cater for the booming timber industry.

The Mapuche

The largest indigenous group in southern South America, the Mapuche take their name from the words for 'land' (*mapu*) and 'people' (*che*). They were known as Araucanians by the Spanish.

Never subdued by the Incas, the Mapuche successfully resisted Spanish attempts at conquest. At the time of the great Mapuche uprising of 1598 they numbered some 500,000, concentrated in the area between the Río Biobío and the Reloncaví estuary. After 1598, two centuries of intermittent war were punctuated by 18 peace treaties. The 1641 Treaty of Quilín recognized Mapuche autonomy south of the río Biobío.

Although tools and equipment were privately owned, the Mapuche held land in common, abandoning it when it was exhausted by repeated use. This relatively nomadic lifestyle helps explain their ability to resist the Spanish. Learning from their enemies how to handle horses in battle, they became formidable guerrilla fighters. They pioneered the use of horses by two men, one of whom handled the animal, while the other was armed with bow and arrows. Horses also enabled the Mapuche to extend their territory to the eastern side of the Andes and the Argentine pampas.

The conquest of the Mapuche was made possible by the building of railways and the invention of new weapons, especially the breach-loading rifle (which had a similarly disquieting effect in Africa and Asia). The settlement of border disputes between Chile and Argentina enabled Argentine troops to occupy border crossings, while the Chileans subjugated the Mapuche.

Under the 1881 treaty, the Mapuche received 500,000 ha from the government, while 5,000,000 ha were kept for Chile. The Mapuche were confined to reservations, most of which were situated near large estates for which they provided a labour force. By the 1930s, the surviving Mapuche, living in more than 3,000 separate reservations, had become steadily more impoverished and dependent on the government.

The agrarian reforms of the 1960s provided little real benefit to the Mapuche since they encouraged private landholding – indeed some communal lands were sold off at this time – and the military government made continued encroachments on Mapuche communities, which remain among the poorest in Chile.

It is estimated that the Mapuche now occupy only about 1½% of the lands they inhabited at the time of the Spanish conquest, mainly in communities south of the Biobío and in reserves in the Argentine *cordillera* around Lago Nahuel Huapi. July 2001 saw repeated clashes with the police over land rights.

The Lake District

Crossing to Argentina

There are five main routes from the Lake District into Argentina:

1) From Curacautín and Lonquimay to Zapala via Paso Pino Hinchado (see page 315).
2) From Pucón and Curarrehue to Junín de los Andes via Paso Tromen (see page 324).
3) From Panguipulli via Choshuenco and Lake Pirehueico to San Martín de los Andes via Paso Huahum (see page 335).
4) From Osorno and Entrelagos via the Parque Nacional Puyehue and Paso Puyehue to Bariloche (see page 349).
5) The lakes route, from Puerto Montt or Osorno via Ensenada, Petrohué and Lago Todos Los Santos to Bariloche (see page 365).

Temuco and around

→ *Phone code: 045. Colour map 4, A2. Population: 225,000.*

At first sight, Temuco may appear a grey, forbidding place. However in reality it is a lively industrial and university town. For visitors, it is perhaps most interesting as a contrast to the more European cities in other parts of Chile. Temuco is proud of its Mapuche heritage, and it is this that gives it a distinctive character, especially around the feria *(outdoor market). North and east of the city are five national parks and reserves, and several hot springs, while to the west, in the valley of the Río Imperial, are the market towns of Nueva Imperial and Carahue and, on the coast, the resort of Puerto Saavedra.*

Ins and outs

Getting there Manquehue Airport is 6 km southwest of city. There are several daily flights north to Santiago and Concepción, and south to Puerto Montt. Taxis from airport to Temuco city centre cost US$4.50; there is no airport bus service. Temuco is the transport hub for the Lake District, and its municipal bus station serves much of the region, as well as the communities towards the coast. There is also a new long-distance terminal on the outskirts of town. The city is easily accessible by bus from Santiago (many daily) and has connections to large towns both north and south, especially Talca, Chillán, Concepción, Valdivia and Puerto Montt (many daily). There is also a nightly train to Santiago. ►► *For further details, see Transport page 318.* **Getting around** Temuco is a large city. *Colectivos* and buses serve the outlying *barrios*. However, the centre is relatively compact, and few places are more than a ½-hr walk away in this area. When looking for a specific address, be careful not to confuse the streets Vicuña MacKenna and Gen MacKenna. **Tourist information Sernatur** ① *Bulnes 586, T045-211969, infoaraucania@sernatur.cl, summer daily 0830-2030, winter Mon-Fri 0900-1200, 1500-1700,* has good leaflets in English. There is also a tourist information kiosk in the municipal market and an office of **CONAF** ① *Bilbao 931, T045-234420.*

Sights

The city is centred on the newly redesigned **Plaza Aníbal Pinto**, around which are the main public buildings including the cathedral and the municipalidad; the cathedral was destroyed by the 1960 earthquake, when most of the old wooden buildings in the city were also burnt down. On the plaza itself is a monument to La Araucanía featuring figures from local history. Nearby are fountains and a small Sala de Exposiciones, which stages exhibitions. More compelling, though, is the huge produce **market** (*feria*) at Lautaro y Aníbal Pinto is always crammed with people (many of them Mapuche), who have come from the countryside to sell their produce (see page 318).

West of the centre, the **Museo de la Araucanía** ① *Alemania 084, Mon-Fri 0900-1700, Sat 1100-1700, Sun 1100-1300, US$1, bus 1 from centre,* houses a well arranged collection devoted to the history and traditions of the Mapuche nation; there's also a section on German settlement.

On the northern edge of the city is the **Monumento Natural Cerro Ñielol** offering views of the city and surrounding countryside. It is a good spot for a picnic. There is an excellent visitors' centre ① *0830-2030, US$1,* run by CONAF and a fine collection of native plants in their natural environment, including the *copihue rojo*, the national flower. Note that the hill has a one-way system for drivers (entry by Prat, exit by Lynch) and that bicycles are only allowed in before 1100.

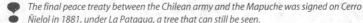

The final peace treaty between the Chilean army and the Mapuche was signed on Cerro Ñielol in 1881, under La Patagua, a tree that can still be seen.

Padre las Casas is a predominantly Mapuche suburb, southeast of the centre, on the other side of the Río Cautín, where you will find the **Casa de la Mujer Mapuche** ① *in the Gymnasium, between Calles Corvalín and Almte Barroso, To9-1694682, Mon-Fri 0930-1300, 1500-1830, bus 8a or 10, colectivo 13a.* Crafts and textiles made by a co-operative of 135 Mapuche weavers are sold here. The items are very good quality, but correspondingly expensive. ►► *For Sleeping, Eating and other listings, see pages 315-319.*

West of Temuco

Chol Chol

To get a flavour of the life of the Mapuche, it is well worth making a trip to this dusty, friendly country town in the heart of Mapuche country. Daily buses, laden with corn, vegetables, charcoal and animals as well as locals make the 30 km journey by paved

Temuco

The Lake District Temuco & around

Sleeping		Eating
Alba Jaramillo 18	Hospedaje Maggi	Artemesa 9
Bayern 1	Alvarado 11	Bahía Perú 1
Casa Blanca 4	Hospedaje Millaray 10	del Sur 7
C'est Bayonne 3	Hostal Argentina 12	La Parrilla de Miguel 2
Continental 5	Nuevo Hotel de	Ñam-Ñam 3
Don Eduardo 6	la Frontera 15	Pizzeria Madonna 4
Espelette 7	Oriente 16	Pront Rapa 5
Flor Acoca 8	Residencial Temuco 17	Quick Biss 6
Hospedaje Aldunate 9	Terraverde 19	Temedors 8
	Tierra del Sur 20	

road from Temuco across rolling countryside, with views of five volcanoes on a clear day. You will see people travelling by ox cart on the tracks nearby, and a few traditional round *rucas*. There are also several cheap bars in the town, as well as a small museum dedicated to Mapuche culture. ▸ *For Sleeping, Eating and other listings, see pages 315-319.*

Towards Puerto Saavedra → *Population: 2,300.*

From Temuco a paved road follows the Río Imperial 35 km west to the market town of **Nueva Imperial**, where cattle auctions are held on Mondays and Tuesdays. From here the road continues to **Carahue**, the site of the Spanish colonial city of Imperial which was destroyed by the Mapuche. It has accommodation, a market, supermarkets and shops. The road continues to **Puerto Saavedra**, which lies behind a sandspit south of the mouth of the Río Imperial. Founded in 1897, the town was destroyed in 1960 by a *maremoto* (tidal wave; see box, page 338). Fortunately the local population were warned of the disaster by the sight of water draining from the bay, and so few people were killed. However, the impact of the *maremoto* on folktales cannot be overestimated. A local man commented to one of the authors of this book, "We thought it was the end of the world, so we spent two months drunk on the hills until the water receded".

After the *maremoto*, the centre of the town moved inland and its former site at **Maule**, 2 km south, became a fishing port. Just beyond Maule is a track to the incredibly narrow sandspit created by the *maremoto*. It stretches several kilometres north to the mouth of the Río Imperial, where there's a beautiful beach and uninterrupted views of the ocean. The third distinct area of Puerto Saavedra is the resort of **Boca Budi**, 4 km south, where's there's an enormous beach.

From Puerto Saavedra a track leads north 2 km to a free ferry crossing over the Río Imperial to **Nehuentue**, on the north bank. From here launches may be chartered up the Río Moncul to the pleasant tour of **Trovolhue**, four hours. There are also beautiful tracks leading north towards the town of **Tirúa**, 70 km away; the route is being widened by mechanical diggers, but is still a long way from being completed and so is best travelled by horse or bicycle. ▸ *For Sleeping, Eating and other listings, see pages 315-319.*

Lago Budi

The only inland saltwater lake in Chile, Lago Budi lies south of Puerto Saavedra and is visited by over 130 species of water bird, including black-necked swans. Although the lake is marked on maps as having an outlet to the sea, this is dried up for most of the year, when there is a continuous track along the expanses of sandy beach from Puerto Saavedra south to Porma and Toltén. This was the old right of way for the Spanish between Concepción and Valdivia before their final defeat of the Mapuche; wild and remote, it passes many isolated Mapuche communities.

On the east shore of Lago Budi, 40 km by road south of Carahue, is **Puerto Domínguez**, a picturesque little town famous for its fishing. On the west shore is **Isla Huapi** (also spelt Guapi), a peninsula with a Mapuche settlement of traditional thatched houses (*rucas*) and fine views of both the lake and the Pacific. This is one of the poorest spots in Chile, but is ideal for camping. It can be reached by ferry (*balsa*) either from about 10 km south of Puerto Saavedra or from Puerto Domínguez (see below).

East of Temuco

Thirty kilometres north of Temuco a paved road branches off the Pan-American Highway and runs east to the Argentine frontier at Pino Hachado, passing through Curacautín and providing access to national parks; there is access to the border from Victoria.

The most famous Chilean film in recent years, 'La Frontera', was filmed in Puerto Saavedra.

A small town situated on the Río Cautín, Curacautín lies 84 km northeast of Temuco and 56 km southeast of Victoria. Deprived by new, stricter deforestation laws of its traditional timber industry (until recently there were several sawmills here), Curacautín is trying to recreate itself as a centre for tourism; it is a useful base for visiting the nearby national parks and hot springs, including the indoor and sadly rundown **Termas de Manzanar** ① *17 km east of Curacautín, open all year, US$5*. On the way, at km 6, the road passes a turn-off to **Laguna Blanca** (25 km north, take fishing gear) and the **Salto del Indio** ① *Km 13, US$1*, a 30-m high waterfall, where there are *cabañas*. Three kilometres beyond Manzanar is the **Salto de la Princesa**, a 50-m waterfall, with camping and *hostería*. ▸▸ *For Sleeping, Eating and other listings, see pages 315-319.*

Parque Nacional Tolhuaca

The beautiful pine-surrounded **Termas de Tolhuaca** ① *open all year, US$2.50-$5*, are 35 km to the northeast of Curacautín by *ripio* road, or 57 km by unpaved road from just north of Victoria; a high-clearance four-wheel drive is essential in winter and autumn. Two kilometres further north is the **Parque Nacional Tolhuaca** ① *open Dec-Apr*, which covers 6,374 ha of the valley of the Río Malleco at altitudes of 850 to 1,830 m and includes the waterfalls of Malleco and Culebra, and two lakes, Laguna Malleco and Laguna Verde. There's superb scenery and good views of the volcanoes from Cerro Amarillo. Park administration is near Laguna Malleco and there is a campsite nearby. Unfortunately, much of the park, together with the neighbouring **Reserva Nacional Malleco**, was damaged by forest fires in 2002, and will take several decades fully to recover.

Reserva Nacional Malalcahuello-Nalcas

Situated northeast of Curacautín, this 31,305 ha park lies on the slopes of the **Lonquimay Volcano** (2,865 m), and is much less crowded than the nearby Parque Nacional Conguillio. Useful information about the park is available from the **CONAF** office on the main road in Malalcahuello (east of Curacautín) and from **La Suizandina** (see Sleeping below), which is also a good base for treks and for the ascent of the volcano. Several marked trails (varying from one hour to two days) leave from the CONAF office. From Malalcahuello it is a one-day hike to the Sierra Nevada (see below), or a two-day hike to Conguillio national park; less experienced climbers should hire a guide.

Los Arenales ski resort ① *Season Jun-Sep, winter access from Lonquimay town only, ski pass US$17*, is at Las Raices Pass on the road from Malalcahuello to Lonquimay town. It is a pleasant, small resort with a nice restaurant and four lifts that go up to 2,500 m with great views. In winter the pass is usually snowed out, and the road from Malalcahuello to Lonquimay town is diverted via the **Túnel Las Raices** ① *toll US$1.50*. This former railway tunnel was, until recently, the longest in South America at 4.8 km. There is talk of repairing the tunnel, but for the moment it is in poor condition. ▸▸ *For Sleeping, Eating and other listings, see pages 315-319.*

Climbing Lonquimay Access is either from Malalcahuello, 15 km south, or from from the ski resort from where it is a one-hour walk to the municipal *refugio* at the base of the mountain. Walk towards the ski lift and from there head to the spur on the left. Allow four hours for the ascent, one hour for the descent. Crampons and ice-axe are necessary in winter, but in summer it is a relatively simple climb.

Parque Nacional Conguillio → *Colour map 4, A3.*

Covering 60,833 ha, the park, situated 80 km east of Temuco, is one of the most popular in Chile though it is deserted outside January and February and at weekends. In the centre is the **Llaima Volcano** (3,125 m), which is still active and can be climbed. There are two

 Lonquimay Volcano began erupting on Christmas Day 1988. The resulting crater is known as Navidad.

craters; the western crater was blown out in 1994 and began erupting again in March 1996. There are two large lakes, Laguna Verde and Lago Conguillio, and two smaller ones, Laguna Arco Iris and Laguna Captrén. North of Lago Conguillio rise the snow-covered peaks of extinct volcano **Sierra Nevada**, which reaches 2,554 m.

Much of the park is covered in forests of southern beech but the park is also the best place in Chile to see native **araucaria forest**, which used to cover extensive areas of land in this part of the country (see box, page 315). Mature araucaria forest can be found around Lago Conguillio and on the slopes of Llaima. Other trees include cypresses and *canelo* (winter's bark). Among the park's wildlife are condors, black woodpeckers, the marsupial *monito del monte*, pumas, foxes, *pudú* and many waterfowl.

There are three **entrances** to the park: the northern entrance is reached by *ripio* road from Curacautín, 28 km north; the southern entrance at Truful-Truful is reached by a *ripio* road from Melipeuco, 13 km southwest, while the western entrance is reached by *ripio* road from Cherquenco (high-clearance vehicle essential). Close by is the **Llaima ski resort** ① *To45-211314, US$10 Mon-Fri, $15 Sat, Sun*, with two ski lifts, a café, restaurant, bar, *refugio* and equipment rental. Each entrance has an information centre. There is also a **visitors' centre** at the park administration by Lago Conguillio ① *open Dec-Mar, park entry US$5*. CONAF runs free slide lectures and short guided walks during the summer, covering flora and fauna, Volcán Llaima and other subjects.

Trails within the park range from 1 km to 22 km in length. Details are available from the park administration or from CONAF in Temuco. One of the best trails is a path round the east side of Lago Conguillio and north towards the Sierra Nevada (allow a full day for the round trip). The first 10 km are reasonably easy, with two or three *miradores* offering spectacular views. After this the going gets much more difficult for the final 5-km climb. From the western entrance it is a two- to three-day hike around Volcán Llaima to Lago Conguillio – a dusty route, but with beautiful views of Laguna Quepe – then on to the Laguna Captrén *guardería*. ⟩⟩ *For Sleeping, Eating and other listings, see pages 315-319.*

Parque Nacional Conguillio

To Curacautín

Termas del Río Blanco

Sierra Nevada

Rio Captrén

Laguna Captrén

Lago Conguillo

Laguna Quepe

Laguna Arco Iris

Laguna Verde

Ski Club Refugio

Volcán Llaima (3,050m)

Rio Calbuco

Parque Nacional Conguillio

Rio Rilpe

Saltos de Truful-Truful

Rio Truful-Truful

To Vicún

To Cunco

Melipeuco

To Argentina via Paso Icalma

N

0 km 5
0 miles 5

□ Park administration posts
⌂ Park warden posts

⦂ The monkey puzzle tree

The Araucaria Araucana, known in Chile as the *araucaria* or *pehuén* and elsewhere called variously the Chilean pine, the umbrella tree, the parasol tree and the monkey puzzle tree, is the Chilean national tree and has flourished in this area for 200 million years. Very slow growing, it can grow up to 40-m high; and live for 1,200 years. The characteristic cones can weigh up to 1 kg so take care sitting underneath! Though its natural habitat is on both sides of the Andes between 37° and 39° south, it is much more widespread in Chile than in Argentina.

The *araucaria* was revered by the Mapuche, who ate both its cones and its sharp leathery leaves. Some isolated trees are still seen as sacred by the Mapuche who leave offerings to the tree's spirit.

Climbing Llaima Climb south from **Guardería Captrén**, avoiding the crevassed area to the left of the ridge and keeping to the right of the red scree just below the ridge. From the ridge it is a straight climb to the summit. Beware of sulphur fumes at the top. Allow five hours to ascend, two hours to descend. Crampons and ice-axe are essential except in summer; less experienced climbers should also hire a guide. Further information on the climb is available from **Guardería Captrén**.

Border with Argentina

The **Paso Pino Hachado** (1,884 m) can be reached either by a paved road 65 km southeast from Lonquimay or by unpaved road 103 km east from Melipeuco. On the Argentine side this road continues to Zapala; some buses from Temuco to Zapala and Neuquén use this crossing. **Immigration and customs** at Liucura ① *22 km west of the frontier, Dec-Mar 0800-2000; Apr-Nov 0800-1800*, involves very thorough searches; two- to three-hour delays have been reported.

An alternative route is via **Paso de Icalma** (1,298 m) reached by *ripio* road, 53 km east of Melipeuco, south of Parque Nacional Conguillio, and continuing on the Argentine side to Zapala. This route is often impassable in winter and permission to cross must be obtained in advance from the **Policía Internacional** in Temuco (Prat 19, T045-293890). **Chilean immigration** ① *open Dec-Mar 0800-2100; Apr-Nov 0800-1900*.

◐ Sleeping

Temuco *p310, map p311*
Many cheaper *residenciales* and pensiones can be found in the market area.
L Terraverde, *Prat 0220, T045-239999, www.panamericanahoteles.cl* This 5-star is the best in town.
AL Nuevo Hotel de la Frontera, *Bulnes 726, T045-200400, www.hotelfrontera.cl* With breakfast, excellent.
A Hotel Don Eduardo, *Bello 755, T045-214133, deduardo@ctcinternet.cl* Parking, suites with kitchen, recommended.
A-B Bayern, *Prat 146, T045-276000, www.interpatagonia.com/hotelbayern* 3-star. Small rooms, clean, helpful.

B C'est Bayonne, *Vicuña MacKenna 361, T045-234119, F045-214915, netchile@entelchile.net* With breakfast, small, modern, German and Italian spoken.
B Luanco, *Aldunate 821, T045-213749, luanco@surnet.cl* Apartments with kitchenette.
B Tierra del Sur, *Bulnes 1196, T/F045-232439.* Pool and sauna.
B Continental, *Varas 708, T045-238973, continental@ifrance.com* Popular with business travellers, old-fashioned building, old beds, excellent restaurant, the bar is popular with locals in the evening, cheaper rooms available without bath.
C Espelette, *Claro Solar 492, T/F045-234805.* Helpful, quiet.
E *Blanco Encalada 1078, T045-234447.* Price per person. Use of kitchen, friendly.

E *Bulnes 1006 y O'Higgins*. Price per person. Good double rooms, hot water, above drugstore, ask for house key otherwise access limited to shop hours.

E **Hostal Argentina**, *Aldunate 864*. Price per person. With breakfast, hot water, clean.

E **Rupangue**, *Barros Arana 182*. Price per person. Hot shower, clean, helpful.

F **Casa Blanca**, *Montt 1306 y Zenteno, T045-277799, www.hostalcasablanca.cl*. Price per person. With breakfast, friendly, slightly run down, but good value for rooms with bath.

F **Hosp Aldunate**, *Aldunate 187, T045-213548*. Price per person. Friendly, cooking facilities, also cheaper dormitory accommodation.

F **Hospedaje 525**, *Zenteno 525, T045-233982*. Price per person. Without breakfast, with bath, large rooms, clean, poor beds but good value. TV lounge.

F **Oriente**, *M Rodríguez 1146, T045-233232, h-oriente@hispavista.com* Price per person. Clean, recommended.

F **Hosp Maggi Alvarado**, *Recreo 209, off Av Alemania, T045-263215*. Price per person. Small rooms, but very clean, friendly, helpful.

G **Hosp Millaray**, *Claro Solar 471. T045-645720*. Price per person. Simple, basic. Other private houses on this street.

G **Res Temuco**, *Zenteno 486, T045-211269*. Price per person. Friendly, clean, hot water.

Puerto Saavedra *p312*

C **Hotel Boca Budi**, *Boca Budi, T045-352990/09-4532107*. With bath and breakfast. Sea views, heating, room service. Tours offered. Mid-price restaurant.

F-G **Lago Los Cisnes**, *Boca Budi, T045-251891*. Cheap option with restaurant.

G **Sra Rita Sandoval Muñoz** *Las Dunas 01511*. Price per person. Lovely, knowledgeable host.

Lago Budi *p312*

F **Hostería Rucaleufú**, *Alessandri 22, Puerto Domínguez*. Price per person. With good meals, clean, lake views. Highly recommended.

The only other accommodation is the **Puaucho** campsite on Isla Huapi.

Curacautín and around *p313*

L-A **Termas de Manzanar**, *Termas de Manzanar, 17 km from Curacautín, T045-881200, termasmanzanar@indecom.cl* Simple rooms with bath. Overpriced.

C **Hostería La Rotunda del Cautín**, *Termas de Manzanar, 17 km from Curacautín, T045-1971478*. Rooms and good mid-range restaurant, friendly.

C **Plaza**, *Yungay 157, main plaza, T045-881256*. Overpriced. Restaurant is good but pricey.

C-E **Hostería Abarzúa**, *Termas de Manzanar, 17 km from Curacautín, T045-870011*. Simple, friendly, cheaper without bath.

D-F, **Anden Rose**, *5km west of Manzanar (km68), on the banks of the river Cautín, T09-8691700*. Price per person. With breakfast, restaurant, bike, horse, kayak rental, tours arranged, camping, German owners.

E **Hostal Las Espigas**, *Miraflores 315, T045-881138, rivaseugenia@hotmail.com* Price per person. Good rooms with bath, kitchen, breakfast, dinner available on request.

F **Hostería Abarzúa**, *T045-870011*. Price per person. Full board, and a campsite.

F **Res Rojas**, *Tarapacá 249*. Price per person. Without bath, good meals. Recommended.

F **Turismo**, *Tarapacá 140, T045-881116*. Price per person. Clean, good food, comfortable, best value.

Parque Nacional Tolhuaca *p313*

AL **Termas de Tolhuaca**, *Termas de Tolhuaca, T045-881164, www.termasdetolhuaca.cl* With full board, includes use of baths and horseriding, very good.

G **Res Roja**, *Termas de Tolhuaca*. Price per person. Hot water, food, camping near the river, good.

RN Malalcahuello-Nalcas *p313*

B-F **La Suizandina**, *Km 28, Curacautín-Lonquimay road (3 km from Malalcahuello), T045-1973735/T09-8849541, www.suizandina.com* Double rooms, hostel accommodation (price per person) and camping. Laundry, homebaked bread, English and German spoken, travellers cheques accepted, good meals. Hiking, horseriding, travel and trekking information. Recommended. Written enquiries to La Suizanda, Casilla 44, Curacautín.

C **Los Arenales**, *at the ski centre, T045-881726*. Price per person, with breakfast, full board also available, open in season.

D-F **Res Los Sauces**, *in Malalcahuello village, on the edge of the park, T09-8837880*. Price per person full board, or cheaper for use of kitchen, hot water. Sra Naomi Saavedra arranges lifts to destinations within the reserve.

F Hostal Lonquimay, *Pinto 500, Lonquimay, T045-891324. Price per person.*

G Hospedaje Navidad, *Caupolicán 915, Lonquimay, T045-891111. Price per person. With restaurant.*

Parque Nacional Conguillio *p313, map p314*

AL-A Camping Los Ñirres, *southern shore of Lago Conguillio, near the visitors' centre, T045-298213.* Campsite with *cabañas* for 4-6 people.

AL-A La Baita, *3 km south of Laguna Verde, T045-416410/09-7332442, www.labaitaconguillio.cl* *Cabañas* with electricity, hot water, kitchen and wood stove. Charming, lots of information, Italian/Chilean owned, recommended. On-line bookings.

D Hostería Hue-Telén, *Aguirre Cerda 1, Casilla 40, Melipeuco, T045-581005.* Good restaurant, also *cabañas* for upto 4 people.

G Hospedaje Icalma, *Aguirre 729, Melipeuco.* Price per person. Spacious, recommended.

Camping

There are several campsites in the park, one on the west side of Laguna Captrén and 5 dotted around Lago Conguillio. All are administered by **CONAF**, *T045-298213* for information and reservations. There is a free municipal campsite in Melipeuco and **Camping Los Pioneros**, *1 km from Melipeuco.* On road to the park, hot water.

❼ Eating

For places to eat in Puerto Saavedra, Curacautín and the national parks, see Sleeping, above.

Temuco *p310, map p311*

Those on a very strict budget should make for the **Mercado Municipal**, *Aldunate y Portales*, where there are several restaurants and fierce touting for business, or the rural bus terminal, where countless restaurants serve very cheap set meals at lunch. *Humitas* are on sale in the street in summer/autumn.

$$ Caletas Restaurante, *Mercado Municipal, Aldunate y Portales.* Fish and seafood.

$$ La Cumbre del Cerro Ñielol, *Cerro Ñielol.* Food and dancing on top of the hill, not always open.

$$ La Parrilla de Miguel, *Montt 1095.* Good for meat and wine .

$$ Pizzeria Madonna, *Montt 670.* Good atmosphere, good pizzas, reasonably priced.

$$ Bahía Peru, *Alemania y Recreo, near the Mall Mirage, about 10 blocks west of centre.* One of several good mid-priced restaurants on Av Alemania (take bus 1), reasonable Peruvian food, good pisco sours.

$$ Las Tranqueras, *Alemania Alemania 0888.* Meat specialists, great grills, but vegetarian options also available.

$ Artemesa, *Aldunate 620, 8th floor.* Vegetarian restaurant with views.

$ Ñam-Ñam, *Portales 802.* Good sandwiches and snacks.

$ Pront Rapa, *Aldunate 421.* For take-away lunches and snacks, recommended.

$ Restaurant del sur, *Portales 921.* Cheap, open 24hrs.

$ Restaurante Temedors, *San Martín 827.* Good-value lunch.

Cafés

Café Marriet, *Prat 451, Local 21.* Excellent coffee.

Cafetería Ripley, *Prat y Varas.* Real coffee.

Dino's, *Bulnes 360.* Good coffee.

Il Gelato, *Bulnes 420.* Delicious ice cream.

❶ Bars and clubs

Temuco *p310, map p311*

Banana bliss, *Montt 1031.* Bar and disco.

El Túnel, *Caupolicán y M Blanco.* Restaurant with dancing.

HBH Bar, *Montt 847.* European-style lager.

Mr Jones, *Bello 844.* Pub-café-disco.

Sol y Luna, *10 km south on road to Pucón.* Late-night disco.

❻ Entertainment

Temuco *p310, map p311*

There is a cinema on the plaza. It is also worth checking out the **Instituto Chileno-Frances**, *Varas 736*, and the **Instituto Chileno-Norte Americano**, *Grl MacKenna 555*, for films and events.

O Shopping

Buy supplies in Temuco, Curacautín or Melipeuco, where they are much cheaper than in the shop in the Parque Nacional Conguillio.

Temuco *p310, map p311*
Crafts
Mapuche crafts and textiles are sold inside and around the **Mercado Municipal**, *Aldunate y Portales*, and also in the **Casa de la Mujer Mapuche** (see Sights above).

Food
Frutería Las Vegas, *Matta 274*. Dried fruit (useful for climbing/trekking).
Las Brisas, *Rodríguez 1100 block*. Supermarket.
Santa Isabel, *Bulnes 279*. Supermarket.
Super, *Rodríguez 1400 block*. Supermarket.
Temuco fería, *Lautaro y Aníbal Pinto*. This is one of the most fascinating markets in Chile, where people from the surrounding countryside come to sell their wares. You will find excellent cheap fruit and vegetables, local spices like *merquén* (made from smoked chillies), fish, grains, cheese and honey; there are many inexpensive bars and restaurants nearby.

▲ Activities and tours

Temuco *p310, map p311*
Most companies in Temuco offer tours to **Parque Nacional Conguillo**, 1 day, US$34; to Puerto Saavedra and Villarrica volcano, but unless you are in a hurry it is better and cheaper to book a tour closer to the destination.
T&S Tour Operador, *Claro Solar 950, Of 404, T045-275445, tts@ctcreuna.cl*
Turismo Gira, *Montt 1027, of 204, T045-406494*.
Turismo Ñielol, *Claro Solar 633, T/F045-239497*.
Turismo Sur de América, *P De Valdivia 0413, T045-317777, myriamhernandez@latinmail.com*

Curacautín and around *p313*
Turismo Christopher, *Yungay 260, T045-882471*.
Turismo Tolhuaca, *Calama 240*.

Temuco *p310, map p311*
Air
LanChile and Sky fly to **Manquehue Airport** from **Santiago**, 1¼ hrs, **Concepción**, 40 mins, **Osorno**, 40 mins, and **Puerto Montt**, 45 mins.

Bus
Local Services to neighbouring towns leave from **Terminal Rural**, *Pinto y Balmaceda* or from bus company offices nearby: **Erbuc**, *Miraflores y Bulnes*; **JAC**, NarBus and Igi Llaima, *Balmaceda y Aldunate*; Tur Bus, *Lagos 549*.
To **Panguipulli**, Power and Pangui Sur, 3 hrs, US$3. Pangui Sur also has services to **Loncoche**, US$1.50, **Los Lagos**, US$2.50, and **Mehuín**, summer only. To **Curacautín** via Lautaro, Erbuc, 4 daily, 2½ hrs, US$2, continuing to **Lonquimay**, 3½hrs, US$3. Narbus has hourly services daily to **Nueva Imperial**, **Carahue** and **Puerto Saavedra**. JAC runs buses to **Villarrica** and **Pucón**, many daily 0705-2045, 1½ hrs, US$3, and to **Coñaripe**, 3 hrs, and **Lican Ray**, 2 hrs. Erbuc and Thiele run buses to **Contulmo**, 2 hrs, US$4, **Cañete**, US$4 and **Lebú**. To **Laguna Captren**, Erbuc, Mon and Fri 1645, 4 hrs, US$3. To **Chol Chol**, Huincabus, 4 daily 1100-1800, 1 hr, US$1.
Long distance The new long-distance terminal is north of city at *Pérez Rosales y Caupolicán*; to get there, take buses 2 or 10 from the centre. To **Santiago** several companies, 9hrs, most overnight, US$8 (*salón cama* US$22); to **Castro**, Cruz del Sur, 3 a day; to **Puerto Montt**, Cruz del Sur, 10 a day, 5½ hrs, US$6; to **Valdivia** 2½hrs, US$3; to **Osorno** 4hrs, US$4; to **Concepción**, Bío Bío, US$5, 4½ hrs; to **Arica**, US$45 (*cama* US$60); to **Antofagasta**, US$45; to **Chillán**, 4 hrs, US$5.
International To **Neuquén** via Pucón, Junín de los Andes and San Martín de los Andes, **Buses San Martín**, 3 a week, US$15. To **Neuquén** via Curacautín, Lonquimay and the Paso Pino Hachado, **Igi Llaima**, Buses Caraza and Buses El Valle, daily between them, US$20; Buses Caraza have connecting services to **Buenos Aires**, **Bahia Blanca** and **Mar del Plata**, US$40. To **Bariloche** via Osorno, Tas Choapa, daily, US$18.

Train

The **station** is at *Barros Arana y Lautaro Navarro, T045-233416*. There is also an additional ticket office at *Bulnes 582, T045-233522*, open Mon-Fri 0900-1300, 1430-1800, Sun 0900-1300. To **Santiago**, overnight service, daily 2030, 12 hrs, *turista* US$13, *salón* US$16, *lower bunk* US$31, *upper bunk* US$25, *double compartment* US$70. The early 1930s dining car (mid-range meals) and the 1929 sleeping car were both built in Germany; the latter features velvet upholstery and hot showers. Note that there are no trains south of Temuco.

Towards Puerto Saavedra *p312*

To **Temuco** (Terminal Rural), Narbus, hourly, 3 hrs, US$1.50.

Lago Budi *p312*

There are **buses** to **Puerto Domínguez** from Temuco, 3 hrs. The *Carlos Schalchli* **ferry** leaves Puerto Domínguez for **Isla Huapi**, Mon and Wed 0900 and 1700, returning 0930 and 1730, free, 30 mins.

Curacautín and around *p313*

The **bus** terminal is on the main street, by the plaza. **Tur Bus** and **Inter Sur** have daily direct services to **Santiago**. **Erbuc** services from Temuco and Los Angeles continue on to **Malalcahuello** and **Lonquimay**, see below.

Parque Nacional Tolhuaca *p313*

There are **bus** services from Victoria to **San Gregorio** (19 km from park entrance) Mon, Wed, Fri 1715; return same day 0645.

RN Malalcahuello-Nalcas *p313*

Erbuc runs **bus** services from Temuco via Lautaro and Curacautín, 4 daily, to **Malalcahuello**, 3 hrs, US$2, and **Lonquimay** town, 3 ½ hrs (or 4hrs via Victoria), US$3.

Parque Nacional Conguillio *p313, map p314*

There are daily buses from Temuco to **Cherquenco**, but no onward public transport into the park. **Taxi** from Curacautín to the **northern entrance**, US$21 one way. Transport to the **southern entrance** can be arranged

from Melipeuco (ask in grocery stores and *hospedajes*), US$20 one way. For touring, hire a 4-WD vehicle in Temuco or join an agency tour, see Activities and tours, above.

❶ Directory

Temuco *p310, map p311*

Airline offices LanChile, *Bulnes 687, on Plaza, T045-272138*; Sky Airline, *T600-600 2828* for information; Varig, *Bello 870, T045-213120*. **Banks and currency exchange** ATMs at several banks on or around Plaza A Pinto also at the new JAC bus terminal. Also try the following casas de cambio: **Christopher**, *Prat 696, Oficina 419*; **Comex**, *Prat 471* ; **Inter-Santiago**, *Bulnes 443, Local 2* ; **Turcamb**, *Claro Solar 733*; also at Bulnes 667, Local 202, and at Prat 427. There are many *cambios* around the Plaza; all deal in dollars and Argentine pesos. **Bicycle repairs** Parts at Oxford, *Andrés Bello 1040, T045-211869*; repairs at *Bulnes 228, Lautaro 1370, Portales 688*. Also many on Balmaceda, nos. 1266, 1294 and 1448. **Car hire** Automóvil Club de Chile, *Varas 687, T045-248903* and at airport; Budget, Lynch 471, T045-214911; Christopher Car, Varas 522, T/F045-215988; Dollar, *at airport, T045-336512*; Euro, *MacKenna 426, T045-210311*, helpful, good value; Full Famas, *at airport and in centre T045-215420*, recommended; Hertz, *Las Heras 999, T045-235385*, US$45 a day. Several others. **Consulates** Netherlands, *España 494*, honorary consul, Germán Nicklas, is friendly and helpful. **Internet** *Gral. MacKenna 445*; several others, generally US$0.75 per hr. **Laundry** Alba, *Zeneto 480*, opposite the church, and at *Aldunate 324* and *Aldunate 842*; Marva, *M Montt 415 and 1099*, Mon-Sat 0900-2030. **Motorbike mechanic** Terremoto, *Claro Solar 358, T045-312828*. **Post office** *Portales 839*. **Telephone** CTC, *A Prat just off Claro Solar and plaza*, open Mon-Sat 0800-2400, Sun and holidays 1030-2400; Entel, *Bulnes 303*. daily 0830-2200; also call centres at *Lautaro 1311* and *Montt 631*.

For an explanation of sleeping and eating price codes used in this guide, see inside the front cover. Other relevant information is found in Essentials, see pages 51-58.

Lago Villarrica and around

Wooded Lago Villarrica, 21 km long and about 7 km wide, is one of the most beautiful lakes in the region, with the active and snow-capped Villarrica volcano (2,840 m) to the southeast. Visitors should note, though, that its resorts are among the priciest in Chile (although those with the money will find them well worth the expense).

Villarrica → *Phone code: 045. Colour map 4, B2. Population: 36,000.*

Pleasantly set at the extreme southwest corner of the lake, Villarrica can be reached by a paved road southeast from Freire, 24 km south of Temuco on the Pan-American Highway, or from Loncoche, 54 km south of Freire, also paved. Less significant as a tourist resort than nearby Pucón, it is also cheaper. Founded in 1552, the town was besieged by the Mapuche in the uprising of 1599: after three years the surviving Spanish settlers, 11 men and 13 women, surrendered. The town was refounded in 1882.

There is a small museum, the **Museo Histórico** ① *Pedro de Valdivia 1050 y Zegers, Mon-Sat 0900-1730, 1800-2200, Sun 1800-2200, reduced hrs in winter, US$0.25,* containing a collection of Mapuche artefacts. Next to it is the **Muestra Cultural Mapuche**, featuring a Mapuche *ruca* and stalls selling good quality handicrafts in summer. The **tourist office** ① *Valdivia 1070, T045-411162, open daily in summer* has information and maps. There are good views of the volcano from the *costanera*; for a different perspective over the lake, go south along Aviador Acevedo and then Poniente Ríos towards the **Hostería La Colina**.► *For Sleeping, Eating and other listings, see pages 324-331.*

Pucón → *Phone code: 045. Colour map 4, B2. Population: 13,000.*

On the southeastern corner of the lake, 26 km east of Villarrica, Pucón is one of the most popular destinations in the Lake District, famous above all as a centre for visiting the Villarrica volcano (2,840 m), which lies to the south. Built across the neck of a peninsula, it has two black sand beaches, which are popular for swimming and watersports. Whitewater rafting is also offered on the nearby rivers and excursions can be made into the Parque Nacional Huerquehue, which lies east of the town.

Ins and outs

Getting there Pucón is served by one or two daily buses from Puerto Montt and several daily from Santiago. There are regular services from Temuco and Villarrica. The airport 2 km east of Pucón on the Caburga road has several flights a week to/from Santiago. **Getting around** Pucón is small enough to walk around on foot. Taxis are useful for out-of-town trips. ► *For further details, see Transport page 331.* **Tourist information** Do not confuse the **Municipal Tourist Office** ① *Municipalidad, O'Higgins 483*, which provides information and sells fishing licences, with the Chamber of Tourism at the entrance to Pucón from Villarrica. The town also has a **CONAF** office ① *O'Higgins 669*.

Sights and excursions

The Pucón of today is very different from the town of 30 years ago, when it was a small, pleasant, quiet village with some seasonal Chilean tourism, but no foreign backpackers. It is now a thriving tourist centre, full of Chileans in summer and gringos in the autumn. Neon signs are forbidden and roadsigns and telephone kiosks are made of wood, but the streets are full of bars, restaurants and *artesanía*. The commercial centre lies between **Avenida O'Higgins**, the main thoroughfare, and the **Gran Hotel Pucón**. Private land (ask for permission at the entrance) leads west from the centre of town to **La Peninsula**, where there are fine views of the lake and volcano, as well as pony rides and golf. There is also a pleasant walk, along the **Costanera Otto Gudenschwager**, starting at the northern end of Calle Ansorena and following the lakeside north.

Boat trips ① *daily 1500 and 1900, summer only, 2 hrs, US$4*, on the lake leave from the landing stage at La Poza at the western end of O'Higgins. Walk a couple of kilometres north along the beach from here to the mouth of the Río Pucón for views of volcanoes. Or take a boat ① *summer only, US$12*, to the mouth of the river from near the Gran Hotel.

Villarrica

Sleeping 🛏
Bungalowlandia **1**
Cabañas Traitraico **2**
Camping du Lac **3**
Camping Los Castaños **4**
Chito Fuentes **7**
El Ciervo **5**
Hospedaje Dalila
 Balboa **8**
Hostería Bilbao **9**
Hostería de la Colina **10**

Hostería Las Rosas del
 Lago **11**
Hotel-Yachting Kiel **12**
La Torre Suiza **13**
Rayhuen **14**
Residencia San
 Francisco **15**
Residencia Victoria **16**
Señora Nelly **17**
Vicente Reyes 854 **18**
Villa Linda **19**

Villarrica **20**

Eating 🍴
El Rey de Mariscos **1**
El Tabor **2**
El Viejo Bucanero **3**
Rapa Nui **4**
Travellers **5**
Treffpunkt **6**

To cross the Río Pucón: head east out of Pucón along the main road, then turn north on an unmade road leading to a new bridge. There are pleasant walks from here along the north shore of the lake to the Mapuche settlement of **Quelhue** and the village of **Trarilelfú**, or northeast towards **Caburga** (the round trip makes a perfect day's outing by mountain bike.) You can also strike up into the hills through farms and agricultural land, with views of three volcanoes and the lake.

From the road to the Villarrica volcano, a *ripio* road branches off for 5 km to some privately managed *cuevas volcanicas* (**volcanic caves**) ① *US$10*, surrounded by a small attractive park with tunnels and a museum, as well as paths through the forest. Entry to the site is expensive, but it's recommended as a bad-weather option. ▸▸ *For Sleeping, Eating and other listings, see pages 324-331.*

East of Lago Villarrica

Within easy reach of Villarrica and Pucón are two more lakes, two national parks and several hot springs. Busy with Chilean tourists in summer, these are among the most dramatic spots in the Lake District, and well worth a visit for those in the area.

Parque Nacional Villarrica: Volcán Villarrica → *Colour map 4, B2.*

This park, which covers 61,000 ha, stretches from Pucón to the Argentine border near Puesco. There are three sectors: Villarrica volcano sector, Quetrupillán volcano sector (see page 324) and the Puesco sector, which includes the slopes of the Lanín volcano on the Argentine frontier. Each sector has its own entrance and ranger station.

The **Villarrica volcano**, 2,840 m high and still active, lies 8 km south of Pucón. Due to accidents, access to this sector ① *US$3.50*, is restricted only to groups with a guide – several agencies offer excursions (see Activities and tours, page 329) – and to individuals who can show proof of membership of a mountaineering club in their own country. Entry is refused if the weather is poor. Good boots, crampons and ice picks are essential; these can be rented for US$4 per day from tour operators. You should also take sunglasses, sun block, plenty of water and chocolate or some other snack; equipment is checked at the park entrance.

It is a three- to four-hour trek to the summit, but you can skip the first 400 m by taking the ski lift (US$4). At the summit look down into the crater at the bubbling molten lava below, but beware of the sulphur fumes; the better tour agencies provide gas masks, otherwise take a cloth mask moistened with lemon juice. On exceptionally clear days you will be able to see six other volcanoes. Conditions permitting, groups may carry ski and snowboard equipment for the descent; otherwise just slide down.

Between July and November it is possible to ski at the **Pucón resort**, which is situated on the eastern slopes of the volcano and reached by a badly maintained track (see page 330). ▸▸ *For Sleeping, Eating and other listings, see pages 324-331.*

Lagos Caburga and Colico

Lago Caburga (spelt locally Caburgua) is a very pretty lake in a wild setting 25 km northeast of Pucón. The lake became famous as the setting for *Oro Verde*, one of Chile's most popular soap operas in recent years. It is unusual for its beautiful white sand beach (other beaches in the area have black volcanic sand), and is supposedly the warmest lake in the Lake District. The western and much of the eastern shores are inaccessible to vehicles, but the village of **Caburga**, at the southern end of the lake, is reached by a turning off the main road to Argentina, 8 km east of Pucón. If walking or cycling, there is a very pleasant alternative route: turn left 3 km east of Pucón, cross the Puente Quelhue, then turn right and follow the track for 18 km through beautiful scenery. Just off the road from Pucón, Km 15, are the **Ojos de Caburga** ① *US$0.50*, beautiful pools fed from

❖ *Rowing boats for the lake may be hired in Caburga for US$3 per hour.*

underground, which are particularly attractive after rainfall. The northern tip of the lake can be reached by a road from Cunco, which runs east along the northern shore of **Lago Colico**. This is one of the less accessible lakes, and lies north of Lago Villarrica in a remote setting. ▸▸ *For Sleeping, Eating and other listings, see pages 324-331.*

Parque Nacional Huerquehue → *Colour map 4, B3.*

ⓘ *open officially Jan-Mar, but you can get in at other times, US$3, parking 1½ km along the track, US$1.*

Located a short distance east of Lago Caburga, Parque Nacional Huerquehue covers 12,500 ha at altitudes rising to 1952 m at the **Picos del Caburga**. It also encompasses about 20 lakes, some of them very small, and many araucaria trees. The entrance and administration is on the western edge, near **Lago Tinguilco**, the largest lake in the park. To get there take the Caburgua road from Pucón; 3km before Caburgua turn right along a ripio road to Paillaco, from which another road leads 7 km to the park administration. From the entrance there is a well-signed track north up a steep hill to **Lago Chico**, where the track divides left to **Lago Verde** and right to **Lago Toro**. The lakes are surrounded by trees and are very beautiful. The tracks rejoin at **Lago Huerquehue**, where a further 20 km of trails begin. None of the routes is particularly taxing, making the park a good warm-up for the volcán Villarrica hike. An adequate map is available at entrance and the warden is very helpful. People in the park rent horses and boats. Take your own food.

Termas de Quimey-Co, de Huife and los Pozones

South of Huerquehue national park, and reached via a turning off the Pucón-Caburga road, are three sets of thermal baths. The most expensive and ostentatious are the **Termas de Huife**ⓘ *Km 33, US$9,* where entry includes the use of one modern, pleasant pool. Closer to Pucón and rather more low-key are the **Termas de Quimey-Co**ⓘ *Km 29, US$5,* while further on are the **Termas los Pozones** ⓘ *Km 35, US$5 per day, US$7 at night,* which have six natural rock pools but little infrastructure and are very popular with travellers. ▸▸ *For Sleeping, Eating and other listings, see pages 324-331.*

Reserva Forestal Cañi

Situated south of Parque Nacional Huerquehue and covering 500 ha, this is a private nature reserve owned by the **Fundación Lahuén** ⓘ *Urrutia 477, Pucón, T045-441660,*

Lagos Villarrica, Caburga & Colico

lahuen@interaccess.cl, and only accessible on a guided tour – it is definitely worth a visit (see page 330). The reserve contains 17 small lakes and is covered by ancient native forests of coigue and lenga; it also has some of the oldest araucaria trees in Chile. From its highest peak, **El Mirador**, (1,550 m) there are panoramic views over neighbouring parts of Argentina and Chile, including four volcanoes: Lanín, Villarrica, Quetrupillán and Llaima. As the reserve is above the snowline, tours are normally restricted to summer, though visits in winter are sometimes possible.

Towards Argentina

From Pucón a road runs southeast along the southern bank of the valley of the Río Traniura to **Curarrehue** and the Argentine border, providing access en route to thermal springs and a number of hikeable waterfalls (*saltos*).

At Km 18, a *ripio* road heads south 10 km to the **Termas de Palguín** ① *US$6*, and the spectacular **Saltos del Puma** and **del León** ① *800 m from the Termas, also accessible at Km 27 on the Pucón-Curarrehue road, US$1.50 for both*. From the springs a rough dirt road runs south to Coñaripe, with access to the Volcán Quetrupillán section of the **Parque Nacional Villarrica**. If you're driving, a high-clearance vehicle is necessary to reach the national park; but travelling on horseback is best. The treks in this sector are not physically demanding. Palguín is also the starting point for a four- to five-day hike to Puesco (see below), with vistas over the Villarrica and Lanín volcanoes.

Back on the Curarrehue road, at Km 23, a turning leads north to the indoor and outdoor pools at **Termas de San Luis** ① *US$9*, from where it is 30 minutes' walk to **Lago del León**. At Km 24, the **Salto Palguín** can be seen (but not reached), and beyond that is the impressive **Salto China** ① *Km 26, US$1*, where there's a restaurant and camping. At Km 35 another turning leads north for 15 km to the **Termas de Pangui** ① *US$10*, where there are three pools beautifully situated in the mountains.

Beyond the small town of Curarrehue, 36 km east of Pucón, the road deteriorates as it turns south to Chilean **immigration and customs** at Puesco ① *16 km from the border, open Dec-March 0800-2100; Apr-Nov 0800-1900*. The road then climbs via **Lago Quellelhue**, to reach the border at **Paso Mamuil Malal** (Paso Tromen). On the Argentine side it runs south to Junín de los Andes, San Martín de los Andes and Bariloche.

To the south of the pass rises the graceful cone of **Volcán Lanín** (3,747 m), one of the world's most beautiful mountains. Although extinct, Lanín is geologically one of the youngest volcanoes in the Andes. It is climbed from the Argentine side. A four-hour hike from Argentine customs (3 km from the border) leads to a *refugio* at 2,400 m. The climb from here to the summit is not difficult but crampons and ice axe are needed.

● Sleeping

Villarrica *p320, map p321*

Price codes are based on high season rates (Jan- Feb); off-season prices are 30-40% lower.
LL **Villarrica Park Lake**, *km 13 on road to Pucón*, *T045-450000, www.villarrica.com/ parklake* 5 star. All rooms have balconies overlooking the lake. Conference rooms, banquet halls, spa with pools, sauna, solarium, fishing trips.
AL-A **El Ciervo**, *Koerner 241, T045-411245*, *www.hotelelciervo.cl* 4-star. German spoken, beautiful location, pool. Recommended.
AL-B **Hostería de la Colina**, *Las Colinas 115*, *overlooking town, T045-411503, aldrich@ entelchile.net* With breakfast, large gardens, good service, good restaurant. Recommended.

A **Hostería Bilbao**, *Henríquez 43*, *T045-411186, www.7lagos.com/bilbao* Clean, small rooms, pretty patio, good restaurant.
A **Hotel y Cabañas El Parque**, *3 km east on Pucón road, T045-411120*, *www.hotelparque.cl* Lakeside with beach, tennis courts, breakfast, good restaurant with set meals. Highly recommended.
A **Hotel-Yachting Kiel**, *Koerner 153*, *T045-411631, www.villarrica.com/yachting* Off season, lakeside, clean, friendly, good.
B **Bungalowlandia**, *Prat 749, T045-411635*, *www.villarrica.com/bungalowlandia* Cabañas for 2, with *comedor*, good facilities.
B **Cabañas Traitraico**, *San Martín 380*, *T/F045-411064*, 100 m from lake, sleep 6, TV, heating, kitchenette, parking.

HOTEL
ANTUMALAL
PUCON · CHILE

Located at 2 kms from Pucón.
Lake side setting.
Panoramic Views of Lake.
Fire place in all the rooms
5 acre private park
Swimming Pool, Tennis court,
Privet Beach &
Docks in premises
Personal Activity Coordination

Tel: 56-45-441011
Fax: 56-45-441013
info@antumalal.com
www.antumalal.com

C Kolping, *Riquelme 399, T/F045-411388*.
Good breakfast, recommended.
F Chito Fuentes, *Vicente Reyes 665,
T045-411595*. Price per person. Basic, restaurant.
F La Torre Suiza, *Bilbao 969, T045-411213,
www.torresuiza.com* Price per person. Excellent
breakfast, kitchen and laundry facilities,
camping, cycle rental, German, English spoken.
F Villa Linda, *Valdivia 678, T045-411392*.
Price per person. Hot water, clean, basic,
cheap, good restaurant.
FRes Victoria, *Muñoz 530*. Price per person.
Cooking facilities. One of several on Muñoz
400 and 500 blocks.
F *Vicente Reyes 854, T045-414457*. Price per
person. Breakfast, limited bathroom facilities.
F Parque Natural Dos Ríos, *13km west of
Villarrica, T09-4198064/09-9581887,
www.dosrios.de* Price per person. Tranquil
40 hectare nature park with *cabañas* on the
banks of the Río Toltén (there is a white sand
beach), horseback riding, bird-watching,
children-friendly, German, English spoken.
F Sra Nelly, *Aviador Acevedo 725,
T045-412299*. Price per person. Hot water all
day, good value, camping, recommended.
G Res San Francisco, *Julio Zegers 646*. Price
per person. Dormitories.

There are also rooms in private homes;
several on Koerner 300 block and O'Higgins
700 and 800 blocks.

Camping
Many sites east of town on Pucón road, but
these are expensive and open in season only.
It may be cheaper to stay in a *hospedaje*;
those nearest to town are **El Edén**, *1 km
southeast of centre, T045-412772*, US$4 per
person, recommended, and **Los Castaños**,
T045-412330, US$11 per site.

Pucón *p320, map, p326*
Rooms may be hard to find in high season
(Dec-Feb), but there are plenty of alternatives in
Villarrica. There are also rooms in private houses
– look for the signs or ask in bars/restaurants.
Price codes are based on high season rates;
off-season prices are 20-40% lower and it's
often possible to negotiate.
LL Antumalal, *2 km west, T045-441011,
www.antumalal.com* Very small, picturesque
chalet-style, magnificent views of the lake,
tennis court, lovely gardens, excellent, with
meals, open year round, pool.

LL-L **Del Lago**, *Ansorena 23, T045-291000, www.hoteldellago.cl* 5 star, pool, health suite, casino, cinema.

LL-L **Gran Hotel Pucón**, *Holzapfel 190, T045-441001, www.granhotelpucon.cl* Restaurant, disco, sports centre shared with **Condiminio Gran Hotel** apartments.

L **Interlaken**, *Caupolicán 270, T045-441276, F441242.* Chalets, recommended, water-skiing, pool, currency exchange (open Nov-Apr), no restaurant.

A **Araucarias**, *Caupolicán 243, T045-441286, www.araucarias.cl* Clean, comfortable, indoor pool.

A **Hostería El Principito**, *Urrutia 291, T045-441200.* Good breakfast, clean.

A **La Posada Plaza-Pucón**, *Valdivia 191, T045-441088, www.hotelplazapucon.cl* With bath, cheaper without, full board available, also spacious cabins.

A **Munich**, *Alderete 275, T/F045-442293.* Modern, spacious, German and English spoken.

A **Oregón**, *Fresia 260, T045-441977, F045-442433.* Clean, good beds.

B **Geronimo**, *Alderete 665, T045-443762, johanavillagran@hotmail.com* Comfortable, friendly, quiet, cable TV, with restaurant, bar and terrace. Recommended.

Pucón

0 metres 100
0 yards 100

Sleeping ⬤
Ainhoa **33** *A3*
Araucarias **1** *B1*
Casa de María **2** *B2*
Casa Eliana **4** *C2*
Casa Richard **5** *C1*

B **Kernayel**, *1 km east at Camino International 1510, T045-442164, www.kernayel.cl* Apartments and *cabañas*, pool, comfortable.

C **Hosp Del Montanés**, *O'Higgins 472, T045-441267*. Clean, TV, central, restaurant.

C **Hostería Milla Rahue**, *O'Higgins 460, T045-441610*. Clean, good restaurant.

C-D **Hosp La Casita**, *Palguín 555, T045-441712, lacasita@entelchile.net* Clean, laundry and kitchen facilities, English and German spoken, large breakfast, garden, motorcycle parking, ski trips, Spanish classes.

C-D **La Tetera**, *Urrutia 580, T045-441462, www.tetera.cl* Rooms with and without bath. Good breakfast with real coffee, German and English spoken, good Spanish classes, book swap, Navimag reservations, informative. Highly recommended, book in advance.

C-F **Hostería école**, *Urrutia 592, T045-441675, www.ecole.cl* Price per person without breakfast, also dormitory accommodation and rooms with bath, discount for Hostelling International members, good vegetarian and fish restaurant, ecological shop, forest treks, rafting, biking, information, language classes, massage, recommended.

F **Hostal Backpackers**, Palguín 695, T045-441373, hostal@politur.com Kitchen facilities, internet, information, 10% discount on Politur excursions.

F **Hostal Carlos Alfredo Richard**, Arauco 171, parque_huerquehue@hotmail.com Price per person. Central location, shared rooms, use of kitchen, internet, also at Parque Huerquehue (see below).

F **Res Lincoyán**, *Av Lincoyán 323, T045-441144, www.lincoyan.cl* Price per person. With bath, cheaper without, clean and comfortable.

F **Tr@vel Pucón**, *Blanco Encalada 190, T045-444093, pucontravel@terra.cl* Price per person. English, German, French spoken, near Turbus terminal, garden, kitchen facilities, Spanish classes.

G **Casa Eliana**, *Pasaje Chile 225, T045-441851*. Price per person. Kitchen facilities.

G **Casa de María**, *General Urrutia 560, T045-443264*. Double rooms, use of kitchen, good position, friendly.

G **Casa Richard**, *Paraguay 140*. Basic but friendly, cooking facilities. Recommended.

G **Hosp El Refugio**, *Lincoyán 348,*

T045-441347. Price per person. With breakfast, good.

G **Hosp Graciela**, *Pasaje Rolando Matus 521 (off Av Brasil)*. Price per person. Comfortable rooms, good food.

G **Hosp Lucía**, *Lincoyán 565, T045-441721*. Friendly, quiet, garden, recommended, cooking facilities.

G **Hosp Sonia**, *Lincoyán 485, T045-441269, hospedajesonia@hotmail.com*. Price per person. Use of kitchen, very noisy and crowded, meals, friendly.

G **Irma Villena**, *Arauco 460*. Price per person. Clean, friendly. Recommended.

G **Roberto y Alicia Abreque**, *Perú 170*. Price per person. Basic, noisy, popular, kitchen and laundry facilities, information on excursions.

Camping

You should buy supplies in Villarrica where they are cheaper.

Ainoha, *12 blocks north of town centre*. Lakeside site.

La Poza, *Costanera Geis 769, T045-441435*. Hot showers, clean, quiet, good kitchen facilities, open all year. Recommended.

L'etoile, *Km 2 towards Volcán Villarrica, T045-442188*. Attractive forest site.

Los Boldos, *Pasaje Las Rosas*. East of town.

Millaray, *Km 7 west of Pucón, T045-212336*. Lakeside campsite.

Saint John, *Km 7 west of Pucón, T045-441165, casilla 154*. Beside Lago Villarrica.

Parque Nacional Villarrica *p322*

There is a refuge without beds 4 km inside the park; it's insecure and in desperate need of renovation. Below is a campsite with drinking water and toilets.

Lagos Caburga and Colico *p322*

L-AL **Trailanqui**, *20 km west of Lago Colico (35 km north of Villarrica), T045-578218, www.trailanqui.com* Luxurious hotel on the riverbank, with suites and restaurant, also fully equipped *cabañas*, campsite, horseriding and golf course.

C **Hostería Los Robles**, *3 km from Caburga village, T045-236989*. Lovely views, good restaurant; also campsite, expensive in season, but cheap out of season.

E **Landhaus San Sebastián**, *east of Lago Caburga, F045-1972360, www.landhaus-chile.com* With bath and breakfast, tasty meals, laundry facilities, good walking base, English and German spoken, Spanish classes.

Camping

The southern end of Lago Caburga is lined with campsites, but there are no shops, so take your own food. There are 2 sites about half-way along north shore of Lago Colico: **Quichelmalleu**, *Km 22 from Cunco, T045-573187.*
Ensenada, *Km 26, T045-221441.*

Parque Nacional Huerquehue *p323*
C-E **Refugio Tinquilco**, *3½ km from park entrance, T02-7777673, patriciolanfranco@entelchile.net* Doubles with bath available, meals served, cooking facilities, heating.
E **Hostal Carlos Alfredo Richard**, *southwest shore of Lago Tinquilco, 2 km from park entrance, parque_huerquehue@hotmail.com* Price per person, breakfast included. Large rooms, private bathrooms with hot water, restaurant, rowboats for hire.
F **Braatz and Soldans**, *southern end of Lago Tinquilco near the park entrance.* 2 German-speaking families offer accommodation, no electricity, food and camping (US$6); they also rent rowing boats on the lake.

Camping

There are 2 campsites at the park entrance, US$8, but no camping is allowed in the park.

Termas de Quimey-Co, de Huife and los Pozones *p323*
L **Hostería Termas de Huife**, *Termas de Huife, T045-1975666, www.termashuife.cl* The most upmarket of the spa hotels.
A **Hotel Termas de Quimey-Co**, *Termas de Quimey-Co, T045-441903.* Also a campsite and two cabins.

Towards Argentina *p324*
AL **Termas de San Luis**, *T045-411388/T045-412880, termasdesanluis@entelchile.net* Cabañas with TV, heating, sauna, restaurant. Pick-up service for hotel guests from Pucón.
A-F **Cabañas La Tranquera**, *Puesco.* Cabins for 6, also dormitory accommodation, restaurant, campsite.

C-D **Hotel Termas**, *Termas de Pangui, contact: O'Higgins 555, of 2, Pucón, T045-442039, ingeluz@yahoo.com* Price per person. Also teepees that sleep 3 and camping facilities. Good vegetarian meals, trekking, aromatherapy, English spoken.
F **Kila Leufu**, *Km 20, Pucón-Curarrehue road, T09-7118064, www.kilaleufu.cl* Price per person. Rooms on the Martínez family farm, contact daughter Margot in advance, friendly, English spoken, full board available including spit-roast lamb in the *ruca*, also offers trekking information, horseriding and mountain bike hire. Recommended.
F **Rancho de Caballos**, *36km SE of Pucón on the dirt road to Coñaripe, T045-441575.* Price per person. Restaurant with vegetarian dishes, laundry and kitchen facilities; also *cabañas* and camping, self-guided trails, horseriding excursions US$50 per day, English and German spoken, recommended.

Camping

There is a CONAF campsite at Puesco and another, 5 km from the frontier near Lago Tromen, free, no facilities.

🅐 Eating

For eating options in the national parks and lakes east of Pucón, see Sleeping, above.

Villarrica *p320, map p321*
$$$ **El Tabor**, *Epulef 1187.* Excellent but pricey.
$$ **El Rey de Mariscos**, *Letelier 1030.* Good seafood.
$$ **Hotel Yandaly**, *Henríquez 401.* Good food. Recommended.
$$ **Rapa Nui**, *Vicente Reyes 678.* Good and cheap end of the range, closed Sun.
$$ **The Travellers**, *Letelier 753.* Varied menu including vegetarian and Asian food, bar, English spoken.
$ **Chito Fuentes**, *Reyes 665.* Chilean fast food.
$ **Café 2001**, *Henríquez 379.* Coffee and ice cream, good.

Pucón *p320, map p326*
For other options see Sleeping, above. Vegetarians should check out the delicatessen at O'Higgins y Fresia, which serves fresh vegetarian food.
$$$ **Ana María**, *O'Higgins 865.* Classic Chilean food.

$$$ **En Alta Mar**, *Urrutia y Fresia*. Fish and seafood, very good.

$$$ **Puerto Pucón**, *Fresia 251*. Spanish, stylish.

$$ **Arabian**, *Fresia 354-B*. Good Arab food.

$$ **Brasil**, *Fresia 477*. Chilean food.

$$ **El Palet**, *Fresia 295*. Authentic local food, clean, friendly service, reasonably priced. Recommended by local people.

$$ **El Refugio**, *Lincoyán 348*. Some vegetarian dishes, expensive wine.

$$ **El Rincón de Los Castaños**, *Colo-Colo 450*. Chilean food.

$$ **La Buonatesta**, *Fresia 243*. Good pizzeria.

$$ **La Maga**, *Fresia 125*. Uruguayan Parillada serving possibly the best steak in Chile.

$$ **Nau Kana**, *Fresia*. Good Oriental food.

$$ **Tijuana**, *Fresia 303*. Mexican.

$ **La Terraza**, *O'Higgins 323*. Pleasant terrace, cheap lunches.

Cafés

Also try **Hostería école**, see Sleeping, above.

Café de la P, *O'Higgins y Lincoyán*. Real coffee.

El Turista, *Fresia y Alderete*. Real coffee.

Holzapfel Backerei, *Holzapfel 524*. German café. Recommended.

La Tetera, *Urrutia 580*. Wide selection of teas, good coffee, snacks, German spoken. Recommended.

Bars and clubs

Pucón *p320, map p326*
At weekends in summer, there are discos 2-3 km east of town: **Kamikaze** and **La Playa**.

Disco For You, *2 km east*. Open all year, there's transport in summer from **Pub for You** (see below).

Mamas and Tapas, *O'Higgins y Arauco*. Drink and snacks.

Pub for You, *Ansorena 370*. English-style pub.

Vagabundo, *Fresia 135*. Pleasant bar, also serves good-value meals.

Festivals and events

Villarrica *p320, map p321*
Many events are organised in Jan and Feb, including music, regattas, triathlon rodeo and the **Festival Cultural Mapuche**, with market, based around the **Muestra Cultural Mapuche**, usually in 2nd week of Feb.

Pucón *p320, map p326*
There is a large handicraft market just south of O'Higgins on Ansorena. Camping equipment is available at **Eltit Supermarket**, *O'Higgins y Fresia*, and from **Outdoors and Travel**, *Lincoyán 361*. **Pucon Express** , *O'Higgins y Colo Colo*, is a 24-hr supermarket.

Activities and tours

Villarrica *p320, map p321*
Tour operators
Prices are fairly standard: to Parque Nacional Villarrica, US$13; to climb Volcán Villarrica, US$30-40; to Valdivia US$25; to Termas de Coñaripe US$22.

Karina Tour, *Letelier 825, T045-412048*.

Politur, *Henriquez 475, T045-414547*.

Turismo Coñaripe, *P Montt 525, T045-411111*.

Turismo Repu-Pehuén, *Pedro de Valdivia 565, T/F045-412065*.

Pucón *p320, map p326*
Aerial sports
Fabrice Pini, *Colo Colo 830, T09-4111072*. Paragliding US$50 for ½ hr; also offers hydrospeed watersports, US$20 for the morning.

Canoeing
Aguaventura expediciones, *Palguín 336, T444246, aguaventura@hotmail.com* Canoe trips on Río Liucura, US$10 per person. French run, English spoken.

Fishing
Pucón and Villarrica are celebrated as bases for fishing on Lago Villarrica and on the beautiful Lincura, Trancura and Toltén rivers. The local tourist office will supply details on licences and open seasons etc. Some tourist agencies also offer trips.

Mario's Fishing Zone, *O'Higgins 581, T045-444259, www.pucon.com/fishing* Expensive, but good fishing guide.

Off Limits, *Fresia 273, T045-441210, offlimitspucon@hotmail.com* Fishing specialists, English spoken, offer fly-fishing excursions US$100 per day, maximum 3 people. Also fishing boat excursions from US$190 for 2 persons.

Horseriding

Horse hire is about US$35 half day, US$55 full day; enquire at **La Tetera** in Pucón, or try **Rancho de Callabos** at the Termas de Palguín; for both see Sleeping above.

Centro de Turismo Ecuestre Huepil *T09-4534212*. Small groups, local excursions and 3-day trips to Argentina.

Skiing

Pucón resort, *35 mins from Pucón on the slopes of the Villarrica volcano, T045-441001, www.granhotelpucon.cl* The resort is owned by **Gran Hotel Pucón**, which can provide information on snow, ski lifts and, perhaps, transport; otherwise consult the tourist office in Pucón. There are 8 lifts (day ticket US$15-25, depending on the season, US$5 to the restaurant), though rarely do more than 2 or 3 work and piste preparation is mediocre. The snow is generally soft and good for beginners, though more advanced skiers can try the steeper areas. The ski centre offers equipment rental (US$15 per day, US$82 per week), ski instruction, first aid, and has a restaurant and bar with wonderful views from the terrace.

Tour operators

All operators can arrange a variety of trips, including climbing Villarrica, 12 hrs, US$30-40 including park entry, equipment provided; ski hire and transport to slopes US$20 per person; tours to Termas de Huife, US$20 including entry. Shop around, prices vary, as well as the quality of guides and equipment. To reach the falls, lakes and *termas* it is cheaper for groups to flag down a taxi and negotiate a price. Also try **Hostería école**, see Sleeping above.

Aguaventura, *Palguín 336, T045-444246, www.aguaventura.com* French-run kayaking and rafting specialists.

Anden Sport, *O'Higgins 535, T045-441048, anden-sport-tours@tie.cl* Skiing specialists.

Politur, *O'Higgins635, T045-441373, www.politur.com.* Good.

Ronco Track, *O'Higgins, esq. Arauco, T045-449597*. Quadbike excursions.

Sol y Nieve *O'Higgins, esq Lincoyán, T/F441070, www.solynieve.cl* Previously held in high esteem, with guides and equipment, but now some mixed reports about organisation. Most guides speak English.

Sur Expediciones, *O'Higgins 660*. New but good.

Watersports

Equipment for water-skiing (US$10 for 15 mins), dinghy sailing (lasers US$11 per hr) and windsurfing (sailboards US$10 per hr) can be hired at Playa Grande, the beach by the **Gran Hotel**. Rowing boats can also be hired for US$4 per hr. The outlets on La Poza beach are more expensive and not recommended.

Whitewater rafting

Very popular on the **Río Trancura**, east of Pucón; many agencies offer trips: Trancura Baja (basic, grade III) US$15; Trancura Alta (advanced, grade IV) US$25.

Parque Nacional Villarrica *p322*

Tours from Pucón cost US$30-40, including park entry, guide, transport to park entrance and hire of equipment (no reduction for those with their own equipment). Bargain for group rates. Travel agencies will not start out if the weather is bad and some travellers have experienced difficulties in obtaining a refund: establish in advance what terms apply in the event of cancellation and be prepared to wait a few days. For information on individual guides, all with equipment, ask for recommendations at the tourist office.

Reserva Forestal Cañi *p323*

Entrance to the reserve is by guided tour only, US$17 per person (take lunch), plus transport. There's also a 2-day tour with basic overnight accommodation, US$34 per person. Contact **Fundación Lahuén**, see p323, or **Hostería école**, see Sleeping, above.

⊖ Transport

Villarrica *p320, map p321*
Bus

The main terminal is at *Pedro de Valdiva y Muñoz*; JAC has 2 terminals, at *Muñoz y Bilbao*, (long-distance) and opposite for Pucón and Lican-Ray (local). Other services leave from the **Terminal Rural**, *Matta y Vicente Reyes*.

Buses to **Santiago**, 10 hrs, US$9, several companies; to **Pucón**, both Vipu-Ray (main terminal) and JAC, every 15 mins in summer, 40-min journey, US$0.75; to **Puerto Montt**, US$6; to **Valdivia**, JAC, 5 a day, 2½ hrs, US$3.50; to **Lican-Ray** services in summer, JAC and Vipu-Ray, US$1; to **Coñaripe**, US$1.50, and **Liquiñe** at 1600 Mon-Sat, 1000 Sun; to

Temuco, JAC, every 30 mins in summer, US$3; to **Loncoche** (Route 5 junction for hitching), US$1.50. There are also occasional direct buses to **Panguipulli**, via Lican Ray.

To Argentina Buses from Temuco to Junín stop in Villarrica en route to the Tromen Pass; fares are the same as from Temuco, see p318. If the Tromen pass is blocked by snow buses go via the paso Carirriñe instead of via Villarrica and Pucón.

Pucón *p320, map p326*
Air
Lan Express flies to **Santiago**, 4 times weekly in summer.

Bus
There is no municipal terminal; each company has its own: JAC, *Uruguay y Palguín*; **Tur Bus**, *O'Higgins 910, east of town*; Igi Llaima and Condor, *Colo Colo y O'Higgins*.
    JAC has services to **Villarrica**, every 15 mins, US$0.50; to **Valdivia**, JAC, 5 daily, US$4.50; to **Temuco** hourly, 2 hrs, US$3, or *rápido*, 1 hr, US$3.50; to **Puerto Montt**, 6 hrs, US$8, daily with **Tur Bus**, or change at Valdivia. To **Santiago**, morning and evening, 10 hrs, US$11; *salón cama* service by **Tur Bus** and JAC, US$30.
    To Argentina Buses from Temuco to **San Martín** arrive in Pucón 1000; fares are the same as from Temuco, see p318. If the Tromen pass is blocked by snow buses go via the paso Carirriñe instead of via Villarrica and Pucón.

Taxi
Cooperative, *T045-441009*.

Lagos Caburga and Colico *p322*
JAC runs buses from Pucón to **Caburga**, several daily, US$1; there are also minibuses every 30 mins from *Ansorena y Uruguay* in Pucón; a taxi day trip costs US$25 return.

Parque Nacional Huerquehue *p323*
JAC buses from Pucón, 3 daily in summer, 2 in winter, 1½ hrs, US$1. Tour agencies arrange transport for groups, US$8. Taxis cost US$34 return. Minibuses from *Ansorena y Brasil*.

Termas de Quimey-Co, de Huife and los Pozones *p323*
A taxi from Pucón costs US$23 return, US$16 one way; **Hostería Termas de Huife** has its own transport and will pick people up from Pucón.

Towards Argentina *p324*
Several minibuses daily to Curarrehue from Pucón. Daily bus from Pucón to border, 1800, 2 hrs, US$2. To Pucón 0700.

❶ Directory

Villarrica *p320, map p321*
Banks There are ATMs at Banco BCI, *Pedro de Valdivia y Alderete*; Banco de Chile, *Pedro de Valdiva y Pedro Montt*; Banco Santander, *Pedro de Valdiva 778*. **Casas de cambio** In general, rates are poor. Carlos Huerta, *Muñoz 417*; Central de Repuestos, *Muñoz 415*, good rates; Cristopher, *Valdivia 1061*, good rates for Tcs; Turcamb, *Henríquez 570*, poor rates for Tcs. **Car hire** Christopher Car, *Pedro de Valdivia 1061, T/045-F413980*; Castillo Propiedades, *Anfion Muñoz 417*, good value. **Bicycle** hire **Mora Bicicletas**, *Körner 760*, helpful. **Internet** Cybercafé Salmon, *Letelier y Henríquez*. **Laundry** Lavacenter, *Alderete 770*; Lavandería y Lavaseco Villarrica, *Andrés Bello 348*; Todo Lavado, *Urrutia 669*. **Post** office *Muñoz y Urrutia*, open Mon-Fri 0900-1300, 1430-1800, Sat 0900-1300. **Telephone** CTC, *Henríquez 544*; Chilesat, *Henriquez 473*; Entel, *Henriquez 440 and 575*.

Pucón *p320, map p326*
Airlines LanChile, *Urrutia 103 y Caupolican, T045-443516, Mon-Sat 1000-1400, 1800-2200*. **Banks** There are ATMs in Banco Santander and Eltit Supermarket, both on O'Higgins, Eltit supermarket also changes TCs but best to change TCs before arriving as rates poor; also at Banco BCI, Fresia y Alderete, and in casino. Several *casas de cambio* on O'Higgins. **Bicycle hire** US$1.50 per hr or US$10 per day from several travel agencies, many on O'Higgins; shop around as quality varies. **Car hire** Prices start at $27 per day; Christopher Car, *O'Higgins 335, T/F045-449013*; Hertz, *Fresia 220, T045-441664*, more expensive; same prices per day at Gran Hotel; Pucón Rent A Car, *Camino Internacional 1395, T045-441922, kernayel@cepri.cl*; Sierra Nevada, *Palguín y O'Higgins*, cars and 4WDs, reasonable. **Internet** *O'Higgins 555*, some computers with Hebrew keyboards; several on the same street. **Laundry** at *Urrutia 520*; *Palguín 460*; *Fresia 224*; *Colo-Colo 475 and 478*, several others. **Post office** *Fresia 183*. **Telephone** CTC, *Gen Urrutia 472*; Entel, *Ansorena 299*.

The Seven Lakes

This group of lakes, situated south of Lago Villarrica, provides a beautiful necklace of water, surrounded by thick woods and with views of distant snows giving a picture-postcard backdrop. Six of the lakes lie in Chile, with the seventh, Lago Lacár, in Argentina. After the final peace settlement of 1882 the area around these lakes was reserved for Mapuche settlements. The southernmost lake, Lago Riñihue, is most easily reached from Valdivia and Los Lagos and is dealt with in a later section (see page 341). Most of the lakes have black-sand beaches, although in spring, as the water level rises, these can all but disappear.

Lago Calafquén

The most northerly of the seven lakes, Lago Calafquén is a popular tourist destination, readily accessible by a paved road from Villarrica, along which there are fine views of the Villarrica volcano. Wooded and dotted with small islands, the lake is reputedly one of the warmest in the region and is good for swimming. A partly paved road runs around the lake.

Lican-Ray → *Phone code: 045. Colour map 4, B2. Population: 1,700.*
Situated 30 km south of Villarrica on a peninsula on the north shore, Lican-Ray is the major resort on the lake and is named after a legendary Mapuche woman (see box page 333). There are two beaches, one on each side of the peninsula. Boats can be hired (US$2 an hour) and there are **catamaran trips** ① *US$3 per hr or US$11 to the islands.* Although crowded in season, Lican-Ray can feel like a ghost town, with most facilities closed by the end of March. Some 6 km to the east is the river of lava formed when the Villarrica volcano erupted in 1971. There is a **tourist office** on the plaza ① *daily in summer, Mon-Fri in winter.* ►► *For Sleeping, Eating and other listings see pages 335-337.*

Coñaripe → *Phone code: 063. Population: 1,250.*
Lying 21 km southeast of Lican-Ray at the eastern end of Lago Calafquén, Coñaripe is another popular Chilean tourist spot. At first sight the village is dusty and nondescript, but its setting, with a black sand beach surrounded by mountains, is very beautiful. Most services in Coñaripe are on the Calle Principal. The **tourist office** on the plaza ① *mid Nov-mid Apr daily; late Apr-early Nov Sat and Sun only*, can arrange excursions to local thermal springs.

From Coñaripe a road (mostly *ripio*) around the lake's southern shore leads to **Lago Panguipulli**, see below, 38 km west, and offers superb views over Volcán Villarrica, which can be climbed from here. Another dirt road heads northeast through the Parque Nacional Villarrica to Pucón, see page 320; high clearance vehicles only.

Southeast of Coñaripe
From Coñaripe a road runs southeast over the steep Cuesta Los Añiques offering views of **Lago Pellaifa**, a tiny lake with rocky surroundings covered with vegetation and a small beach. The **Termas de Coñaripe** ① *Km 16, 2 km from the lakeshore, T063-411407*, has four pools, accommodation, restaurant, cycles and horses for hire.

Further south are the **Termas de Liquiñe** ① *Km 32, T/F063-317377, US$4-7 per person*, with eight thermal springs and accommodation (but little other infrastructure), surrounded by a small native forest. About 8 km north of Liquiñe is a road going southwest (20 km) along the southeast shore of **Lago Neltume** to meet the Choshuenco-Puerto Fuy road.

The legend of Lican-Ray

At the height of the wars between the Spanish and the Mapuche a young Spanish soldier lost the rest of his unit and strayed into the forests near Lago Calafquén. Suddenly he saw a beautiful young Mapuche woman drying her hair in the sun and singing. As he did not want to frighten her he made himself visible at a distance and began to sing along. Singing, smiling and exchanging glances, they fell in love. She called him Allumanche, which means white man in Mapuche, and, pointing to herself, indicated that her name was Lican Rayan, meaning the flower of magic stone. They began to live together near the lake.

Lican Rayan's father, Curtilef, a powerful and fearsome chief, feared she might be dead. One day a boy came to him and said: "Lican Rayan is alive. I have seen her near the lake with a white man but she is not a prisoner: it is clear they are in love".

Lican Rayan saw the warriors coming to look for her. Knowing her father she feared what might happen, so she persuaded the soldier that they should flee. They escaped by riding on logs to one of the islands. There they felt safe, but they could not light a fire against the cold because the smoke would give them away. The weather grew cooler, the north wind blew and it rained heavily. After several days, unable to bear the cold and thinking that the warriors would have given up the search, they lit a fire. The smoke was spotted by Curtilef's men, so Lican Rayan and the solider fled to another island further away but again they were discovered and had to escape. This happened so many times that, although they were never caught, they were never seen again.

In the town of Lican-Ray, it is said that on spring afternoons it is sometimes possible to see a distant column of smoke from one of the islands, where Lican Rayan and the soldier are still enjoying their love after over 400 years.

Abridged and translated from *Lengua Y Costumbres Mapuches* by Orietta Appelt Martin, Imprenta Austral, Temuco, 1995.

The **Paso Carirriñe** across the Argentine border ① *open 15 Oct-31 Aug*, is reached by unpaved road from the Termas de Liquiñe. On the Argentine side the road continues to San Martín de los Andes. ›› *For Sleeping, Eating and other listings see pages 335-337.*

Lago Panguipulli

Covering 116 sq km, Lago Panguipulli, the largest of the seven lakes, is reached either by paved road from Lanco or Los Lagos on the Pan-American Highway or by *ripio* roads from Lago Calafquén. A road leads along the beautiful northern shore, which is wooded with sandy beaches and cliffs, but most of the lake's southern shore is inaccessible by road.

Panguipulli → *Phone code: 063. Colour map 4, B2. Population: 8,326.*

The site of a Mapuche settlement, Panguipulli, meaning 'hill of pumas', is situated on a hillside at the northwest corner of the lake. It grew as a railway terminal and a port for vessels carrying timber from the lakesides, and is now the largest town in the area.

On Plaza Prat is the **Iglesia San Sebastián**, built in Swiss style with twin towers by the Swiss Padre Bernabé; its belltower contains three bells from Germany. The plaza also has a **tourist office** ① *Dec-Feb only.*

From Plaza Prat the main commercial street, Martínez de Rozas, runs down to the lake shore. In summer, catamaran trips are offered on the lake and excursions can be made to Lagos Calafquén, Neltume, Pirehueico and to the northern tip of Lago Riñihue (see page 341). The road east to Coñaripe, on Lago Calafquén, offers superb views of the lake and of the Villarrica volcano. ▶▶ *For Sleeping, Eating and other listings see pages 335-337.*

> ▮ *The streets of Panguipulli are planted with roses: it is claimed that there are over 14,000 in the town.*

Choshuenco and around

Choshuenco lies 45 km east of Panguipulli on the Río Llanquihue, at the eastern tip of the lake and can only be reached by road from Panguipulli or Puerto Fuy. To the south is the **Reserva Nacional Mocho Choshuenco** (7,536 ha), which includes two volcanoes: Choshuenco (2,415 m) and Mocha (2,422 m). On the slopes of Choshuenco the **Club Andino de Valdivia** runs a small ski resort and three *refugios*. (The resort is reached by a turning from the road that goes south from Choshuenco to Enco at the east end of Lago Riñihue, see page 341.) From Choshuenco a road leads east to **Neltume** and **Lago Pirehueico**, via the impressive waterfalls of **Huilo Huilo**. The falls are three hours' walk from Choshuenco, or take the Puerto Fuy bus and get off at **Alojamiento Huilo Huilo,** from where it is a five-minute walk to the falls.

Lago Pirehueico

Lago Pirehueico is a 36-km long, narrow and deep glacial lake surrounded by virgin *lingue* forest. It is beautiful and largely unspoilt, although there are plans to build a huge tourist complex in Puerto Pirehueico.

There are two ports on the lake: **Puerto Fuy** at the northern end and **Puerto Pirehueico** at the southern end. The ports are linked by a ferry service (the crossing is

The Seven Lakes

beautiful; see page 337) and can also be reached by the road that runs east from Neltume to the Argentine border crossing at Paso Huahum. The road south from Puerto Fuy, however, is privately owned and closed to traffic. This is a shame because it is a beautiful route passing around the Choshuenco volcano and through rainforest to Río Pillanleufú, Puerto Llolles on Lago Maihue and Puerto Llifén on Lago Ranco.

Paso Huahum ① *all year, Chilean immigration summer 0800-2100, winter 0800-2000*, is 11 km southeast of Puerto Pirehueico. On the Argentine side the road leads alongside Lago Lacar to San Martín de los Andes and Junín de los Andes.

⊟ Sleeping

Lican-Ray *p332*
There are plenty of options along the north shore of Lago Calafquén towards Coñaripe.
C **Hosp Los Nietos**, *Manquel 125, T045-431078*. Without breakfast.
C **Hostería Inaltulafquen**, *Casilla 681, Playa Grande, T045-431115, F045-410028*. With breakfast and bath, English spoken.
D **Cabañas Cacique Vitacura**, *Urrutia 825, Playa Grande, T02-2355302, tradesic@inter media.cl* For 2, also larger cabins with kitchen.
F **Res Temuco**, *G Mistral 515, Playa Grande, T045-431130*. Price per person, with breakfast. Clean, without bath, good.

ARGENTINA

To Junín de los Andes

Parque Nacional Lanín

Paso Huahum

Lago Lascar   San Martín de los Andes

Camping
There are also 6 sites just west of town.
Foresta, *½ km east of town, T045-211954*. Sites for up to 6 people.
Prado Verde, *1 km east of town, T045-431161*.

Coñaripe *p332*
A **Entre Montañas**, *on the Plaza, T063-408300*. Overpriced, poor food.
F **Hosp Chumay**, *on Plaza, T063-317287 turismochumay@hotmail.com* Price per person. Restaurant, internet, tours.

Camping
There are campsites on both north and south sides of the lake, US$15 per site. Free camping is possible on the beach outside town.
Isla Llancahue, *5 km east, T063-317360*. Campsite with *cabañas* on an island in Río Llancahue.

Southeast of Coñaripe *p332*
A **Termas de Liquiñe**, *Km 32, T/F063-317377*. Price per person, full board, cabins, restaurant, tours offered. There is also accommodation in private houses.

Panguipulli *p333, map p336*
B **Hostal España**, *O'Higgins 790, T063-311166, hostal_espana@elsitio.com* Rooms with breakfast.
B **Hostería Quetropillán**, *Etchegaray 381, T063-311348*. Comfortable.
D **Res La Bomba**, *J M Carrera y R Freire*. Quiet.
F **Hotel Central**, *Valdivia 115, T063-311331/09-8823955*. Price per person. Clean, breakfast.
F *opposite Hotel Quetropillán*. Price per person. Clean private house with beautiful garden.
F *Etchegaray 464*. Price per person. Clean, good breakfast. Suitable for longer stays.
F **Hosp Familiar**, *Los Ulmos 62, T063-311483*. Price per person. English and German spoken, kitchen facilities, helpful, good breakfast.
G **Albergue Juvenil**, *Gabriela Mistral 1112, T063-311282*. Youth hostel opposite bus terminal. Price per person.

There are also 3 sites at Chauquén, 6 km southeast on the lakeside.

Camping Lago Riñihue, *T063-461344, F063-461111.*

El Bosque, *P Sigifredo 241, T063-311489.* Clean, hot water.

Choshuenco and around *p334*

F **Choshuenco**, *Bernabé s/n, T063-318214.* Price per person. Run down but clean, good meals.

F **Hostería Rayen Trai**, *María Alvarado y O'Higgins.* Price per person. Former yacht club serving good food, open all year.

F **Hostería Ruca Pillán**, *San Martín 85, T063-318220, rucapi@telsur.cl* Price per person. English spoken, tours.

F **Restaurant Robles**, *in Neltume, east of Choshuenco.* Price per person without bath.

G **Alojamiento Huilo Huilo**, *Huilo Huilo, nr Neltume.* Price per person. Basic but comfortable and well situated for walks.

Lago Pirehueico *p334*

Beds are available in private houses, and free camping is possible on the beach.

G **Hosp Pirehueico** *Puerto Pirehueico.* Price per person.

G **Restaurant Puerto Fuy**, *Puerto Fuy.* Cold water, good restaurant.

🍴 Eating

For eating options in Coñaripe, Choshuenco and around, see Sleeping, above.

Lican-Ray *p332*

$$-$ **Café Ñaños**, *Urrutia 105.* Very good, reasonable prices, helpful owner.

$$-$ **Restaurant-Bar Guido's**, *Urrutia 405.* Good value.

$ **Coyote**, *on the plaza.* Cheap, open off-season.

Panguipulli *p333, map 336*

There are cheap restaurants on O'Higgins 700 block.

$$ **Didáctico El Gourmet**, *Ramón Freire s/n.* Restaurant linked to a professional hotel school. Excellent food and wine, mid price but high quality, open in school terms only.

$$-$ **Café Central**, *M de Rozas 750.* Good cheap lunches, expensive evening meals.

Panguipulli

N

0 metres 100
0 yards 100

Sleeping
Albergue Juvenil 1
Central 4
El Bosque 9

Etchegaray 464 **8**
Hostal España **5**
Hostería Quetropillán **6**
Residencial La Bomba **7**

Eating 🍴
Didáctico el
Gourmet **1**

$$-$ **El Chapulín**, *M de Rozas 639*. Good food, good value, friendly.

☺ Festivals and events

Panguipulli *p333, map p336*
Last week of Jan is **La Semana de Rosas**, with dancing and sports competitions.

▲ Activities and tours

Coñaripe *p332*
Hospedaje Chumay, see Sleeping, above, organises hikes to Villarica volcano and trips to various thermal springs.

Panguipulli *p333, map p336*
Fishing
Fishing trips on Lago Panguipulli recommended: **Puntilla Los Cipreses** at the mouth of the Río Huanehue, 11 km east of Panguipulli, 30 mins by boat; the mouth of the **Río Niltre**, on east side of lake. Boat hire US$3, licences: the **Municipalidad**, Librería Colón, *O'Higgins 528* or from the **Club de Pesca**.

Rafting
Good rafting opportunities on the **Río Fuy**, grade IV-V; **Río San Pedro**, varying grades, and on the **Río Llanquihue** near Choshuenco.

⊖ Transport

Lican-Ray *p332*
There is no central **bus** terminal; buses leave from offices around plaza. To **Villarrica**, JAC, frequent, 1 hr, US$0.75; to **Santiago**, Tur Bus and JAC, 10 hrs, US$12, *salón cama* in summer US$25; to **Temuco**, JAC 2½ hrs, US$3.50; to **Coñaripe**, 7 daily (4 off season).

Coñaripe *p332*
Buses run to **Panguipulli**, 7 daily (4 off season), US$1.50; to **Villarrica**, 16 daily, US$1; to **Lican-Ray**, 45 mins, US$0.75. Also a nightly bus direct to **Santiago** run by **Tur Bus** and JAC, 10½ hrs, US$12, salón cama in summer US$25.

Panguipulli *p333, map p336*
The **bus** terminal is at *Gabriela Mistral y Portales*. To **Santiago** daily, US$12; to **Valdivia**, Mon-Sat, 4 only on Sun, several companies, 2 hrs, US$3; to **Temuco**, frequent, **Power** and Pangui Sur, US$2; to **Puerto Montt**, US$5; to **Calafquén**, 3 daily at 1200, 1545 and 1600; to **Choshuenco**, **Neltume** and **Puerto Fuy** (3 hrs), 3 daily, US$3; to **Coñaripe**, for connections to Lican-Ray and Villarrica, 7 daily, 4 off season.

Lago Pirehueico *p334*
Bus
Puerto Fuy to **Panguipulli**, 3 daily, 3 hrs, US$3; Puerto Pirehueico via Paso Huahum to **San Martín de los Andes**, daily in summer, weekly in winter (out Sat 0930, back Sun 1330).

Ferry
The *Hua Hum* sails from Puerto Fuy across lake to Puerto Pirehueico, twice daily in summer, daily, other times, 2-3 hrs, foot passengers US$1, cars US$15. For vehicles reserve at the Hotel Quetropillán in Panguipulli.

❶ Directory

Panguipulli *p333, map p336*
Banks Banco de Crédito e Inversiones, *M de Rozas y Matta*, casa de cambio; some shops accept US$ cash, rates poor, TCs not accepted anywhere.

Valdivia and around

→ *Phone code: 063. Colour map 4, B2. Population: 110,000.*

Surrounded by wooded hills, Valdivia is one of the most pleasant cities in southern Chile, a good place to rest after arduous treks in the mountains. With a high student population, it is also one of the best cities for meeting young Chilenos, who will be at the pulse of anything in the way of nightlife in the city. Valdivia lies nearly 839 km south of Santiago at the confluence of two rivers, the Calle Calle and Cruces, which form the Río Valdivia. To the north-west of the city is a large island, Isla Teja, where the Universidad Austral de Chile is situated.

The 1960 earthquake

Southern Chile is highly susceptible to earthquakes: severe quakes struck the area in 1575, 1737, 1786 and 1837, but the tremor that struck around midday on 22 May 1960 caused the most extensive damage throughout southern Chile and was accompanied by the eruption of four volcanoes and a *maremoto* (tidal wave) that was felt as far away as New Zealand and Japan.

Around Valdivia the land dropped by 3 m, creating new lagunas along the Río Cruces to the north of the clty. The *maremoto* destroyed all the fishing villages and ports between Puerto Saavedra in the north and Chiloé in the south. The earthquake also provoked several landslides. The greatest of these blocked the Río San Pedro, near the point where it drains Lago Riñihue, and the lake, which receives the waters of six other lakes, rose 35 m in 24 hours. Over the next two months all available labour and machinery was used to dig channels to divert the water from the other lakes and to drain off the waters of Lago Riñihue, thus averting the devastation of the San Pedro valley.

Ins and outs

Getting there There are daily flights north to Santiago and Concepción. The bus network is very wide, with numerous daily services to Santiago and south to Puerto Montt, as well as to cities such as Temuco, Concepción and Chillán. By road access to the Panamericana is north via Loncoche (toll US$2.50) or south via Paillaco.➤ *For further details, see Transport page 345.* **Getting around** Valdivia is quite sizeable: *colectivos* and buses serving the outlying *barrios*. However, like many Chilean cities, the centre is relatively compact, and few places are beyond walking distance, even those across the river on the Isla Teja. **Tourist information** The tourist office ① *Prat 555, by dock, T063-342300 (ask for "información turistica"), open daily in summer, weekdays only off season*, has good maps of the region and local rivers, a list of hotel prices and examples of local crafts with artisans' addresses. There's also a helpful kiosk in the bus terminal providing travel information and a **CONAF** office① *Ismael Váldez 431, T063-218822.*

History

Valdivia was one of the most important centres of Spanish colonial control over Chile. Founded in 1552 by Pedro de Valdivia, it was abandoned as a result of the Mapuche insurrection of 1599 and was briefly occupied by Dutch pirates. In 1645 it was refounded as a walled city and the only Spanish mainland settlement south of the Río Biobío. The Spanish continued to fortify the area around Valdivia throughout the 1600s, developing the most comprehensive system of defence in the South Pacific against the British and Dutch navies. Seventeen forts were built in total. They were reinforced after 1760, but proved of little avail during the Wars of Indpdendence, when the Chilean naval squadron under Lord Cochrane seized control of the forts in two days. From independence until the 1880s Valdivia was an outpost of Chilean rule, reached only by sea or by a coastal route.

Sights

The city is centred around the tree-lined **Plaza de la República**. In the cathedral, the **Museo de la Cathedral de Valdivia** ① *Independencia 514, Tue-Sun 1000-1300, 1600-1900 in summer; Mon-Fri 1000-1300, 1600-1900, Sat 1000-1300 in winter*, covers four centuries of Christian history. Three blocks east is the **Muelle Fluvial**, the dock for boat trips down the river. From the Muelle Fluvial there is a pleasant walk north along the *costanera* (Avenida Prat) and under the bridge to Isla Teja and on round the bend in the river (where boats can be hired; US$2.50 per hour) as far as the bus terminal.

On the western bank of the river, **Isla Teja** has a botanical garden and arboretum with trees from all over the world. West of the botanical gardens is the **Parque Saval** ① *US$0.50*, which has beautiful flowers in November. Also on the island are two museums. The **Museo Histórico y Antropológico** ① *daily 1000-1300, 1400-2000 in summer; Tue-Sun 1000-1300, 1400-1800 in winter, US$1.50*, is beautifully situated in the former mansion of Carlos Andwandter, a leading German immigrant. Run by the University, it contains sections on archaeology, ethnography and German colonization. Next door, in the former Andwandter brewery, is the **Museo de Arte Moderno** ① *Tue-Sun, 1000-1300, 1400-1800, US$1.50*. Boat trips can be made around Isla Teja, offering views of birds and seals.

The **Kunstmann Brewery** ① *just out of town on the Niebla road, T063-292969, www.cerveza-kunstmann.cl*, offers tours of the working brewery and its beer museum; it also has a good restaurant.

North of Valdivia is the **Santuario de la Naturaleza Río Cruces**, which was flooded as a result of the 1960 *maremoto* and now attracts many bird species. Boat trips to the reserve are available aboard the *Isla del Río*, ① *daily 1415, 6 hrs, US$15 per person*.
▸▸ *For Sleeping, Eating and other listings, see pages 342-346.*

Along the Río Valdivia

The various rivers around Valdivia are navigable: pleasant journeys can be made by rented motor boat south of town on the Ríos Futa and Tornagaleanes around the **Isla del Rey**, while at the mouth of the Río Valdivia are interesting and isolated villages that can be visited by road or by river boat. The two main centres are **Niebla** on the north bank and **Corral** opposite on the south bank, site of two of the most important 17th-century Spanish forts on the río Valdivia (see History, page 338). There is a

Río Valdivia

Santuario de la Naturaleza Río Cruces

Pacific Ocean

Río Cruces

Isla Teja

Valdivia

Río Calle Calle

To Pan-American Highway (North)

To Los Lagos

San Carlos

Los Molinos

Amargos

Niebla

Río Valdivia

Isla Mancera

Corral

Isla del Rey

San Juan

To Valdivia

To Pan-American Highway (South)

0 km 3
0 miles 3

N

Lord Cochrane

Lord Thomas Alexander Cochrane (1775-1860) was born into a Scottish aristocratic family and began his career in the British navy during the Napoleonic Wars, rising rapidly through the officer ranks. He was elected to Parliament in 1806 as MP for Honiton and in 1807 as MP for Westminster. Cochrane had never been on good terms with his naval superiors, and when he used his position in the House of Commons to accuse the naval commander, Lord Gambier, of incompetence, he precipitated his own downfall. Gambier was court-martialled and acquitted; Cochrane was retired on half-pay and spent the next three years exposing corruption and abuses in the navy. His links with a financial scandal in 1814 provided his enemies with an opportunity for revenge: he was dismissed from the navy, expelled from Parliament and sentenced to 12 months' imprisonment.

Cochrane was recruited for the Chilean armed forces by an agent in London and quickly became friendly with Chile's independence leader Bernardo O'Higgins. He was put in command of the new republic's 'navy', a few ill-equipped vessels that relied on foreign adventurers for experienced sailors, and with this fleet harassed the Spanish-held ports along the Chilean coast. His audacious storming of the fortresses of Corral, San Carlos and Amargos led to the capture of the key Spanish base of Valdivia (see page 338).

Later that year Cochrane transported Peruvian liberation troops, led by José de San Martín, along the Pacific coast to invade Peru, but his relations with San Martin were poor and he became very critical of the Peruvian's cautious strategy. Afterwards Cochrane continued to attack Spanish shipping in the Pacific, sailing as far north as Mexico in 1822.

In 1823 the new government of Brazil appointed Cochrane to head its navy in the struggle for independence from Portugal. Once again leading a motley collection of boats manned largely by foreigners, Cochrane drove the colonial fleet from Bahia and pursued it back to Portugal. In 1825 he fell out with the Brazilian government and returned to Britain. Two years later he volunteered to help the Greeks in their struggle for independence from Turkey. He was reinstated in the British navy in 1832, was promoted to Rear-Admiral and spent much of the rest of his life promoting developments in the use of steam power in shipping.

frequent boat service between the two towns. In midstream, between Niebla and Corral is **Isla Mancera**, a small island dominated by the Castillo de San Pedro de Alcántara, the earliest of the Spanish forts. Inside the fort there is a small church and convent. The island is a pleasant place to stop over on the boat trips, but it can get crowded when an excursion boat arrives.

Niebla and around → *Colour map 4, B1.*

Eighteen kilometres west of Valdivia, Niebla is a resort with seafood restaurants and accommodation. To the west on a promontory is the **Fuerte de la Pura y Limpia Concepción de Monfort de Lemus** ① *daily in summer 1000-1900, closed Mon in winter, US$0.75, free on Sun*. It has a museum on Chilean naval history. There's a tourist information office and a telephone office.

Around Niebla the north bank is dotted with campsites and *cabañas*. About 6 km further round the coast is **Los Molinos**, a seaside resort set among steep wooded hills. There is a campsite and lots of seaside restaurants including *La Bahía* which has good food but it's not cheap.

Corral → *Colour map 4, B1. Population 3,600.*

Corral lies 62 km west of Valdivia by road and is the main port serving the city. It is much quieter and more pleasant than Niebla, and its fort, **Castillo de San Sebastian**, has a dilapidated, interesting atmosphere. It was built in 1645 as one of the main fortifications on the estuary, and during the 17th century its 3-m thick walls were defended by a battery of 21 guns. Inside is a museum, and in summer re-enactments of 18th-century battles in period costume are held daily 1530 and 1730. Horses are sometimes found grazing among the ramparts.

Further north near the mouth of the river are pleasant beaches and the remains of two other Spanish colonial forts, the **Castillo San Luis de Alba de Amargos** and the **Castillo de San Carlos**. The coastal walks west and south of Corral, along very isolated and forested roads above the ocean, are splendid and very rarely visited. The friendly tourist office on the pier can provide some trekking information. ▸▸ *For Sleeping, Eating and other listings, see pages 342-346.*

North of Valdivia

On the Río Cruces, 42 km north of Valdivia, lies the small town of **San José de la Mariquina**. From the town an unpaved road leads south along the river to the **Fuerte de San Luis de Alba de Cruces** (22 km), a colonial fortification built in 1647 and largely rebuilt according to the original plans.

West of San José, **Mehuín** is a small, friendly resort and fishing port with a long beach. The fishermen here are usually willing to take people out to see the nearby sealion and penguin colonies, and with a little luck dolphins can also be spotted. A clifftop *ripio* road, with fantastic views north and south along the coastline, leads 6 km north to **Queule**, which has a good beach, but which is dangerous for bathing at high tide because of undercurrents. (Bathing is safer in the river near the ferry.) From Queule, a pretty road leads north again to **Toltén**; numerous small ferry crossings provide access to isolated Mapuche communities and there are wonderful beaches along the coast. ▸▸ *For Sleeping, Eating and other listings, see pages 342-346.*

East of Valdivia

Towards Lago Riñihue

The route east from Valdivia to the lakes passes through what is, perhaps, the least interesting part of the Lake District, consisting largely of wheatfields and dairy farms. Ninety-three kilometres east of Valdivia, beyond Antilhue (where there are picnic sites) and Los Lagos, is **Lago Riñihue** the southernmost of the Seven Lakes. **Riñihue**, a beautiful but small and isolated village at its western end, is worth visiting but the road around the southern edge of the lake from Riñihue to Enco is closed (except to jeeps in summer only) and there is no road around the northern edge of the lake.

Lago Ranco → *Colour map 4, B2.*

South of Lago Riñihue is Lago Ranco, one of the largest lakes, covering 41,000 ha, and also one of the most accessible as it has a road, albeit terrible, round its edge. The road is characterised by lots of mud and animals, including oxcarts. However it is worth taking the opportunity to witness an older lifestyle and to see the beautiful lake, starred with islands, and the sun setting on the distant volcanoes. There is excellent fishing on the southern shore; several hotels organise fishing expeditions.

❖ *If you're travelling to Lago Ranco from the south, access is via La Unión and Río Bueno, which are bypassed by the Pan-American Highway.*

From the Pan-American Highway the lake can be reached from Los Lagos or from a point 18 km further south. These two roads join and meet the road around the lake some 5 km west of **Futrono**. This the main town on the northern shore and has a daily boat service to **Huapi,** the island in the middle of the lake. From Futrono the road curves round the north of the lake to **Llifén,** Km 22, a picturesque place on the eastern shore. From Llifén, it is possible visit **Lago Maihue,** 33 km further east, the south end of which is surrounded by native forests. From Llifén the road around Lago Ranco continues via the Salto de Nilahue (Km 14) to **Riñinahue,** Km 23, at the southeast corner, with access to beaches. Further west is **Lago Ranco,** Km 47, an ugly little town on the south shore, which has a museum with exhibits on Mapuche culture. On the western shore is **Puerto Nuevo,** where there are watersports and fishing on the Río Bueno. Further north, 10 km west of Futrono, is **Coique** , where there are more good beaches. ▸▸ *For Sleeping, Eating and other listings, see pages 342-346.*

● Sleeping

Valdivia *p337, maps p343 and p344.*
Accommodation is scarce during **Semana Valdiviana**. There are many options on Picartea and on A Muñoz opposite bus terminal.
L-AL Puerta del Sur, *Los Lingues 950, Isla Teja, T063-224500, www.hotelpuertadel sur.com* 5 star, all facilities, very good.
A Melillanca, *Alemania 675, T063-212509, www.melillanca.cl* With breakfast, modern.
A Naguilán, *Gen Lagos 1927, T063-212851, cisco@hotelnaguilan.com* Clean, quiet, pool, good restaurant.
A Villa del Río, *España 1025, T063-216292, F063-217851.* Restaurant expensive, rents apartments with kitchen.
B Hostal Torreón, *P Rosales 783, T063-212622, hostorreon@telsur.cl* With breakfast, nice atmosphere, cable TV, parking.

B Palace, *Chacabuco 308 y Henríquez, T063-213319, F063-219133* With breakfast, good, comfortable.
C Prat, *Prat 595, T063-222020.* With good breakfast and bath, cable TV.
C Hosp Universitaria, *Serrano 985, T063-218775.* Breakfast, kitchen facilities, family atmosphere, clean, cheap meals.
C-F Aires Buenos, *Gral Lagos 1036, T063-206304.* Price per person. Some rooms with bath. New, kitchen facilities, bar, internet, tours, Spanish and Tango lessons, Argentinian run, English spoken, recommended.
C-F Hosp Andwandter, *Anwandter 601, T063-218587.* Rooms near the bus terminal with bath and breakfast. Cheaper without.
C-F Hosp Pérez Rosales, *Pérez Rosales 1037, T063-215607, trivinos@surnet.cl* With or without bath and breakfast. Modern, small rooms, good beds, electricity supply shares a circuit with a welding business next door.

Lagos Ranco & Maihue

C-F **Villa Beauchef**, *Beauchef 844,*
T063-216044, beauchef@hotmail.com With
or without bath and breakfast, cable TV.
F **Hosp International**, *García Reyes 660,*
T063-212015. Price per person. With breakfast,
without bath, clean, helpful, use of kitchen.
Recommended; also more expensive rooms
with bath, and *cabañas.*
F **Hostal Casagrande**, *Andtwandter 880,*
T063-202035. Price per person. With
breakfast, more expensive rooms with
bath, cable TV. Attractive old house,
laundry facilities. Recommended.
Near the bus terminal.
G **Hostal del 900**, *Picarte 953, T063-213055.*
Price per person. With breakfast. Near the
bus terminal.
F **Hostal Esmeralda**, Esmeralda 651,
T063-215659. Price per person. With bath,
cheaper without bath, also *cabañas*, parking.
F **Sra Paredes**, *García Reyes 244.* Price per
person. With breakfast, hot water.
Recommended.
G **Albergue Juvenil**, *García Reyes s/n, off*
Picarte. Very cheap youth hostel, open
Jan/Feb only.

G *Aníbal Pinto 1335*. Price per person.
Friendly and cheap.
G *Gen Lagos 874, T063-215946.* Price per
person. With breakfast, old German house,
pleasant family atmosphere. Recommended.
G *Picarte 2625, T063-216750.* Price per person.
Clean, German spoken, recommended.
G **Res Germanía**, *Picarte 873, T063-212405.*
Price per person. With breakfast, without bath,
poor beds, clean, German spoken, Hostelling
International reductions. Near the bus terminal.
G *Riquelme 15, T063-218909.* Price per person.
With breakfast, friendly, clean, good value.

Camping
Camping Centenario, *rowing club on*
España. Overlooking the river.
Isla Teja, *T063-213584.* Views over the river.

Along the Río Valdivia *p339*
B-C **Cabañas Fischer**, *Niebla, T063-282007.*
Cabañas and camping. Worth bargaining
out of season.
C **Hostería Mancera**, *Isla Mancera,*
T/F063-216296. Open Dec-Mar, depending
on weather, no singles, phone first, no
drinking water.

Valdivia

Botanical Gardens

Río Calle-Calle

To the North

Av Costanera

A Prat

Río Valdivia

Caupolicán

Ismael Valdés

16

2

C Andwandter

14

Av Alemania

7

5

Antonio Muñoz

Martí

Torreón de los Canelos

To Universidad Austral,
2 & Niebla

Carampangue

Chacabuco

6

O'Higgins

Picarte

P De Valdivia

17

12

Picarte

9

Condell

Independencia

Plaza de la República

Arauco

G Reyes

5

18

Errázuriz

Pedro Montt

Maipú

B

3

To the South

Museo Histórico y Antropológico & Museo de Arte Moderno

A

10

Esmeralda

Beauchef

Benefícencia

Bertolotto

Museo Cultural Austral

Pérez Rosales

C Henríquez

Y Buenas

Isla Teja

Yungay

1

8

Cochrane

Carrillo

Baquedano

Franciscan Church

19

Torreón del Barro

To Naguilán & 13

To 1

E Riquelme

Santa María

N

0 metres 200
0 yards 200

Sleeping
Aires Buenos 13
Hospedaje
  Andwandter 2
Hospedaje
  Internacional 5
Hospedaje Pérez
  Rosales 1
Hostal Casagrande 7
Hostal del 900 9
Hostal Esmeralda 10
Hostal Montserrat 12
Hostal Torreón 8
Melillanca 14
Prat 16
Puerta del Sur 3
Residencial
  Germanía 17
Villa Beauchef 18
Villa Paulina 19

Eating
Cervecería Kunstmann
  2
La Calesa 1
New Orleans 3
Shanghai 5
Volcán 6

The Lake District Valdivia & around

C-F Villa Santa Clara, *Niebla, T063-282018*. Price per person with breakfast, also *cabañas*, cooking and laundry facilities.
F Hostería Los Alamos, *Corral*. Price per person. Perfect for a quiet life.
F Res Mariel, *Tarapacá 36, Corral, T063-471290*. Price per person. Modern, clean, friendly, good value.

North of Valdivia *p341*
The following are all in Mehuín. There are also two simple *residenciales* in **Queule**.
B El Nogal, *T/F063-451352*. With bath and breakfast, good.
G Hosp Marbella. Price per person. Clean and the cheapest option.

East of Valdivia *p341*
C Hostería Huinca Quinay, *3 km east of Riñihue, Lago Riñihue, T063-461347, F063-461406*. *Cabañas* and restaurant.
C Riñimapu, *Lago Riñihue, T063-311388*. Comfortable, good value, excellent food.

Lago Ranco *p341, map p342*
Houses around the lake are available for let in summer.
AL Hotel Puerto Nuevo, *Puerto Nuevo, 064-375540/064-491376*. Very good.

A Hostería Riñinahue, *Casilla 126, Riñinahue, T063-491379*. Organises fishing expeditions.
B Cabañas Chollinco, *3 km out of Llifén, on the road towards Lago Maihue, T063-1971979*. Limited electricity, swimming pool.
B Huequecura, *Llifén, T09-6535450*. Includes meals and fishing services, good restaurant.
D Hosp Futronhue, *Balmaceda 90, Futrono, T063-481265*. Good breakfast.

Camping
There are campsites all around Lago Ranco as well as several on Lago Maihue, though many are open in summer only and prices are high.
Bahía Coique, *9 km west of Futrono, T063-481264*. Autocamping, US$50 per site in summer, US$35 per site off season.
Bahía Las Rosas, *1 km east of Futrono*. US$18 per site.
Camping Lago Ranco, *Lago Ranco*. US$15 per site.
Maqueo, *eastern shore of Lago Maihue*, US$18 per site.
Nalcahue, *1 km west of Futrono, T063-481663*. US$18 per site.
Playa Ranquil, *Riñinahue*, US$10 per site.

⊕ Eating

For places to eat in the coastal resorts and around the lakes, see Sleeping, above.

Valdivia *p337, maps p343 and p344*.
There are plenty of very cheap restaurants serving good food down by the waterfront, facing the boat dock, and in the market.
$$$ Restaurante Camino de Luna, *Prat s/n*. A floating restaurant next to the *costanera*, unique in Chile.
$$ Cervecería Kunstmann, *on the road to Niebla, T063-292969, www.cerveza-kunstmann.cl* German food, brewery with five varieties of beer, recommended.
$$ Delicias, *Henríquez 372*. Recommended for meals, cakes and real coffee.
$$ La Calesa, *Yungay 735, on the costanera*. Peruvian and international cuisine, plus music and an art gallery. Highly recommended.
$$ Shanghai, *Andwandter y Muñoz*. Pleasant Chinese.

Valdivia centre

Alemania
Carampangue
Buses to Niebla
Independencia
Chacabuco
Municipalidad
O'Higgins
Henríquez
Libertad
Picarte
Cathedral ■
Plaza de la República
Prat
Yungay
Maipú
Arauco
■ Muelle Fluvial
Río Valdivia
Rosales
San Carlos

N

| 0 metres | 100 |
| 0 yards | 100 |

Sleeping 🛏
Palace **1**
Pedro de Valdivia **2**

Eating ⊕
Café Haussmann **2**
Camino de Luna **6**
Entrelagos **4**

$ **Café Aruba**, *Picarte 766*. Good value, filling sandwiches.
$ **Derby**, *Henríquez 314*. Good value.
$ **Restaurant Volcán**, *Caupolicán y Chacabuco, Pichangas, Cazuelas*. Great food at a good price.

Cafés
Café Express, *Picarte 764*. For real coffee and sandwiches.
Café Haussmann, *O'Higgins 394*. Good tea and cakes.
Entrelagos, *Pérez Rosales 622*. Ice cream and chocolates, expensive.
La Baguette, *Libertad y Yungay*. Bakery selling French-style cakes and brown bread. Repeatedly recommended.
La Ultíma Frontera, *Perez Rosales 787 (in Centro Cultural 787)*. Real coffee, homemade cakes and more.

Along the Río Valdivia *p339*
$$ **Las Delicias**, *Niebla, T063-213566*. A restaurant with 'a view that would be worth the money even if the food weren't good'. Also *cabañas* and camping.

❶ Bars and clubs

Valdivia *p337, maps p343 and p344*.
Bataclan, *Henriquez 326*. Live music.
El Cantino, *Andwandter 385*. Brazilian bar/restaurant.
Fuerte de Pedro, *Caupolicán*. Cheap, new restaurant/bar.
La Bomba, *Caupolicán*. Pleasant old Valdivian bar, serves *empanadas*.

❷ Entertainment

Valdivia *p337, maps p343 and p344*.
There's a cinema on Chacabuco 300 block; **Cine Club UACH** on the university campus shows films at the weekend (not in summer).

❸ Festivals and events

Valdivia *p337, maps p343 and p344*.
Semana Valdiviana, in mid Feb, culminates in *Noche Valdiviana* on the Saturday with a procession of elaborately decorated boats which sail past the Muelle Fluvial.

Along the Río Valdivia *p339*
In mid Feb Niebla hosts a **Feria Costumbrista**, with lots of good food including *pullmay, asado* and *paila marina*.

❹ Shopping

Valdivia *p337, maps p343 and p344*.
Bookshops
Librería Andrés Bello, *Independencia 635*.
Librería/Centro Cultural 787, *Pérez Rosales 787*. Old mansion with hip bookstore, café and art exhibitions.
Librería Chiloé, *Caupolicán 410*.

Cameras and film
Fotoquick Agfa, *Picarte 430*.
Fotoquideon, *Picarte 417*.
Kodak, *Picarte 382*.

Supermarketss
Hiper-Unico, *Arauco 697*.
Las Brisas, *Henriquez 522 (on plaza)*.

❺ Transport

Valdivia *p337, maps p343 and p344*.
Air
LanChile several flights daily to/from **Santiago** every day via Temuco or Concepción.

Bus
Terminal at *Muñoz y Prat*, by the river. For local services along the Río Valdivia or to Lago Ranco, see below.

To **Santiago**, several companies, 11 hrs, most services overnight, US$12 *salón cama* US$24; to **Osorno**, every 30 mins, 2 hrs, several companies, US$3; to **Panguipulli**, Empresa Pirehueico, about every 30 mins, US$3; to **Puerto Montt**, many daily, 3 hrs, US$4; to **Castro**, 7 hrs, US$8; to **Temuco**, US$3; to **Puerto Varas**, 2¾ hrs, US$4; to **Frutillar**, 2¼ hrs, US$4; to **Villarrica**, JAC, 6 a day direct, 2½ hrs, US$3.50, continuing to **Pucón**, US$4.50, 3 hrs; to **Mehuin**, 2 hrs, US$2.

To Argentina to **Bariloche** via Osorno, 7 hrs, Bus Norte, US$14; to **Zapala**, Igi-Llaima, Mon, Thu, Sat, 2300, change in Temuco at 0200, arrive Zapala 1200-1500, depending on border crossing, US$34.

In summer there is a regular **steam train** service to **Antilhue**, from the train station on *Equador 2000, T063-214972*, Sun, 1½ hrs, return from Antilhue 2 hrs later, US$4 return. Special additional trips are often made on public holidays; check departure times before travelling.

Along the Río Valdivia *p339*
Boat
The tourist boats to **Isla Mancera** and **Corral**, depart from the Muelle Fluvial, *Av Prat 555, Valdivia*, 1330 daily, US$20 for half-day with meals. Several companies offer trips, including **Catamaran Extasis**, *T063-212464*, US$30 or US$45 with dinner.

There is an hourly ferry service between Niebla and Corral, 30 mins, $US0.75.

Bus
Bus to **Niebla** from *Chacabuco y Yungay*, Valdivia, roughly every 20 mins between 0730 and 2100, 30 mins, US$0.75; the service continues to **Los Molinos**. Also *colectivos*.

Lago Ranco *p341, map p342*
Buses from Valdivia to **Llifén** via Futrono, **Cordillera Sur**, 4 daily, US$2.50; to **Riñihue** via Paillaco and Los Lagos, frequent; from Osorno to **Lago Ranco**, Empresa Ruta 5, 6 daily.

● Directory

Valdivia *p337, maps p343 and p344.*
Airline offices LanChile, *Maipú 271, T063-258840.* **Banks and currency exchange** There is a Redbanc in the Hyperunico Supermarket (see above). **Banco del Estado**, *Camilo Henríquez 562*, huge commission on Tcs; good rates for cash at Banco Santander, *P Rosales 585*; **Corp Banca**, *Picarte 370*, Visa agent, will change cash and Tcs; Banco Santiago, *Arauco 149*, Mastercard agent; Turismo Cochrane, *Arauco 435*; **Casa de Cambio**, *Carampangue 325, T063-213305*; Turismo Austral, *Arauco y Henríquez, Galería Arauco*, accepts TCs. **Car hire** Automóvil Club de Chile, *García Reyes 490, T063-250376*; Autovald, *Henríquez 610, T063-212786*; Hertz, *Picarte 640* and at the airport, *T063-272273/T063-218316*; Turismo Méndez, *Gen Lagos 1335, T063-213205.*
Internet Cafe Phonet, *Libertad 127*, internet cafe, also very cheap call centre; Centro Internet Libertad, *Libertad 7*; **Internet** Letelier, *Letelier 236, of 202*; there are also several internet places on the plaza.
Laundry Au Chic, *Arauco 436*; Lavazul, *Chacabuco 300*; slow; coin laundry at Lavamatic, *Schmidt y Picarte*, Mon-Sat 0930-2030; **Manantial**, *Henríquez 809.*
Public showers In the market, US$1.
Telephone CTC, *Independencia 628, T063-252700*; Entel, *Pérez Rosales 601, T063-225334.*

Osorno and around

→ *Phone code: 064. Colour map 4, B2. Population: 114,000.*
Situated at the confluence of the Ríos Rahue and Damas, 921 km south of Santiago, Osorno is a reasonable base for visiting the southern lakes. Founded in 1553, it was abandoned in 1604 and was refounded by Ambrosio O'Higgins and Juan MacKenna O'Reilly in 1796. It later became one of the centres of German immigration; their descendants are still of great importance in the area. But this is not a touristic city, and is likely to be a place that you will pass through.

Ins and outs
Getting there Osorno is a key crossroads for bus routes in southern Chile. Passengers heading for Bariloche, Neuquén, Coyhaique or Punta Arenas will pass through here before making for the Puyehue Pass into Argentina; buses tend to leave from Puerto Montt, and travellers from Santiago may well change buses here. There are also hourly local services to Puerto Montt, as well as frequent services north to Temuco and Valdivia.

Getting around Osorno is not one of the largest cities in Chile, and most of the places visitors are likely to visit are within easy walking distance. Taxis or *colectivos* may be useful for longer trips. ▸▸ *For further details, see Transport, page 351.* **Tourist information** Information is available from **CONAF** ① *Rosas 430, To64-234393,* and from the provincial government office of **Sernatur** ① *Plaza de Armas, O'Higgins s/n, p 1, left, To64-234104.* The municipal tourist office is based in the bus terminal and in a kiosk on the Plaza de Armas, both open December to February, and offers free city tours ① *Mon-Fri 1500 and 1700, Jan-Feb only, book in advance.*

Sights

On the large **Plaza de Armas** stands the modern, concrete and glass cathedral, with many arches and a tower that is itself an open, latticed arch with a cross superimposed. West of the centre on a bend overlooking the river is the **Fuerte María Luisa**, built in 1793 and restored in 1977; only the river front walls and end turrets are still standing. East of the main plaza along Calle MacKenna are a number of late 19th-century wooden mansions built by German immigrants, now preserved as national monuments. Two blocks south of the Plaza is the **Museo Histórico Municipal** ① *Matta 809, Mon-Sun 1100-1900 in summer; Mon-Fri 0930-1730, Sat 1500-1800 in winter, US$1,* which has displays on natural history, Mapuche culture, the refounding of the city and German colonization. ▸▸ *For Sleeping, Eating and other listings, see pages 349-352.*

North and west of Osorno

Río Bueno, 30 km north, is celebrated for its scenery and fishing. The Spanish colonial fort, dating from 1777, is situated high above the river and offers fine views. Twenty-two kilometres further west on the Río Bueno is **Trumao,** a river port with a

Osorno

The Lake District Osorno & around

river launch service to La Barra on the coast. There are beaches at **Maicolpue**, 60 km west of Osorno, and **Pucatrihue**, which are worth a visit in the summer. Further north is the **Monumento Natural Alerce Costero**, a newly designated park covering 2,307 ha in the coastal mountain range and protecting an area of alerce forest (though a fire in 1975 destroyed some of the forest). Access is by a very poor road (32 km *ripio*, 20 km unpaved), which runs northwest from La Unión. There is a CONAF *guardería* and *refugio* at the entrance, from which a 3-km trail leads to a 3,500-year-old alerce tree.

East of Osorno

From Osorno Route 215 runs east to the Argentine frontier at the Puyehue Pass via the south shore of Lago Puyehue, Anticura and the Parque Nacional Puyehue. The **Auto Museo Moncopulli**, ① *Route 215, T064-204200, 1000-1900 daily, bus towards Entre Lagos*, 25 km east of Osorno is the best motor museum in Chile. Exhibits include a Studebaker collection from 1852 to 1966. There is also a 1950s-style cafeteria.

Lago Puyehue and the Parque Nacional → *Colour map 4, B2.*
Surrounded by relatively flat countryside, 47 km east of Osorno, **Lago Puyehue** extends over 15,700 ha. The southern shore is much more developed than the northern shore, which is accessible only by unpaved road from **Entre Lagos** at the western end. On the opposite side of the lake are the **Termas de Puyehue** ① *0900-2000 daily, US$3.50 outdoor pools, US$15 indoor pools.*

Stretching east from Lago Puyehue to the Argentine frontier, **Parque Nacional Puyehue** covers 107,000 ha, much of it in the valley of the Río Golgol. On the eastern side are several lakes, including Lago Constancia and Lago Gris. There are two volcanic peaks: **Volcán Puyehue** (2,240 m) in the north (access via a private track US$10) and **Volcán Casablanca** (also called Antillanca, 1,900 m). Leaflets on walks and attractions are available from the park administration at Aguas Calientes and from the ranger station at Anticura.

At **Aguas Calientes**, 4 km south of the Termas de Puyehue in a thickly forested valley, is an open-air pool (dirty) with very hot thermal water beside the Río Chanleufú

Lagos Puyehue & Rupanco

From Aguas Calientes the road continues 18 km southeast past three small lakes and through forests to **Antillanca** on the slopes of Volcán Casablanca. In winter a one-way traffic system operates on the last 8 km: ascending traffic from 0800 to 1200 and 1400 to 1730; descending traffic from 1200 to 1400 and after 1730. This is a particularly beautiful section, especially at sunrise, with views over Lago Puyehue to the north and Lagos Rupanco and Llanquihue to the south, as well as the snow-clad peaks of Calbuco, Osorno, Puntiagudo, Puyehue and Tronador forming a semicircle. The tree-line on Casablanca is one of the few in the world made up of deciduous trees (*nothofagus* or southern beech). From Antillanca it is possible to climb Casablanca for even better views of the surrounding volcanoes and lakes; there's no path and the hike takes about seven hours there and back; information from **Club Andino** in Osorno. On the south side of the volcano there are caves (accessible by road, allow five hours from **Hotel Antillanca**).

The paved Route 215 continues from the Termas de Puyehue to **Anticura**, northeast of Aguas Calientes. In this section of the park are three waterfalls, including the spectacular 40-m wide **Salto del Indio**. Legend has it that an Indian, enslaved by the Spanish, was able to escape by hiding behind the falls. Situated just off the road, the falls are on a marked path through dense forest which includes a 800-year-old Coihue tree known as 'El Abuelo'. ▸▸ *For Sleeping, Eating and other listings, see pages 349-352.*

Border with Argentina
The **Chilean frontier** post is 4 km east of Anticura at Pajaritos ① *immigration open second Sat in Oct-second Sat in Mar 0800-2100, otherwise 0800-1900*. From here it's a further 22 km east to the border at **Paso Puyehue**, although this route is liable to closure after snow. For private vehicles entering Chile, formalities are quick (about 15 mins), but include a search for fruit, vegetables and dairy produce. On the Argentine side the road continues to Bariloche.

Lago Rupanco
Lying south of Lago Puyehue and considerably larger, this lake covers 23,000 ha and is far less accessible and less developed for tourism than most of the other larger lakes. Access from the northern shore is via two unpaved roads that branch off Route 215. **El Paraíso** (aka Marina Rupanco), at the western tip of the lake, can be reached by an unpaved road south from Entre Lagos. A 40-km dirt road runs along the southern shore, via **Laguna Bonita**, a small lake surrounded by forest, and **Piedras Negras** to **Bahía Escocia** at the eastern end. From the south, access is from two turnings off the road between Osorno and Las Cascadas. ▸▸ *For Sleeping, Eating and other listings, see pages 349-352.*

● Sleeping

Osorno *p346, map p347*
AL **Del Prado**, *Cochrane 1162, T064-235020.*
Pool, garden, good meals, well-located.
AL-A **Waeger**, *Cochrane 816, T064-233721, PO Box 802, www.interpatagonia.com/waeger*
Comfortable 3-star, with poor restaurant.
A **Gran Hotel Osorno**, *O'Higgins 615, T064-232171, granhotelosorno@entelchile.net*
Cable TV, well furnished.
B **Inter-Lagos**, *Cochrane 515, T064-234695, www.hotelinterlagos.cl* With breakfast, garage, restaurant.

B-C **Pumalal**, *Bulnes 630, T064-242477, pumalal@entelchile.net* With breakfast, modern, airy, clean.
C **Res Riga**, *Amthauer 1058, T064-232945, resriga@telsur.cl* Clean, pleasant. Highly recommended but heavily booked in season.
B **Eduviges**, *Eduviges 856, T/F064-235023.*
Spacious, clean, quiet, attractive, gardens, also *cabañas*. Recommended.
C-D **Hostal Bilbao Express**, *Bilbao 1019, T064-262200, pazla@telsur.cl* With breakfast, parking, restaurant. Also **Res Bilbao II**, *MacKenna 1205, T/F064-264444.*
C-D **Res Hein**, *Errázuriz 1757, T064-234116.*
Old-fashioned, spacious, family atmosphere.

There are lots of cheap options near the bus terminal, including the following:

F *Amunátegui 520*. Price per person. Good.

F **Res Ortega**, *Colón y Errázuriz*. Price per person. Parking, basic, clean, friendly.

F *Anibal Pinto 1758, T064-238024*. Rooms with breakfast.

F **Hosp de la Fuente**, *Los Carrera 1587*. Price per person. Basic, friendly.

F **Res San Diego**, *Los Carrera 1551*. Price per person with breakfast.

G **Res Carillo**, *Angulo 454*. Price per person. Basic, clean.

Camping

Municipal site off Pan-American Highway near southern entrance to city, open Jan-Feb only, poor facilities, US$5 per site.

North and west of Osorno *p347*

D **Hostería Müller**, *Maicolpue, 60 km west of Osorno*. On the beach, clean, with good service, also a recommended campsite.

Lago Puyehue and the Parque Nacional *p348, map p348*

A private house close to the *termas* provides cheap accommodation, either room only or full board.

L **Hotel Termas de Puyehue**, *Termas de Puyehue, T064-232157, F064-371272*. Two thermal swimming pools (one indoors, very clean), theatre, conference centre, well maintained, meals expensive, beautiful scenery, heavily booked Jan-Feb (cheaper May to mid-Dec).

A **Cabañas No Me Olvides**, *Entre Lagos, T064-371633*. Cabins with kitchen.

B **Motel Ñilque**, *on the southern lakeshore, T064-231177*. Cabins (half-price May-Oct), fishing trips, watersports, car hire.

B-C **Hostería Entre Lagos**, *Ramírez 65, Entre Lagos, T064-371225*. Rooms with lake view.

B-C **Hotel Antillanca**, *at foot of Volcán Casablanca, T064-235114*. Includes free mountainbiking and parapenting, access to ski resort, decent restaurant/café, pool, sauna, friendly club-like atmosphere, also *refugio*.

C **Hostería Isla Fresia**, *access from the southern lakeshore, T064-236951*. Located on own island, transport provided.

E **Hosp Millaray**, *Ramirez 333, Entre Lagos, T064-371251*. Price per person with breakfast, excellent, clean, friendly.

F-G **Ruta 215**, *Ramírez 333, Entre Lagos, T064-371251*. Price per person with good breakfast. Clean, friendly, German spoken.

Camping

Camping No Me Olvides, *Km 56, on southern lakeshore*. US$10, also *cabañas*.

Chanleufu, *Aguas Calientes, T064-236988*. US$25 per site with hot water, also *cabañas*, an expensive café and a small shop.

Los Derrumbes, *1 km from Aguas Calientes*. No electricity, US$20 per site.

Playa Los Copihues, *Km 56.5, on southern lakeshore*. Hot showers, good.

There is also a CONAF *refugio* on Volcán Puyehue (check with CONAF in Anticura whether it is open) and a campsite beside the Río Chanleufú (US$4 pp).

Lago Rupanco *p349, map p348*

There is no accommodation on the northern shore of the lake.

L-AL **Puntiagudo Lodge**, *Bahía Escocia, T064-1974731, www.puntiagudolodge.cl* With breakfast, very comfortable, good restaurant, fly fishing, horseriding, boat excursions.

B **Refugio Club de Pesca y Caza**, *sector Islote, 7 km east of Piedras Negras, T064-232056*. Basic *refugio* with breakfast and bath.

Camping

There are several campsites on the southern shore, including at Puerto Rico.

Desague del Rupanco, *just south of El Paraíso*. No facilities.

Puerto Chalupa, *on northern shore, T064-232680, F064-232741*. US$28 per site.

● Eating

For other eating options in the area, see Sleeping, above.

Osorno *p346, map p347*

The bakery at *Ramírez 977* sells good wholemeal bread.

$$ **Dino's**, *Ramírez 898, on the plaza*. Good restaurant upstairs, bar/cafeteria downstairs.

$$ **La Paisana**, *Freire 530*. Arab specialities.

$$ **Peter's Kneipe**, *M Rodríguez 1039*. Excellent German restaurant.

$ **Chung Hwa**, *Matta 517*. Chinese.

$ **Travels**, *bus terminal*. Cheap snacks.

$ **Waldis**, *on Plaza de Armas*. Real coffee.

Lago Puyehue and the Parque Nacional *p348, map p348*

$$ Chalet Suisse, *Km 55, on the southern lakeshore, T064-234073*. Restaurant with excellent food.

$$ Jardín del Turista, *Entre Lagos, T064-371214*. Very good restaurant.

$$ Pub del Campo, *Entre Lagos, F064-371220*. Highly recommended restaurant.

O Shopping

Osorno *p346, map p347*
There is a new mall on *Calle Freire 542* with 3 internet cafes and a bookshop, **CM Books**, which sells some English titles.

Alta Artesanía, *MacKenna 1069*. Excellent handicrafts, not cheap.

Climet, *Angulo 603*. Fishing tackle.

Ekono, *Colón y Errázuriz*. Supermarket.

The Lodge, *Los Carrera 1291, local 5*. Fishing tackle.

▲▲ Activities and tours

Osorno *p346, map p347*
Skiing
Club Andino, *O'Higgins 1073*. Information and advice on skiing in the area.

Hotel Antillanca, see Sleeping, above, is attached to one of the smallest ski resorts in Chile; with three lifts, ski instruction and first aid available. Piste preparation is unreliable. Skiing is not difficult but quality depends on the weather: though rain is common it often does not turn to snow.

Lago Rupanco *p349*
Fishing
Lago Rupanco is very popular for fishing.
Bahía Escocia Fly Fishing offers excursions from the **Puntiagudo Lodge** (see Sleeping, above) advance booking required.

⊙ Transport

Osorno *p346, map p347*
Air
LanChile has flies daily to **Santiago** via Temuco.

Bus
Main terminal 4 blocks from Plaza de Armas at *Errázuriz 1400*, bus from centre, US$0.30. Left luggage open 0730-2030.

To **Santiago**, frequent, 11½ hrs, US$13, *semi cama* US$30; to **Valparaíso** and **Viña del Mar**, Tas Choapa, US$17; to **Arica**, Tas Choapa, US$45; to **Concepción**, US$8; to **Temuco**, US$6; to **Panguipulli**, Buses Pirehueico, 4 a day; to **Pucón** and **Villarrica**, Tur Bus, frequent, US$7; to **Valdivia**, frequent, 2 hrs, several companies, US$3, but Igi Llaima only US$1.80; to **Frutillar**, US$1.50, **Llanquihue**, **Puerto Varas** and **Puerto Montt**, every 30 mins, US$3; to **Puerto Octay**, Vía Octay, 6 daily 0815-1930 (return 0800-1930) Mon-Sat, 5 daily 0800-2000 Sun, (4 return buses), US$2; to **Lago Ranco** (town), 6 a day, Empresa Ruta 5, 2 hrs, US$2; to **Punta Arenas**, several each week, US$55; to **Anticura**, daily at 1620, 3 hrs .

Some local services leave from the **Mercado Municipal terminal**, 1 block west of the main terminal. To **Entre Lagos**, frequent in summer, reduced service off-season, **Expreso Lago Puyehue**, *T064-234919*, and Buses Puyehue, 45 mins, US$1; buses by both companies also continue to **Aguas Calientes**, off-season according to demand, 2 hrs, US$2. To **Puyehue**, 4-5 daily, 1½ hrs, US$2.50. Also frequent buses to **Río Bueno** and daily services to **Maicolpué** and **Pucatrihue** on the coast.

North and west of Osorno *p347*
River launches run between **Trumao** on the Río Bueno, 22 km west of Osorno to **La Barra** on the coast, 0900 Wed and Sat only, 5 hrs, return 0900 Thu and Sun, US$9, no service in winter. For bus services from Osorno, see above.

Lago Puyehue and the Parque Nacional *p348, map p348*
Note that buses from Osorno (see above) to **Entre Lagos** and **Aguas Calientes** do not stop at the lakeside (unless you want to get off at **Hotel Termas de Puyehue** and clamber down). There is no public transport from Aguas Calientes to **Antillanca**; hitching is always difficult, but it is not a hard walk.

Border with Argentina *p349*
Several bus companies run daily services from Puerto Montt via Osorno to **Bariloche** along this route (see p374). Although less scenic than the ferry journey across Lake Todos Los Santos and Laguna Verde (see p) this crossing is far cheaper, reliable and still a beautiful trip. Best views are from the right hand side of the bus.

Lago Rupanco *p349, map p348*
Bus from Osorno to **Piedras Negras** from the
main terminal, leaves 1230 Mon-Fri, 1630 on
Sat, returns from Piedras Negras early morning.

❶ Directory

Osorno *p346, map p347*
Airline offices LanChile, *E Ramirez 802,
T064-314949*. **Banks** ATMs at Banco BCI,
MacKenna 801, **Banco Santiago**, *MacKenna
787*, Visa agent. **Car mechanic**
Automotriz Amthauer, *Amthauer 1250*;
Automotriz Salfa Sur SA, *Fco Bilbao 857*.

Casas de cambio Cambio Tur, *MacKenna
1004*; **Turismo Frontera**, *Ramírez 949, local 11*
(Galería Catedral); if stuck try **Travels** bar
in bus terminal. **Internet** Chat-Mail MP3,
Patricio Lynch 1334; **Dream House**, *Matta
510*, opposite Chung Hwa Restaurant;
Pub Sa Tanca, *Patio Freire 542, local 18*;
Turismo Seis, *Patio Freire 542, local 8*.
Laundry Prat 678, allow at least a day.
Post office O'Higgins 645, also telex.
Telephone Ramírez at central plaza, Juan
MacKenna y Cochrane. **Useful
address** Automóvil Club de Chile, *Bulnes
463, T064-232269*, information and car hire.

Lago Llanquihue

*The second largest lake in Chile and the third largest natural lake in South America, Lago
Llanquihue is one of the highlights of the Lake District. Three snowcapped volcanoes can
be seen across the vast expanse of water: the perfect cone of Osorno (2,680 m), the
shattered cone of Calbuco (2,015 m), and the spike of Puntiagudo (2,480 m), as well as,
when the air is clear, the distant Tronador (3,460 m). On a cloudless night with a full
moon, the snows reflect eerily in the lake and the peace and stillness are hard to match.*

Ins and outs

Getting around The largest towns, Puerto Varas, Llanquihue and Frutillar are all on the
western shore, linked by the Pan-American Highway. Although there are roads around the
rest of the lake the eastern shore is difficult to visit without transport, and beyond Las
Cascadas, the road is narrow with lots of blind corners, necessitating speeds of 20-30
kph at best in places (see below). Beware of lorries that ply the route servicing the salmon
farms. There is almost no public transport on this section and hitching is very difficult.
▸▸ *For further information see Transport, page 362.* **Tourist information** There is no general
information centre for the lake, but each town has its own municipal tourist office.

Puerto Octay → *Phone code: 064. Colour map 4, B2. Population: 2,500*
Puerto Octay is a small town at the north tip of the lake 56 km southeast of Osorno, set
amid rolling hills, hedgerows and German-style farmhouses with views over the
Osorno volcano. Founded by German settlers in 1852, the town enjoyed a boom
period in the late 19th century when it was the northern port for steamships on the
lake: a few buildings survive from that period, notably the church and the enormous
German-style former convent. Since the arrival of railways and the building of roads,
the town has declined. Much less busy than Frutillar or Puerto Varas, Puerto Octay
offers an escape for those seeking peace and quiet.

    Museo el Colono ⓘ *Independencia 591, Tue-Sun 1000-1300, 1500-1900,
Dec-Feb only*, has displays on German colonization. Another part of the museum,
housing agricultural implements and machinery for making *chicha*, is just outside
town on the road towards **Centinela**. This peninsula, about 3 km south (taxi US$1.50
one way) along an unpaved road has accommodation, camping, a launch dock,
bathing beaches and watersports. It is a very popular spot in good weather, especially
for picnics, with fine views of the Osorno, Calbuco and Puntiagudo volcanoes. ▸▸ *For
Sleeping, Eating and other listings, see pages 357-362.*

66 99 On a cloudless night with a full moon, the snows of the volcanoes reflect eerily in Lago Llanquihue, and the peace and stillness of the lake are hard to match.

East of Puerto Octay

The eastern lakeside, with the Osorno volcano on your left is very beautiful. From Puerto Octay two roads run towards Ensenada, one *ripio* along the shore, and one paved. (They join up after 20 km.) At Km 10 along the lakeside route is **Playa Maitén**, a lovely beach, often deserted, with a marvellous view of Volcán Osorno. Continue for another 24 km past **Puerto Fonck**, which has fine 19th century mansions, and you'll reach **Las Cascadas**, surrounded by picturesque agricultural land, old houses and German cemeteries. To reach the waterfalls that give the village its name follow signs along a *ripio* road east to a car park, continue along a footpath over two or three log bridges over a stream, and after a final wade across you will arrive at a 40-m high natural cauldron, with the falls in the middle. The round trip takes about one-and-a-half hours. ➤➤ *For Sleeping, Eating and other listings, see pages 357-362.*

Volcán Osorno → *Colour map 4, C2.*

The most lasting image of Lago Llanquihue is the near perfect cone of Volcán Osorno, situated north of Ensenada on the eastern edge of the lake. Although the peak is on the edge of the Parque Nacional Pérez Rosales (see page 363), it is climbed from the

Lago Llanquihue

To Lago Rapanco

To Osorno

Pan-American Highway to Osorno

Puerto Octay · Playa Maitén
Centinela

Puerto Clocker

Las Cascadas · Volcán Osorno (2,652m)

To Petrohué

Frutillar Alto · Frutillar Bajo

Lago Llanquihue

Refugio La Burbuja

Puerto Oscuro

Saltos de Petrohué

Ensenada

Río Petrohué

Llanquihue

Río Maullín

La Poza

To Ralún, Cochamo, Puelo & Camino Austral

N

Puerto Varas

Volcán Calbuco (2,015m)

Pan-American Highway to Puerto Montt

To Puerto Montt

0 km 5
0 miles 5

western side, which lies outside the park. Access is via two roads that branch off the Ensenada-Puerto Octay road along the eastern edge of Lago Llanquihue: the northern one at Puerto Klocker, 20 km south of Puerto Octay; the other 2 km north of Ensenada (turning unmarked, high clearance vehicle necessary).

Guided ascents of the volcano (organised by agencies in Puerto Varas) set out from the *refugio* at **La Burbuja**. From here it is six hours to the summit. The volcano can also be climbed from the north (La Picada); this route is easier and may be attempted without a guide, although only experienced climbers should attempt to climb right to the top as ice climbing equipment is essential.➤➤ *For further details, see page 361.*

Ensenada
→ *Phone code: 065. Colour map 4, C2.*

Despite its lack of a recognizable centre, Ensenada is beautifully situated at the southeast corner of Lago Llanquihue, almost beneath the snows of Volcán Osorno. A good half-day trip from Ensenada itself is to **Laguna Verde**, about 30 minutes from **Hotel Ensenada**, along a beautiful circular trail behind the lake (take first fork to the right behind the information board), and then down the road to a secluded campsite at Puerto Oscuro on Lago Llanquihue.➤➤ *For Sleeping, Eating and other listings, see pages 357-362.*

The western shore

Frutillar

Lying about half-way along the western side of the lake, Frutillar is in fact two towns: **Frutillar Alto**, just off the main highway, and **Frutillar Bajo**, beautifully situated on the lakeside, 4 km away. The latter is possibly the most attractive and expensive town on the lake, with superb views from the *costanera* over the water with Volcanes Osorno and Tronador in the background. The town's atmosphere is very German and somewhat snobbish, but the **tourist office** ① *on the lakeside, T065-420198, open summer only* is helpful. In the square opposite is an open-air chess board and the **Club Alemán** restaurant. A new concert hall has recently been built on the lakeside to host the town's prestigious music festival in late January (see Festivals and events, below).

Away from the waterfront, the appealing **Museo Colonial Alemán** ① *off Prat, summer 1000-1930 daily; winter 1000-1330, 1500-1800 Tue-Sun, US$2*, is set in spacious gardens, with a watermill,

Frutillar Bajo

N

0 metres 200
0 yards 200

Sleeping 🛏
Casona del 32 **1**
Hospedaje Costa Azul **2**
Hospedaje Tía Clara **4**
Hospedaje Trayén **5**
Hospedaje Vivaldi **6**

Hostería El Arroyo **3**
Klein Salzburg **8**
Nohelia **10**
Pérez Rosales 590 **12**
Residenz/Café am See **13**
Winkler **14**

Eating 🍴
Andes **1**
Casino de Bomberos **2**
Club Alemán **3**
Selva Negra **4**

⁝ German colonization in the Lake District

The most important area of German agricultural colonisation in Chile was around Lago Llanquihue. The Chilean government declared the area as destined for colonisation in 1845, and to encourage settlement and help the new arrivals get started, gave each adult male 75 *cuadras* of land plus an extra 12 *cuadras* for each son, a milking cow, 500 planks of timber, nails, a yoke of oxen, a year's free medical assistance and Chilean citizenship on request.

The first groups of German colonists arrived in the area in 1852: one group settled around Maitén and Puerto Octay, another helped found Puerto Montt. The lives of these early settlers were hard and the risks great, yet within 10 years the settlers had cleared much of the forest round the lake and soon they were setting up small industries. In 1880, when the offer to colonists ended, unsettled land was auctioned in lots of 400-800 ha. By then the lake was ringed by a belt of smallholdings and farms. The legacy of this settlement can be seen in the German-looking farmhouses around Puerto Octay and in many of the older buildings in Frutillar and Puerto Varas.

Valdivia was another centre for German colonisation. A relatively small number of German and Swiss colonists settled in the city, exerting a strong influence on the architecture agricultural methods, education, social life and customs of the area. They established most of the industries that made Valdivia an important manufacturing centre until the 1950s. According to an 1884 survey all the breweries, leatherworks, brickworks, bakeries, machine shops and mills in Valdivia belonged to families with German surnames.

Little of the architectural heritage of this period survived the 1960 earthquake, but the city's German heritage can still be seen in some of its best cafés and restaurants and in the names of its streets.

replicas of two German colonial houses with furnishings and utensils of the period and a blacksmith's shop selling personally engraved horseshoes for US$5. It also has a *campanario*, a circular barn with agricultural machinery and carriages inside, as well as a handicraft shop. At the northern end of the town is the **Reserva Forestal Edmundo Winckler**, run by the Universidad de Chile and extending over 33 ha, with a guided trail through native woods. Named after one of the early German settlers, it includes a very good collection of native flora as well as plants introduced from Europe. ›› *For Sleeping, Eating and other listings, see pages 357-362.*

Llanquihue → *Phone code: 065.*

Twenty kilometres south of Frutillar, Llanquihue lies at the source of the Río Maullín, which drains the lake. The site of a large dairy processing factory, this is the least touristy town on the lake, and makes a cheaper alternative to Puerto Varas and Frutillar. It has uncrowded beaches and hosts a German-style beer festival at the end of January. ›› *For Sleeping, Eating and other listings, see pages 357-362.*

Puerto Varas and around → *Phone code: 065. Colour map 4, C2.*

Situated on the southwestern corner of the lake, Puerto Varas is the commercial and tourist centre of Lago Llanquihue. It also serves as a residential centre for Puerto Montt, 20 km to the south, with a population of 16,000. In the 19th century Puerto Chico (on the southern outskirts) was the southern port for shipping on the lake. With the arrival of the railway the settlement moved to its current location and is now a resort, popular with South American tourists. Despite the numbers of visitors, though, it has a friendly, compact feel, and is one of the best bases for exploring the southern Lake District, near centres for trekking, rafting, canyoning and fly fishing.

Ins and outs

Getting there Puerto Varas is served by many buses from Puerto Montt; there are also connections north to Osorno, and some that contine on to Valdivia and Temuco. A taxi to Puerto Montt airport costs US$16. **Getting around** Puerto Varas is small and easily navigable on foot. ▸▸ *For further details, see Transport page 362.* **Tourist information** The tourist office is in the Municipalidad ① *San Fransisco 413, T065-321330, securismo.puertovaras@ munitel.cl* Other places in town also claim to offer information, but may only give information about their paying members' services.

Sights

Parque Philippi, on top of a hill, is a pleasant place to visit, although the views are a bit restricted by trees and the metal cross at the top is unattractive. Also in the park is an electric clock that chimes the quarter-hours during daylight hours. To reach the summit walk up to **Hotel Cabañas del Lago** on Klenner, cross the railway and the gate is on the right. The centre lies at the foot of the hill, but the town stretches east along the lake to

Puerto Varas

To ② & Parque Philippi

Lago Llanquihue

To ② ② ② ② , Puerto Chico Ensenada & Petrohué

To ③ , Puerto Montt via Pan-American Highway

To ⑤

To Osorno via Pan-American Highway

Cruz del Sur Bus Terminal

0 metres 100
0 yards 100

Sleeping 💤
Agatha Haus **24** C3
Amancay **3** B1
Antonio Varas **1** B2
Bellavista **2** B3

Cabañas Ayentemo **4** B3
Cabañas del Lago **27** A2
Canales del Sur **25** B2
Casa Azul **5** B3
Colonos del Sur **6** B3
Colores del Sur **7** B2
Compass del Sur **8** B1
Del Bosque **9** B3
El Greco **10** B3
Ellenhaus **13** B2
Hospedaje AMAC **15** B2

Hospedaje Don Raúl **12** C1
Hostal Chancerel **16** A1
Hostal Erika **17** B3
Las Dalias **26** B3
Licarayén **19** B2
Loreley **18** B3
Los Alerces **14** B3
Motel Altué **22** B3
Outsider **21** B2
Terrazas del Lago **20** B3
Villa Germania **23** C1

Eating 🍴
Aníbal **1** B2
Dicaruzzo **11** B3
Espigas **3** B2
Ibis **8** B3
La Olla **2** B2, A3
Mediterráneo **6** A2
Merlin **5** B3
Rancho Chico **7** C3
Weiss **4** B2

Puerto Chico, where there are hotels and restaurants. The imposing **Catholic church** was built by German Jesuits in 1918 in Baroque style as a copy of the church in the Black Forest. North and east of the **Gran Hotel Puerto Varas** (1934) are a number of German-style mansions. ►► *For Sleeping, Eating and other listings, see pages 357-362.*

The southern shore

Puerto Varas is a good base for trips around the lake. A paved road runs along the south shore to Ensenada on the southwestern corner of the lake. Two of the best beaches are **Playa Hermosa,** Km 7 and **Playa Niklitschek,** Km 8, where an entry fee is charged. At Km 16 narrow channels overhung with vegetation lead south from Lago Llanquihue to the little lake of **La Poza.** There are boat trips (US$1.50) to the beautiful **Isla Loreley,** an island on the lake, and a channel leads from La Poza to yet another lake, the **Laguna Encantada.** At Km 21 there is a watermill and a restaurant run by the Club Alemán.

● Sleeping

Camping wild and having barbecues are forbidden on the lake shore.

Puerto Octay *p352*
AL **Hotel Centinela**, *T064-391326, www.hotelcentinela.cl* Built in 1913 as a summer mansion, this hotel has been recently restored. It is idyllically situated and has superb views, also *cabañas*, restaurant with grand minstrels' gallery and bar, open all year.
E **Hosp Raquel Mardorf**, *Germán Wulf 712.* Price per person with enormous breakfast, clean, comfortable.
F **Hostería La Baja**, *Centinela, T064-391269/09-1656280.* Price per person, with breakfast and bath. Beautifully situated at the neck of the peninsula.
F **Zapato Amarillo**, *35-mins' walk north of town, T064-391575, www.zapatoamarillo.8k.com* Excellent for backpackers and others, use of spotless kitchen, great breakfasts with homemade bread, very friendly, German and English spoken. Lots of information, mountain bike rental, tours, canoes and sailing boat, luggage storage, phone for free pick up from town. Main house has a grass roof or there's the roundhouse next door . Highly recommended.

Camping
Camping Municipal , *on lakeside, T064-391326.* US$15 per site.
El Molino, *beside lake.* US$5 per person, clean, friendly, recommended.

East of Puerto Octay *p353*
Several farms on the road around the north and east side of the lake offer accommodation; look for signs. Camping is possible at the **Centro de Recreación Las Cascades**, *T064-235377*, and at **Playa Maitén**.
F **Hostería Irma**, *on lake, 2 km south of Las Cascadas.* Price per person. Attractive former residence, good food, very pleasant.

Volcán Osorno *p353*
E There are two *refugios*, both of them south of the summit and reached from the southern access road: **La Burbuja**, the former ski-club centre, 14 km north of Ensenada at 1,250 m) and **Refugio Teski Ski Club**, just below the snow line. Price per person, meals served. **Refugio La Picada** marked on the northern slopes on many trekking maps burned down several years ago.

Ensenada *p354*
LL **Yan Kee Way Lodge**, *T065-212030.* Plush resort specialising in fly-fishing expeditions.
AL-B **Cabañas Brisas del Lago**, *T065-212012, briesen@telsur.cl* On beach, sleep 2-6, good restaurant nearby, supermarket next door. Highly recommended.
AL **Ensenada**, *Casilla 659, Puerto Montt, T065-222017, hotelensenada@surnet.cl* With bath, old-world style, good food, good view of lake and Volcán Osorno, runs tours, hires mountain bikes (guests only). Closed in winter. Also much cheaper *hostal* in the grounds with cooking facilities.
C **Hosp Arena**, *T065-212037.* With breakfast. Recommended.
C **Pucará**, *2 km from town.* With good restaurant (the steaks are recommended).
E **Hosp Ensenada**, *T065-338278.* Price per person. Very clean, excellent breakfast,
E-F **Hotel El Pilar**, south of Ensenada on Puerto Varas road. Price per person, also *cabañas*, situated away from the road with

good views of Volcan Osorno and good service. Recommended.

F Hosp Opazo. Price per person with breakfast, friendly.

D-F Ruedas Viejas, *about 1 km west from Ensenada, T/F065-212050*. Price per person, basic, damp,with hot water. Also *cabañas* and restaurant.

G Hosp Toqui, *above grocery shop*. Price per person. Cheapest in town, basic, quiet, hot water, use of kitchen, beach at the bottom of the back yard, recommended.

Camping

Montaña, *centre of town*. Price per site, good beach space.

Playa Larga, *1 km east of Hotel Ensenada*, US$10 per site.

Puerto Oscuro, *2 km north of Ensenada*, US$8 per site.

Trauco, *4 km west of Ensenada, T065-212033*. Large site with shops, fully equipped, US$4-9 per person.

Frutillar *p354, map p354*.

During the annual music festival accommodation should be booked well in advance; alternatively stay in Frutillar Alto or Puerto Varas. There are several cheap options along Carlos Richter (main street) in Frutillar Alto and at the school in Frutillar Alto in Jan-Feb (sleeping bag required).

AL Hostal Cinco Robles, *1 km north of Frutillar Bajo, T065-421351, eirotec@terra.cl* With breakfast, other meals on request, parking.

AL Salzburg, *Playa Maqui, 7 km north of Frutillar Bajo, T065-421589*. Excellent restaurant, plus sauna, mountain bikes, tours and fishing.

A-B Los Maitenes, *3 km north of Frutillar Bajo, T065-330033, www.interpatagonia.com/losmaitenes* In an old country house in 16 hectares of land by the lake (private beach), fishing trips, free pick-up from terminal.

A Casona del 32, *Caupolicán 28, Frutillar Bajo, T065-421369*. With breakfast, comfortable old house, central heating, English and German spoken. Recommended.

A Residenz/Café am See, *Philippi 539, Frutillar Bajo, T065-421539,*

ciberg@123mail.cl Good breakfast.

C Hostería El Arroyo, *Philippi 989, Frutillar Bajo, T065-421560, alarroyo@surnet.cl* With breakfast. Highly recommended.

C *Philippi 451, Frutillar Bajo, T065-421204*. Clean accommodation and good breakfast.

C Winkler, *Philippi 1155, Frutillar Bajo, T065-421388*. Discount to Hostelling International members, cabins, friendly.

C-D Hosp Costa Azul, *Philippi 1175, Frutillar Bajo, T065-421388*. For families, good breakfasts.

D *Perez Rosales 590, Frutillar Bajo*. Cabañas and excellent breakfast.

E Hosp Vivaldi, *Philippi 851, Frutillar Bajo, T065-421382*. Price per person. Quiet, comfortable, excellent breakfast and lodging, also family accommodation. Recommended.

F Hosp Tia Clara, *Perez Rosales 743, Frutillar Bajo, T065-421806*. Price per person, kitchen facilities, very friendly, good value.

G Hosp Juana Paredes, *Anibal Pinto y Winkler, Frutillar Alto, T065-421407*. Price per person. Recommended, also *cabañas* for up to 5 and parking.

Camping

Los Ciruelillos, *2 km south of Frutillar Bajo, T065-339123*. Most services.

Playa Maqui, *7 km north of Frutillar, T065-339139*. Fancy, expensive site.

Sr Guido González, *Casa 3, Población Vermont, T065-421385*. Recommended site.

Llanquihue *p355*
Camping

Baumbach, *1 km north of Llanquihue, T065-242643*. On lakeside, meals available.

El Totoral, *8 km north of Llanquihue, T065-339123*. Campsite and *cabañas*.

Playa Werner, *2 km north Llanquihue, T065-242114*. On lakeside.

Puerto Varas *p355, map p356*

There are many hotels all along the lake front, but in high season they tend to be tourist traps

L Colonos del Sur, *Del Salvador 24, T065-233369, www.colonosdelsur.cl*. Good views of the lake, decent rooms, good restaurant and tea-room. Has another hotel at *Estación 505*.

King Edward VIII stayed at the Hotel Centinela in Puerto Varas with Mrs Simpson after abdicating the British throne in 1936.

AL **Antonio Varas**, *Del Salvador 322,*
T065-232375, F065-232352. Very comfortable.
AL **Bellavista**, *Pérez Rosales 060,*
T065-232011, www.hotelbellavista.cl. Cheerful
with good views over the lake, restaurant
parking, recommended.
AL **Cabañas del Lago**, *Klenner 195,*
T065-232291, www.cabanasdellago.cl On
Philippi hill overlooking lake, superb views.
Also self-catering *cabañas* sleeping 5 (good
value for groups), cheaper rates in low
season, heating, sauna.
AL-A **Licarayén**, *San José 114, T065-232305,*
F065-232955. Overlooks lake, comfortable,
clean, 'the perfect place for bad weather or
being ill', recommended. Book in season.
A **Los Alerces**, *Pérez Rosales 1281,*
T065-232060, reservalosalerces@hotmail.com.
4-star, with breakfast, also new cabin
complex, attractive.
A **Cabañas Ayentemo**, *Pérez Rosales 0950,*
T065-233412, www.ayentemo.cl Clean,
comfortable, friendly.
A **El Greco**, *Mirador 134, T065-233388,*
www.elgreco.cl Modern, good.
A **Terrazas del Lago**, *Pérez Rosales 1571,*
T/F065-232622. Good breakfast, views over
Osorno volcano, restaurant
B **Del Bosque**, *Santa Rosa 714, T065-232897,*
www.travelsur.com With breakfast,
recommended.
B **Hotel Loreley**, *Maipo 911, T065-232226.*
Homely, quiet. Recommended.
B **The Outsider**, *San Bernardo 318,*
T065-232910, outsider@telsur.net With bath,
real coffee, meals, friendly, comfortable.
German and English spoken, book in advance.
B-C **Agatha Haus**, *Route 5 on southern*
outskirts, T065-232190,
dasagathahaus@hotmail.com Very relaxed,
German spoken.
C **Hostal Chancerel**, *Decher 400,*
T065-234221, www.turismochancerel.com
Also offers tours.
C-F **Las Dalias**, *Santa Rosa 707, T065-233277.*
Doubles with bath or simpler rooms (price
per person). Peaceful , clean, good breakfast
with real coffee, parking, German spoken.
E **Hosp AMAC**, *San Bernardo 313,*
T065-234216. Price per person. Apartment-
style accommodation, clean, comfortable,
heating in lounge, TV, kitchen, hot water.
E **Hosp Carla Minte**, *Maipo 1010,*
T065-232880. Price per person with breakfast,

cable TV, very comfortable.
E **Hosp Las Carmelas**, *Imperial y Rosario.*
Price per person. Excellent, helpful, good
meals, lends books including some in
English. Highly recommended.
F **Amancay**, *Walker Martínez 564,*
T065-232201,
c_bittner_amancay@chile.com Price per
person with breakfast. Some rooms with
bath. Friendly, German spoken, also *cabañas*,
sleep 4. Recommended.
F **Canales del Sur**, *Pasage Ricke 224,*
T065-346121, www.canalesdelsur.com Price
per person, very friendly and helpful, tours
arranged.
F **Casa Azul**, *Manzanal 66 y Rosario,*
T065-232904, www.casaazul.net
German/Chilean owners, homemade muesli
for breakfast, large kitchen, good beds with
duvets, internet, book exchange,
comfortable common area, English and
German spoken, tours organised, friendly,
helpful. Highly recommended.
F **Colores del Sur**, *Santa Rosa 318,*
T065-231850, jurohe@hotmail.com Kitchen
facilities, without breakfast, hospitable, good
meeting place.
F **Compass del Sur**, *Klenner 467,*
T065-232044, compassdelsur.cl
Chilean-Swedish run, kitchen facilities,
internet, cable TV in comfortable lounge,
breakfast with muesli and real coffee,
friendly, helpful, lots of information, tours,
German, English, Swedish spoken, highly
recommended. Also camping.
F **Hosp Imperial**, *Imperial 653, T065-232451.*
Price per person. Clean, including breakfast,
central, recommended.
F **Villa Germania**, *Nuestra Sra del Carmen 873,*
T065-233162. Price per person. Also *cabañas*.
F-G **Ellenhaus**, *Walker Martínez 239,*
T065-233577, ellenhaus@yahoo.com. Price
per person. Kitchen and laundry facilities,
luggage stored, lounge, German and English
spoken, recommended.
F-G **Hosp Don Raúl**, *Salvador 928,*
T065-234174. Price per person. Laundry and
cooking facilities, very friendly, garden with
hammock, clean. Recommended. Camping
by main road.

Camping
Trauco, *Imperial 433, T065-236262.* Expensive
but central.

Camping

Los Troncos, *10 km east of Puerto Varas, T09-9206869*. US$10 per site, no beach access.
Playa Hermosa, *7 km east of Puerto Varas*. Fancy ground, US$20 per site, bargain off season. Recommended. Take own supplies.
Playa Niklitschek, *8 km east of Puerto Varas, T065-338352*. Full facilities.

⊘ Eating

Puerto Octay *p352*

$$ **El Rancho del Espanta-Pajaros** *6 km south on the road to Frutillar, T065-339141*. In a converted barn with wonderful views over the lake, serves all kind of spit roasted meat. All you can eat, with salad bar and drinks included, for US$10. Also arranges horseriding trips. Recommended.
$$ **Fogón de Anita**, *1 km out of town*. Mid-price grill.
$ **Restaurante Baviera**, *Germán Wulf 582*. Cheap and good.
$ **Restaurante La Cabaña**, *Germán Wulf 713*. Good, cheap.

Ensenada *p354*

$$$ **Latitude 42**, *Yan Kee Way resort, T065-212030*. Expensive, excellent and varied cuisine, very good quality wine list.
$ **Canta Rana**. Recommended for bread and *Küchen*.
$ **Donde Juanito**, *west of Ensenada*. Excellent value cheap set lunch.

Frutillar *p354, map p354.*

$$ **Andes**, *Philippi 1057, Frutillar Bajo*. Good set menus and à la carte.
$$ **Club Alemán**, *Av Philippi 747*. Good but not cheap, hostile to backpackers.
$$ **Selva Negra**, *Varas 24 y Philippi, Frutillar Bajo*. Located in a traditional German mill, with scores of toy witches hanging from the ceiling, open 1100-2300.
$ **Casino de Bomberos**, *Philippi 1060, Frutillar Bajo*. Upstairs bar/restaurant, open all year, memorable painting caricaturing the firemen in action. Great value but service can be poor.

Cafés

There are several German-style cafés on Calle Philippi, including **Salón de Te Frutillar** at No 775 and **Guten Apetit** at No 1285.

Puerto Varas *p355, map p356*

The expensive motel restaurants at the end of the *costanera* aren't worth visiting, although service is friendly.

$$$ **Merlin**, *Imperial 0605, on the road east out of town, T065-233105, www.merlinrestaurant.cl* Has the reputation as one of the best restaurants in the Lake District. Often recommended, but some adverse reports.
$$ **La Olla**, *San Bernado y Martinez*. Seafood and traditional Chilean cuisine. Recommended. There is another branch on the *costanera* going east.
$$ **Mediteraneo**, *Santa Rosa 068*. On the lakefront, varied menu, good.
$$ **Dicaruzzo**, *Costanera 01071*. Recommended.
$$ **Espigas**, *Martínez 417, local 3*. Vegetarian.
$$ **Ibis**, *Costanera 1117*. Very good.
$ **Aníbal**, *Del Salvador y Santa Rosa*. Pizzas, cheap, tasty.
$ **Domino**, *Del Salvador 450*. Good, cheap choice.
$ **Donde El Gordito**, *downstairs in market*. Large portions, no set menu, mixed reports.
$ **El Amigo**, *San Bernardo 240*. Large portions, good value. Recommended.
$ **Rancho Chico**, *San Francisco opposite the church*. Menus for US$3.
$ **Weiss**, *San José 415*. Great value, very good meat, seriously cheap.

Cafés

Café Danés, *Del Salvador 441*. Good coffee and cakes.
Coffee Break, *San José 319*. Real coffee.
El Molino, *on road to Ensenada 22 km east* . Café next to an old water mill.

⊙ Bars and clubs

Puerto Varas *p355, map p356*
Barómetro, *San Pedro 418*. Cosy bar serving Kuntstman beer and food.
Pim's, *San Francisco near Calle Imperial*. Spacious US-style pub with food.

 For an explanation of sleeping and eating price codes used in this guide, see inside the front cover. Other relevant information is found in Essentials, see pages 51-58.

⊕ Festivals and events

Frutillar *p354, map p354*
A highly regarded classical **music festival** is held in the town between Jan and early Feb; tickets must be booked well in advance from the Municipalidad, *T065-421290*.

Llanquihue *p355*
A German-style **beer festival** with oom-pah music is held here at the end of Jan.

◯ Shopping

Ensenada *p354*
There are several shop selling basic supplies. Most places are closed off season, other than a few pricey shops, so take your own provisions.

Frutillar *p354, map p354*.
Services and shops are generally much better in Frutillar Alto, although in Frutillar Bajo, seek out **Der Volkladen**, *O'Higgins y Philippi*, for natural products, including chocolates, cakes and cosmetics.

Puerto Varas *p355, map p356*
El Libro del Capitán, *Martiínez 417*. Book shop with a large selection in German and English. Also book swap.
Las Brisas, *Salvador 451*. Supermarket.
Mamusia, *San José 316*. Chocolates.
VYH Meistur, *Walker Martínez*. Supermarket with a good selection, reasonably priced.

▲ Activities and tours

Most tours operate in season only (Sep-May).

Ensenada *p354*
Southern Chile Expeditions, *T065-213030, www.southernchilexp.com* Expensive fly-fishing tours.

Frutillar *p354, map p354*
Viajes Frutillar, *Richter y Alissandre, Frutillar Alto*. Travel and tour agent.

Puerto Varas *p355, map p356*
Fishing
The area around Puerto Varas is popular for fishing. A licence (obligatory) is obtainable from the Municipalidad. Fishing expeditions are organised by many operators (see below). The Río Pescado (25km east of Puerto Varas) is a good easy alternative for those who do not want to hire a guide.

Horseriding
Cabañas Puerto Decher, *Fundo Molino Viejo, 2 km north of Puerto Varas, T065-338033*. Guided tours, horseriding, minimum 2 people, mixed reports.
Campo Aventura, *San Bernardo 318, T065-232710*. English and German spoken, offer 1, 3 and 10-day trips on horseback (see Cochamó, p365).

Tour operators
Alsur, *Del Salvador 100, T065-232300, www.alsurexpeditions.com* Rafting on Rió Petrohue. Official tour operator to the Parque Pumalín. Sells trekking maps.
Andina del Sud, *Del Salvador 72, T065-232811*. Operates 'lakes' trip to Bariloche, Argentina via Lago Todos los Santos, Peulla, Cerro Tronador, plus other excursions.
Aqua Motion, *San Fransisco, T065-232747, www.aquamotion.cl* Rafting, trekking, mountain biking, fishing. Ludwig Godsambassis, owner of Ruedas Viejas, who works for Aqua Motion, also works independently as a trekking guide out of season and is very knowledgeable about flora and fauna.
Kokayak, *San José 320, T065-346433*, French/Chilean run, offers bike hire, white-water rafting and sea kayaking.
Tranco Expeditions, *Santa Rosa 580, T065-311311, www.trancoexpediciones.cl* Trekking, rafting and climbing, Norwegian and English spoken, good equipment.
Travel Art, *Imperial 0661, T065-232198, www.travelart.cl*. Biking and hiking tours.
Turismo Biker, *Café Terranova, on Plaza, turismobiker@yahoo.es*. Specialists in downhill mountain bike trips. Not for the fainthearted.

Volcán Osorno *p353*
Climbing
Weather permitting, agencies in Puerto Varas organise climbing expeditions with a local guide, transport from Puerto Montt or Puerto Varas, food and equipment, US$150 per person, payment in advance (minimum group

2, maximum 6 with 3 guides). Weather conditions are checked the day before and a 50% refund is available if the climb is abandoned due to weather. Those climbing from La Burbuja must register with CONAF at La Burbuja, and show they have suitable equipment. Those climbing from the north (La Picada) are not subject to any checks.

⊖ Transport

Puerto Octay *p352*
Buses to **Osorno**, 9 a day, US$2; to **Las Cascadas** Mon-Fri 1730, return next day 0700. Thaebus runs 5 daily services to **Frutillar**,1 hr, US$0.90, **Puerto Varas**, 2 hrs, and **Puerto Montt**, 2¼ hrs, US$2.

Ensenada *p354*
Frequent minibuses run from **Puerto Varas** in summer. Buses from Puerto Montt via Puerto Varas to **Cochamó** also stop here. Hitching from Puerto Varas is difficult.

Frutillar *p354, map p354.*
Colectivos run between the two towns, 5 mins, US$0.50. Most buses to other destinations leave from opposite the Copec station in Frutillar Alto. Thaebus and others have frequent services to **Puerto Varas**, US$0.75, and **Puerto Montt**, US$1.25. To **Osorno**, Turismosur, 1¼ hrs, US$1.50; to **Puerto Octay**, Thaebus, 5 a day.

Puerto Varas *p355, map p356*
Minibuses to **Ensenada** and **Petrohué** leave from *San Bernardo y Martínez*; regional buses stop on *San Fransisco 500 block*; long distance buses leave from their own terminals.

To **Santiago**, Turbus, Igi Llaima, Cruz del Sur and several others, US$13, *semi cama* US$20, *salón cama* US$30. Thaebus, Full Express and others have services to **Puerto Montt**, every 15 mins, 30 mins, US$0.70; same companies, same frequency to **Frutillar**, 30 mins, US$0.75, and **Osorno**, 1 hr, US$2.50. Same companies hourly to **Petrohue**, US$3. To **Valdivia**, 3 hrs, US$4.50; to **Temuco**, US$8; to **Cochamó** via

Ensenada, 5 a day, US$2. Services from Puerto Montt to **Bariloche** (Argentina) also stop here. For the **Andina del Sud** lakes route via Lago Todos Los Santos, see p367.

⊕ Directory

Frutillar *p354, map p354.*
Banks Banco Santander, *Phillippi, at the lakeside*, with Redbanc ATM taking Visa and other cards. **Car mechanic** Toirkens, *Los Carrera 1260*, highly recommended. **Post office** *San Martín y Pérez Rosales*, Mon-Fri 0930-1230, 1430-1800, Sat 0900-1230. **Telephone** call centre at *Phillippi 883.* **Useful services** Toilet, showers and changing cabins for beach on O'Higgins.

Puerto Varas *p355, map p356*
Banks Redbancs at the following: BBVA, *San Pedro 326*; De Chile, *Salvador 201*; Del Estado, *Santa Rosa 414*; Santiago, *San José 291*; exchange also at Banco Osorno, *Del Salvador 399*, good rates. **Car hire** Adriazola Expediciones, *Santa Rosa 340, T065-233477*; Turismo Nieve, *Gramado 560, T065-346115.* **Camera and film** Foto Kodak, *Del Salvador*; Foto Master, *San José 301.* **Casas de cambio** Exchange Ltda, *Del Salvador 257, local 11*, Travel Sur, *San José 261, local 4*; Turismo Los Lagos, *Del Salvador 257 (Galería Real, local 11)*, open daily 0830-1330, 1500-2100, Sun 0930-1330, accepts TCs, good rates. **Cycle hire** available from many tour operators, see above, for around $US14 per day; check equipment carefully. **Internet** Ciber Service, *Salvador 264, local 6-A*; George's, *San Ignacio 574*; also at *Gramado 560, piso 2* and *San José 380, piso 2.* **Laundry** *Gramado 1090*; Lavanderia Delfin, *Martínez 323*, expensive. **Medical emergencies** Clinica Alemana, *Otto Bader 810, T232336, emergencies T065-232274*, usually has English-speaking doctors. **Post office** *San José y San Pedro; Del Salvador y Santa Rosa.* **Telephone** Bellsouth, *San Bernardo 555*; CTC, *Salvador 320*; Telefónica del Sur, *Del Salvador 314*; Entel, *San José 314.*

Parque Nacional Vicente Pérez Rosales and around

Established in 1926, this is the oldest national park in Chile, stretching east from Lago Llanquihue to the Argentine frontier. The park is covered in woodland and contains a large lake, Lago Todos Los Santos, plus three major volcanic peaks: Osorno, Puntiagudo and Tronador. Several other peaks are visible, notably Casablanca to the north and Calbuco to the south. Near the lake are the Saltos de Petrohué, waterfalls on the Río Petrohué. A memorable journey by road and water takes you through the park from Puerto Montt to Bariloche in Argentina. South of the park is the beautiful Seno de Reloncaví.

Ins and outs

Getting there In season, take one of the hourly minibuses from Puerto Montt and Puerto Varas via Ensenada to Petrohué. It is impossible to reach the national park independently out of season: there are buses only as far as Ensenada, little traffic for hitching and none of the ferries takes vehicles. Entrance to the park is free. **Getting around** A combination of walking and hitching rides in locals' boats is the best way to explore the park. In wet weather many treks in the park are impossible and the road to Puerto Montt can be blocked. ►► *For further details see Transport, page 367.* **Tourist information** CONAF has an office in Petrohué with a visitors' centre, small museum and 3D model of the park. There is also a *guardaparque* office in Puella. No maps of treks are available in the park; buy them from a tour agency in Puerto Varas (see page 361).

Lago Todos los Santos → *There are no roads round the lake and only those people with houses on the lakeshore are allowed access by boat.*

The most beautiful of all the lakes in southern Chile, Lago Todos los Santos is a long, irregularly shaped sheet of emerald-green water, surrounded by a deeply wooded shoreline and punctuated by several small islands that rise from its surface. Beyond the hilly shores to the east are several graceful snow-capped mountains, with the mighty Tronador in the distance. To the north is the sharp point of **Cerro Puntiagudo**, and at the northeastern end **Cerro Techado** rises cliff-like out of the water. The lake is fed by several rivers, including the Río Peulla to the east, the Ríos Techado and Negro to the north, and the Río Blanco to the south. At its western end the lake is drained by the Río Petrohue. The lake is warm and sheltered from the winds, and is a popular location for watersports, swimming and for trout and salmon fishing. The only scheduled vessel on the lake is the **Andina del Sud** service between Petrohue and Peulla, with connections to Bariloche (Argentina; see page 365), but private launches can be hired for trips. ►► *For Sleeping, Eating and other listings, see pages 366-367.*

> ♣ *In the national parks to the east of the Panamerican Highway night-time temperatures can drop as low as -10°C, even in summer.*

Petrohué and around

At the western end of the lake, 16 km northwest of Ensenada, **Petrohué** is a good base for walking tours with several trails around the foot of Volcán Osorno, or to the *miradors* that look over it, such as Cerro Picada. Near the Ensenada-Petrohué road, 6 km west of Petrohué, is the **Salto de Petrohué** ① *US$1.50*, which was formed by a relatively recent lava flow of hard volcanic rock. Near the falls are a snack bar and two short trails, the Sendero de los Enamorados and the Sendero Carileufú. Boat trips from Petrohué visit **Isla**

Margarita, the largest island on the lake, with a lagoon in the middle of it, in summer only, and boats can also be hired to visit the **Termas de Callao** – actually two large Alerce tubs in a cabin – north of the lake. The boat will drop you at the uninhabited El Rincón (arrange for it to wait or collect you later), from where it's a three-and-a-half-hour walk to the baths through forest beside the Río Sin Nombre. The path twice crosses the river by rickety hanging bridges. Just before the baths is a house, doubling as a comfortable *refugio*, where you collect the keys and pay.

Peulla and around

Peulla, at the eastern end of the lake, is a good starting point for hikes in the mountains. The **Cascadas Los Novios**, signposted above the **Hotel Peulla**, are a steep walk away, but are stunning once you reach them. There is also a good walk to **Laguna Margarita**, which takes four hours.

Cayutué and around

On the south shore of Lago Todos Los Santos is the little village of **Cayutué**, reached by hiring a boat from Petrohué, US$30. From Cayutué (no camping on the beach but there are private sites) it is a three-hour walk to **Laguna Cayutué**, a jewel set between mountains and surrounded by forest, where you can camp and swim. From the laguna it is a five-hour hike south to **Ralún** on the Reloncaví Estuary (see page 365): the last half of this route is along a *ripio* road built for extracting timber and is part of the old route used by missionaries in the colonial period to travel between Nahuel Huapi in Argentina and the island of Chiloé.

Parque Nacional Pérez Rosales & the lakes route to Argentina

The lakes route to Bariloche

This popular route from Puerto Montt to Bariloche, involving ferries across Lago Todos Los Santos, Lago Frías and Lago Nahuel Huapi, is outstandingly beautiful. The journey starts by bus via Puerto Varas, Ensenada and the Petrohué falls (20-minute stop) to **Petrohué**, where you board the catamaran service (1¾ hrs) across Lago Todos Los Santos to **Peulla**. During the summer there is a two-hour stop in Peulla for lunch (see Eating, below for options) and for **Chilean customs** ① *summer 0800-2100 daily; winter 0800-2000 daily*, followed by a two-hour bus ride through the **Paso Pérez Rosales** to Argentine customs in **Puerto Frías**. Then it's a 20-minute boat trip across Lago Frías to **Puerto Alegre**, and a short bus journey (15 minutes) to **Puerto Blest**. A catamaran departs from Puerto Blest for the beautiful one-hour trip along Lago Nahuel Huapi to **Puerto Panuelo**, from where there is a final one-hour bus journey to Bariloche. (The bus drops passengers at hotels, camping sites or in the town centre.) ➤➤ *For further details, see Transport, page 367.*

Bariloche ➔ *Phone code: 02944. Argentine phone code: +54. Colour map 4, C3. Population 77,750.*
Bariloche is a popular destination and centre for exploring the Argentine Lake District. Beautifully situated on the south shore of Lago Nahuel Huapi, the streets rise steeply along the edge of a glacial morraine. West of the city on the shores of the lake is the resort of **Llao Llao**, where the famous **Hotel Llao Llao** looks out over chocolate-box scenery. Nearby are two ski resorts. Boat excursions can be made from Bariloche to other parts of the Argentine Lake District. There is a wide range of accommodation as well as air and bus connections to Buenos Aires and other destinations in Argentina.
➤➤ *For more complete details, consult Footprint Argentina or the South American Handbook.*

Seno de Reloncaví

The Seno de Reloncaví situated east of Puerto Montt and south of the Parque Nacional Pérez Rosales, is the northernmost of Chile's glacial inlets. It is a quiet and beautiful estuary, often shrouded in mist and softly falling rain, but stunning nonetheless, and recommended for its wildlife, including sea lions and dolphins, and for its peaceful atmosphere. It is relatively easily reached from Puerto Montt by a road that runs along the wooded lower Petrohué valley south from Ensenada and then follows the eastern shore of the estuary for almost 100 km to join the Carretera Austral. ➤➤ *For Sleeping, Eating and other listings, see pages 366-367.*

Ralún and around ➔ *Colour map 4, C2.*
A small village situated at the northern end of the estuary, Ralún is 31 km southeast from Ensenada by a poorly paved road. There is a village shop and post office, and on the outskirts are **thermal baths** ① *US$2, reached by boat, US$2.50 across the Río Petrohué*. Ralún is the departure point for a five-hour walk north to **Laguna Cayutué** in the Parque Nacional Vicente Pérez Rosales (see above). From Ralún you can either travel along the eastern shore of the estuary to Cochamó (see below) or take the road that branches off and follows the western side of the estuary south, 36 km to Lago Chapo and the Parque Nacional Alerce Andino (see page 406).

Cochamó and further south ➔ *Colour map 4, C2. Population: 1,000.*
Some 17 km south of Ralún along a poor *ripio* road is the pretty village of Cochamó. It's situated in a striking setting, on the east shore of the estuary with the volcano behind, and has a small, frequently deserted waterfront, where benches allow you to sit and admire the view. Cochamó's fine wooden church dates from 1900 and is similar to those on Chiloé. It has a clock with wooden hands and an unusual black statue of Christ.

Further south, on the south bank of the Río Puelo (crossed by a new bridge) is **Puelo**, a most peaceful place. From here the road continues 36 km further southwest to Puelche on the Carretera Austral (see page 407).

Gaucho Trail

The Gaucho Trail east from Cochamó to **Paso León** on the Argentine frontier was used in the colonial period by the indigenous population, Jesuit priests and later by *gauchos*. It runs along Río Cochamó to La Junta, then along the north side of Lago Vidal, passing waterfalls and the oldest surviving Alerce trees in Chile at El Arco. The route takes three to four days by horse, five to six days on foot, depending on conditions and is best travelled between December and March. From the border crossing at Paso León it is a three-hour walk to the main road towards San Carlos de Bariloche.

● Sleeping

Lago Todos los Santos *p363*
The CONAF office in Petrohué can help find cheaper family accommodation.
L Fundo El Salto, *near Salto de Petrohué*, *rioazul@chilesat.net* Very friendly, run by New Zealanders, mainly a fishing lodge, good home cooking, fishing trips arranged.
L Hotel Peulla, *Peulla, T065-258041/ 02-8891032, hpeullareservas@terra.cl* Price includes dinner and breakfast, direct personal reservations, cheaper out of season. Beautiful setting by the lake and mountains, restaurant and bar, poor meals, cold in winter, often full of tour groups (tiny shop at back of hotel).
L-AL Hotel Petrohué, *T/F065-258042*. Burned down in 2002, but is being rebuilt and should be functioning by 2004. With bath, excellent views, log fires, cosy. The owner, Franz Schirmer, is a former climbing guide, who can advise on activities around the lake.
E Res Palomita, *50 m west of Hotel Peulla*. Price per person for half board, lunches available. Family-run, simple, comfortable but not spacious, separate shower, book ahead in season.

Camping

In **Petrohué**, there's a campsite beside the lake, US$4 per site, no services (local fishermen will ferry you across for US$0.50). Camping wild and picknicking is forbidden at Petrohué; car parking US$2 per day.
The campsite in **Peulla** is opposite the CONAF office, US$1.50 per site. There's also a good campsite 1¾ hrs' walk east of of the village, or you could ask the commander of the military garrison near the hotel if you can camp on the beach; no facilities.

Seno de Reloncaví *p365*
Accommodation in Puelo is also available with families.
LL Río Puelo Lodge, *Puelo, T02-2298533, www.rio-puelo-lodge.cl* Plush lodge offering all-in fly fishing packages from about US$380.
A Cabañas Ralún, *Ralún, T/F065-278286.* Cabins for 6.
C Campo Aventura, *4 km south of Cochamó, T065-232910, www.campo-aventura.com* For details of riding and trekking expeditions, see below. Accommodation is offered at the base camp (signpost on road). Price per person with great breakfast, kitchen, sauna. Camping is also possible. Very fresh milk from Campo Aventura's cow, herb garden, expensive but good food using local produce, vegetarian also available, book exchange, Spanish classes. There's another base in a renovated mountain house in the valley of La Junta. Write to **Campo Aventura**, *Casilla 5, Correo Cochamó* for further information.
F Cochamó, *T065-216212.* Price per person. Basic but clean, friendly, often full with salmon farm workers, good meals, recommended.
F Mercado Particular Sabin, *Catedral 20, Cochamó*. One of several *pensiones*, next to Hotel Cochamó.
F Navarrito, *Ralún*. Price per person for lodging. Also restaurant.
F-G Hosp Edicar, *Cochamó*. Price per person with or without breakfast. Without bath, spacious, recommended.
F-G Hosp Maura, *JJ Molina 12, Cochamó*. Price per person with or without bath. Beautifully situated, good food.
G Posada Campesino, *Ralún*. Price per person without breakfast, very friendly, simple, clean.

Camping

Camping Los Castaños, *Cochamó, T065-216212*. Reservations from *Casilla 576, Puerto Montt*.

🍴 Eating

Lago Todos los Santos *p363*

For options see Sleeping, above. There is a small shop in the **Andino del Sud** building in Petrohué, with basic supplies and some of the houses sell fresh bread, but if you're camping it's best to take your own food.

Seno de Reloncaví *p365*

Eateries in Cochamó include **Donde Payi,** opposite the church and **Reloncaví**, on the road down to the waterfront. On the seafront there is a cheap fish/seafood restaurant, which also hires out canoes, US$1 for 30 mins.

🥾 Activities and tours

Seno de Reloncaví *p365*
Horseriding/trekking

Campo Aventura, *Casilla 5, Correo Cochamó, T065-232910, www.campo-aventura.com* Specialises in all-inclusive riding and trekking expeditions with packhorses along the Gaucho trail between the Reloncaví estuary and the Argentine frontier, 2-10 days, US$97 per person, per day; good guides, spectacular scenery, English, French and German spoken, highly recommended. it also organises other activities including combined sea kayaking-horseriding trips with **Kokayak** in Puerto Varas.

Sebastian Contreras, *Calle Morales, Cochamó, T065-216220.* An independent guide who offers tours on horseback and hires out horses, recommended.

⊖ Transport

Lago Todos los Santos *p363*
Boat

The **Andina del Sud** catamaran sails between Petrohué and Peulla, departing Petrohué 1030 Mon-Sat, departing Peulla 1500 Mon-Sat, 2 hrs, US$22 per person one way, bicycles free (book in advance); most seating indoors, no cars carried, commentaries in Spanish and English, expensive refreshments. It is no longer possible to get a day return from Petrohué to Peulla, so you have to stay overnight in Peulla, which is expensive. This is the only public service across the lake and it connects with the **Andina del Sud** tour bus between Puerto Montt and Bariloche (see p375). Local fishermen also make the trip across the lake and for a group this can be cheaper than the public service, allow 3½ hrs.

Bus

Minibuses from **Puerto Varas** to Ensenada continue to **Petrohué** in summer; last return bus from Petrohue to Puerto Varas, 1800. There is a reduced service to **Ensenada** only in winter.

The lakes route to Bariloche *p365*

The trip may be cancelled if the weather is poor; there are reports of difficulty in obtaining a refund. This journey is operated only by **Andina del Sud** (see p375), whose buses depart from company offices in **Puerto Montt** daily at 0800; the fare is US$140 one way (not including lunch in Peulla). From 1 May to 30 Aug this trip is done over 2 days with an overnight stay in Peulla. Add another US$140 to the fare for a double room in the **Hotel Peulla**. Baggage is automatically taken here but for cheaper alternatives see Sleeping, above.

If you have time, it makes sense to buy tickets for the boat section of the journey in Puerto Montt or Puerto Varas and to do the rest of the trip independently, although this will probably involve walking sections of the route since there is little transport for hitching and it is impossible to buy a separate ticket from Peulla to the border, 26 km.

Seno de Reloncaví *p365*
Bus

Buses Fierro and Bohle from Puerto Montt via Puerto Varas and Ensenada, to **Ralún**, **Cochamó** and **Puelo**, 4 daily all year.

Boat

In summer boats sail up the estuary from **Angelmó**. Get a group of people together and convince one of the fishermen to take you. For information on (irregular) scheduled trips, contact the Regional Sernatur office in Puerto Montt.

Puerto Montt and around

→ *Phone code: 065. Colour map 4, C2. Population: 110,139.*

The capital of Región X (Los Lagos), Puerto Montt lies on the northern shore of the Seno de Reloncaví 1,016 km south of Santiago. The jumping-off point for journeys south to Chiloé and Patagonia, it is a busy modern city, the fastest growing in Chile, flourishing with the salmon-farming boom. It was founded in 1853, as part of the German colonization of the area, on the site of a Mapuche community known as Melipulli, meaning four hills. Good views over the city and bay are offered from outside the Intendencia Regional on Av X Region. There is a wide range of accommodation, but some might prefer to stay in Puerto Varas, more picturesque and only 20 minutes' away by bus.

Ins and outs

Getting there El Tepual Airport is 13 km northwest of town, served by **ETM** buses from the bus terminal ① *T065-294292, 1½ hrs before departure, US$1.20*; there's also a minibus service to/from hotels, US$4 per person. There are several daily flights north to Santiago, Concepción and Temuco, and south to Coyhaique and Punta Arenas. Ferries serve Chaitén (four times weekly) and Puerto Chacabuco (four times weekly); there's also a weekly service south to Puerto Natales. Puerto Montt is the departure point for bus services south to Coyhaique and Punta Arenas, and for buses north to Santiago and all the intermediate cities. **Getting around** Puerto Montt is quite a large city, with many *colectivos* and buses serving the *barrios* on the hill above the town. The cental area is down by the port, though, and everything here is within walking distance. ▸▸ *For further details, see Transport page 374.* **Tourist information** Sernatur has an office in the Gobernación Provincial building on Plaza de Armas ① *summer daily 0900-1300, 1500-1900; winter Mon-Fri 0830-1300, 1400-1800*. Ask for information on Chiloé here as this is often difficult to obtain on the island. The regional tourist office is in the Intendencia Regional ① *Av Décima Región 480 (p 3), Casilla 297, T065-254580*. There's also an information kiosk on the Plaza de Armas run by the municipality ① *till 1800 Sat*, which has town maps, but little information on other destinations. **Telefónica del Sur** and **Sernatur** operate a local phone information service (dial 142); you can also dial 149 for chemist/pharmacy information; 148 for the weather and 143 for the news, etc. The service operates throughout the tenth Region. **CONAF** is on Ochogavia 458, but cannot supply details of conditions in the national parks. Information on the Parque Pumalín (see page 408) is available from *Buin 356, T065-250079, www.pumalinpark.org*

> ✦ *If driving north out of Puerto Montt (or Puerto Varas, Frutillar, etc), look for signs to 'Ruta 5'.*

Sights

The **Plaza de Armas** lies at the foot of steep hills, one block north of Av Diego Portales, which runs east-west parallel to the shore. The **Palacio del Arte Diego Rivera** ① *Quillota 116, off the Plaza de Armas, T065-261817*, hosts temporary exhibitions, concerts and plays. Two blocks west of the square is the **Iglesia de los Jesuitas** on Calle Gallardo, dating from 1872, which has a fine blue-domed ceiling; behind it on a hill is the **campanario** (clock tower). Further west, near the bus terminal, is the **Museo Regional Juan Pablo II** ①, *Diego Portales 997, 1030-1800 daily, US$1*, documenting local history. It has a fine collection of historic photos of the city and memorabilia of the Pope's visit in 1988.

The little fishing port of **Angelmó**, 2 km west along Av Diego Portales, has become a tourist centre thanks to its dozens of seafood restaurants and handicraft shops, but it is also the site of an enormous mountain of wood chips that are shipped off to Japan every week and then replenished. The wood chips are a stark reminder of the dangers of deforestation and the accompanying threat of global warming. Launches depart from Angelmó (US$0.50) for the wooded **Isla Tenglo**, offshore from Puerto Montt. It's a

On board the 'Magellanes' to Puerto Natales

"When the boat began loading there was a mild stampede, especially for us economy-class (or dungeon class) passengers: no-one wanted to end up in one of the top bunks, which require elaborate climbing equipment to reach and which give only 3 in of headroom. There were two 24-occupant dungeon-class barracks, each equipped with two toilets and one shower, located at the very bottom of the ship, scattered alongside the engine room, the generator, the anchor-chain-dropping room and the rock-concert-amplifier-testing room. It was loud.

What did we do all day? Not much. The ship felt like an airport waiting room. People read, played cards, drank and slept. The scenery was indeed 'breathtakingly beautiful and rugged' but it was too windy and cold to stay outside for long, so we usually settled for glancing out of the ship's tiny windows. At Puerto Edén we were awakened by the release of the anchor, which, in dungeon class, sounded as though it had been dropped through the ceiling. We weren't sure whether to wake up or abandon ship.

Nearly 200 of us decided to go ashore. We each wore a bright orange life jacket so, naturally, we were easily identifiable to the locals who were eager to do business with us. After a few hours stocking up on souvenirs, we went back to the ship and steeled ourselves for the rough sea crossing. The waves, relative to the boat's size, were not threatening, but they hit the boat directly on her port side and created an impressively nauseating effect. Some passengers took seasickness pills and wandered down to their rooms to pass out. Others drank wine or beer till this had the same effect.

Perhaps the highlight of the trip was a tug-o-war on the upper cargo deck against the crew. The passengers, who had spent too much time sitting around and too little time loading cargo ships, were trounced. Team gringo fared better, however, in the ensuing soccer match: adding to the excitement were the obstacles on the 'pitch': huge metal rivets every few metres and a 20-tonne freight elevator."

favourite place for picnics, with views from the summit. The island is famous for its *curanto*, served by restaurants in summer. Boat trips round the island from Angelmó last for 30 minutes and cost US$8. A longer boat trip (2 hrs) will take you to **Isla Huar**, an island in the Seno de Reloncaví, departing at 1600 and returning from the other end of the island at 0730. If you are lucky you can stay at the church on the island, but it may be best to camp. » *For Sleeping, Eating and other listings, see pages 371-377.*

West of Puerto Montt

The old coast road west from Puerto Montt is very beautiful. **Chinquihue** (the name means 'place of skunks'), beyond Angelmó, has many seafood restaurants, oysters being a speciality. Further south is **Calbuco**, scenic centre of the fishing industry. It is situated on an island linked to the mainland by a causeway and can be visited direct by boat or by road. West of here is the Río Maullín, which drains Lago Llanquihue, and has some attractive waterfalls and good salmon fishing. At its mouth is the little fishing village of **Maullín**, founded in 1602. On the coast to the southeast is **Carelmapu**, with an excellent beach and *cabañas* at Playa Brava, about 3 km away. » *For details of destinations southeast of Puerto Montt, including the Parque Nacional Alerce Andino, see page 406.*

Sea routes south of Puerto Montt

Puerto Montt is the departure point for several popular voyages along the coast of southern Chile. All sailings are from Angelmó; timetables should be checked carefully in advance as schedules change frequently. For shipping offices in Puerto Montt, see Directory below.»» *For ferry routes, refer to the colour maps at the back of the book.*

To Puerto Natales

One of the highlights of many journeys to Chile is the 1,460-km voyage between Puerto Montt and the southern port of **Puerto Natales**, made by the *M/V Magallanes*; it is quicker to fly and cheaper to go by bus via Argentina but the voyage by boat is spectacular. The route south from Puerto Montt crosses the Seno de Reloncaví and

❖ Take seasickness tablets, especially for the stretch of open sea towards the Golfo de Peñas and for the onward journey south of Puerto Edén.

the Golfo de Ancud between the mainland and the large island of Chiloé, then continues south through the Canal Moraleda and the Canal Errázuriz, which separate the mainland from the outlying islands. It then heads west through the Canal Chacabuco to Bahía Anna Pink and across the open sea and the infamous Golfo de Peñas (Gulf of Sorrows) to reach a series of channels – Canal Messier, Angostura Inglesa, Fiordo del Indio and Canal Kirke – which provide one of the narrowest routes for large shipping in the world. There are spectacular views of the wooded fjords, weather permitting, particularly at sunrise and sunset, and a sense of desolate peace pervades everything except the ship, which is filled with cows in transport containers mooing day and night, and people having a good time.

The only regular stop on this route is at the fishing village of **Puerto Edén** on Isla Wellington, one hour south of the Angostura Inglesa. It has three shops (scant provisions), one off-licence, one café, and a *hospedaje* for up to 20 people (open intermittantly). The population of 185, includes five *carabineros* and a few remaining native Alacaluf people. Puerto Edén is the drop-off point for exploring **Isla Wellington**, which is largely untouched, with stunning mountains. If you do stop here, take all food; maps (not very accurate) are available in Santiago. The onward fare to Puerto Natales is US$50.

This is a ferry that also carries cargo (including cattle and sheep) rather than a cruise liner; standards of service and comfort vary, depending on the number of passengers and weather conditions. Economy class accommodation is basic and near the engine room, in 24-berth dormitories (see box, page 369), and although economy class and cabin passengers eat the same food, they are confined to separate areas (economy class is very cramped). The food is variable, and, apart from videos, entertainment on board is limited. Wine is available, but you are welcome to bring your own.»» *For further details, see Transport, page 375*

To Puerto Chacabuco and Laguna San Rafael

A weekly catamaran service sails between Puerto Montt and **Puerto Chacabuco**, 80 km west of Coyhaique. This beautiful voyage passes forested cliffs, seemingly within touching distance, and offers glimpses of distant snows. However, taking this route south means that travellers miss out on the attractions of the Carretera Austral. The Navimag ferry *M/N Edén* also sails this route, continuing (September to April only) from Puerto Chacabuco to visit **Laguna San Rafael**. However, it may well be cheaper, and is certainly more comfortable, to take a catamaran service to the Laguna from Puerto Chacabuco (see page 433) or to charter a small plane from Coyhaique. A luxury alternative is to board *Skorpios II* for a cruise to Chiloe and Laguna San Raphael. Generally service is excellent, the food superb and, at the laguna, you chip ice off the face of the glacier for your whisky. After San Rafael the ship visits **Quitralco fjord**, where

66 99 A sense of desolate peace pervades everything except the ship, which is filled with cows in transport containers, mooing day and night, and people having fun.

there are thermal pools and boat trips. The fare varies according to season, type of cabin and number of occupants. There are also four- to six-day tours from Puerto Montt with **Patagonia Connection,** which visit Puerto Chacabuco, Laguna San Rafael and the Termas de Puyuhuapi (see page 433). ►► *For further details, see Transport, page 376.*

● Sleeping

Puerto Montt *p368, map p373*
Accommodation is expensive in season, much cheaper off season. There are lots of *cabañas*, on the outskirts of the city and in **Pelluco**.
L Gran Hotel Don Vicente, *Varas 447, T065-432900*. With breakfast, some rooms noisy, excellent restaurant, serving seafood, fine views. Recommended.
L-AL Club Presidente, *Portales 664, T065-251666, www.presidente.cl*. Very comfortable 4-star with breakfast, also suites. English spoken. Recommended.
AL Apart Hotel Colón, *Pedro Montt 65, T065-264290, aparthotelcolon@entelchile.net* Fully furbished appartments, good value.
AL Don Luis, *Quillota 146, T065-259001, www.hoteldonluis.cl* Four-star hotel and very good restaurant.
AL Viento Sur, *Ejército 200, T065-258701, www.hotelviento.cl* Excellent 4-star, with good restaurant, sauna, gym and great views.
AL-A Burg, *Pedro Montt 56 y Portales, T065-253941, hotelburg@entelchile.net* Modern, central heating, centrally located, good, interesting traditional food in restaurant.
AL-A O'Grimm, *Gallardo 211, T065-252845, www.ogrimm.com* With breakfast, cosy restaurant with occasional live music, central.
B Le Mirage, *Rancagua 350, T065-255125, F065-256302*. With breakfast, small rooms, clean.
B-C Montt, *Varas 301 y Quillota, T065-253651*. With or without bath, clean, friendly, good value, good restaurant. Helpful.
C Colina, *Talca 81, T065-253502, hotcolina@hotmail.com* Restaurant, bar, car hire, noisy. Recommended.

C Millahue, *Copiapó 64, T065-253829, www.geocities.com/athens/6043/hotelmi1.htm* With breakfast, modern, good restaurant, also apartments at *Benavente 959, T/F065-254592*.
C-E Hostal Pacífico, *J J Mira 1088, T065-256229*. With or without bath, breakfast included, cable TV, parking, comfortable.
C-F Res Urmeneta, *Urmeneta 290, T065-253262*. With or without bath, clean.
D-G Res Embassy, *Valdivia 130, T065-253533*. With or without bath, clean, stores luggage. Recommended.
E-F Res La Nave, *Ancud y Varas, T065-253740*. Price per person with or without bath, clean, inexpensive restaurant.
F *Aníbal Pinto 328*. Price per person with breakfast, popular, laundry facilities, 10-mins' walk from centre. Recommended.
F Casa Perla, *Trigal 312, T065-262104, www.casaperla.com* Price per person with breakfast. Near the bus terminal, helpful, friendly, meals, laundry, internet, pleasant garden, English spoken, Spanish classes offered, good meeting place.
F *Huasco 130*. Cooking facilities, home-made bread. Recommended.
F Hospedaje Erica, *Trigal 309, T065-259923*. Price per person. Kitchen facilities, TV, big bathroom, good views, near the bus terminal.
F Hosp Frente al Mar, *Huasco 6, T065-260126*. Price per person with breakfast, kitchen, also *cabañas*.
F Hosp Nina, *Crucero 1351*. Price per person for small twin rooms, nice kitchen, clean, near the bus terminal.
F Hosp Rocco, *Pudeto 233, T/065-272897, hospedajerocco@hotmail.com* Price per person with breakfast, but without bath, real coffee, English spoken, friendly atmosphere.

F **Hosp Suizo**, *Independencia 231, T/F065-252640*. Price per person, with breakfast. Attractive house near the bus terminal, clean, German and Italian spoken, painting and Spanish classes.

F **Res Calipso**, *Urmeneta 127, T065-254554*. Price per person without bath, clean. Hostelling International discounts.

F **Res Central**, *Lota 111, T065-257516*. Price per person. Clean, use of kitchen, good beds, near the bus terminal. Recommended.

F **Res Emita**, *Miraflores 1281, T065-250725*. Price per person with breakfast, including home-made bread. Some rooms with bath. Clean, friendly, safe, near the bus terminal.

F **Vista Hermosa**, *Miramar 1486, T/F065-268001, vistahermosa@mixmail.com* Price per person without bath, near the bus terminal.

F-G **Alda González**, *Gallardo 552, T065-253334*. Price per person with or without bath, breakfast included, cooking facilities, English and German spoken, good value, near the Plaza de Armas.

F-G **Vista al Mar**, *Vivar 1337, T065-252525*. Price per person. Friendly, helpful, welcoming, good breakfast. Phone for lift from bus terminal.

G **Casa Gladis**, *Ancud y Mira*. Price per person for dormitory beds, some double rooms, kitchen and laundry facilities, near bus terminal.

G **El Tata**, *Gallardo 621*. Price per person for floor space. Very basic but super-cheap and popular, packed in summer.

G **Hosp Leticia**, *Lota 132, T065-256316*. Price per person for dorm beds, basic, safe, cooking facilities, hot showers, near the bus terminal. Recommended.

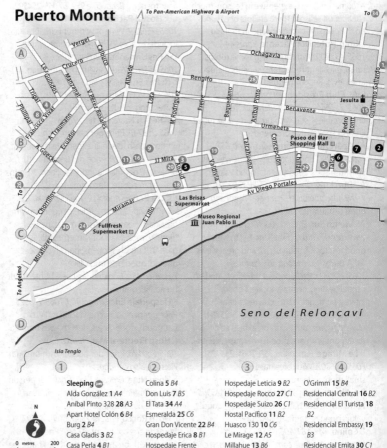

Puerto Montt

Sleeping
Alda González **1** *A4*
Aníbal Pinto 328 **28** *A3*
Apart Hotel Colón **6** *B4*
Burg **2** *B4*
Casa Gladis **3** *B2*
Casa Perla **4** *B1*
Club Presidente **29** *B4*

Colina **5** *B4*
Don Luis **7** *B5*
El Tata **34** *A4*
Esmeralda **25** *C6*
Gran Don Vicente **22** *B4*
Hospedaje Erica **8** *B1*
Hospedaje Frente al Mar **32** *C6*

Hospedaje Leticia **9** *B2*
Hospedaje Rocco **27** *C1*
Hospedaje Suizo **26** *C1*
Hostal Pacífico **11** *B2*
Huasco 130 **10** *C6*
Le Mirage **12** *A5*
Millahue **13** *B6*
Montt **14** *B5*

O'Grimm **15** *B4*
Residencial Central **16** *B2*
Residencial El Turista **18** *B2*
Residencial Embassy **19** *B3*
Residencial Emita **30** *C1*
Residencial La Nave **20** *B2*

Camping

Wild camping is possible along the sea front. There are also several official sites west of Puerto Montt.

Anderson, *11 km west*. American run, hot showers, private beach, home-grown fruit, vegetables and milk products.

El Ciervo, *3 km west*. Good site.

Municipal, *Chinquihue, 10 km west*. Open Oct-Apr, fully equipped with tables, seats, barbecue, toilets and showers, small shop, no kerosene, bus service from town.

West of Puerto Montt *p369*

B **Cabañas El Pangal**, *5 km from Maullín, T065-451244*. Cabins on the beach.

B **Hotel Colonial**, *Calbuco, T065-461546*. One of several decent hotels.

❼ Eating

Puerto Montt *p368, map p372*

For seafood enthusiasts, the only place to go is **Angelmó**, where there are many small, very popular seafood restaurants in the old fishing port by the market, serving excellent lunches only. There is fierce touting for business. Look out for local specialities such as *curanto* and *picoroco al vapor*, a giant barnacle whose flesh looks and tastes like a crab, and ask for *té blanco* (white wine; the stalls are not legally allowed to serve wine). There are more good seafood restaurants on the other side of the city in **Pelluco** (see p406). In Puerto Montt itself, try the following eateries:

$$$ **Balzac**, *Urmeneta y Quillota*. Very good.

$$$ **Centro Español**, *O'Higgins 233*. Expensive but very good.

$$$ **Club Alemán**, *Varas 264*. Old fashioned, good food and wine.

$$$ **Club de Yates**, *Juan Soler s/n*. Excellent, expensive seafood.

$$ **Café Amsel**, *Hotel Burg, Pedro Montt y Portales*. Superb fish, not cheap, real coffee.

$$ **Embassy**, *Ancud 106*. Very good, upper end of range.

$$ **Puerto Café**, *Angelmó 2456 (above Travellers)*. Real coffee, vegetarian dishes, English spoken, recommended.

$ **Café Real**, *Rancagua 137*. For *empanadas, pichangas, congrío frito* and cheap lunches.

$ **Costa de Reloncaví**, *Portales 736*. Good food, moderate prices.

$ **Dino**, *Varas 550*. Restaurant upstairs, snacks downstairs (try the lemon juice).

$ **Plato's**, *Portales 1014, Galería Comercial España*. Cheap and good.

$ **Restaurant de las Antigüedades**, *Av Angelmo*. Attractive and unusual décor, real coffee, interesting menu.

Cheap food is also available at Puerto Montt bus terminal (all credit cards accepted).

Cafés

Asturias, *Angelmó 2448*. Limited menu but often recommended.

Café Alemana, *Rancagua 117*. Real coffee, good.

Café Plaza, *Urmeneta 326*. Good location, friendly, pool/billiards.

$$ **Kiel**, *Chinquihué, T065-255010*. Excellent but not cheap.

⦿ Bars and clubs

Puerto Montt *p368, map p373*
Watch out: several of the 'bars' near the port and along Perez Rosales have more to them than meets the eye.

Star, *Ruta 5 north of the city*. Disco. Several more in Pelluco, east of Puerto Montt.

⦿ Shopping

Puerto Montt *p368, map p373*
Woollen goods and Mapuche-designed rugs can be bought at roadside stalls in Angelmó and on Diego Portales opposite the bus terminal. Prices are much the same as on Chiloé, but quality is often lower.
Fullfresh, *opposite bus terminal*. Supermarket open 0900-2200 daily.
Libros, *Diego Portales 580*. Bookshop with a small selection of English novels, also maps.
Paseo del Mar, *Talca y Antonio Varas*. Large modern shopping mall. A large new mall is also being built on the seafront.
Torres Color, *Rancagua III*. For photo developing and camera repairs, efficient.

▲ Activities and tours

Puerto Montt *p368, map p373*
There are many agencies. Most offer 1-day excursions to **Chiloé** (US$20) and to **Puerto Varas**, Isla Loreley, Laguna Verde, and the Petrohué falls: these tours are cheaper from bus company kiosks inside the bus terminal. Some companies offer 2-day excursions along the Carretera Austral to **Hornopirén**, US$76, with food and accommodation.
Alsur, *Antonio Varas 445, T/F065-287628*. Rafting and water sports
Andina del Sud, *Varas 437 (very close to central tourist kiosk), T065-257797*. Sells a variety of tours, and through its subsidiary Cruce de Lagos (www.lakecrossing.cl) also offers the lakes trip to Bariloche (see p365).
Eureka Turismo, *Varas 449, T065-250412, www.chile-travel.com/eureka.htm* Helpful, German and English spoken.
Kayaking Austral, *T09-6980951, or book through Casa Perla*. Guided sea kayaking.

Patagonia Verde, *Diego Portales 514, T065-286990*. Mountaineering, fishing, trekking, horseriding.
Petrel Tours, *Benavente 327, T065-251780, petrel@telsur.net* Recommended.
Travellers, *Av Angelmó, Casilla 854, T065-262099, www.travellers.cl* Booking office for **Navimag** ferry to Puerto Natales, bespoke excursions, also sells imported camping equipment and runs computerised tourist information service, book swap ("the best south of Santiago"), map display, TV, real coffee, English-run.

West of Puerto Montt *p369*
Marina del Sur (MDS), *T/F065-251958, Chinquihué*. Sailing courses, notice board for crew (*tripulante*) requests, modern building with bar and restaurant. The MDS charters office specialises in chartering boats for cruising the Patagonian channels: US$2,200-8,500 per week depending on size of boat.

⦿ Transport

Puerto Montt *p368, map p373*
Air
LanChile and Sky have several flights daily to **Santiago**, from US$100 return (one way more expensive); to **Balmaceda** for Coyhaique, from US$80 return; to **Punta Arenas**, from US$130 return. In Jan, Feb and Mar you may be told that flights are booked up, however, cancellations are sometimes available from the airport. To **Chaitén**, **Aeropuelche**, daily, US$40. To **Bariloche** and **Neuquén** (Argentina), **TAN**, 2 weekly, 40 mins; to **Port Stanley** (Falkland Islands/Islas Malvinas), from Santiago via Punta Arenas, **LanChile**, Sat, US$600 return.

Bus
The very crowded terminal on the seafront at *Diego Portales y Lota*, has telephones, restaurants, a *casa de cambio* and left luggage (US$1.50 per item for 24 hrs).
Expreso Puerto Varas, Thaebus and Full Express run minibuses every few minutes to **Puerto Varas**, US$0.80, **Llanquihue** and **Frutillar**, US$1.25, and to **Osorno**, US$1.50. Buses and *colectivos* nos 2, 3 and 20 ply the route to **Anglemo**, US$0.30 each way.
To **Ensenada** and **Petrohué**, several companies, hourly; to **Ralún**, **Cochamó** and **Puelo**, Buses Fierro and Buses Bohle, 4 daily

via Puerto Varas and Ensenada; to **Pucón**, several daily, 6 hrs, US$6; to **Santiago**, several companies, 13 hrs, US$13, *semi cama* US$20, *salón cama* US$30; to **Temuco**, US$5; to **Valdivia**, US$4; to **Concepción**, US$9. For services to Chiloé, see page 384.

To **Punta Arenas**, Pacheco and Queilén Bus, 1-3 weekly, 32-38 hrs, approximately US$35 (bus goes through Argentina via Bariloche; take US$ cash to pay for meals etc in Argentina); book well in advance in Jan-Feb and check if you need a multiple-entry Chilean visa; also book any return journey before setting out. To **Coyhaique** via Bariloche, 2 weekly, **Turibus**, US$46.

International To **Bariloche** via Osorno and the Puyehue pass, daily, 7hrs, **Andes Mar**, **Rio de la Plata** and **Tas Choapa**, US$12. **Andes Mar** also has through services to Buenos Aires, Nequén and Bahía Blanca; services are reduced out of season. Buy tickets for international buses from the bus terminal, not through an agency. The best views are from the right hand side of the bus. For the route to Argentina via Lago Todos Los Santos see p365.

To Puerto Natales *p370*
The *Magallanes* sails once a week to **Puerto Natales**, Nov-Apr, departing Puerto Montt Mon 1600, returning from Puerto Natales Fri 0400 (although departures are frequently delayed, or even advanced, by weather conditions), 3 ½ days, economy from US$230 per person (take sleeping bag), private cabin with view US$1513, all prices include meals, 10% discount for ISIC holders in cabin class only, fares 10-20% lower in Nov and Apr. Book well in advance for cabin class departures Dec-Mar (more than 2 weeks in advance in Feb), especially for the voyage south; Puerto Natales to Puerto Montt is less heavily booked; it is worth putting your name on the waiting list for cancellations at busy periods. Tickets can be bought in advance through **Travellers** in Puerto Montt (see Activities and tours, above), from **Navimag** offices in Puerto Montt, Puerto Natales and Punta Arenas, from travel agencies throughout the country, or online at www.navimag.cl

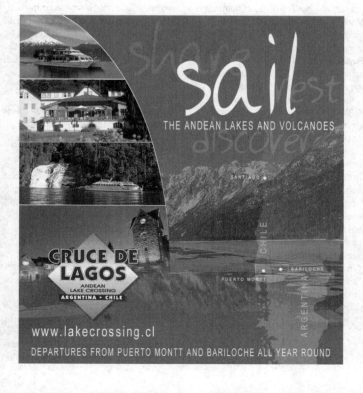
The Lake District Puerto Montt & around

To Puerto Chacabuco and Laguna San Rafael *p370*

Aysen Express operates a weekly catamaran service to **Puerto Chacabuco**, usually depart Puerto Montt Fri, 11 hrs, US$43. The Navimag ferry *M/N Edén* also sails this route throughout the year, once or twice a week, 24 hrs, bunks from US$70, reclining seat US$25, cars US$150, motorcycles US$35, cycles US$20. In the summer (Sep-Apr) the *M/N Edén* continues once a week (usually at the weekend) from Puerto Chacabuco to **Laguna San Rafael**, 21-24 hrs, return fare Puerto Montt-Laguna San Rafael US$325-US$650; for fares from Puerto Chacabuco to Laguna San Rafael see p433.

Skorpios Cruises luxury ship *Skorpios 2* leaves Puerto Montt Sat 1100 for a 6-day cruise to **Laguna San Rafael**, returning to Puerto Montt Fri, double cabin from US$680 per person. For further details (and information about routes sailed by *Skorpios 1* and *3*, consult www.skorpios.cl

Patagonia Connection SA, *Fidel Oteíza 1921, Oficina 1006, Providencia, Santiago, T02-225 6489, www.patagonia-connection.com*, operates all-inclusive 6-day tours, from Puerto Montt to **Laguna San Rafael**, US$1300-2100, including the *Patagonia Express* catamaran service from Puerto Chacabuco via **Termas de Puyuhuapi** (see p413), overnight accommodation at Termas de Puyuhuapi and a day excursion to Laguna San Rafael.

Raymond Weber, *Av Chipana 3435 Pasaje 4, T02-8858250, www.chilecharter.com*, charters two luxury sailing catamarans to visit Golfo de Ancud and Laguna San Rafael.

Other sea routes *p373*

To **Chaitén**, Navimag, 1 ferry weekly, 10 hrs, passengers US$23, *literas* US$33, cars US$90, bicycles US$11; **Transmarchilary**, 3 ferries weekly, prices similar; **Catamaranes del Sur** and **Aysen Express**, 6 weekly between them, catamaran service, 4½ hrs, US$35 including transfer to port from company offices.

To **Río Negro**, Isla Llancahué, Baños Cahuelmó and Fiordo Leptepu/Coman, *m/n Bohemia*, 6 days/5 nights, US$545-720 per person depending on season.

⊕ Directory

Puerto Montt *p368, map p373*

Airline offices Aeropuelche, *Copiapó 106, T065-435827*; LanChile, *O'Higgins 167, T065-253315*; Sky, *T600-600 2828 for information*. **Banks** ATMs at banks including Banco Santiago, *Urmeneta 541*; Banco Santander, *Antonio Varas 501*; also at **Las Brisas supermarket**, in the **Fullfresh** supermarket opposite the bus terminal and in the **Terminal Transbordadores**; for Visa visit **Corp Banca**, *Pedro Montt y Urmeneta*, good rates; commission charges for TCs vary widely. **Bicycle repairs** There are 3 places on Urmeneta, none very well stocked, including Oxford, *Urmeneta 908, T065-272960*. **Car hire** Automotric Angelmó, *Talca 79*, cheap and helpful; Automóvil Club de Chile, *Ensenada 70, T065-254776, and at airport*; Autovald, *Diego Portales 1330, T065-256355*, cheap rates; Avis, *Urmeneta, 1037, T065-253307, and at airport*; Budget, *Gallardo 450, T065-254888 and at airport*; Dollar, *Hotel Vicente Pérez Rosales, Antonio Varas 447*; Egartur, *Benavente 575, loc. 3, T065-257336, egartur@telsur.cl*, good service, recommended, will deliver your car to your hotel for free; First, *Antonio Varas 447, T065-252036*; Full Famas, *Diego Portales 506, T065-258060, F065-259840, and airport, T065-263750*, friendly, helpful, good value, has vehicles that can be taken to Argentina; Hertz, *Antonio Varas 126, T065-259585*, helpful, English spoken; Travicargo, *Urmeneta 856, T065-257137*. **Casas de cambio** Good rates at Galería Cristal, *Varas 595*; Afex, *Portales 516*; La Moneda de Oro, *at the bus terminal*, exchanges Latin American currencies Mon-Sat 0930-1230, 1530-1800; Turismo Los Lagos, *Varas 595, local 13*; Travellers, *Angelmó* (see Activities and tours, above) has exchange facilities. **Consulates** Argentina, *Cauquenes 94, piso 2, T065-253996*, quick visa service; Germany, *Antonio Varas y Gallardo, piso 3, Oficina 306*, Tue-Wed 0930-1200; Netherlands, *Chorillos 1582, T065-253003*; Spain, *Rancagua 113, T065-252557*. **Internet** *Antonio Varas 629*; also upstairs in bus terminal and several on Av Angelmo. **Laundry** Center, *Antonio Varas 700*; Lavatodo, *O'Higgins 231*; Narly, *San Martín 187, Local 6*, high prices, US$7 for 3 kg; Nautilus, *Av Angelmó 1564*, cheaper, good; Unic, *Chillán 149*; Yessil't, *Edif Caracol, Urmeneta 300*, service

(side margin) The Lake District Puerto Montt & around

washes. **Medical services** *Seminario s/n, T065-261134.* **Motorcycle repairs** Miguel Schmuch, *Urmeneta 985, T/F065-258877.* **Post office** *Rancagua 126,* open 0830-1830 Mon-Fri, 0830-1200 Sat. **Shipping offices** Aysen Express, *O'Higgins 167, Of 307, T065-437599, www.aysenexpress.cl*; **Bohemia**, *Antonio Varas 947, T065-254675*; **Catamaranes del Sur**, *Diego Portales 510, T065-267533, www.catamaranesdelsur.cl*; **Navimag**, *Terminal Transbordadores, Av Angelmó 2187, T065-253318, www.navimag.cl*; Skorpios, *Angelmó 1660 y Miraflores (Castilla 588), T065-252619, www.skorpios.cl*; **Transmarchilay**, *Terminal Transbordadores, Angelmó 2187, T065-270416, www.transmarchilay.cl* **Telephone** *Pedro Montt 114* and *Chillán 98*; **Entel**, *Averas between Talca and Pedro Montt*; there is also a cheap call centre at *Rosales 148.*

Introduction

The mysterious archipelago of Chiloé is one of the most fascinating areas of Chile. Consisting of one main island, officially known as Chiloé Grande, and numerous islets, its rolling hills, covered in patchwork fields and thick forest, provide a lasting sense of rural calm. Here you are almost always within sight of the sea, with dolphins playing in the bay and, on a clear day, views across to the twisting spire of Corcovado volcano on the mainland.

There are two main towns, **Ancud** and **Castro**, in which most of the 116,000 people live; there are also many fishing villages. The Cordillera de la Costa runs at low altitudes along the Pacific side of the island; south of Castro a gap in the range is filled by two connected lakes, Lago Huillinco and Lago Cucao. Thick forests cover most of the sparsely populated western and southern parts of the island; elsewhere hillsides are covered with wheat fields and dark green plots of potatoes and the roads are lined with wild flowers in summer. East of the main island are several groups of smaller islands, where the way of life is even more peaceful.

Chiloé is famous for its legends and rich mythology; here witches are said to fly around at night, identifiable as lights in the dark sky. Chiloé is equally well known for its painted wooden churches, some of them dating back to the late colonial period. In January and February, most towns and villages celebrate their annual fiestas; traditional dishes, such as *curanto*, are served and there are rodeos and dancing, as well as much drinking of local *chicha*.

★ **Don't miss...**

❶ **The beach at Cucao** Gallop on horseback along this windswept strand, page 397.

❷ **Parque Nacional Chiloé** Explore the thick forest at the northern end of this remote national park, pages 387 and 397.

❸ **Curanto** Enjoy this and other Chilote specialities in the seafood restaurants by the port at Castro, page 391.

❹ **Chilote churches** Visit any of the fascinating wooden churches based on Jesuit designs, particularly the Iglesia de Quinchao, page 390.

❺ **Quinchao and Lemuy** Explore these beautiful islets between Chiloé Grande and the mainland. They're easy to get to from Dalcahue and Chonchi respectively, pages 390 and 397.

❻ **Fiestas** Celebrated throughout January and February, page 380.

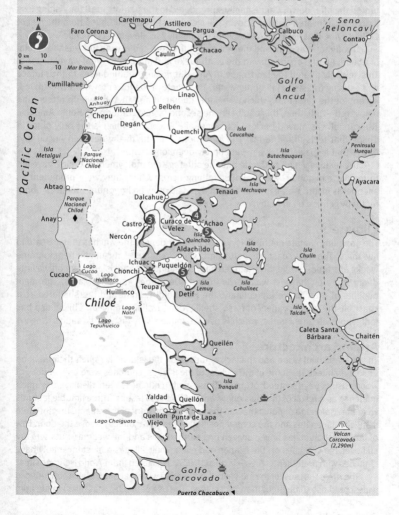

Background

The original Chilotes (inhabitants of Chiloé) were the Chonos tribe, who were pushed south by the Huilliches, invading from the north. The first Spanish sighting of the islands was by Francisco de Ulloa in 1553 and, in 1567, Martín Ruiz de Gamboa took possession of the islands on behalf of Spain. The small settler population divided the indigenous population and their lands between them, but the Huilliche uprising after 1598 drove the Spanish out of the mainland south of the Río Biobío, isolating the 200 Spanish settlers on Chiloé. Following a violent earthquake in 1646, the Spanish population asked the Viceroy in Lima for permission to leave, but this was refused. Much of Chiloé's distinctive character derives from the following 200 years of separation from the mainstream of Spanish colonial development.

The islanders were the last supporters of the Spanish Crown in South America. When the Chilean patriot leaders rebelled, the Spanish Governor fled to the island and, in despair, offered it to Britain. George Canning, the British Foreign Secretary, turned the offer down; Chiloé finally surrendered to the patriots in 1826. Visiting less than a decade later, Charles Darwin still clearly distinguished Chiloé from the rest of Chile, saying that here the Andes were not nearly "so elevated as in Chile".

Throughout the 19th and the first part of the 20th century, Ancud was the capital of Chiloé. All that changed with the earthquake and *maremoto* (tidal wave) of 1960. This severely altered the landscape in Ancud, bringing petrified trees to the surface and causing forests to fall under water. The whole of the lower town was destroyed, except for the cathedral, which was badly damaged and then blown up rather than renovated – until then, this had been the second largest cathedral in South America. The capital was moved back to its former site at Castro, which is the only place in Chiloé that feels urban today. The *maremoto*, and the rivalry between Ancud and Castro that it spawned have never entirely been forgotten.

The relatively high birth rate and the shortage of employment in Chiloé have led to regular emigration, with Chilotes settling across Chile; they were prominent as shepherds in late 19th-century Patagonia and are now an important source of labour for the Argentine oil industry.

Climate

The appalling climate of Chiloé is almost as legendary as the witches that are said to live there. The west coast has particularly vile conditions – it can rain here for three weeks at a time – while the sheltered east coast and offshore islands are only a little drier. Some of the best weather is in early December and late March. The main benefits of the climate are culinary: the Humboldt Current and the sheltered east coast ensure a wide variety of fresh shellfish are available all year. Chiloé also has indigenous elephant garlic, which is used to make a very tasty garlic sauce.

Art and architecture

The availability of wood and the lack of metals on the islands have left their mark on Chilote architecture. Some of the earliest of the islands' churches were built entirely of wood, using pegs instead of nails. These early churches often displayed German influence as a result of the missionary work of Bavarian Jesuits. Three notable features were the *esplanada* or porch that ran the length of the front of the church, the not-quite semi-circular arches and the central position of the tower directly above the door. Few of the oldest churches have survived fire, earthquakes and the weather, but there are still over 150 churches on the islands and even small villages almost invariably have churches with pretty cemeteries – in 2001 UNESCO declared them World Heritage sites.

The *rucas* (houses) of the indigenous population were thatched; thatch continued in widespread use throughout the 19th century. The use of thin *tejuelas* (tiles) made from

Jesuits in Chiloé

The Jesuits arrived in Chiloé in 1608 and the first Jesuit residence was established four years later. Although in Chiloé they established few of the missions for which they became famous in Paraguay, at their expulsion in 1767 there were 79 churches on the island.

The key to the Jesuits' influence lay in their use of *fiscales*: indigenous people who were trained to teach Christian doctrine and to ensure that everyone observed religious duties. One *fiscal* was appointed for every 50 inhabitants. On 17 September each year, two missionaries set sail from Castro in small boats, taking with them statues of saints and other essential supplies. They spent the next eight months sailing round the islands of Chiloé, visiting all the parishes in a set order. In each parish they would spend three days officating at weddings and baptisms, hearing confessions and reviewing the work of the *fiscales*.

Most of the old churches for which Chiloé is famous date from after the expulsion of the Jesuits, but some writers claim that their influence can still be seen, for example in the enthusiasm for education on the island, which has long boasted one of the highest literacy rates in the world. Many villages in Chiloé still have *fiscales* who are, according to tradition, responsible for keeping the church keys.

---

alerce wood was influenced by the German settlers around Puerto Montt in the late 19th century; these tiles, which are nailed to the frame and roof in several distinctive patterns, overlap to form effective protection against the rain. *Palafitos* or wooden houses built on stilts over the water, were once popular in all the main ports, but are now mainly found at the northern end of Castro, to the west of the Panamericana.

The islands are also famous for their traditional handicrafts, notably woollens and basketware, which can be bought in all the main towns and on some of the smaller islands, as well as in Puerto Montt and Angelmó.

Folklore

Chiloé's distinctive history and its maritime traditions are reflected in the strength of its unique folklore. There is widespread belief in a mermaid (*pincoya*), witches, who are said to meet at caves near Quicaví, (between Dalcahue and Quemchi), and a ghost ship, the *Caleuche*, which whisks shipwrecked sailors aboard (see box, page 384). The *Caleuche* is said to transform itself into a log, brought ashore by its crew (who become birds) when it needs repairs. Legend has it that Chiloé's dead are rowed along the reaches of Lago Huillinco and Lago Cucao in a white ship, out into the Pacific. For further information about the myths associated with the islands, read *Casos de Brujos de Chiloé* by Umiliana Cárdenas Saldivia (1989, Editorial Universitaria) and *Chiloé, Manual del Pensamiento Mágico y Creencía Popular* by Renato Cárdenas and Catherine Hall (1989, El Kultrún).

Modern Chiloé

Although fishing and agriculture remain mainstays of the economy, salmon farming has become just as important; seaweed is also harvested for export to Japan. Tourism provides a seasonal income for a growing number of people, especially in Castro, with **agrotourism** increasingly available in rural areas. This consists of staying with local families and sharing their way of life, whether it be farming or fishing. The host families are invariably friendly and welcoming, and the stays are highly recommended as a fascinating way to immerse yourself in Chilote life. Locations of

Chiloé

⁞ Mythical mischiefmakers

Visitors to Chiloé should beware of these four unlikely mythological hazards.

El Trauco A small, ugly and smelly man who wears a small round hat made of bamboo and clothing of the same material; he usually carries a small stone hatchet, with which he is reputed to be able to fell any tree in three strokes. He spends much of his time haunting the forests, sitting on fallen tree trunks and weaving his clothes.

El Trauco specializes in seducing virgins and is – perhaps a little too conveniently – held to be responsible for unwanted pregnancies. He uses his magic powers to give them erotic dreams while they are asleep; they wake and go to look for him in the forest and are seduced by his eyes. Despite his ugliness, he is irresistible and the girl throws herself on the ground. You should be careful not to disturb the Trauco while he is thus occupied: those who do so are immediately deformed beyond recognition and sentenced to die within 12 months.

La Fiura A small ugly woman, who lives in the forests near Hualdes, where she is reputed to bathe in the streams and waterfalls combing her hair with a crystal comb. Known as the indefatigable lover of bachelors, she attracts her victims by wearing colourful clothes. As the man approaches he is put to sleep by her foul breath. After La Fiura has satisfied her desire, the unfortunate man goes insane. Refusing her advances is no escape either: those who do so, whether animals or men, become so deformed that they are unrecognizable.

La Sirena and **El Caleuche** A dangerous double act for those travelling by sea. La Sirena is a mermaid who lies alluringly on rocks and entices sailors to their deaths. Once shipwrecked, sailors are whisked into the bowels of El Caleuche, the ghost ship that is said to patrol the channels of the archipelago. Both the Chilean navy and merchant ships have reported sightings of the Caleuche. The author of this book has also met several people on Chiloé who claim to have seen the ghost ship; but a word of warning was sounded by an old cynic in Castro: 'I knew a fisherman who used to walk along the beach shouting "I've seen La Sirena". All the other fishermen fled, and then he stole their fish.'

families offering agrotourism are mentioned in the text; prices per person are all E/F with breakfast, D/E for half board and C for full board. ① *Reservations should be made in advance directly, or through the group's office in Ancud, To65-628333; more information is available from Sernatur in Ancud, see page 385.*

Ins and outs

Getting there

Ferry and **catamaran** services connect the island with Chaitén and the Carretera Austral (see page 400), but the main sea link is the frequent vehicle ferry service between Pargua on the mainland (55 km southwest of Puerto Montt) across the Chacao straits to Chacao ① *30 mins, cars US$11.40 one way (more expensive at night), foot passengers US$1.* Dolphins often follow the boat.

Frequent **bus** services, which connect with ferry sailings, operate between Ancud and Castro (the main towns on Chiloé) and Puerto Montt. It is possible to travel direct to many cities, including Santiago, Osorno, Valdivia, Temuco and Los Angeles. Inter-urban bus transport is dominated by Cruz del Sur, who also own **Trans Chiloé** and **Regional Sur** and operate from their own terminal in Castro. **Cruz del Sur** also operates its own ferries to the mainland, which give priority to **Cruz del Sur** buses. The only independent bus operator to the island is **Queilen Bus** (cheaper but less regular). Local services are crowded, slow and often wet, but provide a good picture of life in rural Chiloé. Mountain **bikes** and **horses** are ideal for travelling slowly through the more remote parts of the archipelago.

Ancud and around

→ *Phone code: 065. Colour map 4, C1. Population: 23,148.*

Situated on the northern coast of Chiloé, 34 km west of the Straits of Chacao, Ancud lies on a great bay, the Golfo de Quetalmahue. It is a little less characterful than some of the other towns on the island but is nevertheless a good centre for visiting the villages of northern Chiloé. There is a friendly small-town feel; everyone knows each other and everything happens in its own time. Tourism is slowly reviving Ancud's fortunes following the disaster of the maremoto in 1960.

Ins and outs

Getting there   A bridge is planned linking Ancud to the mainland but it is unlikely to be completed for some years yet. In the meantime, there are many buses south to Castro and Quellón (hourly), and also north to Puerto Montt. **Cruz del Sur** have buses continuing north to Valdivia, Temuco and Santiago (several daily). ►► *For further details, see Transport page 389.* **Getting around**   Ancud is big enough for you to want to take the occasional *colectivo*; there are many of these, with their destinations signed on the roof (fares are rarely over US$0.40). There are some buses serving outlying *poblaciones*, but it is unlikely that you will need to use them. **Tourist information** Sernatur ① *Libertad 665, T065-622665, Mon-Fri 0900-1300, 1430-1730.*

Sights

The port is dominated by the **Fuerte San Antonio**, the fort where the Spanish surrendered Chiloé to Chilean troops in 1826. Close to it are the unspectacular ruins of the Polvorín del Fuerte (a couple of cannon and a few walls). A kilometre north of the fort is a secluded beach, **Arena Gruesa**, where public concerts are held in summer. Some 2 km east is a *mirador* offering good views of the island and across to the mainland. The small fishing harbour at Cochrane y Prat is worth a visit, especially in the evening when the catch is landed. On the road west, along the coast, you can see concrete pillars, remnants of the old railway, destroyed by the 1960 earthquake.

❧ *Opposite Hotel Polo Sur on the coast is a kiosk selling many different types of the local artesanal liqueur, known as 'licor de oro'.*

Near the Plaza de Armas is the **Museo Regional** ① *summer daily 1100-1900, winter Tue-Fri 0900-1300, 1430-1830, Sat 1000-1330, 1430-1800, US$1, student reductions*, with an interesting collection on the early history of Chiloé. It also displays a replica of a traditional Chilote thatched wooden house and of the small sailing ship *Ancud*, which claimed the Straits of Chacao for Chile, pipping the French to the post by a day. There's a good craft shop and café on site and activities for children are provided. Excellent wooden toys and clocks are made by **Lucho Troncoso** ① *Prat 342, T09-2639383.*

The **Faro Corona** lighthouse lies 34 km west of Ancud along a beach, which, although unsuitable for swimming (absolutely freezing, quite apart from the dangerous currents), offers good views with interesting birdlife. There isn't much there so take something to eat and drink. ① *Getting there: bus from Ancud 0645; return departure 1730.* To the south is **Fuerte Ahuí**, an old fort with good views of Ancud. ➤➤ *For Sleeping, Eating and other listings, see pages 387-389.*

East of Ancud

Most people travelling to Chiloé will arrive in **Chacao** on the north coast. The town has a small, attractive plaza; and there's a pretty church and old wooden houses in Chacao Viejo, east of the port. Black-necked swans arrive here in summer from their winter habitat in Paraguay and Brazil. The Panamericana heads west from here to Ancud, while a coastal road branches south, towards Quemchi. Turn north off the Panamericana along the coast to reach **Caulín**; the road is only passable at low tide. There are good beaches here; in Caulín you can see many black-necked swans in summer and flamingos in autumn.

❗ *Just outside Chacao, on the road to Ancud, is a shop selling good smoked salmon.*

Ancud

To Polvorín del Fuerte & Playa Arena Gruesa

To Mar Brava, Pumillahue & Faro Corona

Sleeping
Balai 1
Elena Bergmann 3
Galeón Azul 4
Hospedaje Alinar 5
Hospedaje Alto
 Bellavista 2
Hospedaje Capri 6
Hospedaje Miranda 7
Hospedaje O'Higgins 8
Hospedaje Pudeto 331 19
Hospedaje San José 9
Hospedaje Santander 10
Hostal Lluhay 14

Hostería Ahui 11
Hostería Ancud 12
Lacuy 13
Madryn 16
Montserrat 17
Polo Sur 18
Posada Cumelen 23
Residencial Germania 20
Residencial Weschler 21
San Bernardo 22

Eating
Carmen 1
Coral 2
El Cangrejo 3
El Pinguinito 4
El Sacho 5
El Trauco 6
Jardín 7
La Pincoya 8
Lydia 9

Pumillahue

Pumillahue is 27 km southwest of Ancud, on the Pacific coast. About 10 km before Pumillahue is **Mar Brava**, a vast, deserted curved beach, wonderful for horseriding. About 3 km away from Pumillahue there is colony of both Humbolt and Magellanic penguins, situated on an island looked after by the **Otway Foundation** ①️ *To65-315494, otwayfund@ctcinternet.cl, Otway guided tours in English/German US$5, guided tour with local fishermen (in Spanish with exaggerated hand gestures) US$3.50.* The penguins are there from November to early March. The best time to see them is in the early morning or evening. For an account of penguin-watching at Pumillahue, read Ben Richards' *The Mermaid and the Drunks* (Weidengeld, 2003).

Chepu and around

South of Ancud, at junction 26 Km of the Pan-American Highway, a dirt road heads west to the coast at Chepu, famed for its river and sea fishing. It is a base for exploring the drowned forest and the waterways of the Río Chepu and its tributaries (a result of the 1960 *maremoto*). There is a wide range of birdlife here and excellent opportunities for boat trips and horseriding. Chepu is also the entrance to the north part of the Parque Nacional Chiloé (see page 397). At **Río Anguay** (also known as Puerto Anguay), en route from Ancud, there is a campsite and *refugio*. From here, it is a 1½-hour walk to **Playa Aulén**, which has superb forested dunes and an extinct volcano.

Boat trips can be organized in Río Anguay to **Laguna Coluco**, one hour up the Río Butalcura (a tributary of the Río Chepu). Two-day trips, navigating the rivers Grande, Carihueco and Butalcura, usually start further inland and finish at Río Anguay. These can be arranged in Ancud (see page 389). It is possible to reach Chepu on a wild coastal walk from Pumillahue: take the daily bus from Ancud to Pumillahue (0645, return 1330) or hitch. The route is difficult to follow so take food for three days and wear light-coloured clothes in summer to protect against *tavanos* (horseflies). ▸▸ *For Sleeping, Eating and other listings, see below.*

⬤ Sleeping

Ancud *p385, map p386*
In summer the school on Calle Chacabuco is used as a cheap albergue.

AL Cabañas Las Golondrinas, *end of Baquedano at Arena Gruesa, To65-622823, golondri@telsur.cl* Superb views, with kitchenette, overpriced.

AL Galeón Azul, *Libertad 751, To65-622543, galeonazul@telsur.cl* With café.

AL Hostería Ancud, *San Antonio 30, To65-622340, www.hosteriancud.com* Overlooking bay, wonderful views, attractive, very comfortable, friendly and helpful, restaurant, traditional Chilote carvings, English spoken, tours offered.

A-C Playa Gaviotas, *6 km north on R5, Km1103, To9-8830489, playagaviota@hotmail.com* Pool and *cabañas* for up to 6 people. Basic.

B Balai, *Pudeto 169, To65-622541, www.hotelbalai.cl* With heating, laundry, parking, restaurant, cable TV, interesting local paintings, models and artefacts on display. Tours arranged.

B Montserrat, *Baquedano 417, T/F065-622957, hotelmonserrat@hotmail.com* With breakfast, clean, good views, small rooms.

B-C Posada Cumelen, *Quintanilla No 5, just off Pudeto 600 block, T/F065-625677, pcorrea2003@yahoo.com* Comfortable rooms, with bath, heating, laundry, good breakfast, free internet, bar, pool table, great views, friendly, tours arranged, recommended.

C Hostal Chiloe, *O'Higgins 274, To65-622869.* With bath, large doll collection.

C Hostería Ahui, *Costanera 906, To65-622415.* With breakfast, modern, clean, good views, restaurant.

C Lacuy, *Pudeto 219 near Plaza de Armas, T/F065-623019, jyk@entelchile.net* With breakfast, restaurant. Recommended.

C-D Hostal Lluhay, *Cochrane 458, T/F065-622656, hostallluhay@hotmail.com* Meals served, recommended.

C-D Polo Sur, *Costanera 630, To65-622200, www.turismopolosur.cl* With bath, good seafood restaurant, not cheap, avoid rooms overlooking disco next door.

C-D **Res Germania**, *Pudeto 357,*
T/F065-622214, rosemini@entelchile.net With
bath, cheaper without, parking, clean.
C-E **Res Weschler**, *Cochrane 480,*
T065-622318. With bath, cheaper without.
Clean, view of bay.
F **Hosp Alinar**, *Ramírez 348.* Price per person.
Clean, hospitable. Recommended.
F **Hosp Alto Bellavista**, *Bellavista 449,*
T065-622384. Price per person. Good
breakfast, good restaurant.
F **Hosp Austral**, *Aníbal Pinto 1318,*
T065-624847. Price per person with breakfast.
Kitchen and laundry facilities, by bus terminal.
F **Hosp Capri**, *Ramírez 325.* Price per person.
Good breakfast.
F **Hosp Elisabeth Vargas**, *Carreras 821,*
T065-622296. Price per person. Nice house,
clean, friendly, kitchen facilities.
F **Hosp O'Higgins**, *O'Higgins 6, T065-622266.*
Price per person. With breakfast, bath,
spacious, interesting *objets d'art*, near the
sea, nice views, recommended.
F **Hosp Su Casa**, *Los Alerces 841,*
T065-623382. Clean, with bath, TV, with
breakfast, friendly.
F **Hostal Mundo Nuevo**, *Costanera 748,*
T065-628383, www.newworld.cl Sea views,
kitchen facilities, breakfast, bike rental,
English, German spoken, highly
recommended. Price per person.
F **Madryn**, *Bellavista 491, T065-622128,*
www.hotelmadryn.cl Price per person. With
bath, also meals, clean.
F-G **Elena Bergmann**, *Aníbal Pinto 382.* Price
per person. Clean, use of kitchen, parking.
F-G **Hosp Alto Bellavista**, *Bellavista 449,*
T065-622384. Price per person; cheaper if you
sleep in a sleeping bag on the floor.
F-G **Hosp Errázuriz**, *Errázuriz 442.* Price per
person with breakfast, cold water.
F-G **Hosp Lautaro**, *Lautaro 947, T065-*
622980. Price per person. Clean, friendly.
F-G **Hosp Miranda**, *Mocopulli y Errázuriz.*
Price per person with breakfast, comfortable.
F-G **Hosp Mocopulli,** *Mocopulli 710 y*
Ramirez (enter through restaurant). Price per
person. Very friendly, living room full of
plants and flowers, full breakfast, quiet.
F-G **Hosp Pudeto**, *Pudeto 331, T065-622535.*
Price per person without bath, old fashioned.
F-G **Hosp Santander**, *Sgto Aldea 69.* Price
per person. Cheaper without bath, clean.
F-G **Hosp Sra Marta**, *Lautaro 988.* Price per

person with breakfast, TV, kitchen facilities,
good beds, good views from some rooms.
G **Hosp Aguilera**, *Aguilera 756,* Price per
person. Good beds, nice bathroom.
G **Hosp San José**, *Pudeto 619.* Price per person,
with breakfast, large rooms, very friendly,
internet, information, good beds.
G **San Bernardo**, *Errázuriz 395, T065-622657.*
Price per person. Dormitories, clean. Several
others on same street.

Camping

Arena Gruesa, *Arena Gruesa beach, at north*
end of Baquedano, F065-623428
Chiloé, *Arena Gruesa beach, at north of*
Baquedano, T065-622961.
Playa Gaviotas, *5 km north, T09-6538096.*
Also has *cabañas*.
Playa Larga Huicha, *9 km north.* Hot water
and electricity.

Agrotourism

Juan Saldivia and **Corina Huentelicán**,
Guapilacuy, near Faro Corona,
T09-6539422, produce their own cheese,
butter and preserves.

East of Ancud *p386*

AL-B **Hotel Caulín**, *Caulín, 09-6437986.*
Native Chilote trees grow in the garden,
cabañas also available.

Agrotourism

Ariela Bahamonde and **Amador Villagas**,
Pulelo, 2 km south of Chacao, T09-8842421,
T09-8246378. Still use traditional agricultural
techniques and make preserves.

Pumillahue *p387*

AL-C **Pinguinland Cabañas**, *between Mar*
Brava and the penguin colony, T065-627193,
pinguinland@hotmail.com Clean cabañas for
5-7 people, also double rooms and expensive
meals. Spectacular view if weather is good.

Chepu *p387*

Agrotourism

Armando Pérez and **Sonia Díaz**,
T09-6539241. Make cheese, tend cattle and
sheep, and offer good walks in the Chepu
area. To get there from Ancud, travel 26 km
south on Route 5, turn right (east) for 5 km to
Coipomó, there turn left, and after 3½ km
turn right. The farm is on the left after 2 km.

⊘ Eating

Ancud *p385, map p386*
There are excellent cheap seafood restaurants in the market area; the **Hotel Polo Sur** serves good lunches (see above).

$$ Coral, *Pudeto 346*. Good, but not cheap.

$$ Jardín, *Pudeto 263*. Good local food, but not cheap.

$$ Kuranton, *Prat 94*. Serves good *curantos* and seafood.

$$ Lydia, *Pudeto 254*. Chilean and international cuisine.

$$ Patagonia Beef, *main road leading west from Ancúd*. Argentinian restaurant, lots of meat as the name implies.

$ Carmen, *Pudeto 159*. Chilean cooking, including *pasteles*.

$ El Cangrejo, *Dieciocho 155*. Highly recommended for seafood.

$ El Pinguinito, *off Prat, near the market*. Seriously cheap lunches only. Also look in the market area, where there are *colaciones*.

$ El Sacho, *Mercado Municipal, local 7*. Huge portions, not fancy but very reasonable; several similar places in the same arcade.

$ El Timon, *Yungay y Allende*. Small, cheap and good value.

$ El Trauco, *Blanco y Prat*. Excellent seafood. Highly recommended.

$ Hamburguería, *Av Prat*. Much better than name suggests, good seafood.

$ La Pincoya, *Av Prat*. Seafood next to harbour.

$ Mar y Velas, *Serrano 2*. Beautiful views and good food.

$ Retro's Pub, *Maipú 615, off Pudeto*. Appealing ambience, food (including vegetarian fare) and good cocktails. Open Mon-Fri 1100-0300, Sat 2000-0400, Sun 2000-0400 in summer.

East of Ancud *p386*
$$$-$$ Ostras Caulín, *Caulín, T09-6437005*. Excellent, very fresh oysters served in any number of ways.

$$ Restaurant Pilón de Oro, *Chacao*. Good Chilote fare. There's also restaurant and *hospedaje* at Freire 35.

▲ Activities and tours

Ancud *p385, map p386*
Tours are available from the kiosk on the plaza.

Austral Adventures, *Pudeto 22, Ancud, T065-625977, www.austral-adventures.com* Small group tours of the archipelago and northern Patagonia (including Parque Pumalín), hiking or by sea, bilingual guides, US run. Recommended.

Paralelo 42, *Prat 28, T065-622458*. Recommended for tours to the Río Chepu area, including 2-day kayak trips guided by Carlos Oyarzun.

Chepu *p387*
For fishing trips around Chepu, try **Alphonso Bergara**, *T09-5170358*. This area also offers great opportunities for horseriding with long beaches that are perfect for a windswept gallop. Try **Sr Zuñipe** or **Sr Uroa**, US$5 per hour (ask at the *refugio* in Río Anguay).

⊖ Transport

For ferry services between the mainland and Chacao, see p384.

Bus
Local Buses leave Ancud from **Terminal Rural**, *Pedro Montt 538*. To **Pumillahue** and **Mar Brava**, Mon-Sat 0645, Mon-Fri 1200, Sat 1400, Mon-Fri 1600 with **Buses Mar Brava**; to **Quemchi** (via Linao and coast), 2 hrs, US$1.50.

Long distance Terminal on eastern outskirts of Ancud at *Av Prat y Marcos Vera*, reached by bus 1 or **Pudeto colectivos**. To **Castro**, frequent, 1½ hrs, **Cruz del Sur/Regional Sur**, US$2.50, or **Quellen Bus**, US$2; to **Chonchi**, US$3; to **Quellón**, **Cruz del Sur/Regional Sur**, 11 daily, US$5.

To **Santiago**, Cruz del Sur, 24 hrs, US$25, *salón cama* US$36; to **Puerto Montt**, 2 hrs, frequent, with Cruz del Sur, US$4.50, **Regional Sur**, US$4, and Quellen Bus, US$3.50.

➊ Directory

Ancud *p385, map p386*
Banks ATM at Banco BCI, *Ramirez, 1 block from the plaza*; Casa de cambio on same block. **Bicycle hire** *Ramírez 311*, US$1/hr or US$5/day. **Post office** *Pudeto y Blanco Encalada, corner of Plaza de Armas*. **Telephone** *Plaza de Armas*, open Mon-Sat 0700-2200; ENTEL, *Pudeto 219*, with internet; *Los Carreras 823*.

Towards Castro

There are two alternative routes from Ancud to Castro: direct along the Pan-American Highway, crossing rolling hills, forest and agricultural land, or the more leisurely route via the east coast. This is a dramatic journey on unpaved roads that plunge up and down forested hills. The route passes through small farming and fishing communities and offers a real insight into rural life in Chiloé. The two main towns along the coastal route, Quemchi and Dalcahue, can also be reached by roads branching off the Pan-American Highway.

Along the east coast

Quemchi and around → *Colour map 4, C1. Population: 2,000.*

South of Chacao is the small village of **Hueihue**, where fresh oysters can be bought, US$15 for 100. Further south, before Quemchi, is a small lake with model sailing boats. Quemchi itself is a quiet town with long beaches, overlooking a bay speckled with wooded islands; a short walk up the road north towards Linao leads to high ground from where there are views to the temperate rainforest on the mainland. Miniature ornamental boats are made in the village. Some 4 km from Quemchi is **Isla Aucar**, once linked by bridge (now ruined), where black-necked swans can be seen. There is a small tourist information booth in the plaza.

The road from Quemchi to Dalcahue (50 km) passes many places that are the essence of Chiloé. The road rises up and down steep forested hills, rich with flowers, past salmon farms and views of distant bays. Some 20 km from Quemchi is a turn-off to **Quicaví**, legendary as the home to the witches of Chiloé; a further few kilometres brings you to **Tenaún**, a beautiful village with a church dating from 1837, which is now a UNESCO World Heritage Site – trips to neighbouring islands such as Mechuque are easy to arrange here. You will pass numerous small communities with churches and views to the coast before you reach Dalcahue. ▸▸ *For Sleeping, Eating and other listings, see pages 392-396.*

Dalcahue and around → *Colour map 4, C1. Population: 3,000.*

Seventy-four kilometres south of Ancud via the Pan-American Highway, **Dalcahue** is more easily reached from Castro, 30 km further south. The wooden church on the main square dates from the 19th century and is a UNESCO World Heritage Site. There is a tourist kiosk in season. Dalcahue is one of the main ports for boats to the offshore islands, including Quinchao (see below) and the **Chauques Islands**. These are a group of 16 islands east of Dalcahue, interconnected by sandbars, which are crossable at low tide. The largest is **Mechuque** (accessed by bus from Tenaún), which has one village and offers splendid walking country. There are beautiful views of the mainland in good weather.

Quinchao → *Colour map 4, C1. Population: 2,500.*

The island of Quinchao is a short ferry journey from Dalcahue. Passing the pretty village of Curaço de Veléz, you reach the main settlement, **Achao**, 25 km southeast of Dalcahue. This is a large fishing village serving the smaller islands offshore, with a boarding school attended by pupils from outlying districts. Its wooden church, built in 1730, is the oldest surviving church in Chiloé. Saved by a change of wind from a fire that destroyed much of the town in 1784, it is a fine example of Chilote Jesuit architecture and contains a small **museum** ① *US$1.* Achao has a seasonal **tourist office** ① *Serrano y Progreso, Dec-Mar only.* A beautiful road leads 9 km south of Achao to the small village of **Quinchao** in a secluded bay at the foot of a hill; an important religious festival is held in the fine church here on 8 December (see page 394).

: Curanto

Particularly associated with Puerto Montt and Chiloé, *curanto* is a very filling fish, meat and seafood stew, which is delicious despite the rather odd combination of ingredients. Though of pre-Hhispanic origins, it has developed by adding new ingredients according to new influences. In its original pre-Conquest form, a selection of fish was wrapped in leaves and baked over hot stones in a hole – some specialists wonder if this way of cooking may have come from the Pacific islands, where pit baking is still practised. With the arrival of the Spanish, the dish was modified to include pork, chicken and white wine. Today, it is often cooked in a large pan and advertised as *pullmay* or *Curanto en Olla*, to distinguish it from the pit-baked form.

With patience and persistence, boats can be found to take you from Achao to outlying islands, where facilities are basic and shops non-existent but lodging can be found with families; ask around. It is recommended to go with a local friend, if possible.▸▸ *For Sleeping, Eating and other listings, see pages 392-396.*

Castro → *Phone code: 065. Colour map 4, C1. Population: 20,000.*

The capital of Chiloé, Castro lies 88 km south of Ancud on a fjord on the east coast. It is a small, friendly town, full of bars and seafood restaurants where Chilotes from remote regions sit drinking *chicha*, eating *cazuela* and swapping tall stories. The centre is on a promontory, from which there is a steep drop to the port. Castro is the major tourist centre on the island.

Ins and outs

Getting there Castro is Chiloé's transport hub. There are many buses south to Quellón (hourly) and north to Ancud and Puerto Montt. **Cruz del Sur** have buses continuing north to Valdivia, Temuco and Santiago (several daily). Many buses serve the more isolated Chilote communities from the Municipal Bus Terminal. Following disputes with dockworkers in Quellón, Castro is temporarily serving as the main port for passenger services to Chaitén and Puerto Montt.▸▸ *For further details, see Transport, page 395.* **Getting around** There are some *colectivos* and public buses serving the *barrios* high above the town near the *media luna*, but it is unlikely that you will need to use these. It is only a half-hour walk up there in any case. **Tourist information** A kiosk run by local hotels and agencies is located on Plaza de Armas opposite the cathedral. **CONAF** is in Gamboa behind the Gobernación building.

Sights

On the Plaza de Armas is the large wooden **cathedral**, unmissable in bright lilac and orange, designed by the Italian architect, Eduardo Provosoli, and dating from 1906. One block south, on Calle Esmerada, is the **Museo Regional** ① *summer Mon-Sat 0930-2000, Sun 1030-1300, winter Mon-Sat 0930-1300, 1500-1830, Sun 1030-1300,* containing displays on the history, handicrafts and mythology of Chiloé, as well as photos of the effects of the 1960 earthquake. Further south, on the waterfront, is the **Feria de Artesanía**, where local woollen articles, such as hats, sweaters, gloves, can be bought, although many of the articles sold are imported from elsewhere in South America. Nearby are several new *palafito* restaurants, built on stilts above the water. More traditional *palafitos* can be seen on the northern side of town and by the bridge over the Río Gamboa.

There are good views of the city from **Mirador La Virgen** on Millantuy hill above the cemetery. The **Museo de Arte Moderno** ① *T065-632787, daily 1000-1900*, is in the Parque Municipal, about 3 km northwest of the centre, and is reached by following Calle Galvarino Riveros up the hill west of town, from where there are fine views. Passing the Parque Municipal, Calle Galvarino Riveros becomes a small track heading out into the thick forests of the interior, with several small farmsteads. There is also a pleasant two-hour circular walk through woods and fields to **Puntilla Ten Ten** and the Peninsula opposite Castro; turn off the Pan-American Highway, 2 km north of town. **Nercón**, 4 km south, has a wooden church, which was restored in 1996.

● Sleeping

Quemchi *p390*

B-G Caulín, *Centenario 141, T065-691230*. Price per person. Also *cabañas* for up to 5 people.
G Hosp El Embrujo, *Pedro Montt 431, T065-651262*. Price per person.
G Hosp La Tranquera, *Yungay 40, T065-651250*. Price per person without bath, basic.

Agrotourism

Guillermo Hernández and **Bernarda Zúñiga**, *Huite, 4 km north of Quemchi, T09-6539239/6450918*. Part of the agrotourism network, in a beautiful spot.
Juan Dougnac and **Evangelina Cordaro**, *Tubildad, 2 km north of Quemchi, T065-691305*. Salmon fishing in lovely surroundings.
Magali Miranda, *Huite, 4 km north of Quemchi, T09-6539245/5173731*. Produces honey, milk, preserves, and smoked salmon. Great location.

Castro

0 metres 100
0 yards 100

Sleeping ●
Cabañas Nercon **3** *C1*
Cabañas Pleno Centro **1** *C2*
Cabañas Truyen **5** *C1*
Casa Blanca **2** *C2*
Casita Española **4** *B2*
Freire 758 **7** *A1*
Gran Alerce Nativo **9** *A2*
Hilton **10** *B2*
Hospedaje El Mirador **12** *B3*
Hospedaje Polo Sur **14** *B3*
Hospedaje Sotomayor **15** *B2*
Hospedaje América **16** *C3*
Hospedaje El Molo **17** *B3*
Hostería de Castro **18** *C3*
Los Carrera 658 **20** *B2*
Residencial La
Casona **23** *B3*
Serrano 407 **24** *B3*
Unicornio Azul **25** *B3*

Eating ●
Chilo's **1** *B2*
Don Camilo **2** *B2*
Donde Eladio **3** *C3*
Don Octavio **8** *B3*
El Curanto **4** *C3*
Gipsy **5** *B2*
La Playa **6** *C2*
Sacho **7** *C3*

Chiloé Towards Castro

María Soto and Manuel Vásquez, *Tenaún, 32 km south of Quemchi, T09-6539416/ 6476752*. Honey, *chicha* and preserves.
Mirella Montaña and Guido Vásquez, *Tenaún, 32 km south of Quemchi, T09-6539423/6476750*. Butter, preserves, *chicha* and pastries.

Dalcahue and around *p390*
F La Feria, *Rodríguez 17, T065-641293*. Price per person without bath, basic.
F Res Playa, *Rodríguez 9*. Price per person. Basic.
G Hosp Mary, *Tte Merino 10, T065-641260*. Price per person. Also sells handicrafts.
G Hosp Puteman, *Freire 305, T065-641330*. Price per person. Clean, basic.
G Res San Martín, *San Martín 1, T065-641207*. Price per person. Basic, clean, also meals.
   On Mechuque, accommodation is available with the schoolteacher's son or with Sra Dina del Carmen Paillacar, who serves good meals.

Quinchao *p390*
C-F Hostería La Nave, *Prat y Aldea, Achao, T065-661219, hosterialanave@latinmail.com* Breakfast provided, cheaper rooms without bath, restaurant with fine views over bay.
D Plaza, *Plaza de Armas, Achao, T065-661283*. With bath and breakfast, clean, good.
D-E Hosp Chilhue, *Zañartu 021, Achao*. Without bath, with breakfast, clean.
E Hosp Achao, *Serrano 061, Achao, T065-661373*. Without bath, good, clean.
F Hosp Sao Paulo, *Serrano 52, Achao, T065-661245*. Basic, poor beds, hot water.

Agrotourism
There are two options on Quinchao:
Juan Guilquiruca and Luzmira Barrientos, *Huyar Bajo (turn left before Achao en route from Curaço de Velez), T09-7963697*. Butter, preserves and *chicha*.
Ramiro and María Cárcamo, *Matao, southeastern tip of the island, T09-6539424/ 6216548*. Preserves and *chicha*.

Castro *p391, map p392*
AL Cabañas Centro Turístico Nercón, *Km 5 south of Castro, T065-632985*. With bath, hot water, heating, restaurant, tennis court.
AL Cabañas Pleno Centro, *Los Carrera 346, T065-635092*. 2-person cabañas, also larger version with kitchen.

AL-A Hostería de Castro, *Chacabuco 202, T065-632301, www.hosteriadecastro.cl* With breakfast, good restaurant, wonderful views.
A Unicornio Azul, *Pedro Montt 228, T065-632359, F065-632808*. Good views over bay, comfortable, restaurant, English spoken.
A-B Cabañas Trayen, *Km 5 south of Castro, T065-633633*. Cheaper off season, *cabañas* with lovely views.
A-B Gran Alerce Nativo, *O'Higgins 808, 4 km south of Castro, T065-632267, hotelalerc@surnet.cl* Heating, breakfast, also has *cabañas* and restaurant. Helpful.
B Casita Española, *Los Carrera 359, T/F065-635186*. Heating, TV, parking. Recommended.
B-F Casa Blanca, *Los Carrera 308, T/F065-632726*. With breakfast, cheaper without bath, clean, modern, warm, also *cabañas*, sleep 6.
D Hilton, *Ramírez 385*. Good value, friendly, with restaurant.
F *Chacabuco 449*. Price per person. Good beds, clean, quiet, friendly, water only warm.
F *Eyzaguirre 469*. Price per person. Comfortable. Recommended.
F *Freire 758*. Price per person. Breakfast, clean, good value.
F Hosp América, *Chacabuco 215, T065-634364*. Price per person with breakfast. Friendly, very good food – "our tourists arrive thin and leave fat" – cable TV, shared bathrooms.
F Hosp Chiloé, *San Martín 739*. Price per person with breakfast, clean. Recommended.
F Hosp El Mirador, *Barros Arana 127, T065-633795*. Price per person. Good breakfast, kitchen facilities, good views, internet, very clean, recommended.
F Hosp El Molo, *Arana 140, T065-635026*. Price per person. 20-30 beds, use of kitchen.
F Hosp Jessie Toro, *Las Delicias 287*. Price per person with good breakfast, helpful, clean, spacious, good bathrooms, also *cabañas*. Recommended.
F Hosp Sotomayor, *Sotomayor 452, T065-632464*. Price per person with breakfast, quiet, small beds.
F Hosp Tonque, *Pasaje Díaz 170, T065-632773*. Price per person, no breakfast, clean, hot water.
F *Los Carrera 658*. Price per person with breakfast. No sign, clean, friendly.

F **María Zuñiga**, *Barros Arana 140, T065-635026.* Price per person with breakfast, clean, comfortable, cooking facilities, friendly, secure. Recommended.

F *O'Higgins 415, Dpto 41.* Price per person. Quiet, very clean, hot water.

F **Pensión Victoria**, *San Martín 747.* Price per person. Small rooms, clean, pretty.

F **Res Capullito**, *San Martín 709.* Price per person. Clean, friendly, quiet.

F **Res La Casona**, *Serrano 496, T065-632246.* Above TV shop. Price per person with breakfast. Recommended.

F *Serrano 407.* Price per person with breakfast, friendly, warm water.

G **Hosp Polo Sur**, *Barros Arana 169, T065-635212.* Price per person. Cooking facilities, wonderful views, noisy.

G **Lidia Low**, *San Martín 890.* Price per person. With good breakfast, warm showers, use of kitchen.

G *San Martín 879.* Price per person with big breakfast, central, clean. Highly recommended.

Camping

Llicaldad, *Esmeralda 269, Km 6 south of Castro, T065-635080.* One of several sites along road south towards Chonchi. *Cabañas* also available.

Pudu, *10 km north on the Pan-American Highway, T/F632476.* Hot showers, sites with light, water, children's games, also *cabañas*.

❶ Eating

Along the east coast *p390*
$ **Restaurant Centenario**, *Bahamonde 360, Quemchi.* Good, cheap fare.

$ **Restaurant La Dalca**, *Freire 502, Dalcahue.* Serves good, cheap food. Recommended. There are also numerous small restaurants along the harbour and around the market in Dalcahue, serving excellent and cheap seafood. Note that if you ask for 'té', you will be served a mug of white wine.

For restaurant food on Quinchao, try the **Hostería La Nave** (see Sleeping, above), or $ **Restaurant Central**, *Achao.* Simple, good.

Castro *p391, map p392*
You may have difficulty tracking down some breakfast before 0900. *Palafito* restaurants near the Feria Artesanía on the waterfront offer

good food and good value, including **Brisas del Mar**, **La Amistad** and **Rapu Nui**. There are also very cheap restaurants by the municipal bus terminal. In the market, try *milcaos*, fried potato cakes with meat stuffing.

$$ **Anadito**, *Plaza de Armas.* Good pub and restaurant.

$$ **Donde Eladio**, *Lillo 97.* Meat and seafood specialities.

$$ **Gipsy**, *O'Higgins 548.* Chinese.

$$ **La Playa**, *Lillo 441.* Recommended for fish and meat.

$ **Chilo's**, *San Martín 459.* Good lunches.

$ **Don Camilo**, *Ramírez 566.* Good food, not expensive.

$ **Don Octavio**, *Pedro Montt 261.* Good food, good value.

$ **El Curanto**, *Lillo 67.* Seafood including *curanto*. Recommended.

$ **Sacho**, *Thompson 213.* Good sea views. Recommended.

Cafés
La Brújula del Cuerpo, *Plaza de Armas.* Good coffee and snacks.
Stop Inn Café, *Martín Ruiz shopping centre, Gamboa s/n.* Good coffee.

⊛ Festivals and events

Quinchao *p390*
Dia de la Virgen People come to the small village of Quinchao from all over Chiloé on **8 Dec** to watch as a huge model of the Virgin is carried with great reverence to the church.

❍ Shopping

Dalcahue *p390*
Dalcahue weekly **market** is held 0700-1300 Sun. It has good quality goods, but bargaining is practically impossible, and in recent years it has become somewhat overrun with tourists; good for *curantos*, though.

Castro *p391, map p392*
Cassettes of typical Chilote music are widely available around town.
Annay Libros, *Serrano 357.* Books in Spanish on Chiloé, often cheaper than Santiago bookshops.
El Tren Libros, *Thompson 229.* Books in Spanish on Chiloé, often cheaper than Santiago bookshops.

Hiper Beckna, *Sargento Aldea y O'Higgins*. Supermarket with good bakery.

Libros Chiloé, *Blanco Encalada 204*. Books in Spanish on Chiloé, often cheaper than Santiago bookshops.

Mercado Artesanal, *on the wharf*. Good quality woollens at reasonable prices.

Mercado municipal, *Yumbel, off Pilato Samuel Ulloa*. Good fish and vegetables.

▲ Activities and tours

Dalcahue *p390*
Altue Active Travel, *3 km south of Dalcahue, reservations from Encomenderos 83, 2nd floor Las Condes, Santiago, T02- 2321103, www.altue.com* Sea kayaking.

Castro *p391, map p392*
Tour operators usually charge US$25 to Parque Nacional Chiloé, US$37 to Mechuque.

Chiotours, *Blanco 293, T065-639544*. Tours to the Parque Nacional, Quinchao, Lemuy and Queilen. Also boat trips.

Sergio Márquez, *Felipe Moniel 565, T065-632617*. Very knowledgeable local guide with transport.

Turismo Isla Grande, *Thompson 241*, Transmarchilay and Navimag agency.

Turismo Pehuén, *Blanco Encalada 299 y Esmeralda, T065-632361, pehuentr@ entelchile.net* LanChile agents, also horseriding excursions and trips to the National Park, the penguin colony and the smaller islands.

Turismo Queilen, *Gamboa 502, T065-632776*. Recommended tours to Chonchi and to the National Park.

◉ Transport

Dalcahue and around *p390*
Buses to **Castro**, hourly, 40 mins, US$1; also *colectivos* to **Castro** and to **Achao**, US$1.50; daily bus to **Puerto Montt**, via Ancud, US$4.

To reach **Mechuque**, catch the bus from Tenaún, departs Wed 1730, returns Thu, 2½ hrs, US$2.50 one way.

Quinchao *p390*
Arriagada buses to **Ancud**, 5 daily; to **Castro**, 4 daily, US$1.75. There's a frequent ferry service to **Dalcahue**, free for pedestrians and cyclists.

Bus
There are 2 bus terminals. **Cruz del Sur** services depart from **Cruz del Sur terminal**, *San Martín behind the cathedral, T065-632389*. Other services, including most buses to rural communities, leave from the **Municipal Terminal**, *San Martín, 600 block (2 blocks further north)*.

To **Quemchi**, 1 daily, with **Queilen Bus**; to **Dalcahue**, frequent, with **Gallardo** and **Arriagada**, also *colectivos* from San Martín 815; to **Tenaún**, daily 1200; to **Achao** via Dalcahue and Curaço de Vélez, 4 daily Mon-Sat, 3 daily Sun, with **Arriagada**, US$1.75, last return from Achao 1730.

To **Chonchi**, frequent, with **Cruz del Sur**, **Queilén Bus**, minibuses and *colectivos* (from Ramirez y San Martín and Esmeralda y Chacabuco); to **Puqueldón**, 4 daily Mon-Sat, with **Gallardo**, US$1.50; to **Queilen**, 6 daily, with **Queilen Bus**, US$2.50; to **Quellón**, frequent, with **Cruz del Sur/Trans Chiloé**, US$2.

To **Cucao** for the Parque Nacional Chiloé, 6 daily in summer, 1 daily in winter, with **Arroyo** and **Ocean Bus**, US$2.20, avoid Fri, when the service is crowded with schoolchildren.

There are also frequent services to **Ancud**, 1 hr, and **Puerto Montt**, 3 hrs, with Cruz del Sur, Trans Chiloé and Queilen Bus, US$4.50. Cruz del Sur also run to **Osorno**, **Valdivia**, **Temuco**, **Concepción** and **Santiago**. Bus Norte serves **Ancud**, **Puerto Montt**, **Osorno** and **Santiago** daily. Queilen Bus runs a weekly service on Mon to **Punta Arenas**, 36 hrs, US$60.

Ferry
While Quellón ferry port is out of action (see p398), the **Navimag** and **Transmarchilay** services to **Chaitén** on the mainland depart from Castro, 4 per week Dec-early Mar, reduced service off season, 5 hrs, passengers US$16, cars US$85, cycles US$9. Some ships continue from Chaitén to **Puerto Montt**. A faster catamaran service is provided by **Aysen Express** and **Catamaranes del Sur** to **Chaitén**, 2 hrs, US$18, and **Puerto Montt**, 5 per week in summer, less regularly off season. The Transmarchilay ferry *Pincoya* sails to **Puerto Chacabuco**, irregular service, 24 hrs.

Castro *p391, map p392*
Airline offices LanChile, *Blanco 209*.
Banks Banco de Chile, *Plaza de Armas*,
ATM, accepts TCs (at a poor rate); BCI, *Plaza de Armas*, Mastercard and Visa ATM; **Julio Barrientos**, *Chacabuco 286*, cash and TCs, better rates than the banks. **Film supplies** *Blanco 360*; *Gamboa 450*. **Internet** *O'Higgins 486*, US$7 per hr, charged by the min, open 0900-1300, 1600-2200; Cadesof Ltda, *Gamboa 447, 2nd floor*; n@vegue, *San Martín 309*. **Laundry** Clean Centre, *Serrano 440* ; Lavandería Adolfo, *Blanco Encalada 96*, quick, reasonably priced; Lavaseco Unic, *Gamboa 594*. **Medical services** *Muñoz de Las Carreras, near police station*, surgery 1700-2000 Mon-Fri, recommended. **Post office** *West side of Plaza de Armas*. **Telephone** *Latorre 289*; Entel, *O'Higgins between Sotomayor and Gamboa*; also private centres at *Latorre 275* and *Lillo 93*.

Chonchi to Quellón

The Pan-American Highway continues south to Quellón, the southernmost port in Chiloé, with paved side roads leading east to Chonchi and an unpaved track heading west to Cucao. From Chonchi, a partially paved road continues southeast to Queilen. Winding across forested hills, this is probably the most attractive route on the island, especially in autumn; numerous tracks branch off to deserted beaches where you can walk for hours and hear nothing but the splashing of dolphins in the bay. The ferry to Lemuy is caught from a port on this track.

Chonchi and around → *Phone code: 065. Colour map 4, C1. Population: 4,000.*

A picturesque fishing village 23 km south of Castro, Chonchi is a good base for exploring the island. Known as the 'Ciudad de los Tres Pisos', or 'the city built on three levels', it was, until the opening of the Panama Canal in 1907, a stopping point for sailing ships. In the years that followed, it was the cypress capital of Chile: big

Quellón

Sleeping		Eating
Club Deportes Turino 1	Las Brisas 5	El Coral 3
El Chico Leo 2	Melimoyu 6	Fogón Las Quilas 1
G Laris 3	Playa 7	Los Suizos 2
	Residencial Esteban 8	

0 metres 50
0 yards 50

N

fortunes were made in the timber industry and grand wooden mansions were built in the town. In the 1950s, the town boomed as a free port but, in the 1970s, it lost that status to Punta Arenas. Its harbour is now the supply point for salmon farms almost as far south as Coyhaique.

On the main plaza is the **church**, built in neo-classical style in 1880. Its once impressive tower was blown off in a storm in March 2002 and, although reconstruction is planned, it had not begun at the time of writing. There is also a tourist information kiosk here in summer. From the plaza, **Calle Centenario** drops steeply to the harbour, lined with several attractive but sadly neglected wooden mansions. Fishing boats bring in the early morning catch, which is carried straight into the nearby market. The small **Museo de Chonchi Viejo** is located in an old house, with videos on the churches of Chiloé, including the 18th-century church, 5 km north of Chonchi at Vilopulli.

In the bay opposite Chonchi lies the island of **Lemuy**. It covers 97 sq km and offers many good walks along quiet unpaved tracks through undulating pastures and woodland. From the ferry dock, a road runs east across the island, passing a fine 19th-century wooden church at **Ichuac** before reaching **Puqueldón**. This is the main settlement on the island and is built on a very steep hill stretching down to the port. There's a post office and a telephone centre here. From Puqueldón, the road continues a further 16 km on a ridge high above the sea, passing small hamlets, with views of the water and the patchwork of fields. There are old churches at **Aldachildo**, 9 km east of Puqueldón, and at **Detif**, in the extreme south of the island.

Forty-six kilometres southeast of Chonchi, **Queilen** is a pretty fishing village on a long finger-shaped peninsula. On the north side is a sandy beach, which curves round the head of the peninsula, while on the south side is the old wooden pier, which doubles as the port. There are fine views across the straits to Tanqui Island and the mainland. ▶▶ *For Sleeping, Eating and other listings, see pages 398-400.*

The west coast

West of Chonchi at Km 12 is **Huillinco**, a charming village on Lago Huillinco. Beyond here the *ripio* road continues west to **Cucao**, one of only two settlements on the west coast of Chiloé. The immense 20-km-long beach is battered by thundering Pacific surf and dangerous undercurrents, making it one of the most dramatic places along the whole coast of Chile.

Cucao lies at the edge of the southern sector (35,207 ha) of the **Parque Nacional Chiloé** ① *T065-532501/09-9329193, US$2.* The park, which is in three sections, covers extensive areas of the wild and uninhabited western side of the island, much of it filled by temperate rainforest. Wildlife includes the Chiloé fox and pudu deer. There are over 110 species of birds resident here, including cormorants, gulls, penguins and flightless steamer ducks.

You can take a car as far as the administration centre at the entrance ① *1 km north of Cucao, T09-9329193, open daily*, which has limited information and a guest bungalow for use by visiting scientists; applications to CONAF via your embassy. There are also decent camping facilities. The centre provides maps of the park, but they are not very accurate and should not be used to locate *refugios* within the park.

‼ *The northern sector of the park is accessed via Chepu (see page 387); the third section of the park is the small island of Metalqui and is difficult to reach.*

A path, affording great views, runs 3 km north from the administration centre to **Laguna Huelde** and then north for a further 12 km to **Cole Cole**. Once you reach **Río Anay**, 9 km beyond Cole Cole, you can wade or swim across the river to reach a beautiful, secluded beach from where you can enjoy the sight of dolphins playing in the huge breakers. The journey can also be made on horseback; allow nine hours for the round trip. Take lots of water and your own food. There are several other walks in the national park, but signposts are limited and *tavanos* are bad in summer, so wear light-coloured clothing.

Chiloé Chonchi to Quellón

Quellón → *Phone code: 065. Colour map 5, A2. Population: 18,700.*

The southernmost port in Chiloé, located 92 km south of Castro, Quellón has suffered its fair share of misfortunes in recent years. In 2002, the arrival of the lethal *marea roja* micro-organism (see page 69) caused the collapse of the shellfish industry, provoking demonstrations from fishermen and dockworkers who destroyed part of the pier. As a result, there are no passenger ferry services from Quellón to Chaitén and Puerto Montt and it is unclear when services will return to normal. There is not much to interest the traveller here, although the **Museo de Nuestros Pasados** ① *Ladrilleros 225*, includes reconstructions of a traditional Chilote house and mill, and there are pleasant beaches nearby: **Viejo**, 4 km west, where there is an old wooden church; **Punta de Lapa**, 7 km west, and **Yaldad**, 9 km west along a pretty road over the hills. The launch *Puerto Bonito* sails around the bay in summer from the pier, passing Punta de Lapa, Isla Laitec and Quellón Viejo ① *3 times daily in summer, US$12.50*. A trip can be made to **Chaiguao**,11 km east, where there is a Sunday morning market.

Sleeping

Chonchi and around *p396*
There are also a number of *hospedajes* on Irarrázaval.
B-C Cabañas Amankay, *Centenario 410, T065-671367*. Homely, kitchen facilities. Recommended.
B-C Posada Antiguo Chalet, *Irarrázaval s/n, T065-671221*. Cheaper in winter, charming, beautiful location, very good.
D Huildin, *Centenario 102, T065-671388*. Without bath, old fashioned, good beds, also *cabañas*, garden with superb views, parking.
F Baker, *Andrade 184*. Price per person. Clean, friendly.
F Esmeralda by the Sea, *on waterfront 100 m south of the market, T/F065-671328, grady@telsur.cl (Casilla 79)*. Price per person with breakfast, attractive, welcoming, English spoken, kitchen facilities, cheap meals served, good beds, canoe and boat trips offered, also rents bicycles, information. Mixed reports, but often recommended.
F Res Turismo, *Andrade 299, T065-671257*. Without bath. Price per person with breakfast.
G Hosp Mirador, *Alvarez 198, T065-671351*. Price per person with breakfast, friendly, clean, good value. Recommended.
G Refugio Sra, *Fedima, Pedro Aquire Cerda 176*. Price per person. Own sleeping bag required, use of kitchen, friendly.

Agrotourism
There are several options between Chonchi and Queilen.
Ernesto Gamín and **Diana Bahamonde**, *Contuy, 38 km southwest of Chonchi,*

T09-6539206/6449262. Make butter and *chicha* and have cattle and sheep.
Manuel Pérez and **Bertila Díaz**, *Dético (4 km before Queilen turn right and travel a further 6 km), T02-9605558*. Make butter, cheese, honey and *chicha*; the farm is beside a football pitch.

Camping
Los Manzanos, *Aguirre Cerda y Juan Guillermo, T065-671263*.

Lemuy *p397*
F Café Amancay, *Puqueldón*. Basic accommodation and food.
F Restaurant Lemuy. Clean, without bath, good, price per person. Food served only in high season.
Lidia and José Pérez, *Puchilco, 10 km beyond Puqueldón, T09-8842430/8998914/4440252*. Part of agrotourism network; make butter, preserves and *chicha*.
Los Isleños, *1½ km from Puqueldón, Lemuy, T09-6548498*. Campsite.

Queilen *p397*
G Pensión Chiloé is basic, friendly, without bath. There is also accommodation in the big house beside the pier, and cheapish food at **Bar Restaurant El Refugio**.

The west coast *p397*
There's a cheap *residencial* in Huillinco with good food, or you can stay at the Post Office. In the Parque Nacional, there is a *refugio* and camping at Cole Cole and another *refugio* at Anay, 9 km further north. The following accommodation is all in Cucao.
F Casa Blanca, *T065-633040*. Price per person with breakfast.

F **Hosp Paraíso**, *T09-2965465*. Friendly *hospedaje*.

F **Posada Cucao**, *T065-633040/ 09-8969855*. Price per person with breakfast, hot water, meals, friendly.

F **Provisiones Pacífico**. Small grocery store offering full board or *demi-pension*, friendly, good, clean, meals and homemade bread, but no hot water. Price per person. Recommended.

G **Parador Darwin**, *at park entrance, Cucao sector, T065-633040*. Price per person with breakfast, good food with vegetarian options, real coffee. Highly recommended. Camping also available.

Camping

Lago Mar, *2 km east of Cucao, T065-635552*, US$12 per site. One of several campsites in the area; check prices carefully first.

Quellón *p398*
The school becomes a cheap *albuergue* in summer, with dormitory accommodation.

B **Melimoyu**, *Pedro Montt 369, T065-681250*. Clean, good beds, parking.

C-F **El Chico Leo**, *Pedro Montt 325*. *T065-681567, elchicoleo@telsur.cl* Cheaper without bath.

F **G Laris**, *Pedro Montt 45*. Price per person with breakfast.

F **Hosp La Paz**, *La Paz 370, T065-681207*. Price per person with breakfast, hot water.

F **Playa**, *Pedro Montt 427*. Price per person with breakfast, without bath. Clean.

F **Res Esteban**, *Aguirre Cerda 351*. Price per person. Safe, clean.

G **Club Deportes Turino**, *Ladrilleros y La Paz 024*. Price per person. Floor space and camping, cold water, kitchen facilities, basic. Open Dec-Feb only.

G **Las Brisas**, *Pedro Montt 555, T065-681413*. Price per person. Without bath, basic.

Agrotourism

Mercedes Vargas, *10 km north of Quellón on Route 5 (turn right at Candelaria; the farm is 2 km on the right), T09-6539213*. Makes preserves and *chicha*.

Camping

There are 5 sites at Punta de Lapa and sites without services at Chaiguao and Yaldad.

Chonchi and around *p396*
$$ **La Parada**, *Centenario 133*. Very friendly, good selection of wines, erratic opening hours. Recommended.

$ **El Alerce**, *Aguirre Cerda 106*. Excellent value.

$ **El Trébol**, *Irarrazával 187*. Good views over the harbour.

$ **La Quila**, *Andrade 183*. Cheap, good, popular with locals.

The west coast *p397*
Las Luminarias in Cucao sells excellent *empanadas de machas* (*machas* are local shellfish).

Quellón *p398*
$$ **Fogón Las Quilas**, *La Paz 053*, *T065-681206*. Famous for lobster. Recommended.

$$ **Los Suizos**, *Ladrilleras 399*. Swiss cuisine.

$ **El Coral**, *22 de Mayo*. Good, reasonably priced, superb views.

$ **Rucantú**, *Pedro Montt*. Good food and value.

🍸 Bars and clubs

Chonchi and around *p396*
Club 88, *on the waterfront*. Bar/restaurant.

Rockets Disco, *near Copec filling station*. Open weekends; more often in summer.

✹ Festivals and events

La Semana Chonchina, one of the series of Chilote festivals, takes place during the second week of **Feb**.

◯ Shopping

Chonchi and around *p396*
Handicrafts are sold from **Opdech** (Oficina Promotora del Desarrollo Chilote), on the waterfront, and from the parroquia, next to the church (open Oct-Mar only). In the summer many artesanal stalls open, a speciality being traditional woollen clothes.

▲ Activities and tours

The west coast *p397*

Many houses in Cucao rent horses at US$2.50 per hr, US$22 per day. It usually costs US$40 a day for the round trip on horseback to **Río Anay**. Bear in mind that the horses will be of varying tameness, and that if you hire a guide you pay for his horse too.

Quellón *p398*

Horses can be hired US$2.50 per hr; kayaks with a guide, US$2.50 per hr from the beach at Quellon.

⊖ Transport

Chonchi and around *p396*
Bus

Services depart from the main plaza to **Castro**, frequent, US$0.75; to **Puerto Montt**, US$5.50. Services to **Quellón** and **Queilen** (from Castro and Puerto Montt) and to **Cucao** (from Castro) also stop in Chonchi.

There are 4 buses daily Mon-Sat from Castro to **Lemuy**, and 6 daily Mon-Fri, 4 daily Sat, 3 daily Sun, from Castro to **Queilen**, Queilen Bus, 2 hrs, US$2.50.

Ferry

Services to **Lemuy** depart from Puerto Huicha, 4 km south of Chonchi, approximately every 30 mins, foot passengers travel free.

The west coast *p397*

Six buses a day to **Cucao** from Castro via Chonchi in season, US$2.20, last departure 1600, reduced service off season; hitching is very difficult.

Quellón *p398*
Bus

To **Castro**, frequent, 2 hrs, Cruz del Sur, US$3; also services to **Ancud** and **Puerto Montt**, US$7.

Ferry

For services to **Chaitén** and **Puerto Montt**, see Castro transport listings p395. It is possible that normal services will return to Quellón during 2004 or 2005.

● Directory

Chonchi *p396*

Banks Nicolás Alvarez, *Centenario 429*, cash only. **Telephone** *San Martín y Mistral.*

Quellón *p398*

Banks Banco del Estado, *Ladrilleros.* US$12 commission on TCs, credit cards not possible, no commission on US$ cash. **Laundry** Lavandería Ruck-Zuck, *Ladrilleras 392.* **Shipping offices** Navimag, *Pedro Montt 383*; Transmarchilay, *Pedro Montt 457*, *T065-681331.*

For an explanation of sleeping and eating price codes used in this guide, see inside the front cover. Other relevant information is found in Essentials, see pages 51-58.

The Carretera Austral

Introduction

Travelling along the Carretera Austral (also known as the Camino Austral) is one of the greatest journeys South America has to offer. The Carretera is a largely unpaved *ripio* road stretching over 1,000 km through ever-changing spectacular scenery. Before the opening of the carretera, this part of Chile was largely inaccessible; it remains breathtaking. Deep tree-lined fjords penetrate into the heart of a land of spiralling volcanoes and sparkling glaciers, rushing rivers, crystal blue lakes and temperate rainforest rich with southern Chile's unique flora.

The only town of any size, **Coyhaique**, lies in the valley of the Río Simpson. South of Coyhaique are **Lago General Carrera**, the largest lake in Chile, and the **Río Baker**, one of the longest rivers in the country, which reaches the sea at Caleta Tortel. Further south still is **Villa O' Higgins** and the icefields of the **Campo de Hielo Sur**, which feed several magnificent glaciers and prevent further road building, although a route (by boat and on foot or mountain bike) exists that goes on to El Chaltén in Argentina. Coyhaique enjoys good air connections with Puerto Montt and Santiago, while nearby Puerto Chacabuco can be reached by ferry or catamaran from Puerto Montt, Chaitén and Chiloé. The most appealing parts of this region, however, can only be visited by travelling along the Carretera Austral.

★ **Don't miss...**

❶ Parque Pumalin
Not only is it an area of outstanding beauty, it also gives an insight into what is widely regarded as one of the world's most important conservation projects, page 408.

❷ Laguna San Rafael
Sail on a cruise ship right up to the icebergs at the foot of the San Rafael glacier, page 431.

❸ Trekking Especially near Futaleufú in the north and Chile Chico in the south, pages 412 and 426.

❹ Lago General Carrera Take a ferry ride across the huge, deep blue expanse between Puerto Ibañez and Chile Chico, page 428.

❺ Mountain-biking
Take to two wheels along a stretch of the spectacular Carretera Austral itself, page 406.

Background

The original inhabitants of northern Patagonia were Alacalufes (Kaweshour or *canoeros*), who were coast dwellers living off the sea (see page), and Tehuelches (Tzónecas, or Patagones), who lived on the pampa hunting guanacos, *ñandúes* (rheas) and *huemules* (an indigenous deer, now almost extinct; see box, page 430). There are some fine cave paintings in the vicinity of Lago General Carrera, for example at Cueva de la Guanaca, near Lago Lapparent, and Cueva de las Manos, on the Argentine side of the frontier near Chile Chico.

The Spanish called the region Trapalanda, but initially explored little more than the coast. This was the last territory to be occupied by the Chilean state after Independence from Spain. In the late 19th century, expeditions up the rivers led by George Charles Musters (1869) and Enríque Simpson Baeza (1870-72) were followed by a failed attempt to found a settlement at the mouth of the Río Palena in 1884. Fearing that Argentina might seize the territory, the Chilean government appointed Hans Steffen to explore the area. His seven expeditions (1892-1902) were followed by an agreement with Argentina to submit the question of the frontier to arbitration by the British crown.

The Chilean government granted concessions to three large cattle companies in an attempt to occupy the area. One of these ranches, on the Río Baker, was managed by E Lucas Bridges, of the Bridges family from Tierra del Fuego and author of *Uttermost Part of the Earth* (for more details, see *South* by AF Tschiffely). Until the 1920s, there were few settlers; early pioneers settled along the coast and brought supplies from Chiloé. The estimated population of northern Patagonia in 1907 was just 197 people. By 1920, this had risen to 1,660 and, by 1930, 8,886 inhabitants were in the region. Although the first town, Balmaceda, was founded in 1917, followed by Puerto Aisén in 1924, the first road, between Puerto Aisén and Coyhaique, was not built until 1936. It was not until the 1960s, when new roads were built and airstrips were opened, that this region began to be integrated with the rest of the country.

Although the road has helped transform the lives of many people in this part of Chile, the motivation behind its construction was mainly geopolitical. Ever since Independence, Chilean military and political leaders have stressed the importance of occupying the southern regions of the Pacific coast and preventing any incursion by Argentina. Building the Carretera Austral was seen by General Pinochet as a means of achieving this task: a way of occupying and securing territory, just as colonization had been in the early years of the 20th century.

‼ *Most of the villages along the Carretera are of very recent origin and consist of a few wooden houses, some of which offer accommodation and other services to travellers.*

Begun in 1976, the central section of the Carretera Austral, from Chaitén to Coyhaique, was opened in 1983. Five years later, the northern section, linking Chaitén with Puerto Montt, and the southern section, between Coyhaique and Cochrane, were officially inaugurated. Since then, the Carretera has been extended south of Cochrane to Puerto Yungay and Villa O'Higgins. Work is continuing, building branch roads and paving the most important sections.

Despite recent growth, this remains one of the most sparsely populated areas of Chile, with fewer than 100,000 inhabitants, most of whom live in Coyhaique or in nearby Puerto Aisén. Agriculture is limited by the climate and poverty of the soil, but fishing remains important as a source of employment in the inland channels, with salmon farming providing most income. Forestry plays a growing role in the economy: wood is used for construction and is in such demand in towns such as Coyhaique for winter fuel that it costs as much as petrol. Zinc, lead and copper are mined, but only zinc is produced in major quantities. A huge aluminium plant is in the pipeline, which will have both economic and ecological repercussions.

⁝ Tips for travelling along the Carretera Austral

Travelling the length of the Carretera Austral can be quite a challenge. The first, and most important, piece of advice is to take enough cash. While there are Cirrus and Mastercard ATMs in Chaitén and Cochrane, Coyhaique is the only place between Puerto Montt and Villa O'Higgins with Visa ATMs.

Off-season much of the northern section of the Carretera is rendered inaccessible when the Arena-Puelche and Hornopirén-Caleta Gonzalo ferries are suspended. You will have to go to Chaitén directly from Puerto Montt or Chiloé instead. If you are driving, take a four-wheel-drive vehicle and fill up your tank whenever possible. Take spare parts – the road is unforgiving. After heavy rain, parts of the Carretera are liable

to flood, so check the weather carefully and be prepared to be stuck in one place for a few days while conditions improve.

Most of the buses that ply the Camino Austral are minibuses (and in more than one case converted transit vans) operated by small companies and often they are driven by their owners. Services are less reliable than elsewhere in Chile and timetables change frequently as operators go out of business and new ones start up. Booking your ticket in advance means that if your bus does not leave for whatever reason, the company is liable to pay for your accommodation until the bus is ready to depart. Complaints should be directed to SERNAC, the goverment consumer rights department, in Coyhaique.

Geography and climate

South of Puerto Montt the sea has broken through the coastal *cordillerra* and drowned the central valley. The higher parts of the coastal *cordillerra* form a maze of islands, stretching for over 1,000 km and separated from the coast by tortuous fjords and inlets (*senos*). There is no real dry season near the coast, with annual rainfall of over 2,000 mm on the offshore islands. Westerly winds are strong, especially in summer, and temperatures vary little between day and night.

> ⁝ *January and February are probably the best months for a trip to this area of Chile. From April to September it is bitterly cold inland.*

The Andes are much lower than further north and eroded by glacial action: towards the coast they rise in peaks such as San Valentín (4,058 m), the highest mountain south of Talca; inland they form a high steppe around 1,000 m, where the climate is drier, warm in summer and cold during the winter months. The shores of Lago General Carrera enjoy a warm microclimate that allows the production of fruit.

To the south of Coyhaique are two areas of highland covered by ice, known as *campos de hielo* (icefields). The Campo de Hielo Norte, over 100 km from north to south and some 50 km from west to west, includes the glaciers (*ventisqueros*) San Rafael, Montt and Steffens. The Campo de Hielo Sur covers a larger area, stretching south from the mouth of the Río Baker towards Puerto Natales.

Five main rivers flow westwards: from north to south these are the Futaleufú or Yelcho, the Palena, the Cisnes, the Simpson or Aisén and the Baker. The latter, at 370 km, is the third longest river in Chile. The three largest lakes in this region, Lago General Carrera, Lago Cochrane and Lago O'Higgins, are shared with Argentina.

Chilote legend ascribes the creation of the myriad islands and fjords south of Puerto Montt to a war between two serpents, one good (on land) and one evil (in the sea).

The road can be divided into three sections: **Puerto Montt to Chaitén** (242 km), with two or three ferry crossings; **Chaitén to Coyhaique** (435 km); and **Coyhaique to Villa O'Higgins** (582 km), with one ferry crossing. There is also a branch that runs along the southern shore of **Lago General Carrera** from Puerto Guadal to Chile Chico. The Puerto Montt-Chaitén section can only be travelled in summer, when the ferries are operating, but an alternative route, through Chiloé to Chaitén, exists year round (see page 395). The road is paved around Coyaique, from Puerto Chacabuco to Villa Cerro Castillo.

Driving Some sections of the road can be difficult or even impossible after heavy rain or snowfall. Although tourist infrastructure is growing rapidly and unleaded fuel is available all the way to Villa O'Higgins, drivers should carry adequate fuel and spares, especially if intending to detour from the main route, and should protect their windscreens and headlamps.

Hitching This is popular in summer, but extremely difficult out of season, particularly south of Cochrane. Watching the cloak of dust thrown up by the wheels from the back of a pick-up, while taking in the lakes, forests, mountains and waterfalls, is an unforgettable experience, but be prepared for long delays and allow at least three days from Chaitén to Coyhaique.

Cycling The Carretera Austral is highly recommended for cycling as long as you have enough time and are reasonably fit. A good mountain bike is essential and a tent is an advantage. Most buses will take bicycles for a small charge. An excellent online guide to cycling the Carretera, can be found at www.salamandras.cl

Puerto Montt to Chaitén

This 242-km section of the Carretera Austral is perhaps the most inaccessible and secluded stretch along the entire route, passing through two national parks and the private Parque Pumalin. Beautiful old trees close in on all sides, the rivers and streams sparkle and, on (admittedly rare) clear days, there are beautiful views across the Golfo de Ancud to Chiloé.

Ins and outs

This section of the route includes two ferry crossings at La Arena and Hornopirén. Before setting out, it is imperative to check when the ferries are running and, if driving, to make a reservation for your vehicle: do this at the **Transmarchilay** office in Puerto Montt (see Directory page 376), rather than in Santiago. ▸▸ *For further details, see Transport, page 410.* Hitching to Chaitén takes several days, and there is a lot of competition for lifts: you must be prepared for a day's wait if you find yourself out of luck. The experience of riding in the back of a pick-up, however, will make the hanging around worthwhile. An alternative route to Chaitén is by catamaran or ferry from Puerto Montt or Castro/Quellón (see page 395). ▸▸ *For Sleeping, Eating and other listings, see pages 409-411.*

South of Puerto Montt → *Colour map 4, C2.*

The Carretera Austral heads east out of Puerto Montt, through **Pelluco**, where there is a polluted bathing beach with black sand and some good seafood restaurants, and then follows the shore of the beautiful Seno de Reloncaví (Reloncaví estuary; see page 365). Between the sound to the south and west and Lago Chapo to the northeast is **Parque Nacional Alerce Andino** ① *entrances 2½ km from Correntoso (35 km west of Puerto Montt) and 7 km west of Lenca (40 km south of Puerto Montt), US$5.* The park covers 39,255 ha of steep forested valleys rising to 1,500 m and containing ancient alerce trees, some over 1,000 years old (the oldest are estimated to be 4,200 years old). There are also some 50 small lakes and many waterfalls in the park. Wildlife includes *pudú*, pumas, *vizcachas*, condors and black woodpeckers. Lago Chapo (5,500 ha) feeds a hydroelectric power station at Canutillar, east of the park. There are ranger posts at Río Chaicas, Lago Chapo, Laguna Sargazo and at the north entrance. These can provide very little information, but a map is available from CONAF in Puerto Montt.

Forty-six kilometres south of Puerto Montt (allow one hour), **La Arena** is the site of the first ferry, across the Reloncaví estuary to **Puelche**. From Puelche there is an unpaved road north to Puelo, from where transport can be found north to Cochamó and Ralún. ▸▸ *For Sleeping, Eating and other listings, see pages 409-411.*

Hornopirén and around
Also called Río Negro, **Hornopirén** lies 58 km south of Puelche at the northern end of a fjord. Although a branch of the Carretera Austral runs round the edge of the fjord to Pichanco, 35 km further south, that route is a dead-end. There is excellent fishing in the area and Hornopirén is a base for excursions to the Hornopirén volcano (1,572 m) and to Lago Cabrera, which lies further north. It is also the departure point for the second ferry, to Caleta Gonzalo. At the mouth of the fjord is **Isla Llancahué**, a small island with a hotel and thermal springs. The island is reached by boat ① *T09-6424857, US$25 one way shared between group*; look out for dolphins and fur seals on the crossing.

Parque Nacional Alerce Andino

The Carretera Austral Puerto Montt to Chaitén

Sixteen kilometres by *ripio* road east of Hornopirén and covering 48,232 ha, **Parque Nacional Hornopirén** includes the Yates volcano (2,187 m) as well as the basins of two rivers, the Blanco and the Negro. The park protects some 9,000 ha of alerce forest as well as areas of mixed native forest including lenga and coigue. From the entrance a path leads 8 km east up along the Río Blanco to a basic *refugio*. ▶▶ *For Sleeping, Eating and other listings, see pages 409-411.*

Parque Pumalin and around

Situated on the southern edge of the Fiordo Reñihue, **Caleta Gonzalo** is the base for visiting **Parque Pumalin** ① *T/F02-7358034, www.pumalin.org, free.* Created by the US billionaire Douglas Tompkins and seen by many as one of the most important conservation projects in the world, this private reserve extends over 320,000 ha and is in two sectors, one just south of the Parque Nacional Hornopirén and the other stretching south and east of Caleta Gonzalo to the Argentine border. Its purchase aroused controversy, especially in the Chilean armed forces, which saw it as a threat to national sovereignty; initially, Tompkins was frustrated by stonewalling from the Chilean government, but progress has been made and the park now has nature sanctuary status.

Covering large areas of the western Andes, most of the park is occupied by temperate rainforest. The park is intended to protect the lifestyles of its inhabitants as well as the physical environment. Tompkins has established a native tree nursery, producing 100,000 saplings of native endangered species, and developed apiculture; in 2002 the Pumalin bee stations produced 30,000 kg of honey. There are treks ranging from short trails into the temperate rainforest to hikes lasting for several days (these are very arduous). Three marked trails lead to a waterfall, Cascadas Escondidas; to an area of very old alerce trees; and to Laguna Tronador.

The Carretera Austral runs through the park, climbing steeply before reaching two lakes, Lago Río Negro and Lago Río Blanco. The coast is reached at **Santa Bárbara**, 48 km south, where there is a black sand beach, good campsite and swimming. Do not camp close to the water.

Chaitén → *Phone code: 065. Colour map 4, C2. Population: 3,258.*

The capital of Palena province, Chaitén lies in a beautiful spot, with a forest-covered hill rising behind it, and a quiet inlet leading out into the Patagonian channels. The town is important as a port for catamarans and ferries to Puerto Montt and to Chiloé (see page 395), and is a growing centre for adventure tourism. There is excellent fishing nearby, especially to the south in the ríos Yelcho and Futaleufú and in lagos Espolón and Yelcho. Fishing licences are sold at the Municipalidad. Visits are also possible to a sea-lion colony offshore on **Isla Puduguapi**. There are good views over the Corcovado Bay from Avenida Corcovado.

Chaitén

N

0 metres 100
0 yards   100

Sleeping
Brisas del Mar 1
Cabañas Tranqueras del Monte 12
Casa Rita 2
El Triángulo 3
Hospedaje Ancud 14

Hospedaje Hogareño 4
Hospedaje Recoba 5
Hospedaje Watson 13
Hostería Llanos 6
Hostería San Sebastián 11
Los Colonos 7
Mi Casa 8
Residencial Astoria 9
Schilling 10

Eating
Corcovado 448 1
El Quijote 2
Flamengo 3

The price of settlement

In 1937, desperate to encourage settlement in this isolated region, the Chilean government passed a law offering settlers ownership of land provided it was cleared of forest. The people came and smoke from the forest fires which followed could be seen from the Atlantic coast. The legacies of this law are still apparent to the visitor. Firstly, in the large expanses of burnt tree stumps to be seen, especially around the Río Palena and Mañihuales, and also in the shifting of the port facilities from Puerto Aisén to Puerto Chacabuco, as so much soil was washed into the rivers that the Río Aisén silted up, preventing vessels from reaching Puerto Aisén.

Sleeping

South of Puerto Montt *p406*

There are basic *refugios* at Río Pangal, Laguna Sargazo and Laguna Fría in the Parque Nacional Alerce Andino, and campsites at Río Chaicas and the northern entrance; no camping is permitted inside the boundaries of the park.

Hornopirén and around *p407*

There are lots of *cabañas* and *residenciales* here, including the following:

B Termas de Llancahuée, *Llancahue island, T09-6424857*. Full board, good food, pool.
C-D Hornopirén, *Carrera Pinto 388, T065-217256*. Recommended, also *cabañas*.
E Holiday Country, *O'Higgins 637, T065-217220*. Restaurant, also *cabañas*.

Camping

There's a good site next to the **Hostería Setca**, US$14 per site, and four more sites south of Hornopirén on the road to Pichanco.

Parque Pumalín and around *p408*

There is a restaurant, *cabañas* and a campsite in Caleta Gonzalo, as well as a visitors' centre and demonstrations of agricultural techniques in the region. Camping is available in the park at several well-run sites from US$8 per tent.

Chaitén *p408, map p408*

Ferries from Chiloé are met by people offering accommodation.

A Brisas del Mar, *Corcovado 278, T065-731284, cababrisas@telsur.cl* 4-person *cabañas*.
A-B Schilling, *Corcovado 320, T065-731295*.

With breakfast, heating, restaurant.
B Mi Casa, *Av Norte, T065-731285, hmicasa@telsur.cl* On a hill offering fine views. Sauna, gymnasium and restaurant with good-value set meal. Recommended.
C Cabañas Tranqueras del Monte, *Av Norte s/n, T065-731379, tranqer@telsur.cl* Fully furnished, English spoken, recommended.
C Los Colonos, *Juan Todesco 77*. With bath, shabby, without breakfast.
D El Triángulo, *Juan Todesco y Corcovado, T065-731312*. Without bath or breakfast.
F Hosp Watson, *Ercilla 580, T065-731237*. Price per person including use of kitchen. Clean.
F Hostería Llanos, *Corcovado 378, T065-731332*. Price per person with breakfast. Basic, without bath, good beds, friendly, restaurant.
F Hostería San Sebastián, *Riveros 163, T065-731225*. Price per person. Some with bath, with breakfast.
F Res Astoria, *Corcovado 442, T065-731263*. Price per person. Without bath or breakfast.
G Casa Rita, *Rivero y Prat*. Use of kitchen, clean, open all year, heating. Recommended. Camping also available.
G Hosp Ancud, *Libertad 105*. Price per person. Use of kitchen, very friendly.
G Hosp Hogareño, *Pedro de Valdivia 129, T065-731413*. Price per person full board.
G Hosp Recoba, *Libertad 432, T065-731390*. Price per person with breakfast. Clean, friendly, good meals available.
G Martín Ruiz, *Carretera Austral, 1 km north of Chaitén*. Price per person with breakfast. Friendly, nice views.

Camping

Los Arrayanes, *Carretera Austral, 4 km north*. With hot showers and close to sea, good.

South of Puerto Montt *p406*

$$ **Azurro**, *Pelluco, T065-318989*. Italian.

$$ **Pazos**, *Pelluco, T065-252552*. Serves the best *curanto* in the Puerto Montt area.

Chaitén *p408, map p408*

$$ **Las Brisas del Mar**, *Corcovado 278*. Good fish dishes.

$$ *Corcovado 448*. Decent food

$ **El Quijote**, *O'Higgins 42*. Bar snacks.

$ **Flamengo**, *Corcovado 218*. Popular.

▲ Activities and tours

Chaitén *p408, map p408*

Chaitur, *Diego Portales 350, T/F065-731429, nchaitur@hotmail.com*   General travel agent selling bus and boat tickets. Also bespoke excursions, trekking, horseriding, fishing and trips to Pumalín park. English spoken, friendly and helpful. Lots of information and internet access. Highly recommended. Another branch in the bus station, see below. Opposite the bus station is an office of the Parque Pumalín.

⊖ Transport

South of Puerto Montt *p406*

To reach the northern entrance of the **Parque Nacional Alerce Andino**, take **Fierro** or **Río Pato** bus from Puerto Montt to **Correntoso** (or **Lago Chapo** bus which passes through Correntoso), several daily except Sun, then walk. To reach the southern entrance, take any **Fierro** bus to Chaicas, La Arena, Contau and Hornopirén, US$1.50, getting off at **Lenca** sawmill, then walk (signposted).

A **ferry** makes the 30-min crossing, from La Arena to **Puelche**, 10 daily Dec-Mar, reduced service off season. Arrive 30 mins early for a place; buses have priority, cars US$5.

Hornopirén and around *p407*
Bus

Fierro runs 2 buses daily from Puerto Montt. There are no buses south from Hornopirén.

Ferry

In Jan and Feb only, the **Transmarchilay** ferry *Mailen* sails from Hornopirén to **Caleta Gonzalo**, 1600 daily, 6 hrs, return departures

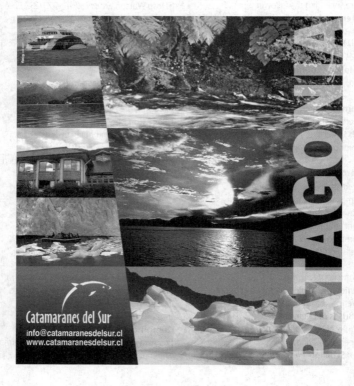

Catamaranes del Sur
info@catamaranesdelsur.cl
www.catamaranesdelsur.cl

PATAGONIA

0900 daily, cars US$83 one way, foot passengers US$13, bicycles US$8. Advance booking required: there can be a 2-day wait. **Chaitur** organizes connecting transport between the ferry port in Caleta Gonzalo and Chaitén (see Activities and tours, above).

Chaitén *p408, map p408*

Air
Flights to **Puerto Montt** by Aerosur, **Aeropuelche** and **Aeromet**, daily 1200, 35 mins, US$50. **Aeroregional** also flies to **Castro**, irregular service. Bookings can be made through **Chaitur** (see Activities and tours).

Bus
Terminal at O'Higgins 67. Several companies run minibuses along the Carretera Austral to **Coyhaique**, most days direct in summer, 2 a week with overnight stop in La Junta or Puyuguapi in winter, departures usually 0800-0900. Minibuses usually travel full, so can't pick up passengers en route. Chaitur acts as an agent for all these services (see Activities and tours, above). Or try **Buses Norte**, *Libertad 432, T065-731390*, with buses to **Coyhaique**, US$20, and intermediate points such as La Junta and Puyuguapi. To **Futaleufú**, Buses Ebenezer, Mon-Sat 1530, Sun 1700, 4 hrs; change here for buses to the Argentine border.

Sea
The ferry port is about 1 km north of town. Schedules change frequently and are infrequent off season.

To **Chiloé**, Navimag and Transmarchilay have ferry services to Castro or Quellón, 4 per week in summer (Dec- Mar), reduced service off season, 5hrs, passengers US$16 one way, cars US$85, bicycles US$9. **Aysen Express** and **Catamaranes del Sur** operate catamaran services on the same route, 5 weekly between them in summer, less regularly off season, 2 hrs, US$18.

To **Puerto Montt**, Navimag and Transmarchilay, 4 weekly, 10 hrs, passengers US$23, car US$93, bike US$9; **Catamaranes del Sur** and **Aysén Express**, 5 weekly, 3 hrs, US$30.

To **Puerto Chacabuco**, Aysén Express 2 weekly, 7 hrs, US$32.

❶ Directory

Chaitén *p408, map p408*
Banks Banco del Estado, *O'Higgins y Libertad*, charges US$10 for changing TCs, ATM accepts Mastercard and Cirrus but not Visa. Rates in general are poor along the Carretera Austral; change money in Puerto Montt. **Shipping offices** Transmarchilay, *Corcovado 266, T065-731273, www.transmarchilay.cl*; Navimag, *Carrera Pinto 108, T065-731570, www.navimag.cl*; Catamaranes del Sur, *Todesco 180, T065-731199, www.catamaranesdelsur.cl*

Chaitén to Coyhaique

This section of the Carretera Austral, 422 km long, runs through long stretches of virgin rainforest, passing small villages, the perfectly still white waters of Lago Yelcho, and the Parque Nacional Queulat, with its glaciers and waterfalls. Roads branch off east to the Argentine frontier and west to Puerto Cisnes. Near Coyhaique, the road passes huge tracts of land destroyed by logging, where only tree-stumps remain as testament to the depredations of the early colonists.

Towards Puerto Cárdenas → *Colour map 5, A3.*
At Amarillo, 25 km south of Chaitén there is a turning to the **Termas de Amarillo** ⓘ *5 km east, US$3*, which consists of two wooden sheds with a very hot pool inside, and an outdoor swimming pool. There is superb salmon fishing in the nearby rivers. From here, it is possible to hike along the old trail to **Futaleufú** (see below); the hike takes four to seven days and is not for the inexperienced; be prepared for wet feet all the way. The trail follows the Río Michinmawida, passing the volcano of the same name,

⦂ Whitewater rafting on the Río Futaleufú

If you want to whitewater raft in Chile, there is no better place than the Río Futaleufú. Only accessible by road since 1982, Futaleufú (big river in the Mapuche language) has quickly grown to be a mecca for kayakers and whitewater rafters. Every year, hundreds of fanatics travel to spend the southern summer here and there is no shortage of operators offering trips.

The river is an incredible deep blue colour and offers everthing from easy grade II-III sections downstream to the extremely challenging grade V Cañon del Infierno (Hell Canyon), surrounded by a dramatic backdrop of spectacular mountain scenery.

to **Lago Espolón** (see below). A ferry with a sporadic schedule crosses the lake, taking cargo, foot passengers and bicycles to Futaleufú.

Situated 46 km south of Chaitén and surrounded by forest, **Puerto Cárdenas** lies on the northern tip of **Lago Yelcho**, a beautiful glacial lake on the Río Futaleufú surrounded by hills and the beautiful Yelcho glacier. The lake is frequented by anglers. At Puerto Cárdenas, there is a police post where you may have to register your passport. Further south at Km 60, a path leads to the **Yelcho glacier**, a two-hour walk. ▸▸ *For Sleeping, Eating and other listings, see pages 414-416.*

Into Argentina via Futaleufú or Palena

→ *Argentine phone code: +54. Colour map 5, A3.*

Southeast of Chaitén the Argentine frontier is reached in two places, Futaleufú and Palena, along a road that branches off at **Villa Santa Lucía** (Km 81), where there are 30 houses, a military camp, one small shop and bread available from a private house. The road to the border is single track, *ripio*, passable in a regular car, but best with a good, strong vehicle; the scenery is beautiful.

At **Puerto Ramírez**, at the southern end of **Lago Yelcho**, the road divides: the north branch runs along the valley of the Río Futaleufú to **Futaleufú**, while the southern one continues to Palena. Futaleufú has established itself as the centre for the finest whitewater rafting in the southern hemisphere. The village, hemmed in by spectacular mountains and the Río Espolón, is peaceful, with wide streets and Chilote-style houses. Tourist information ⓘ *O'Higgins y Prat, T065-721370*. **Lago Espolón**, west of Futaleufú, is reached by a turning 41 km northeast of Puerto Ramírez. It is a beautiful lake and enjoys a warm microclimate: 30°C in the day in summer, 5°C at night. The lake is even warm enough for a quick dip, but beware of the currents.

Chilean immigration is on the border, 8 km east of Futaleufú, at the bridge over the Río Grande. If entering Chile, change money in Futaleufú (poor rates but there is nowhere to change at the border), and then continue from Futaleufú towards Puerto Ramírez; outside Ramírez, take the right turn to Chaitén, otherwise you'll end up back at the border in Palena.

The Chilean immigration post at Palena lies 8 km west of the frontier. Both crossings lead to **Trevelin**, which is 45 km east of Futaleufú, 95 km east of Palena. Trevelin is an offshoot of the Welsh Chubút colony on the Atlantic side of Argentine Patagonia, as featured in Bruce Chatwin's *In Patagonia* (see page 554). It has accommodation, restaurants, tea-rooms and a tourist office, but there is a much wider range of services at **Esquel**, 23 km northeast. Esquel is a base for visiting the Argentine Parque Nacional Los Alerces. There are also transport connections to Bariloche and other destinations in Argentine Patagonia. ▸▸ *For Sleeping, Eating and other listings, see pages 414-416.*

From Villa Santa Lucía, the Carretera Austral follows the Río Frío and then the Río Palena to **La Junta**, a tranquil, non-descript village at the confluence of Río Rosselot and Río Palena, 151 km south of Chaitén. Fuel is available here. Nine kilometres east is **Lago Rosselot**, surrounded by forest and situated at the heart of a *reserva nacional* (12,725 ha). From here, the road continues east, 74 km, to the border crossing at **Lago Verde** ① *summer 0730-2200; winter 0800-2000*, and on to Las Pampas in Argentina. There is also a new road leading northwest from La Junta to **Puerto Raúl Marín Balmaceda** on the coast.

Puyuhuapi and around → *Phone code: 068. Colour map 5, A3. Population: 500.*

From La Junta, the Carretera Austral runs south along the western side of Lago Risopatrón, past several waterfalls, to **Puyuhuapi** (also spelt Puyuguapi), 45 km further south. Located in a beautiful spot at the northern end of the Puyuhuapi fjord, the village is a tranquil stopping place, about halfway between Chaitén and Coyhaique. It was founded by four Sudeten German families in 1935, and its economy is based around fishing, tourism and the factory where Puyuhuapi's famous handmade carpets are produced.

From Puyuhuapi, the road follows the eastern edge of the fjord along one of the most beautiful sections of the Carretera Austral, with views of the **Termas de Puyuhuapi** ① *18 km southwest of Puyuhuapi, US$15 per person, under-12s US$10.* This resort is on the western edge of the fjord and is accessible only by boat. It has several 40°C springs filling three pools near the beach. Take food and drink. The resort can also be visited on a four- or six-day tour with **Patagonia Connection SA** (see pages 414 and 433).

Covering 154,093 ha of attractive forest around Puyuhuapi, the **Parque Nacional Queulat** ① *administration at the CONAF office in La Junta, T067-314128*, is, supposedly, the former location of the legendary Ciudad de los Césares, a fabulously wealthy mythological city built between two hills made of gold and diamonds and inhabited by immortal beings. According to legend, the city was protected by a shroud of fog and hence was impossible for strangers to discover. The Carretera Austral passes through the park, close to **Lago Risopatrón** north of Puyuhuapi, where boat trips are available. Twenty-four kilometres south, a two-hour trek leads to the **Ventisquero Colgante** hanging glacier① *US$3.* From here the Carretera Austral climbs out of the Queulat valley through a series of hairpin bends offering fine views of the forest and several glaciers. Near the pass (500 m) is the **Salto Pedro García** waterfall, with the Salto del Cóndor waterfall some 5 km further on. ►► *For Sleeping, Eating and other listings, see pages 414-416.*

South of the Río Cisnes → *Colour map 5, A3. Population: 1,784.*

Stretching 160 km from the Argentine border to the coast at Puerto Cisnes, the Río Cisnes is recommended for rafting or canoeing, with grand scenery and modest rapids – except for the horrendous drop at Piedra del Gato, about 60 km east of Puerto Cisnes. Good camping is available in the forest. Possibly the wettest town in Chile, **Puerto Cisnes** is reached by a 33-km winding road that branches west off the Carretera Austral about 59 km south of Puyuhuapi. Traditional knitted clothes are made here.

At Km 92, south of **Villa Amengual**, a road branches west 104 km to the **Argentine border** via La Tapera. Chilean immigration is 12 km west of the frontier and is open daylight hours only. On the Argentine side, the road continues to meet up with Route 40, the north-south road at the foot of the Andes.

The **Reserva Nacional Lago Las Torres** is 98 km south of Puyuhuapi and covers 16,516 ha. It includes the wonderful Lago Las Torres, which offers good fishing and a small CONAF campsite. Further south, at Km 125, a road branches east to El Toqui where zinc is mined. From here the Carretera Austral is paved.

Villa Mañihuales, at Km 148, is near the **Reserva Forestal Mañihuales** ① *US$1.* The reserve covers 1,206 ha and encompasses a huemul sanctuary. Fires largely destroyed the forests in the 1940s but the views are good.

Towards Puerto Cárdenas *p411*

L-A **Cabañas Yelcho en La Patagonia**, *Lago Yelcho, 7 km south of Puerto Cardenas, T065-731337*. Cabins and rooms on the lake shore. Also camping and cafeteria.

AL **Cabanas CAVI**, *Lago Yelcho, nr Puerto Cárdenas*. Sauna, restaurant, video room, laundry. Six *cabañas* with private bathrooms, hot water, kitchen facilities. Also campsite with electricity, hot showers, drinking water, laundry facilities, barbecue area and fishing boats for hire. Book via **Turismo Austral Ltda**, *Santa Magdelena 75, of 902, Providencia, Santiago,T02-3341309, F02-3341328*.

B **Termas de Amarillo**, *Termas de Amarillo, T065-731326*. Also camping and *cabañas*.

C **Res Yelcho**, *Puerto Cárdenas, T065-264429*. Clean, full board available.

F **Res Marcela**, *Amarillo, T065-264442*. Also *cabañas* and camping.

Into Argentina via Futaleufú or Palena *p412*

There are *cabañas* and a campsite on the shore of Lago Espolón, US$3.75 for a motor home. Aníbal, who owns the campsite, sells meat, bread, beer and soft drinks and will barbecue lamb.

AL-A **Hostería Río Grande**, *O'Higgins 397, Futaleufú, T065-721320*. This is the best place in town. Comfortable, en-suite bathrooms, friendly, bar, good restaurant, arranges tours and activities.

F **Continental**, *Balmaceda 397, Futaleufú, T065-721222*. Price per person. Basic, hot water, clean. Recommended. Cheap restaurant.

F **Hosp Adolfo**, *O'Higgins 302, Futaleufú, T065-721256*. Nice and friendly, though pretty basic.

F **Res Carahue**, *O'Higgins 332, Futaleufú, T065-721221*. Price per person. Very basic, kitchen facilities.

F **Res Yamara**, *O'Higgins s/n, Futaleufú*. Without bath. Recommended.

G **Sra Rosalía Cuevas de Ruiz**, *No7, Villa Santa Lucía*. Basic, meals available. One of several options on the main street; none has hot water.

In Palena there are simple rooms at:

F **Res La Chilenita**, *Pudeto 681, Palena, T065-741212*. Simple accommodation. Price per person.

Into Argentina via La Junta *p413*

A-B **Hostal Espacio y Tiempo**, *La Junta, T067-314141, www.espacioytiempo.cl*. Attractive garden, English spoken, good restaurant, fishing expeditions.

F **Café Res Patagonia**, *Lynch 331, La Junta, T067-314120*. Price per person. Good meals, small rooms, limited bathrooms.

F **Res Copihue**, *Varas 611, T067-314184*. Price per person. Without bath, with breakfast, good meals, changes money at very poor rates.

F **Res Valdera**, *Varas s/n, T067-314105*. Price per person. With breakfast and bath, very good value.

Puyuhuapi and around *p413*

There's a CONAF campsite at Lago Risopatrón.

LL-L **Hotel Termas de Puyuhuapi**, *T067-325103*. Price depends on season and type of room but always includes use of baths and the boat transfer to the hotel. Good restaurant; full board US$40 extra. Recommended. For reservations contact: **Patagonia Connection SA** (see p433). Boat schedule from jetty, 2 hrs' walk from town, frequent in season, US$3 each way, 10-min crossing. Transport to the hotel may also be arranged independently via hydroplane from Puerto Montt.

L **Cabañas El Pangue**, *north end of Lago Risopatrón, Carretera Austral Norte, Km 240, Parque Nacional Queulat, T067-325128, cpangue@entelchile.net* Cabins sleep 4, private bathrooms, hot water, heating, telephone, parking, swimming pool, fishing trips, horseriding, mountain bikes. Recommended.

AL-A **Cabañas Fiordo Queulat**, *Seno Queulat, Parque Nacional Queulat, T067-233302*. Has a good reputation, offers hikes and fishing trips. Campsite nearby, US$3.50.

C-D **Hostería Alemana**, *Av Otto Uebel 450, T067-325118*. A large, comfortable, wooden house on the main road, owned by Sra Ursula Flack Kroschewski. Highly recommended, closed in winter.

E **Casa Ludwig**, *Av Otto Uebel s/n, south of Puyuhuapi, T067-325220, www.contactchile.cl/casaludwig* Excellent, English and German spoken. Highly recommended. Price per person.

F **Hostería Elizabeth**, *Llautureo y Henriquez*. Clean, good meals but unwelcoming atmosphere. Price per person with breakfast.

F **Sra Leontina Fuentes**, *Llantureo y Circunvalación*. Clean, hot water, good breakfast for US$1. Price per person.

Camping
CONAF, *reservations T067-212125*, runs a basic campsite (cold water) 12 km north of Puyuhuapi on the shores of Lago Risopatrón, and another near the Ventisquero Colgante. There is also a dirty campsite by the fjord behind the general store in Puyuhuapi.

South of the Río Cisnes *p413*
A-C **Cabañas Río Cisnes**, *Costanera 101, Puerto Cisnes, T067-346404*. Cabins sleep 4-8. Owner, Juan Suazo, has a boat and offers good sea trout/salmon fishing.
B **Manzur**, *Dunn 75, Puerto Cisnes, T067-346453. Cabañas*.
D **Pensión** *Carlos Condell y Dr Steffen, Puerto Cisnes*. With breakfast, hot shower, friendly.
F **Hospedaje, Café y Restaurante El Encanto**, *Villa Amengual*. One of several cheap options in the town.
F **Hostería El Gaucho**, *Holmberg 140, Puerto Cisnes, T067-346514*. Price per person. With breakfast, dinner available, hot water.
F **Res Bienvenido**, *Ibar 248, Villa Mañihuales*. Clean, friendly, with a restaurant
F **Villa Mañihuales**, *E Ibar 200, Villa Mañihuales, T067-234803*. Friendly, with breakfast.

● Eating

Puyuhuapi and around *p413*
$$ **Café Rossbach**, *Costanera, Puyuhuapi*. Limited menu, including excellent salmon; also good for tea and Küchen; building is in the style of a German Black Forest inn.
$ **Restaurante Marili**, *Otto Ubel s/n, Puyuhuapi*. Cheaper option. There are also several general stores and a couple of bars.

South of the Río Cisnes *p413*
$ **K-Cos Café Restaurante**, *Prat 270, Puerto Cisnes*. Good snacks.

▲ Activities and tours

Fishing
Isla Monita Lodge, near Puerto Cardenas, offers packages for anglers and non-anglers on a private island on **Lago Yelcho** (see p411), as well as fishing in many nearby

locations; contact **Turismo Grant**, *PO Box 52311, Santiago, T02-6395524, F6337133*.

There are also good opportunities for fishing on **Río Futaleufú** and **Lago Espolón** (see p412; ask for the Valebote family's motorboat on the lake) and in the area around **Puerto Cisnes** (see p413). For the latter, contact **German Hipp**, *Costanera 51, Puerto Cisnes, T067-346587* or **Cabañas Río Cisnes** (see above). Further information on fishing in the area can be obtained from **Turismo Lago Las Torres**, 130 km Carretera Austral Norte, T067-234242.

Into Argentina via Futaleufú or Palena *p412*
All tour operators in Futaleufú can arrange whitewater rafting (see p412). The Hostería Río Grande (see above) also offers good trips.
Earth River, *www.earthriver.com/ futaleufu.htm* Excellent choice for river-rafting and kayaking trips, book in advance.
Expediciones Chile, *www.exchile.com* Offers the best multi-day trips. Book in advance. Day trips can be booked on site.
Futaleufú Expediciones, *O'Higgins 397, Futaleufú, T/F065-258634*. Organize rafting, canyoning, trekking and horseriding expeditions around Futaleufú.

● Transport

Into Argentina via Futaleufú or Palena *p412*
Buses to the **border** depart *Balmaceda 419* in Futaleufú, Mon and Fri 0900 and 1800, 30 mins, US$3; from the Argentine side there are connecting services to **Trevelin** and **Esquel**. Futaleufú to **Chaitén**, daily, 5 hrs.
Transporte Patagonia Norte, *T065-741257*, runs a weekly service from Palena to **Puerto Montt** via Argentina, Mon 0630, 13 hrs, US$28.

Into Argentina via La Junta *p413*
There is no bus terminal in La Junta. To **Puerto Cisnes**, Buses Emanuel, *Manuel Montt, Esq Esmeralda, T067-314198*, Mon and Fri, US$6. To **Coyhaique**, Buses Emanuel, Tue and Sat, US$12; Buses Daniela, *T067-231701*, 2 weekly, US$12; Buses Norte, 3 weekly. To **Chaitén**, Buses Emanuel, Mon to Sat, US$8; Transportes Lago Verde, *Varas s/n, T067-314108*, 3 weekly, US$8; **Buses**

Norte, 3 weekly. To **Lago Verde**, Buses Daniela, 2 weekly. Book all in advance.

Puyuhuapi and around *p413*
Daily buses from Puyuhuapi north to **Chaitén** and south to **Coyhaique**, plus 2 weekly to **Lago Verde**.

South of the Río Cisnes *p413*
Transportes Terra Austral, *T067-346757*, runs services from **Puerto Cisnes** to **Coyhaique**,

Mon-Sat 0600, US$9; **Buses Norte**, *T067-346440* offers the same route once a week, US$8. There are also daily buses to Coyhaique from **Villa Mañihuales**, 1½ hrs.

---

❶ Directory

Into Argentina via Futaleufú or Palena *p412*
Banks Banco de Chile, *Futaleufú*, changes US dollars and Argentine pesos.

Coyhaique and around

→ *Phone code: 067. Colour map 5, B3. Population: 36,376.*
Located 420 km south of Chaitén, Coyhaique (also spelt Coihaique) lies in the broad green valley of the Río Simpson. The city is encircled by a crown of snowcapped mountains and, for a few hours after it has rained, the mountainsides are covered in a fine layer of frost – a spectacular sight. Founded in 1929, it is the administrative and commercial centre of Region XI and is the only settlement of any real size on the Carretera Austral. A lively city in itself, Coyhaique also provides a good base for hiking, skiing and fishing excursions in the area.

Ins and outs

Getting there There are two **airports** in the Coyhaique area: **Tte Vidal** ❶ *5 km southwest of town (including a steep climb up and down to the Río Simpson bridge), taxi US$5*, handles only smaller aircraft; **Balmaceda** ❶ *56 km southeast of Coyhaique via paved road, 5 km from the Argentine frontier at Paso Huemules, taxi 1 hr, US$6*, is the most direct way into Coyhaique from Santiago or Puerto Montt, with three or four flights daily. There's also a weekly flight to Punta Arenas. There is no bus service between Coyhaique and Balmaceda; instead minibuses, known as 'transfers', ply this route, collecting/delivering to hotels; contact **Travell** ❶ *Parra y Moraleda, T067-230010, US$3.50* and **Transfer** ❶ *Lautaro 828, T067-233030, US$3.50*. **Buses** (several weekly) from Puerto Montt have to take the route via Argentina, which is long and expensive. There are also one or two weekly buses to Comodoro Rivadavia and south to Punta Arenas. Within Region XI, Coyhaique is the transport hub. There are minibuses north to Chaitén and south to Cochrane (both daily), as well as minibuses connecting with the ferry at Puerto Ibañez for Chile Chico (five weekly). ▶▶ *For further details, see Transport, page 422.* **Getting around** Coyhaique is small enough to be easily covered on foot; taxis are expensive and only useful for out-of-town excursions. **Tourist information** English is spoken at the very helpful **Sernatur** office ❶ *Bulnes 35, T067-231752, F233949, infoaisen@sernatur.cl, Mon-Fri 0830-1700*, which has bus timetables. There's also a kiosk on the plaza in summer. **CONAF** is at ❶ *Ogana 1060*. Maps (photocopies of 1:50,000 IGM maps) are available from **Dirección de Vialidad** on the plaza.

❦ *Near the city, on the west bank of the Río Simpson, is the Piedra del Indio, a rock outcrop which, allegedly, looks like a face in profile. This is best viewed from the Puente Simpson.*

Sights

Although a visit to the tourist office will throw up far more attractions outside Coyhaique than in the town itself, this is a pleasant, friendly place, perfect for relaxing for a couple of days or as a base for day trips. The town is centred around an unusual pentagonal plaza, on which stand the cathedral, the Intendencia and a handicraft market. The plaza was built in 1945, supposedly inspired by the Place de l'Étoile in Paris. Two blocks northeast of the plaza at Baquedano y Ignacio Serrano, there is a monument to El Ovejero (the shepherd). Further north on Baquedano is a display of old military machinery outside the local regimental headquarters. In the Casa de Cultura the **Museo Regional de la Patagonia Central** ① *Baquedano s/n, Tue-Sun 0900-2000 (summer), 0830-1730 (winter), US$1*, has sections on history, mineralogy, zoology and archaeology, as well as photos of the construction of the Carretera Austral.

There are two national reserves close to Coyhaique: 5 km northwest off the Carretera Austral is **Reserva Nacional Coyhaique**, which covers 2,150 ha of forest (mainly introduced species), while around the valley of the Río Simpson west of Coyhaique (take any bus to Puerto Aisén) is the **Reserva Nacional Río Simpson**, covering 40,827 ha of steep forested valleys and curiously rounded hills rising to 1,878 m. One of these, near the western edge of the park, is known as '*El Cake Inglés*'. There

Coyhaique

0 metres 200
0 yards 200

Anglers' paradise

The rivers around Coyhaique provide the greatest fishing in Chile; each summer the international fishing fraternity converge on the town for the season, which runs from 15 November to 15 April. Rivers range from the typically English slow chalk stream to the fast-flowing Andean snowmelt torrents, requiring a variety of angling techniques.

On the outskirts of Coyhaique, the spectacular **Río Simpson** teems with both rainbow and brown trout, offering over 60 km of world-class angling. It is renowned for its exciting evening hatches (sedge and mayfly), which take place throughout the season. Anglers will find that, pound for pound, these are some of the best fighting fish to be found anywhere. Catches in excess of five pounds are frequent and rainbow trout weighing over 12 pounds have been landed.

Located near the Argentine border, a scenic one-hour drive from Coyhaique, the **Río Nirehuao** is a fly-fisher's dream. Throughout the season the brown trout feed voraciously on grasshoppers and dragonfly. The easy wading and moderate casting distances make this river an all-time favourite.

South of Coyhaique, the **Río Baker** offers anglers a unique fishing experience in its turquoise blue water. The Baker is huge and intimidating, as are its fish: rainbows up to 12 pounds lurk here and anglers regularly take fish in the four to seven pound range. The **Río Cochrane,** a tributary of the Baker, also holds large rainbows and, if it were possible for a river to be clearer than 'gin-clear', this would be it. The Cochrane is mainly a 'sight-fishing' experience, which requires skill, patience and an experienced guide.

are beautiful waterfalls, lovely views of the river and very good fly fishing here, as well as trekking options. Wildlife includes pudú, pumas and huemul, as well as a variety of birds ranging from condors to several species of ducks. Administration is 32 km west of Coyhaique, just off the road.➤➤ *For Sleeping, Eating and other listings, see pages 419-424.*

Border crossings to Argentina

The crossing at **Coyhaique Alto** ① *43 km east of Coyhaique, 6 km west of the frontier, open May-Aug 0800-2000, Sep-Apr 0730-2200*, is reached by a *ripio* road that runs east of Coyhaique past the **Monumento Natural Dos Lagunas** ① *25 km east, entry US$1, camping US$12 per site*, a small park that encompasses Lagos El Toro and Escondido. On the Argentine side, the road leads through Río Mayo and Sarmiento to Comodoro Rivadavia on the Atlantic seaboard. Chilean immigration is at Coyhaique Alto.

❖ *If looking for transport to Argentina, it is worth going to the local Radio Santa María on Bilbao y Ignacio Serrano, and leaving a message to be broadcast.*

The crossing at **Paso Huemules** ① *61 km southeast of Coyhaique, open May-Jul 0800-2000, Sep-Apr daily 0730-2200*, is reached by a paved road, Route 245, which runs southeast from Coyhaique, via Balmaceda airport. There is no accommodation at the frontier or at the airport and no public transport from the frontier to the airport. On the Argentine side, a *ripio* road runs via Lago Blanco (fuel) to join Route 40, 105 km west of Paso Huemules.➤➤ *For details of transport between Coyhaique and both border crossings, see page 422.*

Puerto Aisén and around → *Phone code: 067 Colour map 5, B3. Population: 13,050.*

Puerto Aisén lies at the confluence of the rivers Aisén and Palos. First developed in the 1920s, the town grew as the major port of the region although it has now been replaced by Puerto Chacabuco, 15 km further down the river. Few vestiges of the port remain today: boats lie high and dry on the river bank when the tide is out and the **419** foundations of buildings by the river are now overgrown with fuchsias and buttercups. To see any maritime activity you have to walk a little way out of town to **Puerto Aguas Muertas** where the fishing boats come in.

The town is linked to the south bank of the Río Aisén by the Puente Presidente Ibañez, once the longest suspension bridge in Chile. From the far bank a paved road leads to **Puerto Chacabuco**; a regular bus service runs between the two. There is a helpful **tourist office** in the Municipalidad ① *Prat y Sgto Aldea, Dec-Feb only.*

It is much wetter here than in Coyhaique: local wags say that it rains for 370 days a year. September to January are the driest months.

A good 10 km walk north along a minor road from Puerto Aisén leads to **Laguna Los Palos**, calm, deserted and surrounded by forested hills. En route is a bridge over a deep, narrow river; it's freezing cold but offers the chance for a bracing swim. **Lago Riesco**, 30 km south of Puerto Aisén, can be reached by an unpaved road that follows the Río Blanco. In season, the *Apulcheu* sails regularly to **Termas de Chiconal** ① *US$30*, about one hour west of Puerto Chacabuco on the northern shore of the Seno Aisén, offering a good way to see the fjord; take your own food. ►► *For Sleeping, Eating and other listings, see pages 419-424.*

● Sleeping

Coyhaique *p416, map p416*
The tourist office has a list of all accommodation, but look out for notices in windows since any place with fewer than 6 beds does not have to register with the authorities.
L Hostería Coyhaique, *Magallanes 131, T067-231137*. 4 star set in large gardens, overpriced.
A Cabañas Río Simpson, *Km 3, T067-232183, riosimpsoncab@hotmail.com* Fully equipped cabins for 4-9 people. Horseriding, fishing and tours. Several tame alpacas in the grounds.
A El Reloj, *Baquedano 828, T067-231108, www.aisen.org/elreloj* In a former saw-mill. With good restaurant, nice lounge, conference room, some rooms have wonderful views. English spoken. Highly recommended.
A Los Ñires, *Baquedano 315, T067-232261, www.doncarlos.cl/hotel.htm* With breakfast, small rooms, comfortable, parking.
A San Sebastian, *Baquedano 496, T067-233427*. Small, views, good breakfast, recommended.
A-B Hotel y Apart Hotel Austral, *Colón 203, T067-232522*. Hot water, clean, English spoken, tours arranged, friendly. Recommended.
B Cabañas La Pasarela, Km 1.5, *T067-234520*. Good atmosphere, *comedor*.
B Cabañas Mirador, *Baquedano 848, T067-233191*. Sleep 8.
B Libanés, *Simpson 367, T067-234242, hlibanes@entelchile.net* With television, phones, heating, laundry and café, several small lounges.

B-C Hostal Araucarias, *Vielmo 71, T067-232707*. Large rooms, good view, also hires out cars.
B-C Hostal Bon, *Serrano 91, T067-231189*. With breakfast, friendly, clean, also *cabañas*, good meals served. Recommended.
D Res Licarayen, *Carrera 33A, T067-233377*. With bath and breakfast, no singles, rundown.
D Res Mónica, *Lillo 664, T067-234302*. With bath, breakfast.
E Hosp Lautaro, *Lautaro 532, T067-231852*. Clean, kitchen facilities, large rooms.
F-G Albergue Las Salamandras, 2 km south of town, *T067-211865, www.salamandras.cl* Double rooms, dormitories, *cabañas* and camping in attractive forest location. Kitchen facilities, winter sports, trekking and tours. Maps, including good trekking maps, and cycling information provided. English spoken. Excellent website. Price per person. Highly recommended.
F-G Casa Irene, *12 de Octubre 503*. Breakfast, kitchen and laundry facilities.
F-G Hosp Belén, *Simon Bolivár 616, T067-218517*. With breakfast and cooking facilities. Friendly, comfortable. Recommended.
F-G Hosp Chiloé, *Baquedano 274, T067-235332*. Small rooms, very good, also lets apartments.
F-G Hosp Lautaro 269, *T067-238116*. With parking, internet access and kitchen facilities. English spoken. Recommended.
F-G Hosp Mundaca, *Av Simpson 571*. Friendly, breakfast extra, will heat up pre-prepared food.
F-G Hosp Natti, *Av Simpson 417, T067-231047*. Clean, very friendly, kitchen facilities, breakfast. Highly recommended.

The Carretera Austral Coyhaique & around

F-G **Hosp Ogana**, *Av Ogana Pasaje 8, 185, T067-232353*. With breakfast and cooking facilities, also camping and *cabañas*.

F-G **Hosp Patricio y Gedra Guzmán**, *Baquedano 20, T067-232520*. Room in family home by the river, with use of kitchen, bathroom and laundry facilities. Wonderful views from garden. Friendly, helpful, English spoken, breakfast served with homemade bread, recommended.

F-G **Hosp Pierrot**, *Baquedano 130, T067-231315*. Comfortable, great view, some English spoken, recommended. Also *cabaña* at back of house.

F-G **Hostal San Cayetano**, *Av Simpson 829, T/F067-231555*. Cooking facilities, good.

F-G **Los Cuatro Hermanos**, *Colón 495, T067-232647*. With breakfast, hot water, clean, mixed reports.

F-G **Los Profesores**, *Presidente Errazuriz y Arturo Prat*. Good beds, good showers.

F-G **Sra Elba Araneda**, *Colón 190*. With breakfast.

Campsites

Sernatur in Coyhaique has a full list of all sites in Region XI. There are several campsites in Coyhaique and on the road to Puerto Aisén, including:

Camping Alborada, *Km 1 towards Puerto Aisén, T067-238868*. US$10, with hot shower.

Camping Río Correntoso, *Km 42 towards Puerto Aisén, T067-232005*. US$15, showers and fishing. Automobile Club discount.

In the Reserva Nacional Coyhaique, there are basic campsites, US$4, at Laguna Verde and at Casa Bruja, 4 km and 2 km respectively from the entrance, and a *refugio*, US$1, 3 km from the entrance. There's also a campsite near the turning to Santuario San Sebastián, US$5, in the Reserva Nacional Rio Simpson.

Puerto Aisén and around *p418*

Accommodation can be hard to find, most is geared towards workers in the fishing industry in both ports. There's no campsite but free camping is easy.

LL **Parque Turístico Loberías de Aisén**, *Carrera 50, Puerto Chacabuco, T067-234520*. Recently rebuilt 5-star complex, serving the best food in the area. Climb up the steps direct from port for a drink or a meal overlooking the boats and the mountains before boarding your ferry. Car hire available.

B **Hotel Caicahues**, *Michimalonco 660, Puerto Aisén, T067-336633*. With bath, heating, telephone and internet; book in advance.

F **Hotel Plaza**, *O'Higgins 613, Puerto Aisén, T067-332784*. Price per person. Basic, without breakfast, some rooms with no windows.

F **Mar Clara**, *Carrera 970, Puerto Aisén, T067-330945*. Price per person. More expensive with bath. Basic, clean, thin walls, looks nicer from outside than within.

F **Roxy**, *Aldea 972, Puerto Aisén, T067-332704*. Price per person. Friendly, clean, large rooms, restaurant. Rooms at the back are quieter and have a view. Recommended.

G **Moraleda**, *O'Higgins 82, Puerto Chacabuco, T067-351155*. Price per person, also food.

🍴 Eating

Coyhaique *p416, map p416*

$$$ **Café Restaurant Histórico Ricer**, *Horn 48 y 40 2o Piso*. Regional specialities, historical exhibits, recommended.

$$ **Café Ricer**, *Horn 48*. Good food.

$$ **Casona**, *Vielmo 77*. Traditional food. Recommended.

$$ **El Reloj**, *Baquedano 828*. Uses all local ingredients, recommended.

$$ **La Casona**, *Obispo Vielmo 77*. Good lamb and fish dishes, recommended.

$$ **La Olla**, *Gen Prat 176*. Spanish, excellent cuisine, not cheap, good-value lunches. Highly recommended.

$$ **La Posada del Conejo**, *Km 3 to Teniente Vidal, T067-238335*. Popular. Recommended.

$$ **Loberías de Chacabuco**, *Prat 386*. Basic, slow service.

$ **Casino de Bomberos**, *Gen Parra 365*. Wide range, large portions, very good value.

$ **Don Carlos**, *Baquedano 315*. Good value lunches.

$ **El Mastique**, *Bilbao 141*. Seriously cheap but good. Recommended.

$ **El Quincho**, *Km 6 on road to Puerto Aisén*. Good food. Recommended.

$ **La Fiorentina**, *Prat*. Cheap pizzas, good.

Cafés

Café Alemana, *Condell 119*. Excellent cakes, coffee, vegetarian dishes. Recommended.

Café Kalu, *Prat 402*. Beer, snacks.

Café Oriente, *Condell 201 y 21 de Mayo*. Good bakery, serves tea.

Puerto Aisén *p418*

$$ Café Restaurante Ensenada, *O'Higgins 302, Puerto Chacabuco*. Basic grub.

$$ Restaurante International, *Km 41 between Coyhaique and Puerto Aisén, Villa Los Torreones*. Recommended.

$$ Restaurante La Cascada, *Km 32 between Coyhaique and Puerto Aisén*. Waterfalls nearby. Recommended for meat and fish.

$$ Restaurante Martina, *Av Municipal, near bridge, Puerto Aisén*. Good Chilean fare. Probably the best place to eat in town.

There are many cheap places on Aldea in Puerto Chacabuco, between Municipal and Dougnac.

♦ Bars and clubs

Coyhaique *p416, map p416*
Bar West, *Bilbao y 12 de Octubre*. Western-style bar.
Piel Roja, *Moraleda y Condell*. Friendly, laid-back atmosphere, meals served, not cheap.
Pub El Cuervo, *Parra 72*. Good cocktails and snacks, relaxed ambience, live music.

Puerto Aisén *p418*
Crazzy Pub, *Aldea 1170*. Make up your own mind how 'crazzy' it is.
Dina's, *Carrera 1270*. Disco.
Eko Pub, *Tte Merino 998*. There are a couple of smaller bars on Sargento Aldea; one has a wildly sloping pool table.
Pollo's, *Caupolicán 265*. Nightclub.

✪ Festivals and events

Puerto Aisén *p418*
Local festival of folklore is held during the 2nd week of **Nov**.

⭗ Shopping

Coyhaique *p416, map p416*
Food, especially fruit and vegetables, is more expensive here than in Santiago. For *artesanía* try the **Feria de Artesanía** on the plaza or **Manos Azules**, *Riquelme 435*. **Gun & Rod**, *Horn 47*, sell fishing gear. There are supermarkets at *Magallanes y Bilbao*, *Prat y Lautaro* and *Lautaro y Cochrane*.

Coyhaique *p416, map p416*
A full list of specialist tours and fishing guides is available from **Sernatur**, see above. Excursions and good trekking information is available from **Albergue Las Salamandras** (see Accommodation above).

Fishing
There are excellent opportunities for fishing in the Coyhaique area, especially southwest at Lagos Atrevesado (20 km) and Elizalde (also yachting and camping), and southeast at Lagos Frío, Castor and Pollux. In addition to those listed below, most of the general tour operators offer specialist fishing trips.
Alex Prior, *T067-234732*. Recommended for fly-fishing.
Patagonia Travel Service, *Condell 149, T067-237795*. Offers fishing tours on Lago Riesco and near Puerto Chacabuco.
Turismo Aysén, *Barroso 626, T067-238036, F235294*. Fishing and horseriding tours.

General tours
Andes Patagónicos, *Horn 48 y 40, local 11, T067-216711*. Trips to local lakes as well as Tortel, historically based tours and bespoke trips all year round. Good, but not cheap. Provides general tourist information.
El Puesto Expeditions, *Moraleda 299, T067-233785, elpuesto@entelchile.net* Hiking, fishing, climbing.
Encounter Patagonia, *Colon 166, T067-215001, info@encounterpatagonia.com* Small agency specializing in the XI Region, strong local contacts, ecologically aware, English-speaking guide. Highly recommended.
Expediciones Coyhaique, *Portales 195, T067-232300*. Tours of local lakes and other sights, Laguna San Rafael trips, fishing trips and excursions down the Río Baker.
Geo Turismo, *Lillo 315, T067-237456, www.geoturismo.cl* Offers wide range of tours throughout the region, English spoken, professional, recommended.
Turaustralis, *Moraleda 589, T067-239696, hsaldivia@hotmail.com* Fishing, horseriding, bird watching, trips to the lakes and tours along the Carretera Austral.
Turismo Prado, *21 de Mayo 417, T067-231271, www.turismopradopatagonia.cl* Tours of local lakes and other sights, Laguna

San Rafael trips and historical tours. Also offers general tourist information and accepts TCs.

Turismo Queulat, *21 de Mayo 1231, T067-231441*. Trips to Queulat glacier, adventure and nature tourism, fishing, etc. Tours only operate in summer.

Horseriding

Baltazar Araneda, *T067-231047 or book through Hospedaje Natti (see Accommodation above)*. Horseriding trip to Lagos Palomo, Azul and Desierto, US$240 per person for 4 days, US$300 for 5 days. Recommended.
Cabot, *Dussen 357, T067-230101, Cabot@entelchile.net* Horseriding excursions to Cerro Castillo, US$70 for 2 days, and other tours.

Scenic flights

Patagonia Explorer, *T09-8172172, stonepiloto@hotmail.com* Pilot Willy Stone offers charter flights to the Laguna San Rafael, US$200 per person, recommended.

Skiing

El Fraile, *office in Coyhaique at Dussen y Plaza de Armas 376, T067-231690*. Located 29 km southeast of Coyhaique, near Lago Frío, this ski resort has 5 pistes, 2 lifts, a basic cafetería and equipment hire (season Jun-Sep).

Puerto Aisén *p418*
Turismo Rucaray, *on the plaza, rucaray@entelchile.net* Recommended for local tours. Internet access.

◉ Transport

Coyhaique *p416, map p416*
Air
From **Tte Vidal airport**, Don Carlos flies to **Chile Chico**, Mon-Sat, US$35; to **Cochrane**, Mon and Thu, 45 mins, US$57, and to **Villa O'Higgins**, Mon and Thu, US$85, recommended only for those who like flying, with strong stomachs, or in a hurry. There are also flights to **Tortel**, Wed, US$25, but these are subsidized for residents of the village; foreigners may fly if there's a free seat, but should expect to pay more.

Balmaceda airport is used by LanChile and **Sky** for flights to **Santiago**, several daily, US$130-250 return plus tax (depending on season and flexibility) and **Puerto Montt**,

several daily, US$75-150 return plus tax. **LanChile** also flies to **Punta Arenas**, Sat, US$75-150 return plus tax. One-way fares are usually more expensive than the cheapest return flights. For details of transport to/from the airport, see p416.

Bus
A full listing of bus timetables is posted outside the Sernatur office. The main terminal is at *Lautaro y Magallanes* but many companies use their own offices. In the terminal are: **Bus Sur**, *T067-211460, www.bus-sur.cl*; **Giobbi**, *T067-232607*; **Los Ñadis**, *T067-211460*; **Interlagos**, *www.turismointerlagos.cl*, recommended; **Acuario 13**, *T067-240990*; **Queilén Bus**; **Transportes Terra Austral**, *T067-254475*. Other companies are: **Don Carlos**, *Subteniente Cruz 63, T067-232981*; **Suray**, *Prat 265, T067-238387*; **Turibus**, *Baquedano 1171, T067-231333*; **Bus Norte**, *Parra 337, T067-232167*; **Buses Daniela**, *Baquedano 1122, T067-231701*.

Long distance To **Puerto Montt**, via Bariloche, all year, **Turibus**, Tue and Sat 1700, US$25; **Queilén Bus**, Mon, Thur, US$28, with connections to Osorno, Valdivia, Temuco, Santiago and Castro, often heavily booked. To **Punta Arenas** via Coyhaique Alto and Comodoro Rivadavia, **Bus Sur**, Tue, US$45. To **Comodoro Rivadavia** (Argentina), **Turibus**, Mon, Fri, also **Giobbi**, Tue, Sat, from terminal, 12 hrs, US$25.

Carretera Austral Bus services vary according to demand: north to **Chaitén** via Puyuhuapi and La Junta, **Buses Norte**, Mon, Thu, Sun, approximately 12 hrs, US$20. To **Lago Verde** via La Junta, **Buses Daniela**, Tue, Sat, US$18. To **Puerto Cisnes**, **Transportes Terra Austral**, Mon-Sat, US$9.

South to **Cochrane**, **Interlagos**, 0930 Mon, Wed, Thu, Sat, Sun, US$12, recommended; **Don Carlos**, 0830 Tue, Sat, US$14; **Acuario 13**, 1000 Wed, Sat, US$11; and **Los Ñadis**, 1000 Tue, Thu, Sun, 8 hrs, US$11. Buses to Cochrane stop at **Cerro Castillo**, US$3.50, **Bahía Murta**, US$7, **Puerto Río Tranquilo**, US$8, and **Puerto Bertrand** , US$10.

Local Suray, Interlagos and Don Carlos minibuses run to **Puerto Aisén** every 15 mins, 1 hr, US$2, with connections for Puerto Chacabuco. There are also a few buses daily to **Mañihuales**. *Colectivos* to

Puerto Ibáñez on Lago Gen Carrera will pick you up at 0700 from your hotel to connect with **El Pilchero** ferry to Chile Chico, 2 hrs, book the day before, US$5; operators include **Colectivos Sr Parra**, *T067-251073*, Sat and Sun only; **Minibus Don Tito**, *T067-250280*, daily; **Sr Yarnil**, *T067-250346*, daily.

Taxi
Fares are 50% extra after 2100. *Colectivos* congregate at Prat y Bilbao, fare US$0.50.

Puerto Aisén *p418*
Bus
To **Puerto Chacabuco**, **Suray**, every 20 mins, US$0.75. To **Coyhaique**, Interlagos minibuses, frequent, or **Suray** minibuses every 45 mins, both 1 hr, US$2.

Ferry
Both **Transmarchilay** and **Navimag** have year-round ferry services from Puerto Chacabuco to **Puerto Montt** via the Canal Moraleda once a week in summer, irregular off-season, 24 hrs, US$40. **Aysén Express** also operates a weekly catamaran service to Puerto Montt via Chaitén and Chiloe, 11 hrs, US$43. See also p395.

Several companies offer trips of varying length to **Laguna San Rafael**. It is best to make reservations at the ferry companies' offices in Puerto Montt, Coyhaique or Santiago (or, for **Transmarchilay**, in Chaitén or Ancud). Boat information is posted at **Turismo Rucaray**.

🟢 Directory

Coyhaique *p416, map p416*
Airline offices Sky, *Prat 203*, *T067-240826*, *local calls 600-6002828*; LanChile, *Moraleda 402*, *T067-231188, local calls 600-5262000*; Don Carlos, *SubTte Cruz 63*, *T067-231981*.
Banks Several with Redbanc ATMs in centre,

for dollars, TCs and Argentine pesos. Both the following *casas de cambio* are recommended: Casa de Cambio Emperador, *Bilbao 222*, and Lucia Saldivia, *Baquedano 285*. **Bicycle** hire Figón, *Simpson y Colón, T067-234616*, check condition first, also sells spares; *Bilbao 500 block*, poor supply of spares but good repair service; **Motortech**, *Baquedano 131*; Tomás Enríque, *Madrid Urrea, Pje Foitzick y Libertad, T067-252132*. Bicycle spares are also available from several shops on Simpson. **Books** Library, *Cochrane, near plaza*, good selection of videos on Chile and book exchange (mostly English and German). **Cameras and film** Several outlets on both Condell and Prat. **Car hire** AGS, *Av Ogana 1298, T067-235354, F231511*; Automóvil Club de Chile, *Carrera 333, T067-231649*, rents jeeps and other vehicles; **Automundo AVR**, *Bilbao 510, T067-231621*; Río Baker, *Balmaceda airport, T067-272163*; Sur Nativo Renta Car; *Baquedano 457, T067-235500*; Traeger- Hertz, *Baquedano 457, T067-231648*; Turismo Prado, *21 de Mayo 417, T/F067-231271*. Hire cars may be taken across the border and returned to an office in Argentina, but you should buy fuel at one of the stations in Coyhaique. **Hospital** *Calle Hospital 068, T067-233172*. **Internet** Ciber Patagonia, *21 de Mayo 525*, best value; Entel, *Prat 340*; Hechizos, *21 de Mayo 460*, also cheap; several others. **Language schools** Baquedano International Language School, *Hosp of Sr Guzmán , Baquedano 20, T067-232520, www.patagoniachile.cl/bils* US$300 per week, including 4 hrs one-to-one tuition daily, lodging and all meals, other activities organized at discount rates, friendly, informative, highly recommended.
Laundry Lavaseco Universal, *Gen Parra 55*. QL, *Bilbao 160*. **Mechanic** Automotores Santiago, *Calle Los Ñires 811, T067-238330, T09-6406896*, speak English, can obtain spare parts quickly. **Post office** *Cochrane 202,*

open Mon-Fri 0900-1230, 1430-1800, Sat 0830-1200. **Shipping offices** Aysen Express, *Condell 149, of 203, T067-240956, aysenexpress@123.cl*; Navimag, *Ibáñez 347, T067-233306, www.navimag.cl*; Transmarchilay, *21 de Mayo 447, T067-231971, www.transmarchilay.cl* **Telephone** Several call centres; shop around as prices are relatively expensive.

Puerto Aisén *p418*
Banks Banco de Crédito, *Prat*, for Visa; Banco de Chile, *Plaza de Armas*, only

changes cash, not TCs. There's a Redbanc ATM machine in Puerto Chacabuco. **Post office** *south side of bridge.* **Shipping offices** Agemar, *Tte Merino 909, T067-332716*; the other offices are in Puerto Chacabuco: Catamaranes del Sur, *Carrera 50, T067-351112, www.catamaranesdelsur.cl*; Navimag, *Terminal de Transbordadores, T067-351111, www.navimag.cl*; Transmarchilay, *Av O'Higgins s/n, T067-351144, www.transmarchilay.cl* **Telephone** *Plaza de Armas, next to Turismo Rucuray*; ENTEL, *Libertad 408*, internet access.

Lago General Carrera

The section of the Carretera Austral around the north and western sides of Lago General Carrera is reckoned by many people to be the most spectacular stretch of all. Straddling the frontier with Argentina, this is the largest lake in South America after Lake Titicaca and is now believed to be the deepest lake on the continent; depth soundings in 1997 established its maximum depth as 590 m.

The lake is a beautiful azure blue, surrounded at its Chilean end by predominantly Alpine terrain and at the Argentine end by dry pampa. The region prides itself on having the best climate in southern Chile, with some 300 days of sunshine a year; much fruit is grown as a result, especially around Chile Chico, where rainfall is very low for this area. In general, the climate here is more similar to Argentine Patagonia than to the rest of the Carretera Austral region.

‡ *Fuel (sold in 5 litre containers) is available in Puerto Ibáñez at Luis A Bolados 461 (house with 5 laburnum trees outside).*

The eruption of Volcán Hudson in 1991 (south of Chile Chico) polluted parts of Lago General Carrera and many rivers. Although the waters are now clear, the effects can still be seen in some places where there is a metre-thick layer of ash on the ground. In Argentine Patagonia, the eruption was even more catastrophic: prevailing winds blew the ash onto farmland, blinding and killing many thousands of sheep.

Ins and outs
Getting there The main towns, **Puerto Ibáñez** on the north shore and **Chile Chico** on the south, are connected by a ferry, the *Pilchero*. Overland routes between Coyhaique and Chile Chico are much longer, passing either through Argentina, or along the Carretera Austral, which runs west around the lake. **Getting around** Minibuses run along the Carretera Austral in summer and air taxis link the small towns of the region.

Reserva Nacional Cerro Castillo and around → *Colour map 5, B3.*
Beyond Coyhaique, the Carretera Austral runs southwest through the Reserva Nacional Cerro Castillo, which extends over 179,550 ha. The park is named after the fabulous **Cerro Castillo** (2,675 m), which resembles a fairytale castle with rock pinnacles jutting out from a covering of snow. It also includes Cerro Bandera (2,040 m) just west of Balmaceda and several other peaks in the northern wall of the valley of the Río Ibáñez. There is a *guardería* at the northeastern end of the park near Laguna Chinguay and a CONAF campsite nearby ⓘ *T067-237070, US$5 per site.* At Km 83 the road crosses the Portezuelo Ibáñez (1,120 m) and drops through the Cuesta del Diablo, a series of bends with fine views over the Río Ibáñez.

The principal port on the Chilean section of the lake, **Puerto Ibáñez** (officially Puerto Ingeniero Ibáñez) is reached by taking a branch road, 31 km long, from Bajada Ibañez 97 km south of Coyhaique. There are some fine waterfalls, including the **Salto Río Ibáñez**, 6 km north. Eight kilometres beyond Bajada Ibáñez is **Villa Cerro Castillo**, a village where there are several *residenciales*. Near the village is a small local **museum** ① *2 km south of Villa Cerro Castillo, Dec-Mar 0900-1900*, and the **Monumento Nacional Manos de Cerro Castillo**, where traces of ancient rock paintings, estimated to be 10,000 years old, have been found. Various trekking options are available in this area.

The road climbs out of the valley, passing the emerald-green **Laguna Verde** and the Portezuelo Cofré. It descends to the boggy Manso valley, with a good campsite at the bridge over the river; watch out for mosquitoes. This area was seriously affected by the ash from Volcán Hudson. ▶▶ *For Sleeping, Eating and other listings, see pages 427-429.*

The western shore

Some 5 km from the Carretera Austral, at Km 203, is **Bahía Murta**, situated on the northern tip of the central 'arm' of Lago General Carrera. This village dates from the 1930s, when it exported timber to Argentina via Chile Chico. From here, the road follows the lake's western shore to **Río Tranquilo** at Km 228 from Coyhaique, where the buses stop for lunch and fuel is available. The lake reflects the mountains that surround it and the clouds above. Close to Río Tranquilo is the unusual **Catedral de Mármol**, a peninsula made of marble, with fascinating caves that can be visited by boat ① *10 mins, US$25 to hire a boat with guide.* The village also has an unusual cemetery. A new branch of the Carretera Austral heads northwest from Río Tranquilo to **Puerto Grosse** on the coast at Bahía Exploradores. ▶▶ *For Sleeping, Eating and other listings, see pages 427-429.*

Lago General Carrera

At the southwestern tip of Lago General Carrera, at Km 279, is **El Maitén**, from where a road branches off east along the south shore of the lake towards Chile Chico (see below). South of El Maitén, meanwhile, the Carretera Austral becomes steeper and more winding; in winter this stretch is icy and dangerous. **Puerto Bertrand**, 5 km away, is a good place for fishing. Nearby is a sign showing the 'Nacimiento del Río Baker': the place where the gleaming turquoise Río Baker begins. Beyond Puerto Bertrand, the road climbs up to high moorland, passing the confluence of the rivers Neff and Baker, before winding south along the east bank of the Río Baker to Cochrane. The road is rough but not treacherous and the scenery is splendid all the way. Watch out for cattle and hares on the road (and huemuls in winter) and take blind corners slowly.

The southern shore of Lago General Carrerra

Ten kilometres east of El Maitén, **Puerto Guadal** is a picturesque town that is a centre for fishing. It also has shops, accommodation, restaurants, a post office and petrol. Further east along the shore, just past the village of **Mallín Grande**, Km 40, the road runs through the **Paso de las Llaves**, a 30-km stretch carved out of the rock-face on the edge of the lake. The road climbs and drops, offering wonderful views across the lake and the icefields to the west. At Km 74, a turning runs to **Fachinal**. A further 8 km east, there is an open cast mine, which produces gold and other precious metals.

Chile Chico and around → *Phone code: 067. Colour map 5, B3. Population: 3,757.*

Chile Chico is a quiet, friendly but dusty town situated on the lake shore 122 km east of El Maitén, close to the Argentine border. The town dates from 1909 when settlers crossed from Argentina and occupied the land, leading to conflict with cattle ranchers who had been given settlement rights by the Chilean government. In the showdown that followed (known as the war of Chile Chico) the ranchers were driven out by the settlers, but it was not until 1931 that the Chilean government finally recognized the town's existence.

Now the centre of a fruit-growing region, it has an annual festival at the end of January and a small museum open in summer; outside is a boat that carried cargo on the lake before the opening of the new road along the southern shore. There are fine views from the **Cerro de las Banderas** at the western end of town. The **tourist office** ① *Municipalidad, O'Higgins 333*, can help in arranging tours.

The country to the south and west of Chile Chico provides good walking terrain, through weird rock formations and dry brush scrub. The northern and higher peak of **Cerro Pico del Sur** (2,168 m) can be climbed by the agile from Los Cipres (beware dogs in the farmyard). You will need a long summer's day and the 1:50,000 map. Follow the horse trail until it peters out, then navigate by compass or sense of direction until the volcano-like summit appears. After breaching the cliff ramparts, there is some scrambling and a 10 ft pitch to the summit, from where you'll enjoy indescribable views of the Lake and the Andes.

Twenty kilometres south of Chile Chico towards Lago Jeinimeni is the **Cueva de las Manos**, a cave full of Tehuelche paintings, the most famous of which are the *manos azules* (blue hands). From the road, climb 500 m and cross Pedregoso stream. The path is difficult, and partly hidden, so you're recommended to take a guide.

Reserva Nacional Lago Jeinemeni

① *53 km south of Chile Chico, open all year but access may be impossible between Apr and Oct due to high river levels, admission US$1.50, camping US$3. Getting there: lifts may be possible from Chile Chico; try Juan Núñez, Hernán Trizzando 110, for a lift on a timber truck, or ask in the CONAF office.*

This park covers 160,000 ha and includes two lakes, **Lago Jeinemeni** and **Lago Verde**, which lie surrounded by forests in the narrow valley of the Río Jeinemeni. Impressive cliffs, waterfalls and small glaciers provide habitat for huemul deer, pumas and condors. Activities include fishing for salmon and rainbow trout, trekking and rowing.

Access is via an unpaved road, which branches south off the road to Los Antiguos and crosses five rivers, four of which have to be forded. At Km 42, there is a small lake, **Laguna de los Flamencos**, where large numbers of flamingos can be seen. The park entrance is at Km 53; just beyond is a ranger station, a campsite and fishing area at the eastern end of Lago Jeinemeni. Take all supplies, including a good map.

Into Argentina → *Argentine phone code: +54.*

A road runs 2 km east from Chile Chico to the **Argentine frontier** ① *Chilean immigration open Sep-Apr 0730-2200, May-Aug 0800-2000*, and on for 5 km to **Los Antiguos**. This is another fruit-growing town with an annual cherry festival in mid-January. Salmon fishing is also possible. **Perito Moreno**, 67 km east of the frontier, has a few hotels, a campsite, a restaurant and money exchange services. About 120 km south is the famous **Cueva de las Manos**, where the walls of a series of galleries are covered with painted human hands and animals, 10,000 years old. All but 31 of the 800 hands are left hands.

● Sleeping

Bahía Murta, with good views of Cerro Castillo.

Reserva Nacional Cerro Castillo and around *p425*
B Cabañas Shehen Aike, *Risopatrón 55, Puerto Ibañez, T067-423284.* English spoken.
E Hostería Villaricia, *O'Higgins 59, Villa Cerro Castillo.* Accommodation, good mid-price meals and a grocery store. Cheap meals are also available at **Restaurante La Querencia**, *O'Higgins s/n, Villa Cerro Castillo.*
G Res Ibáñez, *Bertrán Dixon 31, Puerto Ibañez, T067-423227.* Price per person. Clean, warm, hot water. Similar next door at no 29.
G Vientos del Sur, *Bertrán Dixon 282, Puerto Ibañez, T067-423208.* Price per person. Cheap meals available, good.

Camping
Municipal campsite, *Puerto Ibañez, T067-423234.* Open Dec-Mar, US$7 per site.

The western shore *p425*
C Hostal Los Pinos, *2 Oriente 41, T067-411576, Río Tranquilo.* Family run, well maintained, good mid-price meals. Recommended.
F Hostería Carretera Austral, *1 Sur 223, Río Tranquilo, T067-419500.* Price per person. Also serves mid-range/cheap meals.
F-G Cabañas Jacricalor, *1 Sur s/n, Río Tranquilo, T067-419500.* Price per person. Tent-sized *cabañas*.
G Hostería Lago Gen Carrera, *Av 5 de Abril 647 y Colombia, Bahía Murta, public telephone 067-419600.* Price per person. Cheap meals.
G Res Patagonia, *Pasaje España 64, Bahía Murta, public telephone 067-419600.* Price per person. Very basic, without bath.

Free camping is possible by the lake in

El Maitén and south *p426*
L Mallín Colorado, *2 km west of El Maitén, T067-2741807, chile@patagonia-pacific.cl* Cabañas, adventure activities, horseriding, rafting, fishing, English and German spoken.
A-B Hostería Campo Baker, *Puerto Bertrand, T067-411477.* Cabañas, sleeps 5.
F Doña Ester, *Puerto Bertrand.* Rooms in a pink house. Price per person. Good.
F Hostería Puerto Bertrand, *Sector Costanera, Puerto Bertrand, T067-419900.* Price per person. Also meals, *cabañas*, and activities (see below).
F-G Sra Alicia Sobarzo, *Puerto Bertrand.* Price per person.

Chile Chico and around *p426*
C-D Ventura, *Carrera 290, T067-411311.* Modern suites.
D-F Hostería de la Patagonia, *Camino Internacional s/n, T067-411337, F411414.* Price per person; full board available. Clean, excellent food, English, French and Italian spoken, trekking, horseriding and whitewater rafting organized, also camping.
F Plaza, *O'Higgins y Balmaceda, T067-411510.* Price per person. Basic, clean. Recommended.
G Casa Quinta No me Olvides, *Camino Internacional s/n .* Price per person. Without bath. Clean, cooking facilities. Also camping. Tours arranged to Lago Jeinimeni and Cueva de las Manos.
G Hospedaje Alicia, *Ramon Freire 24.* Price per person. Single, double and 3-bed rooms, clean, use of kitchen.
G Res Don Luis, *Balmaceda 175, T067-411384.* Price per person. Clean, meals available.

Camping

Free campsite at **Bahía Jarra**, 5 km from Chile Chico, then 12 km north. Also **Camping del Sol** at the eastern end of the town.

⚙ Eating

Hosterías are your best bet for food in this region (see Sleeping, above), although you may also want to try the following:

Chile Chico and around *p426*
$$ **Café Holiday**, *Calle Gonzalez*. Good coffee, friendly service.
$$ **Cafetería Loly y Elizabeth**, *Gonzalez 25, on the plaza*. Serves coffee, delicious ice cream and cakes.

ⓝ Bars and clubs

Chile Chico and around *p426*
Pub El Minero, *Carrera 205*. Recommended for a drink.
Zebra, *O'Higgins 750 Interior*. This disco is the place to be seen in Chile Chico.

⊛ Festivals and events

Chile Chico and around *p426*
The town hosts the **Festival Internacional de la Voz** in the last week of Jan.

⚑ Activities and tours

The western shore *p425*
El Puesto Expediciones, *Lagos 258, Río Tranquillo, T067-233785, elpuesto@entelchile.net* Fishing trips and other excursions.

El Maitén and south *p426*
Jonathan Leidich, *Puerto Bertrand, T067-411330*. Lives on the edge of the lake, and is highly recommended for rafting, horseriding and other activities.
La Red de Turismo Río Baker, *Hostería Puerto Bertrand, Sector Costanera, Puerto Bertrand, T067-419900*. Organises rafting, horseriding and other activities.
Patagonia Baker Lodges, *Orillas del Río Baker, Puerto Bertrand, T067-411903*. Fishing trips on the lake.
Río Baker Lodges, *T067-411499*. Fishing trips on the lake.

The southern shore *p426*
Hacienda Tres Lagos, *Sector El Maitén, Puerto Guadal, T067-411323*. Fishing trips.
Playa Guadal, *2 km from Puerto Guadal, T067-411443*. Fishing trips.

Chile Chico and around *p426*
Jaime Berrocal, *O'Higgins 501*. Fishing guide

⊖ Transport

Cerro Castillo and around *p425*
Bus
Minibuses run between Puerto Ibáñez and **Coyhaique**, 2 hrs, US$5. There is also a road from Puerto Ibáñez to **Perito Moreno** in Argentina, but no public transport.
Transportes Amin Ali, *O'Higgins s/n, Villa Cerro Castillo, T067-419200*, provides transport from Villa Cerro Castillo to **Coyhaique**, US$5.

Ferry
The car ferry, *El Pilchero*, sails from Puerto Ibáñez to **Chile Chico**, daily Mon, Wed-Fri, Sun 1000, return departures 1700 (Sun 1200), 2¾ hrs, cars US$30, passengers US$3, motorbikes and bicycles US$5. The number of passengers is limited to 70; arrive 30 mins before departure, reservations possible. This is a very cold crossing even in summer: take warm clothing. Buses and jeeps meet the ferry in Puerto Ibáñez for connections to Coyhaique (see above).

Chile Chico and around *p426*
Air
Don Carlos flies to **Coyhaique**, 5 weekly, US$35, from an airstrip just outside Chile Chico.

Bus
Transportes Ales, *T067-411739*, runs minibuses along the south side of the lake to **Puerto Guadal**, Wed, Sat, US$8, and **Cochrane**, US$15. Additional services to Puerto Guadall are provided by **Sr Sergio Haro Ramos**, *T067-411251*, Wed, Sat, US$10, and **Transportes Seguel**, 2 weekly, US$9.

Minibuses from Chile Chico to **Los Antiguos** (Argentina), 45 mins including formalities, US$2 (payable in Chilean pesos only), are run by **Arcotrans**, *T067-411841*, and **Transportes Padilla**, *T067-411904*. The buses depart when they are full – usually about 5 times daily each.

Ferry
For services to Puerto Ibáñez, see above.

Into Argentina *p427*
From Los Antiguos buses run weekdays to **Comodoro Rivadavia** via Perito Moreno, 7 hrs, US$20. There are also direct buses to **Río Gallegos** from Los Antiguos, and one flight a week from Perito Moreno.

Chile Chico and around *p426*
Banks Generally it's best to change money in Coyhaique or Argentina, but dollars and Argentine pesos can be changed in small amounts (at poor rates) at shops and cafés in Chile Chico, including **Café Loly y Elizabeth**. **Camera and films** Rene Villegas, *O'Higgins 424*. **Car hire** Jaime Acuña Vogt, *Grosse 150, T/F067-411553*. **Hospital** *Lautaro s/n, T067-411334*.

Cochrane and further south

The final 224-km stretch of the Carretera Austral from Cochrane to Villa O'Higgins has now been completed. Travelling by bus can be frustrating as you will undoubtedly want to stop every 15 minutes to marvel at the views. From Vagabundo, Km 98, boats sail regularly down the Río Baker to Tortel. This is a beautiful trip through thick forest, with vistas of snow-capped mountains and waterfalls.

Ins and outs
Getting there Cochrane can be reached by aeroplane or bus from Coyhaique, or on a poor unpaved road from Perito Moreno in Argentina. The southern tip of the Carretera at Villa O'Higgins is linked by an erratic ferry service to Calendario Mansilla, from where it is a two-day hike to/from El Chaltén in Argentina. **Getting around** Public transport is scarce. Only two weekly buses ply the route from Cochrane to Villa O'Higgins. Hitching is a possibility in summer, but a four-wheel-drive vehicle will make getting around much easier. Better still, travel by mountain bike. ▶▶ *For further details, see Transport, page 433.* **Tourist information** The office in Cochrane is open only in the summer ⓘ *Mon-Sat 0900-1300, 1430-2000*; in winter go to Cochrane Municipalidad at Esmeralda 398.

Cochrane and around → *Phone code: 067. Colour map 5, C3. Population: 3,000.*
Sitting in a hollow on the northern banks of the Río Cochrane, 343 km south of Coyhaique, Cochrane is a simple place, sunny in summer and good for walking and fishing. There is a small **museum** ⓘ *San Valentín 555, Mon-Fri 0900-1300, 1500-1900*. On the same street is an odd, *maté*-shaped house.

Excursions can be made to **Lago Cochrane**, which straddles the frontier with Argentina (the Argentine section is called Lago Puerredón). The lake, which covers over 17,500 ha, offers excellent fishing all-year round; boats can be hired for US$12 per person. On the northern shores of the lake is the **Reserva Nacional Tamango** ⓘ *Dec-Mar 0830-2100, Apr-Nov 0830-1830, US$3, guided visits to see the huemal, Tue, Thu, Sat, US$60 for a group of 6 people*. The reserve covers 6,925 ha of lenga forest and is home to one of the largest colonies of the rare huemul as well as guanaco, foxes and lots of birds, including woodpeckers and hummingbirds. There are several marked trails affording views over the town, the nearby lakes and even to the Campo de Hielo Norte to the west. Tourist facilities, however, are rudimentary.

Some 17 km north of Cochrane, a road runs east through Villa Chacabuco to enter Argentina at **Paso Roballos** ⓘ *78 km, Chilean immigration open summer 0730-2200,*

⦂ Deer, oh deer

The Andean **huemul** (Hippocamelus bisulcus) is a mountain deer native to the Andes of southern Chile and Argentina. Sharing the Chilean national crest with the Andean condor, the huemul (pronounced 'way-mool') is a medium-sized stocky cervid adapted to survival in rugged mountain terrain. Males grow antlers and have distinctive black face masks. Huemul tend to live in groups of two to five – usually a breeding pair accompanied by offspring. The rutting season peaks in February and March; females give birth to a single fawn in November or December.

Although it used to range from just south of Santiago to the Straits of Magellan, human pressures have pushed the huemul to the brink of extinction. Current numbers are estimated at 1,000-1,500. A small and dwindling group of 60 animals survive in the Nevados de Chillán in central Chile, their northernmost presence. The remaining known populations are scattered across the southern regions of Argentina and Chile.

The huemul is the focal point of both national and international conservation efforts, carried out primarily by CONAF and the Comite pro la Defensa de la Fauna y Flora de Chile (CODEFF). The current focus is on halting and reversing the decline in numbers in central Chile and on determining more precisely numbers and distribution further south.

The huemul is a shy animal that tends to avoid human contact. Your best chance of seeing them is in one of two reserves managed by CONAF: the Reserva Nacional Río Claro, which lies on the southeastern corner of the larger Reserva Nacional Río Simpson just outside Coyhaique, and the Reserva Nacional Tamango, near Cochrane. To visit either of these you will need to be accompanied by a warden: ask in Coyhaique or Cochrane to make sure someone is available.

The Carretera Austral area is also one of the best places for trying to spot the equally rare **pudu**. This miniature creature, around 40 cm tall and weighing only 10 kg, is the smallest member of the deer family in the world. Native to southern Argentina and Chile, the pudu is listed in Chile as vulnerable to extinction, largely due to habitat loss, but also because its unique appearance (the males grow two short spiked antlers) has made it a target for poaching for zoos. Reddish-brown in colour, the pudu is ideally adapted to the dense temperate rainforests of Chile and Argentina, scooting along on trails through the undergrowth, leaving behind minuscule cloven tracks.

winter 0800-2000, before continuing on to Bajo Caracoles. There isn't any public transport along this route and, although the road is passable in summer, it is often flooded in spring. ▸▸ *For Sleeping, Eating and other listings, see pages 432-434.*

Tortel → *Phone code: 067. Colour map 5, C2.*

Built on a hill at the mouth of the river 135 km from Cochrane, Tortel has no streets, only wooden walkways ('*no hay ni una bicicleta*'); its main industries are wood, for trade with Punta Arenas, and shellfish. The village became famous in October 2000 as the place where British Prince William spent three months working for **Operation Raleigh**; it is also where Rosie Swale ended her epic horseback journey through Chile, as recorded in *Back to Cape Horn* (see page 554). A branch of the Carretera Austral, beginning 2 km south of Vagabundo and reaching south to Tortel, was completed in early 2003, so the village is now accessible by road, and the repercussions on its character will be enormous. From Tortel, you can hire a boat to visit two spectacular glaciers: **Ventisquero Jorge Montt**, five hours southwest, or **Ventisquero Steffens**, north on the edge of the Parque Nacional San Rafael. On the Río Baker nearby is the **Isla de los Muertos**, where some hundred Chilote workers died under mysterious circumstances early in the 20th century.

The Carretera continues southwards to **Puerto Yungay**, a tiny village with a military post and a pretty church. This section of the road is hilly and in places very bad; it is not advisable to drive along here at night. From Puerto Yungay, there is a **ferry** crossing to Río Bravo run by the army① *several daily, 45 mins, free, check timetables locally*. If you miss the last boat the *carabineros* will help you find accommodation. After the ferry crossing, the road continues through more spectacular scenery – lakes moors, swamps, rivers and waterfalls – before arriving at its final destination.

Villa O'Higgins → *Phone code: 067. Colour map 5, C3. Population: 500.*

Villa O'Higgins lies 2 km from the northeastern end of an 'arm' of **Lago O'Higgins**, which straddles the Argentine border (it's known as Lago San Martín in Argentina). The people are friendly, and there is still something of a frontier feel about the town. **Tourist information** ① *T067-211849, www.ohiggins.cl*, is available in the plaza in summer or from the Municipalidad, which can also provide trekking guides.

Behind the town, a *mirador* affords spectacular views of nearby mountains, lakes and glaciers. There are large numbers of icebergs in Lago O'Higgins, which have split off the glaciers of the Campo de Hielo Sur to the west. A six-hour trek from the town goes through native forest to the **Mosco Glacier**. Allow two days for a return trip. Fresh water is plentiful and there is a *refugio* on the way, but the route is difficult after heavy rain.

From Villa O'Higgins, the road continues 7 km south to **Bahía Bahamóndez** on the shores of Lago O'Higgins, from where a boat departs ① *every 2 wks in summer, although frequency is likely to increase (contact the Municipalidad in Villa O'Higgins for details)*, to Chilean immigration at Candelario Mancila. From here, it is a two-day walk or one-day mountain bike ride (you will need to carry the bicycle in places) to **El Chaltén** in Argentina. With the opening of this route, it is now possible to travel along the whole of the Carretera Austral and on to Torres del Paine without having to double back on yourself. ⏩ *For Sleeping, Eating and other listings, see pages 432-434.*

Parque Nacional Laguna San Rafael

Situated west of Lago General Carrera and some 200 km south of Puerto Aisén, Laguna San Rafael is one of the highlights for many travellers to Chile. The **Ventisquero San Rafael**, one of many glaciers from the giant **Campo de Hielo Norte**, flows into the laguna, which, in turn, empties into the sea northwards via the Río Tempano. About 45 km in length and towering 30 m above water level, the deep blue glacier groans and cracks as it carves off icebergs, which are carried across the laguna and out to sea. Around the shores of the laguna is thick vegetation and above are snowy mountain peaks.

Laguna San Rafael and the Campo de Hielo Norte are part of the **Parque Nacional Laguna San Rafael**① *entry fee US$6*, which extends over 1,740,000 ha. In the national park are puma, pudu, foxes, dolphins, occasional sea-lions and sea otters, and many species of bird. Walking trails are limited (about 10 km in all) but a lookout platform has been constructed, with fine views of the glacier. There is also a small ranger station that provides information and a pier. The rangers are willing to row you out to the glacier in calm weather, an awsome three-hour adventure, past icebergs and swells created when huge chunks of ice break off the glacier and crash into the laguna.

Sadly, the San Rafael glacier is rapidly disintegrating and is likely to have disappeared entirely by 2011. While this shrinkage is symptomatic of what has happened to many glaciers in Patagonia, some place the blame for the speed of deterioration on the waves created by motorised tourist boats that go too close to the glacier, creating a greater force of erosion against the ice. If the glacier is to be preserved, it is vital that travellers take a pro-active stance on this issue and insist that the boats do not go too close to the glacier and further damage this fragile environment.

● Sleeping

Cochrane p429
In summer it is best to book rooms in advance.

A **Ultimo Paraíso**, *Lago Brown 455, T067-522361*. Regarded as the best place to stay. Also arranges fishing trips.

B **Cabañas Rogery**, *Tte Merino 502, T067-522264*. Cabins sleep 4, with kitchen facilities. Breakfast included.

C **Hotel Wellmann**, *Las Golondrinas 36, T067-522171*. Hot water, comfortable, warm, good meals. Recommended.

E **Res Rubio**, *Tte Merino 4, T067-522173*. Price per person, breakfast included, lunch and dinner extra. With bath. Very good,

E-F **Residencial Cero a Cero**, *Lago Brown 464, T067-522158, ceroacero@ze.cl* Price per person, with breakfast, cheaper without bath, welcoming, recommended.

F **Hosp Cochrane**, *Dr Steffens 451, T067-522377*. Price per person. Good meals, camping available. Recommended.

F **Hosp Paola**, *Lago Brown 150, T067-522215*. Price per person. Also camping.

F **Hostal Latitud 47 sur**, *Lago Brown 564*. Price per person. Clean, hot water, internet, tours offered.

F **Res El Fogón**, *San Valentín 651, T067-522240*. Price per person. Its pub is one of few eating places open in the low season.

F **Res Sur Austral**, *Prat 334, T067-522150*. Price per person with breakfast and hot water.

Camping
In the Reserva Nacional Tamango, there are campsites at **Los Correntadas**, US$10 per site, also *cabañas*, and **Los Coigües**, US$13 per site, also *cabañas*. Details and booking through CONAF, *main plaza in Cochrane, T067-422164*.

Tortel p430
Free accommodation is also available at the **Centro Abierto**, ask at the Municipalidad, *T067-211876*.

D **Doña Berta Muñoz**, *Tortel*. Full board. One guest comments: "Expect fresh mutton meals and if you are squeamish about seeing animals killed don't look out of the window when they butcher the two lambs a day on the front porch."

D-F **Sergio Barrio**, *Tortel*. Full board available, good food.

E-G, **Casa Rural**, *Tortel*. Full board or bed and breakfast.

F **Hospedaje Costanera**, *Tortel, T067-234815*. Price includes breakfast (also open to non-residents). Clean, warm, with attractive garden, recommended.

Villa O'Higgins p431
F **Hospedaje Patagonia**, *T067-234813*. Price per person without bath.

G **Apocalipsis 1:3**, *T067-216927*. Price per person without bath, friendly, serves food.

● Eating

For other eating options in this area, see Sleeping, above.

Cochrane p429
$ **La Costa**, *plaza*. A friendly cheapie. There are also a couple of mid-range options on Tte Merino and San Valentín

Tortel p430
$ **Café Celes Salom**. Basic cheap meals and a disco every Sat with occasional visiting bands.

▲ Activities and tours

Cochrane p429
Excursions can be arranged through Guillermo Paso at **Transportes Los Ñadis** (see below, Transport); fishing tours are available from **Hotel Ultimo Paraíso** (see above, Sleeping).

Don Pedro Muñoz, *T067-522244*. Hires out horses for excursions in the surrounding countryside.

Red de Turismo Río Baker, *San Valentin 438, T067-522646, trural@patagoniachile.cl* Offers tours of all kinds within the region.
Samuel Smiol, *T067-522487*. Offers tours to the icefields and mountains, English spoken.
Siesta Oppi, *3176 Neuenegg, Switzerland, T+41-31-7419192, F7411215*. This Swiss canoe shop organizes canoe trips in the area during Jan and Feb.

Tortel *p430*
Charter boats can be arranged through Viviana Muñoz or Hernán Ovando at the *Municipalidad, T067-211876*. Prices to Ventisquero Jorge Montt speedboat 2 hrs, US$100 per person; *lancha* 5 hrs, US$120. To Ventisquero Steffens speedboat 1 hr, US$60 per person; lancha 2½ hrs, $70.

Villa O'Higgins *p431*
Nelson Henriquez, *Lago Cisnes 201*. Fishing trips on the lake.

⊜ Transport

Cochrane *p429*
Air
Don Carlos flies to Coyhaique, Mon, Thu, US$57, from an airstrip just north of town.

Bus
To Coyhaique, Don Carlos, *Prat 344, T/F067-522150*, 2 weekly, US$14; Inter Lagos, 6 weekly, US$12, recommended; Los Ñadis, *Los Helechos 490, T/F067-522196*, 3 weekly, US$11; Acuario 13, *Río Baker 349, T/F067-522143*, 3 weekly, US$19. To Vagabundo, US$7, Los Ñadis, 3 weekly; Acuario 13, 4 weekly. To Villa O'Higgins, Los Ñadis, 1 weekly, US$8; Acuario 13, 1 weekly, US$11.

Tortel *p430*
Air
Don Carlos to Coyhaique, Mon and Wed, US$25. This is a subsidized price for residents of the village. Other travellers must buy a standby ticket and should expect to pay much more.

Boat
To Vagabundo, Tue, Sun 0900, 5 hrs, US$2 one way; return trip Tue, Sun 1500, 3 hrs. There is a boat once a fortnight from Tortel to Puerto Yungay, or you can arrange a charter for 6-10 people by contacting Viviana Muñoz or Hernán

Ovando at the *Municipalidad, T067-211876*, 8 hrs, US$110 return.

Villa O'Higgins *p431*
Don Carlos air taxi flies to Villa O'Higgins from Coyhaique, via Cochrane, Mon, Thu, US$75. There's also two buses weekly to Cochrane, US$8.

Laguna San Rafael *p431*
Air
Aerohein and Don Carlos provide air taxis from Coyhaique (addresses under Coyhaique), US$200 each for party of 5; some pilots in Puerto Aisén will also fly to the glacier for about US$95 per person, but many are unwilling to land on the rough airstrip. Other air-tour options are available from Coyhaique.

Boats from Puerto Montt
The official cruises from Puerto Montt are run by Skorpios (p370). Various private yachts for 6-12 passengers can also be chartered. Other tour companies include:
Compañía Naviera Puerto Montt, *Diego Portales 882, Puerto Montt, T/F065-252547*. Runs 6-day, 6-night tours to the Laguna, via various ports and channels, on board the *Quellon*, US$900. Office in Santiago at *Alameda B O'Higgins 108, local 120, T02-6330883*, and in Puerto Aisén/Puerto Chacabuco, see below.
Pamar, *Pacheco Altamirano 3100, T065-256220*. Sails Sep-Mar only.
Patagonia Connection SA, *Fidel Oteíza 1921, Oficina 1006, Providencia, Santiago, T02-2256489, F2748111*. Operates a 4-6 day catamaran tour to Laguna San Rafael via Termas de Puyuhuapi (see p413) on board the *Patagonia Express*.

Boats from Puerto Chacabuco
Although it's now nearly as cheap to fly, official cruises to the Laguna are run by Navimag, all year, reduced service off season, 24 hrs, from US$259, and Catamaranes del Sur, 1-3 weekly Sep-Apr, 1-day trips US$299, 3-day trips from $550. For contact details, see p424.
Compañía Naviera Puerto Montt, *Sgto Aldea 679, Puerto Aisén, T067-332908/3511066*. Motorized sailing boats, the *Odisea* and the *Visun*, sail Dec-Mar on 6-day trips to the Laguna San Rafael.

Iceberg Express, *Av Providencia 2331, of 602, Santiago, T02-3350580, F3350581*. 12-hr luxury catamaran cruises.

Local fishing boats from Puerto Chacabuco/Puerto Aisén take about 18-20 hrs each way and charge the same as the tourist boats. Try the following: **Jorge Prado**, ask at the port, takes a minimum of 7, more expensive than others; **Andino Royas**, *Cochrane 129*; **Justiniano Aravena**, *Dr Steffen 703*; **Rodrigo Azúcar**, *Agemar office, T067-332716*; or **Sr Ocuña**, ask at the port. Note that these unauthorized boats may have neither adequate facilities nor a licence for the trip. Trips to Laguna San Rafael out of season are very difficult to arrange, but in Puerto Chacabuco, try **Edda Espinosa**, *Sgto Aldea 943*.

Directory

Cochrane *p429*

Banks Banco del Estado, *on the plaza*, changes dollars. ATM accepts Mastercard and Cirrus but not Visa. **Car hire** Marcel Moya Diaz, *Dr Steffens 147, T067-522276*. Petrol is available at the **Copec** station.
Internet There are 2 on the plaza, one run by nuns (closed Sun). **Supermarket** Melero, *Las Golondrinas 148*.

Tortel *p430*

Banks There is no bank in the village but a mobile bank comes by air twice per month.
Medical services Medical centre staffed by doctors, nurses and dentists visits monthly. **Post office** open Mon-Fri 0830-1330, post leaves Tortel weekly by air.
Telephone *T067-234815*.

 For an explanation of sleeping and eating price codes used in this guide, see inside the front cover. Other relevant information is found in Essentials, see pages 51-58.

The Far South

Introduction

A spectacular land of fragmenting glaciers and teetering icy peaks, southern Patagonia feels like nowhere else on earth. Although Chileans posted here will often say that they are a "long way from Chile", this is the country's most popular destination for visitors. The jewel in the crown is the **Parque Nacional Torres del Paine**, a natural magnet for travellers from all over the world. The 'towers', three distinctive columns after which the park is named, point vertically upwards from the Paine massif like fingers, surrounded by imposing glaciers, turquoise-coloured lakes and thick forests of native trees.

Nearby, **Punta Arenas** is a European-style city with a lively Chilote community and remnants of earlier English and Croatian influences. There are numerous other attractions, notably the glaciers that descend from Monte Balmaceda at the southern end of the **Parque Nacional Bernardo O'Higgins**. On the Argentine side of the frontier lies more spectacular scenery, including the **Perito Moreno Glacier** and the mountainous area around **Cerro Fitz Roy**.

★ Don't miss...

❶ Parque Nacional Torres del Paine Complete the seven-day trek through the national park, passing fields of wild flowers, glaciers, mountains, forests, and white and turquoise lakes, page 455.

❷ Perito Moreno Witness the creaking, heaving mass of this Argentine glacier, from which huge chunks of ice regularly break off into Lago Argentino, page 470.

❸ Cerro Fitz Roy Trek through a stunning part of Argentine Patagonia: "anyone within 500 miles would be a fool to miss it", page 471.

❹ Skiing Punta Arenas is one of the only places in the world where you can ski in sight of the sea, page 447.

❺ Parque Nacional Bernardo O'Higgins Take a boat trip to the glaciers at the bottom of one of the planet's largest non-polar icefields, the Campo de Hielo Sur, page 450.

❻ Seno Otway Pick up a penguin near Punta Arenas, page 443.

The Far South

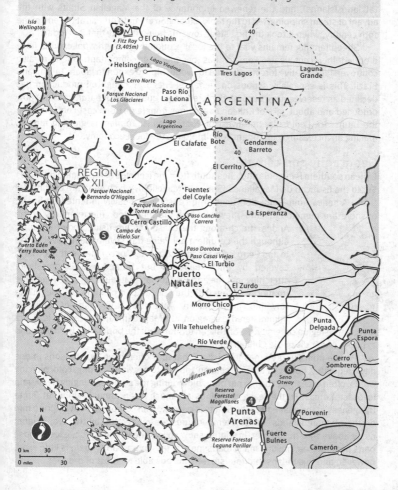

Background

Southern Patagonia was inhabited from the end of the Ice Age, mainly by the Tehuelche people, who roamed from the Atlantic coast to the mountains (see box opposite). The first Europeans did not visit until the 16th century. When Magellan sailed through the Straits in 1520, their strategic importance was quickly recognized: soon Spanish naval and merchant ships were using the route, as were mariners from other countries, including Francis Drake on his world voyage (1578). However, the route became less important after 1616 when the Dutch sailors Jacob le Maire and Cornelius van Schouten discovered a quicker route into the Pacific round Cape Horn.

At Independence, Chile claimed the far southern territories along the Pacific coast. But little was done to carry out this claim until 1843 when, concerned at British activities in the area and at rumours of French plans to start a colony, President Bulnes ordered the preparation of a secret mission. The expedition, on board the vessel *Ancud*, established Fuerte Bulnes; the fort was abandoned in 1848 in favour of a new settlement 56 km north, called Punta Arenas. The development of sheep farming in Patagonia and on Tierra del Fuego (with the help of arrivals from the nearby Falkland Islands), and the renewed importance of the Magellan Straits with the advent of steam shipping, led to the rapid expansion of Punta Arenas at the end of the 19th century, when it took the first steps towards being the city that it is today.

Sheep farming remains vital to the local economy, although wool exports have dropped in recent years. Forestry has become more important, but it is also controversial, as native forests are used for woodchips to export to Japan, Taiwan and Brazil. This is especially serious on Tierra del Fuego. Although oil production has declined as reserves have become depleted, large quantities of natural gas are now produced and about 33% of Chilean coal comes from large open cast coal mines on the Brunswick Peninsula, northwest of Punta Arenas. Tourism is growing rapidly, making an increasingly important contribution to the local economy.

Geography and climate

Chilean southern Patagonia stretches south from the icefields of the Campo de Hielos Sur to the Estrecho de Magallanes (Straits of Magellan), which separate continental South America from Tierra del Fuego. The coastline is heavily indented by fjords; offshore are numerous islands, few of which are inhabited. The remnants of the Andes stretch along the coast, seldom rising above 1,500 m, although the Cordillera del Paine has several peaks over 2,600 m and Cerro Balmaceda is 2,035 m. Most of the western coast is covered by thick rainforest but further east is grassland, stretching into the arid Patagonian plateau across the Argentine frontier. Together with the Chilean part of Tierra del Fuego, Isla Navarino and Chilean Antarctica, this part of Chile is administered as Región XII (Magallanes); the capital is Punta Arenas. The region covers 17.5% of Chilean territory, but the population is only around 171,000, under 1% of the Chilean total.

> ✷ *When travelling in this region, protection against the ultraviolet rays of the sun is essential at all times, but especially in the spring, when the ozone layer all but disappears.*

People from Punta Arenas tell visitors that they often have four seasons in one day. Frequently, however, the only season appears to be winter. Strong, cold, piercing winds, often exceeding 100 km per hour, blow during the summer bringing heavy rain to coastal areas. Further east, the winds are much drier; annual rainfall at Punta Dungeness at the east end of the Straits is only 250 mm compared to over 4,000 mm on the offshore islands. Coastal temperatures are moderated by the sea, seldom rising above 15°C in summer. In winter, snow covers the whole region, except those parts near the sea, making many roads more or less impassable; there is little wind, however, and this means that tourism remains possible for most of the year.

The original big foots

The dry Patagonian plateau was originally inhabited by one principle indigenous group, the **Tehuelches**, who lived along the eastern side of the Andes, as far north as modern-day Bariloche, and were hunters of guanaco and rheas. In the 18th century, they began to domesticate the wild horses of the region and sailed down the Patagonian rivers to reach the Atlantic coast.

The Tehuelches were very large: it is said that when the Spanish first arrived in this area, they discovered Tehuelche footprints in the sand, exclaiming 'qué patagón' ('what a large foot'), hence the name Patagonia.

In the 18th and early 19th centuries, the Tehuelche interacted with European whalers and were patronizingly described as 'semi-civilized'. The granting by the Chilean government of large land concessions in the late 19th century, combined with Argentine President Julio Roca's wars of extermination against Patagonian native peoples in the 1870s, spelled the end for the Tehuelches. They were hunted and persecuted by settlers and only a few survived diseases and the radical change of lifestyle.

Towards the end of the 20th century, a belated sense of moral guilt arose among the colonizers, but it was too late to preserve the Tehuelche way of life. Today only a few isolated groups remain in Argentine Patagonia.

For details of the indigenous groups further south and in the Patagonian fjords, see the chapter on Tierra del Fuego and page 528.

Punta Arenas and around

→ *Phone code: 061. Colour map 7, B1. Population: 120,000.*
Capital of Región XII, Punta Arenas lies 2,140 km due south of Santiago. The city was originally named 'Sandy Point' by the English, but adopted the Hispanic equivalent under Chilean colonization. A centre for the local sheep farming and fishing industries, it is also the home of La Polar, the most southerly brewery in the world. Although Punta Arenas has expanded rapidly, it remains a tranquil and pleasant city. The climate and architecture give it a distinctively northern European atmosphere, quite unlike anywhere else in Chile.

Ins and outs → *Note that many eating places in Punta Arenas are closed on Sunday.*
Getting there Punta Arenas is cut off from the rest of Chile. The only road connections are via Comodoro Rivadavia and Río Gallegos either to Coyhaique and the Carretera Austral (20 hours; one or two buses weekly in summer) or to Bariloche and on to Puerto Montt (36 hours; daily buses in summer); it is quicker, and often cheaper, to take one of the many daily flights to/from Puerto Montt or Santiago instead. Carlos Ibáñez del Campo Airport is 20 km north of town. **Buses Transfer** and **Buses Pacheco** (see Directory below) run services to/from Punta Arenas, scheduled to meet flights, US$2. Buses from Punta Arenas to Puerto Natales will only stop at the airport if they are scheduled to pick up passengers there. A taxi costs US$7. Transport to Tierra del Fuego is on the Melinka ferry to Porvenir (six weekly) or, further north, at Punta Delgada (many daily) to Cerro Sombrero. There are also direct flights to

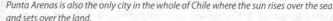
Punta Arenas is also the only city in the whole of Chile where the sun rises over the sea and sets over the land.

Porvenir, Puerto Williams and Ushuaia. Puerto Natales, 247 km north, is easily reached on a paved road (many buses daily). ▸▸ *For further details, see Transport page 447.*
Getting around Calle Pedro Montt runs east-west, while Jorge Montt runs north-south. Buses and *colectivos* in Punta Arenas tend to go either north along the 21 de Mayo-Magallanes-Bulnes axis, south down Chiloe, or east-west up Independencia. In either case, Punta Arenas is not a huge city and walking about is a pleasant way of getting to know it. Buses are plentiful and cheap: a taxi is only really necessary for out-of-town excursions. **Tourist information** Muñoz Gamero ⓘ *near the Plaza, 0830-1745, closed Sat and Sun off season*, is helpful and has lots of information, English spoken. The municipal **tourist office** on the plaza is also good, To61-200610, or there are **Sernatur** ⓘ *Magallanes 960, To61-225385*, and **CONAF** ⓘ *Menéndez 1147, piso 2, To61-223841, open Mon-Fri.* The *Turistel Guide* is available from a kiosk belonging to **Café Garogha** at Bories 831.

History

After its foundation in 1848, Punta Arenas became a penal colony modelled on Australia. In 1867, it was opened to foreign settlers and given free port status. From the 1880s, it prospered as a refuelling and provisioning centre for steam ships and whaling vessels. It also became a centre for the new sheep *estancias* since it afforded the best harbour facilities. The city's importance was reduced overnight by the opening of the Panama Canal in 1914. Most of those who came to work in the *estancias* were from Chiloé, and many people in the city have relatives in Chiloé and feel an affinity with the island (the *barrios* on either side of the upper reaches of Independencia are known as Chilote areas); the Chilotes who returned north took Patagonian customs with them, hence the number of *maté* drinkers on Chiloé.

Sights

Around the attractive **Plaza Muñoz Gamero** are a number of mansions that once belonged to the great sheep-ranching families of the late 19th century. A good example is the **Palacio Sara Braun** ⓘ *Tue-Sun, US$1.50*, built between 1894 and 1905 with materials from Europe; the Palacio has several elegantly decorated rooms open to the public and also houses the **Hotel José Nogueira**. In the centre of the plaza is a statue of Magellan with a mermaid and two Fuegian Indians at his feet. According to local wisdom, those who rub or kiss the big toe of one of the Indians will return to Punta Arenas.

Just north of the plaza is the **Museo de Historia Regional Braun Menéndez** ⓘ *Magallanes 949, To61-244216, museoregional1001@chilnet.cl, Mon-Sat 1030-1700, Sun 1030-1400 (summer) or 1100-1300 (winter), US$1.50, children half-price*, the opulent former mansion of Mauricio Braun, built in 1905. A visit is recommended. Part of the museum is set out as a room-by-room regional history; the rest of the house has been left with its original furniture. Guided tours are in Spanish only, but a somewhat confusing information sheet in English is also available. In the basement there is a café. One block further north is the **Teatro Cervantes**, now a cinema with an ornate interior.

Three blocks east of the plaza, the **Museo Naval y Maritimo** ⓘ *Pedro Montt 981, To61-205479, terzona@armarda.cl, Tue-Sun 0930-1230, 1400-1700, US$1*, houses an exhibition of local and national maritime history; sections on naval instruments, cartography, meteorology , as well as shipwrecks. There is a video in Spanish and an information sheet in English.

West of the plaza Muñoz Gamero on Waldo Seguel are two reminders of British influence in the city: the **British School** and **St James's Anglican Church** next door. Nearby on Calle Fagnano is the **Mirador Cerro de La Cruz** offering a view over the city and the Magellan Straits complete with its various shipwrecks.

North of the centre along Bulnes is the excellent **Museo Regional Salesiano Mayorino Borgatello** ⓘ *Colegio Salesiano, Av Bulnes 374, entrance next to church,*

Tue-Sun 1000-1800, hours change frequently, US$2, which covers the history of indigenous peoples, with sections on local animal and bird life and other interesting aspects of life in Patagonia and Tierra del Fuego. Three blocks further on, the **cemetery** ① *Av Bulnes, 0800-1800 daily*, is one of the most interesting places in the city, with cypress avenues, gravestones in many languages, which bear testimony to the cosmopolitan provenance of Patagonian pioneers, and many mausolea and memorials to pioneer families and victims of shipping disasters. Look out for the

Punta Arenas

0 metres 300
0 yards 300

Port Famine (Puerto Hambre)

In 1582, Felipe II of Spain, alarmed by Drake's passage through the Straits of Magellan, decided to establish a Spanish presence on the Straits. A fleet of 15 ships and 4,000 men, commanded by Pedro Sarmiento de Gamboa, was despatched in 1584. Before the ships had left the Bay of Biscay, a storm arose and scattered the fleet, sinking seven ships and killing 800 people. Further depleted by disease, the fleet of three remaining ships at length arrived at the Straits, with just 300 men on board. Led by Sarmiento this small force founded two cities: Nombre de Jesús on Punta Dungeness at the eastern entrance to the Straits and Rey Don Felipe near Puerto Hambre.

Disaster struck when their only remaining vessel broke its anchorage in a storm near Nombre de Jesús; the ship, with Sarmiento on board, was blown into the Atlantic, leaving many of Sarmiento's men stranded on land.

After vain attempts to re-enter the Straits, Sarmiento set sail for Río de Janeiro where he organized two rescue missions: the first ended in shipwreck, the second in mutiny. Captured by English corsairs, Sarmiento was taken to England where he was imprisoned. On his release by Elizabeth I, he tried to return to Spain via France, but was jailed again. Until his death in 1608, Sarmiento besieged Felipe II with letters urging him to rescue the men stranded in the Straits.

When the English corsair Thomas Cavendish sailed through the Straits in 1587 he found only 18 survivors at Rey Don Felipe. With the English and Spanish at war, only one – Tomé Hernández – would trust Cavendish when he first arrived. A sudden spell of fine weather arose, and Cavendish set sail, leaving the rest of the men to die. He named the place Port Famine as a reminder of their grisly fate.

statue of Indicito, the little Indian, on the northwest side, which is now an object of reverence, bedecked with flowers. Further north still, the Instituto de la Patagonia houses the **Museo del Recuerdo** ⓘ *Av Bulnes 1890, Km 4 north (opposite the zona franca), T061-207056, Mon-Fri 0830-1130, 1430-1815, Sat 0830-1300, US$2, children free*, an open-air museum with artefacts used by the early settlers, pioneer homes and botanical gardens.

On 21 de Mayo ,south of Independencia, is Chile's only Hindu temple, while further along the same street, on the southern outskirts of the city, the wooded **Parque María Behety**, features a scale model of Fuerte Bulnes, a campsite and children's playground, popular for Sunday picnics. In winter, there is an ice rink here.

Reserva Forestal Magallanes ⓘ *7 km west of town, administration at CONAF in Punta Arenas, admission US$2*, known locally as the Parque Japonés, extends over 13,500 ha and rises to 600 m. **Viento Sur** (see Activities and tours, below) offers a scheduled transport service to the reserve, but it can also be reached on foot or by bike: follow Independencia up the hill and take a right turning for Río de las Minas, about 3 km from the edge of town; the entrance to the reserve is 2 km beyond. Here you will find a self-guided nature trail through lenga and coigue trees. The road continues through the woods for 14 km passing several picnic sites. From the top end of the road a short path leads to a lookout over the **Garganta del Diablo** (Devil's Throat), a gorge with views over Punta Arenas and Tierra del Fuego. From here a slippery path leads down to the Río de las Minas Valley and then back to Punta Arenas. ▶▶ *For Sleeping, Eating and other listings, see pages 444-449.*

Fuerte Bulnes and south

Fifty-six kilometres south of Punta Arenas, Fuerte Bulnes is a replica of the wooden fort erected in 1843 by the crew of the Chilean vessel *Ancud*. Built in the 1940s and originally designed to house a museum, nearly all the interesting exhibits and artefacts were moved to museums in Punta Arenas and Santiago in 1986 and now only the empty shells of the various buildings remain. Several agencies run tours to Fuerte Bulnes ① *4 hrs, US$14*, but hitching is not difficult at weekends or in summer, as there are many holiday camps in the area.

Nearby is **Puerto Hambre**, where there are ruins of the church built by Sarmiento de Gamboa's colonists in 1584. This is a very beautiful area with views towards the towering ice mountains near Pico Sarmiento; it was of Puerto Hambre that Darwin wrote: "looking due southward... the distant channels between the mountains appeared from their gloominess to lead beyond the confines of this world". Southern dolphins can often be seen in the straits around this point.

At the intersection of the roads to Puerto del Hambre and Fuerte Bulnes, 51 km south of Punta Arenas, is a small monolith marking the **Centro Geográfico de Chile**, the midway point between Arica and the South Pole. Bypassing Fuerte Bulnes, the road continues past a memorial to Captain Pringle Stokes, Captain of the Beagle before Fitz Roy, who committed suicide here in 1829. The road runs out 5 km further on, at San Juan. From here, it is a two-and-half-day hike to **Cape Froward**, the southernmost point of the continent of South America. There is no path, and a guide is essential (travellers have died attempting the trek alone); **Bruce Willett**, T093-602204, has been recommended. ▸▸ *For Sleeping, Eating and other listings, see pages 444-449.*

Reserva Forestal Laguna Parrillar

About 25 km south of Punta Arenas, there is a fork in the road to the right; 27 km further on is the very peaceful Parrillar reserve, covering 18,814 ha and surrounded by snowcapped hills. It has older forest than the Magallanes Reserve and sphagnum bogs, and offers excellent salmon trout fishing. There is a three-hour walk to the tree-line, as well as along poorly marked, boggy paths, and fine views from the Mirador. Camping is forbidden (although possible in the wild in woods outside the Reserve), but there are sites for cooking on gas stoves. Note that there is no public transport to the reserve and hitching is virtually impossible; a radio taxi will cost about US$50.

North of Punta Arenas

Seventy kilometres north of Punta Arenas, Seno Otway is the site of a colony of Magellanic penguins, which can be visited ① *Oct-mid Mar, US$4*. There are beautiful views across the sound to the mountains to the north and rheas and skunks can also be seen. Several agencies offer trips to the colony, lasting five hours (US$14 at peak season); if you wish to visit independently, a taxi from Punta Arenas will cost US$40 return.

A small island, 30 km northeast, Isla Magdalena is the location of the **Monumento Natural Los Pingüinos**, a colony of 150,000 penguins, administered by CONAF. Deserted apart from during the breeding season from November to early February, Magdalena is one of a group of three islands visited by Drake (the others are Marta and Isabel), whose men killed 3,000 penguins for food. Boat trips to the island are run by **Comapa** ① *Tue, Thu, Sat, 0800 (Dec-Feb), 2 hrs each way, with 2 hrs on the island, US$30, subject to cancellation if windy; full refund given.* Tours are also organized by several operators in Punta Arenas.

Beyond, Route 255 heads northeast via Punta Delgada to the **Argentine frontier** at Kimiri Aike and then along Argentine Route 3 to Río Gallegos, an unappealing city. For routes to Calafate in Argentina, see page 463.

Punta Arenas *p439, map p439*
Hotel prices are substantially lower during winter months (Apr/May-Sep). Most hotels include breakfast in the room price. Accommodation is also available in many private houses; ask at tourist office. There are no campsites in or near the city.
LL Finis Terrae, *Colón 766, T061-228200, www.hotelfinisterrae.com* Modern rooms with safe; some rooms are small, also rooftop café/bar, English spoken, parking.
LL José Nogueira, *Bories 959, in former Palacio Sara Braun, T061-248840, www.hotelnogueira.com* Beautiful *loggia*, good food, lovely dining room, parking, great atmosphere. Probably the best hotel in town. Recommended.
L Isla Rey Jorge, *21 de Mayo 1243, T061-248220, www.islareyjorge.com* Modern, pleasant, pub downstairs.
L Tierra del Fuego, *Colón 716, T061-226200, www.patagoniahotels.com* Good breakfast, parking. Some rooms with kitchenette. Recommended. **Café 1900** is downstairs.
AL Apart Hotel Colonizadores, *Colón 1108, T061-244144, F061-226587.* Clean, fully furnished 2-bedroom apartments for 2 to 5 people, discounts for long stay.
AL Hostería Yaganes, *Camino Antiguo Norte Km 7.5, T061-211600, www.pehoe.cl/yaganes.htm* Cabañas on the shores of the Straits of Magellan, nice setting.
AL Plaza, *Nogueira 1116, piso 2, T061-241300, www.chileaustral.com/hplaza* Pleasant, good breakfast.
A Cóndor del Plata, *Colón 556, T061-247987, F061-241149.* Excellent breakfast.
A Mercurio, *Fagnano 595, T061-242300, mercurio@chileaustral.com* TV and phone, good restaurant and service. Recommended.
A Savoy, *Menéndez 1073, T061-241951, www.hotelsavoy.cl* Pleasant rooms but some lack windows, good place to eat.
A-B Hostal Carpa Manzano, *Lautaro Navarro 336, T061-242296, F061-248864.* Clean, quiet, recommended, but not the most central option.
A-B Hostal de la Avenida, *Colón 534, T061-247532.* Good breakfast, friendly, safe. Recommended.
B Hostal Rubio, *España 640, T061-226458, www.chileaustral.com/hostalrubio* With

bath, parking, laundry facilities, helpful.
B Oro Fueguino, *Fagnano 356, T061-249401, www.orofueguino.cl* Recently refurbished, TV and phone, recommended.
B Ritz, *Pedro Montt 1102, T061-224422.* Old, clean and cosy. Recommended (Bruce Chatwin stayed here: check out his name in the guest book).
B-C Hostal Calafate I, *Lautaro Navarro 850, T061-248415, calafate@entelchile.net* Rooms with TV, cheaper without bath, internet access, clean. **Calafate II**, *Magallanes 926, T061-241281, www.calafate.cl* is the same price but more impersonal.
B-C Hostal Del Estrecho, *Menéndez 1048, T061-241011, www.chileanpatagonia.com/estrecho* With large breakfast and bath (cheaper without), central heating, cable TV.
B-D Monte Carlo, *Colón 605, T061-222120, www.h-montecarlo.com* Traditional, charming, slightly run down, good food. Cheaper rooms without bath.
C Hostal de la Patagonia, *O'Higgins 730, T061-249970, www.ecotourpatagonia.com* Cheaper rooms without bath.
C Hostal del Sur, *Mejicana 151, T061-227249, F061-222282.* Large rooms and excellent breakfast. Recommended.
C Hostal Sonia Kuscevic, *Pasaje Darwin 175 (off Angamos 500 block), T061-248543, www.hostalsk.50megs.com* Price per person, with bath, breakfast, kitchen facilities, hot water, heating, parking. Popular, Hostelling International discounts.
C-D Dinka's House, *Caupolicán 169, T061-226056, fueguino@entelchile.net* With breakfast, use of kitchen, noisy.
C-D Hostal Paradiso, *Angamos 1073, T061-224212.* Rooms with or without bath, breakfast, parking, use of kitchen. Recommended.
C-D Res Central 1, *España 247, T061-222315, r.central@ctcinternet.cl.* Comfortable rooms with or without bath. Also at *Sanhueza 185, T061-222845.*
C-F Hostal El Bosque, *O'Higgins 424, T061-221764, elbosque@patagonia.com* Breakfast included, use of kitchen, laundry facilities; dorm beds available.
D Hostal O'Higgins, *O'Higgins 1205, T061-227999.* With breakfast, very clean.
D-F Lodging, *Sanhueza 933, T061-221035.* With or without bath, clean, heating, modern. Price per person.

E **Hostal Al Fin del Mundo**, *O'Higgins 1026, T061-710185*. Price per person with breakfast, spacious, central, helpful, laundry facilities, internet, English spoken, recommended.

E-F **The Pink House**, *Caupolicán 99, T061-222436, www.chileanpatagonia.com/pinkhouse* Clean rooms with or without bath, breakfast included.

F **Alojamiento Prat**, *Sgto Aldea 0520*. Price per person. Clean, not central. Recommended.

F **Hosp Nena**, *Boliviana 366, T061-242411*. Price per person, with large breakfast. Friendly.

F **Res Centenario**, *Plaza Centenario 105, T061-225710*. Price per person, with breakfast.

F **Res Roca**, *Magallanes 888, T061-243903*. Price per person. Without bath, clean.

F-G **Alojamiento Golondrina**, *Lautaro Navarro 182, T061-229709*. Price per person. Kitchen facilities, meals served, friendly, English spoken, hot water, internet access, good large breakfast. Recommended.

G **Backpackers Paradise**, *Carrera Pinto 1022, T061-246325, backpackersparadise@hotmail.com* Price per person. Dormitories, cooking facilities, limited bathroom facilities, good meeting place, luggage store, internet access. Recommended.

G **Hosp Costanera**, *Correa 1221, T061-240175*. Price per person. Kitchen facilities, large breakfast, friendly, clean.

G **Hosp Huala**, *Maipú 851, T061-244244*. Price per person. Kitchen facilities, laundry, book exchange.

G **Hosp Miramar**, *Almte Senoret 1190, T061-215446*. Price per person. Friendly staff, good views over the bay.

G **Lodging Manuel**, *O'Higgins 648, T061-220567, turmanmi@entelchile.net* Price per person, without breakfast, mostly dormitories, helpful service.

G **Res Independencia**, *Independencia 374, T061-227572, www.chileaustral.com/independencia* Price per person, with breakfast, kitchen facilities, laundry service, and camping.

G **Sra Carlina Ramírez**, *Paraguaya 150, T061-247687*. Motorcycle parking, meals, safe, quiet. Recommended. Price per person.

Very cheap dormitory accommodation may also be available at the **Salvation Army Hostel**, *Bellavista 577*.

● Eating

Punta Arenas *p439, map p441*
Visitors to Punta Arenas and the surrounding region should be especially wary of eating shellfish. In recent years, the nearby waters have been affected by a *marea roja* (red tide) of poisonous algae. While the *marea roja* only affects bivalve shellfish, infected molluscs can kill humans almost instantly. Mussels should not be picked along the shore of Punta Arenas; foreigners who have done this have died. However, all shellfish sold in restaurants have been inspected and so are theoretically safe.

Lobster has become more expensive and there are seasonal bans on *centolla* (king crab) fishing to protect dwindling stocks; do not purchase *centolla* out of season. *Centolla* fishing is banned at other times, too, if the crabs become infected with a disease that is fatal to humans.

$$$-$$ The hotels **Tierra del Fuego** and **José Nogueira** each have excellent restaurants (see Sleeping above).

$$$-$$ **Sotitos**, *O'Higgins 1138*. Good service and excellent cuisine. Elegant, expensive. Recommended.

$$ **Centro Español**, *Plaza Muñoz Gamero 771, above Teatro Cervantes*. Large helpings, limited selection, quite expensive.

$$ **El Estribo**, *Carrera Pinto 762*. Specializes in local and exotic dishes, such as guanaco.

$$ **El Mercado**, *Mejicana 617*. Open 24 hrs, reasonable set lunch, expensive à la carte.

$$ **El Mesón del Calvo**, *Jorge Montt 687*. Excellent, seafood, lamb, small portions, pricey. Recommended.

$$ **Golden Dragon**, *Señoret 908*. Chinese.

$$ **La Luna**, *O'Higgins 974*. Fish and shellfish including local specialities, good.

$$ **Las Asturias**, *Navarro 967*. Basque seafood specialities, good food and atmosphere, recommended .

$$ **Quick Lunch Patagónico**, *Armando Sanhueza 1198, Esquina Errazuriz*. Vegetarian, Mexican and Chinese food.

$$ **Remezón**, *21 de Mayo 1469, T061-220511*. Regional specialities.

$$ **Santino**, *Colón 657, T061-220511*. Good pizzas, large bar, good service.

$$ **Yaganes**, *Camino Antiguo Norte Km 7.5*. Beautiful setting, weekend buffet.

$ **Calypso**, *Bories 817*. Open Sun evening, busy at night, smoky, cheap.

$ **Carioca**, *Menéndez 600 y Chiloé*. Cheap lunches, snacks and beer, good service.

$ **Cocinerías**, *Lautaro Navarro, south of the port entrance*. Stalls serving cheap fish meals.

$ **Dino's Pizza**, *Bories 557*. Good pizzas, huge sandwiches. For something different, try their rhubarb juice. Recommended.

$ **El Quijote**, *Lautaro Navarro 1087*. Good sandwiches and fish dishes. Recommended.

$ **La Casa de Juan**, *O'Higgins 1021*. Spanish.

$ **La Terraza**, *21 de Mayo 1288*. Sandwiches, *empanadas* and beer, cheap and good.

$ **Lomit's**, *Menéndez 722*. Cheap snacks and drinks, open when the others are closed, popular with tourists.

$ **Los Años 60 The Mitchel**, *Chiloé 1231*. One of several along this strip serving economic set lunches.

$ **Lucerna**, *Bories 624*. Excellent meat, reasonably priced, good.

$ **Restaurant de Turismo Punta Arenas**, *Chiloé 1280*. Good, friendly. Recommended. Also serves beer and 26 varieties of sandwiches, open 24 hrs.

$ **Sabores de Chiloé**, *Chiloé esq Balmaceda*. Chilote food as the name implies.

Cafés and snack bars

Café 1900, *Hotel Tierra del Fuego, Colón 716*. See Sleeping above.

Casa del Pastel, *Carrera Pinto y O'Higgins*. Very good pastries.

Kiosco Roca, *(no sign), Roca 875*. Early morning coffee.

La Espiga, *Errázuriz 632*. Bread, pastries and snacks.

Pancal, *21 de Mayo 1280*. Excellent *empanadas*, bread and pastries.

🔊 Bars and clubs

Punta Arenas *p439, map p441*
Note that anywhere that calls itself a 'nightclub' is in fact a brothel.

Bar Lunaticos, *21 de Mayo 1262*. Bit of a dive.

Cuervo, *José Menéndez 756*. Disco.

Drive-In Los Brujos, *Km 7.5, T061-212600*. Large disco north of the city.

Kamikaze, *Bories 655*. Disco.

La Taberna del Club de la Unión, *Plaza Muñoz Gamero y Seguel*. For drinks, more upmarket.

Makanudo, *Ovejero 474*. Bar that's popular with locals.

Olijoe, *Errazuriz 970*. Reasonably plush British-style pub, leather interior, recommended.

Pub 1900, *Av Colón esq. Bories*. Friendly, relaxed atmosphere.

⊛ Festivals and events

Punta Arenas *p439, map p441*
Carnaval de invierno The winter solstice is marked by a carnival on the weekend closest to **21st Jun**.

O Shopping

Punta Arenas *p439, map p441*
Zona Franca, *3½ km north of the centre, on the right-hand side of the road to the airport, take bus E or A from Plaza Muñoz Gamero or a colectivo*. Punta Arenas has certain free-port facilities. Cheap electrical goods are especially worth seeking out, as is camping equipment. The quality of most other goods is low and the prices little better than elsewhere. Open Mon-Sat 1000-1230, 1500-2000.

Cameras

The Zona Franca has a wide range of cameras but a limited range of film, instead try: **Foto Sánchez**, *Bories 768*, for Fuji film and **Fotocentro**, *Bories 789*, for Agfa: all have same-day print-processing service.

Handicrafts and local products

Punta Arenas is famous for the quality of its chocolate. Delicious handmade chocolate is for sale at several shops on Calle Bories.

Artesanía Ramas, *Independencia 799*. Handicrafts.

Casa Diaz, *Bories 712/546*. Handicrafts.

Chile Típico, *Carrera Pinto 1015*. Chilean souvenirs at good prices; also available from outdoor stalls at the bottom of Independencia, by the port entrance.

Patagonia Gourmet, *Mejicana 608*. Local marmalades and other specialities.

Pingüi, *Bories 404*. Crafts and books on Tierra del Fuego, Patagonia and Antarctica.

The Wool House Patagonia, *Fagnano 675, by the plaza*. Good quality, reasonably priced woollen clothes.

Supermarkets

Abu Gosch, *between Magallanes and Bories north of Carrera Pinto.*

Cofrima, *Lautaro Navarro 1293 y Balmaceda.*

Cofrima 2, *España 01375.*

Listo, *21 de Mayo 1133.*

Marisol, *Zenteno 0164.*

Super Norte, *Salvador Allende y Chorillos.*

▲ Activities and tours

Punta Arenas *p439, map p441*

Golf

There's a 9-hole golf course 5 km south of town on the road to Fuerte Bulnes.

Skiing

Cerro Mirador, 9 km west of Punta Arenas in the Reserva Nacional Magallanes, is one of the few places in the world where you can ski with a sea view. Season Jun to Sep, weather permitting. Daily lift-ticket, US$7; equipment rental, US$6 per adult. There's a mid-way lodge with food, drink and equipment. For crosscountry skiing facilities, contact the **Club Andino**, *T061-241479, www.clubandino.tierra.cl* There's also a good 2-hr hike here in summer, the trail is clearly marked and flora is labelled. **Transtur** buses to the ski resort depart 0900 and 1400 from in front of Hotel Cabo de Hornos, US$3 return, taxi US$6.

Skiing is also available at **Tres Morros**.

Tour operators

Most organize tours to Torres del Paine, Fuerte Bulnes and *pingüineras* on Otway sound. Several also offer bespoke tours: shop around as prices vary. Specify in advance if you want a tour in English.

Arka Patagonia, *Magallanes 345, T061-248167, www.arkaoperadora.com* All types of tours, rafting, fishing, etc.

El Conquistador, *Menéndez 556, T061-222896.* Recommended.

Sandy Point, *Pedro Montt 840, T061-222241.* Offer transport to Seno Otway and Fuerte Bulnes with or without guide. Also has airport shuttlebuses that will pick you up from your lodgings, US$3.

Turismo Aonikenk, *Magallanes 619, T061-228332, www.aonikenk.com* Expensive but very good bespoke excursions. Recommended.

Turismo Aventour, *Nogueira 1255, T061-241197, aventour@entelchile.net* English spoken, specialize in fishing trips, also organize tours to Tierra del Fuego.

Turismo Comapa, *Magallanes 990, T061-200200, www.comapa.com.* Tours to Torres del Paine, Tierra del Fuego and Isla Magdalena, also agents for trips to the Falklands/Malvinas, Ushuaia and Cape Horn.

Turismo Nueva Galicia, *Sarmiento 845, T061-220409, www.nuevagalicia.com* Organizes boat trips from Puerto Natales to PN Bernardo O'Higgins (see p450).

Turismo Pehoé, *Menéndez 918, T061-244506, www.pehoe.com* Organizes tours and hotels; enquire here about catamaran services.

Turismo Viento Sur, *Fagnano 565, T061-226930, www.vientosur.com* For camping equipment, fishing excursions, sea kayaking, cycle hire, English spoken, good tours, recommended.

⊖ Transport

Punta Arenas *p439, map p441*

All transport is heavily booked from late Dec through to Mar; advance booking is advised.

Air

Flights to Punta Arenas arrive at **Carlos Ibáñez del Campo Airport**, 20 km north of town. The airport restaurant is good.

National To **Balmaceda** (for Coyhaique), with **LanChile** (LanExpress), Sat, US$80, or daily via Puerto Montt (more expensive). To **Puerto Montt**, with **LanChile** (LanExpress), 3-6 daily, US$150 one way; it's sometimes cheaper to buy a return ticket. To **Santiago**, LanChile (LanExpress), several daily, US$160 return, via Puerto Montt (sit on the right for views). When no tickets are available, go to the airport and get on the standby waiting list. To **Porvenir**, Aerovías DAP, 2 daily Mon-Sat, US$26 one way, plus other irregular flights, with Twin-Otter and Cessna aircraft. To **Puerto Williams**, Aerovías DAP, daily in summer, US$70 one way. There are approximately 2 military flights per month to **Puerto Montt**, US$30, information and tickets from airforce base at the airport, Spanish essential, *T061-213559*; need to book well in advance. It is very difficult to get space during the summer as armed forces personnel and their families have priority over civilians.

International To **Ushuaia** (Argentina), Aerovías DAP, twice weekly in summer, 1 hr, US$110 one way; reserve well in advance from mid-Dec to Feb. To **Falkland Islands/Islas Malvinas**, LanChile, Sat, US$500 return. International Tours & Travel, *T+500-22041, jf.itt@horizon.co.fk*, serve as LanChile agents on the Falkland Islands.

Bus

Buses depart from the company offices as follows: Bus Sur, *Menéndez 565 T061-227145*; Buses Transfer, *Menéndez 631, T061-220766*; Cruz del Sur, Pingüino and Fernández, *Sanhueza 745, T061-242313, www.busesfernandez.com*; Gesell, *Menéndez 556, T061-222896*; Ghisoni, *Lautaro Navarro 971, T061-222078, www.ghisoni.terra.cl*; Los Carlos, *Plaza Muñoz Gamero 1039, T061-241321*; Pacheco, *Colón 900, T061-242174*; Turbus, *Errázuriz 932, T061-225315*.

Services and frequencies change every year, so check on arrival at the helpful Sernatur office. Timetables are also printed daily in *El Austral*. The services detailed below are for high season only.

Fernández, Transfer (cheapest), Buses Pacheco and Buses Sur, all run several services each day to **Puerto Natales**, 3 hrs, last departure 2000, US$4 one way, US$7.50 return (although this means you have to return with the same company). Buses will pick up at the airport with advance notice.

To **Coyhaique**, 20 hrs, Buses Sur, 1 per week via Argentina, US$45, meals not included. Cruz del Sur, Queilen Bus and Pacheco have services through Argentina to **Osorno**, **Puerto Montt** and **Castro**, several weekly, 36 hrs to Castro, US$50.

To **Argentina** To **Río Gallegos**, Pingüino, departs 1245 daily, returns 1300; Ghisoni, 4 weekly, departs 1100; Pacheco, 5 weekly, departs 1130. All cost US$14 and take about 5 hrs. For services to **Buenos Aires** it is cheaper to go to Río Gallegos and buy an onward ticket from there. Pacheco and Ghisoni have buses most days to **Río Grande** via Punta Delgada, 8hrs, US$18, heavily booked. To **Ushuaia** via Punta Delgada, 12-14 hrs, book any return at same time, Tecni Austral, Tue, Thu, Sat, Sun 0800

from Ghisoni office, US$28; **Pacheco**, Mon, Wed, Fri 0715, US$42.

Ferry

All tickets on ships must be booked in advance for Jan and Feb. Visits to the beautiful fjords and glaciers of **Tierra del Fuego** are highly recommended. Comapa runs a fortnightly 22-hr, 320-km round trip to the 30-km fjord d'Agostino, where many glaciers descend to the sea. The luxury cruiser, *Terra Australis*, sails from Punta Arenas on Sat via Ushuaia and Puerto Williams; details from Comapa; advance bookings (advisable) from **Cruceros Australis SA**, *Miraflores 178, piso 12, Santiago, T02-6963211, www.australis.com* For services to **Porvenir**, Tierra del Fuego, see page 481.

Government supply ships are recommended for the young and hardy, but take a sleeping bag, extra food and travel pills. For transport on navy supply ships to **Puerto Williams** and **Cape Horn**, enquire at Tercera Zona Naval, *Lautaro Navarro 1150*, but be prepared to be frustrated by irregular sailings (about 1 every 3 months) and inaccurate information. During the voyage across the Drake Passage, albatrosses, petrels, cormorants, penguins, elephant seals, fur seals, whales and dolphins can all be sighted.

Most cruise ships to **Antarctica** leave from Ushuaia (Argentina). Other than asking in agencies for possible empty berths on the few cruise ships that call in at Punta Arenas, the only possibility is to ask at the Chilean navy (Tercera Zona Naval, see above). A letter of recommendation will probably be necessary; Spanish is essential. The two naval vessels, the *Galvarino* and the *Lautaro*, charge US$80 per person per day. There is no accurate schedule; it may help to go to the port and try to talk to the Captain. Accommodation includes 4 meals a day (2 with meat), laundry facilities. Take twice as much film as you think you'll need.

Taxis

Ordinary taxis have yellow roofs. Reliable service is available from **Radio Taxi Austral**, *T061-247710/244409*. Colectivos (all black) run on fixed routes within the city, US$0.50 for anywhere on the route.

Punta Arenas *p439, map p441*

Airline offices Aerovías DAP, *O'Higgins 891, T061-223340, www.aeroviasdap.cl,* open 0900-1230, 1430-1930; LanChile, *Lautaro Navarro 999, T061-241232, www.lanchile.cl* **Banks** Several on or around Plaza Muñoz Gamero many 24 hrs, all have ATMs. Banks open Mon-Fri 0830-1400, casas de cambio open Mon-Fri 0900-1230, 1500-1900, Sat 0900-1230; outside business hours, try Buses Sur (see above), or the major hotels (lower rates); Argentine pesos can be bought at casas de cambio; good rates at Cambio Gasic, *Roca 915, Of 8, T061-242396.* German spoken; La Hermandad, *Lautaro Navarro 1099, T061-243991,* excellent rates, US$ cash for AmEx TCs and credit cards; Scott Cambios, *Colón y Magallanes, T061-227145;* Sur Cambios, *Lautaro Navarro 1001, T061-225656,* accepts TCs. **Car hire** Bargain if you want to hire a car for several days. Autómovil Club, *O'Higgins 931, T061-243675, F061-243097,* and at airport; Budget, *O'Higgins 964, T061-241696;* Hertz, *O'Higgins 987, T061-229049, F061-244729,* English spoken; also at airport *T061-210096;* Internacional, *Seguel 443* and at airport, *T061-228323, F061-226334,* recommended; Lotus Rentacar, *Mejicana 694, T061-241697, F061-241697;* Lubac, *Magallanes 970, T/F061-242023;* Magallanes Rent a Car, *O'Higgins 949, T/F061-221601;* Paine Rent a Car, *Menéndez 631, T/F061-240852,* try bargaining, friendly; Todoauto, *España 0480, T061-212492, F061-212627;* Willemsen, *Lautaro Navarro 1038, T061-247787, F061-241083,* recommended. **Car mechanic** Automotriz Hoopers, *Boliviana y Chiloé, T061-241239;* Centro automotriz Crisostomo, *Independencia 377, T061-243731.* **Consulates** Argentina, *21 de Mayo 1878, T061-261912,* open weekdays 1000-1530, visas take 24 hrs; Brazil, *Arauco 769, T061-241093;* Belgium, *Roca 817, Oficina 61, T061-241472;* Germany, *Pasaje Korner 1046, T061-241082, Casilla 229;*

Italy, *21 de Mayo 1569, T061-221596;* Netherlands, *Magallanes 435, T061-248100;* Norway, *Magallanes 990, T061-20200;* Spain, *Menéndez 910, T061-243566;* Paraguay, *Bulnes 0928 Dp14 p1, T061-211825;* Sweden, *Errazúriz 891, T061-224107;* United Kingdom, *Catarates de Niaguara 01325, T061-211535,* helpful, with information on Falkland Islands; Uruguay, *José Nogueira 1238, T061-241594.* **Cycle parts** José Aguila Quezada, *Arauco 2675, T061-265399.* **Dentists** Dr Hugo Vera Cárcamo, *España 1518, T061-227510,* recommended; Rosemary Robertson Stipicic, *21 de Mayo 1380, T061-22931,* speaks English. **Hospitals** Hospital Regional Lautaro Navarro, *Angamos 180, T061-244040,* public hospital, for emergency room ask for 'la posta'; Clínica Magallanes, *Bulnes 01448, T061-211527,* private clinic, medical staff the same as in the hospital but fancier surroundings and more expensive; minimum charge US$45 per visit. A list of English-speaking doctors is available from Sernatur. **Internet** Lots of places offer access, including at *Magallanes y Menendez,* and below Hostal Calafate on *Magallanes,* ½ *block north of Plaza.* Prices are generally US$1 per hour. **Laundry** Lavaseco Josseau, *Carrera Pinto 766;* Lavasol, *O'Higgins 969,* the only self-service laundry, Mon-Sat 0900-2030, Sun (summer only) 1000-1800, US$6 per machine, wash and dry, good but busy. **Motorcycle parts** Violic, *Sanhueza 285, T061-241606,* also in the Zona Franca. **Post office** *Bories 911 y Menéndez,* Mon-Fri 0830-1930, Sat 0900-1400.

Shipping offices Comapa (Compañía Marítima de Punta Arenas), *Magallanes 990, T061-200200;* Navimag, *Magallanes 990, T061-244400, www.navimag.cl*

Telephone There are several call centres in the city centre (shop around as prices vary).

For an explanation of sleeping and eating price codes used in this guide, see inside the front cover. Other relevant information is found in Essentials, see pages 51-58.

Puerto Natales and around

→ *Phone code: 061. Colour map 6, B3. Population 20,000.*

From Punta Arenas a good paved road runs 247 km north to Puerto Natales through forests of southern beech and prime pastureland; this is the best area for cattle-raising in Chile. Ñandúes and guanacos can be seen en route. Puerto Natales lies between Cerro Dorotea (which rises behind the town) and the eastern shore of the Seno Ultima Esperanza (Last Hope Sound), over which there are fine views, weather permitting, to the Peninsula Antonio Varas. Founded in 1911, the town grew as an industrial centre and, until recent years, the town's prosperity was based upon employment in the coal mines of Río Turbio, Argentina. Today, Puerto Natales is the starting point for trips to the magnificent Balmaceda and Torres del Paine national parks, and tourism is one of its most important industries; the town centre has a prosperous if somewhat touristy atmosphere.

Ins and outs

Getting there Puerto Natales is easily reached by many daily buses from Punta Arenas, as well as by six daily buses from Río Turbio (Argentina), one or two of which begin in El Calafate. There are also two buses weekly from Río Gallegos. The town is the terminus of the *Magallanes* ship to Puerto Montt (for further details see page 454). If driving between Punta Arenas and Puerto Natales make sure you have enough fuel. **Getting around** Puerto Natales is not a large place and taxis are only needed for journeys out of town. **Tourist office** There is a kiosk on the waterfront ① *Av Pedro Montt y Phillipi, T061-412125*; information is also available from the **Municipalidad** ① *Bulnes 285, T061-411263*, and from **CONAF**, *O'Higgins 584*.

Sights

The colourful old steam train in the main square was once used to take workers to the the biggest meatpacking factory in Patagonia at **Puerto Bories**, 6 km north of town; though much of the old plant was destroyed by fire, the English-style administration buildings and housing can be visited.

The slab-like **Cerro Dorotea** dominates the town, with superb views of the whole Seno Ultima Esperanza. It can be reached on foot or by any Río Turbio bus (recommended, as the hill is farther off than it seems). **Monumento Nacional Cueva Milodón** ① *25 km north, US$4, Buses JB US$5, taxi US$18 return* is the end point of Bruce Chatwin's travelogue *In Patagonia* (see page 554). The cave, a massive 70 m wide, 220 m deep and 30 m high, contains a plastic model of the prehistoric ground-sloth whose remains were found there in 1895. The remains are now in London, although there is some talk of returning them to the site. Evidence has also been found here of occupation by Patagonians some 11,000 years ago. Nearby, there is a visitors' centre, with summaries in English. Most tours to Torres del Paine stop at the cave.

On the Peninsula Antonio Varas, on the western side of the Seno Ultima Esperanza, **Estancia Rosario** ① *T061-411273, estancia_rosario@hotmail.com, US$30 for a full day including transport across the sound*, offers lunches, horseriding and other activities. Book in advance. ▸▸ *For Sleeping, Eating and other listings, see pages 451-455.*

Parque Nacional Bernardo O'Higgins → *Colour map 6, B2.*

Often referred to as the **Parque Nacional Monte Balmaceda**, this park covers much of the Campo de Hielo Sur, plus the fjords and offshore islands further west. A three-hour boat trip from Puerto Natales up the Seno de Ultima Esperanza takes you to the southernmost section, passing the Balmaceda Glacier, which drops from the eastern slopes of **Monte Balmaceda** (2,035 m). The glacier is retreating; in 1986 its where it is a 1-km walk to the base of the Serrano Glacier on the north slope of Monte Balmaceda. On the trip, dolphins, sea-lions (in season), black-necked swans, flightless steamer ducks and cormorants can be seen. Take warm clothes, including a hat and gloves.

There is a route from Puerto Toro along the Río Serrano for 35 km to the Torres del Paine administration centre (see page 458); guided tours are available. It is also possible to travel to the Paine administration centre by boat or zodiac ① *4 hrs, US$60*; details from **Casa Cecilia** in Puerto Natales (see Sleeping below), or from Onas tour operator; advanced booking essential.

● Sleeping

Puerto Natales *p450, map p452*
Most prices include breakfast. Hotels in the countryside are open only in the summer months; specific dates vary. In season, cheaper accommodation fills up quickly after the arrival of the *Magallanes* from Puerto Montt.
LL-AL Costaustralis, *Pedro Montt 262, T061-412000, www.australis.com/ costaustralis* Modern, comfortable, good views, popular cafeteria. Recommended.
L Juan Ladrilleros, *Pedro Montt 161, T061-411652, F412109, aventour@entelchile.net* Modern and clean, with restaurant.
L Martín Guisinde, *Bories 278, T061-412770, www.austrohoteles.cl* Pub, restaurant, modern. Recommended.
AL Glaciares, *Eberhard 104, T061-411208, F411209, glaciares@entelchile.net* New hotel with snack bar.
AL Hostal Lady Florence Dixie, *Bulnes 659, T061-411158, F411943.* Modern, friendly. Recommended.
AL Saltos del Paine, *Bulnes 156, T061-413608.* Excellent.
AL-A Aquaterra, *Bulnes 299, T061-412239/ 09-4499075, www.aquaterrapatagonia.cl* New hotel, with restaurant and alternative therapy centre.
AL-A Hostal Sir Francis Drake, *Phillipi 383, T061-411553.* Good views, quiet, snack bar. Recommended.
B Lago Sarmiento, *Bulnes 90, T061-411542, www.hotellagosarmiento.galeon.com* Good value, good views, restaurant, parking.
C Blanquita, *Carrera Pinto 409.* Quiet, with bath, heating and breakfast, friendly. Recommended.
C Hostal Rey Mar, *Baquedano 414, T061-413610.* With breakfast, good restaurant.

C Natalino, *Eberhard 371, T061-411968.* Clean and very friendly (tours to Milodón Cave arranged), parking.
C-D Res Oasis, *Señoret 332, F411675, resoasis@hotmail.com* Comfortable rooms, with or without bath, cable TV.
C-F Casa Cecilia, *Tomás Rogers 60, T061-411797, redcecilia@entelchile.net* With breakfast, clean, cooking facilities, English, French and German spoken, heating, luggage store, camping equipment rental, information on Torres del Paine, tours organized, bus tickets sold, credit cards accepted. Price per person with or without bath. Warmly recommended.
C-F Concepto Indigo, *Ladrilleros 105, T061-413609, www.conceptoindigo.com* Rooms and dormitory accommodation (price per person), lovely views, rock climbing courses and tours, good meeting place, slide shows, good pizzeria and vegetarian restaurant plus bar. Internet access. Recommended.
E-G La Casona, *Bulnes 280, T061-412562.* Price per person. Dormitories and double rooms. Clean, hot showers, heated lounge, including breakfast, helpful, good.
F Hosp Laury, *Bulnes 222.* Price per person. With breakfast, cooking and laundry facilities, clean, warm, friendly.
F Patagonia Adventure, *Tomás Rogers 179 on Plaza, T061-411028, patagonia_adventure@ terra.cl* Price per person. Dormitory style and private rooms, friendly, clean, use of kitchen, breakfast, English spoken, camping equipment for hire, luggage store, book exchange.
F Res Centro, *Magallanes 258, T061-411996.* Price per person, with bath.
F Res Gabriela, *Bulnes 317, T061-411061.* Price per person. Clean, good breakfast, helpful, luggage store. Recommended.
F Res La Florida, *O'Higgins 431, T061-411361.* Price per person. Luggage store, laundry facilities.

F-G Bulnes, *Bulnes 407, T061-411307*. Price per person, with breakfast, good, laundry facilities, luggage store.

F-G Res Niko's, *Ramirez 669, T061-412810*. Price per person, with breakfast, good meals, also dormitory accommodation, recommended.

F Res Niko's II, *Phillipi 528, T061-411500, residencialnicosii@hotmail.com* Price per person, with breakfast. More expensive rooms with bath and cable TV, English spoken, tours.

F-G Res Carahue, *Bulnes 370, T061-411339*. Price per person, with breakfast, laundry facilities, pleasant.

F-G Res El Mundial, *Bories 315, T061-412476*. Price per person, with or without bath. Use of kitchen, good-value meals, luggage stored. Recommended.

G Casa Teresa, *Esmeralda 463, T061-410472*. Price per person. Good value, warm, cheap meals, quiet, friendly. Tours to Torres del Paine arranged. Recommended.

G El Refugio, *O'Higgins 456, T061-414881*. Price per person. Youthful and lively place to stay. Offers tours. Internet access.

G Hosp Chila, *Carrera Pinto 442, T061-412328*. Price per person. Use of kitchen, welcoming, laundry facilities, luggage store, bakes bread. Recommended.

G Hosp Nancy, *Bulnes 343*. Price per person. Cooking facilities, internet access, helpful, tours and information.

G Los Inmigrantes, *Carrera Pinto 480, T061-413482*. Price per person. Good breakfast, clean, kitchen facilities, equipment rental, luggage store. Recommended.

Puerto Natales

G **Res Asturias**, *Prat 426, T061-412105*. Price per person, with breakfast, kitchen facilities, cosy.
G **Res Dickson**, *Bulnes 307, T061-411871*. Price per person. Good breakfast, clean, helpful, cooking and laundry facilities. Recommended.
G **Res Lago Pingo**, *Bulnes 808, T061-411026*. Price per person. Basic, with breakfast, laundry, use of kitchen, luggage stored, English spoken; similar at *O'Higgins 70, 431* and *Perito 443*.
G **Res Ritz**, *Carrera Pinto 439, T061-412196*. Price per person. Full board available, friendly.
G **Res Sutherland**, *Barros Arana 155, T061-410359*. Price per person. With bath, welcoming, clean, kitchen facilities.
G **Tierra del Fuego**, *Bulnes 23, T061-412138*. Price per person. Clean, parking, will store luggage, good.

Around Puerto Natales *p450*
Along the road from Punta Arenas are several hotels, including:
L **Hostal Río Penitente**, *Km 138, T061-331694*. In an old *estancia*. Recommended.
A **Hostería Río Verde**, *Km 90, east off the highway on Seno Skyring, T061-311122, F241008*. Private bath, heating. Recommended.
B **Hostería Llanuras de Diana**, *Km 215 (30 km south of Puerto Natales), T061-410661*. Hidden from road, beautifully situated. Recommended.
C **Hotel Rubens**, *Km 183, T061-226916*. Popular for fishing.

Options to the north of town include
L-AL **Cisne de Cuello Negro**, *6 km from town, Km 275 near Puerto Bories, for bookings contact: Av Colón 782, Punta Arenas, T061-244506, pehoe1@ctcinternet.cl* Clean, reasonable, excellent cooking. Recommended.
AL-A **Hotel 3 Pasos**, *40 km north, T061-225167*. Simple and beautiful.
A **Cabañas Koten Aike**, *2 km north of town, T061-412581, F225935*. Sleeps 4, modern, very comfortable, great location.

Camping
There is free camping at **Monumento Nacional Cueva Milodón** once the US$4 entrance fee has been paid.

PN Bernado O'Higgins *p450*
Although the park is uninhabited, guest accommodation is available at
L **Hostería Monte Balmaceda,** *T061-220174*.

🍴 Eating

Puerto Natales *p450, map p452*
$$$ **Centro Español**, *Magallanes 247*. Good service, reasonable.
$$ **El Asador Patagonico**, *Prat 158 on Plaza*. Specializes in spit-roast lamb. Recommended.
$$ **El Marítimo**, *Pedro Montt 214*. Seafood and salmon, good views, popular. Recommended.
$$ **El Rincón de Don Chicho**, *Luiz Cruz Martinez 206*. All-you-can-eat *parillada*. Vegetarian options on request. Recommended.
$$ **La Ultima Esperanza**, *Eberhard 354*. Recommended for salmon, seafood, enormous portions, not cheap but worth the experience.
$ **Andrés**, *Ladrilleros 381*. Excellent, good fish dishes, good service.
$ **Club Deportivo Natales**, *Eberhard 332*. Very cheap, decent meals
$ **Cristal**, *Bulnes 439*. Tasty sandwiches and salmon, good value.
$ **Don Alvarito**, *Blanco Encalada 915*. Hospitable.
$ **La Caleta Economica**, *Eberhard 261, T061-413969*. Excellent seafood, also meat and chicken dishes, good value for money.
$ **La Frontera**, *Bulnes 819*. Good value.
$ **La Oveja Negra**, *Tomas Rogers 169, on Plaza*. Typical Chilean dishes, good, book swap.
$ **La Repizza**, *Blanco Encalada 294*. Good value.
$ **Mari Loli**, *Baquedano 615*. Excellent food.
$ **Tierra del Fuego**, *Bulnes 29*. Cheap, good.

Cafés
Aquaterra, *Bulnes 299*. Cosy, good, also a shiatsu and reiki centre.
El Living, *on Plaza*. Cosy, British run, with English newspapers and magazines. Wide variety of cakes, good tea and coffee, wine and vegetarian food. Book exchange.

🎵 Bars and clubs

Puerto Natales *p450, map p452*
There are a couple of discos on Blanco Encalada.
El Bar de Ruperto, *Bulnes 371*. Good, English-run pub with cheap internet access, games and live music at weekends.
Kaweshkar, *Bulnes 43*. Relaxed bar, food served.
La Esquina, *Magallanes y Eberhard*. Good bar.

Puerto Natales *p450, map p452*
Camping equipment
Balfer, *Bulnes y Pedro Montt*. Camping gear and fishing tackle, but more expensive than the Zona Franca in Punta Arenas. Camping gas is available in hardware stores, eg at Baquedano y O'Higgins and at Baquedano y Esmeralda. For equipment rental, see Directory, below.

Food
Food prices are variable so shop around, although everything tends to be more expensive than in Punta Arenas. There's a 24-hr supermarket on the Bulnes 300 block, and at Bulnes 1085. The town markets are also good.

Handicrafts
Ñandu, *Eberhard 586*. Popular craft store. Another branch at *Baquedano y Chorillos*.

▲▲ Activities and tours

Puerto Natales *p450, map p452*
Reports of the reliability of agencies, especially for their trips to Torres del Paine National Park, are very mixed. It is better to book tours direct with operators in Puerto Natales than through agents in Punta Arenas or Santiago, where huge commissions may be charged.

Some agencies offer 1-day tours to the **Perito Moreno** glacier in Argentina (see p470), 14-hr trip, 2 hrs at the glacier, US$50 excluding food and park entry fee; take US$ cash or Argentine pesos as Chilean pesos are not accepted. However, if you have more time it is better to break the trip by staying in Calafate, and organizing a tour from there.
Bigfoot Expediciones, *Bories 206, T061-414611, www.bigfootpatagonia.com* Sea kayaking and ice-hiking trips on the Grey glacier. Recommended.
Chile Nativo, *Barros Arana 176, casilla 42, T061-411835, www.chilenativo.com* Specializes in multi-day and bespoke tours of Torres del Paine and surroundings.
Knudsen Tours, *Blanco Encalada 284, T061-411531*. Recommended.
Onas and **Andescape**, *Eberhard 595, T061-412707, www.onaspatagonia.com, T061-412592, www.andescape.cl* Tours of Torres del Paine and kayak trips. Andescape also runs many *refugios* in the park (see p461).

Sendero Aventura *Hostal Patgonia Adventure, Tomás Rogers 179, T061-415636, sendero_aventura@terra.cl* Trekking to Torres del Paine, boats to Parque Nacional Balmaceda, camping equipment and bike hire. Recommended.
Tour Express, *Bulnes 769, T061-411639, www.tourexpress.cl* Recommended for tours to Torres del Paine.
Turismo 21 de Mayo, *Eberhard 560, T061-411476, www.turismo21demayo.cl* Organizes boat trips to Parque Nacional Bernado O'Higgins, see Transport below.
Turismo Zaahj, *Prat 236, T061-412260, F411355.. 1 day tours of Torre del Paine cost around US$25, excluding park entry.*

⊖ Transport

Puerto Natales *p450, map p452*
Air
Aerovías DAP flies daily in summer to **El Calafate**, US$54.

Bus
Punta Arenas is served by Bus Fernández, *Eberhard 555, T061-411111*; Bus Sur, *Baquedano 534, T061-411325*; and Bus Transfer, *Baquedano 414, T061-421616*; several daily, 3 hrs, US$4, book in advance. Bus Sur runs to **Coyhaique**, Mon, US$45. For details of buses to **Torres del Paine**, see p462.

To Argentina Bus Sur has 3 weekly direct services to **Río Gallegos**, US$14. Lagoper (Baquedano y Valdivia), Turisur, Bus Sur and Cootra run hourly services to **Río Turbio** (change bus at border), 2 hrs (depending on customs), US$4. To **Calafate**, Bus Sur and Zaahj Bus, 5 hrs, US$22; Cootra also runs a service via Río Turbio, 7 hrs, reserve at least 1 day ahead.

Boat
The **Navimag** ferry *Magallanes* sails every Fri in summer to **Puerto Montt**, less frequently off season (see p370); confirmation of reservations is advised.

PN Bernardo O'Higgins *p450*
The cutter *21 de Mayo* and the sailing boat *Nueva Galicia* sail every morning from Puerto Natales to **Parque Nacional Bernardo O'Higgins** in summer and on Sun only in the winter, US$60 per person, minimum 10

passengers. Book through **Casa Cecilia** (see Sleeping above), or directly through **Turismo 21 de Mayo** (see Activities and tours, above). Lunch extra, so take own food; snacks and drinks available on board. The trip can be combined with a visit to Torres del Paine. You have to pay the full return fare on the boat and you need a permit from CONAF.

⊙ Directory

Puerto Natales *p450, map p452*
Banks and casas de cambio Shop around as some casas offer very poor rates (much better to change money in Punta Arenas). Banks offer poor rates for TCs, which cannot be changed into US$ cash. **Banco Santiago**, *Bulnes y Blanco Encalada*, Mastercard and Visa, ATM; **Cambio Stop**, *Baquedano 380*; **Enio America**, *Blanco Encalada 266*, Argentine pesos can be changed here; there are two more at Bulnes 683 and 1087 (good rates, also change Argentine pesos), and others on Prat.
Bicycle hire Casa Cecilia and Patagonia Adventure (for both, see Sleeping, above).
Bicycle repairs El Rey de la Bicicleta, *Ramírez 540*; good, helpful. **Camping equipment** Patagonia Adventure and Casa Cecilia hire out good-quality gear (for

both, see Sleeping, above). Check all equipment and prices carefully. Average charges, per day: tent US$6, sleeping bag US$3-5, mat US$1.50, raincoat US$0.60, also cooking gear US$1-2. Deposits sometimes required: tent US$200, sleeping bag US$100. Note that it is often difficult to hire walking boots. **Car hire** Hire agents can arrange permission to drive into Argentina, but this is expensive and takes 24 hrs to arrange. **Avis**, *Bulnes 632, T061-410775*; **Motor Cars**, *Blanco 330, T061-415593, www.motorcars.cl*; **Ultima Esperanza**, *Blanco Encalada 206, T061-410461*. **Car mechanic** Carlos González, *Ladrilleros entre Bories y Eberhard*, recommended. **Internet** Concepto Indigo, *Hosp María José* (see Sleeping, above). El Rincón de Tata, *Prat 236*, **Patagonianet**, *Blanco 330*. **Laundry** Lavandería Catch, *Bories 218*, friendly service; **Servilaundry**, *Bulnes 513*. **Post office** *Eberhard 417*, open Mon-Fri 0830-1230, 1430-1745, Sat 0900-1230.
Shipping Comapa, *Hotel Coastaustralis, Bulnes y Pedro Montt, T061-414300*; **Navimag**, *Pedro Montt 262, Loc B, Terminal Marítimo, T061-411421*. **Telephone** CTC, *Blanco Encalada 23 y Bulnes*; **Entel**, *Baquedano y Bulnes*, phone and fax service; **Telefonica**, *Blanco Encalada y Phillipi*.

Parque Nacional Torres del Paine

→ *Colour map 6, B2.*
Covering 242,242 ha, 145 km northwest of Puerto Natales, this national park is a UNESCO Biosphere Reserve and a must-visit for its diverse wildlife and spectacular surroundings. Taking its name from the Tehuelche word Paine, meaning 'blue', the park encompasses stunning scenery, with constantly changing views of peaks, glaciers and icebergs, vividly coloured lakes of turquoise, ultramarine and grey, and quiet green valleys filled with wild flowers. In the centre of the park is one of the most impressive mountain areas on earth, a granite massif from which rise oddly shaped peaks of over 2,600 m, known as the Torres (towers) and Cuernos (horns) of Paine.

Background

There are 15 peaks above 2,000 m, of which the highest is **Cerro Paine Grande** (3,050 m); few places can compare to its steep forested talus slopes topped by 1,000-m vertical shafts of basalt with conical caps. These are the remains of frozen magma in ancient volcanic throats, everything else having been eroded. On the western edge of the park is the enormous **Campo de Hielo Sur** icefield; four main **glaciers** (*ventisqueros*): Grey,

Dickson, Zapata and Tyndall branch off it, their meltwater forming a complex series of lakes and streams, which lead into fjords extending to the sea. Two other glaciers, Francés and Los Perros, descend on the western side of the central *massif*.

The park enjoys a micro-climate especially favourable to **plants** and **wildlife**. Over 200 species of plants have been identified and, although few trees reach great size, several valleys are thickly forested and little light penetrates. The grassland here is distinct from the monotony of the *pampa* and dispersed sclerophyl forest. There are

Parque Nacional Torres del Paine

species of birds in the park, including 18 species of waterfowl and 11 birds of prey.
Particularly noteworthy are condors, blacknecked swans, rheas, kelp geese, ibis, flamingos and austral parrakeets. The park is also one of the best places on the continent for viewing rheas and *guanacos*. Apart from the 3,500 *guanacos*, 24 other species of mammals can be seen here, including hares, foxes, skunks, *huemules* (see box page 430) and pumas (the last two only very rarely).

The Far South Parque Nacional Torres del Paine

Sleeping 🛏
Explora **1**
Hostería Lago Grey **3**
Hostería Las Torres **4**
Hostería Mirador del Payne **2**
Hostería Pehoé **5**
Posada Río Serrano **6**

Refugios 🏠
Chileno **1**
Grey (Andescape) **3**
Lago Dickson (Andescape) **2**
Lago Paine **4**
Lago Pehoé (Andescape) **9**
Laguna Amarga **6**
Laguna Verde **7**
Los Cuernos **8**
Pudeto **11**

Camping ⛺
Campamento Británico **1**
Campamento Chileno **3**
Campamento Italiano **4**
Campamento Japonés **5**
Campamento Las Carretas **15**
Campamento Las Guardas **6**
Campamento Las Torres **7**
Campamento Paso **8**
Campamento Pingo **16**
Campamento Zapata **17**
Lago Pehoé **14**
Laguna Azul **9**
Las Torres **10**
Los Perros **11**
Serón **13**
Serrano **12**

Ranger stations (*guarderías*) 🏠

0 km   4

Torres del Paine has become increasingly popular with foreigners and Chileans alike: in 2002 it received around 70,000 visitors, most during the summer months of January and February, which, if possible, should be avoided due to overcrowding, especially at *refugios* and campsites, and the unpredictability of the weather. Many parts of the park are now open all year round; visiting in winter is becoming increasingly popular as, although the temperature is low, there is little wind. Despite efforts to manage the ever-growing number of visitors, the impact of such a large influx is starting to show. Litter has become a problem, especially around *refugios* and camping areas; please take all your rubbish out of the park and remember that this also includes toilet paper.

Ins and outs

Getting there The most practical way to get to Torres del Paine is with one of the many bus or tour companies that leave Puerto Natales daily. If you want to drive, hiring a pick-up from **Budget** in Punta Arenas is an economical proposition for a group (up to 9 people), US$415 for four days. The road from Puerto Natales is being improved; it takes about three hours from Puerto Natales to the administration. Petrol is available at Río Serrano, but fill up in case.► *For further details, see Transport, page 462.* **Getting around** Allow a week or 10 days to see the park properly. Most visitors will find that they get around on foot, however, there are minibuses between the CONAF administration and Guardería Laguna Amarga, as well as boats across Lago Pehoé. Roads inside the park are narrow and bendy with blind corners. Rangers keep a check on the whereabouts of all visitors: you are required to register and show your passport when entering the park or setting off on any hike. **Visitor information** There are entrances at Laguna Amarga, Lago Sarmiento and Laguna Azul, foreigners US$11 (proceeds are shared between all Chilean national parks), climbing fees US$800. The park is administered by CONAF, which has an administration centre at the northern end of Lago del Toro ① *T061-691931, open daily 0830-2000 in summer, 0830-1230, 1400-1830 off season*. It provides a good slide show at 2000 on Saturday and Sunday and there are also excellent exhibitions on the flora and fauna of the park in Spanish and English. There are six ranger stations (*guarderías*) in the park staffed by *guardaparques*, who give advice and also store luggage (not at Laguna Amarga). **Climate** The weather in the park can change in a few minutes. The warmest time is from December to March, although it can be wet and windy. The spring months of October and November are recommended for wild flowers. Rain and snowfall are heavier the further west you go and bad weather sweeps off the Campo de Hielo Sur without warning. Snow may prevent access in winter, but well-equipped hikers can do some good walking, when conditions are stable. For information in Spanish on weather conditions, phone the administration centre.► *For Sleeping, Eating and other listings, see pages 460-463.*

▲ Trekking

There are about 250 km of well-marked trails. Visitors must keep to the trails: cross country trekking is not permitted. It is vital not to underestimate the unpredictability of the weather, nor the arduousness of some stretches on the long hikes. Some paths are confusingly marked and it is all too easy to end up on precipices with glaciers or churning rivers awaiting below; be particularly careful to follow the path at the Paso John Gadner on the *Circuito* (see below). The only means of rescue are on horseback or by boat; the nearest helicopter is in Punta Arenas and high winds usually prevent its operation in the park.

Equipment

It is essential to be properly equipped against cold, wind and rain. A strong, streamlined, waterproof tent is essential if doing El Circuito (although you can hire camping equipment for a single night at most *refugios*). Also essential are protective clothing, strong waterproof footwear, compass, good sleeping bag and sleeping mat. In summer also take shorts and sunscreen. You are strongly advised to bring all necessary equipment and your own food from Puerto Natales and not to rely on availability at the Andescape *refugios* within the park; the small shops at the *refugios* (see below) and at the **Posada Río Serrano** are expensive and have a limited selection. Note that rats and mice are occasionaly a problem around camping sites and the free *refugios*, so do not leave food in your pack (which may be chewed through), instead, the safest solution is to hang food in a bag on a wire. Note that you are not allowed to build fires in the park. A basic map is provided with your park entrance ticket; other maps (US$4) are obtainable at CONAF offices in Punta Arenas or Puerto Natales but most are unreliable. The map produced by **Cartographia Digital** has been recommended as more accurate, as is the one produced by **Patagonia Interactiva**.

El Circuito → *In theory, lone walkers are not allowed on this route.*

The most popular trek is a circuit round the Torres and Cuernos del Paine. It is usually done anticlockwise starting from the *guardería* at **Laguna Amarga** and, although some people complete the route in less time, it normally takes five to six days. The circuit is often closed in winter because of snow; major rivers are crossed by footbridges, but these are occasionally washed away. From Laguna Amarga the route is north along the western side of the Río Paine to **Lago Paine,** before turning west to follow the lush pastures of the valley of the Río Paine to the southern end of **Lago Dickson** (it is possible to add a journey to the *campamento* by the Torres on day one of this route); the *refugio* at Lago Dickson lies in a breathtaking position in front of the icy white lake with mountains beyond. From Lago Dickson the path runs along the wooded valley of the **Río de los Perros**, past the Glaciar de los Perros, before climbing through bogs and up scree to **Paso John Gadner** (1,241 m, the highest point on the route), then dropping steeply through forest to follow the Grey Glacier southeast to **Lago Grey**, continuing to **Lago Pehoé** and the administration centre. There are superb views en route, particularly from the top of Paso John Gadner.

> ⚑ *Some walkers advise doing the route clockwise so that you climb to Paso John Gadner with the wind behind you.*

The longest stretch is between Refugio Laguna Amarga and Refugio Dickson (30 km, 10 hours in good weather; two campsites on the way at Serón and Cairon), but the most difficult section is the very steep, slippery slope from Paso John Gadner down to the Campamento Paso; the path is not well signed at the top of the pass, and some people (including one of the authors of this book!) have got dangerously lost and ended up on the Grey Glacier itself. Camping gear must be carried, as some *campamentos* (including Campamento Paso and Campamento Torres) do not have *refugios*.

The W

A popular alternative to El Circuito, this four- to five-day route can be completed without camping equipment as there is accommodation in *refugios* en route. It combines several of the hikes described separately below. From Refugio Laguna Amarga the first stage runs west via **Hostería Las Torres** and up the valley of the **Río Ascensio** via Refugio Chileno to the base of the **Torres del Paine** (see below). From here return to the Hostería Las Torres and then walk along the northern shore of **Lago Nordenskjold** via Refugio Los Cuernos to Campamento Italiano. From here climb the Valley of the **Río del Francés** (see below) before continuing to Refugio Pehoé. From here you can complete the third part of the 'W' by walking west along the northern shore of **Lago Grey** to Refugio Grey and the Grey Glacier before returning to Refugio Pehoé and the boat back across the lake to the Refugio Pudeto.

Valley of the Río del Francés

From Refugio Pehoé this route leads north across undulating country along the western edge of **Lago Skottberg** to Campamento Italiano and then follows the valley of the Río del Francés, which climbs between Cerro Paine Grande and the Ventisquero del Francés (to the west) and the Cuernos del Paine (to the east) to Campamento Británico; the views from the mirador an hour's walk above Campamento Británico are superb. Allow two and a half hours from Refugio Pehoé to Campamento Italiano, two and a half hours further to Campamento Británico.

Treks from Guardería Grey

Guardería Grey, 18 km west by road from the administration centre, is the starting point for a five-hour trek to Lago Pingo. From the *guardería* follow the **Río Pingo**, via Refugio Pingo and Refugio Zapata (four hours), with views south over Ventisquero Zapata (look out for plenty of wildlife and for icebergs in the lake) to reach the lake. **Ventisquero Pingo** can be seen 3 km away over the lake. Two short signposted walks from Guardería Grey have also been suggested: one is a steep climb up the hill behind the ranger post to **Mirador Ferrier**, from where there are fine views; the other is via a suspension bridge across the Río Pingo to the peninsula at the southern end of **Lago Grey**, from where there are good views of the icebergs on the lakes.

To the base of the Torres del Paine

From Refugio Laguna Amarga, this six-hour route follows the road west to **Hostería Las Torres** (one and a half hours), before climbing along the western side of the **Río Ascensio** via Refugio Chileno (two hours) and Campamento Chileno to Campamento Las Torres (two hours), close to the base of the **Torres del Paine** (be careful when crossing the suspension bridge over the Río Ascensio near Hostería Las Torres, as the path is poorly marked and you can end up on the wrong side of the ravine). The path alongside the Río Ascensio is well marked, and the Campamento Las Torres is in an attractive wood (no *refugio*). A further 30 minutes up the morraine takes you to a lake at the base of the towers themselves; they seem so close that you almost feel you could touch them. To see the Torres lit by sunrise (spectacular but you must have good weather), it's well worth carrying your camping gear up to Campamento Torres and spending the night. One hour beyond Campamento Torres is Campamento Japonés, another good campsite.

To Laguna Verde

From the administation centre follow the road north 2 km, before taking the path east over the **Sierra del Toro** and then along the southern side of **Laguna Verde** to the Guardería Laguna Verde. Allow four hours. This is one of the easiest walks in the park and may be a good first hike.

To Laguna Azul and Lago Paine

This route runs north from Laguna Amarga to the western tip of **Laguna Azul**, from where it continues across the sheltered **Río Paine** valley past Laguna Cebolla to the Refugio Lago Paine at the western end of the lake. Allow eight and a half hours.

● Sleeping

LL **Explora**, *Salto Chico on edge of Lago Pehoé, T061-411247, reservations from Av Américo Vespucci 80, piso 7, Santiago, T02-2066060, www.explora.com* Ugly building but the most luxurious and comfortable hotel in the park, offering spectacular views, pool, gym, tours and transfer from Punta Arenas.
LL **Hostería Lago Grey**, *T061-410220, reservations T061-229512/225986,*

www.austrohoteles.com Small rooms on edge of Lago Grey with views of the Grey Glacier, average restaurant.
LL-L **Hostería Lago Tyndall**, *T061-221303, www.hosterialagotyndall.com* Expensive, cafeteria-style restaurant, electricity during the day only, good views. Not recommended.
LL-AL **Hostería Las Torres**, *head office Magallanes 960, Punta Arenas, T061-710050, www.lastorres.com* Nice rooms, good restaurant, English spoken, horseriding, transport from Laguna Amarga ranger station.

LL-AL **Hostería Pehoé**, *5 km south of Pehoé ranger station, 11 km north of park administration, T061-411390 www.pehoe.com*. On an island with spectacular view across the lake to Cerro Paine Grande and Cuernos del Paine, this place does not make the most of its stunning location, rundown, overpriced. Reservations from **Turismo Pehoé** in Punta Arenas. Closed Apr-Oct.

L **Hostería Mirador del Payne (Estancia Lazo)**, *on the eastern edge of the park, reservations from Fagnano 585, Punta Arenas, T061-226930, F228712, www.miradordelpayne.com* Beautifully situated on Laguna Verde with spectacular views and good fishing, restaurant. Recommended but an inconvenient base for visiting the park; own transport essential, or you can trek to it from within the park.

AL-B **Posada Río Serrano**, *reservations advisable; contact Turismo Río Serrano, Prat 258, Puerto Natales, T061-410684*. An old *estancia*, much improved recently, some rooms with bath, some with shared facilities, breakfast extra, near park administration, with expensive but good restaurant and a shop.

Andescape refugios

Accommodation and meals in the **Andescape** *refugios* should be booked in advance in Puerto Natales, see p454, or by asking staff in one *refugio* to radio another. Prices are all per person (**D**); full board US$38; cheaper for non-residents of Chile paying in US dollars. Good food, clean, modern, closed in winter until 10 Sep, dormitory accommodation (take your own sleeping bag), hot showers (US$2 for non-residents), cooking and laundry facilities, meals served, kiosk with basic food and other supplies, rental of camping equipment (eg US$9 per day for a tent), campsite, advance booking advisable.

Refugio Grey, *on the eastern shore of Lago Grey*. Guided glacier walks including ice climbing, US$50.

Refugio Lago Dickson and **Refugio Los Chilenas**, *valley of the Río Ascensio*.

Refugio Lago Pehoé, *on the northeast arm of Lago Pehoé*. Crowded, unfriendly.

Refugio Los Cuernos, *on the northern shore of Lago Nordenskjold*.

Other refugios

E **Refugio Las Torres**, *Hostería Las Torres (see above)*, meals served, kitchen facilities.

In addition, there are 6 free *refugios*: Zapata, Pingo, Laguna Verde, Laguna Amarga, Lago Paine and Pudeto. Most have cooking areas (wood stove or fireplace) but Laguna Verde and Pingo do not. These two are in very poor condition.

Campsites

The wind tends to increase in the evening so it is a good idea to pitch tents early (by 1600). In addition to sites at the **Andescape** *refugios*, there are the following sites (see map p457 for locations):

Lago Pehoé. Run by Turismo Río Serrano (see Sleeping, above), US$20 per site, maximum 6 persons, hot showers, beware mice.

Laguna Azul. Hot showers.

Las Torres. Run by Estancia Cerro Paine, US$4, hot showers.

Los Perros. Run by Andescape, with shop and hot showers.

The Far South Parque Nacional Torres del Paine

Serón. Run by Estancia Cerro Paine, US$4, hot showers.

Serrano. Run by Turismo Río Serrano (see Sleeping, above), US$15 per site, maximum 6 persons, cold showers, basic.

Free camping is permitted in 7 other locations in the park; these sites are known as *campamentos*. Fires may only be lit at organized campsites, not at *campamentos*. The *guardaparques* expect people to have a stove if camping. These restrictions should be observed as forest fires are a serious hazard. *Guardaparques* also require campers to have a trowel to bury their waste. Equipment can be hired in Puerto Natales (see above).

▲ Activities and tours

Before booking a tour check all the details carefully and get a copy in writing, as there have been increasingly mixed reports of the quality of some tours. Many companies who claim to visit the Grey Glacier, for example, only visit Lago Grey (you see the glacier in the distance). After mid-Mar there is less public transport and trucks are irregular.

Several agencies in Puerto Natales including Servitur, Zaahj, Onas and Tour Express (see p451) offer 1-day tours by minibus, US$25 plus park entry; these give a good impression of the lower parts of the park, although you spend most of the day in the vehicle and many travellers would argue that you need to stay several days, or at least overnight, in the park to appreciate it fully. Cheaper tours are also available, but both guide and vehicle may not be as good as the established operators.

Cascada Expediciones, *T02-861 1777, www.cascada-expediciones.com*, based in Santiago, offers small group tours to Torres del Paine. **Experience Chile**, *T07977 223 326, www.experiencechile.org* Itineraries and accomodation in the region can be arranged by this UK-based operator.

Hostería Grey (see Sleeping, above) provides excusions by boat to the face of the Grey Glacier at 0900 and 1500 daily, 3½ hrs, US$60 per person.

Onas Turismo, (see p454), runs trips to and from the park down the Río Serrano in zodiac boats to the Serrano glacier in the Parque National Bernardo O'Higgins, and from there on the tour boats to Puerto Natales, US$90 each all inclusive. Book in advance.

● Transport

Bus

From early Nov to mid-Apr daily bus services run from Puerto Natales to the park, leaving between 0630 and 0800, and again at around 1430, 2½ hrs to Laguna Amarga, 3 hrs to the administration centre, US$7 1 way, US$12 open return (return tickets are not always interchangeable between different companies); return departures are usually around 1300 and 1800. Generally, buses will drop you at Laguna Amarga and pick you up at the administration centre for the return. The buses wait at Refugio Pudeto until the 1200 boat from Refugio Lago Pehoé arrives. Travel between 2 points within the park (eg Pudeto–Laguna Amarga), US$3. Services are provided by **Bus Sur**, *Baquedano 534, T061-411325*; **JB**, *Prat 258, T061-412824*; and **Fortaleza**, *Prat 258, T061-410595*.

At other times, services by travel agencies are subject to demand; arrange your return date with the driver and try to coincide with other groups to keep costs down; **Luis Díaz** has been recommended, about US$12, minimum 3 persons. In season there are minibus connections from Laguna Amarga to the **Hostería Los Torres**, US$4, and from the administration centre to **Hostería Lago Grey**.

To go from Torres del Paine to **Calafate** (Argentina), either return to Puerto Natales and catch a bus, or take a bus or hitch from the park to Villa Cerro Castillo and try to link with the Natales–Calafate bus schedule. In season, there is a direct bus service from the park to Calafate with **Chaltén Travel**, US$40.

Boat
A boat service runs across Lago Pehoé from Refugio Lago Pehoé to Refugio Pudeto, daily, 30 mins, US$14 1 way with 1 piece of baggage free, tickets available on board. Departures from Pehoé 1000, 1230, 1830; from Pudeto 0930, 1200, 1800. Reduced service off season, no service May-Sep.

Into Argentina

The small Argentine town of El Calafate, *the base for visits to the Parque Nacional Los Glaciares, is a short distance from Puerto Natales and can easily be visited. This little town is situated in a beautiful position on the southern shore of Lago Argentino, the largest lake in Argentina, surrounded by mountains.*

Ins and outs → *Argentine phone code: +54.*
Getting there El Calafate is easily accessible from Puerto Natales in Chile (two buses daily in summer, less frequent in winter) via Río Turbio or Cerro Castillo (both roads *ripio*), or along a smooth metalled road from Río Gallegos near the Atlantic coast (several buses daily). There are poorer roads north to El Chaltén and Perito Moreno. Lago Argentino airport, 22 km east of town, has a paved runway suitable for jet aircraft. **Aerobus** ① *T02902-492492, US$3* runs from the airport to hotels in town; a taxi to the town centre costs US$7. ➤➤ *For further details, see Transport, page 468.* **Getting around** El Calafate is so small that it's easy to get around the town on foot. **Tourist information** The office in the bus terminal ① *T02902-491090, info@calafate.com, Oct-Apr daily 0700-2200*, is very helpful, English spoken, and maintains a complete list of available accommodation. For information on the Parque Nacional los Glaciares, visit the park office ① *Libertador 1302, T02902-491005, apnglaciares@ cotecal.com.ar, Mon-Fri 0800-1500.*

> ❖ *You need the hire company's authorization to take a car into Argentina.*

Argentine border
From Puerto Natales, the Argentine frontier can be crossed at three points, all of which meet Route 40, which runs north to El Calafate. These crossings are open, subject to weather conditions, 24 hrs a day from September to May and 0700 to 2300 daily between June and August.

Paso Casas Viejas This crossing, 16 km east of Puerto Natales, is reached by turning off Route 9 (the Punta Arenas road) at Km 14. On the Argentine side, the road (*ripio*) runs east to meet Route 40, en route to Río Gallegos (or north to El Calafate). This crossing is open all year.

Villa Dorotea This crossing is reached by branching off Route 9, 9 km east of Puerto Natales and continuing north a further 11 km. On the Argentine side, the road (*ripio*) continues north to Route 40 via **Río Turbio**, see page 464.

Cerro Castillo The most northerly of the three crossings, Cerro Castillo is reached by turning off the road north to Torres del Paine at Km 65. Chilean customs and immigration formalities are at Cerro Castillo; Argentine formalities are at Cancha Carrera, 2 km further east. On the Argentine side of the frontier, the road meets Route 40 in a very desolate spot – hitching may be possible, but this route is more feasible if you have your own transport.

Río Turbio → *Phone code: 02902. Population: 8,000.*

Only 30 km northeast of Puerto Natales, Río Turbio is the site of Argentina's largest coalfield. Little visited by travellers, it is a good centre for trekking and horseriding. There is a **tourist office** in the Municipalidad on Calle San Martín. Visits can be made to **Mina Uno** (where the first mine was opened), to the south of the town, and to the present mining and industrial area, on the eastern outskirts, where there is a museum, the **Museo del Carbón** ① *Mon-Fri 0700-1200.* About 4 km south of town is **Valdelén**, a ski resort situated just inside the frontier on the slopes of Sierra La Dorotea (see page 467). ▸▸ *For Sleeping, Eating and other listings, see pages 465-468.*

Towards El Calafate

From the border there are two alternative routes to El Calafate. On clear days both offer fantastic views of Torres del Paine. The longest but easiest route runs north along Route 40 along beautiful valleys with flowers, woods and grazing horses, to Cancha Carrerra (the junction with the border crossing from Cerro Castillo), then follows the Río Coyle to **La Esperanza**, Km 123, where it meets the main El Calafate–Río Gallegos road, 161 km southeast of El Calafate. The shorter route continues northwards from Cancha Carrerra along a very poor, desolate *ripio* road, the continuation of Route 40, which turns off at Km 30 and runs northeast 70 km to meet the El Calafate–Río Gallegos road at **El Cerrito**, 91 km southeast of El Calafate. In winter, both the Cerro Castillo crossing and this shorter route are occasionally closed. For public transport on this route see page 454.

El Calafate and around → *Phone code: 02902. Population: 8,000.*

Founded in 1927, El Calafate has grown rapidly as a tourist centre for the Parque Nacional los Glaciares, 50 km further west. Here you will see no sign of the Argentinian economic crisis. The weakness of the peso has led to a boom in tourism. As a result, El Calafate has a distinctly prosperous feel. Given the town's name, it is no surprise that the surrounding hills abound with small calafate bushes.

A straightforward walk directly behind the town leads up a hill from where there are views of the silhouette of the southern end of the Andes, Lago Argentina and Isla Solitaria. Just west of the town centre is **Bahía Redonda**, a shallow part of Lago Argentino where in winter you can ice-skate and ski. At its eastern edge is **Laguna Nimes**, a bird reserve where there are flamingos, black necked swans and ducks. There is scope for good hill-walking to the south of the town, **Cerro Elefante**, west of Calafate on the road to the Moreno glacier, is good for rock climbing. Further west, **El Galpón** ① *21 km west, T02902-492316, open from 1730 daily* is an *estancia* and bird sanctuary where 43 species of birds have been identified. There are also sheep shearing displays, horseriding and a barbecue; English spoken.

Punta Gualicho, on the shores of Lago Argentino, some 15 km east of town (or 7 km on foot when cutting across the pampa), has badly deteriorated painted caves. The caves are on private property and may soon be closed to the public. There is an entrance fee (US$3). On the same road, 12 km east of El Calafate on the edge of the lake, are fascinating geological formations caused by erosion. Several agencies run two-hour tours to Punta Gualicho for US$6. At **Lago Roca**, 40 km south of El Calafate, there is trout and salmon fishing, climbing, walking and cattle branding in summer.
▸▸ *For Sleeping, Eating and other listings, see pages 465-468.*

The Calafate

According to local lore, whoever eats the fruits of the Calafate, *Berberis buxifolia*, will return to Patagonia. Certainly, he or she is likely to have purple-stained lips and fingers thanks to the plant's edible berries. This spiny, hardy shrub grows to 2 m in height and has single bright yellow/orange flowers dotted along its arching branches in spring. Also known as the Magellan barberry, its wood is used for making red dye.

Sleeping

Argentine border *p463*

AL-A Hostería El Pionero, *Villa Cerro Castillo, 63 km north of Puerto Natales, T061-412911.* With bath, good service, horses available for hire. There are also 2 *hospedajes* in the town.

Río Turbio *p464*

Hotels are almost always full, so reserve your room in advance.

B-F Gato Negro, *T02902-4921226.* Rooms and dormitory accommodation.

E Hostería de la Frontera, *Paraje Mina 1, T02902-421979.* Nice *albergue* at Valdelén.

Towards El Calafate *p464*

F Hotel Fuentes del Coyle, *Fuentes del Coyle, 31 km east of Cerro Castillo.* Cold, dirty.

F Restaurant La Esperanza, *La Esperanza.* Bunk beds, with bath; also *cabañas* at the YPF service station.

El Calafate *p464, map p465*

In summer, accommodation can be hard to find. Ask at the tourist office, which rents out caravans, tents and 4-berth *cabañas*, showers extra. Credit cards are only welcome at hotels, with high commissions. Many hotels are only open Oct to Apr/May.

El Calafate

Sleeping
ACA Hostería
    El Calafate **1**
Albergue Buenos Aires **7**
Albergue del Glaciar **2**
Albergue Lago
    Argentino **3**
Amado **4**

Cabañas del Sol **9**
Cabañas Nevis **5**
Calafate Hostel **16**
Camping Municipal **23**
El Quijote **19**
Hospedaje Alejandra **6**
Hospedaje Cerro Cristal **20**
Hospedaje del Norte **8**

Hospedaje Los
    Dos Pinos **10**
Kapenke **12**
Lago Azul **21**
Lago Roca **22**
La Loma **13**
Las Cabañitas **18**
Los Alamos **14**

Michelangelo **15**
Mirador del Lago **11**
Upsala **17**

Eating
El Rancho **3**
Mi Viejo & Rick's Café **1**
Pizzería Casablanca **2**

N
0 metres   100
0 yards   100

L **El Mirador del Lago**, *Libertador 2047, T02902-491213, www.miradordellago.com.ar* Good accommodation on the lakefront just outside town, restaurant, half-board available.

L **Hostería Kau-Yatún**, *25 de Mayo (10 blocks from town centre), T02902-491059, kauyatun@cotecal.com.ar* Many facilities, old *estancia* house, comfortable, restaurant and barbecues, horseriding tours with guides.

L **Los Alamos**, *Moyano y Bustillo, T02902-491145, www.posadalosalamos.com* Best hotel in town, comfortable, very good service, excellent restaurant, extensive gardens, single-hole golf course. Recommended.

AL **ACA Hostería El Calafate**, *Av del Libertador 1350, T02902-491004, www.ubikt.com.ar/usc/hosteriaelcalafate* Good view, open all year.

AL **El Quijote**, *Gob Gregores 1181, T02902-491017, elquijote@cotecal.com.ar* Modern, comfortable. Recommended.

AL **Kapenke**, *9 de Julio 112, T02902-491093, www.kapenke.com.ar* Modern, with breakfast, good beds, bright, internet access, snackbar, overpriced.

A **La Loma**, *Julio Roca 849, T02902-491016, www.lalomahotel.com* Spacious rooms, breakfast, library, restaurant, tea-room, games room, gardens. Recommended.

A **Michelangelo**, *Espora y Gob Moyano, T02902-491045, www.michelangelo hotel.com.ar* With breakfast, modern, comfortable, excellent restaurant, accepts TCs (poor rates).

B **Upsala**, *Espora 139, T02902-491166, dflella@lacasilla.com.ar* With breakfast, good beds. Recommended.

B-C **Cabañas Del Sol**, *Libertador 1956, T02902-491439, cabadelsol@yahoo.com.ar* Good meals. Recommended.

C **Amado**, *Libertador 1072, T02902-491134, familiagomez@cotecal.com.ar* With bath and breakfast, simple, cable TV.

C **Hosp Cerro Cristal**, *Gob Gregores 979, T02902-491088*. With bath and breakfast, basic.

C **Hosp del Norte**, *Los Gauchos 813, T02902-491117*. Open all year, kitchen facilities, comfortable, owner organizes tours.

C **Las Cabañitas**, *V Feilberg 218, T02902-491118, lascabanitas@cotecal.com.ar* Cabins, hot water, kitchen and laundry facilities, helpful. Recommended.

C **Los Lagos**, *25 de Mayo 220, T02902-491170, loslagos@cotecal.com.ar* Very comfortable, with bath and breakfast, good value. Recommended.

D **Cabañas Nevis**, *about 1 km from town towards glacier, Libertador 1696, T02902-491180*. For 4 or 8, some have lake view, full board available, excellent value.

D **Lago Azul**, *Perito Moreno 83, T02902-491419*. Only 2 double rooms. Highly recommended.

B-F **Albergue del Glaciar**, *Los Pioneros 251, T02902-491243, www.glaciar.com* Discount for ISIC or IYHA members, open mid-Sep to end-Apr. Price per person with dorms, also doubles with bath and without, kitchen facilities, English, German, Italian spoken, internet, also have El Tempano Errante restaurant with good-value fixed menu and vegetarian options, booking service for hotels and transport throughout Patagonia. Recommended. The hostel's tour agency **Patagonia Backpackers**, is a Navimag agent, organizes tours to the Moreno glacier (US$35 per person, good value) and elsewhere, and runs a free shuttle service from the bus station, book in advance in summer.

F-G **Albergue Lago Argentino**, *Campaña del Desierto 1050, T02902-491423, F491139*. Near bus terminal. Price per person for dormitory accommodation, limited bathrooms, kitchen facilities, helpful.

E **Enrique Barragán**, *Barrio Bahía Redonda, Casa 10, T02902-491325*. Accommodation in a private house. Recommended.

F **Apartamentos Lago Viedma**, *Paralelo 158, T02902-491159*. Hostel, 4 bunks to a room, cooking facilities.

F **Calafate Hostel**, *Gob Moyano 1226, 300 m from bus terminal, T02902-492450, www.hostelspatagonia.com* Price per person in dormitories. Also more expensive rooms with bath. Kitchen facilities, internet, often full.

F **Hosp Alejandra**, *Espora 60, T02902-491328*. Price per person. Without breakfast or bath, good value, kitchen facilities, recommended.

F **La Cueva de Jorge Lemos**, *Gob Moyano 839, behind YPF station*. Bunk beds, bathroom, showers, kitchen facilities, popular and cheap.

F-G **Albergue Buenos Aires**, *Buenos Aires 296, 200 m from terminal, T02902-491147*. Kitchen facilities, helpful, good hot showers, luggage store.

G **Hosp Los Dos Pinos**, *9 de Julio 358, T02902-491271*. Price per person for dormitory accommodation, bad beds, cooking and laundry facilities, also cabins (C) and camping. Arranges tours to glacier, popular.

Camping
Municipal campsite, *behind YPF service station*, *T02902-492622, campingmunicipal@ cotecal.com.ar* Hot water, security, bar, *parillada*, open 1 Oct-30 Apr; good meeting place.
Camping Lago Roca, *T02902-499500*. Good campsite in a wooded area beside Lago Roca, US$4 per site, also restaurant/*confitería*.
Camping Río Bote, *35 km, on road to Río Gallegos*.

🍴 Eating

El Calafate *p464, map p465*
There's a good-value fixed-price menu at **Albergue del Glaciar** (see Sleeping, above).
$$ Hotel Los Alamos, *Moyana y Bustillo*. Inventive menu using local ingredients. Recommended.
$$ Michelangelo, *Espora y Gob Moyano*. Magnificent steaks, trout, pastas. Recommended.
$$ Paso Verlika, *Libertador 1108*. Cosy and good value.
$ Bar Don Diego de la Noche, *Libertador 1603*. Lamb and seafood, live music, good atmosphere.
$ El Rancho, *9 de Julio y Gob Moyano*. Good-value, generously sized pizzas, popular, free video shows of the glacier. Highly recommended.
$ La Loma, *see Sleeping, above*. Friendly, home-style food.
$ Maktub, *Libertador 905*. Excellent pastries.
$ Mi Viejo, *Libertador 1111. Parrilla*.
$ Pizzería Casablanca, *Libertador y 25 de Mayo*. Serves good breakfasts.
$ Rick's Café, *Av del Libertador 1105*. Popular *tenedor libre* , US$5.

🎉 Festivals

El Calafate *p464, map p465*
People flock to the rural show on **Día del Lago Argentino** (15 Feb) from all over the vast Provincia de Santa Cruz. Many wear their finest *gaucho* clothes – *bombachas*, *espuelas* and wide-brimmed hats – and camp out. Revelry includes dances, *asados* and *jineteadas* (a type of rodeo, featuring wild horses ridden by wild men). This is a highly recommended insight into Patagonia's 'wild west'.

There are also barbecues and rodeos etc on **Día de la Tradición** on the 10 Nov.

⛰️ Activities and tours

Río Turbio *p464*
Skiing
The ski resort at **Valdelén** has 6 pistes and is ideal for beginners. There is also scope for crosscountry skiing nearby. The season runs from early Jun to late Sep, with floodlights to extend the short winter afternoons.

El Calafate *p464, map p465*
Tour operators
There are many agencies, most of them along Libertador. Most charge the same rates for excursions: to the **Moreno Glacier**, US$18 plus US$3.50 park entry for a trip leaving early morning or around 1400, 3 hrs at glacier (see p474); to **Lago Roca**, depart 0930, return 1700, US$20; to **Cerro Fitz Roy**, depart 0600 return 1900, US$30; to **Punta Gualicho**, 2 hrs, US$10.
Cecilia Scarafoni, *T02902-493196, ecowalks@cotecal.com.ar* Birdwatching walks 2 km from town, 2 hrs, US$5.
Chaltén Travel, *Libertador 1177, T02902-492212, rancho@cotecal.com.ar* Wide range of tours, English spoken, helpful.
Fernández Campbell, *Libertador 867, T02902-491155*. Combined bus and boat tours to the Upsala glacier.
Hielo y Aventura, *Libertador 935, T02902-491053, hieloyaventura@cotecal.com.ar* Organizes 2-hr treks on the Moreno glacier with champagne, US$50, plus US$15 for transport to the glacier. Recommended, book ahead.
Interlagos, *Libertador 1175, T02902-491179*. Daily bus to Moreno glacier.
Leutz, *Libertador 1341, T02902-492316, leutzturismo@cotecal.com.ar* Daily excursion to Lago Roca 1000-1800, US$25 per person, plus US$12 for lunch at Estancia Nibepo Aike.
Santa Cruz, *Campo del Desierto 1695, T02902-493166*. Helpful.

Several hotels organize tours by minibus including **Albergue del Glaciar** (see Sleeping, above), which offers an alternative Moreno glacier tour including some trekking.

🚌 Transport

Río Turbio *p464*
Air
The airport is 15 km southeast near 28 de Noviembre; taxi US$7. **LADE** flies to **Río Gallegos** on Tue, 45 mins, US$30.

To **Puerto Natales**, several daily, 1 hr, US$2, with Cootra, Bus Sur and Zaahj. To **Calafate**, several daily, many companies, 4½ hrs, US$7. To **Río Gallegos**, many companies, 4 hrs, US$5.

El Calafate p464, map p465

Air

Aerolineas Argentinas and AIRG have daily services to **Buenos Aires**. To **Ushuaia**, LADE and Aerolineas Argentinas, several weekly between them, US$50. To **Gob Gregores** and **Perito Moreno**, LADE, weekly, US$35. To **Río Turbio**, LADE, weekly, US$35. LADE also flies twice weekly to **Río Gallegos**, US$40, and **Comodoro Rivadavia**, US$60. To **Puerto Natales**, DAP, daily in summer, US$54. There are many more flights in summer.

Bus

The terminal is on Roca, 1 block from Libertador. Bus schedule changes annually.

To **Perito Moreno Glacier**, Taqsa and Interlagos, daily, $10 return. To **Río Gallegos**, Interlagos and Taqsa, daily, US$11. To **Río Turbio**, several daily, many companies, 4½ hrs, US$7. For **Ushuaia**, **Buenos Aires** and northern destinations go to Río Gallegos and change.

To Chile Cootra runs to **Puerto Natales** via Río Turbio, daily, 6 hrs including tedious border crossing, US$15 (advance booking recommended). **Bus Sur** and **Zaahj** make the journey via Cerro Castillo (a simpler crossing), 5 weekly, 4½-5 hrs, US$15. **Chaltén Travel** runs regular services in summer to Torres del Paine, US$45.

Taxi

Travel by road to the most interesting spots near El Calafate is limited and may require taxis. Tours can be arranged with taxi drivers at the airport who await arrivals. To **Río Gallegos**, 4 hrs, US$100 for up to 5 people.

ⓘ Directory

El Calafate p464, map p465

Airline office LADE, Roca 1004, T02902-491262, www.lade.com.ar **Banks and currency exchange** There are several ATMs in town. Travel agencies such as Interlagos change notes; YPF garage, Chocolate El Calafate and some other shops give good rates for cash; Albergue del Glaciar charges 5% commission on TCs; the Scorpio snack bar on Libertador is reported to give the best rates. Many businesses add 10% for credit card transactions. Remember that US dollar notes are widely accepted. **Bicycle hire** Mountain bikes can be hired from Bike Way, Espora 20, T02902-492180, US$7 per day. **Laundry** El Lavadero, Libertador 1474, US$3 a load, also has internet access. **Post office** Libertador; service is quicker from Puerto Natales (Chile). **Telephone** Open Calafate, Libertador 996, good service, with internet.

Parque Nacional Los Glaciares

This park, the second largest in Argentina, covers more than 660,000 ha. Over a third is covered by the hielos continentales, giant icefields that straddle the border with Chile. Of the 47 major glaciers that flow from the icefields, 13 descend into the park to feed two great lakes, Lago Argentino and Lago Viedma. The Río La Leona, flowing south from Lago Viedma, links the two lakes. There are also 190 other smaller glaciers that aren't even connected to the icefields. East of the icefields are areas of forest, which eventually give way to Patagonian steppe. Here, there are over 100 species of bird, among them the condor, the Patagonian woodpecker, the austral parakeet, the green-backed firecrown as well as blacknecked swans, Andean ruddy ducks and torrent ducks. Guanacos, grey foxes, skunks and rheas can be seen on the steppe, while the endangered huemul inhabits the forest.

Ins and outs

Getting there   There are two sections of the park, around Lago Argentino and the Perito Moreno glacier, and around Cerro Fitz Roy. To get to the former, most people take one of the minibuses that leave daily from El Calafate. To get to the latter, take a daily bus from El Calafate to El Chaltén. ▶▶ *For further details, see Transport, page 475.* **Getting around**   Once in a section of the park, most people walk, but to go from one part of the park to another, it is necessary to return to Calafate first and change buses. **Climate**   Many facilities are

Parque Nacional Los Glaciares

The advance and retreat of the Moreno glacier

The Moreno glacier is frequently said to be in retreat as a result of global warming. Although the glacier no longer blocks Brazo Rico on a three-yearly cycle, such statements must be treated with caution.

Glaciers are usually described by glaciologists as advancing, retreating or stable. However, even a retreating glacier will continue moving slowly forward; its frontage or snout retreats because it melts or breaks up at a faster rate than its forward movement. Although the Moreno glacier no longer behaves as it did up until 1988, it is considered by glaciologists to be stable: its rates of forward movement and break-up are in a rough equilibrium.

One of the most puzzling things about glaciers is the way they change their behaviour. As far as is known, the Moreno glacier did not block Brazo Rico until 1917; according to early scientific studies its snout was 750 m away from the Magallanes Peninsula in 1900, a distance that had dropped to 350 m by 1908. In 1917, the small dam formed by the ice broke after a few weeks; the next time the glacier blocked the fjord was in 1934-5. Between this date and 1988 the glacier moved forward more vigorously; in 1939, when it reached the Magallanes Peninsula again, the waters in Brazo Rico rose 9 m and flooded coastal areas, leading to attempts by the Argentine navy to bomb it from the air. These failed but the waters eventually broke through. After 1939 the glacier reached the Peninsula about every three years until 1988. Its changed behaviour since then may be related to global warming, but we also need to know why the glacier started advancing so vigorously in the first place – one theory is that it was being pushed forward by an unknown glacier on the Campo de Hielos Sur.

closed off season. The climate is variable, depending on altitude and season. The best time to visit is between October and March. Temperatures in summer reach 20-25°C and even 30°C on occasions, so remember your sun block at all times.

Albergue del Glaciar offers tours to the glacier via Estancia Anita, the site of farmworkers massacred during the failed Patagonian Revolution. Consult La Patagonia Rebelde by Osvaldo Bayer for further details.

Rainfall ranges from 2,000 mm in the far west to 400 mm in the east, falling mainly between March and late May. **Visitor information** Trekking information is available in El Chaltén from the **national park office** ⓘ *across the bridge at the entrance to the town, T02962-493004.* The village also has a **tourist office** ⓘ *Guemes 21, T02962-493011, www.el chalten.com, Mon-Fri 0900-2000, Sat and Sun 1300-2000.* Both provide helpful maps of the area, showing paths, campsites, distances and walking times. Lighting fires and camping wild are prohibited throughout the park. Access to the central sector of the park, north of Lago Argentino and south of Lago Viedma, is difficult and there are few tourist facilities, although *estancias*, such as Helsingfors and La Cristina, offer accommodation and excursions. The Helsingfors also offers boat trips to the Viedma Glacier.

Lago Argentino and around

The source of the Río Santa Cruz, one of the most important rivers in Patagonia, Lago Argentino covers some 1,400 sq km. At its western end there are two networks of fjords (*brazos*), fed by glaciers (*ventisqueros*). The major attraction in the park is the **Ventisquero Perito Moreno**, which reaches the water at a narrow point in one of the fjords, opposite Peninsula Magallanes, 80 km, west of Calafate.

: Beware: flying ice

"One or two of the tourists who ignore the prohibition signs and walk down to the rocks overlooking the channel in front of the glacier always get washed away every season. They all think it won't happen to them, but it does; 60 m of ice break off and hit the water just in front of them. But it isn't the water that kills them, it's the chunks of flying ice."

Carlos Dupáez, Superintendent, Parque Nacional Los Glaciares, interviewed in the *Buenos Aires Herald*, 1 November 1997.

Spectacular, especially at sunset, the Moreno glacier is constantly moving and never silent and was, until recently, one of the few in the world still advancing. Five kilometres across, 20 km long and 60 m high, it used to advance across Brazo Rico, blocking the fjord roughly every three years; as the water pressure built up behind it, the ice would break, reopening the channel and sending giant icebergs (témpanos) rushing down the appropriately named Canal de los Témpanos. Since February 1988 this has not occurred, possibly because of global warming.

From the viewing area the glacier stretches back in a sheet of white towards the Chilean frontier. The ice is riven by crevasses; the noise as it cracks and strains can be heard clearly. As pieces break off and collapse into the water, there is a roar. Boardwalks allow a close-up view of the glacier; there is a fine of up to US$250 for leaving the boardwalks, apart from on guided expeditions onto the glacier itself.

The fjords at the northwestern end of Lago Argentino are fed by four other glaciers, including the **Ventisquero Upsala**, which is considered the largest glacier in South America at 60 km long, over 100 m thick and with a frontage 10 km wide. **Spegazzini**, further south, has a frontage 1½ km wide and is 130 m high. In between are **Agassiz** and **Onelli**, both of which feed **Lago Onelli**, a quiet and very beautiful lake, full of icebergs of every size and sculpted shape, surrounded by beech forests on one side and ice-covered mountains on the other.▸▸ *For Sleeping, Eating and other listings, see pages 473-475.*

Cerro Fitz Roy and El Chaltén

In the far north of the park, 230 km north of El Calafate at the western end of Lago Viedma is Cerro Fitz Roy (3,405 m), part of a granite massif that also includes the peaks of Cerro Torre (3,128 m), Poincenot (3,076 m), Egger (2,673 m), Guillaumet (2,503 m), Saint-Exupery (2,600 m), Aguja Bífida (2,394 m) and Cordón Adela (2,938 m). Clearly visible from a distance, Fitz Roy towers above the nearby peaks, its sides normally too steep for snow to settle. Named after the captain of the Beagle who saw it from afar in 1833 (its Tehuelche name was El Chaltén), it was first climbed by a French expedition in 1952.

●*Do not stray from the paths. A map is essential, even on short walks.*

The area around the base of the massif offers fine walking opportunities and stupendous views that anyone within 500 miles would be a fool to miss. Occasionally at sunrise the mountains are briefly lit up bright red for a few seconds: this phenomenon is known as the *amanecer de fuego* ('sunrise of fire').

At the foot of Fitz Roy, 230 km northwest of El Calafate, is this small village of **El Chaltén**. It was founded in 1985 for military reasons – to settle the area and pre-empt Chilean territorial claims, and still has something of a frontier feel about it. Growing rapidly as a centre for some of the best trekking and climbing in Patagonia, it also offers cross country skiing opportunities in winter.

Northwest from El Chaltén, a trail leads via a good campsite with wonderful views at Lago Capri to Campamento Río Blanco and nearby Campamento Poincenot (two to three hours). From here, a path heads up to the blue **Lago de los Tres** and the green

Lago Sucia; it's a two- to three-hour round trip to the lakes from the camps. From Campamento Río Blanco, another trail runs north along the Río Blanco and west along the Río Eléctrico to **Piedra del Fraile** (four hours). From here, you can continue to **Lago Eléctrico** or follow a path south up **Cerro Eléctrico Oeste** (1,882 m) towards the north face of Fitz Roy (two hours); it's a tough climb but there are spectacular views. This route passes through private property: the owner only allows you to walk through.

Heading west from El Chaltén, a trail runs along the Río Fitz Roy to **Laguna Torre** (three hours), beautifully situated at Cerro Torre and fed by the Torre glacier. Southwest from El Chaltén, meanwhile, a badly marked path leads to **Laguna Toro** (six hours) and the southern entrance of the icefields.

The park information centre (see Ins and outs, above) provides photocopied maps of treks, but the best one is published by Zagier and Urruty, 1992, US$6; available in shops in El Calafate and El Chaltén. ▶▶ *For Sleeping, Eating and other listings, see pages 473-475.*

Lago del Desierto
Some 37 km north of El Chaltén and surrounded by forests, this lake is reached by an unpaved road that leads along the Río de las Vueltas via **Laguna Condor**, where flamingos can be seen. A path runs along the east side of the lake to its northern tip, from

The Fitz Roy area

Camping ▲
Campamento Poincenot 1
Campamento Río Blanco 2

where a trail leads west along the valley of the Río Diablo to **Laguna Diablo.** Excursions to Lago del Desierto from El Chaltén are offered by **Chaltén Travel,** daily in summer (see page 467). There are also daily boat trips on the lake on board the *Mariana* ① daily *1030, 1330, 1630, 2 hrs, US$20.*

● Sleeping

In the park *p468, map p469*

L Estancia Helsingfors, *shores of Brazo Sur at the southern end of Lago Viedma, T02902-420719, www.helsingfors.com.ar* With breakfast, full board available (good food), many treks, boat trips on Lago Viedma and flights over glaciers available, also riding, sheep-shearing, daily sailing across Lago Viedma, via the Viedma glacier. Recommended.

L Los Notros, *40 km west of El Calafate on the road to the Moreno glacier, T02902-491437, www.lastland.com* Spacious, rooms with views of the glacier, transport from airport. Breakfast included; other meals extra.

Camping

Apart from those in El Chaltén, all campsites in the national park are free. There are no toilets so bury your waste. A stove is essential for camping as wood is scarce and lighting fires is prohibited in campsites in the national park. Take warm clothes and a good sleeping bag. You can rent equipment in El Chaltén, ask at the park entrance, or from the *artésania* shop on the road past **Albergue Patagonia**.

There are 3 campsites en route from El Calafate to the glacier. Take food to all 3. **Río Mitre**, *near the park entrance, 52 km from El Calafate, 26 km east of the glacier.*

Arroyo Correntoso, *10 km east of the glacier.* No facilities but nice location.

Bahia Escondida, *7 km east of the glacier.* Toilets and hot showers, crowded in summer, free off season but no water.

The campsite at **Piedra del Fraile**, just outside the park, has *cabañas* (with hot showers) and tent pitches, US$5, plus an expensive shop.

El Chaltén *p471, map p472*

L-AL Hostería El Puma, *Lionel Terray 545, T02962-493095, www.elchalten.com/elpuma* With breakfast, comfortable, lounge with log fire, tours arranged. Recommended.

AL La Aldea, *Av M Guemes s/n, T02962-493040, www.patagonia-travel.com/ aldea.html* Fully furnished apartments sleeping 4-6.

A Hotel Lago del Desierto, *T02962-493010, www.elchalten.com/hotellagodeldesierto* Good beds, *comedor*, Italian spoken, camping US$5.

A-D Fitz Roy Inn, *San Martin s/n, T02962-493062, www.elchalten.com/ fitzroyinn* With breakfast and restaurant, Also shared cabins.

A-E Casa de Piedra, *Lago del Desierto s/n, T02962-493015, www.lacasapiedra.com/ lacasadepiedra* Shared cabins, also 4-bed cabins with bath, new restaurant, trekking guides (English, French and Italian spoken).

B Estancia La Quinta, *3 km from Chaltén, T02962-493012, info@estancialaquinta.com.ar* Half-board, no heating, prepares lunch for trekkers. Recommended.

C La Base, *Lago del Desierto 97, T02962-493031, www.elchalten.com/labase* With bath, nice atmosphere, self-service breakfast, kitchen facilities, video rental, hot water, heating, helpful.

D Cabañas Cerro Torre, *Halvorsen 110, T02962-493061, www.elchalten.com/ cerrotorre* Built for the Herzog film *El Grito de la Piedra*, fully equipped cabins sleep 4/6, heating, kitchenette.

E Hostería Los Ñires, *Lago del Desierto s/n, T02962-493009, www.elchalten.com/losnires* Doubles and dormitories, and camping, US$5.

F Albergue Rancho Grande, *San Martín s/n, T02962-493005, rancho@cotecal.com.ar* Price per person in small dormitories, good bathrooms, laundry and kitchen facilities, Hostelling International discounts, English, Italian, French, German spoken, highly recommended, reservations from **Chaltén Travel** in Calafate (see page 467).

F-G Albergue Patagonia, *San Martín 493, T02962-461564, www.elchalten.com/ patagonia* Price per person for dormitory accommodation, kitchen and laundry facilities, TV and video, book exchange, accepts TCs, comfortable, Hostelling International discounts, mountain bike rental US$10 per day, reservations for local excursions (Lago del Desierto, Lago Viedma boat trip, ice trek on Cerro Torre glacier). Highly recommended. Next door is the **Bar de Ahumados**, which serves regional specialities, homemade pasta and local ice cream.

These three campsites in the village all have hot showers. Showers are also available at the **Albergue Patagonia** and at **Confitería La Senyera** for US$2. There is also a campsite at the southern end of the **Lago del Desierto**.
Del Lago, *Lago del Desierto 135, T02962-493010*.
El Refugio, *San Martín s/n*.
El Relincho, *San Martín s/n, T02962-493007*.

🍴 Eating

El Chaltén *p471, map p472*
$$ **El Bodegón**, *San Martín s/n*. Small pub that brews its own beer, also serves reasonable food.
$$ **Josh Aike**. Excellent *confitería*, homemade food, beautiful building. Recommended.
$$ **La Senyera del Torre**. Pub/restaurant, excellent bread. Recommended.
$$ **Ruca Mahuida**, *Lionel Terray s/n*. Imaginative food using local ingredients.
$$ **The Wall Pub**. Breakfasts and meals, plus interesting videos of ascents of Fitz Roy and Cerro Torre.
$ **Las Lengas**, *Güemes y A de Viedma*. Large portions, good value.

🎉 Festivals and events

El Chaltén *p471, map p472*
The **Día de la Tradición** on 10 Nov is celebrated with *gaucho* events, riding and a barbecue (US$5).

⭕ Shopping

El Chaltén *p471, map p472*
There are several small shops selling food, gas and batteries (**Despensa 2 de Abril** is said to be cheapest) but you're better off buying supplies in El Calafate (cheaper and more choice). Many places bake good bread. Fuel is available.
Viento Oeste, *T02962-493021*. Rents and sells mountain equipment.

🔺 Activities and tours

Ventisquero Moreno *p470*
Equip yourself with warm clothes, food and drink for any trip to the glacier.

Tours from El Calafate
In addition to buses by **Interlagos** and **Taqsa** (see p468), many agencies run minibus tours, US$18 return (plus US$3.50 park entry), leaving around 0800 or around 1430, 6-7 hr trip, allowing 3 hrs at the glacier, return ticket valid if you come back next day (student discount available). Several agencies offer walking excursions on the Ventisquero Moreno, usually finishing with champagne or whisky with ice chipped from the glacier. For contact details, see p467. It is also possible to visit from Puerto Natales (see p450), which is cheaper than staying in Argentina.

Out of season, trips to the glacier are difficult to arrange, but you could gather a group and hire a taxi (US$40 for 4 passengers round trip); try **Remise Taxis**, *T02902-491745*. Ask rangers where you can camp out of season; there are no facilities except for a decrepit toilet block.

Boat trips
A boat leaves twice daily to the glacier from near the park entrance. Most of the minibus tours are timed to coincide with departure. The boats (with capacity for up to 60 passengers) take you right up to the face of the glacier, 1 hr, US$10, recommended.

Ventisquero Upsala *p471*
Pay in dollars and take food. Out of season it is extremely difficult to get to the glacier.
Fernández Campbell (see p467) runs daily bus and boat tours in summer to visit the Upsala glacier, Lago Onelli, the Onelli glacier and the Spegazzini glacier (check before going that access to the face of the Upsala glacier is possible). Bus departs 0730 from El Calafate for Punta Bandera, 50 km west, from where the tour boats depart. The price includes bus fares and park entry fees. 1 hr is allowed for a meal at the restaurant near Lago Onelli. Return bus to Calafate at 1930: a tiring day, it is often cold and wet, but memorable.
Upsala Explorer, *9 de Julio 69, T02902-491034/491133, reservascristinaing@cotecal.com.ar* Organizes tours for US$100, including lunch, 4WD trip and guided hikes around Estancia Cristina with amazing views of the glacier. Reservations can be made through several agencies.

Cerro Fitz Roy *p471, map p472*
Climbing
Base camp for climbing Fitz Roy is **Campamento Río Blanco** (see above). Permits for climbing are available at the national park information office. The best time is mid-Feb to end-Mar; Nov-Dec is very windy; Jan is fair; winter is extremely cold. Most of the peaks in the Fitz Roy massif and the Campo de Hielo Continental (continental icefield), which marks the frontier with Chile, are for very experienced climbers only. For the icefields guides are essential; the terrain is ice and rock and should only be tackled by extremely fit climbers. Necessary gear includes double boots, crampons, pickaxe, ropes, winter clothing; ask **Sr Guerra** in El Chaltén about hiring animals to carry equipment.

Fitz Roy Expediciones, *El Chaltén, T02962-493017, www.elchalten.com/fitzroy* Experienced guide Alberto del Castillo organizes adventure excursions, including trekking on the Campo de Hielo Continental and horseriding, English and Italian spoken. Highly recommended.

Horse treks
Prices from El Chaltén to Laguna Capri US$15; Laguna Torre US$20; Río Blanco, Piedra del Fraile and Laguna Toro all US$25 each; contact **Rodolfo Guerra**, *T02962-493020*, or **El Relincho**, *T02962-493007*.

Transport

El Chaltén *p471, map p472*
Bus
To **Calafate**, **Chaltén Travel**, Los Glaciares and Caltur, several daily in summer, less frequent off season, 4 hrs, US$7 one way. Bear in mind that day trips from Calafate involve a lot of travelling and little time to see the area, although some agencies offer deals, for example return travel by regular bus and 1 night's accommodation for US$50.

To **Los Antiguos**, north along Ruta 40, **Chaltén Travel**, 3 weekly, 14 hrs, US$40. Best to book return before departure during high season. Off season, travel is difficult and there's little transport for hitching. Agencies charge US$100 1 way for up to 8 people, US$150 return.

The Far South Parque Nacional Los Glaciares

For an explanation of sleeping and eating price codes used in this guide, see inside the front cover. Other relevant information is found in Essentials, see pages 51-58.

Introduction

Tierra del Fuego really feels like the bottom of the world. The northern area is a desolate land of vast sheep farms, while further south are mountains, icy-blue glaciers, pristine lakes and forests that turn golden in the autumn. Whether you ride a pick-up through the wastes of the north, hike through thick, silent forests, or navigate the Beagle Channel, travel in this region is an unforgettable adventure.

The island is now divided between Argentina and Chile; both are covered in this section. The main centre is the Argentine city of **Ushuaia**, which is a base for visiting the mountains and the starting point for boat trips along the **Beagle Channel**. On the southern shore of the channel is the Chilean island of **Isla Navarino** and the town of Puerto Williams, and to the south of Navarino lies the end of the world at **Cape Horn**.

★ Don't miss...

❶ **Lago Blanco** One of the remotest spots in the whole of Chilean Patagonia with some of the best fishing in the country, page 482.

❷ **Museo Martín Gusinde** A tribute to the lost peoples of Tierra del Fuego, page 484.

❸ **Isla Navarino** Trek around the island for the fantastic views of forests and glaciers, page 484.

❹ **Cape Horn** Cruise through icy, beautiful channels and, on arrival, stand on the cliff above the mist and waves with rain lashing into your face on the back of 100 km per hour winds, page 484.

❺ **Parque Nacional Tierra del Fuego** Take the southernmost train in the world – a must for rail buffs, page 490.

❻ **Estancia Harberton** Gain a sense of the endurance and bravery of the pioneers to Tierra del Fuego, page 489.

Background

Human habitation of Tierra del Fuego dates back some 10,000 years; four indigenous groups inhabited the island until the early 20th century. The most numerous, the Onas (also known as the Selk'nam), were hunter-gatherers in the north, living mainly on guanaco and several species of rodents. The southeastern corner of the island was inhabited by the Haus or Hausch, also hunter-gatherers, of whom very little is known. The Yaganes or Yámanas lived along the Beagle Channel and on the islands further south. A seafaring people who survived mainly on seafood, fish and seabirds, they were physically smaller than the Onas but had a strongly developed upper body for rowing long distances. The fourth group, the Alacalufe, lived in the west of Tierra del Fuego as well as on the Chonos Archipelago, surviving by fishing and hunting seals.

The first Europeans to visit the island came with the Portuguese navigator Fernão Magalhães (Magellan), who, in 1520, sailed through the channel that bears his name. The story is that, seeing fires lit on shore, Magellan and his crew called the place 'Tierra del Fuego' ('the land of fire'). However, as a result of numerous maritime disasters, including the failure of Sarmiento de Gamboa's attempt at colonizing the Straits in 1584, the indigenous population were left undisturbed for three centuries.

Fitzroy and Darwin's visits in 1832 and 1833 were a precursor to determined attempts to convert the indigenous groups. Several disastrous missions followed; the first successful mission was finally established in 1869 and, in 1884, the Reverend Thomas Bridges founded a mission at Ushuaia. Bridges was the first European to learn the Yámana language, which eased his task. He soon had many Yámana settled around Ushuaia and compiled his Yámana-English dictionary for the ease of conversion. Charles Darwin had written that the Yámana language "barely deserves to be called articulate", but Yámana turned out to have an extraordinarily rich vocabulary: the dictionary had 32,000 words, and was not complete at the time of Bridges' death. See also box page 489.

The work of the missionaries was disturbed by two developments: the discovery of gold (see box opposite) and the growth of sheep farming. The Ona were attracted to the 'white guanacos' on their land and hunted them. The colonists responded by offering two sheep for each Ona that was killed (proof was provided by a pair of Ona ears). The indigenous groups were further ravaged by epidemics of European diseases. In a desperate attempt to save the Ona, Salesian missionaries founded three missions in the Magellan Straits in the early 20th century, but, stripped of their land, the Ona lost the will to live; the last Ona died in 1999. The Hausch also died out. One old Yámana lady presently survives near Puerto Williams and there is a handful of Alacalufe at Puerto Edén in the Chonos Archipelago.

Imprecision in the original colonial land division and the greed of the rush southwards led to border disputes between Argentina and Chile. These still rumble on today. The initial settlement of the dispute in 1883 was followed by a desire by both governments to populate the area by allocating large expanses of land for sheep farming. The main beneficiaries of this policy on Tierra del Fuego were the Menendez and Braun families, already established in Punta Arenas.

For many years, the main economic activity of the northern part of the island was sheep farming, but Argentine government tax incentives to companies in the 1970s led to the establishment of new industries in Río Grande and Ushuaia and a rapid growth in the population of both cities; the subsequent withdrawal of incentives has produced increasing unemployment and migration. Tourism is increasingly important in Ushuaia.

For a detailed narrative account of Tierra del Fuego, *Savage – The Life and Times of Jemmy Button* by Nick Hazelwood (Hodder & Stoughton, 2000) is recommended reading. See also page 554.

Gold fever

The Tierra del Fuego Gold Rush began with Julio Popper, a German settler who came to San Sebastián in 1887, where he founded the El Paramó mine. By the time he died in 1893, his company had extracted 600 kilos of gold from El Paramó and from along the Beagle Channel.

After his death, gold mining in Tierra del Fuego became a much larger scale business. Many prospectors came from North America and Europe hoping to get rich. The largest group were Croats from Dalmatia, then part of the Austrian Empire. In 1909, the gold suddenly ran out, but the short-lived gold rush had lasting consequences: many descendants of Croatian prospectors still live in the area.

Geography

Tierra del Fuego is separated from the South American mainland by the Magellan Strait to the north; to the east is the Atlantic Ocean. The Beagle Channel separates Tierra del Fuego from other islands to the south and a complex network of straits divide it from the Pacific Ocean to the west.

The north of Tierra del Fuego is steppe sprinkled with grassland but further south the island is crossed from east to west by the continuation of the Andes, with sub-Antarctic forests growing up to about 600 m. In the Argentine sector peaks rise to around 1,500 m, but in the Chilean part, in the far southwest, there are peaks of well over 2,000 m. The main rivers drain into the Beagle Channel and into Lago Fagnano, the largest lake on

When crossing the border, make sure you get an entry stamp for as long as you require; note that Argentine time is one hour ahead of Chilean time from March to October.

the island, which straddles the frontier between Chile and Argentina. There are numerous other lakes, including Lagos Yehuín and Chapelmuth, just north of Lago Fagnano in Argentine territory, and Lagos Blanco, Chico and Lynch in Chilean territory. Trout and salmon inhabit nearly all the lakes and rivers. One hundred and fifty bird species have been identified on the island, including wild geese and ducks in summer. The Bahía San Sebastián is an important area for migratory birds. Mammals include native guanacos and red foxes, plus introduced species such as musk rats, beaver and rabbits.

Climate

The island's climate is sub-Antarctic. In Ushuaia, southwesterly winds prevail, ranging from 15 kph to 100 kph. September to March are the windy months, while winter is normally calmer. In winter, average daily temperatures hover around zero but in summer they range from 15°C during the day to 5°C at night. Further north, in Río Grande, westerly winds blow up to 200 km per hour almost all year round; average temperatures range from -3°C to 2°C in winter and from 5°C to 15°C in summer. Rainfall is higher in Ushuaia than further north; in Río Grande most rain falls in summer and autumn.

Ins and outs

Getting there

Flights to and from the island are heavily booked in summer, especially in January. There are airports at Porvenir and Puerto Williams (Chile) and at Río Grande and Ushuaia (Argentina). There are also two ferry crossings: Punta Arenas to Porvenir and Punta Delgada to Punta Espora. The latter short crossing is via the Primera Angostura (First Narrows), 170 km northeast of Punta Arenas.

The only legal crossing between the Chilean and Argentine parts of Tierra del Fuego is 142 km east of Porvenir. There are two settlements called San Sebastián, one on each side of the border, but they are 14 km apart and taxis are not allowed to cross the frontier, which means you must travel on one of the scheduled buses or with your own transport. If you are hitching, try to pick up an Argentine lorry at the Punta Delgada ferry crossing. Throughout Tierra del Fuego the roads are narrow and gravelled. The exceptions are San Sebastián (Argentina)-Ushuaia, which is almost all paved, and the road for about 50 km east of Porvenir, which is being widened. Fuel is available in Porvenir, Cerro Sombrero and Cullen (Chile), and Río Grande, Ushuaia and San Sebastián (Argentina). There are scheduled buses linking Punta Arenas, Río Grande and Ushuaia in summer. ▶▶ *For further details, see Transport, pages 486 and 495.*

Tourist information

Information on Chilean Tierra del Fuego is best sought from tour operators in Punta Arenas. The tourist office in Ushuaia is a good source for information on the Argentine side of the island. The international dialling code for Argentina is +54.

Chilean Tierra del Fuego

Chilean Tierra del Fuego forms part of Región XII (Magallanes), the capital of which is Punta Arenas. It is a wild spot, a mixture of rolling pampas, thick forests and imposing glaciers, with views of the Magellan Straits.

Porvenir → *Phone code: 061. Colour map 7, B1. Population: 4,500.*

Chilean Tierra del Fuego has a population of 7,000, most of whom live in Porvenir. Founded in 1894 as a port serving the sheep *estancias* of the island, this is the only town in Chilean Tierra del Fuego. It is quiet and pleasant. Many people are of Croatian descent and the signpost at the port marks the distance to Croatia. There is a small museum, the **Museo Fernando Cordero Rusque** ① *Samuel Valdivieso 402, T061-580098*, with archaeological and photographic displays on the Ona people, as well as sections on natural history and gold mining. There is a small **tourist office** annexed to the museum. ▶▶ *For Sleeping, Eating and other listings, see pages 485-487.*

Beyond Porvenir

About 90 km east of Porvenir, roads head north to San Sebastián and south to **Cameron**. This large farm settlement is the only other community of any size on the Chilean part of the island and lies 149 km southeast of Porvenir on the opposite shore of Bahía Inútil. Nearing Cameron, the southern mountains loom ahead and the road passes secluded canyons and bays, interspersed with a few farms. The road has little traffic, but there are a few vehicles daily in summer, so hitching is possible – although waiting on a windswept plain for hours may not be to everyone's liking.

❧ *If hitching note that the road to Lago Blanco forks east just before Cameron; stranded hitchhikers can shelter at the abandoned police post here.*

From Cameron a road runs southeast past an airfield and on for a further 40 km to a junction, where roads head north to San Sebastián and south to Sección Río Grande (7 km from the junction) and Estancia Vicuña (35 km further on) – there is very little traffic here. The road south climbs into the hills, through woods where guanacos hoot and run off into glades and the banks are covered with red and purple moss. The north shores of **Lago Blanco** can be reached by cutting through the woods from Sección Río Grande, with superb views of the mountains surrounding the lake and the snows in the south, or from Estancia Vicuña. In the centre of the lake is Isla Victoria,

⁝ Shipwrecked in the Magellan Straits

The Estrecho de Magallanes, 534 km long, is a treacherous sea passage with a long history of claiming victims. The hostile conditions are eloquently conveyed in the words of Sir John Narborough: "horrible like the ruins of a world destroyed by terrific earthquakes".

From the Atlantic the first navigational problem facing sailors is simply the difficulty of entering the Straits against the fierce westerly gales that prevail. Once in the Straits the dangers are far from over: many ships have fallen victim to the notorious Williwaws, winds with the ferocity of tornados that spring up from nowhere; no less vicious are the Pamperos, which blow off the land with enough force to capsize a vessel.

Although in 1520 Magellan succeeded in passing through the straits that bear his name, few others managed to do so in the years that followed: of the 17 ships that attempted the passage in the early 16th century, only one, the *Victoria*, succeeded in reaching the Pacific and returning to Europe. Twelve were lost near the eastern entrance and four returned in failure. The reason these early navigators chose to attempt the dangerous voyage was the lure of a short route between Europe and the spices of the East. Even when it became clear that there was no such short route, the Straits still provided a useful means for Europeans to reach the rich Pacific ports of Peru and Chile without disembarking to cross Mexico or Panama overland.

Even with the development of advanced navigation techniques in the 19th century, losses continued: in 1869, for instance, the *Santiago*, an iron paddle-steamer built in Glasgow and owned by the Pacific Mail line, went down off Isla Desolación at the western end of the Straits with a cargo of gold and silver.

While the Panama Canal now provides a shorter route between the Atlantic and Pacific Oceans, the size of modern ships means that the Straits are still a busy shipping route. The most common cargo is now oil; casualties still occur with, of course, the added risk of environmental disaster from oil spillage.

which has accommodation (see Sleeping below). The lake area can be very cold, even in mid-summer; biting winds sweep in from the south, so wrap up warmly.

Beyond Vicuña a horse trail leads south across the Darwin Range to the tiny hamlet of **Yendegaia** on the Beagle Channel. The journey takes 10 to 14 days, across mountains and sphagnum bogs. It is very remote and used almost exclusively by *carabineros* patrolling from Yendegaia, so should only be attempted by experienced riders or hikers. Crossing the border into Argentina from here is not permitted, although it may sometimes be possible to get a berth on one of the navy supply ships that occasionally call in.

Isla Navarino

Situated on the southern shore of the Beagle Channel, Isla Navarino is unspoilt and beautiful, with a chain of rugged snowy peaks, magnificent woods and many animals. Guanacos and condors can be seen inland, as well as large numbers of beavers, which were introduced to the island and have done a lot of damage. The flight from Punta Arenas is beautiful, with superb views of Tierra del Fuego, the Cordillera Darwin, the Beagle Channel and the islands stretching south to Cape Horn.

The only settlement of any size on the island is Puerto Williams, a Chilean naval base situated about 50 km east of Ushuaia (Argentina). Puerto Williams is the southernmost permanently inhabited town in the world; 50 km east-south-east is Puerto Toro, the southernmost permanently inhabited settlement on earth. Some maps mistakenly mark a road from Puerto Williams to Puerto Toro: this does not exist; access is only by sea. Due to the long-running border dispute with Argentina here, Puerto Williams is controlled by the Chilean Navy. Outside the Naval headquarters, you can see the bow section of the *Yelcho*, the tug chartered by Shackleton to rescue men stranded on Elephant Island (see box, page 491).

Museo Martín Gusinde ① *Mon-Thu 1000-1300, 1500-1800, 1500-1800 Sat and Sun, US$1*, known as the Museo del Fin del Mundo ('End of the World Museum') is full of information about vanished indigenous tribes, local wildlife and famous voyages by Charles Darwin and Fitzroy of the *Beagle*. A visit is highly recommended. There is a tourist office near the museum (closed in winter), which can provide maps and information on hiking. A kilometre west of the town is the yacht club (one of Puerto Williams' two nightspots), whose wharf is made from a sunken 1930s Chilean warship. The last of the Yámana people live at **Villa Ukika**, 2 km east of town, where there are beaver dams and waterfalls. ▶ *For Sleeping, Eating and other listings, see pages 485-487.*

Exploring the island

For superb views, climb **Cerro Bandera**, which is reached by a path from the dam 4 km west of the town (three- to four-hour round trip, steep, take warm clothes). A four- to five-day walking circuit, the 'Dientes de Navarino' begins here (information in the tourist office at Puerto Williams). There are views of Cape Horn in clear weather but conditions change quickly and it can snow on the hills, even in high summer.

Beyond Cerro Bandera, a road leads 56 km west of Puerto Williams to Puerto Navarino. There is little or no traffic on this route and it is very beautiful, with forests of lengas stretching right down to the water's edge. At **Mejillones**, 32 km from Puerto Williams, is a graveyard and memorial to the Yámana people. Just before Estancia Santa Rosa (10 km further on), a path is said to cross the forest, lakes and beaver dams to Wulaia (four to six hours), where the *Beagle* anchored in 1833; however, even the farmer at Wulaia gets lost following this track.

> **♦** *No equipment is available for rent on the island; if you plan to explore you should buy food in Punta Arenas.*

At **Puerto Navarino** there are a handful of marines and an abandoned police post, where you may be allowed to sleep. There are beautiful views across to Ushuaia and west to icebound Hoste Island and the Darwin Massif. A path continues to a cliff above the Murray Narrows; blue, tranquil and utterly calm. If trekking alone in wild parts of the island, beware of sinking mud caused by beaver dams; note also that there is quite a high incidence of rabies among domestic and wild animals (including beavers).

Cape Horn

It is possible to catch a boat south from Isla Navarino to Cape Horn (the most southerly piece of land on earth apart from Antartica). There is one pebbly beach on the north side of the island; boats anchor in the bay and passengers are taken ashore by motorized dinghy. A rotting stairway climbs the cliff above the beach, up to the building where three marines run the naval post. A path leads from here to the impressive monument of an albatross overlooking the wild, churning waters of the Drake Passage below. ▶ *For further details, see Transport, page 486.*

> **●** *For an explanation of sleeping and eating price codes used in this guide, see inside the front cover. Other relevant information is found in Essentials, see pages 51-58.*

Isla de los Estados

"This long (75 km) and guarded island lies east of Tierra del Fuego. It is famous in Patagonia as the setting for Jules Verne's novel, *The Lighthouse at the End of the World* – ruins of the lighthouse remain. Except for the caretakers of the lighthouse and an occasional scientist, few people ever set foot on this cloud-shrouded reserve of Fuegian flora and fauna that no longer exist on the main island. During the 18th and 19th centuries, large numbers of ships were wrecked or lost in the treacherous waters surrounding this island. Much gold, silver and relics await salvage." Robert T Cook.

Sleeping

Porvenir *p482*

A Hostería Los Flamencos, *Tte Merino 018, T061-580049*. Comfortable, nice restaurant, best in town.

C Central, *Phillippi 298, T061-580077*. Rooms with hot water.

C Rozas, *Phillippi 296, T061-580088*. With bath, hot water, heating, restaurant and bar, laundry facilities. Recommended.

F España, *Croacia 698, T061-580160*. Price per person. Some rooms with bath, breakfast extra. Good restaurant with fixed-price lunch.

F Miramar, *Santos Mardones 366*. Price per person. Full board also available. Clean, friendly, heaters in rooms, hot water, views, good.

F-G Hosp Guaignio, *Santos Mardones 333, T061-580491, wshere@hotmail.com* Price per person without bath, including breakfast. Friendly and helpful, use of kitchen, clean, good value.

Beyond Porvenir *p482*

If you get stuck in the wilds, note that it is almost always possible to camp or bed down in a barn at an *estancia*.

B-F Hostería de la Frontera, *San Sebastián, T061-224731*. Rooms with bath and decent restaurant. Also basic, dirty accommodation in an annex, sleeping bag essential.

B-F Hostería Tunkelen, *Cerro Sombrero, 46 km south of Primera Angostura*. Rooms and dormitory accommodation. Recommended.

F Posada Las Flores, *Km 127 on the Porvenir-San Sebastián road*. Reservations via Hostal de la Patagonia in Punta Arenas.

G Pensión del Señor Alarcón, *Cerro Sombrero, 46 km south of Primera Angostura*. Good, friendly.

G Refugio Lago Blanco, *Lago Blanco, T061-241197*. The only accommodation on the lake.

Puerto Williams *p484*

You can also stay at private houses. Camping wild is cold but easy.

A-B Hostería Wala, *on the edge of Lauta bay, T061-621114, 2 km out of town*. Splendid walks in the area. Very hospitable.

C Pensión Temuco, *Piloto Pardo 224, T061-621113*. Price per person, including full board, comfortable, good food, hot showers. Slightly overpriced, but recommended.

C-D Hostería Camblor, *T061-621033*. Price per person, including full board.

E Hostal Yagan, *Piloto Pardo 260, T061-621334, hostalyagan@hotmail.com*. Price per person. Single and double rooms. Good meals available. Clean and comfortable, friendly, tours offered.

E Jeanette Talavera, *Maragaño 168, T061-621150, coiron@simltd.com* Small dormitories, kitchen and laundry facilities, also organize sailing trips.

E Res Onashaga, *run by Señor Ortiz - everyone knows him*. Price per person. Cold, rundown, good meals, helpful, full board available.

Eating

Porvenir *p482*

There are many lobster fishing camps nearby, where fishermen will prepare lobster on the spot.

$$ Club Croata, *Senoret y Phillippi*. On waterfront, good food, lively.

$$/$ Restaurante Puerto Montt, *Croacia 1169*. Recommended for seafood.

$ Miramar, *Croacia s/n*. Large portions, good value.

There are several grocery stores; prices are very high because of the remoteness. Beware drinking water from the rivers without purification. Away from the **Club Naútico**, nightlife in Puerto Williams is at the **Dientes de Navarino**, a bar in the plaza.

▲ Activities and tours

Porvenir *p482*
Turismo Cordillera de Darwin, *Croacia 675, T061-580206, www.explorepatagonia.cl* For tours of the island from a day to a week.

Puerto Williams *p484*
Sailing
Captain Ben Garrett offers recommended adventure sailing in his schooner *Victory* in Dec and Jan, including special trips to Ushuaia, cruises in the canals and voyages to Cape Horn, the glaciers, Puerto Montt and Antarctica. Write to Victory Cruises, Annex No 1 Puerto Williams (slow mail service); or call collect to Punta Arenas and leave a message with the Puerto Williams operator.

◉ Transport

Porvenir *p482*
Air
Aerovías DAP, *Señoret s/n, Porvenir, T061-580089, www.aeroviasdap.cl*, fly from Punta Arenas (weather and bookings permitting), twice daily Mon-Sat, US$23 one way. Heavily booked so make sure you have your return reservation confirmed.

Bus
Transportes Gessell, *Duble Almeyda 257, T061-580488* (also in Punta Arenas at *José Menéndez 556, T061-222896*) runs buses to **Río Grande** (Argentina), Tue and Sat 1400, 5 hrs, US$15; return service Wed and Sun 0800.

Local buses run to **Cameron** from C Manuel Señor, Mon and Fri 1700, US$10.

Ferry
The *Melinka* sails from **Tres Puentes** (5 km north of Punta Arenas; catch bus A or E from Av Magallanes, US$1; taxi US$3) to **Bahía Chilota**, 5 km west of Porvenir, Tue-Sun 0900 with an extra afternoon sailing Tue-Thur in season, 2½ hrs, pedestrians US$6, motorbikes

US$10, cars US$35; return from Porvenir in the afternoon Tue-Sun. From the ferry to Porvenir bus terminal, bus US$1.50, taxi US$5.

Timetable dependent on tides and subject to change: check in advance. The crossing can be rough and cold; watch for dolphins. Reservations are essential especially in summer (at least 24 hrs in advance for cars); obtainable from **Transbordadora Austral Broom**, *Bulnes 05075, Punta Arenas, T061-218100, www.tabsa.cl*

There is also a ferry service from **Punta Delgada** on the mainland to **Punta Espora**, 80 km north of Porvenir, usually every 45 mins (schedules vary with the tides), pedestrians US$2, motorbikes US$5, cars US$15. Before 1000 most space is taken by trucks. There is no bus service to or from this crossing; but, if hitching, note that this is the principal route between Ushuaia and mainland Argentina.

Puerto Williams *p484*
Air
Aerovías DAP flies 20-seater Cessna aircraft from Punta Arenas Mon-Sat, departure time varies, US$64 one way. Book well in advance; there are long waiting lists. Luggage allowance 10 kg (US$2 per kg extra). **Aeropetrel** will charter a plane from Puerto Williams to Cape Horn (US$2,600 for 8-10 people).

Ferry
There are no regular sailings from Ushuaia (Argentina). The following boats all depart from **Punta Arenas**.

Austral Broom ferry *Cruz Australis, www.tabsa.cl*, sails once a week, 36 hrs, US$120 for a reclining seat, US$150 for a bunk, meals included.

The *Navarino* sails 3rd week of every month, 12 passengers, US$150 one way; contact the owner, **Carlos Aguilera**, *21 de Mayo 1460, Punta Arenas, T061-228066.*

The *Beaulieu*, a cargo boat carrying a few passengers, sails once a month, US$300 return, 6 days.

In addition, the naval vessel *PSG Micalvi* sails once every 3 months from Punta Arenas to **Cape Horn** via Puerto Williams, and may take passengers to Cape Horn for approximately US$250 (letters of recommendation will help). Navy and port authorities in Puerto Williams may deny any knowledge, but everyone else knows when a boat is due; ask at the *Armada* in Punta Arenas (see p448). Otherwise ask at the yacht club about hitching a ride on a private yacht to Cape Horn.

⊙ Directory

Porvenir *p482*
Currency exchange Availalble at Estrella del Sur, *Santos Mardones*.

Puerto Williams *p484*
Airline offices Aerovías DAP, *Centro Comercial s/n, T061-621051, www.aeroviasdap.cl* **Post office** closes 1900. **Telephone** CTC, Mon-Sat 0930-2230, Sun 1000-1300, 1600-2200.

Argentine Tierra del Fuego

Argentine Tierra del Fuego belongs to the Province of Tierra del Fuego, Antártida y Las Islas del Atlántico Sur, the capital of which is Ushuaia. The population of the Argentine sector is around 85,000, most of whom live in the two towns of Río Grande and Ushuaia. Both bigger and more developed than the Chilean side of the island, it provides good territory for guided explorations of the wilderness.

Río Grande → *Phone code: 02964. Colour map 7, B2. Population: 35,000.*
Situated 87 km south of San Sebastián on the southern edge of the Bahía San Sebastián, Río Grande is the largest settlement in Tierra del Fuego. It is a sprawling modern town set among windy, dust-laden, sheep-grazing and oil-bearing plains. The *frigorífico* (frozen meat) plant and sheep-shearing shed are among the largest in South America.

The town has two small museums: the **Museo de Ciencias Naturales y História** ① *El Cano 225, Tue-Fri 0900-1700, Sat and Sun 1500-2000*, and the **Museo de la**

Río Grande

Sleeping	Hospedaje Noal **3**	Residencial	Eating
Argentino **6**	Isla del Mar **5**	Rawson **8**	Club de Pesca **1**
Atlántida **1**	Posada de los	Villa **9**	Don Rico **2**
Federico Ibarra **2**	Sauces **7**		La Nueva Colonial **3**

Ciudad ① *Alberdi 555, Mon-Fri 1000-1700*, which has exhibits on the history of the pioneers, missions and oil. There's a tourist information kiosk on the plaza in season, otherwise try the Municipalidad, on Elcano.

The Salesian Mission of **La Candelaria** ① *11 km north along Route 3, Mon-Sat 1000-1230, 1500-1900, Sun 1500-1900, US$1.50, afternoon tea US$3*, was founded in 1893 by José Fagnano as one of three missions set up to try to protect the Onas of Tierra del Fuego from marauding gold prospectors and *estancieros* (sheep farmers). However, by the time the mission closed in 1920, the overall Ona population of the island had shrunk from several thousand to only 276. La Candelaria now houses a historical museum with a collection of indigenous artefacts and a natural history section. Nearby is the first parish church of Río Grande. ▸▸ *For Sleeping, Eating and other listings, see pages 490-496.*

Ushuaia → *Phone code: 02901. Colour map 7, C2. Population: 45,000.*

The most southerly town in Argentina, Ushuaia is 234 km southwest of Río Grande by a new road via Paso Garibaldi. Founded in 1884, it is situated on the northern shore of the Beagle Channel, and its streets climb steeply towards snow-covered Cerro Martial to the north. The mainstays of the local economy are fishing and tourism.

Ins and outs
Getting there It is not surprising that Ushuaia is hard to reach. By road, the only scheduled bus connection is the run up to Río Grande, or the direct connections to Punta Arenas. By far the easiest way in is by air, on the daily flights from Buenos Aires, Río Gallegos or Río Grande or the twice-weekly flights from Punta Arenas. ▸▸ *For further details, see Transport, page 495.* **Getting around** Ushuaia is a relatively large town, and it may be worth taking taxis for some of the longer excursions, but everywhere within the central area is easily accessible by foot. **Tourist information** Ushuaia **tourist office** ① *San Martín 674, T02901-432000/1, www.tierradelfuego.org.ar, Mon-Fri 0830-2030, Sat and Sun 0900-2000*, is said to be the 'best in Argentina'. It has literature in English, German and Dutch, helpful staff (English spoken), a large list of hotels, a noticeboard for messages, plus information on travel and staying at Estancia Harberton. The **National Park Office** ① *San Martín between Patagonia y Sarmiento*, has a small map but not much additional information.

Sights
The old prison, **Presidio** ① *Yaganes y Gob Paz, daily 0900-2000, closed winter, US$4, student reductions*, at the back of the Naval Base, houses the **Museo Marítimo**, with models and artefacts from seafaring days, and, in the cells, the **Museo Penitenciario**, which details the history of the prison. Elsewhere in town is **Museo del Fin del Mundo** ① *Maipú y Rivadavia, T02091-421863, daily 1000-1300 and 1500-1930, US$1.50, students US$1*, has small displays on indigenous peoples, missionaries and first settlers, as well as a natural history section, recommended. The building also contains an excellent library with helpful staff. Also recommended for a visit is **Museo Fueguino** ① *Gob Godoy, daily 1100-1800, free*, which has interesting sections on indigenous peoples, plus videos and a library. ▸▸ *For Sleeping, Eating and other listings, see pages 490-496*

> ✎ *You can get an 'end of the world' stamp in your passport at the Museo del Fin del Mundo.*

Around Ushuaia
Seven kilometres behind the town, **Cerro Martial** offers fine views down the Beagle Channel and to the north. There's a chairlift (*Aerosilla*, US$2) to take you to the top, starting from the outskirts of town (follow Magallanes). There is skiing on the glacier in winter, as well as a café and *refugio*.

The Bridges of Harberton

An orphan from Bristol, Thomas Bridges was so named because he was found under a bridge with the letter T on his clothing. Bridges arrived in Tierra del Fuego from the Falkland Islands in 1871 with his wife, young daughter and his adoptive father, Reverend Despard. Until his death in 1898, he lived near the shores of the Beagle Channel, first at Ushuaia and then Harberton. Bridges devoted his life to his work with the Yámanas (Yaganes) and compiled a dictionary of their language, containing 32,000 words, which was not complete at his death. Of his six children the most famous was Lucas (1874-1949), who, after spending his early life among the Yámanas and Onas and learning their languages, chronicled their tragic fate in his memoir, *Uttermost Part of the Earth* (1947).

Away from literature, the main legacy of the Bridges family on Tierra del Fuego is their *estancia*, Harberton, which is still a working farm run by Thomas Bridges' great-grandson, Thomas Goodall. Visitors receive a conducted tour of the farm buildings and immediate surroundings; Thomas, in his dungarees and horn-rimmed glasses, and his wife, Natalie, are usually on hand. Natalie is an internationally recognized expert on whales and dolphins, which accounts for the whale jawbone arch over the garden entrance. The *estancia* incorporates a 'house of bones', where dolphin, whale and seal carcasses are cleaned and labelled for research, and entire skeletons are on display.

Harberton itself is named after the Devonshire village where Thomas Bridges' wife Mary was born. The farmhouse was prefabricated by her carpenter father, and then assembled on a spot chosen by the Yámanas as the most sheltered. The English connection is still evident in the neat garden of lawns between the jetty and the farmhouse. Behind the buildings is a large vegetable garden, a real rarity on the island. Visitors will notice that there is much more wildlife around the *estancia* than in the Tierra del Fuego National Park.

Estancia Harberton ① *85 km to the east of Ushuaia, T02901-422742, www.acatushun.com, open Oct-Apr*, is the oldest *estancia* on the island (see box, above). Run by descendants of its founder, Thomas Bridges, it offers guided walks through protected forest (US$3 per person), plus tours in English of the new **Museo Acatushún**, which has skeletons of South American birds and sea mammals. Refreshments are sold in the Manacatush *confitería*. Access is from a good *ripio* road, which branches off Route 3, 40 km east of Ushuaia and runs past **Lago Victoria**, then 25 km through forest before hitting the open country around Harberton. From the *estancia*, a track continues east along the channel through wild country towards very isolated *estancias*. For excursions to Harberton by boat see below. Other worthwhile destinations include the **Río Olivio falls** and the pristine, wild **Lagos Fagnano** and **Escondido,** 50 km from Ushuaia.

Beagle Channel

A sea trip along the Beagle Channel can be rough but is highly recommended. Destinations include the sea-lion colony at **Isla de los Lobos, Isla de los Pájaros, Les Eclaireurs lighthouse** and the penguin colony on **Isla Martillo.** It is also possible to visit Estancia Harberton by boat, although some agencies imply that their excursions go to the *estancia*, when in fact they only go to Harberton bay; others go by inflatable launch from the main boat to the shore. Check thoroughly in advance. ▶ *For further details, see Activities and tours, page 494.*

Covering 63,000 ha of mountains, lakes, rivers and deep valleys, the park stretches west to the Chilean border and north to Lago Fagnano. Large areas are closed to tourists to protect the environment, although this hasn't prevented the damage caused by introduced species, like rabbits, beavers and musk rats. The lower parts of the park are forested with lenga, ñire and coihue. Birdlife includes several species of geese, as well as ducks, Magellanic woodpeckers and austral parakeets.

❢ Beaver dams can be seen near the Chile border. With much luck and patience you may see the beavers themselves. Stand still and down-wind of them: their sense of smell and hearing are good, but their eyesight is poor.

The park entrance is 12 km west of Ushuaia ① *US$4*; administration is at Lapataia Bay. A Decauville-gauge tourist train currently runs along the shore of the Beagle Channel between the Fin del Mundo station west of Ushuaia and the boundary of the park (see page 496). Be sure to sit on the left on the outbound journey. Run by **Ferrocarril Austral Fueguino**, with new locomotives and carriages, the railway uses track first laid by prisoners to carry wood to Ushuaia. There are plans to extend the line to Lapataia.

Once inside the park, there are several beautiful walks: the most popular ones are an interpreted trail along **Lapataia Bay**, which is particularly good for birdwatching; a 5-km walk along **Lago Roca** to the Chilean frontier at Hito XXIV; and a 2½-km climb to **Cerro Pampa Alta**, which offers fine views. Club Andino in Ushuaia has a booklet explaining routes in the park (in Spanish) with poor maps. There are no recognized crossing points to Chile from the park.

Visitors to the park must be well prepared with suitable clothing; in winter the temperature drops as low as -12°C; in summer it goes up to 25°C, but the weather can still be cold, damp and unpredictable. ▸▸ *For Sleeping, Eating and other listings see pages 490-496.*

● Sleeping

Río Grande *p487, map p487*
Accommodation can be difficult to find if arriving at night.

B **Posada de los Sauces**, *El Cano 839, T02964-432895, posadadelossauces@ arnet.com.ar* With breakfast, good beds, comfortable, good restaurant, bar. Best in town. Recommended.

C **Atlántida**, *Belgrano 582, T02964-431914, atlantida@netcombbs.com.ar* Comfortable, with breakfast, bath, cable TV, restaurant, parking.

C **Federico Ibarra**, *Rosales y Fagnano, T02964-430071.* With breakfast, good beds, large rooms, excellent restaurant.

D **Isla del Mar**, *Güemes 963, T02964-422883, isladelmar@arnet.com.ar* Next to bus terminal, with breakfast, slightly rundown.

E **Res Rawson**, *Estrada 750, T02964-430352.* Cable TV, clean, poor beds.

E **Villa**, *San Martín 277, T02964-422312.* Without breakfast, very warm.

Parque Nacional Tierra del Fuego

N

0 km 5
0 miles 5

Sierra de Beauvoir

Parque Nacional Tierra del Fuego

Lago Fagnano

CHILE

Sierra de Vinciguerra
Lago Alto

Sierra de Valdivieso

Río Pipo

Cascada del Río Pipo

Cerro Martial

Lago Roca
Camping Lago Roca

Camping Río Pipo

Ushuaia

Cerro Cóndor
Laguna Negra

Bahía Lapataia

Canal Beagle

Route 3 to Río Grande

Shackleton and the rescue from Elephant Island

Shackleton's 1914-16 Antarctic expedition is one of the epics of polar exploration. Shackleton's vessel, *Endurance*, which left England in August 1914 with 28 men aboard, became trapped in pack-ice in January 1915. After drifting northwards with the ice for eight months, the ship was crushed by the floes and sank. With three boats, supplies and the dogs, the group camped on an ice floe which continued to drift north for eight months. In April 1916, after surviving on a diet largely of seals and penguins, the party took to the boats as the ice broke up. After seven days at sea they reached Elephant Island. From there Shackleton and five other men sailed 1,300 km in 17 days to South Georgia, where there were whaling stations. On reaching the south shore of South Georgia, Shackleton and two men crossed the island (the first such crossing and achieved without skis or snowshoes) to find help. Shackleton, from whom nothing had been heard by the outside world since leaving the island 18 months before, was not at first recognized.

The British government sent a rescue vessel to Elephant Island, but the delays involved led Shackleton to seek help locally. After ice had prevented three rescue attempts – the first from South Georgia, the second from the Falkland Islands/Islas Malvinas and the third from Punta Arenas – Shackleton persuaded the Chilean authorities to permit a fourth attempt using the tug *Yelcho*. Leaving Punta Arenas on 25 August 1916, the small vessel encountered thick fog but, unusually for the time of year, little ice and it quickly reached Elephant Island where the men, who had endured an Antarctic winter under upturned boats, were down to four daysof supplies.

Although the expedition failed to cross Antarctica, Shackleton's achievement was outstanding: despite the loss of *Endurance*, the party had survived two Antarctic winters without loss of life. Shackleton himself returned to the region in 1921 to lead another expedition but, in January 1922, aged only 47, he suffered a fatal heart attack in South Georgia.

Tierra del Fuego Argentine Tierra del Fuego

F Argentino, *San Martín 64, T02964-422546, www.hostelargentino.com.ar* Price per person, good value, kitchen facilities.
F Hosp Noal, *Rafael Obligado 557*. Lots of bread and coffee for breakfast, cosy. Good value. Recommended.

Camping
Club Náutico Ioshlelk-Oten, *Montilla 1047, 2 km from town on river*. Clean, cooking facilities, camping inside heated building in cold weather. The gym has free hot showers for men, as has the ACA garage on the seafront.

Ushuaia *p488, map p493*
Prices double on 12 Dec and accommodation may be hard to find Dec-Mar. The tourist office will help with rooms in private homes and with campsites.

LL Las Hayas, *Km 3 , road to Martial glaciar, T02901-430710, www.lashayas.com.ar* 5-star resort overlooking the city. Colourful large rooms, full facilities, exceptional views.
L Hotel del Glacier, *Km 3.5, on the road towards Martial glacier, T02901-430640, www.hoteldelglaciar.com* Modern, casino, pool rooms, shuttle to/from *Hotel Albatros*.
AL-A Tolkeyen, *Estancia Río Pipo, 4 km from Ushuaia, T02901-445315, www.tolkeyenhotel.com.ar* Good views, pick-up service from town, good restaurant specializing in spit-roast lamb.
AL Albatros, *Lasserre y Maipú, T02901-423206, albatros@tierradelfuego.org.ar* Modern, includes breakfast, good views.
AL Ushuaia, *Laserre 933, 1 km north of Ushuaia, T02901-430671, hotelushuaia@yahoo.com.ar* With breakfast, restaurant, sauna.

A-B Posada Fin del Mundo, *Valdez 281, T02901-434847, www.posadafindel mundo.com.ar* Family atmosphere, breakfast.

B Las Lengas, *Florencia 1722, T02901-423366, laslengas@tierradelfuego.org.ar* Superb setting, heating, good restaurant.

B-C Cabo de Hornos, *San Martín y Rosas, T02901-422187, cabohornos@arnet.com.ar* Comfortable, good value, often full, restaurant (residents only).

B-C César Hostal, *San Martín 753, T02901-421460, www.hotelcesarhostal.com.ar* Comfortable, including breakfast and bath.

B-C La Posada, *San Martín 1299, T02901-433330, laposada@tierradelfuego.org.ar* With breakfast, good.

C Hostería Alakaluf, *San Martín 146, T02901-436705, alakalufes@arnet.com.ar* With breakfast and bath, internet, kitchen and laundry facilities, quiet.

C Hostería América, *Gobernador Paz 1665, T02901-423358, hosteriaamerica@ arnet.com.ar* With breakfast and bath, cable TV, restaurant, internet, modern.

C Maitén, *12 de Octubre 140, T02901-422745, maiten@tierradelfuego.org.ar* With bath, reasonably basic, 1 km from centre.

C-D Mustapic, *Piedrabuena 230, T02901-421718, mustapic@sinectis.com.ar* With breakfast and bath (or without), poor beds, but great views.

D B&B Nahuel, *25 de Mayo 440, T02901-423068, byb_nahuel@yahoo.com.ar* Delightful house with views over channel, comfortable rooms and good attention from welcoming owner. Great value.

E-G Refugio del Mochilero, *25 de Mayo 237, T02901-436129, refugiodelmochilero@ hotmail.com* Rooms and dormitories. Shared bathrooms, kitchen facilities, internet access.

E-G Res Fernández, *Onachaga 72, T02901-421192.* With breakfast, good beds, with or without bath.

F-G Los Cormoranes, *Kamshen 788, T02901-423459.* Dorms with shared baths. With breakfast, heating, lounge, kitchen, free luggage storage, lockers, book exchange, laundry service, free pick up from the bus stop.

Ushuaia

Sleeping		
Albatros 1	Hostería Alakaluf 8	Posada Fin del Mundo 14
B&B Nahuel 4	Hostería América 9	Refugio del Mochilero 2
Cabo de Hornos 3	Las Lengas 11	Residencial Fernández 6
César Hostal 5	Maitén 10	Torre al Sur 7
	Mustapic 12	Ushuaia 13

0 metres 200
0 yards 200

To Airport & Lapataia

Bahía Encerrada

F-G Torre al Sur, *Gob Paz 1437,*
T02901-430745, torrealsur@speedy.com.ar
Price per person. HI-affiliated (discounts for
members), heating, good atmosphere,
kitchen facilities, some long-term residents.
G Violeta de la Montaña, *Belgrano 236,*
T02901-421884. Price per person. Large
kitchen, helpful.

Accommodation in private homes
List of private accommodation is available
from the tourist office.
D Familia Galeazzi, *Gdor Valdez 323,*
T02901-423213, fbasily@quasarlab.com.ar
In pleasant suburb close to town centre.
Bedrooms in house and 5-bed cabin in
garden, excellent food. Highly
recommended.
D María Navarrete, *25 de Mayo 440,*
T02901-423068. Without bath or breakfast
(US$1.50 extra), hot water, laundry and
cooking facilities.
D Posada de los Angeles, *Paz 1410, opposite*
Torre al Sur. Dormitories, good kitchen.

Bahía Ushuaia

E Silvia Casalaga, *Gob Paz 1380 (Yellow*
Tower), T02901-423202. Without bath, heating,
breakfast extra, no sign. Recommended.

Around Ushuaia *p488*
B Hostería Petrel, *Lago Escondido, 54 km*
north of Ushuaia, on the road to Río Grande
(bus US$4), T02901-433569. Trout fishing
possible, boat rides, friendly staff.
D Cabañas Khami, *Lago Fagnano, T02964-*
15611243, www.cabaniaskhami.com.ar In a
lovely spot, comfortable and well equipped,
nicely decorated rustic cabins. Good value.

Camping
No campsites in town. The following are east
of Ushuaia on Route 3. It is also possible to
camp at **Estancia Harberton.**
Camping Río Pipo, *Ushuaia Rugby Club, Km*
4. Price per person, friendly owners, use of
kitchen, bus No 2 to centre.
Ushuaia Camping Municipal, *Km 8.* Price
per person, toilets, showers.
Camping del Solar del Bosque, *Km 14.* Price
per person, hot showers.
Camping Río Tristen, *Haruwen Winter Sports*
complex, Km 36, T/F02901-424058. Price per
tent, with electricity, bar, restaurant.

Parque Nacional Tierra del Fuego
p490, map p490
Camping Lago Roca, *18 km from Ushuaia,*
Lapataia, entry fee US$5. By forested shore of
Lago Roca, with good facilities, noisy, reached
by bus Jan-Feb, small shop, cafeteria.
    There are also 3 sites with no facilities: **Bahía**
Ensenada Camping, 14 km from Ushuaia;
Camping Las Bandurrias and **Camping**
Laguna Verde, both 21 km from Ushuaia.

🍴 Eating

Río Grande *p487, map p487*
$$ **Club de Pesca**, *El Cano.* Seafood.
$$ **Don Rico**, *Belgrano y Pento Moreno.*
Modern building, interesting, closed Mon.
$$ **La Nueva Colonial**, *Fagnano 669.* Pasta
and pizza, friendly, good.
$ **Leymi**, *25 de Mayo 1335.* Fixed price, popular.

Ushuaia *p488, map p492*
Ask around for *centolla* (king crab) and *cholga*
(giant mussels). Also try the home-made
chocolate sold at a shop at *San Martín 785.*

$$$ **Barcleit 1912**, *Fadul 148 y San Martín*. Cordon bleu cooking at reasonable prices.
$$$ **Kaupé**, *Roca 470*. English spoken, excellent food and wine. Recommended.
$$ **Barcito Ideal**, *San Martín 393*. Good, very popular with travellers.
$$ **Bidu Bar**, *San Martín 898*. Good music, lunches, good meeting place.
$$ **Café de la Esquina**, *San Martín y 25 de Mayo*. Nice view, pleasant, not cheap.
$$ **Los Amigos**, *San Martín 130*. Quick service, some cheaper dishes.
$$ **Mi Viejo**, *Campos 758*. *Tenedor libre* (self-service), good value.
$$ **Moustacchio**, *San Martín 298*. Good fish, good *tenedor libre*, expensive a la carte.
$ **Ushuaia Shopping**, *San Martín 788*. Good-value set lunches at restaurant.
$ **Helados Massera**, *San Martín 270-72*. Good ice cream.

❶ Bars and clubs

Ushuaia *p488, map p493*
El Ñaupe, *Gobernador Paz y Fadul*. Bar with live music.
Siglo, *9 de Julio y Maipú*. A popular disco.

✦ Festivals and events

Río Grande *p487, map p487*
Local festivals are the **Trout Festival**, third Sun in Feb; **Snow Festival**, third Sun in Jul; **Woodsman Festival**, first week of Dec.

Ushuaia *p488, map p493*
The **Founding of Ushuaia** is celebrated with a festival on **12 Oct**.

❍ Shopping

Río Grande *p487, map p487*
Food is cheaper than in Ushuaia.
La Nueva Piedmontesa, *Belgrano y Laserre*. 24-hr food store;
Tia, *San Martín y Piedrabuena*. Supermarket with good selection. Fill up with petrol here.

Ushuaia *p488, map p493*
Bookshop, *Ushuaia Shopping, San Martín y 9 de Julio*.
Kelly, *San Martín y Onas*. Good selection of climbing and trekking clothing at European prices, clean toilets.

La Anónima, *Rivadavia y Gob Paz*. Supermarket.
Stella Maris, *San Martín 443*. Stocks good boots.

⛰ Activities and tours

Ushuaia *p488, map p493*
Boat trips
Various operators offer boat trips along the **Beagle Channel** as follows: to Isla de los Lobos, 2 hrs by catamaran, 4 hrs by boat, US$22; to Isla de los Lobos, Isla de los Pájaros, Les Eclaireurs lighthouse and the Isla Martillo penguin colony, 4½ hrs, US$18; to Isla de los Lobos, Isla de los Pájaros, Isla Martillo penguin colony, Les Eclaireurs lighthouse and Estancia Harberton, 8 hrs round trip on catamaran, Tue, Thur, Sat, US$40, includes packed lunch.

Fishing
Asociación de Caza y Pesca, *Maipú y 9 de Julio*. Provides information about the trout season 1 Nov-31 Mar and licences US$10 per week, US$5 per day. It also has a small museum.
Yishka, *Gobernador Godoy 115*, *T02901-431535, F431230*. Fishing excursions to Lago Fagnano.

Skiing
There's a downhill ski run (beginner standard) on **Cerro Martial**.
  Cerro Castor, *27 km northeast of town*, *T02901-422244, office in Ushuaia at San Martyn 740, www.cerrocastor.com* 17 km of pistes of all levels, good off-piste skiing, 772m vertical drop. Ski school on site, equipment rental from US$7 per day. Ski pass US$17-23 per day. The area is excellent for crosscountry skiing; **Caminante** organizes excursions 'off road'.
  Haruwen Winter Sports, *36 km east on Route 3*. Crosscountry skiing, snow-shoe treks and other activities. Equipment and lessons available.
  Valle Tierra Mayor, *20 km northeast of Ushuai*a. A large flat valley with high-standard facilities for crosscountry skiing, snow-shoeing and snowmobiling; rentals and a cafeteria; bus in the morning and 1400 from *Antartur, San Martín 638*.
  Wallner, *3 km from Ushuaia*. Open Jun-Aug, has lights for night-skiing and is run by **Club Andino**, *Fadul 5*.

Tour operators

All agencies charge the same fees for excursions: **Parque Nacional Tierra del Fuego**, 4 hrs, US$12 (plus US$4 park entry); **Lagos Escondido and Fagnano**, 8 hrs, US$22 with lunch included. Tours by land to **Estancia Harberton** cost US$10; take your own food if not wishing to buy meals at the *estancia*. Ask at the tourist office about cycling tours in the national park, US$30 full day, also 'Eco Treks' and cultural events.

All Patagonia, *Juana Fadul 60, T02901-430725, www.allpatagonia.com* Birdwatching, horseriding, trekking and cruises.

Canal Fun, *Rivadavia 82, T02901-437395, www.canalfun.com* Offers a range of activities, riding, 4WD excursions. Recommended.

Compañía de Guias de Patagonia *El Nido de los Condores, Gob Campos 783 y 9 de Julio, T02901-432642, www.companiadeguias.com.ar* Well-run trekking expeditions for all levels, ice climbing (training and equipment provided) to Cerro del Medio and Cerro Alvear. Recommended.

Rumbo Sur, *San Martín 350, T02901-422275, www.rumbosur.com.ar* Runs a range of tours on water and on land to places as far afield as Calafate and Antarctica. Also organizes bus to ski slope, very helpful, English spoken.

Tolkeyen, *Maipú 237, T02901-437073, pretour@tierradelfuego.org.ar* Recommended operator.

Turismo de Campo, *25 de Mayo 34, T02901-430739, www.turismodecampo.com.ar* Birdwatching, fishing, *estancia* and sailing trips. Bilingual guides.

Ushuaia Marina, *San Martín 788, T02901-424058, www.ushuaiamarina.com.ar* Trips in the yacht Callas in the Beagle Channel and as far as Antarctica.

❷ Transport

Río Grande *p487, map p487*
Air
Airport 4 km west of town, bus US$0.50, taxi US$2. To **Buenos Aires**, Aerolíneas Argentinas and AIRG daily, 3½ hrs direct. To **Ushuaia**, AIRG, 3 weekly. To **Río Gallegos**, LADE, Mon-Fri, 1 hr, US$30 one-way.

Bus
All buses leave from the terminal on Elcano y Güemes except for **Tecni Austral**, which leaves from its own office at Moyano 516. **Gesell** has services to **Porvenir** (Chile), Wed and Sun 0800, 5 hrs including meticulous passport and luggage control at San Sebastián, US$9. To **Punta Arenas** (Chile), via Punta Delgada, Pacheco, Tue, Thu, Sat 0730, 10 hrs, US$15. To **Ushuaia**, 3-4 hrs, **Tecni Austral**, 2 daily US$12, and **Tolkeyen**, 2 daily, US$7. There are also direct buses to **Río Gallegos**.

Hitching
Hitching to Ushuaia is relatively easy in summer, but it is very difficult to hitch to Porvenir or north into Argentina (try the truck stop opposite the bus terminal or the police post 7 km out of town).

Ushuaia *p488, map p493*
For details of transport from Ushuaia to the Parque Nacional Tierra del Fuego, see below.

Air
Services are more frequent in high season as the weather often impedes flights in winter. However, it is sometimes difficult to get a flight out without advance booking in the summer tourist season, in which case it may be worth flying to Río Grande instead. Note that airport tax is charged for all internal flights except to Río Gallegos.

Aerolíneas Argentinas, and **Southern Winds** fly to **Buenos Aires** via Río Gallegos (some via Bariloche) all year round, 4 hrs direct. **LADE** flies once a week to **Comodoro Rivadavia**, US$60 one-way, via Río Gallegos and El Calafate, US$45.

To **Punta Arenas**, **DAP**, once a week, US$100 one way.

Bus
Tecni Austral (book through Tolkar, Roca 157) and **Líder**, *Gob Paz 921, T02901-436421*, run services to **Río Grande**, twice daily, 3½ hrs, US$8. **Tolkeyen**, *Maipú 237, T02901-437073*, runs the same route for US$10. There are no through services to **Río Gallegos**; change at Río Grande and book your connection in advance in Ushuaia. **Pasarela** and **Kaupen** run minibus services to Cerro Martial, several departures daily in summer, US$4 return.

To **Punta Arenas** (Chile), Tecni Austral/Ghisoni, Mon, Wed, Fri 0600, US$23, and **Tolkeyen/Pacheco**, Tue, Thu, Sat, 0630, 12 hrs, US$25, a comfortable and interesting ride via Punta Delgada. Both also have services via Porvenir.

Hitching
Trucks leave Ushuaia for the refinery at San Sebastián Mon-Fri. A good place to hitch from is the police control on Route 3.

Boat
There are no regular sailings from Ushuaia to **Puerto Williams** (Chile) but yachts based at the **Club Náutico**, will sometimes carry charter passengers in summer, US$25-40 one-way, returning the same day.

Luxury cruises around **Cape Horn** via Puerto Williams and several glaciers are operated by **Cruceros Australis**, *Pellegrini 989, p6, Buenos Aires* T011-43258400/ 02-4423110, *www.australis.com*, 3 days or 7/8 return, from US$681 in low season.

Most tourist vessels to **Antarctica** call at Ushuaia and take on passengers, space permitting. Enquire at **Rumbo Sur** or other agencies. All agencies charge a similar price, US$2,200 per person for 8/9 day trip, but last-minute offers are often available.

Parque Nacional Tierra del Fuego
p490, map p490
Bus
In summer, buses and mini-buses, US$3, to the park are run by several companies in Ushuaia: **Pasarela**, *Fadul 5,* T02901-421735, leaving from Maipú y Fadul; **Kaupen**, T02901-434015, leaving from Maipú y 25 de Mayo, and **Eben-Ezer**, T02901-431133, leaving from San Martín y 25 de Mayo. Timetables vary with demand, tourist office has details.

Train
The tourist train to the park boundary departs from the Fin del Mundo station west of Ushuaia, 3 or 4 departures daily (1 or 2 daily off season), 4½ km, return fares US$15 tourist class, US$24 first class, plus US$4 park entrance and US$2 for bus to the station, discounts for children in tourist class. Tickets are sold at the **Tranex** kiosk in the port, T02901-431600, *www.trendelfindelmundo.com.ar*

❶ Directory

Río Grande *p487, map p487*
Airline offices Aerolíneas Argentinas, *San Martín 607,* T02964-425700, *rgagte@ aerolineas.com.ar*; LADE, *Lastarre 425,* T02964-422968, *rgrande@lade.com.ar*
Banks Banco de la Nación Argentina, *San Martín 200*; Banco del Sud, *Rosales 241*, cash advance on Visa; **Superkiosko**, *Piedrabuena y Rosales*, cash only. Exchange is difficult: buy Argentine pesos in Chile or bring US dollars. **Car hire** Hertz, *Libertad 714,* T02964- 426534; Localiza, *at airport,* T02964-430482. **Car mechanic** Viaval SRL, *Pento Moreno 927.* **Laundry** El Lavadero, *P Moreno y 9 de Julio.* **Post office** *Rivadavia 968.* **Tour operators** Yaganes, *San Martín 641,*helpful.

Ushuaia *p488, map p493*
Airline offices Aerolíneas Argentinas, *Roca 116,* T02901-422267, *airport* T02901- 421265, *ushgte@aerolineas.com.ar*; **Aerovias DAP**, *25 de Mayo 64,* T02901-431110, *www.aeroviasdap.cl*; LADE, *San Martín 542, loc 2-B,* T/F02901-421123, *airport* T02901- 421700, *www.lade.com.ar*; AIRG, *25 de Mayo 64,* T02901-432112, F432117. **Tapsa,** *Rumbo Sur, San Martín 342,* T02901-422441/423085. **Banks** Banks open 1000-1500 (in summer); credit cards useful as difficult to change TCs and very high commission (up to 10%); Banco de la Nación Argentina, *Rivadavia y San Martín*, only bank which accepts Chilean pesos; cash advance on Mastercard at **Banco de Tierra del Fuego**, *San Martín 1044*, accepts Amex Tcs; tourist agencies and the Hotel Albatros also give poor rates; try the **Listus record shop**, *San Martín 973*, or sweet shop next door, for better rates for cash. **Car hire** Hertz, *at airport,* T02901-432429, Localiza, *San Martín 1222,* T02901-430739, recommended. Tagle, *San Martín y Belgrano,* T02901-433084, good. **Embassies and consulates** Chile, *Malvinas Argentinas y Jainen, Casilla 21,* T02901-421279; Finland, *Gobernador Paz y Deloqui*; Germany, *Rosas 516*; Italy, *Yaganes 75.* **Internet** Several along San Martín. **Laundry** *Kanip 195*, Mon-Sat 0900-2030, US$2 wash, US$2 dry; *Rosas 139, between San Martín and Deloqui*, open Mon-Fri 0900-2100, US$4. **Post office** *San Martín y Godoy*, open Mon-Fri 0900-1300 and 1700-2000, Sat 0830-1200. **Telephone** Several on San Martín.

Chilean Pacific Islands

Introduction

Far out in the Pacific are two Chilean island possessions, the **Juan Fernández Islands**, famed for Alexander Selkirk's enforced stay in the 17th century (the inspiration for Defoe's Robinson Crusoe), and the Polynesian island of Rapa Nui, better known as **Easter Island**, the most isolated inhabited spot on earth. Both possess dramatic views of the Pacific. Juan Fernández is famous for the huge cliffs that rise sheer from the ocean, while Easter Island is home to hundreds of mysterious and imposing 'moai'. Although the cost of getting to these islands is prohibitive for many visitors to Chile, both can be reached relatively easily by air from Santiago.

Juan Fernández Islands

→ *Phone code: 032. Colour map 3, B2. Population: 500.*

Situated 667 km west of Valparaíso, this group of small volcanic islands is a national park administered by CONAF and was declared a UN World Biosphere Reserve in 1977. There are three islands: Isla Alejandro Selkirk (4,952 ha), the largest; Isla Robinson Crusoe (4,794 ha), and Isla Santa Clara (221 ha), the smallest. The islands enjoy a mild climate and the vegetation is rich and varied: the Juan Fernández palm, previously used widely for handicrafts, is now a protected species, but the sandalo (sandalwood tree), once the most common tree on the islands, is now extinct owing to its overuse for perfumes. Fauna includes wild goats, hummingbirds and seals. The islands are famous for langosta de Juan Fernández *(a pincerless lobster) that is prized on the mainland. In summer, a boat goes once a month between Robinson Crusoe and Alejandro Selkirk if the* langosta *catch warrants it, so you can visit either for a few hours or a whole month.*

Background

The islands are named after Joao Fernández, a Portuguese explorer in the service of Spain, who was the first European to visit them in 1574. For the next 150 years, they were frequented by pirates and *corsairs* resting up before attacking the coast of Spanish America. In 1704, Alexander Selkirk, a Scottish sailor, quarrelled with his captain and was put ashore from HMS *Cinque Ports* on what is now Isla Robinson Crusoe, where he stayed alone until 1709, when he was picked up by a privateer, the *Duke*; his experience became the inspiration for *Robinson Crusoe*.

It was not until after 1750 that the Spanish took steps to defend the archipelago, founding San Juan Bautista and building seven fortresses. During the Wars of Independence the islands were used as a penal colony for Chilean independence leaders captured after the Battle of Rancagua. In 1915, two British destroyers, HMS *Kent* and *Glasgow* cornered the German cruiser, *Dresden*, in Bahía Cumberland. The German vessel was scuttled and still lies on the bottom; a monument on shore commemorates the event and, nearby, unexploded shells are embedded in the cliffs. Some of the German crew are buried in the cemetery.

Isla Robinson Crusoe

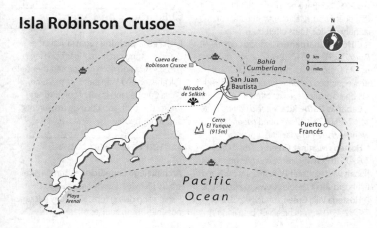

Getting there The best time for a visit is between October and March. Air taxis from Santiago land on an airstrip in the west of the island, from where passengers are taken by boat to San Juan Bautista. (The boat tranfer should be included in the price of the air ticket.) There are also boats to the islands from Valparaíso. ▸▸ *For further details, see Transport, page 501.* **Getting around** Isla Robinson Crusoe is small enough to explore on foot. You will need a boat the other islands. Take insect repellent. **Tourist information** San Juan Bautista has a **CONAF** office ⓘ *Mon-Fri 0800-1800,* with information and advice on the island.

Sights

The only settlement in the archipelago is **San Juan Bautista,** a fishing village of simple wooden frame houses, located on Bahía Cumberland on the north coast of Isla Robinson Crusoe: it has a church, schools, post office, police station and radio station. San Juan Bautista is overlooked by the remains of the **Fuerte Santa Bárbara**, the largest of the Spanish fortresses, while in the village itself is a **Casa de la Cultura** ⓘ *Mon-Fri 1000-1300, 1700-2100,* with exhibition rooms. Nearby are the **Cuevas de los Patriotas,** home to the deported Chilean independence leaders. The island's other famous cave, where Alexander Selkirk spent his years of isolation, is about 4 km north west of the village and can be visited by boat.

South of the village is the **Mirador de Selkirk,** the hill where Selkirk lit his signal fires. A plaque was set in the rock at the lookout point by British naval officers from *HMS Topaze* in 1868; nearby is a more recent plaque placed by Selkirk's descendants. The mirador is the only easy pass between the north and south sides of the island. A footpath leads further south to the anvil-shaped **El Yunque,** 915 m, the highest peak on the island, where Hugo Weber, a survivor from the *Dresden,* lived as a hermit for 12 years: some remains of his dwelling can be seen. The only sandy beach on Robinson Crusoe is **Playa Arenal,** in the extreme southwest corner, two hours by boat from San Juan Bautista.

⊜ Sleeping

Lodging with villagers is difficult.
AL **Hostería El Pangal**, *East of San Juan in the Caleta Pangal, T032-2735209, www.robinsoncrusoetours.cl* Great views, bar and restaurant, best on the island.
B-C **Aldea Daniel Defoe**, *Larraín Alcalde 449, T032-751075.* Price per person. Half board (full board also available), with bath, bar, laundry service, tours offered.
B-C **Hostal Charpentier**, *Ignacio Carrera Pinto 256, F032-751020, yunquea@ hotmail.com.* With bath, kitchen facilities, Also equipped *cabañas* for upto 4, half and full board available, tours offered.
C **Cabañas Dafne Rita**, *Ignacio Carrera Pinto 118, T/F032-751042.* Wooded *cabañas* for 2, with views, laundry facilities.
C **Hostería Martinez Green**, *El Castillo 116, T032-751039, www.hosteriamartinezgreen.cl* Rooms with bath and TV, restaurant (half- and full-board also available), views, tours offered.
D **Hostería Villa Green**, *Larraín Alcalde 246, T/F032-751044.* With breakfast, bath and TV.

E **Hostería Cabañas Paulentz**, *Ignacio Carrera Pinto 120, T032-751108.* Double *cabañas*, comfortable.

⊕ Eating

For eating options on the island, see Sleeping, above.

⊛ Festivals and events

Each Feb, a **yachting regatta** visits the islands; setting out from Algarrobo (see p153) to Isla Robinson Crusoe and thence to Talcahuano and Valparaíso. At this time, Bahía Cumberland is full of colourful and impressive craft, and prices in restaurants and shops double.

▲ Activities and tours

Archipielago Expediciones, *Larraín Alcalde s/n, T032-751030, www.archipielago.cl* Fishing and diving trips. Multi-day packages possible, diving courses offered.

Ecoturismo Aventuras, *Larraín Alcalde s/n,*
T032-751006. Offers horseriding tours, boat
trips and fishing.
Endémica Expeditions, *sector del Muelle s/n,*
T032-751077. Offers diving, fishing and trekking.
Marenostrum, *Larraín Alcalde s/n,*
T032-751023, www.endemica.com. Offers
underwater excursions, as well as
sea-kayaking and trekking, good.
Terranova Tours, *Vicente Gonzales s/n,*
T032-751050. Trekking, boat trips and fishing.

⊖ Transport

Air
Air taxis from **Santiago**, 2½ hrs, are operated
by 2 companies: Transportes Aéreas Isla
Robinson Crusoe (*Av Pajaritos 3030, of. 604,*
Maipú, Santiago, T02-5313772, www.tairc.cl),
depart from Cerrillos (southwest of central
Santiago); Lassa, (*Av Larraín 7941, La Reina,*
Santiago, T02-2734309, lassa@terra.cl), leaves
from Tobalaba Aerodrome in La Reina, on
the eastern ouskirts of the city, Oct-Apr, at
least 3 weekly or daily if demand is sufficient.
Prices are around US$200 one way, US$400
return, luggage allowance 10 kg per person.

Sea
Boats from **Valparaíso** are operated by
Naviera del Sur of Valparaíso (*Blanco*
Encalada 1041, of. 18, Valparaíso,
T032-594304), leaving in the 1st wk of each
month; preference is given to islanders, and
passages are sometimes difficult to obtain.
Also try Agentur, *Esmerada 940, Valparaíso,*
T032-250976.

The Chilean Navy have 4 boats a year to
the islands and may take passengers with
appropriate credentials; contact the **Armada**,
Prat 620, Valparaíso, T032-252094.

To explore the archipelago, it is possible to
charter the municipal launch, *Blanca Luz*,
which goes to different places including
Selkirk Island; contact *Larraín Alcalde 320,*
T032-751001. The fishermen's union has
several launches between them, some of
which can be hired.

❶ Directory

Currency exchange There are no
exchange facilities on the island. No credit
cards, no TCs; only pesos and US$ cash are
accepted. **Post office** *Alcalde Larraín s/n*.

Easter Island

Isla de Pascua or Rapa Nui lies in the Pacific Ocean just south of the Tropic of Capricorn
and 3,790 km west of Chile; its nearest neighbour is Pitcairn Island. The island is
triangular in shape, with an extinct volcano at each corner. The original inhabitants
called the island Te Pito o te Henua, 'the navel of the world'. The unique features of the
island are the many ahu (ceremonial altars) on top of some of which stand 600 (or so)
moai, huge stone figures up to 10 m in height and broad in proportion, representing
the deified ancestors of the Rapa Nui people. The islanders have preserved their
indigenous songs and dances and are extremely hospitable.

Background
It is now generally accepted that the island was colonized from Polynesia about AD
800. Thor Heyerdahl's theories that the first inhabitants came from South America are
less widely accepted than they used to be and South American influence is now
largely discounted.

Indigenous Polynesian society, for all its romantic idylls,
was competitive and it seems that the five clans that originally
had their own lands on Rapu Nui demonstrated their strength by
erecting complex monuments. *Moai* were sculpted at the Rano
Raraku quarry and transported on wooden rollers over more or

Easter Island is always
two hours behind the
Chilean mainland in both
summer and winter time.

less flat paths to their final locations; their red topknots were sculpted at Puna Pau
and then brought to the coast. Rounded pebbles were all collected from the same

Easter Island geology and the making of the *moai*

In geological terms Easter Island is not very old; potassium argon dating shows that its oldest part is under 2.5 million years old. It is located above a tectonic 'hot spot', an active upwelling of liquid rock emerging from beneath the crust of the earth and solidifying. Enough molten rock has poured out to form a mountain nearly 3,000 m high, the altitude of the Easter Island volcano if measured from the sea bed. There are, however, no records of volcanic activity since human occupation of the island began. The three high peaks are all volcanic in origin and consist mainly of basalt. In the cliffs of Rano Kau different layers of basalt can be identified, indicating the existence of distinct lava flows. Caves have been formed where the lava has solidified on the outside but continued to flow downhill on the inside. On Terevaka, where the roofs of some of these caves have collapsed, long caverns up to 10 m high can be seen.

The volcanic nature of the island contributed to the carving of the *moai*. Extremely hard basalt from Terevaka was used to make the tools for carving and sharp-edged implements were fashioned using obsidian, volcanic glass formed by lava cooling very rapidly. The *moai* themselves were carved from tuff, a porous rock much softer than basalt but also volcanic in origin, which can be found at Rano Raruka, a secondary cone on the side of Terevaka.

beach at Vinapu and laid out checkerboard fashion at the *ahu*. The sculptors and engineers were paid out of the surplus food produced by the sponsoring family: thus the unfinished *moai* at Rano Raraku quarry mark the end of the families' ability to pay. Over several centuries, from about AD 1400 onwards, this stonework slowed down and stopped, owing to the deforestation and soil damage of the island caused by roller production and heavy cropping.

European contact with the island began with the visit of the Dutch admiral, Jacob Roggeven, on Easter Sunday 1722, who was followed by the British navigator James Cook in 1774 and the French sailor Le Perouse in 1786. The population of the island remained stable at 4,000 until the 1850s, when Peruvian slavers, smallpox and emigration to Tahiti (encouraged by plantation owners) reduced the numbers. Between 1859 and 1862, over 1,000 islanders were transported as slaves to work in the Peruvian guano trade. The island was annexed by Chile in 1888 and from 1895 to 1952 most of it was leased to a private company, which bred sheep on its grasslands: a wall was built around the Hanga Roa area and the islanders were forbidden to cross.

Nowadays, about half the island of low round hills with groves of eucalyptus, is used for horses and cattle, while the other half constitutes a national park. Of the current population, about 1,000 are from the mainland. Tourism has grown rapidly since the air service began in 1967 and the islanders have profited greatly from the visits of North Americans: a Canadian medical expedition left a mobile hospital on the island in 1966 and, when a US missile-tracking station was abandoned in 1971, vehicles, mobile housing and an electricity generator were left behind.

Unlike most Polynesian islands, Easter Island has no coral reef as winter temperatures are too cold for coral to survive. As a result, the coastline has been eroded in parts to form steep cliffs, around Poike, Rano Kao and on the northern side

● *In 1947, the Norwegian ethnologist Thor Heyerdahl constructed a reed and balsawood boat, the Kon Tiki, and sailed it from the coast of Chile to Easter Island, to prove that such a migration would have been possible.*

of Terevaka. There is no high central plateau and consequently little gully erosion, which would normally lead to the development of streams and rivers. Moreover much of the island's rainfall drains away underground into the huge caverns formed by the collapse of basalt caves. As a result, although annual rainfall is usually above 1,000 mm, there is always a severe shortage of water and in many years several months of drought. The rainy season is March to October, with the wettest weather in May. Average monthly temperatures range from 15-17°C in August to 24°C in February, the hottest month.

> ‡ Anyone travelling to Polynesia or Melanesia from Easter Island will find David Stanley's South Pacific Handbook (Moon Publications Inc) a useful guide to the region.

Ins and outs → Phone code: 032. Population 2,900.

Getting there The tourist season is from September to April. The only way to reach the island is by **Lanchile** plane from Santiago. Easter Island's airport is just south of Hanga Roa. Most flights continue from Easter Island to Tahiti. **Getting around** There are numerous taxis available on the island and an unreliable summer bus service. Horses, bicycles, motorbikes and cars can all be hired. ►► *For further details, see Transport, page 508.* **Tourist information** Sernatur ① *Tu'u Maheke, T032-100255, Mon-Fri 0830-1300, 1400-1730, Sat 1000-1300, 1400-1730.*

Hanga Roa and around

There is one village on the island, **Hanga Roa**, where most of the population live. The **Museo Antropológico Sebastián Englert** ① *T032-551020, www.museorapanui.cl, Tue-Fri 0930-1230, 1400-1730, Sat and Sun 0930-1230, US$1.50, US$0.75 concessions*, has good descriptions of island life, although most of the objects are reproductions, because the originals were removed from the island, and explanations are in Spanish only. Free guided visits are available with advance notice. There is also a cultural centre next to the football field, with an exhibition hall and souvenir stall.

A six-hour walk from Hanga Roa on the west coast passes **Ahu Tahai**, just outside town, where there is a cave house and a *moai* with eyes and topknot in place. Two caves can be reached north from here: the one inland appears to be a ceremonial centre, while the other (nearer the sea) has two 'windows' (take a strong flashlight and be careful). Further north is **Ahu Tepeu**, with a broken *moai* and ruined houses. Beyond here you can join the path to Hanga o Teo (see below), or turn right to **Te Pahu**

(Side text, vertical right margin) Chilean Pacific Islands Easter Island

Rapa Nui – Easter Island

Hanga O Teo
Anakena
Ovahe
Ahu Te Pito Kura
Maunga Kuma
Cave of White Virgins
Motu Tautara
Cave
Te Pahu Cave
Vitea
Rapa Nui National Park
Poike
Ahu Akivi
Tahai
Puna Pau
Rano Raraku
Ahu Tongariki
Motu Maratiri
Ana Kai Tangata
Hanga Roa
Hanga Tetenga
Vaihu
Akahanga
Rano Kau
Vinapu
Orongo
Motu Nui
N

Volcanoes (extinct)

0 km 2
0 miles 2

cave and the seven *moai* at **Akivi**. Either return to Hanga Roa or continue to the **Puna Pau** crater (two hours), where the *moai*'s distinctive red topknots were carved.

South of Hanga Roa is **Rano Kau**, the extinct volcano where the curious Orongo ruins can be seen. The road south out of Hanga Roa passes the two caves of **Ana Kai Tangata**, one of which has paintings, and continues southeast, if, however, you're on foot, take the path just past the CONAF sign for a much shorter route to the Rano Kau crater. A lake with many reed islands lies 200 m below the rim of the crater. On the seaward side of the volcano is **Orongo** ① *US$6*, one of the most important sites on the island with many ruined buildings and petroglyphs, where the bird man cult flourished (see box, page 505). Out to sea are the 'bird islets', Motu Nui, Motu Iti and Motu Kao. It is very windy at the summit, with good views at sunset or under a full moon. It is easy to follow the road back to Hanga Roa in the dark.

> ☻ *Note that street names are rarely used in Hanga Roa. Directions are given by referring to local landmarks such as the church.*

Exploring the rest of the island

A tour of the main part of the island can be done on foot, but this would need at least two days, either camping at Anakena or returning to Hanga Roa and setting out again the next day. For more extensive exploration you could hire either a horse or a vehicle (for both see below). A high-clearance vehicle is better suited to the roads than a normal car. From Hanga Roa, take the road going southeast past the airport; at the oil tanks turn right to **Vinapu**, where there are two *ahu* and a wall whose stones are

Hanga Roa

To Museo Antropológico Sebastián Englert

Pacific Ocean

Caleta Hanga Pilco

Souvenirs

Supermarket

LanChile

Moana Launderette

Kia Koe Tours

Insular

Hertz

Mahinatur

Sunoco Service Station

Sleeping 🛏	**Eating** 🍴	**Bars & clubs** 🍸
Hanga Roa **2** · O'Tai **5**	Ave Rei Pua **1** · Kona Koa **4**	Piriti **7**
Iorana **3** · Poike **8**	Cowboy **2** · Le Pecheur **5**	
Orongo **4** · Topa Ra'a **6**	Ki Tai **3** · Mama Sabina **6**	
Victoria **7**		

0 metres 200
0 yards 200

⁝ Bird man cult of Orongo

Far from being the passive recipient of external influences, Easter Island shows the extent of unique development possible for a people left wholly in isolation. Its older altars (*ahu*) are similar to those of French Polynesia, and its older statues (*moai*) similar to those of the Marquesas Islands, but the very precise stone fitting of some of the *ahu*, and the tall gaunt *moai* with elongated faces and ears for which Easter Island is best known were later developments.

The bird man cult represented at Orongo developed in the early 18th century after the islanders had lost their clan territoriality and were concentrated at Hanga Roa, but still needed a non-territorial way to simulate inter-clan rivalry. The central feature of the birdman cult was an annual ceremony in which the heads of the clans, or their representatives, raced to the islets of Motu Nui, Motu Iti and Motu Kao off the southwest coast of Rapa Nui to obtain the first egg of the sooty tern (known as the Manutara), a migratory seabird that nests there. The winning chief was then named Bird Man, Tangata Manu, for the following year.

It appears that, in the cult, the precious egg of the tern represented fertility, although the actual status of the Tangata Manu on the island is less clear. The petroglyphs at Orongo depict the half-man, half-bird Tangata Manu, the creator god Make Make and the symbol of fertility, Komari.

Chilean Pacific Islands **Easter Island**

joined with Inca-like precision. Head back northeast along the south coast to reach **Vaihu,** an *ahu* with eight broken *moai* and a small harbour, **Akahanga,** an *ahu* with toppled *moai*, and **Hanga Tetenga**, a toppled *moai* and an *ahu*, with bones visible inside. Beyond is **Ahu Tongariki**, once the largest platform on the island, which was damaged by a tidal wave in 1960 and later restored with Japanese aid. Turn left here to **Rano Raraku** (2 km), the volcano where the *moai* were

⁝ *If you are driving, visit the sites from south to north since travel agencies tend to start their tours in the north.*

originally carved (see box, page 505) and where many statues can still be seen. In the crater is a small lake surrounded by reeds; swimming is possible beyond the reeds.

The road heads north past 'the trench of the long ears'; an excursion can be made from here east to **Poike** headland to see the open-mouthed statue that is particularly popular with local carvers. Ask the farmer for permission to cross his land. At the northeast end of the headland is the cave where a virgin was kept before marriage to the victor of ceremonies during the time of the bird man cult; ask someone for directions.

The road along the north coast passes **Ahu Te Pito Kura**, where the 10-m-tall *moai* is one of the largest ever brought to a platform. The road continues to **Ovahe** where there is a very attractive beach with pink sand and some rather recently carved faces and a cave.

From Ovahe, you can return direct to Hanga Roa or continue to the palm-fringed, white-sand beach at **Anakena**, the site of the village of the island's first king, Hotu Matua, and the spot where Thor Heyerdahl landed in 1955; his visit is commemorated with a plaque. The *moai* here has been restored to its probable original state. From Anakena a coastal path of variable quality runs west, passing beautiful cliff scenery and interesting remains. At **Hanga o Teo**, there appears to be a large village complex, with several round houses, while further on is a burial place, built like a long ramp with several ditches containing bones. From Hanga o Teo the path goes west then south, inland from the coast, to meet the road north of Hanga Roa.

● *The runway south of Hanga Roa has been extended to provide an emergency landing site for US space shuttles.*

Hanga Roa and around *p503, map p504*
Unless it is a particularly busy season there is no need to book in advance; mainland agencies make exorbitant booking charges. The accommodation list at the airport information desk only covers the more expensive places. Flights are met by large numbers of hotel and *residencial* representatives but it is cheaper to look for yourself. There are even reports of touts approaching passengers at Santiago airport prior to their flight to the island. Accommodation is much more expensive than anywhere else in Chile, ranging from about US$20-200 per person. Room rates, especially in *residenciales* can be much cheaper out of season and if you do not take full board, but beware of extras such as US$3 charge for hot water.

L **Hanga Roa**, *Av Pont s/n, T032-100299, reshangaroa@panamericanahoteles.cl* Full board, all mod cons, very luxurious. Traditional dancing in the evening.

L **Iorana**, *Policarpo Toro s/n, Ana Magara promontory, 5 mins from airport, T032-100312, ioranahotel@entelchile.net* Friendly, excellent food, convenient for visiting Ana Kai Tangata caves.

L **Orongo**, *Atamu Tekena s/n, T/F032-100294.* Half board (excellent restaurant), good service, nice garden.

L **O'Tai**, *Te Pito Te Henua s/n, T032-100250, otairapanui@entelchile.net* Great location 2 mins from sea, lovely gardens, no meals except breakfast.

L **Res Hanga Roa Reka**, *Simon Paoa s/n, T032-100433.* Full board, good, friendly, camping available.

L **Poike**, *Petero Atamu, T032-100283, ngaeheehe@entelchile.net* 2 star, hot water.

AL **Chez Cecilia**, *near Tahai Moai, T032-100499, www.chezcecilia.co.cl* With breakfast, speaks English and French, excellent food, also cabañas and camping.

A **Res El Tauke**, *Te Pito Te Henua s/n, T032-100253.* Excellent, airport transfers, tours arranged.

AL **Res Maori**, *Te Pito Te Henua s/n, T/F032-100105.* Bed and breakfast.

AL **Res Martín y Anita**, *Simon Paoa s/n, opposite hospital in Hanga Roa, T032-100593.* With breakfast, clean, good food.

A **Res Kaipo**, *Av Pont s/n, T032-100340.* Small, clean, with breakfast, friendly, with hot water.

A **Res Pedro Atán**, *Policarpo Toro, T032-100329.* With breakfast.

A **Res Taheta One One**, *T032-100257.* Motorbike rental, with breakfast or full board.

A **Topa Ra'a**, *Hetereki s/n, 5 mins from Hanga Roa, T032-100225, rapanui@lava.net* Rundown, very helpful, excellent restaurant.

A **Victoria**, *Av Pont s/n, T/F032-100272, jedmonds@entelchile.net* Friendly, with breakfast, helpful owner (speaks English), arranges tours.

B **Res Tahai**, *Sector Tahai s/n, T032-100395.* With breakfast, full board available, nice garden. Recommended.

Camping
Free in eucalyptus groves near the ranger's house at **Rano Raraku** (with water tank), and at **Anakena**, no water, make sure your tent is ant-proof. Officially, camping is not allowed anywhere else, but this does not seem to be strictly enforced. Many people have campsites in their gardens, US$5-10 per person, check availability of water first; some families also provide food. There are also several habitable caves around the coast: for example between Anakena Beach and Ovahe. If you must leave anything behind in a cave, leave only what may be of use to other campers, candles, oil, etc, certainly not rubbish. Camping equipment is for hire at shop near the supermarket.

● Eating

Food, wine and beer are expensive, often twice the price of the mainland, because of freight charges, but local fish, vegetables, fruit and bread are cheap and vegetarians will have no problems on the island. Average prices: coffee/tea US$1, meals about US$10 or more, bread US$2 per kg, beer/cola US$2 in most bars and restaurants. Bring all you can from the mainland, but not fruit.

Most *residenciales* offer full board. Coffee is generally instant. It is worth booking a table in advance for evening meals.

$$$ **Le Pecheur**, *Hanga Roa.* French run, unfriendly, seafood speciality, expensive.

$$$ **Playa Pea**, *Av Apina.* Pricey but pleasant with fine sea views, seafood.

$$ **Ave Rei Pua**, *Hanga Roa.* Limited menu, good tuna and lobster.

Tapati or Semana Rapa Nui

Held each year in late January/early February, Tapati is organized as a huge competition between groups, many of them families, each of which elects a beauty queen. It begins slowly but keeps on getting better as the fortnight goes on. Families score points by participating in a wide variety of competitions, including gastronomy, necklace-making, sculpting *moai*, body painting, dancing, singing, horseracing, swimming, modified decathlon. In the most spectacular event, men, dressed only in the traditional thong and with their bodies painted, compete to slide down the side of a volcano, sitting on a kind of sledge made from the trunks of two banana plants. Only for the tough guys!

Lots of tourists, especially from the Chilean mainland, visit at this time. It is best to stay in Hanga Roa, since it is easy to hitch from here to activities elsewhere on the island.

$$ **Cowboy**, *Hanga Roa*. Good food, not too expensive prices.

$$ **Ki Tai**, *Hanga Roa*. Pizzas and snacks.

$$ **Kona Koa**, *Hanga Roa*. Not cheap but good, with traditional dances.

$$ **Mama Sabina**, *Av Policarpo Toro*. Clean and welcoming.

$$ **Pizzería**, *opposite post office*. Moderately priced pizzas.

❶ Bars and clubs

There are 2 discos in Hanga Roa. Action begins after 0100. Drinks are expensive: a bottle of *pisco* costs US$7, canned beer US$2. **Toroko**, *by the coast in Caleta Hanga Roa*. Open daily.
Piriti, *near airport*. Open Thu-Sat.

❿ Entertainment

There are shows of traditional dancing from the island at **Hotel Hanga Roa** (see Sleeping above) at 2100, and at **Kona Koa Restaurant** (see Eating above) at 2200.

Music at the **church**, *Av Te Pito Ote Henua*, for the 0900 Sunday mass has been described as 'enchanting'.

❀ Festivals and events

Tapati, or **Semana Rapa Nui**, starts at the end of **Jan** and lasts 2 weeks, see box, above.

⦿ Shopping

On **Av Policarpo Toro**, the main street, there are lots of small shops and market stalls, which close when it rains, and a couple of supermarkets; the cheapest are **Kai Nene** or **Tumukai**. Some local produce can be found free, but ask first. This includes wild guava fruit, fish, 'hierba luisa' tea and wild chicken. Film is readily available but cannot be developed on the island.

Handicrafts and souvenirs

Wood carvings and stone *moais* are best bought from the craftsmen themselves, such as **Antonio Tepano Tucki**, **Juan Acka** or **Hipolito Tucki** and his son (who are knowledgeable about the old culture). Good pieces cost between US$30-150. Bargaining is only possible if you pay cash. The municipal market, left of the church, will give you a good view of what is available and there's no compunction to buy.

There are several souvenir shops on Av Policarpo Toro including **Hotu Matuu's Favorite Shoppe** where prices have been described as 'top dollar and she will not bargain', but she does have the best T-shirts. Handicrafts are also sold at Tahai, Vaihu, Rano Raraku and Anakena. The airport shop is expensive.

For an explanation of sleeping and eating price codes used in this guide, see inside the front cover. Other relevant information is found in Essentials, see pages 51-58.

Diving

Orca, *Caleta Hanga Roa, T032-100375, www.seemorca.cl* Offers guided diving trips.

Hiking

Allow at least a day to walk the length of the island, one way, taking in all the sites. It is 5 hrs' easy walk from Hanga Roa to Rano Raraku (camp at ranger station); 5 hrs to Anakena (camp at ranger station, but ask first). You can hitch back to Hanga Roa, especially at weekends, although there are few cars at other times. Anyone wishing to spend time exploring the island would be well advised to speak to **CONAF** first (T032-100236); they also give good advice on special interests (biology, archaeology, handicrafts etc). Maps are sold on Av Policarpo Toro for US$15-18, or at the ranger station at Orongo for US$10.

Riding

This is the best way to see the island, provided you are fit. Horses can be hired for US$25-40 a day (including a guide; cheaper without). The tourist office provides a list of people hiring horses. Try **Emilio Arakie Tepane**, *T032-100504*, who also leads horseback tours of the island (Spanish only); **Ana Rapa**, *T032-100540*, good value, or **Vai Honu**, *T032-100935*.

Tours

Many agencies, *residenciales* and locals arrange excursions around the island, including **Aku-Aku Tours**, Krenia Tucki of **Res Kai Poo** (see Sleeping above), **Fernando and Marcelo León** (Pai Tepano Rano, recommended). Some go in jeeps, others will accompany tourists in hired vehicles (eg US$75 for 3), prices around US$35 each per day. The English of tour guides is often poor.

Archaeological Travel Service, *Tu' U Koihi s/n, T032-100364, archeots@rapanui.cl* Archaeological and scientific tours. English, French, German spoken.

Hanga Roa Travel, *T032-100158, hfritsch@entelchile.net* English, German, Italian and Spanish spoken, good-value all-inclusive tours. Recommended.

Air

LanChile flies from **Santiago**, once a day, Thu-Sun in high season, Wed and Sun only in low season, 5-5½ hrs. Most flights continue to Papeete on Tahiti. Return to Santiago is Mon, Wed, Fri and Sat in high season, Mon and Thu only out of season.

LanChile will not allow you to fly to Easter Island unless you have a confirmed flight off the island (note that planes to Tahiti are more crowded than those back to Santiago). You should reconfirm your booking on arrival on the Island.

The fare in 2003 was approximately US$800 return from Santiago, with occasional special deals available through travel agents. Special deals may be available on flights originating outside Chile, or for those booking in advance. Students studying in Chile are eligible for a 30% discount.

Flying from Santiago to Easter Island incurs the domestic tax of US$13. The airport tax for international flights from Easter Island to Tahiti is US$5. Don't take pesos to Tahiti, they are worthless in French Polynesia.

Sea

There are no passenger services to Easter Island. Freight is brought by sea 3 times a year.

Around the island

There are several **taxis** and, in summer, a **bus** goes from Hanga Roa to Anakena on Sun at 0900, returning in the evening (unreliable). **Bicycles** (some in poor condition) are available for rent for US$12 on main street or from *residenciales*.

Motorbikes can be hired for about US$25 a day plus fuel (Suzuki or Honda 250 are recommended because of the rough roads). **Cars** and **jeeps** are available from main hotels but hire companies tend to have better vehicles. There are many different companies (see Directory below), so shop around. Jeep hire US$50 per day, US$90 with driver. There is no insurance available, drive at your own risk (be careful at night, many vehicles drive without lights). US$5-10 will buy enough fuel for a one-day trip around the island.

● Directory

Airline office LanChile, *Poilcarpo Toro Y Av Pont, T032-100279*. **Banks and currency exchange** US dollars are widely accepted although usually at a poor rate. Prices are often quoted in dollars, but bills can be paid in pesos. Buy Chilean pesos on the mainland as local rates are poor. The bank next to the tourist office, open daily 0900-1200, charges US$15 commission on changing TCs, but you can change as many TCs for this fee as you like (and in different names). Cash can be exchanged in shops, hotels, etc, at about 3% less than in Santiago. Poor rates on AmEx TCs at Sunoco service station but no commission. AmEx TCs also changed by

Kia-Koe Land Operator, Hanga Roa Hotel. AmEx credit cards are widely accepted, but cannot be used to obtain cash (but enquire at Sunoco service station). **Car hire** Many vehicle hire agencies on Policarpo Toro including Insular, *T032-100480*, Tipanie, *T032-100577*, Toki, *T032-100577* and Puna Pau, *T032-100626*. **Medical services** There is a 20-bed hospital as well as 3 resident doctors, a trained nurse and 1 dentist on the island. **Post office** Mon-Fri 0900-1300, 1430-1800, Sat 0900-1200. **Telephone** ENTEL, *Atamu Tekena s/n*. Phone calls from the Chilean mainland are subsidized, at US$0.50 per minute, minimum 3 mins. Calls to Europe cost US$5 for 3 mins.

Background

History

Origins

Some 50,000 years ago, the very first people crossed the temporary land bridge spanning Asia and America at the Bering Straits and began a long migration southwards. They were hunters and foragers, following in the path of huge herds of now extinct animals, such as mammoth, giant ground sloth and ancestors of the camel and horse. The first signs that these people had reached South America date from around 14,000 BC, if not earlier.

As sources of game in forested valleys dried up, some groups settled along the coasts, particularly drawn by the abundance of marine life provided by the cold Humboldt current in the Pacific. Some of the earliest evidence of humans in Chile has been found in the north, both on the coast and in the parched Atacama Desert. The coastal people lived on shellfish gathered by the shore and on fish and sea-lions speared from inflated seal-skin rafts.

One such group, the Las Conchas people, migrated from the inland valleys to the coast near Antofagasta around 7500 BC. They were one of the first peoples in South America to take hallucinogenic drugs. Many graves excavated in this region contain mortars, which may have been used to grind up seeds also found nearby. These seeds contained an alkaloid similar to that found in the ayahuasca plant, which is still used for its hallucinogenic effects by the Shuar in Peru – indeed, the Shuar are believed by some to be descendants of these Atacameño peoples, having migrated to the Amazon in order to hide from the Spanish. Some specialists believe that the many geoglyphs of the Atacama Desert (see box, page 248) – the most famous ones being the Nazca Lines in Peru – were maps for shamans undergoing the hallucinatory experience of flight after taking drugs such as *ayahuasca*. Other objects found in graves include bags, trays and tubes, which were used for inhaling the drug in the form of snuff, a method still employed in curing and divination practices in the Andean region and coastal Brazil. Some of the trays and tubes found were decorated with images of supernatural beings and anthropomorphic figures, such as bird-headed angels, styles that are also common in the Andean regions of present-day Peru and Bolivia (see also box, page 205).

The beginnings of agriculture

Gradually, the settled life of agricultural subsistence took over from the more nomadic hunting lifestyle. Remains of slingshot stones and what seem to be bolas (weights attached to cords used to bring down prey by entangling their legs) have been found alongside bones of mastodons in Monte Verde, near Puerto Montt. Other remains found nearby included agricultural tools and medicinal plants, hearths and house foundations, all indications that the site was inhabited for some time by one community. Crop seeds have also been found, including those of potatoes, evidence of very early contact with cultures from as far afield as the Central Andes. Some of these remains were found in a remarkable condition, owing to being buried in a peat bog; mastodon bones even had traces of meat on them. It is widely agreed that the site was settled 10,000 years ago, although lower levels have been controversially dated from as early as 34,000 years ago.

By about 2500 BC, agriculture was practised throughout much of Chile, as it was across the rest of the continent. Maize, beans and squash have been found in northern Chile from as early as 5,000 BC. However, people in the south only turned definitively to agriculture at a much later date. In Araucanía, horticulture was not practised until around AD 500. These people also had unusual burial practices, placing the body in an urn inside a funerary canoe, perhaps reflecting the local

66 99 Specialists believe that geoglyphs were maps for shamans undergoing the hallucinatory experience of flight after taking drugs, such as ayahuasca.

dependence on fishing for their livelihood. Elaborate artefacts found in some graves, such as stone and copper jewellery and ceramic offerings, suggest a stratified society of both rich and poor.

Northern influences

In the north, the extremely dry climate is a great preservative, allowing archaeologists to build up a detailed picture of early life. The people in the Atacama lived in solidly built adobe houses, arranged in complexes around inner courtyards and corridors, such as can be seen in the village of Tulor near San Pedro de Atacama (see page 228).

These northern peoples had contact with neighbouring highland communities, shown by the presence there of plants and other goods found only in the adjacent regions. The important *altiplano* culture of **Tiahuanaco** in present-day Bolivia is thought to have had particularly close links with northern Chile, helping to stimulate the growth of settlements such as that at San Pedro de Atacama. Trade with Tiahuanaco, through llama caravans bringing highland goods and produce, boosted the wealth and cultural development of the desert people. Some very fine textiles were found in this area, showing distinct design similarities with those of Tiahuanaco. The textiles were hand-spun and coloured with vegetable and cochineal dyes. Clothing and jewellery adornments containing feathers suggested contact even with tropical regions, although these may have been obtained through their *altiplano* intermediaries. Local ceramics were mostly plain and highly polished, but some items decorated with elaborate dragon-like figures had probably been traded with Tiahuanaco.

Mummification was practised from as early as 2,500 BC by coastal peoples and was also common further north in present-day Peru as practised by the Chinchorro people. They buried their dead stretched out straight, in contrast to the foetal position used by other Chilean and Peruvian cultures. Internal organs and the brain were removed and the body was stuffed with a variety of materials to preserve it. Sticks were attached to the limbs to keep them straight. A mask was placed over the face and a wig of real human hair was attached to the head. The body was then coated in a layer of clay and wrapped in animal skins or mats. According to the person's status, they were often buried with their personal possessions: clothing, jewellery, musical instruments and copper items.

In the period AD 500-900 the association between San Pedro de Atacama and Tiahuanaco had become even stronger. In return for trading their agricultural produce and other goods, it is thought that the Tiahuanaco people sought copper, semi-precious stones and the use of grazing lands in northern Chile. As with the Araucanía in the south, some graves from this period contained bodies with more elaborate clothing, jewellery, imported ceramics and other valuables, suggesting the existence of a wealthy elite, which was also common in central Andean cultures.

Following the demise of Tiahuanaco in about AD 1100, a number of cultures arose in the adjacent area bordering southern Bolivia, northern Chile and Argentina, practising derivative agriculture, with terraces and irrigation, and producing ceramics in similar styles. In the Quebrada de Humahuaca in present-day Argentina, several small defensive towns were built with fortified walls and stone houses. Grave remains have revealed that metallurgy was well developed here; some bodies were adorned with pectorals, bracelets, masks and bells, made of copper, silver and gold. Shells from the Pacific and ceramics from present-day Bolivian cultures, such as the Huruquilla, show the existence of widespread trade links.

Inca expansion

The next major empire to touch northern Chile was that of the Incas, which, at the peak of its growth in the 16th century, stretched as far south as the Aconcagua Valley near modern-day Santiago. The advancing armies of Inca Topa Yupanqui suppressed resistance in the valleys of the central region and replaced local structures with their own military administration. They were finally stopped by hostile forest tribes at the Río Maule near present-day Talca. This was the southernmost limit of the Inca Empire, some 3,840 km south of the equator and the deepest that any imperial movement had penetrated into the southern hemisphere.

One major group that survived the Inca incursion and resisted conquest by the Europeans right up until the 19th century was the **Mapuche** (see box, page 309). They were concentrated in the central valley south and east of the Cordillera de Nahuelbuta. The Mapuche were primarily farmers but also hunted and fished, both inland and along the coasts and lake shores. Their large cemeteries contained a variety of burial sites, some in canoes or stone chambers and some in simple earthen graves. Grave goods were plentiful, with elaborate ceramics, wooden and stone artefacts and jewellery made of copper and semi-precious stones.

The far south

Despite the apparently inhospitable conditions, these regions were home to a sizeable population of hunting, fishing and gathering peoples from very early times continuously up to the 19th century AD. Bones of horses and extinct giant sloths, dating from approximately 8,000 BC, have been found near to stone arrowheads in sites such as Fells's Cave and Pali Aike Cave on the Magellan Straits – evidence of the earliest hunters.

Four distinct cultures developed here: the Haush, Ona, Yámana and Alacalufe. The oldest of these was the **Haush**, nomadic hunters of the guanaco mainly confined to the farthest southeastern tip of Tierra del Fuego, in present-day Argentina. The Haush hunted with bows and arrows, using guanaco skins for clothing and sometimes for covering their stick-framed houses. They also gathered shellfish and caught fish by the shore, using spears and harpoons.

The **Ona** people also hunted guanaco, ranging on foot across most of the Isla Grande of Tierra del Fuego in family groups. They were strong runners and tall people, some of them 6 ft tall; in fact, all these hunters and gatherers are thought to have been the tallest of the first South American peoples. They wore guanaco skin robes, fur side out, and also guanaco fur moccasins, known as *jamni*. They made open-topped shelters out of guanaco skins, which were weatherproofed with a coating of mud and saliva, and sometimes painted red. The Ona did not use harpoons or spears and only collected shellfish from beaches at low tide.

The **Yámana** were nomadic coastal hunters, travelling in canoes up and down the coasts of the Beagle Channel and around the islands southwards to Cape Horn. They caught otters, fish and seals, using spears and harpoons, and used slings and snares to catch birds. The Yámana houses were simple, made of sticks and grass, and they wore little clothing, perhaps a small seal skin and skin moccasins in winter.

Like the Yámana, the **Alacalufes** were also nomadic coastal peoples, roaming from Puerto Edén in the Chilean channels, to Yendegaia in the Beagle Channel. There was some contact with the Yámana, with whom they would sometimes exchange goods and inter-marry. The Alacalufes had similar lifestyles to the Yámana but developed various additions, such as raising a sail on their canoes and using a bow and arrow in addition to the sling when hunting birds or guanaco.

A conquistador with a difference

We know that Pedro de Valdivia joined the Spanish army as a young man in 1521, serving in Flanders and Italy, but little else is known of his early life. In 1535, he was sent to Venezuela, where he joined an expedition sent to Peru to reinforce Francisco Pizarro. In 1537, he became *aide de camp* to Pizarro and sided with him in the war between the latter and Diego de Almagro, receiving an award of land and Indians in return. Shortly afterwards, he sold his property to finance an expedition southwards to Chile; setting off in 1540 accompanied by 12 white men, one white woman (Inés de Suárez), 1,000 Indians and a few black slaves. Travelling across the Atacama Desert, he reached the Copiapó Valley and then moved south to the Mapocho Valley, where he founded Santiago. Receiving further supplies and reinforcements from Peru, he travelled north again, founding La Serena. After a brief expedition to Peru in 1547 where he helped in the defeat of Gonzalo Pizarro by troops sent from Spain, he returned to Chile in 1549, founding the cities of Concepción, Valdivia and Villarrica, before being killed in battle with the Mapuche at Fort Tucapel (sited at the modern town of Carahue, near Temuco).

Although Valdivia's military career was typically bloody and brutal, he is seen by many historians as driven more by the spirit of adventure than by the desire to acquire gold and silver, which motivated so many of his fellow *conquistadors*.

Spanish conquest and early settlement

The first Spanish expeditions to Chile were led by **Diego de Almagro** and **Pedro de Valdivia** (see box, page 515), both of whom followed the Inca road from Peru to Salta and then west across the Andes. Almagro's expedition of 1535-37, which included 100 Spaniards, African slaves, crypto-Jews and some thousands of indigenous Americans – many of whom perished – reached the heartland but, bitterly disappointed at not finding gold, returned to Peru almost immediately. Valdivia's expedition then carried out what initially appeared to be a swift and successful conquest, founding Santiago in February 1541 and a series of other settlements in the following years. But, in the 1550s, these Spanish settlements were shaken by a Mapuche rebellion, which led to the death of Valdivia.

The two major indigenous figures in this early resistance to the Spaniards were the *caciques* Lautaro and Caupolicán. Lautaro was an interesting case: initially an adjutant of Pedro de Valdivia (known by the *conquistador* as Felipe), he turned against Validivia and led the expedition that captured him in 1553. Lautaro went on to lead several successful campaigns, before being killed by the Spaniards in the Mataquito Valley in 1557. Caupolicán fought alongside Lautaro, but was eventually captured in the *cordillerra* in 1558 and impaled on a stake by the Spaniards. Nevertheless, the two Mapuche heros had successfully undermined the Spanish colony and their struggles set the tone for the colonial period in Chile. Lacking precious minerals, threatened by the warlike Mapuche and never less than four months' journey from Europe, the colony was of relatively little importance to Spain, except as a frontier zone.

The motivation of these early expeditions – as in Mexico and Peru – was greed. The Spanish crown did nothing to finance the ventures, so all the risk was shouldered by those who participated, who therefore had a pressing need to find silver and gold to recompense themselves. Nevertheless, a fifth of all gold and silver that was found in the New World went into the royal coffers; an influx of precious metal that was urgently needed to prop up the falling value of coinage in Europe at this time.

The greedy motivations of the early arrivals made control in distant Chile difficult for the Castillian crown to exercise. Chile was effectively run by men such as **Francisco de Aguirre**, a conquistador who had accompanied Pedro de Valdivia's initial expedition. As one of the first Spaniards on the scene, Aguirre was made Governor of Tucumán – just across the Andes in modern-day Argentina – and later founded La Serena. He was, however, deeply anti-clerical and proclaimed himself "Pope and King" in Chile, saying that he would rather have a farrier than a priest. The Inquisition eventually caught up with Aguirre in the Río de la Plata in the 1570s and he died poor, bitter and disgraced in La Serena.

In addition to trying to exert effective control over the Spaniards in their territory, one of the main concerns of Chile's Spanish governors after Valdivia was the war against the Mapuche successors to Lautaro and Caupolicán. Known by the Spanish as Araucanos, the Mapuche were fearsome opponents. In 1598, they began a general offensive that destroyed all of the Spanish settlements south of the Río Biobío, revealing the weakness of a colony whose Spanish population was under 8,000. Pushed back into the northern part of the Central Valley, the Spanish were forced to build a string of forts along the Río Biobío, guarded by a frontier army of 2,000 men, the only force of its type in Spanish America, financed by a special subsidy from the viceregal capital of Lima. However, Chile was not important enough to warrant a full-scale Spanish assault on the Mapuche and, for the rest of the colonial period, the Spanish presence south of the river would be limited to the island of Chiloé and to the coastal city of Valdivia.

The Chilean colony

As in the other colonies in the Americas, Chilean society under Spanish rule was not the two-sided world of Spanish settlers and Amerindian peoples that official histories would have us believe. From very early on, two other groups became increasingly important: *marranos* – or forced converts from Judaism to Christianity, who had fled Inquisitiorial persecution in Spain and Portugal – and slaves from West Africa. The *marranos* controlled large parts of the trade in South America and suffered bouts of persecution from the Inquisitional office in Lima (see box, page 518), while the Africans did much of the manual labour in the colony. Although both groups eventually became absorbed into Chile, the legacy of their presence can perhaps be felt today in the widespread stereotyping of Africans and Jews in mainstream Chilean society.

African slaves started arriving from very early on in the colonial period, principally because the Spanish found that the Indians were not hardy enough to do the work required of them. By the end of the 16th century, Africans in Chile were working as cattle ranchers and as *stevedores*, and as blacksmiths, tailors, carpenters and servants in every city. They were mostly sold as contraband, brought over from Buenos Aires instead of through the 'official' port of entry at Cartagena, Colombia, and originated from all parts of the West African coast, from Senegambia to Angola.

By the turn of the 17th century, much of the trade of the fledgling colony was in the hands of the *marranos*, who were prohibited from holding positions of authority. Their main port of entry was Buenos Aires, from where they travelled overland to Potosí and Lima by way of Tucumán.

In the following years, colonial Chile achieved a degree of stability and developed as a compact society; most of its population inhabited the Central Valley and most trade was through Valparaíso. By the end of the 17th century, there were few people of pure indigenous blood, most having died, inter-married or escaped south of the Río Biobío. The majority of the population was *mestizo* (mixed race), though the society was dominated by a small white elite. Chile was, however, highly isolated, being cut off from the rest of the continent in winter. People dared not use the lower passes to the south for fear of the Mapuche, and the high passes near Mendoza and Santiago were blocked by snow for months at a time.

Town planning in the 16th century

Perhaps the most obvious influence of Spanish colonial settlement for a visitor is the characteristic street plan of towns and cities. Colonial cities were founded by means of an official ceremony, which involved tracing the central square and holding a mass. A series of Royal Ordinances issued in Madrid in 1573 laid down the rules of town planning: the four corners of the main plaza had to face the four points of the compass; the plaza and the main streets had arcades and, away from the plaza, the streets were traced out with a cord and ruler in the now-familiar grid-pattern. Once this was done, building lots near the plaza were distributed, allocated by lottery to those settlers who had rights to be there.

The Ordinances specified the principles underlying the distribution of the major public buildings. Churches were to be distant from the plaza and built on high ground, so that they were easy to see and people had to climb up to them on steps, thereby forcing a greater reverence. The *cabildo* and the customs house were to be built nearby, while the hospital of the poor and those sick with non-contagious diseases was to be north-facing, planned so that the inmates could enjoy southern exposure.

The Ordinances also advised settlers on how to deal with local suspicion and hostility: "While the new town is being built the settlers ... shall try to avoid communication and intercourse with the Indians. Nor are the Indians to enter the circuit of the settlement until the latter is complete and in condition for defence and the houses built, so that when the Indians see them they will be filled with wonder and will realize that the Spaniards are settling there permanently and not temporarily."

'Royal Ordinances Governing the Laying Out of New Towns' by Zelia Nuttall, *Hispanic American Historical Review*, May 1922.

During the colonial period, the *hacienda*, or landed estate, was the most important feature of rural society in the Central Valley. In the 17th century, Chilean agriculture expanded to meet demands for wheat, tallow, salted beef and cattle hides from Peru; hides were also sent to Potosí and mules to the great fair in Salta. These exports and the need to feed the frontier army led to the development of large-scale agriculture. As the *haciendas* grew, small farmers and tenants were gradually forced to become *inquilinos*, a class of peasants tied to the land. The *inquilino* is regarded as the ancestor of the *huaso*, the Chilean cowboy, a figure seen as resourceful, astute, cunning and archetypally Chilean.

Although *haciendas* grew in response to food shortages, they were very self contained, with their own supplies of food and clothing, their own vineyards, forges and workshops. Ownership of a *hacienda* was one of the clearest marks of upper-class status, although many were the property of religious orders. The *hacienda* remained at the centre of rural life in the Central Valley and social relations between landowners and *inquilinos* changed little until the Agrarian Reforms of the 1960s. Although no colonial *haciendas* remain, a few dating from the 19th century can be visited, notably Villa Huilquilemu, near Talca (see page 281).

Chile was governed as part of the Viceroyalty of Peru, with its capital in Lima; until the 18th century, all trade with Spain had to pass via Lima and trade with other countries was forbidden. This led to uncontrolled smuggling and, by 1715, there were 40 French vessels trading illegally along the Chilean coast. In 1740, direct trade with Spain was permitted for the first time and, in 1750, Chile was allowed to mint her own currency.

● No one expects the Spanish Inquisition

The activities of the Spanish Inquisition were not restricted to Spain, they spread to every corner of the Spanish Empire during the colonial period. In Latin America, the Inquisition is best known for a few large show trials and burnings. At a conflagration in Lima in 1639, 11 people were burnt and one person was tortured to death. Even beyond these headline events, its influence was pervasive and enduring on colonial life. It operated in every corner of the American continent, persecuting alleged Jews and avowed Protestants for the 'irregularities' of their faith. The Inquisition was not permitted to inquire into the faith of indigenous peoples, as they were not thought to have sufficient 'mental maturity' but its influence on the colonial population was pervasive. As well as engendering fear among the settlers, it was capable of impounding the goods of anyone who was suspected of heresy, thereby affecting payment for goods and services over networks that ranged from Mexico to Chile. The force of the Inquisitorial inquiries at this date has been blamed by some historians for the economic decline in South America at this time. As most people of Judaic origin were merchants, this had a significant knock-on effect in small provincial towns.

Furthermore, the essential requirements of keeping a 'pure' faith were underlined by the processions that took place in every town at three-year intervals on the first Sunday in Lent. Every Spanish settler had to attend the procession, at which Inquisitorial officials, wearing the habit of St Peter, with a green cross encased in silver and a crown hanging from their necks, read out the 'edicts of faith'. The settlers were told that they had to denounce anyone observing Judaic practices, which the Inquisitors would then list.

Genuine crypto-Jews who wished to profess their faith were moved to crisscross the continent in search of sanctuary. Santiago was one of the last significant strongholds of the crypto-Jews in the Spanish American colonies, lasting into the 18th century. Elsewhere, Jews sought sanctuary in Colombia's Antioquia region, Suriname, Curaçao and, for a time, in northern Brazil. Although it was usually the crypto-Jews who suffered the burnings, Protestants were often punished as well; victims included Francis Drake's cousin, John, who spent three years in a monastery near Lima repenting his Lutheran 'crimes' in the late 1580s.

In Chile – as in the whole of Latin America – the Inquisition was finally abolished only at the time of Independence. However, the torture practices of the DINA – the secret police under Pinochet – were eerily resonant of the Inquisition's methods of extracting confessions of heresy. It could be argued that the legacy of the Inquisition once more reared its ugly head in South America during the 1970s, as much of the continent became taken over by repressive regimes, many of which had a penchant for torture.

The War of Independence

Independence came to Spanish America as a direct result of Napoleon's invasion of Spain. As Spanish guerrilla forces fought to drive the French out, these events led the colonial elites to debate where their loyalties lay: to Napoleon's brother Joseph, now officially King? Or to the overthrown king, Ferdinand VII, now in a French prison? Or to the Spanish resistance parliament in Cádiz?

In 1810, a group of leading Santiago citizens appointed a Junta to govern until Ferdinand returned to the throne. Although they protested loyalty to Ferdinand, their move was seen as a challenge to the crown by the viceregal government in Lima, which sent an army to Concepción. War broke out between the Chilean Patriots and the Royalist troops supporting Lima. The defeat of the Patriot army led by **Bernardo O'Higgins** at Rancagua in October 1814 led to a restoration of colonial rule, but O'Higgins was able to escape across the Andes to join forces with Buenos Aires' liberation hero, José de San Martín. The turning point came in 1817, with the invasion of Chile from Mendoza by San Martín's Army of the Andes, a force of 4,000 men, which defeated the Royalists at Chacabuco on 12 February 1817. A Royalist counter-attack was defeated at Maipó, just south of Santiago, on 5 May 1818, putting an end to Royalist power in the Central Valley. The victory of the small Patriot navy led by **Lord Cochrane** (see box, page 340) at Valdivia in January 1820 helped clear the Pacific coast of Royalist vessels and paved the way for San Martín to launch his seaborne invasion of Peru.

Nineteenth-century expansion

In most of former Spanish America, Independence was followed by a period of political turmoil, marked by civil wars and dictatorship, which in some cases lasted until the 1860s. Many Independence heroes had tragic ends: disgusted at the chaos, San Martín retired to France; Simon Bolívar died penniless and in hiding in a boarding house in Santa Marta, Colombia; and O'Higgins was quickly overthrown. O'Higgins' demise was followed by a brief period of instability in Chile but, in 1830, conservative forces led by Diego Portales restored order and introduced the Constitution of 1833, which created a strong government under a powerful president. Portales, a Valparaíso merchant, who never became president, explained his actions thus: "If one day I took up a stick and gave tranquillity to the country it was only so that the bastards and whores of Santiago would let me get on with my work in peace."

Chile became famous throughout Latin America as the great example of political stability: the army was reduced to 3,000 men and kept out of politics; after 1831, four successive presidents served the two five-year terms permitted under the constitution. However, this stability had another side: civil liberties were frequently suspended, elections rigged, opponents exiled and power lay in the hands of a small landowning elite. Neither was the stability perfect: there were short civil wars in 1851, 1859 and 1891.

The latter half of the 19th century saw Chile's great period of expansion. In 1881, when victory over Peru in the War of the Pacific was assured (see box, page 520), the much-enlarged army was sent to put an end to Mapuche independence and thus secure continuous Chilean control over the entire Pacific coastline south of Arica. In the few short years between 1879 and 1883, Chilean territory had expanded both northwards and southwards. However, some Chileans still argue that the victory over Peru and Bolivia came at the price of losing both the region around Mendoza and most of Patagonia to Argentina; according to some, this should, by dint of colonial land divisions under the Viceroyalty, be Chilean territory. It is certainly true that maps from the early 19th century show Chilean territory crossing the Andes and advancing halfway to the Atlantic Ocean, while early colonial documents speak of "the city of Mendoza in Chile".

From the 1860s onwards, conflict between President and Congress became a constant feature of political life. The War of the Pacific brought the Chilean government a new source of income through the tax levied on nitrate exports coming from the new territories of the Atacama (see box, page 212), but it also increased rivalry for control of this income. When, in 1890, Congress rejected the budget, President Balmaceda announced he would use the 1890 budget for 1891. Congressional leaders denounced this as illegal and fled to Iquique, where they

The War of the Pacific, 1879-83

One of the few major international wars in Latin America after Independence, the War of the Pacific had its roots in a dispute between Chile and Bolivia over national boundaries in the Atacama Desert. There had already been one military conflict in 1836-39, when Chile defeated Peru and Bolivia, but relations were further complicated by the discovery of nitrates in the Atacama in the 1860s, particularly in the then-Bolivian province of Antofagasta.

The War also has to be put into the wider international context of the late 1870s. The years 1873-75 saw a serious recession, with plunging commodity prices around the world. This was followed in 1876 by one of the most severe El Niño weather patterns the world has ever seen, leading to the deaths of tens of millions of people from famine. Santiago had its lowest ever barometric reading in 1877, Peru suffered widespread floods and there were devastating droughts in the Bolivian *altiplano*.

The Bolivian government was forced to impose port taxes to support its weak economy and, in 1878, attempted to tax the Chilean-owned Antofagasta Railroad and Nitrate Company. When the company refused to pay, its assets were seized, sparking claims of foul play by the Chilean government. Peru announced that it would honour a secret alliance with Bolivia, so the Chilean president, Aníbal Pinto, declared war on both states.

None of these three countries was prepared for military conflict; they lacked skilled officers and adequate weapons. Control of the sea was vital: when the Chileans blockaded the Peruvian nitrate port of Iquique with two wooden ships, the *Esmeralda*

and the *Covadonga*, Peru retaliatied with her two best iron-clad ships, the *Huáscar* and the *Independencia*. In the Battle of Iquique, 21 May 1879, the *Esmeralda* was sunk, but the *Independencia* ran aground and was captured, thus altering the balance of power between the two navies. Later in October 1879, the two Chilean iron-clads, *Blanco Encalada* and *Cochrane*, captured the *Huáscar* off Angamos, near Antofagasta. (The ship can now be visited in the harbour at Talcahuano.)

Rather than attack the Peruvian heartland, the Chileans invaded the southern Peruvian province of Tarapacá and then took the town of Tacna, in May 1880, before capturing Arica, further south. In January 1881, fresh Chilean armies seized control of Lima. Bolivia signed a ceasefire, giving up her coastal province, and eventually, under the 1883 peace settlement, Peru gave up Tarapacá to Chile. The provinces of Tacna and Arica were occupied by Chile for 10 years, and it was not until 1929 that an agreement was reached under which Tacna was returned to Peru.

The war gave Chile a monopoly over the world's supply of nitrates and enabled her to dominate the southern Pacific coast. Some idea of its importance in official Chilean history can be gained by the number of streets and squares named after the war heroes, especially Arturo Prat and Aníbal Pinto, and after the two Chilean vessels *Esmeralda* and *Blanco Encalada*. Chile's relations with her northern neighbours, however, remain sour. There is widespread racism in Chile towards the indigenous peoples in Peru and Bolivia, while signs in Bolivia proclaim that the Pacific coastline is still Bolivian.

recruited an army, which defeated Balmaceda's forces and seized the capital. Balmaceda took refuge in the Argentine embassy, where he committed suicide. His defeat was important: between 1891 and 1924 Chilean presidents were weak figures and real power lay with Congress, ruled by the elite.

Twentieth-century politics

In the years before the First World War, the income from nitrates helped build a large railway network, roads and ports and the best education system on the continent. However, the collapse of the industry during the First World War led to worker and student unrest, which brought down the constitutional system in 1924 when the military intervened. A new constitution restored the strong presidency, which had apparently served Chile so well in the 19th century, but the Great Depression brought further economic stress, which resulted in a series of short-lived governments, including a military-led 100-day Socialist Republic in 1932.

As economic conditions recovered in the 1930s, Chile once again became a model of political stability. Between 1932 and 1970, Chile developed a complex multiparty system: two left-wing parties, the Socialists and Communists, representing the urban workers and miners; the Conservative and Liberal parties, dating from the 19th century, representing the landowners; and the Radicals, a centre party representing the middle classes. The Radicals became the key to power, winning the presidency in 1938, 1942 and 1946. However, one major group remained excluded from political life: the peasants, whose votes, controlled by their landlords, gave the Liberals and Conservatives their representation in Congress and enabled the landlords to block rural reform.

In the 1958 election, the Socialist **Salvador Allende** (see box, page 522) only narrowly failed to defeat the Conservative Jorge Alessandri. This shook both the right-wing parties and (in the aftermath of the Cuban Revolution), the US government. In 1964, the US and the Chilean right-wing threw their weight behind **Eduardo Frei Montalva**, a Christian Democrat who promised a 'revolution in freedom'. Frei Montalva's achievements in office were impressive: state ownership of 51% of the copper industry; minimum wage and unionization rights for agricultural workers; and the 1967 agrarian reform, which began replacing the *haciendas* with family farms. However, these measures raised hopes that could not be satisfied, especially in the countryside where workers now enjoyed rights and pushed for faster land reform. Hostility from the landowners was reflected in Congress where the National Party, formed in 1966 by the merger of the Conservatives and Liberals, denounced the government. The President's Christian Democrat Party was divided between supporters and opponents of reform. Nevertheless, Frei Montalva has been an enduringly popular President – his memory was widely seen as a key factor in the landslide victory of his son, Eduardo Frei Ruiz-Tagle, in the 1993 presidential elections.

The 1970 election was narrowly won by Salvador Allende, polling just over 36.3% of the vote, with the electorate split in three. Allende headed a left-wing alliance called Unidad Popular, which launched an ambitious programme of reforms: banking, insurance, communications, textiles and other industries were taken over in the first year and the nationalization of copper was completed (this last even with the support of the right-wing parties). After that, the government ran into major problems: the nationalizations had depleted Chile's currency reserves, while hostility by domestic business groups and the US caused capital flight and a US-led boycott on international credit. In Congress, an alliance between the Christian Democrats and National Party impeached several ministers. At grassroots level, a series of anti-government strikes by truck drivers and professional groups brought the country to a halt in October 1972 and again in August 1973, while the supplies in shops were unable to keep pace with the wider purchasing power of many social classes, leading to long queues for foodstuffs and a rise in annual inflation to over 300% in 1973.

Salvador Allende Gossens

Born in 1908 into an upper-middle-class Valparaíso family, Salvador Allende's childhood ambition was to be a doctor, like his grandfather Ramón Allende Padín, a respected Radical politician who became Serene Grand Master of the Chilean freemasons. While studying medicine, Salvador discovered first-hand the appalling living conditions of the poor and the links between poverty and disease. Even before he qualified as a doctor, he became active in politics and was briefly imprisoned during the Ibáñez dictatorship. He was a founder member of the Chilean Socialist party in 1933; at about the same time he also became active in the Freemasons.

Elected to Congress for Valparaíso at the age of 29, he served as Minister of Health in Aguirre Cerda's Popular Front government of 1939-42 and was elected to the Senate in 1945, becoming Senate president in 1965. Allende was a candidate in four presidential elections. In 1952, he gained only 5.45% of the votes but, in 1958, as candidate of the Front for Popular Action, an alliance between the Socialists and Communists,

he lost narrowly to the right-wing candidate, Jorge Alessandri. Easily defeated in 1964 by the Christian Democrat, Eduardo Frei, he finally won the presidency in 1970. However, without a majority in Congress, heading a broad but divided coalition of eight parties, and facing the hostility of much of the Chilean population and of Washington, Allende found himself with increasingly little room for political manoeuvre.

When news of the military revolt came through in the early hours of 11 September 1973, Allende went to the Moneda Palace and spoke twice on the radio before communications were cut. Although he was offered a flight out of the country in return for his resignation, Allende refused, and the Palace was bombed by three Hawker Hunter jets. Most accounts now accept that Allende committed suicide. He was buried in an unmarked grave in Viña del Mar. In September 1990, following the return to civilian rule, his body was exhumed and transported to Santiago for a state funeral, thousands of people lining the route from the coast.

Despite these negative effects, Allende's Socialist experiment did have a measure of success: agricultural production increased and, by 1972, there were 27% more foodstuffs available in Chile than there had been in 1970. However, even this increase in supply was outstripped by the demand caused by a real rise in wages among the poor. This was a sign that Allende's goal of eradicating poverty was bearing some fruit, with per capita consumption rising for all foodstuffs except red meat. The upper and middle classes who bemoaned the queues in the shops were, in fact, venting frustration that their customary position at the head of affairs was finally being usurped.

The Pinochet era

Allende's popularity in some quarters was demonstrated by the March 1973 Parliamentary elections, at which the Unidad Popular polled 43.4% of the vote, 7% more than in 1970. Nevertheless, the coup of 11 September 1973, led by **General Augusto Pinochet** (b1915), was widely expected, the armed forces having received open encouragement from Allende's opponents in Congress, including the Christian Democrats, and from opposition groups on the streets; it later became clear that the CIA had had a major role in fomenting the unrest that led to the pre-coup stand-off.

The brutality of the coup shocked people who were accustomed to Chile's peaceful traditions. Left-wing activists and people mistakenly identified as leftists were arrested, thousands were executed, torture was widespread, with at least 7,000 people held in the national football stadium, and, by 1978, there were 30,000 Chilean exiles in Western Europe alone. With political parties and labour unions banned, the government adopted neo-liberal economic policies under the influence of Milton Friedman and the 'Chicago Boys' – local economists who had been trained in the United States.

Pinochet installed himself as the undisputed head of a military junta. Those who did not approve of his methods often met grisly ends, including the former head of the Army, Carlos Prats, who was assassinated by a car bomb in Buenos Aires. Pinochet increased his hold on power by his control over the regime's notorious secret police, the DINA, which was headed by a close colleague, General Manuel Contreras. Under a new constitution, adopted in 1980, Chile became a 'protected democracy' based on the exclusion of political parties and the 'guardianship' of the armed forces, who put forward a single candidate for an eight-year presidential term in 1981. To no one's surprise that candidate was Pinochet, who, during his second term (1981-1989) became the longest-serving Chilean president. With his stern features enhanced by dark glasses, Pinochet became the stereotype of the South American dictator. Often seen as a bluff, no-nonsense character, he was also noted for his astuteness, his suspicious mind, his ruthlessness and his hatred of democracy.

It would be wrong to see his dominance as merely the result of repression and fear. For many Chileans, who had hated Allende and feared his liberal policies, the human rights abuses and destruction of democracy were seen as a price worth paying. In spite of his widespread vilification in much of the Western press, Pinochet retained popularity among many Chileans, polling 44% of the vote in a plebiscite in 1988. This bid for a further eight-year term was unsuccessful but, when the first results came in, the military government initially tried to maintain that the 'sí' vote (yes to Pinochet) had triumphed. Even when this position became untenable, the constitution of 1980 ensured that Pinochet still had 18 months before he had to relinquish power.

Eventually, presidential and congressional elections were held in 1989. A veteran Christian Democrat politician, Patricio Aylwin Azócar, the candidate of the Coalition of Parties for Democracy (CPD, or Concertación), was elected President and took office in March 1990 in a peaceful transfer of power. General Pinochet remained as Army Commander, although other armed forces chiefs were replaced. The new Congress set about revising many of the military's laws on civil liberties and the economy, but in December 1990, questions in Congress and in the press about financial scandals involving army officers and Pinochet's own son-in-law led the Army Commander to order all troops to report to barracks. In May 1993, Pinochet surrounded the Ministry of Defence with soldiers and ordered generals to wear battle dress to work for a day.

In 1991, the National Commission for Truth and Reconciliation (the RETTIG Commission) published a report detailing those who had been killed under the military regime. The RETTIG commission established that 3,197 people had died as the result of the violation of human rights, but opposition by the armed forces and an amnesty law protecting members of the military prevented mass human rights trials. At this time, prosecution of those guilty of human rights abuses in Chile was widely seen as impossible.

Presidential elections in December 1993 resulted in victory for the Christian Democrat, Eduardo Frei Ruiz-Tagle, candidate of the Concertación coalition but, in congressional elections held at the same time, the Concertación failed to achieve the two-thirds majority required to reform the constitution, replace the heads of the armed forces and end the system of designated senators whose votes enabled the right-wing parties and the military to block reform. As a result Frei's presidency became an exercise in balancing the demands of the parties of the Concertación against the entrenched power of the military and the right-wing. Although the Concertación won a comfortable victory in congressional elections in December 1997, it still failed to achieve the majority necessary to break the deadlock; the position of the military was strengthened in March 1998 when General Pinochet retired as Army Commander-in-Chief and, as a former president who had held office for six years, took up his lifetime seat in the Senate.

In October 1998, General Pinochet was arrested in London at a private clinic, while recovering from a back operation. The arrest warrant had been issued by a Spanish judge, Baltasar Garzón, for murder and torture of Spanish citizens under the military regime. Pinochet's arrest put the Frei government under great pressure: Pinochet's supporters demanded action, while some of the government's supporters, especially those in the Socialist party, were privately delighted. Meanwhile, the families of those who had disappeared during Pinochet's regime continued to demand news of the whereabouts of the victims' corpses, and the prosecution of those responsible. Combined with the worsening economic situation and the choice of the first Socialist to head the Concertación into presidential elections, these dramatic events made the December 1999 poll unexpectedly close. The Concertación candidate, Ricardo Lagos, eventually won with a tiny majority in a second-round ballot against the populist Mayor of Las Condes, Joaquín Lavín (one of the bright young 'Chicago boys' of the 1970s), although Lavín had won more votes in the first round of polling.

The ructions caused by the Pinochet affair were significant. Having allowed the extradition process to continue, Jack Straw, the British Home Secretary, permitted Pinochet to return to Chile on grounds of ill health in March 2000. However, a legal case started by Judge Juan Guzmán Tapia in the Chilean courts in January 1998 meant that Pinochet still faced a legal challenge. In July 1999, the Supreme Court ruled that, in cases where the fact of death could not be certified, amnesty did not apply, thereby laying Pinochet and the military open to charges regarding the 'disappeared'. This was followed in June 2000 by an Appeal Court ruling that stripped Pinochet of his immunity from trial. The decision was confirmed by the Supreme Court in August, and Pinochet was finally indicted by Judge Guzmán on 29th January 2001. The charges of kidnapping and murder related to the infamous 'caravan of death' in 1973, when many political detainees 'disappeared' in the north of the country. However, in July 2001, the court ruled narrowly that Pinochet's worsening health meant that he was not capable of mounting a proper defence and that the case could not be continued. Judge Guzmán was soon forced to take sick leave as a result of stress induced by the case. Although appeals were mounted by the families of victims of the military government, Pinochet eventually won the right not to stand trial under a Supreme Court Ruling in July 2002.

Recent history

The July 2002 ruling allowed some distance finally to be put between Chile and its troublesome former President. For some time Chileans had been cynical about the prospects of 'Pinocchio' ever being brought to justice and the ruling simply confirmed most people's suspicions. Nevertheless, the long, drawn-out legal wranglings have made it impossible for Pinochet to end his life with the respect and authority he spent so long developing.

President Lagos now urgently needed to concentrate on important national economic issues: in particular, the impact of the economic meltdown in neighbouring Argentina – Chile's main trading partner and the source of the majority of its overseas visitors. As political uncertainty increased across the continent – with coups and counter-coups in Venezuela, the collapse of Argentina and the victory of the left in presidential elections in Brazil – 2002 was a difficult year to be steering the Chilean effort to reduce unemployment caused widespread protests, largely because most people's experience of economic realities did not match the government's subsequent statements as to the "improving situation".

The early months of 2003, however, saw Lagos able to reassert his statesmanship through his renewed importance on the global stage: Chile now occupied one of the 15 seats on the UN Security Council. As the international crisis over Iraq reached a head, Lagos did not desert his old support base, with Chile proving to be one of the most intractable of the "six undecided council members", and putting forward a strong case against pre-emptive military invasion. This resistance to pressure from the 'yanquis' and the Brits reflected the mood in the country and enhanced Lagos's popularity. But opposition to war in Iraq did not come without a price; the Americans subsequently postponed signing a free trade agreement with Chile.

Modern Chile

An overview

The Pinochet affair forced Chileans to confront their recent past. Although old wounds reopened, the increasing political apathy of the young, which was apparent in the early 1990s, was nipped in the bud. While the presidencies of the Concertación continued the Pinochetista neo-liberal policies that made Chile such a banker's favourite in the 1980s, these have been accompanied by a genuine attempt at more inclusive government, including significant increases in the national minimum wage, at rates well above that of inflation. With a pension system on which countries such as Britain have modelled their own 'stakeholder' schemes, urban Chile is now, for the most part, modern and dynamic.

There are, however, several problems that the government needs to address. While there has been a limited rise in living standards among the inhabitants of Santiago's *callampas* (shanty towns), urban poverty remains widespread. Problems in Santiago are due in large part to the over-centralization of the country: over a third of the population live in the capital or the surrounding Región Metropolitana, and Chile's unusual geography means that Santiago is a natural focal point, on which the rest of the country is all too dependent.

Meanwhile, the newspapers and TV stations are full of talk of Chile's '*crisis económica*'. Unemployment in Gran Santiago is up to 15% and everywhere people are talking about the difficulty of finding – and keeping – work. Although Chile's economy remains the most stable in South America, there is no doubt that the period of constant growth and prosperity that characterized the 1990s is over. This is largely the result of weaknesses among Chile's main trading partners: the crisis in the Far East had major ramifications in Chile, while the devaluation in Brazil, followed by the subsequent economic crisis in Argentina, led to the rise of the US dollar against the Chilean peso in 2001 and beyond. The government did extremely well to stave off the inflationary pressures of these developments, but there have been significant economic consequences, not least the arrival of Argentines looking for work in Santiago, adding to the existing employment problems. With the economic situation of the lower and middle classes worse than it has been for many years, the chances of a populist emerging from the right to win the next presidential election in December 2005 must be high.

Chile's income tax system is symptomatic of the country's traditional conservatism. Direct income tax is exceptionally low and business tax, at 17%, is less than half the rate applied in most developed countries. While Chile's lower and middle classes can clearly not afford to pay more income tax, this is far from true of the country's upper classes. The inability of President Lagos's government to tackle this subject is evidence both of the oligarchic stranglehold that the Chilean aristocracy retains on the state and of the taboo status of even the slightest economic redistribution – thanks to the 'anti-Communist wars' waged by the military government in the 1970s and 1980s and to the psychological scars caused by the Allende government's economic policies and their consequences.

Perhaps the most fundamental long-term problem, however, is that Chile's wealth depends in part on the ongoing rape of its extensive natural resources, often by multinational companies; industries such as logging and intensive fishing, while successful at present, have the potential to ruin Chile's future. An example is the ongoing plan of a Canadian multinational to build a vast aluminium smelting plant in the Aysen region in the far south, which would contaminate the pristine ecosystems of Chilean Patagonia; there has been widespread local opposition (see www.noalumysa.cl for more details). According to one estimate, Chile lost 80% of its marine life in the 1980s and its native forests continue to disappear at alarming rates. Environmentalists have joined forces with farmers to highlight the environmental damage caused by introduced species such as the eucalyptus, which extracts most of the goodness from the soil, and by plantations of pine, which acidify the soil. The desire of the Chilean government to join the North American Free Trade Agreement, along with the USA, Canada and Mexico, is not seen as beneficial in all quarters.

However, these moves are symbolic of Chile's increasingly outward-looking mentality. After four centuries characterized by isolation and insularity, the ramifications of Chile's recent history have put the country onto the international map in an unprecedented manner. Whereas, until recently, Chileans compared themselves to Europeans, they now take increasing national pride in their own achievements. Even though Pinochet was not put on trial in Chile, the case and its consequences mean that the country is at the vanguard of one of the most significant human rights movement, in history; one that, in a short space of time, has already had repercussions for repressive former heads of state in the Central African Republic and Yugoslavia.

Constitution and government

Chile is governed under the 1980 Constitution, introduced by the military government of General Pinochet and approved in a plebiscite on 11 September 1980, although important amendments were made during the transition to civilian rule in 1989-90. The constitution provided for an eight-year non-renewable term for the President of the Republic, a bicameral legislature with a Congress and a Senate and an independent judiciary and central bank, although it was only after the rejection of Pinochet in the 1988 vote that most of the provisions of the constitution come into operation. A two-thirds majority in both houses of legislature is required to reform the constitution. In February 1994, the legislature cut the presidential term of office from eight years to six.

The legislature is composed of a 120-seat Chamber of Deputies and a 47-seat Senate, eight of whose members are nominated rather than elected. Among the nominated senators is one former head of each of the armed forces and any former presidents who have completed a full six-year term (such as Pinochet). The existence of nominated senators has enabled the right-wing opposition parties to block constitutional reform, and their abolition has been a major aim of civilian governments since 1990.

The dominant political party in Chile is the Christian Democrats, a centre party which grew rapidly after its foundation in 1957. The Christian Democrats welcomed the overthrow of Allende but later became the focus of opposition to the dictatorship. Not strong enough to rule on its own, since 1990 the party has contested elections in an alliance known as the **Concertación**. The other members are the Socialists, a

66 99 After four centuries characterized by isolation and insularity, Chile's recent history has put it onto the international map in an unprecedented manner.

centre-left party traditionally split between the Radicals and the Partido por la Democracía, a centre-left grouping led by ex-Socialists. The main opposition to the Concertación comes from the right wing, which is divided into two main parties, Renovación Nacional and the Unión Democrática Independiente. For the 1993 and 1999 elections, they formed an alliance called the **Unión por el Progreso.**

Chile is divided into 13 regions, usually referred to by Roman numerals (although they also have names). The government of each region is headed by an Intendent, who is appointed by the President.

Economy

Chile's economy is dependent on the mining sector. Mineral ores account for half of total export revenue. Copper is the most important mineral, with Chile being the world's largest producer. Although the Pinochet government of 1973-90 sold off most state-run industries to the private sector, CODELCO (the state copper mining company) was not touched. The biggest new mine is La Escondida, where production began in 1990, which produces an output of 800,000 tonnes a year, making it the world's leading mine (see page 229). Other mineral resources in Chile include a quarter of the world's known molybdenum ore reserves and around 40% of the world's lithium reserves. Fluctuations in world prices for minerals can have a great impact on the country's balance of payments.

The country's diverse environment means that agriculture is also of great importance. Traditional crops, such as cereals, pulses, potatoes and industrial crops, such as sugar beet, sunflower seed and rape seed, account for about a third of the value of agriculture, while vegetables account for a quarter. Fruit growing has expanded rapidly, with fresh fruit now accounting for over US$1 billion in exports a year, while timber and wood products make up the third place in exports. Chile is the most important fishing nation in Latin America and the largest producer of fishmeal in the world; it is also one of the world's leading salmon farmers.

Chile is fortunate in possessing reserves of oil, natural gas and coal, and abundant hydroelectricity potential. Almost all the country's hydrocarbon reserves are in the extreme south, on Tierra del Fuego, in the Strait of Magellan. Two pipelines are planned and six new gas-fired power plants have recently been built. Manufacturing activity is mostly food processing, metalworking, textiles, footwear and fish processing.

The Government follows anti-inflationary policies, accompanied by structural adjustment and reform. Privatization has been widespread, although certain key companies, such as Codelco, remain in state hands. Rising investor confidence brought economic growth throughout the late 1980s and most of the 1990s and the Chilean model has been held up as an example for other debtor countries.

However, in 1999, Chile experienced negative economic growth for the first time in more than 15 years, as a result of drought and the financial crisis in the Far East. The subsequent world recession limited economic recovery and, in 2002, growth was only 2.1%. By March 2003, inflation in the consumer sector had risen to the equivalent of 15% – a five-year high – but, given the global and local economic situation, observers agree that Chile is weathering the storm relatively well.

Background Modern Chile

Chile is a deeply conservative country: it was the first newly independent state in Latin America fully to embrace the Catholic church and has the most stable 'democratic' (or, until the 1950s, oligarchic) tradition in the region.

There is less racial diversity in Chile than in most Latin American countries. Over 90% of the population of 14.2 million is *mestizo* (mixed race). There are hardly any people of African origin – in sharp contrast to, say, Brazil or Colombia – and there has been much less immigration from Europe than in Argentina and Brazil. The German, French, Italian and Swiss immigrants came mostly after 1846 as small farmers in the forest zone south of the Biobío. Between 1880 and 1900, gold-seeking Serbs and Croats settled in the far south and the British took up sheep farming and commerce in the same region.

There is disagreement over the number of indigenous people in Chile. Survival International estimate the **Mapuche** population to be one million, but other statistics – including the official ones – put it at much less. There are also 15,000-20,000 **Aymara** in the northern Chilean Andes and 1,200 **Rapa Nui** on Easter Island. A political party, the Party for Land and Identity, unites many Indian groupings, and legislation is proposed to restore indigenous people's rights.

The population is far from evenly distributed: Middle Chile, from Copiapó to Concepción, consisting of 18% of the country's area, is home to 77% of the population, with the Metropolitan Region of Santiago containing, on its own, about 39% of the total. Population density in 1995 ranged from 377 per sq km in the Metropolitan Region to 0.8 per sq km in Región XI (Aisén). Since the 1960s, heavy migration from the countryside has led to rapid urbanization. By 1995, 85.8% of the population lived in urban areas.

According to the 1992 census the population is 76.7% Catholic and 13.2% Protestant. Membership of Evangelical Protestant churches has grown rapidly in recent years. There are also small Jewish communities in Santiago and Temuco especially.

Chilean literacy rates are higher than those of most other South American states; according to the 1992 census over 95% of the population above the age of 15 is literate. Census returns also indicated that, among the over-25s, 8% had completed higher education, 42% had completed secondary education and 44% had only completed primary education. Higher education provision doubled in the 1980s through the creation of private universities.

Chile is the only country in the world in which divorce does not exist. Couples that want to separate have to go through the farcical process of getting a notary to swear that they were married in an inappropriate municipality and that their marriage certificate is therefore invalid. This is manageable for those on reasonable incomes but the upshot for impoverished rural populations is that divorce – and remarriage – becomes impossible. Although a divorce law is currently being mooted, this has been met by attacks in the conservative press, with long articles by Catholic bishops appearing in *El Mercurio* lamenting this shift to a permissive society.

Culture

Chilean culture is rooted in the nation's hybrid soul. European guitars blend with panpipes and *queñas*; religious art flourishes alongside traditional crafts; literature scales the heights of modernism, while never losing track of the natural beauty from which it is born.

Chile's traditional crafts are often specific to particular places and all have a long history. Present-day handicrafts represent either the transformation of utilitarian objects into works of art, or the continued manufacture of pieces that retain symbolic value. A number of factors threaten these traditions: the loss of types of wood and plant fibres through the destruction of forests; the mechanization of farm labour, reducing the use of the horse; other agricultural changes, which have, among other things, led to reductions in sheep farming and wheat growing; and migration from the countryside to the city. On the other hand, city dwellers and tourists have created a demand for 'traditional' crafts so their future is to some degree assured.

Basketry Mapuche basketry is made for domestic, agricultural and fishing uses in Lago Lanalhue and the Cautín region. Apart from the Mapuche areas, one of the great centres of basket-making is Chimbarongo, just south of San Fernando in the Central Valley. Here, weaving is done in almost every household, usually by the men. One of the main materials used is willow, which is collected in June when it is still green and then soaked in water for four months, at the end of which the bark peels off. The lengths of willow are split into four and finished with a knife. Baskets, chairs and lamps are the most common objects made. Willow is not the only fibre used. Many items are made from different types of straw, including little boxes made of wheat; although the latter are produced throughout the country, the most famous are from La Manga, Melipilla. Note also the yawl made for fishing, typical of Chiloé. Other important centres of basket-making are Ninhue-Hualte in Ñuble (Región VIII), Hualqui, 24 km south of Concepción, and San Juan de la Costa, near the coast of Osorno, Región X.

Carving and woodwork The people of the Atacama region edge trays with cactus wood and make little churches – traditionally the doors of the old churches were made of cactus – and they also use cactus for drums, while bamboo is used for flutes of various sizes. Different types of wood are used in the construction of guitars, guitarrones, harps and *rabeles* (fiddles), mainly in the Metropolitan Region. Villarrica (see page 320) is a major producer of wooden items: plates, kitchen utensils, but especially decorative objects like animals and birds, jointed snakes and *picarones* (small figures, which, when picked up, reveal their genitals). Wooden ships in bottles are made in Coronel, while in Loncoche, south of Temuco, a workshop specializes in fine carvings, in native wood, of country and Mapuche scenes. Another craft from the Mapuche region is the carving of horn or antler (*asta*) in Temuco, to make animals, birds, cups, spoons etc.

Ceramics The two most famous places for ceramics are Quinchamalí near Chillán (see page), where the traditional black ware is incised with patterns in white, and Pomaire, west of Santiago (see page 118), which is renowned for heavy terracotta household items that are used in many Chilean homes. Less well known is the pottery of the Atacama zone, the clay figures of Lihueimo (Región VI), the household items, clay figurines and model buildings of Pilén de Cauquenes-Maule (Región VII) and the scented pottery of the nuns of the Comunidad de Santa Clara (Convento de Monjas Claras in Santiago and Los Angeles). These highly decorated pieces have been made since colonial times, when they achieved great fame.

Cowboy equipment and clothing Items can be found in any part of the country where there are *huasos*: San Fernando, Chillán, Curicó, Colchagua, Doñihue and also in Santiago. Saddles of leather, wood and iron, carved wooden stirrups in the old style, leather reins, spurs (some of them huge and very elaborate – *huasos* are always proud of their spurs) and hats of straw or other materials are the types of equipment you will see. The clothing comprises ponchos (long, simple in colour and design, often with one or two coloured stripes), *mantas* (shorter, divided into four with a great variety of colour), *chamantos* (luxurious *mantas*, double-sided, decorated with fine patterns of vines, leaves, flowers, small birds etc) and sashes/*fajas* (either single or tri-coloured, made to combine with *mantas* or *chamantos*).

Knitwear and textiles Chiloé is famous for its woollen goods, hand-knitted and coloured with natural dyes. With the atrocious weather, clothing (such as sweaters, knitted caps, mantas, socks) is very popular; this and rugs, blankets and patch dolls are all sold locally and in Puerto Montt. The main knitting centres are Quinchao, Chonchi and Quellón. Other crafts of Chiloé are model boat building and basketware from Quinchao and Quellón, where mats and figurines such as birds and fish are also made.

The Mapuche are also weavers of sheep's wool, making ponchos, mantas, sashes (*fajas*), reversible rugs (*lamas*) with geometric designs and bedspreads (*pontros*). The colours come from natural dyes. The main producing areas are around Lago Lanalhue, Chol Chol, Nueva Imperial and other small settlements in the Mapuche heartland between Temuco and the coast (see pages 296 and 311).

Silverware Although silverware is one of the traditional crafts of the Mapuche, its production is in decline owing to the cost of the metal. Traditional women's jewellery includes earrings, headbands, necklaces, brooches and *tupus* (pins for fastening the *manta* or shawl). Nowadays, the most common items to be found for sale are *chawai* (earrings), but these are smaller and in simpler shapes than those traditionally worn by Mapuche women. It is a matter of debate whether Mapuche silversmiths had perfected their skills before the arrival of the Spaniards; certainly the circulation of silver coins in the 18th century gave great impetus to this form of metalwork. The Universidad Católica in Temuco is in charge of a project to ensure the continuance of the art.

Specialist crafts The Mapuche make musical instruments: the *trutruca*, a horn 1½ to 4 m long; *pifilka* (or *pifüllka*), a wooden whistle; the *kultrún* drum; *cascahuilla*, a string of bells; and *trompe*, similar to a Jew's harp. The village of Rari, near the Termas de Panimávida, some 25 km northeast of Linares (Región VII), specializes in beautiful, delicate items made from dyed horsehair: bangles and brooches in the shape of butterflies, little hats, flowers, etc.

Mined in the Cordillera de Ovalle, lapis lazuli is a blue stone, only found otherwise in Afghanistan. It is set in silver to make earrings, necklaces and bracelets. Many shops in Santiago sell the gemstone and objects that incorporate it. Of growing popularity in recent years, combarbalita is a smooth, marble-like stone found only around the remote town of Combarbalá in Regió IV. A very beautiful stone, it is used to make everything from jewellery and cutlery holders to bedside tables and can be very good value.

Fine art and sculpture

The colonial period

There was little home-grown art during the colonial period in Chile but trade with other regions was extensive and Santiago in particular has good collections of non-Chilean art. The Catholic church inevitably dominated fine art and sculpture; the new religious foundations needed images of Christ and the saints to reassure Christian settlers and also to instruct new converts. The importation of works from Spain was very costly, so most patrons relied instead on the major colonial artistic centres of Cusco, Potosí and Quito.

The churches and monasteries of Santiago give a vivid sense of the thriving art market in colonial Spanish America: sculptures were shipped down the coast from Lima and from Quito via Guayaquil; canvasses were carried across the Andes on mule trains from Cusco and Potosí; and occasionally an itinerant Spanish-trained artist would pass through in search of lucrative commissions. Extensive cycles of the lives of Christ, the Virgin and selected saints were popular: a cycle of 40 or 50 large canvasses representing the exploits of, say, St Francis, provided instant cover for large expanses of bare plaster, a good clear narrative and an exemplary life to follow.

San Francisco in Santiago (see page 86) has a cycle of 53 paintings of the life of St Francis painted in Cusco in the late 17th century. These are based on a similar cycle in the Franciscan monastery in Cusco by the Indian artist Basilio de Santa Cruz Pumacallao, which is in turn derived from a series of European engravings. One of the Santiago paintings, the Funeral of St Francis of 1684, is signed by **Juan Zapaca Inca**, an indigenous artist and follower of Santa Cruz, who probably oversaw production of the whole series. Wherever possible the artist has introduced bright-coloured tapestries and rich fabrics embellished with lace and gold embroidery, a mark of the continuing importance of textiles in Andean culture. This is a typical pattern for colonial art: a set of European engravings forms the basis for a large painted cycle which in turn becomes the source for further copies and derivatives. The narrative content and general composition remain constant, while the setting, attendant figures, costume and decorative detail are often translated into an Andean idiom.

There are, of course, many different categories of colonial art. The big painted cycles were produced more for the educated inhabitants of the monastic establishments than for a lay audience, and were intended for edification rather than devotion. Popular devotion tends to create increasingly decorated and hieratic images. A good example is that of the so-called Cristo de Mayo. Early in the 17th century Pedro de Figueroa, a friar of the Augustinian monastery in Santiago, carved a figure of the crucified Christ, which still hangs in the church of **San Agustín** (Estado 170, not far from Cerro Santa Lucía). This passionate, unusually defiant image was credited with miraculous powers after it survived a serious earthquake in Santiago in May 1647 (hence the popular name de Mayo). The only damage was that the crown of thorns slipped from Christ's head and lodged around his neck. A cult quickly grew up around the image, creating a demand for painted copies, which are identifiable by the upward gaze, the distinctive necklace of thorns and the evenly distributed lash marks across the body. The Carmelite convent of San José has a locally produced 18th-century example of the Cristo de Mayo that includes attendant saints and garlands of bright flowers, the latter like pious offerings. The Jesuits established a school of sculpture on Chiloé, where, up until the late 19th century, native craftsmen continued to produce boldly expressive Christian images.

After Independence

In the 19th century, Chile's distance from the old colonial centre of viceregal power worked to its advantage in the field of art. The Lima-born artist **José Gil de Castro** (died 1841), known as El Mulato Gil, accompanied Bernardo O'Higgins on the campaign for Chilean Independence from 1814, working both as engineer and map-maker and as a portrait painter. His portrait of O'Higgins of 1820 in the **Museo Histórico Nacional** in Santiago represents the hero as a towering giant of a man, immovable as the rocky mountains behind him. Another 1818 painting in the **Municipalidad of La Serena** shows San Martín standing beside a writing desk, his hand inside his jacket in a distinctively Napoleonic pose.

The 19th century also brought European traveller-artists to Chile, who helped to confirm the Chilean landscape, peoples and customs as legitimate subjects for paintings, including the German Johann Moritz Rugendas, who lived in Chile from 1833 to 1845, and the Englishman Charles Wood (in Chile from 1819 to 1852). Examples of both artists' work can be seen in the **Museo Nacional de Bellas Artes** (see page 84). The Frenchman Raymond Monvoisin also spent many years in Chile, from 1843 to 1857. His perceptive portraits of members of the government and the literary élite are interesting for the way in which they link the Chilean tradition of Gil de

Castro with European sources. After his return to France he produced the first major painting dedicated to an event from colonial history, the Mapuche hero Caupolicán taken prisoner by the Spaniards (1859). Caupolicán was celebrated in Chile 10 years later in a bronze statue by Nicanor Plaza (1844-1914) erected on the Cerro Santa Lucía in Santiago, and although it originated as an entry for a competition organized by the US government for a statue to commemorate the Last of the Mohicans, it represents the incorporation of indigenous people into the national mythology.

The **Chilean Academy of Painting** was founded in 1849 and, although its first presidents were mediocre European artists, they too helped to make Chilean subject matter respectable. The Academy also acted as a focus for aspiring young artists. **Antonio Smith** (1832-77) rebelled against the rigidity of the academic system, working as a political cartoonist as well as a painter, but his dramatic landscapes grew out of the gradual awakening of interest in Chilean scenery. He transformed the picturesque view into a heroic vision of mountains and valleys, full of air and space and potential. Cosme San Martín (1850-1906), Pedro León Carmona (1853-99), Pedro Lira (1845-1912), Alfredo Valenzuela Puelma (1856-1909) and English-born Thomas Somerscales (1842-1927) extended the range of possible national subjects in the fields of landscape, portraiture, history and genre. The late 19th century saw a number of important commissions for nationalistic public statuary including the peasant soldier 'El Roto Chileno' in Santiago's Plaza Yungay by Nicanor Plaza's pupil Virginio Arias (1855-1941), and several monumental works by Rebecca Matte (1875-1929).

The 20th century

From the later 19th century until well into the 20th century, Chilean painting was dominated by refracted versions of Impressionism. Artists such as **Juan Francisco González** (1853-1933) and **Alfredo Helsby** (1862-1933) introduced a looser technique and more luminous palette to create landscapes full of strong contrasts of sunlight and shadows, a tradition continued by, for example, **Pablo Burchard** (1873-1964), **Agustín Abarca** (1882-1953), **Arturo Gordon** (1883-1944) and **Camilo Mori** (1896-1973).

The Chilean avant garde has been dominated by artists who have lived and worked for long periods abroad, many as political exiles. After studying with Le Corbusier in Switzerland and encountering the Surrealists in Paris, **Roberto Matta** (born 1911) moved to New York in 1939 and began painting uniquely unsettling space-age monsters and machines that circulate in a multi-dimensional chaos; he is perhaps the most famous artist to have come from Chile. **Nemesio Antúnez** (1918-93) developed more earth-bound abstractions of reality: volcanic landscapes viewed through flames and falling rocks, or milling crowds, faceless and powerless.

The younger generation includes **Eugenio Dittborn** (born 1943), who sends 'Airmail Paintings' around the world in an exploration of ideas of transition and dislocation and, because many contain photographs of victims of political violence, of anonymity and loss. **Alfredo Jaar** (born 1956) creates installations using maps and photographs to document the destructive exploitation of the world's resources, both human and natural – most recently focusing on the aftermath of the Rwandan genocide.

In recent years many exiles have returned home and Santiago is now a cultural centre of growing importance, with women particularly well represented (for example **Carmen Valbuena**, born 1955, and **Bernarda Zegers**, born 1951). Chile is the home of an interesting ongoing project called **'Cuerpos Pintados'** (Painted Bodies), whereby artists from Chile and other Latin American countries are invited to Santiago to paint nude models in the colours and designs of their choice. It is worth watching out for exhibitions of the stunning photographs that are the project's permanent outcome; and also for one-off exhibitions up and down the country of the many very talented local artists (especially in cultural centres such as Concepción and La Serena).

From colonial times to Independence

The long struggle of the Spaniards to conquer the lands south of their Peruvian stronghold inspired one of the great epics of early Spanish American literature, *La Araucana* by **Alonso de Ercilla y Zúñiga** (1533-94). Published in three parts (1569, 1578 and 1589), the poem tells of the victories and defeats of the Spaniards. Nothing like an apologia, the work endures because it recognizes the brutal actions of the Spaniards. Like a subsequent work, *Arauco domado* (1596), by the *criollo* **Pedro de Oña** (1570-1643), the point of view is that of the conquering invader, not a celebration of Chilean, or American identity, although Ercilla does show that the people who resisted the Spaniards were noble and courageous. After Ercilla, literature written in what was to become Chile concentrated on chronicling either the physical or the spiritual conquest of the local inhabitants.

Writers in the 18th and early 19th centuries tended to mirror the colonial desire to consolidate the territory that was in Spanish, rather than Mapuche hands. Post-Independence, the move was towards the establishment of the new republic. To this end, the Venezuelan **Andrés Bello** (1781-1865) was invited to Santiago from London in 1829 to oversee the education of the new elite. Already famous for his literary journals and strong views on Romantic poetry, Bello made major contributions to Chilean scholarship and law. His main work was *Gramática de la lengua castellana destinada al uso de los americanos* (1847). As Jean Franco says, "He was one of the first of many writers to see that a general literary Spanish could act as an important cohesive factor, a spiritual tie of the Hispanic peoples".

A cultural haven

Chile's relative political stability in the 19th century helped Santiago to become a cultural centre that attracted many foreign intellectuals, such as the Argentine Diego Sarmiento and the Nicaraguan Rubén Darío. At this time, Chilean writers were establishing a national literary framework to replace the texts of the colonial era. This involved the spreading of *buenas costumbres*, a movement to shift literary subject matter onto Chilean territory, a republican education for the middle classes and the founding of a national identity. Realist fiction captured the public interest. **José Victorino Lastarria** (1817-88) wrote *costumbrista* stories, portraying national scenes and characters, while **Alberto Blest Gana** (1829-1904) enjoyed two periods of success as a novelist, heavily influenced by Balzac. His most popular novel was *Martín Rivas* (1862), the love story of a young man who wins a wife of a higher class. For some, Blest Gana's presentation of Santiago and its class structure is a worthy imitator of the French *comédie humaine*; for others, his realism fails either to unite his themes to his sketches of Chilean life or to rise above a pedestrian style.

Twentieth-century prose writing

Realism remained the dominant mode of fiction until well into the 20th century, but it appeared in several guises. **Baldomero Lillo** (1867-1923) wrote socialist realist stories about the coal miners of Lebu: *Sub terra* (1904) and *Sub sole* (1907). Lillo and other regionalist writers shifted the emphasis away from the city to the countryside and the miserable conditions endured by many Chileans. Other novelists, including **Luis Orrego Luco** (1866-1948) and **Joaquín Edwards Bello** (1887-1968), concentrated on the crisis of aristocratic values and the gulf between the wealthy and the deprived.

Another strand was *criollismo*, a movement seeking to portray Chile and the tribulations of Chileans without romanticism, championed especially by short story writers like **Mariano Latorre** (1886-1955). His main interest was the Chilean landscape, which he described almost to the point of overwhelming his characters.

534 A different emphasis was given to regionalism and *criollismo* by **Augusto d'Halmar** (Augusto Goeminne Thomson, 1882-1950), whose stories in *La lámpara en el molino* (1914) were given exotic settings and were labelled *imaginismo*. D'Halmar's followers, the Grupo Letras (1920s and 1930s), became openly antagonistic towards the disciples of Latorre: **Luis Durand** wrote books in the 1920s and 1940s that described *campesino* life in detail. Another branch of realism was the exploration of character through psychology in the books of **Eduardo Barrios** (1884-1963), such as *El niño que enloqueció de amor* (1915), *El hermano asno* (1922) and *Los hombres del hombre* (1950).

The anti-fascist views of a group of writers known as the Generation of 1938 (**Nicomedes Guzmán**, 1914-65, **Juan Godoy**, **Carlos Droguett**, born 1915, and others) added a politically committed dimension, which coincided with the rise to power of the Frente Popular, a Socialist movement. At the same time, *Mandrágora*, a journal principally dedicated to poetry, introduced many European literary ideas, notably those of the surrealists. Its influence, combined with a global decline in Marxist writing after the Second World War and the defeat of the Frente Popular, contributed to the rise of a new generation of writers in the 1950s, whose main motivation was the rejection of all the '*ismos*' that had preceded it. These novelists, short story writers and dramatists were characterized by existential individualism and political and social scepticism. Many writers started publishing in the 1950s; among them was **Volodia Teitelboim** (born 1916), a communist exiled to the USSR after 1973, whose novels *Hijo del salitre* (1952) and *La semilla en la arena* (1957) were portrayals of the struggles of the Chilean masses. In 1979 he published *La guerra interna*, which combined real and imaginary characters in a vision of post-coup Chile.

From the 1920s on, a significant development away from *criollismo* was the rise of the female voice. The first such novelist to achieve major recognition was **Marta Brunet** (1901-67), who brought a unique perspective to the rural themes she handled (including the need to value women), but who has also been described as a writer of the senses (by Nicomedes Guzmán). Her books include *Montaña adentro* (1923), *Aguas abajo* (1943), *Humo hacia el sur* (1946) and *María Nadie* (1957). Also born in 1901, **María Flora Yáñez** wrote about the alienation of women with great emphasis on the imagination as an escape for her female protagonists from their routine, unfulfilled lives (*El abrazo de la tierra*, 1934; *Espejo sin imágen*, 1936; *Las cenizas*, 1942). **María Luisa Bombal** (1910-80) took the theme of alienated women even further (*La última niebla*, 1935; *La amortajada*, 1938, and various short stories): her narrative and her characters' worlds spring from the subconscious realm of female experience and are expressed through dreams, fantasies and journeys loaded with symbolic meaning.

Manuel Rojas (1896-1972) was brought up in Argentina, but his family moved to Chile in 1923. His first short stories, such as *Hombres del sur* (1926), *Travesía* (1934) and the novel *Lanchas en la bahía* (1932) were undoubtedly *criollista* in outlook, but he devoted a greater importance to human concerns than his *criollista* contemporaries. By 1951, Rojas' style had changed dramatically, without deserting realism. *Hijo de ladrón* (1951) was perhaps the most influential 20th-century Chilean novel up to that time. It describes the adventures of Aniceto Hevía, the son of a Buenos Aires jewel thief, who crosses the Andes to Valparaíso, ending up as a beachcomber. Nothing in his life is planned or motivated by anything other than the basic necessities. Happiness and intimacy are only brief moments in an unharmonious, disordered life. Aniceto's adventures are continued in *Mejor que el vino* (1958), *Sombras contra el muro* (1963) and *La obscura vida radiante* (1971). To describe the essential isolation of man from the inside, Rojas relaxes the temporal structure of the novel, bringing in memory, interior monologue and techniques to multiply the levels of reality (to use Fernando Alegría's phrase).

The demise of *criollismo* coincided with the influence of the US Beat Generation and the culture epitomized by James Dean, followed in the 1960s by the protest movements in favour of peace, and black and women's rights. The Cuban Revolution inspired Latin American intellectuals of the left and the novel-writing 'boom' gained momentum. At the same time, the national political process which led ultimately to Salvador Allende's victory in 1970 was bolstered by writers, folk singers and painters who questioned everything to do with the Chilean bourgeoisie.

José Donoso (1924-96) began publishing stories in 1955 (*Veraneo y otros cuentos*), followed two years later by his first novel, *Coronación*. This book describes the chaos caused by the arrival of a new maid into an aristocratic Santiago household and introduces many of Donoso's recurring themes: the closed worlds of old age and childhood, madness, multiple levels of reality, the inauthenticity of the upper classes and the subversion of patriarchal society. The stories in *Charleston* (1960), *El lugar sin límites* (1966), about a transvestite and his daughter who live in a brothel near Talca, and *Este domingo* (1966) mark the progression from *Coronación* to *El obsceno pájaro de la noche* (1970), a labyrinthine novel (Donoso's own term) narrated by a schizophrenic, throwing together reality, dreams and fantasy, darkness and light. Donoso achieved the same status as Gabriel García Márquez, Julio Cortázar and Mario Vargas Llosa with this, his most experimental novel. Between 1967 and 1981 he lived in Spain; in the 1970s he published several novels, including *Casa de campo* (1978), which relates the disintegration of a family estate when the children try to take it over. Back in Chile, he published, among others, *El jardín de al lado* (1981), which chronicles the decline of a middle-aged couple in exile in Spain, *Cuatro para Delfina* (1982), *La desesperanza* (1986) about the return of a left-wing singer from Paris to the daily horrors of Pinochet's regime.

Another writer who describes the bad faith of the aristocracy is **Jorge Edwards** (born 1931). His books include *El patio* (1952), *Los convidados de piedra* (1978), *El museo de cera* (1980), *La mujer imaginaria* (1985) and *Fantasmas de carne y hueso* (1993). His book *Persona non grata* (1973) describes his experiences as a diplomat, including his expulsion from Cuba. **Fernando Alegría** (born 1918) spans all the movements since 1938, with a variety of work including essays, highly respected literary criticism, poetry and novels. He was closely associated with Salvador Allende and was his cultural attaché in Washington 1970-73. *Recabarren* was published in 1938, after which followed many books, among them *Lautaro, joven libertador del Arauco* (1943), *Caballo de copas* (1957), *Mañana los guerreros* (1964), *El paso de los gansos* (1975), about a young photographer's experiences in the 1973 coup, *Coral de guerra* (1979), also about brutality under military dictatorship, *Una especie de memoria* (1983), Alegría's own memoir of 1938 to 1973, and *Allende: A Novel* (1992). Having been so close to Allende, Alegría could not write a biography, he had to fictionalize it, he said. But the rise and fall of Allende becomes a realization that history and fiction are intimately related, particularly in that Chilean epoch.

The death of Salvador Allende in 1973, and with it the collapse of the left's struggle to gain power by democratic means, was a traumatic event for Chilean writers. Those who had built their careers in the 1960s and early 1970s were for the most part exiled, forcibly or voluntarily, and thus were condemned to face the left's own responsibility in Allende's failure. René Jara says that before 1970 writers had not managed to achieve mass communication for their ideas and 1970-73 was too short a time to correct that. Once Pinochet was in power, the task became how to find a language capable of expressing the usurping of democracy without simplifying reality. Those in exile still felt part of Chile, a country temporarily wiped from the map, where their thought was prohibited.

There are many other contemporary male novelists who deserve mention: **Antonio Skármeta** (born 1940) was exiled in Germany until 1980, writing short stories and novels and directing theatre and film. His short-story collections include *El* entusiasmo (1967), *Desnudo en el tejado* (1969), *Tiro libre* (1973) and his novels *Soñé que la nieve ardía* (975), *No pasó nada* (1980), *Ardiente paciencia* (1985) and *Match-ball* (1989). *Ardiente paciencia*, retitled *El cartero de Neruda* after its successful filming as *Il postino*, is a good example of Skármeta's concern for the enthusiasms and emotions of ordinary people, skilfully weaving the love life of a postman and a bar owner's daughter into the much bigger picture of the death of Pablo Neruda and the fall of Allende. A different take entirely on the legacy of Neruda and Chilean letters in general is provided by **Roberto Bolaño** – also an exile – whose satirical novel *Nocturno de Chile* (2003 – English translation, *By Night in Chile*) provides both an understanding of the fate of the Chilean literary world under Pinochet and of the nature of that world itself.

Another famous Chilean exile is **Ariel Dorfman** (see box, page 537), whose work exemplifies the struggle of the exile to find a bridge between their social reality overseas and their Chilean identity. His prolific output includes the novels *Moros en la costa*, 1973, (Hard Rain), *La última canción de Manuel Sendero*, 1982 (The Last Song of Manuel Sendero), *Mascara*, 1988, *Viudas*, 1981, (Widows), *Konfidenz*, 1995 and *The Nanny and the Iceberg*, 1999; the plays *Death and the Maiden*, *Reader* (1995), *Widows* (1997) and two further dramas co-written with his son Rodrigo; several volumes of essays and many poems (some collected in English as *Last Waltz in Santiago and other poems of Exile and Disappearance*, (1988). Most of Dorfman's work is currently in print in English.

The most successful Chilean novelist today is **Isabel Allende** (born 1942). Her book *La casa de los espíritus* (1982) was a phenomenally successful novel worldwide. Allende, a niece of Salvador Allende, was born in Peru and went into exile in Venezuela after the 1973 coup. *The House of the Spirits*, with its tale of the dynasty of Esteban Trueba interwoven with Chilean history throughout much of the 20th century, ends with a thinly disguised description of 1973. It was followed in 1984 by *De amor y de sombra*, a disturbing tale set during the Pinochet regime. The main motivation behind these novels is the necessity to preserve historical reality (see the brief prologue to *Of Love and Shadows*, "Here, write it, or it will be erased by the wind"). The same thing applies in *Paula* (1994), Allende's letter to her daughter in a coma, where possible salvation from the devastation of not being able to contact Paula comes through the "meticulous exercise of writing". She has also written *Eva Luna* (1987) and *Los cuentos de Eva Luna* (1990), about a fictional Venezuelan storyteller and her stories, *El plan infinito* (1991), *Daughter of Fortune* (1998), and her most recent novel, *Portrait in Sepia* (2002).

Like her predecessors, Allende employs the marvellous and the imaginary to propose alternatives to the masculine view of social and sexual relations. The same is true of **Lucía Guerra** (born 1942), who published *Más allá de las máscaras* in exile in 1984. Another example might be **Daniela Eltit** (born 1949), who did not leave Chile after 1973 and was actively involved in resistance movements. Her provocative, intense fiction confronts issues of exploitation, violence, the oppression of women and volatile mental states. In *Vaca sagrada* (1991) at least, the protagonist's vulnerability is expressed through her body, by her blood, her two lovers' effects upon it, the brutality inflicted upon it and her obsession with her heartbeat. The main characters live out their obsessions and fears in a city in which there are no jobs and no warmth. Three earlier novels, *Lumpérica* (1983), *Por la patria* (1986) and *El cuarto mundo* (1988) maintain the same experimental, challenging approach to contemporary Chilean society.

Twentieth-century poetry

In many ways, poetry is the lifeblood of Chilean culture; the country's poetic output is prodigious, with poetry circles thriving even in remote rural areas. In the first half of the 20th century, four figures dominated Chilean poetry, Gabriela Mistral, Vicente

Ariel Dorfman

As expressed in the subtitle of his fascinating recent memoir, *Heading South, Looking North* (1998), the literary and political career of Ariel Dorfman has taken the form of a 'bilingual journey', between the United States and South America, between English and Spanish. Born in Buenos Aires in 1942, as the son of Russian Jewish immigrants, Dorfman and his family were expelled from Argentina in the mid-1940s due to his father's political activism. They took up residence in New York, until McCarthyism sent the Dorfmans once more south in 1954, this time to Chile. Here, the monolingual, English-speaking adolescent gradually focused his attention on the Spanish language and on Chilean politics and culture, until the military coup of 1973 drove Dorfman once again into exile, where he became one of the most articulate, bilingual voices against the military regime.

Since the return to civilian government in 1990, Dorfman has divided his time between Santiago and a professional post at Duke University, writing and broadcasting in both Spanish and English. Dorfman's work, as a poet, novelist, short story writer, essayist, playwright and more recently scriptwriter, is concerned, in his words, with, "on the one hand, the glorious potential and need of human beings to tell stories and, on the other, the brutal fact that in today's world, most of the lives that should be telling those stories are generally ignored, ravaged and silenced". He is perhaps best known for his early critique of US cultural imperialism, *How to Read Donald Duck* (1971) and for *Death and the Maiden* (1990), later filmed by Roman Polanski, which deals with torture and resistance.

He often adapts his own work to different genres: *Widows* started as a poem, became a novel and later a play. Much of the work focuses on torture, disappearance, censorship and the exile condition, but also demonstrates staunch rebellion and resistance and optimism for our future. For further details, see page 554.

Background Culture

Huidobro, Pablo Neruda (see box, page 539) and Pablo de Rokha. The three men were all socialists, but their politics and means of expression followed different trajectories. Neruda overshadows all other Chilean poets on an international level, and for this reason he is discussed in the accompanying box.

Gabriela Mistral wrote poetry that rejected elaboration in favour of a simple style using traditional metre and verse forms. Her poetry derives from a limited number of personal roots: she fell in love with Romelio Ureta who blew his own brains out in 1909. This inspired the *Sonetos de la muerte* (1914), which were not published at the time. She never lost the grief of this tragic love, which was coupled with her love of God and her "immense martyrdom at not being a mother". Frustrated motherhood did not deprive her of tenderness, nor of a deep love for children. The other main theme was her appreciation of nature and landscape, not just in Chile, but also in North and South America and Europe, which she visited as a diplomat. Her three principal collections are *Desolación* (1923, but re-edited and amplified frequently), *Tala* (1938) and *Lagar* (1954). She also wrote many poems for children.

If Gabriela Mistral relied on tradition and verse to present her unique view of a lone woman trying to find a place in a male-oriented world, **Vicente Huidobro** (1893-1948) wanted to break with all certainties. He made grand claims for the poet's role as nothing short of a quest for the infinite and for the language to liberate it. From

Santiago he moved to Buenos Aires, then Paris, where he joined the Cubists, collaborated with Apollinaire and others, began to write in French and got involved in radical politics. Between the 1920s and 1940s he moved from Europe to the USA to Chile, back to Spain during the Civil War, before retiring to Llolleo to confront time and death in his last poems, *Ultimos poemas*, 1948. Huidobro considered himself at the forefront of the avant garde, formulating *creacionismo*, a theory that the poet is not bound by the real world, but is free to create and invent new worlds through the complete freedom of the word. Nevertheless, all the experimentation and imagery which "unglued the moon", was insufficient to achieve the language of revelation. So in 1931 he composed *Altazor*, a seven-canto poem which describes simultaneously the poet's route to creation and the ultimate frustration imposed by time and the human condition.

Pablo de Rokha (Carlos Díaz Loyola, 1894-1968) was deeply concerned for the destiny of the Chilean people and the advance of international socialism. His output was an uncompromising epic search for Chilean identity and through his work, for all its political commitment, there runs a deep sense of tragedy and inner solitude (especially true in *Fuego negro*, 1951, written after the death of his wife). *Los gemidos* was his first major book (1922); others included *Escritura de Raimundo Contreras* (1929), a song of the Chilean peasant, *Jesucristo* (1933) and *La morfología del espanto* (1942).

Although these poets, and Neruda especially, furthered the Chilean poetic tradition, those who came after were not necessarily keen to emulate his style or his politics. From the 1950s, poets were still critical of society but, taking their cue from **Nicanor Parra**, they did not elevate the writer's role in denouncing inhumanity, alienation and the depersonalization of modern life. Instead writer and reader are placed on the same level; rhetoric and exuberant language are replaced by a conversational, ironic tone. **Parra** (born 1914; see also box, page 544), a scientist and teacher, called this attempt to overcome the influence of Neruda *antipoesía* (antipoetry). In the poem 'Advertencia al lector' in *Poemas y antipoemas* (1954), he writes:

> *According to the doctors of the law this book should not be published:*
> *The word rainbow does not appear in it,*
> *Let alone the word grief,*
> *Chairs and tables, yes, there are aplenty,*
> *Coffins! Writing utensils!*
> *Which fills me with pride*
> *Because, as I see it, the sky is falling to bits.*

Obra gruesa anthologizes his work to 1969, followed by *Emergency Poems* (1972, bilingual edition, New York), which contain a darker humour and satire, but remain compassionate and socially committed, *Artefactos* (1972) and *Artefactos II* (1982), *Sermones y prédicas del Cristo de Elqui* (1979) and *Poesía política* (1983).

The adherents of *antipoesía* continually sought new means of expression, so that the genre never became institutionalized. There are too many poets to list here, but **Gonzalo Rojas** (born 1917), **Enríque Lihn** (1929-88), **Armando Uribe** (born 1933) and **Miguel Arteche** (born 1926) are perhaps the best known.

Another poetic development of the 1950s onwards was *poesía lárica*, or *de lares*, poetry of one's place of origin (literally, of the gods of the hearth). Its founder and promoter was **Jorge Teillier** (1935-96), whose poems describe a precarious rural existence, wooden houses, fencing, orchards, distant fires, beneath changing skies and rain. The city dweller is an exile in space and time who returns every so often to the place of origin. See especially 'Notas sobre el último viaje del autor a su pueblo natal', which evokes the lost frontier of his youth, the changed countryside and his city life. As for the future, "if only it could be as beautiful as my mother spreading the

Pablo Neruda

Pablo Neruda was born in Parral on 12 June 1904 as Ricardo Neftalí Reyes. Two months later, his mother died and his father and stepmother subsequently moved the family to Temuco. Neruda's childhood memories were dominated by nature and, above all, rain, "my only unforgettable companion", as he described it in *Confieso que he vivido*. Among his teachers in Temuco was Gabriela Mistral. In 1921, he went to study in Santiago, but he had already decided on a literary career. His first book of poems *Crepusculario* (1923), was published under the pseudonym Neruda, borrowed from a Czech writer; it was postmodernist in style but did not yet reveal the poet's own voice. His next volume, *Veinte poemas de amor y una canción desesperada* (1924) catapulted him into the forefront of Latin American poetry. The freedom of the style and the natural, elemental imagery invoking the poet's two love affairs, made the collection an immediate success. Three books followed in 1926 before Neruda was sent to Rangoon as Chilean consul in 1927. His experiences in the Orient, including his first marriage, inspired one of his finest collections, *Residencia en la tierra*, in which the inherent sadness of the *Veinte poemas* becomes despair at the passing of time and human frailty. Reinforcing this theme is a kaleidoscope of images, seemingly jumbled together, yet deliberately placed to show the chaos and fragmentary nature of life.

In the 1930s, Neruda moved to Spain, where he met many poets. The Civil War, especially the death of Federico García Lorca, affected him deeply and his poetic vision became more direct, with a strong political orientation. 'Explico algunas cosas' in *Tercera residencia* (1947) explains the move towards militancy.

Between 1938 and the election of Videla to the Chilean presidency, Neruda worked with the Frente Popular and was consul general in Mexico. He also composed his epic poem of Latin American and Chilean history, from a Marxist stance, *Canto general* (1950). Its 15 cantos chronicle the natural and human life of the Americas, from the conquered pre-Columbian inhabitants to the 20th-century labourers. One of its most famous sections is 'Alturas de Machu Picchu', which mirrors the poet's own development: from the universal to 'minuscule life', from introspection to a new-found role as the voice of the oppressed.

'Canto general' defined Neruda's subsequent enormous output. The political commitment remained but did not submerge his respect for and evocation of nature in *Odas elementales* (1954), *Nuevas odas elementales* (1957) and *Tercer libro de odas* (1959), which begins with 'El hombre invisible'. He also never tired of writing lyric verse, such as *Los versos del capitán* (1950), *Cien sonetos de amor* (1959), and wrote memoirs such as *Memorial de Isla Negra* (1964) and *Confieso que he vivido* (1974). *Extravagaria* (1958), whose title suggests extravagance, wandering and variety, is full of memory, acceptance and a world-weary joy.

Neruda was awarded the Nobel Prize in 1971 but died of cancer two years' later. His death was hastened by the coup and the military's heartless removal of him from Isla Negra to Santiago. The poet's three houses were either ransacked or shut up by the dictatorship, but many of the Chileans for whom the poet spoke visited Isla Negra to leave messages of respect, love and hope until democracy returned. (See Ariel Dorfman's 'Afterword' in *The House in the Sand*, translated by Dennis Maloney and Clark Zlotchew, 1990, Milkweed).

sheets on my bed", but it is only an unpaid bill; "I wish the UFOs would arrive." In his later poems, the violence of the city and the dictatorship invade the *lares*. Among Teillier's books are *Para angeles y gorriones* (1956), *Para un pueblo fantasma* (1978), *Cartas para reinas de otras primaveras* (1985) and *Los dominios perdidos* (1992). A variation on this type of poetry comes from **Clemente Riedemann** (born 1953), whose *Karra Maw'n* deals with the Mapuche lands and German immigration in the area.

Many poets left Chile after 1973 but others stayed to attack the dictatorship from within through provocative, experimental works. In a country with such a strong poetic tradition and such a serious political situation, poets understood that their verses had to mutate in order to reflect and comment on their contemporary realities. A more experimental and opaque poetry developed as a result, dealing with themes such as the reaffirmation of colloquialism, the city (developed through the slang of *antipoesía*), and poetry itself, unravelling contexts and bridging the past and the present. Several writers were members of the Grupo Experimental de Artaud, including Daniela Eltit (see above), Eugenia Brito, Rodrigo Cánovas and **Raúl Zurita**, perhaps the most celebrated poet in Chile today: his verse is a complex and at times difficult union of mathematics and poetry, logical, structured and psychological. *Purgatorio* (1979) had an immediate impact and was followed by *Anteparaíso* (1982), *El paraíso está vacío* (1984), *Canto a su amor desaparecido* (1986) and *El amor de Chile* (1987). 'Pastoral de Chile' in *Anteparaíso* reveals most of Zurita's obsessions: Chilean landscapes, love, Chile's distress, sin and religious terminology.

Other significant poetic works of the 1980s include *La Tirana* (1985) by **Diego Maquieira**, a complex, multireferential work, dealing with a Mapuche virgin, surrounded by a culture that oppresses her and with which she disguises herself. It is irreverent; a 'black mass', threatening to the régime. Carmen Berenguer's *Bobby Sands desfallece en el muro* (1983) is a homage to the IRA prisoner and thus to all political prisoners. She also wrote *Huellas del siglo* (1986) and *A media asta* (1988). Carla Grandi published *Contraproyecto* in 1985, an example of feminine resistance to the coup.

Poetry continues to be significant in Chile. There are numerous workshops and organizations for young poets; the Taller de Poesía de la Fundacion Pablo Neruda is particularly influential. There are also important underground literary movements. Interesting young contemporary poets include **Carolina Cerlis** and **Javier del Cerro**, both maintaining the experimental and free verse tradition of Zurita and others.

Cinema

Not many months after the first screening organized by the Lumière brothers in Paris in December 1895, moving pictures were exhibited in Chile on 25 August 1896. Initially all the films were imported, but from 1902 local artists and entrepreneurs began to produce short documentaries. The first narrative movie, *Manuel Rodríguez*, was screened in September 1910. From about 1915, with European production semi-paralysed by war, the pre-eminence of Hollywood cinema was established. The modern dreams of Hollywood were often more complex, technologically superior and more entertaining than the products of rudimentary national cinemas. The historian of Chilean silent films, Eliana Jara Donoso, quotes a publicity handout for a local movie that read, "it's so good that it doesn't seem Chilean".

But despite the overwhelming presence of Hollywood, local film-makers in the silent era could still establish a small presence in the market. In the main they made documentaries, for this was a niche free of international competition: regional topics, football competitions, civic ceremonies, military parades. Almost 100 feature films were also made, but these are the domain of the film historian, since only one such movie has survived (carefully restored by the University of Chile in the early 1960s): *El húsar de la muerte* (The Hussar of Death), directed by Pedro Sienna in 1925. It was, like many movies in Latin America at the time, a historical melodrama, exploring the fight for Chilean independence from Spanish rule in the 1810s through the heroic exploits of the legendary Manuel Rodríguez. It achieved great box office success in a year when 16 Chilean films were screened. Never again would so many national movies be produced annually.

The coming of synchronized sound created a new situation in Latin America. In those countries with a large domestic market – in particular Mexico, Argentina and Brazil – investment was made in expensive machinery, installations and rudimentary studios. Elsewhere, and Chile is a telling example, sound devastated local production due to its cost and complexity. Local entrepreneurs were usually unwilling to make the risky capital investment, and the history of Chilean cinema thereafter is littered with tales of self-sacrifice on the part of cast and crew. The first non-silent film made in Chile was *Norte y Sur*, directed by **Jorge Délano** in 1934, telling the story of a love triangle where a woman is the object of the attentions of a Chilean and an American engineer. It was a rare example of sophisticated cinema at a time when Chilean film output was reverting to often formulaic stories of young men seducing innocent ladies, or the naïve idealization of rural landscapes. Délano stood out in this age – another film of his, *Escándalo* (1940) was almost unique in dealing with the lives of the middle class, rather than those of the aristocracy or the peasantry. Nevertheless, Tobías Barros, an important director of the time, summed up the mood when he sarcastically described his *Río Abajo* as a film "where there are neither illegitimate nor lost children".

An attempt was made in the 1940s to stimulate cinema through state investment. The state agency CORFO saw cinema as an important growth industry and in 1942 gave 50% finance to set up **Chile Films**. Costly studios were erected, but the plan proved over-ambitious and Argentine film-makers ended up using most of the facilities; by 1947 Chile Films had collapsed. In 1959, however, the Universidad de Chile set up a Centre for Experimental Cinema under the direction of a documentary film-maker Sergio Bravo, which trained aspirant directors from Chile and elsewhere in Latin America (notably the Bolivian Jorge Sanjinés).

Cinema became intricately involved in the wider political discussions of the 1960s. The years 1968-69 saw the maturity of Chilean cinema. Five features came out: **Raúl Ruiz**'s *Tres tristes tigres* (Three Sad Tigers); Helvio Soto's *Caliche sangriento* (Bloody Nitrate); Aldo Francia's *Valparaíso mi amor* (Valparaíso My Love); Miguel Littín's *El chacal de Nahueltoro* (The Jackal of Nahueltoro) and Carlos Elsesser's *Los testigos* (The Witnesses). These film-makers came from different ideological and aesthetic tendencies, from the inventive maverick Raúl Ruiz to the sombre neo-realism of Francia, but they can be seen as a group, working with very scarce resources: the films by Ruiz, Elsesser, Francia and Littín were made, consecutively, with the same camera; furthermore, many of the directors sought to break down the traditionally melodramatic themes of Chilean cinema, employing more realistic language and situations more reflective of everyday social problems. Aldo Francia, a doctor by profession, also organized a famous 'Meeting of Latin American Film-makers' at the Viña del Mar film festival in 1967. This would be one of the key events to cause growing awareness of cineastes across the continent that they were working with similar ideas and methods, producing 'new cinemas'.

The narrow victory of the Popular Unity parties in the election of 1970 was greeted by film-makers with an enthusiastic manifesto penned by **Miguel Littín**; Littín himself was put in charge of the revived state institution Chile Films. He lasted for only 10 months, tiring of bureaucratic opposition and inter-party feuding, as the different members of Popular Unity all demanded a share of very limited resources. Few films were made between 1970 and 1973; Raúl Ruiz was the most productive film-maker of the period, with a number of films in different styles. Littín was working on an historical feature *La tierra prometida* (The Promised Land) when the 1973 coup occurred and post-production took place in Paris.

Background Culture

The most ambitious film to trace the radicalization of Chile in 1972 and 1973 was Patricio Guzmán's three-part documentary *La batalla de Chile* (The Battle of Chile), which was edited in exile in Cuba. In the first years of exile, this film became Chile's most evocative testimony abroad and received worldwide distribution. Paradoxically, Chilean cinema, which had little time to grow under Popular Unity, strengthened in exile.

Policies following the coup practically destroyed internal film production for several years. Film personnel were arrested, tortured and imprisoned and many escaped into exile. Severe censorship was established: even *Fiddler on the Roof* was banned for displaying Marxist tendencies. It is from the exiled directors that the continuity of film culture can be seen. Littín took up residence in Mexico, supported by Mexican President, Echeverría, and became an explicit spokesman for political Latin American cinema, making the epic *Actas de Marusia* (Letters from Marusia) in 1975 and several other features in Mexico and later in Nicaragua. In the mid-1980s he returned clandestinely to Chile with several foreign film crews to make the documentary *Acta General de Chile* in 1986, a perilous mission documented by Gabriel García Márquez in his reportage *Clandestine in Chile* (1986). Raúl Ruiz took a less visible political role, but since his exile to France, he has produced a body of work that has earned him a reputation as one of the most innovative directors in Europe, the subject of a special issue in 1983 of France's distinguished journal *Cahiers du Cinéma*. He makes movies with great technical virtuosity and often great speed: on a visit to Santiago to celebrate the return to civilian rule in 1990, he shot a film, entitled *La telenovela errante* (The Wandering Soap Opera), in less than a week for US$30,000. Other exile directors to make their mark include Ruiz's wife Valeria Sarmiento, Gastón Ancelovici and Carmen Castillo, all based in France, Patricio Guzmán in Spain, Marilú Mallet in Canada, Angelina Vásquez in Scandinavia, Sebastián Alarcón in the Soviet Union and Antonio Skármeta in Germany.

Inside Chile, the output under censorship varied from maritime adventures such as *El Último Grumete* to Silvio Caiozzi's *Julion comienza en julio* (Julio begins in July, 1979), one of the first films made in the period, set carefully in a turn-of-the-century historical location and self-financed through Caiozzi's work in commercials. It would take him a further 10 years to produce a second feature, *La luna en el espejo* (The Moon in the Mirror), evocatively set in Valparaíso, which was screened in 1990. An example of increased critical debate within Chile in the last years of the Pinochet régime can be found in Pablo Perelman's *Imagen latente* (Latent Image, 1987) which tells of a photographer's search for a missing brother who disappeared after the coup; although the film was not released in Chile until 1990, it was possible to make the film in the country in the mid-1980s. Another case is that of *Hijos de la Guerra Fría* by Gonzalo Justiniano (1985), which is replete with metaphors of a society asphyxiated by a repressive system.

The return to civilian rule had some benefits for film-makers, most notably the easing of censorship. The Viña del Mar Film Festival was symbolically reinstated after 20 years and saw the emotional return of many exiled directors, but that, in itself, could not solve the problems of an intellectual community dispersed around the world and the chronic underfunding and under-representation of Chilean films in the home market. New names have emerged and some internationally successful films have been made, most notably Ricardo Larraín's *La Frontera* (The Frontier, 1991), one of the best Chilean films ever made, which tells of a school teacher's internal exile in the spectacular scenery of southern Chile in the late 1980s, which as Gustavo Graef-Marino's *Johnny Cien Pesos* (1993), which deals with violence in Chilean society. The latter was produced by Chile Films, a short-lived production company made up of film directors and producers financed by a State Bank credit loan. The loan was withdrawn, however, when other productions failed at the box office.

Facing the music

There are many famous Chilean groups whose music is still widely distributed and available internationally. These include Illapu, Inti Illimanni, Quilapayún and the late Victor Jara. All these groups were involved in some way in the movement of 'la nueva canción' (see page 545), and went into exile after the military coup.

One of the best albums is Illapu's *Despedida del Pueblo*, of which the most popular and resonant song is 'Vuelvo', dealing with the emotions of the returning exile. Compilations of Victor Jara are usually good, and the collection of *Cantos de Pueblos Andinos* by Inti Illimanni is a haunting, melodic introduction to their music.

Among the standard bearers of 'nueva canción' and one of Inti Illimanni's most popular songs was 'El pueblo unido jamás será vencido' ('The people, united, will never be divided') – a good old-fashioned protest song. Later Inti Illimanni music demonstrates the influence of dance rhythms from the Caribbean, yet retains its Chilean roots – a good example is 'Andadas'.

As far as pop music goes, the Chilean national scene has been dominated in recent years by the rock band La Ley. Los Prisioneros, an older band, were more political, producing music that expressed the feelings of the Chilean youth that grew up in the 1980s under the Pinochet dictatorship.

The last few years have seen the screening of one or two Chilean features a year, the best received being the political thriller *Amnesia* (1994), directed by Gonzalo Justiniano, Andrés Wood's vogue-ish *Historias de Futbol* (1997) and Sergio Castillo's 1997 *Gringuito*, which focuses on the problems of children brought up in exile, returning as foreigners to Chile. This gentle comedy of reintegration has been made to seem somewhat tame by the demonstrations in Chile surrounding the Pinochet extradition process. Larraín's latest feature *El entusiasmo* (Enthusiasms, 1999) did not live up to its title among local audiences but it garnered international recognition, as did Andrés Wood's new films, *El Desquite*, and most recently *Loco Fever*, an engaging comedy about two conmen's frenzied search for as many "locos" – the shellfish, not the crazies – as possible. With the increasing globalization of the culture industry, however, the pattern of scarce local production is likely to continue.

Music and dance

Traditional forms

As far as traditional dance goes, at the very heart of Chilean music is the *cueca*, a courting dance for couples, both of whom make great play with a handkerchief waved aloft in the right hand. The man's knees are slightly bent and his body arches back; in rural areas, he stamps his spurs together for effect. Guitar and harp are the accompanying instruments, while handclapping and shouts of encouragement add to the atmosphere. The dance has a common origin with the Argentine *zamba* and Peruvian *marinera* via the early 19th-century *zamacueca*, in turn descended from the Spanish fandango. The most traditional form of song is the *tonada*, with its variants the *glosa*, *parabienes*, *romance*, *villancico* (Christmas carol) and *esquinazo* (serenade), in common with the *custon* in Argentina, this may be heard in the form of a *contrapunto* or *controversia*, a musical duel. Among the most celebrated groups are **Los Huasos Quincheros**, Silvia Infante with **Los Condores** and the **Conjunto Millaray**,

⁝ Violeta Parra

Violeta Parra was brought up in Chillán as one of 11 children. Her father, Nicanor, was a music teacher, while her mother, Clarisa, was a seamstress who played the guitar and sang. Most of the children were artistic in some way. Violeta sang with her sister Hilda in Santiago bars for several years. She also worked in the circus. Another child, Nicanor, became a professor of maths and physics, and a poet (see page 538).

Violeta travelled the length of Chile and abroad with the Chilean poet Pablo de Rokha (see page 538), collecting material and promoting their idea of Chilean-ness. While de Rokha expressed himself in the lyrical epic, Violeta sang, wrote songs, made tapestries, ceramics, paintings and sculpture. All her work was based on a philosophy of helping those in need. In France she was recognized as a great artist and her works were exhibited in the Louvre in 1964, but at home recognition was only grudgingly given.

In the 1960s Violeta set up La Carpa de la Reina as a centre for popular art in the capital. It was here, in February 1967, that she committed suicide, her head resting on her guitar. The national grief at her funeral far outweighed the acclaim given her during her life. Neruda called her 'Santa Violeta'; the Peruvian novelist Jose Maria Arguedas described her as 'the most Chilean of all Chileans I could possibly know, but at the same time the most universal of all Chile'.

For Violeta, folklore was a form of class struggle. Her influence on a whole generation of Latin American folk singers was enormous and long-lasting. Without her, Salvador Allende would not have had the folkloric backing of Victor Jara, Inti-Illimani, Los Quilapayún and the Parras themselves. After Violeta's death, her brother Nicanor published *Décimas*, a sort of autobiography in verse, full of simple humanity.

all of which are popular at rural dances, with their poignant combination of formal singing and rousing accordian music. Famous folk singers in this genre are the **Parra family** from Chillán (see box, page 544), **Hector Pávez** and **Margot Loyola**.

In the north of the country the music is Amerindian and closely related to that of Bolivia. Groups called 'Bailes' dance the *huayño*, *taquirari*, *cachimbo* or *rueda* at carnival and other festivities as well as pre-Columbian rites like the *cauzulor* and *talatur*. Instruments are largely wind and percussion, including *zampoñas* (pan pipes), *lichiguayos*, *pututos* (conch shells), *queñas* (flutes) and *clarines*. There are some notable religious festivals that attract large crowds of pilgrims and include numerous groups of costumed dancers. The most outstanding of these festivals are those of the **Virgen de La Tirana** near Iquique (see box, page 247), the **Virgen de la Candelaria** of Copiapó (see page 191) and the **Virgen de Andacollo** (see page 167).

In the south the Mapuche nation have their own songs, dance-songs and magic and collective dances, accompanied by wind instruments like the great long *trutruca* horn, the shorter *pifilka* and the *kultrún* drum. Further south still, Chiloé has its own unique musical expression: wakes and other religious social occasions include collective singing, while the recreational dances, all of Spanish origin – such as the *vals*, *pavo*, *pericona* and *nave* – have a heavier and less syncopated beat than in central Chile. Accompanying instruments here are the *rabel* (fiddle), guitar and accordion.

Nueva canción

The most famous Chilean movement on the international stage was that of the *nueva canción*, or new song, which arose in the late 1960s and early 1970s under such luminaries as **Violeta Parra** (see box, page 544) and **Victor Jara**. This movement, which scorned commercialism and sought to give a political meaning to its songs – whether overt or suggested – gave a whole new dimension to the Chilean musical scene, and was part of a wider movement across the continent, involving people such as Mercedes Sosa in Argentina and Sílvio Rodríguez in Cuba.

Beginning as an underground movement, faraway from the usual round of publicity and radio stations, the *nueva canción* protagonists rose to prominence during the 1970 election campaign, which resulted in the victory of Salvador Allende. Although related to folk rhythms, the movement sought to be dynamic and not confined to any particular style. Violeta Parra's suicide and the subsequent coup of 1973 forced its protagonists into exile – Inti Illimanni to Italy, Illapu to France. But Victor Jara was imprisoned in the National Stadium after the coup and was hauled to his death, singing Violeta Parra's famous song, 'Gracias a la vida' (I give thanks to life).

Land and environment

Chile is smaller than all other South American republics except Ecuador, Paraguay, Uruguay and the Guianas. It is 4,329 km long and, on average, no more than 180 km wide. In the north Chile has a short (150 km) east-west frontier with Peru. In the far north its eastern frontier is with Bolivia – 750 km long – but from San Pedro de Atacama south to Tierra del Fuego it shares over 3,500 km of frontier with Argentina. In the main this frontier follows the crest of the Andes but, in the far south, where the Andes are lower, there have been frequent frontier disputes with Argentina; these still rumble on. Chilean sovereignty over the islands south of Tierra del Fuego gives it control over Isla Navarino, on which Puerto Williams is the most southerly permanent settlement in the world (apart from scientific bases in Antarctica). Various island archipelagos in the Pacific, including Easter Island/Rapa Nui and the Juan Fernández group, are under Chilean jurisdiction.

Geology

The Quaternary Period, 1.6 million years ago, was marked by the advance and retreat of the Antarctic Ice Sheet which, at its maximum extent, covered all of the Chilean Andes and the entire coastline south of Puerto Montt. However, although there are surface remnants of older rock formations, most have disappeared with the dramatic creation of the Andes, which started around 80,000 years ago and continues to this day. The South American Plate, moving westwards, meets the Nazca and Antarctic Plates, which are moving eastwards and sinking below the continent. These two plates run more or less parallel between 26°S and 33°S and the friction between them creates a geologically unstable zone, marked by frequent earthquakes and volcanic activity. The area of Concepción has been particularly susceptible to both land and undersea quakes and the city was twice destroyed by tidal waves in the 18th century before being moved to its present site.

All of the Chilean Pacific islands were formed by underwater volcanoes associated with fracture zones between the Nazca and Antarctic Plates. Easter Island gained its characteristic triangular shape from the joining together of three lava flows.

Northern desert

Northern Chile has a similar form to Peru immediately to the north: the coastal range rises to 1,000-1,500 m; inland are basins known as *bolsones*, east of which lie the

Andes. The Atacama Desert is, by most measures, the driest area on earth, and some meteorological stations near the coast have never reported precipitation. Water is therefore at a premium as far south as Copiapó; it is piped in from the east and, in the Andean foothills, streams flow into alluvial fans in the inland basins, which can act as reservoirs and may be tapped by drilling wells. One river, the Río Loa, flows circuitously from the Andes to Calama and then through the coastal range to the coast; however, for most of its length it is deeply entrenched and unsuitable for agriculture. East of Calama and high in the Andes are the geysers of El Tatio, more evidence of volcanic activity, which are fed by the summer rains that fall in this part of the Andes.

In the past, notably as the ice sheets retreated, there were many lakes in the depressions between the Coastal Range and the Andes. These dried out, leaving one of the greatest concentrations of salts in the world, rich in nitrates: there has been extensive mining activity here since the late 19th century.

Central Chile

South of Copiapó the transition begins between the Atacama and the zone of heavy rainfall in the south. At first, the desert turns to scrub and some seasonal surface water appears. The Huasco and Elqui rivers follow deep trenches to reach the sea, allowing valley bottoms inland to be irrigated for agriculture. Further south, near Santiago, the Central Valley between the Coastal Range and the Andes reappears, the rivers flowing westwards across it to reach the Pacific. Further south is the Lake District, with its many lakes formed by glaciation and volcanic activity, its attractive mountain scenery, its rich volcanic soils and fertile agricultural land.

Southern Chile

South of Valdivia, the Coastal Range becomes more broken until near Puerto Montt it becomes a line of islands as part of a 'drowned coastline' that extends all the way south to Cape Horn. The effects of glaciation can be seen in the U-shaped valleys and the long deep fjords stretching inland. This is a land of dense forests with luxuriant undergrowth that is virtually impenetrable and difficult to clear owing to the high water content. Further south in Chilean Patagonia, coniferous forests are limited in expanse because glaciers have stripped the upper slopes of soil. Some of the remaining glaciers reach sea level, notably the San Rafael, which breaks off the giant icefields of the Campo de Hielo Norte.

The Andes

The whole of Chile is dominated by this massive mountain range, which reaches its highest elevations in the border region between Chile and Argentina. In the north, near the Peruvian border, the ranges that make up the Andes are 500 km wide, but the western ranges, which mark the Chilean border, are the highest. Sajama, the highest peak in Bolivia, lies only 20 km east of the border, along which are strung volcanoes including Parinacota (6,330 m). Further south, to the southeast of San Pedro de Atacama, lies the highest section of the Andes, which includes the peaks of Llullaillaco (6,739 m) and Ojos del Salado (altitude 6,864 m, 6,879 m or 6,908 m depending on your source). Still further south, to the northeast of Santiago and just inside Argentina, lies Aconcagua (6,960 m).

South of Santiago, the Andes begin to lose altitude. In the Lake District, the mountain passes are low enough in places for crossing into Argentina. South of Puerto Montt, the Andes become more inhospitable, however, as lower temperatures bring the permanent snowline down from 1,500 m at Volcán Osorno near Puerto Montt to 700 m on Tierra del Fuego. Towards the southern end of the Andes stand Mount Fitzroy (3,406 m) – in Argentina – and the remarkable peaks of the Paine massif in Chilean territory.

Climate

It is only to be expected that a country that stretches over 4,000 km from north to south will provide a wide variety of climatic conditions. Annual rainfall varies from zero in northern Chile to over 4,000 mm on the offshore islands south of Puerto Montt. Rainfall is heavier in the winter months (May to August) throughout the country, except for in the northern *altiplano* where January and February are the wettest months.

Variations in the Chilean climate are concentrated by two significant factors: altitude and the cold waters of the Humboldt Current. The Andes, with their peaks of over 6,000 m, are rarely more than 160 km from the coastline. On average, temperatures drop by 1°C for every 150 m you climb. The Humboldt Current has perhaps even more impact. The current flows in a northeasterly direction from Antarctic waters until it meets the southern coast of Chile, from where it follows the coastline northwards. Cold polar air accompanies the current on its journey, eventually colliding with warmer air moving in from the southwest. The lighter warm air is forced to rise over the dense cold air, bringing rainfall all year round to the area south of the Río Biobío and rain in winter further north in the Central Valley.

Paradoxically, the ocean also has a moderating effect on temperatures, which are not generally extreme and decrease less than might be expected from north to south. As a result of the Humboldt Current, temperatures in northern Chile are much lower than they are for places at corresponding latitudes, such as Mexico. In the far south, the oceans have the opposite effect and temperatures rarely fall below -6°C despite the high latitude. Detailed temperature and rainfall patterns are given in the text.

Flora

The diversity of Chilean flora reflects the geographic length and climatic variety of the country. Although the Andes constitute a great natural barrier, there are connections between the flora of Chile and that of the eastern side of the mountain range, most notably in the far north with the Bolivian *altiplano* and in the south with the temperate forests of Argentina.

Far North

The arid central plain of northern Chile forms one of the driest areas on earth. Vegetation is limited to cacti, among them the *cardon* (Echinopsis atacamensis) and, in the Pampa de Tamarugal around Iquique, the *tamarugo* (Proposis tamarugo), a tree specially adapted to arid climates. On the western slopes of the Andes, ravines carry water, which has permitted the establishment of small settlements and the planting of crops. The only native tree of this area, *queñoa* (Polylepis tomentella) – heavily overexploited in the past – grows in sheltered areas, mainly near streams, at altitudes between 2,000 and 3,500 m. Among cacti are the *candelabros* (genus Browningia) and, at higher altitudes (between 3,000 and 4,000 m) the *ayrampus* (genus Opuntia).

The northern *altiplano* supports only sparse vegetation. Many plants found in this area, such as the *llareta* (genus Laretia) and the *tola* (genus Baccharis) have deep root systems and small leaves. Near streams, there are areas of spongy, wet salty grass, known as *bofedales*.

To the west of the central plain, the Pacific coastal area is almost complete desert, although in places the influence of the Humboldt Current is offset by the *camanchaca*, an early morning coastal fog that comes off the sea and persists at low altitudes, permitting the growth of vegetation, notably in the Parque Nacional Pan de

Glacial landscapes

Southern Chile provides some of the best examples of glacial landscapes on earth. One common sign of the region's glacial past is the U-shaped valleys. Good examples can be seen throughout the south, but perhaps one of the best is the Río Simpson between Coyhaique and Puerto Aisén. High above these valleys, sharp mountain ridges can often be seen, which have been caused by the eroding action of the ice on two or more sides. In some places, the resulting debris or 'moraine' formed a dam, blocking the valley and creating a lake, as in the Lake District at Lagos Calafquén, Panguipulli and Riñihue.

The drowned coastline south of Puerto Montt also owes its origin to glaciation. The ice that once covered the southern Andes was so heavy that it depressed the relatively narrow tip of South America. When the ice melted and the sea level rose, water broke through, leaving the western Andes as islands and creating the Chilean fjords, glaciated valleys carved out by the ice and now drowned.

Azúcar, north of Chañaral, and around Poposo, south of Antofagasta, where about 170 flowering plants, including shrubs, bromeliaceae and cacti can be found.

Norte Chico

Lying between the northern deserts and the matorral of central Chile, the Norte Chico is a transition zone: here annual rainfall averages from 30 to 100 mm, increasing southwards. In the main dry areas native flora, such as *pingo-pingo* (Ephedra andina), *jarilla* (Larrea nitida) and *brea* (Tessaria absinthoides) can be found. On the rare occasions when there is spring rainfall, the desert comes to life in a phenomenon known as the 'flowering of the desert' (see box, page 188). The central plain is crossed by rivers; in the valleys irrigation permits the cultivation of fruit, such as chirimoya, papaya and grapes.

On the coast near Ovalle, sea mists support a forest of evergreen species, including the *olivillo* (Aextoxicon punctatum), *canelo* or winter's bark (Drimys winteri) and *arrayán* (Luma chequen or Myrtus chequen) in the Parque Nacional Fray Jorge.

Central Chile

The Central Valley, with its dry and warm summers and mild winters, is home to the *matorral*, a deciduous scrubland ecologically comparable to the chaparral in California and consisting of slow-growing drought-resistant species with deep roots and small spiny sclerophyllous leaves. The original plant cover has been modified by human impact, particularly in the form of livestock agriculture, charcoal-burning and irrigation. In many areas, from the Río Limarí in the north to the Río Laja in the south, the result is *espinal* (Acacia cavan), usually considered to be a degraded form of the original matoral and characterized by open savanna scattered with *algarrobo* trees (Prosopis chilensis). Along ravines and on western facing slopes, there are areas of evergreen sclerophyllous trees, including the *peumo* (Cryptocarpa alba), *litre* (Lithrea caustica) and *boldo* (Peumos boldos) and, along the banks of the great rivers, the *maiten* (Maytenus boaria or Maytenus chilensis) and a local species of willow can be found.

Towards the coast more hygrophilous species grow on hills receiving coastal fogs: among these are *avellano*, *lingue* (Persea lingue), *belloto* or northern acorn (Beilschmiedia miersii) and *canelo* as well as bromeliads and epiphytic lichens and mosses. Species of southern beech (Nothofagus) and the formerly endemic Chilean or ocoa palm (Jubea chilensis), grow under protection in the Parque Nacional La Campana between Santiago and Valparaíso.

Subantarctic temperate forests

As a result of the fragmentation of the great landmass of Gondwana some 120 million years ago, some of the species in these forests (Araucaria araucana, Nothofagus and Podocarpus salingus) share affinities with flora found in Australia and New Zealand as well as with fossils uncovered in Antarctica. Similar affinities of some insect groups have also been established. However the isolation of these subantarctic forests, with the nearest neighbouring forests 1,300 km away in northwestern Argentina, has led to the evolution of many unique endemic species, with volcanic activity also having had an important influence.

Nowadays these forests are mainly of broad-leafed evergreen species; in contrast to temperate forests in the northern hemisphere there are few species of conifers. The dominant genus is the Nothofagus or southern beech, of which eight species are found in Chile. In the Maule area *roble* (Nothofagus obliqua) and *hualo* (Nothofagus glauca) can be found, while further south there is a gradual transitional change via the Valdivian rainforest (see below), to the southern deciduous Nothofagus forests. The latter, which can also be found at higher altitudes along the Andes, include the Patagonian and Magellanic forests. From the Valdivian forest south to the Magellanic forests all species of Nothofagus attract fungis from the genus Cyttaria and, especially in the south, the *misodendron* or South American mistletoe.

Around the Río Biobío, the Valdivian rainforest predominates. This is a complex and diverse environment, which includes ferns, bromeliads, lichens including old man's beard, and mosses, as well as a variety of climbing plants including the *copihue* or Chilean bell flower (Lapageria rosea), the national flower of Chile. Colourful flowering plants that can easily be identified include the firebush or *ciruelillo* (Embothrium coccineum), several species of alstroemeria and berberis and the fuschia. Near the Andes, for example in the Parque Nacional Puyehue, the forests are dominated by two species of Nothofagus, the evergreen *coihue* or *coigüe* (Nothofagus dombeyi) and the deciduous *lenga* (Nothfagus pumilio) as well as by the Podocarpus (Podocarpus salingus) and, near water, myrtle trees like the *arrayán*. The under-storey is dominated by tall *chusquea* bamboos. However many of these endemic species of flora are currently under threat from the proposed damming of the Río Biobío by Endesa, the Chilean electricity company, in violation of a law of 1993 which safeguards people from signing away their lands if they do not want to.

In the northern parts of the Valdivian forest, at altitudes mainly between 900 m and 1,400 m, there are forests of monkey puzzle trees (Araucaria araucana), Chile's national tree. The most important of these forests are in the Parque Nacional Nahuelbuta in the coastal *cordillera* and in the Parque Nacional Huerquehue in the Andean foothills (see also box, page 315).

Other species include the giant larch (Fitzroya cupressoides), known as the *alerce* or *lahuén*, which has some of the oldest individual specimens on earth (3,600 years). Athough this conifer grew extensively as far south as the 43° 30' south, excessive logging has destroyed most of the original larch forest. Some of the best examples of *alerce*, which is now a protected species, can be seen in the Parque Nacional Andino Alerce and in the Parque Pumalin.

The Patagonian and Magellanic forests are less diverse than their Valdivian counterpart, mainly due to lower temperatures. The Magellanic forest, considered the southernmost forest type in the world, includes the evergreen Nothofagus betuloides, the deciduous *lenga* (Nothofagus pumilio) and Nothofagus antarctica, and the *canelo*. Firebush and berberis can also be found, as well as several species of orchids and beautiful species of Calceolaria or slipper plants. Shrubland in the south is mainly characterized by mounded shrubs, usually found in rocky areas. Common species include *mata barrosa* (Mullinum spinosum), a yellow-flowered shrub, and *mata guanaco* (Anartrophyllum desideratum), a red-flowered shrub of the legume family.

In both the Juan Fernández Islands and Easter Island there are endemic species. In the forests of the Juan Fernández Archipelago, at altitudes above 1,400 m, important species of ferns can be found, as well as tree species such as *luma*, *mayu-monte*, giant naranjillo and the *yonta* or Juan Fernández palm, which, along with the ocoa palm, is one of only two palms native to Chile. The native forests of Easter Island were destroyed, first by volcanic activity and later by human impact, leaving land covered partially with pasture. Although native species, such as the *toromiro*, can be found, introduced species, such as the eucalyptus, are more common.

Fauna

Chile is an ecological island. Fauna that is commonplace in neighbouring countries has not been able to migrate here because of the Andes, the desert, the ice and the sea. This explains why there are no land tortoises, squirrels, jaguars or poisonous snakes in the country. Surrounded by natural barriers on all sides, its isolation has contributed to a range of endemic wildlife – something that Darwin glimpsed in microcosm on Chiloé in 1835, when he observed a fox unique to that island.

The one geographical constant from top to bottom of the country is the **Pacific Ocean**, the world's richest ocean for marine species. Coldwater species live near Chile's mainland, feeding off the rich nutrients in the Humboldt Current, while subtropical species inhabit the warmer waters around the Juan Fernández archipelago, and tropical species can be found in the waters around Easter Island. This explains the diversity of Chilean marine life, from hake, swordfish, bream and bass to countless shellfish, such as abalones, mussels, sea urchins, lobsters and a variety of crabs. Nine of the world's 18 species of **penguins** also live in Chile. The Humboldt penguins can be found between Arica and Chiloé, while the King, Adelia and Emperor penguins live solely in Antarctica. There are numerous colonies of sea-lions up and down the coast; dolphins are often seen off the shore of Chiloé and even killer whales abound.

Inland, there are some 680 species of mammals, amphibians, reptiles and birds. In the north, the **camelids** predominate among mammals: the alpacas, guanacos, llamas and vicuñas, with the guanaco also being found as far south as Tierra del Fuego. These South American camels are adapted for the mountainous terrain by having narrower feet than the desert forms of the species. All four species can be seen in Chile, although three are found only in the north. Like horses and donkeys, all the camelids can breed with one another, arising to some confusion as to their origins. There is a long-held view that both the llama and the alpaca are descended from wild guanaco.

Guanaco, coffee coloured with a dark head and tail and weighing up to 55 kg, were once found throughout Chile except in rainforest areas. Both grazers and browsers, they live in deserts, shrub land, savannah and occasionally on forest fringes. In many areas hunted to extinction, an estimated 20,000 now survive in the far north, especially in the Parque Nacional Lauca, in coastal areas between Antofagasta and Lago Rapel and in parts of the far south, such as the Parque Nacional Torres del Paine.

Vicuña, weighing up to 20 kg, are like half-sized guanaco, although with a yellower coat and coffee-coloured head and tail. Hunted almost to extinction, there were only around 400 in Chile in 1970. Protection has increased their numbers to around 12,000, mainly in the far north at altitudes of 3,700-4,800 m.

Alpaca are domesticated animals, weighing 20-30 kg, but seeming to be much larger because of their wool. Colours vary between black, coffee coloured, mahogany, grey and white. An estimated 20,000 can be found in drier parts of the northern altiplano.

⋮ 'The tangled Chilean forest'

Under the volcanoes, beside the snow-capped mountains, among the huge lakes, the fragrant, the silent, the tangled Chilean forest... My feet sink down into the dead leaves, a fragile twig crackles, the giant rauli trees rise in all their bristling height, a bird from the cold jungle passes over, flaps its wings, and stops in the sunless branches. And then, from its hideaway, it sings like an oboe... The wild scent of the laurel, the dark scent of the boldo herb, enter my nostrils and flood my whole being... The cypress of the Guaitecas blocks my way... This is a vertical world: a nation of birds, a plenitude of leaves... I stumble over a rock, dig up the uncovered hollow, an enormous spider covered with red hair stares up at me, motionless, as huge as a crab... A golden carabus beetle blows its mephitic breath at me, as its brilliant rainbow disappears like lightning... Going on, I pass through a forest of ferns much taller than I am: from their cold green eyes 60 tears splash down on my face and, behind me, their fans go on quivering for a long time... A decaying tree trunk: what a treasure!... Black and blue mushrooms have given it ears, red parasite plants have covered it with rubies, other lazy plants have let it borrow their beards, and a snake springs out of the rotted body like a sudden breath, as if the spirit of the dead trunk were slipping away from it... Farther along, each tree stands away from its fellows... They soar up over the carpet of the secretive forest, and the foliage of each has its own style, linear, bristling, ramulose, lanceolate, as if cut by shears moving in infinite ways... A gorge; below, the crystal water slides over granite and jasper... A butterfly goes past, bright as a lemon, dancing between the water and the sunlight... Close by, innumerable calceolarias nod their little yellow heads in greeting... High up, red copihues dangle like drops from the magic forest's arteries... The red copihue is the blood flower, the white copihue is the snow flower... A fox cuts through the silence like a flash, sending a shiver through the leaves, but silence is the law of the plant kingdom... The barely audible cry of some bewildered animal far off... The piercing interruption of a hidden bird... The vegetable world keeps up its low rustle until a storm churns up all the music of the earth.

Anyone who hasn't been in the Chilean forest doesn't know this planet.

From Pablo Neruda, *Memoirs*, Penguin (1977) pages 5-6.

Background Land and environment

Llama are also domesticated and are usually found with alpacas. Larger than alpacas and weighing up to 55 kg, their wool varies in colour but is shorter than that of alpacas. They are found only in the area of their domestication, which first occurred around Lake Titicaca some 4,000-5,000 years ago. Used as pack animals, males can carry loads of up to 40 kg. There are some 40,000 in the Tarapacá and Antofagasta regions of Chile.

Perhaps surprisingly, the north is also one of the avian capitals of Chile, with three of the world's six species of **flamingo** – the James, Chilean and Andean – all to be found around the saltpans of the Atacama. The **Parque Nacional Lauca** is also exceptional for birdlife, with over 120 species of either resident or migrant birds (see box, page 262).

As the land becomes more humid, south of the desert, there are naturally many changes in wildlife. One of the few constants is the famous **puma**, which is found in the *cordillerra* all the way from Arica to the Straits of Magellan, albeit in increasingly small numbers; the puma is understandably shy of humans, and is rarely spotted. There are several species of fox, particularly in the mountains, and the Central Valley is also a haven for spiders, including dangerous black widows and tarantulas.

Further south, in the lush forests of the Lake District and down towards the Carreterra Austral, two of the most interesting creatures are the **huemul** and the **pudú**. Both are species of deer. The huemul's northernmost group is found around Chillán; it is a medium-sized stocky creature, well adapted for the rigours of life in the mountains. The pudú is an extraordinary creature, a deer just 40 centimetres high, very shy and extremely difficult to spot, although it can sometimes be seen in the more remote parts of Chiloé and the Carreterra Austral (see box page 430).

The **Parque Torres del Paine** is a haven for wildlife, sheltering guanacos, condors, pumas and foxes. In Seno Otway near Punta Arenas there is a famous Magellanic penguin colony, while Isla Navarino has a colony of beavers (unintentionally introduced from Canada), as well as some fantastic birdlife including petrels and even – on a good day – albatrosses.

Wine

Chile is a major producer and exporter of fine wines. The wine-producing area stretches from the valley of the Río Aconcagua in the north to the Biobío Valley in the south. Grapes are also produced outside this area, notably around Ovalle and in the Elqui Valley near La Serena, which is the main production centre for pisco, a clear distilled spirit commonly drunk with lemon as *pisco sour* (see box, page 57), although the distillery that many hold to be the best is Alto del Carmén, in the upper reaches of the Huasco Valley.

The great majority of Chilean wines come from the Central Valley. The hot, dry summers guarantee exceptionally healthy fruit. Chilean wine is famous for being free from diseases such as downy mildew and phylloxera. As a result, growers are spared the costs of spraying and of grafting young vines onto phylloxera-resistant rootstocks.

Legislation in 1979 and 1985 established the current system of five denominated wine-growing regions, based around the valleys of the Ríos Aconcagua, Maipo, Rapel, Maule and Biobío. The heartland of Chilean wine production is the Maipo Valley, just south of Santiago, which is home to many of the most prestigious names in Chilean wine. Although the Maipo produces far less wine than the regions to the south, it is considered by many experts to produce the best wines in Chile as a result of the lime content of its soils. For visits to vineyards in this area, see page 119.

The main harvest period begins at the end of February, for early maturing varieties such as Chardonnay, and runs through to the end of April for Cabernet Sauvignon, although there are regional variations. Harvest celebrations are often accompanied by two drinks: *chicha*, a partly fermented grape juice, and *vino pipeño*, an unfiltered young wine which contains residue from the grapes and dried yeast.

Although the vine was introduced to Chile in the mid-16th century by the Spanish, the greatest influence on Chilean vineyards and wine making has been exerted by the French. In the 1830s, one prominent Frenchman, Claudio Gay, persuaded the Chilean government to establish the Quinta Normal in Santiago as a nursery for exotic botanical specimens including vines. In the 1970s domestic consumption of wine dropped and wine prices fell, leading to the destruction of many vineyards. In the last two decades, however, large-scale investment, much of it from the United States and Europe has led to increases in wine production, increasingly of quality wines destined for export. Chilean wines are now widely available around the world; they are also very popular within Latin America.

Chilean wine: an aristocratic tradition

The cultivation of grapes in Chile dates back almost to the Spanish conquest, the first recorded vineyard being established in 1551 in La Serena by Francisco de Aguirre. One of the major motives for early vine-growing was to supply wine for the celebration of mass. In the 18th century, the efforts of Madrid to restrict the planting of new vines in order to prevent competition with Spanish wines were largely ignored and vineyards became common on *haciendas* and villages throughout the Central Valley as far south as the Río Biobío.

Some of the most famous Chilean wines are closely associated with major names in the Chilean elite of the 19th century, among them the Errázuriz, Cousiño, Subercaseaux and Undurraga families. With the introduction of direct steamship services to Europe, the heads of many of these families travelled to France and returned with French and German grape varieties. New cultivation techniques were also introduced from France. French experts were employed to design the cellars with double walls to prevent temperature fluctuations; some of them can be visited today. The largest and most famous of these vineyards were situated just south of Santiago in the floodplains of the Ríos Pirque and Maipo, which were adapted for commercial agriculture by the building of a network of canals.

Defended by natural frontiers, the Pacific, the Andes and the Atacama Desert, Chile also benefited by being one of the very few wine-growing areas in the world not to suffer the devastation of the phylloxera louse, which destroyed the vineyards of Europe after 1863.

There is a marked distinction between export wines and wines grown for domestic consumption. The most commonly planted grape variety is the dark-skinned Pais, found only in Chile, and thought to be a direct descendant of cuttings imported by Spanish colonists. Many of the vines known in Chile as Sauvignon are not the familiar Sauvignon Blanc, but rather Sauvignon Vert or Sauvignon Gris. Although Chilean wines, especially those produced for export, are typically very clean and fruity, they have only recently developed a full-bodied structure. Most export wines are red Cabernet and white Chardonnay.

Four large companies now account for 80% of all the wine sold inside Chile: Concha y Toro, Santa Rita, San Pedro and Santa Carolina. A few others, among them Errázuriz/Caliterra, Undurraga, Cánepa and Manquehue, supply most of the rest of the domestic market. Many of the smaller wineries, however, specialize in exports. Although a few wineries, including Cousiño-Macul, Los Vascos, Montes, Portal del Alto, Santa Monica and Santa Inés, use only their own grapes, this practice is rare and most companies buy in grapes.

● '120', one of Chile's most popular wines, commemorates the 120 patriot soldiers, who hid
● in the Santa Rita cellars in 1814 after their defeat at Rancagua. 'Casillero del Diablo', meanwhile, was a favourite wine of the founder of the Concha y Toro company, who kept intruders away from his cellar by spreading the rumour that it was haunted by the devil.

Background Land and environment

Further reading

Travelogues

Beckett, Andy, *Pinochet in Piccadilly* (2002), Faber. Part travelogue, part reprise of almost two centuries of relations between England and Chile, seen through the prism of the Pinochet affair. One of the best books by an English writer on Chile for a long time – highly recommended.

Chatwin, Bruce, *In Patagonia* (1977), Pan. A modern classic for those visiting the far south, although it concentrates mainly on Argentina.

Cooper, Marc, *Pinochet and Me* (2001), Verso. Fascinating account of the 1973 coup by Salvador Allende's English translator, intermingled with his account of Chile today and the coup's legacy.

Darwin, Charles, *The Voyage of the Beagle* (1989), Penguin. Still fascinating reading of the great naturalist's voyage and adventures from Cape Horn to Copiapó in the 1830s.

Giménez Hutton, Adrian, *La Patagonia de Chatwin* (1999), Editorial Sudamericana. Interesting Argentine perspective on Chatwin and Patagonia (both Argentine and Chilean).

Green, Toby, *Saddled with Darwin* (2000), Phoenix House. One of the authors of this book retraces Darwin's route in South America on horseback.

Keenan, Brian and McCarthy, John, *Between Extremes*, (2000), Black Swan. The 2 friends from Lebanon travel together again, this time through Chile.

Lucas Bridges, E, *Uttermost Part of the Earth* (1948), Hodder & Stoughton. Brilliant and beautiful account of his adventurous life in Tierra del Fuego with the Yámana and Ona peoples; the classic text on Tierra del Fuego.

Pilkington, John, *An Englishman In Patagonia* (1991), Century. Heavily critical of Chatwin.

Souhami, Diana, *Selkirk's Island* (2001), Weidenfeld & Nicolson. The extraordinary story of Alexander Selkirk and his island, inspirations for Robinson Crusoe and for the community of San Juan Bautista on modern-day Isla Robinson Crusoe. A prizewinning account.

Swale, Rosie, *Back to Cape Horn* (1988), Fontana. Swale tells of her epic journey from Antofagasta to Cape Horn on horseback.

Wheeler, Sara, *Travels in a Thin Country* (1994), Little, Brown & Co. Popular account of the author's 6-month stay in Chile.

Fiction and poetry

Allende, Isabel, The doyenne of modern Chilean letters. Her books include: *The House of the Spirits* (1994), Black Swan. Brilliant, evocative, allegorical magical-realist account taking the reader through 20th-century Chilean history. *Of Love and Shadows* (1988), Black Swan. Painful story about a journalist uncovering evidence of military atrocities under the military regime. *Paula* (1996), Flamingo. A beautiful 'letter' written from Allende to her daughter, who is stuck in a coma after a car accident, taking in the modern history of Chile and Allende's emotional roots. More recent books include *Daughter of Fortune* (2000), Flamingo, and *Portrait in Sepia* (2002), Flamingo, both of which are lyrical prequels to the story that made Allende's name: *The House of the Spirits*.

Bolaño, Roberto, *By Night in Chile* (2003), Harvill. A caustic, brilliant novel, as an ageing Chilean priest lives through the last night of his life, and recalls teaching Marxism to General Pinochet and various surreal encounters with the Chilean literary establishment – thereby exposing the complicity of so many in the 'normality' that accompanied the military government. If you read one novel about Chile, make sure it's this one.

Donoso, José, *The Garden Next Door* (1994), Grove Press. Evocative novel that deals with the ageing process of a couple in Spain. *The Obscene Bird of the Night* (1995), Grove Press. Donoso's most famous, experimental novel, which gained him international acclaim across Latin America.

Dorfman, Ariel, *Death and the Maiden* (1996), Nick Hern Books (also in the collected volume *The Resistance Trilogy*; 1998). Subtle, moving tale of torture and resistance, an allegory for the state of Chile. *The Nanny and the Iceberg* (1999), Sceptre. Cross-cultural story of Chile and North America told with Dorfman's usual eloquence.

Neruda, Pablo, *Selected Poems* (trans/ed Ben Bellit (1961), New York Grove Press. Bilingual anthology of the master's work.

Richards, Ben, *The Mermaid and the Drunks* (2003), Weidenfeld & Nicolson. A recent English novel set in Chile, which gives an entertaining picture of modern Chile from the perspective of a longtime friend of the country.

Skármeta, Antonio, *Il Postino* (The Postman, 1996), Bloomsbury. Beautiful novel about the relationship between Neruda and his postman while the poet is in exile in Italy, made into a famous film. *Watch Where the Wolf is Going* (1991), Readers' International. Another novel in Skármeta's trademark style of eloquence and emotional honesty.

Adventure sports

Biggar, John, *The High Andes*, (1996), Castle Douglas, Kirkudbrightshire. Andes contains three chapters with information on Chilean peaks.

CONAF, *Guía de Parques Nacionales y Otras Areas Silvestres Protegidas de Chile*, US$12, a very useful guide to the main parks, with information on access, campsites, flora and fauna. They also publish *Chile Forestal*, a monthly magazine with articles on the parks and ecological issues.

Fagerstrom, René Peri, *Cuentos de la Carretera Austral*, on the Camino Austral. *Regata*, a monthly sailing magazine. Climbers will also find *Cumbres de Chile* of interest: two books with accompanying tapes, each covering 20 peaks.

Mantellero, Alberto, *Una Aventura Navegando Los Canales del Sur de Chile*, a guide to sailing the southern coast, with maps.

Reference and background

Almarza V, Claudio, *Patagonia* (Punta Arenas: GeoPatagonia). A book of photographs, with text, on the region.

Araya, B and Millie, G, *Guía de Campo de Las Aves de Chile*. Bird-lovers will appreciate this guide to Chile's feathered population.

Earth Island (1992), Thames and Hudson. A comprehensive appraisal of Easter Island's archaeology.

Cárdenas Saldivia, Umiliana, *Casos de Brujos de Chiloé* (1989), Editorial Universitaria. Fascinating tales of witchcraft on Chiloé.

Castillo, Juan Carlos (ed) *Islas Oceánicas Chilenas* (1987), Ediciones Universidad Católica de Chile. Much information on the natural history and geography of Juan Fernández and Easter Islands.

Clissold, Stephen, *Chilean Scrapbook* (1952), The Cresset Press. Gives an evocative historical picture of Chile, region by region.

Collier, S and Sater, WF, *A History of Chile 1808-1994* (1996), Cambridge University Press. Examination of Chile's recent history.

Coña, Pascal, *Memorias de un Cacique Mapuche* (1930), publisher unmarked. An account of Mapuche traditions and history by a Mapuche chief in his 70s.

Constable, Pamela and Valenzuela, Arturo, *Chile: A Nation of Enemies* (1991), Norton. Excellent on the Pinochet years.

Dorfman, Ariel, *Unending Terror: The Incredible Unending Trial of General Augusto Pinochet* (2003), Pluto Press. A gripping account of the Pinochet affair from one of the most perceptive living writers on Chile. His memoir *Heading North, Looking South* (1998) is also essential reading.

Goni, Uki, *The Real Odessa: How Perón Brought the Nazi War Criminals to Argentina* (2002), Granta. Although based on the Argentine hiding of Nazi war criminals, this book has a continent-wide significance, as it reveals how this movement shaped the fascist attitudes of military governments of the 1970s.

Hazlewood, Nick, *Savage: The Life and Times of Jemmy Button* (2001), Sceptre. Interesting if hyperbolic history of Jemmy's tale.

Heyerdahl, Thor, *Aku-Aku, The Art of Easter Island* (1975), New York: Doubleday.

Montecino, Sonia, *Historias de Vida de Mujeres Mapuches* (1985), Centro de Estudios de la Mujer. Interviews with Mapuche women giving a real insight into their lives.

O'Shaughnessy, Hugh, *Pinochet: The Politics of Torture* (2000), Latin American Bureau. Informed and up-to-date analysis of the whole Pinochet affair.

Porteous, J Douglas, *The Modernization of Easter Island* (1981), Department of Geography, University of Victoria, BC, Canada. A very thorough illustrated book.

Read, Jan, *The Wines of Chile* (1994), Mitchell Beazley. A gazetteer of the vineyards and wineries of Chile, ideal for the discerning specialist.

South American Explorers Club, *The South American Explorer* (126 Indian Creek Road, Ithaca, New York 14850, USA). This journal regularly publishes articles on Chile including Easter Island.

Spooner, MH, *Soldiers In A Narrow Land* (1994), University of California Press. A readable account of the Pinochet dictatorship by a North American journalist resident in the country at the time.

Wearne, Philip, *Return of the Indian: Conquest and Revival in the Americas* (1996), Cassell/Latin America Bureau. Information on the Mapuche within the entire Amerindian context.

Maps and guidebooks

The **Turistel** guide, **Turiscom**, *Av Santa Maria 0120, Providencia, Santiago, T02-3658800, F3658801, turiscom@chilesat.net* is very useful for roads and town plans, but not all distances are exact. It is published annually in three parts, *Norte*, *Centro*, and *Sur* (in Spanish only), alongside a separate volume listing campsites. It contains a wealth of maps covering the whole country and neighbouring tourist centres in Argentina, and is well worth getting, particularly for those with their own transport. Each volume costs around US$10, but buying the whole set is better value. Available from bookshops and from newspaper kiosks in the centre of Santiago or directly from the publisher.

Sernatur publishes a free *Guía Turistica/ Tourist Guide* in Spanish and English, with good maps, useful text, while **CONAF** publishes a series of illustrated booklets in Spanish/English on Chilean trees, shrubs and flowers, as well as *Juventud, Turismo y Naturaleza*, which lists national parks, their facilities and the flora and fauna of each.

A recommended series of general maps are published by **International Travel Maps** (ITM), *345 West Broadway, Vancouver, V5Y 1P8, Canada, T604-8793621*, compiled with historical notes, by Kevin Healey.

Footnotes

Basic Spanish for travellers

Learning Spanish is a useful part of the preparation for a trip to Latin America and no volumes of dictionaries, phrase books or word lists will provide the same enjoyment as being able to communicate directly with the people of the country you are visiting. It is a good idea to make an effort to grasp the basics before you go. As you travel you will pick up more of the language and the more you know, the more you will benefit from your stay.

General pronunciation
Whether you have been taught the 'Castilian' pronunciation (*z* and *c* followed by *i* or *e* are pronounced as the *th* in *think*) or the 'American' pronunciation (they are pronounced as *s*) you will encounter little difficulty in understanding either. Regional accents and usages vary, but the basic language is essentially the same everywhere.

Vowels
a   as in English *cat*
e   as in English *best*
i   as the *ee* in English *feet*
o   as in English *shop*
u   as the *oo* in English *food*
ai as the *i* in English *ride*
ei as *ey* in English *they*
oi as *oy* in English *toy*

Consonants
Most consonants can be pronounced more or less as they are in English. The exceptions are:
g   before *e* or *i* is the same as *j*
h   is always silent (except in *ch* as in *chair*)
j   as the *ch* in Scottish *loch*
ll as the *y* in *yellow*
ñ   as the *ni* in English *onion*
rr trilled much more than in English
x   depending on its location, pronounced *x*, *s*, *sh* or *j*

Spanish words and phrases

Greetings, courtesies
hello	*hola*
good morning	*buenos días*
good afternoon/evening/night	*buenas tardes/noches*
goodbye	*adiós/chao*
pleased to meet you	*mucho gusto*
see you later	*hasta luego*
how are you?	*¿cómo está?¿cómo estás?*
I'm fine, thanks	*estoy muy bien, gracias*
I'm called...	*me llamo...*
what is your name?	*¿cómo se llama? ¿cómo te llamas?*
yes/no	*sí/no*
please	*por favor*
thank you (very much)	*(muchas) gracias*
I speak Spanish	*hablo español*
I don't speak Spanish	*no hablo español*
do you speak English?	*¿habla inglés?*
I don't understand	*no entiendo/no comprendo*
please speak slowly	*hable despacio por favor*
I am very sorry	*lo siento mucho/disculpe*
what do you want?	*¿qué quiere? ¿qué quieres?*
I want	*quiero*
I don't want it	*no lo quiero*
leave me alone	*déjeme en paz/no me moleste*
good/bad	*bueno/malo*

Basic questions and requests

have you got a room for two people?	*¿tiene una habitación para dos personas?*
how do I get to_?	*¿cómo llego a_?*
how much does it cost?	*¿cuánto cuesta? ¿cuánto es?*
I'd like to make a long-distance phone call	*quisiera hacer una llamada de larga distancia*
is service included?	*¿está incluido el servicio?*
is tax included?	*¿están incluidos los impuestos?*
when does the bus leave (arrive)?	*¿a qué hora sale (llega) el autobús?*
when?	*¿cuándo?*
where is_?	*¿dónde está_?*
where can I buy tickets?	*¿dónde puedo comprar boletos?*
where is the nearest petrol station?	*¿dónde está la gasolinera más cercana?*
why?	*¿por qué?*

Basic words and phrases

bank	*el banco*
bathroom/toilet	*el baño*
to be	*ser, estar*
bill	*la factura/la cuenta*
cash	*el efectivo*
cheap	*barato/a*
credit card	*la tarjeta de crédito*
exchange house	*la casa de cambio*
exchange rate	*el tipo de cambio*
expensive	*caro/a*
to go	*ir*
to have	*tener, haber*
market	*el mercado*
note/coin	*el billete/la moneda*
police (policeman)	*la policía (el policía)*
post office	*el correo*
public telephone	*el teléfono público*
shop	*la tienda*
supermarket	*el supermercado*
there is/are	*hay*
there isn't/aren't	*no hay*
ticket office	*la taquilla*
travellers' cheques	*los cheques de viajero/los travelers*

Getting around

aeroplane	*el avión*
airport	*el aeropuerto*
arrival/departure	*la llegada/salida*
avenue	*la avenida*
block	*la cuadra*
border	*la frontera*
bus station	*la terminal de autobuses/camiones*
bus	*el bus/el autobús/el camión*
collective/fixed-route taxi	*el colectivo*
corner	*la esquina*
customs	*la aduana*
first/second class	*la primera/segunda clase*
left/right	*izquierda/derecha*
ticket	*el boleto*
empty/full	*vacío/lleno*
highway, main road	*la carretera*
immigration	*la inmigración*
insurance	*el seguro*
insured person	*el asegurado/la asegurada*

to insure yourself against	*asegurarse contra*
luggage	*el equipaje*
motorway, freeway	*el autopista/la carretera*
north, south, west, east	*el norte, el sur, el oeste (occidente), el este (oriente)*
oil	*el aceite*
to park	*estacionarse*
passport	*el pasaporte*
petrol/gasoline	*la gasolina*
puncture	*el pinchazo/la ponchadura*
street	*la calle*
that way	*por allí/por allá*
this way	*por aquí/por acá*
tourist card/visa	*la tarjeta de turista/visa*
tyre	*la llanta*
unleaded	*sin plomo*
waiting room	*la sala de espera*
to walk	*caminar/andar*

Accommodation

air conditioning	*el aire acondicionado*
all-inclusive	*todo incluido*
bathroom, private	*el baño privado*
bed, double/single	*la cama matrimonial/sencilla*
blankets	*las cobijas/mantas*
to clean	*limpiar*
dining room	*el comedor*
guesthouse	*la casa de huéspedes*
hotel	*el hotel*
noisy	*ruidoso*
pillows	*las almohadas*
power cut	*el apagón/corte*
restaurant	*el restaurante*
room/bedroom	*el cuarto/la habitación*
sheets	*las sábanas*
shower	*la ducha/regadera*
soap	*el jabón*
toilet	*el sanitario/excusado*
toilet paper	*el papel higiénico*
towels, clean/dirty	*las toallas limpias/sucias*
water, hot/cold	*el agua caliente/fría*

Health

aspirin	*la aspirina*
blood	*la sangre*
chemist	*la farmacia*
condoms	*los preservativos, los condones*
contact lenses	*los lentes de contacto*
contraceptives	*los anticonceptivos*
contraceptive pill	*la píldora anticonceptiva*
diarrhoea	*la diarrea*
doctor	*el médico*
fever/sweat	*la fiebre/el sudor*
pain	*el dolor*
head	*la cabeza*
period/sanitary towels	*la regla/las toallas femininas*
stomach	*el estómago*
altitude sickness	*el soroche*

Family

family	*la familia*
brother/sister	*el hermano/la hermana*
daughter/son	*la hija/el hijo*
father/mother	*el padre/la madre*
husband/wife	*el esposo (marido)/la esposa*
boyfriend/girlfriend	*el novio/la novia*
friend	*el amigo/la amiga*
married	*casado/a*
single/unmarried	*soltero/a*

Months, days and time

January	*enero*
February	*febrero*
March	*marzo*
April	*abril*
May	*mayo*
June	*junio*
July	*julio*
August	*agosto*
September	*septiembre*
October	*octubre*
November	*noviembre*
December	*diciembre*
Monday	*lunes*
Tuesday	*martes*
Wednesday	*miércoles*
Thursday	*jueves*
Friday	*viernes*
Saturday	*sábado*
Sunday	*domingo*
at one o'clock	*a la una*
at half past two	*a las dos y media*
at a quarter to three	*a cuarto para las tres/a las tres menos quince*
it's one o'clock	*es la una*
it's seven o'clock	*son las siete*
it's six twenty	*son las seis y veinte*
it's five to nine	*son cinco para las nueve/las nueve menos cinco*
in ten minutes	*en diez minutos*
five hours	*cinco horas*
does it take long?	*¿tarda mucho?*

Numbers

one	*uno/una*
two	*dos*
three	*tres*
four	*cuatro*
five	*cinco*
six	*seis*
seven	*siete*
eight	*ocho*
nine	*nueve*
ten	*diez*
eleven	*once*
twelve	*doce*
thirteen	*trece*
fourteen	*catorce*

fifteen	*quince*
sixteen	*dieciséis*
seventeen	*diecisiete*
eighteen	*dieciocho*
nineteen	*diecinueve*
twenty	*veinte*
twenty-one	*veintiuno*
thirty	*treinta*
forty	*cuarenta*
fifty	*cincuenta*
sixty	*sesenta*
seventy	*setenta*
eighty	*ochenta*
ninety	*noventa*
hundred	*cien/ciento*
thousand	*mil*

Food

avocado	*el aguacate*
baked	*al horno*
bakery	*la panadería*
banana	*el plátano*
beans	*los frijoles/las habichuelas*
beef	*la carne de res*
beef steak or pork fillet	*el bistec*
boiled rice	*el arroz blanco*
bread	*el pan*
breakfast	*el desayuno*
butter	*la mantequilla*
cake	*el pastel*
chewing gum	*el chicle*
chicken	*el pollo*
chilli pepper or green pepper	*el ají/el chile/el pimiento*
clear soup, stock	*el caldo*
cooked	*cocido*
dining room	*el comedor*
egg	*el huevo*
fish	*el pescado*
fork	*el tenedor*
fried	*frito*
garlic	*el ajo*
goat	*el chivo*
grapefruit	*la toronja/el pomelo*
grill	*la parrilla*
guava	*la guayaba*
ham	*el jamón*
hamburger	*la hamburguesa*
hot, spicy	*picante*
ice cream	*el helado*
jam	*la mermelada*
knife	*el cuchillo*
lime	*el limón*
lobster	*la langosta*
lunch	*el almuerzo/la comida*
meal	*la comida*
meat	*la carne*
minced meat	*el picadillo*
onion	*la cebolla*
orange	*la naranja*

pepper	*el pimiento*
pasty, turnover	*la empanada/el pastelito*
pork	*el cerdo*
potato	*la papa*
prawns	*los camarones*
raw	*crudo*
restaurant	*el restaurante*
salad	*la ensalada*
salt	*la sal*
sandwich	*el bocadillo*
sauce	*la salsa*
sausage	*la longaniza/el chorizo*
scrambled eggs	*los huevos revueltos*
seafood	*los mariscos*
soup	*la sopa*
spoon	*la cuchara*
squash	*la calabaza*
squid	*los calamares*
supper	*la cena*
sweet	*dulce*
to eat	*comer*
toasted	*tostado*
turkey	*el pavo*
vegetables	*los legumbres/vegetales*
without meat	*sin carne*
yam	*el camote*

Drink

beer	*la cerveza*
boiled	*hervido/a*
bottled	*en botella*
camomile tea	*té de manzanilla*
canned	*en lata*
coffee	*el café*
coffee, white	*el café con leche*
cold	*frío*
cup	*la taza*
drink	*la bebida*
drunk	*borracho/a*
firewater	*el aguardiente*
fruit milkshake	*el batido/licuado*
glass	*el vaso*
hot	*caliente*
ice/without ice	*el hielo/sin hielo*
juice	*el jugo*
lemonade	*la limonada*
milk	*la leche*
mint	*la menta/la hierbabuena*
rum	*el ron*
soft drink	*el refresco*
sugar	*el azúcar*
tea	*el té*
to drink	*beber/tomar*
water	*el agua*
water, carbonated	*el agua mineral con gas*
water, still mineral	*el agua mineral sin gas*
wine, red	*el vino tinto*
wine, white	*el vino blanco*

Glossary

adobe a sun-dried mixture of silt and clay used as a building material in the country

alfajores flaky biscuits filled with *manjar* (caramelised condensed milk)

almuerzo lunch

altiplano the high plateau found in the northern Andes

cabaña chalet, usually rented out to families in the south and on the coast

cama bed

carabineros police

cerro hill

chicha type of homemade fermented drink, usually made of apples (in the south) or grapes (in the north)

Codec National Petrol Company

Codeff national body campaigning to protect flora and fauna

colectivo a collective taxi

comedor dining room

CONAF national body overseeing the running and administration of Chile's national parks and reserves

congrio not to be confused with conger eel (although Iberian Spanish uses *congrio* in this way). It is, in fact, a type of ling

cordillera mountain range

costanera waterfront

cuadra block (in a city)

curanto stew from Chiloé with shellfish, pork and potatoes

estancia sheep farm in the far south

fundo old-style farm in the Central Valley

huasos Chilean cowboys

humitas crushed corn paste stuffed into corn leaves, often sweetened

kuchen cakes in German style (usually found in the south)

pampa flat, desert or semi-desert landscape (found in the Atacama and also in Patagonia)

pebre spicy chilli and tomato sauce found in any restaurant worthy of the name as a relish

peñas restaurant or bar with live folkloric performances

pudu small indigenous deer, very rare, found in the southern Andes

restaurant bailable restaurant with live music and dancing. Sometimes it is necessary to pay a cover to enter.

seno gulf, inlet

Sernatur National Tourist Board, usually very helpful

tábanos horseflies (found in the south)

Index

Shorts index

Map index

Advertisers' index

Credits

Footprint credits

Editor: Sophie Blacksell
Map editor: Sarah Sorensen

Publisher: Patrick Dawson
Editorial: Alan Murphy, Sarah Thorowgood, Claire Boobbyer, Caroline Lascom, Felicity Laughton, Davina Rungasamy, Laura Dixon
Proofreading: Sarah Chatwin
Cartography: Robert Lunn, Claire Benison, Kevin Feeney
Series development Rachel Fielding
Design: Mytton Williams and Rosemary Dawson (brand)
Advertising: Debbie Wylde
Finance and administration: Sharon Hughes, Elizabeth Taylor

Photography credits

Front cover: Imagestate (Moai at Rano Raraku, Easter Island)
Back cover: Imagestate (Signage in Punta Arenas)
Inside colour section: Alamy, Christabelle Dilks, Jamie Marshall, Robert Harding Picture Library, South American Pictures (p7 Lago Grey, Patagonia), Karen Ward

Print

Manufactured in Italy by LegoPrint
Pulp from sustainable forests

Footprint feedback

We try as hard as we can to make each Footprint guide as up to date as possible but, of course, things always change. If you want to let us know about your experiences – good, bad or ugly – then don't delay, go to www.footprintbooks.com and send in your comments.

Publishing information

Footprint Chile
4th edition
© Footprint Handbooks Ltd
January 2004

ISBN 1 903471 76 1
CIP DATA: A catalogue record for this book is available from the British Library

® Footprint Handbooks and the Footprint mark are a registered trademark of Footprint Handbooks Ltd

Published by Footprint

6 Riverside Court
Lower Bristol Road
Bath BA2 3DZ, UK
T +44 (0)1225 469141
F +44 (0)1225 469461
discover@footprintbooks.com
www.footprintbooks.com

Distributed in the USA by
Publishers Group West

Neither the black and white nor coloured maps are intended to have any political significance.

Every effort has been made to ensure that the facts in this guidebook are accurate. However, travellers should still obtain advice from consulates, airlines etc about travel and visa requirements before travelling. The authors and publishers cannot accept responsibility for any loss, injury or inconvenience however caused.

Acknowledgements

Many people have helped in making this book as thorough and relevant as possible. Fulsome thanks go to all the regional SERNATUR offices from Iquique to Punta Arenas, as well as to the CONAF and municipal tourist offices, all of whom gave their time, expertise and local knowledge to ensure that information on their area was thorough and complete.

Janak Jani would like to thank the following for providing help and information: Ross Moorehouse in Arica; Martin and everyone at Cosmo Andino in San Pedro; Marco Velasquez for putting us up in Antofagasta; Lucas in the Elqui Valley; everyone at Casa Chueca, Talca; Alex in Talca for a great city tour; Alejandro in Constitución for an unforgettable ride along the Putú sand dunes; Hans in Pucón; Nadia and Armin in Puerto Octay; Mauro and Malin in Puerto Varas; Nicholas in Chaitén; Santi and Chus in Coyhaique; Umberto in Villa O'Higgins; Christian for giving me both a lift along 500 km of the Carreterra Austral and the shortest-ever tour of Tortel; and Werner and Cecilia in Puerto Natales. Thanks also to Lorena for holding the fort and travelling with me to the north.

Toby Green would like to thank the Chilean Embassy in London, Janak Jani, the libraries at the University of Birmingham and the British Library.

Thanks to Sophie Blacksell and all at Footprint for working tirelessly on the production of this book and, finally, to the countless readers whose letters have make this guide as up to date as possible.

Bibliography

Sources for the section on Arts and Crafts are: Artesanía tradicional de Chile, Serie El Patrimonio Cultural Chileno, Ministerio de Educación, 1978; 'Visión estética de la cerámica de Quinchamalí', by Luis Guzmán Molina, Atenea, No 458 (Universidad de Concepción, 1988), pages 47-60; Mapudungun, lengua y costumbres Mapuches, by Orietta Appelt Martín (Temuco: Magin, 1995); Arts and Crafts of South America, by Lucy Davies and Mo Fini (Bath: Tumi, 1994). Tumi, a Latin American Craft Centre in Britain, specializes in Mexican and Andean products and produces cultural and educational videos for schools: at 23/24 Chalk Farm Road, London NW1 8AG, 8/9 New Bond Street Place, Bath BA1 1BH, 1/2 Little Clarendon Street, Oxford OX1 2HJ, 82 Park Street, Bristol BS1 5LA.

A great many sources have been consulted in the preparation of the section on Literature. Apart from those already mentioned, reference is made to: Cedomil Goic, La novela chilena. Los mitos degradados (Santiago: Universitaria, 1991); Kenneth Fleak, The Chilean Short Story. Writers from the Generation of 1950 (New York: Peter Lang, 1989); René Jara, El revés de la arpillera, perfil literario de Chile (Madrid: Hiperión, 1988); Jean Franco, Spanish American Literature since Independence (London: Ernest Benn, 1973); Eugenia Brito, Campos minados. Literatura post-golpe en Chile (Santiago: Mujeres Cuarto Propio, 1990); Poesía chilena de hoy. De Parra a nuestros días, selected by Erwin Díaz (Santiago: Ediciones Documentas, 1989); Lautaro Silva, Vida y obra de Gabriela Mistral (Buenos Aires: Andina, 1967); Gordon Brotherston, The Emergence of the Latin American Novel (1977) and Latin American Poetry. Origins and Presence (Cambridge University Press, 1975); Darío Villanueva y José María Viña Liste, Trayectoria de la novela hispanoamericano actual (Madrid: Austral, 1991); Jason Wilson, Traveller's Literary Companion: South and Central America (Brighton: In Print, 1993); Gerald Martin, Journeys through the Labyrinth (London: Verso, 1989); Poesía Chilena Para el Siglo XXI (Dirección de Bibliotécas, Archivos y Museos, 1996). A key text for English readers is Steven White's Poets of Chile (Unicorn Press, 1986).

What the papers say...

"I carried the South American Handbook from Cape Horn to Cartagena and consulted it every night for two and a half months. I wouldn't do that for anything else except my hip flask."
Michael Palin, BBC Full Circle

"My favourite series is the Handbook series published by Footprint and I especially recommend the Mexico, Central and South America Handbooks."
Boston Globe

"If 'the essence of real travel' is what you have been secretly yearning for all these years, then Footprint are the guides for you."
Under 26 magazine

"Who should pack Footprint—readers who want to escape the crowd."
The Observer

"Footprint can be depended on for accurate travel information and for imparting a deep sense of respect for the lands and people they cover."
World News

"The guides for intelligent, independently-minded souls of any age or budget."
Indie Traveller

Mail order

Available worldwide in bookshops and on-line. Footprint travel guides can also be ordered directly from us in Bath, via our website www.footprintbooks.com or from the address on the imprint page of this book.

Check out...

www...

Map 1

PERU

Visviri

Tacora (5,988m)

Putre

Pomerape (6,282m)

Parinacota

Geoglifos de Lluta

Parque Nacional Lauca

Acotango (6,050m)

Parinacota (6,342m)

Paso Tambo Quemado

Capurata (5,990m)

Guallatiri (6,060m)

Arica

Poconchile

Belén

Guallatiri

Geoglifos de Azapa

Río Lluta

Río Azapa

Tignamar

Tignamar Viejo

Reserva Nacional Las Vicuñas

Codpa

Salar de Surire

Monumental Natural Salar de Surire

Surire

Río Camarones

Parque Nacional Volcán Isluga

Isluga (5,530m)

Cuya

Colchane

Geoglifos de Chiza

Camiña

Isluga

Geoglifos de Tiliviche

British Cemetery

Cariquima

Pisagua

REGION I

Reserva Nacional Pampa del Tamarugal

Chusmisa

Cta Buena

Giante del Atacama

Alto Toroni (5,982m)

Huara

Tarapacá

Humberstone

Mamiña

Iquique

Pozo Almonte

La Tirana

Salar de Huasco

Reserva Nacional Pampa del Tamarugal

Salar de Pintados

Pica

Matilla

Puerto Patillos

Geoglifos de Pintados

Salar de Coposa

San Marcos

Salar de Llamara

BOLIVIA

Ollagüe

Buenaventura

Salar de Carcote

Ollagüe (5,863m)

Pacific Ocean

Cebollar

Quillagua

Ascotán

Salar de Ascotán

Conchi Viejo

San Pedro

Inacaliri

Tocopilla

Conchi

Punta Blanca

Río Loa

Lasana

Baños de Turi

Línzor

Mantos de la Luna

Ayquina

Toconce

Gatico

María Elena

Chuquicamata

Chiu Chiu

Caspana

El Tatio Geysers

Cobija

Pedro de Valdivia

Calama

Michilla

Salar Miraje

Río Grande

Puritama

Hornitos

Catarpe

Lincancábur (5,916m)

Zapaleri (5,653m)

Sierra Gorda

Pukará Quitor

San Pedro de Atacama

Mejillones

Chacabuco

Tulor

Reserva Nacional Los Flamencos

Bolsico

Carmen Alto

Toconao

Salar de Quisquiro

Paso de Jama

Juan Lopez

La Portada

Baquedano

Salar de Atacama

Talabre

La Chimba

Camar

Lascar (5,154m)

Antofagasta

REGION II

Peine

Socaire

Paso de Guaitiquina

Laguna Miscanti

Reserva Nacional Los Flamencos

Tilopozo

Tilomonte

Laco

Paso de Sico

Map 2

N

0 km 30

0 miles 30

① ② ③

Ⓐ Ⓑ Ⓒ

Map symbols

Administration

□ Capital city
○ Other city/town
～ International border
～ Regional border
～ Disputed border

Roads and travel

— Main road (National highway)
— Unpaved or *ripio* (gravel) road
- - - - 4WD track
······ Footpath
＋■ Railway with station
✈ Airport
🚌 Bus station
Ⓜ Metro station
- - - - Cable car
╫╫╫ Funicular
⛴ Ferry

Water features

River, canal
Lake, ocean
Seasonal marshland
Beach, sand bank
Waterfall

Topographical features

Contours (approx)
Mountain
Volcano
Mountain pass
Escarpment
Gorge
Glacier
Salt flat
Rocks

Cities and towns

Main through route
Main street
Minor street
Pedestrianized street

⊃⊂ Tunnel
→ One way street
Steps
⇌ Bridge
Fortified wall
Park, garden, stadium
● Sleeping
❷ Eating
● Bars & clubs
⊙ Entertainment
Building
▫ Sight
✝ Cathedral, church
Chinese temple
Hindu temple
Meru
Mosque
△ Stupa
✡ Synagogue
Tourist office
🏛 Museum
✉ Post office
Police
Ⓢ Bank
@ Internet
☎ Telephone
Market
Hospital
Ⓟ Parking
Petrol
Golf
A Detail map
A Related map

Other symbols

Archaeological site
National park, wildlife reserve
Viewing point
Campsite
Refuge, lodge
Castle
Diving
Deciduous/coniferous/palm trees
Hide
Vineyard
Distillery
Shipwreck
Historic battlefield

Complete title listing

Footprint publishes travel guides to over 150 destinations worldwide. Each guide is packed with practical, concise and colourful information for everybody from first-time travellers to travel aficionados. The list is growing fast and current titles are noted below.
Available from all good bookshops and online

www.footprintbooks.com

(P) denotes pocket guide

Latin America and Caribbean
Argentina
Barbados (P)
Bolivia
Brazil
Caribbean Islands
Central America & Mexico
Chile
Colombia
Costa Rica
Cuba
Cusco & the Inca Trail

Dominican Republic
Ecuador & Galápagos
Guatemala
Havana (P)
Mexico
Nicaragua
Peru
Rio de Janeiro
South American Handbook
Venezuela

North America
Vancouver (P)
New York (P)
Western Canada

Africa
Cape Town (P)
East Africa
Libya
Marrakech & the High Atlas
Marrakech (P)
Morocco
Namibia
South Africa
Tunisia
Uganda

Middle East
Egypt
Israel
Jordan
Syria & Lebanon

Australasia
Australia
East Coast Australia
New Zealand
Sydney (P)
West Coast Australia

Asia
Bali
Bangkok & the Beaches
Cambodia
Goa
Hong Kong (P)
India
Indian Himalaya
Indonesia
Laos
Malaysia
Nepal
Pakistan
Rajasthan & Gujarat
Singapore
South India
Sri Lanka
Sumatra
Thailand
Tibet
Vietnam

Europe
Andalucía
Barcelona
Barcelona (P)
Berlin (P)
Bilbao (P)
Bologna (P)
Britain
Copenhagen (P)
Croatia
Dublin
Dublin (P)
Edinburgh
Edinburgh (P)

England
Glasgow
Glasgow (P)
Ireland
Lisbon (P)
London
London (P)
Madrid (P)
Naples (P)
Northern Spain
Paris (P)
Reykjavík (P)
Scotland
Scotland Highlands & Islands
Seville (P)
Spain
Tallinn (P)
Turin (P)
Turkey
Valencia (P)
Verona (P)

Also available
Traveller's Handbook (WEXAS)
Traveller's Healthbook (WEXAS)
Traveller's Internet Guide (WEXAS)

For a different view of Europe, take a Footprint

❝❞ Superstylish travel guides – perfect for short break addicts.
Harvey Nichols magazine

Discover so much more...
Listings driven, forward looking and up to date. Focuses on what's going on right now. Contemporary, stylish, and innovative approach, providing quality travel information.